Non-Smokers' Guide to Bed & Breakfasts

1993-1994 Edition

Non-Smokers' Guide to Bed & Breakfasts

1993-1994 Edition

Julia M. Pitkin, *Editor*

RUTLEDGE HILL PRESS
NASHVILLE, TENNESSEE

In the course of producing a book of this scope, the help of many people has been required. I would like to acknowledge the following.

Thanks to David Taylor, the Assistant Editor, for rolling up his sleeves and keeping the project moving.

Thanks are due to Stephen Woolverton for his technical expertise, and for resolving many dilemmas that arose while bringing this volume to completion.

Thanks also to Tracey Menges for making the time among her many responsibilities to go beyond the call of duty. This book would not have been possible without her help.

Finally, thanks to the following people for their help in the production of this volume: Ron Pitkin, Nancy Malman, Lisa Duvall, Jennifer Bruer, Marty Molpus, Grace Monk, and Tom Noser.

Julia M. Pitkin

Published in Nashville, Tennessee, by Rutledge Hill Press, Inc., 211 Seventh Avenue North, Nashville, Tennessee 37219

Cover design and book design by Harriette Bateman
Maps and selected illustrations by Tonya Pitkin Presley

Manufactured in the United States of America
1 2 3 4 5 6 — 96 95 94 93

Contents

Introduction. vii
Alabama 1
Alaska. 3
Arizona. 19
Arkansas 31
California 39
Colorado 115
Connecticut. 133
Delaware. 153
District of Columbia. 157
Florida. 165
Georgia. 173
Hawaii. 179
Idaho. 219
Illinois. 223
Indiana 235
Iowa 241
Kansas. 247
Kentucky. 249
Louisiana. 251
Maine 259
Maryland. 281
Massachusetts 307
Michigan. 365
Minnesota. 375
Mississippi 381
Missouri 387
Montana 403
Nebraska. 407
Nevada 409
New Hampshire 411

New Jersey 427
New Mexico 435
New York 447
North Carolina 483
North Dakota 491
Ohio 493
Oklahoma 495
Oregon 501
Pennsylvania. 507
Rhode Island. 543
South Carolina 551
South Dakota 557
Tennessee 559
Texas. 569
Utah 581
Vermont 585
Virginia. 603
Washington 625
West Virginia 651
Wisconsin 655
Wyoming 663
Alberta 667
British Columbia. 669
Manitoba. 677
New Brunswick 681
Nova Scotia. 683
Ontario 684
Prince Edward Island 689
Quebec 690
Puerto Rico. 693
Virgin Islands 694

Introduction

Welcome to the second edition of *The Non-Smokers' Guide to Bed & Breakfasts*. This directory is a collection of bed and breakfasts and small inns across the country that are smoke-free. Specifically, they do not allow smoking indoors, although some allow smoking on porches or lawns.

While assembling this directory, the editor and publisher received a few letters proclaiming strong disagreement with non-smoking policies. However, many more bed and breakfast owners cheered for and encouraged the printing of this resource for non-smokers, making clear the need for such a directory.

This non-smokers' guide has been patterned after *The Annual Directory of American Bed & Breakfasts*, using the same format for quick reference and efficient travel planning. Each listing is presented alphabetically by state, city, and establishment name. **Note:** The descriptions have been provided by the hosts. The publishers have not visited these B&Bs and are not responsible for inaccuracies.

Following the description is information that will be helpful when choosing a bed and breakfast. With this fact list, seen in the example below, you can quickly determine the number of rooms available, the number with private baths (PB), the number with shared baths (SB), and the cost range for two people sharing a room. Tax may or may not be included. Also, the "Credit Cards" and "Notes" correspond to the list at the bottom of each page. You may notice that the "Notes" are not in sequence. Number 7, which represents smoking, has been eliminated.

GREAT TOWN _____

Favorite Bed and Breakfast

123 Main Street, 10000
(800) 555-1234

This quaint bed and breakfast is surrounded by five acres of award-winning landscaping and gardens. There are four guestrooms, each individually decorated with antiques. It is close to antique shops, restaurants, and outdoor activities. Breakfast includes homemade specialties and is served in the formal dining room at your leisure.

Hosts: Sue and Jim Smith
Rooms: 4 (2 PB; 2 SB) $65-80
Full Breakfast
Credit Cards: A, B
Minimum stay: 2 nights
Notes: 2, 5, 8, 10, 11, 12, 13

Tips for B&B Travel

After choosing a bed and breakfast that appeals to you, it is important to call ahead for reservations and for information that may not be included in the description. For example, ask about local taxes, as city and state taxes vary. Ask if dietary needs you may have can be accommodated. Confirm that your children or pets will be welcome. And ask for directions as many bed & breakfasts are off the beaten path.

Because many B&Bs are home to the hosts, remember to be respectful of their property and busy schedules. Most do not have the luxury of a large staff and have established certain policies to assure each guest a pleasant stay.

It is hoped that with *The Non-Smokers' Guide to Bed & Breakfasts* you will discover great places to visit and revisit; places where your desire for clean, breathable air will be respected; and places where your room will more often be filled with the aroma of baked-goods and fresh coffee than with the stale odor of tobacco smoke. It is hoped, too, that this guide will help you have a pleasant, memorable trip, whether it be a family vacation, a romantic getaway, or a business meeting.

Non-Smokers' Guide to Bed & Breakfasts

1993-1994 Edition

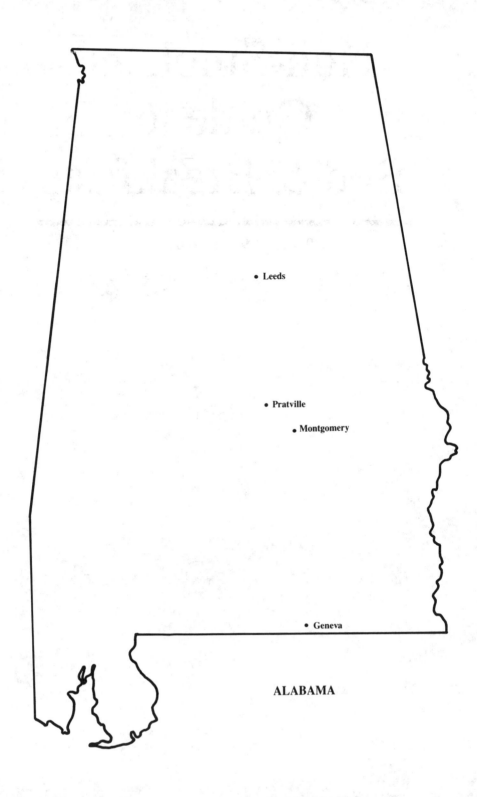

• Leeds

• Pratville

• Montgomery

• Geneva

ALABAMA

Alabama

Live Oaks of Geneva

GENEVA

Live Oaks of Geneva

307 South Academy Street, 36340
(205) 684-2489

Beautifully restored 1918 home situated one block from downtown Geneva in southeast Alabama, this bed and breakfast offers comfortable bedrooms with private baths and TV. Enjoy the large porch, sun room, and livingroom as a family member. A private entrance allows guests to come and go as they wish. No pets in bedrooms. Children welcome.

Hosts: Horace and Pamela Newman
Rooms: 3 (PB) $40
Continental Breakfast
Credit Cards: None
Notes: 2, 5, 8, 12

LEEDS

Country Sunshine

Route 2, Box 275, 35094
(205) 699-9841

A four and one-half-acre secluded retreat with a quiet country atmosphere. Barn and pasture to board guests' horses. Ranch-style house with four bedrooms and four baths, TV den, fireplace, formal dining room, country dining room, outside screened patio. Guided fishing, camping, horseback riding in the area. Twenty minutes south of Birmingham, near the Botanical Gardens, Vulcan Park, and Oak Mountain State Park.

Host: Kay Red House
Rooms: 4 (PB and SB) $50-65
Full Breakfast
Credit Cards: None
Notes: 2, 3, 4, 5, 8 (over 13), 14

MONTGOMERY

Red Bluff Cottage

551 Clay Street, P. O. Box 1026, 36101
(205) 264-0056

The Waldos built Red Bluff Cottage in 1987 high above the Alabama River in Montgomery's historic Cottage Hill District. A raised cottage, all guest rooms are on the ground floor, with easy access to off-street parking, gazebo, and fenced play

Red Bluff Cottage

NOTES: Credit cards accepted: A Master Card; B Visa; C American Express; D Discover Card; E Diner's Club; F Other; 2 Personal Checks accepted; 3 Lunch available; 4 Dinner available; 5 Open all year; 6 Pets welcome; 8 Children welcome; 9 Social drinking allowed; 10 Tennis available; 11 Swimming available; 12 Golf available; 13 Skiing available; 14 May be booked through travel agents.

yard. Upstairs, guests will enjoy pleasantly light and airy public rooms, including dining, living, music (piano and harpsichord), and sitting (TV) rooms, plus a deep porch overlooking downtown, the state capitol, and river plain.

Hosts: Ann and Mark Waldo
Rooms: 4 (PB) $55
Full Breakfast
Credit Cards: None
Notes: 2, 5, 8, 9, 14

PRATTVILLE _____

Plantation House Bed and Breakfast Inn

752 Loder Street, 36067
(205) 361-0442

Plantation House is a beautiful 161-year old antebellum home surrounded by more than four acres of beautiful grounds. There are two large guest rooms with queen beds and fireplaces, one features a Jacuzzi and a fireplace in an adjoining bath. The romantic atmosphere and quiet surroundings afford an ideal hideaway. A continental breakfast consists of homemade muffins, breakfast souffle or quiche, juice, and beverage. Special requests, within reason, are granted.

Hosts: John and Bernice Hughes
Rooms: 3 (1 PB; 1 or 2 SB) $50-65
Continental Breakfast
Credit Cards: None
Notes: 2, 5, 9, 11, 14

NOTES: Credit cards accepted: A Master Card; B Visa; C American Express; D Discover Card; E Diner's Club; F Other; 2 Personal Checks accepted; 3 Lunch available; 4 Dinner available; 5 Open all year;

Alaska

Alaskan Bed and Breakfast

320 East 12th Avenue, 99501
(907) 279-3200

Suite with both TV and phone; two rooms with TV and phone with shared bath. View of downtown Anchorage. Walking distance to central business district. Visit Portage Glacier, Alyeska Ski Resort. Tour of historic Anchorage. Fishing, wildlife bird sanctuary, Mount McKinley, bicycling, sightseeing, or just relaxing.

Host: Joy Young
Rooms: 3 (SB) $55-65
Continental Breakfast
Credit Cards: A, B, C, D, E, F
Notes: 2, 5, 8, 9, 11, 13, 14

All the Comforts of Home

12531 Turk's Turn, 99516-3309
(907) 345-4279; FAX (907) 345-4761

Receive a warm welcome at this renowned establishment. Retreat just ten minutes beyond urban bustle to a secluded slice of country living. Five wooded acres at 1,100-foot elevation provide magnificent views of greater Anchorage, Mount McKinley, active volcanos, and distant glaciers. Pioneer hostess serves full breakfast in a 14-foot bay window that overlooks it all. The outdoor hot tub is heated year-round, sheltered by towering evergreens.

Host: Sydnee Mae Stiver
Rooms: 3 (1 PB; 2 SB) $85-125
Full Breakfast

Credit Cards: A, B, C, D, E, F
Notes: 2, 5, 9, 10, 11, 12, 13, 14

Accommodations in Alaska AC

The Friendly Lodging Choice
P. O. Box 110624, 99511-0624
(907) 345-4761

Enjoy the solitude and landscaping of this spacious yard brimming with summer flowers. This traditional homestay is situated in a quiet, exclusive neighborhood close to downtown. Three guest rooms are offered with queen or double beds, one with private bath. Situated near health and fitness facilities, shopping, and restaurants. Christian hostess serves a variety of breakfasts, choice of full or continental. Resident dog. Free parking. $75-90

All the Comforts of Home

6 Pets welcome; 8 Children welcome; 9 Social drinking allowed; 10 Tennis available; 11 Swimming available; 12 Golf available; 13 Skiing available; 14 May be booked through travel agents.

Juneau

Gustavus

Tok

Fairbanks

Gakona

Valdez

Hatcher Pass

Talkeetna

Wasilla

Delta Junction

Healy

Eagle River

Anchorage

Sterling

Seward

Willow

Homer

Soldotna

Anchor Point

McGrath

ALASKA

Accommodations in Alaska AF

The Friendly Lodging Choice
P. O. Box 110624, 99511-0624
(907) 345-4761

This custom-built home nestled in the trees on three landscaped acres offers a variety of accommodations. Rooms with king, queen, or double beds, shared or private bath, two with Jacuzzis, one with a VCR, rock fireplace, and sauna. Personable hostess serves delicious full breakfasts in the formal dining room. Furnished with Alaskan artifacts and trophies, this traditional homestay offers intriguing opportunities to learn more about the area. Free parking. $95-175.

Accommodations in Alaska AH

The Friendly Lodging Choice
P. O. Box 110624, 99511-0624
(907) 345-4761

The innkeepers here enjoy watching the moose and bald eagles from their large sun deck. Tall evergreens surround this traditional homestay in south Anchorage. The two guest rooms share a bath. A family room adjoins the guest rooms complete with cable TV, VCR, rock fireplace, and mini-kitchen. Guests may also enjoy the electric sauna. Weather permitting, full breakfasts are served on the deck. Free parking. Resident dog. $75-100

Accommodations in Alaska AK

The Friendly Lodging Choice
P. O. Box 110624, 99511-0624
(907) 345-4761

Between downtown and the airport, this large home has facilities for outdoor pets on approval. Recently remodeled, this traditional homestay fits the needs of many visitors to Alaska. Near parks, a free tennis court and popular fitness trail. Accommodations are on the lower level and offer private and shared baths. Twin or double beds. Full breakfast. Sauna. Resident dogs. Free parking. $75-90.

Accommodations in Alaska AN

The Friendly Lodging Choice
P. O. Box 110624, 99511-0624
(907) 345-4761

There are two knowledgeable hostesses at this traditional homestay near the Chugach foothills. Hostesses enjoy restoring antique furniture. Situated in a family-oriented neighborhood, with library, restaurants, theaters, and supermarket nearby. Twin with shared bath or suite with private bath. The wilderness of Chugach State Park is just blocks away. Return from your expedition to a cozy fire and hot cocoa. Continental breakfast. Resident dog. Free parking. $65-85.

Accommodations in Alaska AP

The Friendly Lodging Choice
P. O. Box 110624, 99511-0624
(907) 345-4761

This hostess is well traveled and interested in meeting visitors from around the world. The oversize livingroom affords a good view of the Chugach Mountains to the east. Visitors interested in sporting events will appreciate the proximity to Anchorage's major sports complex. A traditional homestay offering king and queen beds, suites or shared bath. Hostess enjoys scuba diving and cooking; host is an amateur radio operator. Resident dog. Free parking. $70-85.

Accommodations in Alaska AT

The Friendly Lodging Choice
P. O. Box 110624, 99511-0624
(907) 345-4761

NOTES: Credit cards accepted: A Master Card; B Visa; C American Express; D Discover Card; E Diner's Club; F Other; 2 Personal Checks accepted; 3 Lunch available; 4 Dinner available; 5 Open all year; 6 Pets welcome; 8 Children welcome; 9 Social drinking allowed; 10 Tennis available; 11 Swimming available; 12 Golf available; 13 Skiing available; 14 May be booked through travel agents.

This hostess is a native-born Alaskan. Her renowned traditional homestay features full breakfasts accompanied by generous helpings of tall tales. Designed as a bed and breakfast, this rustic establishment is decorated in Alaskana and treasures collected from all corners of the world. Year-round outdoor hot tub and wood-burning sauna. 360-degree view on five wooded acres is at 1,100 feet elevation, overlooking everything. Outdoor dogs and cats. Free parking. $85-125.

Accommodations in Alaska BB

The Friendly Lodging Choice
P. O. Box 110624, 99511-0624
(907) 345-4761

This Christian family offers a traditional homestay with privacy in mind. This is a popular accommodation, as families can economize. The suite includes two bedrooms with queen-size beds, a double Hide-a-bed, and private bath. There is also a TV, microwave, and refrigerator. Free parking is provided in the carport near the private entrance. Free tennis and basketball courts are nearby. Hostess, a professional baker, serves heavenly breakfasts. Resident dog. $85.

Accommodations in Alaska BG

The Friendly Lodging Choice
P. O. Box 110624, 99511-0624
(907) 345-4761

Guest rooms are named after bear species in this traditional homestay near both military bases. Two rooms have half-baths, and one room has a three-quarter-bath. Innkeepers have an amazing collection of old Alaskana to enjoy. The family practices a self-sufficient lifestyle and enjoys gathering wild berries, gardening, hunting, fishing, and clamming. Full breakfast including wild game may be served by request. Free parking. $75-80.

Accommodations in Alaska CA

The Friendly Lodging Choice
P. O. Box 110624, 99511-0624
(907) 345-4761

An abundance of summer vegetables and flower gardens enhances this traditional homestay, situated in a quiet neighborhood. A stream borders this oversize property. Two professionally decorated suites, each with a private bath. Each suite has room for four guests, with a queen-size bed and two twin beds. Near health care facilities, the university, and shopping. Easy access to major highway routes. Full breakfast is served with fresh Alaska honey. Free parking. $75-85.

Accommodations in Alaska CE

The Friendly Lodging Choice
P. O. Box 110624, 99511-0624
(907) 345-4761

This traditional homestay is just 100 feet from the shoreline in a quiet downtown neighborhood, a few steps from the popular Coastal Trail. Enjoy sunsets from the deck. Two nicely appointed guest rooms with queen or twin beds share a bath. The cozy suite has a queen bed, private entrance, private bath, and kitchenette. The innkeeper of this 7,500-square-foot home is a professional chef. Gourmet continental breakfast. Free parking. $85-100.

Accommodations in Alaska CG

The Friendly Lodging Choice
P. O. Box 110624, 99511-0624
(907) 345-4761

This modest homestay is near Merrill Field, a popular small-plane airport near downtown Anchorage. Two friendly outdoor German shepherds and their professionally employed hostesses enjoy company and look forward to guest's visit. Their location is also close to health care facilities and the

NOTES: Credit cards accepted: A Master Card; B Visa; C American Express; D Discover Card; E Diner's Club; F Other; 2 Personal Checks accepted; 3 Lunch available; 4 Dinner available; 5 Open all year;

university. The guest room has a double bed and shared bath. Continental breakfast. Free parking. $65.

Accommodations in Alaska CM

The Friendly Lodging Choice
P. O. Box 110624, 99511-0624
(907) 345-4761

Three shy house cats assist in hosting this elegant home filled with quality furnishings. Both guest rooms have private baths. The hostess serves a full breakfast in the formal dining room. This traditional homestay has easy access to all major highways, yet is isolated from traffic noise. Enjoy the unobstructed view of the Chugach Mountains from the sun deck. Free parking. $85-100.

Accommodations in Alaska CR

The Friendly Lodging Choice
P. O. Box 110624, 99511-0624
(907) 345-4761

These hosts enjoy getting acquainted with visitors from around the world in this traditional homestay a few blocks south of major hotels. Three guest rooms with queen, double, and twin beds reflect varied traveling experiences of this professionally employed couple. Flowers abound in the landscaped yard. A popular fitness trail is nearby. Full secretarial services complete with computers, FAX, laser printer, and copier. Continental breakfast. Free parking. $85.

Accommodations in Alaska CW

The Friendly Lodging Choice
P. O. Box 110624, 99511-0624
(907) 345-4761

The innkeepers at this cozy Cape Cod-style home serve homemade jams and jellies with the tasty continental breakfast. This traditional homestay caters to hikers,

cyclists, pilots, rafters, and all types of outdoor adventurers. Three rooms with shared baths. Twin, queen, or king size beds. Situated in an older neighborhood convenient to Merrill Field, Sears Mall, theaters, recreational facilities, the university, and restaurants. Easy freeway access. Free parking. $75.

Accommodations in Alaska FX

The Friendly Lodging Choice
P. O. Box 110624, 99511-0624
(907) 345-4761

One of the prettiest lawns in Anchorage surrounds this traditional homestay near the Chugach Mountains. Your oversize room has a double bed and private bath. Hosts enjoy Alaska's great outdoors and have traveled extensively in Latin America. Continental breakfast includes homemade breads. Resident dogs. Free parking. $75.

Accommodations in Alaska GH

The Friendly Lodging Choice
P. O. Box 110624, 99511-0624
(907) 345-4761

This guest room has a king size bed, private bath, and sauna. The friendly hostess prepares a delicious full breakfast and serves it with a smile. This traditional homestay is a custom redwood home, nestled on 1.5 wooded acres. There is a large yard offering a chance to relax and enjoy the flowers. This quiet established neighborhood is convenient to the airport, downtown, and all the local attractions. Free parking. $100.

Accommodations in Alaska HO

The Friendly Lodging Choice
P. O. Box 110624, 99511-0624
(907) 345-4761

Guests are invited to join the family around the antique pump organ for musical inter-

6 Pets welcome; 8 Children welcome; 9 Social drinking allowed; 10 Tennis available; 11 Swimming available; 12 Golf available; 13 Skiing available; 14 May be booked through travel agents.

ludes at this traditional homestay. All beds are queen-size, one bedroom with a private bath. The delicious Alaskan breakfast may include fresh salmon or many other house specialties. Hungarian and Polish spoken. Free parking. $60-85.

Accommodations in Alaska HS

The Friendly Lodging Choice
P. O. Box 110624, 99511-0624
(907) 345-4761

These pioneer hosts are weekend gold prospectors and invite you to share their modern custom home near the airport. This traditional homestay is out of the flight path, situated on an oversize lot with plenty of lawn and flower gardens to enjoy. Families are welcome. Variety of beds with shared bath, and queen-size bed with private bath and Jacuzzi. Full breakfast. Free parking in garage. $85-125.

Accommodations in Alaska LS

The Friendly Lodging Choice
P. O. Box 110624, 99511-0624
(907) 345-4761

Accommodations on the ground floor of this custom-designed home include a private entrance, laundry facilities, fireplace, TV, VCR, microwave, refrigerator, queen-size beds, shower, bidet, and oversize Jacuzzi. The 14-foot picture windows overlook the Chugach Mountains and 150 feet of private lake frontage. Situated in an exclusive neighborhood near shopping, restaurants, and recreational facilities. Continental breakfast is served to the suite each morning. Resident dog. Free parking. $100.

Accommodations in Alaska MB

The Friendly Lodging Choice
P. O. Box 110624, 99511-0624
(907) 345-4761

A creek meanders through six wooded acres of this 1953 log homestead. Twenty minutes south of Anchorage on a peaceful hillside, this traditional homestay is popular with travelers who appreciate quiet adult atmosphere. Both suites have a private entrance, private bath, and queen-size bed. The upper suite has a kitchenette, romantic wood stove, and queen Hide-a-bed for a party of four. Friendly hostess serves full breakfast. Free parking. $85-100.

Accommodations in Alaska MN

The Friendly Lodging Choice
P. O. Box 110624, 99511-0624
(907) 345-4761

A modern home decorated with three generations of antiques. Gothic stained-glass windows enhance the romantic livingroom, which sometimes serves as a wedding chapel. Two rooms, one with balcony and Jacuzzi. Close to tourist attractions, shopping, and restaurants. Full breakfast served by knowledgeable hostess. Resident dog and cat. Free parking. $85-100.

Accommodations in Alaska PC

The Friendly Lodging Choice
P. O. Box 110624, 99511-0624
(907) 345-4761

These innkeepers have lived in Alaska for 45 years and welcome families. This homestay offers four accommodations, shared bath to private suite with private entry, deck, and laundry and cooking facilities. All have queen-size beds. Convenient to both military bases. Easy access to Fairbanks and Denali Highway. Host provides freshly caught seafood as part of the full breakfast. Resident dog. Free parking. $75-95.

Accommodations in Alaska RH

The Friendly Lodging Choice
P. O. Box 110624, 99511-0624
(907) 345-4761

The Christian hostess is an accomplished seamstress and craftswoman. This homestay is decorated in tasteful and sometimes whimsical antiques, as well as her own clever creations. Hillside location offers a respite from downtown hustle and bustle. Three guest rooms with double and queen-size beds, private or shared bath. Close to wilderness hiking trails. Easy freeway access for guests traveling either direction. Continental breakfast. Outdoor dog. Free parking. $75-95.

Accommodations in Alaska SF

The Friendly Lodging Choice
P. O. Box 110624, 99511-0624
(907) 345-4761

This traditional homestay has one room with shared bath and queen-size bed, and offers a fenced back yard that can accommodate friendly traveling canines. Hostess enjoys many crafts and has added loving touches to the guest room. Situated within walking distance of shopping and dining. Also close to health-care facilities and the university. Convenient to city bus routes. Continental breakfast. Resident dogs. Free parking. $75.

Accommodations in Alaska SH

The Friendly Lodging Choice
P. O. Box 110624, 99511-0624
(907) 345-4761

Bring bathing suits no matter what the season. This homestay offers magnificent views of the Chugach Mountains from the large Jacuzzi spa in the sun room. Enjoy a game of billiards on the antique table. Or just relax by the fireplace and browse through the library. Three guest rooms with twins, doubles, or queen, all with private baths. Resident dog. Free parking. $85-100.

Accommodations in Alaska SL

The Friendly Lodging Choice
P. O. Box 110624, 99511-0624
(907) 345-4761

Easy access to the major airports at this homestay near the Coastal Trail, a paved hiking and biking trail about three miles from downtown. Relax in the spacious livingroom enhanced by a 30-foot-wide stone fireplace that reaches the vaulted ceiling. Three guest rooms with queen-size beds and shared bath. Continental breakfast. Resident cats and dogs. Free parking. $85.

Accommodations in Alaska SN

The Friendly Lodging Choice
P. O. Box 110624, 99511-0624
(907) 345-4761

Fishing and swimming ponds are in walking distance to this homestay with easy access to all freeways. Situated near Anchorage airports, yet out of the flight path, four guest rooms share two baths. One suite with a private bath. Guests are invited to use the family recreation room, complete with microwave, refrigerator, TV, VCR, and wet bar. Full breakfast is served. Eggs Benedict is a house specialty. Resident dog. Free parking. $65-85.

6 Pets welcome; 8 Children welcome; 9 Social drinking allowed; 10 Tennis available; 11 Swimming available; 12 Golf available; 13 Skiing available; 14 May be booked through travel agents.

Accommodations in Alaska SW

The Friendly Lodging Choice
P. O. Box 110624, 99511-0624
(907) 345-4761

This custom home is designed to resemble a swan in flight. Guests will find the history and design fascinating; from the 127 windows to the jade and black walnut fireplace mantle, nothing is left unaddressed. Offering three distinctive guest rooms with private or shared bath, this traditional homestay overlooks downtown. Hot tub, gourmet continental breakfast. Indoor dog. Free parking. $100-195.

Accommodations in Alaska TS

The Friendly Lodging Choice
P. O. Box 110624, 99511-0624
(907) 345-4761

A world away, tucked into treetops on two secluded acres, this hideaway is the top floor of a private home. This traditional homestay can comfortably accommodate a party of six. There's a wood stove, full kitchen, laundry facilities, and private bath. Full breakfast is served in the suite, or on the sun deck overlooking the abundant gardens. Free parking. $125.

Accommodations in Alaska 419

The Friendly Lodging Choice
P. O. Box 110624, 99511-0624
(907) 345-4761

This downtown cottage has a colorful past that reaches back into the 1920s. Your suite includes a mini-kitchen, three-quarter-bath, bedroom and livingroom. Breakfast at this traditional homestay includes nutritional whole foods and good coffee. The hostess is interested in Alaskan wildflowers, therapeutic massage, and natural health. Free parking. $100.

ANCHOR POINT

Accommodations in Alaska OF

The Friendly Lodging Choice
P. O. Box 110624, 99511-0624
(907) 345-4761

This homestay sits on seven wooded acres near the best fishing in the state. Two guest rooms are offered, one with private bath. Each has room for four guests. Christian hostess can provide information about her favorite fishing and beachcombing spots. Wood-burning sauna. Complimentary laundry facilities. Freshly caught crab, scallops, shrimp, halibut, and salmon are for sale. Full breakfast. Resident dog and cat. Free parking. $60-80.

DELTA JUNCTION

Accommodations in Alaska TB

The Friendly Lodging Choice
P. O. Box 110624, 99511-0624
(907) 345-4761

This homestay is midway between Tok and Fairbanks. Wildlife abounds in the black spruce, willow, and birch forest surrounding this modern log home. Two guest rooms are offered; one has shared bath, the other private. Choice of bed sizes. The innkeepers enjoy relaxing around their outdoor fireplace in the evenings. The hostess cooks "heart healthy" full breakfasts and serves them by the wood stove. Outdoor dogs. Free parking. $75-90.

DENALI NATIONAL PARK

Accommodations in Alaska DH

The Friendly Lodging Choice
P. O. Box 110624, 99511-0624
(907) 345-4761

Healy, a community of 500, is situated 12 miles north of Denali Park. This homestay is a unique structure: a four-story geodesic dome on two and one-half wooded acres. This active family of five invites guests to enjoy mountain views from livingroom windows. Two guest rooms with queen beds are available, each with a private bath. Indoor sauna. Continental breakfast features tasty homemade cinnamon rolls. Resident dog. Free parking. $60-80.

EAGLE RIVER

Accommodations in Alaska AW
The Friendly Lodging Choice
P. O. Box 110624, 99511-0624
(907) 345-4761

This lovely log home at a 2,000-foot elevation has an impressive view of mountains, valleys, water, islands, and volcanoes. Just 12 miles north of Anchorage, this homestay has two guest rooms with private baths. Free laundry. Limited German spoken. Well-traveled hosts serve continental breakfast. Resident dog and cat. Free parking. $85.

Accommodations in Alaska CC
The Friendly Lodging Choice
P. O. Box 110624, 99511-0624
(907) 345-4761

Enjoy a soak in the stainless steel hot tub after a day of business or pleasure. This homestay is in an exclusive neighborhood of custom-built homes. The Christian family of six welcomes children. One room with space for four has a queen-size bed, futon, and private bath. Full breakfast including breads made with 65-year-old sourdough starter. Resident dog. Free parking. $85.

Accommodations in Alaska CH
The Friendly Lodging Choice
P. O. Box 110624, 99511-0624
(907) 345-4761

This traditional homestay, just twelve miles north of Anchorage, offers privacy from the host family if preferred. New in 1992, the accommodations include a private bath with an oversize Jacuzzi, a wood stove, kitchen, living and dining room. The hostess, who is fluent in German, serves a lovely full breakfast. This bed and breakfast can comfortably host a party of six. Resident dog. Free parking. $80-125.

Accommodations in Alaska LH
The Friendly Lodging Choice
P. O. Box 110624, 99511-0624
(907) 345-4761

A cozy log lodge with a view overlooking the surrounding countryside. Custom-built with a spectacular native stone fireplace, this traditional homestay offers a choice of two rooms with private or shared bath and a generous full breakfast. The 1.5 acre yard abounds with blooming flowers, which means moose visit often. Grill the catch of the day on the stone barbeque. Resident dog. Free parking. $85-100.

Country Garden Bed and Breakfast
8210 Frank Street, 99518
(907) 344-0636

Country Garden is a small, uniquely warm and friendly bed and breakfast owned and operated by a long-time Alaskan couple. Throughout the house, antiques and hand-stincilled walls mix tastefully with casual country decor. Fresh flowers for the bedrooms are cut daily from flower gardens. The beautifully landscaped yard set in a wooded lot, received rave reviews on the 1990 Anchorage Garden Tour. In the eveningthere is the opportunity for dessert and conversation, then awake the next morning to a delicious homemade full breakfast Alaska-style.

6 Pets welcome; 8 Children welcome; 9 Social drinking allowed; 10 Tennis available; 11 Swimming available; 12 Golf available; 13 Skiing available; 14 May be booked through travel agents.

Hosts: Kay and Jim Heafner
Rooms: 3 (SB) $60-70
Full Breakfast
Credit Cards: None
Notes: 2, 5, 10, 12, 13, 14

Green Bough
Bed and Breakfast

3832 Young Street, 99508
(907) 562-4636

Anchorage's oldest independent bed and breakfast home was opened in 1981. The hosts have developed the art of complementing spacious, smoke-free lodgings with warm hospitality. Slip into freshly ironed sheets at night and awaken to aromas of coffee and cinnamon. Guests represent the world and most walks of life. Freezer space, storage, public transportation, a convenient location, and on-site laundry. Two resident cats.

Hosts: Jerry and Phyllis Jost
Rooms: 5 (2 PB, 3 SB) $45-70
Continental Breakfast
Credit Cards: None
Notes: 2, 5, 8, 10, 11, 12, 13, 14

Wright's Bed and Breakfast

1411 Oxford Drive, 99503
(907) 561-1990

Jack and Marilyn Wright's mid-town Anchorage home is a split level "typical Alaskan home," with two bedrooms available for guests. One room features a queen-size bed, while the other boasts a double bed and both rooms share a bath. There is a sitting area with cable television and a refrigerator for guest use. Also included are full Alaskan breakfasts, airport, train or tour bus pick-up.

Hosts: Jack and Marilyn Wright
Rooms: 2 (SB) $45-55
Full Breakfast
Credit Cards: A, B
Notes: 2, 5, 9, 10, 12, 13

FAIRBANKS

Accommodations in Alaska MD

The Friendly Lodging Choice
P. O. Box 110624, 99511-0624
(907) 345-4761

The first level of this homestay is dedicated to the guest rooms. Three rooms share baths. The central location is convenient to all downtown attractions, shopping, and restaurants. The 20 hours of summer sunshine help keep the yard filled with blooming flowers. Innkeepers are longtime Alaskans with a desire to assist in making their guests' visit special. Continental breakfast. Free parking. $65-80.

Alaska's 7 Gables
Bed and Breakfast

P. O. Box 80488, 99708
(907) 479-0751; FAX (907) 479-ABBY

Historically, Alaska's 7 Gables was a fraternity house within walking distance to the UAF campus, yet near the river and airport. The spacious 10,000-square-foot, Tudor-style home features a floral solarium, antique stained glass in the foyer with an indoor waterfall, cathedral ceilings, a wedding chapel, wine cellar, and rooms with dormers. A gourmet breakfast is served daily. Other amenities include cable TV and phone in each room, laundry facilities, Jacuzzi, bikes, and canoes.

NOTES: Credit cards accepted: A Master Card; B Visa; C American Express; D Discover Card; E Diner's Club; F Other; 2 Personal Checks accepted; 3 Lunch available; 4 Dinner available; 5 Open all year;

Hosts: Paul and Leicha Welton
Rooms: 9 (4 PB; 5 SB) $40-95
Full Breakfast
Credit Cards: A, B, C, D, E
Notes: 2, 5, 8, 9, 11, 13, 14

Hillside Bed and Breakfast

310 Rambling Road, 99712
(907) 457-2664

Authentic Alaskan decor and hospitality in contemporary comfort. Relax and enjoy this quiet hillside location, spacious guest rooms, in-room TV, laundry facilities, and fully equipped private kitchen. Family and extended-stay rates available. Enjoy sharing experiences with the hosts, who have lived several years in the Alaskan bush as well as in Fairbanks. Full sourdough breakfasts feature delicious items such as sourdough pancakes, reindeer sausage, home-ground wheat bread, and lowbush cranberry muffins. Established in 1987.

Hosts: Tim and Debra Vanasse
Rooms: 2 (SB) $45-55
Full Breakfast
Credit Cards: None
Notes: 2, 5, 6, 8, 14

GAKONA

Accommodations in Alaska BC

The Friendly Lodging Choice
P. O. Box 110624, 99511-0624
(907) 345-4761

Enjoy a view of the Wrangell Mountains from ten acres of natural wilderness. This traditional homestay is twelve miles from Glenallen, a major crossroad in Alaska's highway system. A full breakfast is served in this two story saltbox by the friendly host who will pester with his incessant airplane banter. Walking distance to fishing spots and the Alyeska Pipeline. Two rooms share a bath. German spoken. Free parking. Freezer available. $75.

GUSTAVUS

Glacier Bay Country Inn

P. O. Box 5, 99826
(907) 697-2288; FAX (907) 697-2289
Winter: (801) 673-8480; FAX (801) 673-8481

Peaceful storybook accommodations away from the crowds in a wilderness setting. Cozy comforters, warm flannel sheets. Superb dining features local seafood, garden-fresh produce, home-baked breads, spectacular desserts. Enjoy fishing, whale watching, sightseeing, hiking, bird watching, photography. Rates include three meals, airport transfers, and use of bicycles. Glacier Bay boat/plane tours.

Hosts: Al and Annie Unrein
Rooms: 9 (8 PB; 1 SB) $140-218 (American Plan)
Full Breakfast, Lunch, Dinner
Credit Cards: None
Notes: 2, 3, 4, 8, 9, 14

Glacier Bay Country Inn

A Puffin's Bed and Breakfast

Box 3-NS, 99826
(907) 697-2260; FAX (907) 697-2258

A cozy Alaskan cabin, nestled among tall spruce and hemlock trees on our five-acre homestead carpeted in soft moss, wildflowers and berries. Bicycles available. Come to the new picturesque central lodge for breakfast, socializing and watching new video tapes of Gustavus, Glacier Bay and

6 Pets welcome; 8 Children welcome; 9 Social drinking allowed; 10 Tennis available; 11 Swimming available; 12 Golf available; 13 Skiing available; 14 May be booked through travel agents.

Icy Strait. Full travel services for the area include reservations for Alaska Marine Highway. Tour boats, charters for fishing, kayaking, flightseeing and kayak rentals.

Hosts: Chuck and Sandy Schroth
Rooms: 5 (PB) $60-75
Full Breakfast
Credit Cards: A, B
Notes: 2, 5, 6, 8, 14

HATCHER PASS

Accommodations in Alaska HP
The Friendly Lodging Choice
P. O. Box 110624, 99511-0624
(907) 345-4761

These log cabins are newly constructed, warm, and cozy. They have individual heat and electricity and are decorated with artifacts reminiscent of yesteryear, right down to the functional water pitchers and basins. Each of the three cabins has indoor chemical toilets. Running water for showers at main home. Outdoor summer hot tub. Full breakfast. Resident dog. Free parking. $55-70.

HEALY

Accommodations in Alaska HH
The Friendly Lodging Choice
P. O. Box 110624, 99511-0624
(907) 345-4761

Situated in Healy, a community twelve miles north of Denali's entrance, is a unique bed and breakfast offering. Select a traditional homestay with innkeepers or choose one of their new cabins on a nearby ridge. These units are self-contained with full utilities and kitchens stocked and equipped to prepare breakfast at leisure. Free parking. Fully licensed. $90-180.

HOMER

Accommodations in Alaska BR
The Friendly Lodging Choice
P. O. Box 110624, Anchorage, 99511-0624
(907) 345-4761

Year-round travelers have come to rely on this downtown homestay for good value and friendly hospitality. An outdoor hot tub was recently added for the enjoyment of guests. Five guest rooms with a variety of sleeping arrangements share two baths in this log home. A full breakfast is served in the spacious kitchen and may feature fresh seafood. Free parking. $75-85.

Accommodations in Alaska RB
The Friendly Lodging Choice
P. O. Box 110624, 99511-0624
(907) 345-4761

Two acres of tall spruce surround this three-story cedar home, 15 minutes from downtown. Observation windows span 36 feet for Kachemak Bay views. This inn offers two suites with color TV, phone, and private baths. Ground-floor suite has wood stove and kitchenette. Third-story guest room offers a private balcony and king-size bed. Continental breakfast features homemade breads. Resident dog. Free parking. $75-100.

JUNEAU

Dawson's Bed and Breakfast
1941 Glacier Highway, 99801
(907) 586-9708

Comfortable, modern home on the bus line located two miles from downtown. Full breakfast, laundry facilities, customer parking and courtesy pick-up available from 7 A.M. until 10 P.M. with a stay of two days or longer. Beautiful view, open year-round.

NOTES: Credit cards accepted: A Master Card; B Visa; C American Express; D Discover Card; E Diner's Club; F Other; 2 Personal Checks accepted; 3 Lunch available; 4 Dinner available; 5 Open all year;

Hosts: Velma and Dave Dawson
Rooms: 5 (3 PB; 2 SB) $50-75
Full Breakfast
Credit Cards: A, B
Notes: 2, 5, 9, 14

The Lost Chord

2200 Fritz Cove Road, 99801
(907) 789-7296

The hosts' music business has expanded to become a homey bed and breakfast on an exquisite private beach. Breakfast is with the proprietors, who have been in Alaska since 1946. Situated in the country 12 miles from Juneau; a car is suggested.

Hosts: Jesse and Ellen Jones
Rooms: 4 (1 PB; 3 SB) $35-65
Full Breakfast
Credit Cards: None
Notes: 2, 5, 6 (by arrangement), 8, 9, 10, 11, 12, 13, 14

Pearson's Pond Luxury Bed and Breakfast

4541 Sawa Circle, 99801
(907) 789-3772

Alaskan luxury invites you to watch wild mallards landing on a glacial pond as you relax in a steaming spa tucked in a forest just steps from your deck. Deluxe suites with all amenities, including private entries, phones, VCR, stereo, and extra space beckon you to enjoy a long, leisurely stay. Barbeque, rowboat, bikes, freezer, wildlife, and majestic views of Mendenhall Glacier, and close to airport, ferry, shopping, and trails. Self-serve breakfast provided in adjoining kitchenette. Free travel/tour arrangements. Three diamond award.

Hosts: Steve and Diane Pearson
Rooms: 3 (1 suite PB; 2 SB) $79-149
Full/Self-serve Breakfast
Credit Cards: A, B, E, F
Notes: 2, 5, 8 (over 3), 9, 13, 14

MATANUSKA

Yukon Don's Bed and Breakfast Inn

HC31 5086, 99654
(907) 376-7472

This extraordinary Alaskan inn has a 270-degree view of the surrounding mountains and upper Knik arm. The five rooms each have a specific decor theme such as Hunting Room, Fishing Room, Iditarod Room. In addition, there is a 900-square foot guest lounge, complete with 25 years of collectible Alaskana. Selected as one of the top 50 inns in America in 1991 by *Inn Times*.

Hosts: Art and Diane Mongeau
Rooms: 5 (1 PB; 4 SB) $60-80
Continental Breakfast
Credit Cards: None
Notes: 2, 5, 8, 9, 12, 13, 14

MCGRATH

Accommodations in Alaska FO

The Friendly Lodging Choice
P. O. Box 110624, 99511-0624
(907) 345-4761

Depending on the season, complimentary pickup at the airstrip may be by truck, 3- or 4-wheeler, or dog sled! Situated on the Iditarod Trail, this unique lodging experience is a small cabin right on the Kuskokwim River. The innkeepers live next door. Double bed, propane stove. Running water for laundry, showers across the street. Full breakfast. Outdoor dogs. $75.

SEWARD

Swiss Chalet Bed and Breakfast

P. O. Box 1734, 99664
(907) 224-3939

6 Pets welcome; 8 Children welcome; 9 Social drinking allowed; 10 Tennis available; 11 Swimming available; 12 Golf available; 13 Skiing available; 14 May be booked through travel agents.

Pioneer Alaskans offer gracious hospitality catering to adults only. Shared or private baths. Situated a block off the Seward Highway, it is near the road to Seward's spectacular Exit Glacier and a short ride to the small boat harbor in magnificent Resurrection Bay where tours and charters originate.

Host: Charlotte Freeman-Jones
Rooms: 4 (2 PB; 2 SB) $50-75
Continental Breakfast
Credit Cards: A, B
Notes: 2, 9, 14

The White House Bed and Breakfast

P. O. Box 1157, 99664
(907) 224-3614

Nestled in a mountain panorama. The home's intrigue is country charm—quilts and hand-crafts abound. Breakfast is self-serve buffet in guest kitchen. Cable TV in guest common area. Attractions close by: Resurrection Bay/Kenai Fjords National Park, historical Iditarod Trail (cross-country skiing or dog mushing), Exit Glacier.

Hosts: Tom and Annette Reese
Rooms: 5 (3 PB; 2 SB) $51-77
Continental Breakfast
Credit Cards: A, B
Notes: 2, 5, 8, 9, 13, 14

SOLDOTNA

Accommodations in Alaska LV

The Friendly Lodging Choice
P. O. Box 110624, 99511-0624
(907) 345-4761

This spacious log home is on a lake near the heart of the Kenai Peninsula. The full breakfast includes homemade cinnamon buns, and upon request breakfast may include wild game. This traditional bed and breakfast is furnished with many trophies won by the host. Sauna and freezer space for registered guests. Three rooms. The dormitory is popular with local fisherman. Indoor cats and dogs. Free parking. $75-100.

STERLING

Accommodations in Alaska SR

The Friendly Lodging Choice
P. O. Box 110624, 99511-0624
(907) 345-4761

A real Alaskan log home close to the Kenai National Wildlife Refuge and popular Kenai River. On 15 acres with a nice view of the Chugach Mountains, this homestay offers five guest rooms with twins or doubles, and shared baths. One room has a king-size bed with a private bath. There is a place to clean the day's catch and freeze a few. Full breakfast is served. No alcohol. Free parking. $65-80.

TALKEETNA

Accommodations in Alaska BA

The Friendly Lodging Choice
P. O. Box 110624, 99511-0624
(907) 345-4761

Three miles from beautiful downtown Talkeetna is this brand new log home with stone fireplace. A breathtaking view of Mount McKinley, which is just a few minutes away. This homestay offers three guest rooms on the upper level with rustic open log-beam ceilings throughout. Two shared baths. Innkeepers are eager to share the beauty of Alaska with guests. Continental breakfast. Free parking. $75.

TOK

Accommodations in Alaska ST

The Friendly Lodging Choice
P. O. Box 110624, 99511-0624
(907) 345-4761

Rough edges on this rustic setting fool travelers. Log buildings are surrounded by barrels and buckets of colorful blooming plants. A full bath is shared by two guest

NOTES: Credit cards accepted: A Master Card; B Visa; C American Express; D Discover Card; E Diner's Club; F Other; 2 Personal Checks accepted; 3 Lunch available; 4 Dinner available; 5 Open all year;

rooms with queen- and king-size beds. The guest cabin is a non-threatening "wilderness experience." Breakfasts are home-cooked and delicious. The innkeeper of this unique homestay also boards horses. Resident dog. Free parking. $55-85.

VALDEZ

Accommodations in Alaska BZ

The Friendly Lodging Choice
P. O. Box 110624, 99511-0624
(907) 345-4761

One of the best breakfasts in town is elegantly served at this homestay near downtown and the ferry terminal. The hosts' attend to every need and serve memorable meals. Three rooms with shared baths. Near indoor pool, tennis, hiking, and shopping. Resident dog. Free parking. $75-95.

WASILLA

Accommodations in Alaska CL

The Friendly Lodging Choice
P. O. Box 110624, 99511-0624
(907) 345-4761

This active family includes the host, combination bread baker/chief pilot at this home-stay and sightseeing operation. Floatplanes are docked at the front door on a quiet canal of Lake Wasilla. Two guest rooms share a bath. Two acres provide many bird watching opportunities. Full breakfast includes freshly baked bread. Resident dogs and cats. Free parking. $65.

6 Pets welcome; 8 Children welcome; 9 Social drinking allowed; 10 Tennis available; 11 Swimming available; 12 Golf available; 13 Skiing available; 14 May be booked through travel agents.

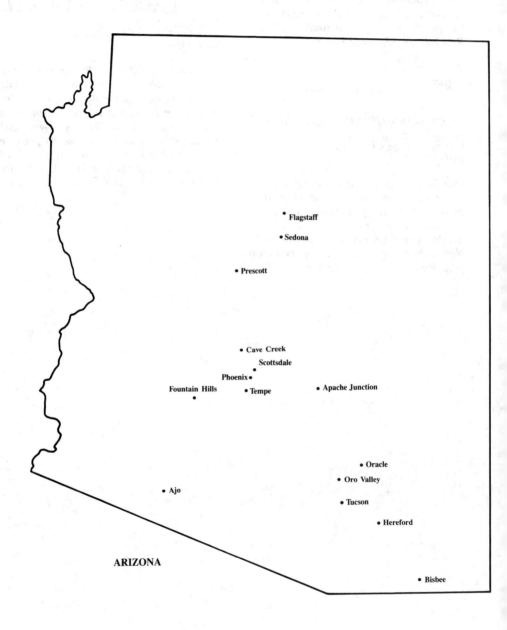

Flagstaff

Sedona

Prescott

Cave Creek

Scottsdale

Phoenix

Fountain Hills

Tempe

Apache Junction

Oracle

Oro Valley

Ajo

Tucson

Hereford

ARIZONA

Bisbee

Arizona

AJO

Bed and Breakfast Scottsdale and the West 104

P. O. Box 3999, Prescott, 86302-3999
(602) 776-1102

Enjoy this 1925 mining corporation executive home near Organ Pipe Cactus National Monument, just 50 minutes from Mexico. Three guest rooms with private baths. Full breakfast. $59-69 plus tax.

APACHE JUNCTION

Bed and Breakfast Scottsdale and the West 116

P. O. Box 3999, Prescott, 86302-3999
(602) 776-1102

This small bed and breakfast features two guest rooms, with a microwave oven and refrigerator in each. Next to Superstition Mountains Wilderness Area, it is an ideal place for enjoying desert flora and fauna. $71 plus tax (add $10 for one night stay).

BISBEE

The Greenway House

401 Cole Avenue, 85603
(602) 432-7170; (800) 253-3325

Craftsman-style mansion built in 1906 and it's carriage house contain eight guest rooms furnished with antiques. All feature private baths and kitchenettes, and are stocked with provisions and refreshments for a continental breakfast. Homebaked blueberry muffins are delivered to the door in the morning. Game-room with pool table, patio with a barbecue, air conditioning and other amenities make this a unique stop. AAA, Mobil approved.

Hosts: Dr. George S. Knox and Joy O'Clock
Rooms: 8 (PB) $75-125
Continental Breakfast
Credit Cards: A, B
Notes: 2, 5, 8 (in carriage house suites), 9, 10, 12

The Schoolhouse Inn

818 Tombstone Canyon, P. O. Box 32, 85603
(602) 432-2996; (800) 537-4333

An old schoolhouse built in 1918 and converted into lovely large rooms and suites with 12-foot ceilings and private baths. Situated high up Tombstone Canyon, the 5,600 foot elevation provides spectacular scenery, clean air, and a relaxing retreat. A full breakfast is served on the shaded patio or in a spacious family room. The inn is close to mine tours, art galleries, antique shops, hiking, bird-watching, and much more.

The Schoolhouse Inn

NOTES: Credit cards accepted: A Master Card; B Visa; C American Express; D Discover Card; E Diner's Club; F Other; 2 Personal Checks accepted; 3 Lunch available; 4 Dinner available; 5 Open all year; 6 Pets welcome; 8 Children welcome; 9 Social drinking allowed; 10 Tennis available; 11 Swimming available; 12 Golf available; 13 Skiing available; 14 May be booked through travel agents.

Hosts: Marc and Shirl Negus
Rooms: 9 (PB) $40-65
Full Breakfast
Credit Cards: A, B , C
Notes: 2, 5, 12

Arizona Mountain Inn

CAVE CREEK

Bed and Breakfast Scottsdale and the West 072

Box 3999, Prescott, 86302-3999
(602) 776-1102

Stay on ten acres of lush desert with cactus and trees, and hike to old Indian sites. This bed and breakfast has a queen bed and private bath. Continental breakfast is served; Minimum stay is two nights. $50.

Park Place Bed and Breakfast

Old Pueblo Homestays
P. O. Box 13603, Tucson, 85732
(800) 333-9RSO

No visit to Arizona is complete without seeing the historical old mining town of Bisbee, some 25 miles from Tombstone. Cool in the summer and far enough south to have mild winters. Park Place is a 1920-vintage, well-cared for, two-story Mediterranean-style home with spacious bedrooms, balconies, terraces, library, and sun room.

Two guest rooms have queen beds and adjoining baths. Two other bedrooms share hall bathroom. Minimum stay is two nights. $40-60.

FLAGSTAFF

Arizona Mountain Inn

685 Lake Mary Road, 86001
(602) 774-8959

The Old English Tudor-style inn and cottages are situated about three miles from Flagstaff. There are 13 wooded acres surrounded by national forest. The rooms are decorated in antiques, crystal, and lace in a beautiful mix of European charm and classic southwestern elegance.

Hosts: The Wanek family
Rooms: 5 (1 PB; 4 SB) $70-100
Full Breakfast
Credit Cards: A, B, D
Notes: 2, 5, 9, 12, 13

Bed and Breakfast Scottsdale and the West 107

Box 3999, Prescott, 86302-3999
(602) 776-1102

Situated in quiet neighborhood backing onto the forest. Accommodations include bedroom, family room, kitchenette, and private bath. Continental breakfast is served, and spa is available. $75.

Bed and Breakfast Scottsdale and the West 113

Box 3999, Prescott, 86302-3999
(602) 776-1102

Three private cottages, each with two bedrooms, kitchen, bath, livingroom, wood burning stove, washer/dryer, cable TV, and bicycles. Continental breakfast is provided. $80; $100 for three or more.

NOTES: Credit cards accepted: A Master Card; B Visa; C American Express; D Discover Card; E Diner's Club; F Other; 2 Personal Checks accepted; 3 Lunch available; 4 Dinner available; 5 Open all year;

FOUNTAIN HILLS

Bed and Breakfast Scottsdale and the West 070

Box 3999, Prescott, 86302-3999
(602) 776-1102

Enjoy this luxurious 6,500-square-foot Spanish contemporary home with lush tropical courtyard, gazebo, and 40-foot pool. Three magnificent levels and a tennis court. Full breakfast; private bath. Fireplace. $110.

HEREFORD

Ramsey Canyon Inn

31 Ramsey Canyon Road, 85615
(602) 378-3010

Capture the romantic spirit of country living with a warmth and graciousness that is traditionally Arizona. Situated in the Huachuca Mountains at an elevation of 5,400 feet, Ramsey Canyon is truly a hummingbird haven with fifteen recorded species. The inn is on a winding mountain stream and surrounded by sycamore, maple, juniper, oak, and pine trees. Wildlife abounds, and the average summer temperature is 75 degrees. Discover the rich history of Cochise County.

Ramsey Canyon Inn

Hosts: Ronald and Shirlene De Santis
Rooms: 6 (PB) $75-105
Cottages: 2 (PB)
Full Gourmet Breakfast
Credit Cards: None
Notes: 2, 5, 8 (over 12), 10, 11, 12 (all nearby)

ORACLE

Villa Cardinale

Old Pueblo Homestays
P. O. Box 13603, Tucson, 85732
(800) 333-9RSO

A Spanish hideaway with red tile roofs and courtyard with fountain. Just 35 minutes from Tucson but a world away from the city's fast pace. Catalina Mountain country with spectacular views and clear, starry nights. Spacious rooms, private entrance, fireplace, baths. A full country breakfast is included. Minimum stay is two nights. Children over 16. $55.

ORO VALLEY

Desert Adventure

Old Pueblo Homestays
P. O. Box 13603, Tucson, 85732
(800) 333-9RSO

Large adobe ranch-style home on one acre in northwest foothills. Fenced yard with pool and mountain views. Two large bedrooms with private bath. Tiled and carpeted. Guest sitting room with fireplace and TV. Kitchen privileges on the weekdays with breakfast supplies provided. Resident cat. Minimum stay is two nights. Children welcome. $45.

PAGE

Bed and Breakfast Scottsdale and the West 112

Box 3999, Prescott, 86302-3999
(602) 776-1102

---

6 Pets welcome; 8 Children welcome; 9 Social drinking allowed; 10 Tennis available; 11 Swimming available; 12 Golf available; 13 Skiing available; 14 May be booked through travel agents.

This inn offers cliffside views of Lake Powell and canyonlands. On the quiet edge of town, this bed and breakfast has a shared bath, pool, and Jacuzzi. Full breakfast is provided. Seven miles to Wahweap Marina. $60 plus tax.

PHOENIX

Bed and Breakfast Scottsdale and the West 082
Box 3999, Prescott, 86302-3999
(602) 776-1102

Near West Thunderbird and 35th Avenue, this bed and breakfast is a short drive from Metro Center and various shopping malls. Enjoy a leisurely day by the pool, or get walking exercise on one of the nearby golf courses. Pet in residence. $45.

Bed and Breakfast Scottsdale and the West 105
Box 3999, Prescott, 86302-3999
(602) 776-1102

This is a popular home with bed and breakfast travelers. Featured in *Arizona Highways Magazine* and highlighted by antiques and glass, it has a spa and private bath. Full breakfast. Near golf and tennis. $55; $5 surcharge for one-night stays.

Westways Private Resort Inn
Valley of the Sun, Box 41624, 85080
(602) 582-3868

In northwest Phoenix, Westways is a jewel situated among executive estate homes, surrounded by mountain preserve, convenient to I-17, Thunderbird Park, and Arrowhead Country Club. Arizona room with large-screen TV, VCR, games, library, and fireplace; guest wet bar/refrigerator, and microwave available. Radio, TV, and sitting area in each deluxe queen-size bed guest room; diving pool, whirlpool, courtyard for guest use. Use of country club facilities. Casual western comfort with a touch of class where guests preserve their privacy. Rated as one of the fifty best inns in America. Other attractions include a pool, hot tub, bicycles, country club privileges, golf, tennis and a health club. Reservations necessary.

Host: Darrell Trapp
Rooms: 6 (PB) $49-122; special rates available
Full Breakfast
Credit Cards: A, B, C
Notes: 2, 3, 4, 5, 9, 10, 11, 12, 14

PRESCOTT

Bed and Breakfast Scottsdale and the West 083
Box 3999, 86302-3999
(602) 776-1102

Rural luxury with a 25-acre lot. Decks, spa, and volleyball available. Full breakfast is provided. Private baths. $55-65; $85 suites.

Bed and Breakfast Scottsdale and the West 084
Box 3999, 86302-3999
(602) 776-1102

Magnificently restored historic register home on Nob Hill near Courthouse Plaza and Whiskey Row. Full breakfast. $85-110.

Bed and Breakfast Scottsdale and the West 087
Box 3999, 86302-3999
(602) 776-1102

This restored historic home is centrally situated to downtown and the Center House Plaza. Features double and twin beds, with golf courses nearby. $35-45.

NOTES: Credit cards accepted: A Master Card; B Visa; C American Express; D Discover Card; E Diner's Club; F Other; 2 Personal Checks accepted; 3 Lunch available; 4 Dinner available; 5 Open all year;

SCOTTSDALE

Bed and Breakfast Scottsdale and the West 060

Box 3999, Prescott, 86302-3999
(602) 776-1102

This charming guest house is near Camelback Corridor and golf club. Hosts raise Arabians and Beagles. Private baths; continental breakfast; pool. $50.

Bed and Breakfast Scottsdale and the West 066

Box 3999, Prescott, 86302-3999
(602) 776-1102

A three-year old contemporary-style home just off Shea Boulevard is the perfect spot for a refreshing getaway weekend or longer. Features king and twin beds, a pool, and is close to Wright's Taliesin and the Mayo Clinic West. $55-75.

Bed and Breakfast Scottsdale and the West 095

Box 3999, Prescott, 86302-3999
(602) 776-1102

This charming bed and breakfast is near Scottsdale Fashion Square and the Phoenician Golf Club. Large four-poster canopy beds and French doors to the pool make it special. Private bath; continental breakfast. $75, seasonal; $10 surcharge for one-night stays.

Bed and Breakfast Scottsdale and the West 110

Box 3999, Prescott, 86302-3999
(602) 776-1102

This guest house is a great value. Near Scottsdale and Lincoln, walk to the Borgata, Hilton Village, and new Crazy Gold center. Private bath; continental breakfast; pool. Near golf and tennis. $75; $10 surcharge for one-night stays.

Valley O' The Sun Bed and Breakfast

P. O. Box 2214, 85252
(602) 941-1281

Within walking distance of Arizona State University, this charming homes offers its guests a variety of activities. Golfers will enjoy two courses nearby, and a driving range to practice on before taking to the links. Swimmers will delight in Big Surf, while shoppers will be enchanted with a weekend of browsing at Park and Swap Flea Market. The home itself is ranch-style, with two patios from which guests can enjoy a beautiful view of the Papago Buttes. Airport pickup and delivery is available.

Host: Kathleen Curtis
Rooms: 2 (SB) $35
Full and Continental Breakfast
Credit Cards: None
Notes: 5, 9, 10, 11, 12, 14

SEDONA

Bed and Breakfast at Saddle Rock Ranch

255 Rock Ridge Drive, 86336
(602) 282-7640

History, romance, antiques, and elegance centrally situated historic landmark estate with panoramic vistas. Romantic rooms feature private baths, canopied beds, field-stone fireplaces, and superb views. Hillside grounds feature a sparkling pool with Jacuzzi spa, view decks, flower gardens, and wildlife. Guest refrigerator, micro-wave, plenty of ice, and a barbecue available. The warm, friendly hosts provide a scrumptious breakfast and afternoon

6 Pets welcome; 8 Children welcome; 9 Social drinking allowed; 10 Tennis available; 11 Swimming available; 12 Golf available; 13 Skiing available; 14 May be booked through travel agents.

snacks. Hiking, horseback riding, fishing, tennis, and golf nearby. Five minutes to shops, galleries, and restaurants.

Hosts: D. F. Bruno and F. G. Bruno
Rooms: 3 (PB) $95-125
Full Breakfast
Credit Cards: None
Notes: 2, 5, 9, 10, 11, 12, 13

Bed and Breakfast Scottsdale and the West 097

Box 3999, Prescott, 86302-3999
(602) 776-1102

This large home offers a choice of four separate rooms or a private suite. A large buffet breakfast is served. $68-$98 seasonal, plus tax; $5 surcharge for one-night stays.

Country Elegance Bed and Breakfast

P. O. Box 1257, 86336
(602) 634-4470

Country Elegance Bed and Breakfast offers French ambience in a beautiful, secluded country setting. Ideally situated between majestic Sedona and historic Jerome, the inn's elegant decor is the work of designer innkeeper, Rita Sydelle. It features well-appointed rooms with mountain views that allow guests to retreat to the "understated luxury and tranquility" of country life. A private library and the Arizona Room offer relaxation after a day of touring. Country Elegance is also a mini-farm with organic vegetable gardens, and fruit and nut trees. A full gourmet country breakfast is served that can include crepes, stuffed French toast, quiche, blintzes, garden egg dishes, breads and muffins, and triple chocolate brownies. AAA approved.

Hosts: Rita Sydelle
Rooms: 3 (2 PB; 1 SB) $65-85
Full Breakfast
Credit Cards: F (travelers checks, cash)
Notes: 2, 5, 11, 12

The Cozy Cactus

80 Canyon Circle Drive, 86336-8673
(602) 284-0082

Cozy Cactus Bed and Breakfast is situated at the foot of Castle Rock between Sedona's red rock cliffs and Wild Horse Mesa. Cozy Cactus is a ranch-style home comfortably furnished with family heirlooms and theatrical memorabilia. Each room has a private bath, and each pair of bedrooms shares a sitting room with a fireplace. Breakfasts are served in the great room. Guests have direct access into Coconino National Forest for hiking, bird-watching, and photography.

Hosts: Bob and Lynne Gillman
Rooms: 4 (PB) $90
Full Breakfast
Credit Cards: A, B
Notes: 2, 5, 8 (over 6), 9, 10, 12, 13, 14

The Graham Bed and Breakfast Inn

150 Canyon Circle Drive, 86336
(602) 284-1425

The Graham Bed and Breakfast Inn was built specifically as an inn, and is situated with views of the red rock formations that have made Sedona famous. There are six unique guest rooms, all with private balconies and baths, some with Jacuzzi and fireplace. Sculptures and paintings by local artists add to the beauty of the inn. The beautifully landscaped grounds with pool, spa, and fountain invite guests to enjoy the outdoors. Guests experience comfortable elegance and memorable breakfasts.

Hosts: Carol and Roger Redenbaugh
Rooms: 6 (PB) $98-190
Full Breakfast
Minimum stay weekends: 2 nights; Holidays 2-3 nights
Credit Cards: A, B
Notes: 2, 5, 8, 9, 10, 11, 12, 14

TEMPE

Mi Casa Su Casa Reservation Service

P. O. Box 950, 85250-0950
(602) 990-0682; (800) 456-0682

More than 160 approved, friendly homestays, guest cottages, ranches, and inns in Arizona, Utah, Nevada and New Mexico. Some of the listings are sistuated in Ajo, Apache Junction, Bisbee, Cave Creek, Clarksdale, Dragoon, Flagstaff, Page, Paradise Valley, Patagonia, Payson, Phoenix, Pinetop, Prescott, Scottsdale, Sedona, Tempe, Tubac, Tucson, Wickenburg and Yuma in Arizona; Albuquerque, Algodones, Chimaye, Las Cruces, Ramah, Santa Fe, and Taos in New Mexico; Moab, Monroe, Monticello, Salt Lake City, Springsdale, St. George, and Tropic in Utah; and Las Vegas, Nevada.

Coordinator: Ruth Young
Rooms: 400 (350 PB; 50 SB) $35-150
Full Breakfast (usually); Continental Breakfast (occasionally)
Credit Cards: None
Notes: 5, 8, 10, 11, 12, 13, 14

TUCSON

Adobe House

Old Pueblo Homestays
P. O. Box 13603, 85732
(800) 333-9RSO

This home is in the foothills between the Santa Catalina Mountains and midtown Tucson. Private bath and sitting room with TV and radio. Outside is a covered porch complete with swing and a patio. Beautiful mountain views can be enjoyed during the day. Continental breakfast served outside, weather permitting, and includes freshly squeezed juice. Minimum stay is two nights. No children. $60.

Bed and Breakfast Scottsdale and the West 073
Box 3999, Prescott, 86302-3999
(602) 776-1102

Luxury Santa Fe adobe inn built in 1929. Five custom-designed suites are available. Gourmet breakfast and afternoon tea are served. Private bath. Close to golf and tennis. $90-110, plus tax. Also, a $10 surcharge for one-night stays.

Bed and Breakfast Scottsdale and the West 088
Box 3999, Prescott, 86302-3999
(602) 776-1102

Find gracious Southwest living in this restored 1870s home in El Presidio historic district. There is a garden courtyard with fountains. Private bath; continental breakfast. $85-95, plus tax; $10 surcharge for one-night stays.

Bed and Breakfast Scottsdale and the West 089
Box 3999, Prescott, 86302-3999
(602) 776-1102

Private home in residential northeast Tucson. Featuring a garden patio and private entrance. Private bath; continental breakfast. $50; $5 surcharge for one-night stays.

6 Pets welcome; 8 Children welcome; 9 Social drinking allowed; 10 Tennis available; 11 Swimming available; 12 Golf available; 13 Skiing available; 14 May be booked through travel agents.

Bed and Breakfast Scottsdale and the West 102

Box 3999, Prescott, 86302-3999
(602) 776-1102

There are several rooms to choose from in this spacious hacienda-style home with central courtyard. Near the University of Arizona and three miles northeast of the City Center. Private bath; continental breakfast; pool. Close to golf and tennis. $75; $5 surcharge for one-night stays.

Bed and Breakfast Scottsdale and the West 114

Box 3999, Prescott, 86302-3999
(602) 776-1102

Choose from accommodations in an adobe-style hacienda built in the 1870s, or one with a Japanese hot tub. Convenient for downtown walking and shopping. Full breakfast. $70-120, plus tax; $10 surcharge for one-night stays.

Casa Alegre Bed and Breakfast Inn

316 East Speedway, 85705
(602) 628-1800

This distinguished 1915 home between the University of Arizona and downtown Tucson has four uniquely decorated guest rooms with private baths. A scrumptuous breakfast is served in the formal dining room or poolside on the serene patio. Casa Alegre allows easy access to Tucson's many historic, cultural, and recreational attractions, state and national parks, as well as great shopping and fantastic eateries.

Host: Phyllis Florek
Rooms: 4 (PB) $70-80
Full Breakfast
Credit Cards: A, B
Notes: 2, 5, 9, 10, 11, 12, 14

Casa Tierra Adobe Bed and Breakfast Inn

11155 West Calle Pima, 85743
(602) 578-3058

Casa Tierra is on five acres of beautiful Sonoran desert thirty minutes west of Tucson. This secluded area has hundreds of saguaro cactus, spectacular mountain views, and brilliant sunsets. The rustic adobe house features entryways with vaulted brick ceilings, an interior arched courtyard, Mexican furnishings, and a hot tub overlooking the desert. Great hiking and birding. Near Desert Museum, Saguaro National Monument, and Old Tucson.

Hosts: Karen and Lyle Hymer-Thompson
Rooms: 3 (PB) $65-75
Full Breakfast
Credit Cards: None
Notes: 2, 8, 9, 14

Cloud House

Old Pueblo Homestays
P. O. Box 13603, 85732
(800) 333-9RSO

This inn is a southwestern Santa Fe design home, nestled in the Catalina Foothills above the city. A blend of southwestern decor tastefully appoints each room. Two of the rooms feature queen-size beds, and one has a double bed. The TV or VCR can be enjoyed in the family room, while the stereo can be enjoyed by the fireplace in the livingroom. $85-95.

The Desert Yankee

Old Pueblo Homestays
P. O. Box 13603, 85732
(800) 333-9RSO

Family residence is in a quiet neighborhood. Five rooms, all with private baths, offer a variety of bed sizes. Lovely courtyard, great room, and pool available. Continental breakfast served in the dining

NOTES: Credit cards accepted: A Master Card; B Visa; C American Express; D Discover Card; E Diner's Club; F Other; 2 Personal Checks accepted; 3 Lunch available; 4 Dinner available; 5 Open all year;

room or courtyard. Withing walking distance of the university. Pets are allowed, as there are two cats in residence. Children are $10 extra. $75-85.

Double K Ranch

Old Pueblo Homestays
P. O. Box 13603, 85732
(800) 333-9RSO

Bird watcher's paradise! Private guest facility with Ben Franklin stove, private shower, and patio. Color TV, radio, tape player, phone, western books, and games. Jacuzzi and pool available. Experience splendid bird watching, explore ancient Hohokam sites on private trail, or venture off on nearby national forest trails. The ranch is home to many animals. Tennis is five minutes away, and bicycles are loaned to guests. Children welcome. $55.

El Presidio
Bed and Breakfast Inn

297 North Main Street, 85701
(602) 623-6151

A Victorian adobe, this inn is a splendid example of American-Territorial style and is listed on the National Register of Historic Places. Close to downtown and within walking distance of the best restaurants, museums, and shopping. Guests enjoy true southwestern charm in spacious suites, two with kitchens that open onto large courtyards and gardens, fountains, and lush floral displays. A tranquil oasis with the ambiance of Old Mexico. Three-star rating in the Mobile Travel Guide, 1991, 1992.

Host: Patti Toci
Rooms: 4 (PB) $65-105
Full Breakfast
Credit Cards: None
Notes: 2, 5, 9, 10, 11, 12, 13, 14

Ford's Bed and Breakfast

Old Pueblo Homestays
P. O. Box 13603, 85732
(800) 333-9RSO

A warm welcome awaits at this air-conditioned home situated in a residential cul-de-sac on Tucson's northeastern side. Guests enjoy a bird's-eye view of the mountains from their own private patio. Suite consists of two bedrooms, small sitting room with TV, refrigerator, private bath, and separate entrance. Expanded continental breakfast served. Visit Saguaro Monument East, Sabino Canyon, Colossal Cave, and scenic drives. Minimum stay is two nights. Children over 12. $50.

Fort Escalante

Old Pueblo Homestays
P. O. Box 13603, 85732
(800) 333-9RSO

A mile from Sahuaro National Monument, this French Chateau-styled home offers you a breathtaking, unobstructed view of the beautiful Sonoran Desert. Guest quarters feature a furnished livingroom with a TV, satellite, VCR, radio and phone, full bath, separate bedroom with a double bed, and a sofa that will turn into a king-size bed or two twin beds. Also available in the main house is a bedroom decorated in blue with a king-size bed. Children over 12. $45-55.

Gable House

Old Pueblo Homestays
P. O. Box 13603, 85732
(800) 333-9RSO

The picturesque style of Santa Fe Pueblo Indian with Mexican influence is found throughout this home, built in 1930. Situated in a quiet residential neighborhood in Tucson, it features southwestern decor

6 Pets welcome; 8 Children welcome; 9 Social drinking allowed; 10 Tennis available; 11 Swimming available; 12 Golf available; 13 Skiing available; 14 May be booked through travel agents.

and air conditioning. Massages are available on the premises, as the hostess is a licensed massage therapist. A continental breakfast is served in the dining room or on the patio. Two rooms feature shared baths, while one boasts a private bath, and all feature modern amenities. $50-70.

Katy's Hacienda

Old Pueblo Homestays
P. O. Box 13603, 85732
(800) 333-9RSO

Charming home filled with antiques. Hostess entertains with home privileges. Colorful, restful back yard. A choice breakfast is served. Within walking distance of Park Mall, theaters, and many fine restaurants. Close to bus line. One room with private bath. Resident dog. Minimum stay is two nights. Children over 12. $45.

La Casita

Old Pueblo Homestays
P. O. Box 13603, 85732
(800) 333-9RSO

Town house set in lush desert growth area. Hostess is a former travel agent. One room with a king-size waterbed and private bath. Pool adjacent to the house for enjoyment in the hot summer, and another pool is heated during the winter. Jacuzzi is heated year-round. Continental breakfast. Near La Paloma, Vantana Canyons, and resort golf courses. Minimum stay is two nights. $60.

La Posada Del Valle

1640 North Campbell Avenue, 85719
(602) 795-3840

An elegant 1920s inn nestled in the heart of the city with five guest rooms with private baths and outside entrances. Mature orange trees perfume the air as guests enjoy a gourmet breakfast and sip tea each afternoon on the patio overlooking the garden.

Hosts: Charles and Debbi Bryant
Rooms: 5 (PB) $90-115
Full Breakfast weekends; Continental Breakfast
  week-days
Credit Cards: A, B
Notes: 2, 4, 5, 8 (over 12), 9, 10, 11, 12, 14

Mesquite Retreat

Old Pueblo Homestays
P. O. Box 13603, 85732
(800) 333-9RSO

Offering desert quiet near the base of Mount Lemmon, yet easy access to the city—five minutes to fine dining. This spacious ranch-style home is decorated with a blend of traditional and many antiques. Two guest rooms feature antique beds and share a bath. Living area shared with host has TV and fireplace. Mountain view patio with pool and spa. Full or light breakfast served. Resident dog. Children over 12. $50.

Prickly Pear Casa

Old Pueblo Homestays
P. O. Box 13603, 85732
(800) 333-9RSO

This hostess from England and her Ohio-born husband welcome guests to their spacious ranch-style house on four desert acres. All rooms have cable TV and share a large hall bath, plus two powder rooms. Enjoy the view of the Catalina Mountains or relax by the pool. Close to fine dining, shopping, and Catalina State Park. Two cats and two dogs in residence. Choice of king, queen, or twin beds. No children. $65-75.

Quail's Vista

Old Pueblo Homestays
P. O. Box 13603, 85732
(800) 333-9RSO

Panoramic view of the Catalina Mountains makes this Santa Fe-style, rammed-earth solar structure home give guests the feeling

NOTES: Credit cards accepted: A Master Card; B Visa; C American Express; D Discover Card; E Diner's Club; F Other; 2 Personal Checks accepted; 3 Lunch available; 4 Dinner available; 5 Open all year;

of true desert living. Guest room has a queen-sized bed with private full hall bath. Swim-stream spa, and hostess' membership at private country club with golf, tennis, and aerobics available to guests. Continental breakfast. No pets or children. $60-85.

Redbud House

Old Pueblo Homestays
P. O. Box 13603, 85732
(800) 333-9RSO

In a quiet neighborhood within walking distance to parks, shops, and good restaurants, as well as transportation. Cozy atmosphere with mountain views, use of livingroom with fireplace. Two cheerful bedrooms with private bath and TV. Full or light breakfast offered. Use of barbecue, patio, books, games, and bicycles. Minimum stay is two nights. $50.

Rimrock West

Old Pueblo Homestays
P. O. Box 13603, 85732
(800) 333-9RSO

A southwestern hacienda of two talented artists situated on twenty acres in the foothills of the Santa Catalina Mountains, two miles from city limits. Two rooms in main house with private baths open onto courtyard with fountain. Separate adobe guest house near pool area has livingroom, full kitchen, bedroom. Breakfast is informal and plentiful, including freshly baked muffins and interesting conversation. Minimum stay is two nights. $85-105.

Roadrunner

Old Pueblo Homestays
P. O. Box 13603, 85732
(800) 333-9RSO

Stay in a home with a spectacular view of the mountains. The great room provides

reading material, TV, and piano for guests. All rooms are light and cheerful, tastefully furnished with antiques and Oriental rugs. Private baths, one with Jacuzzi. Full gourmet breakfast with a special of cracked broiled whole-wheat served with delicious desert honey and syrup. Four rooms available. $45-110.

Timrod

Old Pueblo Homestays
P. O. Box 13603, 85732
(800) 333-9RSO

Desert living at its best. Beautiful home set in a lovely rural area with mountain vistas. A self-contained four-room suite. Private bath, full kitchen, separate entrance. Hostess stocks refrigerator with breakfast foods. Second suite with two bedrooms and bath. Pool is heated at additional charge. Pottery lessons available by hostess. Resident dog. Minimum stay is two nights. Children over 15. $60-80.

Travelers Rest

Old Pueblo Homestays
P. O. Box 13603, 85732
(800) 333-9RSO

A neighborhood park surrounded by pleasant homes is the setting for this special offering. One room with twin beds, private bath, and separate entrance. Private patio for relaxing. Close to shopping, restaurants, churches, theaters, and doctors. Neighborhood pool available late spring and summer. Three miles to University of Arizona. Resident dog. Minimum stay is two nights. $40.

Tucson Mountain Hideaway

Old Pueblo Homestays
P. O. Box 13603, 85732
(800) 333-9RSO

6 Pets welcome; 8 Children welcome; 9 Social drinking allowed; 10 Tennis available; 11 Swimming available; 12 Golf available; 13 Skiing available; 14 May be booked through travel agents.

This home offers a relaxed, friendly atmosphere. Three rooms with shared bath. Queen bedroom with private bath. Hostess sets out a very special continental breakfast. Easy access to desert and mountain trails, community center, downtown Tucson, and the University of Arizona. Share family room, TV, and pool. Minimum stay is two nights. Children over 12. $40-50.

Vista Montana

Old Pueblo Homestays
P. O. Box 13603, 85732
(800) 333-9RSO

An unobstructed view of the Santa Catalina Mountains beckons from this charming private home in the foothills. The luxurious bedroom has twin beds, phone, and TV. Adjoining bath has private access to an enclosed patio with lap pool that can be used most of the year. Luscious breakfast of your choice is served in the shade of a ramada by the pool. This adobe brick home is 15 minutes from the University of Arizona, and close to shopping centers, outstanding art galleries, and restaurants. Resident dog. Minimum stay is two nights. $65.

Arkansas

Arkansas and Ozarks Bed and Breakfast ACR01

HC 61, Box 72, 72519
(501) 297-8764; (501) 297-8211

Contemporary home in a secluded woodland setting offers a full delicious breakfast, large family room, satellite TV and games, a hot tub in the sunroom, and pool table. Beautiful stained-glass creations by the hostess and collectibles from around the world make this a delightful setting. Garage parking is available, and children are welcome. $40.

Arkansas and Ozarks Bed and Breakfast ACR02

HC 61, Box 72, 72519
(501) 297-8764; (501) 297-8211

Two log cabins surrounded by the Ozark National Forest, decorated with the past in mind but offering modern comforts. A sleeping loft in each cabin sleeps two; downstairs has a Hide-a-bed and wood stove in the living area, kitchen, and bath. The cabins are unhosted for maximum privacy but provided with coffee, milk, cereal, and homemade fruit bread. Relax on the front porch and enjoy a panoramic view of river, forest, and ever-present wildlife. Only minutes from town, the Ozark Fold Center, Blanchard Springs Caverns, antique shops, and live music shows or dinner theaters. $48.

Arkansas and Ozarks Bed and Breakfast ACR03

HC 61, Box 72, 72519
(501) 297-8764; (501) 297-8211

Original 1923 hotel within walking distance of two boat docks, one block from Main Street. Continental breakfast provided. Furnishings include antiques and collectibles of the 1920s. Handmade jewelry shop on premises. $35-48.

Arkansas and Ozarks Bed and Breakfast ACR04

HC 61, Box 72, 72519
(501) 297-8764; (501) 297-8211

Forest home lodge is perched on a 300-foot bluff overlooking the beautiful, clear White River. A large country breakfast, including homemade breads and a hearty main dish, is served on a deck outside your room. The contemporary home, decorated with stained glass, has a large three-keyboard organ, satellite TV, and video games in the spacious livingroom for the guests' enjoyment. The Ozark Folk Center, Blanchard Caverns, craft shops, antique shops, and hiking trails are only minutes away. $45.

The May House Inn

101 Railroad Avenue, 72830
(501) 754-6851

Lovely Victorian home overlooking downtown historic Clarksville, offering turn-of-the-century charm. Features spacious bed-

- Eureka Springs
- Rogers
- Fayetteville
- Jasper
- Norfork
- Clarksville

Gassville
- Calico Rock
- Hardy

- Little Rock
- Hot Springs

ARKANSAS

The May House Inn

rooms with beautiful antiques, finest
amenities, and the Ozark Ritz Tea Room.
Situated on I-40 at Highway 64 and scenic
Highway 21 (the gateway to the Ozarks),
the area is a mountain lovers' paradise.

Hosts: Robin and Jayanne Courser
Rooms: 3 (SB) $55-65
Full Breakfast
Credit Cards: A, B
Notes: 2, 5, 9, 10, 11, 12

CROSSETT

The Trieschmann House Bed and Breakfast

707 Cedar, 71635
(501) 364-7592

Built in 1903 for an official of the Crossett
Company, this lovely bed and breakfast is
nine miles from the Felsenthal Refuge for
good fishing and hunting. Front porch with
wicker swing and furniture; common room
with a wood-burning stove, cable television, and games. Full breakfast is served in
the kitchen, and the home is furnished with
furniture from the past. Guests are invited
to go back in time.

Hosts: Pat and Herman Owens
Rooms: 3 (1 PB; 2 SB) $40-45
Full Breakfast
Credit Cards: A, B
Notes: 2, 5, 12

EUREKA SPRINGS

Bridgeford House Bed and Breakfast

263 Spring Street, 72632
(501) 253-7853

Nestled in the heart of Eureka Springs' historic residential district, Bridgeford House
is an 1884 Victorian delight. Outside are
shady porches that invite guests to pull up a
chair and watch the world go by on Spring
Street. Each room has a private entrance,
antique furnishings, and private bath. Fresh
coffee in your suite, a selection of fine teas,
color TV, air conditioning, and a mouth-
watering breakfast.

Hosts: Michael and Denise McDonald
Rooms: 4 (PB) $75-95
Full Breakfast
Credit Cards: A, B
Notes: 2, 5, 7 (outside), 9, 10, 11, 12, 14

The Trieschmann House

Crescent Cottage Inn

211 Spring Street, 72632
(501) 253-6022

Famous "Painted Lady" on the National
Register of Historic Places, this Victorian
House was built in 1881 for the first
Arkansas governor after the Civil War.
Two veranda porches overlook mountains

NOTES: Credit cards accepted: A Master Card; B Visa; C American Express; D Discover Card; E Diner's
Club; F Other; 2 Personal Checks accepted; 3 Lunch available; 4 Dinner available; 5 Open all year; 6 Pets welcome; 8 Children welcome; 9 Social drinking allowed; 10 Tennis available; 11 Swimming available; 12 Golf
available; 13 Skiing available; 14 May be booked through travel agents.

Crescent Cottage Inn

for the best view in town. Two sleeping areas have separate double Jacuzzi spas and their own verandas. One two-room suite is also available. All accommodations have private baths. Easy walk to town on historic loop lined with maples and flowers. Superb antiques throughout this home, and truly memorable breakfasts. Adjacent to the trolley stop.

Hosts: Ralph and Phyllis Becker
Rooms: 4 (PB) $70-105
Full Breakfast
Credit Cards: A, B, D
Notes: 2, 5, 8 (over 14), 9, 11, 12

The Heartstone Inn and Cottages

35 Kings Highway, 72632
(501) 253-8916

Nationally acclaimed, award-winning bed and breakfast inn. Antiques, quilts, all private baths, private entrances, cable TV, and full gourmet breakfasts. Licensed massage therapist on duty. "Best breakfast in the Ozarks," the *New York Times*. In historic district and on trolley route. Off-street parking.

Hosts: Iris and Bill Simantel
Rooms: 10 (PB) $58-105
Cottages: 2 (PB)
Full Breakfast
Credit Cards: A, B, C, D
Closed Christmas
Notes: 2, 8, 9

Ridgeway House

28 Ridgeway, 72632
(501) 253-6618; (800) 477-6618

Prepare to be pampered! Sumptuous breakfasts elegantly served in a completely restored 1908 Colonial Revival home, with luxurious rooms, antiques, flowers, desserts, and quiet streets. Just a five minute walk from historic downtown and one block from the trolley. Porches, decks, and a Jacuzzi suite for honeymoons or special occasions. All guests are VIPs!

Host: Linda Kerkera
Rooms: 5 (3 PB; 2 SB) $69-99
Full Breakfast
Credit Cards: A, B, C
Notes: 2, 5, 8, 9, 11, 14

Singleton House Bed and Breakfast

11 Singleton Street, 72632
(501) 253-9111; (800) 833-3394

This country Victorian home is an old-fashioned place with a touch of magic. Each guest room is whimsically decorated with a delightful collection of antiques and folk art. Breakfast is served on the balcony overlooking the fantasy wildflower garden below, with its goldfish pond and curious

The Heartstone Inn

Hosts: Dale and Cecelia Thompson
Rooms: 3 (SB) $40
Full Breakfast
Credit Cards: None
Notes: 5

Hill Avenue

birdhouse collection. A honeymoon cottage with a Jacuzzi for two at a separate location is also available. Situated in the historic district. Guests park and walk a secluded pathway to Eureka's shops and cafes.

Host: Barbara Gavron
Rooms: 5 (4 PB; 1 SB) $55-65
Cottage: 1 (PB) $95 (no breakfast)
Full Breakfast
Credit Cards: A, B, C, D
Notes: 2, 5, 8, 9, 11, 12, 14

FAYETTEVILLE

Hill Avenue Bed and Breakfast
131 South Hill Avenue, 72701
(501) 444-0865

This two-story older home in a residential neighborhood is the only registered bed and breakfast in Fayetteville. It is near the University of Arkansas, Walton Art Center, and the town square. Guests will find comfortable, nonsmoking accommodations. A hearty country breakfast is served in the dining room or on the large porch.

GASSVILLE

Arkansas and Ozarks Bed and Breakfast AGV01
HC 61, Box 72, Calico Rock, 72519
(501) 297-8764; (501) 297-8211

This 100-year-old former health lodge has been lovingly restored with added gift shop featuring the hosts' own fine handicrafts. Breakfast is served in the dining room or large, screened front porch. On 39 acres of meadows and woods, it reflects the original lodge in character. Near the White and Buffalo rivers and between Bull Shoals and Norfork dams. An ideal location. No alcoholic beverages. $40-45.

Arkansas and Ozarks AGV01

6 Pets welcome; 8 Children welcome; 9 Social drinking allowed; 10 Tennis available; 11 Swimming available; 12 Golf available; 13 Skiing available; 14 May be booked through travel agents.

Arkansas and Ozarks AHA01

HARDY

Arkansas and Ozarks Bed and Breakfast AHA01

HC 61, Box 72, Calico Rock, 72519
(501) 297-8764; (501) 297-8211

This newly renovated stone house used as a boarding house in the depression is only a short walk from handicraft and antique shops and the Spring River. The rock formations in its walls and fireplace provide an interesting background for its antiques, collectibles, and locally handcrafted decor. Music shows, golfing, tennis, horseback riding, and canoeing are available nearby. $45 weekdays; $55 Friday and Saturday.

Olde Stonehouse Bed and Breakfast Inn

511 Main Street, 72542
(501) 856-2983

Historic Arkansas stone house with large porches lined with jumbo rocking chairs is comfortably furnished with antiques and features central heat and air, ceiling fans, queen-size beds, and private baths. One block from Spring River and the shops of old Hardy town. Three country music theaters, golf courses, horseback riding, canoeing, and fishing nearby. Local attractions include Mammoth Spring State Park, Grand Gulf, Evening Shade, Arkansas, and Arkansas Traveller Theater.

Host: Peggy Johnson
Rooms: 5 (PB) $55
Full Breakfast
Credit Cards: A, B, D
Notes: 2, 5, 9, 10, 11, 12, 14

HOT SPRINGS

Williams House Bed and Breakfast Inn

420 Quapaw Avenue, 71901
(501) 624-4275

Listed on the National Register of Historic Places, in 1980 this 1890 brownstone and brick Victorian became the first bed and breakfast in the state. Attention to detail and comfort are important, as is guest privacy. Antiques, plants, romance, and good food. Only four blocks to the Hot Springs National Park headquarters and hiking trails. Minimum two-day stay on weekends in March, April, October, and holidays.

Hosts: Mary and Gary Riley
Rooms: 5 (PB); $60-85
Continental Breakfast, Monday-Friday; Full
   Breakfast, Saturday and Sunday
Credit Cards: A, B, C
Notes: 2, 5, 9, 10, 11, 12, 14

Williams House

JASPER

Brambly Hedge Cottage

HCR 31, Box 39, 72641
(501) 446-5849

Breakfast above the clouds at this mountaintop home right on Scenic Highway 7.

NOTES: Credit cards accepted: A Master Card; B Visa; C American Express; D Discover Card; E Diner's Club; F Other; 2 Personal Checks accepted; 3 Lunch available; 4 Dinner available; 5 Open all year;

Gorgeous view "clear to Missouri" overlooks Buffalo River Valley. Country French-Victorian elegance in the rugged Ozarks. "Absolutely charming," *National Geographic Traveller,* 1991. Thick-walled livingroom is a homestead log cabin. Lovely upstairs guest room. Minutes from Buffalo National River float trips, hiking trails, Dogpatch, craft shops; short distance to Eureka Springs; Branson, Missouri; major lakes. 4.2 miles south of Jasper.

Hosts: Jacquelyn Smyers and Louise Hudson
Rooms: 3 (PB) $55-65
Full Breakfast
Credit Cards: None
Notes: 2, 5, 9

LITTLE ROCK

Quapaw Inn

1868 South Gaines, 72206
(501) 376-6873; (800) 732-5591

This 1905 Colonial Revival house is just four blocks from the Arkansas Governor's Mansion, former residence of President Bill Clinton, Hillary, Chelsea, and Socks the cat. Tour this historic neighborhood just 10 blocks from the central business district and 10 minutes from the airport. Stay in the Clinton Suite. Private, secluded, king bed, television, VCR, wood fireplace, and many more amenities.

Host: Dottie Woodwind
Rooms: 4 (2 PB; 2 SB) $60-130
Full or Continental Breakfast
Credit Cards: A, B, C, F
Notes: 2, 4, 5, 8, 9, 14

NORFORK

Arkansas and Ozarks Bed and Breakfast ANF01

HC 61, Box 72, Calico Rock, 72519
(501) 297-8764; (501) 297-8211

A mountain retreat with a country club setting, this lodge sits on the banks of the

White River and overlooks the beauty and serenity of the Ozark National Forest. In the large, antique-furnished dining room, family-style home-cooked meals (including hand selected meats, fowl, fish, vegetables, freshly baked breads, and European desserts) are served. A complete breakfast is included with your lodging. The bedrooms have their own entrances into an open-air courtyard. $68.

OZARK

Arkansas and Ozarks Bed and Breakfast AOZZ01

HC 61, Box 72, Calico Rock, 72519
(501) 297-8764; (501) 297-8211

This 1880s in is beautifully restored with original wood floors, stained glass, crystal chandeliers, and a winding staircase. A hammered dulcimer and piano add to the enjoyment. A luxurious breakfast is served on china, crystal, and silver, with an evening dessert provided. The romantic honeymoon anniversary suite offers a candlelight dinner served in the room. Selected lovely furnishings and local handcrafts are for sale. $50 to $75.

Arkansas and Ozarks Bed and Breakfast AOZ02

HC 61, Box 72, Calico Rock, 72519
(501) 297-8764; (501) 297-8211

This brick home, overlooking the Arkansas River, provides queen-size beds and personal TVs in each lovely decorated guest room. Enjoy a full breakfast in front of the fireplace, in the large family dining room, or relax in the hot tub. The River View suite is available, with dinner served in your room. $35-75.

6 Pets welcome; 8 Children welcome; 9 Social drinking allowed; 10 Tennis available; 11 Swimming available; 12 Golf available; 13 Skiing available; 14 May be booked through travel agents.

ROGERS

Arkansas and Ozarks Bed and Breakfast ARO01

HC 61, Box 72, Calico Rock, 72519
(501) 297-8764: (501) 297-8211

This country charmer for adult travelers is nestled among oak, dogwood, and redbud trees. Queen-size beds, private baths, fruit, and homemade candy are just a few of the features. A full breakfast is served in the spacious country dining room or on the veranda where birds, wildlife, and natural beauty may also be enjoyed. The hosts delight in providing special arrangements for birthdays, anniversaries, and other occasions. Only minutes from boating, fishing, swimming, golf, and a variety of shopping and craft areas. $40-55.

Old Washington Jail

WASHINGTON

The Old Washington Jail Bed and Breakfast

P. O. Box 179, Conway and Jackson Street, 71862
(501) 983-2461

Forty minutes east of Texarkana, near Hope, Arkansas. Originally constructed as a jail in 1872 and partially rebuilt in 1918, it was completely renovated in 1982. Guest rooms are furnished in period antiques, with each containing a private bath. Enjoy one of three sitting rooms, or one of two porches furnished with rocking chairs. Morning coffee is served.

Hosts: Hugh and Ruth Erwin
Rooms: 7 (5 PB; 2 SB) $55
Full Breakfast
Credit Cards: None
Notes: 2, 5, 9

YELLVILLE

Arkansas and Ozarks Bed and Breakfast AYV01

HC 61, Box 72, Calico Rock, 72519
(501) 297-8764; (501) 297-8211

This elegant Victorian home is beautifully and lovingly restored to its stately charm. There are six rooms in this spacious inn, and a "honeymoon suite" for those special celebrations. Also available are sitting rooms, a large dining room with a breakfast buffet of "make-it-yourself" Belgian waffles. Homemade cakes and other delights are served as snacks. Major credit cards accepted. Children over 5 welcome. $40; $55 honeymoon suite.

Arkansas and Ozarks Bed and Breakfast AYV02

HC 61, Box 72, Calico Rock, 72519
(501) 297-8764; (501) 297-8211

Two bedrooms, each with a double bed, bath, guest parlor, full kitchen, formal dining room, enclosed sunroom, and two-car covered carport. Children welcome; high chair provided. Piano, books, games, and TV. Local telephone service. House is unhosted. $68; $11 for each additional person.

California

Garratt Mansion
900 Union Street, 94501
(510) 521-4779

This 1893 Victorian makes time stand still on the tranquil island of Alameda. Only 15 miles to Berkeley or downtown San Francisco. The hosts will help maximize guests vacation plans or allow privacy to regroup. Rooms are large and comfortable, and breakfasts are nutritious and filling.

Hosts: Royce and Betty Gladden
Rooms: 6 (3 PB; 3 SB) $75-125
Full Breakfast
Credit Cards: A, B, C, E
Notes: 2, 5, 8, 10, 11, 12, 14

ALTADENA

Eye Openers Bed and Breakfast Reservations
P. O. Box 694, 91003
(213) 684-4428; (818) 797-2055
FAX (818) 798-3640

A reservation service that matches guest requests with bed and breakfast homestays and inns throughout California. One hundred and fifty accommodations to choose from, with private and shared baths. Many situated near tourist attractions, tennis, golf, skiing and swimming.

Garratt Mansion

ANAHEIM

Anaheim Bed and Breakfast
1327 South Hickory, 92805
(714) 533-1884

Anaheim Bed and Breakfast is less than one mile from Disneyland and the Anaheim Convention Center. It is situated in a residential area close to the I-5 Santa Ana freeway, and the neighborhood is one of the oldest in the city. The owner of the home lives on the premises, and speaks English and German fluently.

Host: Margot E. Palmgren
Rooms: 3 (SB) $40
Full Breakfast
Credit Cards: None
Notes: 2, 5, 8

Anaheim Country Inn
856 South Walnut Street, 92802
(800) 755-7801

Step back in time and enjoy the Anaheim Country Inn. Graced by beveled, leaded-

6 Pets welcome; 8 Children welcome; 9 Social drinking allowed; 10 Tennis available; 11 Swimming available; 12 Golf available; 13 Skiing available; 14 May be booked through travel agents.

CALIFORNIA

McCloud

Trinidad

Eureka
Ferndale

Anderson

Westport
Yuba City
Portola
Little River
Mendocino
Nevada City
Elk
Ukiah
Truckee
Point Arena
Lucerne
Tahoe City
Gualala
Cloverdale
Camino
Lake Tahoe
Healdsburg
Hope Valley
Geyserville
Calistoga
Woodland Hills
St. Helena
Santa Rosa
Yountville
Sutter Creek
Freestone
Napa
Inverness
Guerneville
Lodi
Murphys
Bridgeport
Point Reyes Station
Sausalito
Point Richmond
Columbia
Sonoma
Brentwood
Sonora
Groveland
San Francisco
Alameda
Yosemite
Montara
Fremont
Half Moon Bay
Fish Camp
San Gregorio
Capitola-by-the-Sea
Davenport
Santa Cruz
Aptos
Pacific Grove
Sequoia
Monterey
Carmel
Carmel Valley
Springville

Cambria
Morrow Bay
San Luis Obispo
Los Osos

Arroyo Grande
Santa Monica
Muir Beach
Thousand Oaks
Calabassas
Santa Barbara
Manhattan Beach
Solvang
Burbank
Camarillo
Carpinteria
Toluca Lake
Ventura
Altadena
Pasadena
Fawnskin
Sunset Palisades
Skyforest
Sherman Oaks
Malibu
North Hollywood
West Covina
Venice
Mar Vista
Palm Springs
Whittier
Beverly Hills
Anaheim
Northridge
Marina Del Ray
Orange
Los Angeles/Hollywood
Santa Ana
Long Beach
Newport Beach
Ranchos Palos Verdes
Avalon
Temecula
Westchester
Laguna Beach
Capistrano
Seal Beach
Garden Grove
Encintas
San Diego
Coronado Island

glass windows, and charming turn-of-the-century furnishings, it is situated on spacious grounds in a quiet residential neighborhood near Disneyland and the Anaheim Convention Center. Off-street parking and a hot tub are available.

Hosts: Lois Ramont and Marilyn Watson
Rooms: 9 (6 PB; 3 SB) $55-80
Full Breakfast
Credit Cards: A, B, C, D
Notes: 2, 5, 9, 10, 12, 14

Bed and Breakfast International #501

P. O. Box 282910, San Francisco, 94128-2910
(415) 696-1690; FAX (415) 696-1699

Perfect location for visiting Disneyland, Knott's Berry Farm, and other tourist attractions in Southern California. This large two-story home is ideal for a family. Guest room has a queen bed, private bath, plus a queen sofa bed in an adjacent sitting room with a fireplace and balcony. Breakfast at this house lasts all day. $55.

Bed and Breakfast International #504

P. O. Box 282910, San Francisco, 94128
(415) 696-1690; FAX (415) 696-1699

This traditional southern California home is centrally situated for tourists, close to Disneyland, Universal Studios, and Knott's Berry Farm. There is a lovely pool and gazebo in back, and one room offers a private entrance. Host can offer a 35 percent discount on tickets to Disneyland with advanced notice. $60-80.

Bed and Breakfast Los Angeles 7-6

3924 East 14th Street, Long Beach, 90804
(310) 498-0552; (800) 383-3513

Less than a mile from Disneyland, three guest rooms share two baths. The hosts are German and Scandinavian. Family rates are available. Affordable rates.

Bed and Breakfast Los Angeles 7-7

3924 East 14th Street, Long Beach, 90804
(310) 498-0552; (800) 383-3513

Just five miles from Disneyland, this beautiful, contemporary house is set on one-quarter acre, with a view of the hills from the pool and spa. Three nice guest rooms share two baths. Affordable rates.

Eye Openers Bed and Breakfast Reservations AN-A9I

P. O. Box 694, Altadena, 91003-0694
(213) 684-4428; (818) 797-2055
FAX (818) 798-3640

Beautifully restored and decorated, this 1910 Princess Anne Victorian, now a friendly bed and breakfast, is surrounded by lovely gardens and is situated in a residential area convenient to most Orange County attractions with local bus service. Hearty breakfast and afternoon refreshments. Nine guest rooms with private and shared baths. $65-100 plus tax.

Eye Openers Bed and Breakfast Reservations AN-P3

P. O. Box 694, Altadena, 91003-0694
(213) 684-4428; (818) 797-2055
FAX (818) 798-3640

This bed and breakfast, with its country kitchen and full breakfast, offers comfort, convenience, economy, and good location

NOTES: Credit cards accepted: A Master Card; B Visa; C American Express; D Discover Card; E Diner's Club; F Other; 2 Personal Checks accepted; 3 Lunch available; 4 Dinner available; 5 Open all year; 6 Pets welcome; 8 Children welcome; 9 Social drinking allowed; 10 Tennis available; 11 Swimming available; 12 Golf available; 13 Skiing available; 14 May be booked through travel agents.

near restaurants and public transportation. Bicycles, hot tub, and complimentary transport to Disneyland are available. Children welcome. Two guest rooms with private and shared baths. $35-55.

Eye Openers Bed and Breakfast Reservations AN-W3

P. O. Box 694, Altadena, 91003-0694
(213) 684-4428; (818) 797-2055
FAX (818) 798-3640

One mile to Disneyland and Anaheim Convention Center. Hearty breakfast served with special attention from European host in the large family room or dining room. Three guest rooms with shared bath. $45-55 plus tax.

Eye Openers Bed and Breakfast Reservations GG-04

P. O. Box 694, Altadena, 91003-0694
(213) 684-4428; (818) 797-2055
FAX (818) 798-3640

Convenient to Orange County attractions, this bed and breakfast features large comfortable rooms, full breakfast, and TV room with fireplace. Four guest rooms with private and shared baths. $40-55.

Eye Openers Bed and Breakfast Reservations OR-C3

P. O. Box 694, Altadena, 91003-0694
(213) 684-4428; (818) 797-2055
FAX (818) 798-3640

Enjoy a delicious country-style breakfast in a contemporary wood-and-glass bed and breakfast. Relax in the outdoor pool, Jacuzzi, livingroom, or interesting family

room. Convenient to Disneyland, Anaheim Convention Center and Stadium. Handicapped accessible with adaptive equipment. Three guest rooms. $55-60.

Eye Openers Bed and Breakfast Reservations SA-D1

P. O. Box 694, Altadena, 91003-0694
(213) 684-4428; (818) 797-2055
FAX (818) 798-3640

Older home in a lovely neighborhood has been restored by young hosts. Antique accents are featured in the guest room and the livingroom. One guest room with private bath is available, and generous continental breakfast served. This bed and breakfast is convenient to the Anaheim Convention Center and Disneyland. Cats in residence. $55.

Kids Welcome 7-5

3924 East 14th Street, Long Beach, 90804
(310) 498-0552; (800) 383-3513

The guest wing of this spacious house in Anaheim has room for the entire family, with a livingroom with a fireplace, balcony, kitchen, and private bath. Livingroom couch converts to a bed for the kids. Two downstairs guest rooms share a bath. Enjoy the spa and patio, as well as a full country breakfast. Pets welcome. Affordable rates.

ANDERSON

The Plantation House

1609 Ferry Street, 96007
(916) 365-2827

The Plantation House, a two-story Victorian home offers a tranquil, romantic step into the past. Hosts Vi and Bob, dressed in authentic *Gone With The Wind*

NOTES: Credit cards accepted: A Master Card; B Visa; C American Express; D Discover Card; E Diner's Club; F Other; 2 Personal Checks accepted; 3 Lunch available; 4 Dinner available; 5 Open all year;

The Plantation House

costumes, greet their guests with true southern hospitality. After a tour of the antique-filled home, guests are shown to their rooms. Each bedroom is furnished in breathtaking splendor, complete with television, radio, VCR, phone, chilled wine, fruit, nuts, and candy. Guests are also served elaborate hors d'oeuvres and a full breakfast in the morning.

Hosts: Bob and Vi Webb
Rooms: 2 (PB) $50
Suite: 1 (PB) $90
Full Breakfast
Credit Cards: None
Notes: 2, 5, 9, 10, 11, 12, 13, 14

APTOS

Apple Lane Inn
6265 Soquel Drive, 95003-3117
(408) 475-6868

Apple Lane Inn is a historic Victorian farmhouse restored to the charm and tranquility of an earlier age. It is situated just south of Santa Cruz on two and one-half acres of grounds, with gardens, a romantic gazebo, and fields. Explore the many miles

of beaches within walking distance. Golf, hiking, fishing, shopping, and dining are all close by.

Hosts: Doug and Diana Groom
Rooms: 5 (3 PB; 2 SB) $70-125
Full Breakfast
Credit Cards: A, B, D
Notes: 2, 5, 8, 9, 10, 11, 12, 14

ARROYO GRANDE

Arroyo Village Inn
407 El Camino Real, 93420
(805) 489-5926

Romantic, award-winning Victorian offering a delightful blend of yesterday's charm and hospitality with today's comforts and conveniences. Spacious suites are decorated with Laura Ashley prints and antiques with private baths, window seats, and balconies. Situated in the heart of California's Central Coast, halfway between Los Angeles and San Francisco. Near beaches, wineries, mineral spas, San Luis Obispo; less than one hour to Hearst Castle. "The best kept secret on the Central Coast," *Los Angeles Times.*

Hosts: John and Gina Glass
Rooms: 7 (PB) $95-165
Full Breakfast
Credit Cards: A, B, C, D, E
Notes: 2, 5, 8 , 9, 10, 11, 12, 14

Arroyo Village Inn

6 Pets welcome; 8 Children welcome; 9 Social drinking allowed; 10 Tennis available; 11 Swimming available; 12 Golf available; 13 Skiing available; 14 May be booked through travel agents.

Megan's Friends #15
Bed and Breakfast Reservation Service
1776 Royal Way, San Luis Obispo, 93405
(805) 544-4406

Welcome to Casa de Colores, a joyful, colorful home on seven acres of rural Arroyo Grande. This architectural masterpiece features international folk art and Mexican and Italian tile collections. Surrounded by a magnificent view of the mountains and fields, just 20 minutes from Cal-Poly University. Stay includes gourmet breakfasts, wine and hors d'oeuvres in the evening, complimentary wine, fresh fruit, and homemade treats in the cabin. Each accommodation, with either king, queen or twins beds, also features a private bath, an Inca "birthday cake" fireplace, patio, and shared central courtyard. Relax or work out in the 80-foot lap pool, ride mountain bikes, or shop the Casa de Colores Boutique. $125-150.

AVALON

The Garden House Inn
125 Third Street, P. O. Box 851, 90704
(310) 510-0356

1923 historic home is situated 100 feet from Avalon Bay on Catalina Island. Nine lovely rooms are available, many have ocean views and private terraces. All have private tiled baths, queen-size beds, and overstuffed upholstered furnishings. Buffet breakfast and wine hour daily. Large gardens run along the ocean side of the house, and the inn is within walking distance to all of Avalon. Come and enjoy our romantic, relaxed atmosphere. Call about the midweek season discount.

Hosts: Jon and Cathy Olsen
Rooms: 9 (PB) $95-250
Continental Plus Breakfast
Credit Cards: A, B, C
Notes: 2, 5, 10, 11, 12, 14

Gull House
344 Whittley Avenue, Box 1381, 90704
(310) 510-2547

Bed and breakfast with a touch of class for honeymooners and those celebrating anniversaries. AAA-approved contemporary house with swimming pool, spa, barbecue, gas-log fireplaces, morning room with refrigerator, cable TV. Close to bay beaches and all water activities. Deposit or full payment in advance reserves taxi pickup and return. Ask about the guest rooms.

Hosts: Bob and Hattie Michalis
Suites: 2 (PB) $135-145
Guest room: $110-125
Continental Breakfast
Minimum stay: 2 nights
Credit Cards: None
Notes: 2, 8, 9, 10, 11, 12, 14

BERKELEY

Gramma's Rose Garden Inn
2740 Telegraph Avenue, 94705
(510) 549-2145; FAX (510) 549-1085

Two turn-of-the-century Tudor-style mansions, garden, cottage, and carriage houses set amid English country gardens. Rooms furnished with antiques; many have fireplaces, decks, porches, and/or views. Near the University of California, Berkeley, shops, parks, and museums.

NOTES: Credit cards accepted: A Master Card; B Visa; C American Express; D Discover Card; E Diner's Club; F Other; 2 Personal Checks accepted; 3 Lunch available; 4 Dinner available; 5 Open all year;

Host: Barry Cleveland
Rooms: 40 (PB) $85-175
Full Breakfast
Credit Cards: A, B, C, E
Notes: 2, 5, 8, 9, 10, 11, 12, 14

Hillegass House

2834 Hillegass Avenue, 94705
(510) 548-5517

Light-filled house, circa 1904, situated two blocks from many excellent shops and restaurants. Large, comfortable guest rooms furnished with antiques. One room features a whirlpool bath. Common areas include two large parlors and an elegant deck overlooking the garden. Telephone and voice mail furnished. Breakfast is served in the dining room. Walk to the University of California, BART to San Francisco, and just a one-hour drive to the wine country.

Host: Richard Warren
Rooms: 4 (PB) $75-90
Full Breakfast
Credit Cards: None
Notes: 2, 5, 8, 9, 10, 11, 14

BEVERLY HILLS _____

Bed and Breakfast Los Angeles 2-6

3924 East 14th Street, 90804
(310) 498-0552; (800) 383-3513

This spacious condo includes a guest room with twin beds, TV, and garden view. Great location in a delightful setting. Moderate rates.

Bed and Breakfast Los Angeles 2-7

3924 East 14th Street, Long Beach, 90804
(310) 498-0552; (800) 383-3513

Tucked behind the host's home, this quaint cottage features twin beds, private bath, refrigerator, and TV. Affordable rates.

Eye Openers Bed and Breakfast Reservations BH-N1

P. O. Box 694, Altadena, 91003-0694
(213) 684-4428; (818) 797-2055
FAX (818) 798-3640

In the heart of Beverly Hills, this bed and breakfast offers a guest cottage in the garden area for ultimate privacy and comfort. Cottage has microwave, refrigerator, and choice of continental or full breakfast. Public transportation available. Private bath. $45-50.

BIG BEAR LAKE (FAWNSKIN) _____

The Inn at Fawnskin Bed and Breakfast

880 Canyon Road, P. O. Box 378, 92333
(714) 866-3200

Beautiful custom log home nestled in its own private pine forest, just steps away from lake and forest trails. Livingroom with big rock fireplace, baby grand piano, comfy furniture, decks with lake and forest views. Dining room with big rock fireplace, delicious homemade breakfast. Large game room—50-inch TV screen, pool table, game table, stereo, wet bar. Gazebo with Jacuzzi. Basketball court. Breathtaking master suite. Comforters and plush robes. Exceptional hospitality provided by owner/operators.

Hosts: G. B. and Susie Sneed
Rooms: 4 (2 PB; 2 SB) $75-155
Full Breakfast
Credit Cards: A, B
Notes: 2, 3, 4, 5, 9, 10, 11, 12, 13

BISHOP_____

The Matlick House

1313 Rowan Lane, 93514
(619) 873-3133

6 Pets welcome; 8 Children welcome; 9 Social drinking allowed; 10 Tennis available; 11 Swimming available; 12 Golf available; 13 Skiing available; 14 May be booked through travel agents.

A 1906 ranch house, completely renovated, nestled at the base of the eastern Sierra Nevada Mountains. Close to year-round fishing, hiking, skiing, trail rides. Telephones available, air conditioning, wine and hors d'oeuvres; antiques throughout.

Host: Nanette Robidart
Rooms: 5 (PB) $55-75
Full Breakfast.
Credit Cards: None
Notes: 2, 5, 8 (over 14), 9, 10, 11, 12, 13

BOONVILLE

The Toll House

P. O. Box 268, 15301 Highway 253, 95415
(707) 895-3630

In the heart of Mendicino's wine country just 125 miles north of San Francisco. This charming bed and breakfast offers some of northern California's most beautiful land. The secluded 300-acre ranch offers five guest rooms, each individually furnished with elegant antiques and artwork. Stroll through the lovely gardens, hike dramatic hills, picnic among magnificent black oaks or spend a leisurely afternoon with a good book. The Toll House Restaurant features superb cuisine, wines and champagne. The executive chef prepares menus using only the freshest ingredients. Wild game is offered seasonally, and catering on- and off-site is available.

Host: Barry Ingram
Rooms: 5 (4 PB; 1 SB) $115-190
Full Breakfast
Credit Cards: A, B, D
Notes: 2, 4, 9, 10, 11, 12, 14

BRENTWOOD

Eye Openers
Bed and Breakfast
Reservations LA-S1

P. O. Box 694, Altadena, 91003-0694
(213) 684-4428; (818) 797-2055
FAX (818) 798-3640

Brentwood town house features lovely livingroom with appointed antiques and French doors that open onto a patio facing a green belt complete with eucalyptus grove. A quiet retreat in the midst of busy, exciting Brentwood. Continental breakfast. Public transportation available. One guest room with private bath. $45-50.

BRIDGEPORT

The Cain House

11 Main Street, 93517
(619) 932-7040; (800) 433-CAIN

Situated in a small valley with a view of the rugged eastern Sierras, the Cain House has blended European elegance with a western atmosphere. Every amenity has been provided, including wine and cheese in the evenings. After breakfast, the pristine beauty of the valley, lakes, and streams await for a day of hiking, boating, fishing, hunting, and cross-country skiing. Three-diamond AAA, ABBA, and Mobil approved.

Hosts: Chris and Marachal Gohlich
Rooms: 6 (PB) $80-135
Full Breakfast
Credit Cards: A, B, C, D, E
Notes: 2, 9, 10

BUELLTON

Megan's Friends #19

Bed and Breakfast Reservation Service
1776 Royal Way, San Luis Obispo, 93405
(805) 544-4406

Rancho Simpatico, a three-year old contemporary situated on a hilltop near the Santa Ynez Valley, is a unique design oriented to the site on 20 acres. The guest suite has a queen-size bed, small kitchenette, and private patio with a small waterfall and pond. Adjacent to the guest suite is a Jacuzzi-swim spa. Guests have use of the satellite TV, telephone, garage, elevator,

NOTES: Credit cards accepted: A Master Card; B Visa; C American Express; D Discover Card; E Diner's Club; F Other; 2 Personal Checks accepted; 3 Lunch available; 4 Dinner available; 5 Open all year;

and the livingroom area of the home. A full breakfast is served, with beverages offered at sunset. $75.

BURBANK

Bed and Breakfast Los Angeles 3-7

3924 East 14th Street, Long Beach, 90804
(310) 498-0552; (800) 383-3513

This charming cottage has a pool, barbecue, and wet bar. Guest room has trundle beds and private bath. Quarters also have handicapped facilities. Affordable rates.

CALABASSAS

Kids Welcome 11-1

3924 East 14th Street, Long Beach, 90804
(310) 498-0552; (800) 383-3513

The friendly Scottish hostess opens her beautiful, three-level home to families with children over age seven. Just fifteen minutes from Malibu, two guest rooms on the top floor share a bath. A family room, a library, and heated pool are at the doorstep. Affordable rates.

CALISTOGA

Calistoga Country Lodge

2883 Foothill Boulevard, 94515
(707) 942-5555

This 1917 farmhouse, set among 100-year-old oaks, has been restored in a southwestern style. Rooms feature whitewashed pine floors, custom lodgepole furnishings, and one-of-a-kind Navajo rug wall hangings. A large, stone fireplace and Georgia O'Keefe-style artifacts draw guests to the spacious common area. A colorful breakfast buffet overlooks the patio and heated pool, where guests can relax and enjoy the views.

Host: Rae Ellen Fields
Rooms: 6 (4 PB; 2 SB) $95-125
Expanded Continental Breakfast
Credit Cards: A, B, C
Notes: 2, 5, 9, 10, 11, 12

The Elms Bed and Breakfast Inn

1300 Cedar Street, 94515
(707) 942-9476; (800) 235-4316

This elegant three-story French Victorian has been included in the National Register of Historic Places. The inn is on a quiet street, less than a block from town beside a park. Situated at the northern end of the wine country, the town features spas, mud baths, fine restaurants, and shops. The inn is decorated with antiques, canopy beds and down comforters, fireplaces, and TV. Full gourmet breakfasts served, with wine and cheese served in the afternoon.

Host: Elaine Bryant
Rooms: 5 (PB) $95-145
Full Breakfast
Credit Cards: A, B, C
Notes: 2, 5, 9, 11, 12, 14

Foothill House

3037 Foothill Boulevard, 94515
(707) 942-6933; (800) 942-6933

"The most romantic inn of the Napa Valley," according to the *Chicago Tribune* travel editor. In a country setting, Foothill House offers spacious suites individually decorated with antiques, each with private bath and entrance, fireplace, and small refrigerator. Private cottages, some with Jacuzzi, also available.

Hosts: Doris and Gus Beckert
Rooms: 3 (PB) $115-220
Full Breakfast
Credit Cards: A, B, C
Notes: 2, 5, 9, 10, 11, 12, 14

---

6 Pets welcome; 8 Children welcome; 9 Social drinking allowed; 10 Tennis available; 11 Swimming available; 12 Golf available; 13 Skiing available; 14 May be booked through travel agents.

The Pink Mansion

1415 Foothill Boulevard, 94515
(707) 942-0558

A 116-year-old Victorian in the heart of the Napa Valley wine country. Within biking distance to several wineries; walking distance to Calistoga's many spas and restaurants. Fully air-conditioned; complimentary wine and cheese. Each room has a wonderful view and private bath.

Host: Jeff Seyfried
Rooms: 5 (PB) $85-155
Full Breakfast
Minimum stay weekends and holidays: 2 nights
Credit Cards: A, B
Notes: 2, 5, 8 (over 12), 9, 10, 11, 12

Quail Mountain Bed and Breakfast Inn

4455 North Street, Helena Highway, 94515
(707) 942-0316

Quail Mountain is a secluded luxury bed and breakfast situated on 26 wooded and vineyard acres. Three guest rooms, each with king bed, private bath, and private deck. Complimentary wine, pool, spa. Full breakfast. Close to Napa Valley wineries and restaurants.

Hosts: Don and Alma Swiers
Rooms: 3 (PB) $90-125
Full Breakfast
Credit Cards: A, B
Notes: 2, 5, 9, 10, 11, 12, 14

CAMARILLO

Kids Welcome 3-14

3924 East 14th Street, Long Beach, 90804
(310) 498-0552; (800) 383-3513

This four-acre ranch in Camarillo has stables, fruit trees, a spa, and hiking trails. The two guest wings have a total of five rooms, which is perfect for a large family. Affordable rates.

CAMBRIA

Bed and Breakfast Homestay

P. O. Box 326, 93428
(805) 927-4613

Bed and Breakfast Homestay has been providing travelers with quality overnight accommodations in quiet, residential homes for more than 12 years. Accommodations consist of a private floor, room, or suite with bath. All homestays include a full or continental breakfast. Guests will be hosted by very friendly, active people, who enjoy meeting other people and sharing the Cambria experience. This service is listed in AAA of Southern California.

Eye Openers Bed and Breakfast Reservations CA-P31

P. O. Box 694, Altadena, 91003-0694
(213) 684-4428; (818) 797-2055
FAX (818) 798-3640

Just south of Hearst Castle at the ocean, this bed and breakfast features rooms with fireplaces, private patios, and bath en suite. A full breakfast is served with an ocean view. Three guest rooms. Private bath. $75 plus tax.

Eye Openers Bed and Breakfast Reservations CA-B51

P. O. Box 694, Altadena, 91003-0694
(213) 684-4428; (818) 797-2055
FAX (818) 798-3640

Contemporary A-frame bed and breakfast inn on the beach has antique furnishings, ocean views, and outdoor decks. Continental breakfast. Five guest rooms. Private bath. $105-135 plus tax.

NOTES: Credit cards accepted: A Master Card; B Visa; C American Express; D Discover Card; E Diner's Club; F Other; 2 Personal Checks accepted; 3 Lunch available; 4 Dinner available; 5 Open all year;

Eye Openers Bed and Breakfast Reservations CA-D1

P. O. Box 694, Altadena, 91003-0694
(213) 684-4428; (818) 797-2055
FAX (818) 798-3640

English couple hosts an elegant bed and breakfast with a relaxed atmosphere near Hearst Castle and mid-coast beaches. First floor is guest's domain and includes a large sitting room/bedroom with a fireplace and wet bar. Continental breakfast with jams and jellies from homegrown berries. One guest room with private bath. $90.

Eye Openers Bed and Breakfast Reservations CA-O61

P. O. Box 694, Altadena, 91003-0694
(213) 684-4428; (818) 797-2055
FAX (818) 798-3640

Each guest room in this 1873 Greek Revival-style historic inn is decorated differently, but all have antiques from the 1800s. Full breakfast. Six guest rooms. Private bath. $85-115 plus tax.

Megan's Friends #08

1776 Royal Way, San Luis Obispo, 93405
(805) 544-4406

This retreat is situated in the pines above West Village. It has two bedrooms with queen or twin beds and a shared bath, and provides radios and books. Continental breakfast is served on the deck, in the dining room, or in the breakfast area. A five-minute drive to the village shops and art galleries. Pack a lunch and walk along the craggy beaches nearby off Highway 1, where picnic tables are conveniently situated. $65.

Megan's Friends #09

1776 Royal Way, San Luis Obispo, 93405
(805) 544-4406

Two cabins are available for guests: the Blue Cabin and the Brown Cabin, both with double beds, showers, color TV, VCR, microwave ovens, and refrigerators. Each cabin has a deck outside with a shared barbecue. Expanded continental breakfast. No children, please. $70.

Megan's Friends #10

1776 Royal Way, San Luis Obispo, 93405
(805) 544-4406

Luxurious, architect-designed home close to the Pacific Ocean. Guests are provided with a spacious bedroom, king-size bed, and private bath. An extra room can be available with a shared bath. Private entrance. Refreshments upon arrival. Full breakfast. $78.

Megan's Friends #12

1776 Royal Way, San Luis Obispo, 93405
(805) 544-4406

Beautiful cottage in quiet area. Kitchen with refrigerator, fully supplied with coffee maker, toaster oven, utilities. Fireplace and color TV. French doors open to a deck and patio. Twenty-minute walk to Pacific Ocean. Welcome basket and continental breakfast. $75.

The Olallieberry Inn

2476 Main Street, 93428
(805) 927-3222

Romance and charm, served with local wine, evening hors d'oeuvres, and a full breakfast in a historic 1873 inn. The six beautifully appointed guest rooms, three with fireplaces, all have private baths and some feature oversized tubs. Walk to

6 Pets welcome; 8 Children welcome; 9 Social drinking allowed; 10 Tennis available; 11 Swimming available; 12 Golf available; 13 Skiing available; 14 May be booked through travel agents.

restaurants and shops. Seven miles from Hearst Castle. Framed by beautiful gardens and the Santa Rosa Creek, the Olallieberry Inn is the perfect romantic getaway. Handicapped accessible.

Hosts: Peter and Carol Ann Irsfeld
Rooms: 6 (PB) $85-115
Full Breakfast
Credit Cards: A, B
Notes: 2, 4, 5, 10, 12, 14

The Pickford House Bed and Breakfast
2555 MacLeod Way, 93428
(805) 927-8619

Only eight miles from Hearst Castle, Pickford House is decorated with antiques reminiscent of the golden age of film. Eight rooms have king or queen beds, private baths, fireplaces, and a view of the mountains. Parlor with an 1860 bar is used for wine and tea bread at 5:00 P.M. TV in rooms. All have claw-foot tubs and showers in rooms. Well-behaved children welcome. Extra person, $20. Crib or rollaway bed available.

Host: Anna Larsen
Rooms: 8 (PB) $85-120 plus tax
Full Breakfast
Credit Cards: A, B
Notes: 5, 8, 9, 11, 14

CAMINO

Camino Hotel: The Seven Mile House
4103 Carson Road, P. O. Box 1197, 95709
(916) 644-7740

Situated in the Apple Hill region of California's Gold Country at an elevation of 3,000 feet along the historic Carson Wagon Trail, the Camino Hotel is within walking or biking distance of several apple ranches, wineries, antiques, and dining. For years, the town of Camino has been a haven for loggers and weary wayfarers.

Today it continues this tradition of offering hospitality to travelers from around the world.

Hosts: Paula Nobert and John Eddy
Rooms: 10 (3 PB; 7 SB) $65-85
Expanded Continental Breakfast
Credit Cards: A, B, C, D
Notes: 2, 5, 8, 9, 11, 12, 13, 14

CAPISTRANO

Bed and Breakfast Los Angeles 6-8
3924 East 14th Street, Long Beach, 90804
(310) 498-0552; (800) 383-3513

This classic little Spanish inn sits on the beach in San Juan Capistrano. Individually decorated rooms feature wood-burning fireplaces, wet bars, refrigerators, and private patios. Continental breakfast includes croissants and jam. Moderate rates.

CAPITOLA-BY-THE-SEA

The Inn at Depot Hill
250 Monterey Avenue, 95010
(408) 462-3376

Sophistication and elegance describe The Inn at Depot Hill in the quaint Mediterranean-style, beach-side resort of Capitola. A ticket to romance, illusion, and escapism. Travel the world, make stops at Portofino, Stratford-on-Avon, Delft, Sissinghurst, or Paris. Capture a dream in Cote d'Azur, or come home to America in the contemporary Capitola beach room. Each of the eight suites has a fireplace and private bath. All are unique—so varied that it will be difficult to decide where the journey will begin or end.

Host: Suzie Lankes
Rooms: 8 (PB) $155-250
Full Breakfast
Credit Cards: A, B, C
Notes: 2, 5, 9, 10, 11, 12, 14

NOTES: Credit cards accepted: A Master Card; B Visa; C American Express; D Discover Card; E Diner's Club; F Other; 2 Personal Checks accepted; 3 Lunch available; 4 Dinner available; 5 Open all year;

CARMEL

Bed and Breakfast International #203

P. O. Box 282910, San Francisco, 94128-2910
(415) 696-1690; FAX (415) 696-1699

Large contemporary home with several decks surrounded by hills ten minutes from Carmel. There is a studio guest house with a queen-size lodgepole pine bed, wood-burning fireplace, and private entrance. There is a hot tub on one of the decks for guests to use. Breakfast is brought to the guest house by the host. $88.

Bed and Breakfast International #205

P. O. Box 282910, San Francisco, 94128-2910
(415) 696-1690; FAX (415) 696-1699

Spacious modern home has four fireplaces, and is very contemporary in design, just minutes from downtown Carmel. The guest room has a charming and cozy decor with professional decorator touches. There is a private entrance, fireplace in the room, private bath, and view of Point Lobos. Breakfast is prepared by the host in the main house. $95.

Bed and Breakfast International #207

P. O. Box 282910, San Francisco, 94128-2910
(415) 696-1690; FAX (415) 696-1699

Contemporary town house with fine art and tasteful furnishings situated on the east side of Highway 1, five minutes from Carmel Beach. The guest room is large and has a queen bed and private bath. There is a pool available for guests' use. $78.

Eye Openers Bed and Breakfast Reservations CA-C251

P. O. Box 694, Altadena, 91003-0694
(213) 684-4428; (818) 797-2055
FAX (818) 798-3640

Charming country inn offers twenty-five large, nicely decorated guest rooms with fireplace, full breakfast, afternoon and evening refreshments. Convenient to all Carmel area attractions. Private bath. $105-180 plus tax.

Eye Openers Bed and Breakfast Reservations CA-G191

P. O. Box 694, Altadena, 91003-0694
(213) 684-4428; (818) 797-2055
FAX (818) 798-3640

Close to the beach in a quiet neighborhood, this 1926 refurbished inn has a lush garden setting. Buffet breakfast and afternoon refreshments. Nineteen guest rooms. Private bath. $85-150 plus tax.

Happy Landing Inn

Box 2619, 93921
(408) 624-7917

Delightful little bed and breakfast inn in the heart of downtown Carmel. Beautiful antiques, stained-glass windows, fresh flowers. Breakfast served in your room. This inn looks like a page out of a Beatrix Potter book.

Hosts: Robert Ballard and Dick Stewart
Rooms: 7 (PB) $90-145
European Breakfast
Minimum stay weekends: 2 nights
Credit Cards: A, B
Notes: 2, 5, 8 (over 12), 9, 10, 12

Monte Verde Inn

P. O. Box 394, Ocean Avenue and Monte Verde, 93921
(408) 625-6046; (800) 328-7707

6 Pets welcome; 8 Children welcome; 9 Social drinking allowed; 10 Tennis available; 11 Swimming available; 12 Golf available; 13 Skiing available; 14 May be booked through travel agents.

A charming country inn nestled in the heart of Carmel and surrounded by lovely gardens and terraces as well as decks. The inn has ten uniquely furnished warm rooms with either king or queen beds, all with private baths. Some rooms have spectacular ocean views, while others have wood-burning fireplaces. Only three short blocks to the shimmering Pacific Ocean. With a courteous staff, this little inn is one many would like to keep secret.

Hosts: Willa and Ernest Aylaian
Rooms: 10 (PB) $85-145
Continental Breakfast
Credit Cards: A, B, C
Notes: 2, 5, 8, 9, 10, 11, 12, 14

Sea View Inn

P. O. Box 4138
Camino Real between 11th and 12th, 93921
(408) 624-8778

The Sea View Inn, a simple country Victorian, has been welcoming guests for over 70 years. A quiet, cozy bed and breakfast, the Sea View has eight individually decorated rooms, six with private baths. Situated near the village and the beach, the Sea View provides a welcoming retreat. A generous continental breakfast and afternoon tea are complimentary.

Host: Diane Hydorn
Rooms: 8 (6 PB; 2 SB) $80-110
Expanded Continental Breakfast
Credit Cards: A, B
Notes: 2, 5, 9, 10, 11, 12

CARPINTERIA

Carpinteria Beach Condo

1825 Cravens Lane, 93013
(805) 684-1579

Situated in a lush flower-growing valley. Across the street from "the world's safest beach." Unit has mountain view. Tropical island decor has a sunset wall mural, fully furnished kitchen, queen bed, and color cable TV. Pool, spa, and gas barbecue on complex. Self-catering with beverage provided and fruit from host's ranch. Sleeps four. Eleven miles south of Santa Barbara. Hosts available for tennis, bridge, or tour of their semitropical fruit ranch and orchid farm.

Hosts: Bev and Don Schroeder
Suite: Rooms 2 (SB) $60-65
Continental Breakfast
Credit Cards: None
Notes: 2, 5, 8, 9, 10, 11, 12

CLOVERDALE

Vintage Towers Bed and Breakfast Inn

302 North Main Street, 95425
(707) 894-4535

This lovely Queen Anne Victorian mansion was built in 1901 with three architecturally unique towers that now house some of the guest suites. Situated near 52 wineries in the serene Sonoma Valley and the Russian River Basin. Gourmet breakfast prepared by a French pastry chef.

Hosts: Jim Mees and Garrett Hall
Rooms: 7 (5 PB; 2 SB) $80-115
Full Breakfast
Credit Cards: A, B, C, D
Notes: 2, 7 (limited), 8, 9, 10, 11, 12, 14

Ye Olde Shelford House Bed and Breakfast

29955 River Road, 95425
(800) 833-6479

This circa 1885 country Victorian home is situated in the wine country, with a wrap-around porch, hot tub, pool, bicycles, and recreation room. Guest rooms are filled with antiques, flowers, homemade quilts and dolls. Horse-drawn surrey rides ($60) or antique car wine tours ($55) with a picnic lunch are available.

Hosts: Ina and Al Sauder
Rooms: 6 (PB) $85-110
Full Breakfast
Credit Cards: A, B, D
Notes: 2, 8, 9, 10, 11, 12, 14

NOTES: Credit cards accepted: A Master Card; B Visa; C American Express; D Discover Card; E Diner's Club; F Other; 2 Personal Checks accepted; 3 Lunch available; 4 Dinner available; 5 Open all year;

COLUMBIA

Columbia City Hotel
P. O. Box 1870, 95310
(209) 532-1479

Centrally situated in Columbia, a historic
Gold Rush town preserved and protected
by the state of California, this impeccable
inn is surrounded by relics of the past. All
rooms have been restored to reflect the
1850s. Downstairs, the highly acclaimed
restaurant and always inviting What Cheer
Saloon provide a haven for travelers seeking comfort and gracious hospitality. All
rooms have half-baths; hall showers.

Host: Tom Bender
Rooms: 10 (PB) $70-90
Full Breakfast
Credit Cards: A, B, C
Notes: 2, 3, 4, 5, 7, 8, 9, 10, 11, 12, 13, 14

Columbia City Hotel

Fallon Hotel
Washington Street, 95310
(209) 532-1470

Since 1857, the historic Fallon Hotel has
provided a home-away-from-home to
countless visitors. Authentically restored to
its Victorian grandeur, most of the furnishings are original to the inn. Several rooms
have private balconies, and all rooms have
half-baths. Baskets of toiletries, robes, and
slippers are provided for the showers off
the hallway. One handicapped room available. Centrally situated in a state-restored
Gold Rush town. Adjacent to the Fallon
Theatre which provides year-round productions. Call or write for price information.

Host: Tom Bender
Rooms: 14 (SB) $55-90
Continental Breakfast
Credit Cards: A, B, C
Notes: 2, 5, 8, 11, 12, 13, 14

CORONADO ISLAND

Bed and Breakfast Los Angeles 8-4
3924 East 14th Street, Seal Beach, 90804
(310) 493-6837; (800) 383-3513

Not just a bed and breakfast, but a weekend
experience. This hostess also teaches fitness and dance classes. The 1894 historic
landmark home features Balanchine, Bary-
shnikov, and Fred and Ginger rooms.
Breakfast includes Armenian eggs and
baklava. Cooking classes available, too.
Luxury rates.

DAVENPORT

New Davenport Bed and Breakfast
31 Davenport Avenue, 95017
(408) 425-1818; (408) 426-4122

Halfway between Carmel-Monterey and
San Francisco on Coast Highway 1. Small,
rural, coastal town noted for whale watching, wind surfing, Ano Nuevo Elephant
Seal State Reserve, hiking, bicycling, and
beach exploration. Wonderful restaurant
and gift store with unusual treasures and
jewelry.

6 Pets welcome; 8 Children welcome; 9 Social drinking allowed; 10 Tennis available; 11 Swimming available;
12 Golf available; 13 Skiing available; 14 May be booked through travel agents.

Hosts: Bruce and Marcia McDougal
Rooms: 12 (PB) $60-110
Full Breakfast
Credit Cards: A, B
Notes: 2, 3, 4, 5, 8 (limited family rooms), 9

DEL MAR

Eye Openers Bed and Breakfast Reservations DM-R101

P. O. Box 694, Altadena, 91003-0694
(213) 684-4428; (818) 797-2055
FAX (818) 798-3640

Romantic getaway in a lovely seaside village just north of San Diego offers a choice of ten rooms, many with an ocean view and one with a fireplace. Enjoy an extended continental breakfast, afternoon refreshments, a walk on the beach, or a trip to the racetrack or nearby reknown flower-growing areas. Private and shared baths. $80-135 plus tax.

Gull's Nest

12930 Via Esperia, P. O. Box 1056, 92014
(619) 259-4863

Gull's Nest rustic hideaway is a contemporary wood home surrounded by pines with a beautiful ocean and bird sanctuary view from two upper decks. Home is decorated with many paintings, mosaics, and wood carvings. Five minutes from La Jolla and Del Mar. Close to I-5, and just 20 minutes from the San Diego Zoo and airport.

Hosts: Mike and Connie Segel
Rooms: 2 (PB) $60-85
Full Breakfast
Credit Cards: F
Notes: 2, 10, 11, 12

ELK

Elk Cove Inn

6300 South Highway 1, P. O. Box 367, 95432
(707) 877-3321

An 1883 Victorian atop a bluff with spectacular ocean views. Some cabins with fireplaces. Full gourmet breakfast is served in the ocean-view dining room. Ready access to an expansive, driftwood-strewn beach. Beds have the subtle luxury of sun-dried linens. Romantic atmosphere in rural coastal village. New addition provides dormers, window seats, and ocean-view deck.

Host: Hildrun-Uta Triebess
Rooms: 7 (PB) $108-148
Cabins: 4 (PB)
Full Breakfast
Credit Cards: None
Notes: 2, 5, 8 (over 12), 9, 10, 11, 12

ENCINITAS

Eye Openers Bed and Breakfast Reservations EN-C41

P. O. Box 694, Altadena, 91003-0694
(213) 684-4428; (818) 797-2055
FAX (818) 798-3640

Situated in Encinatas, a renowned flower-growing area in California, this new family-run bed and breakfast with ocean views has large rooms, a Southwest decor, and a relaxed atmosphere. Continental breakfast. Three rooms and one suite. Private bath. $75-95 plus tax.

EUCALYPTUS HILL

Kids Welcome 11-3

3924 East 14th Street, Long Beach, 90804
(310) 498-0552; (800) 383-3513

This hilltop home with ocean views has a pool, spa, and two guest rooms, both with private entrances and private baths. Breakfast is served poolside. Friendly golden retriever will greet guests. Moderate rates.

NOTES: Credit cards accepted: A Master Card; B Visa; C American Express; D Discover Card; E Diner's Club; F Other; 2 Personal Checks accepted; 3 Lunch available; 4 Dinner available; 5 Open all year;

EUREKA

Old Town
Bed and Breakfast Inn
1521 Third Street, 95501
(707) 445-3941; (800) 331-5098

Historic 1871 Victorian in Eureka's famous Old Town district. Small, cozy, uniquely warm, plush, original art and period antiques. Tubs and showers; Teddy bears, rubber duckies; full breakfast. "The quintessence of world-class bed and breakfast."

Hosts: Leigh and Diane Benson
Rooms: 7 (5 PB; 2 SB) $75-185
Full Breakfast
Credit Cards: A, B, D
Notes: 2, 5, 8 (over 10), 9, 10, 11, 12, 14

FERNDALE

The Gingerbread Mansion
400 Berding Street, 95536
(707) 786-4000

The Gingerbread Mansion Bed and Breakfast Inn is well known as one of America's most photographed homes. Its striking Victorian architecture trimmed with gingerbread, its colorful peach and yellow paint, and its surrounding English gardens all make the Gingerbread Mansion a photographer's delight. It is an understatement to say that the interiors are also spectacular.

Host: Ken Torbert
Rooms: 9 (PB) $70-185
Continental Breakfast
Credit Cards: A, B
Notes: 2, 5, 9, 12, 14

FISH CAMP

Karen's Bed and Breakfast
Yosemite Inn
1144 Railroad Avenue, P. O. Box 8, 93623
(800) 346-1443

Experience the splendor of each season in Yosemite National Park. Only two miles from the south entrance, Karen's is open year-round offering cozy country comfort. Nestled amid the towering pines and whispering cedars at 5,000 feet, it blends contemporary and country living. Innkeepers will assist in planning guests' visit while in the Yosemite area to assure maximum enjoyment.

Hosts: Karen Bergh and Lee Morse
Rooms: 3 (PB) $85
Full Breakfast
Credit Cards: None
Notes: 2, 5, 8, 10, 11, 12, 13, 14

FORT BRAGG

Avalon House
561 Stewart Street, 95437
(707) 964-5555

A 1905 Craftsman house built completely of redwood and extensively remodeled in 1988, Avalon House is furnished with a mix of antiques and willow furniture. The emphasis here is on luxury and comfort: fireplaces, whirlpool tubs, down comforters and pillows, good bedside lights, as well as mood lights to create a romantic ambience. The inn is in a quiet residential area three

The Gingerbread Mansion

6 Pets welcome; 8 Children welcome; 9 Social drinking allowed; 10 Tennis available; 11 Swimming available; 12 Golf available; 13 Skiing available; 14 May be booked through travel agents.

blocks from the Pacific Ocean and one block from Highway 1. The Skunk Train depot is two blocks away.

Host: Anne Sorrells
Rooms: 6 (PB) $70-135
Full Breakfast
Credit Cards: A, B, C, D
Notes: 2, 5, 8, 9, 14

The Grey Whale Inn

The Grey Whale Inn

615 North Main Street, 95437
(707) 964-0640; (800) 382-7244

Handsome four-story Mendocino Coast landmark since 1915. Cozy rooms to expansive suites, all private baths. Ocean, garden, or hill and city views. Some have fireplace, some have TV, one has whirlpool tub, all have phones. Recreation area: pool table, books, fireside lounge, TV theater. Conference room (16 persons). Complimentary buffet breakfast features Colette's Blue-ribbon coffee cakes. Friendly, helpful staff. Relaxed seaside charm, situated six blocks from beach. Celebrate special occasions on the fabled Mendocino Coast! Mobil three-star rating. AB & BA three crowns.

Host: Colette Bailey
Rooms: 14 (PB) $80-160
Full Breakfast
Credit Cards: A, B, D
Notes: 2, 5, 9, 10, 11, 12, 14

Pudding Creek Inn

700 North Main Street, 95437
(707) 964-9529

Two Victorian homes built in 1884 by a Russian count, connected by a lush enclosed garden. All rooms are comfortably decorated in Victorian style; all have private baths, and some have fireplaces. Exceptional accommodations with personal service, friendly hospitality, and yet special emphasis on privacy. Within walking distance of Glass Beach, Pudding Creek, downtown shops and restaurants, logging museum, Skunk Train depot.

Hosts: Garry and Carole Anloff
Rooms: 10 (PB) $65-125
Full Breakfast
Credit Cards: A, B, C
Notes: 2, 5, 8, 10, 11, 12, 14

FREMONT

Lord Bradley's Inn

43344 Mission Boulevard, 94539
(415) 490-0520

This Victorian is nestled below Mission Peak, adjacent to the Mission San Jose. Numerous olive trees on the property were planted by the Ohlone Indians. Common room, garden, patio. Parking in rear. Take the bus or Bay Area Rapid Transit to San Francisco for a day.

Pudding Creek Inn

Hosts: Keith and Anne Bradley Medeiros
Rooms: 8 (PB) $65-75
Continental Breakfast
Credit Cards: A, B, D
Notes: 2, 5, 6, 9, 14

FREESTONE

Green Apple Inn

520 Bohemian Highway, 95472
(707) 874-2526

An 1860s New England-style farmhouse set in a meadow backed by redwoods. This inn is situated on five acres in the designated historic district of Freestone between Bodega Bay and the Russian River. There are several excellent restaurants and small family wineries in the area. In the village itself are many unique shops.

Hosts: Rogers and Rosemary Hoffman
Rooms: 4 (PB) $82-92
Full Breakfast
Credit Cards: A, B
Notes: 2, 5, 6, 8 (over 6), 10, 11, 12, 14

GARDEN GROVE

Kids Welcome 7-4

3924 East 14th Street, Long Beach, 90804
(310) 498-0552; (800) 383-3513

Kids are really welcome in this lovely older home in Garden Grove. There are three guest rooms; one has a fireplace and a balcony, and another one has a TV and small refrigerator. All have private baths. The hostess is a weaver and doll collector. Affordable rates.

Rent-A-Room

11531 Varna Street, 92640
(714) 638-1406

This is a referral service that books private homes between Los Angeles and San Diego. No inns are on the list; these bed and breakfasts are in the British tradition.

Most offerings are close to Southern California attractions, such as Disneyland, Knott's Berry Farm, San Diego Zoo, Sea World, Universal Studios, Anaheim Convention Center, and beaches. One to three guest rooms in each home. All rooms have private baths. Full breakfast is served in all bookings. Personal checks accepted. Open year-round; children welcome. Swimming nearby. $45-65.

GEYSERVILLE

Campbell Ranch Inn

1475 Canyon Road, 95441
(707) 857-3476

Thirty-five-acre country setting in the heart of Sonoma County wine country. Spectacular view, beautiful gardens, tennis court, swimming pool, hot tub, bicycles. Full breakfast served on the terrace; homemade evening dessert. Teenagers welcome. Color brochure available.

Hosts: Mary Jane and Jerry Campbell
Rooms: 5 (PB) $100-145
Full Breakfast
Minimum stay weekends: 2 nights; major holiday
    weekends: 3 nights
Credit Cards: A, B
Notes: 2, 5, 9, 10, 12, 11, 14

GLEN ELLEN

JVB Vineyards

14335 Sonoma Highway, P. O. Box 997, 95442
(707) 996-4533

Two private little Spanish-style adobe haciendas overlooking the vineyard. Queen beds, hot tub, beautiful patio. Great waffles for breakfast. Thirty-seven wineries and champagne cellars in historic Sonoma Valley. Site of raising of the Bear Flag, author Jack London's Wolf House, last mission on the California trail, and home of General Vallejo.

Hosts: Beverly and Jack Babb
Rooms: 2 (PB) $85
Full Breakfast
Credit Cards: None
Notes: 2, 5, 9, 11, 12, 14

GROVELAND

Bed and Breakfast International #401

P. O. Box 282910, San Francisco, 94128-2910
(415) 696-1690; FAX (415) 696-1699

Contemporary wood home with deck situated on the top of one of the hills in an area called Pine Mountain Lake. Home has a view of the lake below and the mountains of Yosemite in the distance. It is 25 miles to the entrance of Yosemite. There are three rooms with private baths. Hosts serve excellent breakfasts, sometimes with a South-of-the-border flair. $60.

Lee's Middle Fork Resort and Motel

11399 Cherry Oil Road, 95321
(209) 962-7408; (800) 626-7408

Small resort/bed and breakfast motel features cabins with kitchens, motel rooms, and rooms in the lodge. Situated on the river, with swimming, fishing, hiking, and hunting in the middle of a national forest. Owner operated, just 10 miles outside Yosemite National Park, West Gate, Highway 120.

Hosts: Kathy and Ed Niedeals
Rooms: 24 (23 PB; 1 Suite) $49-98
Continental Breakfast
Credit Cards: A, B, C, D, E, F
Notes: 2, 3, 5, 8, 9, 10, 11, 12, 14

GUALALA

North Coast Country Inn

34591 South Highway 1, 95445
(707) 884-4537; (800) 995-4537

A cluster of rustic redwood buildings with ocean views. Rooms feature queen beds, fireplaces, kitchenettes, private baths, decks, and private entries. The inn has a hot tub and gazebo. Full breakfast is served in guest rooms. Nearby golf, hiking, horseback riding, fishing, and beaches.

Hosts: Loren and Nancy Flanagan
Rooms: 4 (PB) $135
Full Breakfast
Credit Cards: A, B, C
Notes: 2, 5, 9, 10, 12, 14

Whale Watch Inn

35100 South Highway 1, 95445
(707) 884-3667; (800) WHALE42

Romance on the rugged northern California coast. Oceanfront, cliff-side accommodations on two acres of gardens and a private stairway to the beach. Luxurious contem-porary rooms and suites, ocean views and secluded decks, sixteen with fireplaces, and eight with a two person Jacuzzi, are available. Skylights provide moon and star viewing, and gourmet breakfast is delivered to the room. Situated three hours north of San Francisco and ranked among the top fifty romantic California getaways.

Hosts: Jim and Kazuko Popplewell
Rooms: 18 (PB) $160-275
Full Breakfast
Credit Cards: A, B, C
Notes: 2, 5, 9, 10, 12

GUERNEVILLE

Bed and Breakfast International #304

P. O. Box 282910, San Francisco, 94128-2910
(415) 696-1690; FAX (415) 696-1699

An estate situated among rolling hills in one of Northern California's most beautiful wine country areas. Very peaceful atmosphere, high quality decor, and full breakfasts. Nine rooms, all with private baths, and furnished in antiques and other fine

NOTES: Credit cards accepted: A Master Card; B Visa; C American Express; D Discover Card; E Diner's Club; F Other; 2 Personal Checks accepted; 3 Lunch available; 4 Dinner available; 5 Open all year;

pieces. Lots of fresh flowers. Swimming pool and hot tub available. $115-150.

HALF MOON BAY

Bed and Breakfast Los Angeles 13-8

3924 East 14th Street, Long Beach, 90804
(310) 498-0552; (800) 383-3513

These British-born hosts offer complimentary wine and a wood-burning stove in their perfectly restored Queen Anne-style home. They have seven rooms, including a Garden Suite featuring an in-room hot tub, and a refrigerator stocked with goodies. The hostess collects rare herbs and invites guests to share in her cuttings. Two children still live at home. Moderate-luxury rates.

Bed and Breakfast Los Angeles 13-10

3924 East 14th Street, Long Beach, 90804
(310) 498-0552; (800) 383-3513

The original home of the town's first city planner still stands in the town of Half Moon Bay. Sumptuous buffet is served in the morning. Beverages are served around the fire at night. Nine rooms with private baths, some with Jacuzzis and/or fireplaces, are available to guests with well-behaved children, or those who want to leave the children at home. Luxury rates.

Old Thyme Inn

779 Main Street, 94019
(415) 726-1616

This 1890s Victorian is on historic Main Street and has an herbal theme. Guests are invited to stroll in Marcia's English herb garden and take cuttings. Everybody loves

George's buttermilk scones with herb tea for breakfast. Some rooms have double-size whirlpool tubs; fireplaces and antiques are everywhere.

Hosts: Marcia and George Dempsey
Rooms: 7 (PB) $65-210
Full Breakfast
Credit Cards: A
Notes: 2, 5, 9, 10, 12, 14

HEALDSBURG

Bed and Breakfast San Francisco #16

P. O. Box 420009, San Francisco, 94142
(415) 479-1913; FAX (415) 921-BBSF

Jane's place is situated in the heart of wine country, just minutes from some of California's finest wineries, close to the Russian River beaches and resorts and only one-half hour from the Pacific coast. There are three quaintly furnished rooms with private baths on an estate overlooking vineyards. Home-cooked breakfast. $85.

Healdsburg Inn on the Plaza

110 Matheson Street, P. O. Box 1196, 95448
(707) 433-6991

A 1900 brick Victorian, formerly a Wells Fargo stagecoach express station, now restored and elegantly furnished as a bed and breakfast. Bay windows view old town plaza; fireplaces; central heat and air, solarium/roof garden for afternoon snacks, popcorn, wine, music. Coffee and tea available all day. Champagne breakfasts on weekends. TV, VCR, phone, and gift certificates available. Family owned and operated, close to everything.

Hosts: Genny Jenkins and Dyanne Celi
Rooms: 9 (PB) $75-155
Full Breakfast
Credit Cards: A, B
Notes: 2, 5, 9, 10, 11, 12

6 Pets welcome; 8 Children welcome; 9 Social drinking allowed; 10 Tennis available; 11 Swimming available; 12 Golf available; 13 Skiing available; 14 May be booked through travel agents.

HOLLYWOOD

Bed and Breakfast Los Angeles 2-1

3924 East 14th Street, Long Beach, 90804
(310) 498-0552; (800) 383-3513

Just north of Sunset Boulevard, this upstairs suite has two bedrooms, two baths, and a sun deck. Hosts live downstairs and speak seven languages. Affordable rates.

Eye Openers Bed and Breakfast Reservations LA-G2

P. O. Box 694, Altadena, 91003-0694
(213) 684-4428; (818) 797-2055
FAX (818) 798-3640

1910 California bungalow on a quiet palm-lined street close to Hollywoods well-known attractions. There are two second-floor guest rooms, one with a sun deck overlooking the spacious garden. Hosts speak several languages. Continental breakfast. Good public transportation. Resident dog. Private bath. $40-45.

Eye Openers Bed and Breakfast Reservations LA-M1

P. O. Box 694, Altadena, 91003-0694
(213) 684-4428; (818) 797-2055
FAX (818) 798-3640

Bed and breakfast inn lovingly decorated by host offers guest livingroom with fireplace, dining room, kitchen, and laundry privileges. Relax in the backyard garden, or walk to nearby studios and restaurants. Good public transportation nearby. Host is a scientist who enjoys traveling and folk dancing. Two guest rooms. Shared bath. $30-40 plus tax.

Kids Welcome 2-3

3924 East 14th Street, Long Beach, 90804
(310) 498-0552; (800) 383-3513

Cute three-bedroom, two-bathroom bungalow can be rented by the room or by the whole house. West Hollywood location includes livingroom (with fireplace), dining room, and kitchen. Hostess brings breakfast from the house next door. Affordable rates.

HOPE VALLEY

Sorensen's Resort

14255 Highway 88, 96120
(916) 694-2203; (800) 423-4949

Sorensen's is an all-season resort situated in Hope Valley 20 minutes south of Lake Tahoe and offering 30 cozy cabins—three of which are bed and breakfast. The restaurant serves breakfast, lunch, and dinner daily. A wood-burning sauna is available for guests.

Hosts: John and Patty Brissenden
Rooms: 30 (28 PB; 2 SB) $60-225
Continental Breakfast
Credit Cards: A, B
Notes: 2, 3, 4, 5, 8, 9, 10, 11, 12, 13, 14

IDYLLWILD

Wilkum Inn

Box 1115, 92549
(909) 659-4087

Nestled among the pines in a rustic mountain village, this two-story shingle-sided inn offers rooms that are individually furnished with the innkeepers' antiques and collectibles. Knotty-pine paneling and a river-rock fireplace enhance the hospitality of the common room.

Hosts: Annamae Chambers and Barbara Jones
Rooms: 5 (3 PB; 2 SB) $65-95
Expanded Continental Breakfast
Credit Cards: None
Notes: 2, 5, 9, 11, 14

NOTES: Credit cards accepted: A Master Card; B Visa; C American Express; D Discover Card; E Diner's Club; F Other; 2 Personal Checks accepted; 3 Lunch available; 4 Dinner available; 5 Open all year;

INVERNESS

Dancing Coyote Beach

P. O. Box 98, 94937
(415) 669-7200

Four charming cottages set on a private beach surrounded by Point Reyes National Seashore, each with fireplace, decks, and bay views. Stroll along the beach, linger over breakfast in the morning sun on your private deck, walk into the village of Inverness, or simply relax by the fire.

Rooms: 4 (PB) $95-125
Full Breakfast
Credit Cards: None
Notes: 2, 5, 6, 9

Fairwinds Farm
Bed and Breakfast Cottage

P. O. Box 581, 94937
(415) 663-9454

Large, secluded, cozy cottage high atop Inverness Ridge surrounded by 68,000-acre National Seashore (direct access). Ocean view from hot tub. Livingroom, fireplace, fully equipped kitchen, full bath with tub and shower. Sleeps six comfortably. TV, stereo, VCR, movies, library, guitar. Generous country breakfast plus homemade tea treats. Private garden with ponds and swing, barnyard animals, and playhouse. A private hideaway, adjacent to hiking, biking, beaches, whale watching, horseback riding.

Host: Joyce H. Goldfield
Cottage: 1 (PB) $125
Full Breakfast
Credit Cards: None
Notes: 2, 5, 8, 9, 11

Sandy Cove Inn

12990 Sir Francis Drake Boulevard, P. O. Box 869, 94937
(415) 669-1233; FAX (415) 669-7511

Relax in an inside-outside smoke-free environment, with spring water and clean air. On pristine Tomales Bay in West Marin County, just 35 miles north of San Francisco. Swimming, windsurfing, kyacking, tidepooling, beachcombing, bird watching, bicycling, and picnicking can be enjoyed from Sandy Cove Inn. Sailing, whale watching, ocean beaches, horseback riding, galleries, parks, and nature preserves are all nearby. A hearty, healthy full breakfast is served in the solarium.

Hosts: Kathy and Gerry Coles
Rooms: 3 (PB) $115
Full Breakfast
Credit Cards: A, B, C
Notes: 2, 5, 10, 11, 14

IONE

The Heirloom

214 Shakeley Lane, 95640
(209) 274-4468

Travel down a country lane into a romantic English garden, where a petit Colonial mansion (circa 1863) is shaded by century-old trees and scented by magnolias and gardenias. Fireplaces and balconies. Breakfast has a French flair. Enjoy gracious hospitality.

Hosts: Patricia Cross and Melisande Hubbs
Rooms: 6 (4 PB; 2 SB) $50-80
Full Breakfast
Credit Cards: None
Closed Thanksgiving and Dec. 24-25
Notes: 2, 8 (over 10), 9, 10, 11, 12, 14

KERNVILLE

Kern River
Bed and Breakfast

119 Kern River Drive, P. O. Box 1725, 93238
(619) 376-6750

A warm, charming country-style inn on the wild and scenic Kern River in a quaint western town within Sequoia National

6 Pets welcome; 8 Children welcome; 9 Social drinking allowed; 10 Tennis available; 11 Swimming available; 12 Golf available; 13 Skiing available; 14 May be booked through travel agents.

Kern River

Forest in the southern Sierra Nevada Mountains. Six individually decorated country bedrooms reflect the charm of Kern River Valley; all offer river views, and some have fireplaces or whirlpool tubs. Breakfast features home-baked cinnamon rolls, special blend cereals, sweetheart waffles, muffins, fresh fruit, juices, coffee, tea, and stuffed French toast. Year-round activities include rafting, fishing, golf, hiking, biking, and skiing. Fine restaurants, antique shops, and museum are within walking distance.

Hosts: Mike and Marti
Rooms: 6 (PB) $79-89 plus tax
Full Breakfast
Credit Cards: A, B
Notes: 5, 9, 14

LAGUNA BEACH

Bed and Breakfast Los Angeles 6-1

3924 East 14th Street, Long Beach, 90804
(310) 498-0552; (800) 383-3513

This getaway by the sea has a private entry, spacious room with four-poster bed, sitting room with sofa bed, TV, private bath, refrigerator, microwave, and a very large sun deck with a 180-degree ocean view. Breakfast is served on the deck or dining room. Children over eight. Moderate rates.

Bed and Breakfast Los Angeles 6-7

3924 East 14th Street, Long Beach, 90804
(310) 498-0552; (800) 383-3513

This hilltop home has sweeping views of the ocean. Two guest rooms share one bath. Downstairs suite includes pool table, bar, deck, and private bath. Children over eight, please.

Eye Openers Bed and Breakfast Reservations LA-J1

P. O. Box 694, Altadena, 91003-0694
(213) 684-4428; (818) 797-2055
FAX (818) 798-3640

Sitting room, bedroom, bath, and large deck with panoramic ocean views make this suite for guests with private entrance. Suite has refrigerator, microwave, TV, VCR and a full breakfast. Guest cottage has a living room kitchen, loft bedroom, deck, Jacuzzi tub, and continental breakfast. Walk to the beach. Private bath. $85-100.

Eye Openers Bed and Breakfast Reservations LG-B2

P. O. Box 694, Altadena, 91003-0694
(213) 684-4428; (818) 797-2055
FAX (818) 798-3640

Hilltop bed and breakfast has an ocean view, hot tub, and sauna. European hostess can accommodate up to eight guests. Full or continental breakfast is served. Resident dog. Two guest rooms. Privare and shared bath. $60-80.

Eye Openers
Bed and Breakfast
Reservations LG-C201

P. O. Box 694, Altadena, 91003-0694
(213) 684-4428; (818) 797-2055
FAX (818) 798-3640

Charming Spanish-style bed and breakfast inn with unique guest rooms and suites provides a generous buffet breakfast and evening refreshments in the library or poolside. Nineteen guest rooms and one cottage. Private bath. $95-155 plus tax.

Eye Openers
Bed and Breakfast
Reservations LG-E121

P. O. Box 694, Altadena, 91003-0694
(213) 684-4428; (818) 797-2055
FAX (818) 798-3640

Rooms in lovely continental-style bed and breakfast in the heart of Laguna are set around a courtyard, complete with fountain, flowers, tables, and chairs, where guests can enjoy breakfast and lounging. The beach is just outside the back gate. Eleven guest rooms and one suite. Private bath. $95-150 plus tax.

Eye Openers
Bed and Breakfast
Reservations LG-S2

P. O. Box 694, Altadena, 91003-0694
(213) 684-4428; (818) 797-2055
FAX (818) 798-3640

Contemporary seaside getaway in Laguna offers expansive view from an outdoor deck. Self-hosted apartment. Bedroom and living room with small kitchen have ocean views. Quiet area of bustling renowned seaside art colony. Self-catered breakfast. $110-140.

LAKE ARROWHEAD

Eagle's Landing

12406 Cedarwood, Box 150, Blue Jay, 92317
(909) 336-2642

The interesting architecture (Mountain Gothic), tower, stained glass, 26-foot ceilings and walls of glass with grand views of Lake Arrowhead, make Eagle's Landing a landmark. The three beautiful rooms are decorated with art, antiques and crafts collected from around the world. The suite is cabin-like, and done in Early California style.

Hosts: Dorothy Stone and Jack
Rooms: 4 (PB) $95-195
Full Breakfast
Credit Cards: A, B, D
Notes: 2, 5, 9, 10, 11, 13, 14

LAKE TAHOE

Bed and Breakfast
Los Angeles 18-2

3924 East 14th Street, Long Beach, 90804
(310) 498-0552; (800) 383-3513

Pine trees and serenity surround you at this historic lodge on the west shore of Lake Tahoe. The Fireplace Room and Studio can accommodate four people. The cottage and family suites are better for three or four people. Features include a hearty breakfast, Scandinavian sauna, and one of the nicest beaches on the lake. The main house is always open for games, piano playing, or lounging by the fire. Moderate rates.

Eye Openers
Bed and Breakfast
Reservations LT-C3

P. O. Box 694, Altadena, 91003-0694
(213) 684-4428; (818) 797-2055
FAX (818) 798-3640

6 Pets welcome; 8 Children welcome; 9 Social drinking allowed; 10 Tennis available; 11 Swimming available; 12 Golf available; 13 Skiing available; 14 May be booked through travel agents.

Lakefront 1928-style Tahoe stone house bed and breakfast has contemporary decor with antique accents. Continental or full breakfast. Three rooms plus a guest house. Private and shared baths. $90-110 plus tax.

Eye Openers Bed and Breakfast Reservations LT-C71

P. O. Box 694, Altadena, 91003-0694
(213) 684-4428; (818) 797-2055
FAX (818) 798-3640

This 1938 Old Tahoe-style with European pine furniture offers cottage suites and large rooms, full breakfast, afternoon refreshments, private beach with a dock, and winter ski packages. Private bath. $80-100 plus tax.

Eye Openers Bed and Breakfast Reservations LT-R41

P. O. Box 694, Altadena, 91003-0694
(213) 684-4428; (818) 797-2055
FAX (818) 798-3640

Inn decorated with Laura Ashley fabrics has pine walls and lake view. Full breakfast. Four guest rooms. Private bath. $100-150 plus tax.

LITTLE RIVER

Victorian Farmhouse Inn

7001 North Highway One, 95456
(707) 937-0697

On the coast just two miles south of Mendocino, this inn was built in 1877 and has been completely renovated and furnished in period antiques, wall coverings, lace curtains, and handmade quilts. All rooms feature either king- or queen-size beds and private baths, some with fire-places. Breakfast is delivered to the room each morning, and sherry is served in the parlor room every evening. Enjoy the apple orchards, flower gardens, School House Creek, and the nearby Pacific Ocean.

Hosts: Carole and George Molnar
Rooms: 10 (PB) $80-130
Full Breakfast
Credit Cards: A, B
Notes: 2, 5, 8, 9, 10, 11, 12, 14

LODI

Wine and Roses Country Inn

2505 West Turner Road, 95242
(209) 334-6988

Converted to a romantic country inn with nine nostaligic guest rooms and one "special occasion" two-room suite, antiques, and fresh flowers, the 1902 estate is secluded on five acres of towering trees and old-fashioned flower gardens. Afternoon tea and cookies, evening wine, delightful breakfast, library, "wine country" dining. "Casually elegant" restaurant featuring California cuisine. Five minutes to wine-tasting, golf, tennis, health club. The 1,000-mile Delta waterway is 15 minutes away; museums, performing arts, Sacramento, and gold country within 30 minutes. Full restaurant that serves lunch Tuesday-Friday, dinner Wednesday-Saturday, and brunch on Sunday. Cocktails and full bar also available. San Francisco one and one-half hours; Lake Tahoe and Yosemite two and one-half hours.

Hosts: Kris Cromwell; Del and Sherri Smith
Rooms: 10 (PB) $85-115
Full and Continental Breakfast
Credit Cards: A, B, C
Notes: 2, 4, 5, 9, 10, 11, 12, 14

LONG BEACH

Bed and Breakfast Los Angeles 5-8

3924 East 14th Street, 90804
(310) 498-0552; (800) 383-3513

NOTES: Credit cards accepted: A Master Card; B Visa; C American Express; D Discover Card; E Diner's Club; F Other; 2 Personal Checks accepted; 3 Lunch available; 4 Dinner available; 5 Open all year;

Deep pastels swath this 1903 home on a hill in Long Beach. Two guest rooms (one with kid's beds, and toys) share one and one-half baths, a large wooden deck, a hot tub, an old-fashioned garden. Less than one mile from the airport. Affordable rates.

Eye Openers Bed and Breakfast Reservations LB-A51

P. O. Box 694, Altadena, 91003-0694
(213) 684-4428; (818) 797-2055
FAX (818) 798-3640

Newly refurbished inn with handcrafted features is centrally located in Long Beach. Nicely decorated with antiques and artwork, rooms offer comfort and privacy. Continental-plus breakfast. Five guest rooms. Private bath. $50-75 plus tax.

Eye Openers Bed and Breakfast Reservations LB-M1

P. O. Box 694, Altadena, 91003-0694
(213) 684-4428; (818) 797-2055
FAX (818) 798-3640

This bed and breakfast is three short blocks from the beach, with one guest room and one suite with kitchen. Continental breakfast. Weekly rates available. Private bath. $50-75.

Eye Openers Bed and Breakfast LB-H3

P. O. Box 694, Altadena, 91003-0694
(213) 684-4428; (818) 797-2055
FAX (818) 798-3640

This 1912 California bungalow in the historic Bluff Park area is close to beaches, the park, and museum. Friendly, helpful hosts. Comfortable, quiet, airy rooms, and full breakfast await guests. Pet dog. $50-55.

Lord Mayor's Inn

435 Cedar Avenue, 90802
(213) 436-0324

Originally the home of the first mayor of Long Beach, this elegant Edwardian home has been beautifully restored. The home is well kept, filled with antiques, and has been presented with awards for excellence in restoration. The inn has five rooms, all with private baths, and guests enjoy a full breakfast served in the dining room. In addition, there are covered porches and decks to enjoy Southern California weather, beaches, entertainment; Queen Mary and convention centers are nearby.

Hosts: Laura and Reuben Brasser
Rooms: 5 (PB) $85-95
Full Breakfast
Credit Cards: A, B, C
Notes: 2, 5, 7, 8, 14

LOS ANGELES

Bed and Breakfast Los Angeles 1-1

3924 East 14th Street, Long Beach, 90804
(310) 498-0552; (800) 383-3513

Lush gardens and a shaded patio in the Los Feliz Hills, minutes from the heart of the city. Three guest rooms, each with a balcony. One private bath; one shared. Friendly hosts donate all proceeds to United Cerebral Palsy. Moderate rates.

Bed and Breakfast Los Angeles 1-3

3924 East 14th Street, Long Beach, 90804
(310) 498-0552; (800) 383-3513

Time stands still in this 1902 mansion near downtown Los Angeles. Leaded windows, period furnishings, full breakfast, and complimentary wine. Five rooms, private baths, library, game room. Secure parking. Older children only, please. Moderate-luxury rates.

6 Pets welcome; 8 Children welcome; 9 Social drinking allowed; 10 Tennis available; 11 Swimming available; 12 Golf available; 13 Skiing available; 14 May be booked through travel agents.

Bed and Breakfast
Los Angeles 1-6
3924 East 14th Street, Long Beach, 90804
(310) 498-0552; (800) 383-3513

A whole house is available to you. Two bedrooms, one and one-half baths, kitchen, dining room, livingroom (with fireplace), laundry room, and deck. Mid-Wilshire location. Hosts live next door. Affordable rates.

Bed and Breakfast
Los Angeles 1-8
3924 East 14th Street, Long Beach, 90804
(310) 498-0552; (800) 383-3513

Close to the USC campus, this 1910 Craftsman historic register home has two upstairs guest rooms, with a bath between them. There is a shaded porch in front, a sunny deck in the rear, and a smaller sun porch off one guest room. Affordable rates.

Bed and Breakfast
Los Angeles 2-4
3924 East 14th Street, Long Beach, 90804
(310) 498-0552; (800) 383-3513

Spacious high-rise near UCLA campus has two guest rooms, each with a private bath. Hostess speaks many languages. Older children only, please. Moderate rates.

Bed and Breakfast
Los Angeles 4-2
3924 East 14th Street, Long Beach, 90804
(310) 498-0552; (800) 383-3513

Cozy family home in a quiet neighborhood has two guest rooms that share one and one-half baths. Close to the beach, and hosts will pick guests up at the airport. Babies or children over five please. Affordable rates.

Eye Openers
Bed and Breakfast
Reservations LA-B1
P. O. Box 694, Altadena, 91003-0694
(213) 684-4428; (818) 797-2055
FAX (818) 798-3640

Five minutes from the Marina and LAX and walking distance to parks, tennis courts, golf, and restaurants, this cozy bed and breakfast is also near public transportation. Continental breakfast. One guest room. Shared bath. $35-45.

Eye Openers
Bed and Breakfast
Reservations LA-C2
P. O. Box 694, Altadena, 91003-0694
(213) 684-4428; (818) 797-2055
FAX (818) 798-3640

Beautifully restored Craftsman-style house on the National Register of Historic Places is close to USC and civic and convention centers. Two comfortable guest rooms, lovely gardens and patio are available for guests to enjoy. Shared and private baths. $40-50.

Eye Openers
Bed and Breakfast
Reservations LA-D1
P. O. Box 694, Altadena, 91003-0694
(213) 684-4428; (818) 797-2055
FAX (818) 798-3640

Spacious West Los Angeles apartment with elegant hospitality, interesting artifacts, and a location near most West Side destinations makes this a good bed and breakfast at a modest price. Swimming pool available. Continental breakfast. Two guest rooms. Private bath. $50-55.

NOTES: Credit cards accepted: A Master Card; B Visa; C American Express; D Discover Card; E Diner's Club; F Other; 2 Personal Checks accepted; 3 Lunch available; 4 Dinner available; 5 Open all year;

Eye Openers
Bed and Breakfast
Reservations LA-D2

P. O. Box 694, Altadena, 91003-0694
(213) 684-4428; (818) 797-2055
FAX (818) 798-3640

Convenient to L.A. International Airport, this comfortable, homey bed and breakfast with two spacious guest rooms has full exercise equipment room and hearty American breakfast. Spanish is spoken. Private and shared baths. $40-45.

Eye Openers
Bed and Breakfast
Reservations LA-H1

P. O. Box 694, Altadena, 91003-0694
(213) 684-4428; (818) 797-2055
FAX (818) 798-3640

Quite residential area near the airport and Marina has good public transportation. Share comfortable livingroom with fireplace, lovely yard, and a full or continental breakfast with hosts whose interests are folk instruments and music. One guest room. Shared bath. $32-38.

Eye Openers
Bed and Breakfast
Reservations LA-P1

P. O. Box 694, Altadena, 91003-0694
(213) 684-4428; (818) 797-2055
FAX (818) 798-3640

Walk to Westwood and UCLA from this attractive Wilshire Boulevard bed and breakfast. Enjoy an ample continental breakfast on the balcony prepared by French-speaking host. Good public transportation nearby. One guest room with private bath. $60.

Eye Openers
Bed and Breakfast
Reservations LA-S1

P. O. Box 694, Altadena, 91003-0694
(213) 684-4428; (818) 797-2055
FAX (818) 798-3640

Centrally located, spacious 800-square-foot, three-room apartment with patios is a good location for vacationing sightseers, business people, and people interested in relocating to the Los Angeles area. Breakfast is self-catered. Private bath. Weekly rates available. $65-75.

Eye Openers
Bed and Breakfast
Reservations LA-S3

P. O. Box 694, Altadena, 91003-0694
(213) 684-4428; (818) 797-2055
FAX (818) 798-3640

Two-story Art Deco-style architect-designed bed and breakfast nestled in the beautiful Los Feliz Hills near Griffith Park and the Greek Theatre. Offering a quiet, comfortable setting convenient to fine restaurants, entertainment, and tourist attractions. Two guest rooms and private bath. Public transportation available. $55-120.

Eye Openers
Bed and Breakfast
Reservations LA-S51

P. O. Box 694, Altadena, 91003-0694
(213) 684-4428; (818) 797-2055
FAX (818) 798-3640

Antique-decorated, restored 1908 Craftsman home provides the setting and mood of an earlier era. A marvelous, full gourmet breakfast and evening refreshments are served. Convenient to the University of Southern California, Civic

6 Pets welcome; 8 Children welcome; 9 Social drinking allowed; 10 Tennis available; 11 Swimming available; 12 Golf available; 13 Skiing available; 14 May be booked through travel agents.

Center, Hollywood, and tourist attractions. Five guest rooms. Shared and private bath. $70-95, plus tax.

Eye Openers Bed and Breakfast Reservations LA-T51

P. O. Box 694, Altadena, 91003-0694
(213) 684-4428; (818) 797-2055
FAX (818) 798-3640

Close to the Los Angeles Convention Center, this stately 1902 bed and breakfast inn with period furnishings offers a lovely setting. Full breakfast and afternoon tea or wine is served in the parlor or library. Five guest rooms. Private bath. $75-105.

Kids Welcome 1-5

3924 East 14th Street, Long Beach, 90804
(310) 498-0552; (800) 383-3513

Five minutes from Music Center, this Silverdale apartment easily accommodates five. Full kitchen, TV, private entrance, situated in the hills above downtown. Moderate rates.

Kids Welcome 3-5

3924 East 14th Street, Long Beach, 90804
(310) 498-0552; (800) 383-3513

This retired couple in a quiet neighborhood has two guest rooms and one bath in their upstairs suite. Toys, crib, and TV, and you can walk to Universal Studios. Affordable rates.

LOS OSOS

Gerarda's

1056 Bay Oaks Drive, 93402
(805) 528-3973

The ideal place to stop between San Francisco and Los Angeles. On the coast with ocean and mountain views. Close to Hearst Castle, Morro Bay, and San Luis Obispo; golf, tennis, hiking, and shopping. Dutch hospitality; your host speaks several languages.

Host: Gerarda Ondang
Rooms: 3 (1 PB; 2 SB) $45
Full Breakfast
Credit Cards: None
Notes: 2, 5, 8, 9, 10, 11, 12

Megan's Friends #06

Bed and Breakfast Reservation Service
1776 Royal Way, San Luis Obispo, 93405
(805) 544-4406

A large hillside house with a stunning view of the valley, mountains, bay, and Pacific Ocean. There is a bedroom with a queen bed and separate entrance, and a twin bedroom adjacent for two couples traveling together. Meticulous Dutch housekeeping and hospitality. Two miles from the sand dunes and Montana de Oro State Park. Full breakfast served in the dining room. $50-60.

Megan's Friends #07

Bed and Breakfast Reservation Service
1776 Royal Way, San Luis Obispo, 93405
(805) 544-4406

This Austrian-style guesthouse is on an ocean bluff, with deer and raccoons for neighbors. The guest house is a separate unit with pegged oak floors, large windows with a view of the ocean, and features king and double beds. Perfect for honeymooners and couples. A full breakfast is provided in the kitchen for guests to serve themselves. No children under 10. $60-$75.

Megan's Friends #14

Bed and Breakfast Reservation Service
1776 Royal Way, San Luis Obispo, 93405
(805) 544-4406

NOTES: Credit cards accepted: A Master Card; B Visa; C American Express; D Discover Card; E Diner's Club; F Other; 2 Personal Checks accepted; 3 Lunch available; 4 Dinner available; 5 Open all year;

Cozy home near the bay, with a secluded patio for a full breakfast, weather permitting. The friendly English hostess, an art collector, offers her guests a queen-size bed, cable TV, and private bath. There are several good restaurants within walking distance. $50-60.

LUCERNE

Kristalberg

P. O. Box 1639, 95458
(707) 274-8009

1985 Cape Cod 800 feet above Clear Lake. Magnificent 30-mile view of lake and countryside. Three rooms elegantly furnished with antiques; two have private baths and balcony on lake side; master bath has whirlpool tub. Breakfast in formal dining room includes fresh fruit and home-baked items. Afternoon wine and after-dinner brandy. Hiking and biking from front door. Boating, fishing, antique shops, wineries, good restaurants. German and Spanish spoken.

Host: Merv Myers
Rooms: 3 (2 PB; 1 SB) $55-150
Expanded Continental Breakfast
Credit Cards: None
Notes: 2, 5, 9, 14

McCLOUD

Stoney Brook Inn

309 West Colombero, P. O. Box 1860, 96057
(916) 964-2300; (800) 369-6118

On the south side of majestic Mount Shasta in the heart of the Shasta Cascade wonderland is the historic Stoney Brook Inn. It is fully restored, yet retains its homey character. Enjoy its soothing atmosphere. Relax in the outdoor hot tub, sauna, or on the spacious front porch. Unwind with a therapeutic massage, or lounge by the fire in the winter. Group and individual retreats available.

Host: Adrian Naylor
Rooms: 17 (14 PB; 3 SB) $32-58
Full Breakfast
Credit Cards: A, B
Notes: 2, 4, 5, 8, 11, 12, 13, 14

MALIBU

Bed and Breakfast Los Angeles 4-10

3924 East 14th Street, Long Beach, 90804
(310) 498-0552; (800) 383-3513

The entire second floor of this spacious house in Malibu is reserved for guests. Master room has a king-size bed, private bath, and balcony that looks out over the mountains. Sitting room loft can accommodate the kids and two other rooms share a bath. No toddlers, please. Affordable rates.

Bed and Breakfast Los Angeles 4-11

3924 East 14th Street, Long Beach, 90804
(310) 498-0552; (800) 383-3513

This charming cottage has views through the canyon all the way to the ocean. Bedroom, livingroom, small kitchen, full

Kristalberg

---

6 Pets welcome; 8 Children welcome; 9 Social drinking allowed; 10 Tennis available; 11 Swimming available; 12 Golf available; 13 Skiing available; 14 May be booked through travel agents.

bath, deck. Breakfast on weekends only. Children over 12. Moderate rates.

Eye Openers Bed and Breakfast Reservations MA-S3

P. O. Box 694, Altadena, 91003-0694
(213) 684-4428; (818) 797-2055
FAX (818) 798-3640

Folk art and a 180-degree view of the Pacific Ocean at a bright, cheerful bed and breakfast. Outdoor decks for sunning and viewing. Continental breakfast. $55-65.

MANHATTAN BEACH

Eye Openers Bed and Breakfast Reservations MB-C2

P. O. Box 694, Altadena, 91003-0694
(213) 684-4428; (818) 797-2055
FAX (818) 798-3640

Walk to the beach, shops, and restaurants from this restored beach bungalow. Ocean view from upstairs guest room. Continental breakfast; other amenities available. Two guest rooms. Private and shared baths. $45-75.

Eye Openers Bed and Breakfast Reservations MB-L2

P. O. Box 694, Altadena, 91003-0694
(213) 684-4428; (818) 797-2055
FAX (818) 798-3640

Beachfront bed and breakfast is the entire first floor of this lovely home on the Strand. Private entrance, living/dining room area with fireplace, wet bar, and guest parking are some of the amenities offered. Continental breakfast. Two guest rooms. Private bath. $75-85.

MARINA DEL REY

Eye Openers Bed and Breakfast Reservations MR-Z1

P. O. Box 694, Altadena, 91003-0694
(213) 684-4428; (818) 797-2055
FAX (818) 798-3640

Large apartment in Marina Del Rey offers privacy and comfort, contemporary decor, full kitchen, living/dining room area, and self-catered continental breakfast. Walk to the beach, and short ten minutes from Los Angeles International Airport. Weekly rates available. Private bath. $55-75.

Eye Openers Bed and Breakfast Reservations PL-D2

P. O. Box 694, Altadena, 91003-0694
(213) 684-4428; (818) 797-2055
FAX (818) 798-3640

Set on a hillside near the beach, this three-story Tudor-style bed and breakfast offers the first story as guest quarters with guest livingroom and patio. Gourmet, continental, or full breakfast served. Two guest rooms. Private bath. $60-80.

MARIPOSA

Oak Meadows, too.

5263 Highway 140N, P. O. Box 619, 95338
(209) 742-6161

Situated in the historic Gold Rush town of Mariposa, this bed and breakfast has turn-of-the-century charm. New England architecture; rooms decorated with handmade quilts, wallpaper, and brass headboards. Close to Yosemite National Park. The California State Mining and Mineral Museum is nearby.

NOTES: Credit cards accepted: A Master Card; B Visa; C American Express; D Discover Card; E Diner's Club; F Other; 2 Personal Checks accepted; 3 Lunch available; 4 Dinner available; 5 Open all year;

Hosts: Frank Ross and Karen Black
Rooms: 6 (PB) $69-89
Continental Breakfast
Credit Cards: A, B
Notes: 2, 5, 13, 14

The Headlands Inn

MENDOCINO

The Headlands Inn

P. O. Box 132, 95460
(707) 937-4431

The Headlands Inn is an 1868 Victorian, centrally situated within Mendocino village on California's scenic north coast minutes from redwoods and wineries. Full gourmet breakfasts are served in the room. All rooms have wood-burning fireplaces and spectacular ocean views overlooking an English-style garden. King or queen beds. Two parlors, many period antiques. Afternoon tea service with mineral waters, cookies, and mixed nuts.

Hosts: David and Sharon Hyman
Rooms: 5 (PB) $103-172
Full Breakfast (served in room)
Credit Cards: None
Notes: 2, 5, 8, 9, 10, 11, 12

John Dougherty House

571 Ukiah Street, P. O. Box 817, 95460
(707) 937-5266

Historic John Dougherty House was built in 1867 and is one of the oldest houses in Mendocino. Situated on land bordered by Ukiah and Albion streets, the inn has some of the best ocean and bay views in the historic village of Mendocino; steps away from great restaurants and shopping, but years removed from 20th-century reality. The main house is furnished with period country antiques and will take guests back to 1867. Enjoy quiet peaceful nights seldom experienced in today's urban living.

Hosts: David and Marion Wells
Rooms: 6 (PB) $95-155
Full Breakfast
Credit Cards: None
Notes: 2, 5, 9, 10, 11, 14

Joshua Grindle Inn

44800 Little Lake Road, P. O. Box 647, 95460
(707) 937-4143

Situated on two acres in the historic village of Mendocino overlooking the ocean, the Joshua Grindle Inn is a short walk to the beach, art center, shops, and fine restaurants. Stay in the lovely two-story Victorian farmhouse, a New England-style cottage, or a three-story water tower. Six rooms have fireplaces; all have private baths, antiques, and comfortable reading areas. Enjoy a full breakfast served around a ten-foot 1830s harvest table.

Hosts: Jim and Arlene Moorehead
Rooms: 10 (PB) $90-135
Full Breakfast
Credit Cards: A, B, D
Notes: 2, 5, 9, 10

Kids Welcome 16-7

3924 East 14th Street, Long Beach, 90804
(310) 498-0552; (800) 383-3513

These hosts raised a total of twelve children in their Victorian home before they started taking in bed and breakfast guests. They have four guest rooms, all with private baths, and the house has plenty for kids to do and all the necessities a parent could ask for. Kids stay free in parents' room. Breakfast is not included. Affordable rates.

6 Pets welcome; 8 Children welcome; 9 Social drinking allowed; 10 Tennis available; 11 Swimming available; 12 Golf available; 13 Skiing available; 14 May be booked through travel agents.

Mendocino Village Inn

Mendocino Village Inn

Box 626, 95460
(707) 937-0246

Watertower suite, 1882 Victorian, frog pond. Eclectic coast whimsy, fireplaces, fine music, and hearty breakfasts. Beach trails, migrating whales, and feline frolics. "Your home on the north coast."

Hosts: Bill and Kathleen Erwin
Rooms: 13 (11 PB; 2 SB) $65-195
Full Breakfast
Credit Cards: None
Notes: 2, 5, 9, 10, 12

S.S. Seafoam Lodge

Box 68, 95460
(707) 937-1827

Guests enjoy spectacular ocean views from every room. Situated on six forested acres along a dramatic stretch of Mendocino coastline, each charming stateroom features a private bath, private deck, TV, and in-room coffee. Ocean view conference facility available for private parties, meetings or retreats. Beach access at adjacent Buckhorn Cove. Close to golf, tennis, and gourmet dining. Children and pets welcome.

Hosts: Rick and Ligaya Sublett
Rooms: 24 (PB) $85-200
Continental Breakfast
Credit Cards: A, B
Notes: 2, 5, 6, 8, 10, 12

Stanford Inn by the Sea

P. O. Box 487, Highway 1 and Comptche-Ukiah Road, 95460
(707) 937-5615; (800) 331-8884

Elegantly rustic lodge situated on a meadow sloping to the sea. Accommodations with wood-burning fireplaces, down comforters, and the amenities expected at the finest hotels, including VCRs, remote control television, refrigerators, wine, coffee makers. A true country inn, the Stanford Inn is the home of California Certified Organic Big River Nurseries and Big River Llamas. The finest canoes, kayaks, and bicycles available for exploring. Indoor swimming pool, sauna, and spa.

Hosts: Joan and Jeff Stanford
Rooms: 26 (PB) $145-160
Expanded Continental Breakfast
Credit Cards: A, B, C, D, E, F
Notes: 2, 5, 6, 8, 9, 10, 11, 12

Whitegate Inn

Box 150, 499 Howard Street, 95460
(707) 937-4892

Everything you look for in a bed and breakfast experience: antiques, fireplaces, ocean views, and private baths. Elegant 1880 Victorian, in the center of the historic preservation village of Mendocino. Shops, galleries, and nationally acclaimed restaurants are just steps away. A perfect setting for romance, weddings, or rest and relaxation.

Hosts: Carol and George Bachtloff
Rooms: 6 (PB) $90-130
Full Breakfast
Credit Cards: None
Notes: 2, 5, 9, 10, 11, 12

MONTARA

Bed and Breakfast San Francisco #15

P. O. Box 420009, San Francisco, 94142
(415) 479-1913; FAX (415) 921-BBSF

Twenty miles south of San Francisco on California's famous Highway 1 lies the

NOTES: Credit cards accepted: A Master Card; B Visa; C American Express; D Discover Card; E Diner's Club; F Other; 2 Personal Checks accepted; 3 Lunch available; 4 Dinner available; 5 Open all year;

small beach community of Montara. The hosts offer a very romantic hide-a-away suite with a sitting room, fireplace, and ocean view. Montara is well known for its terrific beach, hiking trails, and horseback riding. Deep sea fishing and whale-watching excursions leave from nearby Princeton. Moderate-luxury rates. $85.

The Goose and Turrets Bed and Breakfast

835 George Street, P. O. Box 937, 94037-0937
(415) 728-5451

A 1908 Italian villa in a quiet garden offers comfort and four-course breakfasts. Thirty minutes to San Francisco; 20 minutes from San Francisco airport; one-half mile to the beach. Near restaurants, horseback riding, tide pools, galleries, golf. Pickup at local harbor and airport. French spoken.

Hosts: Raymond and Emily Hoche-Mong
Rooms: 5 (PB) $93.15-109.65
Full Breakfast
Credit Cards: A, B, C, D
Notes: 2, 5, 8, 9, 10, 11, 12, 14

Montara Bed and Breakfast

P. O. Box 493, 94037
(415) 728-3946

Just 20 miles south of San Francisco on the scenic California coast. Semi-rural area with nearby hiking, beaches, and horseback riding. Private entrance, private bath, ocean view, fireplace, TV, stereo, telephone, sun deck. Business travelers welcome.

Hosts: Bill and Peggy Bechtell
Room: 1 (PB) $85
Full Breakfast
Credit Cards: A, B
Notes: 2, 5, 9, 11, 12, 14

MONTEREY

B and B International #204

P. O. Box 282910, San Francisco, 94128-2910
(415) 696-1690; FAX (415) 696-1699

Three homes situated on the southern end of Monterey, all modestly priced. Two have views of the bay. There are six rooms that offer twin, queen, and double beds. All have shared baths. Excellent breakfasts are prepared by experienced hosts. $50-60.

B and B International #206

P. O. Box 282910, San Francisco, 94128-2910
(415) 696-1690; FAX (415) 696-1699

Contemporary two-story redwood home situated in one of Monterey Peninsula's most exclusive areas and one block to the ocean. The home is spacious with much glass. The breakfast room is a glass semicircle extending into the garden. There is a fireplace and a view of the ocean from the living room. Two rooms with private baths. $98.

Del Monte Beach Inn

1110 Del Monte Avenue, 93940
(408) 649-4410

The only one of its kind on the Monterey Peninsula, the Del Monte Beach Inn offers guests all of the charm and comfort of a quaint European bed and breakfast at comfortably affordable rates in an ideal location. Walk across the boulevard to the beach and the bike and walking trail. Only minutes from Fisherman's Wharf, Cannery Row, Historic Monterey, and the Aquarium.

Host: Lisa Glover
Rooms: 18 (2 PB; 16 SB) $40-75
Continental Breakfast
Credit Cards: A, B
Notes: 2, 5, 8, 9, 10, 11, 12, 14

MORROW BAY

Bed and Breakfast Los Angeles 12-7

3924 East 14th Street, Long Beach, 90804
(310) 498-0552; (800) 383-3513

6 Pets welcome; 8 Children welcome; 9 Social drinking allowed; 10 Tennis available; 11 Swimming available; 12 Golf available; 13 Skiing available; 14 May be booked through travel agents.

This Dutch hostess offers three bedrooms, one with a private bath and two with shared baths. Rates are very low, breakfast is sumptuous, and pets are welcome. Hostess speaks five languages. Affordable rates.

Dunbar House, 1880

Megan's Friends #05
Bed and Breakfast Reservation Service
1776 Royal Way, San Luis Obispo, 93405
(805) 544-4406

This beautiful home in a quiet area overlooks the bay and the Pacific Ocean. Sit on the deck and watch the sailboats on the Bay, the herons nesting in their rookery, or deer silhouetted on the dunes in the evening. There is a large upstairs room with a king-size bed, private shower, and a separate entrance. Downstairs there is a suite with a king-size bed, private bath/shower, and a second bedroom with a queen-size bed with shared bath and shower. Crib available. The state park, a golf course, and the Museum of Natural History are all close by. Charter fishing, kayak and bicycle rentals available. It is just a half hour drive to Hearst Castle. $75; suite $125.

MUIR BEACH

Bed and Breakfast San Francisco #22
P. O. Box 420009, San Francisco, 94142
(415) 479-1913; FAX (415) 921-BBSF

A lovely bedroom suite with private entrance, fireplace, and private bath that overlooks the Pacific Ocean and beach. Muir Beach is a quiet community 45 minutes from downtown San Francisco. Full breakfast. $95.

MURPHYS

Dunbar House, 1880
271 Jones Street, P. O. Box 1375, 95247
(209) 728-2897

Explore Gold Country during the day and enjoy a glass of lemonade or local wine on the wide porches in the afternoon. Inviting fireplaces and down comforters in your antique-filled room; cedar room has a two-person whirlpool bath. All rooms have tulvers and classic video library. Breakfast may be served in the guest room, the dining room, or in the century-old gardens.

Hosts: Bob and Barbara Costa
Rooms: 4 (PB) $105-145
Full Breakfast
Credit Cards: A, B
Notes: 2, 5, 9, 10, 11, 12, 13, 14

NAPA

Beazley House
1910 First Street, 94559
(707) 257-1649; (800) 559-1649 in California

Stroll past verdant lawns and bright flowers, and sense the hospitality of Beazley House. The landmark 1902 mansion is a chocolate brown masterpiece. The view from each room reveals beautiful gardens, and some rooms feature a private spa and fireplace. Napa's first bed and breakfast is still the best. Call for a color brochure.

Hosts: Jim and Carol Beazley
Rooms: 10 (PB) $105-175
Full Breakfast
Credit Cards: A, B
Notes: 2, 5, 9, 10, 11, 12, 14

NOTES: Credit cards accepted: A Master Card; B Visa; C American Express; D Discover Card; E Diner's Club; F Other; 2 Personal Checks accepted; 3 Lunch available; 4 Dinner available; 5 Open all year;

Full Breakfast
Credit Cards: A, B
Notes: 2, 5, 9, 10, 11, 12, 14

Hennessey House
1727 Main Street, 94559
(707) 226-3774

Queen Anne Victorian situated in downtown Napa, the gateway to the historic
wine country. Main house and carriage
house. All rooms are furnished in antiques
and have private baths. Selected rooms
have fireplaces and whirlpool tubs. Full
breakfast is served in unique dining room
that features a beautiful hand-painted,
stamped tin ceiling. Listed on National
Register of Historic Places. Sauna, bike
rentals on premises. Complimentary wine
on weekend evenings.

Hosts: Andrea Weinstein and Lauriann Delay
Rooms: 10 (PB) $75-155
Full Breakfast
Credit Cards: A, B, C
Notes: 2, 5, 9, 12, 14

Beazley House

Bed and Breakfast International #303
P. O. Box 282910, San Francisco, 94128
(415) 696-1690; FAX (415) 696-1699

Situated in Old Town Napa, this English
country home was built in 1892 and is
close to many wineries. The house has been
renovated and furnished with heirloom-
quality antiques. $85-105.

Churchill Manor
485 Brown Street, 94559
(707) 253-7733

A magnificent 1889 mansion resting on an
acre of beautiful gardens, Churchill Manor
is listed on the National Register of Historic Places. Elegant parlors boast carved
wood ceilings and columns, leaded-glass
windows, Oriental rugs, brass and crystal
chandeliers, four fireplaces, and a grand
piano. Ten guest rooms are individually
decorated with gorgeous antiques. Guests
enjoy afternoon fresh-baked cookies and
lemonade, evening wine and cheese recep-
tion, and a full gourmet breakfast served in
a mosaic-floored sun room. Complimentary
tandem bicycles and croquet.

Host: Joanna Guidotti
Rooms: 10 (PB) $75-145

Churchill Manor

Napa Inn
1137 Warren Street, 94559
(707) 257-1444

The Napa Inn is a beautiful Queen Anne
Victorian situated on a quiet tree-lined
street in the historic section of the town of

Napa. The inn is furnished in turn-of-the-century antiques in the five guest rooms, large parlor, and formal dining room. Each spacious guest room has its own private bath and two suites feature fireplaces. The inn is conveniently situated to the Napa, Sonoma, and Carneros wine regions. Also many other activities: hot air ballooning, gliding, biking, hiking, golf, tennis, many fine restaurants, and the Napa Valley Wine Train.

Hosts: Doug and Carol Morales
Rooms: 5 (PB) $100-160
Full Breakfast
Credit Cards: A, B, D
Closed Christmas
Notes: 2, 10, 12, 14

Napa Valley Reservations Unlimited

1819 Tanen Street, Suite B, 94559
(707) 252-1985; (800) 6272

This reservation service specializes in accommodations in and around the Napa Valley. Using the travel dates and other information provided by guests, such as price range, bed size, city or county, agents will arrange for suitable accommodations. More than 1,000 rooms are represented, ranging from $65-600. This is a no-fee service.

The Old World Inn

1301 Jefferson Street, 94559
(707) 257-0112; (800) 966-6624

For a holiday of romance and plentiful gourmet delights, plan a stay at this charming Victorian inn. Relax in the outdoor spa or choose a room with a sunken spa tub. Be pampered with home-baked treats from morning until bedtime. Enjoy the afternoon tea, unwind during the wine and cheese social, induldge in a chocolate lover's dessert buffet, and top the morning with a gourmet breakfast.

Host: Diane Dumaine
Rooms: 8 (PB) $97-137
Expanded Continental Breakfast
Credit Cards: A, B, C, D
Notes: 2, 5, 9, 14

Wine Country Reservations

P. O. Box 5059, 94581-0059
(707) 257-7757

Many unique accommodations in the wine country offered. Let Wine Country help arrange a memorable stay while visiting the many attractions the Valley has to offer. There are no fees for helping select the right bed and breakfast. Advanced reservations are advised. There is also a wedding consultant available for those who wish to get married in the wine country. Open daily from 9:00 A.M. to 9:00 P.M. (PST). Usually closed on major holidays, but voice mail is available.

Owner: Mary Foux
Rooms: $65-300
Continental or Full Breakfast

NAPA VALLEY

Bartels Ranch and Country Inn

1200 Conn Valley Road, St. Helena, 94574
(707) 963-4001; FAX (707) 963-5100

Situated in the heart of the world-famous Napa Valley wine country. Secluded, romantic, elegant country estate overlooking a "100-acre valley with a 10,000-acre view." Honeymoon "Heart of the Valley" suite with sunken Jacuzzi, sauna, shower, stone fireplace and private deck. Spacious, award-winning accommodations, expansive entertainment room, pool table, fireplace, library and terraces overlooking the vineyard. Poolside lounging, bicycles available to ride to nearby lake, refrigerator, TV and telephone available. Personalized itinerary provided; champagne and afternoon refreshments served. Close to wineries, golf, tennis, fishing, boating, and mineral spas.

Host: Jami Bartels
Rooms: 4 (PB) $98-275
Continental Breakfast
Credit Cards: A, B, C, D
Notes: 2, 3, 4, 5, 9, 10, 11, 12, 14

Bed and Breakfast Los Angeles 15-1

3924 East 14th Street, Long Beach, 90804
(310) 498-0552; (800) 383-3513

This rural 1930s farmhouse has three suites with fireplaces, kitchens, and redwood decks. The family cottage can accommodate up to six. It has a refrigerator stocked with goodies and French doors that open onto the vineyards. Moderate rates.

Bed and Breakfast Los Angeles 15-4

3924 East 14th Street, Long Beach, 90804
(310) 498-0552; (800) 383-3513

Victorian furniture and stained-glass windows adorn this elegant 1893 Queen Anne mansion. Hosts offer six rooms. Breakfast is served in the sun room, and complimentary wine tastings are available in the cellar. Babies or older children only, please. Luxury rates.

Eye Openers Bed and Breakfast Reservations NA-C91

P. O. Box 694, Altadena, 91003-0694
(213) 684-4428; (818) 797-2055
FAX (818) 798-3640

Bed and breakfast in the heart of wine country is offered in the 1889 mansion that has been designated as a national historic landmark. Each room is individually decorated. Enjoy an extended continental breakfast, and relax on the veranda with evening refreshments. Nine guest rooms. Private baths. $75-145 plus tax.

Eye Openers Bed and Breakfast Reservations SH-D21

P. O. Box 694, Altadena, 91003-0694
(213) 684-4428; (818) 797-2055
FAX (818) 798-3640

Secluded in a forest above the vineyards, yet near the town, this small bed and breakfast offers a peaceful retreat for its guest rooms, one with a fireplace. Large continental breakfast is served, and a swimming pool is available for guests to enjoy. Two guest rooms. Private bath. $95-125 plus tax.

Kids Welcome 15-3

3924 East 14th Street, Long Beach, 90804
(310) 498-0552; (800) 383-3513

This hostess truly loves and welcomes children. She has a crib and toys available, and her 1900 farmhouse overlooks Napa Valley's best vineyards. One room has a fireplace and wet bar. Breakfast is served by the pool, and wine and cheese is served in the afternoon. Luxury rates.

NEVADA CITY

Downey House Bed and Breakfast

517 West Broad Street, 95959
(916) 265-2815; (800) 258-2815

Eastlake Victorian, circa 1870, restored to its original elegance with lovely garden and water falling into a lily pond by new arbor with tables where guests may eat breakfast. Situated one block from fine shops and restaurants, live theater, museums, art galleries, and horse-drawn carriages. Soundproofed rooms. Near historic gold mines, lakes, streams, tennis, golf, skiing, horseback riding, and more,

6 Pets welcome; 8 Children welcome; 9 Social drinking allowed; 10 Tennis available; 11 Swimming available; 12 Golf available; 13 Skiing available; 14 May be booked through travel agents.

Host: Miriam Wright
Rooms: 6 (PB) $75-90
Full Breakfast
Credit Cards: A, B
Notes: 2, 5, 8, 10, 11, 12, 13, 14

Grandmere's

449 Broad Street, 95959
(916) 265-4660

1856 Colonial Revival situated on Nobob Hill. Beautiful garden, suitable for weddings or receptions. Seven rooms, each with private bath and down comforters, are decorated in elegant country French decor. A full breakfast is served at 9:00 A.M. in the dining room.

Hosts: Doug and Geri Boka
Rooms: 7 (PB) $100-150
Full Breakfast
Credit Cards: A, B
Notes: 2, 5, 8, 9, 10, 11, 12, 13, 14

Piety Hill Inn

523 Sacramento Street, 95959
(916) 265-2245

The inn consists of eight cottages surrounding a lush garden. Featured are pre-Civil War to early 20th-century furnishings, king beds, refrigerators, wet bars, TV, and breakfast in bed. Nearby are quaint shops, theater, music, excellent restaurants, hiking, swimming, and winter sports.

Host: Linda
Rooms: 8 (PB) $75-125
Full Breakfast
Credit Cards: A, B
Notes: 2, 5, 8, 9, 10, 11, 12, 13, 14

NEWPORT BEACH

Bed and Breakfast Los Angeles 6-3

3924 East 14th Street, Long Beach, 90804
(310) 498-0552; (800) 383-3513

Stained glass, bricks, and wood add to the charm of this unusual house just minutes

from the beach in Newport. Upstairs room is a loft with a private bath, mini-kitchen, and stairs to the rooftop deck. Downstairs guest room also has a private bath. Not safe for toddlers. Moderate rates.

Eye Openers Bed and Breakfast Reservations NP-D2

P. O. Box 694, Altadena, 91003-0694
(213) 684-4428; (818) 797-2055
FAX (818) 798-3640

Crow's-nest with 360-degree view tops this tri-level beach home. Third level is a large guest deck with barbecue and refrigerator. Stained glass is featured throughout the house. Perfectly located for beach and bay activities; bicycle and beach chairs available. Full or continental breakfast and afternoon refreshments. Two rooms. Private bath. $50-75.

Eye Openers Bed and Breakfast Reservations NP-D101

P. O. Box 694, Altadena, 91003-0694
(213) 684-4428; (818) 797-2055
FAX (818) 798-3640

A very special beachfront bed and breakfast inn has spacious antique-decorated guest rooms, each with its own fireplace and some with Jacuzzis. Delicious continental breakfast is served in the room, on the patio, or in the parlor. Ten guest rooms. Private bath. $135-275 plus tax.

Eye Openers Bed and Breakfast Reservations NP-W2

P. O. Box 694, Altadena, 91003-0694
(213) 684-4428; (818) 797-2055
FAX (818) 798-3640

NOTES: Credit cards accepted: A Master Card; B Visa; C American Express; D Discover Card; E Diner's Club; F Other; 2 Personal Checks accepted; 3 Lunch available; 4 Dinner available; 5 Open all year;

Stunning, well-decorated bed and breakfast on the water's edge has a guest den with retractable roof, lounge chairs, refrigerator, and grassy yard for sun bathing. Take the shuttle or bike to unique shops and restaurants. Continental breakfast. Minimum stay is two nights. Resident dog. Two guest rooms. Private bath. $80-85.

The Little Inn on the Bay
617 Lido Park Drive, 92663
(714) 673-8800

This is the only property on the waterfront in Newport Beach. Each room in this charming country inn is oriented to beautiful Newport Bay. Rooms are elegant, comfortable, and relaxing. Stroll to restaurants, antiques, boutiques, and the ocean beach. Complimentary bicycles, wine and cheese, hors d'oeuvres, and milk and cookies are offered.

Hosts: Mike and Laura Palitz
Rooms: 29 (PB) $100-150
Continental Breakfast
Credit Cards: A, B, C
Notes: 5, 9, 11, 12

NORTH HOLLYWOOD

Bed and Breakfast Los Angeles 3-2
3924 East 14th Street, Long Beach, 90804
(310) 498-0552; (800) 383-3513

Spacious guest wing in a North Hollywood home has a lovely yard, pool, and decorator whimsy. Private bath and TV. Affordable rates.

NORTHRIDGE

Bed and Breakfast Los Angeles 3-4
3924 East 14th Street, Long Beach, 90804
(310) 498-0552; (800) 383-3513

Stained glass, art, and country decor grace this Northridge home on one-half acre with trees, pool, and paddle tennis court. Guest room, sitting room, private bath, and TV. Affordable rates.

ORANGE

Country Comfort Bed and Breakfast
5104 East Valencia Drive, 92669
(714) 532-2802

Situated in a quiet residential area, this house has been furnished with comfort and pleasure in mind. It is handicapped accessible with adaptive equipment available. Amenities include a swimming pool, cable TV and VCR, atrium, fireplace, piano, and the use of bicycles, one built for two. Breakfast often features delicious Scotch eggs, stuffed French toast, and hash, as well as fruits and assorted beverages. Vegetarian selections also available. Disneyland and Knotts Berry Farm are less than seven miles.

Hosts: Geri Lopker and Joanne Angell
Rooms: 3 (PB) $50-60
Full Breakfast
Credit Cards: None
Notes: 2, 5, 8, 9, 11, 14

PACIFIC GROVE

Bed and Breakfast Los Angeles 13-3
3924 East 14th Street, Long Beach, 90804
(310) 498-0552; (800) 383-3513

Soak in the hot tub at this elegant Cape Cod-style home, built originally as a convent in 1910. Hosts emphasize comfort, tranquility, and attention to every detail. Accommodations range from a canopied, double-bedded room with an ocean view and a crib to a spacious two-room cottage that can accommodate four. Breakfast

6 Pets welcome; 8 Children welcome; 9 Social drinking allowed; 10 Tennis available; 11 Swimming available; 12 Golf available; 13 Skiing available; 14 May be booked through travel agents.

includes champagne. Three miles from Monterey. Older kids only. Luxury rates.

Eye Openers
Bed and Breakfast
Reservations PG-C201

P. O. Box 694, Altadena, 91003-0694
(213) 684-4428; (818) 797-2055
FAX (818) 798-3640

Century-old Victorian boarding house is a refurbished award-winning bed and breakfast inn. Beautifully decorated rooms, delicious breakfast, and afternoon refreshments. Shared and private baths. $75-175 plus tax.

Eye Openers
Bed and Breakfast
Reservations PG-G11I

P. O. Box 694, Altadena, 91003-0694
(213) 684-4428; (818) 797-2055
FAX (818) 798-3640

1888 Queen Anne-style mansion-by-the-sea has a panoramic view of Monterey Bay. Delicious breakfast and afternoon refreshments. Shared and private baths. $95-155.

Eye Openers
Bed and Breakfast
Reservations PG-G21I

P. O. Box 694, Altadena, 91003-0694
(213) 684-4428; (818) 797-2055
FAX (818) 798-3640

Beautifully preserved 1887 Victorian on the National Register of Historic Places can now be enjoyed as a bed and breakfast inn. Wonderful breakfast, afternoon hors d'oeuvres, and wine or tea served. $95-155 plus tax.

Eye Openers
Bed and Breakfast
Reservations PG-G81

P. O. Box 694, Altadena, 91003-0694
(213) 684-4428; (818) 797-2055
FAX (818) 798-3640

1884 Victorian with ocean views was renovated and opened its doors in the summer of 1990 to become a Pacific Grove bed and breakfast inn close to the beach. Each room is uniquely decorated and features views or sun decks. Delicious full breakfast and afternoon refreshments are provided. Private bath. $95-155.

Gatehouse Inn

225 Central Avenue, 93950
(800) 753-1881

Built in 1884, this historic residence greets you with light and airy, lovingly restored guest rooms. These eight unique bedrooms offer private baths, and many have fireplaces and private patios. A full buffet breakfast is served each morning, with wine and hors d'oeuvres served in the afternoon. Situated in the quaint Victorian town of Pacific Grove on California's Central Coast, the Gatehouse Inn is within easy walking distance of Cannery Row, the Monterey Bay Aquarium, many shops, and restaurants.

Hosts: Doug and Kristi Aslin
Rooms: 8 (PB) $95-170
Full Breakfast
Credit Cards: A, B, C
Notes: 2, 5, 12, 14

The Martine Inn

255 Ocean View Boulevard, 93950
(408) 373-3388

Surpassed only by the beauty of Monterey Bay, the Martine Inn complements the rugged terrain with a timeless sense of graciousness. Don and Marion Martini have filled this Victorian-turned-Mediterranean

---

NOTES: Credit cards accepted: A Master Card; B Visa; C American Express; D Discover Card; E Diner's Club; F Other; 2 Personal Checks accepted; 3 Lunch available; 4 Dinner available; 5 Open all year;

mansion, built in the 1890s, with an extensive collection of antiques. The all-private bath bedrooms offer richness in history and tradition, many of which offer incredible ocean views or a wood-burning fireplace. Enjoy the spectacular bay vistas. Breakfast, evening wine, and hors d'oeuvres served on Old Sheffield silver, fine china, and crystal.

Hosts: Marion and Don Martine
Rooms: 19 (PB) $115-225
Full Breakfast
Credit Cards: A, B
Notes: 2, 3, 5, 8, 9, 10, 11, 12, 14

The Old Saint Angela Inn

321 Central Avenue, 93950
(408) 372-3246

A 1910 Cape Cod-style Victorian home overlooking Monterey Bay. Full breakfast is served daily; late afternoon refreshments are served in the garden solarium. Truly an experience in comfort. Monterey Bay Aquarium, Cannery Row, Fisherman's Wharf, and restaurants are within walking distance.

Host: Don and Barbara Foster
Rooms: 9 (6 PB; 3 SB) $90-150
Full Breakfast
Credit Cards: A, B
Notes: 2, 5, 9, 10, 11, 12, 14

Roserox Country Inn by-the-Sea

557 Ocean View Boulevard, 93950
(408) 373-7673

Historic country mansion set on the edge of the Pacific shoreline. Built at the turn of the century, the inn is an intimate four-story inn with original patterned oak floors, high ceilings, high brass beds, imported soaps and French water, designer linens, ocean sounds, and a special gift for each guest. A full country breakfast and wine and cheer hour. The Shoreline Trail to Cannery Row, Monterey Bay Aquarium, world-renown

shops and restaurants, as well as swimming beach, bicycling, and fishing, are within 30 feet of the inn.

Host: Dawn Vyette Browncroft
Rooms: 8 (S2B) $125-205
Full Breakfast
Credit Cards: None
Notes: 2, 5, 9, 10, 11, 12, 14

PACIFIC PALISADES

Bed and Breakfast Los Angeles 9-1

3924 East 14th Street, 90804
(310) 498-0552; (800) 383-3513

This 1930s family-style inn, situated in the center of town, has several units with kitchens, patios, and fireplaces. The courtyard has a nice pool, spa, and big, old fruit trees. Affordable rates.

PALM SPRINGS

Casa Cody Bed and Breakfast Country Inn

175 South Cahuilla Road, 92262
(619) 320-9346

Romantic, historic hideaway in the heart of Palm Springs village. Beautifully redecorated in Santa Fe decor, with kitchens, wood-burning fireplaces, patios, two pools, and a spa. Close to the Desert Museum, Heritage Center, and Moorten Botanical Gardens. Nearby hiking in Indian canyons, horseback riding, tennis, golf. Polo, ballooning, helicopter, and desert Jeep tours. Near celebrity homes, date gardens, and Joshua Tree National Monument.

Host: Therese Hayes
Rooms: 17 (PB) $45-160
Continental Breakfast
Credit Cards: A, B, C
Notes: 2, 5, 6, 8, 9, 10, 11, 12, 14

6 Pets welcome; 8 Children welcome; 9 Social drinking allowed; 10 Tennis available; 11 Swimming available; 12 Golf available; 13 Skiing available; 14 May be booked through travel agents.

Eye Openers
Bed and Breakfast
Reservations PS-C51

P. O. Box 694, Altadena, 910034-0694
(213) 684-4428; (818) 797-2055
FAX (818) 798-3640

New Japanese-style inn, with decor that creates a relaxed bed and breakfast stay. Shoji doors slide open to the pool. Shiatsu massage, kimonos, and additional amenities available. Continental breakfast. $45-75 plus tax.

PASADENA _____

Eye Openers
Bed and Breakfast
Reservations AL-C2

P. O. Box 694, Altadena, 91003-0694
(213) 684-4428; (818) 797-2055
FAX (818) 798-3640

A special 1926 French Normandy farmhouse in a lovely neighborhood has two-story livingroom and open-hearth fireplace. Enjoy an elegant continental breakfast in the garden patio or dining room. Good hiking trails, museums, and libraries nearby. Short drive to Los Angeles. Two guest rooms. Private and shared baths. $55.

Eye Openers
Bed and Breakfast
Reservations AL-J1

P. O. Box 694, Altadena, 91003-0694
(213) 684-4428; (818) 797-2055
FAX (818) 798-3640

View of nearby mountains from this second floor, private two-room suite provides the illusion of living in a tree house. Continental breakfast is served in the fami-ly dining room, garden, or bridge overlooking the garden. Private bath. $75.

Eye Openers
Bed and Breakfast
Reservations AL-J1B

P. O. Box 694, Altadena, 91003-0694
(213) 684-4428; (818) 797-2055
FAX (818) 798-3640

Poolhouse with small kitchen offers privacy and comfort. Contemporary bed and breakfast on a cul-de-sac is across from the golf course and has good local hiking. Fifteen to 20-minute drive to the LA Civic Center or Hollywood. Continental breakfast. Private bath. $45-55.

Eye Openers
Bed and Breakfast
Reservations AL-P8

P. O. Box 694, Altadena, 91003-0694
(213) 684-4428; (818) 797-2055
FAX (818) 798-3640

Enjoy an extended continental breakfast near the fountain in this beautifully landscaped, walled garden of a stately, Spanish-style home, hosted by a yoga teacher and amateur astronomer. Two guest rooms. Shared bath. $45-55.

Eye Openers
Bed and Breakfast
Reservations AL-R2

P. O. Box 694, Altadena, 91003-0694
(213) 684-4428; (818) 797-2055
FAX (818) 798-3640

Large, contemporary home with Old World wine cellar has Angeles National Forest as its backyard. Enjoy a continental or full breakfast on the deck overlooking pool and

NOTES: Credit cards accepted: A Master Card; B Visa; C American Express; D Discover Card; E Diner's Club; F Other; 2 Personal Checks accepted; 3 Lunch available; 4 Dinner available; 5 Open all year;

view of the valley. Host teaches wine classes and is a gourmet cook. Two guest rooms. Private bath. $55-60.

Eye Openers
Bed and Breakfast
Reservations AL-S1

P. O. Box 694, Altadena, 91003-0694
(213) 684-4428; (818) 797-2055
FAX (818) 798-3640

Large, well-landscaped yard in a quiet, residential community is a wonderful retreat at the end of the day. A delicious continental breakfast is served One guest room, with private bath. $50-55.

Eye Openers
Bed and Breakfast
Reservations AL-W2

P. O. Box 694, Altadena, 91003-0694
(213) 684-4428; (818) 797-2055
FAX (818) 798-3640

A Cape Cod-style bed and breakfast appointed with early American antiques. Situated on one of Altadena's loveliest streets. Hosted by horse enthusiasts. There is a large yard with a pond. Continental breakfast. Private baths. Resident dog. $50-55.

Eye Openers
Bed and Breakfast
Reservations AR-P2

P. O. Box 694, Altadena, 91003-0694
(213) 684-4428; (818) 797-2055
FAX (818) 798-3640

Horserace and garden enthusiasts will be close to Santa Anita Racetrack and the Los Angeles County Arboretum while enjoying the hospitality at this large, well-decorated, contemporary home. Enjoy a continental

breakfast by the pool or in the family room. Resident dog. Two guest rooms. Private and shared baths. $45-50.

Eye Openers
Bed and Breakfast
Reservations AR-W2

P. O. Box 694, Altadena, 91003-0694
(213) 684-4428; (818) 797-2055
FAX (818) 798-3640

Quiet cul-de-sac near the Santa Anita racetrack, LA County Arboretum, Huntington Library, golf courses, and the beautiful San Gabriel Mountains is the setting for this bed and breakfast. Host loves to garden, hike, and travel. Enjoy a continental breakfast on the pool patio. Two guest rooms with private and shared baths. $35-45.

Eye Openers
Bed and Breakfast
Reservations PA-G2

P. O. Box 694, Altadena, 91003-0694
(213) 684-4428; (818) 797-2055
FAX (818) 798-3640

Large two-story Spanish-style bed and breakfast in the Cal Tech area of lovely old Pasadena has a swimming pool, Jacuzzi, and full country breakfast prepared by a gourmet cook. Two guest rooms. Private bath. $70-90.

Eye Openers
Bed and Breakfast
Reservations PA-H1

P. O. Box 694, Altadena, 91003-0694
(213) 684-4428; (818) 797-2055
FAX (818) 798-3640

Near the Huntington Hotel, which is now the Ritz-Carlton, this contemporary bed and breakfast is hosted by a retired school administrator. Enjoy the lovely garden room, where

6 Pets welcome; 8 Children welcome; 9 Social drinking allowed; 10 Tennis available; 11 Swimming available; 12 Golf available; 13 Skiing available; 14 May be booked through travel agents.

an ample continental breakfast is served. Convenient to all local tourist attractions. Resident cat. One guest room with private bath. $45-50.

Eye Openers Bed and Breakfast Reservations PA-P2

P. O. Box 694, Altadena, 91003-0694
(213) 684-4428; (818) 797-2055
FAX (818) 798-3640

Sprawling ranch-style house in Colonial style has a large livingroom and book-lined library, both with a fireplace. A full scrumptious breakfast is served on the sunny patio or formal dining room. Host is concert pianist, organist, and harpsichordist. Close to Los Angeles and most tourist attractions. Two guest rooms. Private and shared baths. $55.

Eye Openers Bed and Breakfast Reservations PA-R2

P. O. Box 694, Altadena, 91003-0694
(213) 684-4428; (818) 797-2055
FAX (818) 798-3640

This cheerful bed and breakfast is in one of Pasadena's well-known neighborhoods of tree-lined streets and well-kept homes. Continental breakfast, hot tub, private bath Two guest rooms. $45-50.

Eye Openers Bed and Breakfast Reservations PA-R3

P. O. Box 694, Altadena, 91003-0694
(213) 684-4428; (818) 797-2055
FAX (818) 798-3640

Short walk to Pasadena Civic and Convention Center, this bed and breakfast is an older, well-kept California bungalow with

second-floor guest accommodations, as well as a separate, private apartment. Hosts who enjoy traveling have lived abroad and speak Swedish. Continental or full breakfast. Private and shared baths. $35-75.

Eye Openers Bed and Breakfast Reservations PA-S9

P. O. Box 694, Altadena, 91003-0694
(213) 684-4428; (818) 797-2055
FAX (818) 798-3640

Gracious hosts interested in art offer very private guest quarters make up the entire first floor of this contemporary hillside home with guest livingroom and patio. Garden and pool lend an Oriental atmosphere, and a delicious full breakfast served along with a view of the city makes this bed and breakfast a special place to stay. Two guest rooms. Shared bath. $55-72.

Eye Openers Bed and Breakfast Reservations PA-W1

P. O. Box 694, Altadena, 91003-0694
(213) 684-4428; (818) 797-2055
FAX (818) 798-3640

Half-timbered Tudor-style home was designed and built by the host, who is a magician, yoga enthusiast, and vegetarian gourmet cook. Lovely community with good hiking is close to museums and tourist attractions. One guest room with private bath. $55-60.

Eye Openers Bed and Breakfast Reservations SP-P1

P. O. Box 694, Altadena, 91003-0694
(213) 684-4428; (818) 797-2055
FAX (818) 798-3640

NOTES: Credit cards accepted: A Master Card; B Visa; C American Express; D Discover Card; E Diner's Club; F Other; 2 Personal Checks accepted; 3 Lunch available; 4 Dinner available; 5 Open all year;

400-square-foot redwood guest house shares patio and Jacuzzi with host's home, which faces Arroyo Seco natural recreation area. Horse stable, par three golf course, racquetball, and tennis courts are within walking distance. Cottage has cooking facilities and TV. Twelve minute drive to Los Angeles. Private bath. $55-75.

PASO ROBLES

Megan's Friends #02

Bed and Breakfast Reservation Service
1776 Royal Way, San Luis Obispo, 93405
(805) 544-4406

Early 1900s California farmhouse with modern comforts. Peace and quiet in your own separate cabin yet close to town on a well-paved country road with easy access to wineries and wine tasting rooms. Lakes Nacimiento and San Antonio, less than an hour away, for water skiing, fishing, and sailing. Cabin has two bedrooms with bath and a country kitchen supplied with breakfast foods and juices. Nature trails over 40 acres of farmland. $75.

Megan's Friends #03

Bed and Breakfast Reservation Service
1776 Royal Way, San Luis Obispo, 93405
(805) 544-4406

This is an elegant, gated hilltop estate in the Paso Robles wine country. It is a large, traditional home on more than six acres with a 360-degree view and a pool, spa, and gazebo. There are three guest rooms, one with private bath; two share a bath. Gourmet breakfast is served. Each room comes with a fruit basket and a local wine, and robes are provided. No children please. $100-125.

Megan's Friends #16

Bed and Breakfast Reservation Service
1776 Royal Way, San Luis Obispo, 93405
(805) 544-4406

Separate wing in a large, contemporary home on 20 acres of gently sloping terrain. The area surrounding the house is completely landscaped with lawn, trees, garden and patios. The two bedrooms have queen-size beds with private baths. There is a large game room with a fireplace, games, TV and VCR. Continental breakfasts are provided, with use of the microwave oven and refrigerator. $75.

POINT ARENA

Coast Guard House

695 Arena Cove, 95468
(707) 882-2442; (800) 524-9320

On the beautiful Mendocino Coast, this historic Coast Guard lifesaving station, built in 1901, was authentically restored by the owners/hosts. Furnishings are from the studio Arts and Crafts period of American design (1870-1920), a style characterized by fine craftsmanship and simple, elegant lines. Nearby beaches, whale watching, and fishing are but a few of the coastal activities available.

Hosts: Merita Whatley and Richard Wasserman
Rooms: 6 (4 PB; 2 SB) $75-145
Continental Breakfast
Credit Cards: A, B
Notes: 2, 5

POINT REYES STATION

Ferrandos Hideaway

12010 Highway 1, 94956
(415) 663-1966

Rich and homey bed and breakfast one mile north of Point Reyes Station. Private cottage with fully equipped kitchen and two rooms in main house. Hot tub, private baths, wood-burning stoves, vegetable garden, chickens. Close to Point Reyes National Seashore, hiking, biking, bird watching, horseback riding, whale watching, and miles of sandy beaches.

6 Pets welcome; 8 Children welcome; 9 Social drinking allowed; 10 Tennis available; 11 Swimming available; 12 Golf available; 13 Skiing available; 14 May be booked through travel agents.

Hosts: Greg and Doris Ferrando
Rooms: 2 plus cottage (PB) $95-120
Continental Breakfast
Credit Cards: None
Notes: 2, 5, 12, 14

Jasmine Cottage

11561 Coast Route One, 94956
(415) 663-1166

This charming guest cottage was built in 1879 for the original Point Reyes schoolhouse. Secluded, romantic cottage sleeps four, has a library, wood-burning stove, full kitchen, beautiful pastoral views, private patios, and gardens. Five-minute walk down the hill to town; five-minute drive to spectacular Point Reyes National Seashore. A crib and highchair are available.

Host: Karen Gray
Cottage: 1 (PB) $115 plus
Full Breakfast
Credit Cards: None
Notes: 2, 5, 6, 8, 9, 11, 14

Marsh Cottage Bed and Breakfast

Box 1121, 94956
(415) 669-7168

The privacy of your own peaceful bayside retreat near Inverness and spectacular Point Reyes National Seashore. Exceptional location and views, tasteful interior, fireplace, fully equipped kitchen, complete bath. Breakfast provided in the cottage. Ideal for romantics and naturalists. Hiking nearby.

Host: Wendy Schwartz
Room: 1 (PB) $95-110
Full Breakfast
Minimum stay weekends and holidays: 2 nights
Credit Cards: None
Notes: 2, 5, 8, 9, 10, 11

The Neon Rose

P. O. Box 632, 94956
(415) 663-9143

A unique guest cottage overlooking Tomales Bay is available for dreams, private moments and quiet times. One bedroom, livingroom, fully equipped kitchen, Jacuzzi, wood-burning stove, cable television, stereo, and a private garden with direct access to Point Reyes National Seashore. Breakfast foods available for guest preparation.

Host: Sandy Fields
Room: 1 (PB) $125-150
Continental Breakfast
Credit Cards: A, B
Notes: 2, 5

Thirty-nine Cypress

39 Cypress Road, 94956
(415) 663-1709

This small redwood inn overlooking a 500-acre ranch, marshlands, and the upper reaches of Tomales Bay offers spectacular views for guests to enjoy. Furnished with family antiques, Oriental rugs, original art, and an eclectic library, each of the rooms

Marsh Cottage

NOTES: Credit cards accepted: A Master Card; B Visa; C American Express; D Discover Card; E Diner's Club; F Other; 2 Personal Checks accepted; 3 Lunch available; 4 Dinner available; 5 Open all year;

opens onto its own private patio. An outdoor spa overlooking the views is available, and this is a favorite spot for bird watchers. Near Point Reyes National Seashore, with its splendid beaches and 140 miles of hiking trails.

Host: Julia Bartlett
Rooms: 3 (SB) $100-115
Full Breakfast
Credit Cards: A, B
Notes: 2, 5, 9, 14

there are board games, puzzles, and popcorn for relaxing. Walk to the railroad museum, restaurants, wild and scenic river, and national forest. Only one hour from Reno entertainment.

Hosts: Jon and Lynne Haman
Rooms: 6 (SB) $40 plus tax
Full Breakfast
Credit Cards: None
Notes: 2, 5, 6, 8, 9, 10, 11, 12, 13

POINT RICHMOND

East Brother Light Station, Inc.
117 Park Place, 94801
(510) 233-2385

Formed as a non-profit organization in 1979 for the preservation and restoration of the light station. Overnight guests will enjoy an innovative four-course dinner expertly prepared and four guest rooms comfortably appointed with Victorian furnishings, brass beds, and fresh flowers. Situated on an island in the San Francisco Bay. Guests are treated to a demonstration of the restored diaphone foghorn after an exquisite breakfast. Accommodations are available Thursday through Sunday nights only.

Hosts: John and Lore Barnett
Rooms: 4 (2 PB; 2 SB) $295
Full Breakfast and Dinner
Credit Cards: None
Notes: 2, 3, 4, 5, 9

PORTOLA

Upper Feather Bed and Breakfast
256 Commercial Street, 96122
(916) 832-0107

Small-town comfort and hospitality in casual country style. No TV or radio, but

RANCHO PALOS VERDES

Bed and Breakfast Los Angeles 5-1
3924 East 14th Street, Long Beach, 90804
(310) 498-0552; (800) 383-3513

Ocean breezes and a panoramic view are part of everyday life in this Rancho Palos Verdes home. Two comfortable guest rooms, both with private baths, are available to families. Older children only. Moderate rates.

Hartley House Bed and Breakfast Inn
700 22nd Street, 95816
(916) 447-7829; (800) 831-5806

A stunning, turn-of-the-century mansion surrounded by elm trees and stately old homes in midtown Sacramento. We have exquisitely appointed rooms are conveniently located near the Capitol, Old Town, Convention Center, and the city's finest restaurants, coffee and dessert shops. There is even a cookie jar fully stocked with fresh-baked cookies.

Hosts: Margarita and Michele
Rooms: 5 (PB) $99-125
Full Breakfast
Credit Cards: A, B, C, D, E, F
Notes: 2, 5, 9, 10, 11, 12, 13, 14

6 Pets welcome; 8 Children welcome; 9 Social drinking allowed; 10 Tennis available; 11 Swimming available; 12 Golf available; 13 Skiing available; 14 May be booked through travel agents.

ST. HELENA

Ambrose Bierce House

1515 Main Street, 94574
(707) 963-3003

Built in 1872, this house combines history, romance, and pampering. Queen-size beds, claw foot tubs, and armoires decorate the former home of the writer Ambrose Bierce. Suites are named for historical figures whose presence touched Bierce and Napa Valley in the late 1800s. Convenient location, walking distance to restaurants, shops, and wineries. A gourmet continental breakfast is complimentary, as is the hospitality.

Host: Jane Gibson
Rooms: 3 (PB) $99-139
Continental Breakfast
Credit Cards: None
Notes: 2, 5, 9, 12, 14

Cinnamon Bear Bed and Breakfast

1407 Kearney Street, 94574
(707) 963-4653

Classic Arts and Craft house, built in 1910 and furnished in that style with lots of bears. Close to downtown shops and restaurants; air-conditioned. Afternoon socializing with snacks, beverages, TV, phone. Family-owned and operated; full breakfast.

Host: Genny Jenkins
Rooms: 4 (PB) $75-145
Full Breakfast
Credit Cards: A, B
Notes: 2, 5, 9, 10, 11, 12

Erika's Hillside

285 Fawn Park, 94574
(707) 963-2887

Guests will be welcomed with warm European-style hospitality when they arrive at this hillside chalet. Just two miles from St. Helena, it has a peaceful, wooded country setting and view of the vineyards and wineries. The grounds (three acres) are nicely landscaped. The rooms are spacious, bright, and airy, with private entrances and bath, fireplace, and hot tub. Continental breakfast and German specialities are served on the patio or in the garden room. More than 100 years old, the structure has been remodeled and personally decorated by German-born innkeeper.

Host: Erika Cunningham
Rooms: 3 (PB) $65-165
Continental Breakfast
Credit Cards: C
Notes: 2, 5, 8, 9, 10, 11, 12, 14

Hilltop House Bed and Breakfast

P. O. Box 726, 94574
(707) 944-0880

Poised at the very top of the ridge that separates the famous wine regions of Napa and Sonoma, Hilltop House is a country retreat with all the comforts of home, and a view that must be seen to be believed. The contemporary home was built with the mountain panorama in mind, and the vast deck allows guests to enjoy it at their leisure. From this vantage point, sunrises and sunsets are simply amazing.

Hosts: Bill and Annette Gevarter
Rooms: 3 (PB) $95-165
Full Breakfast
Credit Cards: A, B, C
Notes: 2, 5, 9, 14

Oliver House Bed and Breakfast Country Inn

2970 Silverado Trail, 94574
(707) 963-4089; (800) 682-7888

Nestled against the foothills of Glass Mountain overlooking Napa Valley's finest vineyards rests Oliver House Country Inn. Here Indians camped under the spreading branches of the 400-year-old oak tree, and obsidian rocks are found in abundance on it's lovely four acres. Today, sheep graze peacefully beneath it's branches, while guests enjoy the pastoral, romantic setting. In 1871 this property was sold by Charles Krug and his wife for $200 in U.S. gold coins.

Hosts: Richard and Clara Oliver
Rooms: 4 (PB) $75-205
Full Breakfast
Credit Cards: A, B, C
Notes: 5, 10, 11, 12, 14

Oliver House

SAN DIEGO

Bed and Breakfast Los Angeles 8-1
3924 East 14th Street, Long Beach, 90804
(310) 498-0552; (800) 383-3513

Small beachfront cottages can accommodate a family of four; the two-bedroom apartments have room for six. Kitchens are stocked with goodies for breakfast. Great weekend and monthly rates are available. Affordable rates.

Blom House
1372 Minder Drive, 92111
(619) 427-0890

Blom House is a charming cottage situated less than 10 minutes from the beach, downtown, and all the local tourist attractions. The 65-foot deck features a spa, and a superb view of the lights from the Hotel Circle below. Bedrooms and guest lounge have 14-foot ceilings, antique furnishings and fresh flowers. All accommodations have color television, VCR, refrigerators with wine and cheese, bathrobes and private baths. A four-course breakfast, kitchen privileges and two-for-one dining cards are included. Dinner is available Sunday through Thursday for a cost of $6.50 per person.

Hosts: John and Betty Blom
Rooms: 3 (PB) $45-85
Full Breakfast
Credit Cards: C
Notes: 2, 3, 4, 5, 8, 9, 10, 11, 12, 14

The Cottage
3829 Albatross Street, 92103
(619) 299-1564

Situated between the zoo and Sea World, the Cottage is a quiet retreat in the heart of a downtown residential neighborhood. The turn-of-the-century furnishings throughout evoke visions of a bygone era. Each morning guests will be served a breakfast of freshly baked bread, juice, and beverage.

Hosts: Robert and Carol Emerick
Rooms: 2 (PB) $59-75
Continental Breakfast
Credit Cards: A, B, C
Notes: 2, 5, 8, 9, 14

Erene's Inn
3776 Hawk Street, 92103
(619) 295-5622

This charming, circa 1900, Mission Hills home close to Balboa Park, Gaslamp district, and Old Town, welcomes with its pillared porch and French doors. Original paintings, enamels, and ceramics comple-

6 Pets welcome; 8 Children welcome; 9 Social drinking allowed; 10 Tennis available; 11 Swimming available; 12 Golf available; 13 Skiing available; 14 May be booked through travel agents.

ment Greek antiques, English armoires, Oriental wares, and Turkish rugs. Coffee and tea around the fireplace or on the sunny deck, fresh flowers on the breakfast table and tiny surprises under the pillow are some of the cordial gestures guests enjoy.

Host: Erene Rallis
Rooms: 2 (1 PB; 1 SB) $40-50
Continental Breakfast
Credit Cards: None
Notes: 2, 4, 5, 6 (outside), 8, 9, 10, 11, 12

Eye Openers
Bed and Breakfast
Reservations DD-P2

P. O. Box 694, Altadena, 91003-0694
(213) 684-4428; (818) 797-2055
FAX (818) 798-3640

Japanese ambience characterizes this two-bedroom guest house and numerous outdoor areas. Views of nearby mountain lakes and surrounding mountains can be enjoyed from the decks, livingroom with fireplace, and upstairs bedroom. Indoor hot tub, choice of full or continental breakfast. Twenty minutes inland from San Diego near Escondido. Only a short drive to several beach cities. $70-115.

Eye Openers
Bed and Breakfast
Reservations FA-B2

P. O. Box 694, Altadena, 91003-0694
(213) 684-4428; (818) 797-2055
FAX (818) 798-3640

Large country French chateau is nestled on a working avocado ranch. Relax and unwind poolside in a peaceful hilltop setting. Antiques are throughout this pretty bed and breakfast, and the guest room overlooks the garden. Full breakfast. Wineries, antique shops, and golf courses are nearby. Resident cats and dogs. Two guest rooms with private and shared baths. $60-75.

Eye Openers
Bed and Breakfast
Reservations SD-E1

P. O. Box 694, Altadena, 91003-0694
(213) 684-4428; (818) 797-2055
FAX (818) 798-3640

Separate guest house with turn-of-the-century furnishings assures privacy in central San Diego and offers a bedroom, sitting room with wood-burning stove, and dining area where a delicious continental breakfast is served. Additional guest room in the house is available. Private bath. $45-60 plus tax.

Eye Openers
Bed and Breakfast
Reservations SD-H3

P. O. Box 694, Altadena, 91003-0694
(213) 684-4428; (818) 797-2055
FAX (818) 798-3640

Self-hosted three-bedroom beachfront home can accommodate two to eight guests. Weekly and monthly rates also available. Three guest rooms. Private baths. $120-220.

Eye Openers
Bed and Breakfast
Reservations SD-H41

P. O. Box 694, Altadena, 91003-0694
(213) 684-4428; (818) 797-2055
FAX (818) 798-3640

Beautifully restored, tastefully decorated inn with large rooms and views is in the Golden Hill area of San Diego, convenient to downtown and many tourist attractions. Large rooms have sitting areas, and one has a fireplace. Extended continental breakfast is served in the formal dining room. There are several outdoor areas for sunning and relaxation. Four guest rooms with shared bath. $50, plus tax. Cottages available, $75 plus tax.

NOTES: Credit cards accepted: A Master Card; B Visa; C American Express; D Discover Card; E Diner's Club; F Other; 2 Personal Checks accepted; 3 Lunch available; 4 Dinner available; 5 Open all year;

Eye Openers Bed and Breakfast Reservations SD-S2

P. O. Box 694, Altadena, 91003-0694
(213) 684-4428; (818) 797-2055
FAX (818) 798-3640

Clairmont area above Misson Bay is the convenient locale of this bed and breakfast, with spacious suite and second guest room. Near most tourist attractions, there is bus transportation nearby. A full breakfast is served in the dining room. The host, an amateur winemaker, enjoys showing off his wine cellar. Resident dog. One guest room and suite. Private baths. $46-56.

Eye Openers Bed and Breakfast Reservations SD-H61

P. O. Box 694, Altadena, 91003-0694
(213) 684-4428; (818) 797-2055
FAX (818) 798-3640

Tri-level bed and breakfast inn with a harbor view and garden is near Balboa Park, Sea World, and the zoo. Continental breakfast. Six guest rooms. Private baths. $60-95 plus tax.

Eye Openers Bed and Breakfast Reservations SD-H91

P. O. Box 694, Altadena, 91003-0694
(213) 684-4428; (818) 797-2055
FAX (818) 798-3640

1889 Victorian antique-furnished bed and breakfast inn is in a restored village convenient to tourist attractions. Full breakfast, candlelight dinners, and special amenities available. Nine guest rooms. Private baths. $85-125 plus tax.

Eye Openers Bed and Breakfast Reservations SD-P1

P. O. Box 694, Altadena, 91003-0694
(213) 684-4428; (818) 797-2055
FAX (818) 798-3640

Condominium bed and breakfast near San Diego Stadium with excellent freeway access to all tourist attractions. Continental breakfast, swimming pool, Jacuzzi, kitchen, and laundry facilities. One room with private bath. $75.

Eye Openers Bed and Breakfast Reservations SD-Q21

P. O. Box 694, Altadena, 91003-0694
(213) 684-4428; (818) 797-2055
FAX (818) 798-3640

Converted San Diego Trolley Car and four-room guest cottage, beautifully restored and decorated with memorabilia and appointed antiques, are located near a quiet ravine in a natural setting in central San Diego close to Balboa Park. Lushly landscaped patios are a quiet retreat after a busy day of sightseeing. Self-hosted continental-plus breakfast and afternoon refreshments are provided. Private bath. $65-75 plus tax.

Heritage Park Bed and Breakfast Inn

2470 Heritage Park Row, 92110
(619) 299-6832

A splendid Queen Anne in San Diego's unique setting for romantic overnight lodging, a 7.8-acre Victorian Park in the heart of historic Old Town. Accommodations include eight distinctive guest chambers, each carefully furnished with authentic period antiques, Victorian wall coverings, and nostalgic trimmings of a century ago. Full homemade breakfast buffet is served

---

6 Pets welcome; 8 Children welcome; 9 Social drinking allowed; 10 Tennis available; 11 Swimming available; 12 Golf available; 13 Skiing available; 14 May be booked through travel agents.

in the dining room and may be enjoyed on the veranda. Evening social hour and nightly vintage movies.

Hosts: Nancy and Charles Helsper
Rooms: 8 (4 PB; 4 SB) $80-120
Full Breakfast
Credit Cards: A, B
Notes: 2, 4, 5, 8 (over 12), 9, 14

Vera's Cozy Corner

2810 Albatross Street, 92103
(619) 296-1938

This crisp white Colonial with black shutters sits in a quiet cul-de-sac overlooking San Diego Bay. Comfortable guest quarters consist of a separate cottage with private entrance across a flower-filled patio. Vera offers freshly squeezed orange juice from her own fruit trees in season as a prelude to breakfast, which is served in the dining room. The house is convenient to local shops and restaurants, beaches, and is one mile from the San Diego Zoo.

Host: Vera V. Warden
Room: 1 (PB) $45-50
Continental Breakfast
Credit Cards: None
Notes: 2, 5, 9, 10, 11, 12, 14

SAN FRANCISCO

Bed and Breakfast International-TNN-CALIFORNIA

P. O. Box 282910, 94128-2910
(415) 696-1690; (800) 872-4500

Part of the Bed and Breakfast National Network, Bed and Breakfast International offers bed and breakfast not only in California but also in many other cities and states across the country. The members of this network adhere strictly to the standards set by TNN, such as getting to know the guests personally, having an established cancelation and refund policy, and following a thorough inspection and approval

process for all properties rented. This is because each member of the network is dedicated to ensuring guests comfort, pleasure, and personal needs while staying at one of these "homes away from home."

B&B International #101

P. O. Box 282910, 94128-2910
(415) 696-1690; FAX (415) 696-1699

Situated in the heart of San Francisco on Russian Hill, this charming three-story Victorian Row house is close to the cable car line, and within walking distance of Chinatown, Union Square, and North Beach. It has original woodwork and is furnished with antiques. The guest room offers a panoramic view of San Francisco. $90.

B&B International #102

P. O. Box 282910, 94128-2910
(415) 696-1690; FAX (415) 696-1699

Ideally situated second-floor home in a modernized Victorian building near the North Beach area on Telegraph Hill. Walking distance to Fisherman's Wharf and many restaurants. Cable car is three blocks away. Two rooms share a bath. $55-68.

B&B International #104

P. O. Box 282910, 94128-2910
(415) 696-1690; FAX (415) 696-1699

Exceptionally clean and well-decorated guest room, studio, or carriage house in the back garden of an 1880 Victorian. Room has a double bed, private bath, and private entrance. Studio has queen bed, fireplace, fully equipped kitchen, and deck. Two-story carriage house has fireplace, grand piano, formal dining room, and fully equipped kitchen. Continental breakfast items are left for the guests. $65-175.

B&B International #105

P. O. Box 282910, 94128-2910
(415) 696-1690; FAX (415) 696-1699

This 1876 Victorian is "eccentrically, eclectically, and very tastefully decorated." This home is truly "San Francisco" and is close to shops and restaurants in popular Pacific Heights. There is a room with private bath, mini-kitchen, and sitting room. In the back garden, there is a guest cottage that affords privacy and opens onto the patio. $85.

B&B International #107

P. O. Box 282910, 94128-2910
(415) 696-1690; FAX (415) 696-1699

Four homes all built around the 1920s furnished in antiques and situated near many interesting shops and restaurants on Haight Street. All homes have back decks for guests to enjoy. Situated about 15 minutes from downtown and walking distance to Golden Gate Park. Ten rooms with all types of bed sizes. All have shared baths. Host prepares breakfast. $50-58.

Bed and Breakfast Los Angeles 14-5

3924 East 14th Street, Long Beach, 90804
(310) 498-0552; (800) 383-3513

This three-story mansion has four guest rooms and two baths, all of which are upstairs. Features include full American breakfast, afternoon wine and munchies, fireplaces, antique furnishings, and off-street parking. Moderate-luxury rates.

Bed and Breakfast Los Angeles 14-6

3924 East 14th Street, Long Beach, 90804
(310) 498-0552; (800) 383-3513

Secluded on a hill, but close to Golden Gate Park, this cute cottage has twin beds, a fireplace, kitchen and bath, as well as a full view of the city. Hosts require a three-night minimum stay. Moderate rates.

Bed and Breakfast Los Angeles 14-7

3924 East 14th Street, Long Beach, 90804
(310) 498-0552; (800) 383-3513

This 1910 Edwardian home is located near the University of California Medical Center and Golden Gate Park, and has four guest rooms that share two baths. Cribs are available. Continental breakfast is served. Affordable rates.

B&B San Francisco #06

P. O. Box 420009, 94142
(415) 931-3083; FAX (415) 921-BBSF

One of San Francisco's most beautiful neighborhoods. The homes on Russian Hill offer wonderful views of the bay and Golden Gate Bridge. It's a wonderful walk down the hill to Fisherman's Wharf and North Beach. Cable cars are just one block away. The host has two guests rooms, both offering a bay view. $75-85.

B&B San Francisco #07

P. O. Box 420009, 94142
(415) 931-3083; FAX (415) 921-BBSF

A scenic location in San Francisco with a panoramic view. Three guest rooms, each facing west, allow a lovely sunset view overlooking the Glen Canyon Park with its beautiful eucalyptus grove. Mt. Davidson towers majestically over the canyon in full view from each guest room. Each room has a TV. Two bathrooms for guest use. Breakfast is a gourmet treat. Family accommodations available. $55-95.

---

6 Pets welcome; 8 Children welcome; 9 Social drinking allowed; 10 Tennis available; 11 Swimming available; 12 Golf available; 13 Skiing available; 14 May be booked through travel agents.

B&B San Francisco #08
P. O. Box 420009, 94142
(415) 931-3083; FAX (415) 921-BBSF

A wonderful warm San Francisco neighborhood. Lots of excellent local shops and restaurants on 24th Street. This lovely bed and breakfast is on the J-Church streetcar line only 20 minutes from downtown. Full breakfast; shared bath. $55.

B&B San Francisco #09
P. O. Box 420009, 94142
(415) 931-3083; FAX (415) 921-BBSF

Quiet, spacious, tastefully decorated room with fireplace, fresh flowers, and fruit basket. Breakfast served by the bay window, king-size bed, and TV. Second room has antique double bed. Fisherman's Wharf and cable cars are only two blocks away. Full breakfast; shared bath. $55-65.

B&B San Francisco #11
P. O. Box 420009, 94142
(415) 931-3083; FAX (415) 921-BBSF

Pines Mews, a Victorian treasure, sits in San Francisco's most prestigious neighborhood, Pacific Heights. The three accommodations, the Carriage House, the Studio, and the Guest Quarter, have been splendidly restored, and some modern amenities have been added. Full breakfast is provided. $65-200.

B&B San Francisco #13
P. O. Box 420009, 94142
(415) 931-3083; FAX (415) 921-BBSF

A new private addition onto a charming old San Francisco home. If guests prefer privacy, this unhosted, charming, and quiet bed and breakfast is most enjoyable. Large bedroom has a view of North Beach; excellent Italian restaurants in the neighborhood.

Fisherman's Wharf and Chinatown are a short walk away. Crib available. Full breakfast. $125; $10-15 extra for children.

B&B San Francisco #18
P. O. Box 420009, 94142
(415) 931-3083; FAX (415) 921-BBSF

The quaint town of Larkspur is where this bed and breakfast is situated. The hostess offers her guests an entire floor with a livingroom, two bedrooms, bath, and a wonderful private patio. Pool available during the summer months. Muir Woods, Stenson Beach, and the rugged California coast are just a short drive away. Full breakfast. $95-115.

B&B San Francisco #19
P. O. Box 420009, 94142
(415) 931-3083; FAX (415) 921-BBSF

The hosts offer San Francisco hospitality in their contemporary Russian Hill home. The quaint, quiet street offers the true flavor of the city, and cable cars, Fisherman's Wharf, and Chinatown are only a short walk away. They offer two guest rooms, one with a queen-size bed, and the other with a pair of twin beds. Both rooms share a full bath. The livingroom has a fireplace. Full breakfast is served. $65-75.

B&B San Francisco #20
P. O. Box 420009, 94142
(415) 931-3083; FAX (415) 921-BBSF

High atop charming Russian Hill sits a two-bedroom Victorian flat with a beautiful view of San Francisco Bay. This is a great place for two couples or a family. Off the livingroom is a sunny solarium, a full kitchen, and a bath. One bedroom has a double bed, and the other bedroom offers a queen-size bed. A futon is available. The livingroom has a TV, fireplace, and phone. Cable cars are just around the corner, and

NOTES: Credit cards accepted: A Master Card; B Visa; C American Express; D Discover Card; E Diner's Club; F Other; 2 Personal Checks accepted; 3 Lunch available; 4 Dinner available; 5 Open all year;

the Wharf is just a short distance away. Special rates for stays longer than seven days. $125-150.

Bock's Bed and Breakfast
1448 Willard Street, 94117
(415) 664-6842

This lovely 1906 Edwardian home has been a bed and breakfast since 1980. Situated in Parnassus Heights, guests enjoy beautiful city views, decks, private phones, television, and coffee or tea served in each room. Golden Gate Park and the University of California Medical Center are just two blocks away. Cafes, shops, and restaurants are nearby, and there is excellent public transportation. Two-day minimum stay.

Host: Laura J. Bock
Rooms: 3 (1 PB; 2 SB) $50-65 plus tax
Continental Breakfast
Credit Cards: None
Notes: 2, 5, 8, 9, 10, 11

Casa Arguello
225 Arguello Boulevard, 94118
(415) 752-9482

Comfortable rooms in a cheerful, spacious flat ten minutes from the center of town. Situated in a desirable residential neighborhood near Golden Gate Park and the Presidio. Restaurants and shops within walking distance. Excellent public transportation.

Hosts: Emma Baires and Marina McKenzie
Rooms: 5 (3 PB; 2 SB) $52-77
Expanded Continental Breakfast
Credit Cards: None
Notes: 2, 5, 8, 9, 10, 11, 12, 14

Chateau Tivoli
1057 Steiner Street, 94115
(415) 776-5462; (800) 228-1647
FAX (415) 776-0505

The Chateau Tivoli is a landmark mansion that was the residence of the owners of San Francisco's world-famous Tivoli Opera House. Guests experience a time-travel journey back to San Francisco's golden age of opulence, the 1890s. The chateau is furnished with antiques from Cornelius Vanderbilt, Charles de Gaulle, J. Paul Getty, and famous San Francisco madam Sally Stanford.

Hosts: Rodney Karr and Bill Gersbach
Rooms: 5 (PB) $80-125
Suites: 2 (PB) $160-200
Expanded Continental Breakfast
Credit Cards: A, B, C
Notes: 2, 5, 8, 9, 10, 11, 12, 14

Cornell Hotel
715 Bush Street, 94108
(415) 421-3154

The Cornell Hotel, a six-story Victorian under French management, offers elegant rooms, comfortably appointed and individually decorated. Its restaurant, Jeanne d'Arc, replete with tapestries, statues, and artifacts, provides fine French-country cuisine. Ideal low Nob Hill location in the heart of the city. Call about special rates.

Host: Claude H. Lambert
Rooms: 8 (2 PB; 6 SB) $55-85
Full Breakfast
Credit Cards: A, B, C, E
Notes: 4, 5, 10, 11, 12, 14

Eye Openers Bed and Breakfast Reservations SF-A3
P. O. Box 694, Altadena, 91003-0694
(213) 684-4428; (818) 797-2055
FAX (818) 798-3640

Victorian with Old World decor offers friendly hospitality and excellent location in the Marina District. Good public transportation. Continental breakfast. Three guest rooms and studio. Shared and private bath. $60-100, plus tax.

6 Pets welcome; 8 Children welcome; 9 Social drinking allowed; 10 Tennis available; 11 Swimming available; 12 Golf available; 13 Skiing available; 14 May be booked through travel agents.

Eye Openers Bed and Breakfast Reservations SF-B1

P. O. Box 694, Altadena, 91003-0694
(213) 684-4428; (818) 797-2055
FAX (818) 798-3640

Unique small cottage to the rear of the host home atop one of San Francisco's highest points near Golden Gate Park has fireplace and kitchen. Continental breakfast is self-catered. Car essential. Minimum stay is three nights. Private bath. $75-85.

Eye Openers Bed and Breakfast Reservations SF-K51

P. O. Box 694, Altadena, 91003-0694
(213) 684-4428; (818) 797-2055
FAX (818) 798-3640

Victorian bed and breakfast features three guest rooms with fireplace, rooftop deck with Jacuzzi, and full breakfast. Excellent location with good transportation to all tourist attractions and business meetings. Five guest rooms. Private and shared baths. $75-125 plus tax.

Eye Openers Bed and Breakfast Reservations SF-H1

P. O. Box 694, Altadena, 91003-0694
(213) 684-4428; (818) 797-2055
FAX (818) 798-3640

This 1892 restored Victorian in the Noe Valley area offers a spacious suite with a private entrance, lovely decor, full breakfast, and many more amenities. Good public transportation. $85.

Eye Openers Bed and Breakfast Reservations SF-L1

P. O. Box 694, Altadena, 91003-0694
(213) 684-4428; (818) 797-2055
FAX (818) 798-3640

Centrally located Victorian condo is well-decorated with period pieces and offers privacy in lovely surroundings. Continental breakfast. Five guest rooms. Self-hosted apartment. $100.

Eye Openers Bed and Breakfast Reservations SF-M1

P. O. Box 694, Altadena, 91003-0694
(213) 684-4428; (818) 797-2055
FAX (818) 798-3640

Upstairs guest room in a well-maintained garden apartment is in a quiet neighborhood three miles from Golden Gate Park, five miles from downtown, and provides a continental-plus breakfast. One guest room with shared bath. $45-500.

Eye Openers Bed and Breakfast Reservations SF-M2

P. O. Box 694, Altadena, 91003-0694
(213) 684-4428; (818) 797-2055
FAX (818) 798-3640

1910 vintage Victorian near Golden Gate Park and UC Medical Center offer inexpensive, friendly hospitality. Good public transportation. Continental breakfast. Four guest rooms with shared baths. $39-69 plus tax.

Eye Openers Bed and Breakfast Reservations SF-M301

P. O. Box 694, Altadena, 91003-0694
(213) 684-4428; (818) 797-2055
FAX (818) 798-3640

Four-story Victorian hotel, now a Marina District bed and breakfast inn, features four-poster beds and modern amenities. Continental breakfast. Thirty guest rooms. Private bath. $65-85 plus tax.

Eye Openers Bed and Breakfast Reservations SF-P261

P. O. Box 694, Altadena, 91003-0694
(213) 684-4428; (818) 797-2055
FAX (818) 798-3640

Sister inns, one French Country and the other formal English, are two blocks from Union Square and offer beautifully appointed rooms, friendly hospitality, afternoon refreshments, and wonderful breakfast. Twenty-six guest rooms. Private bath. $105-195 plus tax.

Eye Openers Bed and Breakfast Reservations SF-P3

P. O. Box 694, Altadena, 91003-0694
(213) 684-4428; (818) 797-2055
FAX (818) 798-3640

Hilltop home in Diamond Heights area has glorious view of the bay and city from the two-story livingroom. Enjoy a full breakfast in the Scandinavian-furnished dining area. Each of three guest rooms has a balcony. Two shared baths. $35-45.

The Inn at Union Square

440 Post Street, 94102
(415) 397-3510; (800) AT-THE-INN
(800) 753-5911; FAX (415) 989-0529

The Inn at Union Square is an elegant small hotel in the heart of downtown San Francisco. The financial and theater districts are a short walk from the door. The city's famed cable car is less than a block away, and can make traveling to view historic sites convenient and fun. The inn provides breakfast of flaky croissants, muffins, fresh juice, and coffee served in bed or in the lobbies situated on each floor. Enjoy afternoon tea served with fresh cakes and crisp cucumber sandwiches, or hors d' oeuvres and wine served every day.

Host: Brooks Bayly
Rooms: 30 (PB) $110-180; $145-400 suites
Continental Breakfast
Credit Cards: A, B, C, E
Notes: 2, 5, 8, 9, 11, 14

Kids Welcome 14-1

3924 East 14th Street, Long Beach, 90804
(310) 498-0552; (800) 383-3513

Walk to Golden Gate Park from this three-story Victorian that is geared toward traveling families. Two guest rooms share one bath on each floor. Full breakfast is provided, and guests are welcome to use the kitchen, fireplace, and even the playpen. Host's teenage daughter is willing to babysit. Family rates are available. Moderate rates.

Monica and Ed Widburg

2007 15th Avenue, 94116
(415) 564-1751

This charming home in a quiet residential area has an ocean view and ample parking. There is one bed and breakfast room, but for groups up to four guests, additional accommodations are available in an adjacent room. Queen beds in both rooms. The park, museums, and zoo are close by.

6 Pets welcome; 8 Children welcome; 9 Social drinking allowed; 10 Tennis available; 11 Swimming available; 12 Golf available; 13 Skiing available; 14 May be booked through travel agents.

Public transportation is easily available to downtown and Fisherman's Wharf. Reservations required.

Hosts: Monica and Ed Widburg
Room: 1 (PB) $75
Full Breakfast
Credit Cards: None
Notes: 2, 5, 10, 11, 12

The No Name Victorian Bed and Breakfast

P. O. Box 420009, 94142
(415) 479-1913; FAX (415) 921-BBSF

Situated in one of the most photographed areas of an Francisco, the historic district of Alamo Square, this bed and breakfast is close to the Civic Center, Opera House, Davies Symphony Hall, Union Square, and all the sites that make the city famous. Most of the guest rooms feature private baths and fireplaces. One room features an antique Chinese wedding bed. A sumptuous breakfast is served every morning. In the evening help yourself to wine and relax in the hot tub, where many a guest has received a surprise visit from "Nosey" the raccoon. $65-105.

Pine Mews

P. O. Box 282910, 94128-2910
(415) 696-1690

Exceptional accommodations in back of an 1880 Victorian. All three guest quarters have private entrances and open onto the garden. There is a spacious, elegantly appointed carriage house with a grand piano, fireplace, and formal dining area. A large studio with a fireplace facing the sleeping area is also available, along with a smaller guest room with a private bath. Situated in one of the city's nicest neighborhoods, Pacific Heights, it is close to wonderful shops and restaurants on Union and Fillmore streets.

Host: Sharene Z. Klein
Rooms: 3 (PB) $65-175
Continental Breakfast
Credit Cards: A, B
Notes: 5, 9, 14

Red Victorian Bed and Breakfast Inn

1665 Haight Street, 94117
(415) 861-7264

Built at the turn of the century as a country resort hotel serving nearby Golden Gate Park, the Red Victorian enjoys an international clientele of globally minded people. From the aquarium bathroom to the Redwood Forest Room to the Peace Gallery where breakfast is served among Transformational paintings, the Red Victorian exudes color and joy.

Host: Sami Sunchild
Suite: 1 (PB) $135
Rooms: 13 (3 PB; 10 SB) $55-100
Expanded Continental Breakfast
Credit Cards: A, B, C
Notes: 2, 5, 10, 11, 12, 14

Washington Square Inn

1660 Stockton Street, 94133
(415) 981-4220; (800) 388-0220
FAX (415) 397-7242

Situated in the heart of the city's Italian district on historic Washington Square, the inn offers imaginatively and tastefully furnished rooms, with French and English antiques and an intimate parlor with fireplace where complimentary tea and hors d'oeuvres are served. Within walking distance to Telegraph Hill, Fisherman's Wharf, Chinatown, financial district, restaurants, shops, markets, and cable car line. Concierge service available.

Hosts: Brooks Bayly
Rooms: 15 (10 PB; 5 SB) $85-180
Continental Breakfast
Credit Cards: A, B, C, E
Notes: 2, 5, 8, 9, 14

NOTES: Credit cards accepted: A Master Card; B Visa; C American Express; D Discover Card; E Diner's Club; F Other; 2 Personal Checks accepted; 3 Lunch available; 4 Dinner available; 5 Open all year;

SAN GREGORIO

Rancho San Gregorio

Route 1, Box 54, 94074
(415) 747-0810

Five miles inland from the Pacific off Highway 1 in a rural valley, Rancho San Gregorio welcomes travelers to share relaxed hospitality. This country getaway has 15 acres, an old barn, creek, gardens, decks, and gazebo. Full country breakfast features home-grown specialities. Forty-five minutes from San Francisco, Santa Cruz, and the bay area.

Hosts: Bud and Lee Raynor
Rooms: 4 (PB) $65-135
Full Breakfast
Credit Cards: A, B, C
Notes: 2, 5, 8, 9, 11, 12, 14

SAN LUIS OBISPO- SEE ALSO ARROYO GRANDE

Eye Openers Bed and Breakfast Reservations LO-03

P. O. Box 694, Altadena, 91003-0694
(213) 684-4428; (818) 797-2055
FAX (818) 798-3640

Well-traveled, multilingual host offers comfortable accommodations. Livingroom has a view of Morro Rock. Delicious breakfast. Three guest rooms. Shared and private bath. $35-50, plus tax.

Eye Openers Bed and Breakfast Reservations PB-S301

P. O. Box 694, Altadena, 91003-0694
(213) 684-4428; (818) 797-2055
FAX (818) 798-3640

Contemporary inn on the beach in the midst of twenty-three miles of unspoiled sand and surf. Continental breakfast delivered to your room. Twenty-five guest rooms. Private bath. $65-165 plus tax.

Eye Openers Bed and Breakfast Reservations SL-G131

P. O. Box 694, Altadena, 91003-0694
(213) 684-4428; (818) 797-2055
FAX (818) 798-3640

This 1887 Italianate Queen Anne Victorian recently restored to its orginal splendor is an elegant and friendly bed and breakfast. Full breakfast served. Close to the beaches and attractions of the Central Coast. Nine guest rooms and four suites. Private bath. $80-160, plus tax.

Megan's Friends

Bed and Breakfast Reservation Service
1776 Royal Way, San Luis Obispo, 93405
(805) 544-4406

For the single, traveling woman, we have a charming, cozy and comfortable home in its surrounding gardens with emphasis on nature. A quiet place for reading, sunbathing, and use of a cozy campfire. Easy access to all of San Luis Obispo. Visit Mission San Luis de Tolosa (fifth in a network of 21 California missions) situated downtown. Every Thursday evening, Farmers' Market attracts residents and visitors alike on Higuera Street and shops are open, while barbecued food is served by local restaurants. Madonna Mt. and Bishop's Peak are pleasantly viewed from the small bedroom provided by the hostess. Extra-long twin bed; shared bathroom. $50.

SAN PEDRO

Bed and Breakfast Los Angeles 5-5

3924 East 14th Street, Long Beach, 90804
(800) 383-3513

Sprawling over a hillside, this house in colorful San Pedro offers three rooms with

6 Pets welcome; 8 Children welcome; 9 Social drinking allowed; 10 Tennis available; 11 Swimming available; 12 Golf available; 13 Skiing available; 14 May be booked through travel agents.

private baths. One room has a crib. Visit the tide pools nearby. Affordable rates.

SANTA BARBARA

Bath Street Inn

1720 Bath Street, 93101
(805) 682-9680; (800) 788-2284

An 1873 Queen Anne Victorian in the heart of historic Santa Barbara. Scenic downtown is within walking distance. Rooms have views, balconies, and private baths. Breakfast is served in the dining room or garden; bikes are available; evening refreshments.

Host: Susan Brown
Rooms: 10 (PB) $90-150
Full Breakfast
Credit Cards: A, B, C
Notes: 2, 5, 8, 9, 10, 11, 12, 14

Bed and Breakfast at Valli's View

340 North Sierra Vista Road, 93108
(805) 969-1272

This beautiful home is nestled in the foothills of Montecito. The guest room overlooks the mountains and has a color TV. Spacious back patios offer lounges for sunning and a porch swing for relaxing. Shady fern gardens surround the hillside deck with a magnificent view. The livingroom offers a fireplace and grand piano. Awaken to songbirds and the aroma of Dutch babies in the oven.

Hosts: Valli and Larry Stevens
Rooms: 1 (PB) $65
Full Breakfast
Credit Cards: None
Notes: 2, 5, 6 (outside), 8, 9, 10, 11, 12

Bed and Breakfast Los Angeles 11-2

3924 East 14th Street, Long Beach, 90804
(310) 498-0552; (800) 383-3513

On a perfect hill in Santa Barbara, this little bed and breakfast features one spacious guest room with room for a daybed, two decks, a porch swing, a fireplace, and a grand piano. Hosts will pick you up at the train station or airport, and they pride themselves on turning strangers into friends. Moderate rates.

Bed and Breakfast Los Angeles 11-4

3924 East 14th Street, Long Beach, 90804
(310) 498-0552; (800) 383-3513

Set among the ancient oaks, this private little bed and breakfast has one cottage (bedroom, livingroom with roll-away bed, small bath, and refrigerator), and two guest rooms in the main house (one with a sitting room, fridge, and private bath). Guests are provided with lots of goodies for self-catered breakfast. Walk to the Mission, Botanical Gardens, and Natural History Museum. Affordable rates.

Blue Quail Inn and Cottages

1908 Bath Street, 93101
(805) 687-2300; (800) 549-1622 (CA)
(800) 676-1622 (USA)

Relax and enjoy the quiet country atmosphere of the Blue Quail Inn and Cottages, just three blocks to Sansum Clinic and Cottage Hospital. Linger over a delicious full breakfast including home-baked goods served on the patio or in the main house dining room. Take a picnic lunch for a day of adventure on the inn's bicycles, then return for afternoon wine and light hors d'oeuvres. Sip hot spiced apple cider in the evening before enjoying a restful sleep in a cottage, suite, or guest room.

Host: Jeanise Suding Eaton
Rooms: 9 (PB) $74-165
Full Breakfast
Credit Cards: A, B, C
Notes: 2, 3, 5, 8, 9, 10, 11, 12, 14

NOTES: Credit cards accepted: A Master Card; B Visa; C American Express; D Discover Card; E Diner's Club; F Other; 2 Personal Checks accepted; 3 Lunch available; 4 Dinner available; 5 Open all year;

Cheshire Cat Inn

36 West Valerio Street, 93101
(805) 569-1610; FAX (805) 682-1876

Victorian elegance in a Southern California seaside village. The Cheshire Cat is conveniently situated near theaters, restaurants, and shops. Decorated exclusively in Laura Ashley papers and linens, the sunny guest rooms have private baths; some with fireplaces, spas, balconies. Collectibles, English antiques, and fresh flowers enhance one's stay in beautiful Santa Barbara.

Hosts: Christine Dunstan and Midge Goeden
Rooms: 14 (PB) $79-249
Full Breakfast
Credit Cards: A, B
Notes: 2, 5, 8, 9, 10, 11, 12, 14

Eye Openers
Bed and Breakfast
Reservations SB-B1

P. O. Box 694, Altadena, 91003-0694
(213) 684-4428; (818) 797-2055
FAX (818) 798-3640

Centrally located and filled with country charm, this inn is on beautiful grounds that provide a feeling of seclusion. Delicious full breakfast and evening refreshments. Bicycles available. Eight rooms. Private and shared baths. $82-120 plus tax.

Eye Openers
Bed and Breakfast
Reservations SB-R1

P. O. Box 694, Altadena, 91003-0694
(213) 684-4428; (818) 797-2055
FAX (818) 798-3640

Architect-designed contemporary home is nestled among oaks near Santa Barbara Mission and five minutes to the beach and shopping. Choice of full or continental breakfast. One room. Private bath. $45-50.

Eye Openers
Bed and Breakfast
Reservations SB-C110

P. O. Box 694, Altadena, 91003-0694
(213) 684-4428; (818) 797-2055
FAX (818) 798-3640

Luxurious Victorian inn with a wide choice of uniquely decorated guest rooms is centrally located and offers an excellent breakfast. Eleven rooms. Private bath. $108-150 plus tax.

Eye Openers
Bed and Breakfast
Reservations SB-H91

P. O. Box 694, Altadena, 91003-0694
(213) 684-4428; (818) 797-2055
FAX (818) 798-3640

Situated near the beach, this elegant inn is decorated with French and English antiques and has a country feeling. Full breakfast and afternoon tea. Nine rooms. Private bath. $85-185 plus tax.

Eye Openers
Bed and Breakfast
Reservations SB-O61

P. O. Box 694, Altadena, 91003-0694
(213) 684-4428; (818) 797-2055
FAX (818) 798-3640

Delicious, elegant breakfast, comfortable rooms, and friendly hospitality are found at this conveniently located inn near beaches and Mission. 1904 Craftsman-style bungalow with individually decorated rooms, several with private decks. Beach towels and chairs provided. Six rooms and one guest cottage. Private bath. $85-120 plus tax.

6 Pets welcome; 8 Children welcome; 9 Social drinking allowed; 10 Tennis available; 11 Swimming available; 12 Golf available; 13 Skiing available; 14 May be booked through travel agents.

Eye Openers Bed and Breakfast Reservations SB-R51

P. O. Box 694, Altadena, 91003-0694
(213) 684-4428; (818) 797-2055
FAX (818) 798-3640

This 1886 restored Victorian inn decorated with antiques is close to Mission and shops. Continental breakfast with homemade breads. Bikes available. Five guest rooms. Private and shared baths. $75-100, plus tax.

The Old Yacht Club Inn

431 Corona Del Mar Drive, 93103
(805) 962-1277; (800) 549-1676 (CA)
(800) 676-1676 (USA)

The Old Yacht Club Inn has nine guest rooms in two houses: a 1912 California Craftsman and a 1920s Early California-style building. The inn opened as Santa Barbara's first bed and breakfast in 1980 and is now world-renowned for its hospitality and warmth in comfortable surroundings, and for its fine food. The inn is within a block of the beach and close to tennis, swimming, boating, fishing, and golf. Bikes and beach chairs available.

Hosts: Nancy Donaldson, Lu Caruso, and Sandy Hunt
Rooms: 9 (PB) $80-140
Full Breakfast
Credit Cards: A, B, C, D
Notes: 2, 3 4 (Sat. only), 5, 8, 9, 10, 11, 12, 14

The Olive House

1604 Olive Street, 93101
(805) 962-4902; (800) 786-6422

Enjoy quiet comfort and gracious hospitality in a lovingly restored and richly furnished 1904 Craftsman-style house replete with redwood paneling, bay windows, window seats, coffered ceilings, and a fireplace and studio grand piano in the livingroom. Richly refurbished in 1990. Breakfast is served in the large, sunny dining room that also houses a studio grand piano. Enjoy mountain and ocean views from the sun deck and several guest rooms.

Host: Lois Gregg
Rooms: 6 (PB) $105-155
Expanded Continental Breakfast
Credit Cards: A, B
Notes: 2, 5, 9, 10, 11, 12, 14

Simpson House Inn

Simpson House Inn

121 East Arrellaga, 93101
(805) 963-7067; (800) 676-1280

This 1874 Victorian estate is secluded on an acre of beautifully landscaped gardens, yet only a five-minute walk to historic downtown. Cottages, suites, and guest rooms are decorated with antiques, Oriental rugs, and English lace. They feature fireplaces, private decks, Jacuzzis, televisions and VCRs. Spacious common area opens onto large porches overlooking the gardens. A full gourmet breakfast, wine and hors d'oeuvres, and afternoon tea are served on the veranda. Bicycles and croquet are available.

Host: Gillean Wilson
Rooms: 13 (PB) $75-225
Full Breakfast
Credit Cards: A, B, C, D
Notes: 2, 5, 8, 10, 11, 12, 14

The Tiffany Inn

1323 De la Vina, 93101
(805) 963-2283

NOTES: Credit cards accepted: A Master Card; B Visa; C American Express; D Discover Card; E Diner's Club; F Other; 2 Personal Checks accepted; 3 Lunch available; 4 Dinner available; 5 Open all year;

This 1898 Victorian inn is filled with antiques and is a great romantic hideaway. Downtown is only two blocks away, where guests can enjoy shopping, movies, theater and restaurants. A full vegetarian breakfast and nightly refreshments offered. Guests can relax in the Victorian garden or sit by the fire during winter months. After guests come back from dinner, they can enjoy our homemade cookies and brownies. The staff prides itself on customer service, and try hard to ensure their happiness.

Hosts: Carol and Larry MacDonald
Rooms: 7 (5 PB; 2 SB) $75-175
Full Breakfast
Credit Cards: A, B, C
Notes: 2, 5, 12

SANTA CRUZ

Babbling Brook Inn

1025 Laurel Street, 95060
(408) 427-2437; (800) 866-1131
FAX (408) 427-2457

A waterwheel and meandering brook are in the gardens of this 12-room inn with French decor. Each room has a private bath, telephone, TV, fireplace, private deck, private entrance. Two have deep soaking bathtubs. Walk to beaches, the boardwalk, a garden mall, or tennis. Full breakfast and complimentary wine and cheese. Romantic garden gazebo for weddings.

Host: Helen King
Rooms: 12 (PB) $85-150
Full Breakfast
Credit Cards: A, B, C, D, E
Notes: 2, 5, 8 (over 11), 9, 10, 11, 12, 14

Bed and Breakfast International #201

P. O. Box 282910, San Francisco, 94128
(415) 696-1690; FAX (415) 696-1699

This home is in a spectacular setting overlooking the Santa Cruz Mountains. Guests have full use of the two-bedroom house with fireplace, deck, and hot tub. $125.

Bed and Breakfast International #202

P. O. Box 282910, San Francisco, 94128
(415) 696-1690; FAX (415) 696-1699

Guest quarters are in a former carriage house behind an 1875 Victorian home just a few minutes from the ocean and Santa Cruz by car. The house features patios, hot tub, and fireplaces. $80-95.

B&B San Francisco #21

P. O. Box 420009, 94142
(415) 931-3083; FAX (415) 921-BBSF

This Frank Lloyd Wright-designed home is in the beautiful Santa Cruz Mountains, only seven miles from the popular Santa Cruz Beach. One bedroom has a mountain view, private entrance, and private bath. Another bedroom features a mountain view and shared bath. Full breakfast. Minimum stay is three nights. $65-75.

SANTA MARIA

Hunters Inn

1514 South Broadway, 93454
(805) 922-2123; (800) 950-2123
FAX (805) 925-1523

This 70-unit motel in the middle of town is situated only eight miles from the ocean. Close to Solvang (Danish Town), Hearst Castle, and half-way between Sab Francisco and Los Angeles. Coffee served always, with danish and coffee in the morning. Perfect for family reunions and company seminars. Barbecue available for guest use.

Hosts: Lee and Nita Hilarides
Rooms: 70 (PB) $39-95
Continental Breakfast
Credit Cards: A, B, C, D, E, F
Notes: 2, 5, 6, 8, 9, 12, 14

6 Pets welcome; 8 Children welcome; 9 Social drinking allowed; 10 Tennis available; 11 Swimming available; 12 Golf available; 13 Skiing available; 14 May be booked through travel agents.

SANTA MONICA

Bed and Breakfast International #502

P. O. Box 282910, San Francisco, 94128
(415) 696-1690; FAX (415) 696-1699

Guest quarters are an addition, with a deck
on the second floor of a renovated 1920s
California bungalow. Contemporary furnishings in blue and white with natural
wood. Close to Venice boardwalk and
Santa Monica pier. $75.

Bed and Breakfast Los Angeles 4-4

3924 East 14th Street, Long Beach, 90804
(310) 498-0552; (800) 383-3513

This sunny studio apartment looks out onto
the ocean in Santa Monica. Walk to the
shops or borrow the owner's bikes.
Moderate rates.

Bed and Breakfast Los Angeles 4-5

3924 East 14th Street, Long Beach, 90804
(310) 498-0552; (800) 383-3513

This contemporary home is near Santa
Monica and has two rooms, each designed
for a single guest. Two bathrooms are
shared with the hosts. Nice patio and bikes
are available. Children over five welcome.
Affordable rates.

Channel Road Inn

219 West Channel Road, 90402
(310) 459-1920

Elegant inn one block from the beach in
Santa Monica. "One of the most romantic
places in Los Angeles"—*LA* magazine.
Views and bicycles. Two miles from the J.
Paul Getty Museum.

Hosts: Kathy Jensen and Susan Zolla
Rooms: 14 (PB) $85-195
Full Breakfast
Credit Cards: A, B
Notes: 2, 5, 8, 9, 10, 11, 12, 14

Eye Openers Bed and Breakfast Reservations SM-H1

P. O. Box 694, Altadena, 91003-0694
(213) 684-4428; (818) 797-2055
FAX (818) 798-3640

Economically priced bed and breakfast in
Santa Monica offers large guest room.
Hosts have interesting collection of folk
instruments and a large library. Good public transportation nearby. Continental
breakfast. Resident cat and dog. Private
bath. $40-45.

Eye Openers Bed and Breakfast Reservations VE-V10I

P. O. Box 694, Altadena, 91003-0694
(213) 684-4428; (818) 797-2055
FAX (818) 798-3640

Turn-of-the-century beach estate is now a
lovely bed and breakfast inn. Guest rooms
and suites are individually decorated with
antiques and hand-detailed furnishings.
Large continental breakfast and evening
refreshments are served. Ten guest rooms.
Shared and private bath. $85-140 plus tax.

SANTA ROSA

Melitta Station Inn

5850 Melitta Road, 95409
(707) 538-7712

Late 1800s restored railroad station, this
American country bed and breakfast is on a
country road in the Valley of the Moon in
the center of wine country. Next to three
state parks, hiking, biking, horseback riding,

hot air balloons, gliders, hot baths, and massages. Within minutes of many fine restaurants and wineries.

Hosts: Vic and Diane
Rooms: 6 (4 PB; 2 SB) $75-90
Full Breakfast
Credit Cards: A, B
Notes: 2, 5, 8 (prior arrangement) 10, 12

SAUSALITO

B&B International #108

P. O. Box 282910, San Francisco, 94128-2910
(415) 696-1690; FAX (415) 696-1699

Try a new way to stay at a bed and breakfast. Three houseboats docked in Sausalito, five minutes north of the Golden Gate Bridge and close to interesting shops and restaurants in downtown Sausalito. Two have beautiful views of the bay from the decks, and all are beautifully furnished in fine furniture and art. Two are unhosted leaving guests much privacy. The third comes with a home-cooked breakfast. $96-125.

B&B San Francisco #04

P. O. Box 420009, 94142
(415) 931-3038; FAX (415) 921-BBSF

The Marin County picturesque village of Sausalito offers wonderful restaurants, quaint shops, and romantic views of San Francisco. Stay aboard a houseboat, a permanently moored home on the bay. Decks on three sides, livingroom with a fireplace, king-size bed, full kitchen, and full bath. The home is unhosted, but all breakfast items are in the kitchen for a self-catered breakfast. Enjoy a glass of wine while watching the city lights come on and the sun slips behind Mt. Tamalpias. $125.

SEAL BEACH

Eye Openers
Bed and Breakfast
Reservations SB-B2

P. O. Box 694, Altadena, 91003-0694
(213) 684-4428; (818) 797-2055
FAX (818) 798-3640

Large villa on the sand with colorful gardens beach-side beckons you to indulge in water sports, sun on the dunes, or relax on an enclosed balcony with an ocean view. Indoor Jacuzzi, continental-plus breakfast. Two guest rooms. Private bath.

Eye Openers
Bed and Breakfast
Reservations SB-S241

P. O. Box 694, Altadena, 91003-0694
(213) 684-4428; (818) 797-2055
FAX (818) 798-3640

A bed and breakfast inn with the look and ambience of an elegant European inn is surrounded by lovely gardens. Inn has a brick courtyard, pool, library, and gracious dining room for large continental breakfast and evening refreshments. Twenty-four guest rooms all have individual decor and private baths. This lovely, quiet beach community is a well-kept secret. $108-155 plus tax.

Seal Beach Inn and Gardens

212 Fifth Street, 90740
(310) 493-2416; (800) HIDEAWAY

Situated just one block from the beach are 23 elegant and comfortable guest rooms, featured in a restored vintage inn with lush, peaceful gardens. A gourmet breakfast is served in the French tea room. Complimentary wine, cheese, and crackers are served in the library during the evening.

6 Pets welcome; 8 Children welcome; 9 Social drinking allowed; 10 Tennis available; 11 Swimming available; 12 Golf available; 13 Skiing available; 14 May be booked through travel agents.

A swimming pool and board games are available. Nearly 20 restaurants are within walking distance.

Host: Marjorie Bettenhausen Schmaehl
Rooms: 23 (PB) $98-155
Full Breakfast
Credit Cards: A, B, C, D, E, F
Notes: 2 (advance payment only), 3, 4, 5, 9, 10, 11, 12, 14

SEQUOIA

Eye Openers Bed and Breakfast Reservations TR-C1

P. O. Box 694, Altadena, 91003-0694
(213) 684-4428; (818) 797-2055
FAX (818) 798-3640

Enjoy an architect designed cottage with kitchen facilities. Beautiful views of the mountains from this community near the entrance to Sequoia National Park. Hot tub available. Private bath. $75.

SHERMAN OAKS

Bed and Breakfast Los Angeles 3-6

3924 East 14th Street, Long Beach, 90804
(310) 498-0552; (800) 383-3513

Drive through an enchanting garden to a private suite, that includes a bedroom, sitting room, bath, TV, and refrigerator. This home also features a pool, Jacuzzi, and deck, as well as a crib, highchair, and a laundry room. Moderate rates.

SOLVANG

Megan's Friends #01

Bed and Breakfast Reservation Service
1776 Royal Way, San Luis Obispo, 93405
(805) 544-4406

Lovely home graciously furnished in contemporary style blended with Oriental accessories and original oil paintings, in one of the major tourist meccas nestled between the Santa Ynez and San Rafael mountain ranges. The twin-bedroom suite has a sumptuous dressing room and private bath. The patio offers a view of the Santa Ynez hills and garden. In the valley is Santa Ynez Mission with its impressive museum with a wide array of Indian artifacts, wall murals, and its Chapel of the Madonnas. $60.

SONOMA

B&B International #301

P. O. Box 282910, San Francisco, 94128-2910
(415) 696-1690; FAX (415) 696-1699

Situated in the heart of Sonoma, in walking distance to the plaza and wineries, is an old stonecutter's cottage. It has a king/twin bed with bath and large deck. There is a Franklin stove in the cottage. In a garden setting surrounded by countryside studded with giant oaks. Breakfast is served in the main house. $100.

Eye Openers Bed and Breakfast Reservations HE-C61

P. O. Box 694, Altadena, 91003-0694
(213) 684-4428; (818) 797-2055
FAX (818) 798-3640

This 1869 Italianate Victorian town house on one-half acre has landscaped grounds with pool and large antique-filled guest rooms. Breakfast with fresh baked breads and afternoon refreshments are served. Six guest rooms. Shared and private baths. $75-115 plus tax.

NOTES: Credit cards accepted: A Master Card; B Visa; C American Express; D Discover Card; E Diner's Club; F Other; 2 Personal Checks accepted; 3 Lunch available; 4 Dinner available; 5 Open all year;

Eye Openers Bed and Breakfast Reservations HE-F2

P. O. Box 694, Altadena, 91003-0694
(213) 684-4428; (818) 797-2055
FAX (818) 798-3640

Seventy-acre grape ranch in Sonoma County's spectacular Dry Creek Valley near many wineries and restaurants is a family-run bed and breakfast. Enjoy charming antique decorated guest rooms, tranquil vineyard setting, and walks, swimming pool, garden terrace, and wildlife pond. Full breakfast. Two guest rooms. Private bath. $90.

Eye Openers Bed and Breakfast Reservations HE-G71

P. O. Box 694, Altadena, 91003-0694
(213) 684-4428; (818) 797-2055
FAX (818) 798-3640

This 1902 Queen Anne Victorian offers an elegant return to a bygone era. Upstairs rooms have roof windows and view of the lovely grounds. Full country breakfast. Seven guest rooms. Private bath. $85-105 plus tax.

SONORA

Kids Welcome 17-2

3924 East 14th Street, Long Beach, 90804
(310) 498-0552; (800) 383-3513

Play with the llamas at this creek-side guest ranch in the country. Amenities include hot tub and sauna, music room/library (with lots of kids' games), and gracious Southern hospitality. Moderate rates.

SOQUEL

Blue Spruce Inn

2815 Main Street, 95073
(408) 464-1137; (800) 559-1137

The O'Brien's 1873 farmhouse blends the flavor of yesterday with the luxury and privacy of today. Situated on the crest of Monterey Bay, guests can easily enjoy the beaches as well as unique shops and dining in this distinctive destination. There are excellent local wineries, many antique shops, and state parks with miles of biking or hiking trails. The hosts offer a bountiful breakfast to fuel guests for the activities of the day and recommend the hot tub under the stars for the perfect day's end.

Hosts: Pat and Tom O'Brien
Rooms: 5 (PB) $80-125
Full Breakfast
Credit Cards: A, B, C
Notes: 2, 5, 8, 9, 12, 14

Blue Spruce Inn

SPRINGVILLE

Annie's Bed and Breakfast

33024 Globe Drive, 93265
(209) 539-3827

Situated on five acres in the beautiful Sierra foothills, this inn features beautiful antiques, feather beds, and handmade

6 Pets welcome; 8 Children welcome; 9 Social drinking allowed; 10 Tennis available; 11 Swimming available; 12 Golf available; 13 Skiing available; 14 May be booked through travel agents.

quilts. Full country breakfast is prepared on an antique wood cookstove. Close to golf, tennis, river, boating, lakes, hiking, swimming, and redwoods. The host has a custom saddle shop and horse training facility on the property. Guests are welcome to come out and watch. Annie's is a great place to relax and enjoy the peace and quiet of country life.

Hosts: Annie and John Bozanich
Rooms: 3 (PB) $85
Full Breakfast
Credit Cards: A, B, C, E
Notes: 2, 4, 5, 9, 10, 11, 12, 14

SUNSET PALISADES

Megan's Friends #04

Bed and Breakfast Reservation Service
1776 Royal Way, San Luis Obispo, 93405
(805) 544-4406

Serene ocean view form the livingroom of this spacious home with beach access. Breakfast overlooking the surf from the deck. Nearby attractions: Avila Plunge, massage, spa, hot tubs. Super breakfasts (special diets on request), and dinner for $5 or $6 with wine with advance notice. Even bridge games, if guests are inclined. $60.

SUTTER CREEK

Sutter Creek Inn

75 Main Street, P. O. Box 385, 95685
(209) 267-5606

The inn has 19 rooms with private baths, electric blankets, and air conditioning. Ten rooms feature fireplaces, and four have swinging beds that can be stabilized. The large, old livingroom is filled with books, games, and a piano. A hot breakfast is served by the fireplace. A one-half-acre lawn surrounds the inn with garden furniture and hammocks. Handwriting analysis, massage, and reflexology upon request.

Host: Jane Way
Rooms: 19 (PB) $45-97
Full Breakfast
Credit Cards: None
Notes: 2, 5, 9, 10, 11, 12, 13, 14

TAHOE CITY

Bed and Breakfast International #404

P. O. Box 282910, San Francisco, 94128
(415) 696-1690; FAX (415) 696-1699

This large, alpine-style house has beautiful views of Lake Tahoe. Guest rooms are on the second floor. Close to casinos, ski areas, and lakefront. $75.

Mayfield House

236 Grove Street, P. O. Box 5999, 96145
(916) 583-1001

Snug and cozy 1930s Tahoe home, one-half block from the beach. Premium skiing within five miles. Full breakfast, home-made baked goods. Within walking distance of shops and restaurants in Tahoe City. Off-street parking.

Hosts: Cynthia and Bruce Knauss
Rooms: 6 (SB) $70-105
Full Breakfast
Credit Cards: A, B
Notes: 2, 5, 8, 9, 10, 11, 12, 13, 14

TEMECULA

Eye Openers Bed and Breakfast Reservations TE-S61

P. O. Box 694, Altadena, 91003-0694
(213) 684-4428; (818) 797-2055
FAX (818) 798-3640

Situated in Southern California's wine country, this lovely bed and breakfast has six uniquely decorated guest rooms. Full country breakfast. Six rooms. Private bath. $75-95 plus tax.

NOTES: Credit cards accepted: A Master Card; B Visa; C American Express; D Discover Card; E Diner's Club, F Other; 2 Personal Checks accepted; 3 Lunch available; 4 Dinner available; 5 Open all year;

Loma Vista
Bed and Breakfast
33350 La Serena Way, 92591
(714) 676-7047

Loma Vista, in the heart of Temecula wine country, is conveniently situated to any spot in Southern California. This beautiful new mission-style home is surrounded by citrus groves and premium vineyards. All six rooms have private baths; most have balconies.

Hosts: Betty and Dick Ryan
Rooms: 6 (PB) $95-125
Full Breakfast
Credit Cards: A, B, D
Closed Thanksgiving, Christmas, New Year's
Notes: 2, 9, 10, 11, 12, 14

Megan's Friends
Bed and Breakfast Reservation Service
1776 Royal Way, San Luis Obispo, 93405
(805) 544-4406

Off scenic Highway 46 between Paso Robles and Cambia. This small cottage in an oak forest is near wineries and private trails. Includes a queen-size hideaway bed, single bed, and three window bunks. Large shower, microwave oven, coffee maker, wood stove, and refrigerator. Guests receive welcome basket; continental breakfast. $90-150.

THOUSAND OAKS

Bed and Breakfast
Los Angeles 3-13
3924 East 14th Street, Long Beach, 90804
(310) 498-0552; (800) 383-3513

Overlooking a regional nature center, this beautiful Thousand Oaks home has a gorgeous view, pool, deck, and spa. Guest room has twin beds and a shared bath. Affordable rates.

Bed and Breakfast
Los Angeles 3-15
3924 East 14th Street, Long Beach, 90804
(310) 498-0552; (800) 383-3513

This luxury condo has a view of the hills and great recreational facilities. Retired hosts offer one guest room with a private bath. Older children only. Affordable rates.

TOLUCA LAKE

Bed and Breakfast
Los Angeles 3-1
3924 East 14th Street, Long Beach, 90804
(310) 498-0552; (800) 383-3513

This southwestern-style home in Toluca Lake features two guest rooms, private baths, private entrances, TV's, pool, decks, and spa. One room even has a full line of baby equipment. Moderate rates.

TRINIDAD

Trinidad Bed and Breakfast
Box 849, 95570
(707) 677-0840

A Cape Cod-style home overlooking beautiful Trinidad Bay. The inn offers spectacular views of the rugged coastline and fishing harbor from two suites, one with a fireplace, and two upstairs bedrooms, all with private baths. Surrounded by beaches, trails, and redwood parks. Within walking distance of restaurants and shops. The suites enjoy breakfast delivered. The other two rooms enjoy breakfast at a family-style table.

Hosts: Paul and Carol Kirk
Rooms: 4 (PB) $105-145
Full Breakfast
Credit Cards: A, B, D
Notes: 2, 9, 10, 12

6 Pets welcome; 8 Children welcome; 9 Social drinking allowed; 10 Tennis available; 11 Swimming available; 12 Golf available; 13 Skiing available; 14 May be booked through travel agents.

TRUCKEE

The Truckee Hotel

10007 Bridge Street, 96161
(800) 659-6921

This circa 1873 Victorian bed and breakfast is in Truckee's historical district. Begin the day with a continental breakfast, and enjoy the sights and activities that our beautiful Sierra location offers. In-house dining at The Passage offers fine wine and cuisine. Relax fireside in the parlor before turning in for the night. Shopping and dining are outside the door and Amtrak is close by. Come visit by train.

Host: Brenda Schwartz
Rooms: 37 (8 PB; 29 SB) $80-130
Expanded Continental Breakfast
Credit Cards: A, B, C
Notes: 2, 5, 8, 13

UKIAH

Kids Welcome 16-8

3924 East 14th Street, Long Beach, 90804
(310) 498-0552; (800) 383-3513

The champagne baths are the center of this parklike resort at the foot of the Mendocino Hills. Twelve individually decorated rooms with private baths date from the 1860s, while the two free-standing cottages (with modern kitchens) were built in 1854. Wildlife abounds in the 700 acres of woods, meadows, streams, and falls that surround the ranch. Sailing, wind-surfing, jet-skiing, and salmon fishing are all within easy reach, and naturally carbonated hot tubs are at the doorstep. Moderate-luxury rates.

Oak Knoll
Bed and Breakfast

858 Saanel Drive, 95482
(707) 468-5646

A large redwood contemporary home with spectacular views of hills, valleys, vineyards, and sheep. Spacious deck. Lovely furnishings of Oriental pieces and chandeliers. Two rooms with shared bath, adjacent sitting room, TV, and movies on a 40-inch screen in the family room. Full breakfast in the dining room or on the deck in summer. Hiking, golf, and boating are nearby.

Host: Shirley Wadley
Rooms: 2 (SB) $70
Full Breakfast
Credit Cards: None
Notes: 2, 5, 9, 10, 11, 12, 14

Vichy Springs Resort

2605 Vichy Springs Road, 95482
(707) 462-9515

Vichy Springs is a delightful two-hour drive north of San Francisco in Ukiah, Mendocino County. The 1854 resort reflects the country lifestyle of the 1800s, with the modern conveniences of today. Vichy Springs features naturally sparkling 90-degree mineral baths, a communal 104-degree pool, Olympic-size pool (in-season), Swedish massage, and herbal facials along with 700 private acres with trails, and roads for hiking and picnicking. A quiet, healing environment describes Vichy's idyllic setting.

Hosts: Gilbert Ashoff
Rooms: 14 (PB) $95-150
Continental Breakfast
Credit Cards: A, B, C, D, E, F
Notes: 2, 8, 9, 10, 11, 12, 14

VALLEY CENTER

Lake Wohlford
Bed and Breakfast

27911 North Lake Wohlford Road, 92082
(619) 749-1911

The Lake Wohlford Bed and Breakfast promotes the appreciation of Southern California's native plants and natural terrain. The inn is situated 30 miles north of

---

NOTES: Credit cards accepted: A Master Card; B Visa; C American Express; D Discover Card; E Diner's Club; F Other; 2 Personal Checks accepted; 3 Lunch available; 4 Dinner available; 5 Open all year;

San Diego, and 120 miles south of Los Angeles. A two-story log home completed just this year, rests on 48 acres of undeveloped terrain. In addition to a full gourmet breakfast, guests can enjoy on-site nature trail walks and learn the native plant names and history, as well as activities at the nearby lake.

Host: Tatiana Ovanessoff
Rooms: 5 (3 PB; 2 SB) $98-128
Full Breakfast
Credit Cards: A. B
Notes: 2, 5, 8, 12, 14

La Mer

VENICE

Venice Beach House

15 30th Avenue, 90291
(310) 823-1966; FAX (310) 823-1842

A nine-room California Craftsman-style home constructed in 1911. Siutuated less than a block from Venice Beach, with a combination of casual and traditional in a warm and gracious atmosphere. A scrumptious breakfast is served daily, with home-baked breads, coffee cakes, and fresh squeezed juices and fruit. There are tea and cookies in the afternoon. All rooms have direct dial telephones and cable television. There is parking available on the premises. Reserve in advance.

Host: Betty Lou Weiner
Rooms: 9 (5 PB; 4 SB) $80-150
Continental Breakfast
Credit Cards: A, B, C
Notes: 5, 9, 14

VENTURA

Eye Openers
Bed and Breakfast
Reservations VE-B171

P. O. Box 694, Altadena, 91003-0694
(213) 684-4428; (818) 797-2055
FAX (818) 798-3640

Three blocks from the beach, this inn with Mediterranean decor offers comfort and convenience. Full breakfast and afternoon refreshments. Seventeen rooms. Private bath. $75-120, plus tax.

La Mer European
Romantic Get-a-Way

411 Poli Street, 93001
(805) 643-3600

La Mer, three blocks from the beach on a hillside overlooking the Pacific coastline, is a Victorian Cape Cod historical landmark built in 1890. Each accommodation represents a European country. The inn is decorated with European antiques, and features private entrances. There is complimentary wine or champagne upon arrival. Midweek packages are available with therapeutic massages, European dinners, and carriage rides.

Host: Gisela Flender Baida
Rooms: 5 (PB) $80-155
Full Breakfast
Credit Cards: A, B
Notes: 2, 3, 5, 9, 10, 11, 12, 14

WESTCHESTER

Bed and Breakfast
Los Angeles 2-12

3924 East 14th Street, Long Beach, 90804
(310) 498-0552; (800) 383-3513

This remodeled Craftsman bungalow is close to the airport with easy access to the

6 Pets welcome; 8 Children welcome; 9 Social drinking allowed; 10 Tennis available; 11 Swimming available; 12 Golf available; 13 Skiing available; 14 May be booked through travel agents.

beach. Two nice guest rooms share a bath in hall. Airport pick-up is possible. Affordable rates.

Kids Welcome 2-13

3924 East 14th Street, Long Beach, 90804
(310) 498-0552; (800) 383-3513

Country-style cottage near the airport in Westchester has one guest room, which shares a bath with your host. Close to restaurants, tennis, and golf. Affordable rates.

WEST COVINA

Hendrick Inn

2124 East Mercer Avenue, 91791
(810) 919-2125

This large, rambling house provides a real taste of the California lifestyle with its gorgeous deck, swimming pool, Jacuzzi. Centrally situated for visiting Disneyland, the mountains, and the desert. Only 45 minutes to airport; 20 to Ontario Airport.

Hosts: Mary and George Hendrick
Rooms: 4 (2 PB; 2 SB) $35-60
Full Breakfast
Credit Cards: None
Notes: 2, 4 (with notice), 5, 8 (over 5), 9, 10, 11, 12

WEST LAKE

Bed and Breakfast Los Angeles 3-11

3924 East 14th Street, Long Beach, 90804
(310) 498-0552; (800) 383-3513

On a quiet cul-de-sac, this Spanish-style home has one guest room with a private bath. Guests are welcome to use their neighborhood recreation area. Affordable rates.

WESTPORT (SEE ALSO MENDOCINO)

DeHaven Valley Farm

39247 North Highway 1, 95488
(707) 961-1660

The inn, a Victorian farmhouse built in 1875, is situated on 20 acres of meadows, hills and streams across from the Pacific Ocean. Guests enjoy various farm animals, exploring the tide pools, and soaking in the hot tub. Restaurant serves delicious four-course dinners complimented by home-grown herbs and vegetables. The inn is ideally situated to visit the gigantic redwoods 25 miles to the north, or the artist colony of Mendocino 25 miles to the south.

Hosts: Jim and Kathy Tobin
Rooms: 8 (6 PB; 2 SB) $85-125
Full Breakfast
Credit Cards: A, B, C
Closed Jan.
Notes: 2, 4, 8, 9

DeHaven Valley Farm

Howard Creek Ranch

40501 North Highway One, Box 121, 95488
(707) 964-6725

A historic 1867 farm on 20 acres, only 100 yards from the beach. A rural retreat adjoining wilderness. Suite and cabins; views of ocean, mountains, creek, or gardens; fireplace/wood stoves; period furnishings; wood-heated hot tub, sauna, pool, horseback riding nearby. Gift certificates available.

Howard Creek Ranch

Hosts: Charles (Sunny) and Sally Grigg
Rooms: 8 (5 PB; 3 SB) $50-115
Full Breakfast
Credit Cards: A, B
Notes: 2, 5, 6 (with prior arrangement), 9

WHITTIER

Coleen's California Casa
P. O. Box 9302, 90608
(310) 699-8427

Take the children to Disneyland, Knott's Berry Farm, and Universal Studios, then come back to a luxurious home. Bedrooms are decorator designed with elegant private baths, one with Jacuzzi tub. From the deck one can see Los Angeles, Long Beach, and Catalina Island. The host will help plan tours, provide baby-sitting, and pick guests up at the airport for a charge.

Host: Coleen Davis
Rooms: 4 (3PB; 1 SB) $55-65
Full Breakfast
Credit Cards: None
Notes: 2, 3, 4 (by arrangement), 5, 7, 8, 9, 10, 11, 12, 14

WOODLAND HILLS

Kids Welcome 3-10
3924 East 14th Street, Long Beach, 90804
(310) 498-0552; (800) 383-3513

This traditional home is graced with a grand piano and delightful brick patio with a firepit. Two guest rooms share one bath; family rates are available. Affordable rates.

YOSEMITE

Bed and Breakfast Los Angeles 18-5
3924 East 14th Street, Long Beach, 90804
(310) 498-0552; (800) 383-3513

This small bed and breakfast is the only bed and breakfast in Yosemite. It consists of one guest room in the main house and one free-standing cottage, both with private baths. Breakfast is full at the hostess' cafe. Redwoods surround the area. Moderate rates.

Eye Openers Bed and Breakfast Reservations YG-C2
P. O. Box 694, Altadena, 91003-0694
(213) 684-4428; (818) 797-2055
FAX (818) 798-3640

Get away to this large A-frame house with open-beamed ceilings on a tree-filled hillside above a private lake twenty minutes west of Yosemite. Loft bedroom/sitting room and two other guest rooms available. Full breakfast served on deck with view of the Sierra Nevadas. Private bath. $60-70.

YOUNTVILLE

Bordeaux House
6600 Washington Street, 94599
(707) 944-2855

A charming English-French country inn nestled in the heart of Napa Valley with lush gardens. Wood-burning fireplaces, spacious rooms, wonderful continental breakfast served. All rooms air-conditioned.

6 Pets welcome; 8 Children welcome; 9 Social drinking allowed; 10 Tennis available; 11 Swimming available; 12 Golf available; 13 Skiing available; 14 May be booked through travel agents.

Rooms: 6 (PB) $95-120
Continental Breakfast
Credit Cards: A, B, C, D, E
Notes: 5

Oleander House

Oleander House

7433 St. Helena Highway, P. O. Box 2937, 94599-2937
(707) 944-8315

Country French charm, situated at the entrance to the wine country. Spacious, high-ceiling rooms done in Laura Ashley fabric and wallpaper and antiques. Breakfast is served in the large dining room on the main floor. All rooms have fire-places, private baths, and their own decks.

Hosts: John and Louise
Rooms: 4 (PB) $115-160
Full Breakfast
Credit Cards: A, B
Notes: 2, 5, 9, 10, 11, 12, 14

YUBA CITY

Harkey House
Bed and Breakfast

212 C Street, 95991
(916) 674-1942

1864 Victorian Gothic, queen beds, fire-places, TV/VCR/CD, telephones. Breakfast served in dining room or on patio. Spa, air conditioning in all rooms, basketball court, pool, chess, game table, library, original art work, piano. Near museums, hiking, and fishing. Fresh flowers, down comforters. A romantic getaway. Reservation deposit required. Five-day cancellation notice. $10 cancellation fee. Business rates available.

Hosts: Bob and Lee Jones
Rooms: 4 (PB) $75-100 plus tax
Continental Breakfast
Credit Cards: A, B, D
Notes: 2, 5, 8, 9, 11, 12, 13, 14

Colorado

Cottonwood Inn
Bed and Breakfast
and Gallery

123 San Juan Avenue, 81101
(719) 589-3882; (800) 955-2623

Lovely turn-of-the-century Craftsman-style inn, decorated with antiques and local artwork, many pieces of which are for sale. Near the Cumbres-Toltec Scenic Railway, Great Sand Dunes, wildlife refuges, Adams State College, cross-country skiing, and llama trekking. Delicious breakfasts featuring freshly ground coffee, homemade baked goods, and fresh fruit. Famous for their green chili strata and raspberry pancakes. Innkeepers are well informed about the San Luis Valley.

Hosts: Julie Mordecai and George Sellman
Rooms: 6 (4 PB; 2 SB) $56-75
Full Breakfast
Credit Cards: A, B, E
Notes: 2, 5, 8, 9, 10, 11, 12, 14

ARVADA

On Golden Pond
Bed and Breakfast

7831 Eldridge, 80005
(303) 424-22961

For European hospitality and a relaxing blend of country comfort, join us at our secluded 10-acre retreat only 15 miles from downtown Denver. Enjoy dramatic views of the mountains, prairies and downtown Denver. Each room has a large sliding door that opens onto a spacious deck. Four rooms feature Jacuzzis. Outdoor swimming pool, hot tub, nearby horseback riding, golf, tennis, skating and fishing in the pond.

Hosts: Kathy and John Kula
Rooms: 5 (PB) $50-100
Full Breakfast
Credit Cards: A, B
Notes: 2, 5, 6 (outside), 8, 9, 11, 12, 14

The Tree House

6600 Simms, 80004
(303) 431-6352

A charming guest house in the middle of a 10-acre forest. Squirrels, rabbits, and birds abound, breaking the quiet serenity of the setting. Balconies on the front and back of the house provide a lovely view of the forest and a perfect spot for breakfast. Guest rooms with wood-burning fireplaces are furnished with brass beds, handmade quilts, and lovely antiques. A common area with fireplace and oak and leather furniture can be used for small meetings or just to relax. Perfect for weddings, anniversaries, and family reunions.

Host: Sue Thomas
Rooms: 5 (PB) $49-79
Full Breakfast
Credit Cards: A, B
Notes: 2, 5, 9, 11, 12, 13, 14

ASPEN

Boomerang Lodge

500 West Hopkins, 81611
(303) 925-3416; (800) 992-8852

Unique ski lodge situated in Aspen's quiet West End within walking distance to the

6 Pets welcome; 8 Children welcome; 9 Social drinking allowed; 10 Tennis available; 11 Swimming available; 12 Golf available; 13 Skiing available; 14 May be booked through travel agents.

COLORADO

music festival or downtown. All Boomerang rooms and fireplace apartments have a sunny patio or a balcony, thanks to the handsome design that was influenced by the owner-architect's teacher, Frank Lloyd Wright. Thoughtful touches include continental breakfast, pool, whirlpool, and sauna. Additional winter amenities include afternoon tea and town courtesy van. Discover why devoted guests return to Boomerang.

Hosts: Charles and Fonda Paterson
Rooms: 35 (PB) $93-174
Continental Breakfast
Credit Cards: A, B, C, E
Notes: 2, 5, 8, 11, 13, 14

C.C.'s

Bed and Breakfast Vail Ski Areas
P. O. Box 491, 81658
(303) 949-1212; (800) 748-2666

Hot tub under a star-filled sky warms guests after a long day on the slopes. Hosts are restaurateurs who serve a hearty breakfast. Five minutes to Snowmass Mountain and 15 minutes to downtown Aspen. On bus route. $65.

Little Red Ski Haus

118 East Cooper Street, 81611
(303) 925-3333

Charming 100-year-old Victorian three blocks from the center of town. No TV, but always interesting conversation. One could travel the world just sitting in the living room. The house is very popular with Australians. Exceptionally clean and friendly, especially suited to those traveling alone. Dinner is available on Wednesdays for $8.

Hosts: Marge Riley and Jeannene Babcock
Rooms: 16 (3 PB; 13 SB) $22-110
Full Breakfast winter; Continental summer
Credit Cards: A, B, C
Closed April 10 - May 31
Notes: 4, 5, 8, 9, 10, 11, 12, 13, 14

Main Street

Bed and Breakfast Vail Ski Areas
P. O. Box 491, 81658
(303) 949-1212; (800) 748-2666

All rooms are richly appointed, opening up to a center room lounge. They offer wet bars, refrigerators, cable TV, and phones. On the premises is a heated pool, Jacuzzi, and parking lot. A river rock fireplace cascades the lounge where a continental breakfast and a wine and cheese party is served daily. Great for traveling couples.

Slice of Heaven

Bed and Breakfast Vail Ski Areas
P. O. Box 491, 81658
(303) 949-1212; (800) 748-2666

Hot tub, snowmobile rentals, snowmobile tours atop Aspen Mountain. Airport pickup. This converted barn has open-beamed rooms individually decorated with antiques, old-fashioned claw foot tubs, and huge fireplaces. Secluded, cozy, and restful. $80 summer; $120 winter.

Little Red Ski Haus

What A View!

Bed and Breakfast Vail Ski Areas
P. O. Box 491, 81658
(303) 949-1212; (800) 748-2666

For the feel of being in the mountains with great view, this is it! A former home that

NOTES: Credit cards accepted: A Master Card; B Visa; C American Express; D Discover Card; E Diner's Club; F Other; 2 Personal Checks accepted; 3 Lunch available; 4 Dinner available; 5 Open all year; 6 Pets welcome; 8 Children welcome; 9 Social drinking allowed; 10 Tennis available; 11 Swimming available; 12 Golf available; 13 Skiing available; 14 May be booked through travel agents.

has been renovated into four units, this apartment was the family's patio overlooking Aspen highlands and Maroon Bells. Located within walking distance of downtown Aspen, the room offers plenty of privacy with a lock-off master bedroom suite and a sunken. Japanese tub in the bathroom. A warm and comfortable stay. $65-75.

BRECKENRIDGE

Breckenridge Inn #1

Bed and Breakfast Vail Ski Areas
P. O. Box 491, 81658
(303) 949-1212; (800) 748-2666

Two blocks from downtown shops and restaurants on the free shuttle bus during ski season, this inn offers free parking and ski storage. In the historic section of this Victorian mining town, this inn offers guests comfortable accommodations and use of a central livingroom with TV, games, books, and fireplace. Summer activities include hiking, backpacking, bicycling, four-wheeling, sailing, horseback riding, golf, and rafting. If meeting people and spending time with travelers who want a true bed and breakfast experience is appealing, guests will enjoy staying at this inn.

Mountain Crest

Bed and Breakfast Vail Ski Areas
P. O. Box 491, 81658
(303) 949-1212; (800) 748-2666

This lovely, contemporary cedar home sits in a large, peaceful forest one and one-half miles south of the Breckenridge ski area. With a private entrance guests have a large sitting room with a full-size pool table, color TV, and wood-burning stove. Full breakfast on weekends; continental on weekdays. Cross-country skiing available

from the front door in winter; hiking trails to lakes in summer. $80-85.

CARBONDALE

The Ambiance Inn

66 North 2nd Street, 81623
(303) 963-3597

Enjoy Aspen, Glenwood Springs, and the beautiful Crystal Valley from this spacious chalet-style home featuring vaulted ceilings throughout. The 1950s ski lodge decor of the very large Aspen Suite or the Victorian elegance of the Sonoma Room featuring a romantic four-poster bed are ideal for your getaways. The Santa Fe Room is alive with the warmth of the Southwest. Island ambience is the Kauai Room, with a double Jacuzzi tub.

Hosts: Norma and Robert Morris
Rooms: 4 (PB) $60-80
Full Breakfast
Credit Cards: A, B
Notes: 2, 5, 9, 10, 11, 12, 13, 14

Van Horn House

0318 Lions Ridge Road, 81623
(303) 963-3605

This country home, filled with antiques and family heirlooms, is situated in the Aspen Roaring Fork Valley, and within minutes of Aspen, Snowmass, and Sunlight ski areas. The historic towns of Redstone, Marble, and Glenwood Springs are also nearby. Each room features a beautiful view of Mount Sopris. Two rooms have private balconies, and the guest lounge, furnished in wicker, has snacks, games, telephones, and its own balcony.

Hosts: Jack and Jane E. Van Horn
Rooms: 4 (2 PB, $65; 2 SB, $50)
Full Breakfast
Credit Cards: A, B
Notes: 2, 8 (over 12), 10, 11, 12, 13, 14

Black Forest

COLORADO SPRINGS

Black Forest Bed and Breakfast

11170 Black Forest Road, 80908
(719) 495-4208; FAX (719) 495-0688

Picture a massive log home built on the highest point of the Rockies. This rustic mountain setting is complete with 20 rolling acres of Ponderosa Pine, a wonderful location for a peaceful, relaxing time away. Two guest rooms with private baths, and separate one-bedroom apartment above the log barn. Continental-plus breakfast or create your own in the guest kitchen.

Hosts: Robert and Susan Putnam
Rooms: 3 (PB) $65-75
Continental Breakfast
Credit Cards: A, B
Notes: 2, 5, 8, 9, 10, 11, 12, 13, 14

Hearthstone Inn

506 North Cascade, 80903
(719) 473-4413; (800) 521-1885
FAX (719) 473-1322

The Hearthstone Inn is an elegantly restored 1885 mansion near the heart of Colorado Springs. The 23 rooms, with private baths, are furnished with Victorian antiques. Three rooms feature private porches, and three have wood-burning fireplaces. A conference room is available for seminars and executive retreats of about 35 people. Full gourmet breakfast, which changes daily, is part of the warmth and friendliness of this in-town country inn.

Hosts: Dot Williams and Ruth Williams
Rooms: 25 (23 PB, 2 SB) $60-130
Full Breakfast
Credit Cards: A, B, C
Notes: 2, 5, 10, 11, 12, 13, 14

Holden House—1902 Bed and Breakfast Inn

1102 West Pikes Peak Avenue, 80904
(719) 471-3980

A 1902 storybook Victorian and a 1906 carriage house filled with antiques and heirlooms. Immaculate accommodations in a quiet area near historic district and central to the Pikes Peak region. Enjoy the parlor, livingroom with fireplace, or veranda with mountain views. Guest rooms boast queen beds, down pillows, and private baths. Honeymoon suites with tubs for two, fireplaces, and more! Complimentary refreshments. Friendly resident cats named Muffin and Mingtoy. "Experience the Romance of the Past with the Comforts of Today." AAA and Mobil approved.

Hosts: Sallie and Welling Clark
Rooms: 2 (PB) $65
Suites: 3 (PB) $90
Full Gourmet Breakfast
Minimum stay holidays, special events weekends & high season, 2 - 3 nights
Credit Cards: A, B, C, D
Notes: 2, 5, 9, 10, 11, 12, 14

Holden House—1902

6 Pets welcome; 8 Children welcome; 9 Social drinking allowed; 10 Tennis available; 11 Swimming available; 12 Golf available; 13 Skiing available; 14 May be booked through travel agents.

Creede Hotel

CREEDE

Creede Hotel

Box 284, 81130
(719) 658-2608

The hotel is a landmark in Creede, dating back to the wild days of the silver boom. Four rooms, all with private baths, have been individually restored. The hotel dining room is open to the public and noted for its delicious food. Guests will love Creede and the hotel! "Warm hospitality. . .capturing the lure of the 1890s."

Hosts: Cathy and Rich Ormsby
Rooms: 4 (PB) $59
Full Breakfast
Credit Cards: A, B, D
Notes: 2, 3, 4

DENVER

Castle Marne

1572 Race Street, 80206
(303) 331-0621; (800) 92-MARNE

Come fall under the spell of one of Denver's grandest historic mansions. Built in 1889, the Marne is on both the local and national historic registers. A stay here is a unique experience in pampered luxury. Minutes from the finest cultural, shopping, sightseeing attractions, and the convention center. Only 12 minutes from Stapleton International Airport. Ask about the candle-light dinners.

Host: The Peiker family
Rooms: 9 (PB) $80-155
Full Breakfast
Credit Cards: A, B, C, E
Notes: 2, 4, 5, (with reservation only), 9, 10, 11, 12, 14

Queen Anne Inn

2147 Tremont Place, 80205
(303) 296-6666; (800) 432-INNS reservations only
FAX (303) 296-2151

Award-winning inn in the downtown historic district. Two side-by-side Victorians of 1879 and 1886 facing Benedict Park Already named "Best Bed and Breakfast in Town" and "Colorado Company of the Year." Listed by several editors as one of "America's Top 10" Features chamber music, fresh flowers, air conditioning, phones, free parking. Walk to business district, 16th Street Pedestrian Mall, and other attractions.

Host: Tom King
Rooms: 14 (PB) $75-150
Expanded Continental Breakfast
Credit Cards: A, B, C, D
Notes: 2, 5, 10, 13, 14

Castle Marne

NOTES: Credit cards accepted: A Master Card; B Visa; C American Express; D Discover Card; E Diner's Club; F Other; 2 Personal Checks accepted; 3 Lunch available; 4 Dinner available; 5 Open all year;

Queen Anne Inn

DOLORES

Mountain View
Bed and Breakfast

28050 County Road P, 81323
(303) 882-7861

Mountain View is situated in the "four cor-ners area," and is one mile from the gate-way to the San Juan Skyway, a designated national 238 mile scenic loop, and twelve miles from the entrance to Mesa Verde National Park. Mountain View includes 22 acres with walking trails, cottonwood-lined stream and canyon. Situated on the west slope of the San Juan Mountains at an ele-vation of 6,500-feet, overlooking the beau-tiful Montezuma Valley.

Hosts: Brenda and Cecil Dunn
Rooms: 7 (PB) $45-55
Full Breakfast
Credit Cards: A, B
Notes: 2, 5, 8, 11, 12, 13, 14

DURANGO

Country Sunshine
Bed and Breakfast

35130 Highway 550N, 81301
(303) 247-2853; (800) 383-2853

Nestled below rocky bluffs, there's a spec-tacular view of the San Juan Mountains from this spacious ranch home. Enjoy the sound of the Animas River flowing by or the sight of abundant wildlife from the deck. The bed and breakfast has spacious common areas, serves full hearty break-fasts, and is centrally situated to many area attractions.

Hosts: Jim and Jill
Rooms: 6 (PB) $85-100
Full Breakfast
Credit Cards: A, B
Notes: 2, 5, 8, 9, 11, 12, 13, 14

River House
Bed and Breakfast

495 Animas View Drive, 81301
(303) 247-4775

River House is a large, sprawling, south-western home facing the Animas River. Guests eat in a large atrium filled with plants, a water fountain, and eight sky-lights. Antiques, art, and artifacts from around the world decorate the six bed-rooms, snooker and music room, and com-mon room with fireplace and large-screen TV. Comfort, casualness, and fun are themes.

Host: Crystal Carroll
Rooms: 6 (PB) $45-65
Full Breakfast
Credit Cards: A, B, D
Notes: 2, 5, 8, 9, 10, 11, 12, 13, 14

Scrubby Oaks
Bed and Breakfast Inn

P. O. Box 1047, 81302
(303) 247-2176

Situated on 10 acres overlooking the spec-tacular Animas Valley and surrounding mountains. Just three miles from downtown Durango and 30 minutes from Purgatory ski resort. Rooms are spacious and fur-nished with antiques, art work, and good books. Beautiful gardens and patios frame the inn outside, with large sitting areas inside for guest use.

6 Pets welcome; 8 Children welcome; 9 Social drinking allowed; 10 Tennis available; 11 Swimming available; 12 Golf available; 13 Skiing available; 14 May be booked through travel agents.

Host: Mary Ann Craig
Rooms: 7 (3 PB; 4 SB) $65-75
Full Breakfast
Credit Cards: None
Notes: 2, 5, 8, 9, 10, 11, 12, 13, 14

EATON

The Victorian Veranda Bed and Breakfast

515 Cheyenne Avenue, P. O. Box 361, 80615
(303) 454-3890

Wood-framed, two-story Queen Anne-style house with a wraparound porch that overlooks a mountain view. All three rooms are very comfortable and are furnished with antiques of the 1800s. Guests enjoy relaxing in a private whirlpool tub, riding the bicycles built for two, or listening to the baby grand player piano. One bedroom has a wood-burning fireplace and a balcony. A large picnic area is available in the backyard for guests to cook their own lunch and dinner.

Hosts: Dick and Nadine White
Rooms: 3 (1 PB; 2 SB) $40-55
Full Breakfast
Credit Cards: None
Notes: 2, 5, 8, 9, 12, 13

ESTES PARK

RiverSong Inn

P. O. Box 1910, 80517
(303) 586-4666

Once the summer home of the very rich, this nine-room inn lies secluded at the end of a country road on 30 forested acres. A veritable wildlife sanctuary with its private ponds, wildflower gardens, hiking trails in the forest, the inn also has a "heart-stopping" view of the snow-capped peaks of Rocky Mountain National Park. All of the rooms have private baths, some with Jacuzzi whirlpool tubs in front of fireplaces. With no guest phones or TV's but only the sounds of a rushing trout stream to

lull guests to sleep, it's easy to see why RiverSong is so very popular as a romantic escape.

Hosts: Gary and Sue Mansfield
Rooms: 9 (PB) $85-160
Full Breakfast
Credit Cards: A, B
Notes: 2, 4, 5, 14

FRISCO

Naomi's Nook

Bed and Breakfast Vail Ski Areas
P. O. Box 491, 81658
(303) 949-1212; (800) 748-2666

Situated in a quiet neighborhood, this one bedroom suite has a private entrance and bath with laundry facilities. Guests basically have the whole floor to themselves, although hosts enjoy talking and visiting with guests and would be happy to sit and talk in front of the wood-burning stove. Breakfast is served either upstairs or downstairs in the suite. Great central location for the wide variety of ski mountains that Summit County offers.

Woods Inn

205 South 2nd Avenue, P. O. Box 1302, 80443
(303) 668-3389

Built of pine logs in 1938, the Woods Inn sits at 9,500 feet in the heart of Summit County. A unique bed and breakfast with a variety of bedrooms, each warmly decorated with a homespun flair. Three sitting rooms and a spacious outdoor deck featuring an all-season spa. The surrounding lakes, rivers, and mountain peaks offer year-round activities. Three of the state's prime ski areas are only minutes away. "Check us out!"

Hosts: Murray and Sue Bain
Rooms: 7 (SB) $35-85
Full Breakfast, winter; Continental Breakfast, summer
Credit Cards: A, B
Notes: 2, 3, 5, 8, 9, 10, 11, 12, 13, 14

NOTES: Credit cards accepted: A Master Card; B Visa; C American Express; D Discover Card; E Diner's Club; F Other; 2 Personal Checks accepted; 3 Lunch available; 4 Dinner available; 5 Open all year;

GLENWOOD SPRINGS

The Kaiser House

932 Cooper Avenue, 81601
(303) 945-8827; FAX (303) 945-8826

In the center of the "Spa of the Rockies," The Kaiser House features turn-of-century charm with 20th-century conveniences. Situated on the corner of 10th and Cooper, The Kaiser House features seven bedrooms, each with attached baths, and each uniquely decorated in Victorian style. In the winter, before hitting the ski slopes, enjoy a gourmet breakfast in the spacious dining room or the sunny breakfast area. In the summer, enjoy brunch on the private patio. From the Kaiser House, it's an easy walk to parks, shopping, fine restaurants, and to the Hot Springs Pool and Vapor Caves.

Hosts: Ingrid and Glen Eash
Rooms: 7 (PB) $55-115
Full Breakfast
Credit Cards: A, B, D
Notes: 2, 5, 9, 10, 11, 12, 13, 14

GUNNISON

Mary Lawrence Inn

601 North Taylor Street, 81230
(303) 641-3343

Make this Victorian home the center of your excursions through Gunnison County. The mountains, river, and lakes are extraordinary. Golf, swimming, rafting are accessible. The inn is furnished with antiques and collectibles. Breakfasts are bountiful and imaginative. Great ski package offered for Crested Butte skiing.

Hosts: Jan Goin
Rooms: 3 (PB) $63
Suite: 2 (PB) $78
Full Breakfast
Credit Cards: A, B
Notes: 2, 5, 8, 10, 11, 12, 13, 14

LAKE CITY

The Crystal Lodge

P. O. Box 246, 81235
(303) 944-2201

This beautiful mountain retreat offers a quiet and secluded retreat from city life. The hosts are dedicated to good taste in accommodations, guest rooms, apartments, and cottages. As a guest, one will be served delicious foods in the charming restaurant. Enjoy the heated swimming pool, biking, and hiking. The biking and hiking trails are right outside the front door.

Hosts: The Crystal Lodge Family
Rooms: 19 (PB) $54-95
Credit Cards: None
Notes: 2, 4, 6 (prior arrangements), 8, 11, 13

OURAY

Main Street
Bed and Breakfast

322 Main Street, P. O. Box 641, 81427
(303) 325-4871

These two superbly renovated, turn-of-the-century residences offer three suites, three rooms, and a two-story cottage. All accommodations have private baths, queen-size beds, and cable TV. Five of the units have decks with spectacular views of the San Juan Mountains. Three units have fully equipped modern kitchens. Guests who stay in rooms without kitchens are served a full breakfast on antique china. Guests also have exclusive use of a landscaped courtyard and play area.

Hosts: Lee and Cathy Bates
Rooms: 7 (PB) $53-80
Full Breakfast
Credit Cards: A, B
Notes: 2, 8, 9, 11

6 Pets welcome; 8 Children welcome; 9 Social drinking allowed; 10 Tennis available; 11 Swimming available; 12 Golf available; 13 Skiing available; 14 May be booked through travel agents.

St. Elmo Hotel
426 Main Street, P. O. Box 667, 81427
(303) 325-4951

Listed in the National Register of Historic
Places, established in 1898 as a miners'
hotel, and now fully renovated with stained
glass, antiques, polished wood, and brass
trim throughout. An outdoor hot tub and an
aspen-lined sauna are available, as well as a
cozy parlor and a breakfast room.

Hosts: Sandy and Dan Lingenfelter
Rooms: 9 (PB) $58-90
Full Breakfast
Credit Cards: A, B, D
Notes: 4, 5, 7 (limited), 8, 10, 11, 13 (XC) , 14

The Wiesbaden
P. O. Box 349, 81427
(303) 325-4845

Built in 1879, the Wiesbaden is known for
its "incredibly comfortable elegance."
Individually decorated rooms, some with
kitchens, some with fireplaces. Continually
flowing hot springs (84 to 134 degrees),
vaporcave, sauna, outdoor swimming pool,
private outdoor spa, and float tank.
Massage, facials, reflexology, and acupres-
sure available. Health-oriented, no pets.
Reviewed in *Travel & Leisure, National
Geographic Traveler, Colorado Homes &
Lifestyles, Sunset and Shape*, and the *New
York Times*.

Host: Linda Wright-Minter
Rooms: 20 (19 PB) $70-125
Coffee and Tea Only; Available at all times
Credit Cards: A, B
Notes: 2, 5, 8, 10, 11, 13

PAGOSA SPRINGS

Royal Pine Inn
4760 W. Highway 60, 81157
(303) 731-4179

This inn is an eight-year-old building
designed in the old Tudor fashion. Offering
five bedrooms, three with private baths.

Two bedrooms share an extra large full
bath with a half bath across the hall.
Bedrooms are large and spacious and decorated in Laura Ashley style. All rooms have
their own TV and breathtaking views.
During winter months, the inn serve a full
breakfast of waffles, French toast, and eggs
to order. June through September we serve
our continental breakfast that features
freshly baked pastries, jams, fresh fruit, and
cold cereal. Coffee, juice, and herbal tea
are always available.

Hosts: Kathy and Roy
Rooms: 5 (3 PB; 2 SB) $45.55-60
Full Breakfast
Credit Cards: A, B
Notes: 3, 4, 5, 7 (downstairs only), 8, 9, 10, 11, 12, 13

REDSTONE

Avalanche Ranch Country Inn & Cabins
12863 Highway 133, 81623
(303) 963-2846

Avalanche Ranch is situated on 45 acres of
lush countryside overlooking the Crystal
River at the base of Mt. Sopris (elev.
12,953). The inn is decorated with an
eclectic collection of early country antiques
and folk art. Its 14 cozy log cabins feature
different amenities. Each cabin is fully
equipped with a kitchen and bathroom.
Avalanche Ranch provides an ideal setting
for romantic getaways, family reunions,
and weddings. While the hosts have taken
great care to create an interesting yet comfortable atmosphere for their guests, it is
their philosophy that "The ornament of a
house is the friends who frequent it"
(Emerson).

Hosts: Sharon and Jim Mollica
Rooms: 4 (2 PB; 2 SB) $75-95
Cabins: 14 (PB) $75-118
Continental Breakfast
Credit Cards: A, B, D
Notes: 2, 5, 6 (in cabins), 8 (in cabins), 9, 13, 14

SILVERTON

Christopher House
Bed and Breakfast

821 Empire Street, P. O. Box 241, 81433
(303) 387-5857 (June-Sept)
(904) 567-7549 (Oct-May)

Traditional Irish bed and breakfast hospitality amid the scenic splendor of the Rocky Mountains. The charming 1894 Victorian home features original woodwork and fireplace, sturdy antiques. Comfortable, carpeted rooms with mountain view and fresh flowers. Within walking distance of shops, restaurants, riding stable, stage coach, and narrow-gauge train station. Reasonable rates.

Hosts: Eileen and Howard Swonger
Rooms: 4 (1 PB; 3SB) $42-52
Full Breakfast
Credit Cards: None
Closed Sept. 16-May 30
Notes: 2, 8, 9, 10, 14

STEAMBOAT SPRINGS

Easy Access

Bed and Breakfast Vail Ski Areas
P. O. Box 491, 81658
(303) 949-1212; (800) 748-2666

TV in rooms, whirlpool, fully stocked library, bumper pool, or movie watching are just a few of the amenities offered here. Simply decorated and affordable, this is great for skiers wanting comfortable accommodations. Within walking distance to downtown shops and restaurants, this bed and breakfast is located three miles from the ski area.

Inn Town

Bed and Breakfast Vail Ski Areas
P. O. Box 491, 81658
(303) 949-1212; (800) 748-2666

In the heart of downtown with restaurants, shops; hot mineral springs within walking distance. Each room has unique antique decor. Phone, TV, HBO. Kids stay free. Continental breakfast. $57-119 seasonal.

Vista Verde Guest Ranch, Inc.

P. O. Box 465, 80477
(303) 879-3858; (800) 526-7433

This small, highly regarded western guest and cattle ranch offers a secluded, picturesque setting and an active program of riding, hiking, rock climbing, rafting, and more. In winter, there is ski touring, sleigh rides, dog sleds, and other similar activities. In all seasons enjoy superbly prepared cuisine served family style. Relax in the authentic, elegantly furnished log cabins with fireplaces or in the hot tub and sauna. Minimum stays required by season.

Rooms: 8 cabins (PB) $240-360
Full Breakfast
Credit Cards: None
Notes: 2, 3, 4, 8, 9, 10, 11, 12, 13, 14

TELLURIDE

Alpine Inn
Bed and Breakfast

P. O. Box 2398, 440 West Colorado Avenue, 81435
(303) 728-6282

This restored Victorian Inn built in 1907 is in historic downtown Telluride. The Inn has seven rooms with both shared and private baths. Within walking distance of ski lifts and summer festival activities, the inn is furnished with antiques, Victorian accents, and quilts. Full breakfast is served daily in the large sunroom, which offers a panoramic view of the mountains. Hot tub with a mountain view is also available for guests to use. Under new management as of May, 1992

Hosts: Johnnie and Jay Weaver
Rooms: 7 (3-PB; 4 SB) $60-155

6 Pets welcome; 8 Children welcome; 9 Social drinking allowed; 10 Tennis available; 11 Swimming available; 12 Golf available; 13 Skiing available; 14 May be booked through travel agents.

Full Breakfast
Credit Cards: A, B, C
Notes: 2, 5, 13, 14

Johnstone Inn

403 West Colorado, Box 546, 81435
(303) 728-3316; (800) 752-1901

A true 100-year-old restored Victorian boarding house, this bed and breakfast is in the center of Telluride and the spectacular San Juan Mountains. Rooms are warm and romantic, with Victorian marble and brass private baths. Full breakfast is served each morning, and the winter season includes après ski refreshments. A sitting room fireplace and outdoor hot tub complete the amenities. Nordic and Alpine skiing, jeep tours, and loafing are within walking distance of the Inn.

Rooms: 8 (PB) $70-145
Full Breakfast
Credit Cards: A, B, C
Notes: 2, 9, 12, 13, 14

San Sophia

330 West Pacific Avenue, P. O. Box 1825, 81435
(800) 537-4781

Elegant, luxurious accommodations for the discriminating traveler. Indoor and outdoor dining areas, huge bathtubs for two, brass beds, handmade quilts, dramatic view of the surrounding 13,000-foot mountains. Common areas include an observatory, library, and gazebo with Jacuzzi. "One of the most luxurious and romantic inns in America"—*Inside America*. Complimentary refreshments each afternoon.

Hosts: Dianne and Gary Eschman
Rooms: 16 (PB) $85-175
Full Breakfast
Credit Cards: A, B
Closed April 8-May 4 and Oct. 25-Nov. 24
Notes: 2, 9, 10, 11, 12, 13, 14

VAIL

Alpen Haus

Bed and Breakfast Vail Ski Areas
P. O. Box 491, 81658
(303) 949-1212; (800) 748-2666

This Austrian-flavored home is one bus stop from Vail village on the golf course. Great views from each bedroom, one overlooking the Gore Range and Vail village; the other looks out on tall pines and aspens. Common gathering room available for après ski with TV, VCR, and library. Kitchenette with microwave and refrigerator. $105-115.

Aspen Haus

Bed and Breakfast Vail Ski Areas
P. O. Box 491, 81658
(303) 949-1212; (800) 748-2666

If guests would like to be pampered, then this is the house for them . Set on a hillside, surrounded by trees, the suite has a delightful, homey feeling with a great view. There is a TV, phone, and large couch to snuggle into when one wants to relax. The bath is situated in the suite for extra privacy. Breakfast is served upstairs in the European decorated home. High ceilings and wonderful German artifacts grace the sunny kitchen area. The hosts offer a ski locker in town at the base of the the mountain, as well as an athletic club membership, discounted parking tickets, and ski tickets (limited availability) . Wine and cheese are served each afternoon. $125.

Aunt Em's Bed and Breakfast

Bed and Breakfast Vail Ski Areas
P. O. Box 491, 81658
(303) 949-1212; (800) 748-2666

Just three short miles from the base of Beaver creek snuggled on the Eagle River is this Victorian town house full of warmth

---

NOTES: Credit cards accepted: A Master Card; B Visa; C American Express; D Discover Card; E Diner's Club; F Other; 2 Personal Checks accepted; 3 Lunch available; 4 Dinner available; 5 Open all year;

and comfort. A cozy, homey feeling is what guests feel when they walk in the door. Aunt Em's is appointed with turn of the century antiques, homemade quilts, and a wood-burning stove that will entice any guest in the winter. In summer, exercise at the athletic facility. The room has an outdoor deck, and is finely decorated with an antique sleigh bed, TV, VCR, microwave, and private bath. Each night before turning in, choose breakfast from the menu provided. Discounted Vail parking and young children welcome. $60-75.

BB Inn

Bed and Breakfast Vail Ski Areas
P. O. Box 491, 81658
(303) 949-1212; (800) 748-2666

This inn is everything one would expect from a Rocky mountain getaway. Situated on Gore Creek, this handcrafted log inn with an enormous main room has a cozy fire, great views, and warmth beyond compare. Breakfast features baked breads, rolls, muffins, fruits in season, and a daily gourmet creation. Après-ski snacks and appetizers are also served daily. $80-175.

Bluebird

Bed and Breakfast Vail Ski Areas
P. O. Box 491, 81658
(303) 949-1212; (800) 748-2666

This wonderful mountain home offers warmth and charm to all guests who stay here. The hostess offers quaint rooms, each with its own decor. Additional children are welcome in the room or on the futon for an extra $10-15. Microwave and refrigerator are available for guests to use. Views of Vail and surrounding mountains are spectacular. In summer, relax on the outside sunny deck while feasting on breakfast. Bus stops at the end of the street, and free shuttle to downtown. $80-95.

Colorado Comfort

Bed and Breakfast Vail Ski Areas
P. O. Box 491, 81658
(303) 949-1212; (800) 748-2666

This comfortable two story town house offers beautiful views of Aspen and the pine trees while overlooking a challenging golf course. The room is high vaulted with an electric blanket, humidifier, TV, and bathroom in the room. Cross country skiing outside the back door in the winter, and golf in the summer. Guests are welcome to relax in the home when shopping and touring are finished. $8-11 discount lift tickets and Vail parking is available. (excluding Christmas and New Year's) $80-85.

Columbine Chalet
Bed and Breakfast of Vail

P. O. Box 1407, 81658
(303) 476-1122

Stay in this American-style chalet nestled in the pines of an exclusive neighborhood at the edge of the Vail Golf Course. Enjoy a hearty breakfast, afternoon refreshments, outdoor hot tub, games, books, and puzzles. A recreation path outside the front door serves cross country skiers in the winter, and bicyclists and hikers in the summer. Just one bus stop away from the town of Vail and its award-winning slopes.

Hosts: Pat Funk and Ruthie Bopes
Rooms: 3 (PB) $40-150
Full Breakfast
Credit Cards: A, B
Notes: 2, 5, 8, 9, 10, 12, 13, 14

Cottonwood Falls

Bed and Breakfast Vail Ski Areas
P. O. Box 491, 81658
(303) 949-1212; (800) 748-2666

Sunny, secluded location conveniently situated on free bus route; cross-country skiing and bike path nearby; tennis courts within walking distance. Rock fireplace, kitchen,

6 Pets welcome; 8 Children welcome; 9 Social drinking allowed; 10 Tennis available; 11 Swimming available; 12 Golf available; 13 Skiing available; 14 May be booked through travel agents.

private entrance, parking, VCR available. Fully stocked kitchen, but gourmet breakfast is served with hosts. $125-150.

Dave's Domain

Bed and Breakfast Vail Ski Areas
P. O. Box 491, 81658
(303) 949-1212; (800) 748-2666

Situated on Vail's free bus shuttle, this self-contained apartment is perfect for two traveling couples or a family of four. Full kitchen, private entrance, TV, small living room. Host lives upstairs. Five minutes from downtown Vail and close to shopping and skiing. $90-125.

Elk View

Bed and Breakfast Vail Ski Areas
P. O. Box 491, 81658
(303) 949-1212; (800) 748-2666

This gorgeous townhome is nestled on the hillside of Beaver creek is six levels with breathtaking view of Beaver Creek Mountain. Each room has a charm of its own, and the house is impeccably furnished. In summer, breakfast can be enjoyed on one of the three outside decks, and in the winter, after a long day of skiing, relax in the outside hot tub. Perfect for honeymoon couples and guests wanting to relax with the locals. $85 and up.

Fairway House

Bed and Breakfast Vail Ski Areas
P. O. Box 491, 81658
(303) 949-1212; (800) 748-2666

This beautiful rustic mountain home lies very close to the ski mountain. The room is cozy, with a stucco fireplace and magnificent view of Gore Range. Adjoining living room with fireplace, TV, VCR, wet bar, library, pool table. Two blocks from free bus route. Continental breakfast. $100.

Game Creek House

Bed and Breakfast Vail Ski Areas
P. O. Box 491, 81658
(303) 949-1212; (800) 748-2666

Situated between Vail and Beaver Creek, this private home is situated on nine acres and is surrounded on three sides by forest service land. Near four local favorite restaurants. Refrigerator, laundry, fireplace, TV, VCR. Many outdoor activities. Breakfast is served in the kitchen with beautiful mountain view. $75.

Kay's Corner

Bed and Breakfast Vail Ski Areas
P. O. Box 491, 81658
(303) 949-1212; (800) 748-2666

This brand-new home, nestled in a corner lot, offers a great view and serenity. Bedroom is spacious with TV, refrigerator, and a great view. Host is a ski instructor. Continental breakfast. $80.

Matterhorn

Bed and Breakfast Vail Ski Areas
P. O. Box 491, 81658
(303) 949-1212; (800) 748-2666

TVs in rooms, phone nearby, snow tires suggested for driveway. Enjoy a hearty breakfast with a magnificent view of the Gore Valley. A European family (all speak German—daughter is bilingual) offers a comfortable, cozy home. Box lunch is provided for early rising convention attendants. Great for single travelers. $60-75.

Minturn Meadows

Bed and Breakfast Vail Ski Areas
P. O. Box 491, 81658
(303) 949-1212; (800) 748-2666

NOTES: Credit cards accepted: A Master Card; B Visa; C American Express; D Discover Card; E Diner's Club; F Other; 2 Personal Checks accepted; 3 Lunch available; 4 Dinner available; 5 Open all year;

The upstairs room in this home is cozy, bright, and private. Hosts share the general living area and offer genuine warmth and care. Perfect for avid skiers. Full breakfast. Resident pets. $60-65.

Mountain Chalet

Bed and Breakfast Vail Ski Areas
P. O. Box 491, 81658
(303) 949-1212; (800) 748-2666

Ski out the front door to cross-country terrain, or summers, just walk on the Vail golf course. This beautiful Bavarian mountain chalet is wonderfully decorated with antiques. Large moss-rock fireplace and sitting room with TV and stereo. On bus route. Full breakfast. $185 for two rooms.

Mountain Hideaway

Bed and Breakfast Vail Ski Areas
P. O. Box 491, 81658
(303) 949-1212; (800) 748-2666

Guests should bring bathing suits so that they can sooth their weary bones in the hot tub while sipping on a glass of wine or cappuccino and enjoying après-ski refreshments. Situated on a wooded lot overlooking a creek, this spacious mountain home beckons. Newly renovated with high vaulted ceilings and a beautiful glassed-in kitchen nook, guests will find countless hours of relaxation here. Close to the village on the free bus route, the host family hospitality is incomparable. Discounted Vail parking is available. $90-125.

Mt. Retreat

Bed and Breakfast Vail Ski Areas
P. O. Box 491, 81658
(303) 949-1212; (800) 748-2666

If guests are looking for an out-of-the-way spectacular home with an unsurpassed view, this bed and breakfast will meet their needs. Guests will need a car to get there, because it is not on any of the bus routes, but once they arrive, they will never want to leave. The hostess pampers every need with breakfast served on fine china and crystal. A hot tub room is available so guests can soak while enjoying the views of Beaver Creek and Arrowhead mountains. The room is impeccably decorated and offers another great view. $100-125.

Mountain Weavery

Bed and Breakfast Vail Ski Areas
P. O. Box 491, 81658
(303) 949-1212; (800) 748-2666

This spacious, child-free, single family home on the fourth fairway of the Vail Golf Course offers great hospitality, magnificent views and is steps away from the free bus shuttle. The hostess is an nationally known designer and weaver and welcomes guests into her studio. Guests are also offered use of the microwave to make evening dinner and snacks.

Mr. B's

Bed and Breakfast Vail Ski Areas
P. O. Box 491, 81658
(303) 949-1212; (800) 748-2666

The location and the cost cannot be beat for a stay at this wonderful mountain, situated just five minutes from cross country and downhill skiing. Bright and airy, guests enjoy a room with a private entrance and a bath with a fridge in the room. The bus stop is only two houses away. For comfort and easy access, guests will love this home.

Outdoorsman

Bed and Breakfast Vail Ski Areas
P. O. Box 491, 81658
(303) 949-1212; (800) 748-2666

6 Pets welcome; 8 Children welcome; 9 Social drinking allowed; 10 Tennis available; 11 Swimming available; 12 Golf available; 13 Skiing available; 14 May be booked through travel agents.

Overlooking a lake and the majestic mountains, this beautifully appointed condo is decorated with an abundance of antiques and special color blends. Full breakfast. $65-75.

Plum House

Bed and Breakfast Vail Ski Areas
P. O. Box 491, 81658
(303) 949-1212; (800) 748-2666

This small, cozy mountain home is at the base of Shrine Mountain Pass, a favorite of cross-country skiers. Relax in the hot tub, enjoy the library, or warm up in front of the wood-burning stove. Hostess is a gourmet chef. Full breakfast. $60.

Sis's

Bed and Breakfast Vail Ski Areas
P. O. Box 491, 81658
(303) 949-1212; (800) 748-2666

This comfortable condo, situated on the creek and a wooded lot, will meet all needs. The free bus stops right outside the door, and guests are whisked into the village in no time. The hostess, a ski instructor, loves to entertain, and her warmth and home are unmatched anywhere. Relaxing in the living room with the fireplace and overlooking the creek will sooth tired bones after a hard day of skiing or hiking. Perfect for traveling couples or a family of four.

Sportsman's Haven

Bed and Breakfast Vail Ski Areas
P. O. Box 491, 81658
(303) 949-1212; (800) 748-2666

Surrounded by pine trees and nestled on a creek, this home is a warm, spacious mountain home that beckons guests to snuggle in in during the winter, or lounge on the sunny, private sun decks in summer. The hosts offer a ski home with two rooms. One is bright and cheery with pine trees outside

every window, and the downstairs room has a private bath with a sauna and offers an adjoining family room with TV, pool table, shuffleboard, and fireplace. The home is easy walking distance from the free bus. Discounted parking tickets available if one should decide to drive. $70-80.

Streamside

Bed and Breakfast Vail Ski Areas
P. O. Box 491, 81658
(303) 949-1212; (800) 748-2666

This town house is conveniently situated just a few minutes west from Vail Village. The bus stop is only a few steps away so guests don't even need a car. The hosts are a young couple and avid skiers, and are eager to share their life in Vail with guests. On cold afternoons, guests can look forward to a warm or cold après-ski drink, heat some popcorn in the microwave, or store drinks in the fridge. Upstairs, they can relax by the fire in the main living room to watch TV or read a book. This property is perfect for two couples travelling together or for a young family. $70-85.

Tortilla Flats

Bed and Breakfast Vail Ski Areas
P. O. Box 491, 81658
(303) 949-1212; (800) 748-2666

Bordered by forest land with a spectacular view of Meadow Mountain, this bed and breakfast has immediate access to cross-country, hiking, and mountain biking trails. This cozy suite features a sitting room and bedroom with a private bath and is furnished with antique oak and brass. An extra day bed is also available for a family with a child. Continental breakfast is served in the private dining area. Within walking distance to Minturn's restaurants and galleries. Private parking and entrance allow for secluded, quiet retreat. $85.

NOTES: Credit cards accepted: A Master Card; B Visa; C American Express; D Discover Card; E Diner's Club; F Other; 2 Personal Checks accepted; 3 Lunch available; 4 Dinner available; 5 Open all year;

Vail View Bed and Breakfast

Bed and Breakfast Vail Ski Areas
P. O. Box 491, 81658
(303) 949-1212; (800) 748-2666

Begin the morning with a spectacular view of the Gore Range while sipping on coffee. Check out the weather, and decide a course of action while staring into the mountains. What a way to start the day! The hosts and cats welcome guests to their home, offering comfortable home away from home accommodations. The room has a TV and stereo for days that guests prefer to stay at home and relax, and breakfasts at this terrific bed and breakfast are great. $70-75.

Village Artist

Bed and Breakfast Vail Ski Areas
P. O. Box 491, 81658
(303) 949-1212; (800) 748-2666

Centrally situated, on the free bus route, right in the heart of Vail. Within walking distance of the village, slopes, Vail's nightlife, Vista Bahn, and Lionshead Gondola. Share the living area, TV, fireplace, and kitchen with hostess. Full or continental breakfast. $75-85.

Whiskey Hill

Bed and Breakfast Vail Ski Areas
P. O. Box 491, 81658
(303) 949-1212; (800) 748-2666

If guests are looking for a quiet, secluded, romantic bed and breakfast room, here it is. The bedroom has a rock fireplace, private bath, and private entrance. Near shops, restaurants, and Beaver Creek. Continental breakfast. $80.

WINTER PARK

Alpen Rose Bed and Breakfast

244 Forest Trail, P. O. Box 769, 80482
(303) 726-5039

Surrounded by aspen and pine trees with a spectacular view of the front range. Situated in a sporting paradise, two miles from nation's fifth largest ski area and 40 minutes from Rocky Mountain National Park, the Alpen Rose reflects the owners' love of Austria and feels like an Austrian chalet. The inn features an outdoor hot tub and five rooms with Austrian furnishings, down puffs, and handmade quilts make guests feel at home. A memorable breakfast with Austrian specialties awaits in the morning; crackling fire, hot tea, and cookies beckon you home after an enjoyable day in the Rockies.

Hosts: Robin and Rupert Sommerauer
Rooms: 5 (PB) $65-95
Full Breakfast
Credit Cards: A, B, C
Notes: 2, 9, 13, 14

Engelmann Pines Bed and Breakfast

P. O. Box 1305, 80482
(303) 726-4632

Engelmann Pines is a contemporary mountain home furnished with European and American antiques, Oriental rugs, and art. Beds have European down comforters and handmade quilts. This spacious home provides a TV room, reading room, and kitchen for guests to use. A full gourmet breakfast, that includes Swiss specialities is served. Nestled among the pines, high in the Rocky Mountains, close to Winter Park Ski Resort, Pole Creek Golf Course, and Rocky Mountain National Park.

Hosts: Margaret and Heinz Engel
Rooms: 6 (2 PB; 4 SB) $55-95
Full Gourmet Breakfast
Credit Cards: A, B, C
Notes: 2, 5, 8, 9, 10, 11, 12, 13, 14

6 Pets welcome; 8 Children welcome; 9 Social drinking allowed; 10 Tennis available; 11 Swimming available; 12 Golf available; 13 Skiing available; 14 May be booked through travel agents.

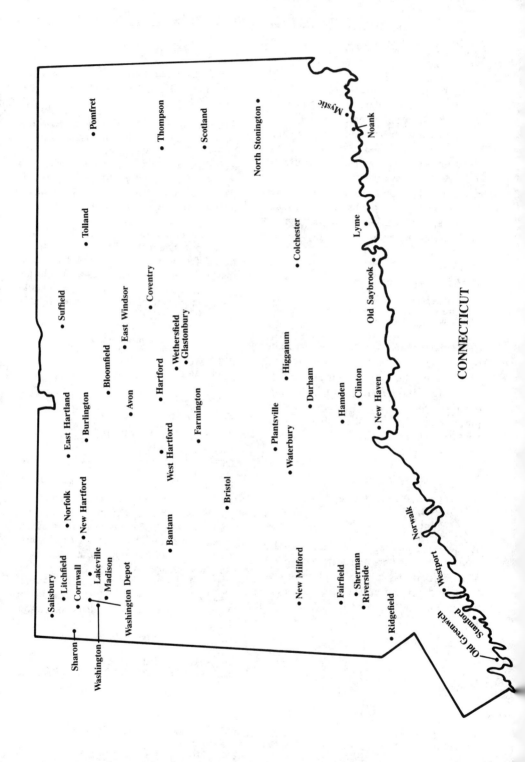

CONNECTICUT

Connecticut

Nutmeg Bed and Breakfast Agency #414

P. O. Box 1117, West Hartford, 06107
(203) 236-6698

This bright, spacious contemporary has a solarium, deck, and lovely grounds including a Japanese garden with a pond and a waterfall. One room has a cathedral ceiling and skylight; adjacent studio. Six languages spoken here. Continental breakfast and afternoon tea served. Children welcome; baby-sitting available.

BANTAM

Nutmeg Bed and Breakfast Agency #319

P. O. Box 1117, West Hartford, 06107
(203) 236-6698

Deer Island Guest House on Bantam Lake with a lake view in back, front on road; rustic but comfortable. One bedroom with twin beds, fireplace, chairs, table for dining in a completely equipped kitchen, bath with a shower; kitchen stocked for breakfast; canoe rentals nearby, restaurant nearby. Continental breakfast, children allowed, no pets in the guest house.

BARKHAMSTED

Covered Bridge

P. O. Box 447, Norfolk, 06058
(203) 542-5944

Rustic Victorian lake lodge features fireside concerts on the antique grand piano, wraparound porch with a commanding view of woods, and crystal clear lake. Feel free to borrow the canoe, relax on the private beach, or enjoy a country walk. Three guest rooms, one with a balcony overlooking the lake, share a bath and a half. $80-95.

BLOOMFIELD

Nutmeg Bed and Breakfast Agency #407

P. O. Box 1117, West Hartford, 06107
(203) 236-6698

A 1920s farmhouse, this bed and breakfast has its own duck pond. Three guest rooms share one full bath and two half baths. Guests enjoy country English livingroom with a lovely deck. Private apartment available for long-term guests. Continental breakfast. Children 10 and over welcome.

Nutmeg Bed and Breakfast Agency #467

P. O. Box 1117, West Hartford, 06107
(203) 236-6698

NOTES: Credit cards accepted: A Master Card; B Visa; C American Express; D Discover Card; E Diner's Club; F Other; 2 Personal Checks accepted; 3 Lunch available; 4 Dinner available; 5 Open all year; 6 Pets welcome; 8 Children welcome; 9 Social drinking allowed; 10 Tennis available; 11 Swimming available; 12 Golf available; 13 Skiing available; 14 May be booked through travel agents.

This 1958 ranch-style house has spacious rooms, wide hallways, and wheelchair accommodations. There are three rooms with a choice of king, double, or single beds. All share a bath. Convenient to the University of Hartford, Loomis Chaffee, the University of Connecticut, and the airport. Three minutes to public transportation, off-street parking available. Continental breakfast served to the room if desired. Children welcome.

BRISTOL

Chimney Crest Manor
5 Founders Drive, 06010
(203) 582-4219

Experience quiet elegance in this splendid 32-room Tudor mansion. Chimney Crest was built in 1930 in the Federal Hill Historic District just minutes away from the Litchfield Hills, where guests will find antiques, wineries, parks, art galleries, museums, and restaurants. Stay in the spacious suites, for pleasure or on business. Guests will be treated with warm, attentive hospitality set in the splendor and style of a bygone era.

Hosts: Dan and Cynthia Cimadamore
Suites: 5 (PB) $69.89-112
Full Breakfast
Credit Cards: A, B, C
Notes: 5, 8 (7 and over), 10, 11, 12, 13, 14

Chimney Crest Manor

Nutmeg Bed and Breakfast Agency #433
P. O. Box 1117, West Hartford, 06107
(203) 236-6698

Visitors to Bristol's clock museum and history lovers will especially enjoy a stay in the Dutch Colonial home of the city historian. Large lawns and gardens surround this lacy home in a residential area. One guest room with private bath. Full breakfast.

BURLINGTON

Nutmeg Bed and Breakfast Agency #478
P. O. Box 1117, West Hartford, 06107
(203) 236-6698

This ranch-style home has a screened porch, pool, and lovely gardens. There is a room with twin beds, private bath, livingroom, porch, and deck for guests' use. Convenient to Avon Old Farms, Miss Porter's, and the University of Connecticut Medical Center. Full breakfast. No children. Dogs on premises.

CLINTON

Captain Dibbell House
221 Commerce Street, 06413
(203) 669-1646

This 1866 Victorian, situated on a historic residential street, is two blocks from the harbor and features a century-old, wisteria-covered iron truss bridge. Rooms are furnished with a comfortable mix of heirlooms, antiques, auction finds, and a growing collection of original art by New England artists. Bicycles are available.

Hosts: Helen and Ellis Adams
Rooms: 4 (PB) $75-85
Full Breakfast
Credit Cards: A, B, C, D
Closed January
Notes: 2, 8 (over 14), 9, 10, 11, 12, 13, 14

NOTES: Credit cards accepted: A Master Card; B Visa; C American Express; D Discover Card; E Diner's Club; F Other; 2 Personal Checks accepted; 3 Lunch available; 4 Dinner available; 5 Open all year;

Captain Dibbell House

COLCHESTER

Nutmeg Bed and Breakfast Agency #438

P. O. Box 1117, West Hartford, 06107
(203) 236-6698

Situated on the town green, this 1776 home is on the historic register. Four rooms with private baths, one with Jacuzzi. Two carriage house apartments available. Biking, a picnic, and good restaurant meal can be arranged. Country American antique shop is open in the barn. Continental breakfast. Children over eight welcome.

CORNWALL

Covered Bridge 1C

P. O. Box 447, Norfolk, 06058
(203) 542-5944

1808 Colonial farmhouse set on 20 acres adjoining Mohawk State Forest. The guest livingroom has a large old Colonial fireplace and wood stove. Breakfast is served in the country kitchen or on the terrace. Three bedrooms decorated in period antiques with shared full and half baths. $85.

Covered Bridge 2C

P. O. Box 447, Norfolk, 06058
(203) 542-5944

Enjoy warm, quiet hospitality at this custom-designed stone home set on a 64-acre private estate with breathtaking views of the countryside. Hearty full breakfasts are served before the library fireplace or on the terrace. All of the rooms are decorated in antiques. Two guest rooms with private baths. $95.

COVENTRY

Nutmeg Bed and Breakfast Agency #458

P. O. Box 1117, West Hartford, 06107
(203) 236-6698

Pink towered Victorian with a well-traveled hostess who collects antique toys; shop and museum in addition to bed and breakfast dining area with picture windows and skylights, solarium with potted plants. House is air-conditioned; two guest rooms have private baths, one has a queen-size bed and the other a pair of twin beds; both have access to large guest balcony overlooking the garden. Another twin bedded room share a bath with hosts. Full breakfast, children allowed, no pets.

Nutmeg Bed and Breakfast Agency #463

P. O. Box 1117, West Hartford, 06107
(203) 236-6698

Fully modernized colonial built in 1731 on three and one-quarter acres with a pool, Jacuzzi, maple trees with hammocks, three fireplaces, four guest rooms with double beds share one upstairs and one downstairs bath. Rollaway available. Full breakfast, infants and children over five allowed. Dog in residence.

6 Pets welcome; 8 Children welcome; 9 Social drinking allowed; 10 Tennis available; 11 Swimming available; 12 Golf available; 13 Skiing available; 14 May be booked through travel agents.

DURHAM

Nutmeg Bed and Breakfast Agency #516

P. O. Box 1117, West Hartford, 06107
(203) 236-6698

Enjoy the swimming pool and the rural setting of this two-story Colonial. It has a large entrance hall downstairs and a lovely sitting room. Three guest rooms share a bath and are comfortably furnished. A roll-away and crib are available. Air-conditioned. Continental breakfast. Children welcome.

EAST HARTLAND

Nutmeg Bed and Breakfast Agency #480

P. O. Box 1117, West Hartford, 06107
(203) 236-6698

Guest house adjacent to Colonial farmhouse built in 1700s. Private entrance to sitting room with working fireplace, double Murphy bed, complete kitchen, full bath, and beautiful setting with horses, stone fences, and hills beyond. Full breakfast served in antique-filled main dining room or in guest house. 20 minutes from airport; hiking, skiing, biking, fishing minutes away. Children allowed. No pets in guest house.

EAST LYME

Nutmeg Bed and Breakfast Agency #517

P. O. Box 1117, West Hartford, 06107
(203) 236-6698

This 1760 Colonial has exposed beams, wide oak floor boards, seven fireplaces, a root cellar, an original goose pen, and a host and hostess who bake and make jelly. One guest room with private bath, and one guest room with a shared bath. Afternoon tea or apple cider is served in season. Full breakfast is served on the outdoor deck in good weather.

EAST WINDSOR

Nutmeg Bed and Breakfast Agency #410

P. O. Box 1117, West Hartford, 06107
(203) 236-6698

This beautifully restored 1837 home has a pond and two goats. Four guest rooms, one with private oak bathroom and Jacuzzi. Antiques, family art, and stenciled walls and floors make this the perfect country getaway. Full breakfast and afternoon tea are served. Children over nine welcome.

FAIRFIELD

Nutmeg Bed and Breakfast Agency #110

P. O. Box 1117, West Hartford, 06107
(203) 236-6698

Nestled in two acres of woods, this English cottage is the perfect spot for a cozy getaway. Guest room with private bath is furnished with a blend of country English and antiques. In nice weather, continental breakfast is served on patio overlooking a pond.

Nutmeg Bed and Breakfast Agency #112

P. O. Box 1117, West Hartford, 06107
(203) 236-6698

This early 1950s custom-built ranch has a large screened porch, comfortable antique furnishings, and off-street parking or garage. There are two double bedrooms, or one double and one single as needed. Both rooms share a bath. A full breakfast is served. No children, no pets on premises.

NOTES: Credit cards accepted: A Master Card; B Visa; C American Express; D Discover Card; E Diner's Club; F Other; 2 Personal Checks accepted; 3 Lunch available; 4 Dinner available; 5 Open all year;

FARMINGTON

The Farmington Inn

827 Farmington Avenue, 06032
(203) 677-2821; (800) 648-9804 (US)

Two-story, 72-room facility built in 1966 and completely renovated in 1988. All rooms feature private baths and remote control televisions with cable and VCR hook-up. The room decor is cozy country or elegant traditional. Farmington Inn is located in the center of scenic and historic Farmington.

Host: Elisa Aiello
Rooms: 72 (PB) $69-105
Continental Breakfast
Credit Cards: A, B, C, D, E
Notes: 2, 5, 8, 10, 11, 12, 13, 14

GLASTONBURY

Butternut Farm

1654 Main Street, 06033
(203) 633-7197

An 18th-century architectural jewel that is furnished in museum-quality period antiques. Estate setting with ancient trees, herb gardens, prize dairy goats, barnyard chickens, and pigeons. Just 10 minutes from Hartford. All Connecticut is within one and one-half hours.

Host: Don Reid
Rooms: 5 (PB) $65-85
Full Breakfast
Credit Cards: A, B, C
Notes: 2, 5, 8, 9, 10, 11, 12, 13

Udderly Woolly Acres

581 Thompson Street, 06033
(203) 633-4503

Stay the night in a suite of rooms in an 1820 farmhouse set on 20 acres in East Glastonbury. Look out on a pastoral scene with sheep, goats, and geese on a working homestead. Farm-fresh vegetables, fruit, milk, eggs, and cheese in season. Lodging includes breakfast.

Hosts: Joan and Tom Kemble
Rooms: 1 Suite (PB) $75
Full Breakfast
Credit Cards: None
Notes: 2, 5, 8, 9

HAMDEN

Nutmeg Bed and Breakfast Agency #207

P. O. Box 1117, West Hartford, 06107
(203) 236-6698

A pool and lovely deck add to your enjoyment of this comfortable home. Situated right outside New Haven, this house has one guest room with shared bath, perfect for the single traveler. Continental breakfast. Children welcome.

HARTFORD

Nutmeg Bed and Breakfast Agency #428

P. O. Box 1117, West Hartford, 06107
(203) 236-6698

Classical musician husband and wife host this elegant late Victorian bed and breakfast. Authentic stained glass and hand-done stenciling add charm to this city home. One guest room with shared bath. Pull-out bed for children. Close to Trinity, the Bushnell, the Civic Center, and the bus line. Enjoy a continental breakfast with hosts or privately. Children welcome. German and some French spoken.

Nutmeg Bed and Breakfast Agency #453

P. O. Box 1117, West Hartford, 06107
(203) 236-6698

6 Pets welcome; 8 Children welcome; 9 Social drinking allowed; 10 Tennis available; 11 Swimming available; 12 Golf available; 13 Skiing available; 14 May be booked through travel agents.

Lovely Victorian home in an exclusive residential section has a third-floor room with king bed, private bath with shower, seating area with sofa which opens into queen bed, TV, clock radio, terry robe, two telephone jacks; second-floor room with double bed and bath shared with hosts, small TV. Kitchen and laundry privileges for long-term stay. Two-night minimum for weekends in summer and fall (Memorial Day through end of October). Continental plus breakfast, no children, cat and dog in residence.

HIGGANUM

Nutmeg Bed and Breakfast Agency #521

P. O. Box 117, West Hartford, 06107
(203) 236-6698

This Dutch Colonial home is in a very secluded setting on a wooded two-acre lot. There is a second-floor king bedroom with a private bath across the hall, and a single bed is available in the next room for a child. There is a sauna and shower in the basement. Full breakfast is served. Children are allowed. No pets.

KENT

Covered Bridge 1K

P. O. Box 447, Norfolk, 06058
(203) 542-5944

Charming 18th-century house is one of the oldest in Kent and is a splendid example of Federal architecture and decor. Livingroom with fireplace is available for guests; upstairs suite has an ornately carved four-poster canopy bed and private bath. Continental breakfast. $85-120.

Covered Bridge 2K

P. O. Box 447, Norfolk, 06058
(203) 542-5944

This 1860 Colonial set on two acres is close to Kent Falls. The owner, who also has an antique shop on the grounds, has decorated all of the rooms with period furniture. There is a livingroom and a den with a fireplace and TV. Continental breakfast. Three guest rooms, shared and private bath. $85-95.

Nutmeg Bed and Breakfast Agency #322

P. O. Box 1117, West Hartford, 06107
(203) 236-6698

Friendly hospitality awaits at this 1860s Colonial bed and breakfast home. Unwind in the romantic rose stenciled room with beamed ceiling or the country blue room with carved Victorian headboard, both with private baths. Relax by the fireplace in the cozy den or walk the lovely grounds and view St. John's Ledges. After a continental breakfast in the charming dining room, visit the adjoining antique shop. Nearby to hiking, skiing, canoeing, museums, and many fine restaurants. Children over 12 welcome.

LAKEVILLE

Nutmeg Bed and Breakfast Agency #320

P. O. Box 1117, West Hartford, 06107
(203) 236-6698

The smell of blueberry muffins and warm hospitality await you when you stay at this bed and breakfast. The three comfortable guest rooms have private and semi-private baths. Enjoy the screened-in porch in the evenings or sit before the cozy fireplace in the sitting room. Close to Lime Rock, private schools, and many fine restaurants. Children over 10 are welcome.

NOTES: Credit cards accepted: A Master Card; B Visa; C American Express; D Discover Card; E Diner's Club; F Other; 2 Personal Checks accepted; 3 Lunch available; 4 Dinner available; 5 Open all year;

Nutmeg Bed and Breakfast Agency #328

P. O. Box 1117, West Hartford, 06107
(203) 236-6698

Set along a lovely lake, this 15-room turn-of-the-century bed and breakfast is filled with antiques and charm. Guests may choose guest rooms with a Sleigh or a Spool bed, each with its own private bath. After a sumptuous continental breakfast enjoy some of the many area attractions: Lime Rock Park, Music Mountain, and Mohawk Ski Area. Children over 8 are welcome.

Nutmeg Bed and Breakfast Agency #330

P. O. Box 1117, West Hartford, 06107
(203) 236-6698

High on a peaceful hill this stately home sits on beautifully landscaped acreage. Guests will find flowers in their room, fresh from the greenhouse, and terry-cloth robes to snuggle in after bathing in an old-fashioned claw foot tub. The three guest rooms are lovingly furnished with antiques and have private and semi-private baths. Guests have a private entrance and share their own sitting room with fireplace. Children over 10 are welcome.

LITCHFIELD

Covered Bridge

P. O. Box 447, Norfolk, 06058
(203) 542-5944

Pre-Revolutionary War Colonial set on more than 200 acres. In summer, guests can enjoy a full breakfast overlooking a rolling view towards a wooded brook. There are three guest rooms, one on the first floor with a queen bed and private bath, and two king bedrooms on the second floor with a bath between the rooms. $90.

Nutmeg Bed and Breakfast Agency #333

P. O. Box 1117, West Hartford, 06107
(203) 236-6698

Situated on a quiet country road outside the historic village of Litchfield, this bed and breakfast features three guest rooms—one with private entrance, queen-size bed, and private bath, and two with king-size beds which share a bath. The house is a pre-Revolutionary Colonial, shaded by century-old sugar maples. Horses and sheep graze in the pasture. Guests will enjoy a full breakfast on the stone terrace or the covered porch in warm weather where they can overlook a rolling view of a wooded brook. Children over 12 welcome.

LYME

Covered Bridge LY

P. O. Box 447, Norfolk, 06058
(203) 542-5944

A 1765 Colonial set on four acres and surrounded by stone walls, gardens, and terraces. Relax in the living room with fireplace and the original beehive oven or choose a book from the library. Full breakfast. Two guest rooms with private bath. $95.

Covered Bridge 2LY

P. O. Box 447, Norfolk, 06058
(203) 542-5944

European charm and antiques make this Colonial set on fourteen acres a very special retreat. A full breakfast is served in the elegant dining room or in the sitting room that has a wood-burning stove and offers a lovely view of the grounds. Several pieces of furniture have been hand-painted by the hostess, reflecting her Swiss heritage, and both of the queen guest rooms, each with a private bath, have handmade quilts. $85.

6 Pets welcome; 8 Children welcome; 9 Social drinking allowed; 10 Tennis available; 11 Swimming available; 12 Golf available; 13 Skiing available; 14 May be booked through travel agents.

Nutmeg Bed and Breakfast Agency #512

P. O. Box 117, West Hartford, 06107
(203) 236-6698

This new center-chimney Colonial is on several acres of woods and has its own walking trail and horseshoe court. Two guest rooms with private baths are accented by family pieces and European furnishings. Convenient to the Old Lyme Art Center, all the shoreline attractions, and many restaurants. Full breakfast.

MADISON

Nutmeg Bed and Breakfast Agency #520

P. O. Box 1117, West Hartford, 06107
(203) 236-6698

Lovely center chimney Colonial about 20 years old, large livingroom for guests, lovely dining room, pool, comfortably large eat-in kitchen, fireplace in family room, pool, patio for breakfast on nice days; about 5 minutes from beach. Two second-floor guest rooms share bath; one has double spool bed, wicker chaise, chest, large closet, shuttered windows overlooking pool; one has twin beds, bedroom chair, chest, large closet. Continental breakfast. No children. No pets.

MYSTIC

Covered Bridge -1M

P. O. Box 447, Norfolk, 06058
(203) 542-5944

This 150-year-old restored Victorian farmhouse is situated on two acres of lovely, landscaped grounds with old stone walls, fruit trees, and an outdoor eating area for guests' enjoyment. A full breakfast is served in the dining room, and a Scottish tea is served in the afternoon. There are five guest rooms, one with a fireplace and a private bath. $75-125.

Covered Bridge-2M

P. O. Box 447, Norfolk, 06058
(203) 542-5944

This 1800s Colonial in a village setting offers a quiet retreat only minutes from the center of Mystic. There is a pleasant livingroom with a fireplace and a large dining room where a full breakfast is served. There are four guest rooms in the main house, three with fireplaces, and four guests rooms in the carriage house, two with whirlpool tubs. All rooms have queen-size beds and private baths. $98-125.

Comolli's House

36 Bruggeman Place, 06355
(203) 536-8723

Ideal for vacationers touring historic Mystic or the business person who desires a homey respite while traveling. This immaculate home, situated on a quiet hill overlooking the Mystic Seaport complex, is convenient to Olde Mistic Village and the aquarium. Sightseeing, sporting activities, shopping, and restaurant information is provided by your hosts. Off-season rates are available.

Host: Dorothy M. Comolli
Rooms: 2 (PB) $60-90
Continental Breakfast
Credit Cards: C
Notes: 2, 5

Nutmeg Bed and Breakfast Agency #513

P. O. Box 1117, West Hartford, 06107
(203) 236-6698

Built in 1837, this large farmhouse is surrounded by fruit trees and strawberry beds.
Five guest rooms, one with private bath,
four sharing two baths. There is also a spacious dining room and a warm family
room. The home-cooked breakfast with
specialty muffins is amply satisfying. Full
breakfast. Children over 11 welcome.

Nutmeg Bed and Breakfast Agency #522

P. O. Box 1117, West Hartford, 06107
(203) 236-6698

Lovely, bright house convenient to downtown
Mystic and Seaport but in a nice residential
neighborhood. Guest bedroom on the first floor
with double spool bed, private full bath. Small
upstairs room available for child. Livingroom
available for guests. Continental breakfast.
Children allowed. Cat in residence.

Red Brook Inn

P. O. Box 237, 06372
(203) 572-00349

The Red Brook Inn welcomes guests to the
charm and beauty of early New England.
Two Colonial buildings are situated on
seven acres of woodlands and surrounded
by ancient stone walls. Eleven guest rooms
are furnished with period American
antiques, and some feature canopy beds.
Seven rooms boast working fireplaces.

Host: Ruth Keyes
Rooms: 11 (PB) $95-179
Full Breakfast
Credit Cards: A, B
Notes: 2, 4, 5, 8, 9, 10, 11, 12

Steamboat Inn

73 Steamboat Wharf, 06355
(203) 536-9300

Luxurious lodging directly on the Mystic
River in downtown Mystic Village. Many
shops, restaurants, and historic homes are

just steps away. All rooms feature a river
view, fireplace, and personal whirlpool.

Host: Kitty Saletnik
Rooms: 6 (PB) $95-185
Continental Breakfast
Credit Cards: A, B, C
Notes: 2, 5, 8, 9, 11, 12, 14

NEW HARTFORD

Covered Bridge -1NH

P. O. Box 447, Norfolk, 06058
(203) 542-5944

A grand, 14-gabled Victorian in a very
secluded setting yet not far from a very
charming village on the Farmington River.
There is a sitting room with TV and also a
livingroom with a fireplace that guests are
welcome to enjoy. A continental breakfast
is served in the elegant dining room or, in
the summer, on the huge porch overlooking
the grounds. All four guest rooms are tastefully decorated in antiques. The guest
rooms can be taken as suites with a bath in
between two rooms, or two rooms with a
private bath. $75-95.

Covered Bridge - 2NH

P. O. Box 447, Norfolk, 06058
(203) 542-5944; (800) 488-5690

Featured in *Country Living*, this 1700s
Colonial farmhouse is set on 40 acres. The
grounds include a spring-fed pond for
swimming and fishing, a barn for horses,
chickens, and pigs, and beautiful flower
gardens. Enjoy old brick fireplaces, living
room with sun porch, and country kitchen.
Full breakfast. Five guest rooms. $95-125.

NEW HAVEN

Bed and Breakfast, Ltd.

P. O. Box 216, 06513
(203) 469-3260 Sept-June: after 5 P.M. weekdays
and anytime on weekends; July-August: anytime

6 Pets welcome; 8 Children welcome; 9 Social drinking allowed; 10 Tennis available; 11 Swimming available;
12 Golf available; 13 Skiing available; 14 May be booked through travel agents.

Bed and Breakfast, Ltd. offers over 125 listings of selected private homes and small inns throughout Connecticut, from elegantly simple to simply elegant. It provides personal service and great variety to the budget conscious traveler. A quick phone call assures one of up-to-the-minute availability and descriptions, all designed to meet guests' needs and price range.

Host: Jack M. Argenio, Director
Rooms: 125 (60 PB; 65 SB) $55-75
Continental Breakfast or Full Breakfast

Nutmeg Bed and Breakfast Agency #208

P. O. Box 1117, West Hartford, 06107
(203) 236-6698

Catch a game at the Yale Bowl or the bus downtown from this bed and breakfast in the Westville section. This English Tudor has two guest rooms with shared bath. Help yourself to continental breakfast. Children welcome.

Nutmeg Bed and Breakfast Agency #210

P. O. Box 1117, West Hartford, 06107
(203) 236-6698

Walk to Yale from this gracious Victorian home set in the residential section of New Haven. A newly decorated third-floor suite consists of a bedroom with a large private bath and a smaller bedroom. A guest room is also available on the second floor. Continental breakfast. Children welcome.

Nutmeg Bed and Breakfast Agency #212

P. O. Box 1117, West Hartford, 06107
(203) 236-6698

This beautiful home has a livingroom with grand piano, fireplace, central air. One guest room has twin pineapple four-poster beds, large closet, balcony, view of East

Rock, and feather comforters; the other guest room has a single bed and sofa, TV and VCR, large closet, beautiful printed coverlet; both rooms share a bath. Continental breakfast. Infants and children over 5 allowed. No resident pet.

Nutmeg Bed and Breakfast Agency #214

P. O. Box 1117, West Hartford, 06107
(203) 236-6698

A 1926 Colonial style with large porch; master bedroom with private bath (Jacuzzi and shower shared with hosts); cable TV, private deck, king bed; two blocks from public transportation. Continental breakfast, children allowed. No pets.

NEW MILFORD

Covered Bridge 1NM

P. O. Box 447, Norfolk, 06058
(203) 542-5944

Vista for viewing, woods for walking, hills for cross-country skiing, streams for fishing, flower gardens, and a pool are some of the attractions of this sprawling estate three miles outside of town. First-floor guest room with private bath and an upstairs guest room. $60-95.

Nutmeg Bed and Breakfast Agency #315

P. O. Box 1117, West Hartford, 06107
(203) 236-6698

A delightfully restored reverse wood tobacco barn, this bed and breakfast is beautifully landscaped with a pool and tennis court. Private and shared bath. Continental breakfast includes homegrown berries, homemade jams, popovers, and muffins prepared by former chef. Children welcome.

NOTES: Credit cards accepted: A Master Card; B Visa; C American Express; D Discover Card; E Diner's Club; F Other; 2 Personal Checks accepted; 3 Lunch available; 4 Dinner available; 5 Open all year;

NOANK

The Palmer Inn

25 Church Street, 06340
(203) 572-9000

Take a step back in time and enjoy gracious seaside lodging. Craftsmen skillfully built this elegant mansion at the turn of the century. Guests enjoy afternoon tea in the Victorian parlor. Antique furnishings, fireplaces, mahogany staircase, original wall coverings, stained-glass windows, and individually decorated guest rooms will enhance every stay. It is situated just two miles from Mystic shopping and other attractions.

Host: Patricia White
Rooms: 6 (PB) $105-175
Continental Breakfast
Credit Cards: A, B
Notes: 2, 5, 10, 11, 12

NORFOLK

Covered Bridge 2N

P. O. Box 447, Norfolk, 06058
(203) 542-5944

Early 1900s Victorian estate on five acres in a very secluded setting. There is a large living room with fireplace and a spacious sun porch for guests' use. A full breakfast is served in each of the three guest rooms. Two guest rooms have fireplaces, and one includes a livingroom. $90-150.

Manor House

Maple Avenue, P. O. Box 447, 06058
(203) 542-5690

Victorian elegance awaits you at this historic Tudor/Bavarian estate. Antique-decorated guest rooms, several with fireplaces, canopies, and balconies, offer a romantic retreat. Enjoy a sumptuous breakfast in the Tiffany-windowed dining rooms or indulge in breakfast in bed. Designated Connecticut's Most Romantic Hideaway, and included in *Fifty Best Bed and Breakfasts in the USA.*

Host: Hank and Diane Tremblay
Rooms: 9 (PB) $85-160
Full Breakfast
Credit Cards: A, B, C
Notes: 2, 5, 8 (over 12), 9, 10, 11, 12, 13, 14

NORTH STONINGTON

Antiques and Accommodations

32 Main Street, 06359
(203) 535-1736

A warm welcome awaits you at this beautifully restored 1861 Victorian home furnished in the Georgian manner, with formal antique furniture and accessories, canopy beds, and private baths. Begin the day with a four-course candlelight breakfast, relax on the porches and patios, and stroll among the extensive gardens. The 1820 house has two suites, each with three bedrooms, living room, and kitchen; it is ideal for families or groups traveling together. A small antique shop is in the Victorian barn. Easy access from I-95.

Hosts: Tom and Ann Gray
Rooms: 4 (3 PB; 1 SB) $95-145
Suites: 2 $125 midweek; $185 weekends
Full Breakfast
Credit Cards: A, B
Notes: 2, 5, 8, 9, 10, 11, 12, 14

Covered Bridge 1NS

P. O. Box 447, Norfolk, 06058
(203) 542-5944

Two 1861 and 1820 Victorian houses are linked by a courtyard and set in a charming, historic seacoast town close to Mystic. The hosts furnished this home in the Georgian manner with formal antique furniture and accessories, many of which are offered for sale. The four guest rooms in the 1861 house have four-poster canopy beds. Full English breakfast. $90-150.

6 Pets welcome; 8 Children welcome; 9 Social drinking allowed; 10 Tennis available; 11 Swimming available; 12 Golf available; 13 Skiing available; 14 May be booked through travel agents.

Nutmeg Bed and Breakfast Agency #506

P. O. Box 1117, West Hartford, 06107
(203) 236-6698

This beautiful village Victorian, built in 1861, has a covered porch and lovely flower and herb gardens. The rooms are beautifully furnished, and a gourmet breakfast is served in the elegant dining room with silver and china. There are four guest rooms; two with private baths, some with four-poster canopy beds. Mystic Seaport is just ten minutes away, and Rhode Island beaches are close by, as are Stonington Village and local vineyards. Full breakfast.

NORWALK

Nutmeg Bed and Breakfast Agency #115

P. O. Box 1117, West Hartford, 06107
(203) 236-6698

Fifty-year-old Cape Cod with two-room suite, private entrance, bedroom with double bed, private bath, livingroom with color TV; air conditioning for summer and electric blanket for winter. Phone and small refrigerator in livingroom, cot available. Continental breakfast, children allowed. No pets.

Nutmeg Bed and Breakfast Agency #118

P. O. Box 1117, West Hartford, 06107
(203) 236-6698

Contemporary home with private first floor guest room with high rise bed, desk, TV, and ample storage space. Full private bath with tub and shower. Continental breakfast, no children, no dogs on premises.

OLD GREENWICH

Nutmeg Bed and Breakfast Agency #120

P. O. Box 1117, West Hartford, 06107
(203) 236-6698

On Long Meadow Creek, an open, airy beach house with a dock on the tidal inlet off Greenwich Cove. Walking distance to the village and train to NYC, and about a mile off I-95. First floor room with queen-size sofa bed (open when quests arrive), wicker sofa, TV, private bath with shower. Full breakfast, ask about children, cats on premises.

OLD SAYBROOK

Nutmeg Bed and Breakfast Agency #503

P. O. Box 1117, West Hartford, 06107
(203) 236-6698

A lovely southern hostess greets guests at this 1740 Colonial on the historic register. This house is seven blocks from the Long Island Sound. There are two guest rooms sharing a bath, plus a suite with a private entrance and a kitchenette. High tea is served in the afternoon upon request. Continental breakfast. Children welcome.

PLANTSVILLE

Nutmeg Bed and Breakfast Agency #465

P. O. Box 1117, West Hartford, 06107
(203) 236-6698

This eleven-room central-chimney Colonial, circa 1740, is situated on a beautifully landscaped acre with a pool and surrounded by centuries-old maple trees.

NOTES: Credit cards accepted: A Master Card; B Visa; C American Express; D Discover Card; E Diner's Club; F Other; 2 Personal Checks accepted; 3 Lunch available; 4 Dinner available; 5 Open all year;

There are four fireplaces and a Dutch oven in the great room. One guest room has a king-size bed and a private bath; another has queen-size bed, shared bath, and working fireplace. Both rooms are air-conditioned. Full breakfast is served. Children are allowed, smoking is restricted, and there is a cat and dog on the premises.

POMFRET

The Covered Bridge
P. O. Box 447, Norfolk, 06058
(203) 542-5944

Set on over 6 acres, this 18-room Victorian cottage offers a very secluded country getaway. All of the common rooms and guest rooms are exquisitely decorated with Oriental rugs and antiques. There is a large livingroom with a fireplace and a very elegant dining room. There are two guest rooms with private baths and a two-bedroom suite with a bath. Several rooms also have fireplaces. A full breakfast and afternoon tea are served. $75-110.

RIDGEFIELD

Nutmeg Bed and Breakfast Agency #301
P. O. Box 117, West Hartford, 06107
(203) 236-6698

Combine a trip into history with the pleasures of an active getaway at this 200-year-old bed and breakfast. Complimentary tickets to Keeler Tavern, the historical society's showcase, and bicycles for a tour of the nearby nature trails. Two guest rooms with a shared bath. Wine and cheese served upon arrival. Robes, heated spa, and Jacuzzi provided. Children welcome.

Nutmeg Bed and Breakfast Agency #352
P. O. Box 1117, West Hartford, 06107
(203) 236-6698

An elegant historical home on three and a half beautifully landscaped acres, pool, sun room available for guests. Two guest rooms with queen beds and private baths. Rooms may be booked together as a suite. Convenient to NYC and airports; swimming, hiking, cycling, golfing nearby. Full breakfast, children allowed. Two dogs on premises.

RIVERSIDE

Nutmeg Bed and Breakfast Agency #105
P. O. Box 1117, West Hartford, 06107
(203) 236-6698

These active hosts have decided to share their lovely country-style Cape home. Guest room has private bath. New York City is only one hour away. Full breakfast. Children welcome.

SALISBURY

Covered Bridge 1S
P. O. Box 447, Norfolk, 06058
(203) 542-5944

An 1810 Colonial set on two private, landscaped acres in the center of town. There is a large livingroom with a fireplace and a study with a TV for guests. A full breakfast is served. Two guest rooms. $85.

---

6 Pets welcome; 8 Children welcome; 9 Social drinking allowed; 10 Tennis available; 11 Swimming available; 12 Golf available; 13 Skiing available; 14 May be booked through travel agents.

Nutmeg Bed and Breakfast Agency #324

P. O. Box 117, West Hartford, 06107
(203) 236-6698

Among the oldest in Salisbury, this attractive home is a fine example of early Federal period architecture. There are three guests rooms with private and semi-private baths. A continental breakfast is served in the dining room. There is a special Sunday half-day option for those who want to stretch their weekend. No children. Pets on the premises.

Nutmeg Bed and Breakfast Agency #337

P. O. Box 117, West Hartford, 06107
(203) 236-6698

This 1813 Colonial is in the historic district of Salisbury, one of Connecticut's most charming villages. There are two guest rooms with private baths. Enjoy breakfast in the dining room or the stone terrace in warm weather. Walk to fine restaurants, shopping, and antiquing. Convenient to Lime Rock and the Appalachian Trail. Children welcome. Pets on the premises.

Nutmeg Bed and Breakfast Agency #338

P. O. Box 117, West Hartford, 06107
(203) 236-6698

An elegant country retreat perched on top of a high hill. Watch the geese land on beautiful Lake Wononscopomuc while you eat your full homemade breakfast. The guest room has twin beds and a private bath. No children. Pets on the premises.

Nutmeg Bed and Breakfast Agency #339

P. O. Box 117, West Hartford, 06107
(203) 236-6698

A restored 1774 home with period furnishings that has three guest rooms with a shared bath. Full gourmet breakfasts are served. Near Music Mountain, antique shops, boating, hiking, and skiing. Children are welcome. Pets on the premises.

SCOTLAND

Nutmeg Bed and Breakfast Agency #454

P. O. Box 1117, West Hartford, 06107
(203) 236-6698

A 1797 Colonial-style country inn with a large sitting room for guests, keeping room, and kitchen for breakfast. Also a TV room with fireplace. double bedroom, and queen bedroom with fireplace. Both share a bath. Full breakfast, children over 10 allowed, cat in residence.

SHARON

Covered Bridge 1SH

P. O. Box 447, Norfolk, 06058
(203) 542-5944

Beautifully situated in a secluded setting, this lovely contemporary home is decorated throughout with antiques. Guests are welcome to enjoy the large living room, sun porch, and deck. Within walking distance of the village green and the Sharon Playhouse. Reserve a suite or just ask for the bedroom. $85-125.

NOTES: Credit cards accepted: A Master Card; B Visa; C American Express; D Discover Card; E Diner's Club; F Other; 2 Personal Checks accepted; 3 Lunch available; 4 Dinner available; 5 Open all year;

SHERMAN

Covered Bridge 1SHR

P. O. Box 447, Norfolk, 06058
(203) 542-5944

Circa 1835, this restored bed and breakfast was a rest stop for travelers throughout the 1800s. There is a pleasant living room for guest use and a Jacuzzi on the deck overlooking the secluded grounds. Acres of woods and fields for hiking or cross-country skiing. Three guest rooms with private baths. Full breakfast. $85-95.

Nutmeg Bed and Breakfast Agency #321

P. O. Box 1117, West Hartford, 06107
(203) 236-6698

This superbly restored 1835 Colonial farmhouse has three air-conditioned guest rooms that are furnished with antiques and have private baths. After a full country breakfast, guests are invited to enjoy the outdoor Jacuzzi, game room or sitting room with television. One mile from Candlewood Lake, boating, fishing, swimming, and cross country skiing nearby. Children over 10 are welcome.

STAMFORD

Nutmeg Bed and Breakfast Agency #116

P. O. Box 1117, West Hartford, 06107
(203) 236-6698

This Nantucket Colonial is 50 to 60 years old and has 4 bedrooms, two and a half baths on the sandy beach, Shippan Point. Ten minutes from railroad station. Tastefully furnished, gorgeous water view, breakfast on sun porch. One double bedroom with built-in bunk beds, one single bedroom with shared bath with double room, one queen bedroom with private bath. Full breakfast. One child allowed. No pets on premises.

Nutmeg Bed and Breakfast Agency #117

P. O. Box 1117, West Hartford, 06107
(203) 236-6698

1960s ranch-style inn has a family room with fireplace, country kitchen, screened porch. The first floor bedroom trundle bed can be single or double. Private bath, TV. Continental breakfast. No children. One dog on premises.

SUFFIELD

Nutmeg Bed and Breakfast Agency #474

P. O. Box 1117, West Hartford, 06107
(203) 236-6698

An 1825 Federal Colonial near the town green on Main Street; it is a five-minute walk to the grocery, library, pharmacy, movies, and restaurants. There is a choice of a bedroom with attached bath with tub and shower, double four-poster bed, chest, easy chair, and a large built-in closet, or a bedroom not attached to bath with old Victorian double bed, princess dresser, easy chair, bookcase, two closets, sink. Will rent either room but not both; guests have use of livingroom, dining room, kitchen, and yard. There is a TV with HBO in one room. It is 10 minutes to Bradley; host will provide transportation to and from airport with advance notice. Long term only. No children. No resident pets.

---

6 Pets welcome; 8 Children welcome; 9 Social drinking allowed; 10 Tennis available; 11 Swimming available; 12 Golf available; 13 Skiing available; 14 May be booked through travel agents.

THOMPSON

Nutmeg Bed and Breakfast Agency #468

P. O. Box 1117, West Hartford, 06107
(203) 236-6698

This new post-and-beam two-story home is situated in a wooded area with lake frontage and three acres. The inn offers cable TV, VCR, telephone. Two bedrooms, one double one twins, share a bath and large sitting room, private entrance, queen Hide-a-bed in the sitting room, rollaways, and a refrigerator available to guests. Convenient to Sturbridge Village, Woodstock Fair, Thompson Raceway. Pets welcome. Full breakfast, children welcome, dogs in residence.

TOLLAND

The Tolland Inn

63 Tolland Green, 06084-0717
(203) 872-0800

Built in 1800, the Tolland Inn stands in the northwest corner of the Tolland village green, one-half mile from I-84. Situated midway between Boston and New York City, the inn is convenient to the University

The Tolland Inn

of Connecticut, Old Sturbridge, Caprilands, Hartford, and Brimfield Fair. The inn also features a fireplace in the common room, and a sun porch.

Hosts: Susan and Stephen Beeching
Rooms: 7 (5 PB; 2 SB) $56-78.40
Suites: $78.40-134.40 (one with fireplace and spa)
Full Breakfast
Credit Cards: A, B, C
Notes: 2, 5, 8 (over 10), 9, 10, 11, 12, 14

WASHINGTON

Nutmeg Bed and Breakfast Agency #313

P. O. Box 1117, West Hartford, 06107
(203) 236-6698

This serene bed and breakfast is a true working farm. There is a brook, a small lake, a pool, and cross-country skiing on the property. Nearby guests will find canoeing, hiking, and good biking trails. Relax over a glass of wine before retiring to one of three guest rooms. A single loft room is also available. Full breakfast of farm-fresh eggs and homemade breads starts the day. Children welcome.

WASHINGTON DEPOT

Nutmeg Bed and Breakfast Agency #348

P. O. Box 1117, West Hartford, 06107
(203) 236-6698

A lovely contemporary home overlooking lawns, fields, woodlands, and a small pond has a completely private guest house with nicely furnished sitting room (cable TV and VCR), spacious double bedroom, private bath with shower, separate sleeping alcove with built-in single bed, and small porch. There is a small refrigerator in the guest house and picnic table in pine grove next to the pond. Continental breakfast. Children allowed. Cat on premises.

NOTES: Credit cards accepted: A Master Card; B Visa; C American Express; D Discover Card; E Diner's Club; F Other; 2 Personal Checks accepted; 3 Lunch available; 4 Dinner available; 5 Open all year;

WATERBURY

Covered Bridge 1WAT

P. O. Box 447, Norfolk, 06058
(203) 542-5944

An 1888 Victorian house on the National Register of Historic Places set on an acre in a historic district. There are several common rooms, including an antique-decorated livingroom with a fireplace. All of the guest rooms are decorated with antiques. Full breakfast and high tea are served. $75-150.

House on the Hill Bed and Breakfast

92 Woodlawn Terrace, 06710-1929
(203) 757-9901

A gracious 1888 Victorian listed on the National Register of Historic Places and beautifully furnished with antiques and flowers, House on the Hill is perched on an acre and a half of gardens and woodlands. Six fireplaces, sunny wraparound porches, and renowned breakfasts have made this inn the choice of experienced business and leisure travelers. Elegant setting for weddings, corporate entertaining, and special events. Featured in *Victoria Magazine*, *Yankee Magazine*, *Connecticut Magazine*, and *Fodor's Guide*. One mile from I-84. AAA approved.

Host: Marianne Vandenburgh
Rooms: 5 (4 PB; 1 SB) $65-100 plus tax
Full Breakfast
Credit Cards: None
Notes: 2, 4 (by arrangement), 5, 8, 9, 14

WEST HARTFORD

Nutmeg Bed and Breakfast Agency #441

P. O. Box 1117, West Hartford, 06107
(203) 236-6698

The single-story home is furnished with a blend of modern, traditional, and antique. One guest room with TV and private bath. Continental breakfast. Hungarian spoken. Children welcome.

Nutmeg Bed and Breakfast Agency #455

P. O. Box 1117, West Hartford, 06107
(203) 236-6698

This center hall Colonial has a year-round sunroom. On the bus line and within walking distance to University of Connecticut, West Hartford branch, and St. Joseph's College. Small child in house. Second floor bedroom with double bed and bath shared with the family. Long term preferred. Continental breakfast. Children allowed. No pets.

Nutmeg Bed and Breakfast Agency #473

P. O. Box 1117, West Hartford, 06107
(203) 236-6698

This apartment is situated on the first floor in back of the house with private entrance, bedroom with two closets and queen bed, sitting room with TV, and table for dining, fully equipped kitchen with storage, bath with tub and shower, and small hallway. Central air, weekly laundering of linens, periodic cleaning with cleaning fee. Long term only; no breakfast, no children, no pets on premises.

Nutmeg Bed and Breakfast Agency #482

P. O. Box 1117, West Hartford, 06107
(203) 236-6698

6 Pets welcome; 8 Children welcome; 9 Social drinking allowed; 10 Tennis available; 11 Swimming available; 12 Golf available; 13 Skiing available; 14 May be booked through travel agents.

Ranch-style home with facilities for handi-capped. Guest bedroom with private bath, attractive furnishings, three windows, car-peted, queen bed, ample storage; second bedroom with twin beds, a full bath (both used for a family traveling together). Continental breakfast (full on request), children allowed, no pets on premises.

A large Colonial surrounded by many old trees on hilly, wooded acre just outside of town. The original part of the house was built in 1740; guest quarters with separate entrance, bedroom with separate sitting room, double bed, Hide-a-bed in sitting room. Full private bath; parking in front lot. Pool and spa for guests, dog pen avail-able. Continental breakfast. Children allowed. Dogs on premises.

WESTPORT

Nutmeg Bed and Breakfast Agency #111
P. O. Box 1117, West Hartford, 06107
(203) 236-6698

Breathtaking setting overlooking Long Island Sound, this home combines rural beauty with metropolitan sophistication. Guest wing is private with its own sitting room, fireplace, and entrance. Three guest rooms with private and shared bath. Enjoy the beach during summer. Continental breakfast. Children welcome. $60 plus.

Nutmeg Bed and Breakfast Agency #113
P. O. Box 1117, West Hartford, 06107
(203) 236-6698

An Italianate Victorian on 3 acres. Formal garden, grape arbor, brook, terrace, sculp-ture studio (hosts are professional artists). Double bed, private bath with tub and shower, beautiful furnishings. Full break-fast. No children. Dogs on premises.

Nutmeg Bed and Breakfast Agency #114
P. O. Box 1117, West Hartford, 06107
(203) 236-6698

WETHERSFIELD

Nutmeg Bed and Breakfast Agency #408
P. O. Box 1117, West Hartford, 06107
(203) 236-6698

Nestled in the historic village of Old Wethersfield, this classic Greek Revival brick house has been lovingly restored to provide a warm and gracious New England welcome to all travelers. Built in 1830, it boasts five airy guest rooms furnished with period antiques. Three rooms have private baths; two rooms share a bath. Fresh flow-ers, cozy livingroom and parlor, afternoon tea, and elegant continental breakfast buf-fet. Children over 11 welcome.

Nutmeg Bed and Breakfast Agency #429
P. O. Box 1117, West Hartford, 06107
(203) 236-6698

This attractive Colonial home is rich in the history of the town. The hostess, a member of the historical society, offers one guest room with private bath. A small room suit-able for a child available. Close to a park and safe for walking. Full breakfast. Children welcome.

NOTES: Credit cards accepted: A Master Card; B Visa; C American Express; D Discover Card; E Diner's Club; F Other; 2 Personal Checks accepted; 3 Lunch available; 4 Dinner available; 5 Open all year;

WINDSOR

Nutmeg Bed and Breakfast Agency #469

P. O. Box 1117, West Hartford, 06107
(203) 236-6698

Charming Victorian home dating to 1860s, renovated with an addition in 1890. Lovely antique furniture, large front porch, three second floor bedrooms, 2 with extra long double beds, one with extra long twin beds, all with private baths. Convenient to airport, University of Hartford, Loomis Chaffee. Full breakfast. Children over 12. Dog on premises.

Nutmeg Bed and Breakfast Agency #479

P. O. Box 1117, West Hartford, 06107
(203) 236-6698

A 10-year-old Colonial in a nice residential neighborhood. Bright first floor room with private front and rear entrances; private bath with stall shower. Tiny kitchenette for snacks. Two twin four-poster beds. Private phone line for local or calling card calls. Access to screened porch overlooking the garden and woods. Airport transportation available if pre-arranged. Continental breakfast. Children over 12 allowed. Cat on premises.

6 Pets welcome; 8 Children welcome; 9 Social drinking allowed; 10 Tennis available; 11 Swimming available; 12 Golf available; 13 Skiing available; 14 May be booked through travel agents.

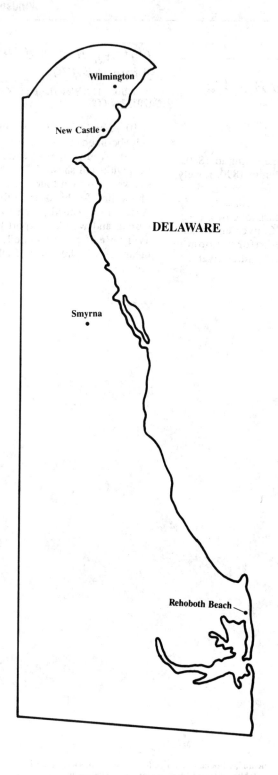

Wilmington

New Castle

DELAWARE

Smyrna

Rehoboth Beach

Delaware

DAGSBORO

Bed and Breakfast of Delaware #30

Box 177, 3650 Silverside Road,
  Wilmington, 19810
(302) 479-9500

This is the oldest existing residence in Dagsboro, circa 1850. Parkhurst, the original builder or owner was also a postmaster, with the post office located in the inn. The rooms have a warm, comfortable country theme. Guests can relax with a book or have a friendly conversation in front of the two fireplaces. There are three guest rooms with private baths.

DOVER

Bed and Breakfast of Delaware #23

Box 177, 3650 Silverside Road,
  Wilmington, 19810
(302) 479-9500

The charm of Historic Dover's Victorian era is found in this 1880s home filled with antiques. There are four bedrooms with private baths. Full breakfast is served.

LAUREL

Bed and Breakfast of Delaware #25

Box 177, 3650 Silverside Road,
  Wilmington, 19810
(302) 479-9500

Step back in time and enjoy the charm of this 18th-century country manor listed in the National Register of Historic Places. There are four spacious rooms and one suite with authentic period furnishings and fireplaces. Bicycles and picnic lunches are available to explore the Eastern Shore.

LEWES

Bed and Breakfast of Delaware #26

Box 177, 3650 Silverside Road,
  Wilmington, 19810
(302) 479-9500

This cottage is about 150 years old. All rooms have pieces from the 17th, 18th, and 19th centuries. The bathrooms are totally modern, and there is a large screened porch comfortably furnished in rattan and old pine. One mile from the Delaware bay and five minutes by car from the Atlantic Ocean. Continental breakfast is served.

MILFORD

Bed and Breakfast of Delaware #31

Box 177, 3650 Silverside Road,
  Wilmington, 19810
(302) 479-9500

This Greek Revival mansion, built in 1763 and on the National Register of Historic Places, has been home to two former governors, Rogers (1797-1799) and Causey

NOTES: Credit cards accepted: A Master Card; B Visa; C American Express; D Discover Card; E Diner's Club; F Other; 2 Personal Checks accepted; 3 Lunch available; 4 Dinner available; 5 Open all year; 6 Pets welcome; 8 Children welcome; 9 Social drinking allowed; 10 Tennis available; 11 Swimming available; 12 Golf available; 13 Skiing available; 14 May be booked through travel agents.

(1855-1859). It is situated on three and one-half acres in downtown Milford. The original slave quarters are still on the property. There are queen and twin bedrooms. A full country breakfast is served.

NEW CASTLE

Bed and Breakfast of Delaware #20

Box 177, 3650 Silverside Road, Wilmington, 19810
(302) 479-9500

This bed and breakfast is on the Delaware River just southeast of Wilmington. The cobblestone streets date from the Colonial era. This historic home has four lovely rooms with queen-size beds and all with private baths. Decorated in Laura Ashley prints, with Oriental rugs. A gourmet continental breakfast is served.

The Terry House Bed and Breakfast

130 Delaware Street, 19720
(302) 322-2505

The Terry House, situated in the center of historic New Castle, is an 1860s Federal town house. It offers four large bedrooms with private baths and cable TV. The rooms overlook the Delaware River and Battery Park, and the porches are the perfect spot to sit and relax after a day of shopping and sightseeing.

Host: Brenda Rogers
Rooms: 5 (PB) $60-80
Continental Breakfast
Credit Cards: A, B, C, D
Notes: 2, 5, 10, 11, 14

ODESSA

Bed and Breakfast of Delaware #22

Box 177, 3650 Silverside Road, Wilmington, 19810
(302) 479-9500

This circa 1840 home has been beautifully restored and furnished with period antiques. There are two bedrooms with private baths, and a suite with a queen-size bed, whirlpool bath, and lovely view of the town.

REHOBOTH BEACH

Tembo Bed and Breakfast

100 Laurel Street, 19971
(302) 227-3360

Tembo, situated 750 feet from the beach in a quiet, residential area offers a casual atmosphere with warm hospitality. Relax among Early American furnishings, antiques, oil paintings, waterfowl carvings, and Gerry's elephant collection. Clean bedrooms that have firm beds.

Hosts: Don and Gerry Cooper
Rooms: 6 (1 PB; 5 SB) $55-100
Continental Breakfast
Minimum stay weekends: 2 nights; holidays: 3 nights
Credit Cards: None
Notes: 2, 5, 6 (11/31-3/31), 8 (over 12), 9, 10, 11, 12

SELBYVILLE

Bed and Breakfast of Delaware #28

Box 177, 3650 Silverside Road, Wilmington, 19810
(302) 479-9500

This turn-of-the-century Victorian home displays family heirlooms, Oriental carpets, crystal chandeliers and antiques. Enjoy the cozy Victorian parlor or read a book in a rocking chair on the breezy verandas. The guest rooms have high ceilings. Just nine miles from Ocean City or Fenwick Island, the estate is close enough to get to the beach, but far enough away to avoid the hustle.

Bed and Breakfast of Delaware #29

Box 177, 3650 Silverside Road,
   Wilmington, 19810
(302) 479-9500

This Irish bed and breakfast is in a lovely quiet area and offers a swimming pool, two adult bicycles, tennis courts, and racquets. There are five bedrooms with two shared baths. Five miles to Bethany Beach and Fenwick Island. Convenient to state and national parks.

SMYRNA

The Main Stay

41 South Main Street, 19977
(302) 653-4293

This early 1800s white clapboard Colonial town house is in the heart of the downtown historic area. It is furnished with Oriental rugs and antique furniture and is accented with needlework and handmade quilts. Each bedroom has twin beds and shares a bath. Breakfast may include homemade muffins, bread, scones, or hot cakes.

Host: Phyllis E. Howarth
Rooms: 3 (SB) $50
Continental Breakfast
Credit Cards: None
Closed June 1-Nov. 1
Notes: 8, 9, 10, 12

WILMINGTON

Bed and Breakfast of Delaware: A Reservation Service

3650 Silverside Road, Box 177, 19810
(302) 479-9500

Accommodations in private homes and small historic inns throughout Delaware, Maryland, and Virginia's Chesapeake Bay, Pennsylvania's Brandywine Valley Wyeth, Hagley, Winterthur, Nemours Museum, and Longwood Gardens.

Host: Mille Alford, director
Rooms: 45 homes in registry; $55-160
Full or Continental Breakfast
Credit Cards: A, B
Notes: 5, 8, 10, 11, 12

Bed and Breakfast of Delaware #21

Box 177, 3650 Silverside Road,
   Wilmington, 19810
(302) 479-9500

A lovely Cape Cod in a quiet suburban neighborhood, this inn has beautiful award-winning landscaped grounds and three double rooms with private baths furnished with fresh flowers and fruit. In the winter the mature hedges and unusual shrubs are decorated for the holidays. Five minutes north of downtown Wilmington, 27 miles south of the center of Philadelphia. Minutes to Brandywine Valley museums, colleges, and industry. A full breakfast is served.

6 Pets welcome; 8 Children welcome; 9 Social drinking allowed; 10 Tennis available; 11 Swimming available; 12 Golf available; 13 Skiing available; 14 May be booked through travel agents.

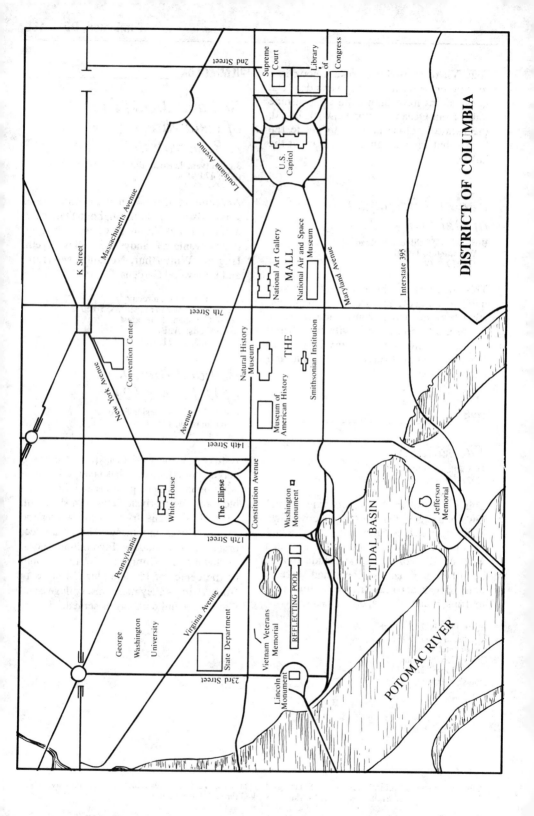

DISTRICT OF COLUMBIA

Supreme Court
Library of Congress
2nd Street
Louisiana Avenue
U.S. Capitol
Massachusetts Avenue
K Street
National Art Gallery
MALL
National Air and Space Museum
Maryland Avenue
Interstate 395
Convention Center
7th Street
New York Avenue
Natural History Museum
THE
Smithsonian Institution
Avenue
Museum of American History
14th Street
White House
The Ellipse
Pennsylvania
Constitution Avenue
Washington Monument
17th Street
TIDAL BASIN
Jefferson Memorial
George Washington University
Virginia Avenue
Vietnam Veterans Memorial
REFLECTING POOL
State Department
23rd Street
Lincoln Monument
POTOMAC RIVER

District of Columbia

Adams Inn

1744 Lanier Place, NW, 20009-2118
(202) 745-3600

Convenient, comfortable, home-style atmosphere in a neighborhood with over 40 American and ethnic restaurants to choose from. Near the bus lines, shopping, Metro, museums, government buildings, and convention sites. Economical for the tourist and business traveler. Both private and shared bathrooms available.

Hosts: Gene and Nancy Thompson; Anne Owens
Rooms: 25 (12 PB; 13 SB) $55-95
Continental Breakfast
Credit Cards: A, B, C, D, E
Notes: 2, 5, 8, 14

Adams Inn

Bed and Breakfast Accommodations, Ltd. TNN DC

P. O. Box 12011, 20005
(202) 328-3510; FAX (202) 332-5999

Part of the Bed and Breakfast National Network, Bed and Breakfast Accommodations, Ltd. of Washington D.C. offers bed and breakfast not only in the District of Columbia, but also in many other cities and states across the country. The members of this network adhere strictly to the standards set by TNN, such as getting to know the guests personally, having an established cancellation and refund policy, and following a thorough inspection and approval process for all properties rented. This is because each member of the network is dedicated to ensuring comfort, pleasure, and personal needs while guests are staying at one of these "homes away from home."

Bed and Breakfast Accommodations, Ltd. #100

P. O. Box 12011, 20006
(202) 328-3510; FAX (202) 332-5999

This 100-year-old Victorian was built by John Shipman as his personal residence and has been carefully and extensively restored by its present owners who have added exterior landscaping, gardens, terrace, and fountains to the existing town

NOTES: Credit cards accepted: A Master Card; B Visa; C American Express; D Discover Card; E Diner's Club; F Other; 2 Personal Checks accepted; 3 Lunch available; 4 Dinner available; 5 Open all year; 6 Pets welcome; 8 Children welcome; 9 Social drinking allowed; 10 Tennis available; 11 Swimming available; 12 Golf available; 13 Skiing available; 14 May be booked through travel agents.

house. The house has been featured on the Logan Circle House Tour and was written up in *Washington Gardener Magazine, The Washington Post,* and *The Philadelphia Inquirer.* Accommodations offer either a queen or double bed, and have both shared and private baths. Parking must be arranged in advance. $55-85.

Bed and Breakfast Accommodations, Ltd. #111
P. O. Box 12011, 20005
(202) 328-3510; FAX (202) 332-3885

Situated on General's Row, a row of town houses constructed in the late 1880s. This house is just three blocks from Dupont Circle, second only to Georgetown as a neighborhood for the trendy. Dupont Circle offers good restaurants, boutiques, and theaters, and the Dupont Circle Metro Subway is three blocks away. Four guest rooms have either double or pair of twin beds, and both shared and private baths are available. The hostess is an artist with a MA from the University of Alabama. Resident cat. $60-75.

Bed and Breakfast Accommodations, Ltd. #120
P. O. Box 12011, 20005
(202) 328-3510; FAX (202) 332-3885

This upper Northwest Washington residence is tastefully appointed with crafts, flowers, and comfortable furniture. The fashionable neighborhood offers elegant shopping, close access to all the attractions in downtown Washington, and other major activity areas in Maryland. The host family has lived in Washington D.C. for 25 years, and he is an urban planner, which makes him an excellent resource on Washington attractions. $55-65.

Bed and Breakfast Accommodations, Ltd. #122
P. O. Box 12011, 20005
(202) 328-3510; FAX (202) 332-3885

This unhosted apartment has a prestigious address set back from Wisconsin Avenue in its own park-like environment. Situated in upper Georgetown, it is close to major attractions, yet posses an air of being miles from city life. The efficiency has a double-size, fold-out sleep sofa, a kitchen with microwave, dishwasher, and European-styled cabinetry, TV, telephone, and washer and dryer. $70-75.

Bed and Breakfast Accommodations, Ltd. #123
P. O. Box 12011, 20005
(202) 328-3510; FAX (202) 332-3885

Designed in 1891 by famous Washington architect Franklin Schneider, this house was recently renovated by its present owner, an attorney who has traveled all over the United States, Europe, and the Far East. Accommodations include a queen-size reproduction of a Victorian iron and brass bed, private hall bath, and separate sitting room. There is also a front study with extensive bookcases and a sun porch that guests are welcome to use. $75-85.

Bed and Breakfast Accommodations, Ltd. #125
P. O. Box 12011, 20005
(202) 328-3510; FAX (202) 332-3885

This Victorian town house was built in 1990 and is filled with an eclectic mix of period pieces, Oriental, and contemporary art. Four gracefully appointed bedrooms share two baths on the second floor. A third floor two room suite adjoins a private bath and can accommodate up to four people.

Conveniently situated in the heart of the city, this home is situated one mile north of the White House and six blocks of Dupont Circle Metro Stop on the Red Line. No children. $65-75.

Bed and Breakfast Accommodations, Ltd. #126

P. O. Box 12011, 20005
(202) 328-3510; FAX (202) 332-3885

This house is a Georgian-style brick Colonial with a slate roof. Situated on a wide, tree-lined avenue in a residential neighborhood, Tenley Circle is conveniently situated between Georgetown and Chevy Chase, Maryland. Guests have easy access to downtown business areas and major bus routes, and within two blocks are many restaurants, shops, movie theaters, tennis courts, and an indoor pool. Two large guest rooms, each have a private bath with a tiled shower. Pets are not permitted. $70-80.

Bed and Breakfast Accommodations, Ltd. #129

P. O. Box 12011, 20005
(202) 328-3510; FAX (202) 332-3885

This red-brick former schoolhouse, circa 1880, was converted about four years ago into condominiums. It features enormous windows and 15-ceilings. Situated four and one-half blocks from Union Station. The guest room was designed by the hostess, an avid collector of antiques. It has an Old World-style bed built into an existing alcove, and an entertainment center and appliances are all operated by remote control so that a tired guest can prop himself against a pillow and never have to move. Walking distance to charming cafes and restaurants that line Massachusetts Avenue. $60, single only.

Bed and Breakfast Accommodations, Ltd. #130

P. O. Box 12011, 20005
(202) 328-3510; FAX (202) 332-3885

Built in 1892, this home was one of the early gracious row houses of Capitol Hill. The house has been renovated, but the original architectural details have been retained. A spacious guest room on the English Basement level has a comfortable queen-size, half cherry poster bed, comfortable sitting chairs, a bookshelf full of American history books, cable TV, and a private entrance. Situated two blocks from the host's home is Capitol South Metro (Blue Line) and many good restaurants. $75-85.

Bed and Breakfast Accommodations, Ltd. #131

P. O. Box 12011, 20005
(202) 328-3510; FAX (202) 332-3885

This Federal-style brick home was custom-designed by the owners and built in 1982. The house has two guest rooms, each with a private bath and double bed. Between Connecticut and Wisconsin Avenues, the house is convenient to numerous restaurants, movie theaters, and elegant shopping. The Metro subway is a brief three and one-half blocks away, and buses arrive regularly at stops on Wisconsin and Connecticut Avenues. $65-75.

Bed and Breakfast Accommodations, Ltd. #136

P. O. Box 12011, 20005
(202) 328-3510; FAX (202) 332-3885

This unhosted apartment on a quiet residential street of three-story town houses is only a few blocks away from Metro stops to the White House, Woodley Park/Zoo, excellent area shops and restaurants, and the Sheraton Washington and Connecticut Avenue. This

6 Pets welcome; 8 Children welcome; 9 Social drinking allowed; 10 Tennis available; 11 Swimming available; 12 Golf available; 13 Skiing available; 14 May be booked through travel agents.

completely self-contained one-bedroom apartment occupies one floor of the town house. It has been professionally decorated, has a queen-size bed, full bath, fully equipped kitchen and livingroom with cable TV, VCR, stereo, and private patio. Roll-away bed, laundry facilities, and weekly maid service available. $90-100.

Bed and Breakfast Accommodations, Ltd. #137

P. O. Box 12011, 20005
(202) 328-3510; FAX (202) 332-3885

Seven blocks behind the Capitol, walking distance to the Supreme Court and Library of Congress, and a ten-minute walk to both Eastern Market Metro and Union Station. This house, built in 1902, has been restored to its present condition by the owner, a fashion designer whose renovations have been featured in *Better Homes and Gardens* and *The Washington Post*. Two guest rooms are available, each with a double bed, color TV, telephone, and shared bath. $65-75.

Bed and Breakfast Accommodations, Ltd. #145

P. O. Box 12011, 20005
(202) 328-3510; FAX (202) 332-3885

This quintessentially Washington-style town house is situated in a prestigious district on Captiol Hill. The elegant restorations and decor of this 13-room residence has four guest accommodations with a variety of bed sizes and both private and shared baths. All rooms have a color TV and a telephone. This home is original and exudes great warmth and hospitality. Resident cats. $65-85.

Bed and Breakfast Accommodations, Ltd. #155

P. O. Box 12011, 20005
(202) 328-3510; FAX (202) 332-3885

A 19th century inn situated in historic Virginia, just 45 minutes from downtown, has been lovingly restored as a cozy and beautiful bed and breakfast. There are 14 unique rooms furnished with antiques and reproductions, with each named for a note-worthy Virginian. The dining room was inspired by Belvoir, the home of William Fairfax. Gardens designed to reflect the era when the inn was constructed have been added to both the front and back of the building. Full breakfast and high tea are both served. $115-250.

Bed and Breakfast Accommodations, Ltd. #171

P. O. Box 12011, 20006
(202) 328-3510; FAX (202) 332-3885

This split-level home is situated in a country setting, with a county park across the street that has a nature trail leading to the Potomac River. Two guest rooms, both with double bed and a shared bath, are available. Iron, laundry facilities, parking, telephone, and color TV with VCR and cable are offered as well. Pets can be accommodated in the garage. $40-60.

Bed and Breakfast Accommodations, Ltd. #196

P. O. Box 12011, 20006
(202) 328-3510; FAX (202) 332-3885

This house, a new Victorian-style, has a wrap-around porch and decks for sitting or sunning. Situated in Silver Springs, an old established community adjacent to Washington, D.C. The guest rooms are comfortably furnished and share one large bathroom. Guests will also enjoy relaxing in the huge spa on the deck that looks out toward the woods. The general area has a large variety of interesting restaurants and shopping malls, and major downtown attractions are only thirty minutes away via

NOTES: Credit cards accepted: A Master Card; B Visa; C American Express; D Discover Card; E Diner's Club; F Other; 2 Personal Checks accepted; 3 Lunch available; 4 Dinner available; 5 Open all year;

Metro, which is three miles away with ample parking. Resident dog. $60-70.

The Bed and Breakfast League, Ltd. #1
P. O. Box 9490, 20016
(202) 363-7767

The Park House is a late Victorian house that overlooks the Folger Park, three blocks from the U.S. Capitol and the Capitol South Metro stop. The master bedroom has a king bed, sitting area with TV, desk, phone, and private bath. Two other bedrooms share a bath. The hostess, a lobbyist, serves a self-serve continental breakfast. Children over 12 welcome. $65-100.

The Bed and Breakfast League, Ltd. #2
P. O. Box 9490, 20016
(202) 363-7767

The Madison House, situated just across the street from the Madison Building of the Library of Congress, was built in 1850 and retains its original woodwork and mantels. It is elegantly decorated with antiques and reproductions. Two suites and a master bedroom with private bath and Jacuzzi are available. Breakfast is served in the dining room with a fireplace or on the deck in good weather. Children welcome in some rooms. $70-160.

The Bed and Breakfast League, Ltd. #3
P. O. Box 9490, 20016
(202) 363-7767

The charming turn-of-the-century Victorian was lovingly rescued and restored by the hostess. It is decorated with period furnishings, beautiful wallpaper and linens, and

antiques. Six guest rooms share three baths. Relax in the parlor or library, or on the deck in good weather. A five-minute walk to all the shops and restaurants of Connecticut Avenue, and a ten-minute walk to the DuPont Circle Metro stop. Continental breakfast. Children over 11 welcome. $65-70.

The Bed and Breakfast League, Ltd. #4
P. O. Box 9490, 20016
(202) 363-7767

This Federal-style Victorian house is hosted by an independent film producer, an energy consultant, and their children. The third-floor guest area consists of two bedrooms, a shared bath, and a small kitchen. Breakfast is served in the dining room with a fireplace. A number of antiques, Oriental rugs, and an art collection decorate the house. A 10- to 12-minute walk to the Woodley Park/Zoo Metro stop and to major hotels. Children welcome. $60-65.

The Bed and Breakfast League, Ltd. #5
P. O. Box 9490, 20016
(202) 363-7767

The Inver House is an elegant Georgian home in an area close to many embassy residences. A short walk from two major convention hotels and the Woodley Park Zoo. Metro stop, the house is decorated with antique furniture, Oriental rugs, and porcelains. The spacious guest rooms include a master bedroom with a king bed, private attached bath, and private deck. Other guest rooms have either a king or queen bed and private or shared baths, depending on the room. All rooms include color TV and private telephone lines. Children over 12 welcome. Ample free parking. $65-150 plus tax.

6 Pets welcome; 8 Children welcome; 9 Social drinking allowed; 10 Tennis available; 11 Swimming available; 12 Golf available; 13 Skiing available; 14 May be booked through travel agents.

The Bed and Breakfast League, Ltd. #6

P. O. Box 9490, 20016
(202) 363-7767

The Capitol Hill Suite is part of a Victorian house situated on one of the prettiest blocks in the Capitol Hill District. It is three blocks from the Eastern Metro stop and eight blocks east of the U.S. Capitol, the Supreme Court, and the Library of Congress. The guest area contains a bedroom/sitting room with a queen bed, dining area, private bath, kitchen, and private deck. The suite is beautifully and comfortably decorated and includes color TV and private telephone. Parking is on the street and easily available. $60-85, plus tax.

The Bed and Breakfast League, Ltd. #7

P. O. Box 9490, 20016
(202) 363-7767

Georgetown is the oldest section of the city, home of some of the city's best restaurants, and renown for its world class shopping. After a full day of touring, return to this quiet and secluded suite and relax in the sitting room before walking out for dinner. In addition to the sitting room with color TV, there is a wet bar, bedroom with queen bed, and private bath. The host stocks the wet bar for a continental breakfast. All the shops and restaurants are within easy walking distance, as are Georgetown University and Dumbarton Oaks Museum and Gardens. $75-85, plus tax.

The Bed and Breakfast League, Ltd. #8

P. O. Box 9490, 20016
(202) 363-7767

This unhosted, one-bedroom apartment is just eight blocks east of the U.S. Capitol, and two blocks from the oldest remaining farmers' market in the city. Accommodations include one bedroom with private bath, large closet, living/dining room with a queen-size pull-out bed, and a Pullman kitchen with washer and dryer. The kitchen is stocked for a continental breakfast. $60-105.

The Bed and Breakfast League, Ltd. #9

P. O. Box 9490, 20016
(202) 363-7767

Situated just ten minutes from Georgetown and five minutes from American University and the Potomac River is this handsome house built on a hillside. Two guest rooms with private baths (one bath in hall), and use of den and wet bar. Close to bus service to downtown and the mall. $60-70.

Kalorama Guest House at Woodley Park

2700 Cathedral Avenue, 20008
(202) 328-0860

This charming Victorian inn provides a cozy home away from home. Situated on a quiet, tree-lined street in a lovely downtown residential neighborhood, the inn is just a short stroll from the Metro (subway), and a host of fine restaurants and shops. Guest rooms have been tastefully decorated in period. Enjoy a complimentary continental breakfast in the sun-filled breakfast room, and an aperitif at day's end. The hospitality and personal service here is nationally known. Most tourist attractions are only 10 minutes away.

Rooms: 19 (12 PB; 7 SB) $45-95
Continental Breakfast
Credit Cards: A, B, C, E
Notes: 2, 5, 9, 10, 11, 14

NOTES: Credit cards accepted: A Master Card; B Visa; C American Express; D Discover Card; E Diner's Club; F Other; 2 Personal Checks accepted; 3 Lunch available; 4 Dinner available; 5 Open all year;

The Reeds
P. O. Box 12011, 20005
(202) 328-3510

A 100-year-old Victorian mansion that has been carefully and extensively restored. Original wood paneling, stained glass, chandeliers, porch. Each room has a color TV and phone; laundry facilities are available. Adjoins Logan Circle Historic District, with excellent transportation and easy parking. This beautiful home was selected as a part of the "Christmas at the Smithsonian" festivities and was featured in the *Washington Post* in December when it was decorated for Christmas. Ten blocks from the White House. The hosts speak English and French.

Hosts: Charles and Jackie Reed
Rooms: 5 (SB) $55-82.50
Continental Breakfast
Credit Cards: A, B, C, E
Notes: 2 (two weeks in advance), 5, 8, 9

The Reeds

6 Pets welcome; 8 Children welcome; 9 Social drinking allowed; 10 Tennis available; 11 Swimming available; 12 Golf available; 13 Skiing available; 14 May be booked through travel agents.

FLORIDA

Havana

Amelia Island

Saint Augustine

Coleman

Tarpon Springs

Saint Petersburg Beach

Palm Beach Gardens
Lake Park
Lantana
Delray Beach
Boca Raton
Deerfield Beach

Key West

Key Largo

Florida

Florida House Inn

20 and 22 South Third Street, P. O. Box 688, 32034
(904) 261-3300; (800) 258-3301
FAX (904) 277-3831

Situated on Amelia Island in the heart of the 50-block historic district of Fernandina, it was built in 1857 as a tourist hotel. Today's guests can enjoy the same large porches and 11 rooms, some with fireplaces, all with private baths. Country pine and oak antiques, cheerful handmade rugs and quilts found in each room. A pub and full service restaurant is also situated on the premises. Airport pickup available; bikes; FAX machine; handicapped access.

Hosts: Bob and Karen Warner
Rooms: 11 (PB) $65-125
Full Breakfast
Credit Cards: A, B, C, E
Notes: 2, 3, 4, 5, 8 (limited), 9, 10, 11, 12, 14

Florida House Inn

Camino Real #10

Open House Bed and Breakfast Registry
P. O. Box 3025, Palm Beach, 33480
(407) 842-5190

This neoclassic home is a decorator's delight. From the king-size bedroom, the sliding glass doors open to the landscaped patio and pool. Enjoy your ample breakfast with the morning newspaper. Other amenities include TV with remote control, room telephone, and an electric tea kettle in the room for tea, coffee, or soup any time. Five-minute drive to the ocean. $75.

Suburban Ranch #11

Open House Bed and Breakfast Registry
P. O. Box 3025, Palm Beach, 33480
(407) 842-5190

A comfortable home west of Florida's Turnpike and near mall restaurants and shopping. Guests are welcome to use the barbecue and refrigerator on the patio. From the pool, relax and enjoy looking at the lush greens of a local golf course. Choose between a corner queen-size bedroom or a single bedroom. Continental breakfast. $40-60.

NOTES: Credit cards accepted: A Master Card; B Visa; C American Express; D Discover Card; E Diner's Club; F Other; 2 Personal Checks accepted; 3 Lunch available; 4 Dinner available; 5 Open all year; 6 Pets welcome; 8 Children welcome; 9 Social drinking allowed; 10 Tennis available; 11 Swimming available; 12 Golf available; 13 Skiing available; 14 May be booked through travel agents.

COLEMAN

The Son's Shady Brook Bed and Breakfast

P. O. Box 551, 33521
(904) PIT-STOP (748-7867)

A refreshing change. This modern home has comfortable beds with private baths. Overlooks spring-fed creek on 21 secluded, wooded acres. A relaxing retreat for elderly, handicapped, newlyweds, and others. Air conditioning, heat, sound system throughout rooms; piano, library, and more. Solitude and tranquility with therapeutic, scenic, picturesque surroundings. Rural setting, easy to find. Within 100 miles of Central Florida attractions. Good fishing nearby. Brochure available.

Host: Jean Lake Martin
Rooms: 4 (PB) $50-60
Full Breakfast
Credit Cards: A, B, C
Notes: 2, 3 (prior arrangement), 4 (prior arrangement), 5, 10, 12

DEERFIELD BEACH

Parkland #14

Open House Bed and Breakfast Registry
P. O. Box 3025, Palm Beach, 33480
(407) 842-5190

A country home in the suburbs on 1 1/4 acres invites guests to sun by the pool or stroll across the grounds to the private pond. A footbridge and waterfall are part of the garden landscape. Some French is spoken by the hosts, a professional couple. They will prepare extra breakfast treats on weekends. A small dog will greet guests. $45-55.

DELRAY BEACH

A Petit Salon #12

Open House Bed and Breakfast Registry
P. O. Box 3025, Palm Beach, 33480
(407) 842-5190

The name accurately describes this artist's home. The hostess' talents carry through to her lush tropical garden. Double or twin bedrooms, each with a private bath, are available. One and one-half miles from the beach. Children welcome, bikes provided. Resident cats. Continental breakfast. $55.

FT. LAUDERDALE

Beach Front

Open House Bed and Breakfast Registry
P. O. Box 3025, Palm Beach, 33480
(407) 842-5190

Enjoy the ocean view from the expansive terrace and lawn of this contemporary home. Two guest rooms are offered, one double and one twin or king-size bedroom. Each has a private bath. A continental breakfast is offered, along with kitchen privileges and use of beach chairs. A gas barbecue grill is available for guest use. $90.

HAVANA

Harrington House Bed and Breakfast

5626 Gulf Drive, 34217
(813) 778-5444

The charm of old Florida architecture and the casual elegance of beachfront living are beautifully combined at the Harrington House, a one-of-a-kind bed and breakfast guest house on Anna Maria Island. Built in 1925, this lovingly restored home has eight charming bedrooms, each with private bath. Most rooms have French doors leading to balconies overlooking the pool, the beach, and the blue-green Gulf of Mexico. Guests are served a full breakfast in the dining room as they enjoy stimulating conversation with other guests. Relax by the pool, take a moonlit stroll on the beach, or listen to the surf. AAA rated, Mobil Guide rated; American Bed and Breakfast Association rated.

NOTES: Credit cards accepted: A Master Card; B Visa; C American Express; D Discover Card; E Diner's Club; F Other; 2 Personal Checks accepted; 3 Lunch available; 4 Dinner available; 5 Open all year;

Harrington House

Hosts: Frank and Jo Adele Davis
Rooms: 8 (PB) $79-149
Full Breakfast
Credit Cards: A, B
Notes: 2, 5, 9, 11, 14

KEY LARGO

Jules' Undersea Lodge

51 Shoreland Drive
P. O. Box 3330, 33037
(305) 451-2353; FAX (305) 451-3909

Dive, dine, and dream at five fathoms in "the world's first and only underwater hotel." Situated at Key Largo Undersea Park in Florida. Resort courses available for non-certified divers, packages for $195 to $295 per person. Includes dinner, breakfast, unlimited diving, refreshments, 42-inch windows, stereo sound system, microwave, refrigerator, and global communications.

Host: Neil Monney and Ian Koblick
Rooms: 2 (SB) $195-295
Full Breakfast and Dinner
Credit Cards: A, B, D
Notes: 4, 5, 11, 14

KEY WEST

Whispers
Bed and Breakfast Inn

409 William Street, 33040
(305) 294-5969

The owner-managers take great pride in their service, hospitality, and the romance of their historic 1866 inn. Each room is unique and appointed with antiques. Included in the room rate is a full gourmet breakfast served in the tropical gardens.

Hosts: Les and Marilyn Tipton
Rooms: 7 (1 PB; 6 SB) $69-150
Full Breakfast
Credit Cards: A, B, C
Notes: 5, 7, 9, 10, 11, 12

Whispers

6 Pets welcome; 8 Children welcome; 9 Social drinking allowed; 10 Tennis available; 11 Swimming available; 12 Golf available; 13 Skiing available; 14 May be booked through travel agents.

LAKE PARK

Classic Comfort #16

Open House Bed and Breakfast Registry
P. O. Box 3025, Palm Beach, 33480
(407) 842-5190

Situated in a suburban community seven
miles north of West Palm Beach and five
minutes from the beautiful ocean beaches
of Singer Island, this comfortable bungalow offers a standard double bedroom, or a
twin bedded room. The hosts serve freshly
squeezed orange juice from citrus trees on
the premises with continental breakfast.
Children over four welcome. Family rates
available. $45.

LANTANA

Lagoon Setting #06

Open House Bed and Breakfast Registry
P. O. Box 3025, Palm Beach, 33480
(407) 842-5190

Twenty minutes south of Palm Beach
International airport and west of I-95, this
sprawling ranch home is secluded yet near
good restaurants and ten minutes from the
ocean. If traveling with family or friends, a
choice of double, king, or twin bedrooms.
Children over five welcome. Family rates.
Relax on the screened patio and by the
pool. Continental breakfast. $55.

NAPLES

Inn by the Sea

287 11th Avenue South, 33940
(813) 649-4124; (813) 244-2978

Inn by the Sea is a bed and breakfast inn
offering five guest rooms. Situated just two
blocks from the beach, the inn is a "beach
house" in a tropical setting. Coconut Palms,
White Bird of Paradise, Bougainvillea and
numerous other local plantings surround

the home, which is listed on the National
Register of Historic Places. Bountifully
appointed with casually elegant decor,
there is an abundance of wicker, floral print
fabrics, white iron and brass beds and ceiling fans. Each room is named after a local
island in an effort to instill awareness about
the history natural resources of out area.
Activities include swimming, sailing, fishing, boating, golf and tennis. Jump on one
of the inn's beach cruisers and pedal
through Port Royal, Naples' most prestigious neighborhood.

Hosts: Catlin Maser
Rooms: 5 (PB)
Continental Breakfast
Credit Cards: A, B
Notes: 2, 5, 9, 10, 12, 14

PALM BEACH GARDENS

Decorator's Town House

Open House Bed and Breakfast Registry
P. O. Box 3025, Palm Beach, 33480
(407) 842-5190

From the twin bed room, step out onto the
private balcony overlooking the beautifully
landscaped patio. The colorful livingroom
boasts a wood-burning fireplace. Situated
near the Interstate, and within easy walking
distance of the shopping mall and restaurants. A full breakfast is served. $55.

Heron Cay #17

Open House Bed and Breakfast Registry
P. O. Box 3025, Palm Beach, 33480
(407) 842-5190

Water, boats, sun, and fun describe this
unique hideaway on two acres facing the
Intracoastal Waterway. Explore the private
island or hop into the pool or hot tub.
Weekly guests may enjoy a cruise on your
host's 48-foot Sportsfisherman. Inside,
relax by the stone fireplace in the Victorian
parlor, or try your luck on the pinball
machine in the game room. Guest rooms
have either a king or double bed with bal-

conies for a beautiful view of the inlet. Full breakfast; dinner served at extra charge. Resident dog and cats. $80-125.

ORLANDO

Perri House
Bed and Breakfast Inn

10417 State Road 535, 32836
(407) 876-4830; (800) 780-4830

Perri House is a quiet, private, secluded country estate conveniently situated in the backyard of the Walt Disney World Resort area. Because of its outstanding location, Perri House provides easy access to all that Disney World and Orlando has to offer. An upscale continental breakfast awaits each morning to start the day. The hosts offer a unique blend of cordial hospitality, comfort, and friendship to all their guests.

Hosts: Nick and Angie Perretti
Rooms: 4 (PB) $65-75
Continental Breakfast
Credit Cards: A, B, C, D
Notes: 2, 5, 8, 9, 10, 11, 12, 14

ST. AUGUSTINE

Carriage Way
Bed and Breakfast

70 Cuna Street, 32084
(904) 829-2467

An 1883 Victorian in the historic district, within walking distance of the waterfront, shops, restaurants, and historic sites. Complimentary cordial, newspaper, cookies, bicycles, and breakfast. The atmosphere here is leisurely and casual.

Hosts: Bill and Diane Johnson
Rooms: 9 (PB) $49-105
Full Breakfast
Credit Cards: A, B, D
Notes: 2, 3, 4, 5, 8, 9, 10, 11, 12, 14

Casa de Solana
Bed and Breakfast Inn

21 Aviles Street, 32084
(904) 824-3555

Built circa 1763, this inn has four antique-filled suites with cable TV, private bath, enclosed courtyard. Full breakfast is served in the formal dining room; a decanter of sherry is presented on arrival. The inn is downtown, with all the quaint shops, museums, restaurants, and horse and buggies to help tour St. Augustine, the nation's oldest city. A fee of $10 is charged for each additional person. AAA approved.

Host: Faye McMurry
Rooms: 4 (PB) $125
Full Breakfast
Minimum stay weekends and holidays: 2 nights
Credit Cards: A, B, C, D
Notes: 2, 5, 9, 10, 11, 12

Casa de Solana

Old City House
Inn and Restaurant

115 Cordova Street, 32084
(904) 826-0113

In the heart of town sits the Old City House, in a building that has been called a classic example of Colonial Revival architecture. Carefully restored in 1990 by its current owners, the premises include five bed-and-breakfast rooms and a full service

6 Pets welcome; 8 Children welcome; 9 Social drinking allowed; 10 Tennis available; 11 Swimming available; 12 Golf available; 13 Skiing available; 14 May be booked through travel agents.

Old City House

award winning restaurant. It commands a view of some of the most beautiful, historic architecture in northeastern Florida. Queen-size beds, private baths, full breakfast.

Hosts: Bob and Alice Compton
Rooms: 5 (PB) $60-95 weekends and holidays;
  reduced weekdays
Full Breakfast
Credit Cards: A, B, C
Notes: 2, 3, 4, 5

ST. PETERSBURG ISLAND

Bernard's Swanhome

8690 Gulf Boulevard, 33706
(813) 360-5245

Casual, laid back, lazy Florida living. Fish off of our dock, sun on deck, lounge in spa, or wander one-half mile to milk-white sandy gulf beach. Kitchen and laundry privileges (seventh night free). Fishing poles, beach chairs, mats, and towels provided. Golf, tennis, major league sports, Dali Museum, Busch Gardens all nearby. Enjoy dancing, fabulous dining, and glorious sunsets nightly on the charming island. Mrs. Bernard also operates a reservation service representing many waterfront homes with docks.

Host: Mrs. "Danie" Bernard
Rooms: 3 (1 PB; 2 SB) $45-80
Continental Breakfast served
Full Self-serve Breakfast
Credit Cards: C (deposit only)
Notes: 5, 8, 9, 10, 11, 12, 13 (water), 14

SINGER ISLAND

Waterfront

Open House Bed and Breakfast Registry
P. O. Box 3025, Palm Beach, 33480
(407) 842-5190

This spacious home is situated by a navigable canal, just a short walk to the beautiful ocean beach. Each of the two bedrooms has a private bath and balcony facing the water. A full breakfast is included, with cooking privileges available in the ultramodern kitchen. Living areas include a library, livingroom, and TV room with a six-foot screen and elaborate stereo system. Relax outdoors by the lily pond, on the patios or the dock lounges. Close to fine beachfront restaurants and tennis courts. $75-85.

TARPON SPRINGS

Spring Bayou Bed and Breakfast Inn

32 West Tarpon Avenue, 34689
(813) 938-9333

A large, elegant home built 1905 in center of historical district. Enjoy beautiful Spring Bayou, downtown antique shops, and area attractions of small Greek village. Excellent restaurants nearby, and short drive to the beach. Well-appointed rooms with antique furnishings and modern conveniences. Complimentary glass of wine and baby grand piano in lovely parlor, spacious wraparound front porch.

Hosts: Ron and Cher Morrick
Rooms: 2 (PB) $70-95
Expanded Continental Breakfast
Credit Cards: None
Notes: 2, 9, 10, 11, 12

NOTES: Credit cards accepted: A Master Card; B Visa; C American Express; D Discover Card; E Diner's Club; F Other; 2 Personal Checks accepted; 3 Lunch available; 4 Dinner available; 5 Open all year;

WEST PALM BEACH _____

Sterling House

Open House Bed and Breakfast Registry
P. O. Box 3025, Palm Beach, 33480
(407) 842-5190

This charming California-style house offers a view of the Intracoastal and the island of Palm Beach. Miles of landscaped paths for strolling, biking, and jogging. Walk to shops and restaurants; just two blocks to city bus stop. Relax on the spacious old brick terrace, surrounded by lush tropical foliage. Female only. Guest shares bath with hostess. Full breakfast. $45.

GEORGIA

Georgia

Honeysuckle Hill

Atlanta Hospitality Bed and Breakfast Service
2472 Lauderdale Drive, 30345
(404) 493-1930

Enjoy rustic ambience and southern hospitality in a cozy log home furnished with antiques and collectibles. Guests will be welcomed by the hosts, both Georgia natives, who are experienced in nature and nature crafts. Enjoy a generous breakfast of homemade breads, muffins, juice, herb teas, coffee, and fresh fruits on the partially-covered deck. Box lunches available with advanced notice; fruit basket and flowers in the rooms. Just 45 minutes north of Atlanta, and 45 minutes to Dahlongena and the scenic North Georgia Mountains. The hosts are Pat and Len, along with the resident K-9, Sugar. Affordable rates.

ATLANTA

Atlanta Hospitality Bed and Breakfast Service

2472 Lauderdale Drive, 30345
(404) 493-1930

Atlanta Hospitality Bed and Breakfast Services is a reservation agency that places guests in charming, safe homes with caring hosts. From the budget-minded to the affluent, quality accommodations can be provided to the degree desired. Accommodations are reserved upon receipt of a Reservation Request with a $20 deposit, which is credited to the bill. If the visit is cancelled, the deposit remains good for one year, and may be used at any time during the year. Full payment is due upon arrival, and hosts can only accept travelers checks or cash. $20-75.

Bed & Breakfast Atlanta D1

1801 Piedmont Avenue NE, Suite 208, 30324
(404) 875-0525

This traditional two-story house with swimming pool is situated on 12 beautifully wooded acres in Druid Hills. Two guest rooms, each with queen bed, share one bath. One room has handmade quilts and an antique doll collection. The other provides a wonderful view of the pool, woods, and flowers. An expanded continental breakfast is served in the charming downstairs dining room. One of the hosts builds beautiful reproduction furniture; an impressive silver chest in the front entry is evidence of his skill. $52.

Bed & Breakfast Atlanta D2

1801 Piedmont Avenue NE, Suite 208, 30324
(404) 875-0525

This 36-year-old Colonial brick home is in the heart of the Morningside, one of Atlanta's most desirable neighborhoods. There is a spacious bedroom with a queen-size bed and a bath with a shower. There are several sitting areas downstairs and a lovely outdoor deck overlooking a large walled yard. Guests may choose a continental or full breakfast, served in the sunlit dining room. Public transportation is excellent, and many restaurants, shops, and points of interest are within walking distance. Resident dog and cat. $72. Suite $80.

Bed & Breakfast Atlanta E1

1801 Piedmont Avenue NE, Suite 208, 30324
(404) 875-0525

Fully renovated, spacious 1960s brick ranch-style home offers one sunny antique-furnished double with adjoining bath and one spacious, bright twin-bed room with private bath down the hall. A single-bed studio room with full view of the patio and garden is sometimes available. Host couple serves nutritious breakfasts featuring home-baked breads, and lively hospitality completes. Within walking distance of Emory University. Kosher dietary laws observed. $60.

Bed & Breakfast Atlanta I1

1801 Piedmont Avenue NE, Suite 208, 30324
(404) 875-0525

This restored 1816 house was the honeymoon cottage for Robert Woodruff, the Coca-Cola magnate. The large livingroom displays a cherished Persian rug. Guest rooms include a private room and full bath downstairs—lace curtains, antique double iron bed. The upstairs suite has two bedrooms, a large sitting room with a built-in single bed, and a renovated full bath. One bedroom has an antique double sleigh bed, and the other has twin beds. High ceilings, heart-pine floors, wonderful old family furniture, and a gracious host welcome the guest. Relax along with the family cats on the screened porch overlooking an urban park. Continental or full breakfast. $68.

Bed & Breakfast Atlanta L1

1801 Piedmont Avenue NE, Suite 208, 30324
(404) 875-0525

This French Regency-style Victorian house (circa 1872) was saved from demolition in 1990 and restored by the current owners. There are front and rear porches where breakfast is served when the weather permits, as well as a downstairs sitting room. Gourmet breakfast is served in the dining room, with careful attention given to low-fat ingredients and special dietary needs. Four guest rooms are available, one with king-size bed and three with queen-size beds, all with private baths. $76-100.

Bed & Breakfast Atlanta L1

1801 Piedmont Avenue NE, Suite 208, 30324
(404) 875-0525

An intimate bed and breakfast just one block off the square in Decatur, the house was built in 1937. There are two bedrooms for guests. The gourmet breakfasts include homemade breads, muffins, fresh fruit or fruit smoothies, freshly ground coffee, imported tea, and sweet, dark honey gathered from hives in the lower garden. There is a hot tub and a nearby pool available to guests. The city of Decatur is one of Atlanta's most historic and well maintained neighborhoods. It is less than six miles from downtown Atlanta and three miles from Emory University, the CDC, and the American Cancer Society. $52-60.

Bed & Breakfast Atlanta M1

1801 Piedmont Avenue NE, Suite 208, 30324
(404) 875-0525

This early 1900s neighborhood is on the historic register and has special appeal for walkers and joggers. Nearby are the Woodruff Arts Center, High Museum, Botanical Gardens, Piedmont Park, and Colony Square with many appealing restaurants and shops. Public transit is excellent. Host couple resides in Dutch Colonial home with private cottage in rear. Bright, cheery, spacious unit has bedroom alcove with double bed and desk. The living/dining space has a double sleep sofa, chair, and breakfast table. New full bath and galley kitchen. Cable TV and phone available. Self-catered breakfast. $80.

Bed & Breakfast Atlanta S1

1801 Piedmont Avenue NE, Suite 208, 30324
(404) 875-0525

This authentic 1830s white two-story farmhouse was moved and carefully reassembled on this site in 1984. The house has porches on all sides. In the main house there is a terrace room with a private entry, king-size poster bed, antique furniture, a fireplace, and a large full bath. The carriage house has a suite with a large livingroom, dining room with a wet bar, undercounter refrigerator, microwave oven, and large screen TV. The bedroom features a king-size canopied bed and more interesting antiques. The private bath has a shower only. There is a queen sleep sofa in the livingroom, and a Port-a-Crib is available. $80.

Guesthouse

Atlanta Hospitality Bed and Breakfast Service
2472 Lauderdale Drive, 30345
(404) 493-1930

Situated behind the home of the owners in northwest Atlanta, this cottage is a self-contained bed and breakfast in the woods. Furnished with a sleeper sofa, chairs, desk, and refrigerator stocked with breakfast treats. A telephone, TV, and air conditioning are also included. Reasonable rates.

Inman Park

Atlanta Hospitality Bed and Breakfast Service
2472 Lauderdale Drive, 30345
(404) 493-1930

Inman Park has survived as a suburban oasis close to downtown Atlanta (two

miles). Many of the amenities the Victorians thought desirable are also here. The two cottages, Oakwood House and Woodruff Cottage, feature quaint touches from yesteryear, along with the modern amenities of today. Close to the state capitol, The Omni, Georgia Dome Stadium, and Underground Atlanta. MasterCard and Visa accepted. $60-90.

Lilburn Bed and Breakfast

Atlanta Hospitality Bed and Breakfast Service
2472 Lauderdale Drive, 30345
(404) 493-1930

Conveniently situated four miles east of Stone Mountain Park, yet only 30 minutes from downtown Atlanta. Here you will find plenty of southern hospitality and information on surrounding areas. The large guest room features a private bath, and is furnished with antiques. There is a separate sitting room and a sun porch. Continental breakfast. Children welcome; no pets. $50.

AUGUSTA _____

Into the Woods
Bed and Breakfast

176 Longhorn Road, Hephzibah, 30815
(706) 554-1400

This house was built in the late 1800s in Waynesboro and relocated to Hephzibah, fifteen minutes away. Relax in the Victorian parlor, step out onto one of the porches, or pull up a rocker and have a cookie from the kitchen. All of the guest rooms have good firm beds. Guests can take a short drive to Augusta for for a lovely walk on the Riverwalk along the Savannah River, or visit the restaurants and shops.

Host: Mr. and Mrs. Robert L. Risser
Rooms: 4 (2 PB; 2 SB) $55-65
Full Country Breakfast
Credit Cards: A,B
Notes: 2, 5, 8, 12

---

6 Pets welcome; 8 Children welcome; 9 Social drinking allowed; 10 Tennis available; 11 Swimming available; 12 Golf available; 13 Skiing available; 14 May be booked through travel agents.

CHICKAMAUGA (SEE ALSO CHATTANOOGA, TENNESSEE)

Gordon-Lee Mansion

217 Cove Road, 30707
(706) 375-4728; (800) 487-4728

Step back in time and enter this antebellum plantation house of museum quality, circa 1847. Used during the battle of Chickamauga as a Union headquarters and hospital, the mansion is furnished with period antiques in the atmosphere of early southern aristocracy. It is listed on the National Register of Historic Places. The seven-acre setting is just three miles from the Chickamauga-Chattanooga National Military Park, and 20 minutes from scenic downtown Chattanooga, Tennessee. Complimentary wine and tea served on the verandas.

Host: Richard Barclift
Rooms: 5 (4 PB; 1 SB) $65-90
Expanded Continental Breakfast
Credit Cards: A, B
Notes: 2, 5, 9, 10, 12, 14

DAHLONEGA

Mountain Top Lodge at Dahlonega

Route 7, Box 150, 30533
(706) 864-5257

Share the magic of a secluded bed and breakfast inn surrounded by towering trees and spectacular views. Enjoy antique-filled rooms, cathedral-ceiling, great room, spa, decks, heated outdoor spa, some rooms with fireplaces, whirlpool tubs, and porches. Generous country breakfast with home-made biscuits.

Host: David Middleton
Rooms: 11 (PB) $66.60-88.80
Deluxe Rooms: 2 (PB) $127.65-138.75
Full Breakfast
Minimum stay holidays: 2 nights
Credit Cards: A, B, C, D
Notes: 2, 5, 8 (over 11), 9, 14

Worley Homestead

410 West Main Street, 30533
(706) 864-7002

Built circa 1845 during America's first gold rush, the Worley Homestead bed and breakfast is situated in the beautiful north Georgia mountains. The inn is restored to it's late 1800s facade, and is furnished with antique furniture. Every effort is made to make guests feel like they have traveled back in time 100 years without leaving behind modern conveniences.

Hosts: Bill and Mary Scott
Rooms: 8 (PB) $49-75 (seasonal)
Full Breakfast
Credit Cards: A, B
Notes: 2, 5, 9, 14

FORT OGLETHORPE (SEE ALSO CHATTANOOGA, TENNESSEE)

Captain's Quarters Bed and Breakfast

13 Barnhardt Circle, 30742
(706) 858-0624

Built in 1902, this home has been completely restored. Great attention has been paid to detail to retain the charm of yesterday and add the convenience of today. Situated adjacent to Chickamauga-Chattanooga Military Park, and only twenty minutes from all the attractions in downtown Chattanooga, Tennessee, including the new Tennessee Aquarium, this quiet haven is convenient to many tourist attractions but restful when the day of sightseeing is done.

Host: Pam Humphrey and Ann Gilbert
Rooms: 6 (PB) $50-75
Full Breakfast
Credit Cards: A, B, C
Notes: 2, 5, 14

NOTES: Credit cards accepted: A Master Card; B Visa; C American Express; D Discover Card; E Diner's Club; F Other; 2 Personal Checks accepted; 3 Lunch available; 4 Dinner available; 5 Open all year;

GAINESVILLE

The Dunlap House
Bed and Breakfast Inn

635 Green Street, 30105
(706) 536-0200

The Dunlap House is north Georgia's luxury bed and breakfast inn. Built in 1910, the 10-room inn provides a grand introduction to the charming elegance of the Old South. Each uniquely decorated room has a private bath, telephone, remote control television, and either king- or queen-size beds.

Hosts: Ann and Ben Ventress
Rooms: 9 (PB) $85-115
Continental Breakfast
Credit Cards: A, B, C
Notes: 2, 5, 12, 14

HAMILTON

Wedgwood
Bed and Breakfast

P. O. Box 115, 31811
(706) 628-5659

Situated five miles south of Callaway Gardens. Stately 1850 home decorated in Wedgwood blue with white stenciling. Enjoy the piano in the livingroom, a classic movie on the VCR in the den, read in the library, swing on the screened porch, or doze in a hammock in the gazebo under pecan trees. Roosevelt's Little White House is nearby.

Host: Janice Neuffer
Rooms: 3 (PB) $63-73
Full Breakfast
Credit Cards: None
Notes: 2, 5, 8, 9, 10, 11, 12, 14

ST. MARYS

Goodbread Inn
Bed and Breakfast

209 Osborne Street, 31558
(912) 882-7490

This 1875 Victorian inn is in the historic district of a quaint fishing village nine miles east of I-95, 30 miles north of Jacksonville and 30 miles south of Brunswick. The Cumberland Island Ferry is within walking distance. Each antique-filled room has its own large bath, fireplace and ceiling fan. Large porches, with wine served upon arrival. Guests are treated to a seated deluxe continental breakfast.

Hosts: Betty and George Krauss
Rooms: 4 (PB) $65 plus tax
Continental Breakfast
Credit Cards: None
Notes: 2, 5, 9, 12, 14

SAUTEE

The Stovall House

Route 1, Box 1476, 30571
(404) 878-3355

This 1837 farmhouse beckons for a country experience in the historic Sautee Valley near Helen. The award-winning restoration and personal touches here will make quests feel at home. Enjoy mountain views in all directions. The restaurant, recognized as one of the top 50 in Georgia, features regional cuisine with a fresh difference.

Host: Ham Schwartz
Rooms: 5 (PB) $70
Continental Breakfast
Credit Cards: A, B
Notes: 2, 4, 5, 7, 8, 9, 10, 11, 12

SAVANNAH

Joan's on Jones
Bed and Breakfast

17 West Jones Street, 31401
(912) 234-3863

In the heart of the historic district, two charming bed and breakfast suites in the garden level of this three-story Victorian private home. Each suite has a private entry, off-street parking, bedroom, sitting room, kitchen, bath, private phone, and cable TV. Note the original

6 Pets welcome; 8 Children welcome; 9 Social drinking allowed; 10 Tennis available; 11 Swimming available; 12 Golf available; 13 Skiing available; 14 May be booked through travel agents.

heart-pine floors, period furnishings, and Savannah grey brick walls. Innkeepers Joan and Gary Levy, former restaurateurs, live upstairs and invite guests for a tour of their home if staying two nights or more.

Host: Joan Levy
Rooms: 2 suites (PB) $85-95
Continental Breakfast
Credit Cards: None
Notes: 2, 5, 6 (limited), 8, 9

SENOIA

The Veranda

252 Seavy Street, P. O. Box 177, 30276-0177
(404) 599-3905; FAX (404) 599-0806

Beautifully restored spacious Victorian rooms in a 1907 hotel on the National Register of Historic Places. Just 30 miles south of Atlanta airport. Freshly prepared southern gourmet meals by reservation. Unusual gift shop featuring kaleidoscopes. Memorabilia and 1930 Wurlitzer player piano pipe organ. One room has a whirlpool bath; all have private baths and air conditioning.

Hosts: Jan and Bobby Boal
Rooms: 9 (PB) $80-100
Full Breakfast
Credit Cards: A, B, C
Notes: 2, 3*, 4, 5, 8*, 10*, 12*, 14 (*with advance inquiry)

THOMSON

1810 West Inn

254 North Seymour Drive NW, 30824
(706) 595-3156

1810 West Inn is a rambling Piedmont Plainstyle restored farmhouse and accompanying renovated houses with 19th century ambience and 20th century conveniences. Just off I-20, the inn is in the historic classic south, near Augusta. Relax among antique furnishings, an inviting country kitchen and large screened veranda overlooking 12 landscaped acres.

Host: Virginia White
Rooms: 10 (PB) $45-65
Continental Breakfast
Credit Cards: A, B, C
Notes: 2, 9, 10, 11, 12, 14

VILLA RICA

Twin Oaks Bed and Breakfast Farm Vacation

Atlanta Hospitality Bed and Breakfast Service
2472 Lauderdale Drive, 30345
(404) 493-1930

This country bed and breakfast is situated on a 23-acre farm just 30 minutes from Atlanta. Featuring a completely private guest cottage separate from the main house, it has 12-foot ceilings and 10 and one-half foot windows across the front for viewing pleasure. Decorated in Victorian, the cottage includes a sitting area, sunroom, kitchen, and bathroom. Other amenities include several domestic animals, walking trails, swimming pool, and horseback riding. Continental breakfast served. $85.

Hawaii

Halfway to Hana House

P. O. Box 675, 96708
(808) 572-1176

A 15-minute drive from Paia town on the Hana road, this cozy, private studio has a spectacular location with a 180 degree wraparound ocean view. The studio has a double bed, mini-kitchen, bath and breakfast patio shaded by a bamboo grove that looks through a lush green valley to the ocean. Freshwater pools and waterfalls are one-half mile away. The host, who has lived on Maui for 24 years, delights in graceful touches like chocolate covered macadamia nuts on the pillow, dazzling arrangements of tropical fruit at breakfast and homemade Hawaiian coconut pudding. She is helpful in planning adventure trips, and may invite guests to go snorkeling on Sunday morning.

Host: Gail Pickholz
Rooms: 1 (PB) $65
Continental Breakfast
Credit Cards: None
Notes: 5, 9, 11, 12, 14

HAWAII—CAPTAIN COOK

Bed & Breakfast Hawaii H35

P. O. Box 449, Kapaa, 96746
(808) 822-7771

This bed and breakfast home is situated above the little town of Captain Cook. The accommodations offered are three bedrooms that share a bath. The home is an expanse of emerald lawn with many palms and exotic fruit trees. Guests are welcome to use the pool or watch TV. The hosts are helpful and interesting. $60.

HAWAII—HILO

Bed & Breakfast Hawaii H1

P. O. Box 449, Kapaa, 96746
(808) 822-7771

A large Hawaiian type house about two miles north of Hilo overlooking Hilo Bay, this home has a yard so private that if guests decide to take a swim in the pool, only the birds will know. There are two bedrooms available to guests, each with a pair of twin beds, one that converts to a king-size bed, if desired. Not only is the yard beautifully landscaped around the pool, a lovely mile walk past the surfing beach meanders through a tropical forest. $55.

Bed & Breakfast Hawaii H1A

P. O. Box 449, Kapaa, 96746
(808) 822-7771

This host home is situated right next door to host home H1, and guests are more than welcome to use the pool. The home is perched on the cliffs overlooking Hilo Bay and the Big Island's premier surfing spot. The house is small, and guests can choose a room with a private entrance and queen-size bed or a room with two twin beds. The bathroom between the two rooms is shared. Breakfast is served on the outdoor patio where guests can enjoy watching the sunrise, surfers, and ships. $45-55.

6 Pets welcome; 8 Children welcome; 9 Social drinking allowed; 10 Tennis available; 11 Swimming available; 12 Golf available; 13 Skiing available; 14 May be booked through travel agents.

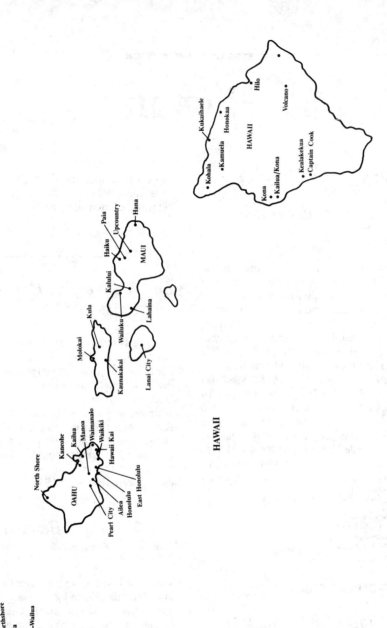

HAWAII

KAUAI: Hanalei, Princeville, Kilauea, Anahola, Northshore, Kapaa, Wailua, Poipu, Koloa, Kalaheo

OAHU: North Shore, Kaneohe, Kailua, Manoa, Waimanalo, Waikiki, Hawaii Kai, Pearl City, Aiea, Honolulu, East Honolulu

Molokai: Kaunakakai, Kula

MAUI: Haiku, Upcountry, Paia, Hana, Kahului, Wailuku, Lahaina

Lanai City

HAWAII: Kukuihaele, Hilo, Kohala, Kamuela, Honokaa, Volcano, Kealakekua, Kailua/Kona, Captain Cook, Kona

Bed & Breakfast Hawaii H2

P. O. Box 449, Kapaa, 96746
(808) 822-7771

Hale Paliku, which means "house against the cliff," is the name of this home originally built in the 1930s. Situated three blocks from downtown Hilo, guests share the TV, tape deck, microwave, and refrigerator. Two rooms with shared bath are available, one with ocean view and private balcony. Each room has down pillows, comforters, shuttered windows, and a table for two. Hosts live downstairs. $55-65.

Bed & Breakfast Hawaii H3

P. O. Box 449, Kapaa, 96746
(808) 822-7771

Relax on a grand scale in this large, modern, Hawaiian-style home surrounded by nearly four acres of parklike setting on an oceanfront bluff. With a spectacular view of Wailea Bay, this is the perfect spot for a peaceful haven. A tennis court and a municipal beach park are within walking distance, and the world-famous Akaka Falls is a short drive away. A spacious one-bedroom apartment includes bedroom, private bath, fully equipped kitchenette, and livingroom with cable TV, radio, piano, and day beds. Children over eight welcome. $75.

Bed & Breakfast Hawaii H3A

P. O. Box 449, Kapaa, 96746
(808) 822-7771

A charming little beachfront cottage surrounded by swaying coconut palms awaits guests. There is a nice beach and boat launch for guests to explore in a quiet, private setting. Guests can enjoy sitting out on the big lanai with ocean view or sitting on the rocks dangling their toes in the water while watching fishermen and sailboats. Two guest rooms with private bath. Resident dog. Two-night minimum stay. $75.

Bed & Breakfast Hawaii H4C

P. O. Box 449, Kapaa, 96746
(808) 822-7771

This bed and breakfast home is just three miles south of Hilo, near the zoo and equestrian center, on nine acres of parklike property. The home is in a secluded, private setting. Guests have a separate entrance to the cottage, which has light cooking facilities and a small glass fireplace. Breakfast supplies are provided. Three-night minimum stay. $75.

Bed & Breakfast Hawaii H5

P. O. Box 449, Kapaa, 96746
(808) 822-7771

A charming bed and breakfast host home that offers guests a view of Hilo Bay and Hilo town just ten minutes from the airport and 10 minutes to Richardson Beach. Guests are offered a choice of two rooms, both of which have private baths and ocean views. Breakfast is served in the breakfast nook or dining room, which is tastefully decorated with antiques. Children over eight are welcome. $65.

Bed & Breakfast Hawaii H7

P. O. Box 449, Kapaa, 96746
(808) 822-7771

Right on a bluff overlooking the ocean, the home offers an oceanfront pool with Jacuzzi and a view of a popular surfing beach. Large, covered, comfortably furnished decks face the ocean where you can watch the whales and cruise ships. This modern home is just two miles from downtown Hilo but quiet and private. Three guest rooms with private baths are separated by a family room with TV, VCR, and a private entrance to the pool. The master suite is sometimes available. Minimum stay is three nights. $95.

NOTES: Credit cards accepted: A Master Card; B Visa; C American Express; D Discover Card; E Diner's Club; F Other; 2 Personal Checks accepted; 3 Lunch available; 4 Dinner available; 5 Open all year; 6 Pets welcome; 8 Children welcome; 9 Social drinking allowed; 10 Tennis available; 11 Swimming available; 12 Golf available; 13 Skiing available; 14 May be booked through travel agents.

Bed & Breakfast Hawaii H8

P. O. Box 449, Kapaa, 96746
(808) 822-7771

Paradise Place is the name of this accommodation on a rural acre just one-half mile from the ocean in Keaau. Accommodations are downstairs with a private entrance and consist of a two-room suite with a double bed in the bedroom, sofa sleeper in the livingroom, and private bath with a shower. This area also has a TV with VCR, microwave, small refrigerator, and table where host puts all the fixings for a leisurely breakfast served on a quiet landscaped patio. This area is a central location for a guest to explore the fresh lava flows and Volcano National Park. The seventh night is free. $50-55.

Bed & Breakfast Hawaii H33

P. O. Box 449, Kapaa, 96746
(808) 822-7771

A rain forest retreat just south of Hilo is waiting next to an orchid nursery. The hostess tends the orchids and boards horses on her property as well as accommodates bed and breakfast guests. A private studio complete with a king-size bed, private bath, and light cooking appliances (refrigerator, hot plate, and toaster oven). Guests are welcome to use the hot tub. This retreat is only thirty minutes away from Hilo and Volcano National Park. $45-60.

Bed & Breakfast Hawaii H42

P. O. Box 449, Kapaa, 96746
(808) 822-7771

Nestled in a tropical area in Pahoa, two studios can accommodate handicapped guests. Premises have a swimming pool, abundant fruit trees, flowers, and wild turkeys, pigs, and squabbling pigeons. The ranch unit has queen-size bed, private bath, air conditioning, TV, radio, private patio, and a refriger-

ator stocked with goodies. Hosts are former hoteliers on the main island and aim to please. Minimum stay is two nights. $65.

Bed & Breakfast Hawaii H45

P. O. Box 449, Kapaa, 96746
(808) 822-7771

Just between Hilo and Volcano, and twenty minutes from each. Guests are invited to stay with a charming hostess originally from England. An attractive two-story home with a portico and nicely landscaped grounds set in the rural area of Pahoa offers accommodations with twin beds and a private bath. Delicious breakfast is served in the dining room. Minimum stay is two nights. $50.

Bed & Breakfast Hawaii H63

P. O. Box 449, Kapaa, 96746
(808) 822-7771

A detached studio apartment has a private bath and kitchenette. Hosts own an eight acre lot at 1,500-foot elevation above and three miles from Hawi. The view of the ocean is unobstructed, and access to the Alenuihaha Channel to Halaekala on Maui. The main house and the guest house are situated on the property. The guest house is furnished with a sofa bed and a double bed, color TV, and radio. Sliding glass doors overlook the view of the ocean. The kitchen is fully equipped for preparing all meals, and breakfast fixings are stocked in the refrigerator. Another studio attached to the main house has a separate entrance and private bath. $50-75.

Bed and Breakfast Honolulu (Statewide) KEGLS

3242 Kaohinani Drive, Honolulu, 96817
(808) 595-7533; (800) 288-4666
FAX (808) 595-2030

NOTES: Credit cards accepted: A Master Card; B Visa; C American Express; D Discover Card; E Diner's Club; F Other; 2 Personal Checks accepted; 3 Lunch available; 4 Dinner available; 5 Open all year;

A five-minute walk to the center of Hilo, this home offers two guest rooms that share a bath. Livingroom for guests has TV, microwave, refrigerator, and ocean-mountain view. Breakfast is served on an enclosed porch. Children over 12. From $45.

Bed and Breakfast Honolulu (Statewide) MILLS

3242 Kaohinani Drive, Honolulu, 96817
(808) 595-7533; (800) 288-4666
FAX (808) 595-2030

Large cedar home with four guest rooms (doubles and kings) just outside Hilo is within walking distance to shops and cafes. The king room has a private bath. All guest rooms have private lanais to enjoy a tropical view and the stream that runs through the half-acre tropical setting. Common room for guests has a TV, fireplace, and piano. Hearty breakfast served. Children over 11. From $40.

Bed and Breakfast Honolulu (Statewide) MERCE

3242 Kaohinani Drive, Honolulu, 96817
(808) 595-7533; (800) 288-4666
FAX (808) 595-2030

Two guest rooms with private baths in a pretty country setting are five minutes outside Keaau and a twenty-minute drive to Hilo. Guests are welcome to use the spacious livingroom and enjoy the lovely views. Full breakfast is served. No small children. Hosts speak French and some Italian. From $40.

Bed and Breakfast Honolulu (Statewide) LANNA

3242 Kaohinani Drive, Honolulu, 96817
(808) 595-7533; (800) 288-4666
FAX (808) 595-2030

Two miles out of Hilo on a cliff overlooking Hilo Bay, this Hawaiian-type home has a private yard with a lovely pool. Two bedrooms are available. A full bath and a half bath are reserved for guests. The yard is beautifully landscaped, and there's also a charming tea house on the grounds. From $55.

Bed and Breakfast Honolulu (Statewide) SMALM

3242 Kaohinani Drive, Honolulu, 96817
(808) 585-7533; (800) 288-4666
FAX (808) 595-2030

This house, with a stone fireplace and screened Japanese tea room, was once the home of a Japanese ambassador. Across the street from the ocean. $60.

HAWAII—HONOKAA

Bed & Breakfast Hawaii H11

P. O. Box 449, Kapaa, 96746
(808) 822-7771

The hostess of this large plantation estate enjoys having guests share its beauty and tranquility. With ocean views on three sides, the estate is built on an ocean point at the 1,200-foot level just outside of Honokaa. The main house offers three guest accommodations; a large suite with fireplace, an adjoining bedroom, private lanai, and private bath; a queen room with private bath, 12-foot ceilings, and tongue-and-groove woodwork. There are also two cottages on the property. Lighted tennis courts, gazebo, macadamia orchard, fruit trees, and lush tropical flowers throughout the estate. $75-200.

HAWAII—KAILUA-KONA

Bed & Breakfast Hawaii H10

P. O. Box 449, Kapaa, 96746
(808) 822-7771

6 Pets welcome; 8 Children welcome; 9 Social drinking allowed; 10 Tennis available; 11 Swimming available; 12 Golf available; 13 Skiing available; 14 May be booked through travel agents.

These warm-hearted hosts have a spacious home surrounded by tropical foliage about a five-minute drive from the ocean. The downstairs accommodation includes a private lanai with an ocean view and a separate entrance through glass doors to the bedroom. The room is large and has a mini-refrigerator, a microwave oven, TV, and phone. A tasty continental breakfast is served. Two-night minimum stay. $65.

Bed & Breakfast Hawaii H23

P. O. Box 449, Kapaa, 96746
(808) 822-7771

Guests are invited to share the magnificent panoramic view from this hillside home. Bed and breakfast guests can choose between the Hula Room, with queen-size bed and large, private lanai, and the Garden Room, with two twin beds. Both have TV, microwave, and small refrigerator. $50-55.

Bed & Breakfast Hawaii H26

P. O. Box 449, Kapaa, 96746
(808) 822-7771

Escape to the peaceful hillside of Hualalai Mountain overlooking the Kona coast. The interior of this lovely 2,500-square-foot home is meticulously furnished. The guest quarters are on the first level and have two bedrooms, with one bath and a kitchen and living area. There is a large deck for guests' exclusive use. Breakfast fixings are provided. Two-night minimum stay. $65.

Bed & Breakfast Hawaii H29

P. O. Box 449, Kapaa, 96746
(808) 822-7771

Guests can stay at this peaceful bed and breakfast just two miles from the middle of Kailua-Kona town and the ocean. A large covered lanai offers ocean views and comfortable seating for breakfast. The accom-modation is furnished with twin beds, which can convert to a king-size bed, and a private bath. The hosts are recently retired and enjoy serving breakfast and meeting new people. $40-55.

Bed & Breakfast Hawaii H32A

P. O. Box 449, Kapaa, 96746
(808) 822-7771

Right on the beach in Kona is this luxurious and comfortable oceanfront home. Two rooms are available; one is oceanfront with a queen-size bed, and the other is ocean, view with a queen-size bed. Both have full private baths and a color TV. Hostess loves to play tennis and meet new people. $70-90.

Bed & Breakfast Hawaii H34

P. O. Box 449, Kapaa, 96746
(808) 822-7771

Situated just 12 minutes from the airport and 15 minutes from Kailua Village in the cool Kaloko Mauka area is this beautiful new home on five acres. It offers an attractive separate apartment at garden level with two bedrooms, bath, and sitting room with TV and limited cooking facilities. Guests may choose to breakfast with their hosts or on their own. After a busy day of sports, shopping, or sightseeing, sit on the lanai high above the Kona coast and enjoy the magnificent sunset. Resident dog, cats, and llamas. Two-night minimum stay. $75.

Bed & Breakfast Hawaii H46

P. O. Box 449, Kapaa, 96746
(808) 822-7771

Elegant, brand new, with an ocean view. Guests will enjoy this accommodation in Kona separate from the main house. One bedroom with a queen bed and full bathroom, plus a sitting area with TV, is decorated in off-white with rose-colored accents. There is also a dining area with a refrigerator and wet bar. Private deck. Two-night minimum stay. $75.

Bed & Breakfast Hawaii H50

P. O. Box 449, Kapaa, 96746
(808) 822-7771

This bed and breakfast has a private entrance on the lower level of this beautiful, brand-new, two-story Art Deco home. Guests have a choice of two large bedrooms, with access to the gardens that offer a beautiful ocean view. A special aloha breakfast is served in the family room that is furnished with a piano, pool, and Ping-Pong tables, and big-screen TV. A great location for two couples traveling together. $50-80.

Bed & Breakfast Hawaii H59

P. O. Box 449, Kapaa, 96746
(808) 822-7771

Guests can experience one of the many breathtaking sunsets from this bed and breakfast overlooking the coastline just above Kona Village. Situated on a three-acre estate, the accommodations for guests are private and self-contained. A separate apartment features one bedroom with a queen-size bed, livingroom with a fold-out sofa, private bath, kitchen, TV, private entrance, and lanai with a barbecue. A queen-size futon is also available. The building is designed like a dome with open beam ceilings. $65-85.

Bed and Breakfast Honolulu (Statewide) FREIS

242 Kaohinani Drive, Honolulu, 96817
(808) 595-7533; (800) 288-4666
FAX (808) 595-2030

Beautiful new two-story home overlooking the ocean with three large guest rooms (queen, king and twin beds). King room has a private bath; queen and twin rooms share a bath. Special Aloha breakfast is served in the family room, which is furnished with a piano, pool table, Ping Pong, big screen TV, wet bar, and refrigerator for drinks or snacks. Great for couples traveling together. No children. From $50.

Kailua Plantation House

75-5948 Alii Drive, Kailua-Kona, 96740
(800) 329-3727

Kailua Plantation House is a tropical haven for travelers seeking luxurious accommodations with the coziness of an oceanfront bed and breakfast inn. Each individually decorated suite in this lovely mansion boasts a private lanai. Complete with its own outdoor dipping pool and spa, both overlooking the Pacific Ocean, Kailua Plantation House is an elegant lodging choice for island guests. Situated less than a mile from the town of Kona, the inn is a short drive or walk from fine restaurants, shops, snorkeling, and diving establishments. The innkeeper can provide arrangements for wedding ceremonies.

Host: Rosanna V. Singarella
Rooms: 5 (PB) $120-175
Continental Plus Breakfast
Credit Cards: A, B, C
Notes: 2, 5, 10, 11, 12

HAWAII—KAMUELA

Bed & Breakfast Hawaii H27A

P. O. Box 449, Kapaa, 96746
(808) 822-7771

The host and hostess have a 4,000-square-foot home and have used about 800 square feet of it for a completely separate apartment for guests. Guest quarters include a bedroom, private bath, and livingroom. There is

6 Pets welcome; 8 Children welcome; 9 Social drinking allowed; 10 Tennis available; 11 Swimming available; 12 Golf available; 13 Skiing available; 14 May be booked through travel agents.

also a sink and small refrigerator. The home borders a stream and has a 360-degree view of the Kohala Mountains, Pacific Ocean, and the famous Mauna Kea and Mauna Loa. Three-night minimum stay. $80-90.

Bed & Breakfast Hawaii H41

P. O. Box 449, Kapaa, 96746
(808) 822-7771

In the historic area of North Kohala just about seven miles from lush Pololu Valley and the rugged coastline of beautiful Hawaii, guests can enjoy the rural atmosphere and cooler climate. The home is set back from the road and is a modified A-frame. Accommodations include a self-contained studio under the main house with a separate entrance, limited kitchenette, private bath, and double bed. Two-night minimum stay. $50.

Bed & Breakfast Hawaii H57

P. O. Box 449, Kapaa, 96746
(808) 822-7771

This newly built guest house with 1,900 square feet is situated at the top of Knob Hill, and within walking distance to Kamuela. It offers beautiful views of twenty-five miles of coastline, Mauna Kea and Mauna Loa, and the accommodations border Parker Ranch. Two bedrooms, with queen and king beds, full bathroom, 300-square-foot deck, color TV, library, washer/dryer. Three night minimum stay. $125.

Bed and Breakfast Honolulu (Statewide) BATEG

3242 Kaohinani Drive, Honolulu, 96817
(808) 595-7533; (800) 288-4666
FAX (808) 595-2030

Parker Ranch country. This Hawaiian missionary-style home is by a quiet, meandering stream. Completely private guest quar-

ters contain bedroom, livingroom, light cooking facilities, and a full bath. Guests have a 360-degree view of famous Mauna Kea and Mauna Loa mountains and the blue Pacific. Hosts are widely traveled. He is a sailing enthusiast, and she spins, weaves, and does basketweaving. From $65.

Bed and Breakfast Honolulu (Statewide) HORNJ

3242 Kaohinani Drive, Honolulu, 96817
(808) 795-7533; (800) 288-4646
FAX (808) 595-2030

This renovated 50-year old home has four guests rooms, and sits on more than an acre of tropical gardens. Enjoy sunning at the pool or the ocean view from the gazebo. $50.

HAWAII—KEALAKEKUA

Bed & Breakfast Hawaii H28A

P. O. Box 449, Kapaa, 96746
(808) 822-7771

This bed and breakfast home is about thirty minutes from the airport at a 1,300-foot elevation overlooking the Pacific Ocean, Kailua-Kona, Kailua Bay, and the western slopes of Hualalai. The garden-level accommodations are large and offer a suite with two bedrooms, each with a queen-size bed, a livingroom with cable TV, full bathroom, and a large dressing table. The unit has a separate lanai and entrance. Breakfast is served upstairs on the host's lanai, which also provides beautiful views of the ocean and towns below. Minimum stay is two nights. $50-55.

Bed & Breakfast Hawaii H38

P. O. Box 449, Kapaa, 96746
(808) 822-7771

This is an unusual and beautifully designed home with hardwood floors, decks, and lots of windows with screens. This two-story home is just 200 yards from Napoopoo Bay, a great area for swimming and snorkeling. Downstairs, two separate bedrooms with private baths and queen-size beds share a sitting room with a covered deck that views the ocean. $75.

Bed & Breakfast Hawaii H52

P. O. Box 449, Kapaa, 96746
(808) 822-7771

This privately owned Hawaiian compound, which is fully contained on eight acres of lush tropical fruit trees, has a large rambling ranch house with an annex for guests. One room offers a queen-size bed, and the other offers two twin beds. A bathroom situated between the two rooms is shared. Cottages for families are also available. The grounds feature outdoor barbecue pit, tropical grass huts for picnics, sand volleyball court, tennis courts and a large pool. Host's lanai, where breakfast is served, has a spectacular view of the ocean. Two-night minimum stay. $65-100.

HAWAII—KOHALA

Bed and Breakfast Honolulu (Statewide) AROSP

3242 Kaohinani Drive, Honolulu, 96817
(808) 795-7533; (800) 288-4666
FAX (808) 595-2030

On the north shore of the big island, this large, landscaped old plantations manager's home has two guest rooms, one with a private entrance and shared bath. $50.

HAWAII—KONA

Bed and Breakfast Honolulu (Statewide) BOONW

3242 Kaohinani Drive, Honolulu, 96817
(808) 595-7533; (800) 288-4666
FAX (808) 595-2030

This home is on an expanse of emerald lawn with palms and exotic fruit trees. It is fenced along the road with head-high poinsettias and is surrounded by a wall of banana trees among groves of coffee and macadamias. Take a swim in the pool, play tennis nearby, or go to one of the nearby beaches. Three rooms share a bath. Generous continental breakfast includes homemade breads. Enjoy bicycling, Ping-Pong, or hiking with the hosts. Resident dog. From $55.

Bed and Breakfast Honolulu (Statewide) CANNT

3242 Kaohinani Drive, Honolulu, 96817
(808) 795-7533; (800) 288-4666
FAX (808) 595-2030

This is a complete studio on the Kona coast. Enjoy a private view of the blue Pacific from the lanai. $60.

Bed and Breakfast Honolulu (Statewide) DEFAC

3242 Kaohinani Drive, Honolulu, 96817
(808) 595-7533; (800) 288-4666
FAX (808) 595-2030

This Kona-style home is on the slopes above the City of Refuge. King bed, bath, and refrigerator for snacks are in the separate guest quarters on the ground level. Breakfast is served upstairs on the 50-foot lanai with a panoramic view of the ocean. Enjoy the cool, quiet, private half-acre of gardens. From $60.

6 Pets welcome; 8 Children welcome; 9 Social drinking allowed; 10 Tennis available; 11 Swimming available; 12 Golf available; 13 Skiing available; 14 May be booked through travel agents.

Bed and Breakfast Honolulu (Statewide) MCDAJ

3242 Kaohinani Drive, Honolulu, 96817
(808) 795-7533; (800) 288-4666
FAX (808) 595-2030

Accommodations include a main house and apartment, with a separate entrance. All rooms have private baths. $45.

Bed and Breakfast Honolulu (Statewide) OBERJ

3242 Kaohinani Drive, Honolulu, 96817
(808) 795-7533; (800) 288-4666
FAX (808) 595-2030

Right at the Captain Cook monument is a brand-new accommodation with one bedroom and adjacent sitting room. Two night stay minimum. $65.

Bed and Breakfast Honolulu (Statewide) RITZA

3242 Kaohinani Drive, Honolulu, 96817
(808) 595-7533; (800) 288-4666
FAX (808) 595-2030

This lovely home is situated on the slopes above the City of Refuge in Hanaunau. View of the ocean from the dining lanai and the hot tub. Hosts offer four rooms, two on the garden level with TV, VCR, refrigerator, microwave, and private bath and entrance. The room on the main level has a queen bed and shares a bath with the loft room. Rooms decorated with local art. From $55.

Bed and Breakfast Honolulu (Statewide) ROSEJ

3242 Kaohinani Drive, Honolulu, 96817
(808) 795-7533; (800) 288-4666
FAX (808) 595-2030

In the Captain Cook area is this bed and breakfast with a kitchen stocked with items for a hearty continental breakfast for guests to enjoy at their leisure. Near shopping and restaurants. $50.

Bed and Breakfast Honolulu (Statewide) TOYJ

3242 Kaohinani Drive, Honolulu, 96817
(808) 795-7533; (800) 288-4666
FAX (808) 595-2030

This completely private apartment has a sweeping view of Kona's sunsets. The breakfast alcove has a toaster oven, refrigerator and microwave oven. Kona coffee, tropical fruit and local specialties are furnished. $60.

HAWAII—KUKUIHAELE

Bed and Breakfast Honolulu (Statewide) HUNTK

3242 Kaohinani Drive, Honolulu, 96817
(808) 595-7533; (800) 288-4666
FAX (808) 595-2030

Privacy! An unhosted home with a fantastic view in a small village above Waipio Valley. Walk 15 minutes to Waipio lookout, take a hiking adventure in the valley, or go horseback riding and come home to a hot tub. The home includes a livingroom with queen bed, futon upstairs, a fireplace, and kitchen. Watch the whales and the sunset. Listen to the year-round stream. Very romantic! Large screened porch. From $60.

HAWAII—VOLCANO

Bed & Breakfast Hawaii H51

P. O. Box 449, Kapaa, 96746
(808) 822-7771

NOTES: Credit cards accepted: A Master Card; B Visa; C American Express; D Discover Card; E Diner's Club; F Other; 2 Personal Checks accepted; 3 Lunch available; 4 Dinner available; 5 Open all year;

Conveniently situated just two miles from Volcanoes National Park at 3,500-foot elevation. Helpful hosts offer a king-size bedroom with its own entrance and private bath. A futon can be put down for a third person. Great breakfasts are served every morning to get guests off to a good start for exploring the park. $55.

Bed & Breakfast Hawaii H51A

P. O. Box 449, Kapaa, 96746
(808) 822-7771

Also available in this lodging are three cottages. Guests check in with hosts and receive keys. The refrigerator and kitchen are stocked with breakfast foods more than ample for a week's stay. Choose from one of three cottages: The Dome, Grand Cedar, or Cedar One. All are plush and beautifully furnished with fireplaces, TV with VCR, and stereos. $85-125.

Bed and Breakfast Honolulu (Statewide) TUTTM

3242 Kaohinani Drive, Honolulu, 96817
(808) 795-7533; (800) 288-4666
FAX (808) 595-2030

At Volcano Village is this complete three-bedroom cottage, with well-equipped kitchen, large livingroom, covered deck and hibachi. Hiking, picnics and gold nearby. $55.

Bed and Breakfast Honolulu (Statewide) PEDES 1

3242 Kaohinani Drive, Honolulu, 96817
(808) 795-7533; (800) 288-4666
FAX (808) 595-2030

Situated just one mile from Volcano National Park, this bed and breakfast is surrounded by fruit trees and many native trees. Rooms feature a lovely view of this natural setting. $56.

Kilauea Lodge

P. O. Box 116, 96785
(808) 967-7366; FAX (808) 967-7367

Charming mountain lodge situated one mile from Volcanoes National Park. Full service dining room with excellent wine list. Full breakfast readies guests for an active day of hiking and viewing the wonders of Pele, the volcano goddess. All private baths. Twelve rooms, six rooms with fireplace. Common area.

Rooms: 12 (PB) $85-125
Full Breakfast
Credit Cards: A, B
Notes: 2, 4, 5, 8, 9, 12

Kilauea Lodge

HAWAII—VOLCANO VILLAGE

Chalet Kilauea at Volcano

P. O. Box 998, 96785
(808) 967-7786; (800) 937-7786

A bed and breakfast inn at its best. Choose from unique theme rooms, the Treehouse Suite, and deluxe vacation homes. Relax by the fireplace, peruse the library, and enjoy the Jacuzzi. Tempt your appetite with a two-course, full gourmet breakfast and afternoon tea. Chalet Kilauea offers amenities not found at other bed and breakfasts. The inn is situated less than two miles from Hawaii Volcanoes National Park, a wonder in itself!

Hosts: Lisha and Brian Crawford
Rooms: 9 (5 PB; 3 SB) $75-145
Full Breakfast
Credit Cards: A, B, D
Notes: 2, 5, 8, 9, 12, 14

6 Pets welcome; 8 Children welcome; 9 Social drinking allowed; 10 Tennis available; 11 Swimming available; 12 Golf available; 13 Skiing available; 14 May be booked through travel agents.

HAWAII—WAIPIO

Bed & Breakfast Hawaii H22

P. O. Box 449, Kapaa, 96746
(808) 822-7771

Step back in time and experience the gracious hospitality of a 1938 sugar plantation home, renovated to preserve its character. Each bedroom is individually decorated with antique furniture, Chinese rugs, and exquisite hand-painted silk drapes. Breakfast includes pure Kona coffee and fine Stash teas. $85.

KAUAI—ANAHOLA

Bed & Breakfast Hawaii K67

P. O. Box 449, Kapaa, 96746
(808) 822-7771

Wake up in beautiful tropical surroundings at Anahola Beach abundant with flowers, fresh fruit, singing birds, and sounds of the ocean. Enjoy beautiful views and beach atmosphere in this bright studio with private yard and entrance, full bath, and breakfast facilities. The home is situated across the street from a beach great for swimming, snorkeling, boogie boarding, and wind surfing. Convenient to all Kauai attractions. Tropical continental breakfast fixings provided. Two-night minimum stay. $75.

Bed and Breakfast Honolulu (Statewide) SKAGJ

3242 Kaohinani Drive, Honolulu, 96817
(808) 595-7533; (800) 288-4666
FAX (808) 595-2030

On the beach for a peaceful vacation or a romantic honeymoon! Private studio with TV, laundry facilities, and ready for light cooking. Continental breakfast fixings are provided. Centrally situated for sightseeing

and touring. The beach is reef-protected for swimming. Sun on the white sands, sit in the private yard and enjoy the tropical birds, flowers, trees, and the mountain view, or take a walk in the hills and valleys behind the home. Adults preferred. From $70.

KAUAI—HANALEI

Bed & Breakfast Hawaii K13

P. O. Box 449, Kapaa, 96746
(808) 822-7771

The hosts' brand new and beautiful house is built on one and one-half acres. The community offers a 45-hole golf course, clubhouse, athletic club, tennis, swimming, and driving range just minutes away. Breakfast is served in the dining room or on the decks overlooking the Pacific. All rooms have private entrances, ceiling fans, refrigerators, and color TVs. Choose from three rooms—one a honeymoon suite with whirlpool tub, one a penthouse with whirlpool and balcony. Two-night minimum stay. $85-190.

Bed & Breakfast Hawaii K21

P. O. Box 449, Kapaa, 96746
(808) 822-7771

This hostess offers to share her beach house right on Anini Beach with visitors. She is a world traveler and has a natural affinity for travelers. Her home is halfway between Kilauea and Hanalei, and the room offered has a double bed, shared bath. There is large covered porch for relaxing and viewing the sunsets of the north shore. Two-night minimum stay. $40.

Bed & Breakfast Hawaii K32

P. O. Box 449, Kapaa, 96746
(808) 822-7771

This accommodation is a little backwards: the hosts live in the apartment above the garage while the guests stay in the main house. Just steps from the beach, a beautiful two-mile crescent-shaped bay surrounded by lush mountains and waterfalls. Two bedrooms share one and one-half baths, plus an outdoor shower for after the beach. The livingroom has open beam ceilings, wood floors, rattan furniture, cable TV, and a complete library. Five-night minimum stay. $100.

Bed & Breakfast Hawaii K45

P. O. Box 449, Kapaa, 96746
(808) 822-7771

This bed and breakfast accommodation is situated 100 yards from the gorgeous Hanalei Bay. Perfect for hiking, watersports, sightseeing, golf, sunbathing, or just long walks in a quaint, unpretentious town. Sunsets from the lanai are breathtaking. A two-story home with 1,000 square feet of deck surrounding the second floor and providing a partial ocean view and a mountain view of waterfalls. A continental breakfast of fresh island fruit, juice, and breads is served on the second-story lanai. $55-75.

Bed & Breakfast Hawaii K46

P. O. Box 449, Kapaa, 96746
(808) 822-7771

This spacious new country home and guest quarters offer comfort and a spectacular view of the Hanalei Valley. Enjoy the sunsets, the mountain waterfalls, and the peace of this special location. The guest bedroom has a king bed, a microwave oven, sink, refrigerator, and private bath. On five and one-half acres. Three-night minimum stay. $70.

Bed and Breakfast Honolulu (Statewide) BARNC

3242 Kaohinani Drive, Honolulu, 96817
(808) 595-7533; (800) 288-4666
FAX (808) 595-2030

This lovely home has three units. The guest room with private bath and queen bed; a downstairs one-bedroom apartment with light cooking facilities, TV, private patio, and garden with ocean view; and the third-floor unit that sleeps four. View Hanalei Bay. Sunset and waterfall views are dramatic through the cathedral windows. Livingroom TV is available for guests. The beach is 100 yards away. Bright and airy with pine and wicker. Children over 12 welcome. Three-night minimum stay. From $70.

KAUAI—KALAHEO

Bed & Breakfast Hawaii K19

P. O. Box 449, Kapaa, 96746
(808) 822-7771

Three bedrooms open onto a swimming pool flanked by flowering hibiscus, gardenias, and bougainvillaeas in this home nestled in the hills of South Kauai. Out back, a second-story wooden porch overlooks sugar cane fields, jungle, and the National Botanical Gardens. It is only a 7- to 20-minute drive to beaches. All rooms have private baths, and one room is handicapped accessible. The hostess is proud of her breakfast that includes homemade bread and hot muffins, Hawaiian fruits, and Hawaiian coffee. $55-75, seasonal.

Bed and Breakfast Hawaii K84

P. O. Box 449, Kapaa, 96746
(808) 822-7771

A serene landscape in Lawai is the setting for this separate one-room cottage set apart from the main house. Inside is a separate little kitchenette and private bath. The livingroom features a brand-new Serta queen size sofa-bed and a full-size futon. Hostess is an activities director, so she can give great sight seeing tips. $65-75.

6 Pets welcome; 8 Children welcome; 9 Social drinking allowed; 10 Tennis available; 11 Swimming available; 12 Golf available; 13 Skiing available; 14 May be booked through travel agents.

Bed and Breakfast Hawaii K85

P. O. Box 449, Kapaa, 96746
(808) 822-7771

Mango Hills Cottage is situated on two and
one-half acres in Kalaheo overlooking the
ocean and many acres of coffee fields. The
hostess is an interior designer, and her
attention to details inside the cottage is
apparent. The livingroom has a pull-out
queen-size sofa bed, cable TV, and an
adjoining full kitchen with counter seating.
The bedroom has a mountain view and a
queen-size bed with adjoining bath. Hosts
invite guests to swim in their pool or relax
in a hammock under flowering trees.
Minimum stay is three nights. $65.

Classic Vacation Cottages

2687 Onu Place, P. O. Box 901, Kalaheo, 96741
(808)332-9201

Minutes away from major attractions in the
countryside of Kalaheo on the garden
island of Kauai are delightful, self-contained cottages. These unique units feature
antique stained-glass leaded windows and
all the comforts of home. Fully furnished,
complete kitchens, TVs, and daily linen
service. Ten minutes by car to the golden
beaches of the sunny south shore of Poipu.
Five minutes to Kukuiolono Golf Course.

Hosts: Richard and Wynnis Grow
Cottages: 4 (PB) $55-65
Continental Breakfast
Credit Cards: None
Notes: 2, 5, 8, 9, 10, 11, 12, 14

KAUAI—KAPAA

Bed & Breakfast Hawaii K1

P. O. Box 449, 96746
(808) 822-7771

A secluded oceanfront home on beautiful
Anahola Bay where guests can enjoy a
large studio apartment detached from the
main house. Accommodations include

queen-size bed and private bath with a garden shower, color cable TV, and a kitchenette. Breakfast fixings are provided for
the first three days. Occasionally a honeymoon room with a deep Jacuzzi is available. Enjoy the oceanfront amenities and
privacy of the property. Three-day minimum stay. Weekly rates. $85; $125 honeymoon room.

Bed & Breakfast Hawaii K3

P. O. Box 449, 96746
(808) 822-7771

Stay in a brand-new 600-square-foot, one-
bedroom guest cottage nestled on the lush
mountainside of Wailua Homesteads.
Views of the wettest spot on earth can be
seen from the deck. The kitchenette is great
for preparing light meals and snacks and is
stocked with breakfast fixing, for the first
morning only. Private bath, color TV, and
phone. Children welcome. $70.

Bed & Breakfast Hawaii K3A

P. O. Box 449, 96746
(808) 822-7771

Cloud Nine Holiday is a spacious apartment that is completely private with its
own entrance. It comes equipped with a
color cable TV, a microwave, a small
refrigerator, and all the breakfast fixings.
The lanai overlooks a beautifully landscaped "bird of paradise" tropical garden
perfect for romantic sunrise or sunset
strolls. Situated near the beach and public
tennis court. $60-100.

Bed & Breakfast Hawaii K4

P. O. Box 449, 96746
(808) 822-7771

Enjoy traditional bed and breakfast in this
lovely two-story cedar home. Guests have a

choice of two rooms, each with their own private bath, queen-size bed, and TV. Each morning, wake up to the smell of fresh-baked bread and Kona coffee, which is served in the glassed-in lanai area that offers views of Mt. Waialeale in the background. Five minutes to the beach. $40-45.

Bed & Breakfast Hawaii K6

P. O. Box 449, 96746
(808) 822-7771

These three fresh and comfortable accommodations overlook a horse pasture skirted by Opaekaa Stream. Waterfalls are often visible in the distance from the lanai. Private entrances open to all suites decorated in wicker and rattan. All rooms feature king- or queen-size beds, kitchen areas, and private baths. $50-100.

Bed & Breakfast Hawaii K7

P. O. Box 449, 96746
(808) 822-7771

On a quiet country road in the hills of Keapana Valley, this hostess offers guest rooms in a pastoral setting. Beautifully landscaped and architect-designed by the hostess herself, the property has panoramic views of the ocean and mountains. Three guest rooms, one with private bath, two with shared bath. A solar hot tub is available as well as a refrigerator. There is a spacious lanai with rattan furniture and hammocks in a tropical, adult-only environment. Just five minutes from restaurants and beaches. $40-60.

Bed & Breakfast Hawaii K16

P. O. Box 449, 96746
(808) 822-7771

Three rooms on the coconut coast of Kauai, just two blocks inland from the beach. Two rooms in the main house have private baths.

A third room is separate from the main house. Enjoy breakfast with the hosts or choose self-serve. All the rooms have hand-painted art done by the hostess. $50.

Bed & Breakfast Hawaii K26A

P. O. Box 449, 96746
(808) 822-7771

Peace and quiet, mountain and ocean views, central location, and fabulous breakfast all characterize this home that offers guests one of two accommodations. A separate cottage with a livingroom/dining room and kitchen can comfortably sleep four and has a king- and queen-size bed. A downstairs one-bedroom apartment with a deck and private entrance offers a kitchenette with light cooking appliances. Minimum stay is three nights. $85.

Bed & Breakfast Hawaii K53

P. O. Box 449, 96746
(808) 822-7771

This lovely one-bedroom cottage overlooks several acres of what was once a nursery area for exotic tropical plants. Although the cottage is under the same roof as the main house, it offers private entrance and its own separate lanai where the hosts serve a continental breakfast each morning. The livingroom has color TV and cable with a VCR and stereo, and light meals can be prepared in the kitchenette or barbecue area. The bedroom has a queen-size bed, and the cottage has a full private bath. Children are welcome, and comfortable futons are available for extra bedding. $65.

Bed & Breakfast Hawaii K73

P. O. Box 449, 96746
(808) 822-7771

Enjoy a room and private bath in this rambling two-story Victorian home. Set against

6 Pets welcome; 8 Children welcome; 9 Social drinking allowed; 10 Tennis available; 11 Swimming available; 12 Golf available; 13 Skiing available; 14 May be booked through travel agents.

the backdrop of Sleeping Giant Mountain, two guest facilities are offered. One area is a screened lanai; upstairs there is a king-size bed with an adjoining private bath with sunken tub. For parties of three, a room on the east side of the house has queen-size bed and two twins with a bath across the hall. Good beaches are a five minute drive. $45-60.

Bed & Breakfast Hawaii K82

P. O. Box 449, 96746
(808) 822-7771

Hosts built an extra two-story house on their mountain view plateau property just for bed and breakfast guests. Accommodations for guests are two separate units downstairs. One unit has a queen-size bed, private bath, living area with queen-size sofa bed, color TV, wet bar, refrigerator, and microwave. Another larger unit includes a bedroom with a pair of twin beds, spacious living area with a queen-size sofa bed, large private bath, color TV, wet bar, refrigerator, and microwave. Each area has its own lanai and entrance. Breakfast is served upstairs in the breakfast nook, and a gazebo with a sauna and Jacuzzi is on premises. $75-105.

Bed and Breakfast Honolulu (Statewide) BAUMT

3242 Kaohinani Drive, Honolulu, 96817
(808) 795-7533; (800) 288-4666
FAX (808) 595-2030

Just past Opaekaa Falls is this new 600-square foot guest cottage with a deck. Falls can be seen from the deck. Breads and fruit provided for breakfast. Light cooking facilities. $65.

Bed and Breakfast Honolulu (Statewide) LOWYT

3242 Kaohinani Drive, Honolulu, 96817
(808) 595-7533; (800) 288-4666
FAX (808) 595-2030

This private mountain bed and breakfast is behind Sleeping Giant Mountain on a lovely landscaped half acre. The rooms have private baths with tubs and showers. Continental breakfast is served, and the fruit fresh off the trees surrounding the house. Well-lit off-street parking. Five minutes to Wailua Bay. From $50.

Bed and Breakfast Honolulu (Statewide) SCHEJ

3242 Kaohinani Drive, Honolulu, 96817
(808) 795-7533; (800) 288-4666
FAX (808) 595-2030

This studio is under the eyebrow of the sleeping giant and very private. Guests enjoy the best of both the mountains and the sea. Only five minutes from Lydgate Park. $55.

Bed and Breakfast Honolulu (Statewide) SMITR

3242 Kaohinani Drive, Honolulu, 96817
(808) 595-7533; (800) 288-4666
FAX (808) 595-2030

Above Opaekaa Fall, a home situated in the restored Wailua Homestead area offers two guest rooms. This plantation home is decorated in a country motif with antiques. One room has a king-size bed, and the other room has a queen and twins. Both have private baths, and the mountain and valley views from the porch are breathtaking. Hosts also offer two one-bedroom condos on the beach. Guests can enjoy the peaceful sounds of the Pacific from the lanais adjoining the condos, and the bedrooms have queen-size beds. $50 and up.

NOTES: Credit cards accepted: A Master Card; B Visa; C American Express; D Discover Card; E Diner's Club; F Other; 2 Personal Checks accepted; 3 Lunch available; 4 Dinner available; 5 Open all year;

Bed and Breakfast Honolulu (Statewide) TAYLG

3242 Kaohinani Drive, Honolulu, 96817
(808) 795-7533; (800) 288-4666
FAX (808) 595-2030

Three acres of rolling hills overlook the ocean and mountains. The large solar Jacuzzi offers green mountain vistas. The grounds have ample space for solitude. $45.

KAUAI—KILAUEA

Bed & Breakfast Hawaii K31

P. O. Box 449, Kapaa, 96746
(808) 822-7771

A private, north shore of Kauai guest house is the perfect setting for getting away from it all. Accommodations include a light cooking area, full bath, queen bed, and a sitting area. Overlooking the beautiful Kilauea River and "rainbow valley," named for the brilliant rainbows that stretch from the lush recesses of the valley floor to the ocean. A private hiking trail takes guests down to a secluded, semiprivate sandy beach. The main house has a pool available to guests. $115.

KAUAI—KOLOA

Bed and Breakfast Honolulu (Statewide) GOOCK

3242 Kaohinani Drive, Honolulu, 96817
(808) 795-7533; (800) 288-4666
FAX (808) 595-2030

Centrally situated, only five miles from the beaches of Poipu and 15 minutes from downtown Lihue. Loan of beach and sports equipment. Light cooking facilities. $65.

KAUAI—NORTHSHORE

Bed & Breakfast Hawaii K01

P. O. Box 449, Kapaa, 96746
(808) 822-7771

This suite is surrounded by what the hosts call "real Hawaii." The river that adjoins the property has been beautifully landscaped, has its own waterfalls, and is perfect for a swim. Two outdoor hot tubs, eight-person Jacuzzi, and massage are also available to guests. The accommodation is a private guest house with a loft bed, kitchen, and queen-size brass bed on the main level. Living area has a VCR and stereo CD/cassette player. Indoor and outdoor showers also available. $95-120.

Bed & Breakfast Hawaii K20

P. O. Box 449, Kapaa, 96746
(808) 822-7771

Heart Song Inn welcomes you to the magical healing beauty of Kauai. Two bedrooms with a private bath in the hall are offered for a group of one to four people. Breakfast is served out on the deck where the view of the valley is breathtaking. A lower deck offers a hot tub and a view of the Kilauea waterfalls. Minimum stay is three nights. $65-115.

Bed & Breakfast Hawaii K28

P. O. Box 449, Kapaa, 96746
(808) 822-7771

Guests have the pleasure of staying at this new home at the river's edge in Kilauea. Guest accommodations are in separate wing with a private balcony overlooking the river. The bedroom has a queen-size bed, plus a fold-out sofa bed. A private full bath adjoins the room, plus small kitchen appliances for light cooking make this accommodation perfect for longer stays. $70.

6 Pets welcome; 8 Children welcome; 9 Social drinking allowed; 10 Tennis available; 11 Swimming available; 12 Golf available; 13 Skiing available; 14 May be booked through travel agents.

Bed & Breakfast Hawaii K35

P. O. Box 449, Kapaa, 96746
(808) 822-7771

Guests are invited to come and enjoy this lush tropical paradise overlooking the Kilauea Valley. The bedroom overlooks one of the most spectacular views of the island, and the room is newly remodeled with its own private entrance and bath. Upon awakening, step out onto the cedar deck and take in the view of the mountains, mist, and lush valley below, while smells of Kona coffee, baked goods, and fresh local fruits for continental breakfast fill the air. Minimum stay is two nights. $65.

Bed & Breakfast Hawaii K39A

P. O. Box 449, Kapaa, 96746
(808) 822-7771

Situated on the north shore of Kauai in Kalahiwai, hosts offer a room with a private entrance and adjoining bath. This home with three acres, horses, and golden retrievers, adjoins a 600-acre guava orchard. The accommodations are elegant, large, and sound-proofed, and include a king-size bed, double-head tiled shower, color TV and VCR, and a bay window that overlooks the grounds. Hosts encourage guests to explore the quiet, uninhabited grounds with waterfalls and streams that surround their lovely home. Minimum stay is 3 nights. $70-80.

Bed & Breakfast Hawaii K45

P. O. Box 449, Kapaa, 96746
(808) 822-7771

This bed and breakfast accommodation is perfect for guests who enjoy hiking, water sports, sightseeing, golf at Princeville, sunbathing, or long walks in a quiet unpretentious Hawaiian-style town. The house is a stylish two-story home on grounds abundant with coconut, plumeria, and papaya trees, and the views from 1,000-square-foot deck and the lanai are breathtaking. One will instantly feel at home in any of the rooms, which all feature queen-size beds and private baths. Continental breakfast of fresh fruit, juice, and warm breads is served each morning on the second-story lanai that views Mt. Waialeale. $55-75.

Bed & Breakfast Hawaii K60

P. O. Box 449, Kapaa, 96746
(808) 822-7771

This brand-new, spacious accommodation is completely separate from the main house and a block from the beach. Sit out on the deck and enjoy the view of Bali Hai Mountain, or enjoy the ocean view with breakfast in the dining area. Full kitchen, Jacuzzi tub, bedroom with queen-size bed and skylights make this guest area private and spacious. Livingroom also has a queen-size sofa bed for extra guests. Another accommodation is a separate bedroom in the main house with its own private entrance, patio area, and unique private bath. Minimum stay is three nights. $50-100.

Bed & Breakfast Hawaii K64

P. O. Box 449, Kapaa, 96746
(808) 822-7771

This private, handcrafted redwood cottage is carefully and comfortably equipped for any length of stay. It includes a kitchenette, a private full bath, queen-size bed in the bedroom, and a livingroom with a large futon couch. French doors open to deck that offers distant mountain, ocean and sunset views, and the area surrounding the cottage is full of thoroughbred horse farms and organic fruit, flower, and vegetable farms. Children welcome. $75.

Bed & Breakfast Hawaii K74

P. O. Box 449, Kapaa, 96746
(808) 822-7771

A slightly rustic accommodation on a working farm is a great way to relax in Kauai. Hosts have added onto their barn by building a bedroom, efficiency kitchen, and private bath on the second-story. Comfortable king-size bed and double sofa bed furnish the room. Grounds have a pineapple patch and orchid greenhouse that guests are welcome to explore. Children are welcome. $65.

Bed & Breakfast Hawaii K81

P. O. Box 449, Kapaa, 96746
(808) 822-7771

This full apartment in Hanalei town is just 200 feet from the bay. Hostess lives in the upstairs half of a new two-story house across the street from the ocean. The whole downstairs portion of the house is for guests to enjoy. Guests have a private entrance, queen-size bed in the bedroom, private bath with tub and shower, fully equipped kitchen, and cozy livingroom. No breakfast is served here. Minimum stay is three nights. $90.

KAUAI—POIPU

Bed & Breakfast Hawaii K11A

P. O. Box 449, Kapaa, 96746
(808) 822-7771

Enjoy a luxury one-bedroom bed and breakfast with first-class accommodations on acres of gardens and tropical flowers just a five-minute walk to Poipu Beach. Guests have use of the main bedroom with king bed, color TV, sliding glass doors to the lanai, and private bath. A delicious breakfast is served on the lanai overlooking tropical gardens. Take advantage of the pool, tennis courts, and Jacuzzi on the condominium premises. Three-night minimum stay. $75-92.

Bed & Breakfast Hawaii K22

P. O. Box 449, Kapaa, 96746
(808) 822-7771

Bed and breakfast is available in this plantation house with two lovely rooms with private baths. Relax in the screened-in lanai or in the common livingroom. Tropical continental breakfast is served in the formal dining room or on the lanai. Two-night minimum is preferred. $65-75.

Bed & Breakfast Hawaii K23

P. O. Box 449, Kapaa, 96746
(808) 822-7771

Right in Poipu and three blocks from Shipwreck Beach are two accommodations in one. The entire downstairs of this architect's home is devoted to bed and breakfast and has a suite and a bedroom available for guests. The suite offers a private bath with a queen-size bed and a sitting area with a queen-size sofa sleeper. The suite also has a kitchenette with a dishwasher, microwave, and refrigerator. The bedroom offers a queen-size bed, adjoining private bath and sliding glass doors to a sitting area. A walk-in closet has a small refrigerator for storing drinks. Breakfast is served each morning. Both rooms have TV. $65-85.

Bed & Breakfast Hawaii K24

P. O. Box 449, Kapaa, 96746
(808) 822-7771

Poipu Plantation is more a small inn than a bed and breakfast accommodation because twenty people can be accommodated. Nine rooms feature a variety of bed sizes, face the garden or ocean, and have their own

6 Pets welcome; 8 Children welcome; 9 Social drinking allowed; 10 Tennis available; 11 Swimming available; 12 Golf available; 13 Skiing available; 14 May be booked through travel agents.

telephone lines. Two of the units are two-bedroom, two-bath suites. Guests are welcome to pick any fruit in season, and a barbecue, sunning area, and laundry facilities are available to guests. $75-125.

Bed & Breakfast Hawaii K25

P. O. Box 449, Kapaa, 96746
(808) 822-7771

This unhosted property is a two-bedroom condo at Makahuena. The condo has no ocean view, even though the complex is situated on the oceanfront at Makahuena Point. Two bedrooms, two baths, fully equipped kitchen, TV, telephone, and swimming pool and tennis courts on premises make this a perfect spot for families. Walk along the cliffs to Shipwreck Point or down the street to Poipu Beach Park. No breakfast is served. $85.

Bed & Breakfast Hawaii K29

P. O. Box 449, Kapaa, 96746
(808) 822-7771

Brand-new one-bedroom apartment overlooking the shore of Kauai is just minutes from the beach and centrally located in O'mao. Hosts have lived in Kauai over fifteen years and can share information about beaches, dining, and shopping. The apartment is upstairs through a private entrance and has a kitchen, telephone, cable TV, queen-size bed in the bedroom, private bath, and sofa bed in the livingroom. Guests can enjoy ocean view from their own private deck, and breakfast fixings are in the refrigerator. Minimum stay is three nights. $60.

Bed & Breakfast Hawaii K61

P. O. Box 449, Kapaa, 96746
(808) 822-7771

Enjoy a quiet, relaxing stay in lush surroundings on the South Shore of Kauai in a beautifully furnished room with a king-size bed, reading area, and breakfast nook with a coffee maker, small refrigerator, and microwave for light snacking. The bedroom is cool and airy with an adjoining private bath, and the home is within walking distance of the National Tropical Botanical Gardens. The host is a third-generation-born Hawaiian. $65.

Bed & Breakfast Hawaii K71

P. O. Box 449, Kapaa, 96746
(808) 822-7771

Japanese decor is the theme for this 900-square-foot cottage in Poipu. Guests will enjoy the Shoji screen doors, as well as the miniature gardens at the entrance and in the bathroom. Sofa bed in the livingroom, kitchenette, and queen-size bed in the bedroom offer a guest plenty of living area. Although there is no ocean view, a five-minute walk will take guests to the Poipu Beach Park. No breakfast is served at this accommodation. Minimum stay is four nights. $100; $600 per week.

Bed and Breakfast Honolulu (Statewide) JOHNJ

3242 Kaohinani Drive, Honolulu, 96817
(808) 795-7533; (800) 288-4666
FAX (808) 595-2030

This deluxe master bedroom has a cathedral ceiling, king bed and color television. Enjoy the view of the ocean from a private lanai in a lush green setting with beautiful landscaping. $65.

Bed and Breakfast Honolulu (Statewide) LEVII

3242 Kaohinani Drive, Honolulu, 96817
(808) 795-7533; (800) 288-4666
FAX (808) 595-2030

NOTES: Credit cards accepted: A Master Card; B Visa; C American Express; D Discover Card; E Diner's Club; F Other; 2 Personal Checks accepted; 3 Lunch available; 4 Dinner available; 5 Open all year;

This apartment has two bedrooms with private entrances and a shared bath. The home sits in a tropical setting, with an array of Hawaiian foliage and sweeping ocean and mountain views. $75.

Bed and Breakfast Honolulu (Statewide) NAKAS

3242 Kaohinani Drive, Honolulu, 96817
(808) 595-7533; (800) 288-4666
FAX (808) 595-2030

Centrally situated for sightseeing. The room has twin beds, private entrance and bath, a small refrigerator, TV, and a private patio. The tropical setting is complete with running stream. Three-night minimum stay. From $45.

KAUAI—PRINCEVILLE

Bed and Breakfast Honolulu (Statewide) BARNC 1

3242 Kaohinani Drive, Honolulu, 96817
(808) 795-7533; (800) 288-4666
FAX (808) 595-2030

A lovely home in the Hanalei area offers three units, including an apartment with light cooking. Sunset and waterfall views are dramatic from the cathedral windows. Only 100 yards to the beach. $60.

Bed and Breakfast Honolulu (Statewide) FISHJ

3242 Kaohinani Drive, Honolulu, 96817
(808) 795-7533; (800) 288-4666
FAX (808) 595-2030

Three guest rooms all have private baths, and one features a private entrance. This condominium is situated on the third hole of the golf course. Walk to town or the ocean. $55.

KAUAI—WAILUA

Bed & Breakfast Hawaii K30

P. O. Box 449, Kapaa, 96746
(808) 822-7771

The Fern Grotto Inn is perfectly situated on the only private property in the middle of the Wailua River State Park. Breakfast is served on elegant English china in the Plantation Dining Room with its many windows providing a view of the Wailua River. Drift off to sleep in one of the three bedrooms on queen beds with designer sheets and comforters piled high with white goose down pillows. European down/feather beds are provided for added comfort and luxury. Elegant adjoining private bath. $70-100.

Bed & Breakfast Hawaii K36

P. O. Box 449, Kapaa, 96746
(808) 822-7771

Experience the magic of Kauai while staying in this A-frame cottage on the hosts' half-acre property in Wailua. Set back from the main home, there is plenty of privacy and space. A large deck fronts the cottage. Inside through French doors is an oversize all-glass family room. The kitchen is stocked with breakfast fixings. Two bedroom areas sleep up to four. Children welcome. Two-night minimum stay. $75.

Bed & Breakfast Hawaii K47

P. O. Box 449, Kapaa, 96746
(808) 822-7771

A spectacular 360-degree view of the ocean, Sleeping Giant, and Mount Waialeale can be seen from this bilevel cottage that sleeps up to six people. The bedroom has a queen bed, and there is a queen-sofa bed in the livingroom. A private bath, livingroom, large screened-in lanai, and loft complete the accommodations. The

6 Pets welcome; 8 Children welcome; 9 Social drinking allowed; 10 Tennis available; 11 Swimming available; 12 Golf available; 13 Skiing available; 14 May be booked through travel agents.

hosts live in the main house. Children welcome. Baby equipment is available. Three-night minimum stay. $65.

Bed & Breakfast Hawaii K62

P. O. Box 449, Kapaa, 96746
(808) 822-7771

The Orchid Hut is a modern cottage situated on a bluff overlooking the north fork of the Wailua River. The front door opens into a sitting room with color TV and kitchenette. Dine at the outdoor table or just relax and enjoy the scenic view of nature and the meticulously landscaped tropical garden. Perfect for couples and honeymooners, this beautifully furnished unit is just three minutes from the mouth of the Wailua River for water skiing, the beach, restaurants, and shopping. Three-night minimum stay. $75.

KAUAI—WAIMEA

Bed & Breakfast Hawaii K42

P. O. Box 449, Kapaa, 96746
(808) 822-7771

In the heart of old Waimea and within walking distance of the store, pier, restaurants, and shops, this home is perfect for those who want to hike the Waimea Canyon and explore Kokee State Park. There is a private entrance into the cozy bedroom, sitting area, and light cooking area. Private bath. A prepared continental breakfast is left in the refrigerator. Three-night minimum stay. $50.

Kamalo Plantation

Star Route, Box 128, 96748
(808) 558-8236

Across the road from Father Damien's historic St. Joseph Church lies Kamalo

Plantation, a five acre lime orchard and tropical garden at the foot of Mt. Kamakou. Ancient Hawaiian stone ruins beside the plantation offer a unique sense of peace and tranquility. Stay at the country cottage with fully equipped kitchen, or in the main house that has two rooms and a shared bath available. Enjoy a healthy aloha breakfast, including fresh tropical fruits and freshly baked breads. A natural stop over on the way to or from Halawa Valley.

Hosts: Akiko and Glenn Foster
Rooms: 3 (1 PB; 2 SB) $60-75
Continental Breakfast
Credit Cards: None
Notes: 5, 9, 11, 12

LANAI—LANAI CITY

Bed & Breakfast Hawaii L1

P. O. Box 449, Kapaa, 96746
(808) 822-7771

Two of the bedrooms in this retired nurse's home are available for guests visiting the small, fairly remote island of Lanai. One room offers a double and single bed, while the other has a queen-size bed. There is a full and a half-bath shared by both hostess and guests. Both of the bedrooms are good-size and well-furnished. Hostess is an artist and has a fascinating collection of bottles and shells. $45-55.

Bed and Breakfast Honolulu (Statewide) COLEP

3242 Kaohinani Drive, Honolulu, 96817
(808) 595-7533; (800) 288-4666
FAX (808) 595-2030

Two rooms are offered to guests in this bed and breakfast, one with a double bed and one with a pair of twins. Host provides coffee for guests, but no breakfast. Restaurants and convenience stores are nearby, and hostess' kitchen is available to guests for $5 a day. From $57.

NOTES: Credit cards accepted: A Master Card; B Visa; C American Express; D Discover Card; E Diner's Club; F Other; 2 Personal Checks accepted; 3 Lunch available; 4 Dinner available; 5 Open all year;

MAUI—HAIKU

Bed and Breakfast Honolulu (Statewide) DOWNN

3242 Kaohinani Drive, Honolulu, 96817
(808) 595-7533; (800) 288-4666
FAX (808) 595-2030

Pleasant hosts offer a spacious one bedroom cottage in the heart of windsurfing country. Five minutes from Hookai Park, twenty minutes from the airport, and ten minutes from Paia, this ocean-view home has a quiet rural setting and an all-electric kitchen with washer/dryer, ice-maker, and garbage disposal. No children. From $55.

MAUI—HANA

Bed and Breakfast Honolulu (Statewide) KAIAJ 1

3242 Kaohinani Drive, Honolulu, 96817
(808) 795-7533; (800) 288-4666
FAX (808) 595-2030

Guests may roam the gardens of this working fruit and flower farm, or even pull a few weeds. Kerosene lamps, no electricity, television or phone. $60.

MAUI—KIHEI

Bed and Breakfast Hawaii M16

P. O. Box 449, Kapaa, 96746
(808) 822-7771

This a large home situated on the edge of of Ulapalakua Ranch is totally surrounded by decks. Breakfast is served on the upper deck, which provides a great place to whale-watch, and accommodations include two bedrooms decorated with Japanese antique furnishings. Both share a bath across the hall, and one has an ocean view, while the other views a tropical garden. A studio with a kitchenette, private entrance, and private bath, and a cottage with one bedroom both offer more room and more privacy for families. $55-85.

Bed & Breakfast Hawaii M17

P. O. Box 449, Kapaa, 96746
(808) 822-7771

Tennis buffs could not ask for a better place to vacation than sunny Kihei, with courts available right outside their door. The accommodation is a full apartment with one bedroom, private bath, kitchenette, living/dining room, cable TV. The home has an ocean view and is a short drive to beaches, golf, and restaurants. Three-night minimum stay. $65-100.

Bed & Breakfast Hawaii M20

P. O. Box 449, Kapaa, 96746
(808) 822-7771

Guests have a choice of accommodations in the home of these busy hosts. A guest cottage can sleep four people comfortably, and includes a private deck, full kitchen, large room with a fold-out futon couch bed that also serves as the living area, and a full bath. The other accommodation is in the downstairs of the main house, has its own private entrance, kitchenette, bath, and queen-size bed. Breakfast foods are left in the units each morning for guests. Children over 12. Minimum stay is three nights. $75-120.

Bed & Breakfast Hawaii M28

P. O. Box 449, Kapaa, 96746
(808) 822-7771

Luxuriate in the privacy of one of three guest rooms in this large home. One accommodation is a suite with two bedrooms, queen-size beds, mini-kitchen, and one and one-half baths. A third bedroom has a king-size bed that can convert to

6 Pets welcome; 8 Children welcome; 9 Social drinking allowed; 10 Tennis available; 11 Swimming available; 12 Golf available; 13 Skiing available; 14 May be booked through travel agents.

twins, and a loft bed, private entrance, and private bath with a huge all-tile sunken tub. Minimum stay is three nights. $85-110.

Bed & Breakfast Hawaii M32

P. O. Box 449, Kapaa, 96746
(808) 822-7771

This beautiful home offers a bedroom with a private bath and private entrance off the deck. The room has a queen bed and color TV. Another single bedroom is next door. Breakfast is usually served on the lanai where guests can enjoy a view of a well-landscaped tropical garden. The hostess loves to treat her guests to some delicious breakfast treats. Three-night minimum stay. $55; $30 for additional room.

Bed & Breakfast Hawaii M32A

P. O. Box 449, Kapaa, 96746
(808) 822-7771

This accommodation is a large garden-level apartment with fully equipped kitchen and two bedrooms with one bath. Ideal for a small family. The unit has lots of windows that afford an excellent ocean view. The hostess serves breakfast on the lanai upstairs. One-week minimum stay. $80; $100 for four.

Bed & Breakfast Hawaii M38

P. O. Box 449, Kapaa, 96746
(808) 822-7771

This bed and breakfast accommodation offers two bedrooms on the second level of this oceanfront home. Each bedroom has a private entrance, private full bath, small refrigerator, color TV, and a queen-size bed. Breakfast is served downstairs, and guest rooms share a covered deck that overlooks the ocean and islands of Kahoolawe and Molokini. Minimum stay is

two nights. Children over 12. Resident dog. $70.

Bed & Breakfast Hawaii M62

P. O. Box 449, Kapaa, 96746
(808) 822-7771

Guests have their choice of a variety of accommodation at this large house. Queen-size beds are available, and private baths are in all accommodations. Breakfast is served on the deck, and the views are magnificent. No breakfast is included with a stay in the cottage. Minimum stay is two nights. $55-130.

Bed and Breakfast Honolulu (Statewide) LOWRP

3242 Kaohinani Drive, Honolulu, 96817
(808) 595-7533; (800) 288-4666
FAX (808) 595-2030

This hostess offers a studio with a queen bed, a cottage with a queen bed in the loft and a Hide-a-bed in the livingroom, and two rooms in her home that share a bath. Her home has an ocean view, and the islands of Lanai and Kahoolwe can be seen from her lanai. Five-minute drive to the beach, and a pool on premises. Breakfast is provided in the bed and breakfast room, and the studio and cottage have light cooking facilities. From $55.

Bed and Breakfast Honolulu (Statewide) SOUCZ

3242 Kaohinani Drive, Honolulu, 96817
(808) 795-7533; (800) 288-4666
FAX (808) 595-2030

The guest room has a sliding glass door leading to a private patio. Refrigerator is stocked with food for guests to enjoy at their leisure. $45.

NOTES: Credit cards accepted: A Master Card; B Visa; C American Express; D Discover Card; E Diner's Club; F Other; 2 Personal Checks accepted; 3 Lunch available; 4 Dinner available; 5 Open all year;

Bed and Breakfast Honolulu (Statewide) SVENC

3242 Kaohinani Drive, Honolulu, 96817
(808) 595-7533; (800) 288-4666
FAX (808) 595-2030

This single-family Hawaiian-style pole home in Kihei offers a panoramic view of the ocean and the slopes of Haleakala from the lanai. It has two rooms on the ground floor—the hosts live upstairs. Cable TV, ceiling fan, twin beds or king, private bath, and a refrigerator for cold drinks. There are many shops and restaurants in Kihei, and the ocean is only a mile from the house. Two-bedroom cottage also available. From $90.

Bed and Breakfast Honolulu (Statewide) FEKEJ

3242 Kaohinani Drive, Honolulu, 96817
(808) 595-7533; (800) 288-4666
FAX (808) 595-2030

This large studio with private entrance and bath has light cooking facilities. Just six blocks to the beach. Full breakfast is served. Ocean view and wheelchair accessible. From $65.

MAUI—KULA

Bed & Breakfast Hawaii M53

P. O. Box 449, Kapaa, 96746
(808) 822-7771

Enjoy an elegant and comfortable stay with charming, gracious hosts. Up on the slopes of the dormant volcano, Haleakala, guests can enjoy two separate bedrooms with private baths and separate entrances to the sunny courtyard where breakfast is served. The home is new and specially designed with a bed and breakfast in mind. About 30 minutes by car to the beaches and 40 minutes to the airport, this is truly a quiet,

relaxing place to enjoy Maui. Three-night minimum stay. $57.

Bloom Cottage Bed and Breakfast

Rural Route 2, Box 229, 96790
(808) 878-1425

A romantic getaway situated one-third of the way up Haleakala Crater. Spectacular view, cool mountain climate, surrounded by herb and flower gardens. There is an antique Hawaiian quilt on four-poster bamboo bed, old wicker in breakfast nook, original art on the walls. The two-bedroom 700-square-foot cottage has a fully stocked kitchen, large livingroom with fireplace, breakfast nook, bathroom. Hosts stock the refrigerator; guests fix their own breakfast.

Hosts: Herb and Lynne Horner
Cottage: $92.65
Continental Breakfast
Minimum stay: 2 nights
Credit Cards: None
Notes: 2, 5, 9, 14

MAUI—LAHAINA

Bed & Breakfast Hawaii M2A

P. O. Box 449, Kapaa, 96746
(808) 822-7771

Two different accommodations are offered to suit guests' needs. There is a room with a private bath in the main house with a window overlooking the ocean just steps away. Easy access to the sea-wall through a private porch. Also an attached cottage, Ohana House, just 50 feet from the ocean. The cottage has a kitchenette and private bath and entrance. The refrigerator will be stocked with fresh fruit and juice. Two-night minimum stay. $55-75.

Bed & Breakfast Hawaii M5

P. O. Box 449, Kapaa, 96746
(808) 822-7771

---

6 Pets welcome; 8 Children welcome; 9 Social drinking allowed; 10 Tennis available; 11 Swimming available; 12 Golf available; 13 Skiing available; 14 May be booked through travel agents.

This guest house is a private home created for those who appreciate a restful, relaxed holiday. Every guest room offers optimum privacy with color TV, refrigerator, ceiling fan, and air conditioning. All rooms have private baths, and one includes a Jacuzzi tub. The shared family room has a VCR, and the livingroom has a 350-gallon marine aquarium. A short walk to shops and restaurants as well as the beach, or relax beside the pool at the guest house. $75-95.

Bed and Breakfast Honolulu (Statewide) SWANT

3242 Kaohinani Drive, Honolulu, 96817
(808) 595-7533; (800) 288-4666
FAX (808) 595-2030

A place for relaxation! A cottage, plus three guest rooms and a family suite. Most offer private entrance, bath, TV, refrigerator, air conditioning, and lanai. One has a Jacuzzi. Near old whaling village and Kaanapali resort area. Quiet rooms and generous continental breakfast. Decked pool. Beach and picnic gear available. Beach park is two blocks away. From $60.

Lahaina Hotel

127 Lahainaluna Road, 96761
(808) 661-0577; (800)-669-3444

The Lahaina Hotel's three parlor suites and 10 standard double guest rooms capture the intimacy and romance of the late 1800s with antique wood, brass, iron beds, Oriental rugs and wooden wardrobe closets from the past. Modern amenities include new private baths, air conditioning, balconies with ocean or mountain views and telephones. A Continental breakfast is served each morning on the hall sideboard. Guests may enjoy breakfast in bed or from the comfort of wicker rockers on their balconies. Conveniently situated in the heart of the old whaling town, the hotel is near

Lahaina's renown shopping, dining, and entertainment.

Host: Ken Eisley
Rooms: 13 (PB) $89.99-129
Continental Breakfast
Credit Cards: A, B, C, D, F
Notes: 3, 4, 5, 11, 12, 14

MAUI—PAIA

Bed & Breakfast Hawaii M4A

P. O. Box 449, Kapaa, 96746
(808) 822-7771

This charming inn was built in 1850 for Maui's first doctor who came with the pineapple cannery. Newly refurbished, it sits among nearly one and one-half acres of pineapple fields and pine trees. Situated just 700 feet above sea level and just down the road from Hookipa Beach, this bed and breakfast includes full breakfast, twin or queen-size beds, and private baths in all rooms. Four rooms. Open from October through May. $80.

Bed & Breakfast Hawaii M12

P. O. Box 449, Kapaa, 96746
(808) 822-7771

Right on the beach and centrally situated for sightseeing all of Maui, this large plantation-style home is in an exclusive neighborhood adjacent to the Maui Country Club. It offers a large guest room with a private bath. There is no ocean view from the home, but a short walk will lead to a stretch of white, sandy beach good for walking. Usually the hosts' friendly dog will come along. $70.

MAUI—UPCOUNTRY

Bed & Breakfast Hawaii M9

P. O. Box 449, Kapaa, 96746
(808) 822-7771

NOTES: Credit cards accepted: A Master Card; B Visa; C American Express; D Discover Card; E Diner's Club; F Other; 2 Personal Checks accepted; 3 Lunch available; 4 Dinner available; 5 Open all year;

A delightful bed and breakfast with an ocean view setting, this studio is attached to the host's home in a quiet and private setting. The accommodation offers a separate entrance and is furnished with rattan furniture. Unit includes a double bed, private bath, ceramic tile floors, and a mini kitchen with a microwave, toaster, coffee maker, and refrigerator. The host serves a delicious Aloha-style breakfast on the patio that has an exquisite ocean view. $55-65.

Bed & Breakfast Hawaii M15

P. O. Box 449, Kapaa, 96746
(808) 822-7771

For the free-spirited, this glass gazebo is perched on the cliff overlooking Waipio Bay on Huelo Point. Inside is fully carpeted with a futon on the floor; nicely appointed with a stereo, small refrigerator, and coffee maker. The half-bath is hidden behind all-glass sliding doors. The hot/cold shower is outside in the newly landscaped gardens, and the large cement patio includes a hot tub shared with the hosts who live in the main house. Hosts will rent the entire home when they are away. Three-night minimum stay. $85.

Bed & Breakfast Hawaii M18A

P. O. Box 449, Kapaa, 96746
(808) 822-7771

This accommodation in the Upcountry area is for guests who want a special experience and care little about the cost. As guests enter the home, they encounter a small interior stream and fish pond that is situated in the living area. The bedroom uses glass to create an open feeling and adjoins a private bath that offers a view of the Kula landscape from the shower. Above that room up a small circular staircase is the Moon Room. This room is made entirely of glass and has a bed that rotates 360 degrees. Guests breakfast by the stream that runs through the home and across a cantilevered deck. Hot tub available also. $75-95.

Bed & Breakfast Hawaii M26

P. O. Box 449, Kapaa, 96746
(808) 822-7771

Named Halemanu, which is Hawaiian for birdhouse, this home is perched 3,500 feet above the town of Kula and provides an awesome view of the island of Maui. The home is new and has lots of windows and decks. The guest room has its own private deck, private full bath, and queen-size bed. Breakfast is served in a sunny spot on the deck or in the dining area. $70.

Bed & Breakfast Hawaii M55

P. O. Box 449, Kapaa, 96746
(808) 822-7771

Real island-style living can be enjoyed while staying here, just five minutes from Hookipa, the windsurfing beach of Maui. Overlooking pineapple fields, this studio has a separate entrance and sun deck with tropical flowers and fruit trees. The artwork was done by a famous Maui artist. Three-night minimum stay. $55.

Bed & Breakfast Hawaii M56

P. O. Box 449, Kapaa, 96746
(808) 822-7771

This modern cedar chalet is built on about two acres on the beautiful green slopes of Haleakala crater near Makawao. The home is tastefully decorated, and offers two bedrooms, one with twin beds and one with a queen-size bed, that share a bath. A hearty breakfast is served. No children. Minimum stay is three nights. $60.

6 Pets welcome; 8 Children welcome; 9 Social drinking allowed; 10 Tennis available; 11 Swimming available; 12 Golf available; 13 Skiing available; 14 May be booked through travel agents.

Bed and Breakfast Honolulu (Statewide) FOXF

3242 Kaohinani Drive, Honolulu, 96817
(808) 595-7533; (800) 288-4666
FAX (808) 595-2030

Situated in the quiet country hillside at the base of Mt. Haleakala, this 100-year-old Hawaiian plantation house was recently renovated with antiques. This house has one and one-half acres of spacious lawn, with banana, mango, and poinciana trees. Breakfast includes fresh fruit, banana bread, and Kona coffee. The beach is two miles away, and the airport is twelve miles away. From $80.

Bed and Breakfast Honolulu (Statewide) HOPKJ

3242 Kaohinani Drive, Honolulu, 96817
(808) 595-7533; (800) 288-4666
FAX (808) 595-2030

Enjoy a panoramic view of Mount Haleakala and the ocean from two secluded acres. Two guest rooms with private entrance and bath: one with a king bed; one with twins. Eight minutes to windsurfing and beaches. The hostess enjoys talking about "her" island. From $60.

Bed and Breakfast Honolulu (Statewide) HORNH

3242 Kaohinani Drive, Honolulu, 96817
(808) 595-7533; (800) 288-4666
FAX (808) 595-2030

This two-bedroom cottage is surrounded by herb and flower gardens. It contains a queen and twin room, livingroom with fireplace and TV, fully equipped kitchen, and breakfast nook. Watch a sunset from the private front porch. Smell the fresh-brewed Kona coffee, and enjoy homemade muffins, fresh fruit, and juice. From $70.

Bed and Breakfast Honolulu (Statewide) MCKAS

3242 Kaohinani Drive, Honolulu, 96817
(808) 795-7533; (800) 288-4666
FAX (808) 595-2030

This 1,000-square foot cottage at the 4,000-foot level on the slope of Haleakala is beautifully decorated, and has a full kitchen, fireplace, and lanai with barbecue. $95.

Bed and Breakfast Honolulu (Statewide) POWEN

3242 Kaohinani Drive, Honolulu, 96817
(808) 595-7533; (800) 288-4666
FAX (808) 595-2030

Enjoy paradise in the cool Upcountry. A modern cedar chalet home in paniolo (cowboy) country. Two rooms share a bath. The host provides beach and picnic supplies—or warm clothing for trips to the Haleakala Crater. Enjoy a tropical setting from a comfortable lanai. From $55.

MAUI—WAILUKU

Bed & Breakfast Hawaii M14

P. O. Box 449, Kapaa, 96746
(808) 822-7771

This comfortable home is only a few minutes from the Kaului airport. Two bedrooms, each with private entrance and shared bath. Outdoor patio is shared and includes a pool. No children. Two-night minimum stay. $50.

MOLOKAI—KAUNAKAKAI

Bed & Breakfast Hawaii MO2

P. O. Box 449, Kapaa, 96746
(808) 822-7771

NOTES: Credit cards accepted: A Master Card; B Visa; C American Express; D Discover Card; E Diner's Club; F Other; 2 Personal Checks accepted; 3 Lunch available; 4 Dinner available; 5 Open all year;

This five-acre parklike property lies at the foot of Molokai's highest mountain. Surrounding the charming guest cottage is a variety of tropical foliage and flowering trees and shrubs. The cottage is fully furnished and includes everything guests need to feel at home. Breakfast items are stocked in the kitchen area so that guests can eat when they please. There are many coves and beaches nearby, and hosts invite guests to use the lawn chairs, snorkel masks, and a good selection of Hawaiian records. Minimum stay is three nights. $60.

Bed & Breakfast Hawaii M04

P. O. Box 449, Kapaa, 96746
(808) 822-7771

This home is situated only ten miles from the airport and three miles past the town of Kaunakakai. The deluxe quiet bedroom has a private bath, private entry, and a small lanai facing the east Molokai Mountains. The ocean is 35 steps away, and a swimming pool, snorkels, masks, and kayaks are available for those experienced in watersports. Continental breakfast is served each morning. $95.

Bed and Breakfast Honolulu (Statewide) LENNN

3242 Kaohinani Drive, Honolulu, 96817
(808) 595-7533; (800) 288-4666
FAX (808) 595-2030

This cedar home is next to a park in Kaunakakai. The host offers a continental breakfast on the deck overlooking the ocean toward Lanai. The deck has been said to have a million-dollar view. The guest room does not face the ocean. It has TV, double bed, couch, and private bath. It is 300 feet to the ocean (not a swimming beach), three miles to town, and 13 miles to a swimming beach. From $65.

Bed and Breakfast Honolulu (Statewide) NEWHJ

3242 Kaohinani Drive, Honolulu, 96817
(808) 595-7533; (800) 288-4666
FAX (808) 595-2030

Surrounded by the lush native plants of Molokai and an easy walk to the beach, Honomuni House offers a personal and unique Hawaiian holiday. The cottage is nestled in a tropical garden and lulled by the sound of the surf. Evidence of the early Hawaiians abounds in Honomuni Valley— ancient stonework, taro terraces, and house foundations. Breadfruit, bananas, mango, ginger, coffee, coconut, and guava plum still grow wild in the tropical forest. Prawns and native freshwater fish can be seen in nearby streams. Waterfalls and refreshing pools await the ambitious hiker. Full bath, plus outdoor Hawaiian shower. From $65.

Bed and Breakfast Honolulu (Statewide) PAUHA

3242 Kaohinani Drive, Honolulu, 96817
(808) 595-7533; (800) 288-4666
FAX (808) 595-2030

Pau Hana ("done work") and it's time to relax. This rustic, unspoiled, truly Hawaiian hideaway is a favorite of many islanders. The inn offers all the comforts of a full-service hotel with restaurant, bar, pool, daily room service, and a staff that welcomes all visitors with genuine warmth and aloha. It leaves no doubt that Molokai is the friendly island. Forty rooms, some along the ocean or facing the pool. Some with kitchenettes and some separate cottages. The oceanfront suite has a view spanning the spindrift surf of the Molokai channel and the lush islands of Lanai and Maui. Just 25 air-minutes from Honolulu, yet 30 years behind. From $49.

6 Pets welcome; 8 Children welcome; 9 Social drinking allowed; 10 Tennis available; 11 Swimming available; 12 Golf available; 13 Skiing available; 14 May be booked through travel agents.

Bed and Breakfast Honolulu (Statewide) SWENYL

3242 Kaohinani Drive, Honolulu, 96817
(808) 595-7533; (800) 288-4666
FAX (808) 595-2030

Hosts are pleased to offer this one-bedroom cottage on the beach near good fishing and snorkeling. Bedroom has king or pair of twin beds, and the livingroom has a couch bed. The cottage is completely equipped, right down to the dishes, and offers privacy. A two-bedroom house on the beach is also available to accommodate large parties. No breakfast is provided at either accommodation. From $55.

Bed and Breakfast Honolulu (Statewide) WRIGH

3242 Kaohinani Drive, Honolulu, 96817
(808) 595-7533; (800) 288-4666
FAX (808) 595-2030

Hale Kawaikapu ("house of sacred waters") has two rentals, totally separated. Eighteen miles to town, it is situated on a tropical garden estate of 250 acres stretching from sea to mountaintop. The spectacular seaward view of Maui and Kahoolawe is matched by the magnificent mountains and valleys. Reef protected for safe swimming, snorkeling, fishing, and wind surfing. Hike along a Jeep trail to the top of the mountain for a four-island view. The two-bedroom, two-bath home has a private lanai and is fully equipped. The A-frame has a lanai open to the gardens and ocean. Washer and dryer are included. Caretaker on grounds. $150 security deposit payable in advance. From $120.

Kamalo Plantation

Star Route, Box 128, 96748
(808) 558-8236

Across the road from Father Damien's historic St. Joseph Church lies Kamalo Plantation, a five-acre lime orchard and tropical garden at the foot of Mt. Kamakou. Ancient Hawaiian stone ruins beside the plantation offer a unique sense of peace and tranquility. Stay at the country cottage with fully equipped kitchen, or in the main house that has two rooms and a shared bath available. Enjoy a healthy aloha breakfast, including fresh tropical fruits and freshly baked breads. A natural stop over on the way to or from Halawa Valley.

Hosts: Akiko and Glenn Foster
Rooms: 3 (1 PB; 2 SB) $60-75
Continental Breakfast
Credit Cards: None
Notes: 5, 9, 11, 12

OAHU—AILEA

Bed and Breakfast Honolulu (Statewide) NEESB

3242 Kaohinani Drive, Honolulu, 96817
(808) 595-7533; (800) 288-4666
FAX (808) 595-2030

This Oahu home is about two miles from Pearl Harbor and the Arizona Memorial. Two rooms are available. Kitchen privileges, laundry facilities, and color TV. The host loves Hawaii and enjoys sharing information with visitors. Children accepted. From $35.

OAHU—EAST HONOLULU

Bed & Breakfast Hawaii O40

P. O. Box 449, Kapaa, 96746
(808) 822-7771

This lovely condominium on the water is hosted by a single lady who knows quite a bit about Oahu and can give guests good recommendations on what to do and where to go. Situated close to Hanauma Bay, there are two single beds that can form a king bed. The room shares a bath in the hall. $40.

NOTES: Credit cards accepted: A Master Card; B Visa; C American Express; D Discover Card; E Diner's Club; F Other; 2 Personal Checks accepted; 3 Lunch available; 4 Dinner available; 5 Open all year;

Bed & Breakfast Hawaii 054

P. O. Box 449, Kapaa, 96746
(808) 822-7771

Spectacular bird's-eye views of Diamond Head and the entire Honolulu coastline can be seen from the deck of this little studio. The studio has its own private entrance, and sliding glass doors off the lanai open into an air conditioned bedroom with a king-size bed and a private bath. The hosts stock the mini-fridge with breakfast fixings. Preferred minimum stay is three nights. $65.

Bed & Breakfast Hawaii 065

P. O. Box 449, Kapaa, 96746
(808) 822-7771

This artist's home is perfect for exploring Honolulu without being in the heart of Waikiki. Swim in the pool, and enjoy views of the ocean and Diamond Head. Accommodations include a two room suite with a full-size waterbed, private sitting room, and private bath. Breakfast is normally served poolside. Minimum stay is two nights. $70.

OAHU—HAWAII KAI

Bed & Breakfast Hawaii 019

P. O. Box 449, Kapaa, 96746
(808) 822-7771

The hosts, mother and daughter, are from England and combine Old World charm with New World aloha to make sure their guests have a good time. In this home there is a spacious, airy bedroom with private bath, color TV, and sliding door leading to the swimming pool. Breakfast is served in the dining room with the hosts. Two-night minimum stay. $55.

Bed & Breakfast Hawaii 026

P. O. Box 449, Kapaa, 96746
(808) 822-7771

Stay in this beautiful home in the best part of town, and enjoy a spectacular ocean view from this hillside setting. The whole downstairs level of the house is devoted to bed and breakfast and accommodates up to six people. Sliding glass doors facing the ocean run the length of each room. Two-night minimum stay. $50.

Bed & Breakfast Hawaii 040

P. O. Box 449, Kapaa, 96746
(808) 822-7771

This home is three blocks from the ocean in a quiet residential neighborhood. Handy to stores, the bus line, a beach park, restaurants, and tennis courts. Two rooms available with shared bath. Hosts accept only one group at a time. Continental breakfast. Children welcome. Two-night minimum stay. $45.

Bed and Breakfast Honolulu (Statewide) ABEB

3242 Kaohinani Drive, Honolulu, 96817
(808) 595-7533; (800) 288-4666
FAX (808) 595-2030

The hosts came from England where bed and breakfast started. They have two guest rooms, one with private bath, TV, and refrigerator. The other has a TV and shared bath. The hearty continental breakfast is served in the dining room. On a bus line. Seven-minute drive to swimming beaches and Hanauma Bay. Enjoy the pool, or shop in the on-premises gallery of items collected from around the world. Adults only. Two-night minimum stay. From $50.

6 Pets welcome; 8 Children welcome; 9 Social drinking allowed; 10 Tennis available; 11 Swimming available; 12 Golf available; 13 Skiing available; 14 May be booked through travel agents.

Bed and Breakfast Honolulu (Statewide) BRUCB

3242 Kaohinani Drive, Honolulu, 96817
(808) 595-7533; (800) 288-4666
FAX (808) 595-2030

These hosts offer two renovated guest rooms with a shared bath. A queen-size bed is in one of the rooms, and a pair of twins that can convert to a king is in the other. Each room has a private entrance through a garden and patio area, TV, radio-alarm clock, ceiling fans, and small refrigerator. Guests are welcome to eat, sunbathe, or use the grill on the marina side of the house. Near Hanauma Bay, Sandy Beach, shopping, and restaurants. Nine miles to Waikiki, eleven miles to Ala Moana shopping center. Breakfast included if requested. From $55.

Bed and Breakfast Honolulu (Statewide) CRIPS

3242 Kaohinani Drive, Honolulu, 96817
(808) 595-7533; (800) 288-4666
FAX (808) 595-2030

On a high ridge, the bedrooms offer a beautiful view of the ocean and Koko Marina. They are large with private baths. Hanauma Bay, Oahu's best snorkeling beach, two shopping centers, and other tourist attractions, are a five-minute drive away. Coffee and doughnuts are served weekday mornings; a special breakfast is served on weekends. The comforts of home and more. From $55.

OAHU—HONOLULU

Bed & Breakfast Hawaii O22

P. O. Box 449, Kapaa, 96746
(808) 822-7771

Outstanding views characterize this home situated on the edge of the beach and near local tourist attractions. Two upstairs suites with private baths and lanai are available for bed and breakfast guests. The Mauka Suite has an antique bed and a view of Diamond Head; the Makai Suite has two double beds and view of the garden. $75-100.

Bed & Breakfast Hawaii O30

P. O. Box 449, Kapaa, 96746
(808) 822-7771

This large family home is situated on the hillside of Manoa Valley. It is quiet, cool, and surrounded with birds. The guest room has a queen-size bed, futon, and shared bath. Breakfast is served in the dining room with a wraparound view of Waikiki, Honolulu, and Manoa Valley or on the spacious and sunny front deck. Close to the bus stop. $45.

Bed & Breakfast Hawaii O53

P. O. Box 449, Kapaa, 96746
(808) 822-7771

Built on a hillside about one-fifth of a mile from the University of Hawaii at Manoa, this home has two bed and breakfast rooms available for guests. Guests are encouraged to sit on the large deck and enjoy the city's skyline and ocean below. One room offers a queen-size bed and a private bath with a shower, and the other room offers extra-long twin beds and a private one-half bath connected to a shared shower. Children over 10 years old. Minimum stay is three nights. $55-65.

Bed & Breakfast Hawaii O53A

P. O. Box 449, Kapaa, 96746
(808) 822-7771

The downstairs of this lovely home offers a peaceful, two-bedroom retreat ten minutes from Waikiki and Ala Moana Shopping Center. No breakfast is served here, but 1,150 square feet of living space provides a family with a perfect vacation accommodations. The sleeping porch area has a queen-size bed, and the two bedrooms have double beds. Area includes livingroom, dining room, fully equipped kitchen, and full bath. Minimum stay is three nights. Discount for weekly stay. $95.

OAHU—KAILUA

Affordable Paradise Bed and Breakfast Reservations

226 Pouli Road, 96734
(808) 261-1693; (800) 925-9065
FAX (808) 261-7315

Situated on the Island of Oahu and serving all of the major Hawaiian islands. Representing bed and breakfast homes, private studios, one-bedroom suites, cottages, and entire homes. All accommodations are on private property, inspected and approved. Listed are more than 300 hosts, with daily rates starting at $40. Affordable Paradise guarantees is that if guests are not satisfied, their deposit money will be refunded. The experienced staff has been in the reservations service for over ten years.

Beachline Bed and Breakfast

156-C, North Kalaheo Avenue, 96734
(808) 263-4297

Situated only steps from the beach. Comfortable accommodations include two rooms, as well as a new light and airy studio with kitchenette. Host: Eileen Palmer. $45-55.

Bed & Breakfast Hawaii O6

P. O. Box 449, Kapaa, 96746
(808) 822-7771

A great location for enjoying Lanakai Beach, this accommodation in the downstairs area of a beautiful A-frame cedar home offers a kitchenette, dining area, living area, and bedroom with a queen-size bed and queen-size futon, and private full bath. Light cooking can be done in the kitchenette, and an extra futon for a child is also available. A nice breakfast of fruit, fresh croissants, and coffee is provided. Minimum stay is three nights. $85.

Bed & Breakfast Hawaii O8A

P. O. Box 449, Kapaa, 96746
(808) 822-7771

Within walking distance of Kailua Beach on the canal, this studio apartment is perfect for longer stays. The bedroom area has a queen bed, there is a kitchenette for light cooking, and the bathroom has a two-person Jacuzzi. Share the pool with the host family. The hostess enjoys interaction with guests. Five-night minimum stay. $65 daily; $395 weekly.

Bed & Breakfast Hawaii O9A

P. O. Box 449, Kapaa, 96746
(808) 822-7771

This delightful accommodation is just across the street from one of the most beautiful beaches in Hawaii. A fully furnished garden studio in a tropical setting includes a private lanai. The apartment is beautifully furnished and includes a queen-size bed and large bath. Enjoy breakfast on the private patio. Three-night minimum stay. $55.

Bed & Breakfast Hawaii O12

P. O. Box 449, Kapaa, 96746
(808) 822-7771

6 Pets welcome; 8 Children welcome; 9 Social drinking allowed; 10 Tennis available; 11 Swimming available; 12 Golf available; 13 Skiing available; 14 May be booked through travel agents.

This accommodation allows guests to lounge by the swimming pool and enjoy a leisurely breakfast or sit in the hot tub after a day of sightseeing. One mile from Kailua Beach, this home gives guests their choice of two rooms with a shared bath between them. One room has a double bed, and the other has a twin bed. Guests are welcome to use the host's refrigerator to keep light snacks, and a crib is available. One-night stays have an extra $5 surcharge. $40-45.

Bed & Breakfast Hawaii O13A

P. O. Box 449, Kapaa, 96746
(808) 822-7771

Imagine waking up after a good night's sleep on a raised bamboo frame, all-cotton futon bed, and seeing the incredible blue waters and white sandy beach right outside the windows. This studio in Lanakai offers a private entrance, private bath, sitting area with a full ocean view, and wet bar. Minimum stay is three nights. $125.

Bed & Breakfast Hawaii O16

P. O. Box 449, Kapaa, 96746
(808) 822-7771

A gracious home on a private access road one-half block from a safe swimming beach. There are two large bedrooms with adjoining bath. This is ideal for couples traveling together. Two covered lanais surrounded by tropical foliage and a separate refrigerator are for guests. A neighborhood shopping center and restaurants are within walking distance. Adults only. $65.

Bed & Breakfast Hawaii O17

P. O. Box 449, Kapaa 86746
(808) 822-7771

This contemporary home, a short five-minute drive from the beach, offers guests two bedrooms that share a bath. Breakfast

is usually served on the lush and secluded lanai. Two-night minimum. $45.

Bed & Breakfast Hawaii O25

P. O. Box 449, Kapaa, 96746
(808) 822-7771

This delightful host home in Kailua offers two rooms, each with a private bath and air conditioning. Hosts have a beautiful garden with a covered patio and pool for guests to enjoy. Breakfast features something different and delicious every day. Guests have a bedroom with a queen-size bed that looks out toward the pool area. An additional bedroom with a queen-size bed is available for two couples traveling together. Minimum stay is two nights. $65.

Bed & Breakfast Hawaii O27

P. O. Box 449, Kapaa 86746
(808) 822-7771

This home has easy access to the expansive Kailua Beach. The hosts offer an attractive studio apartment with a new screened-in lanai. The interior is furnished with twin beds and a loft. It has light kitchen facilities and an outdoor barbecue. Continental breakfast includes coffee, tea, fresh fruit, rolls, and juice. Resident pets. Three-night minimum stay. $60.

Bed & Breakfast Hawaii O31

P. O. Box 449, Kapaa, 96746
(808) 822-7771

An elegant oceanfront home opens in front on a large pool with Jacuzzi and in back opens to the ocean. The home is spacious and has comfortable areas for guests to relax after a day of sightseeing. Bedrooms have private bath and private entrance from the pool/courtyard area. Each is decorated with an antique and tropical mixture. A deluxe continental breakfast is served. $120.

Bed & Breakfast Hawaii O32

P. O. Box 449, Kapaa, 96746
(808) 822-7771

This bed and breakfast apartment is attached to the host's home, but has a private entrance and private porch with a two-person swing. The unit consists of a livingroom, bedroom with a queen-size bed, and a private full bath. The unit also has a microwave, refrigerator, toaster, coffee maker, TV, and radio. Kailua Beach is a five-minute drive. No breakfast is included in this accommodation. $55.

Bed & Breakfast Hawaii O42

P. O. Box 449, Kapaa, 96746
(808) 822-7771

A block away from Kailua Beach, guests have two newly remodeled bedrooms available with private baths, TV, microwave, and refrigerator, plus use of the swimming pool. Breakfast supplies for three days are stocked to use at your leisure. Three-night minimum stay. $50-60.

Bed & Breakfast Hawaii O44

P. O. Box 449, Kapaa, 96746
(808) 822-7771

Situated one block from Kailua Beach, hosts offer three sets of accommodations. The first is a separate one-bedroom cottage with a complete kitchen, two double beds, color TV, and a private bath and patio area. The second accommodation is a studio attached to the house with a kitchenette, private bath, private patio, and private entrance. The third and newest studio can sleep only two in a double bed and also has a light kitchenette and color TV. Minimum stay is four nights. No breakfast is served. $55-75.

Bed & Breakfast Hawaii O57

P. O. Box 449, Kapaa, 96746
(808) 822-7771

Within walking distance from Kailua Beach is this two-bedroom apartment on the ground level of a two-story home. Two bedrooms, a private bath, and complete kitchenette. The livingroom is complete with TV and rattan furniture and has sliding glass doors to the patio and fenced yard. Perfect for a family of four. $75; $100 for four.

Bed and Breakfast Honolulu (Statewide) BURRT

3242 Kaohinani Drive, Honolulu, 96817
(808) 795-7533; (800) 288-4666
FAX (808) 595-2030

This one-bedroom cottage is one block from the beach, with direct beach access. The cottage has a kitchen, washer/dryer, queen bed and television. Easy access to golf, tennis, restaurants, and shopping. $69.

Bed and Breakfast Honolulu (Statewide) DIMOH

3242 Kaohinani Drive, Honolulu, 96817
(808) 595-7533; (800) 288-4666
FAX (808) 595-2030

This home is 50 yards from the beach, with private room and bath. Lovely patio and yard for guest use. Breakfast on a covered lanai. A 10 percent discount for a two-week stay. Also, separate fully furnished private studio with private entrance and bath. From $60.

Bed and Breakfast Honolulu (Statewide) ISAAC

3242 Kaohinani Drive, Honolulu, 96817
(808) 595-7533; (800) 288-4666
FAX (808) 595-2030

6 Pets welcome; 8 Children welcome; 9 Social drinking allowed; 10 Tennis available; 11 Swimming available; 12 Golf available; 13 Skiing available; 14 May be booked through travel agents.

Two hundred yards from the ocean, this accommodation has two bedrooms available for guests. One room has a pair of twin beds that can be made into a king, and the other room has a king-size bed. Both rooms have private entrances, private bath, microwave, coffee maker, and small refrigerator. Guests are welcome to use the pool, and breakfast is provided for the first three days of stay. Tropical gardens surround the pool and premises in a very private setting. No children under sixteen. From $50.

Bed and Breakfast Honolulu (Statewide) NELMP

3242 Kaohinani Drive, Honolulu, 96817
(808) 795-7533; (800) 288-4666
FAX (808) 595-2030

The upstairs unit has light cooking facilities, while the larger guest room has a private bath and entrance. Ten-minute walk to the beach of Kailua town. Breakfast provided first day of stay only. $55.

Bed and Breakfast Honolulu (Statewide) SASAE

3242 Kaohinani Drive, Honolulu, 96817
(808) 595-7533; (800) 288-4666
FAX (808) 595-2030

One-bedroom detached cottage. A five-minute walk to Kailua Beach and adjacent to a cool, lush tropical park. Bedroom air conditioned, with king bed. Livingroom has twin beds. Small kitchen for light cooking. Furnished in white rattan. Phone, cable TV, radio available. Children welcome. From $65.

Bed and Breakfast Honolulu (Statewide) SHEEP

3242 Kaohinani Drive, Honolulu, 96817
(808) 795-7533; (800) 288-4666
FAX (808) 595-2030

The guest suite has a private entrance and bath, a queen bed, sitting room and kitchenette. A second room has a private entrance and bath. Walk to beach or town. $65.

Bed and Breakfast Honolulu (Statewide) WARMM

3242 Kaohinani Drive, Honolulu, 96817
(808) 795-7533; (800) 288-4666
FAX (808) 595-2030

Enjoy a private entrance and on-site parking, refrigerator, microwave oven, toaster oven, glassware, dishes, phone and tourist information. $55.

Bed and Breakfast Honolulu (Statewide) WIEDP

3242 Kaohinani Drive, Honolulu, 96817
(808) 795-7533; (800) 288-4666
FAX (808) 595-2030

Enjoy the peace and privacy of this cottage in an exclusive residential area, adjacent to Wailea. Five minutes from beaches and golf, tennis, shops and restaurants. $50.

Bed and Breakfast Honolulu (Statewide) WOODLO

3242 Kaohinani Drive, Honolulu, 96817
(808) 795-7533; (800) 288-4666
FAX (808) 595-2030

Kailua Beach Park is one-half mile away. Continental breakfast is served in the family room, or on the lanai overlooking a golf course and mountain range. Guests may borrow beach equipment. Two night stay minimum. $45.

Kailua Beach Bed and Breakfast

570 Wanaao Road, 96734
(808) 262-5481

NOTES: Credit cards accepted: A Master Card; B Visa; C American Express; D Discover Card; E Diner's Club; F Other; 2 Personal Checks accepted; 3 Lunch available; 4 Dinner available; 5 Open all year;

Relax by the pool in a friendly atmosphere. Chose from two rooms or a private studio, featuring a kitchenette. Just a 10-minute walk to the beach, dining or shopping. Host: Maria Wilson. $40-45.

Kailua Kottages

362 Kailua Road, 96734
(808) 262-2212

Right in the heart of Kailua, a short walk to the beach and shopping. Host offers brand new accommodations. Private one bedroom suite, a spacious studio and detached one bedroom cottage. All offer private lanais and cooking facilities. Host: Vikki Patterson. $55-65

OAHU—KANEOHE

Bed & Breakfast Hawaii O24

P. O. Box 449, Kapaa, 96746
(808) 822-7771

Wake up to the cool Kaneohe breeze as birds in the forest behind the guest cottage sing. Enjoy the large deck and private pool. Situated on a separate level from the hosts' residence, providing great privacy. The unit sleeps four comfortably, is ideal for a family, and includes a kitchenette. Some of the finest beaches in Hawaii are on the windward side of Oahu, just a few minutes from this home. Two-night minimum stay. $55.

Bed & Breakfast Hawaii O56

P. O. Box 449, Kapaa, 96746
(808) 822-7771

This bed and breakfast is a luxuriously furnished private home with beautiful views of Kanehoe Bay from the livingroom, dining room, and swimming pool area. The hosts offer two bedrooms, each of which has a private bath. One room offers twin

beds with a bath across the hall, and the other room offers a double bed and has an adjoining bath. Ample, relaxed breakfasts are served each morning. Tea is served in the late afternoon. $50-55.

Bed and Breakfast Honolulu (Statewide) LAKEC

3242 Kaohinani Drive, Honolulu, 96817
(808) 795-7533; (800) 288-4666
FAX (808) 595-2030

Two guest rooms share a bath, ideal for couples traveling together. The home is three minutes from Winward Mall and restaurants are nearby. Continental breakfast. Children welcome. $55.

Bed and Breakfast Honolulu (Statewide) MUNRD

3242 Kaohinani Drive, Honolulu, 96817
(808) 595-7533; (800) 288-4666
FAX (808) 595-2030

This bed and breakfast overlooks Kanehoe Bay and the historic Heeia fish pond on windward Oahu. Furnished with antiques, this home is ideally situated for exploring the windward and north shore, yet is only thirty minutes away from Waikiki, one block to the bus, and convenient to many restaurants and shops. Continental breakfast is served by the pool. One room has a double bed, and the other room has a pair of twins. Both have private baths. From $65.

Bed and Breakfast Honolulu (Statewide) RAYB

3242 Kaohinani Drive, Honolulu, 96817
(808) 595-7533; (800) 288-4666
FAX (808) 595-2030

Beautiful, quiet Japanese/Hawaiian home with pool. Windward Oahu. Two guest rooms with king beds and private garden baths with dressing rooms. A guest refrigerator by the pool cabana. Two miles to beach, shopping, and cafes. Watch TV in the den. Adults only. Cheese and wine served poolside 5:00-6:00 P.M. Resident cats. From $65.

OAHU—LANIKAI

Bed and Breakfast Honolulu (Statewide) EASTJ

3242 Kaohinani Drive, Honolulu, 96817
(808) 795-7753; (800) 288-4666
FAX (808) 595-2030

This studio is on the beach, and has a private entrance, small refrigerator, microwave oven and coffee pot. Fixings are provided for breakfast on the first day only. $60.

Bed and Breakfast Honolulu (Statewide) MAXEM

3242 Kaohinani Drive, Honolulu, 96817
(808) 795-7533; (800) 288-4666
FAX (808) 595-2030

A delightfully furnished garden studio is across the street from one of the most beautiful swimming and windsurfing beaches on Oahu. Continental breakfast is stocked for guests to enjoy at their leisure. $55.

OAHU—MANOA

Bed and Breakfast Honolulu (Statewide) CADEM

3242 Kaohinani Drive, Honolulu, 96817
(808) 595-7533; (800) 288-4666
FAX (808) 595-2030

University area, 15-minute drive to Waikiki beaches. Manoa Valley is blessed with passing showers and tradewinds. Host offers master bedroom with private bath,

queen bed, and TV. Beautiful view of Diamond Head from the sun deck. Second room has twin beds and a half bath with shared shower. Continental breakfast. Resident cat. Children welcome. $55.

OAHU—NORTH SHORE

Bed & Breakfast Hawaii O46

P. O. Box 449, Kapaa, 96746
(808) 822-7771

A perfect spot on the ocean and one-half mile from the Polynesian Cultural Center, this home invites guests to enjoy a bedroom with a king-size bed and an additional bedroom with a twin bed. The bathroom is shared between the two rooms and has a tub and shower. Breakfast is prepared and waiting when guests awake, and the hosts suggest dining by the beach. Preferred three-night minimum stay. $45-75.

Bed and Breakfast Honolulu (Statewide) FRASJ

3242 Kaohinani Drive, Honolulu, 96817
(808) 595-7533; (800) 288-4666
FAX (808) 595-2030

In a rural area on north shore and windward Oahu, two units nestled against the Ko'olau Mountains are a three-minute walk to the beach, shopping, or post office. Units have private baths, full cooking facilities, and ocean views. Host stocks the kitchen for a plentiful breakfast. Everything, including hibachi and picnic supplies, is provided. The upstairs unit has a private deck and an ocean view. From $60.

Bed and Breakfast Honolulu (Statewide) RICHN

3242 Kaohinani Drive, Honolulu, 96817
(808) 595-7533; (800) 288-4666
FAX (808) 595-2030

NOTES: Credit cards accepted: A Master Card; B Visa; C American Express; D Discover Card; E Diner's Club; F Other; 2 Personal Checks accepted; 3 Lunch available; 4 Dinner available; 5 Open all year;

The warm, spunky hostess is a 45-year resident, an artist and author of a Hawaiian cookbook. She offers two large guest rooms. The master bedroom has a queen bed, air conditioning, and TV. The other room has twins beds and shared bath. Guests are welcome to watch the livingroom TV or enjoy the pool. Continental breakfast is served on the patio. Enjoy the serene view of the sweeping mountains and valleys. Five-minute drive to North Shore's famous beaches; 40 minutes to the airport. Much of "Old Hawaii" is here—like going back in time. From $65.

OAHU—PEARL CITY

Bed & Breakfast Hawaii O1A

P. O. Box 449, Kapaa, 96746
(808) 822-7771

This bed and breakfast home is situated just eight miles from Honolulu International Airport and offers an outstanding accommodation for its guests. The home is situated near the Pearl City Golf Course. The unit is a garden-level apartment with a separate entrance and private bath. A large pool is just outside the door. Children who know how to swim are welcome. $60.

OAHU—WAIKIKI

Bed and Breakfast Honolulu (Statewide) SHEAR

3242 Kaohinani Drive, Honolulu, 96817
(808) 595-7533; (800) 288-4666
FAX (808) 595-2030

Two blocks to beach, this tasteful condo has two guest rooms. The master bedroom has king bed and private bath. The other room has a king or two twin beds and a shared bath. View downtown Waikiki and the beach in the day, the beautiful stars and

sunsets in the evening. Continental breakfast. An easy walk to shopping, restaurants, shows, and local tour agencies. Take a quiet stroll by the Ala Wai Canal. From $45.

Bed and Breakfast Honolulu (Statewide) WATTM

3242 Kaohinani Drive, Honolulu, 96817
(808) 595-7533; (800) 288-4666
FAX (808) 595-2030

This lovely penthouse is close to the beach. Three units with refrigerators, hot plates, air conditioning, and full baths. No food is provided, but facilities for light cooking are available. One unit has a private entrance, and the others enter from the hall. Parking by prearrangement. From $65.

OAHU—WAIMANALO

Bed & Breakfast Hawaii O15A

P. O. Box 449, Kapaa, 96746
(808) 822-7771

Two separate accommodations are offered. The Mauka Suite has a large bedroom done in Polynesian-style and includes a small refrigerator, TV, and spacious bathroom. A private entrance opens to a fenced, secluded garden and lanai. Also, the elegant Ocean Suite with sleeping/livingroom, private bath, and separate entrance that opens to its own garden and lanai. Both units have access to a safe white-sand swimming beach. Breakfast is served each morning. Five-night minimum stay. $65-75.

VOLCANO VILLAGE

Chalet Kilauea at Volcano

P. O. Box 998, 96785
(808) 967-7786; (800) 937-7786

6 Pets welcome; 8 Children welcome; 9 Social drinking allowed; 10 Tennis available; 11 Swimming available; 12 Golf available; 13 Skiing available; 14 May be booked through travel agents.

A bed and breakfast inn at its best! Choose from unique theme rooms, the Treehouse Suite and deluxe vacation homes. Relax by the fireplace, peruse the library or enjoy the Jacuzzi. Tempt your appetite with a two-course full gourmet breakfast and afternoon tea. Chalet Kilauea offers amenities not found at other bed and breakfasts. Situated one and one-half miles from Hawaii Volcanoes National Park, it is a wonder in itself. Come experience the true aloha spirit.

Hosts: Lisha and Brian Crawford
Rooms: 9 (5 PB; 3 SB) $75-145
Full Breakfast
Credit Cards: A, B, D
Notes: 2, 5, 8, 9, 12, 14

Idaho

Greenbriar Inn

315 Wallace, 83814
(208) 667-9660

Built in 1908, the Greenbriar is Coeur d'Alene's only nationally registered inn. Just four blocks from downtown and five blocks from the lake, the Greenbriar reflects the residential charm of years gone by. Surrounded by 40-foot-high maples, guests enjoy the spa outside, the wine and tea hour late in the afternoon, and a famous three-course gourmet breakfast in the morning.

Host: Kris McIlvenna
Rooms: 8 (4 PB; 4 SB) $55-85
Full Breakfast
Credit Cards: A
Notes: 2, 4, 5, 8, 9, 10, 11, 12, 13, 14

Katie's Wild Rose Inn

E. 5150 Coeur d'Alene Lake Drive, 83814-9403
(208) 765-9474; (800) 328-WISH

Bordered by tall pine trees and overlooking beautiful Lake Coeur d'Alene, Katie's Wild Rose Inn welcomes all who enjoy a cozy, quiet atmosphere. An enjoyable breakfast may be served beside the wide windows or on the scenic deck. The guests will find relaxation in a game of pool or walk 1,000 yards down the road to a public dock and swimming area.

Hosts: Lee and Joisse Knowles
Rooms: 4 (2 PB; 2 SB) $55-85 plus 7% tax
Full Breakfast
Credit Cards: A, B, C
Notes: 2, 5

Warwick Inn

Warwick Inn
Bed and Breakfast

303 Military Drive, 83814
(208) 765-6565

This beautifully restored home (circa 1905) is located in a quiet residential area known as the Old Fort Grounds of Fort Sherman. Just three houses from Lake Coeur d'Alene and steps to everything else in town. A small but discriminating inn, the Warwick offers many amenities, from fluffy robes to complimentary refreshments in the evening. Proclaimed by *Pacific Northwest Magazine* as a "Preferred Establishment" and CDA Chamber of Commerce bestowed its "Excellence in Lodging" award. A delicious full breakfast is served, with special attention to dietary needs as requested.

Host: Bonnie Warwick
Rooms: 3 (1 PB; 2 SB) $ 75-95
Full Breakfast
Credit Cards: A, B, C
Notes: 2, 3 (picnic), 5, 6 (on premises), 9, 10, 11, 12, 13, 14

Riverside Inn
and Hot Springs

255 Portneut, P.O. Box 127, 83246-0127
(208) 776-5504; (800) 733-5504

6 Pets welcome; 8 Children welcome; 9 Social drinking allowed; 10 Tennis available; 11 Swimming available; 12 Golf available; 13 Skiing available; 14 May be booked through travel agents.

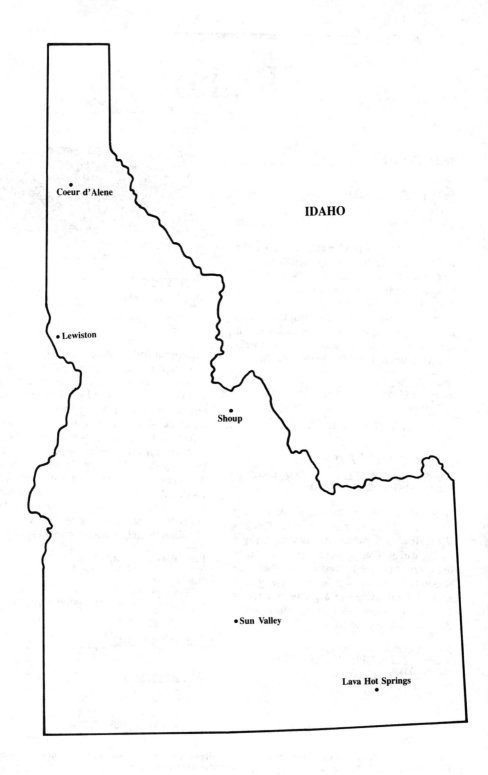

IDAHO

Coeur d'Alene

Lewiston

Shoup

Sun Valley

Lava Hot Springs

This inn was built in 1914 and quickly labeled "The Honeymoon Hotel" for it's elegance. The newly renovated Riverside Inn offers a quiet, relaxing atmosphere and free private hot mineral baths to its guests. A continental breakfast is served in the lobby, and there is a gracious porch overlooking the river. Also included in the lobby is a color television and library. An easy walk to restaurants.

Hosts: Duke and Joan Walden
Rooms: 16 (12 PB; 4 SB) $35-85
Continental Breakfast
Credit Cards: A, B, D
Notes: 5, 6 (some restrictions), 8, 9, 10, 11, 12, 13, 14

LEWISTON

Shiloh Rose
Bed and Breakfast
3414 Selway Drive, 83501
(208) 743-2482

The Shiloh Rose, decorated in a warm, country-Victorian style, offers a spacious three-room suite as a home away from home. Lace curtains, fragrant potpourri, and fresh roses in season invite you to linger. Have morning coffee in the sitting room with a real wood-burning stove. Browse through the overflowing bookshelves, enjoy the TV and VCR, or the grand piano. A complete gourmet breakfast is served in the dining room or on the deck overlooking the valley. The view is fantastic!

Host: Dorothy A. Mader
Rooms: 1 Suite (SB) $65
Full Breakfast
Credit Cards: A, B
Notes: 2, 5, 9, 10, 11, 12, 13

SHOUP

Smith House
Bed and Breakfast
49 Salmon River Road, 83469
(208) 394-2121; (800) 238-5915

Charming log cabin with all the comforts of home. Five distinctively furnished guest rooms with a large covered redwood deck and breathtaking view of the Salmon River. Complimentary beverages in addition to full country breakfast featuring homemade jams and fruit. Guest house includes kitchen, sleeps six (ideal for families).

Hosts: Aubrey and Marsha Smith
Rooms: 5 (1 PB; 4 SB) $35-54
Bed and Breakfast or Modified American Plan
Credit Cards: A, B, D
Notes: 2, 6, 8, 9, 14

SUN VALLEY

The River Street Inn
P. O. Box 182, 83353
(208) 726-3611

Listen to the rippling Trail Creek from the spacious parlor room, and watch the sun come up over snowcapped mountains. The friendly staff will pamper guests and make them feel at home. Relax in the bathroom's Japanese soaking tub or under the umbrella on the deck. Sun Valley's shops, restaurants, and galleries are but a stone's throw from this quiet, central location.

Hosts: Virginia Van Doren and Gun Taylor
Rooms: 9 (PB) $115-155
Full Breakfast
Credit Cards: A, B, C, D
Notes: 2, 5, 6, 8, 9, 10, 11, 12, 13, 14

NOTES: Credit cards accepted: A Master Card; B Visa; C American Express; D Discover Card; E Diner's Club; F Other; 2 Personal Checks accepted; 3 Lunch available; 4 Dinner available; 5 Open all year; 6 Pets welcome; 8 Children welcome; 9 Social drinking allowed; 10 Tennis available; 11 Swimming available; 12 Golf available; 13 Skiing available; 14 May be booked through travel agents.

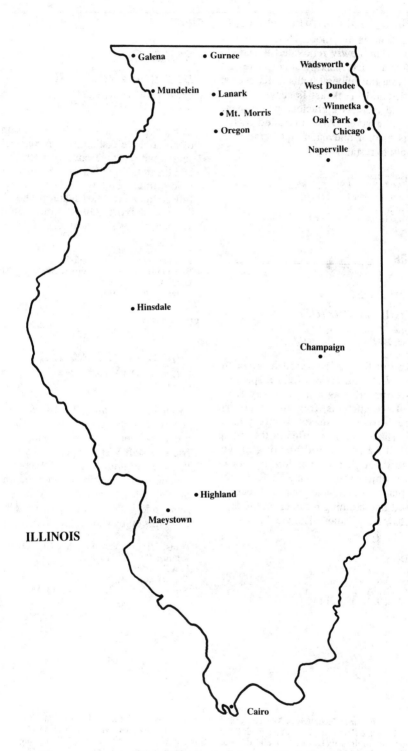

Galena • Gurnee •

Wadsworth •

Mundelein • West Dundee •

Lanark • Winnetka •

Mt. Morris • Oak Park • Chicago •

Oregon •

Naperville •

Hinsdale •

Champaign •

Highland •

Maeystown •

ILLINOIS

Cairo •

Illinois

B & B Midwest Reservations #02052

P. O. Box 95503, Hoffman Estates, 60195-0503
(800) 342-2632

This 120-year-old home sits on Million-aire's Boulevard in this historic town. The Ohio and Mississippi rivers converge at this point, making Cairo a peninsula overlooking Kentucky and Missouri. Civil War buffs will be in awe at the local history, antiques, and mementos from President Grant's stay in this town. The interior of the home has been completely restored and is filled with period antiques. The hostess can answer all questions about the history of the area. All rooms have double beds. Open year-round. Personal checks, Visa, MasterCard, and Discover accepted. Private bath, $80; shared bath, $65-$70.

Barb's Bed and Breakfast

606 South Russell, 61821
(217) 356-0376

This cozy cottage is situated in a quiet, attractive neighborhood with quick access to the University of Illinois. The comfortable guest rooms feature antiques, ceiling fans, and handmade quilts, and they share a parlor with a fireplace. Delicious breakfasts are served in the dining room. The twin cities and nearby communities offer a wide variety of things to see and do. Antique shops, theaters, museums, walking/biking trails, fishing lakes, swimming, and golf are all nearby.

Hosts: Barbara and Merle Eyestone
Rooms: 2 (SB) $45 plus tax
Continental Breakfast
Credit Cards: None
Notes: 2, 9, 10, 11, 12

Annie's

Bed & Breakfast/Chicago, Inc.
P. O. Box 14088, 60614-0088
(312) 951-0085; FAX (312) 649-9243

This comfortable, completely furnished studio apartment has a fully equipped kitchen, queen-size bed, and private bath. Close to some of Chicago's best restaurants and fine shopping. Air conditioning, TV. $75.

Bed and Breakfast/ Chicago, Inc.

P. O. Box 14088, 60614-0088
(312) 951-0085; FAX (312) 649-9243

This reservation service includes guest rooms in private homes, and self-contained apartments primarily in the center of Chicago and the North Shore. Offerings include a converted mansion close to Lake Michigan, or guests may prefer a high-rise condo with a panoramic view of the city, even a handsome guest room with a four-poster bed in historic Old Town.

NOTES: Credit cards accepted: A Master Card; B Visa; C American Express; D Discover Card; E Diner's Club; F Other; 2 Personal Checks accepted; 3 Lunch available; 4 Dinner available; 5 Open all year; 6 Pets welcome; 8 Children welcome; 9 Social drinking allowed; 10 Tennis available; 11 Swimming available; 12 Golf available; 13 Skiing available; 14 May be booked through travel agents.

Rooms: 120 (100 PB; 20 SB) $65-150
Continental Breakfasts
Credit Cards: A, B, C
Notes: 2, 5, 8, 9, 10, 11, 14

Bed & Breakfast/ Chicago, Inc. #2

P. O. Box 14088, 60614-0088
(312) 951-0085; FAX (312) 649-9243

This historic Kenwood home was recently restored by the architect/owner and her co-host who is a public television producer. Its Prairie-style architecture is wonderfully harmonized with antique furniture for an Old World European charm. $55 single and $65 double.

Bed & Breakfast/ Chicago, Inc. #3

P. O. Box 14088, 60614-0088
(312) 951-0085; FAX (312) 649-9243

This self-contained one-bedroom garden apartment is in a renovated frame building. Recently decorated, it is furnished with a four-poster queen bed and sleeper sofa, and offers kitchen and private bath. Guests may have breakfast in the lovely garden, weather permitting. The host family lives upstairs; he is a TV reporter and she owns Bed and Breakfast-Chicago, Inc. $85.

Bed & Breakfast/ Chicago, Inc. #5

P. O. Box 14088, 60614-0088
(312) 951-0085; FAX (312) 649-9243

A traditionally furnished three-story town house offers an extra guest room with twin beds and a shared bath with host. Guests are welcome to enjoy the family room, fireplace, and other homey comforts provided. The host has been with Bed and Breakfast/Chicago for over 5 years. Easily accessible to public transportation. Air conditioning, TV. $55 single; $65 double.

Bed & Breakfast/ Chicago, Inc. #8

P. O. Box 14088, 60614-0088
(312) 951-0085; FAX (312) 649-9243

This renovated Victorian brick building offers several possibilities. There are both guest rooms and self-contained apartments available. There is a twin guest room with a private bath available in the apartment of the owner. Other guest rooms include queen and double rooms with a shared bath. Guests also have access to livingroom and kitchen. This unit can also be rented as a self-contained two-bedroom apartment. The owner has just finished rehabbing a one bedroom unit with twins or a king bed, sleeper sofa in the livingroom, and a Jacuzzi bath. Air-conditioning and TV. $55 single; $65 double; $95 one-bedroom apartment; $135 two-bedroom apartment.

Bed & Breakfast/ Chicago, Inc. #9

P. O. Box 14088, 60614-0088
(312) 951-0085; FAX (312) 649-9243

This self-contained one-bedroom garden apartment has been recently decorated and offers a queen bed, bath, full kitchen, and a livingroom. Air conditioning, TV. $85.

Bed & Breakfast/ Chicago, Inc. #12

P. O. Box 14088, 60614-0088
(312) 951-0085; FAX (312) 649-9243

A 60-year-old replica of a French chateau. The guest area is on the third floor and has a separate entrance. Two rooms, both with private baths, are available. Guests may use exercise room, full kitchen, and share a sitting room. Coffee, tea, and muffins. $65-75 single; $75-85 double.

NOTES: Credit cards accepted: A Master Card; B Visa; C American Express; D Discover Card; E Diner's Club; F Other; 2 Personal Checks accepted; 3 Lunch available; 4 Dinner available; 5 Open all year;

Bed & Breakfast/ Chicago, Inc. #17

P. O. Box 14088, 60614-0088
(312) 951-0085; FAX (312) 649-9243

Relax and enjoy the modern comforts of this forty-year-old home renovated by an architect and brightly decorated in Southwest style. Downstairs guest room on same level as your hosts' bedroom, offers double bed and private bath (shower and tub). Upstairs guest room offers queen futon on frame, private attached bath with bathtub (hand-held shower) and sitting area. Pleasant, outdoor deck off front of house offers excellent place for lounging. TV, air conditioning. The hostess is in advertising/public relations and the host does cancer research at Northwestern University Medical School. $55-65 single; $65-75 double.

Bed & Breakfast/ Chicago, Inc. #27

P. O. Box 14088, 60614-0088
(312) 951-0085; FAX (312) 649-9243

Situated five miles from the Loop, on the border between the Gold Coast and Old Town, this self-contained apartment is in a renovated Victorian brick three-flat, occupied by the hosts. The apartment offers two bedrooms, two baths, fully equipped kitchen, fireplace, and washer/dryer. No breakfast. Air conditioning, TV. $150 daily; $2,000 monthly.

Bed & Breakfast/ Chicago, Inc. #29

P. O. Box 14088, 60614-0088
(312) 951-0085; FAX (312) 649-9243

This high-rise apartment offers a guest room in the spacious condominium of a public relations professional. The guest room in this stylish, contemporary home is furnished with a double bed and has a private bath. The building has a health club. Air conditioning, TV. $65-75.

Bed & Breakfast/ Chicago, Inc. #35

P. O. Box 14088, 60614-0088
(312) 951-0085; FAX (312) 649-9243

This centrally located accommodation is just two blocks from Northwestern University, Kendall College, and the Chicago "el" (elevated train). Only five minutes away, downtown Evanston and Lake Michigan are also easily accessible. This second-floor apartment offers two comfortable guest rooms, one with twin beds (placed together), and the other with a single bed. Enjoy a welcoming glass of sherry, assorted contemporary magazines, classical music, TV and VCR in a tastefully decorated environment. Terry bathrobes and other amenities add to the homey feeling. Shared bath. Continental breakfast consists of seasonal fruits or juices, and delectable scones, muffins, or croissants from Evanston's premier bakers. $65 single; $75 double.

Bed & Breakfast/ Chicago, Inc. #37

P. O. Box 14088, 60614-0088
(312) 951-0085; FAX (312) 649-9243

Elegantly furnished country French home on 3/4 of an acre offers charm and sophistication, in a beautiful area just 10 blocks from Lake Michigan. This home has been written up in several local and city publications and features beautiful gardens, Olympic-size swimming pool, large game room with a 50-inch TV, marble entryway, and many antiques. Three guest rooms are offered: king bed with private hall bath, queen bed with private attached bath with Jacuzzi, and twin beds with private

6 Pets welcome; 8 Children welcome; 9 Social drinking allowed; 10 Tennis available; 11 Swimming available; 12 Golf available; 13 Skiing available; 14 May be booked through travel agents.

attached bath with Jacuzzi. Air conditioning. Deluxe breakfast. $70-90.

Bed & Breakfast/ Chicago, Inc. #41

P. O. Box 14088, 60614-0088
(312) 951-0085; FAX (312) 649-9243

This ground-floor, self-catering apartment in a two-flat building comes fully equipped for a short or long-term stay (three-night minimum), and consists of two bedrooms, one bath, livingroom, dining room, eat-in kitchen, porch, and private phone line. On a quiet residential street, it is close to public transportation in southeast Evanston. For short-term stays, continental breakfast is provided, and is self-serve. The hosts, a retired professor and a teacher, live downstairs in their own apartments. $75 daily; $400 weekly; $900 monthly.

Bed & Breakfast/ Chicago, Inc. #43

P. O. Box 14088, 60614-0088
(312) 951-0085; FAX (312) 649-9243

This single-family home has just been rehabbed. The host, who has traveled extensively and loves staying in bed and breakfast accommodations, lives in a coach house behind this accommodation. Offered are three guest rooms with private baths. Breakfast is self-serve from the kitchen. This is an ideal arrangement for groups traveling together or visitors in Chicago for an extended time who want to settle in and feel they've found a home away from home. Air conditioning, TV. $65-75; weekly and monthly rates are available.

Bed & Breakfast/ Chicago, Inc. #52

P. O. Box 14088, 60614-0088
(312) 951-0085; FAX (312) 649-9243

This three-story Victorian house on a beautiful residential street, studded with elm trees, is situated one block west of Northwestern's campus and three blocks from the "el." Accommodations include one guest room with a double bed and another with twin beds. A private, unattached bath (no shower) is shared with other bed and breakfast guests. The hosts, a family with two daughters, two cats, a cocker spaniel, and two guinea pigs, warmly welcome guests to relax and watch TV in their first-floor livingroom. $55 single; $65 double.

Bed & Breakfast/ Chicago, Inc. #54

P. O. Box 14088, 60614-0088
(312) 951-0085; FAX (312) 649-9243

Spacious, self-contained one-bedroom garden apartment, one block from St. Francis Hospital on Ridge, offers queen bed in bedroom plus a trundle bed in livingroom, kitchen, private bath/shower. Air conditioning. The hosts, an employee of the federal government and a vice president of education/training in health care, live on the premises in their own apartment. $75 daily.

Bed & Breakfast/ Chicago, Inc. #56

P. O. Box 14088, 60614-0088
(312) 951-0085; FAX (312) 649-9243

This Victorian home in Evanston's Lake Shore Historic District is conveniently situated one mile south of Northwestern University and a short walk from fine restaurants and public transportation. Featured in several local and national magazines, it is furnished with a blend of lovely antiques and art. One double room and one single room are available on the third floor. Shared bath when other guest room is occupied. A generous continental breakfast

NOTES: Credit cards accepted: A Master Card; B Visa; C American Express; D Discover Card; E Diner's Club; F Other; 2 Personal Checks accepted; 3 Lunch available; 4 Dinner available; 5 Open all year;

is provided. Individuals or married couples only. $55 single; $65 double.

Bed & Breakfast/ Chicago, Inc. #64

P. O. Box 14088, 60614-0088
(312) 951-0085; FAX (312) 649-9243

This renovated mansion in prime Lincoln Park offers a double bedded guest room with a private, unattached bath. The Victorian home has been rehabbed to maintain the original feeling with antiques, wicker furniture, etc. Also available is a self-contained one-bedroom apartment on the third floor of the home. This unit is a large loft-like space with light wood floors, an island kitchen, and more contemporary furnishings. Guest room is $65 single; $75 double; apartment $125.

City View Inn

Bed and Breakfast/Chicago, Inc.
P. O. Box 14088, 60614-0088
(312) 951-0085; FAX (312) 649-9243

This lovely 22-room property was originally a private club. Situated on the 40th floor of a building in the financial district, the rooms all have king-size beds and marble baths and gorgeous views. Included in the rate is use of the first-class health club located in the building. Parking, and continental breakfast. This is ideal for small group meetings. $105-155.

River Plaza

Bed and Breakfast/Chicago, Inc.
P. O. Box 14088, 60614-0088
(312) 951-0085; FAX (312) 649-9243

These self-contained convertible studio apartments are among the most popular accommodations. Situated in a high-rise building with a full grocery store, restau-rants, health club with indoor/outdoor pool, and other amenities. Each apartment has a double or queen bed, sleeper sofa, complete kitchen, and a fabulous view of the skyline. Walk to business appointments, shops on Michigan Avenue, the lakefront, the Merchandise Mart and the galleries of River North. The "host" is Bed and Breakfast/Chicago. Coffee, tea, and muffins only. Air conditioning, TV. $95-125.

ELIZABETH

B & B Midwest Reservations #22013

P. O. Box 95503, Hoffman Estates, 60195-0503
(800) 342-2632

This 1921 country school has been renovated over the years. Once home to Thomas Locker, a local artist, the home offers a spectacular view overlooking 10 miles of Rush Creek Valley near Galena. Four guest accommodations with either king or queen-size beds and private baths. Only 30 minutes to Galena, and 15 minutes from Savannah. Near Mississipppi River towns and antique shops. A hearty continental breakfast is included. $60-89.

GALENA

Avery Guest House

606 South Prospect Street, 61036
(815) 777-3883

Situated within Galena's historic district, this pre-Civil War home is a short walk from antique shops and historic buildings. Enjoy the scenic view from the porch swing; feel free to play the piano or just visit. Breakfast is served in the sunny dining room with a bay window overlooking the Galena River valley.

6 Pets welcome; 8 Children welcome; 9 Social drinking allowed; 10 Tennis available; 11 Swimming available; 12 Golf available; 13 Skiing available; 14 May be booked through travel agents.

Hosts: Flo and Roger Jensen
Rooms: 4 (2SB) $40-60
Continental Breakfast
Minimum stay weekends and holidays: 2 nights
Credit Cards: A, B
Notes: 2, 5, 8, 9, 10, 11, 12, 13

B & B Midwest Reservations #01012

P. O. Box 95503, Hoffman Estates, 60195-0503
(800) 342-2632

A beautiful farm home six miles south of
Galena is overlooked by Chestnut
Mountain. The original structure is 150-
years old, with additions built 75 and 25
years ago. The home, filled with antiques,
offers three guest rooms. Queen waveless
waterbed with a private bath, and double
brass bed with a shared bath. Light continental breakfast included. Easy drive to
Galena activities. Personal checks,
MasterCard, Visa, and Discover accepted.
$55-75.

B & B Midwest Reservations #06059

P. O. Box 95503, Hoffman Estates, 60195-0503
(800) 342-2632

A restored farmhouse secluded in the hills
near Galena. This inn has air conditioning,
a large front porch, and beautiful views of
the countryside. The Early American flavor
is carried throughout the suite. Suite consists of queen bed with Jacuzzi, loft with
king mattress and private porch at the farmhouse. Other free-standing locations in the
Territories and Eagles Ridge include lovely
homes with two bedrooms, one and one-
half or two baths, livingroom with fireplace. Open year-round. Children welcome.
Enjoy tennis, swimming, golf and skiing.
Can accommodate up to five people. A
honeymoon or anniversary package including champagne, flowers, and breakfast in
room is available. MasterCard, Visa, and
Discover accepted. $195-315.

Brierwreath Manor Bed and Breakfast

216 North Bench Street, 61036
(815) 777-0608

Circa 1884 Queen Anne house with wraparound porch only one short block from
historic Main Street. Cable TV, early morning coffee buffet, and full breakfast are
only a few of the comforts to experience.
The manor has three large suites with sitting areas and private baths. Each is furnished with an eclectic blend of antiques
and modern comforts. Special packages
available.

Hosts: Mike and Lyn Cook
Suites: 3 (PB) $80
Full Breakfast
Credit Cards: None
Notes: 2, 5, 9, 11, 12, 13

Belle Aire Mansion Guest House

11410 Route 20 West, 61036
(815) 777-0893

Belle Aire Mansion is a pre-Civil War
home set on 16 beautiful acres only minutes from historic Galena. The rooms are
large and comfortable. Guests say, "It's just
like visiting friends."

Belle Aire Mansion

NOTES: Credit cards accepted: A Master Card; B Visa; C American Express; D Discover Card; E Diner's
Club; F Other; 2 Personal Checks accepted; 3 Lunch available; 4 Dinner available; 5 Open all year;

Hosts: Jan and Lorraine Svec
Rooms: 5 (PB) $70.85-147.15
Minimum stay weekends holidays and special
   weekends: 2 nights
Credit Cards: A, B, C
Closed Christmas
Notes: 2, 8, 9, 11, 12, 13

Park Avenue Guest House

208 Park Avenue, 61036
(815) 777-1075; (800) 359-0743

An 1893 Queen Anne with original "painted lady" woodwork. Walk to town. Ample parking. Queen beds. Antique furniture. Shaded garden with gazebo. Wraparound screened porch. Central air conditioning, cable TV, and second parlor.

Host: Sharon Fallbacher
Rooms: 4 (PB) $50-95
Continental Breakfast
Credit Cards: A, B, D
Notes: 2, 5, 9, 11, 12, 13

GURNEE

B & B Midwest Reservations #10030

P. O. Box 95503, Hoffman Estates, 60195-0503
(800) 342-2632

"Wonderful" describes this cozy country farm home, 1/2 mile from Great America in Gurnee. Handmade quilts, feather comforters, and antiques throughout make staying in one of the three guest rooms a special experience. Accommodations in a large queen room with sitting area, queen fourposter bed with private bath; family two-room suite sleeping up to five. Separate cottage with queen and twins with a kitchenette and fireplace. Open year-round. Children welcome. Short drive to discount mall and skiing, or feed the llama and sheep. Full breakfast included. MasterCard, Visa, and Discover accepted. $85-105.

HIGHLAND

Phyllis' Bed and Breakfast

801 Ninth Street, 62249
(618) 654-4619

A remodeled bungalow about 100 years old, this bed and breakfast has a place for all seasons. A fireplace for winter wards off the cold, and a deck in the summer lets you watch the birds and squirrels. Just 25 minutes from St. Louis's many sights, Highland has a town square with antique shops, band concerts in the gazebo, and many festivals. There is plenty to do, or just enjoy a quiet, peaceful visit. There is a gift shop on the premises.

Hosts: Bob and Phyllis Bible
Rooms: 5 (3 PB; 2 SB) $50-55
Full Breakfast
Credit Cards: A, B
Notes: 2, 5, 8 (over 12), 10, 11, 12

HINSDALE

B & B Midwest Reservations #19079

P. O. Box 95503, Hoffman Estates, 60195-0503
(800) 342-2632

Beautiful antique-filled home in affluent suburb features a suite with a queen-size bed and an additional queen Hide-a-bed. Private bath with a shower. Family room has a fireplace, and a sun room is available. Only 30 minutes to downtown Chicago (by expressway or train), mall shopping, Brookfield Zoo and the Western Open Golf Course. Rates include continental breakfast. Personal checks, MasterCard, Visa, and Discover accepted . $75.

6 Pets welcome; 8 Children welcome; 9 Social drinking allowed; 10 Tennis available; 11 Swimming available; 12 Golf available; 13 Skiing available; 14 May be booked through travel agents.

LANARK

Standish House
Bed and Breakfast

540 West Carrol Street, 61046
(815) 493-2307; (800) 468-2307

Traditional English bed and breakfast. Situated on Route 52, 120 miles west of Chicago. Relaxing small town atmosphere. Walking distance to business district and restaurants. Myles Standish heritage carried throughout with 18th-century English antiques, canopy beds, paintings, and decor. Dining room highlighted by antique portraits, rich, dark furniture, and formal chandelier. Full air conditioning. The owner, Norman Standish, is a direct descendant of Myles Standish.

Host: Eve Engles
Rooms: 5 (1 PB; 4 SB) $55-65
Full Breakfast
Credit Cards: A, B
Notes: 2, 5, 9, 12, 13

MAEYSTOWN

Corner George Inn

P. O. Box 103, Corner of Main and Mill, 62256
(618) 458-6660; (800) 458-6020

A frontier Victorian structure built in 1884, the Maeystown Hotel and Saloon is now the Corner George Inn. Situated 45 minutes south of St. Louis, the inn has five painstakingly restored, antique-filled guest rooms, two sitting rooms, a wine cellar, and an elegant ballroom. Maeystown is a quaint, 19th-century village with shops and a restaurant. Nearby are Fort de Chartres, Fort Kaskaskia, and the scenic bluff along the Mississippi.

Hosts: David and Marcia Braswell
Rooms: 5 (PB) $65-95
Full Breakfast
Credit Cards: A, B
Notes: 2, 5, 14

MT. MORRIS

B & B Midwest
Reservations #16021

P. O. Box 95503, Hoffman Estates, 60195-0503
(800) 342-2632

This newly redecorated and refurbished country inn in Mt. Morris is situated on nine wooded acres in the center of a public golf course. The inn is fully air conditioned and offers one- and two-bedroom suites, some with parlors, phones, color TVs, VCRs, mini-refrigerators, and microwave ovens. All six rooms have queen beds; some have private baths. Light continental breakfast included. $35-65.

MUNDELEIN

B & B Midwest
Reservations #12049

P. O. Box 95503, Hoffman Estates, 60195-0503
(800) 342-2632

This grand old red house, built in the early 1900s, features 44 windows throughout. Situated halfway between Chicago and Milwaukee, it is convenient to Long Grove Village, Ravinia Park, Lamb's Farm and more. Old-fashioned decor and a musical theme are woven together throughout this Victorian home. Three guest rooms share two full baths; two twin beds, a queen bed and a king with private porch. Two rooms have private baths and double beds. Open year-round. Children welcome; skiing available. Personal checks, MasterCard, Visa, and Discover accepted. $40-110.

Round Robin
Bed and Breakfast Inn

231 East Maple, Route 176, 60060
(708) 566-7664

Situated halfway between Chicago and Milwaukee, this grand old house takes guests back to another era. Within are rooms with charm and a musical theme. The hostess often serenades breakfast guests at the piano. Only a few minutes away from Long Grove Historical Village and Gurnee Mills World's Largest Outlet Mall.

Hosts: George and Laura Loffredo
Rooms: 5 (2 PB; 3 SB) $40-65
Full Breakfast
Credit Cards: A, B
Notes: 2, 5, 8, 9, 10, 12, 14

NAPERVILLE

Harrison House Bed and Breakfast

26 North Eagle Street, 60540
(708) 420-1117

Harrison House Bed and Breakfast, circa 1911, is situated 25 miles west of Chicago in historic Naperville. Five antique-filled, air-conditioned guest rooms with private baths, one with Jacuzzi. Walk to downtown restaurants, historic sites, quaint shops, and Centennial Beach. Homemade chocolate chip cookies, fresh flowers, gourmet coffee, and scrumptious breakfast. Business or pleasure. Relax and be pampered.

Host: Neal and Lynn Harrison
Rooms: 5 (3 PB; 2 SB) $68-138

Harrison House

Full Breakfast
Credit Cards: A, B, C
Notes: 2, 5, 9, 10, 11, 12, 13, 14

OAK PARK

B & B Midwest Reservations #15990

P. O. Box 95503, Hoffman Estates, 60195-0503
(800) 342-2632

Queen Anne Victorian home situated in a prominent historic suburb of Chicago. The home, built in 1885, is air conditioned and accommodates guests in one room with a large queen-size bed, private bath, and Victorian-style antiques. A second choice offers either twin beds with a private sitting room and television, or a queen bedroom. Either room may be selected as shared or private bath. Enjoy a light continental breakfast. Open year-round. Children welcome. Home is one block from Frank Lloyd Wright's home and studio. Just 20 minutes from Chicago. Personal checks, Master-Card, Visa, and Discover accepted. $55.

B & B Midwest Reservations #19111

P. O. Box 95503, Hoffman Estates, 60195-0503
(800) 342-2632

Truly for followers and admirers of Frank Lloyd Wright, the architect of this beautiful home. Furnished entirely with his signed pieces and in keeping with his choice of decor. Stay in one of three guest rooms, twin or double with shared bath for $75 per night, or king suite with private bath and sitting area for $125 per night. Enjoy a continental breakfast in the morning. The outdoor whirlpool in the summer or the large fireplace for the winter are available for guests' enjoyment. Open year-round. Personal checks, MasterCard, Visa, and Discover accepted. Children welcome.

6 Pets welcome; 8 Children welcome; 9 Social drinking allowed; 10 Tennis available; 11 Swimming available; 12 Golf available; 13 Skiing available; 14 May be booked through travel agents.

OREGON

B & B Midwest Reservations #16059

P. O. Box 95503, Hoffman Estates, 60195-0503
(800) 342-2632

This 120-year-old Italianate country villa situated in Oregon boasts 12 rooms and seven marble fireplaces, 11-foot ceilings, arched doorways, and antique Parisian wallpaper all adding to the charm. Rooms include a Victorian king with fireplace, private bath, and Jacuzzi, $165; two queen or king rooms with private bath and fireplaces, $110 each; three-room suite with double bed, queen bed, two half-baths, shower, and sitting room, $145 per night. Open year-round. Children welcome. Two-night minimum stay on weekends. Rates include an extensive gourmet breakfast. Special packages and baskets available. Chocolate Fest, winter sports, Christmas tree farm, and river boat cruises available (in season), swimming, golf and skiing. Personal checks, MasterCard, Visa, and Discover accepted.

WADSWORTH

B & B Midwest Reservations #02051

P. O. Box 95503, Hoffman Estates, 60195-0503
(800) 342-2632

This private home allows an entire lower-level floor for their guests. The bedroom offers a queen bed while living area provides a couch, fireplace, kitchenette, dining area, spa, and private bath. The home sits on a large lot where the guests may enjoy a small man-made lake for fishing or rowboating. Open year-round. Just minutes from The Pyramid House, Great America, skiing, or the Gurnee Mills Manufacturers' Discount Mall. MasterCard, Visa, and Discover accepted. $75.

WEST DUNDEE

B & B Midwest Reservations #08040

P. O. Box 95503, Hoffman Estates, 60195-0503
(800) 342-2632

Step back into the early 1900s when visiting this newly renovated historical site in West Dundee. This mansion is filled with antiques and royal hospitality, and convenient shopping malls, interstate highways, and business districts are within a few minutes' drive. The six uniquely decorated rooms range from smaller country-style to formal Colonial doubles to a Victorian suite with a Jacuzzi. Several rooms have shared baths with Jacuzzis for guests. Accommodations include kings, queens, doubles, and twins. Open year-round. Extended continental breakfast included. Children welcome. Golf nearby. $49-179.

Chateau des Fleurs

WINNETKA

Chateau des Fleurs

552 Ridge Road, 60093
(708) 256-7272

Chateau des Fleurs is an elegant respite from the world that welcomes guests with light, beauty, warmth, and lovely views of magnificent trees, gardens, and a swimming pool. A French country home filled with antiques, four fireplaces, 50-inch television, and a grand piano. Situated by a private road for jogging or walking, it is only four blocks from shops and restaurants and a 30-minute train ride to Chicago's Loop. Just 10 minutes from Northwestern University.

Host: Sally H. Ward
Rooms: 3 (PB) $80-90
Full Breakfast
Minimum stay weekends and holidays: 2 nights
Credit Cards: A, B
Notes: 2, 5, 8 (over 11), 9, 10, 11, 12, 14

Bristol •

• Middlebury

South Bend

• Goshen

• Nappanee

• Syracuse

• Warsaw

• Fowler

• Huntington

• Tippecanoe

• Indianapolis

• Knightstown

• Decatur

• Nashville

Corydon
•

INDIANA

Indiana

BRISTOL

Tyler's Place
19562 State Road 120, 46507
(219) 848-7145

Adjoining a 27-hole golf course at the edge of Crystal Valley, Tyler's Place offers a pleasant view of the rolling course and plenty of warm Hoosier hospitality. The Common Room is decorated with an Amish flavor. Full breakfast is served in the sun room, and evenings are enjoyed in the backyard around the fire ring.

Hosts: Esther and Ron Tyler
Rooms: 4 (1 PB; 1 SB) $45
Full Breakfast
Credit Cards: None
Notes: 2, 5, 7, 10, 11, 12, 13

CORYDON

Kintner House Inn
101 South Capitol Avenue, 47112
(812) 738-2020

Completely restored inn, circa 1873, a national historical landmark, with 15 rooms, each with private bath, furnished in Victorian and country antiques. Serves full breakfast. Also, three apartment suites adjacent to inn, completely furnished and decorated, that are ideal for families. Unique shops, fine restaurants, antique malls, first state capitol, and excursion train all within walking distance of the inn. Sports available. Rated AAA and Mobil. A hideaway for romantics. Lower rates Sunday through Thursday.

Host: Mary Jane Bridgewater
Rooms: 18 (PB) $39-89
Full Breakfast
Credit Cards: A, B, C, D, E
Notes: 2, 5, 8, 9, 10, 11, 12, 14

DECATUR

Cragwood Inn Bed and Breakfast
303 North Second Street, 46733
(219) 728-2000

Enjoy the ambience of the past and the conveniences of the present in this beautiful Queen Anne home, circa 1900. Magnificent woodwork and beveled leaded glass windows reflect the craftsmanship of a bygone era. Fireplaces in two rooms, several mystery dinners are offered during the year. Chocolate lovers' weekends are held in March and October. Decatur, a delightful small town just south of Fort Wayne, has a large antique mall. Convenient to Michigan and Ohio.

Hosts: George and Nancy Craig
Rooms: 5 (PB) $45-65
Full Breakfast (weekends); Continental Breakfast (weekdays)
Credit Cards: A, B
Notes: 2, 5, 9, 10, 11, 12

FOWLER

Pheasant Country Bed and Breakfast
900 East Fifth Street, 47944
(317) 884-0908

NOTES: Credit cards accepted: A Master Card; B Visa; C American Express; D Discover Card; E Diner's Club; F Other; 2 Personal Checks accepted; 3 Lunch available; 4 Dinner available; 5 Open all year; 6 Pets welcome; 8 Children welcome; 9 Social drinking allowed; 10 Tennis available; 11 Swimming available; 12 Golf available; 13 Skiing available; 14 May be booked through travel agents.

Purviance House

Situated on a quiet, tree-lined brick street in a small town decorated with quaint shops. Guest rooms are handsomely decorated, and guests may relax in the common room, read a book from the library, play the piano, watch television, play games, go for a walk or just sit and visit. Homemade breads, pastry and gourmet coffee and tea, along with a full breakfast, are served in the formal dining room. The 1940 two-story Colonial is furnished with fine antiques, and situated just 30 minutes from Purdue University.

Host: Julie Gaylord
Rooms: 3 (2 SB) $50-55
Full or Continental Breakfast
Credit Cards: B
Notes: 2, 3, 4, 5, 8, 9, 10, 11, 12, 14

GOSHEN

Timberidge

16801 State Road 4, 46526
(219) 533-7133

This Austrian chalet log home, nestled in the beauty of quiet woods, welcomes guests into a serene setting with a uniquely furnished suite with a private bath and private entrance. A continental breakfast is served in front of the large windows where the beauty of the countryside can be enjoyed. There is a walking path through the woods, and area attractions are nearby Amish and Mennonite communities.

Hosts: Edward and Donita Brookmyer
Rooms: 1 suite (PB) $55
Continental Breakfast
Credit Cards: None
Notes: 2, 5, 8, 10, 11, 12

HUNTINGTON

Purviance House Bed and Breakfast

326 South Jefferson, 46750
(219) 356-4218; (219) 356-9215

Freshly baked breads, a pot of coffee or tea, and fresh fruits welcome guests to a homey atmosphere with a TV, kitchen privileges, and well-stocked bookshelves. Comfortable beds and tasty breakfasts add to the warm ambience of a lovingly restored 1859 Greek Revival-Italianate home listed on the National Register of Historic Places. Features include a winding cherry staircase, parquet floors, ornate ceiling designs, four unique fireplaces, quilts, antiques, and period furnishings. Near lakes and nature trails.

Hosts: Bob and Jean Gernand
Rooms: 4 (2 PB; 2 SB) $40-55 plus tax
Full Breakfast
Credit Cards: None
Notes: 2, 5, 9, 10, 11, 12

INDIANAPOLIS

Friendliness With A Flair

5214 East 20th Place, 46218
(317) 356-3149

Clean, tastefully furnished, strictly private. Full breakfast served in an outside, screened glass Florida room, season permitting. Just 15 minutes from the heart of the city in a residential area. Adequate drive-way parking. Gift certificates available.

Host: Loretta Whitten
Rooms: 2 (PB) $40-45
Full Breakfast
Credit Cards: F
Notes: 2, 5

NOTES: Credit cards accepted: A Master Card; B Visa; C American Express; D Discover Card; E Diner's Club; F Other; 2 Personal Checks accepted; 3 Lunch available; 4 Dinner available; 5 Open all year;

KNIGHTSTOWN

Bed and Breakfast Midwest Reservations #12121

P. O. Box 95503, Hoffman Estates, 60195-0503
(800) 342-2632

This historic country home situated midway between Indianapolis and Richmond, Indiana, provides four rooms for guests with easy access to I-70. Guest rooms include king and queen beds with a fireplace, and queen and pair of twins, each of which has a private bath. This beautiful inn overlooks Hoosier farmland and a beautiful golf course that guests may use. A short drive to a quaint small town and four hours from Chicago, this home is in Antique Alley. Enjoy an extended continental breakfast before beginning the day's activities. Open year-round. Children welcome. Golf packages available. Skiing nearby. Personal checks, MasterCard, Visa, and Discover accepted.

MIDDLEBURY

Bee Hive Bed and Breakfast

Box 1191, 46540
(219) 825-5023

Come home to the farm. Enjoy country life, snuggle under a handmade quilt, and wake to the smell of freshly baked muffins. Situated in the heart of Amish country. Enjoy the shops, flea markets, and antique stores in the area. Right off the Indiana Turnpike.

Hosts: Herb and Treva Swarm
Rooms: 4 (1 PB; 3 SB) $49.95-60
Full Breakfast
Credit Cards: A, B
Notes: 2, 5, 8, 10, 11, 12, 13

NAPPANEE

Amish Acres Bed and Breakfast Reservation Service

1600 West Market Street, 46550
(219) 773-4188; (800) 800-4942

Historic Amish Acres in Nappanee provides a unique bed and breakfast service that offers overnight accommodations in private, northern Indiana Amish country homes. Most accommodations are in two-story frame houses on large farms in Elkhart Country area. Most hosts are members of the Mennonite, German Baptist, and Old Order or conservative Amish faiths. Many Old Order homes do not have electricity and do not accept reservations for Saturday or Sunday. Continental breakfast is served, although some offer full breakfast. $50-60.

NASHVILLE

Russell's Roost Bed and Breakfast

Route 4, Box 68-A, 47448
(812) 988-1600

A newly constructed east bedroom offers a king size bed and private deck facing the lake, with an outdoor hot tub. The room also features a queen sofa-bed for additional guests. The west bedroom boasts a queen size, four-poster bed, and indoor Jacuzzi. The room opens onto a deck with a porch swing facing the lake. Brown County, situated three miles north of Nashville, is known for its 200 craft shops. The house is furnished in Norwegian and English themes on 17 acres of woodlands.

Hosts: Gene and Mary Lou Russell
Rooms: 2 (PB) $75-95
Full Breakfast
Credit Cards: None
Notes: 2, 5, 8, 9, 11, 12

6 Pets welcome; 8 Children welcome; 9 Social drinking allowed; 10 Tennis available; 11 Swimming available; 12 Golf available; 13 Skiing available; 14 May be booked through travel agents.

Story Inn

SCHERERVILLE

Sunset Pines

862 Sunset Drive, 46375-2991
(219) 322-3322

Three wooded acres of country comfort are hidden away in the city, situated less than a mile from the "Crossroads of America," at U.S. Routes 30 and 41. Only 15 minutes from the Star Theater at I-65, 35 miles from the Chicago Loop, and 20 miles from Indiana State Dunes. In-ground pool and other outdoor activities are available.

Hosts: Clay and Nikki Foster
Rooms: 2 (1 PB; 1 SB) $40-50
Continental Breakfast
Credit Cards: None
Notes: 2, 5, 8, 9, 10, 11, 12, 13, 14

SOUTH BEND

The Book Inn

508 West Washington Street, 46601
(219) 288-1990

Second Empire home in downtown South Bend. Designers' showcase—every room beautifully decorated. Fresh flowers, silver, fine china, and candlelight. The hosts

emphasize service for the business person as well as leisured guests. The inn also houses a quality used bookstore, and guest rooms include the Louisa May Alcott, Jane Austen, and Charlotte Brontë rooms.

Hosts: Peggy and John Livingston
Rooms: 5 (PB) $75
Continental Breakfast
Credit Cards: A, B, C
Notes: 2, 5, 9, 14

STORY

Story Inn

P. O. Box 64, Nashville, 47448
(812) 988-2273

Situated on the southern edge of the Brown County State Park, this historic Dodge City-style general store is now a country inn, housing a critically acclaimed full-service restaurant. Overnight lodging is available upstairs, and in the surrounding village cottages. Rooms are furnished with period antiques, original artwork, fresh flowers, private baths, and air conditioning. Reservations required.

Hosts: Benjamin and Cyndi Schultz
Rooms: 17 (PB) $65-85
Full Breakfast
Credit Cards: A, B, C, D
Notes: 3, 4, 5, 6, 8, 9, 10, 11, 12, 13

SYRACUSE

Anchor Inn
Bed and Breakfast

11007 North State Road 13, 46567
(219) 457-4714

Anchor Inn is a turn-of-the-century, two-story home filled with period furniture and antiques. Features of the home include: claw foot tub, pier mirror, transomed doorways, hardwood floors, and a large, inviting front porch that overlooks the greens of an 18-hole public golf course. Halfway between South Bend and Fort Wayne in Indiana's lake region and directly across

NOTES: Credit cards accepted: A Master Card; B Visa; C American Express; D Discover Card; E Diner's Club; F Other; 2 Personal Checks accepted; 3 Lunch available; 4 Dinner available; 5 Open all year;

Anchor Inn

the highway from Lake Wawasee (Indiana's largest natural lake). Nearby attractions include Amish communities of Nappanee and Shipshewanna, several antique shops, flea markets, two live theater groups, stern-wheeler paddle boat rides, 101 lakes in Kosciusko County, and a 3,400-acre game preserve. Air conditioned for comfort.

Hosts: Robert and Jean Kennedy
Rooms: 7 (5 PB; 2 SB) $50-65
Full Breakfast
Credit Cards: A, B, D
Notes: 2, 5

TIPPECANOE

Bessinger's Hillfarm Wildlife Refuge Bed and Breakfast

4588 S. R. 110, 46570
(219) 223-3288

This cozy log home overlooks 143 acres of rolling hills, woods, pasture, fields, and marshes with 41 islands. It is ideal for geese and deer year-round. This farm features hiking trails with beautiful views, picnic areas and benches tucked away in a quiet area. Varied seasons make it possible

to canoe, swim, fish, bird watching, hike and cross-country ski. Start with a country breakfast and be ready for an unforgettable experience.

Rooms: 3 (PB) $55-65
Full Breakfast
Credit Cards: None
Notes: 2, 3, 4, 5, 11, 13

WARSAW

Candlelight Inn

503 East Fort Wayne Street, 46580
(219) 267-2906; (800) 352-0640

The Candlelight Inn offers a gentle reminder of the past with the comforts and convenience of the present. In-room phones, TV, and private baths. Antiques return guests to the 1860s. Many lakes and antique shops provide great relaxation and sport. Close to Amish country.

Hosts: Bill and Debi Hambright
Rooms: 6 (PB) $70-90 (corporate rates available)
Full Breakfast
Credit Cards: A, B, C
Notes: 2, 5, 8, 9, 10, 11, 12, 13 (XC), 14

Bessinger's Hillfarm Wildlife Refuge

6 Pets welcome; 8 Children welcome; 9 Social drinking allowed; 10 Tennis available; 11 Swimming available; 12 Golf available; 13 Skiing available; 14 May be booked through travel agents.

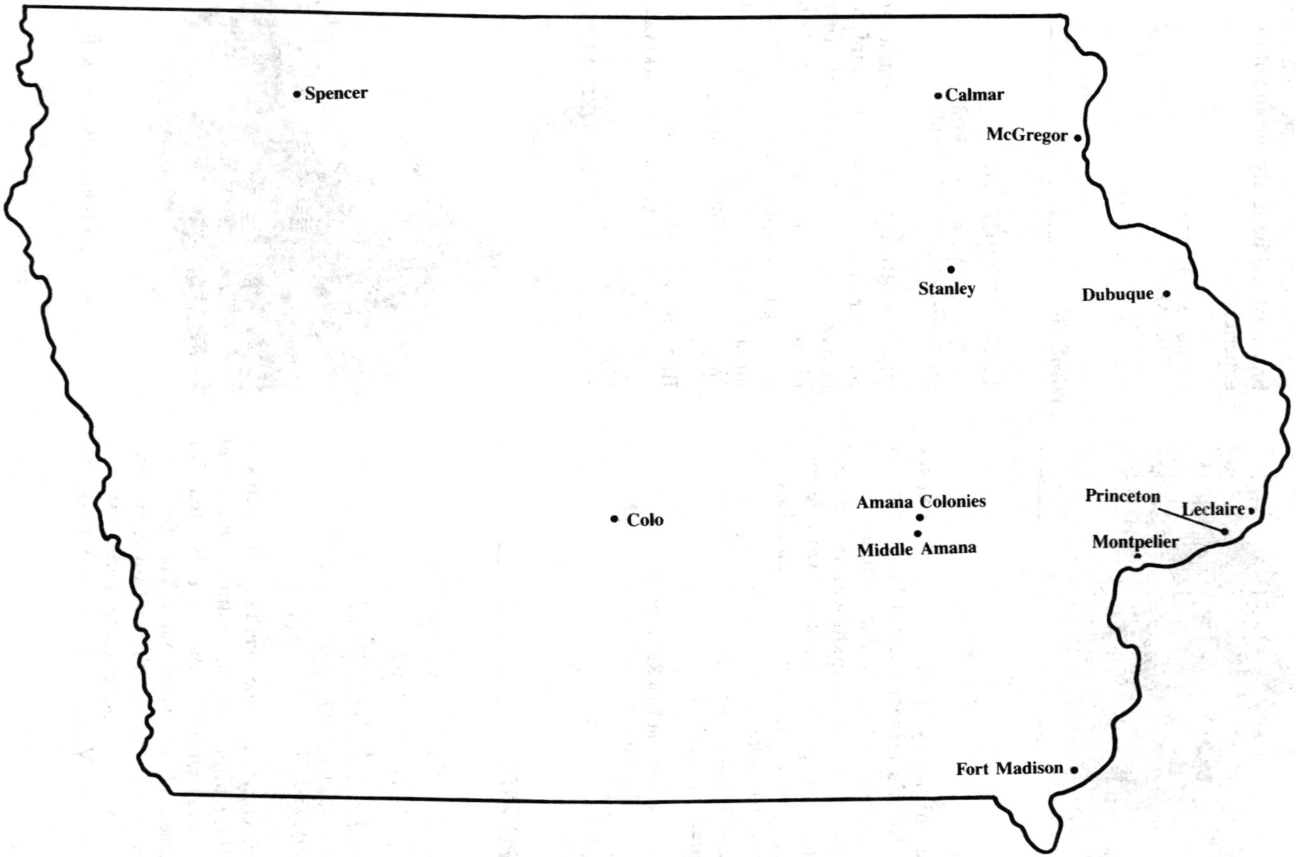

IOWA

Spencer

Calmar
McGregor

Dubuque

Stanley

Amana Colonies
Middle Amana

Princeton
Leclaire
Montpelier

Fort Madison

Colo

Iowa

Die Heimat Country Inn

AMANA COLONIES

Die Heimat Country Inn

Main Street, Homestead, 52236
(319) 622-3937

Die Heimat (German for "the home place") has 19 rooms, all furnished with Amana walnut and cherry furniture, private baths, TVs, and air conditioning. Colony heirlooms and antiques are found throughout the inn. Some rooms have Amana walnut canopy beds. Nature trail, golf course, wineries, woolen mills, and restaurants are all nearby.

Hosts: Don and Sheila Janda
Rooms: 19 (PB) $36.95-65.95
Continental Breakfast
Credit Cards: A, B, D
Notes: 2, 5, 6, 7, 8, 9, 10, 11, 12, 13 (XC)

CALMAR

Calmar Guesthouse

Rural Route 1, Box 206, 52132
(319) 562-3851

Newly remodeled Victorian home with many antiques, situated near Luther College and NITI Community College. Close to world-famous Bily Clocks in Spillville, Niagara Cave, Lake Meyer, and much more. Wake up to a fresh country breakfast. Air-conditioned. Good variety of restaurants in the area.

Hosts: Art and Lucille Kruse
Rooms: 5 (1 PB; 4 SB) $35-45
Full Breakfast
Credit Cards: A, B
Notes: 2, 5, 7, 8, 9, 10, 11, 12, 13

COLO

Martha's Vineyard Bed and Breakfast

620 West Street, 50056
(515) 377-2586

Just 15 minutes east of US 35, this bed and breakfast is a working farm on the edge of town. Homemade and homegrown food is served at meals, and the hostess is a retired home-economics teacher. This fourth-generation 1920 family home has been lovingly restored and is furnished with antiques and collectibles throughout. A wildlife area and an old-fashioned flower garden add quiet beauty. Open May through October.

Hosts: Narb and Martha Kash
Rooms: 2 (PB) $40-45 plus tax
Full Breakfast
Credit Cards: None
Notes: 2, 8, 9, 10, 11, 12, 14

NOTES: Credit cards accepted: A Master Card; B Visa; C American Express; D Discover Card; E Diner's Club; F Other; 2 Personal Checks accepted; 3 Lunch available; 4 Dinner available; 5 Open all year; 6 Pets welcome; 8 Children welcome; 9 Social drinking allowed; 10 Tennis available; 11 Swimming available; 12 Golf available; 13 Skiing available; 14 May be booked through travel agents.

Mandolin Inn

DUBUQUE

Mandolin Inn

199 Loras Boulevard, 52001
(319) 556-0069; (800) 524-7996

Tarry awhile amid Edwardian columns, beveled and stained-glass windows, parquet and mosaic floors. A perfect place to kindle and rekindle romance. Enjoy a sumptuous breakfast served to strains of Mozart in a magnificent dining room of oil wall paintings, floor-to-ceiling china cabinet, and Italian tile fireplace. Perfect for weddings, receptions, family reunions, and business meetings. Corporate rates available. Ideally situated downtown near shopping, riverboat gambling and skiing.

Host: Jan Oswald
Rooms: 8 (4 PB; 4 SB) $65-125
Full Breakfast
Credit Cards: A, B, C, D
Notes: 2, 5, 8, 9, 10, 11, 12, 13, 14

Richards House
Bed and Breakfast

1492 Locust Street, 52001
(319) 557-1492

Relax in this 1883 stick-style Victorian mansion with original interior, over 80 stained-glass windows, embossed wallcoverings, period furnishings, and more. Most rooms include working fireplaces, concealed TVs, and phones. A full breakfast is served in the formal dining room. Easy access with plenty of parking.

Host: Michelle Delaney
Rooms: 5 (4 PB; 1 SB) $35-75
Full Breakfast
Credit Cards: A, B, C, D, E
Notes: 2, 5, 8, 9, 12, 13, 14

FORT MADISON

Kingsley Inn

707 Avenue H on Highway 61, 52627
(319) 372-7074; (800) 441-2327

Yesterday's charm and today's luxury describes this historic Victorian inn on the Mississippi River. Walk to the faithfully restored 1808 Old Fort Madison, Train Depot Museum, Steam Engine Park, unique shops, and galleries. Stately nineteenth-century residential district is nearby, and guests are a 10-minute drive to historic Nauvoo, Illinois, which has been called the "Williamsburg of the Midwest," with 40 restored 1840s shops and homes. Rooms have private baths, some of which are

Richards House

Kingsley Inn

whirlpools. CATV, air conditioning, phones, sprinklers, and alarms. Elevator and FAX machine available.

Host: Myrna Reinhard
Rooms: 14 (PB) $65-105
Continental Breakfast
Credit Cards: A, B, C, D, E
Notes: 2, 5, 9, 14

KEOSAUQA

Mason House Inn of Bentonsport

Route 2, Box 237, 52565
(319) 592-3133

The Mason House Inn of Bentonsport is the only steamboat inn still functioning as such in Iowa. It was built in 1846 by Mormon craftsmen, who stayed in Bentonsport one year while making their famous trek to Utah. Half of the original appointments remain, including a bed with a nine-foot headboard, foot-warming stoves, a nine-foot mirror, memorial hair wreath, and a Murphy copper-lined bathtub. Guests will find a jar of homemade cookies in every room.

Hosts: Sheral and Bill McDermet
Rooms: 9 (5 PB; 4 SB) $49-74
Full Breakfast
Credit Cards: A, B
Notes: 2, 3, 4, 5, 8, 9

LECLAIRE

The Monarch Bed and Breakfast Inn

303 South 2nd Street, 52753
(319) 289-3011; (800) 772-7724

The Monarch Bed and Breakfast Inn was built in the late 1850s and has been restored. It boasts wood floors, high ceilings, and is decorated with antiques and mementos. Overlooking the mighty Mississippi River on the point where the rapids once began, LeClaire is a quaint historical town, and the birthplace of Buffalo Bill. River cruises are available May through October. Handicapped accessible. Two miles north off I-80, Exit 306. French and Polish spoken here.

Hosts: David and Emilie Oltman
Rooms: 3 (PB)
Suites: 1 (PB) $45-65
Full and Continental Breakfast
Credit Cards: A, B
Notes: 2, 5, 8, 12

MCGREGOR

River's Edge Bed and Breakfast

12 Main Street, 52157
(319) 873-3501

Cozy, comfortable rooms overlooking the Mississippi River. Fully equipped kitchen, dining room provided for guest use. Each

Mason House Inn of Bentonsport

6 Pets welcome; 8 Children welcome; 9 Social drinking allowed; 10 Tennis available; 11 Swimming available; 12 Golf available; 13 Skiing available; 14 May be booked through travel agents.

room features a private bath and cable television. Spacious family room, patio. and second level deck are available. Come visit the area's varied recreational opportunities, quaint restaurants, and antique shops.

Host: Rita Lange
Rooms: 3 (PB) $50
Continental Breakfast
Credit Cards: A, B
Notes: 2, 5, 8, 9, 10, 11, 12, 13

MIDDLE AMANA

The Rettig House

P. O. Box 5, 52307
(319) 622-3386

The Rettig House is conveniently situated in peaceful Middle Amana, one of seven historic Amana villages. The quiet and restful setting lends itself to relaxation in comfortable, spacious rooms, all furnished with authentic Amana beds, antiques and family heirlooms. Take an enjoyable stroll around the large yard and Germanic courtyard. Stay amidst the charm and old-world atmosphere of the Amana Colonies.

Hosts: Ray and Marge Rettig
Rooms: 5 (3 PB; 2 SB) $46-50
Continental Breakfast
Credit Cards: None
Notes: 2, 10, 11, 12

MONTPELIER

Varners' Caboose Bed and Breakfast

204 East 2nd, P. O. Box 10, 52759
(319) 381-3652

Come stay in a real Rock Island Lines caboose. Set on its own track behind the hosts' house, the caboose is a self-contained unit with bath, shower, and complete kitchen. It sleeps four, with a queen-size bed and two twins in the cupola. There is color TV, central air and heat, plus plenty of off-street parking. A fully prepared country breakfast is left in the caboose

kitchen to be enjoyed by guests whenever they choose. On Route 22, halfway between Davenport and Muscatine, Iowa.

Hosts: Bob and Nancy Varner
Room: 1 (PB) $55
Full Breakfast
Credit Cards: None
Notes: 2, 5, 8

NEWTON

La Corsette Maison Inn

629 First Avenue East, 50208
(515) 792-6833

Historic turn-of-the-century mission-style mansion. Charming French bedchambers; fireplaces; gourmet dining in a style of elegance. On I-80, 30 minutes from Des Moines. Close to horse track and Adventureland. Listed on the National Register of Historic Places.

Host: Kay Owen
Rooms: 5 (PB) $55-135
Full Breakfast
Credit Cards: C
Notes: 2, 4, 5, 6 (call), 8 (call), 9, 10, 11, 12, 14

PRINCETON

The Woodlands

P. O. Box 127, 52768
(319) 289-3177; (319) 289-4661

A secluded woodland escape that can be as private or social as guests prefer. The Woodlands bed and breakfast is nestled among pines on 26 acres of forest and meadows in a private wildlife refuge. Guests delight in an elegant breakfast by the swimming pool or by a cozy fireplace while viewing the outdoor wildlife activity. Boating and fishing on the Mississippi River, golfing, cross-country skiing, and hiking are available. A short drive to the Quad City metropolitan area, shopping, art galleries, museums, theater, and sporting events.

NOTES: Credit cards accepted: A Master Card; B Visa; C American Express; D Discover Card; E Diner's Club; F Other; 2 Personal Checks accepted; 3 Lunch available; 4 Dinner available; 5 Open all year;

Hosts: Betsy Wallace and E. Lindebraekke
Rooms: 3 (2 PB; 1 SB) $75-115
Full Breakfast
Credit Cards: A, B
Notes: 2, 3, 4, 5, 7, 8, 9, 10, 11, 12, 13, 14

SPENCER

Hannah Marie Country Inn

Rural Route 1, Highway 71 South, 51301
(712) 262-1286; (712) 332-7719

A lovingly restored farm home offering a good night's rest, morning juice/beverage to the room, and a hearty gourmet breakfast. Be pampered by private baths, air conditioning, softened water, relaxing whirlpool or hot shower. Lunches and afternoon desserts served Tuesday to Saturday. Iowa Great Lakes are only 20 miles away.

Hosts: Mary and Dave Nichols
Rooms: 3 (PB) $63-68.25
Full Breakfast
Credit Cards: A, B, C
Closed Dec.-April
Notes: 2, 3, 4, 6 (in barn), 8, 9 (limited), 10, 11, 12, 14

STANLEY

Sawtooth Hotel

West End of Ace of Diamonds, Box 52, 83278
(208) 774-9947

Stanley's first bed and breakfast. Warm western hospitality with an uninterrupted view of the Sawtooth Mountains, with their endless recreational opportunities. Enjoy world-famous sourdough pancakes and cinnamon rolls, country-style ham, sausage or bacon, fresh fruit, and other delights.

Hosts: Steve and Kathy Cole
Rooms: 8 (SB) $35-50
Full Breakfast
Credit Cards: A, B
Notes: None

Hannah Marie Country Inn

Wakeeney

Peabody

KANSAS

Kansas

Jones Sheep Farm
Bed and Breakfast

Rural Route 2, Box 185, 66866
(316) 983-2815

Enjoy a turn-of-the-century home in a pastoral setting. Situated on a working sheep farm "at the end of the road," the house is furnished in 1930s style (no phone or TV). Quiet, private. Historic small town nearby. Country breakfast featuring fresh farm produce served.

Hosts: Gary and Marilyn Jones
Rooms: 2 (SB) $45
Full Breakfast
Credit Cards: None
Notes: 2, 5, 6, 10, 11, 12

Thistle Hill
Bed and Breakfast

Route 1, Box 93, 67672
(913) 743-2644

A comfortable, secluded, cedar farm home halfway between Kansas City and Denver along I-70. Experience farm life and visit Castle Rock. Self-guided prairie wildflower walks through a 60-acre prairie restoration project. Enjoy a hearty country breakfast by the fireplace or on the summer porch overlooking the herb garden.

Hosts: Dave and Mary Hendricks
Rooms: 3 (2 PB; 1 SB) $50
Full Breakfast
Credit Cards: None
Notes: 2, 5, 8, 9, 10, 11, 12

NOTES: Credit cards accepted: A Master Card; B Visa; C American Express; D Discover Card; E Diner's Club; F Other; 2 Personal Checks accepted; 3 Lunch available; 4 Dinner available; 5 Open all year; 6 Pets welcome; 8 Children welcome; 9 Social drinking allowed; 10 Tennis available; 11 Swimming available; 12 Golf available; 13 Skiing available; 14 May be booked through travel agents.

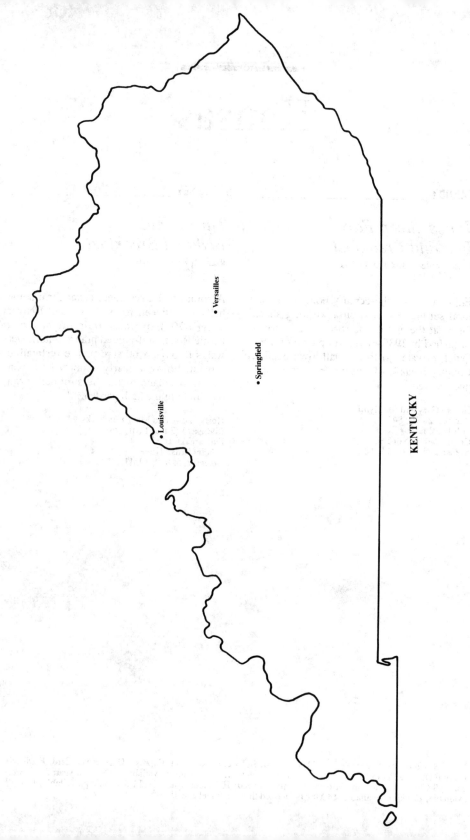

KENTUCKY

• Versailles

• Springfield

• Louisville

Kentucky

The Victorian Secret Bed and Breakfast

1132 South First Street, 40203
(502) 581-1914

In historic old Louisville guests will find a three-story brick mansion appropriately named the Victorian Secret Bed and Breakfast. Its 14 rooms offer spacious accommodations, high ceilings, 11 fireplaces, and original woodwork. Recently restored to its former elegance, the 110-year-old structure provides a peaceful setting for enjoying period furnishings and antiques.

Hosts: Nan and Steve Roosa
Rooms: 3 (1 PB; 2 SB) $53-68
Continental Breakfast
Credit Cards: None
Notes: None

SPRINGFIELD

Maple Hill Manor

2941 Perryville Road, 40069
(606) 336-3075

This circa 1851 brick Revival home with Italianate detail is a Kentucky landmark home on the National Register of Historic Places. It features ceilings more than 13-feet high, 10-foot doors, a cherry spiral staircase, stenciling in the foyer, a large parlor, and formal dining room with fireplace, hardwood floors, and period furnishings. Seven bedrooms with private baths.

Honeymoon accommodation has Jacuzzi, canopy bed, and private entrance. Homemade dessert, and beverages in the evenings.

Hosts: Bob and Kay Carroll
Rooms: 7 (PB) $60-80
Full Breakfast
Credit Cards: A, B
Notes: 2, 5, 8, 9, 14

VERSAILLES

Bluegrass Bed and Breakfast Reservation Service

Route 1, Box 263, 40383
(606) 873-3208

One call does it all! We represent 25 accommodations in Lexington and nearby areas. Fireplaces, four-poster beds, horse farms and even log cabins available. All with breakfast. Call for a brochure.

Host: Betsy Pratt
Rooms: 25 (PB) $54-100
Full and Continental Breakfast
Credit Cards: A, B
Notes: 2, 5 (except Christmas), 9, 12

Shepherd Place

31 Heritage Road at U.S. 60, 40383
(606) 873-7843

Marlin and Sylvia encourage guests to make themselves comfortable in this pre-Civil War home. Rest in spacious, beautifully decorated bedrooms, or relax in the parlor. Enjoy the scenery while sitting in

NOTES: Credit cards accepted: A Master Card; B Visa; C American Express; D Discover Card; E Diner's Club; F Other; 2 Personal Checks accepted; 3 Lunch available; 4 Dinner available; 5 Open all year; 6 Pets welcome; 8 Children welcome; 9 Social drinking allowed; 10 Tennis available; 11 Swimming available; 12 Golf available; 13 Skiing available; 14 May be booked through travel agents.

the porch swing, or stroll up to the barn. Brochures, menus, and plenty of ideas will be available for a stay in the Bluegrass.

Hosts: Marlin and Sylvia Yawn
Rooms: 2 (PB) $60-70
Full Breakfast
Credit Cards: A, B
Notes: 2, 5, 12

Shepherd Place

Louisiana

BATON ROUGE

Southern Comfort Reservations LBR08

P. O. Box 13294, New Orleans, 70185-3294
(504) 861-0082; (800) 749-1928

Guest cottage with living/dining room, kitchen, bath, one bedroom, TV, phone. Sleeps four. FAX, copy machine, computer are available in host's home. Ideal for business people. $75.

CARENCRO

La Maison de Campagne, Lafayette

825 Kidder Road, 70520
(318) 896-6529; (800) 368-7308

This Victorian home, circa 1900, is in a beautiful country setting with 200-year-old oak trees on nine acres. Come enjoy life the way it used to be. The inn offers private baths, antique-furnished rooms, a swimming pool, and three great Cajun restaurants and attractions five minutes away. A gourmet, full country Cajun breakfast is served with the hospitality of the award-winning chef/hostess. Enjoy early morning or late afternoon walks or just relax on the sweeping wraparound veranda or the upstairs balcony. Guests will want to come back again and again.

Hosts: Joann and Fred McLemore
Rooms: 3 (PB) $75 and up
Full Breakfast
Credit Cards: A, B
Notes: 2, 5, 11, 14

COVINGTON

Southern Comfort Reservations LCOV1

P. O. Box 13294, New Orleans, 70185-3294
(504) 861-0082; (800) 749-1928

This is a delightful nonworking farm situated 35 miles across Lake Pontchartrain north of New Orleans in the piney woods of St. Tammany Parish. Enjoy the landscaped gardens and dockside activities on the Tchefuncte River, including fishing and swimming. Comfortable guest cottage includes a livingroom with TV, full kitchen, twin, double, and king rooms, and one bath. Continental breakfast.

JACKSON

Southern Comfort Reservations LJSN1

P. O. Box 13294, New Orleans, 70185-3294
(504) 861-0082; (800) 749-1928

Built in 1825-1836, this property on the national register has been a home, a bank, was occupied by Union troops, and is now totally restored. Bedroom and private bath on the first floor. One two-bedroom-and-bath suite on the second floor. Children welcome. Full breakfast; 10 percent senior citizen discount. Picnic lunches and private sightseeing tours may be arranged. $65-130.

6 Pets welcome; 8 Children welcome; 9 Social drinking allowed; 10 Tennis available; 11 Swimming available; 12 Golf available; 13 Skiing available; 14 May be booked through travel agents.

LAFAYETTE

Southern Comfort Reservations LLF01

P. O. Box 13294, New Orleans, 70185-3294
(504) 861-0082; (800) 749-1928

This authentic Acadian-raised mansion's Victorian carriage house is furnished with Louisiana antiques. Breakfast is a Cajun feast served on a glassed-in porch overlooking the Old New Orleans-style courtyard, or in the dining room, with its original fireplace. In the evening, after-dinner drinks and chocolates are offered. Fishing and duck hunting trips or swamp tours can be arranged. Handicapped accessible. One double room, one queen room $85; suite $95-145.

MADISONVILLE

Southern Comfort Reservations LMA01

P. O. Box 13294, New Orleans, 70185-3294
(504) 861-0082; (800) 749-1928

This 100-year-old house is just seven miles from the 26-mile Lake Pontchartrain Causeway leading to New Orleans. Its big porches, wide hallways, high ceilings, and bright rooms provide a casual atmosphere. Just steps to the beautiful river, where you can enjoy crabbing, fishing, and many water sports. Three bedrooms, shared bath. Full breakfast may include crab omelets or popovers.

MONROE

Southern Comfort Reservations LMN01

P. O. Box 13294, New Orleans, 70185-3294
(504) 861-0082; (800) 749-1928

Situated 15 miles south of Monroe, this cottage is all that remains of a once-magnificent plantation. Its guest house has one spacious room with antique four-poster and a single sleigh bed, private bath. There's a cozy corner with reading lamp, TV, and VCR. Garconniere has one room with private bath, antiques, double bed. Full breakfast.

NEW IBERIA

Southern Comfort Reservations LNI02

P. O. Box 13294, New Orleans, 70185-3294
(504) 861-0082; (800) 749-1928

Contemporary home on three-acre estate overlooking Bayou Tech. Duck pond on the front lawn, unique house with glassed-in porch, large screened patio, and lighted tennis court combine to make visiting a delight. Two guest rooms, one with twins and one with queen bed, have bayou view and private baths and are connected by a large sitting room with TV and phone. Continental breakfast; children welcome. $65.

NEW ORLEANS

Architectural Gem

Bed and Breakfast, Inc.
1021 Moss Street, Box 52257, 70152-2257
(504) 488-4640; (800) 729-4640

NOTES: Credit cards accepted: A Master Card; B Visa; C American Express; D Discover Card; E Diner's Club; F Other; 2 Personal Checks accepted; 3 Lunch available; 4 Dinner available; 5 Open all year; 6 Pets welcome; 8 Children welcome; 9 Social drinking allowed; 10 Tennis available; 11 Swimming available; 12 Golf available; 13 Skiing available; 14 May be booked through travel agents.

Remaining true to the original design, this wonderful guest cottage has been of primary concern to the owners. They have overseen the renovation project from top to bottom, paying careful attention not to disturb the historic detail of this building. Thick exposed brick walls and three brick fireplaces, used in the 1830s as the kitchen facilities for the main house, reflect the authenticity of this historic restoration. Uniquely designed private baths adjoin each of the two cozy bedrooms. Self-serve continental breakfast is provided for guests to enjoy at their leisure. $75-150.

Bed and Breakfast Southern Comfort Reservation Service

P. O. Box 13294, 70185-3294
(504) 861-0082; (800) 749-1928

Let the South's reservation resource make a visit to the deep South a memorable one. With one call to the South's premiere toll free reservation service, one can choose from the finest of Southern bed and breakfasts. From river plantations to country cottages, Southern Comfort brings the gracious lifestyle of the South to guests. Accepts personal checks, MasterCard, Visa, and American Express.

Bourbon Street Suite

Bed and Breakfast Inc.
1021 Moss Street, Box 52257, 70152-2257
(504) 488-4640; (800) 729-4640

Guests enjoy this private, first-floor suite opening onto world-famous Bourbon Street. The host is a New Orleans native and shares his vast knowledge of the special spots not to miss. One bedroom, private bath, continental breakfast. $75-100.

Chartres Marigny Bed and Breakfast, Inc.

1021 Moss Street, Box 52257, 70152-2257
(504) 488-4640; (800) 729-4640

At the edge of the French Quarter sits this 1830s town house where the hosts are enjoying the painstaking restoration of the property. Ask the host for the renovation tour. Seeing the different phases of a renovation in progress is a mini course in the building and architectural styles of New Orleans. The charming guest cottage is tastefully furnished, has a private entrance, four-poster antique bed, baths and kitchenette. Self-serve continental breakfast is provided for guests to enjoy at their leisure. $75-100.

Dauphine Street Suite

Bed & Breakfast Inc.
1021 Moss Street, Box 52257, 70152-2257
(504) 488-4640; (800) 729-4640

In the heart of the residential part of the French Quarter, this guest suite is nestled in the courtyard of an 1840s Creole cottage. The second-story suite is off the charming brick courtyard and has a private entrance, horse-hair double bed, and bath. Self-serve continental breakfast is provided. $75-100.

Designer Guest Cottage

Bed and Breakfast Inc.
1021 Moss Street, Box 52257, 70152-2257
(504) 488-4640; (800) 729-4640

Originally the studio of a famous southern sculptor, the cottage displays his artistic creativity while preserving its historic past. A short streetcar ride to galleries, antiques, restaurants, and the French Quarter. One bedroom with private bath; continental breakfast. $95-135.

NOTES: Credit cards accepted: A Master Card; B Visa; C American Express; D Discover Card; E Diner's Club; F Other; 2 Personal Checks accepted; 3 Lunch available; 4 Dinner available; 5 Open all year;

Galleried Home

Bed and Breakfast Inc.
1021 Moss Street, Box 52257, 70152-2257
(504) 488-4640; (800) 729-4640

Historians delight in this French Plantation-style home. The guest suite is just off the host's livingroom and opens onto the front balcony. The suite offers a sitting room, bedroom with four-poster double bed, and bath. The lush garden below provides a tropical approach. Lovely antiques; continental breakfast. $95-110.

Garden District Guest Suite

Bed and Breakfast Inc.
1021 Moss Street, Box 52257, 70152-2257
(504) 488-4640; (800) 729-4640

Three lovely antique twin beds grace a nicely decorated suite. Comfortably spacious with a livingroom and kitchen. Enjoy the special flavors of New Orleans-style cooking at the nearby famous bistros. Two bedrooms with private bath; continental breakfast supplies provided. $50-80.

Guest Suite in Greek Revival Cottage

Bed and Breakfast Inc.
1021 Moss Street, Box 52257, 70152-2257
(504) 488-4640; (800) 729-4640

Greek Revival cottage offers a well-appointed guest apartment with its own private entrance overlooking the swimming pool. Hosts have tastefully decorated their home. The streetcar ride to downtown is just 10 minutes. A short walk leads to other attractions. One bedroom with private bath; continental breakfast. $50-90.

La Maison Marigny

Bed and Breakfast Inc.
1021 Moss Street, Box 52257, 70152-2257
(504) 488-4640; (800) 729-4640

Situated in the French Quarter, this petite bed and breakfast inn was just completely renovated down to window dressings and dust ruffles. Each of the three guest rooms has a private entrance and modern bath. Enjoy a continental breakfast downstairs or outside in the traditional walled garden and patio. $75-100.

The Lanaux House

Bed and Breakfast Inc.
1021 Moss Street, Box 52257, 70152-2257
(504) 488-4640; (800) 729-4640

The historic Lanaux House was constructed in 1879 and has been restored by the hostess. A private entrance leads to the second-floor guest suite. Guests enjoy their own lovely livingroom, bedroom with antique brass double bed, bath, and kitchenette. Self-serve continental breakfast. $100-150.

Lincoln Ltd. #7

P. O. Box 3479, Meridian, Mississippi 39303
(601) 482-5483 information
(800) 633-MISS reservations

Lovely historic home furnished in antiques. Six beautifully appointed bedrooms with private baths. Situated conveniently close to the Garden District and public transportation. Continental breakfast served. $75-125.

Le Garconiere Guest Suite

Bed and Breakfast Inc.
1021 Moss Street, Box 52257, 70152-2257
(504) 488-4640; (800) 729-4640

A charming couple welcomes guests to their historic home in the French Quarter. Antique shops, restaurants, and jazz clubs are just a short walk from this quiet neighborhood. Private, two-story guest cottage overlooking the tropical courtyard with a balcony and full kitchen. Experience the streetcar along the Mississippi River. Continental breakfast. $75-100.

6 Pets welcome; 8 Children welcome; 9 Social drinking allowed; 10 Tennis available; 11 Swimming available; 12 Golf available; 13 Skiing available; 14 May be booked through travel agents.

Mechlings 1860s Mansion Bed and Breakfast

2023 Esplanade Avenue, 70111
(504) 943-4131; (800) 725-4131

This 1860s historical mansion is situated on beautiful Esplanade Avenue. Experience the ambience of the Victorian era; stroll through the French Quarter or the city park; public transportation is just outside the door. Spacious, beautifully decorated rooms all offer private baths, and complimentary breakfast is served on the veranda or in the rooms. Original marble mantels, gasoliers, slave quarters, cisterns, wine cellars, and a historical oak tree that spans 100-feet are available for guests to view. Guests are welcome to tour this restored home.

Hosts: Keith and Claudine Mechling
Rooms: 6 (PB) $75-155
Full Breakfast
Credit Cards: A, B, C
Notes: 2, 5, 9, 14

New Orleans First Bed and Breakfast

3660 Gentilly Road, 70122
(504) 947-3401

Live oak trees shade this quiet, family oriented area. Two cross-town buses offer easy transportation to popular areas. New Orleans First Bed and Breakfast offers a large master bedroom, with king bed, and an art deco double bedroom, both with private baths. A continental breakfast is served in the dining room. Off-street parking and discount coupons for activities are available.

Host: Sarah Margaret Brown
Rooms: 3 (2 PB; 1 SB) $55-125
Continental Breakfast
Credit Cards: A, B, C, D
Notes: 2, 5, 6, 8, 9

P.J. Holbrook's Olde Victorian Inn

914 North Rampart Street, 70116
(504) 522- 2446; (800) 725-2446

Once an 1800s bordello, this inn is situated in the historic French Quarter. Recently restored, it is now New Orleans' most elegant guest house. Seven period guest rooms all have private baths, and most have fireplaces. Three also feature balconies. Beautiful courtyard for dining, and an elegant gathering room invites conversation. Specializes in honeymoons, anniversaries, and family reunions.

Host: P. J. Holbrook
Rooms: 7 (PB) $100-150
Full Breakfast
Credit Cards: A, B, C
Notes: 2, 5, 9, 14

St. Charles Avenue Home

Bed and Breakfast Inc.
1021 Moss Street, Box 52257, 70152-2257
(504) 488-4640; (800) 729-4640

Hosts love sharing their enthusiasm for New Orleans in a historic, homespun setting. Walking distance to the interesting Riverbend area with its specialty shops, coffee houses, and popular restaurants. The host was born in this house that boasts some of the original antiques. Two bedrooms with hall bath; continental breakfast. $50-60.

Southern Comfort Reservations LNO01

P. O. Box 13294, New Orleans, 70185-3294
(504) 861-0082; (800) 749-1928

Carrollton Cottage near universities, parks, museums. Easy access to all highways, French Quarter, downtown. Hostess speaks fluent Spanish. No children; private bath, king or twin beds; continental breakfast. $45-50.

NOTES: Credit cards accepted: A Master Card; B Visa; C American Express; D Discover Card; E Diner's Club; F Other; 2 Personal Checks accepted; 3 Lunch available; 4 Dinner available; 5 Open all year;

Southern Comfort Reservations LN005

P. O. Box 13294, 70185-3294
(504) 861-0082; (800) 749-1928

This house was built 148 years ago as a river boat captain's inn. It has been lovingly restored and now offers bed and breakfast with delightful hosts who have moved here from California. Since its restoration, the house has been filmed in two segments of *Unsolved Mysteries* TV Series.

The Uptown Home

Bed and Breakfast Inc.
1021 Moss Street, Box 52257, 70152-2257
(504) 488-4640; (800) 729-4640

Guests enjoy this residential neighborhood, with its shady trees and historic homes. Close to universities, restaurants, antique shops, art galleries, and the streetcar line, which can take you to many attractions. Each of the three bedrooms has a double bed and shared bath. Great for the budget-minded. Continental breakfast. $40-60.

NEW ROADS _____

Lincoln Ltd. #38

P. O. Box 3479, Meridian, Mississippi 39303
(601) 482-5483 information
(800) 633-MISS reservations

This attractive Creole cottage is wonderful for a weekend getaway or a special fishing trip. Group accommodations by special request. The hostess is knowledgeable about the history of this Mississippi River town and can offer many ideas about special places to see (plantation homes, fishing, etc.). A continental breakfast is served each morning by the hostess/owner. Six guest rooms. $40.

Southern Comfort Reservations LNR01

P. O. Box 13294, New Orleans, 70185-3294
(504) 861-0082; (800) 749-1928

Newly restored Victorian; seven bedrooms and baths with antiques and wicker; spacious porches. Experienced bed and breakfast hostess pampers guests with wake-up coffee and afternoon high tea. Near scenic Oxbow Lake and public boat launch. Good fishing, water sports, hiking.

PORT VINCENT _____

Tree House in the Park

16520 Airport Road, Prairieville, 70769
(800) LE CABIN

A Cajun cabin in the swamp. Large bedrooms with Jacuzzi tub, queen waterbed, private hot tub on sun deck, heated pool on lower deck. Boat slip, fishing dock, double kayak float trip on Amite River. Three acres of ponds, a footbridge to an island with a gazebo, cypress trees, ducks, and fish. Complimentary supper on arrival.

Hosts: Fran and Julius Schmieder
Rooms: 2 (PB) $60-100
Full Breakfast
Credit Cards: A, B
Notes: 2, 4, 5, 11, 14

SHREVEPORT _____

Fairfield Place Bed and Breakfast

2221 Fairfield Avenue, 71104
(318) 222-0048

Built before the turn of the century, Fairfield Place has been beautifully restored to bring all the charm of a bygone era. Conveniently situated near downtown, I-20, the medical centers, and Louisiana Downs. Within walking distance of fine

6 Pets welcome; 8 Children welcome; 9 Social drinking allowed; 10 Tennis available; 11 Swimming available; 12 Golf available; 13 Skiing available; 14 May be booked through travel agents.

restaurants and unique shops. Breakfast includes rich Cajun coffee and freshly baked croissants, served in the privacy of the room, the balcony, porch, or courtyard.

Host: Jane Lipscomb
Rooms: 6 (PB) $65-145
Full Breakfast
Credit Cards: A, B, C
Notes: 2, 5, 9, 10, 11, 12

2439 Fairfield Bed and Breakfast

2439 Fairfield Avenue, 71104
(318) 424-2424

The 2439 Fairfield is a lovely restored three-story Victorian mansion situated in the Highland Historical District. The delightful guest rooms are furnished with English antiques, Amish quilts, feather beds, down pillows and comforters. Each room also features a private balcony that overlooks the landscaped gardens below. Each bath has a whirlpool tub. A hearty English breakfast is served in the morning room.

Hosts: Jimmy and Vicki Harris
Rooms: 4 (PB) $85-125
Full or Continental Breakfast
Credit Cards: A, B, C, E
Notes: 2, 5, 9, 12, 14

SLIDELL

Southern Comfort Reservations LSLD3

P. O. Box 13294, New Orleans, 70185-3294
(504) 861-0082; (800) 749-1928

Spacious 100-year-old Victorian on a four-acre plot full of azaleas and camellias, has five bedrooms with private baths, and antiques throughout. Guests enjoy several common areas and the glassed-in porch where breakfast is served. It is 35 miles on I-10 from New Orleans. $75-95; honeymoon or anniversary packages include champagne on arrival and breakfast in bed.

Maine

ANDOVER

Andover Arms Family Style Bed and Breakfast

Newton Street, P. O. Box 387, 04216
(207) 392-4251

Discover Maine the way it used to be. Stay in this comfortable 1800s farmhouse in the village, and feel right at home with warm hospitality, country breakfasts, and cozy guest rooms with oil lamps for added charm. Relax by the wood stove or play the piano. Snowmobiling and cross-country skiing at the door. Only 20 minutes to downhill ski areas, including Sunday River. Excellent hunting, fishing, biking, and foliage.

Hosts: Pat and Larry Wyman
Rooms: 4 (1 PB; 3 SB) $50
Full Breakfast
Credit Cards: A, B, C, D
Notes: 2, 5, 6, 8, 9, 10, 11, 12, 13, 14

AUGUSTA

Maple Hill Farm Inn

Outlet Road, Rural Route 1, Box 1145, Hallowell, 04347
(207) 622-2708

A charming country inn with quiet, relaxed elegance. Situated on more than 60 acres of unspoiled rural beauty. Central to Maine's lake regions, mountains, and coast. Near national historic district offering unique shopping, dining, and antiques. Rooms are tastefully furnished with antiques and overlook rolling meadows, woods and gardens; private suite with whirlpool available.

Experience the freedom of open skies and country solitude for an intimate weekend, or as an alternative to everyday business accommodations, just minutes from the Maine Turnpike.

Hosts: Scott Cowger and Robert Audet
Rooms: 7 (4 PB; 3 SB) $50-80
Full Breakfast
Credit Cards: A, B
Notes: 2, 5, 8, 9, 11, 12, 13, 14

BAILEY ISLAND

Captain York House Bed and Breakfast

Route 24, P. O. Box 32, 04003
(207) 833-6224

Enjoy true island atmosphere on scenic Bailey Island, an unspoiled fishing village, accessible by car over the only cribstone bridge in the world. Near Brunswick, Freeport, Portland. Former sea captain's home tastefully restored to original charm, furnished with antiques. Informal, friendly atmosphere, eye-popping ocean views from every room. From the deck, enjoy the sight

Maple Hill Farm

6 Pets welcome; 8 Children welcome; 9 Social drinking allowed; 10 Tennis available; 11 Swimming available; 12 Golf available; 13 Skiing available; 14 May be booked through travel agents.

MAINE

Stratton

Rangeley

Brooksville

Mt. Desert

Prospect Harbor

Eastport

Lubec

Searsport

Belfast

Buccksport

Milbridge

Augusta

Waldoboro

West Gouldsboro

Northeast Harbor

Waterford

Camden

Bar Harbor

Newcastle

Southwest Harbor

Wiscasset

Vinalhaven

Naples

Freeport

Isle Au Haut

South Thomaston

Capitol Island

Thomaston

Damariscotta

Boothbay Harbor

South Harpswell

Bailey Island

Kennebunk

Kennebunkport

Ogunquit

York Beach

Kittery

of local lobstermen hauling traps and the most memorable sunsets on the coast. Nearby fine dining/summer nature cruise.

Hosts: Charles and Ingrid Di Vita
Rooms: 3 (1 PB; 2 SB) $55-75
Full Breakfast
Credit Cards: None
Notes: 2, 5, 9, 14

Katie's Ketch

P. O. Box 105, 04003
(207) 833-7785

Situated on Bailey Island, a lobster fishing community connected to "The Maineland" by the only cribstone bridge in the world. Guests can enjoy fishing, swimming, hiking, sailing, beach combing, ferry rides, antique shops, and the famous L.L. Bean establishment. The host is a retired lobsterman of 40 years, who hand-carves duck decoys. Enjoy a hearty breakfast while watching the lobstermen haul in their traps.

Hosts: Albert and Katie Johnson
Rooms: 2 (1 PB; 1 SB) $60-75 (plus ME state tax)
Full Breakfast
Credit Cards: None
Notes: 2, 8, 10, 11, 12

BAR HARBOR

Castlemaine Inn

39 Holland Avenue, 04609
(207) 288-4563

Castlemaine Inn is nestled on a quiet side street in the village of Bar Harbor, which is surrounded by the magnificent Acadia National Park. The rooms are well appointed, with canopy beds and fireplaces. A delightful continental buffet-style breakfast is served.

Hosts: Terence O'Connell and Norah O'Brien
Rooms: 13 (PB) $80-135 seasonal
Continental Breakfast
Credit Cards: A, B
Open May-Oct.
Notes: 2, 8 (over 13), 9, 10, 11, 12

Cleftstone Manor

92 Eden Street, 04609
(207) 288-4951; (800) 962-9762

Cleftstone Manor is a distinguished 33-room Victorian "cottage," set on a hill amid formal gardens, offering gracious accommodations in one of nature's magnificent meetings of land and sea, Mount Desert Island. The manor offers cozy fireside chats, a library, games, a lavish full breakfast buffet, and the peace of country living.

Hosts: Don and Pattie Reynolds
Rooms: 16 (PB) $95-180
Full Breakfast
Credit Cards: A, B, D
Closed Nov.-April
Notes: 2, 8 (over 7), 10, 11, 12, 13 (XC)

Graycote Inn

40 Holland Avenue, 04609
(207) 288-3044

Step back in time into this painstakingly restored 19th century Victorian cottage. Savor the ambience of large guest rooms with king canopy or queen beds and a choice of fireplace, sunroom, or balcony. Enjoy fresh ground coffee, muffins, fresh fruits, and cereals surrounding a main dish of the day on the sunny breakfast porch. Only a five minute walk to downtown, or a

Graycote Inn

NOTES: Credit cards accepted: A Master Card; B Visa; C American Express; D Discover Card; E Diner's Club; F Other; 2 Personal Checks accepted; 3 Lunch available; 4 Dinner available; 5 Open all year; 6 Pets welcome; 8 Children welcome; 9 Social drinking allowed; 10 Tennis available; 11 Swimming available; 12 Golf available; 13 Skiing available; 14 May be booked through travel agents.

five minute drive to the pristine beauty of Acadia National Park. Come join us in Bar Harbor.

Hosts: Joe and Judy Losquadro
Rooms: 12 (PB) $80-140
Full Breakfast
Credit Cards: A, B
Notes: 2, 9, 10, 11, 12

Hearthside

Hearthside

7 High Street, 04609
(207) 288-4533

Built at the turn of the century as the residence for Dr. George Hagerthy, Hearthside is now a cozy and comfortable bed and breakfast. Hearthside is conveniently situated on a quiet side street in Bar Harbor. All of the newly decorated rooms have queen-size beds and private baths; some have private porches and working fireplaces. Each morning a lavish breakfast buffet is served, and lemonade and homemade cookies are offered each afternoon. Off-season rates available.

Hosts: Susan and Barry Schwartz
Rooms: 9 (PB) $75-110
Full Breakfast

Credit Cards: A, B
Notes: 2, 5, 9

Long Pond Inn

Pond's End, 04660
(207) 244-5854

Centrally situated on the shore of beautiful Long Pond near the quaint village of Somesville, Long Pond Inn offers one of the quietest choices in country lodging on Mount Desert Island. The inn's four guest rooms are charmingly appointed, featuring queen-size beds and private baths; one with a Jacuzzi. A hearty continental breakfast of fresh seasonal fruits and homemade muffins awaits. Stroll the lavish herb, vegetable, and flower gardens, or enjoy a swim or canoe outing on Long Pond. The Long Pond family inlcudes two Springer spaniels. Guest's pets are not allowed.

Hosts: Bob and Pam Mensink
Rooms: 4 (PB) $70-85
Continental Breakfast
Credit Cards: A, B
Notes: 2, 11, 12

The Maples Inn

16 Roberts Avenue, 04609
(207) 288-3443

Built in early 1900, the Maples Inn originally housed the wealthy summer visitors to Mount Desert Island. It is on a quiet, res-

The Maples Inn

NOTES: Credit cards accepted: A Master Card; B Visa; C American Express; D Discover Card; E Diner's Club; F Other; 2 Personal Checks accepted; 3 Lunch available; 4 Dinner available; 5 Open all year;

idential, tree-lined street. Away from the traffic of Bar Harbor, yet within walking distance of attractive boutiques, intimate restaurants, and the surrounding sea. For the perfect romantic getaway, reserve the White Birch Suite, complete with a beautiful, working fireplace. Guests will be treated to gourmet delights each morning in the bay-windowed dining room. Acadia National Park is minutes away.

Host: Susan Sinclair
Rooms: 6 (PB) $60-130 seasonal
Full or Continental Breakfast
Credit Cards: A, B, D
Notes: 2, 3 (picnic), 5, 9, 12, 13

Town Motel and Guest House

12 Atlantic Avenue, 04609
(207) 288-5548; (800) 458-8644

The Town Guest House provides comfort, convenience, and relaxation in a quiet in-town neighborhood. Relax amid the Victorian comfort of period furnishings, marble sinks, porches, and working fireplaces. Enjoy the spacious, well-shaded grounds, drink morning coffee on the front porch or gazebo. Open May through October, with lower off-season rates. Breakfast served all season.

Hosts: Joe and Paulette Paluga
Rooms: 9 (PB) $75-125
Continental Breakfast
Credit Cards: A, B, C, D
Notes: 2, 8, 9, 10, 11, 12, 14

Wayside Inn

11 Atlantic Avenue, 04609
(207) 288-5703; (800) 722-6671

A beautifully decorated early Victorian inn offering private and semi-private rooms with fireplaces. Full gourmet breakfast served. On a quiet side street in historic district within walking distance to all in town activities. Open all year. Lower rates available off-season.

Hosts: Steve and Sandi Straubel
Rooms: 8 (4 SB; 4 PB) $55-135
Full Breakfast
Credit Cards: A, B
Notes: 2, 5, 8, 9, 10, 11, 12, 13, 14

BELFAST

Adaline Palmer House

7 Franklin Street, Corner of Cedar Street, 04915
(207) 338-5790

A warm welcome awaits guests in this rambling Greek Revival Cape, circa 1850, close to harbor, shops, theaters, and restaurants. The home features tile and terra cotta fireplaces, detailed woodwork, pine floors, a glass-enclosed breakfast porch, and spacious twin or queen bedrooms with private baths.

Hosts: Bob and Carol Lentilhon
Rooms: 3 (PB) $45-50
Full Breakfast
Credit Cards: None
Notes: 2, 9, 10, 11, 12

Bed and Breakfast Inns of New England ME-840

329 Lake Drive, Guilford, CT 06437
(800) 582-0853

This Greek Revival house was built around 1845 during Belfast's period of great architectural activity. Guests are welcome to use the beautiful formal livingroom with ornate tiled fireplace. Three large bedrooms with pine floors and a variety of bed sizes are available. All have private baths. There is a screened and glassed-in porch overlooking a garden where breakfast is usually served. Complimentary afternoon wine is served in the livingroom. No pets, but children over 10 are welcome. $45.

The Jeweled Turret Inn

16 Pearl Street, 04915
(207) 338-2304; (800) 696-2304 (in state)

6 Pets welcome; 8 Children welcome; 9 Social drinking allowed; 10 Tennis available; 11 Swimming available; 12 Golf available; 13 Skiing available; 14 May be booked through travel agents.

Step back into 1898, when lace, elegant furnishings, and afternoon tea were an everyday necessity. The inn is named for the grand staircase that winds up the turret, lighted by stained- and leaded-glass panels with jewel-like embellishments. Lots of antiques, woodwork, fireplaces, public rooms, and two verandas available for relaxation. Mornings welcome guests with gourmet breakfasts. Afternoon tea is served off season. Situated in historic district; shops, restaurants, and waterfront close by.

Hosts: Carl and Cathy Heffentrager
Rooms: 7 (PB) $65-85
Full Breakfast
Credit Cards: None
Notes: 2, 5, 9, 10, 11, 12, 13, 14

Arcady Down East

BLUE HILL

Arcady Down East
HC 63, Box 40, 04614
(207) 374-5576

Experience yesteryear in the warmth and elegance of this late-1800s Victorian inn. Listed on the National Historic Register, it is equally suited for honeymoons, family vacations, or family reunions. Come sit on the porch swing and have a pink lemonade or apricot ice tea on the sunporch.

Hosts: Bertha and Gene Wiseman
Rooms: 7 (5 PB; 2 SB) $75-110
Full Breakfast
Credit Cards: A, B, C
Notes: 2, 5, 8, 9, 10, 11, 12, 13, 14

Kenniston Hill Inn

BOOTHBAY

Kenniston Hill Inn
Route 27, P. O. Box 125, 04537
(207) 633-2159; (800) 992-2915

Built in 1786, this rambling clapboard home is the oldest inn in Maine's popular Boothbay Harbor Region. It features 10 rooms, all with private baths and working fireplaces. When there's a nip in the air, antique-filled rooms are cozy and crackling with fires, and candlelight dining is available by the open hearth November through April. A delectable country breakfast is served each morning.

Hosts: David and Susan Straight
Rooms: 10 (PB) $65-95
Full Breakfast
Credit Cards: A, B
Notes: 2, 4, 5, 10, 11, 12, 14

BOOTHBAY HARBOR

Anchor Watch Bed and Breakfast

3 Eames Road, 04538
(207) 633-7565

A shorefront location on a scenic, quiet lane, the Anchor Point is just a short walk to town for shopping, dining, and boat trips. From the breakfast room lobstermen hauling their traps, lighthouses flashing, and ducks feeding along the shore can be seen. Country charm, nautical decor, and a bit of Monhegan Island history add to the cozy comfort of this small seaside inn.

Hosts: Diane and Bob Campbell
Rooms: 4 (PB) $65-95
Full Breakfast
Credit Cards: A, B
Notes: 2, 5, 9, 10, 11, 12, 14

The Atlantic Ark Inn

64 Atlantic Avenue, 04538
(207) 633-5690

An intimate bed and breakfast inn, offering lovely views of the harbor and only a five-minute stroll to town over a historic footbridge. This 100-year-old Maine home has been lovingly restored and tastefully furnished with antiques and Oriental rugs. Guest rooms are adorned with fresh flowers, floor-length drapes, queen-size poster beds, and private baths. Each morning a full breakfast features home-baked goods and a specially prepared entree for that day. Recommended by Stephen Birnbaum in *Good Housekeeping*, August 1990.

Host: Donna Piggott
Rooms: 5 (PB) $65-90
Full Breakfast
Credit Cards: A, B, C
Notes: 2, 9

Five Gables Inn

P. O. Box 75, Murray Hill Road, East Boothbay, 04544
(207) 633-4551; (800) 451-5048

Five Gables Inn is a completely restored Victorian, circa 1865, situated on Linekin Bay. All rooms have an ocean view and five have fireplaces. A gourmet breakfast is served in the large common room or on the spacious wraparound veranda. Minimum stay is two nights on weekends, three days on holidays.

Hosts: Ellen and Paul Morissette
Rooms: 15 (PB) $80-130
Full Breakfast
Credit Cards: A, B
Closed Nov. 16-May 15
Notes: 2, 8 (over 12), 9, 10, 11, 12, 14

BROOKSVILLE

Breezemere Farm Inn

Box 290, Breezemere Farm Road, 04617
(207) 326-8628

Picturesque 1850 farmhouse plus seven cottages on 60 acres on Orcutt Harbor, East Penobscot Bay. Spruce to smell, islands to explore, water to sail, trails to hike, berries to pick, mussels to rake. Bikes, beach, boats. Bed sizes available include twins, doubles, and queens. Full breakfast daily. Open May through October. Free brochure.

Hosts: Joe and Linda Forest
Rooms: 7 (4 PB; 3 SB) $65-95
Cottages: 7 (PB) $110-125
Full Breakfast
Credit Cards: A, B
Closed Nov. 1-April
Notes: 2, 4 (Monday-Thursday), 8 (cottages), 9, 10, 11, 12, 14

6 Pets welcome; 8 Children welcome; 9 Social drinking allowed; 10 Tennis available; 11 Swimming available; 12 Golf available; 13 Skiing available; 14 May be booked through travel agents.

BRUNSWICK

Harpswell Inn

Rural Route 1, Box 141, Lookout Point, South
  Harpswell, 04079
(207) 833-5509; (800) 843-5509

Situated by the sea in Harpswell, this historic 1761 inn at Lookout Point dominates a knoll overlooking a quaint cove that serves as a snug harbor for lobster boats. Explore the local islands and villages, and enjoy interesting day trips to historical sites and attractions. Freeport shopping is only 25 minutes away, with Bowdoin College and Brunswick Summer Theater just 10 minutes away. Fine restaurants, swimming, boating, and bicycling available.

Hosts: Bill and Susan Menz
Rooms: 12 (3 PB; 9 SB) $58-110
Full Breakfast
Credit Cards: A, B
Notes: 2, 5, 9, 10, 11, 14

BUCKSPORT

The River Inn
Bed and Breakfast

210 Main Street, P. O. Box 1657, 04416-1657
(207) 469-3783

Spacious old sea captain's home on the Penobscot River in historic Bucksport. Conveniently situated at the northern tip of

River Inn

Penobscot Bay, Bucksport offers easy access to east and west bay tour areas. Antiquing, auctions, crafts, golf, water, and winter sports are some of the activities available for guests. Public boat launch is nearby, as are mooring rentals. Large deck offers panoramic river views, and a rare player grand piano will interest guests. Breakfast features fruit plates. Children over 12.

Host: The Stone family
Rooms: 3 (1 PB; 2 SB)
Full Breakfast
Credit Cards: None
Notes: 2, 5, 6, 9, 12, 13, 14

CAMDEN

Blackberry Inn

82 Elm Street, 04843
(207) 236-6060; (800) 833-6674
FAX (207) 236-4117

Blackberry Inn is a restored Italianate Victorian with large, spacious rooms decorated in period style, most with queen-size beds and private bath. Some have whirlpools, fireplaces, and cable TV. Stroll to Camden's harbor and fine restaurants, or relax in the comfortable parlors and enjoy afternoon wine and cheese. Wonderful full breakfast in the dining room or courtyard. Featured in *Daughters of Painted Ladies: America's Resplendent Victorians*. "A delightful bed and breakfast," says the *Miami Herald*.

Hosts: Vicki and Edward Doudera
Rooms: 10 (8 PB; 2 SB) $53.50-144.45 (seasonal)
Apartments: 1 (PB) $75-155
Full Breakfast
Credit Cards: A, B
Notes: 2, 4, 5, 8, 9, 10, 11, 12, 13, 14

The Camden Maine Stay Inn

22 High Street, 04843
(207) 236-9636

A comfortable bed, a hearty breakfast, and a friendly innkeeper will be found in this old Colonial home. In Camden's historic

NOTES: Credit cards accepted: A Master Card; B Visa; C American Express; D Discover Card; E Diner's Club; F Other; 2 Personal Checks accepted; 3 Lunch available; 4 Dinner available; 5 Open all year;

Camden Main Stay Inn

district, a short walk to harbor, shops, restaurants, and state park. Recommended by the *Miami Herald, Lewiston Journal, Watterville Sentinel, Country Inns* and *Country Living* magazines.

Hosts: Peter and Donny Smith; Diana Robson
Rooms: 8 (4 PB; 4 SB) $75-100
Full Breakfast
Credit Cards: A, B
Notes: 2, 5, 8 (over 10), 9, 10, 11, 12, 13, 14

Hawthorn Inn

9 High Street, 04843
(207) 236-8842

An elegant family-run Victorian inn with harbor view, spacious grounds, and a large deck. Walk through the back garden to shops and restaurants. Full breakfast and afternoon tea served. Carriage house bedrooms with private Jacuzzi and balconies.

Hosts: Pauline and Bradford Staub
Rooms: 10; 2 apartments (PB) $70-225

Hawthorn Inn

Full Breakfast
Closed January - February
Minimum stay July and Aug: 2 nights
Credit Cards: A, B
Notes: 2, 5, 8, 9, 10, 11, 12, 13, 14

A Little Dream

66 High Street, 04843
(207) 236-8742

Sweet dreams and little luxuries abound in this lovely, white Victorian, with a wrap-around porch. Noted for its delicious breakfasts, beautiful rooms, and charming atmosphere, A Little Dream's English Country Victorian decor has been featured in *Country Inns* magazine and *Glamour's 40 Best Getaways Across The Country*. Situated in the affluent coastal community of Camden, it is close to the harbor and shops.

Hosts: Joanna Hall and Bill Fontana
Rooms: 5 (PB) $89-139
Full Breakfast
Credit Cards: A, B, C
Notes: 2, 5, 10, 11, 12, 13

Albonegon Inn

CAPITOL ISLAND

Albonegon Inn

Capitol Island, 04538
(207) 633-2521

Built in the 1880s, the Albonegon is one of the last old cottage-style inns. It is perched

---

6 Pets welcome; 8 Children welcome; 9 Social drinking allowed; 10 Tennis available; 11 Swimming available; 12 Golf available; 13 Skiing available; 14 May be booked through travel agents.

on the edge of the rocks and offers a delightful view of the Boothbay Harbor area and outer islands. It is a very quiet spot, four miles from downtown.

Hosts: Kim and Bob Peckham
Rooms: 15 (3 PB; 12 SB) $65-100
Continental Breakfast
Credit Cards: None
Notes: 2, 8, 10, 11

DAMARISCOTTA

Brannon-Bunker Inn
HCR 64, Box 045X, 04543
(207) 563-5941

Intimate, relaxed country bed and breakfast in an 1820 Cape, 1880 converted barn, and 1900 carriage house. Seven rooms furnished in themes reflecting the charm of yesterday with the comforts of today. Ten minutes to lighthouse, fort, beach, antique, and craft shopping. Antique shop on the premises.

Hosts: Jeanne and Joe Hovance
Rooms: 7 (4 PB; 3 SB) $53.50-69.55
Continental Breakfast
Credit Cards: A, B, C
Notes: 2, 5, 8, 9, 10, 11, 12, 13, 14

EASTPORT

Weston House
26 Boynton Street, 04631
(207) 853-2907

Built in 1810, this imposing Federal-style house overlooks Passamaquoddy Bay across to Campobello Island. Listed on the National Register of Historic Places; situated in a lovely down east coastal village. Grounds include an expansive lawn suitable for croquet and a flower garden for quiet relaxation. Picnic lunches available.

Hosts: Jett and John Peterson
Rooms: $48.15-69.55
Full Breakfast
Credit Cards: None
Notes: 2, 3, 4, 5, 9, 10, 12

Atlantic Seal

FREEPORT

Atlantic Seal Bed and Breakfast
25 Main Street, P. O. Box 146, 04078
(207) 865-6112

Lovely harbor views year-round from each cozy room of this 1850s Cape Cod home on Freeport Harbor. Antiques and nautical collections of a seafaring family. Rooms feature sea breezes, fresh flowers, candlelight, thick towels, comfortable beds, homemade quilts, and down comforters. Shared and private baths, one with Jacuzzi. Down east hospitality, beverages in old-fashioned parlor. Enjoy a hearty sailors breakfast. Just a five-minute drive to L.L. Bean and other outlet stores. Resident dog and cat.

Hosts: Captain Thomas and Gaila Ring
Rooms: 3 (PB and SB) $55-125
Full Breakfast
Credit Cards: None
Notes: 2, 5, 8 (mature), 9, 10, 11, 12, 13 (XC), 14

The Bagley House
Rural Route 3, Box 269C, 04032
(207) 865-6566

Peace, tranquility, and history abound in this magnificent 1772 country home. Six acres of fields and woods invite nature lovers, hikers, berry pickers, and cross-country skiers. The kitchen's hand-hewn beams and enormous free-standing fire-

NOTES: Credit cards accepted: A Master Card; B Visa; C American Express; D Discover Card; E Diner's Club; F Other; 2 Personal Checks accepted; 3 Lunch available; 4 Dinner available; 5 Open all year;

place with beehive oven inspire mouth-watering breakfasts. A warm welcome awaits guests.

Host: Sig Knudsen
Rooms: 5 (PB) $80-100
Full Breakfast
Credit Cards: A, B, C, D
Notes: 2, 5, 8, 9, 10, 11, 12, 13, 14

Captain Josiah Mitchell House (Nonsmoking Inn)

188 Main Street, 04032
(207) 865-3289

Famous, historic ship captain's home, circa 1779. The 1866 miraculous survival-at-sea story of Captain Mitchell of the ship Hornet is a classic. Mark Twain, then a young newspaperman, wrote about it. Restored more than 25 years ago by present owners, the house is filled with antiques. Beautiful grounds and only a five-minute walk to L.L. Bean. Eleventh year as an inn. Off-season (winter) rates available.

Hosts: Alan and Loretta Bradley
Rooms: 6 (PB) $73-85
Full Breakfast
Credit Cards: A, B
Notes: 5, 9, 11, 12, 13, 14

Country at Heart Bed and Breakfast

37 Bow Street, 04032
(207) 865-0512

Enjoy staying in a cozy 1870 country home with handmade crafts, antiques, and repro-duction furnishings. Choose one of the country-decorated rooms, the Shaker Quilt or Teddy Bear. A full breakfast is served on an eight-foot oak dining table. After breakfast, browse through Kim's Kraft Korner, a gift shop with country crafts and antiques. Park and walk to more than 100 outlet stores, restaurants, and L.L. Bean just two blocks away.

Hosts: Rogert and Kim Dubay
Rooms: 3 (PB) $65-75

Country at Heart

Full Breakfast
Credit Cards: None
Notes: 2, 5, 8, 9, 12, 14

181 Main Street Bed and Breakfast

181 Main Street, 04032
(207) 865-1226

Comfortably elegant, antique-filled 1840 Cape. Just a five-minute walk to L.L. Bean and Freeport's luxury outlets. Hosts pro-vide a renowned breakfast, New England hospitality, and information on all that Maine has to offer, on and off the beaten path. In-ground pool; ample parking. Featured in *Country Home* magazine. American Bed and Breakfast Association and AAA approved.

Rooms: 7 (PB) $75-95
Full Breakfast
Credit Cards: A, B
Notes: 2, 5, 9, 11, 12, 13 (XC), 14

GOULDSBORO

Bed and Breakfast Inns of New England ME-850

329 Lake Drive, Guilford, CT 06437
(800) 582-0853

The grounds of this bed and breakfast home border Jones Pond. Guests can enjoy swimming, fishing, and canoeing in warm

6 Pets welcome; 8 Children welcome; 9 Social drinking allowed; 10 Tennis available; 11 Swimming available; 12 Golf available; 13 Skiing available; 14 May be booked through travel agents.

months, and cross-country skiing, ice skating, and ice fishing in winter months. Artistic and photographic opportunities abound all year. Common rooms in this late Victorian home include a large dining room, a comfortable double parlor, and an inviting sun porch. Seven spacious bedrooms with shared baths are spread over three floors. Four of these rooms have ocean views and a fifth overlooks the pond. Resident pets, but no guest pets, please. Children are welcome.$59-69.

HARRISON

Tolman House Inn
Tolman Road, 04040
(207) 583-4445

Situated in a recently converted carriage house, nine guest rooms, each with private bath, are tastefully decorated with brass and antique beds and furnishings. Stroll leisurely through the formal gardens, which enhance the eight acres of our lovely country setting. A full homebaked country breakfast is served each morning in the gracious and comfortable dining area. Brunches, lunches, and dinners are available with advanced notice. Catering for special occasions.

Hosts: Kenneth and Louise Donisi
Rooms: 11 (9 PB; 2 SB) $60-85
Full Breakfast
Credit Cards: A, B
Notes: 2, 3, 4, 5, 8, 9, 10, 11, 12, 13

ISLE AU HAUT

The Keepers House
P. O. Box 26, 04645
(207) 367-2261

Remote island lighthouse station in the undeveloped wilderness area of Acadia National Park. Guests arrive on the mail boat from Stonington. No phones, cars, TV,

or crowds. Osprey, seal, deer, rugged trails, spectacular scenery, seclusion, and inspiration. Three elegant meals included in rate.

Hosts: Jeff and Judi Burke
Rooms: 6 (SB) $225, includes meals
Minimum stay July-Aug.: 2 nights
Credit Cards: None
Closed Nov. 1-April 30
Notes: 2, 3, 4, 8, 9, 11

KENNEBUNK

Arundel Meadows Inn
P. O. Box 1129, 04043
(207) 985-3770

This 165-year-old farmhouse, two miles north on Route 1 from the center of Kennebunk, combines the charm of antiques and art with the comfort of seven individually decorated bedrooms with sitting areas—two are suites, three have fireplaces, some have cable television, and all have private bathrooms and summer air conditioning. Full homemade breakfasts and afternoon teas are prepared by co-owner Mark Bachelder, a professionally trained chef. The inn is open year-round.

Hosts: Mark Bachelder and Murray Yaeger
Rooms: 7 (PB) $75-110
Full Breakfast
Credit Cards: A, B
Notes: 2, 5, 9

The Keepers House

Bed and Breakfast Inns of New England ME-810

329 Lake Drive, Guilford, CT 06437
(800) 582-0853

Step back in time when welcomed to this 1756 farmhouse set on six acres of rolling hills. Common rooms, including a colonial kitchen, are furnished with period antiques, stenciled walls, pumpkin pine floors, and six fireplaces. Continental breakfast is served on the sun porch each morning. Three rooms with double beds are available, two included private bath and one has a fireplace. Resident pets, but no guest pets, please. Children over 14 are welcome. $70.

English Meadows Inn

141 Port Road, 04043
(207) 967-5766

English Meadows is an 1860 Victorian farmhouse that has been operating as an inn for more than 80 years. It is a 10-minute stroll of the village of Kennebunkport. Enjoy scrumptuous breakfasts amid charming antiques, and rooms appointed in the taste of rural New England. English Meadows offers a friendly and comfortable place to visit.

Host: Charlie Doane
Rooms: 13 (9 PB; 4 SB) $65-90
Full Breakfast
Credit Cards: A, B
Notes: 2, 5, 8 (over 9), 10, 11, 12

KENNEBUNKPORT

Captain Fairfield Inn

P. O. Box 1308, 04046
(207) 967-4454

A gracious 1813 sea captain's mansion in Kennebunkport's historic district is only steps to the village green and harbor. A delightful walk to sandy beaches, Dock Square Marina, shops, and excellent restaurants. Situated on the corner of Pleasant and Green streets. Gracious and elegant, the bedrooms are beautifully decorated with antiques and period furnishings that lend an atmosphere of tranquility and charm. Several bedrooms have fireplaces, and guests are welcome to relax in the livingroom, study, or enjoy the tree-shaded grounds and gardens. Awake to birdsong, fresh sea air, and the aroma of gourmet coffee. Come and enjoy a refreshing, comfortable, memorable stay.

Hosts: Bonnie and Dennis Tallagnon
Rooms: 9 (PB) $75-135
Full Breakfast
Credit Cards: A, B, C
Notes: 2, 5, 9, 10, 11, 12, 14

The Captain Lord Mansion

P. O. Box 800, 04046
(207) 967-3141; (800) 522-3141

The Captain Lord Mansion is an intimate 16-room luxury country inn situated at the head of a sweeping lawn, overlooking the Kennebunk River. The inn is famous for its warm, friendly hospitality, attention to cleanliness, and hearty breakfasts served family-style in the big country kitchen.

Hosts: Bev Davis and Rick Litchfield
Rooms: 16 (PB) $75-115
Full Breakfast
Credit Cards: A, B, D
Notes: 2, 5, 9, 10, 11, 12

1802 House

Locke Street, P. O. Box 646-A, 04046
(207) 967-5632

1802 House is a 19th-century inn tucked away in a quiet section of the quaint seaside village of Kennebunkport. The inn is bounded by the Cape Arundel Golf Club, nestled along the fifteenth green, yet is only a ten-minute walk to bustling Dock Square. Each of the six guest rooms is furnished with antiques, all have private bathrooms, and two guest rooms offer working fireplaces. A full gourmet breakfast awaits each morning.

6 Pets welcome; 8 Children welcome; 9 Social drinking allowed; 10 Tennis available; 11 Swimming available; 12 Golf available; 13 Skiing available; 14 May be booked through travel agents.

Hosts: Ron and Carol Perry
Rooms: 6 (PB) $85-125
Full Breakfast
Credit Cards: A, B, C
Notes: 2, 4, 5, 9, 10, 11, 12, 14

Inn on South Street

Box 478A, 04046
(207) 967-5151

Relax in the comfortable elegance of this early 19th-Century Greek Revival home. The hosts take a special interest in your comfort and enjoyment. The three beautiful guest rooms and one apartment suite, each with private bath and telephone, are available year-round, by the day or week. Rates include Eva's sumptuous breakfast.

Hosts: Jacques and Eva Downs
Rooms: 4 (PB) $85-175
Full Breakfast
Credit Cards: A, B
Notes: 2, 5, 10, 11, 12, 13, 14

KITTERY

Bed and Breakfast Inns of New England ME-805

329 Lake Drive, Guilford, CT 06437
(800) 582-0853

A romantic ambience and elegant antique furnishings await at this 1890 Princess Anne Victorian bed and breakfast. Enjoy a full breakfast of gourmet coffees, omelettes, and pastries in the garden or on the sun deck. Six guest rooms are available with double and queen beds, shared and private baths. Resident pets, and guest pets are welcome. Children are welcome. $69-89.

Gundalow Inn

6 Water Street, 03904
(207) 439-4040

Brick Victorian on the town green, a stroll across the bridge from colonial Portsmouth.

Romantic guestrooms, wallpapers, antiques, and water views. Friendly innkeepers prepare and serve fresh, hearty breakfasts and see to every need. They've furnished the inn for comfort and the pleasures of another era. Situated halfway between Boston and Portland, it is only a short drive to beaches and outlets and just minutes on foot to the harbor, museums, theaters, shops, and restaurants. Recommended by the *New York Times*.

Hosts: Cevia and George Rosol
Rooms: 6 (PB) $75-95 plus tax
Full Breakfast
Credit Cards: A, B
Notes: 2, 5, 9, 10, 11, 12, 13 (XC)

LUBEC

Breakers by the Bay

37 Washington, 04652
(207) 733-2487

One of the oldest houses in the 200-year-old town of Lubec, a small fishing village. Three blocks to Campobello Island, the home of Franklin D. Roosevelt. All rooms have hand-crocheted tablecloths and hand-quilted bedspreads. Five rooms have private decks for viewing the bay. All rooms that share a bath have their own washstands.

Host: E. M. Elg
Rooms: 5 (4 PB; 1 SB) $64.20
Full Breakfast
Credit Cards: None
Notes: 2, 10, 12

Gundalow Inn

MILBRIDGE

Bed and Breakfast Inns of New England ME-855
329 Lake Drive, Guilford, CT 06437
(800) 582-0853

This large Victorian has outstanding views of the bay and Narraguagus River. Common rooms include a sitting room, formal livingroom, dining room, and sun porch. This bed and breakfast is in a rural village with restaurants, light shopping, and an inexpensive movie theater a short walk from the doorstep. Full breakfast includes a bottomless cup of coffee or tea. Six guest rooms with a variety of bed sizes and shared and private baths are available. Children over 12 are welcome. No guest pets. $45-55.

MT. DESERT

Reibers Bed and Breakfast
P. O. Box 163, Somesville, 04660
(207) 244-3047

Handsome 150-year old Colonial homestead with antique furnishings on four acres, with tidal creek and meadows on the outskirts of historic village. Centrally located, a short drive to Bar Harbor and Acadia National Park. Homebaked goods, open year-round. French spoken.

Hosts: Gail and David Reiber
Rooms: 2 (1 PB; 1 SB) $60-70
Full Breakfast
Ctedit Cards: None
Notes: 2, 5, 8, 10, 11, 12, 13

NAPLES

Inn at Long Lake
P. O. Box 806, 04055
(207) 693-6226; (800) 437-0328

Enjoy romantic elegance and turn-of-the-century charm at the Inn at Long Lake, nestled amid the pines and waterways of the beautiful Sebago Lakes region. The inn has 16 restored rooms with TVs, air conditioners, and private baths. Situated one minute's walk from the Naples Causeway. Four-season activities and fine dining nearby. This three-diamond AAA facility is worth the trip. Midweek discounts available.

Hosts: Maynard and Irene Hincks
Rooms: 16 (PB) $63-100 seasonal
Continental Breakfast
Credit Cards: A, B, D
Notes: 2, 5, 8, 9, 11, 12, 13, 14

Inn at Long Lake

NEWCASTLE

The Newcastle Inn
River Road, 04553
(207) 563-5685; (800) 832-8669

A romantic country inn on the Damariscotta River, in an unspoiled part of Maine. Rooms have river views, and some have canopy beds. Enjoy the changing tide while sitting on the glassed and screened sun porch. In the dining room, nationally acclaimed four-star candlelight dinners and multicourse breakfasts are served. The feeling of warmth, friendship and quiet seclusion make this a retreat where guests can relax and unwind.

Hosts: Ted and Chris Sprague
Rooms: 15 (PB) $70-125
Full Breakfast
Credit Cards: A, B
Notes: 2, 4, 5, 10, 11, 12, 13 (XC), 14

6 Pets welcome; 8 Children welcome; 9 Social drinking allowed; 10 Tennis available; 11 Swimming available; 12 Golf available; 13 Skiing available; 14 May be booked through travel agents.

Harbourside Inn

Northeast Harbor, 04662
(207) 276-3272

Peace and quiet, flower gardens at the edge of the forest, and woodland trails into Acadia National Park add to the delights of this genuine 1888 country inn. Spacious rooms and suites, all with private baths, many with king or queen beds. Beautiful antiques, working fireplaces in all first- and second-floor rooms. Walk or drive into nearby Acadia National Park. Sailing, deep-sea fishing, and carriage rides in the park are nearby. Reservations accepted for two nights or more.

Host: The Sweet family
Rooms: 11 plus 3 suites (PB) $85-210
Continental Breakfast
Credit Cards: None
Notes: 2, 10, 11, 12

OGUNQUIT

Beauport Inn

102 Shore Road, P. O. Box 1793, 03907
(207) 646-8680

A cozy nonsmoking bed and breakfast furnished with antiques offers four rooms, all of which have private baths. Pine-paneled livingroom with a fireplace and piano. Baked goods by the host. Antique shop on the premises.

Host: Dan Pender
Rooms: 4 (PB) $75-85
Continental Breakfast
Credit Cards: A, B, C
Closed January and February
Notes: 2, 8 (over 12), 9, 10, 11, 12

PORTLAND

Inn on Carleton

46 Carleton Street, 04102
(207) 775-1910; (800) 639-1779

The Inn on Carleton, a graciously restored 1869 Victorian townhouse in the city's historic West End, is situated on a quiet, tree-lined street in a unique residential neighborhood. Close to downtown and the business district, it is a short walk to the Portland Museum of Art and the Performing Arts Center. Casco Bay's Calendar Islands are nearby, as well as the international ferry to Nova Scotia and the Old Port, with its cobbled streets, colorful shops, and fine restaurants.

Hosts: Phil and Sue Cox
Rooms: 7 (3 PB; 4 SB) $60-90
Full Breakfast
Credit Cards: A, B, D
Notes: 2, 5, 8, 10, 11, 12, 13

PROSPECT HARBOR

Oceanside Meadows Inn

P. O. Box 90, 04669
(207) 963-5557

This lovely 19th-century home overlooks Sand Cove in scenic Prospect Harbor. Seven rooms, including one suite await the weary traveler, along with a private sand beach and refreshing, cool sea breezes. Whether an individual guest or an entire family, Oceanside Meadows will provide a memorable seaside experience.

Hosts: Norm and Marge Babineau
Rooms: 7 (1PB; 6 SB) $50-70
Full Breakfast
Credit Cards: A, B, F
Notes: 2, 5 (May 1 - Oct. 31), 6, 8, 11, 12

RANGELEY

Northwoods

Main Street, P. O. Box 79, 04970
(207) 864-2440

An historic 1912 home of rare charm and easy elegance, Northwoods is centrally located in Rangeley Village. With spacious rooms, a lakefront porch, expansive grounds, and private boat dock, Northwoods provides superb accommodations. Golf, tennis, water sports, hiking, and skiing are a few of the many activities offered by the region.

Host: Carol Scofield
Rooms: 4 (3 PB; 1 SB) $60-75
Full Breakfast
Credit Cards: None
Notes: 2, 9, 10, 11, 12, 13, 14

SACO

Crown 'n' Anchor Inn

121 North Street, P. O. Box 228, 04072-0228
(207) 282-3829

This beautiful, two-story Greek Revival house was built circa 1827. The ornate Victorian furnishings, double parlors with twin mirrors, and bountiful country breakfast afford many memories for guests. All rooms at the inn are furnished with period antiques, many collectibles, and private facilities. Nearby attractions include the York Institute Museum, Thornton Academy, and the Dyer Library.

Hosts: John Barclay and Martha Forester
Rooms: 5 (PB) $65-85
Full Breakfast
Credit Cards: A, B
Notes: 2, 5, 6 (small), 8 (over 12), 9, 10, 11, 14

SEARSPORT

Brass Lantern Inn

Route 1, P. O. Box 407, 04974
(207) 584-0150

Nestled at the edge of the woods, this gracious Victorian Inn, circa 1850, overlooks Penobscot Bay. All of the comfortable guest rooms have private baths. Enjoy a hearty breakfast with friendly hospitality. Open all year, the Brass Lantern will be lit to welcome guests!

Hosts: Pat Gatto; Dan and Lee Anne Lee
Rooms: 4 (PB) $65-70 seasonal
Continental Plus Breakfast
Credit Cards: A, B
Notes: 2, 5, 8, 14

Weskeag at the Water

SOUTH THOMASTON

Weskeag at the Water

Route 73, P. O. Box 213, 04858
(207) 596-6676

The Weskeag Inn is a mid-coast Maine bed and breakfast in an exceptional setting, at the reversing falls of the Weskeag Estuary. From the deck guests often see lobstermen tending their traps and osprey fishing. Birch Point State Park and Owls Head Transportation Musem are nearby, along with a wealth of seaside activities. It's also a perfect respite between Freeport and Acadia National Park.

Hosts: Gray and Lynne Smith
Rooms: 8 (2 PB; 6 S3B) $55-75
Full Breakfast
Credit Cards: None
Notes: 2, 5, 8, 9, 10, 11, 12, 13

SOUTHWEST HARBOR

Harbour Cottage Inn

P. O. Box 258, 04679-0258
(207) 244-5738

This elegant but informal inn is situated in the heart of Acadia National Park. Private baths offer either whirlpools or steam showers and hair dryers. Harbor-facing guest rooms have individual heat and ceiling fans. Hikers, bikers, boaters, skiers, and tourists are welcome to enjoy the warm, friendly hospitality.

6 Pets welcome; 8 Children welcome; 9 Social drinking allowed; 10 Tennis available; 11 Swimming available; 12 Golf available; 13 Skiing available; 14 May be booked through travel agents.

Hosts: Ann and Mike Pedreschi
Rooms: 8 (PB) $60-125
Full Breakfast
Credit Cards: A, B, C, D
Notes: 2, 5 (closed Nov.), 9, 10, 11, 12, 13, 14

Harbour Woods Lodging

P. O. Box 1214, 04679
(207) 244-5388

Relaxing, intimate bed and breakfast. Comfortable traditional furnishings accented with fresh flowers, family keepsakes, and candlelight. Spacious guest rooms with large private baths offer harbor and garden views. Full breakfast, served on fine china, made with the freshest ingredients and imaginatively prepared and presented. Situated at the edge of the village, surrounded by Acadia National Park and the sparkling waters of one of Maine's most picturesque harbors. Special off-season packages. Cottages also available May through October.

Hosts: Margaret Eden and James Paviglionite
Rooms: 3 (PB) $55-105
Full Breakfast
Credit Cards: None
Notes: 2, 5, 9, 10, 11, 12, 13, 14

The Island House

Box 1006, 04679
(207) 244-5180

Relax in a gracious, restful seacoast home on the quiet side of the island. Island House favorites such as blueberry coffee cake and sausage/cheese casserole are served for breakfast. Charming, private loft apartment available. Acadia National Park is just a five-minute drive away. The house is across the street from the harbor, with swimming, sailing, biking, and hiking nearby.

Host: Ann Gill
Rooms: 5 (1 PB; 4 SB) $55-100
Full Breakfast
Credit Cards: None
Closed Jan. 1-Mar. 31
Notes: 2, 8 (over 12), 9, 10, 11, 12, 14

Island Watch Bed and Breakfast

Freeman Ridge Road, P. O. Box 1359, 04679
(207) 244-7229

Overlooking the harbor of Mount Desert Island and the village of Southwest Harbor, Island Watch sits atop Freeman Ridge on the quiet side of the island. The finest panoramic views, privacy, and a short walk to Acadia National Park and the fishing village of Southwest Harbor.

Host: Maxine M. Clark
Rooms: 6 (PB) $65
Full Breakfast
Credit Cards: None
Notes: 5, 8 (over 11), 9, 10, 11, 12, 13, 14

The Kingsleigh Inn

100 Main Street, Box 1426, 04679
(207) 244-5302

Situated in the heart of Acadia National Park overlooking the picturesque harbor is a romantic, intimate inn that will surround guests with charm the moment they walk through the door. Many rooms enjoy spectacular harbor views, and all are tastefully decorated.

Hosts: Tom and Nancy Cerelli
Rooms: 8 (PB) $55-155
Full Breakfast
Credit Cards: A, B, C, D
Notes: 2, 5, 8 (over 12), 9, 11, 12

The Island House

NOTES: Credit cards accepted: A Master Card; B Visa; C American Express; D Discover Card; E Diner's Club; F Other; 2 Personal Checks accepted; 3 Lunch available; 4 Dinner available; 5 Open all year;

Lindenwood Inn

P. O. Box 1328, 04679
(207) 244-5335

Built at the turn-of-the-century as a sea captain's home, the inn derives it's name from the stately Linden trees that line the front lawn. Recently remodeled, each room is individually decorated and has a private bath. Many feature harbor views from sun-drenched balconies. Relax and unwind at one of the inn's elegant sitting rooms or on the large shaded front porch, while listening to the sounds of the harbor just a few steps away.

The Kingsleigh Inn

Hosts: Jim, Brennan, and Britanie King
Rooms: 9 (PB) $55-125 (seasonal)
Full Breakfast
Credit Cards: None
Notes: 2, 5, 9, 10, 11, 12, 13, 14

STRATTON

The Widow's Walk

171 Main Street, P. O. Box 150, 04982
(207) 246-6901

The steamboat gothic architecture of this Victorian home led to a listing in the National Register of Historic Places. Nearby Bigelow Mountain, the Appalachian Trail and Flagstaff Lake present many opportunities for boating, fishing and hiking. In the winter, Sugarloaf USA, Maine's largest ski resort, offers both alpine and cross-country skiing, as well as dogsled rides. Dogs and cats in residence.

Hosts: Mary and Jerry Hopson
Rooms: 6 (SB) $30; $44 in winter
Full Breakfast
Credit Cards: A, B
Notes: 2, 5, 8, 9, 11, 12, 13

VINALHAVEN

Bed and Breakfast Inns of New England ME-830

329 Lake Drive, Guilford, CT 06437
(800) 582-0853

Stay at this comfortable, affordable bed and breakfast in a fishing village by Carver's Harbor. Explore uncrowded woodlands, visit seaside nature preserves and parks, and feast on Maine's freshest seafood caught daily in the surrounding waters. Each morning starts with a continental breakfast, and guests can prepare a picnic in the guest kitchen for the day's adventures. Available are six guest rooms, all with shared baths. Children over 10 are welcome. Resident dog, no guest pets, please. $40-60.

WALDOBORO

The Roaring Lion

Box 756, 04572
(207) 832-4038

A 1905 Victorian home with tin ceilings; elegant woodwork throughout. The Roaring Lion caters to special diets and serves miso soup, sourdough bread, homemade jams and jellies. Hosts are well traveled and lived two years in West Africa. Their interests include books, gardening, art, and cooking. Gallery and giftshop on premises.

---

6 Pets welcome; 8 Children welcome; 9 Social drinking allowed; 10 Tennis available; 11 Swimming available; 12 Golf available; 13 Skiing available; 14 May be booked through travel agents.

Hosts: Bill and Robin Branigan
Rooms: 4 (1 PB; 3 SB) $53.50-64.20
Full Breakfast
Credit Cards: None
Notes: 2, 5, 8, 10, 11, 12, 13, 14

WATERFORD

Lake House

Routes 35 and 37, 04088
(207) 583-4182; (800) 223-4182 outside ME

Lake House is one of 21 buildings in Waterford "Flat" listed on the national historic register. The inn was established in the 1790s. For much of the 19th century it served as the Maine Hygienic Institute for Ladies. From the 1890s to 1940, it was operated as a hotel.

Hosts: Michael and Suzanne Uhl-Myers
Rooms: 5 (PB) $69-125
Full Breakfast
Credit Cards: A, B
Notes: 2, 4, 5, 9, 10, 11, 12, 13, 14

The Parsonage House

The Parsonage House Bed and Breakfast

Rice Road, P. O. Box 116, 04088
(207) 583-4115

The Parsonage House, built in 1870 for the Waterford Church, overlooks Waterford Village, Keoka Lake, and Mount Tirem. Situated in a four-season area, it provides many opportunities for outdoor enthusiasts. The Parsonage is a haven of peace and quiet. Double guest rooms or private suite available. A full breakfast is served on the screen porch or in the large farm kitchen beside a glowing wood stove.

Hosts: Joseph and Gail St. Hilaire
Rooms: 3 (1 PB; 2 SB) $50-75
Full Breakfast
Credit Cards: None
Notes: 2, 3, 5, 8, 11, 12, 13

WEST GOULDSBORO

The Sunset House

Route 186, 04607
(207) 963-7156

This late Victorian home offers a choice of seven spacious bedrooms over three floors. Four feature ocean views, a fifth overlooks Jones Pond. Common rooms include a large dining room, comfortable double parlor and sun porch. Sunset House is situated on the Schoodic Peninsula, the quiet side of Acadia National Park.

Hosts: Carl and Kathy Johnson
Rooms: 7 (SB) $39-69
Full Breakfast
Credit Cards: A, B, D
Notes: 2, 5, 8, 9, 11, 12, 13

WISCASSET

The Squire Tarbox Inn

Rural Route 2, Box 620, 04578
(207) 882-7693

Clean, casual, comfortable, and all country, this is a handsome old farmhouse on a back road near mid-coast Maine harbors, beaches, antique shops, museums, and lobster shacks. Listed on the National Register of Historic Places. The inn offers a proper balance of history, quiet country, good food, and relaxation. Serves a delicious fresh goat cheese by the fire before dinner. Known primarily for rural privacy and five-course dinners.

NOTES: Credit cards accepted: A Master Card; B Visa; C American Express; D Discover Card; E Diner's Club; F Other; 2 Personal Checks accepted; 3 Lunch available; 4 Dinner available; 5 Open all year;

The Squire Tarbox Inn

Hosts: Karen and Bill Mitman
Rooms: 11 (PB) $62-132
Continental Breakfast
Credit Cards: A, B, C, D
Notes: 2, 4, 7, 8 (over 14), 9, 14

YORK BEACH _____

Homestead Inn
Bed and Breakfast

8 South Main Street (Route 1A), 03910
(207) 363-8952

A converted 1905 summer boarding house, the inn is situated at Short Sands Beach. Individually decorated rooms have ocean views. Walk to beach, enjoy sunsets; visit local Nubble Lighthouse. Historic landmarks; fine restaurants. Relax, be pampered, and let the seashore entertain.

Hosts: Dan and Danielle Duffy
Rooms: 4 (S2B) $49-59
Continental Breakfast
Credit Cards: None
Notes: 2, 10, 11, 12

6 Pets welcome; 8 Children welcome; 9 Social drinking allowed; 10 Tennis available; 11 Swimming available; 12 Golf available; 13 Skiing available; 14 May be booked through travel agents.

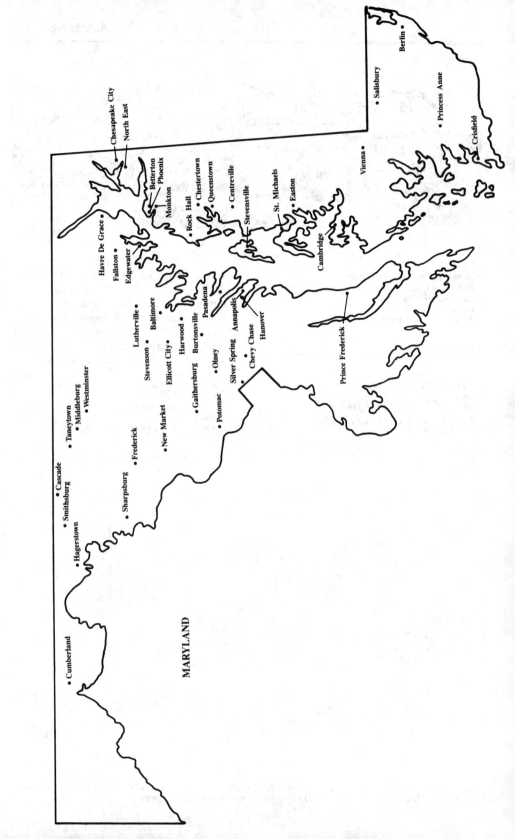

Maryland

Amanda's Bed and Breakfast #139

1428 Park Avenue, Baltimore, 21217
(410) 225-0001; (410) 383-1274

Choose from five historic locations in downtown Annapolis that all accurately reflect early architecture. Some even include dining rooms, taverns, and conference space. Continental breakfast. $85-200.

Amanda's Bed and Breakfast #163

1428 Park Avenue, Baltimore, 21217
(410) 225-0001; (410) 383-1274

This ten-room bed and breakfast is on the main street in downtown Annapolis just steps away from the docks, shops, and historic buildings. As the inn is above a fantastic and famous deli, and meals may be chosen from a special bed and breakfast menu. One room (PB). Full breakfast. $65-85.

Amanda's Bed and Breakfast #182

1428 Park Avenue, Baltimore, 21217
(410) 225-0001; (410) 383-1274

This beautiful, modern condo on the water looks out onto a marina. Location is just 15 minutes (3 miles) from downtown historic Annapolis. Continental breakfast. One queen bed. $85.

Amanda's Bed and Breakfast #191

1428 Park Avenue, Baltimore, 21217
(410) 225-0001; (410) 383-1274

With pleasant Laura Ashley decor, this bright 1830s renovation is conveniently situated near the waters of East Port. Historic Annapolis docks and the Naval Academy are within walking distance. Added benefits include a view of the water, spacious parking, and water taxi. Four rooms (2 PB, 2 SB). Continental breakfast. $65-75.

Amanda's Bed and Breakfast #200

1428 Park Avenue, Baltimore, 21217
(410) 225-0001; (410) 383-1274

This fully furnished historic home is very close to the docks and the historic district of Annapolis. Feel free to walk to restaurants, shops, and the Naval Academy. Special features include modern kitchen, three working fireplaces, four bedrooms, three baths, TV, a washer/dryer, and central heat and air conditioning. Whole house rental. Sleeps 6 to 8. Self-catered breakfast. $300.

Amanda's Bed and Breakfast #218

1428 Park Avenue, Baltimore, 21217
(410) 225-0001; (410) 383-1274

These three homes—Berman, Lauren, and Patterson House—are situated in the heart

NOTES: Credit cards accepted: A Master Card; B Visa; C American Express; D Discover Card; E Diner's Club; F Other; 2 Personal Checks accepted; 3 Lunch available; 4 Dinner available; 5 Open all year; 6 Pets welcome; 8 Children welcome; 9 Social drinking allowed; 10 Tennis available; 11 Swimming available; 12 Golf available; 13 Skiing available; 14 May be booked through travel agents.

of the historic district of Annapolis. There a total of 20 guest rooms (SB) and two suites to choose from. Parlors, dining, and meeting rooms are all lovingly furnished with beautiful antiques. $78-98.

Amanda's Bed and Breakfast #232

1428 Park Avenue, Baltimore, 21217
(410) 225-0001; (410) 383-1274

Across the street from the Naval Academy's Gate 3. Conveniently situated close to the docks, historic sites, shopping, and restaurants. Reservations only for the entire house on a two-night minimum. Four bedrooms. Three baths. Self-catered breakfast. $385.

Amanda's Bed and Breakfast #258

1428 Park Avenue, Baltimore, 21217
(410) 225-0001; (410) 383-1274

A luxury 55-foot yacht on a lovely creek has every amenity. Put worries to rest in the lounging area that adjoins the master stateroom. A spacious aft deck and fly bridge are also included for guests' enjoyment. Historic Annapolis city docks and restaurants are just minutes away with the help of a water taxi. Continental breakfast. Queen beds, $150. Twin beds, $125.

Amanda's Bed and Breakfast #259

1428 Park Avenue, Baltimore, 21217
(410) 225-0001; (410) 383-1274

This cozy cottage is just seven miles from Annapolis on two acres with a large garden, pool, and tennis courts surrounded by magnificent trees and a view towards the bay. A private deck faces the pool, and there are skylights and a loft upstairs. A boat is available for scenic tours. Private bath. Self-catered breakfast. $125.

Chez Amis Bed and Breakfast

85 East Street, 21401
(410) 263-6631

Renovated 70-year-old corner store offers three guest rooms combining yesteryear ambience with today's conveniences—central air conditioning, TVs, beverage centers. The 19th-century American antiques, original oak store counter, tin ceilings, and Georgia pine floors blend with European art and South American artifacts in a setting of West Coast pastels. Centrally situated in the historic district one block from city dock, state capital, and US Naval Academy. Enjoy romance and warm hospitality in America's sailing capital at "The Place of Friends."

Hosts: Tom and Valerie Smith
Rooms: 3 (PB) $75-90
Continental Breakfast
Credit Cards: None
Notes: 2, 5, 8, 14

Gibson's Lodgings

110 Prince George Street, 21401
(301) 268-5555

Historic 20-room inn with a new conference room for business and private gatherings. Situated half a block from the city dock.

Gibson's Lodgings

NOTES: Credit cards accepted: A Master Card; B Visa; C American Express; D Discover Card; E Diner's Club; F Other; 2 Personal Checks accepted; 3 Lunch available; 4 Dinner available; 5 Open all year;

Hosts: Jeanne Schrift
Rooms: 20 (7PB; 13SB) $68-120
Continental Breakfast
Credit Cards: A, B, C
Notes: 2, 5, 8, 9, 12

Shaw's Fancy Bed and Breakfast

161 Green Street, 21404
(301) 263-0320

Welcome to this 1902 Victorian Four-square in the heart of the historic district. Midweek, business, or romantic getaway packages are available. The hosts pamper guests with terry robes, special soaps, and gourmet chocolates. Enjoy the front porch swing or garden hot tub. Two-night minimum.

Hosts: Lilith Ren and Jack House
Rooms: 3 (2 PB; 1 SB) $75-105
Full Breakfast
Credit Cards: None
Notes: 2, 5, 9, 12, 14

The Traveller in Maryland TNN-MARYLAND

P. O. Box 2277, 21404-2277
(410) 269-6232; FAX (410) 263-4841

Part of the Bed and Breakfast National Network, The Traveller in Maryland offers bed and breakfast not only in Maryland, but also in many other cities and states across the country. The members of this network adhere strictly to the standards set by TNN, such as getting to know the guests personally, having an established cancellation and refund policy, and following a thorough inspection and approval process for all properties rented. This is because each member of the network is dedicated to ensuring comfort, pleasure, and personal needs while guests are staying at one of these "homes away from home."

The Traveller In Maryland # 105

P. O. Box 2277, 21404
(410) 269-6232

This ranch-style contemporary home is on a quiet residential street within walking distance of the Naval Academy football stadium and a hearty walk to the historic district and waterfront. The home was built by the owners and is comfortably furnished in contemporary pieces that give a real sense of home and relaxation. Guests are welcome to enjoy a livingroom and a den area with a TV, and an outdoor deck is a fine place to read a book or watch nature unfold. Two guest rooms are available. Continental breakfast. $50-55.

The Traveller In Maryland # 107

P. O. Box 2277, 21404
(410) 269-6232; FAX (410) 263-4841

This Victorian Italianate villa, circa 1864, is a charming piece of architecture situated in the middle of the historic district. A circular staircase greets guests in the entry hallway and flows up to the second floor guest room area. Furnished with period antiques and some reproductions, and numerous objects of art, this bed and breakfast has a livingroom with a baby grand piano and bay window with a nice view of the historic streets. The dining room overlooks the side gardens of the home. Three guest rooms are available. Full breakfast. $50-85.

The Traveller In Maryland # 109

P. O. Box 2277, 21404
(410) 269-6232; FAX (410) 263-4841

This turn-of-the-century home is on Spa Creek and is easy walking distance to the

6 Pets welcome; 8 Children welcome; 9 Social drinking allowed; 10 Tennis available; 11 Swimming available; 12 Golf available; 13 Skiing available; 14 May be booked through travel agents.

hospital. Convenient to all attractions in the historic district, this large and gracious home is filled with antiques and family heirlooms. A warm second floor glassed-in sun porch is great for relaxing with an interesting book or magazine. The rear yard has a terrace where guests can watch the sailboats quietly slip by on their way out to the bay. Two rooms available. Full breakfast. $60-70.

The Traveller In Maryland # 111
P. O. Box 2277, 21404
(410) 269-6232; FAX (410) 263-4841

This three-story home in the historic district adjacent to St. John's College and the US Naval Academy was built in 1880 and is a comforting example of southwestern culture. Hardwood floors coupled with many art objects and paintings, all personally created by the owner, offer a nice contrast to the traditional lifestyle found just outside. Guests are encouraged to enjoy a quiet moment beside the koi pond on the brick patio or relax by the crisp fire in the livingroom on colder months. Three sets of accommodations are available. Continental plus breakfast. $75-90.

The Traveller In Maryland # 115
P. O. Box 2277, 21404
(410) 269-6232; FAX (410) 263-4841

From subtle sunrises to fiery sunsets, the views from this waterfront contemporary are spectacular. This three-story home is nicely furnished with antiques and contemporary pieces that have been carefully selected during the owner's trips abroad. A comfortable livingroom with a fireplace offers open views of the South River, and a large wooden deck opens onto the river, where a large hot tub and large swimming pool are available for guests. Two rooms, both of which have private baths, are available. Continental breakfast. $65-75.

The Traveller In Maryland # 119
P. O. Box 2277, 21404
(410) 269-6232; FAX (410) 263-4841

This restored horse barn, circa 1860, is quietly nestled on a secluded cove off the Severn River. Just two miles from the historic district, this bed and breakfast invites guests to relax in the country surroundings of plank flooring and a stone fireplace. Added touches include handmade quilts, farm tools, and work pieces, and an outdoor deck is most inviting on a warm sunny day. Two bedrooms adjoin each other, and each room has a private half-bath. Full breakfast. $55-65.

The Traveller In Maryland # 121
P. O. Box 2277, 21404
(410) 269-6232; FAX (410) 263-4841

This unhosted three-story home is centrally situated in the historic district, three blocks from the city dock and two blocks from the US Naval Academy. The home was built in the early 1900s and has a comfortable lived-in feeling. A rear brick patio surrounded by a 10-foot high brick wall adds privacy. The first floor has a livingroom, dining room, and large rear kitchen; the second floor has two bedrooms, each with a double bed; and the third floor has a dormer room with a single bed, and window air conditioning. Three-night minimum. $275 per night.

The Traveller
In Maryland # 125
P. O. Box 2277, 21404
(410) 269-6232; (410) 263-4841

This lovely two-story home is furnished with antiques and beautiful accessories. A five-minute drive from the historic district, this home offers three guest rooms on the second floor, a large formal livingroom and family room, screen porch, and in-ground swimming pool. Carefully hidden in a residential neighborhood, this home provides a feeling of the past in present-day, contemporary surroundings. Three rooms are available for guests. Full breakfast is served. $50-80.

The Traveller
In Maryland # 127
P. O. Box 2277, 21404
(410) 269-6232; FAX (410) 263-4841

On a quaint street in downtown Annapolis, three blocks from the city dock, this bed and breakfast is within walking distance to fine restaurants and shopping. Historical sites and tours, and the Naval Adademy are nearby. This Victorian home has comfortable accommodations, shared and private baths, a nicely furnished livingroom, and a brick patio in the rear yard. One queen suite is available. Continental breakfast. $90.

The Traveller
In Maryland #129
P.O. Box 2277, 21404
(410) 269-6232; FAX (410) 263-4841

This three-story Georgian Revival-style brick home is just outside the main entrance of the United States Naval Academy. Three rooms are available; one can accommodate up to six people, one has a fireplace, and two overlook the private garden featuring a southern magnolia tree. A full breakfast is served on the patio. $70-85.

The Traveller
In Maryland # 131
P. O. Box 2277, 21404
(410) 269-6232; FAX (410) 263-4841

This unique grey and white eight-sided home sits on a two-acre wooded lot 100 feet above the South River. As the name Dogwood Hills implies, the woods are full of dogwood trees. The home is situated in a quiet neighborhood called Southaven, but it is minutes from a major shopping center, downtown Annapolis, B.W.I. airport, and a half hour from Washington, D.C. Two spacious, second-floor bedrooms are available. Full breakfast is served. $63-68.

The Traveller
In Maryland # 133
P. O. Box 2277, 21404
(410) 269-6232; FAX (410) 263-4841

This contemporary town house offers the pleasures of home away from home. Comfortable furnishings make this bed and breakfast home well-liked by travelers. Walking distance to several sailing schools and the historic district, or journey by water taxi to the city dock. Seafood restaurants and taverns are minutes away. Off-street parking is available and one upstairs guest room has twin beds and a private hall bath. Continental breakfast is served. $55-60.

The Traveller
In Maryland # 135
P. O. Box 2277, 21404
(410) 269-6232; (410) 263-4841

This rambling country-style home sits on three acres of land on the outskirts of Annapolis. Eclectic furnishings blend well with the seasoned traveler. The livingroom and den have a TV. Outdoor deck is available. Annapolis is eight miles away, and Washington, D.C. is just 16 miles away.

6 Pets welcome; 8 Children welcome; 9 Social drinking allowed; 10 Tennis available; 11 Swimming available; 12 Golf available; 13 Skiing available; 14 May be booked through travel agents.

This is a great area for sightseeing. The double bedroom or twin bedroom have one and a half baths and both rooms have a shared bath option. Full breakfast is served. $50-55.

The Traveller In Maryland # 139

P. O. Box 2277, 21404
(410) 269-6232; (410) 263-4841

A recently renovated 70-year-old corner store features three guest rooms that combine yesteryear ambience (original tin ceiling and oak counter) with contemporary conveniences (coffee makers, TVs). Accommodations are decorated in West Coast pastels, turn-of-the-century furnishings, and art accents from Europe and South America. This central location is just two minutes from the city dock and Naval Academy. First floor Traveler's Room has a king-size bedroom with sofa (suitable for third person) and private bath en suite. Turn-of-the-century style on the second floor has a queen-size bedroom and bath in suite. Stage Coach Room offers double bed and a private hall bath. Extended continental breakfast is served. $75-90.

The Traveller In Maryland # 141

P. O. Box 2277, 21404
(410) 269-6232; (410) 263-4841

Historic Annapolis is just five minutes from this waterfront contemporary home. Guests can enjoy covered waterview deck or may visit with boat owners at the small dock nearby in the spring, summer, or fall. The house is furnished with a comfortable country feel. Large shade trees in the yard offer peaceful setting. The Blue Room has a double bed and private hall bath. The Cabin is a ground floor with large open room offering a livingroom with working fireplace and microwave. A third person can stay in the cabin. Private bath, air conditioning and private entrance are available. Full breakfast is served. $65-90.

The Traveller In Maryland # 145

P. O. Box 2277, 21404
(410) 269-6232; FAX (410) 263-4841

This contemporary home is nestled on the banks of the Church Creek, next to the South River. Quietness and serenity abound here. The gardens are landscaped for seclusion. Two of the water-view bedrooms, making up one entire level of the home, have queen beds, and a private livingroom is available. Guests are also invited to use the patio, garden, and family room. The historic district is just 10 minutes away. Both rooms have a private or shared bath. Air conditioning and convenient parking are also available. Full breakfast is served. $75.

The Traveller In Maryland # 147

P. O. Box 2277, 21404
(410) 269-6232; FAX (410) 263-4841

Elegant multi-room suites are a part of this brick town home that is nestled between the US Naval Academy and St. John's College. The "Annapolitian" has a fireplace, Laura Ashley decor, and private entrance through the ivy-covered courtyard. The "Colonial" has superb Orientals, antiques, and views of the Academy. Many personal touches and amenities have been added. A "breakfast out" option is available. Two-night minimum. A continental breakfast is served. $120-140.

The Traveller In Maryland # 149

P. O. Box 2277, 21404
(410) 269-6232; FAX (410) 263-4841

This restored foursquare home, built in 1908, offers distinctly appointed rooms with a mix of antiques. The third-floor suite has dormer ceilings, large sitting area, and whirlpool. The entry foyer with open stairway is flanked by crystal chandeliers and art work. The elegant common room has a working fireplace. Small groups are welcome. Amenities include queen-size beds, shared or private baths, fold-out sofa bed, off-street parking, air conditioning, wet bar setup in the common room, and full breakfast. $75-120.

The Traveller In Maryland # 151

P. O. Box 2277, 21404
(410) 269-6232; FAX (410) 263-4841

This restored pre-Revolutionary Georgian Colonial, built in 1747, has three beautifully decorated bedrooms furnished with period reproductions. Sip coffee in one of the parlors or have breakfast on the brick patio surrounded by seasonal flowers. Walk out the back door to the harbor, US Naval Academy, Main Street shopping and restaurants. Private bath, air conditioning, and resident cat, Muffin, are also included. Continental breakfast is served. $100.

BALTIMORE

Amanda's Bed and Breakfast #102

1428 Park Avenue, 21217
(410) 225-0001; (410) 383-1274

This beautifully restored four-story row house is decorated with antiques. Only minutes away from the inner harbor, shopping, restaurants, and bars. Choose from four lovely guest rooms (2 double, 1 twin, 1 king). Convenient to public transportation. Owners operate a card and gift shop on first floor. Continental breakfast. $65.

Amanda's Bed and Breakfast #104

1428 Park Avenue, 21217
(410) 225-0001; (410) 383-1274

This restored 1830 Federal town house is downtown in the historic Mt. Vernon district. It has a delightful courtyard and spacious guest rooms that are decorated with antiques and have different themes. Convenient parking. Four rooms (SB). Full breakfast. $75.

Amanda's Bed and Breakfast #108

1428 Park Avenue, 21217
(410) 225-0001; (410) 383-1274

In the suburbs just five minutes from the Baltimore Beltway and 20 minutes from the inner harbor, this quiet getaway is decorated with antiques, handmade furniture, and a garden. Owners are native Baltimoreans who love guests, cooking, and vegetable gardening. Full breakfast. One double. One twin. Swimming pool. $65.

Amanda's Bed and Breakfast #109

1428 Park Avenue, 21217
(410) 225-0001; (410) 383-1274

A colorful 18th-century community, Fells Point is the location for this wonderfully renovated urban inn at the water's edge. All 38 rooms (PB) are individually designed and decorated with antiques and period reproductions. Other attractions include an English pub and elegant dining room. $85 and up.

6 Pets welcome; 8 Children welcome; 9 Social drinking allowed; 10 Tennis available; 11 Swimming available; 12 Golf available; 13 Skiing available; 14 May be booked through travel agents.

Amanda's Bed and Breakfast #110

1428 Park Avenue, 21217
(410) 225-0001; (410) 383-1274

Tudor-style guest house, near Johns Hopkins University Homewood campus, is just minutes from the inner harbor, convention center, and stadium. Our residential neighborhood is bordered by two parks and a lake. Biking, fitness track, and public golf course are all within walking distance. Full breakfast. One queen. One twin (SB). $60-75.

Amanda's Bed and Breakfast #111

1428 Park Avenue 21217
(410) 225-0001; (410) 383-1274

Federal-style town house offers two delightful guest rooms and is within walking distance of inner harbor. Convention center, other hotels, financial district, sports arena, Harbor Place, galleries, museums, theaters, and restaurants are all nearby. One double (SB). One twin (SB). $60.

Amanda's Bed and Breakfast #113

1428 Park Avenue, 21217
(410) 225-0001; (410) 383-1274

Federal Hill town home, just a short distance from the inner harbor and convention center, has a third-floor suite. Host will accommodate long-term at reasonable rates. Double (PB). $60.

Amanda's Bed and Breakfast #117

1428 Park Avenue, 21217
(410) 225-0001; (410) 383-1274

Restored 18th-century town house in historic Fells Point, a waterfront community that is full of unique shops and restaurants. Inner harbor is just one mile away either by walking, water taxi, or trolley. Full breakfast. Three double (PB). One twin (PB). $75-85.

Amanda's Bed and Breakfast #119

1428 Park Avenue, 21217
(410) 225-0001; (410) 383-1274

Elegant Victorian mansion is decorated with imported antiques and is in historic Mt. Vernon near antique row. All 15 rooms/suites offer private baths, kitchenettes, and meeting facilities. The inner harbor is just 10 blocks away and fine dining is nearby. Continental breakfast. $95-105.

Amanda's Bed and Breakfast #131

1428 Park Avenue, 21217
(410) 225-0001; (410) 383-1274

Downtown historic neighborhood town house is furnished with antiques and is on a quiet street facing a park. Public transportation, cultural center, and churches are all nearby. The guest room is a large suite with all the amenities. King with private kitchenette. Swimming pool/club privileges. $85.

Amanda's Bed and Breakfast #132

1428 Park Avenue, 21217
(410) 225-0001; (410) 383-1274

A romantic retreat in Baltimore's historic neighborhood of Fells Point, the oldest maritime area of the city. Just one mile from the inner harbor with water taxi ser-

NOTES: Credit cards accepted: A Master Card; B Visa; C American Express; D Discover Card; E Diner's Club; F Other; 2 Personal Checks accepted; 3 Lunch available; 4 Dinner available; 5 Open all year;

vice in the summer or other transportation options all year. The roof deck overlooks the harbor. Full breakfast. $110-150.

Amanda's Bed and Breakfast #147

1428 Park Avenue, 21217
(410) 225-0001; (410) 383-1274

Californian charm and comfort offered at this historic bed and breakfast with romantic, airy, Roland Park Victorian-style. Tastefully decorated with deck, three wood-burning fireplaces, Jacuzzi, and skylights. Continental breakfast in gourmet kitchen overlooking woods. Nicely landscaped, rejuvenating setting. Two-night minimum. Double (PB)-$75. Master suite-$120.

Amanda's Bed and Breakfast #166

1428 Park Avenue, 21217
(410) 225-0001; (410) 383-1274

Urban inn and restaurant has European charm and warm hospitality. Each room has been tastefully appointed with rich Baltimorean artwork, antique furniture, and brass beds. The inn has a full restaurant and piano bar, lots of parking in lot next door, and free van service to inner harbor. Continental breakfast. $85 up.

Amanda's Bed and Breakfast #186

1428 Park Avenue, 21217
(410) 225-0001; (410) 383-1274

Restored Victorian town house nestled in the Union Square historic district and just minutes away from the inner harbor, convention center, and the new sports complex in Camden Station. The rooms (double,

PB) are decorated with period furnishings. Full breakfast. $90.

Amanda's Bed and Breakfast #190

1428 Park Avenue, 21217
(410) 225-0001; (410) 383-1274

Charmingly historic, intimate waterfront retreat is situated in Fells Point. This bed and breakfast is listed in the National Register of Historic Places. Includes English garden, marina, and period furnishings. Restaurants and shops are within walking distance and a water taxi is available from May to October. Continental breakfast. All rooms have PB, some with water view. $150.

Amanda's Bed and Breakfast #195

1428 Park Avenue, 21217
(410) 225-0001; (410) 383-1274

An attractive Federal Hill row house, just a block and a half from the science center and inner harbor, within walking distance to sites, attractions, restaurants, and shopping. Water taxi is available for rides around harbor. The guest room has a queen-size bed (PB) and is bright and airy. Great breakfast. $75.

Amanda's Bed and Breakfast #197

1428 Park Avenue, 21217
(410) 225-0001; (410) 383-1274

The hostess speaks French, Italian, and Arabic at this Charles Village row house near Johns Hopkins University and the Baltimore Art Museum. The house is a showcase of modern Egyptian art. Great full breakfasts. Double (PB). $60.

6 Pets welcome; 8 Children welcome; 9 Social drinking allowed; 10 Tennis available; 11 Swimming available; 12 Golf available; 13 Skiing available; 14 May be booked through travel agents.

Amanda's Bed and Breakfast #216

1428 Park Avenue, 21217
(410) 225-0001; (410) 383-1274

Beautiful restored town home in historic Federal Hill is furnished in antiques and Oriental rugs and is just six blocks from the inner harbor. Historic sites, shopping, restaurants, and public transportation are all close. Continental breakfast. Double (PB) and suite. $100.

Amanda's Bed and Breakfast #225

1428 Park Avenue, 21217
(410) 225-0001; (410) 383-1274

In Charles Village near Johns Hopkins University. The decor spans a century of-styles from the Victorian to the contemporary. All rooms have brass fixtures, English soaps, amenities, hair dryers, alarm clocks, air conditioning, and color TVs. Continental breakfast served to room. Double (PB). $69-129.

Amanda's Bed and Breakfast #226

1428 Park Avenue, 21217
(410) 225-0001; (410) 383-1274

Built in 1897, the official guest house of the city of Baltimore is comprised of three town houses in historic Mt. Vernon. Guests are treated to personalized service, private baths, ornate and unusual decor. Great location with guest parking. Continental breakfast. $100-125.

Amanda's Bed and Breakfast #265

1428 Park Avenue, 21217
(410) 225-0001; (410) 383-1274

This federal-style town house was built in 1982. Features include three stories, patio, garden in back, fireplace in den and living-room. A springer spaniel, Rocky, loves people. Continental breakfast is served in the dining room. $65-75.

Betsy's Bed and Breakfast

1428 Park Avenue, 21217-4230
(410) 383-1277

This four-story "petite" estate in downtown Bolton Hill is on a tree-lined street with white marble steps and brass rails. This spacious home features a hallway laid in alternating strips of oak and walnut, ceiling medallions, six marble mantles, and a center staircase that rises to meet a skylight. The expansive walls are hung with handsome brass rubbings and family heirloom quilts. Guests may relax in a hot tub shaded by a large pin oak tree.

Host: Betsy Grater
Rooms: 3 (PB) $75
Full Breakfast
Credit Cards: A, B, C, D
Notes: 2, 5, 8, 9, 11, 14

Celie's Waterfront Bed and Breakfast

Historic Fell's Point, 1714 Thames Street, 21231
(410) 522-2323

Situated on Baltimore harbor. Ideal for business or pleasure. Seven air-conditioned guest rooms, one wheelchair accessible, with access to a private garden and harbor view roof deck. Some with whirlpools, fireplaces, private balconies, and harbor views, in a relaxed atmosphere. Private telephones, televisions, marina, and conference space available. Minutes to Harbor Place, central business district, and Orioles Stadium by water taxi.

Host: Celie Ives
Rooms: 7 (PB) $90-140
Continental Breakfast
Credit Cards: A, B, C, D
Notes: 2, 5, 8 (over 10), 9, 14

NOTES: Credit cards accepted: A Master Card; B Visa; C American Express; D Discover Card; E Diner's Club; F Other; 2 Personal Checks accepted; 3 Lunch available; 4 Dinner available; 5 Open all year;

Celie's Waterfront

Mr. Mole Bed and Breakfast

1601 Bolton Street, 21217
(410) 728-1179

In the city on historic Bolton Hill amid quiet, tree-lined streets. An 1870s row house with 14-foot ceilings, marble fireplaces, and many antiques. Concert grand piano in music room. Suites, some with two bedrooms and sitting room. Attached garage parking, with automatic door openers included. Walk to symphony, opera, Antique Row, and Metro. Close to Johns Hopkins University, University of Baltimore, University of Maryland Medical School, and the inner harbor, but without congestion. Handicap accessible.

Hosts: Collin Clarke and Paul Bragaw
Rooms: 5 (PB) $85-125
Continental Breakfast
Credit Cards: A, B, C
Notes: 2, 5, 9, 14

The Traveller In Maryland # 157

P. O. Box 2277, 21404
(410) 269-6232; FAX (410) 263-4841

Experience the charm and character of this 200-year-old town home situated one-half block from the waterfront of historic Fell's Point. Recently restored, and great care was taken to preserve much of the original woodwork and fireplace mantels. Truly a grand example of a bygone era. The waterfront, several restaurants and pubs are all within walking distance. Trolley is available for a trip downtown. Amenities include four guest rooms, two livingrooms, and a private patio terrace. A continental breakfast is served. $75-85.

The Traveller In Maryland # 159

P. O. Box 2277, 21404
(410) 269-6232; FAX (410) 263-4841

Originally an 1830 Federal town house, this home later took on an Italiate appearance with the addition of cornice work to the exterior. The complete restoration

Mr. Mole

6 Pets welcome; 8 Children welcome; 9 Social drinking allowed; 10 Tennis available; 11 Swimming available; 12 Golf available; 13 Skiing available; 14 May be booked through travel agents.

exemplifies leaded glass transoms and entrance fan windows. A modern bathroom and two beautiful bedrooms were created on each of the second and third floors. A delightful courtyard was created by the construction of a wall at the rear of the building. Amenities include sitting room with grand piano, fireplace, and banquet table with two chairs (1790) where a sumptuous full breakfast is served. $75.

The Traveller In Maryland # 163

P. O. Box 2277, 21404
(410) 269-6232; FAX (410) 263-4841

Situated in historic Bolton Hill, this grand 1870s house provides gracious accommodations for discriminating persons visiting Baltimore. The neighborhood is quiet, has tree-lined streets and warm, spacious, brick row houses. The home is decorated in a comfortable English-style with many 18th- and 19th-century antiques. On the first floor, the livingroom, breakfast room, and music room with 14-foot ceilings, bay windows, and marble fireplaces reflect the ambience of past times. A nine-foot concert grand piano is available for guests in the music room. Amenities include private baths, individual room decorations, air conditioning, phones, and on-site garage. A Dutch Continental breakfast is served. $75-115.

The Traveller In Maryland # 165

P. O. Box 2277, 21404
(410) 269-6232; FAX (410) 263-4841

This majestic estate is quietly nestled on 45 acres of wooded land, offering the elegant lifestyle of the early 1900s. Guests will enjoy fireplaces, suites, Jacuzzis in bedrooms, gourmet breakfast, expansive porches, pool, tennis court, woodland trails

and stream, and flower and herb gardens. Abundant history is associated with the house through its builder Alexander J. Cassatt, owner of the Pennsylvania Railroad and brother of Mary Cassatt, the American impressionist. Later it was owned by the Brewster family, descendants of Benjamin Franklin and important in government. In the 1950s it became the Koinonia Foundation, a predecessor of the Peace Corps. Amenities include double or king-size beds, private baths, some suites with separate livingroom and porches, family room, and library. $90-115.

The Traveller In Maryland # 168

P. O. Box 2277, 21404
(410) 269-6232; FAX (410) 263-4841

Situated on a large working farm in the serene Piedmont countryside of Maryland, this Georgian-style country house has a Victorian addition and a hide-away guest house. The property is part of a 3,000-acre tract of land called Runnymeade Enlarged, patented prior to the American Revolution by Dr. Upton Scott. Enjoy the livingroom setting with a large fireplace, dining room, and wraparound porch with rocking chairs overlooking Bear Branch. Each room, with air conditioning, has a pleasant view of lawns, pastures, creeks, or woods. One suite has a private screened porch. One hundred yards across the wide and shaded lawn lies the guest house with two large bedrooms, a livingroom, and a kitchenette. The guest house, with air conditioning, affords a comfortable and very private getaway. Full breakfast is served. $55-100.

The Traveller In Maryland #169

P. O. Box 2277, Annapolis, 21404
(410) 269-6232; FAX (410) 263-4841

NOTES: Credit cards accepted: A Master Card; B Visa; C American Express; D Discover Card; E Diner's Club; F Other; 2 Personal Checks accepted; 3 Lunch available; 4 Dinner available; 5 Open all year;

This small Victorian inn was built in 1827 in Baltimore's earliest fashionable residential area, the Mt. Vernon district. Each of the guest rooms are individually decorated, styled with antiques throughout the house that have been lovingly hand-picked. The Victorian era wallpaper patterns and borders were custom designed for the guest rooms so that no two are alike. Rich Baltimore artworks grace the walls and even small details like porcelain doorknobs are much in evidence. Guest rooms are spacious; and fabrics, rich woods, brass accents and bouquets of flowers and plants all lend to a feeling of graciousness. Amenities include accessibility for handicapped, off-street parking, TV, and phones. Continental breakfast is served. $80-140.

The Traveller In Maryland # 170

P. O. Box 2277, Annapolis, 21404
(410) 269-6232; FAX (410) 263-4841

This is a stately Federal period stone farmhouse situated on two acres with a pond near the historic mill town, Ellicott City. Continuing with the tradition of a lighted candle in each window, indicating the availability of rooms. The candles remain lighted as a nostalgic reminder of the inn's past. Off the center hall the parlor invites guests to read and relax. In the winter months a fire in the fireplaces encourages guests to linger over a game of chess or checkers. Amenities include double and queen-size beds, parlor, and dining room. Continental breakfast is served.

Twin Gates Bed and Breakfast Inn

308 Morris Avenue, Historic Lutherville, 21093
(410) 252-3131; (800) 635-0370

Experience serene elegance in this Victorian mansion near the National Aquarium in Baltimore, Harbor Place, and Maryland hunt country. Friendly hosts, wine and cheese, and gourmet breakfast.

Hosts: Gwen and Bob Vaughan
Rooms: 7 (5 PB; 2 SB) $95-125
Full Breakfast
Minimum stay weekends and holidays: 2 nights
Credit Cards: A, B, C
Notes: 2, 5, 9, 10, 12, 14

BERLIN

Merry Sherwood Plantation

8909 Worchester Highway, 21811
(410) 641-2112

Merry Sherwood Plantation, circa 1859, was listed on the National Register of Historic Places in 1991. A wonderful blend of Greek Revival, Classic Italianate, and Gothic architecture, this elegant 27 room mansion has Victorian-style, nine fireplaces, private baths, ballroom, 19 acres of 19th-century landscaping, and authentic period antiques. Convenient to Ocean City and many historic and resort attractions.

Hosts: Kirk and Ginny Burbage
Rooms: 8 (6 PB; 2 SB)
Full Breakfast
Credit Cards: A, B
Notes: 2, 5, 9, 10, 11, 12, 13, 14

Merry Sherwood Plantation

The Traveller In Maryland # 171

P. O. Box 2277, Annapolis, 21404
(410) 269-6232; FAX (410) 263-4841

6 Pets welcome; 8 Children welcome; 9 Social drinking allowed; 10 Tennis available; 11 Swimming available; 12 Golf available; 13 Skiing available; 14 May be booked through travel agents.

Built in 1895, this restored Victorian is situated in the heart of Berlin's historic district. Antique shops and museums are within easy walking distance. Ocean City and Assateague National Seashore are just eight miles away. A four-star restaurant and piano lounge are on-site. $60-108.

BETTERTON

Lantern Inn

115 Ericson Avenue, 21610
(410) 348-5809

A restored 1904 inn in a quiet town on Maryland's Eastern Shore. One and one-half blocks to a nice sand beach on Chesapeake Bay. Near historic Chestertown, hiking trails, three wildlife refuges. Miles of excellent hiking roads. Antiquing and good seafood restaurants abound.

Hosts: Ken and Ann Washburn
Rooms: 7 (2 PB; 5 SB) $65-80
Continental Breakfast
Credit Cards: A, B, D
Notes: 2, 5, 9, 10, 11, 14

BURTONSVILLE

The Traveller In Maryland # 204

P. O. Box 2277, Annapolis, 21404
(410) 269-6232; FAX (410) 263-4841

Lantern Inn

The contemporary charm of the guest house features an airy living/dining area highlighted by a yellow pine interior, cathedral ceilings, and an expansive picture window offering an uninterrupted view of the natural surroundings. Guests can enjoy sunny mornings on the outdoor deck, afternoon tea in the greenhouse, or cool nights by the fireplace. Each of its two guest rooms has access to a private bath and is furnished with a unique sleep system that allows guests to achieve their own comfort level. Come enjoy life on a working horse farm and equestrian center, tour the 18th-century log cabin with herb and flower gardens—a local historic landmark. Stroll along the miles of wooded trails bordering the Rocky Gorge reservoir, and get a glimpse of the deer, waterfowl and other natural wildlife occupying more than 1,000 acres of adjacent wooded watershed. Full breakfast is served. $75-105.

CAMBRIDGE

Amanda's Bed and Breakfast #192

1428 Park Avenue, Baltimore, 21217
(410) 225-0001; (410) 383-1274

Three-story brick-and-clapboard with high ceilings, six fireplaces, mahogany stair rails, and deep, old-fashioned window seats are but a few of the features of this historic inn that faces the water. Other attractions include Palladian windows, Oriental rugs, and 18th-century reproductions. Fine seafood restaurants are nearby. Continental breakfast. Eight rooms (PB and SB). $90 and up.

The Glasgow Inn Bed and Breakfast

1500 Hambrooks Boulevard, 21613
(410) 228-0575

NOTES: Credit cards accepted: A Master Card; B Visa; C American Express; D Discover Card; E Diner's Club; F Other; 2 Personal Checks accepted; 3 Lunch available; 4 Dinner available; 5 Open all year;

Experience life in a classic Colonial riverside plantation (circa 1760) and seven-acre park. Listed on the National Register of Historic Places, it is ideal for hiking, birding, sailing and hunting. Near Blackwater Wildlife Refuge. Excellent for corporate retreats, reunions, weddings, receptions, writer's retreats and private parties. Air conditioning, fireplaces.

Hosts: Louise Lee Roche and Martha Ann Rayne
Rooms: 7 (1 PB; 6 SB) $90-100 plus tax
Full Breakfast
Credit Cards: A, B
Notes: 2, 5, 9, 10

CASCADE

Amanda's Bed and Breakfast #261

1428 Park Avenue, Baltimore, 21217
(410) 225-0001; (410) 383-1274

Visit the Blue Ridge Summit and Cascade, the undiscovered summer hideaway. Explore Gettysburg or Frederick, ski, or hike. This elegant 1900 manor house on the Mason Dixon line offers gracious old-fashioned porches, luxury, and beauty. Four rooms available. Fireplace. Jacuzzi. $95-115.

CENTREVILLE

Amanda's Bed and Breakfast #280

1428 Park Avenue, Baltimore, 21217
(410) 225-0001; (410) 383-1274

The Centerville Male Academy, built in 1804, is one of the oldest schoolhouses in the state of Maryland. It has been transformed into a charming bed and breakfast with 17th- and 18th-century antiques and paintings throughout. Two rooms available. Private baths. Continental breakfast.

CHESAPEAKE CITY

Amanda's Bed and Breakfast #269

1428 Park Avenue, Baltimore, 21217
(410) 225-0001; (410) 383-1274

This large Victorian, built in 1868, is in the historic district and offers views of the canal from inside and outside the house. Architectural details are original, and the house is furnished with antiques. Shops and restaurants are within walking distance. Six rooms, all with private baths, are available. Continental breakfast. $85.

Inn At the Canal

Inn at the Canal

104 Bohemia Avenue, P. O. Box 187, 21915
(410) 885-5995

This elegant 1870 Victorian inn sits in the midst of the quaint historical district on the banks of the busy Chesapeake and Delaware Canal. Private baths, six antique-filled rooms, a full breakfast, and some of the best ocean-going and pleasure boat watching are all to be found at the inn.

Hosts: Mary and Al Ioppolo
Rooms: 6 (PB) $70-105
Full Breakfast
Credit Cards: A, B, C, D
Notes: 2, 5, 9, 14

6 Pets welcome; 8 Children welcome; 9 Social drinking allowed; 10 Tennis available; 11 Swimming available; 12 Golf available; 13 Skiing available; 14 May be booked through travel agents.

CHESTERTOWN

Amanda's
Bed and Breakfast #152

1428 Park Avenue, Baltimore, 21217
(410) 225-0001; (410) 383-1274

This large 1725 brick house is one-half
mile from colonial Chestertown on a small
estate that has some interesting plantings,
among them a century-old boxwood. The
1725 brick house features a unique spiral
staircase rising from a large center hallway
to the third floor. Two rooms with double
beds and private baths are available. Full
breakfast. $70.

Amanda's
Bed and Breakfast #205

1428 Park Avenue, Baltimore, 21217
(410) 225-0001; (410) 383-1274

This waterfront Georgian manor is situated
at the mouth of the Fairlee Creek on chesapeake Bay. Stroll through twelve acres of
landscaped grounds, or enjoy a private
sandy beach for swimming and rafting.
Tennis courts, golf available, dinner available. 25 rooms. Private bath. $125.

CHEVY CHASE

Chevy Chase
Bed and Breakfast

6815 Connecticut Avenue, 20815
(301) 656-5867

Enjoy gracious hospitality and the convenience of being close to the sights of
Washington, D.C. in a charming beamed-
ceiling, turn-of-the-century house and garden in historic Chevy Chase. Furnished
with rare tapestries, Oriental rugs, and
native crafts from around the world.
Special breakfasts of homemade breads,
jams, and coffee.

Host: S. C. Gotbaum
Rooms: Single (PB) $50-55; Double (PB) $60-65
Continental Breakfast
Credit Cards: None
Notes: 2, 5, 8, 10, 11, 12

CRISFIELD

Amanda's
Bed and Breakfast #256

1428 Park Avenue, Baltimore, 21217
(410) 225-0001; (410) 383-1274

The Southeastern Shore is low, flat, and
sandy, covered with evergreens and fertile
farmland. A region of the tidal creeks, vast
wetlands, and wildlife refuges offers picturesque views along the chesapeake. Two
rooms share a bath, and continental breakfast is served. $50.

EASTON

Ashby 1663

27448 Ashby Drive, 21601
(410) 822-4235

This magnificent colonial mansion is on the
Miles River of Maryland's Eastern Shore.
The estate features a heated swimming pool
with a spa, lighted tennis court, exercise
room with a tanning bed, canoe, jogging
and bicycling path, volleyball, croquet, and

Ashby 1663

NOTES: Credit cards accepted: A Master Card; B Visa; C American Express; D Discover Card; E Diner's
Club; F Other; 2 Personal Checks accepted; 3 Lunch available; 4 Dinner available; 5 Open all year;

badminton. The waterfront towns of Oxford and St. Michael's are within a few minutes' drive. guests may secure their craft at the dock, which provides a six-foot MLW depth. Easton airport is a five-minute drive for visitors arriving by air.

Hosts: Cliff Meredith and Jeanie Wagner
Rooms: 4 (PB) $250-575
Full Breakfast
Credit Cards: A, B
Notes: 2, 5, 9, 10, 12

The Traveller In Maryland # 179

P. O. Box 2277, Annapolis, 21404
(410) 269-6232

This charming Victorian home, circa 1890, is in the center of the historic district of Easton. Easton is renowned as the Colonial capital of Maryland's Eastern Shore. The inn has a high octagonal tower, a hipped roof with dormers, both of which add some very interesting findings on the inside, and a southern wraparound porch for a relaxing afternoon or evening rest. Historic points and restaurants are within easy walking distance. Available for small meetings and seminars. Continental breakfast is served. $60-70.

EDGEWATER

Amanda's Bed and Breakfast #187

1428 Park Avenue, Baltimore, 21217
(410) 225-0001; (410) 383-1274

This contemporary waterfront home is ten minutes from Annapolis and can accommodate a group of four or six. Oriental and European antiques furnish this home, and guests have use of a private sitting room and terrace. Rowboat available for guests to use. Two rooms with private baths. Continental breakfast. $75.

Amanda's Bed and Breakfast #194

1428 Park Avenue, Baltimore, 21217
(410) 225-0001; (410) 383-1274

From subtle sunrises to fiery sunsets, the view from this riverfront, two-story house is spectacular. Furnished in contemporary and Oriental themes. Guests are welcome to use the pool, hot tub, boat dock, and waterfront balcony. This bed and breakfast is a luxurious and serene retreat for visitors from Annapolis. Two rooms, both with private baths and one with a waterfront view, are available. Continental breakfast.

ELLICOTT CITY

The Wayside Inn

4344 Columbia Road, 21042
(410) 461-4636

The Wayside Inn is a stately Federal-period stone farmhouse situated on two acres with a pond, near the historic mill town of Ellicott City. The inn, built between 1800 and 1850, continues the tradition of a lighted candle in each window indicating availability of rooms. It has two suites with private baths; two rooms with working fire-

The Wayside Inn

6 Pets welcome; 8 Children welcome; 9 Social drinking allowed; 10 Tennis available; 11 Swimming available; 12 Golf available; 13 Skiing available; 14 May be booked through travel agents.

places, shared baths. Air conditioning, antiques, and reproduction pieces. Convenient to historic Ellicott City, Columbia, Baltimore. Short commute to Annapolis and Washington, D.C.

Hosts: Margo and John Osantowski
Rooms: 4 (2 PB; 2 SB) $70-90
Continental Breakfast
Credit Cards: A, B, C
Notes: 2, 5, 12, 14

FALLSTON

Amanda's Bed and Breakfast #174

1428 Park Avenue, Baltimore 21217
(410) 225-0001; (410) 383-1274

In the heart of Maryland's "hunt" country on forty acres, this new Georgian-style house offers a pool and beautiful gardens for guests to enjoy. Wind down from a busy day by relaxing on our shady trellised patio overlooking the pond. Nice location for weddings. Five rooms available. Private and shared baths. Continental breakfast. $70-85.

FREDERICK

Middle Plantation Inn

9549 Liberty Road, 21701
(301) 898-7128

A rustic bed and breakfast built of stone and log. Drive through horse country to the village of Mount Pleasant. Several miles east of Frederick, on 26 acres. Each room has furnishings of antiques, with private bath, air conditioning, and TV. Nearby are antique shops, museums, and many historic attractions.

Hosts: Shirley and Dwight Mullican
Rooms: 4 (PB) $85-95
Continental Breakfast (15 % discount without breakfast
Credit Cards: A, B
Notes: 2, 5, 9, 10, 11, 12, 14

Spring Bank, A Bed and Breakfast Inn

7945 Worman's Mill Road, 21701
(301) 694-0440

Built in 1880 and listed on the National Register of Historic Places, this 16-room country house is filled with antiques. Five spacious guest rooms, parlor with fireplace, and library of early books on Maryland history. Situated on ten acres of lawn, walking paths, and crop land. Frederick's charming historic district, with its excellent restaurants, is within a 10-minute drive. Whitetail and Ski Liberty are within a 40 minutes drive.

Hosts: Beverly and Ray Compton
Rooms: 5 (1 PB; 4 SB) $70-85
Continental Breakfast
Credit Cards: A, B, C, D
Notes: 2, 5, 9, 10, 11, 12, 13 (within 40 minutes), 14

GAITHERSBURG

Gaithersburg Hospitality Bed and Breakfast

18908 Chimney Place, 20879
(301) 977-7377

In Montgomery Village near restaurants, shopping, and recreation, this luxury home is ideally situated in a residential neighborhood, offers all amenities, and is a thirty-minute ride to Washington, D.C. via the car or Metro. It is conveniently near I-270 for a

Middle Plantation Inn

Lewrene Farm

drive north to Harper's Ferry, Gettysburg, and Antietam. Hosts delight in catering to travel needs with home cooking and spacious cozy comfort.

Hosts: Joe and Suzanne Danilowicz
Doubles: (PB) $52
Singles: (PB) $42
Full Breakfast
Credit Cards: None
Notes: 2, 8, 10, 11, 12, 14

The Traveller In Maryland # 198

P. O. Box 2277, Annapolis, 21404
(410) 269-6232

Two-story brick contemporary home near community lake. Residential streets provide quiet walks. Ten minutes to Metro stop. Restaurants nearby. Beautifully furnished, this bed and breakfast has two rooms with double beds and private baths. Full breakfast served. Screened porch overlooks nicely landscaped yards; TV, laundry facilities. Also, a large, sunny third room with twin beds. $55.

HAGERSTOWN

Lewrene Farm Bed and Breakfast

9738 Downsfield Pike, 21740
(301) 582-1735

Spacious colonial country farm home near I-70 and I-81. Large livingroom, fireplace, piano, antique family heirlooms. Deluxe bedrooms with canopy poster beds and other antique beds. Bedside snacks, shared and private baths, one of which has a whirlpool. Full breakfast. Home away from home for tourists, business people, families. Children welcome. Peacocks, old-fashioned swing, gazebo. Quilts for sale. Antietam battlefield, Harper's Ferry, C&O Canal, and antique malls nearby. Washington and Baltimore, 70 miles away.

Hosts: Lewis and Irene Lehman
Rooms: 6 (3 PB; 3 SB) $50-80
Full Breakfast
Credit Cards: None
Notes: 2, 5, 8, 10, 11, 12, 13

HANOVER

Amanda's Bed and Breakfast #154

1428 Park Avenue, Baltimore, 21217
(410) 225-0001; (410) 383-1274

The "Woods of Love" is a large new house situated in the woods. The front faces south and is a passive solar. The house has a sunken great room, huge kitchen, game room, greenhouse, a racquet ball court, and fruit trees. A one-room suite with a pair of twin beds and private bath is available. Full breakfast. $75.

HARWOOD

Amanda's Bed and Breakfast #151

1428 Park Avenue, Baltimore, 21217
(410) 225-0001; (410) 383-1274

An elegant early-19th-century manor house, circa 1840, is surrounded by lawns, terraced gardens, and shaded by towering poplar, hickory, and maple trees on seven acres. Furnished with antiques and a blaze

6 Pets welcome; 8 Children welcome; 9 Social drinking allowed; 10 Tennis available; 11 Swimming available; 12 Golf available; 13 Skiing available; 14 May be booked through travel agents.

Spencer Silver Mansion

of color in the spring, with daffodils, irises, and forsythia, this bed and breakfast offers two rooms that share a bath. Continental breakfast. $60-65.

Hosts: Carol and Jim Nemeth
Rooms: 4 (2 PB; 2 SB) $60-85
Full Breakfast
Credit Cards: None
Notes: 2, 5, 8, 9, 10, 11, 12

Amanda's Bed and Breakfast #158
1428 Park Avenue, Baltimore, 21217
(410) 225-0001; (410) 383-1274

This guest room has a balcony that overlooks a working farm. Ample parking area for a boat trailer or camper. Two rooms share a bath. Continental breakfast. $60.

HAVRE DE GRACE

Spencer Silver Mansion
200 South Union Avenue, 21078
(410) 939-1097

Built in 1896, this grand Victorian mansion has been restored to its splendor. The spacious bedrooms are romantically decorated with period antiques. The inn is situated just two blocks from the water in the historic district of Havre de Grace. Excellent restaurants are a short walk away, as are many antique, decoy and other specialty shops. A delicious full breakfast is served at the inn, situated just two miles from I-95.

LUTHERVILLE

Amanda's Bed and Breakfast #128
1428 Park Avenue, Annapolis, 21217
(410) 225-0001; (410) 383-1274

Serene elegance surrounds this romantic Victorian mansion. Each room is decorated in a different theme from the owner's favorite places. Charming and spacious with a lavish breakfast. Seven rooms, five with private baths; two share a bath. Full breakfast. $95-125.

MIDDLEBURG

Bowling Brook Country Inn
6000 Middleburg Road, 21757
(404) 848-0353

Steeped in the rich tradition of horse racing, Bowling Brook Country Inn represents a mansion built in 1837. Appreciate the Georgian architecture, while relaxing in the quiet surroundings of country elegance. All bedrooms feature a private bath and

NOTES: Credit cards accepted: A Master Card; B Visa; C American Express; D Discover Card; E Diner's Club; F Other; 2 Personal Checks accepted; 3 Lunch available; 4 Dinner available; 5 Open all year;

Bowling Brook

color television, while two rooms include a large Jacuzzi and king-size canopy bed. Enjoy afternoon tea, evening wine and cheese and a full country breakfast.

Hosts: Dave and Gina Welsh
Rooms: 4 (4 PB) $85-140
Full Breakfast
Credit Cards: A, B, C
Notes: 2, 5, 8, 9, 11, 12, 13

MONKTON

Amanda's Bed and Breakfast #209

1428 Park Avenue, Baltimore, 21217
(410) 225-0001; (410) 383-1274

Warm hospitality and exceptional accommodations are offered on this working farm. Pond with fishing privileges (catch and throw back), bike and hike trails, and tubing on Gunpowder River. Near North Central Railroad, Ladew Gardens, and Amish Country. One room is offered to guests and it features a private bath. Continental breakfast. $85.

NEW MARKET

National Pike Inn

9 West Main Street, P.O. Box 299, 21774
(301) 865-5055

The National Pike Inn offers five air conditioned guest rooms, each decorated in a different theme. Private baths are available, and our large Federal sitting room is available for guests to use. Our private enclosed courtyard is perfect for a quiet retreat outdoors. Founded in 1793, New Market offers 30 specialized antique shops, old fashioned general stores and fine dining within walking distance. An Old Fashioned General Store is everyone's favorite, and Mealey's, well known for dining excellence, is a few steps away.

Hosts: Tom and Terry Rimel
Rooms: 5 (3 PB; 2 SB) $75-125
Full Breakfast
Credit Cards: A, B
Notes: 2, 5, 8 (over 10), 10, 12, 13

OLNEY

Thoroughbred Bed and Breakfast

16410 Batchellor's Forest Road, 20832
(301) 774-7649

This is a beautiful 175-acre estate. Many fine racehorses were raised here. Full breakfast is served. In addition, there is a hot tub, swimming pool, pool table, and piano all available to guests. Guests may choose to stay in the main house or the quaint renovated 1900 farmhouse with whirlpool tubs. Just six miles from Metro and 12 miles from Washington, D.C.

National Pike Inn

6 Pets welcome; 8 Children welcome; 9 Social drinking allowed; 10 Tennis available; 11 Swimming available; 12 Golf available; 13 Skiing available; 14 May be booked through travel agents.

Host: Helen M. Polinger
Rooms: 13 (7 PB; 6 SB) $65-115
Full and Continental Breakfast
Credit Cards: A, B
Notes: 2, 10, 11, 12, 14

PASADENA

Amanda's Bed and Breakfast #231

1428 Park Avenue, Baltimore, 21217
(410) 225-0001; (410) 383-1274

A lovely setting on the water, this waterfront community called Sunset Knoll is on 1 and 1/2 acres on the Magothy River about fifteen minutes from downtown Annapolis. Quiet and convenient to Annapolis, Washington, D.C., or Baltimore. Two rooms, both with queen-size beds and private baths, are available for guests. Full breakfast. $85.

PHOENIX

Amanda's Bed and Breakfast #121

1428 Park Avenue, Baltimore, 21217
(410) 225-0001; (410) 383-1274

This unique post/beam home is set in the rolling countryside north of Baltimore. Comfortable rooms with antiques in a private wooded setting make this a special stay for guests. Continental breakfast. Private bath. $75.

PITTSFIELD

Country Hearts Bed 'N' Breakfast

52 Broad Street, 01201
(413) 499-3201

Centrally located, Country Hearts is easily accessible to all Berkshire attractions.

Nestled on a quiet residential street well known for its collection of beautifully restored "aristocrats," this lovely "painted lady" is waiting to open her doors for you.

Hosts: Jan and Steve Foose
Rooms: 3 (1 PB; 2 SB) $45-95
Continental Breakfast
Credit Cards: A, B
Notes: 2, 5, 8, 9, 10, 11, 12, 13

POTOMAC

Amanda's Bed and Breakfast #198

1428 Park Avenue, Baltimore, 21217
(410) 225-0001; (410) 383-1274

Early American furnishings complement the charm of this forested, single-family dwelling situated in Maryland's suburbs of Washington, D.C. Two rooms, both of which have a private bath, are available. Continental breakfast. $65.

PRINCE FREDERICK

Amanda's Bed and Breakfast #153

1428 Park Avenue, Baltimore, 21217
(410) 225-0001; (410) 383-1274

This century-old farmhouse with a wrap-around porch is in a country setting of fields, woods, and a view of the river. The private suite for guests includes a parlor and separate entrance. Situated near Chesapeake Bay, Broomes Island, and Cypress Swamp. A full breakfast is served each morning. $70-85.

QUEENSTOWN

Amanda's Bed and Breakfast #167

1428 Park Avenue, Baltimore, 21217
(410) 225-0001; (410) 383-1274

NOTES: Credit cards accepted: A Master Card; B Visa; C American Express; D Discover Card; E Diner's Club; F Other; 2 Personal Checks accepted; 3 Lunch available; 4 Dinner available; 5 Open all year;

This bed and breakfast sits on a quiet harbor that becomes active in the afternoon with sail boats that come in for safe anchorage. Blue herons stalk the soft crabs along the creek bed. Breakfast is served overlooking the water. Close to outlet shopping, boating, and biking.

The Traveller In Maryland # 173

P. O. Box 2277, Annapolis, 21404
(410) 269-6232; FAX (410) 263-4841

Situated on Main Street in a quaint historic village, this home is conveniently accessible to Annapolis, Washington, Baltimore, Easton, Chestertown, and other areas of the Eastern Shore. Each of the four rooms is comfortably and tastefully decorated and includes private bath. A large family room is a spacious gathering place for guests to unwind and meet new acquaintances. It also opens onto the large screened porch overlooking flower gardens. Amenities include TV, reading/work area, off-set parking, and handicapped facilities. Continental breakfast is served. $65.

The Traveller In Maryland # 175

P. O. Box 2277, Annapolis, 21404
(410) 269-6232; FAX (410) 263-4841

The "Cottage" is a gracious suite in a garden setting, with a spacious living-dining room with a view of your own fountain. Perhaps you would rather try the the "Carriage House" in its country setting. Awake refreshed to breakfast in the privacy of your own cottage. Ocean is easily accesible, and fishing, hunting, bird watching, biking, antique shopping, and Blackwater National Wildlife Refuge are nearby. $75-85. Weekly $450-517.

The Traveller In Maryland # 180

P. O. Box 2277, Annapolis, 21404
(410) 269-6232; FAX (410) 263-4841

Circa 1800, 50-acre waterfront farm offers the ultimate in peace and privacy. Comfortably restored Bay Hundred farmhouse and St. James Church (a property saved through historic preservation by the owners) offers the ambience and serenity of a waterman's retreat. Waterfowl and wildlife abound. Antiquing, boating, biking, bird watching, fine restaurants, and museums are but minutes away. Other features include French doors, deck, water views, private bath, marsh, and creek. Continental breakfast is served in this non-smoking environment. $115.

ROCK HALL

Amanda's Bed and Breakfast #203

1428 Park Avenue, Baltimore, 21217
(410) 225-0001; (410) 383-1274

This gracious waterfront manor house on 58.4 acres is one mile south of Rock Hall. Near the water, wildlife, and hunting, six rooms, all with private baths, are available in this quiet country setting. Continental breakfast. $75-145.

ST. MICHAELS

Parsonage Inn

210 North Talbot Street, Route 33, 21663
(800) 394-5519

Late Victorian bed and breakfast, circa 1883, lavishly restored in 1985 with eight guest rooms, private baths, king or queen brass beds with Laura Ashley linens. Parlor and dining room in European tradition. Gourmet restaurant receiving rave reviews next door. Two blocks to Chesapeake Maritime Museum, shops, harbor. Fifteen percent off midweek for AARP or retired officers. Mobil and AB&B approved.

Hosts: Peggy and Bill Parsons
Rooms: 8 (PB) $82-114
Complete Gourmet Breakfast
Credit Cards: A, B
Notes: 2, 5, 8, 9, 10, 12

Parsonage Inn

SCOTLAND

St. Michael's Manor Bed and Breakfast

St. Michael's Manor and Vineyard, 20687
(301) 872-4025

The land belongs to St. Michael's Manor (1805) and was originally patented to Leonard Calvert in 1637. The house, situated on Long Neck Creek, is furnished with antiques. Boating, canoeing, bikes, swimming pool, and wine-tasting are available. Near Point Lookout State Park, Civil War monuments, and historic St. Mary's City.

Hosts: Joseph and Nancy Dick
Rooms: 4 (SB) $50-65
Full Breakfast
Credit Cards: None
Notes: 2, 5, 7, 8, 9, 10, 11

SHARPSBURG

Amanda's Bed and Breakfast #268

1428 Park Avenue, Baltimore, 21217
(410) 225-0001; (410) 383-1274

This inn sits amidst the hallowed ground of the Civil War's Antietam Battlefield. Furnishings of Victorian vintage define a gentler way of life, and the pastoral surroundings of the misty Blue Ridge Mountains can be seen from a wraparound porch. Four rooms have private baths. Continental breakfast. $105-125.

SILVER SPRING

Amanda's Bed and Breakfast #281

1428 Park Avenue, Baltimore, 21217
(410) 225-0001; (410) 383-1274

This beige and brick Cape Cod is close to Washington, D.C. and a large park with trails for walking and biking. Minutes to the Metro with a large pool for guests to enjoy, this bed and breakfast offers two guest rooms that share a bath. Continental breakfast. $75.

The Traveller In Maryland # 185

P. O. Box 2277, Annapolis, 21404
(301) 269-6232; FAX (410) 263-4841

This English Tudor home, built of brick with a steep slate roof, sits alone on one acre of landscaped gardens including two patios that overlook the creek and woods. Situated inside the Beltway on Sligo Creek, and a Metro station is within a reasonable walk or a brief drive. The home is secluded among 50-foot beech and oak trees, with private bath and a nice view of the woods. Continental breakfast is served. $65.

NOTES: Credit cards accepted: A Master Card; B Visa; C American Express; D Discover Card; E Diner's Club; F Other; 2 Personal Checks accepted; 3 Lunch available; 4 Dinner available; 5 Open all year;

The Traveller
In Maryland # 187

P. O. Box 2277, Annapolis, 21404
(301) 269-6232; FAX (410) 263-4841

The house is new Victorian-style with wraparound porches and decks for sitting or sunning. At the end of a residential street and backed up to a wooded area, it is so secluded that sometimes it is difficult to realize that Washington, D.C., is only a few miles away. Amenities include livingroom, TV, fireplace, huge spa, and wooded overlook. Full breakfast is served. $55-65.

SMITHSBURG

Blue Bear Bed and Breakfast

22052 Holiday Drive, 21783
(301) 824-2292

Country charm and warm, friendly hospitality await you at the Blue Bear. There are two beautifully decorated and air conditioned rooms with a shared bath. Enjoy a delicious breakfast of fresh fruits, breads and pastries, and quiche. Feel at home here.

Host: Ellen Panchula
Rooms: 2 (SB) $40-45
Continental Breakfast
Credit Cards: None
Notes: 2, 5, 8 (over 12), 10, 11, 12, 13

STEVENSON

Amanda's
Bed and Breakfast #115

1428 Park Avenue, Baltimore, 21217
(410) 225-0001; (410) 383-1274

Historic 45-acre estate offers elegant living. 1900-style fireplaces, Jacuzzi, gourmet breakfast, swimming pool, tennis, woodland trails and streams, flowers and herb gardens all make this majestic estate a special place to stay. Three guest rooms, all with private baths and fireplaces, are available. Full breakfast. $100-110.

STEVENSVILLE

Amanda's
Bed and Breakfast #180

1428 Park Avenue, Baltimore, 21217
(410) 225-0001; (410) 383-1274

This historic manor is situated on Kent Island on the Eastern Shore side of the Bay Bridge. This grand mansion, circa 1820, is on the Maryland Historic Register and is surrounded by 226 acres of land. A mile and a half from the waterfront with rooms decorated in Victorian style that will make your stay here memorable. Restaurant has a four-star rating. Continental breakfast.

TANEYTOWN

Amanda's
Bed and Breakfast #161

1428 Park Avenue, Baltimore, 21217
(410) 225-0001; (410) 383-1274

This restored 1844 mansion sits on 24 acres, with clay tennis courts, croquet, gardens, a view of the Catoctin Mountains, and gourmet dinners provided with reservations. Winner of "Baltimore's Most Romantic Getaway," this inn offers six rooms, all with private baths and fireplaces. Full breakfast. $150-225.

VIENNA

Amanda's
Bed and Breakfast #172

1428 Park Avenue, Baltimore, 21217
(410) 225-0001; (410) 383-1274

This Victorian inn built of brick in 1861 on the banks of the scenic Nanticoke River offers a view of the river from most rooms. The river is a refuge for waterfowl, osprey,

6 Pets welcome; 8 Children welcome; 9 Social drinking allowed; 10 Tennis available; 11 Swimming available; 12 Golf available; 13 Skiing available; 14 May be booked through travel agents.

eagles, and other birds and animals. House maintains the original character and details. Four rooms with both shared and private baths are available. Continental breakfast. $65-85.

WESTMINSTER

Amanda's Bed and Breakfast #219
1428 Park Avenue, Baltimore, 21217
(410) 225-0001; (410) 383-1274

This Victorian inn is a former schoolhouse forty-five minutes from northwest Baltimore. All guest rooms have a queen-size bed and a Jacuzzi tub. Hearty breakfast buffet, and an athletic club available to guests, which includes, swimming, jogging, racquetball, and weight machines. Historic Union Hills Homestead and museums are all nearby. $110-155.

Massachusetts

Allen House Victorian Bed and Breakfast Inn

599 Main Street, 01002
(413) 253-5000

An authentic 1886 Queen Anne-style Victorian, this home features spacious bed chambers with private baths. Period antiques, decor, art, and wallcoverings are historically and accurately featured. In the heart of Amherst on three scenic acres and within walking distance to the Emily Dickinson House. Amherst College, the University of Massachusetts, fine galleries, museums, theatres, shops, and restaurants are nearby. Free busing throughout this five college area. A full formal breakfast and afternoon tea is served. Brochure available. 1991 Historic Commission Award winner.

Hosts: Alan and Anne Zieminski
Rooms: 5 (PB) $45-95
Full Breakfast
Credit Cards: None
Notes: 2, 5, 8 (over 10), 9, 10, 11, 12, 13

The American Country Collection #120

4 Greenwood Lane, Delmar, NY 12054
(518) 439-7001

This in-town Victorian with wraparound veranda is conveniently situated on a quiet tree-lined street within walking distance to the college, university, and downtown. The decor is pristine and uncluttered, with shiny hardwood floors, lush green plants, fresh flowers, antique oak dressers, and rocking chairs. The first-floor suite is actually a self-contained flat with bath and full kitchen with eating area. A new second-floor guest quarters contains two bedrooms and shared bath, plus kitchen and eating area. Breakfast foods are in the individual suites for guests to enjoy at their convenience. $55-85.

Bed and Breakfast Accommodations 120

984 Gloucester Place, Schenectady, NY 12309
(518) 370-4948

This in-town Victorian with wraparound veranda for outdoor relaxation is situated on a quiet, tree-lined street within walking distance to the college, university, and downtown. The decor is pristine and uncluttered, with shiny hardwood floors, lush green plants, fresh flowers, antique oak dressers, and rocking chairs. The first-floor suite is actually a self-contained flat with bath and full kitchen. New second-floor guest quarters contain two bedrooms, shared bath, plus kitchen. Continental breakfast; children welcome. $60-85 one-night stay; $55-80.

Berkshire Bed and Breakfast Homes PV17

P. O. Box 211, Williamsburg, 01096
(413) 268-7244

This 1968 Garrison Colonial is decorated with traditional and antique furnishings. Twin beds and a semiprivate bath and parlor are available. Continental breakfast; children welcome. $50-55.

6 Pets welcome; 8 Children welcome; 9 Social drinking allowed; 10 Tennis available; 11 Swimming available; 12 Golf available; 13 Skiing available; 14 May be booked through travel agents.

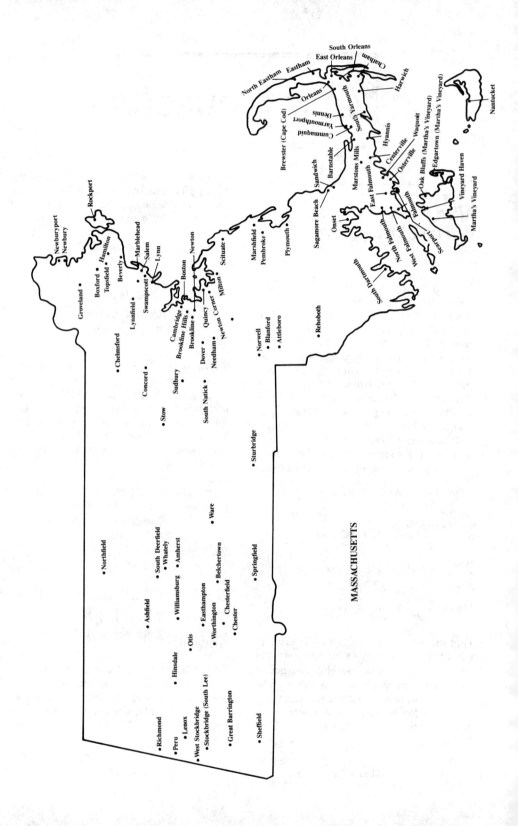

MASSACHUSETTS

Berkshire Bed and Breakfast Homes PV38

P. O. Box 211, Williamsburg, 01096
(413) 268-7244

An 1810 Colonial farmhouse on three acres. The common room and queen room with private bath are decorated with country and antique furnishings. Continental breakfast; children over 10 welcome. $60-65.

ASHFIELD

Bed and Breakfast/Inns of New England MA-1010

Guilford, CT 06437
(800) 532-0853

With its stately hilltop setting, this majestic Georgian-Colonial house with large porches is decorated in Victorian furnishings. The eight spacious rooms are named after local landmarks, with floral wall coverings, ruffle curtains, lacy sheets, period furniture, and loomed rugs. Each of the large bathrooms are shared by two rooms. A continental breakfast is served weekday mornings, and a full breakfast is served on weekends. Children welcome. $85.

The American Country Collection #084

4 Greenwood Lane, Delmar, NY 12054
(518) 439-7001

Flower and herb gardens set the stage for this beautifully restored 18-room Georgian Colonial mansion on nine acres overlooking Ashfield Lake. Featuring a grand livingroom, cozy guest library with TV and VCR, foyer with impressive grand staircase, and a dining room, all available to guests. Spacious bedrooms, three with a lake view, are appointed with antique beds and dressers, and at least one easy chair or rocker. Floral arrangements, reading lamps, antique fixtures, and full bath amenities. Continental breakfast weekdays; full English breakfast weekends. Dinner available Friday and Saturday; mid-week by special request. Children welcome. $55-95. $20 extra person in room.

ATTLEBORO

Bed and Breakfast Associates #CW875

P. O. Box 57166, Babson Park Branch
Boston, 02157-0166
(617) 449-5302; FAX (617) 449-5958

Nestled in a quiet country neighborhood, this Colonial reproduction home offers pleasant accommodations for guests attending concerts at Great Woods or visiting Wheaton College, both only 10 minutes away. Providence is only a 15-minute drive. Two guest rooms on the second floor share a bath. Full breakfast; children welcome. $55-70; family and monthly rates available.

BARNSTABLE (CAPE COD)

Bed and Breakfast Cape Cod #14

Box 341, West Hyannisport, 02672
(508) 775-2772; FAX (508) 775-2884

This circa-1821 barn has been converted into a comfortable home with a natural country feeling. Three guest rooms with private baths feature Victorian decor and furnishings. Children over 12 welcome. $75-85.

NOTES: Credit cards accepted: A Master Card; B Visa; C American Express; D Discover Card; E Diner's Club; F Other; 2 Personal Checks accepted; 3 Lunch available; 4 Dinner available; 5 Open all year; 6 Pets welcome; 8 Children welcome; 9 Social drinking allowed; 10 Tennis available; 11 Swimming available; 12 Golf available; 13 Skiing available; 14 May be booked through travel agents.

Bed and Breakfast Cape Cod #27

P. O. Box 341, West Hyannisport, 02672-0341
(508) 775-2772; FAX (508) 775-2884

A few steps off Old King's Highway, this 1852 renovated Victorian home offers four rooms. Each is complete with decorative wall coverings, period furnishings, and fresh flowers. All have private baths, and room #4 on the third floor is especially private, with a king-size bed. Perfect for honeymooners. Outside, a wraparound porch provides a place for relaxation after a day at the beach or shopping. $65-70.

Bed and Breakfast Cape Cod #35

P. O. Box 341, West Hyannisport, 02672-0341
(508) 775-2772; FAX (508) 775-2884

Not many bed and breakfast travelers have a chance to stay in a house built in 1635. This charming old building was part of the Cape Cod designer's tour of homes in 1989. The owner has two bedrooms used for bed and breakfast, with a king-size bed in one room and a pair of twins in the other. The rooms share one bath. The grounds are like a rural wooded setting with great trails for walking. A parlor is available on the first floor for guests to use. Children over 12 welcome. $60.

BELCHERTOWN

Berkshire Bed and Breakfast Homes PV5

P. O. Box 211, Williamsburg, 01096
(413) 268-7244

Enjoy this 1839 Victorian in a small New England town. Two guest rooms, one with private bath, and livingroom are available to guests. Overlooks the town common.

Continental breakfast; children over 12 welcome. $30-60.

Berkshire Bed and Breakfast Homes PV8

P. O. Box 211, Williamsburg, 01096
(413) 268-7244

This 1989 modern contemporary home has a Scandinavian decor. There is a parlor, deck, and pool for guest use. Enjoy the British hospitality of the hosts. The guest room has twin beds and a private bath. Continental breakfast; children welcome; resident pets. $65.

Berkshire Bed and Breakfast Homes PV29

P. O. Box 211, Williamsburg, 01096
(413) 268-7244

This 1850 Federal-Greek Revival is on 13 acres. Two guest rooms share a bath and the parlor and den have antique furnishings. Full breakfast; children welcome. $45-55.

BEVERLY

Lady Slippers Bed and Breakfast

Bed and Breakfast Marblehead and North Shore
P. O Box 35, Newtonville, 02160
(617) 964-1606; (800)832-2632
FAX (617) 332-8572

Dutch Colonial, antique-furnished attractive family home facing ocean. One or more teenage sons at home. The hostess is a retail merchandiser and is particularly interested in local history and politics. She speaks some Spanish and Hebrew. Four guest rooms available. Continental breakfast. Children welcome. Dog in residence. Baby-sitting by prior arrangement. $45-75.

Next Door Inn Bed and Breakfast

Bed and Breakfast Marblehead and North Shore
P. O. Box 35, Newtonville, 02160
(617) 964-1606; (800) 832-2632
FAX (617) 332-8572

A beautifully decorated, cozy, Colonial-style home offers guests use of kitchen facilities, color TV in livingroom, enclosed sun porch, telephone, and off-street parking. There are three attractive guest rooms: a room with a queen-size bed and private bath, another room with a double bed and a fireplace, and a third room with a pair of twins. (Second and third rooms share a bath). In hot weather, common areas have air conditioning, and the guest rooms have fans. Continental breakfast. $50-75.

BLANFORD

Berkshire Bed and Breakfast Homes SC5

P. O. Box 211, Williamsburg, 01096
(413) 268-7244

A 1768 central-chimney Colonial on six acres. Guest rooms share a bath, and all have Colonial furniture. Parlor with open fireplace and view of the woods. Full breakfast; children welcome. $50-60.

BOSTON

Architect's Home

Host Homes of Boston
P. O. Box 117, 02168
(617) 244-1308; FAX (617) 244-5156

Pleasant and private fourth-floor guest room with queen sofa bed, roof deck. Near Park Plaza and Tufts Medical Center. Air conditioning, private bath, TV. $68.

Around the Corner

Host Homes of Boston
P. O. Box 117, 02168
(617) 244-1308

Great location and exceptional decor in this hosts' lovely 1826 Federal town house. Guest suite two flights up has two small single bedrooms, a sitting room, TV, and bath. Single guest room with bath on the lower level also. Near the State House, Massachusetts General Hospital, major hotels, MIT, Harvard, restaurants and shops. $85.

Back Bay Condo

Host Homes of Boston
P. O. Box 117, 02168
(617) 244-1308; FAX (617) 244-5156

Comfy and casual home in the heart of elegant Back Bay offers a guest room with a queen bed, VCR, and Jacuzzi bath. Steps away from Copley Square, Hynes Convention Center, and Boston Common. $85.

Bed and Breakfast Associates #M128

P. O. Box 57166, Babson Park Branch, 02157-0166
(617) 449-5302; FAX (617) 449-5958

This 1835 Federal town house has all its original architectural details. Guests enjoy the private use of the entire second floor that consists of a bedroom, sitting room, and bath. The two decorative fireplaces add a warm coziness to this peaceful urban retreat. Continental breakfast served in the room; children welcome. $90.

Bed and Breakfast Associates #M131

P. O Box 57166, Babson Park Branch, 02157-0166
(617) 449-5302; FAX (617) 449-5958

---

6 Pets welcome; 8 Children welcome; 9 Social drinking allowed; 10 Tennis available; 11 Swimming available; 12 Golf available; 13 Skiing available; 14 May be booked through travel agents.

In Boston's prestigious Beacon Hill and adjacent to the historic Massachusetts State House, this inn is a loving restoration of two attached 1830s townhouses. The fine period furnishings include four-poster and canopied beds, decorative fireplaces, and reproduction desks. New private baths throughout, and guests are always welcome to use the kitchen, the dining room, and the parlors. $85-99.

Bed and Breakfast Associates #M133

P. O. Box 57166, Babson Park Branch, 02157-0166
(617) 449-5302; FAX (617) 449-5958

A fourth-floor guest room with cathedral ceiling and rooftop deck overlooks this quiet street behind the State House and near the Faneuil Hall Waterfront area. This special retreat awaits atop an 1863 brick town house. Continental, self-serve breakfast; children welcome. $95.

Bed and Breakfast Associates #M136

P. O. Box 57166, Babson Park Branch, 02157-0166
(617) 449-5302; FAX (617) 449-5958

This handsome 46-room mansion at the foot of Beacon Hill is within walking distance of many Boston attractions. Modern amenities have been incorporated into this careful restoration, and rooms include phone lines, private baths, color TVs, kitchenettes, and individual climate controls. Elevator and handicapped access is available. The gracious double parlor with working fireplace and period furnishings serves as the lobby, and reproduction furnishings create a warm and elegant atmosphere. Continental breakfast. Laundry and valet. $90-130.

Bed and Breakfast Associates #M230

P. O. Box 57166, Babson Park Branch, 02157-0166
(617) 449-5302; (800) 347-5088

Situated on a quiet Back Bay street adjacent to the Hynes Convention Center and the Christian Science Center, this family offers one private guest room in this spacious 1880 Victorian brownstone. This sunny room has been lovingly prepared for guests seeking top quality accommodations with bathroom ensuite and private deck. Affordable rates.

Bed and Breakfast Associates #M240

P. O. Box 57166, Babson Park Branch, 02157-0166
(617) 449-5302; FAX (617) 449-5958

Lovely Victorian town house in the Back Bay just steps from the Prudential Center and Copley Place. This warm and hospitable couple offer their guests full use of their second floor with two charming guest rooms and a bath. They also offer a garden-level efficiency with a new kitchenette and private bath. Continental breakfast; children welcome. $60-80.

Bed and Breakfast Associates #242

P. O. Box 57166, Babson Park Branch, 02157-0166
(617) 449-5302; (800) 347-5088

This restored Victorian brownstone adjacent to the famed Symphony Hall and Christian Science Center, offers two guest rooms with pretty country decor. Twin beds or queen bed available. Parking behind the house, $6 per day. Just a block to Massachusetts Avenue bus and subway. $68.

NOTES: Credit cards accepted: A Master Card; B Visa; C American Express; D Discover Card; E Diner's Club; F Other; 2 Personal Checks accepted; 3 Lunch available; 4 Dinner available; 5 Open all year;

Bed and Breakfast Associates #M314

P. O. Box 57166, Babson Park Branch, 02157-0166
(617) 449-5302; FAX (617) 449-5958

Attention to detail and gracious hospitality are the hallmark of this bed and breakfast. Selected as one of the 100 best bed and breakfast in the country, this 1863 townhouse is set in the historic district right next to Boston's famed Copley Square. Each impeccable guest room offers unique decorative features that include wide-pine floors, bow windows, marble fireplaces, queen-size brass beds, Chinese rugs, and private baths. Sumptuous breakfast served in the penthouse dining room. $97-110.

Bed and Breakfast Associates #M319

P. O. Box 57166, Babson Park Branch, 02157-0166
(617) 449-5302; FAX (617) 449-5958

This 19th-century brick town house is on a pretty, quiet street near Copley Square. The hostess, an artist who also restores antique needlework, has tastefully blended her Victorian and contemporary furnishings. Two guest rooms, one with private bath. Continental breakfast; children over six welcome. $65-78.

Bed and Breakfast Associates #M322

P. O. Box 57166, Babson Park Branch, 02157-0166
(617) 449-5302; FAX (617) 449-5958

This congenial couple offers two lovely guest rooms (one queen and one double bed) with charming antique decor, private baths, and central air. Their beautifully restored Victorian bow-front townhouse is situated on a quiet street. Private parking $10. $85.

Bed and Breakfast Associates #M323

P. O. Box 57166, Babson Park Branch, 02157-0166
(617) 449-5302; (800) 347-5088

This 1869 Victorian town house is close to the city's newest restaurant area, and five blocks from Copely Square. Guest room features gracious bay window and antique furnishings. Continental breakfast. $68-85.

Bed and Breakfast Associates #M324

P. O. Box 57166, Babson Park Branch, 02157-0166
(617) 449-5302; FAX (617) 449-5958

This large family home in Boston's South End has reserved the fourth floor for guests. Situated near Prudential Center with reserved parking ($10/day), two guest rooms, one with a queen bed, and one with a double bed plus a queen sleeper sofa, are available and share a bath. Buffet breakfast is served in the formal dining room. $75.

Bed and Breakfast Associates #M346

P. O. Box 57166, Babson Park Branch, 02157-0166
(617) 449-5302; FAX (617) 449-5958

This newly restored brick bow-front townhouse has lovely traditional decor, spacious guest rooms, private baths, and period architectural details. Choose from a pair of twin, king, or double-size beds. This home is situated on a quiet street three blocks from Copley Square, the John Hancock Tower, and many fine shops and restaurants. $95.

Bed and Breakfast Associates #M355

P. O. Box 57166, Babson Park Branch, 02157-0166
(617) 449-5302; FAX (617) 449-5958

6 Pets welcome; 8 Children welcome; 9 Social drinking allowed; 10 Tennis available; 11 Swimming available; 12 Golf available; 13 Skiing available; 14 May be booked through travel agents.

A friendly young family welcomes guests to their guest room with its Laura Ashley decor and sunlight through lace curtains. This renovated town house is situated three blocks from the Prudential Center. Enjoy the continental breakfast cafe-style by a private bay window. Semiprivate bath. Children welcome. $75.

Bed and Breakfast Associates #M356

P. O. Box 57166, Babson Park Branch, 02157-0166
(617) 449-5302; (800) 347-5088

This third-floor apartment offers a bedroom, livingroom with queen sleeper sofa, and fully equipped kitchen. Continental self-serve breakfast. $75.

Bed and Breakfast Associates #M357

P. O. Box 57166, Babson Park Branch, 02157-0166
(617) 449-5302; (800) 347-5088

This 1860s bowfront town house is four blocks from Copely Square, and regularly featured on historic house tours. It is furnished with Federal period antiques and boasts 12-foot ceilings. Continental breakfast. $68.

Bed and Breakfast Associates #M412

P. O. Box 57166, Babson Park Branch, 02157-0166
(617) 449-5302; FAX (617) 449-5958

The hostess and her daughter are pleased to welcome guests to Boston in their waterfront condo with lovely decor. Master bedroom has desk and TV. Second bedroom has twin beds, shared bath, and a feminine decor. Enjoy a nice view of Boston Harbor from the balcony. Continental breakfast; children over 13 welcome; $80.

Bed and Breakfast Associates #M510

P. O. Box 57166, Babson Park Branch, 02157-0166
(617) 449-5302; FAX (617) 449-5958

A wonderful 12-room Victorian in the Jamaica Pond area near the Farber, Children's, and Brigham hospitals. Very large third-floor guest room provides privacy, and its furnishings include a desk and a sofa. A private bath and a full private kitchen adjoin. Drive 10 minutes to downtown Boston. Self-serve continental breakfast. $70; monthly rates available.

Coach House

Host Homes of Boston
P. O. Box 117, 02168
(617) 244-1308; FAX (617) 244-5156

Converted to a private home in 1890, the original structure of this bed and breakfast housed twelve coaches and staff. Here, on a quiet gas-lit street, this host family offers two well-appointed guest rooms on the second (single) and third (double) floors. Both rooms have private baths. Near Freedom Trail, hotels, restaurants, and "Cheers." Resident cats. $85-100.

Downtown Duplex

Host Homes of Boston, P. O. Box 117, 02168
(617) 244-1308; FAX (617) 244-5156

Boston's past and present meet here amid Faneuil Hall, waterfront, and downtown. Host's fifth- and sixth-floor walk-up has brick and beam decor, balcony, antiques. Guest room has double bed and skylights. Walk to Quincy Market, financial district, North End, and Freedom Trail. Air conditioning, TV, private bath. $68.

On the Hill

Host Homes of Boston, P. O. Box 117, 02168
(617) 244-1308; FAX (617) 244-5156

NOTES: Credit cards accepted: A Master Card; B Visa; C American Express; D Discover Card; E Diner's Club; F Other; 2 Personal Checks accepted; 3 Lunch available; 4 Dinner available; 5 Open all year;

This brick Federal town house (1790) on the Hill's loveliest street offers exceptional third-floor quarters—livingroom, bedroom, modern bath, kitchen, and dining room where breakfast is served. Near Freedom Trail, hotels, State House. Air conditioning, TV. $85-95.

Victoriana

Host Homes of Boston
P. O. Box 117, 02168
(617) 244-1308; FAX (617) 244-5156

Host's 1860 Victorian home in historic neighborhood has a second floor guest room with a pair of twin beds and antiques. This home is on a quiet street near Copley Square, Convention Center, and Amtrak. $68.

BOXFORD

Day's End Bed and Breakfast

Bed and Breakfast Marblehead and North Shore
P. O. Box 35, Newtonville, 02160
(617) 964-1606; (800) 832-2632
FAX (617) 332-8572

A beautiful architect-designed contemporary home in a country setting, with swimming pool and large grounds. The four guest rooms can be rented individually or as a separate entrance suite. In addition to the efficiency kitchenette and sitting room, the first-floor livingroom has facilities for entertaining, available for a fee. Open year-round. Continental breakfast. Children welcome. $55-70; weekly and monthly rates available.

BREWSTER (CAPE COD)

Antique Inn and Cottage

Bed and Breakfast of Greater Boston and Cape Cod
P. O. Box 35, Newtonville, 02160
(617) 964-1606; (800) 832-2632
FAX (617) 332-8572

A completely restored 18th-century sea captain's house offers seven guest rooms, all with private baths, air conditioning, and antique furnishings. Award-winning gardens surround the house and full breakfast is served each morning. Children over 12 welcome. $82-108.

Bed and Breakfast Associates #CC675

P. O. Box 57166, Boston, 02157-0166
(617) 449-5302; FAX (617) 449-5958

A quiet neighborhood setting, abundant gardens, and an easy drive to the National Seashore await you at this cozy little bed and breakfast. Enjoy a full country breakfast with eggs from chickens raised by the hosts. This sparkling fresh and charming home has two guest rooms that share a bath. Full breakfast. $70.

Bed and Breakfast Cape Cod #17

P. O. Box 341, West Hyannisport, 02672-0341
(508) 775-2772; FAX (508) 775-2884

Situated along the banks of Cape Cod Bay in historic Brewster is this 1750 sea captain's house. Six hundred yards from the house is a public beach where swimming and fishing are available. A continental breakfast on the patio with an ocean view is served each morning. Double or twin beds available. Golf, Nickerson State Park, and the village are less than a mile away. $65.

Bed and Breakfast Cape Cod #41

P. O. Box 341, West Hyannisport, 02672-0341
(508) 775-2772; FAX (508) 775-2884

In an antique village, this lovely home was rebuilt in 1973 and has all amenities, including air conditioning, TV, and traditional decor. A short walk takes you to shops, bay beaches, and other points of interest. A large second floor private bath/ bedroom has a king-size bed, and four other rooms with either double or queen-size beds are also available. Big gourmet breakfast served each morning. $68-98.

Captain Freeman Inn

Captain Freeman Inn

15 Breakwater Road, 02631
(508) 896-7481

Charming old sea captain's mansion offers luxury suites with balcony, private spa, fireplace, canopy bed, TV, air conditioning. Spacious rooms with canopy beds and private baths and rooms with shared bath. Enjoy the wraparound porch, outdoor pool, bikes, and full breakfast. Centrally situated on Cape Cod's historic north side, close to beaches, restaurants, and shopping.

Host: Carol Covitz
Rooms: 12 (9 PB; 3 SB) $50-185
Full Breakfast
Credit Cards: A, B, C
Notes: 2, 5, 8 (over 10), 9, 10, 11, 12, 14

Ocean Gold

74 Locust Lane, 02631
(508) 255-7045; (800) 526-3760

This residential bed and breakfast is in a restful setting next to Nickerson State Park,

with miles of blacktop trails and ponds nearby. Hosts raise chickens for fresh eggs, and offer homemade breads, jams, and berries. Breakfast is served in the formal dining room.

Hosts: Marge and Jim Geisler
Rooms: 3 (1 PB; 2 SB) $65-95
Full Breakfast
Credit Cards: None
Notes: 2, 5, 10, 11, 12, 13, 14

Old Sea Pines Inn

2553 Main Street, 02631
(508) 896-6114

Lovely turn-of-the-century mansion, once the Sea Pines School of Charm and Personality for Young Women, now a newly renovated and redecorated country inn. Furnished with antiques, some of the rooms have working fireplaces. Situated on three and one-half acres of land, with a wraparound porch looking out over the lawn, trees, and flowers. Complimentary beverage on arrival.

Hosts: Stephen and Michele Rowan
Rooms: 16 (PB) $45-90
Full Breakfast
Credit Cards: A, B, C, E
Notes: 2, 5, 8 (over 8), 9, 10, 11, 12, 14

Old Sea Pines Inn

NOTES: Credit cards accepted: A Master Card; B Visa; C American Express; D Discover Card; E Diner's Club; F Other; 2 Personal Checks accepted; 3 Lunch available; 4 Dinner available; 5 Open all year;

BROOKLINE

Beale House

Host Homes of Boston, P. O. Box 117, 02168
(617) 244-1308; FAX (617) 244-5156

This 1872 registered historic town house has been restored by hosts. The friendly family offers a small third-floor guest room with double bed (private bath on weekends). Resident cat. One block to Green Line-C. Near Boston College, Boston University, Back Bay, and restaurants. $54.

Bed and Breakfast Associates #M617

P. O. Box 57166, Babson Park Branch,
  Boston, 02157-0166
(617) 449-5302; FAX (617) 449-5958

Just three blocks from Commonwealth Avenue, near Boston University, this Victorian bed and breakfast is a haven for guests visiting both Boston and Cambridge. The restful decor is enhanced by the 19th-century American antiques throughout the house. Three second-floor guest rooms with shared bath. Full breakfast; children welcome. $55-62, single; $68-72, double.

Bed and Breakfast Associates #M642

P. O. Box 57166, Babson Park Branch,
  Boston, 02157-0166
(617) 449-5302; (800) 347-5088

Sparkling, bright and cheerful, this spacious condominium occupies the second floor of a fine Old World-style brownstone in the Washington Square area. Full breakfast. $75.

Briarwood

Host Homes of Boston, P. O. Box 117, 02168
(617) 244-1308; FAX (617) 244-5156

Historic 1875 landmark home combines Early American antiques with modern amenities. Exceptional first-floor guest wing with private entrance, queen bed, two twins, skylights, alcove with dining table, and light cooking facilities. Second-floor guest room with double bed. Guests prepare own breakfast in room. One block to Boston College campus. Three blocks to Green Line-D. Air conditioning, TV. $68-75.

The Carriage House

Greater Boston Hospitality
P. O. Box 1142, 02146
(617) 277-5430

This home is listed exclusively with Greater Boston Hospitality. On a separate guest floor of a carriage house, there are two bedrooms — one with a queen bed and the second with twin beds, a bath, and den with piano. Each room leads out onto a large patio exclusively for guest use. Parking included.

Host: Lauren Simonelli
Rooms: 2 (SB) $63
Full Breakfast
Credit Cards: None
Notes: 2, 5, 9, 10, 11, 12, 14

Greater Boston Hospitality

P. O. Box 1142, 02146
(617) 277-5430

Situated throughout the greater Boston area, this reservation service has Federal, Colonial, and Georgian private homes, unhosted apartments, and small, intimate inns in the Back Bay, Beacon Hill, Waterfront areas, as well as Brookline, Cambridge, and suburbs. Many include parking; many are on the subway system; all include breakfast.

Coordinator: Lauren Simonelli
Rooms: 180 (120 PB; 60 SB) $50-150
Continental Breakfast
Credit Cards: A, B, C
Notes: 2, 5, 8, 9, 10, 11, 12, 14

---

6 Pets welcome; 8 Children welcome; 9 Social drinking allowed; 10 Tennis available; 11 Swimming available; 12 Golf available; 13 Skiing available; 14 May be booked through travel agents.

Heath House

Host Homes of Boston, P. O. Box 117, 02168
(617) 244-1308; FAX (617) 244-5156

Country atmosphere close to city in classic Colonial on rolling lawn. English hostess offers two second-floor guest rooms (queen with air conditioning and twins). Children welcome. Near Pine Manor, Boston College, Longwood medical area. Boston five miles. Green Line-D one-half mile. $61-68.

Sarah's Loft

Host Homes of Boston, P. O. Box 117, 02168
(617) 244-1308; FAX (617) 244-5156

Bright and spacious third-floor suite with private entrance. Guest quarters include queen bedroom and smaller room with queen sofa bed. Also, a large living area with skylights, stereo, dining table (where breakfast is served), refrigerator, microwave, and extra sofa bed. Children are welcome. Green Line-C, village two blocks. Fenway Park, Boston one mile. Air conditioning, crib, private bath, TV. $71.

Studio Apartment

Host Homes of Boston, P. O. Box 117, 02168
(617) 244-1308; FAX (617) 244-5156

Colonial home (1620 Salem house replica) on quiet cul-de-sac offers above-ground basement room with double bed, sofa, galley kitchen, patio, and private entrance. Choice of breakfast on tray or self-serve. Five blocks to Green Line-C. Ten minutes to Copley Square. TV, private bath. $68.

Town and Country

Host Homes of Boston, P. O. Box 117, 02168
(617) 244-1308; FAX (617) 244-5156

Elegant 1916 French Riviera-style home in Boston's estate area has walled garden, skyline view. Spacious second-floor guest room (king or twin beds) with fireplace. Near Museum of Fine Arts, Longwood medical area, Boston College, Boston University, Back Bay. Green Line-D one mile. Boston one-half mile. Private bath. $68.

BROOKLINE HILLS

Brookline Hills

Host Homes of Boston
P. O. Box 117, Boston, 02168
(617) 244-1308

This historic 1890 Queen Anne home has been lovingly maintained and preserved throughout. Guests can enjoy the large family kitchen and veranda in summer. Roomy second-floor suite features a twin and single bed with connecting bath. Just three miles from Boston, and a 10-minute walk to the Green Line-D. $75.

The Treehouse

Host Homes of Boston, P. O. Box 117, 02168
(617) 244-1308; FAX (617) 244-5156

Meg's modern town house with traditional decor has a sweeping view from the glass-walled livingroom and deck. Two second floor guest rooms (double and twins). Also, in season, a king room with air conditioning and private bath. Two Siamese cats. Near Back Bay, Boston College, Boston University. Ten minutes to Hynes Convention Center via Green Line-C and D three blocks. Private bath, TV. $57-75.

BROOKLINE VILLAGE

Historic Row

Host Homes of Boston, P. O. Box 117, 02168
(617) 244-1308; FAX (617) 244-5156

NOTES: Credit cards accepted: A Master Card; B Visa; C American Express; D Discover Card; E Diner's Club; F Other; 2 Personal Checks accepted; 3 Lunch available; 4 Dinner available; 5 Open all year;

The National Register of Historic Places lists this 1928 Williamsburg attached house. Three large second-floor guest rooms (two queens and twins) each with color TV. Resident cat and dog. Near Boston College, Boston University, Longwood Medical center. Green Line-D three blocks. 10 minutes to Back Bay and convention center. TV, shared bath. $57.

Situated on the northern perimeter of Harvard, this Victorian offers comfort and convenience. Between them, your host couple speak Italian, French, Spanish, German, Russian, Mandarin, Cantonese, and Japanese. Three guest rooms, one with private bath, on the second floor. Generous continental breakfast; children welcome. $55-62, single; $68-72, double.

CAMBRIDGE

Bed and Breakfast Associates #M804

P. O. Box 57166, Babson Park Branch
Boston, 02157-0166
(617) 449-5302; FAX (617) 449-5958

Near Harvard Yard, this impeccable Philadelphia-style Victorian, circa 1890, is situated on a quiet street among the finest homes in Cambridge. The two-room suite features a spacious sitting room with sleeper sofa, fireplace, writing table, TV, and balcony. Continental breakfast; children welcome. $85-100.

Bed and Breakfast Associates #M813

P. O. Box 57166, Babson Park Branch,
Boston, 02157-0166
(617) 449-5302; (800) 347-5088

This 60-year old home has been newly renovated, maximizing light and natural wood while preserving the original design. Continental breakfast. $60-65, single; $65-70, double.

Bed and Breakfast Associates #M817

P. O. Box 57166, Babson Park Branch
Boston, 02157-0166
(617) 449-5302; FAX (617) 449-5958

Bed and Breakfast Associates #M825

P. O. Box 57166, Babson Park Branch,
Boston, 02157-0166
(617) 449-5302; (800) 347-5088

A private three-room apartment, secluded in the rear of a large (circa 1820) Federalist estate off Brattle Street in West Cambridge. Enjoy a private entry, full kitchen, and bedroom with queen-size bed. Cable TV, telephone, and air conditioning are also included. Caution, low ceilings in some rooms make this cozy unit best for guests under six-feet tall. Single, $75; double, $85.

Bed and Breakfast Associates #M885

P. O. Box 57166, Babson Park Branch,
Boston, 02157-0166
(617) 449-5302; FAX (617) 449-5958

This congenial hostess, a Boston attorney, shares her cozy Greek Revival home (circa 1853) just outside Harvard Square. Her decor is accented by a refreshing mix of country antiques and her quiet urban neighborhood provides a convenient setting for activities in Boston or Cambridge. Two second-floor guest rooms share a bath. Full breakfast upon request; children welcome. $55-75.

6 Pets welcome; 8 Children welcome; 9 Social drinking allowed; 10 Tennis available; 11 Swimming available; 12 Golf available; 13 Skiing available; 14 May be booked through travel agents.

Bed and Breakfast Associates #M900

P. O. Box 57166, Babson Park Branch
Boston, 02157-0166
(617) 449-5302; (800) 347-5088

Newly opened 18-room inn just north of Harvard Square. This fully restored property has lovely furnishings and offers both standard rooms and suites. All rooms feature private baths, telephones, TV, and central air. Reserved parking available at no charge. $95-135 plus tax.

Blue Hawthorne

Host Homes of Boston
P. O. Box 117, Boston, 02168
(617) 244-1308; FAX (617) 244-5156

This 100-year-old Victorian home off Brattle Street is a quiet oasis near bustling Harvard Square. The host offers two first-floor guest rooms (queen and twins) with private baths, phone, and TV. Shady side garden. Three blocks to the square, Red Line, Charles Hotel, restaurants, and shops. Air conditioning, TV. $75

Cambridge Suite

Host Homes of Boston
P. O. Box 117, Boston, 02168
(617) 244-1308; FAX (617) 244-5156

This large home (1855) is on a quiet road only three blocks from bustling Harvard Square. The first-floor guest suite has a queen bedroom, sitting room with sofa, desk. Breakfast served in the dining room. Near William James Hall and law school. Red Line three blocks. Air conditioning. $81.

The Missing Bell

Host Homes of Boston
P. O. Box 117, Boston, 02168
(617) 244-1308; FAX (617) 244-5156

Antiques, extraordinary detailed woodwork in this large Victorian (1883) on a quiet street. Young, welcoming hosts offer two spacious second-floor guest rooms with queen and double beds. Dining room with a fireplace, guest parlor. Close to restaurants, shops, Harvard Square, and the Red Line subway. $85.

True Victorian

Host Homes of Boston
P. O. Box 117, Boston, 02168
(617) 244-1308; FAX (617) 244-5156

Host's Victorian jewel sits on a quiet hill near Massachusetts Avenue between Harvard and Porter squares. Three second-floor guest rooms—two with double bed, TV, and desk; king room. Only two rooms booked at a time. Shared family bath. Hearty breakfast in sunny kitchen, often self-serve on weekdays. Red Line and train at Porter Square three blocks. TV. $61.

CENTERVILLE

Bed and Breakfast Cape Cod #43

P. O. Box 341, West Hyannisport, 02672-0341
(508) 775-2772; FAX (508) 775-2884

This quiet bed and breakfast overlooks Lake Wequaquet, the largest fresh water lake on Cape Cod. The second floor has been set aside for guests, featuring two rooms that share a bath. A first-floor room offers a king-size bed and a private bath. Continental breakfast. $55-65.

Long Dell Inn

436 South Main Street, 02632
(508) 775-2750

Situated just a five minute walk away from the famous Craigville Beach, and a 10

NOTES: Credit cards accepted: A Master Card; B Visa; C American Express; D Discover Card; E Diner's Club; F Other; 2 Personal Checks accepted; 3 Lunch available; 4 Dinner available; 5 Open all year;

minute ride to ferries, trains and the bus. Honeymoon packages and off-season specials available, featuring beautiful apartments, each with a private deck. Off-street parking, canopy beds, and a personally served three-course full breakfast await.

Hosts: Joy and Roy Swayze
Rooms: 6 plus apartment (PB) $75-90
Full Breakfast
Credit Cards: None
Notes: 2, 5, 8, 9, 10, 11, 12, 14

CHATHAM

Bed and Breakfast Associates #CC475

P. O. Box 57166, Babson Park Branch
  Boston, 02157-0166
(617) 449-5302; FAX (617) 449-5958

This hostess invites guests to share her sprawling Cape-style home with its Early American decor. This wooded setting is perfect for country walks. Nearby is the village of Chatham, renowned for its treasure trove of galleries, shops, ice cream parlors, and restaurants in a gracious old-fashioned seaside setting. Three guest rooms, some with private baths, and a studio apartment. Continental breakfast; children welcome. No breakfast served for apartment. $68-93.

Bed and Breakfast Cape Cod #12

P. O. Box 341, West Hyannisport, 02672-0341
(508) 775-2772; FAX (508) 775-2884

This reproduction of an Early American Cape Cod Home offers a first-floor room with a private bath, queen-size bed; the second floor offers two rooms with double beds. (These rooms are never rented separately, so they share a "private" bath.) Continental breakfast. A short walk to the village, fish pier, and the beach. $65.

Bed and Breakfast Cape Cod #48

P. O. Box 341, West Hyannisport, 02672-0341
(508) 775-2772; FAX (508) 775-2884

This eighteen-room country inn was built in the 1830s and painstakingly restored in 1989. All guest rooms are air conditioned, have private baths, and are filled with antiques and tasteful accents. Continental breakfast is served from 8:30 until 10:00 A.M., and cocktails are served in the Schooner Tavern on the premises. $102-145.

Bed and Breakfast Cape Cod #49

Box 341, West Hyannisport, 02672-0341
(508) 775-2772; FAX (508) 775-2884

This 25-year old Cape Cod-style home features wide-board floors, two fireplaces, and a den for guest use. Rooms are furnished in traditional decor. View the lighthouse in the distance. Children over 12 welcome. $65-75.

Bed and Breakfast Cape Cod #60

Box 341, West Hyannisport, 02672-0341
(508) 775-2772; FAX (508) 775-2884

This two-story Garrison Colonial stands three miles from the village center along the warm water sound. The rear deck overlooks a saltwater marsh. Children over four welcome. $55-60.

Bed and Breakfast Cape Cod #78

P. O. Box 341, West Hyannisport, 02672-0341
(508) 775-2772; FAX (508) 775-2884

6 Pets welcome; 8 Children welcome; 9 Social drinking allowed; 10 Tennis available; 11 Swimming available; 12 Golf available; 13 Skiing available; 14 May be booked through travel agents.

Built in 1985, this lovely host home offers a second-floor suite that has a large bedroom with a double bed and a pair of twins, sitting area, TV, and private bath with a shower. A generous continental breakfast with homemade breads and muffins is served in the country room or patio. The home is half mile from town and 3/4 mile from the harbor. $55-65.

Classic Cape Bed and Breakfast

Bed and Breakfast Greater Boston and Cape Cod
P. O. Box 35, Newtonville, 02160
(617) 964-1606; (800) 832-2632
FAX (617) 332-8572

Classic Cape Cod-style home in a quiet area within walking distance of the historic Chatham village center. The spacious guest room is on the second floor, separate from the hosts. It includes one double and two twin beds and a sitting area. Private bath. Generous continental breakfast. Children over 12 welcome. $65-70

Moses Nickerson House

Moses Nickerson House Inn

364 Old Harbor Road, 02633
(508) 945-5859; (800) 628-6972

Quiet, elegant, romantic. Built in 1839 by whaling captain Moses Nickerson, this small inn has seven individually decorated guest rooms featuring canopy beds, fireplaces, and Oriental rugs. Glass-enclosed

breakfast room. Walk to the quaint village of Chatham with its fine shops, galleries, and restaurants or turn right at the end of the driveway and walk to the beach or fishing pier.

Hosts: Elsie and Carl Piccola
Rooms: 7 (PB) $79-149
Full Breakfast
Credit Cards: A, B, C
Notes: 2, 5, 9, 10, 11, 12, 14

Cranberry Inn at Chatham

359 Main Street, 02633
(508) 945-9232; (800) 332-4667

Chatham's oldest inn, completely renovated. Conveniently situated in the heart of the historic village district within steps of shopping, dining, and beautiful beaches. Each of the 18 guest rooms is individually appointed and furnished with antiques and reproductions. All private baths; rooms with fireplaces, balconies, and wet bars available. Spacious, deluxe suite available with fireplace and loft. Hospitable hosts and staff.

Hosts: Peggy DeHan and Richard Morris
Rooms: 18 (PB) $88-165
Continental Breakfast
Credit Cards: A, B, C
Notes: 2, 8 (over 12), 9, 10, 11, 12, 14

The Old Harbor Inn

22 Old Harbor Road, 02663
(508) 945-4434; (800) 942-4434

Casually elegant English Country-style inn featuring king, queen, and twin beds, full private baths and decorator fabrics and

Old Harbor Inn

linens. Delectable buffet breakfast served in sunroom or out on the deck. Short walk to all attractions, including seaside village beaches, shops, galleries, museums, sports, theater, festivals and antiques. AAA Three Diamond rating.

Hosts: Tom and Sharon Ferguson
Rooms: 6 (PB) $95-155
Continental Plus Breakfast
Credit Cards: A, B, D
Notes: 2, 5, 9, 10, 11, 12, 14

CHELMSFORD

Westview Landing

4 Westview Avenue, P. O. Box 4141, 01824
(508) 256-0074

Westview Landing is a large contemporary home set on a tranquil pond. Unwind on a private beach with swimming, boating and fishing. Bicycling and hot spa are available. Situated three miles from Routes 495 and 3, just 30 miles north of Boston, and 15 miles south of Nashua, New Hampshire. Close to historic Lexington, Concord, and Lowell.

Hosts: Lorraine and Robert Pinette
Rooms: 2 (SB) $50
Full Breakfast
Credit Cards: None
Notes: 2, 5, 6, 8 ,9, 10, 11, 12, 13, 14

Westview Landing

CHESTER

Berkshire Bed and Breakfast Homes SC3

P. O. Box 211, Williamsburg, 01096
(413) 268-7244

This unhosted 1990 Colonial-style home is on 168 acres. It is furnished with country and Colonial decor. There is a parlor with a TV, a fully equipped kitchen with microwave, bath with shower, a double bed, and four adult-size bunk beds. All air conditioned. Continental breakfast; children welcome. $65-125.

CHESTERFIELD

Berkshire Bed and Breakfast Homes PV36

P. O. Box 211, Williamsburg, 01096
(413) 268-7244

Unhosted cottage built 175 years ago in Cape Cod-style. It sits on 25 acres of land with forest, beaver dams, mountain views, and small meandering river. The accommodations have a fully equipped kitchen, dining room, parlor, full bath, three bedrooms, wood-burning stove, gas grill, and picnic table. Full breakfast supplies; children welcome. $85-150.

CONCORD

Bed and Breakfast/Inns of New England MA-1009

329 Lake Drive, Guilford, CT 06437
(800) 582-0853

This 1775 center-chimney Colonial has hand-hewn beams, gunstock posts, handsome six-over-six windows, and 18th-century paneling or molding. Guest rooms have double beds and queen beds; all have private bathrooms,

6 Pets welcome; 8 Children welcome; 9 Social drinking allowed; 10 Tennis available; 11 Swimming available; 12 Golf available; 13 Skiing available; 14 May be booked through travel agents.

direct-dial telephone, color TV, and individual climate control. The inn is two miles from Walden Pond and within a one-minute walk from the Concord Fitness Center, where guests can stretch, swim, and sauna as a guest of the inn. No pets. $65-75.

Colonel Roger Brown

1694 Main Street, 01742
(508) 369-9119; (800) 292-1369

This 1775 Colonial home is on the historic register and situated close to the Concord and Lexington historic districts, 15 miles west of Boston and Cambridge. Five rooms with air conditioning, private baths, TV, and telephones. Continental breakfast and complimentary beverages at all times.

Host: Kate Williams
Rooms: 5 (PB) $65-75
Continental Breakfast
Credit Cards: A, B, C, D
Notes: 2, 5, 8 (over 12), 9, 10, 11, 12, 13, 14

Hawthorne Inn

462 Lexington Road, 01742
(508) 369-5610

Built circa 1870 on land once owned by Ralph Waldo Emerson, Nathaniel Hawthorne, and the Alcotts. Situated alongside the "battle road" of 1775 and within walking distance of authors' homes, battle sites, and Walden Pond. Furnished with antiques, handmade quilts, original artwork, Japanese prints, and sculpture.

Hosts: G. Burch and M. Mudry
Rooms: 7 (PB) $75-150
Continental Breakfast
Credit Cards: None
Notes: 2, 5, 7, 8, 9, 10, 11, 12, 13 (XC), 14

1775 Colonial Inn

Bed and Breakfast Greater Boston and Cape Cod
P. O. Box 35, Newtonville, 02160
(617) 964-1606; (800) 832-2632
FAX (617) 332-8572

Just 20 miles west of Boston with easy access to main highways, this meticulously restored Colonial inn offers five guest rooms, all with private baths, color TV, air conditioning, and telephones. Hearty continental buffet breakfast is served in the mornings, and afternoon tea or sherry is served by the fireplace in the 200-year-old sitting room. Fitness club facilities only a short walk from the inn. $65-75.

CUMMAQUID

Bed and Breakfast Cape Cod #61

P. O. Box 341, West Hyannisport, 02672-0341
(508) 775-2772; FAX (508) 775-2884

Just east of Barnstable, this house built in 1950 is a typical Cape Cod-style home with several acres of manicured grounds. Three rooms with private baths are available for guests. Hostess serves a full country breakfast with a Scandinavian flair. Hyannis and the ferry to Nantucket or Martha's Vineyard is four miles away. No children. $65-90.

CUMMINGTON

Hidden Brook

South Street in Plainfield, 01026
(413) 634-5653

Private country carriage-shed studio with deck and well-stocked kitchenette for breakfast at your leisure. Light arrival supper of homemade bread and soup or salad included. Refreshing, romantic escape in the Berkshire Hills for a family or honeymooners, with miles of country roads and trails to hike, bike, or ski lined with gnarled old maples, jewelwood, trillium, and many other wildflowers. Children welcome. Call for a brochure with map.

Hosts: Harold Hofreiter and Jody Kerssenbrock
Apartment: 1 (PB) $60
Full or Continental Breakfast and light Dinner
Credit Cards: None
Notes: 2, 4, 5, 7, 8, 9, 11, 13

Windfields Farm

154 Windsor Bush Road, 01026
(413) 684-3786

Secluded Federal homestead on a dirt road
amid fields and forests. Guests have their
own entrance, book-lined livingroom, fireplace, piano, and dining room. Family
antiques, paintings, and flowers.
Windfields' organic produce, eggs, maple
syrup, raspberries, and wild blueberries
enhance the hearty breakfasts. Near
Tanglewood and six colleges.

Hosts: Carolyn and Arnold Westwood
Rooms: 2 (SB) $45-60
Full Breakfast
Credit Cards: None
Closed March and April
Notes: 2, 8 (over 12), 9, 11, 13

DENNIS

Bed and Breakfast Cape Cod #4

P. O. Box 341, West Hyannisport, 02672-0341
(508) 775-2772; FAX (508) 775-2884

Restored several years ago with Victorian
antiques, this lovely home is now an elegant bed and breakfast, offering three guest
rooms with private baths. Twin or double
beds are available, and the village shops,
restaurants, and summer theater are within
walking distance. Breakfast is served from
8:00 until 10:00 A.M. and is full of house
specialties. No children. $65-95.

DUXBURY

Black Friar Brook Farm

636 Union Street, 02332
(617) 834-8528

This 1708 Saltbox farmhouse is a warm
and welcoming bed and breakfast. It is furnished with many period antiques. Share a
warm fire in the livingroom, or relax on the
brick patio. The host will serve his famous
blueberry pancakes. Walk our famous
beach; visit Boston and Cape Cod, which
are only a short distance away.

Hosts: Ann and Walter Kopke
Rooms: 2 (1 PB; 1 SB) $50-55
Full Breakfast
Credit Cards: None
Notes: 2, 5, 8, 11, 12

DOVER

1802 House

Locke Street, 04046
(207) 967-5632

On Cape Arundel Golf Course, 1802 House
provides peace and quiet, yet is within
walking distance of Dock Square. A pleasant and cozy interlude that guests will long
remember is the legacy of the 1802 House.

Hosts: Ron and Carol Perry
Rooms: 6 (PB) $75-125
Full Breakfast
Credit Cards: A, B, C
Notes: 2, 5, 9, 10, 11, 12, 13, 14

EASTHAM

Bed and Breakfast Cape Cod #72

P. O. Box 341, West Hyannisport, 02672-0341
(508) 775-2772; FAX (508) 775-2884

This sixty-year-old beach home is built in
the heart of what is now Cape Cod National
Seashore Park. Enter from a private
entrance to a livingroom with TV, library,
and sitting area. Two bedrooms, one with a
queen and one with a pair of twins, share
the suite's bath. Casual eclectic decor adds
to the relaxed-style of this popular beach
setting. Continental breakfast from 7:30-
9:30 A.M. Ocean view. $90.

6 Pets welcome; 8 Children welcome; 9 Social drinking allowed; 10 Tennis available; 11 Swimming available;
12 Golf available; 13 Skiing available; 14 May be booked through travel agents.

Bed and Breakfast Cape Cod #84

Box 341, West Hyannisport, 02672-0341
(508) 775-2772; FAX (508) 775-2884

Standing in the midst of a grove of tall pines is a 1983 contemporary home built by the owners. There is a ground floor suite, with a king-size bed and a private bath with shower. There is also a sitting area with a television and sliders to a private porch. The private entrance makes this a special place for visitors. The Cape Cod bike trail is 100 yards from the house. Breakfast is continental. $65.

Bed and Breakfast/Inns of New England MA 1050

329 Lake Drive, Guilford, CT 06437
(800) 582-0853

A traditional two-story home situated in the secluded area on the shore of Great Pond. There is a 1927 Chickering Grand Piano in the music room. The large master bedroom and bath on the second floor has a queen-size bed and color TV. A second large bedroom with pond view has twin beds. A private bathroom is directly across from the bedroom. A continental breakfast is served on the deck or in the dining room. No children; no pets. $75-80.

EAST FALMOUTH

Bed and Breakfast Cape Cod #44

P. O, Box 341, West Hyannisport, 02672-0341
(508) 775-2772; FAX (508) 775-2884

This picturesque modern home on Cape Cod features cathedral ceilings, glass walls, and a magnificent waterview of Waquoit Bay. A large solarium with antique wicker furniture and a spa can accommodate up to six people. Another room offers a king-size bed and shares a bath with third room that has a double and single bed. Children over 11. $85.

EASTHAMPTON

Berkshire Bed and Breakfast Homes PV35

P. O. Box 211, Williamsburg, 01096
(413) 268-7244

This 1902 Victorian on three-fourths acre has a view of the Connecticut River and Mount Tom. One guest room with private bath, two share a bath. Full breakfast; no children over eight. $50-65.

EAST ORLEANS

Bed and Breakfast Cape Cod #18

Box 341, West Hyannisport, 02672-0341
(508) 775-2772; FAX (508) 775-2884

This Salt Box Cape home home was built in 1963 in a quiet section of East Orleans, not far from the pounding surf of Nauset Beach on the Atlantic Ocean. A suite with a queen-size bed, private bath and tub and shower has a wide window overlooking the grounds. A private entrance and a study with desk, chairs, and library complete this very special accommodation. Continental breakfast is available in the room or outside on the grounds. Spacious grounds, beautiful flowers, and a restful setting make the stay special. $95

Nauset House Inn

143 Beach Road, Box 774, 02643
(508) 255-2195

The Nauset House Inn is a place where the gentle amenities of life are still observed, a place where sea and shore, orchard and field all combine to create a perfect setting for tranquil relaxation. The Nauset House Inn is ideally situated near one of the world's great ocean beaches, yet is close to antique and craft shops, restaurants, art galleries, scenic paths, and remote places for sunning, swimming, and picnicking.

Hosts: Diane and Al Johnson, Cindy and John
Vessella
Rooms: 14 (8 PB; 6 SB) $64-104
Full Breakfast; Continental available for lesser rate
Credit Cards: A, B
Closed Nov. 1-March 31
Notes: 2, 7, 9, 10, 11, 12

The Parsonage Inn

202 Main Street, P. O. Box 1501, 02643
(508) 255-8217

Originally a parsonage, circa 1770, this full Cape home is now a cozy, romantic inn less than two miles from one of Cape Cod's most beautiful beaches, Nauset Beach. All seven rooms are decorated with country antiques, quilts, and stenciling. A bountiful breakfast is served either in the dining or under sunny skies on the patio. Appetizers are served in the evening in the parlor, where guests can peruse menus of many fine restaurants.

Hosts: Ian and Elizabeth Browne
Rooms: 7 (PB) $55-95
Continental Breakfast
Credit Cards: A, B
Notes: 2, 5, 8 (over 5), 9, 10, 11, 12, 14

The Parsonage Inn

EDGARTOWN, MARTHA'S VINEYARD ___

Bed and Breakfast Nantucket/ Martha's Vineyard #204

P. O. Box 341, West Hyannisport, 02672-0341
(508) 775-2772; FAX (508) 775-2884

This 1840s sea captain's house offers 11 rooms with private baths, some with fireplaces. The decor is Victorian, and a continental breakfast is served each morning. Transportation to the beach is right outside the door, and a short walk leads to the village shops and restaurants. No children under 12. $65-175.

The Edgartown Inn

56 North Water Street, 02539
(508) 627-4794

Historic inn built in 1798 as the home for whaling Captain Worth. Early guests included Daniel Webster, Nathaniel Hawthorne, and Charles Summer. Later, John Kennedy stayed here as a young senator. Completely restored over the last 150 years, today it is filled with antiques. Convenient to beaches, harbor, and restaurants. Famous for breakfast, including homemade breads and cakes.

Hosts: Liliane and Earle Radford
Rooms: 20 (16 PB; 4 SB) $85-145
Full and Continental Breakfast
Credit Cards: None
Notes: 2, 9, 10, 11, 12

EGREMONT _____

American Country Collection 138

4 Greenwood Lane, Delmar, NY 12054
(518) 439-7001

This 1700s Victorian rural farm is on 500 acres of rolling hills, woods, and fields. It is furnished with antiques and Oriental rugs. There are four guest rooms, one with

6 Pets welcome; 8 Children welcome; 9 Social drinking allowed; 10 Tennis available; 11 Swimming available; 12 Golf available; 13 Skiing available; 14 May be booked through travel agents.

a private bath. Tanglewood, Norman Rockwell Museum, Berkshire Festival, and skiing are all within fifteen minutes. There is an in-ground pool available for guest use, Full breakfast; children over 10 welcome; resident dog. $65-80.

Berkshire Bed and Breakfast Homes SC8
P. O. Box 211, Williamsburg, 01096
(413) 268-7244

An 1803 country farmhouse on three acres. Guest rooms with private baths and parlor are furnished with antiques. Air-conditioned. Full breakfast; children over 16 welcome. $75-100.

FALMOUTH

Bed and Breakfast Cape Cod #38
P. O. Box 341, West Hyannisport, 02672-0341
(508) 775-2772; FAX (508) 775-2884

Built in 1880, this home on the road to Woods Hole has been restored comfortably, offering four guest rooms with private baths. Enjoy a full breakfast served in the dining room, and a nice parlor for reading or relaxing is also available. The village shops in Falmouth are a mile away, and the ferry is one and one half miles. Children over seven. $60-85.

Bed and Breakfast Cape Cod #42
P. O. Box 341, West Hyannisport, 02672-0341
(508) 775-2772; FAX (508) 775-2884

Built in 1822 on the beautiful village green in Falmouth is this gracious Federal Colonial style home. Through the years this prominent home has been photographed several times as a reflection of the architecture of picturesque New England. Offers two bedrooms with private baths, air conditioning, and a four-poster canopy bed. A continental breakfast is served. Walk to the bus, Martha's Vineyard Ferry, or stroll across the green to shops and fine restaurants. No children under 12. $65-80.

Bed and Breakfast Cape Cod #50
P. O. Box 341, West Hyannisport, 02672-0341
(508) 775-2772; FAX (508) 775-2884

This gracious Cape-style home was built in 1950 in the Waquoit section of Falmouth. It is near the bay, with glimpses of the water from the property. The house features four private bedrooms with bath on either of two floors. The breakfast is extensive and continental. A short drive takes one to the ferry, Martha's Vineyard, or to the village center. This lovely three-acre estate has grounds for walking or relaxing near the river on the property. A great location and wonderful hosts. $70-90.

Capt. Tom Lawrence House
75 Locust Street, 02540
(508) 540-1445

Beautiful 1861 Victorian, former whaling captain's residence in the historic village of Falmouth. Comfortable, spacious corner guest rooms. Firm beds—some with canopies. Steinway piano and working fireplace. Gourmet breakfast consists of fresh fruit, breads, pancakes made from freshly ground organic grain, and a variety of other delicious specialties. German spoken.

Host: Barbara Sabo-Feller
Rooms: 6 (PB) $75-99
Full Breakfast
Credit Cards: A, B
Notes: 2, 5, 9, 10, 11, 12

NOTES: Credit cards accepted: A Master Card; B Visa; C American Express; D Discover Card; E Diner's Club; F Other; 2 Personal Checks accepted; 3 Lunch available; 4 Dinner available; 5 Open all year;

Grafton Inn

Grafton Inn

261 Grand Avenue South, 02540
(508) 540-8688; (800) 642-4069
FAX (508) 540-1861

Oceanfront Victorian with a breathtaking view of Martha's Vineyard and Nantucket Sound. Thirty steps to the beach. Gourmet breakfast served at private tables on a lovely enclosed porch. Private baths, airy, comfortable rooms furnished with queen-size beds, period antiques, and ceiling fans. Fresh flowers, homemade chocolates, and other thoughtful amenities. Bicycles, beach chairs, and ample parking. Short walk to the ferry, shops, and restaurants.

Hosts: Liz and Rudy Cvitan
Rooms: 11 (PB) $65-115
Full Breakfast
Credit Cards: A, B, C
Notes: 2, 5, 9, 10, 11, 12, 14

Mostly Hall Bed and Breakfast Inn

27 Main Street, 02540
(508) 548-3786; (800) 682-0565

Romantic 1849 southern plantation-style Cape Cod home with wraparound veranda and widow's walk. Set back from the road on an acre of beautiful gardens with a gazebo. Close to restaurants, shops, beaches, island ferries. Spacious corner rooms with queen-size canopy beds, central air conditioning, gourmet breakfast, bicycles, private baths.

Hosts: Caroline and Jim Lloyd
Rooms: 6 (PB) $80-115
Full Breakfast
Minimum stay Memorial Day-Columbus Day: 2 nights
Credit Cards: A, B
Closed Jan.-mid Feb.
Notes: 2, 8 (over 15), 9, 10, 11, 12

The Palmer House Inn

81 Palmer Avenue, 02540-2857
(508) 548-1230; (800) 472-2632

Turn-of-the-century Victorian bed and breakfast in the historic district. Antique furnishings return guests to the romance of a bygone era. Full gourmet breakfast featuring pain perdue, Belgian waffles and Finnish pancakes. Close to island ferries, beaches, shops. Bicycles available.

Hosts: Ken and Joanne Baker
Rooms: 8 (PB) $65-115
Full Breakfast
Credit Cards: A, B, C, D, E
Notes: 5, 8 (over 12), 10, 11, 12, 14

Village Green Inn

40 West Main Street, 02540
(508) 548-5621

Gracious old Victorian, ideally situated on historic Village Green. Walk to fine shops and restaurants, bike to beaches, tennis, and the picturesque bike path to Woods Hole. Enjoy 19th-century charm and warm hospi-

The Palmer House Inn

tality in elegant surroundings. Four lovely guest rooms and one romantic suite all have private baths. Discount rates from November to May.

Hosts: Linda and Don Long
Rooms: 5 (PB) $75-110
Full Breakfast
Credit Cards: A, B, C
Notes: 2, 5, 8 (over 16), 9, 10, 11, 12

GLOUCESTER

Bed and Breakfast Associates #NS500

P. O. Box 57166, Babson Park Branch
  Boston, 02157-0166
(617) 449-5302; FAX (617) 449-5958

Just steps from the Atlantic, this white frame house in the little village of Lanesville (five miles from Gloucester and Rockport) offers three guest rooms with a shared bath and a separate cottage. Your hostess is an energetic woman who has done much of the interior renovation of her attractive New England-style home. Continental breakfast; children over 10 welcome. $60; family and winter rates available.

GREAT BARRINGTON

The American Country Collection #053

4 Greenwood Lane, Delmar, NY 12054
(518) 439-7001

This house, designed for visitors in 1907, features wraparound porches with a panoramic view of the Berkshire Hills. The dairy barn, renovated in 1987, dates from the 1920s. These two structures comprise an eight-room bed and breakfast inn. Five individually decorated guest rooms are in the house, each with Laura Ashley prints, antique furniture, art, and an extensive book collection. The dairy barn contains a fabulous hay loft renovation with two air-

conditioned luxury suites and private baths. Guests can choose from an extensive country menu for breakfast at any time they wish. Close to Tanglewood, Berkshire Theater, the Norman Rockwell Museum, and other attractions. Two resident dogs; horses welcome, and "stall bed and breakfast" available with advance reservation. $65-135. Surcharge of $15-20 for in-season weekend one night stay.

Baldwin Hill Farm Bed and Breakfast

Rural Delivery 3, Box 125, 01230
(413) 528-4092

A Victorian farm homestead of 450 acres on a spectacular Berkshire mountaintop with panoramic views. Warm hospitality and full country breakfasts. A quiet country setting with a pool, screened porch, gardens, orchards, wildlife, and walks. Close to restaurants and all area attractions. Near golf, tennis, lake, skiing, Tanglewood, museums, drama, concerts, shops, and trails. Hiking and biking maps available. Open year-round.

Hosts: Richard and Priscilla Burdsall
Rooms: 4 (1 PB; 3SB) $65-95 plus tax
Full Breakfast
Credit Cards: A, B
Notes: 2, 5, 8 (over 10), 9, 10, 11, 12, 13, 14

Bed and Breakfast Accommodations 053

984 Gloucester Place, Schenectady, NY 12309
(518) 370-4948

This classic hilltop farmhouse was designed for visitors in 1907 and features wraparound porches with panoramic views of the Berkshire Hills. The dairy barn, renovated in 1987, dates from the 1820s. The main house has five bedrooms decorated with Laura Ashley prints, antique furniture, art, and an extensive book collection. The dairy barn has a hayloft renovation contain-

NOTES: Credit cards accepted: A Master Card; B Visa; C American Express; D Discover Card; E Diner's Club; F Other; 2 Personal Checks accepted; 3 Lunch available; 4 Dinner available; 5 Open all year;

ing two air-conditioned luxury suites with private baths. Guests choose from an extensive country menu for breakfast at any time they wish. Children over 16 welcome. $65-135; $15-20 surcharge for in-season weekends, one-night stays.

Bed and Breakfast/Inns of New England MA 1020

329 Lake Drive, Guilford, CT 06437
(800) 582-0853

A circa 1800 farmhouse built by the Indians early in the last century. It has been added to over the years until it assumed its present rambling shape. There are five brightly furnished guest rooms, each with its own private bath. Bathrobes are found in the bedroom closets for the guests to use. All bedrooms are air-conditioned and equipped with telephones and clock radios.

Berkshire Bed and Breakfast Homes SC12

P. O. Box 211, Williamsburg, 01096
(413) 268-7244

An 1898 Victorian on one-half acre. Victorian and antique furnishings in parlor and guest rooms. Private and semiprivate baths. Situated in residential neighborhood. Continental breakfast; children welcome. $80-95 summer; $60-80 winter.

Covered Bridge 1GBMA

P. O. Box 447A, Norfolk, CT 06058
(203) 542- 5944

Charming Victorian farmhouse in a rural setting. A full breakfast is served in the dining room. There are three large rooms, each with private bath, cable TV, and air conditioning. Two of the rooms have queen beds, and one has twins. A barn on the grounds has also been converted into a two-bedroom cottage. $85-110.

Covered Bridge 2GBMA

P. O. Box 447A, Norfolk, CT 06058
(203) 542-5944

A 1907 farmhouse set on 16 acres offers a lovely retreat. There is a large, formal parlor available for guest use, and a full breakfast is served in the country kitchen. In the main house there are six guest rooms with double and twin beds that share three baths. The hayloft of the dairy barn has been converted into a charming two bedroom, two bath apartment. $75-85; $115-300 dairy barn.

Elaine's Bed and Breakfast and Inn Reservation Service

4987 Kingston Road, Elbridge, NY 13060
(315) 689-2082

Charming 1800s farmhouse updated for comfort, yet retaining antique ambience. Situated on eight acres near a pond, five brightly furnished guest rooms offer private baths. A full gourmet breakfast is served in the dining room or on the screened porch. Terry robes. Open year-round. Just a short drive to Tanglewood and all Berkshire attractions. $85.

Nutmeg Bed and Breakfast Agency #346

P. O. Box 1117, West Hartford, CT 06107
(203) 236-6698

A newly restored Victorian of the 1890s, with lovely old maples and a wraparound front porch. Secluded yet within walking distance to shops, theaters, and restaurants. The three lovely guest rooms with private and semiprivate baths have bay windows and antiques. Close to Stockbridge, Tanglewood, and major ski areas. A full breakfast with home-baked bread is included. Children welcome.

6 Pets welcome; 8 Children welcome; 9 Social drinking allowed; 10 Tennis available; 11 Swimming available; 12 Golf available; 13 Skiing available; 14 May be booked through travel agents.

Round Hill Farm

17 Round Hill Road, 01230
(413) 528-6969

A delightful 19th-century hilltop horse farm overlooking 300 spectacular acres and the glorious panorama of the Berkshires. Tended fields, trails, and trout stream. Tanglewood and Norman Rockwell. Less than three miles from Routes 7 and 23. Call for a complete brochure.

Hosts: Anthony Blair and Rebecca Tillinghast
Rooms: 3 (2 PB; 1 SB) $75-200
Full Breakfast
Credit Cards: A, B, C
Notes: 2, 5, 8 (over 16), 9, 10, 11, 12, 13, 14

Seekonk Pines Inn

142 Seekonk Cross Road, 01230
(413) 528-4192; (800) 292-4192

This restored 1830s homestead, set amid lovely flower and vegetable gardens, offers a large guest livingroom with a fireplace and grand piano. A full country breakfast is different every day, and special diets can be accommodated. Convenient to Tanglewood and other cultural events, museums, shops, golf, and hiking. Features antique quilts, stencilling, original artwork, gardens, picnic tables, in-ground pool, and guest pantry. Seen in the *Boston Globe, Philadelphia Inquirer, Los Angeles Times,* and the August 1992 issue of *Country Inns* magazine.

Hosts: Linda and Chris Best
Rooms: 6 (PB) $65-95
Full Breakfast
Credit Cards: A, B, C
Notes: 2, 5, 8, 9, 10, 11, 12, 13

The Turning Point Inn

3 Lake Buel Road, 01230
(413) 528-4777

An 18th-century former stagecoach inn. Full, delicious breakfast. Featured in *The New York Times, Boston Globe, Los Angeles Times.* Adjacent to Butternut Ski Basin; near Tanglewood and all Berkshire attractions. Hiking, cross-country ski trails. Sitting rooms with fireplaces, piano, cable TV. Groups and families welcome.

Hosts: The Yosts
Rooms: 8 (6 PB; 2 SB) $80-100
Full Breakfast
Credit Cards: A, B, C
Notes: 2, 5, 8, 9, 10, 11, 12, 13, 14

GROVELAND

Seven Acre Farm Bed and Breakfast

Bed and Breakfast Marblehead and North Shore
P. O, Box 35, Newtonville, 02160
(617) 964-1606; (800) 832-2632
FAX (617) 332-8572

A charming country farmhouse, built in 1987, offers three guest rooms. Enjoy the peace and tranquility of quiet walks through the seven acres of land that was once an herb farm. This bed and breakfast is furnished with antiques and has beautiful wood floors, Oriental rugs, atrium, skylights, and a cozy wood-burning stove. Three guest rooms share one and one half baths. Easy access to highways leading to Maine, New Hampshire, and Vermont. Generous continental breakfast. Children welcome. $55-75.

HAMILTON

The Dudley Pickman House

Bed and Breakfast Marblehead and North Shore
P. O, Box 35, Newtonville, 02160
(617) 964-1606; (800) 832-2632
FAX (617) 332-8572

A large gracious 1720s Colonial on one acre of land with herb and vegetable gardens. This home is two miles away from Crane's Beach. Three guest rooms, all with private baths, are included, and two guest rooms have working fireplaces. Generous continental breakfast included. Children welcome. Laundry facilities available.

Miles River Country Manor

Host Homes of Boston
P. O. Box 117, Waban Branch, 02168
(617) 244-1308

This 200-year old estate in Cape Ann horse country near Crane's Beach has many delights. Boasting 30 acres of lawns, gardens, woods, and wetlands, this vintage Colonial with 24 rooms, 12 fireplaces, and four parlors, also features eight guest rooms with twin and double beds, and two queen rooms with private baths. A full breakfast is served. Only 30 minutes to Boston. $61-85.

HARWICH

Bed and Breakfast Cape Cod #7

P. O. Box 341, West Hyannisport, 02672-0341
(508) 775-2772; FAX (508) 775-2884

This Cape-style home is 100 yards from a freshwater pond and offers two bedrooms, one with a double bed and the other a pair of twins. The bath is shared, and a full breakfast served in the dining room features home baked specialties. The pond is available for swimming or fishing, and the beach is close to this pleasant accommodation. Children over 11. $60.

Bed and Breakfast/Inns of New England MA 1047

329 Lake Drive, Guilford, CT 06437
(800) 582-0853

Set on one and one-half acres with flower and vegetable gardens, the main house was built in 1835. A contemporary wing has since been added. Upstairs there are twin beds with a shared bath. Downstairs there is a king-size bed with private bath and entrance. This room boasts five windows

and is especially delightful in the summer. An extra small room with a twin bed for a third guest is available, with a shared bath. A continental breakfast is served each morning. No children; no resident cat. $30-50.

HARWICH PORT

Bed and Breakfast Associates #CC370

P. O. Box 57166, Babson Park Branch, Boston, 02157-0166
(617) 449-5302; FAX (617) 449-5958

White wicker rocking chairs and hanging geraniums on a wraparound porch beckon you to this Victorian home situated less than a mile from the beach. There are five guest rooms with brass beds, fine period furnishings, and pleasing pastel wallpapers. Shops and restaurants are within easy walking distance. A continental breakfast is served. $95. Family and monthly rates available.

HINSDALE

Berkshire Bed and Breakfast Homes NC7

P. O. Box 211, Williamsburg, 01096
(413) 268-7244

A 100-year-old, remodeled Colonial home on ten acres. Guest room with private bath has private entrance. Parlor and deck available to guests. Full breakfast; children welcome. $65-70.

Berkshire Bed and Breakfast Homes NC10

P. O. Box 211, Williamsburg, 01096
(413) 268-7244

6 Pets welcome; 8 Children welcome; 9 Social drinking allowed; 10 Tennis available; 11 Swimming available; 12 Golf available; 13 Skiing available; 14 May be booked through travel agents.

This 1770 central-hall Colonial on six acres has antique and country furnishings throughout guest rooms with shared bath. One room with private bath; three with a shared bath. Parlor and glass porch for guest use. Full breakfast; children welcome. $55-70.

HYANNIS

The Inn on Sea Street

358 Sea Street, 02601
(508) 775-8030

A small, elegant 1849 Victorian inn with fireplace, just steps from the beach. Antiques, canopy beds. Persian rugs and objets d'art abound in this unpretentious, hospitable atmosphere where no detail has been overlooked to assure your comfort. A full breakfast of home-baked delights and fruit is served at individual tables set with the hosts' finest silver, china, crystal, and fresh flowers. One-night stays welcome.

Rooms: 9 (7 PB; 2 SB) $70-90
Full Breakfast
Credit Cards: A, B, C, D
Notes: 2, 9, 10, 11, 12

LANESBORO

Berkshire Bed and Breakfast Homes NC9

P. O. Box 211, Williamsburg, 01096
(413) 268-7244

Late 1800s Colonial farmhouse on three acres. This home was once a turkey farm and has a view of Mount Greylock. Guest rooms with semiprivate baths and parlor have country furnishings. Full breakfast; children over eight welcome. $70-80.

LEE

Applegate

279 West Park Street, 01238
(413) 243-4451

A circular driveway leads to this pillared Georgian Colonial home set on six peaceful acres. Applegate is special in every way, with canopy beds, antiques, fireplaces, pool, and manicured gardens. Its mood is warm, hospitable, and relaxed. Enjoy complimentary wine and cheese in the library-style livingroom, complete with a baby grand piano. Near Norman Rockwell museum and Tanglewood in the heart of the Berkshires.

Applegate

Hosts: Nancy Begbie-Cannata and Richard Cannata
Rooms: 6 (PB) $80-190
Expanded Continental Breakfast
Credit Cards: A, B
Notes: 2, 5, 7, 8 (over 12), 9, 10, 11, 12, 13

Berkshire Bed and Breakfast Homes SC11

P. O. Box 211, Williamsburg, 01096
(413) 268-7244

1780 Garrison Colonial on four acres features antique and formal furnishings, TV room, porch, and patio. This home offers one bedroom with a queen-size bed and private bath, and two other bedrooms that share a bath and have double beds. $75-100.

Berkshire Bed and Breakfast Homes SC21

P. O. Box 211, Williamsburg, 01096
(413) 268-7244

1989 Colonial on 1.3 acres offers three rooms with a variety of bed sizes and choice of either private or semi-private bath. The home is furnished in antiques, with a parlor for guest use, and golf and tennis nearby. Children over 12 welcome. $80-95.

LENOX

The American Country Collection 154

4 Greenwood Lane, Delmar, NY 12054
(518) 439-7001

A Berkshire tradition since 1780, this gracious country home has 14 guest rooms, three with a Jacuzzi and private porch, two with a fireplace, and all with private baths. Rooms are cozy and comfortable. The 72-foot swimming pool is available for guest use. A full breakfast is served daily. Children over 12 welcome. $65-170 (seasonal).

Brook Farm Inn

15 Hawthorne Street, 01240
(413) 637-3013

There is poetry here. Large library, poets on tape. Near Tanglewood (Boston Symphony), theater, ballet, shops. Pool, gardens and fireplaces. Cross-country and downhill skiing close by in winter. Relax and enjoy.

Hosts: Joe and Anne Miller
Rooms: 12 (PB) $70-165
Continental Breakfast
Credit Cards: A, B
Notes: 2, 5, 8 (over 14), 9, 10, 11, 12, 13

Covered Bridge

P. O. Box 447, Norfolk, CT 06058
(203) 542-5944

This historic Colonial, within walking distance of the center of town, is very convenient to the Berkshires. There is a sitting room for guest use and a large wraparound porch to enjoy in the summer. There are seven guest rooms, two with private baths and five with shared baths. $65-100.

Elaine's Bed and Breakfast and Inn Reservation Service

4987 Kingston Road, Elbridge, NY, 13060
(315) 689-2082

An absolutely gorgeous classic Victorian inn dating back to the 1830s. Fifteen newly decorated rooms, all with private bath, antiques, and some with fireplaces. Spacious public rooms, verandas, porches, and lawn. Just a step from shops, restaurants, and Tanglewood. Many different rates; children welcome. Cribs, high chairs available.

Forty-four Saint Anne's Avenue

P. O. Box 718, 01240
(413) 637-3381

Enjoy Lenox, Tanglewood, and the Berkshires from our charming bed and breakfast, situated in the center of Lenox Village. Each of the rooms has a private bath, air conditioning, and a truly comfortable bed. The elegant, expanded Continental breakfast includes fresh fruit, fresh orange juice, homemade muffins, pastries, granola, tea, and coffee. The enthusiastic hosts have a desire to assist newcomers in their discovery of the cultural and scenic joys of the Berkshires.

Hosts: Barbara and Milton Kolodkin
Rooms: 3 (PB) $ 80-170

6 Pets welcome; 8 Children welcome; 9 Social drinking allowed; 10 Tennis available; 11 Swimming available; 12 Golf available; 13 Skiing available; 14 May be booked through travel agents.

Continental Breakfast
Credit Cards: None
Notes: 2, 9, 10, 11, 12

Walker House Inn

74 Walker Street, 01240
(413) 637-1271; (800) 235-3098

This historic Federal mansion was constructed in 1804 and offers eight spacious
rooms, all named for composers and furnished with antiques. Some offer canopy
beds and fireplaces, and a large parlor with
a grand piano and games, well-stocked
library with seven-foot-wide screen where
good films, operas, plays, and special television programs can be enjoyed. The dining room contains two large sociable tables
where complimentary breakfast and afternoon tea is served. Two verandas, one open
and another closed, are available for admir-
ing the landscaped grounds. Walker House
is within walking distance to several good
restaurants, shops, and galleries.

Hosts: Peggy and Richard Houdek
Rooms: 8 (PB) $50-160
Continental Plus Breakfast
Credit Cards: None
Notes: 2, 5, 6 (with approval), 8 (over 12), 9, 10, 11,
   12, 13

LOWELL

Bed and Breakfast Associates #CN300

P. O. Box 57166, Babson Park Branch
Boston, 02157-0166
(617) 449-5302; FAX (617) 449-5958

This beautiful Victorian home with its
wraparound porch and stained glass is
meticulously maintained and is graced by
many authentic architectural details and
tasteful period furnishings. Two guest
rooms on the second floor share a bath.
Expanded continental breakfast; children
welcome. $50-55; family rates available.

Caron

LYNN

Caron Bed and Breakfast

142 Ocean Street, 01902
(617) 599-4470

This 1912 Georgian-style mansion sits on
one-half acre in Boston's North Shore,
which is known as "Lynn's Diamond
District." This was once the private estate
of P. J. Harney, a Lynn shoe manufacturer.
Features include a gracious foyer and staircase winding its way up three floors, a spacious livingroom and banquet dining room,
both with working fireplaces. The large
veranda overlooks the gardens and sports
an ocean view. Antiques and collectibles
are seen throughout the house. A short
walk to Three Mile Beach, with jogging
and biking paths. Walk to restaurants and
shopping.

Hosts: Sandra and Jerry Caron
Rooms: 5 (3 PB; 2 SB) $70-80
Continental Plus Breakfast
Credit Cards: A, B, C
Notes: 2, 5, 6, 8, 11, 14

LYNNFIELD

Willow Tree Farm Bed and Breakfast

Bed and Breakfast Marblehead and North Shore
P. O. Box 35, Newtonville, 02160
(617) 964-1606; (800) 832-2632
FAX (617) 332-8572

Antique house circa 1802 features cozy single and double bedrooms with both shared

NOTES: Credit cards accepted: A Master Card; B Visa; C American Express; D Discover Card; E Diner's
Club; F Other; 2 Personal Checks accepted; 3 Lunch available; 4 Dinner available; 5 Open all year;

and private baths. A hearty breakfast is served in the post-and-beam dining room that overlooks the gardens, farmstead and wooded preserve. Easy access to other North Shore towns and tourist attractions. Extended stays welcome at special rates. $55-70.

MARBLEHEAD

Bed and Breakfast Associates #NS261

P. O. Box 57166, Babson Park Branch
Boston, 02157-0166
(617) 449-5302; FAX (617) 449-5958

Just two blocks to beaches, antique shops and restaurants, this restored Federal property offers beamed cathedral ceilings and a cozy, charming decor. Two guest rooms on the second floor share a bath. Continental breakfast; children welcome. $75-80.

1890 Marblehead Victorian

Bed and Breakfast Marblehead and North Shore
P. O. Box 35, Newtonville, 02160
(617) 964-1606; (800) 832-2632
FAX (617) 332-8572

This gracious Victorian, with its wainscot foyer and stairwell, offers three beautifully decorated guest rooms (two with queen beds, and the other with a pair of twins), that share a bath in the hall. An extra half-bath is available on the first floor, and a separate guest cottage that sleeps two to four people has a private bath. A wonderful breakfast, featuring home-baked breads, muffins, and granola cereal, is served in the breakfast room, or the gardens, weather permitting. Close to beaches and Old Town Marblehead. Children welcome. $75-100.

Harborside House

23 Gregory Street, 01945
(617) 631-1032

This handsome 1850 home in the historic district overlooks Marblehead Harbor. Enjoy water views from a fireplaced parlor, period dining room, third-story sun deck, and summer breakfast porch. Walk to historic sights, excellent restaurants, and unique shops. Generous breakfast includes juice, fresh fruit, homebaked goods and cereal. Hostess is a professional dressmaker and nationally ranked competitive swimmer.

Host: Susan Livingston
Rooms: 1 (PB) $85
Continental Breakfast
Credit Cards: None
Notes: 2, 5, 8 (over 10), 10, 11

The Nesting Place

16 Village Street, 01945
(617) 631-6655

This charming 19th-century home is conveniently situated in historic Marblehead, and within walking distance of the renowned harbor, beaches, historic homes, galleries, eateries, shops, and famous parks. A relaxing, refreshing home away from home. Two comfortably furnished guest rooms featuring a healthful breakfast, and an outdoor hot tub, will be found at The Nesting Place. One half hour from Boston, or one hour from New Hampshire. Day trips by car or bicycle are possible.

Harborside House

6 Pets welcome; 8 Children welcome; 9 Social drinking allowed; 10 Tennis available; 11 Swimming available; 12 Golf available; 13 Skiing available; 14 May be booked through travel agents.

Host: Louise Hirshberg
Rooms: 2 (SB) $55-65, seasonal rates available
Semi-full Breakfast
Credit Cards: A, B
Notes: 2, 5, 8, 9, 10, 11, 12

State Street Pilot House

Bed and Breakfast Marblehead and North Shore
P. O. Box 35, Newtonville, 02160
(617) 964-1606; (800) 832-2632
FAX (617) 332-8572

Attractively restored and situated among Old Town's quaint antique and gift shops, this historic inn was originally the home of John Adams. The inn offers two comfortable guest rooms, both with private baths, and is close to Marblehead's famous harbor and many good restaurants. Children over 12 welcome. $85.

Stillpoint

Stillpoint

27 Gregory Street, 01945
(617) 631-2433

Nicely appointed 1840s home is open all year, graciously landscaped, and filled with antiques, fireplace, piano, books, no TV, and quiet, refreshing ambience. Three spacious bedrooms share two full baths (the option of a private bath is available), and a hearty, healthy continental breakfast is served in the morning on the deck overlooking Marblehead Harbor in good weather. Within walking distance of shops, restaurants, beaches, and public transportation. Twenty minutes

north of Boston, near Logan airport, and an hour south of Maine/ New Hampshire border. Trips to Concord, Lexington Sturbridge Village shopping outlets, and New Hampshire ski slopes are feasible.

Host: Sarah Lincoln-Harrison
Rooms: 7 (PB) $70-90
Continental Breakfast
Credit Cards: A, B
Notes: 2, 5, 10, 11, 13

Tidecrest Bed and Breakfast

Bed and Breakfast Marblehead and North Shore
P. O, Box 35, Newtonville, 02160
(617) 964-1606; (800) 832-2632
FAX (617) 332-8572

Minutes by car to Old Town, this Mediterranean-style villa with spectacular view of the ocean offers two accommodations, both with private baths and ocean views. Breakfast is served on a large sun porch overlooking the ocean. Open weekends only, Memorial Day through Columbus Day. Children over six welcome. $100-150.

Victorian Rose
Bed and Breakfast

72 Prospect Street, 01945
(617) 631-4306; (800) 225-4306

Built at the turn of the century, the Victorian Rose welcomes guests to its

Victorian Rose

NOTES: Credit cards accepted: A Master Card; B Visa; C American Express; D Discover Card; E Diner's Club; F Other; 2 Personal Checks accepted; 3 Lunch available; 4 Dinner available; 5 Open all year;

Victorian wainscot foyer and stairwell. You will fancy spacious bedrooms with high ceilings, brass or antique beds, in a rose accented decor. Share the family room, where one play billiards or relax with an intriguing book. Guests will also find that the Victorian Rose is at the edge of Marblehead's historic Old Town, featuring many historic sights and close to its renowned picturesque harbor.

Hosts: Robert and Denise Campbell
Rooms: 4 (1 PB; 3 SB) $65-95
Continental Breakfast
Credit Cards: A, B
Notes: 2, 8, 9, 10, 11, 14

MARSHFIELD

Bed and Breakfast Associates #SS350

P. O. Box 57166, Babson Park Branch
Boston, 02157-0166
(617) 449-5302; FAX (617) 449-5958

What enthusiasm and hospitality this retired couple bring to hosting! Their New England farm-style home is one block from Marshfield Beach. Built in 1875, it is furnished with warmth and charm; guests will find this bed and breakfast a welcoming retreat. Three guest rooms with private baths. Full breakfast; children welcome. $50-60, single; $60-70, double. Family rates available.

Island Retreat

Be Our Guest Bed and Breakfast
P. O. Box 1333, Plymouth, 02362
(617) 837-9867

This lovely custom-built home is at the point of a small island overlooking salt marshes and the North River. Enjoy beautiful view from the decks and a dock at the back of the home. The east wing of the home offers three guest rooms with a shared bath. All tastefully decorated, there

is a room with a pair of twin beds, a room with a single, and a room with a double. Continental breakfast is served on the deck, weather permitting. Children welcome. $75.

The Little Inn

Be Our Guest Bed and Breakfast
P. O. Box 1333, Plymouth, 02362
(617) 837-9867

This 200-year old Federal Colonial offers three guest rooms furnished in antiques with queen, double, and a pair of twin beds, and private and shared baths. Less than one mile to the beach, the inn is set on a scenic road centrally and conveniently situated to Boston, Plymouth Center, and the Mid-Cape. Full breakfast is served in the fireplaced dining room. Children welcome. $40-60.

Oceanside

Be Our Guest Bed and Breakfast
P. O. Box 1333, Plymouth, 02362
(617) 837-9867

Just step out the door and cross the street to a long stretch of sandy beach and the Atlantic Ocean. Set on a cliff above the water, this charming beach house offers two guest rooms that share a common bath. One room has a pair of twin beds and the other has a double bed. A full breakfast is served in the dining room. Resident dogs. $40-60.

Woodlands

Be Our Guest Bed and Breakfast
P. O.Box 1333, Plymouth, 02362
(617) 837-9867

This lovely Cape is hidden in the woods and surrounded by lush gardens with a scenic ocean view. Guests should be "animal friendly," as the hosts have chickens,

6 Pets welcome; 8 Children welcome; 9 Social drinking allowed; 10 Tennis available; 11 Swimming available; 12 Golf available; 13 Skiing available; 14 May be booked through travel agents.

sheep, and a pony. One guest room is available offering a queen-size bed and private bath. A full breakfast is served, and garden tours are available upon request. $75.

MARSTONS MILLS

Bed and Breakfast Cape Cod #34

P. O. Box 341, West Hyannisport, 02672-0341
(508) 775-2772; FAX (508) 775-2884

Built in 1986 in a quiet residential neighborhood, this ranch-style house has all the extras one could ask for. One room has queen-size bed, private deck, and private entrance. The other room has a queen-size bed and semi-private bath. The beach is two miles away and the ferry to Martha's Vineyard or Nantucket is three miles away. Children over 11 welcome. $65-75.

MARTHA'S VINEYARD ISLAND

Thorncroft Inn

Box 1022, 278 Main Street, 02568
(508) 693-3333

Thirteen antique-appointed rooms in two restored buildings. Private baths, working fireplaces, air conditioning, two-person Jacuzzis or private hot tub. Fine dining. Romantic and intimate. Four-diamond rating from AAA. Named one of the top inns in the country by *Glamour* magazine, September 1990. On three and one-half landscaped acres in an exclusive residential neighborhood, 150 yards from the ocean.

Hosts: Karl and Lynn Buder
Rooms: 13 (PB) $99-299
Full Breakfast
Minimum stay weekends and holidays in-season: 3 nights
Credit Cards: A, B, C, D, F
Notes: 2, 4, 5, 9, 11, 12, 14

MIDDLETON

Bed and Breakfast Associates #CN501

P. O. Box 57166, Boston, 02157-0166
(617) 449-5302; (800) 347-5088

A special retreat for those seeking a romantic getaway. This 1692 antique Saltbox is set on beautifully landscaped grounds just eight miles from Salem and the northern coast of Boston. Two private guest rooms are available, each with a theme decor created by the hostess. The Victorian Room features a working fireplace and is furnished entirely in period pieces with an antique double bed and private bath. The Twenties Room, with private entrance and cathedral ceiling recreates the "Roaring 20s" in every detail. With a double bed and private bath (including a whirlpool for two), this unique space is just the place for a true escape weekend or a fun base for touring the north of Boston area. $100.

MILTON

Historic Country House

Host Homes of Boston
P. O. Box 117, Boston, 02168
(617) 244-1308; FAX (617) 244-5156

This 1780 country home restored by architect/owners blends heirlooms and modern amenities for a special stay. Second-floor guest room offers a pair of twin beds, and the grounds offer a swimming pool and a barn. Situated near I-93, Route 128, and I-95. $68.

NANTUCKET

Bed and Breakfast Cape Cod #102

P. O. Box 341, West Hyannisport, 02672
(508) 775-2772; FAX (508) 775-2884

This 16-room inn is situated close to the harbor in the village. From the widow's walk on the top floor there is a panoramic view of Nantucket Harbor. All guest rooms have private baths. Children over 11 welcome. $80-130.

Bed and Breakfast Nantucket/ Martha's Vineyard #102

P. O. Box 341, West Hyannisport, 02672-0341
(508) 775-2772; FAX (508) 775-2884

This 16-room bed and breakfast is close to the harbor in the village. From the widow's walk on the third floor, there is panoramic view of the Nantucket harbor. All guest rooms have private baths, and two suites are also available. Breakfast is served in the large dining room on the first floor. Children over 12 welcome. $80-130.

Bed and Breakfast Nantucket/Martha's Vineyard #103

P. O. Box 341, West Hyannisport, 02672-0341
(508) 775-2772; FAX (508) 775-2884

Situated in the heart of the village, this guest house has seven bedrooms, five with private bath, queen-size beds, and one with twin beds. Each room has a small refrigerator, coffee maker, cable TV, and are decorated in traditional furnishings. No breakfast is served, but several fine restaurants are nearby. Close to all village points of interest. No children under 12. $65-115.

Cobblestone Inn

5 Ash Street, 02554
(508) 228-1987

This 1725 home is situated on a quiet street in Nantucket's historic district, just a short walk from the steamboat wharf, museums,

shops, and restaurants. Guests can walk to nearby beaches or explore others by taking a bike path. Relax in the yard, sun porch, and livingroom.

Hosts: Robin Hammer-Yankow and Keith Yankow
Rooms: 5 (PB) $50-130
Continental Breakfast
Credit Cards: A, B
Notes: 2, 5, 8, 9, 10, 11, 12

Eighteen Gardner Street Inn

18 Gardner Street, 02554
(508) 228-1155

Guests are warmly welcomed to the circa 1835 home of Captain Robert Joy. Built from the wealth of the whaling era, this island home includes amenities such as fireplaced bedrooms, canopy bed, private baths, and spacious common rooms for the leisure hours of your stay. Whether guests choose the cozy Garden Room or a deluxe suite, they'll be attended by a courteous staff serving a full Nantucket breakfast and assisting with all their holiday enjoyment.

Hosts: Roger and Mary Schmidt
Rooms: 17 (PB) $65-185
Full Breakfast
Credit Cards: A, B
Notes: 2, 5, 8, 9, 10, 11, 12, 14

The Quaker House Inn and Restaurant

5 Chestnut Street, 02554
(508) 228-0400

The Quaker House Inn is a charming 19th century inn situated in the heart of Nantucket's historic area. Each of the eight guest rooms is decorated with antiques and period furnishings, yet with the convenience of queen beds and modern private baths. Its quaint restaurant is popular and highly recommended by reviewers.

Hosts: Caroline and Bob Taylor
Rooms: 8 (PB) $75-125 (plus breakfast)
Full Breakfast
Credit Cards: A, B
Notes: 2, 4, 9, 10, 11, 12, 14

6 Pets welcome; 8 Children welcome; 9 Social drinking allowed; 10 Tennis available; 11 Swimming available; 12 Golf available; 13 Skiing available; 14 May be booked through travel agents.

NEEDHAM

Brock's Bed and Breakfast
60 Stevens Road, 02192
(617) 444-6573

The Brock home is the first Royal Barry
Wills house designed in 1922 when Wills
was an architecture student at Massachusetts Institute of Technology. It is
Cape-style, with nooks and crannies, built-
ins, original high ceilings, flagstone walk,
landscaping, and Williamsburg decor, all
done by the Brocks. Breakfast is served in
the dining room from 7 until 9 A.M. Three
miles from Wellesley College, and four
miles from Boston College. Twenty minutes by public transportation to historic
Boston.

Hosts: Anne and Frank Brock
Rooms: 3 (SB) $55; (PB) $65
Full Breakfast
Credit Cards: None
Notes: 2, 5, 9, 10, 12

The Thistle Bed and Breakfast
Host Homes of Boston
P. O. Box 117, Boston, 02168
(617) 244-1308; FAX (617) 244-5156

Typical, cozy Cape Cod on a quiet street
has a fireplaced livingroom for guests and
two second-floor guest rooms with doubles
or twins and private and shared baths. A
few blocks from Route 128/ I-95, within
walking distance of the train. $44-61.

NEWBURY

Dolan Antique Colonial
Bed and Breakfast Marblehead and North Shore
P. O. Box 35, Newtonville, 02160
(617) 964-1606; (800) 832-2632
FAX (617) 332-8572

This restored Colonial farmhouse is surrounded by five acres of fields and perennial gardens. Convenient to beaches, downtown Newburyport, and Maudsley State
Park, the bed and breakfast offers one
large, sunny guest room with a double and
single bed, private bath, skylights, and
color TV. Guests may relax in the family
room or screened porch, and continental
breakfast offers home-baked goodies. $45-
55.

NEWBURYPORT

Bed and Breakfast/Inns of New England MA 1000
329 Lake Drive, Guilford, CT 06437
(800) 582-0853

Built in 1806 by Captain William Hoyt,
this estate typifies the three-story square
style of the Federal period. Among its
many fine architectural features are cor-
nices, mantles, balustrades, and a graceful
hanging staircase. There are summer and
winter porches, a formal front parlor, and
library. Many special events are offered
throughout the year, including weekend
murder mysteries, fashion shows, weddings, and corporate conferences. Just a
five-minute walk from downtown
Newburyport, a seaport area. There are
nine guest rooms on the inn's three floors,
all furnished in antiques and some with
canopied beds. Children 12 and older welcome. $50-77.

Morrill Place Inn
209 High Street, 01950
(508) 462-2808

This gracious 1806 Federal sea captain's
mansion is in Historic New England's seaport. Enjoy our cozy library, elegant dining
room, formal music parlor, and our summer
and winter porches. Each of the nine guest
rooms is appointed with fine antiques,
canopy four poster, or sleigh beds.

NOTES: Credit cards accepted: A Master Card; B Visa; C American Express; D Discover Card; E Diner's
Club; F Other; 2 Personal Checks accepted; 3 Lunch available; 4 Dinner available; 5 Open all year;

Host: Rose Ann Hunter
Rooms: 9 (3 PB; 6 SB) $60-90
Continental Breakfast
Credit Cards: None
Notes: 2, 5, 6, 9, 10, 11, 12

The Windsor House in Newburyport

38 Federal Street, 01950
(508) 462-3778; FAX (508) 465-3443

Built as a wedding present, this 18th-century Federal mansion offers a rare blend of Yankee hospitality and the English tradition of bed and breakfast. Designed as a residence/ship's chandlery, the inn's spacious rooms recall the spirit of an English country house. Situated in a historic seaport near a wildlife refuge. Whale watching, museums, theater, and antiques. Rates include afternoon tea, English cooked breakfast, tax, and service. Evening meal available November to May.

Hosts: Judith and John Harris
Rooms: 6 (3 PB; 3 SB) $75-115
Full Breakfast
Credit Cards: A, B, D
Notes: 2, 4, 5, 6, 8, 10, 11, 12, 13, 14

NEWTON

Beazie's on the Charles

Host Homes of Boston
P. O. Box 117, Boston, 02168
(617) 244-1308; FAX (617) 244-5156

In a sylvan setting along the Charles River, this Colonial is replete with Early Americana. Breakfast is served in the "Sturbridge" dining room. A second-floor guest room with view of river and woods. Also, single room if same party. Five blocks to village, Green Line-D, air conditioning, private bath, TV. $68.

Bed and Breakfast Associates #31

P. O. Box 57166, Boston 02157-0166
(617) 449-5302; (800) 347-5088

Guests enter from a driveway through a private entrance into a hideaway in the separate wing of this spacious 1876 antique Revival home. Large cathedral ceilings, queen-size beds, two studio beds, dining area, private bath, skylight, TV, refrigerator, microwave oven, and other amenities. $80.

Bed and Breakfast Associates #107

P. O. Box 57166, Boston, 02157-0166
(617) 449-5302; (800) 347-5088

Double four-poster, mahogany bed with private bath and many antiques in this small but comfortable room on the second floor of this home owned by a delightful couple, their son, and a great dog. Makings for a contiental breakfast stocked in the room. Plenty of parking available. $75.

Bed and Breakfast Associates #IW265

P. O. Box 57166, Babson Park Branch
Boston, 02157-0166
(617) 449-5302; FAX (617) 449-5958

This hostess will proudly show guests the distinctive interior and spectacular landscaping of the ranch-style home that her architect husband designed. Large windows afford delightful views of the seasonal splendor. This is one of Boston's best suburban neighborhoods. One guest room with private bath and a single den rented with guest room. Full breakfast; children over ten welcome. $50-80.

Bed and Breakfast Associates #IW270

P. O. Box 57166, Babson Park Branch,
Boston, 02157-0166
(617) 449-5302; FAX (617) 449-5958

6 Pets welcome; 8 Children welcome; 9 Social drinking allowed; 10 Tennis available; 11 Swimming available; 12 Golf available; 13 Skiing available; 14 May be booked through travel agents.

Situated on one acre in a neighborhood little changed since the 1890s, this grand home, furnished with 18th- and 19th-century antiques, is only 15 minutes from downtown Boston via the Massachusetts Pike. The dining room is graced with a beautiful fireplace as are both guest rooms. Full breakfast; children welcome. $60-65; family rates available.

Breamore by the Pike

Host Homes of Boston
P. O. Box 117, Boston, 02168
(617) 244-1308; FAX (617) 244-5156

Large, authentic Victorian home (1898) offers double and twin rooms. Both, if same party. This retired educator and vegetable gardener bakes fruit breads for breakfast. Three blocks to restaurants, express bus (11 minutes to Boston). Easy drive to airport, Cambridge. Air conditioning, private bath. $61-112.

The Carriage House

Bed and Breakfast Greater Boston & Cape Cod
P. O. Box 35, Newtonville, 02160
(617) 964-1606; (800) 832-2632
FAX (617) 332-8572

A charming, renovated private studio in a suburb just west of Boston. The first level has comfortable sitting area; second level has fully equipped kitchenette, private bath, sitting area with a comfortable double futon, two couches, wood-burning stove, color TV, air conditioning, and phone. Rate includes breakfast provided by host and self-served by guest. Weather permitting, guests may use the host's barbecue and back yard deck. Easy access by car or public transportation to Boston/Cambridge. Short walk to village shopping area with movie theater. Special rates for extended stays. $75.

Crescent Avenue Bed and Breakfast

Bed and Breakfast Greater Boston and Cape Cod
P. O. Box 35, Newtonville, 02160
(617) 964-1606; (800) 832-2632
FAX (617) 332-8572

In a lovely suburb just west of Boston with easy access to Boston/Cambridge, this gracious twelve-room Greek Revival circa late 1800s has a pool and lovely gardens. Two guest rooms with a private bath and separate entrance are available, and a generous continental breakfast is served in the dining room or the screened porch. $75-90.

The Evergreens

Host Homes of Boston
P. O. Box 117, Boston, 02168
(617) 244-1308; FAX (617) 244-5156

Older Colonial is filled with host's pottery and Mexican art collection. Two second-floor guest rooms share bath. Cozy screened porch. Five minutes walk to Boston College or Green Line-B to Boston University, Back Bay and Downtown. Air conditioning, shared bath. $46-57.

Meadowbrook Run

Host Homes of Boston
P. O. Box 117, Boston, 02168
(617) 244-1308; FAX (617) 244-5156

These hosts offer old-fashioned hospitality in their contemporary home on a quiet road. Enjoy a game of billiards in the den. First-floor guest room. Resident cat. Village, Green Line-D one mile. Near Boston College. Boston seven miles. Air conditioning, TV, private bath. $57.

Rockledge

Host Homes of Boston
P. O. Box 117, Boston, 02168
(617) 244-1308; FAX (617) 244-5156

NOTES: Credit cards accepted: A Master Card; B Visa; C American Express; D Discover Card; E Diner's Club; F Other; 2 Personal Checks accepted; 3 Lunch available; 4 Dinner available; 5 Open all year;

Stately 1882 Victorian in prime location. Cordial hosts offer bright, spacious rooms, antiques, trees, gardens. Three second-floor guest rooms, but only two booked at a time. Ceiling fans. Second-floor guest parlor. Resident cat. Two blocks to lake, village, and subway. Older children welcome. Shared bath, TV. $57.

The Suite at Chestnut Hill

Bed and Breakfast Greater Boston and Cape Cod
P. O. Box 35, Newtonville, 02160
(617) 964-1606; (800) 832-2632
FAX (617) 332-8572

This gorgeous furnished efficiency, situated in a neighborhood of very beautiful homes, offers easy access by public transportation to Boston/Cambridge. Efficiency has a kitchen area, full bath, color TV, phone, air conditioning separate dining, and sitting areas, and a queen bed. Self-catered breakfast provided. $90.

NEWTON CORNER

The Berry Patch

Bed and Breakfast Greater Boston and Cape Cod
P. O. Box 35, Newtonville, 02160
(617) 964-1606; (800) 832-2632
FAX (617) 332-8572

This three-story brick Colonial offers easy access to Boston/Cambridge by car or public transportation. The main guest room has a queen bed and private bath, and a second guest room has a pair of twins with a shared bath. Host serves a wonderful breakfast that features natural foods and home-baked goodies, and in July, fresh berries from the back yard berry patch. Children over 12 welcome. $55-70.

NORTH EASTHAM

Bed & Breakfast/Inns of New England MA-1051

329 Lake Drive, Guilford, CT 06437
(800) 582-0853

This house, a half-Cape with saltbox addition, is decorated with quilts and collectibles. In a quiet neighborhood less than a mile from Cape Cod National Seashore Visitor's Center, it is minutes from bay beaches, fresh water ponds, and two ocean beaches. Two guest rooms are available, both with shared baths. The first floor room has a king bed, and the upstairs room has a double bed. Resident dog; no guest pets. $50-60.

The Quilted Pineapple

Chester Avenue, P. O. Box 89, 02651
(508) 255-3709

For travelers looking for a cozy retreat, yet close to swimming and biking on Cape Cod, The Quilted Pineapple is the place. Situated less than a mile from the National Seashore Visitor's Center, Cape Cod Rail Trail, and the ocean. Bay or freshwater swimming is nearby. A substantial continental breakfast, including homemade breads and muffins, is served in the homey country kitchen.

Hosts: Emily and David Laribee
Rooms: 2 (SB) $55-65
Continental Breakfast
Credit Cards: None
Notes: 2, 5, 9, 10, 11, 12

NORTH FALMOUTH

Bed and Breakfast Cape Cod #45

Box 341, West Hyannisport, 02672
(508) 775-2772

6 Pets welcome; 8 Children welcome; 9 Social drinking allowed; 10 Tennis available; 11 Swimming available; 12 Golf available; 13 Skiing available; 14 May be booked through travel agents.

This 14-year old Cape Cod-style home was built amid tall trees and flourishing growth, featuring a parlor with a televison and fireplace. The ferry to Martha's Vineyard is 10 minutes away. Children over nine welcome. $55-60

Bed and Breakfast Cape Cod #57

P. O. Box 341, West Hyannisport, 02672
(508) 775-2772

This 1806 restored farmhouse captures the flavor of a bygone era. The second floor suite is available for guests. Two beaches are within a mile of the house. No children. $80.

NORTHFIELD

Berkshire Bed and Breakfast Homes PV14

P. O. Box 211, Williamsburg, 01096
(413) 268-7244

This 1890 Colonial home on two acres has country and Colonial furnishings. There is a parlor for guests' use, and a gift and craft shop on the premises. There are two guest rooms, one with a king-size bed and one with a queen-size bed. Both have private baths. Full breakfast. Children welcome. Resident pets. $55-65.

NORWELL

Bed and Breakfast Associates #SS330

P. O. Box 57166, Babson Park Branch
    Boston, 02157-0166
(617) 449-5302; FAX (617) 449-5958

Situated in the pretty suburban town of Norwell, this country home was built in

1810. The house features beamed ceilings, Oriental rugs, and antiques. Three guest rooms share a bath. Full breakfast; children welcome. $63.

OAK BLUFFS, MARTHA'S VINEYARD

Bed and Breakfast Nantucket/ Martha's Vineyard #201

P. O. Box 341, West Hyannisport, 02672-0341
(508) 775-2772; FAX (508) 775-2884

This 1872 Victorian cottage has six bedrooms for bed and breakfast and is one city block from the beaches. Bedrooms with private baths and king or double beds are available. Continental breakfast is served from 8:00 until 10:00 AM. Public tennis and public transportation to other parts of the island are two blocks away. $75-125.

ONSET

Bed and Breakfast Cape Cod #62

P. O. Box 341, West Hyannisport, 02672
(508) 775-2772; FAX (508) 775-2884

The upper Cape offers a world of beautiful beaches, great restaurants and water views. Built in 1880, this small inn is directly on Onset Bay. The 12 guest rooms are available with private or semi-private baths. Children over 11 welcome. $95-130.

ORLEANS

Bed and Breakfast Cape Cod #8

P. O. Box 341, West Hyannisport, 02672-0341
(508) 775-2772; FAX (508) 775-2884

This dramatic contemporary home is built on high ground and overlooks five acres of

NOTES: Credit cards accepted: A Master Card; B Visa; C American Express; D Discover Card; E Diner's Club; F Other; 2 Personal Checks accepted; 3 Lunch available; 4 Dinner available; 5 Open all year;

wooded land. The large deck is next to an in-ground pool. Interior features include a soaring cathedral ceiling, Oriental carpets, wood-burning fireplaces, and spiral staircase. Bedrooms have queen-size beds and private baths, and Nauset Beach is two miles away. A cottage is also available. Full breakfast. Children over 11 welcome. $90.

OSTERVILLE

Bed and Breakfast Cape Cod #65

P. O. Box 341, West Hyannisport, 02672-0341
(508) 775-2772; FAX (508) 775-2884

This house, built in 1730, was at one time the town's first library. Two upstairs bedrooms share a bath; one room has a double bed and the other room has a pair of twin beds. Only one party at a time accepted. This beautifully restored home is owned by a surgeon's wife and has lovely private gardens. Short walk to the village and the beach. $65.

OTIS

Berkshire Bed and Breakfast Homes SC6

P. O. Box 211, Williamsburg, 01096
(413) 268-7244

A 100-year-old country farmhouse on 15 acres. Antique furnishings throughout parlor and guest rooms with king and queen beds and semiprivate baths. Attic room available with private bath. Full breakfast; children over 10 welcome. $75-135.

PEABODY

1660 Antique Colonial

Bed and Breakfast Marblehead and North Shore
P. O. Box 35, Newtonville, 02160
(617) 964-1606; (800) 832-2632
FAX (617) 332-8572

This beautifully restored historic home provides you with comfortable accommodations in a home listed on the National Register of Historic Places. Furnished with wonderful antiques, the two guest suites each have a sitting room, private bath, fireplace, and air conditioning. Breakfast is served in the country kitchen, sun room, or terrace. By prior arrangement, the host will prepare dinner. $75-90.

PEMBROKE

Serenity

Be Our Guest Bed and Breakfast
P. O. Box 1333, Plymouth, 02362
(617) 837-9867

This beautiful circa 1700 antique Cape is completely restored and decorated with many fine antiques and works of art. There is one guest room with a fireplace, double bed, and private bath. Outside there are many beautiful plantings and trees around the corral that houses two horses. A full breakfast is served in either the dining room or the screened porch. $40-60.

PERU

The American Country Collection #069

4 Grenwood Lane, Delmar, NY 12054
(518) 439-7001

Built in 1830 as the town parsonage, this private homestay features the original wide-plank floors and floor-to-ceiling win-

6 Pets welcome; 8 Children welcome; 9 Social drinking allowed; 10 Tennis available; 11 Swimming available; 12 Golf available; 13 Skiing available; 14 May be booked through travel agents.

dows that look out onto old stone walls and 13 acres of woods. Guests dine in the sunroom with bay windows and French doors that lead out onto a patio. Two guest rooms on the second floor; one features a double bed and private bath, while the other has two twin beds and a private bath. Close to Tanglewood, Jacob's Pillow, Ski Berkshire Snow Basin, and other area attractions. No children. Resident cat. Breakfast available. $55-60.

Bed and Breakfast Accommodations 069

984 Gloucester Place, Schenectady, NY 12309
(518) 370-4948

Built in 1830 as the town parsonage, this private homestay features the original wide-plank floors and floor-to-ceiling windows that look out onto old stone walls and 13 acres of woods. Guests dine in a sun room with bay windows and French doors that lead onto a patio. The decor is French country, and the home is furnished with antiques and colorful Waverly and Laura Ashley chintz fabrics. Three excellent cross-country centers and one downhill ski area are within an eight-mile radius. Two bedrooms with private baths. $55; $60 6/1-10/31.

Berkshire Bed and Breakfast Homes NC8

P. O. Box 211, Williamsburg, 01096
(413) 268-7244

1815 Federal-style home on the historic register is on 13 acres. Guest rooms with private and semiprivate baths share a sun room and patio. Continental breakfast; children over 13 welcome. $55-65.

Berkshire Bed and Breakfast Homes NC13

P. O. Box 211, Williamsburg, 01096
(413) 268-7244

A 1970 Garrison-style apartment on 160 acres of land. Country and colonial furnishings. The apartment contains sitting room with TV, kitchenette, full bath, queen and twin rooms. Pond on premises and lots of hiking. Continental breakfast supplies; children welcome. $50-95.

PLYMOUTH

Bed and Breakfast Associates #SS795

P. O. Box 57166, Babson Park Branch
   Boston, 02157-0166
(617) 449-5302; (800) 347-5088

This spectacular restoration of an 1820 Cape-style home provides gracious accommodations with American and English antiques. The home is set on 40 acres, just six minutes from Plymouth Rock. Full breakfast. $68.

Brookside Farm

Be Our Guest Bed and Breakfast, Ltd.
P. O. Box 1333, 02362
(617) 837-9867

This lovely contemporary home is situated on nine acres that provide privacy. A guest room with twin beds is beautifully decorated with hand stenciling. A full breakfast is served in a true country kitchen. Walk through the meticulously groomed gardens that surround a running stream. Easy access to Plymouth (15 minutes), and Boston (50 minutes). $45.

NOTES: Credit cards accepted: A Master Card; B Visa; C American Express; D Discover Card; E Diner's Club; F Other; 2 Personal Checks accepted; 3 Lunch available; 4 Dinner available; 5 Open all year;

Center Street Bed and Breakfast

Be Our Guest Bed and Breakfast, Ltd.
P. O. Box 1333, 02362
(617) 837-9867

This historic Colonial, built in 1735, has many period features throughout the house. Minutes off the highway and five miles to Plymouth Center. Two adjoining guest rooms, each with a double bed, share a bath. Beautifully decorated, these rooms will make you feel right at home. A full breakfast is served. Ideal for families and parties traveling together. $50.

Country Living

Be Our Guest Bed and Breakfast, Ltd.
P. O. Box 1333, 02362
(617) 837-9867

Only a 20-minute drive from Boston, this lovely 136-year-old farmhouse is accessible from the highway for easy travel to Plymouth Center in 20 minutes and the Cape in 45 minutes. A twin guest room shares a bath with the hosts. Beautifully decorated, this cozy country retreat displays the host's talent for flower arranging throughout. Full breakfast is served. Many fine restaurants nearby. $50.

Foxglove Cottage

Be Our Guest Bed and Breakfast, Ltd.
P. O. Box 1333, 02362
(617) 837-9867

Situated less than a mile from Plymouth Plantation, this lovely Cape circa 1820 has been carefully restored. Two guest rooms share a common bath and are decorated in Laura Ashley and Waverly prints. One room offers a double bed and another room offers a pair of twins. A full breakfast is served on the deck overlooking acres of conservation land. $65.

The Little Inn

Be Our Guest Bed and Breakfast, Ltd.
P. O. Box 1333, 02362
(617) 837-9867

This 200-year-old Federal Colonial offers three guest rooms. A white-wicker room has a queen bed and private bath. The brass room has an antique double bed and shares a bath with an adjoining room, furnished with twin mahogany sleigh beds. Built in 1785, the home has fireplaces throughout and many antique furnishings. Close to the beach, the Little Inn is set on a scenic road 40 minutes south of Boston and 20 minutes north of Plymouth Center. The mid-Cape is less than an hour's drive. A full breakfast is served in the fireplaced dining room. Children welcome. $60.

Main Street Bed and Breakfast

Be Our Guest Bed and Breakfast, Ltd.
P. O. Box 1333, 02362
(617) 837-9867

Equally close to Boston and Plymouth, this beautiful contemporary home offers a quiet escape from their hustle and bustle. Enjoy a guest suite with a loft bedroom and queen bed, private bath with Jacuzzi, and living area that opens out to a deck. The host, a gourmet cook, offers a hearty full breakfast. Close to shopping and restaurants. $60.

Marshview

Be Our Guest Bed and Breakfast, Ltd.
P. O. Box 1333, 02362
(617) 837-9867

This Cape-style home offers beautiful views of the marshland. Only 40 minutes south of Boston and 25 minutes north of Plymouth, the location is ideal for seeing both. A guest wing offers two guest rooms. The rooms share one and one-half baths

6 Pets welcome; 8 Children welcome; 9 Social drinking allowed; 10 Tennis available; 11 Swimming available; 12 Golf available; 13 Skiing available; 14 May be booked through travel agents.

and a sitting room with a TV. A private entrance opens out to a large deck overlooking the marsh. A full breakfast is served on the deck, weather permitting. Ideal for families. $50.

QUINCY

Quincy Adams Bed and Breakfast

Host Homes of Boston
P. O. Box 117, Boston, 02168
(617) 244-1308; FAX (617) 244-5156

This elegant turn-of-the-century home near the ocean has fireplaces, canopy beds, and a den with a TV and hot tub. There are three guest rooms; two have queen-size beds and the third-floor maid's quarters has a double. Near Bayside Expo Center, restaurants, and historic mansions. Boston is 15 minutes away, and the Red Line is one block away. $68-75.

REHOBOTH

Gilbert's Bed and Breakfast

30 Spring Street, 02769
(508) 252-6416

A 150-year-old New England Cape home with authentic hardware, wood floors, and

Gilbert's

windows. Situated on 100-acre tree farm only 12 miles east of Providence, Rhode Island. Guests may enjoy in-ground pool, hiking and pony cart rides. Delicious full country breakfasts.

Hosts: Jeanne and Peter Gilbert
Rooms: 3 (SB) $45-50
Full Breakfast
Credit Cards: None
Notes: 2, 5, 6 (horses $15/night), 8, 9, 10, 11, 12, 14

RICHMOND

Berkshire Bed and Breakfast Homes SC17

P. O. Box 211, Williamsburg, 01096
(413) 268-7244

A Geodesic-style home built by the owners. This dome-shaped home is on three rural acres and is furnished with country collectibles. There is a king-size bed and a private bath. A Hide-a-bed is also available. Continental breakfast. Children welcome. $65.

ROCKPORT

Bed & Breakfast/Inns of New England MA-1005

329 Lake Drive, Guilford, CT 06437
(800) 5882-0853

An intimate, welcoming guest house open year-round, situated only one block from Main Street and the T-Wharf, which is full of shops, galleries, and restaurants. Leave the car and walk to everything. A spacious sun deck is reserved for guests. Television, games, magazines, and books are available. Guests have use of their own refrigerator. Seven rooms are available. Children welcome. Resident cat; no guest pets. $58-70.

NOTES: Credit cards accepted: A Master Card; B Visa; C American Express; D Discover Card; E Diner's Club; F Other; 2 Personal Checks accepted; 3 Lunch available; 4 Dinner available; 5 Open all year;

Bed & Breakfast/Inns of New England MA-1006

329 Lake Drive, Guilford, CT 06437
(800) 582-0853

A small, centrally located inn limited to non-smokers, this 1987 facility is within a five-minute walk from Rockport's art galleries, Headlands beach, restaurants, and shops. Three ground-floor larger-than-average rooms with private bathrooms are available with king or queen beds; all three have private bathrooms. All rooms have controlled air conditioning and heat, cable TV, refrigerators, and microwaves. No children. No pets. $85 (June 12 to September 14); $80 off season.

The Inn on Cove Hill

37 Mount Pleasant Street, 01966
(508) 546-2701

A friendly atmosphere with the option of privacy, this painstakingly restored 200-year-old Federal home is two blocks from the harbor and shops. Meticulously appointed, cozy bedrooms are furnished with antiques, and some have canopy beds. Wake up to the delicious aroma of hot muffins, and enjoy a continental breakfast at the umbrella tables in the Pump Garden.

Hosts: John and Marjorie Pratt
Rooms: 11 (9 PB; 2 SB) $47-95
Continental Breakfast
Credit Cards: None
Notes: 2, 9, 11, 12

Mooringstone for Nonsmokers

12 Norwood Avenue, 01966
(508) 546-2479

A ground-floor wing has been added to this home for our guests to enjoy a private bath and room-controlled air conditioning. Each room has comfortable beds, private baths, room-controlled-air conditioning,

cable TV, refrigerator, microwave oven, parking, etc. Breakfast includes delicious homemade muffins and breads. Park and walk to the beach, restaurants, shops, art galleries, and picturesque headlands, or take day trips to the many special places in this area. Ten to 50 percent off for longer stays. No room tax.

Hosts: David and Mary Knowlton
Rooms: 3 (PB) $70-79
Continental Breakfast
Credit Cards: A, B, C
Notes: 2, 9, 10, 11, 12, 14

The Seafarer

Be Our Guest Bed and Breakfast, Ltd.
P. O. Box 1333, Plymouth, 02362
(617) 837-9867

Just 45 minutes north of Boston in the quaint seaside community of Rockport, this lovely bed and breakfast offers six guest rooms. Each room is unique, and each has an ocean view. Some rooms are equipped with kitchenettes, all have TVs and refrigerators. An apartment is also available on a weekly basis. A lovely continental breakfast is served on the deck overlooking the bay. Within walking distance of the village and the beach. $60-80.

SAGAMORE BEACH

Bed and Breakfast Cape Cod #36

Box 341, West Hyannisport, 02672
(508) 775-2772; FAX (508) 775-2884

Situated on the banks of beautiful Cape Cod Bay is this lovely two-story beach house with spectacular water views. It is only a short drive to fine restaurants and shops. Breakfast is served with home-baked goods in the dining room overlooking the ocean. $75-95.

6 Pets welcome; 8 Children welcome; 9 Social drinking allowed; 10 Tennis available; 11 Swimming available; 12 Golf available; 13 Skiing available; 14 May be booked through travel agents.

SALEM

Amelia Payson House

16 Winter Street, 01970
(508) 744-8304

Built in 1845, this fine example of Greek
Revival architecture is situated in the heart
of Salem's historic district. Guest rooms
are furnished with canopy or brass beds
and antiques. A five-minute stroll to downtown shopping, historic houses, museums,
Pickering Wharf's waterfront dining, and
train station. Brochures available.

Hosts: Ada and Donald Roberts
Rooms: 4 (PB) $75-85
Continental Breakfast
Credit Cards: A, B, C
Notes: 5, 8 (over 12), 9, 10, 11, 12

Essex Street Bed and Breakfast

Bed and Breakfast Marblehead and North Shore
P. O. Box 35, Newtonville, 02160
(617) 964-1606; (800) 832-2632
FAX (617) 332-8572

This turn-of-the-century wood frame house
is in the McIntyre historic district of Salem.
The hosts have lovingly labored to restore
their home to its former elegance and
charm. One guest room with private bath,
separate entrance, and air conditioning is
available. Continental breakfast is served.
Children welcome. $75-85.

The Inn at Seven Winter Street

7 Winter Street, 01970
(508) 745-9520

The inn is situated in the heart of historic
Salem, within walking distance of all that
the town's rich heritage has to offer —
including museums, shops, and quaint
restaurants. The building is a magnificently
restored French Second Empire home built

in 1870 by a wealthy merchant. All rooms
have something wonderfully unique, such a
working marble fireplaces, canopy beds, or
Victorian bath. Breakfast is served in the
main parlor.

Hosts: Sally Flint, Dee and Jill Coté
Rooms: 9 (PB) $65-125
Continental Breakfast
Credit Cards: A, B, C, D
Notes: 2, 5, 8, 9, 10, 11, 12, 13

The Schoolhouse Bed and Breakfast

Bed and Breakfast Marblehead and North Shore
P. O. Box 35, Newtonville, 02160
(617) 964-1606; (800) 832-2632
FAX (617) 332-8572

A beautifully decorated home in a turn-of-
the-century school converted to a condominium, featuring skylights and cathedral
ceilings. This bed and breakfast is a short
walk from the Salem commuter rail station.
One guest room with private bath and TV.
Continental breakfast. Attractive livingroom with TV and designated parking. Air
conditioning. Children welcome if over
five or infants. No pets. $65-75.

The Suite at the Tannet Woods House

Bed and Breakfast Marblehead and North Shore
P. O. Box 35, Newtonville, 02632
(617) 964-1606; (800) 832-2632
FAX (617) 332-8572

The Inn at Seven Winter Street

Built in 1799, the Tannet Woods House was originally a four-room carpenter shop. The guest area includes a completely furnished three-room suite with modern kitchen and bath, color TV, sun deck, separate guest entrance, and parking. It has heat and air conditioning for year-round comfort. The hosts provide a generous supply of breakfast foods, self-prepared by the guest. Easy access by computer rail to Boston and other North Shore locations. Sleeps up to three adults. Children welcome. $85-100.

SANDWICH

Bed and Breakfast Cape Cod #1

P. O. Box 341, West Hyannisport, 02672-0341
(508) 775-2772; FAX (508) 775-2884

This elegant Victorian-style house was built in 1849 and meticulously restored in 1987. The five guest rooms have private baths and are furnished with antiques. The first-floor common rooms for dining and reading are available for guest use. A continental breakfast is served each morning in the dining room. Convenient to many fine restaurants, Heritage Plantation, Sandwich Glass Museum, and the beach. No children under 12. $65-110.

Bed and Breakfast Cape Cod #20

Box 341, West Hyannisport, 02672
(508) 775-2772; FAX (508) 775-2884

Overlooking a beautiful pond, across the street from the oldest house on Cape Cod, this circa-1920 home is a choice bed and breakfast location. Nicely restored and beautifully maintained, it features a four-room second floor suite complete with full kitchen, television, and an air conditioned bedroom. Convenient to local shops, historical sites, and fine restaurants, this interesting accommodation is ideal for guests with infants and older children. $80.

Bed and Breakfast Cape Cod #22

P. O. Box 341, West Hyannisport, 02672-0341
(508) 775-2772; FAX (508) 775-2884

This elegant Victorian-style house in the heart of Sandwich has six bedrooms, most of which offer private baths. In the center of the oldest village on Cape Cod, this inn is within walking distance of fine restaurants, beaches, trails, museums, and parks. A continental breakfast is served in the large dining room. Children over five welcome. $55-85.

Bed and Breakfast Cape Cod #31

P. O. Box 341, West Hyannisport, 02672-0341
(508) 775-2772; FAX (508) 775-2884

The design of this 1699 built home reflects the charm of early America. Three bedrooms with private baths are furnished with antiques or furniture with an Early American design. Across the street from a saltwater marsh full of birds, this bed and breakfast is short walk to many restaurants and shops. A continental breakfast is served in a keeping room with a beehive oven. Children over 12 welcome. $65-75.

Bed and Breakfast Cape Cod #55

P. O. Box 341, West Hyannisport, 02672-0341
(508) 775-2772; FAX (508) 775-2884

This beautiful contemporary home overlooks the Cape Cod Canal. Three spacious guest rooms offer private baths, ocean views, TV, refrigerators, phones, and spe-

6 Pets welcome; 8 Children welcome; 9 Social drinking allowed; 10 Tennis available; 11 Swimming available; 12 Golf available; 13 Skiing available; 14 May be booked through travel agents.

cial touches that enhance any holiday stay. One bedroom has a whirlpool tub for two and a king-size bed. A continental breakfast is served each morning from 8:00-10:30 A.M. in the guest's room, on the deck, or in the dining area. No children. $100-150.

Capt. Ezra Nye House

152 Main Street, 02563
(508) 888-6142; (800) 388-2278

Comfort and warmth, amid antique-filled rooms, some with fireplaces and canopies, make your stay a treat in this 1829 Federal home. Museums, lake, restaurants within a block. Featured in *Glamour* and *Innsider* magazines. "Thank you for opening your hearts and your home to us. . . You have made our first trip to Cape Cod a memorable one!"

Hosts: Elaine and Harry Dickson
Rooms: 7 (4 PB; 2 SB) $55-90
Suite: 1(PB)
Full Breakfast
Credit Cards: A, B, C, D
Notes: 2, 5, 8 (over 5), 9, 10, 11, 12, 14

The Summer House

158 Main Street, 02563
(508) 888-4991

Elegant circa 1835 Greek Revival bed and breakfast featured in *Country Living* magazine, in the heart of historic Sandwich Village, Cape Cod's oldest town (settled 1637). Antiques, hand-stitched quilts, fireplaces, flowers, large sunny rooms, English-style gardens. Close to dining, museums, shops, pond, and gristmill, boardwalk to beach. Bountiful breakfast, elegantly served. Afternoon tea in the garden included.

Hosts: David and Kay Merrell
Rooms: 5 (1 PB; 4 SB) $50-75
Full Breakfast
Credit Cards: A, B, C, D
Notes: 2, 5, 8 (over 6), 9, 10, 11, 12, 14

SCITUATE

Bed and Breakfast Associates #SS250

P. O. Box 57166, Babson Park Branch
  Boston, 02157-0166
(617) 449-5302; FAX (617) 449-5958

Situated just one mile from the ocean, this pretty home affords visitors to the South Shore the opportunity to relax and enjoy nearby tennis, yacht club, pool, and clam digging. The hosts are active tennis players. Two guest rooms, one with private bath. Full breakfast on weekends; children welcome. $50-55; family and monthly rates available.

Bed and Breakfast Associates #SS260

P. O. Box 57166, Babson Park Branch
  Boston, 02157-0166
(617) 449-5302; FAX (617) 449-5958

Offered by a gourmet caterer and her husband, this circa 1905 home is a scant two-minute walk from Scituate Harbor. They have lovingly remodeled their fine bed and breakfast and filled it with period furniture, classical music, and English-style hospitality. Guests will make themselves comfort-

The Summer House

NOTES: Credit cards accepted: A Master Card; B Visa; C American Express; D Discover Card; E Diner's Club; F Other; 2 Personal Checks accepted; 3 Lunch available; 4 Dinner available; 5 Open all year;

able in the cheerful parlor, indulge in the fabulous gourmet breakfast (or ask for a low-cal or "happy heart" diet), relax before the Edwardian fireplace, or gaze out at the yachts in the bustling harbor. A short stroll will lead to local shops and seafood restaurants. Three guest rooms, two with private baths. Full breakfast; children over 16 welcome. $79-89.

Bed and Breakfast Cape Cod #64

P. O. Box 341, West Hyannisport, 02672-0341
(508) 775-2772; FAX (508) 775-2884

Ocean views and English elegance characterize this 1905 Victorian-style inn. Four guest rooms feature queen or double-size beds and water views; two rooms have a private bath and two other rooms share a bath. These English hosts serve a full gourmet breakfast in the morning, and afternoon tea at 5:00 P.M. each day. Breakfast is served in the Victorian dining room or on a porch overlooking the harbor. No children. $65-95.

Bed and Breakfast Cape Cod #76

Box 341, West Hyannisport, 02672
(508) 775-2772

From the windows of this 1973 contemporary home, built directly on the harbor at Scituate, there is a 180 degree view of the ocean. The house has a queen size bedroom with a private tub and shower bath. A full breakfast is served in a dining area with water views. Cable TV is also available. The location is ideal for a 35 minute bus ride to downtown Boston, or drive in the opposite direction to Plymouth and on to Cape Cod. Bring bikes for use on the trails near the water. $75.

Harborside

Be Our Guest Bed and Breakfast, Ltd.
P. O. Box 1333, Plymouth, 02362
(617) 837-9867

Commanding ocean views from every angle. This contemporary-style beach house overlooks the open ocean on one side and picturesque Scituate Harbor on the other. One air-conditioned guest room and a private bath. Continental breakfast is served. Resident dog. $45-65.

Sycamore

Be Our Guest Bed and Breakfast, Ltd.
P. O. Box 1333, Plymouth, 02362
(617) 837-9867

Conveniently situated between Boston and Plymouth, this ranch-style home is within walking distance of the harbor. Beautifully decorated with a blend of contemporary and antiques. A lovely lace-filled guest room with a queen bed, private bath, and deck. A second twin room, again decorated beautifully, shares a bath with the hosts. A full breakfast is served. Walk to shops and restaurants. $50.

SEARSPORT

Homeport Inn

Box 647, East Main Street, Route 1, 04974
(207) 548-2259

Homeport, listed on the National Register of Historic Places, is a fine example of a New England sea captain's mansion situated on beautifully landscaped grounds, with flower gardens and pond that extends to the ocean. This elegant home is furnished with family heirlooms and antiques. There are ten guest rooms, six with private baths. A Victorian cottage is also available. A visit offers a rare opportunity to vacation or be an overnight guest in a warm, homey, hospitable atmosphere without the customary travelers commercialism.

6 Pets welcome; 8 Children welcome; 9 Social drinking allowed; 10 Tennis available; 11 Swimming available; 12 Golf available; 13 Skiing available; 14 May be booked through travel agents.

Hosts: Edith and George Johnson
Rooms: 10 (6 PB; 4 SB) $55-75
Cottage: $450
Full Breakfast
Credit Cards: A, B, C, D, F
Notes: 2, 5, 8, 9, 10, 11, 12, 13, 14

SHEFFIELD

Berkshire Bed and Breakfast Homes SC19

P. O. Box 211, Williamsburg, 01096
(413) 268-7244

An 1815 Colonial on five acres. Formal furnishings. Parlor, screened-in porch, and in-ground pool for guests. One king room with private bath; other rooms share a bath. Full breakfast; children over 16 welcome. $85-150. Closed November to May.

Covered Bridge 1SHMA

P. O. Box 447A, Norfolk, CT 06058
(203) 542-5944

This charming log home, with a sweeping view of the Berkshires, is the perfect spot for an idyllic pastoral retreat. A horse grazes nearby, and it's a short walk across the fields to the swimming pond. A full breakfast is served in the kitchen or on the porch. The host, an actress, has traveled extensively and is also well informed about area activities. There are two double guest rooms that share a bath. $85.

Covered Bridge 2SHMA

P. O. Box 447A, Norfolk, CT 06058
(203) 542-5944

This 1771 Colonial set in the village of Sheffield is surrounded by antique shops and close to Tanglewood. There are several common rooms for guests to enjoy as well as a tree-shaded terrace. A full breakfast is served in the dining room. The guest rooms are decorated with antiques. Three

rooms share a bath, and one room has a private bath. $80-90.

Ramblewood Inn— A Unique Bed and Breakfast

Box 729, Undermountain Road, 01257
(413) 229-3363

This stylish country house, furnished for comfort and romance, is situated in a beautiful natural setting of mountains, pine forests, and a serene private lake for swimming and canoeing. Private baths, fireplaces, central air, lovely gardens, and gourmet breakfasts. Convenient to all Berkshire attractions: Tanglewood, drama and dance festivals, antiques, Lime Rock Racing, skiing, and hiking.

Hosts: June and Martin Ederer
Rooms: 6 (PB) $95-110
Full Breakfast
Minimum stay weekends and holidays: 2 days
Credit Cards: A, B
Notes: 5, 8, 9, 10, 11, 12, 13

SOMMERVILLE

Bed and Breakfast Associates #IN176

P. O. Box 57166, Babson Park Branch
   Boston, 02157-0166
(617) 449-5302; (800) 347-5088

This pleasant modern two-bedroom apartment has a full kitchen, livingroom, dining area, and small balcony. Continental self-serve breakfast. $85.

SOUTH DARTMOUTH

The Little Red House

631 Elm Street, 02748
(508) 996-4554

A charming gambrel Colonial home situated in the lovely coastal village of

NOTES: Credit cards accepted: A Master Card; B Visa; C American Express; D Discover Card; E Diner's Club; F Other; 2 Personal Checks accepted; 3 Lunch available; 4 Dinner available; 5 Open all year;

Pandanaram is beautifully furnished with country accents, antiques, fireplace, luxurious four-poster or brass and iron beds. The backyard gazebo offers a perfect setting for relaxing moments. Breakfast in the romantic candlelit dining room is a delectable treat. Close to the harbor, beaches, restaurants, historic sites, New Bedford, Newport, Plymouth, Boston, and Cape Cod.

Host: Meryl Scully
Rooms: 2 (SB) $65
Full Breakfast
Credit Cards: None
Notes: 2, 5, 11, 12, 14

SOUTH DEERFIELD

Bed & Breakfast/Inns of New England MA-1015

329 Lake Drive, Guilford, CT 06437
(800) 582-0853

This old country house is in the heart of a historical and cultural area and is set on the site of the Bloody Brook Massacre of 1675. Furnished with period antiques, it is just four miles from historic Deerfield and ten minutes from the five college area. Three air-conditioned guest rooms, one with a private bath, are available. Children age ten and over are welcome. No pets. $70-85 (in season); $40-65 (off season).

SOUTH NATICK

Bed and Breakfast Associates #IW545

P. O. Box 57166, Babson Park Branch
Boston, 02157-0166
(617) 449-5302; FAX (617) 449-5958

This striking home in a rural setting features a light and airy guest room with double bed and private attached bath. Turret staircase leads to this second-floor room and the third-floor den. Generous continental breakfast; children over ten welcome. $75-95; weekly and monthly rates available.

SOUTH ORLEANS

Bed and Breakfast Cape Cod #80

P. O. Box 341, West Hyannisport, 02672-0341
(508) 775-2772; FAX (508) 775-2884

On high ground above Pleasant Bay, this 1973 Cape Cod-style home offers three bedrooms. One is a large room with a queen-size bed and private bath, and the other two share a bath and have a queen-size or a pair of twins. This lovely home is convenient to both Chatham and Orleans shops and restaurants. The deck is great for relaxing after spending the day at the beach. $55-70.

SPRINGFIELD

Berkshire Bed and Breakfast Homes GS6

P. O. Box 211, Williamsburg, 01096
(413) 268-7244

An 1896 Greek Revival on one-fourth acre. Colonial and antique furnishings in guest rooms with shared baths and parlor. Porch is also available to guests. View of the local park. Continental breakfast; children welcome. $45-75.

STOCKBRIDGE—SEE ALSO SOUTH LEE

Berkshire Bed and Breakfast Homes SC9

P. O. Box 211, Williamsburg, 01096
(413) 268-7244

An 1865 Federal-style home on three acres with antique-furnished guest rooms, private baths, and canopy beds. Swimming pool, patio, and parlor for guests. Full breakfast. $90 winter (continental breakfast); $150 summer.

6 Pets welcome; 8 Children welcome; 9 Social drinking allowed; 10 Tennis available; 11 Swimming available; 12 Golf available; 13 Skiing available; 14 May be booked through travel agents.

Merrell Tavern Inn

Merrell Tavern Inn

Route 102, Main Street, South Lee, 01260
(413) 243-1794; (800) 243-1794

This 200-year-old brick stagecoach inn situated in a small New England village along
the banks of the Housatonic River is listed
on the National Register of Historic Places.
Rooms with fireplaces, canopy beds, and
antique furnishings. Full breakfast is served
in the original tavern room. Smoking is not
allowed on the first floor or any of the public rooms. One mile to Norman Rockwell's
beloved Stockbridge.

Hosts: Charles and Faith Reynolds
Rooms: 9 (PB) $55-140
Full Breakfast
Credit Cards: A, B,
Notes: 2, 5, 8, 9, 11, 12, 13

STOW

Bed and Breakfast Associates #CW325

P. O. Box 57166, Babson Park Branch
  Boston, 02157-0166
(617) 449-5302; FAX (617) 449-5958

Authentic Colonial farmhouse circa 1734
features romantic guest rooms. Honeymoon

suite has a sitting room, Jacuzzi in the bath,
queen-size canopy bed. All guest rooms
have hand-made quilts, decorative fireplaces, and antique furnishings. $75-100.

STURBRIDGE

Berkshire Bed and Breakfast Homes ST2

P. O. Box 211, Williamsburg, 01096
(413) 268-7244

This contemporary home built in 1986 sits
on two and one-half acres and is furnished
in antiques. There is a parlor and a ground-
floor atrium with a sitting area and a TV
for guests. There are two bedrooms, one
with a double bed and one with twin beds,
and a semiprivate bath. Continental breakfast is served. Children over ten welcome.
$65.

Berkshire Bed and Breakfast Homes ST3

P. O. Box 211, Williamsburg, 01096
(413) 268-7244

A 1971 Dutch Colonial on one acre. One
guest room with private bath; others share a
bath. Country and antique furnishings
throughout. High English tea by reservation
only. Full breakfast; children welcome.
$65-75.

SUDBURY

Bed and Breakfast Associates #CW640

P. O. Box 57166, Babson Park Branch
  Boston, 02157-0166
(617) 449-5302; (800) 347-5088

This exquisite 1929 Dutch Colonial features a world-class collection of antique

carousel horses tastefully integrated with traditional furnishings. Set on several acres with an in-ground pool. Continental breakfast. $95.

Carousel House

Host Homes of Boston
P. O. Box 117, Boston, 02168
(617) 244-1308; FAX (617) 244-2700

This countryside estate, isolated on a hilltop near Concord offers three guest rooms with outstanding amenities. Second-floor Victorian and Green rooms have queen beds, Jacuzzi, and shower baths, and the third-floor Rose room has a pair of twin beds and a shower bath. Grounds include a private golf course and swimming pool, and antique carousel horses artfully blend with traditional decor to make this a special place to stay. $95.

Vine Cottage

Host Homes of Boston
P. O. Box 117, Waban Branch, 02168
(617) 244-1308; FAX (617) 244-5156

In quaint Sudbury Center near the village green, the host's carriage house (circa 1900) combines antiques with modern comfort. The guest entrance leads to a spacious parlor where a buffet breakfast is served. The second-floor features two large bedrooms, one king and one with two doubles. Near historic Concord and country restaurants. Just 15 minutes to I-95 and 30 minutes to Boston. $81-95.

SWAMPSCOTT

Bed and Breakfast Associates #NS200

P. O. Box 57166, Babson Park Branch
Boston, 02157-0166
(617) 449-5302; FAX (617) 449-5958

Just two and one-half blocks to a sandy beach. This hostess collects antiques, refinishes furniture, and enjoys quilting. As a tour escort around New England, she has a wealth of information to share with her guests. Her small Colonial home in a quiet neighborhood is neat and clean. Three guest rooms share a bath. Full breakfast; children over 12 welcome. $50-60; family and monthly rates available.

Harborview Victorian

Bed and Breakfast Marblehead and North Shore
P. O. Box 35, Newtonville, 02160
(617) 964-1606; (800) 832-2632
FAX (617) 332-8572

This lovely Victorian offers a marvelous view of the ocean. Four guest rooms share two baths, and two of the rooms have ocean views. Each room has a color TV, and a guest refrigerator and phone are provided in the guest hallway. Five-minute walk to bus or train for easy access to Boston, Salem, or Marblehead. Hosts will also provide airport pickup by prior arrangement. Children over six welcome. $65-75.

Ocean View

Host Homes of Boston
P. O. Box 117, Waban Branch, 02168
(617) 244-1308; FAX (617) 244-5156

Built on a land grant from the king of England, this sprawling country-style Victorian has the best ocean view in town. Down the hill are fine restaurants, shops, beaches, and the bus to Boston, and two lovely second-floor guest rooms, one with a queen bed and the other a double bed, are available. Fireplaced kitchen, and ground and deck with a view add to the amenities this bed and breakfast offers. Children welcome. $75-85.

6 Pets welcome; 8 Children welcome; 9 Social drinking allowed; 10 Tennis available; 11 Swimming available; 12 Golf available; 13 Skiing available; 14 May be booked through travel agents.

TOPSFIELD

The Wild Berry Bed and Breakfast

Bed and Breakfast Marblehead and North Shore
P. O. Box 35, Newtonville, 02160
(617) 964-1606; (800) 832-2632
FAX (617) 332-8572

A Greek Revival home with all the modern amenities in an area of large properties. This bed and breakfast is close to Hood's Pond, where guests may swim. In winter, guests may use cross-country ski trails behind the house. Livingroom with large stone fireplace and TV. Two guest rooms, one with private bath. Full breakfast. Children welcome. Pets in residence. Guest pets by prior arrangement. $60-85.

VINEYARD HAVEN, MARTHA'S VINEYARD

Bed and Breakfast Nantucket/Martha's Vineyard #205

P. O. Box 341, West Hyannisport, 02672-0341
(508) 775-2771; FAX (508) 775-2884

This house was built nearly 100 years ago as a private home. Later it was used for 40 years as a guest house. It was restored several years ago, and the present owner uses eight rooms for bed and breakfast. Each room has a private bath, and all are clean and bright with tasteful decor. The continental breakfast is served in a common room where guests meet and greet one another. Walk to all Vineyard Haven shops, stores, and restaurants. Bike rental available on the premises. $75-150.

Twin Oaks Inn

8 Edgartown Road, P. O. Box 1767, 02568
(508) 693-8633; (800) 696-8633 (MA only)

This cozy turn-of-the-century farmhouse is decorated with antiques, romantic floral prints, and pastel colors. Walking distance to the ferry, town, shopping, recreation. Four rooms share full baths in the main house, and a one-bedroom apartment with a fireplace and sun room is also available. Nightly and weekly rates are available. Off-season rates. Open year round.

Host: Doris L. Stewart
Rooms: 4 (SB) $75-95; apartment-$160; in season
Continental Breakfast
Credit Cards: A, B
Notes: 2, 5, 8, 9, 10, 11, 12, 14

WAQUOIT

Mariners Cove Bed and Breakfast

Host Homes of Boston
P. O. Box 117, Waban Branch, 02168
(617) 244-1308; FAX (617) 244-5156

Contemporary on the water, with glass walls, cathedral ceilings, view of Vineyard Sound. Two second-floor guest rooms with decks. Passive solarium, bubbling spa. Children over 11 welcome. Near Falmouth and Hyannis. Summer only. Shared bath; private beach. $85; weekly $550.

WARE

Berkshire Bed and Breakfast Homes PV22

P. O. Box 211, Williamsburg, 01096
(413) 268-7244

This 1880 Colonial with colonial furnishings offers five guest rooms sharing baths and a parlor. Full breakfast; children welcome. $50-75.

The Wildwood Inn

121 Church Street, 01082
(413) 967-7798

NOTES: Credit cards accepted: A Master Card; B Visa; C American Express; D Discover Card; E Diner's Club; F Other; 2 Personal Checks accepted; 3 Lunch available; 4 Dinner available; 5 Open all year;

A homey, welcoming 1880 Victorian furnished in American primitive antiques, handmade heirlooms, new quilts, and early cradles greet guests as they drive up a maple canopied street, with stately Victorian homes. Relax in the hammock, swing, or rock on the wraparound front porch. Try a jigsaw puzzle or board game. Play croquet, frisbee, or sit under the fir trees and read. Wander in the 110-acre park. Canoeing, bicycling, and skiing nearby. An easy drive to the five college area, Old Sturbridge, and Deerfield, the Basketball Hall of Fame. This inn's motto is "The NO-LUNCH breakfast."

Hosts: Fraidell Fenster and Richard Watson
Rooms: 7 (SB) $38-74
Full Breakfast
Credit Cards: C
Notes: 2, 5, 8 (over 6), 9, 10, 11, 12, 13, 14

WELLESLEY

Washington Place

Host Homes of Boston
P. O. Box 117, Boston, 02168
(617) 244-1308; FAX (617) 244-5156
  GSC (617) 244-5156

A warm welcome awaits in this 1920 Colonial near the village. The hostess offers two second-floor guest rooms and parlor with books, TV, stereo. Route 128 one mile. Boston 12 miles. Seven minute walk to commuter train weekdays. Shared bath. $57.

WEST FALMOUTH

Bed and Breakfast Cape Cod #70

Box 341, West Hyannisport, 02672
(508) 775-2772

Four blocks from the Old Silver Beach on Buzzards Bay stands a Cape Colonial house that the hosts have been using as a great bed and breakfast host home. A suite with a private entrance has a double bed,

private bath, and sitting area with couch and television. Appointed in traditional decor. On the second floor is a bedroom with two twin beds and a third with one twin bed. The two rooms are always rented to the same party, thus insuring a private bath for guests. The full country breakfast is served in the dining room, and will fill up even the hungriest traveler. Children under eight welcome. $65-75.

WEST HARWICH

Bed and Breakfast Cape Cod #16

Box 341, West Hyannisport, 02672
(508) 775-2772

Three blocks from the warm water beaches of Nantucket Sound stands this Ranch-style private home with one wing set aside for accommodations. The home is immaculate in every respect. No children. $70.

WEST NEWTON

The Carriage House

Bed and Breakfast Greater Boston & Cape Cod
P. O. Box 35, Newtonville, 02160
(617) 964-1606; (800) 832-2632
FAX (617) 332-8572

A charming, renovated private studio in a suburb just west of Boston. The first level has comfortable sitting area; second level has fully equipped kitchenette, private bath, sitting area with a comfortable double futon, two couches, wood-burning stove, color TV, air conditioning, and phone. Rate includes breakfast provided by host and self-served by guest. Weather permitting, guests may use the host's barbecue and back yard deck. Easy access by car or public transportation to Boston/Cambridge. Short walk to village shopping area with movie theater. Special rates for extended stays. $75.

6 Pets welcome; 8 Children welcome; 9 Social drinking allowed; 10 Tennis available; 11 Swimming available; 12 Golf available; 13 Skiing available; 14 May be booked through travel agents.

WESTON

Webb-Bigelow House

863 Boston Post Road, 02193

This spacious 1827 Federal house in Weston's exclusive community has been maintained as an elegant private residence on three acres since Judge Bigelow first built here. Today family antiques, portraits, library, and fireplaces give guests a unique New England experience. Amenities add comfort to this hideaway situated within 20 minutes of Boston and its many area colleges. A full breakfast is served either in the magnificent formal dining room or on-deck by the pool. Fine dining nearby and public transportation to Boston in this quiet residential suburb in a National Historic Preservation District.

Hosts: Robert and Jane Webb
Rooms: 3 (2 PB; 1 SB) $80 off season; $90 in season
Full Breakfast
Credit Cards: None
Notes: 2, 5, 10, 11, 14

WEST STOCKBRIDGE

Bed and Breakfast Accommodations 109

984 Gloucester Place, Schenectady, NY 12309
(518) 370-4948

Built in 1830 and recently renovated, this immaculate home boasts shiny hardwood floors, lace curtains, oak dining table, and artwork by the host's father. Guests are welcome to use the livingroom, dining room, or front porch for relaxation and conversation. Four guest rooms, two with private baths. Just miles from Tanglewood. Children over 10 welcome. $75-100 in-season; $50-65 off-season (Nov. 1-June 30).

Berkshire Bed and Breakfast Homes SC10

P. O. Box 211, Williamsburg, 01096
(413) 268-7244

A 1982 contemporary on five acres. Modern antique touches throughout the guest rooms, with private and semiprivate baths. Family room, formal livingroom, and deck with view of Berkshire Hills. Full breakfast; children over ten welcome. $80-85.

Berkshire Bed and Breakfast Homes SC15

P. O. Box 211, Williamsburg, 01096
(413) 268-7244

An 1830 Colonial on one-half acre. The parlor and porch are available for guest use. The hosts teach yoga and relaxation and cater to health-conscious guests. A double room has a private bath, and two queen bedrooms and a double bedroom have shared baths. Full breakfast. Children welcome. $75-100.

Card Lake Inn

29 Main Street, 01266
(413) 232-0272

This Colonial inn features eight charmingly restored guest rooms, four with private baths, four semi-private. Its tavern and restaurant, situated on the premises, offers a hearty American fare at reasonable prices. Situated in the heart of the Berkshires, it is only minutes away from Tanglewood. Rates include a complimentary breakfast.

Hosts: Edward and Lisa Robbins
Rooms: 8 (4 PB; 4 SB)
Full Breakfast
Credit Cards: A, B, D
Notes: 2, 3, 4, 5, 8, 9, 10, 11, 12, 13, 14

NOTES: Credit cards accepted: A Master Card; B Visa; C American Express; D Discover Card; E Diner's Club; F Other; 2 Personal Checks accepted; 3 Lunch available; 4 Dinner available; 5 Open all year;

WESTWOOD

Bed and Breakfast Associates #IW725

P. O. Box 57166, Babson Park Branch,
Boston, 02157-0166
(617) 449-5302; FAX (617) 449-5958

This country house and barn are graced by an inviting brick patio with a large in-ground pool. The first floor has been redesigned to provide a view of the grounds through walls of glass. Three guest rooms on the second floor share a bath. A Boston tour guide, this hostess claims there is a "friendly ghost" in the house. Full breakfast; children welcome. $50-55; family rates available.

Bed and Breakfast Associates #IW726

P. O. Box 57166, Babson Park Branch
Boston, 02157-0166
(617) 449-5302; FAX (617) 449-5958

This private hideaway is a converted schoolhouse. A party of five can enjoy the two-story apartment with two bedrooms, two full baths, a kitchen, dining area, livingroom, and deck. Sleeping space includes an antique double bed, two twins that can be made up as a king, and one single. Full breakfast; children welcome. $150 for four adults; $120 for family of four.

Woods Abloom

Host Homes of Boston
P. O. Box 117, Boston, 02168
(617) 244-1308; FAX (617) 244-5156

A tree grows through the roof of this 1958 redwood contemporary in the woods. Stunning blend of antiques, modern art, pottery, and porcelain collection. Stone walls and sculptured patio. Both rooms available to same party. Twelve miles southwest of Boston near I-95/128. Air conditioning; private bath; TV. $68.

WHATELY

Berkshire Bed and Breakfast Homes PV21

P. O. Box 211, Williamsburg, 01096
(413) 268-7244

An 1870 sprawling farmhouse on 50 acres. Guest rooms with semiprivate baths and a parlor are available. Antique furnishings. Berry picking nearby. Full breakfast; children over 10 welcome. $50-85.

WILLIAMSBURG

Berkshire Bed and Breakfast Homes PV2

P. O. Box 211, 01096
(413) 268-7244

This 100-year-old Victorian on one acre is a short walk to town center. Guest rooms share a bath and private sitting room. Two-night minimum stay in winter. Full breakfast; children over eight welcome. $45-55.

Berkshire Bed and Breakfast Homes PV3

P. O. Box 211, 01096
(413) 268-7244

A 200-year-old restored farmhouse on 27 acres. Guest rooms furnished with antique and brass share a bath. A porch and sitting room are offered to guests. Full breakfast; children welcome. $45-60; plus $5 surcharge for one-night stay.

Berkshire Bed and Breakfast Homes PV18

P. O. Box 211, 01096
(413) 268-7244

This 1864 restored Victorian town house is a short walk to town center. Guest rooms share a bath and livingroom with fireplace. Full breakfast; children welcome. $45-50.

WORTHINGTON

Berkshire Bed and Breakfast Homes PV20
P. O. Box 211, Williamsburg, 01096
(413) 268-7244

This 1780 Colonial is furnished with antiques, Oriental rugs, five fireplaces, and wide-pine floors. Rooms with private baths and parlor are available. Full breakfast; children over four welcome. $90.

Hill Gallery
HC 65, Box 96, 01098
(413) 238-5914

Situated on a mountaintop in the Hamp shire Hills on 25 acres. Enjoy relaxed country living in an owner-built contemporary home with art gallery, fireplaces, and swimming pool. Self-contained cottage also available.

Hosts: Ellen and Walter Korzec
Rooms: 2 (PB) $60
Full Breakfast
Minimum stay holidays: 2 nights
Credit Cards: None
Notes: 2, 5, 8 (over 5), 9, 10, 11, 12, 13

YARMOUTH PORT

Bed and Breakfast Cape Cod #11
P. O. Box 341, West Hyannisport, 02672-0341
(508) 775-2772; FAX (508) 775-2884

This host home has an adjacent carriage house built with a second-floor suite expressly for bed and breakfast guests. It is spacious and air-conditioned and has a sitting area with a couch, chairs, TV, and refrigerator stocked with beverages. There is a king size bed or twin beds. A pull-out is available for a third person. No children under 12. $110.

Bed and Breakfast Cape Cod #47
P. O. Box 341, West Hyannisport, 02672
(508) 775-2772; FAX (508) 775-2884

This 1964 contemporary home built in a wooded area near Bass River has a marvelous enclosed indoor swimming pool. The luxurious appointments include two bedrooms, each with king size beds. The wing with the two guest rooms is rented to only one party at a time, insuring total privacy for guests. The 70-foot deck is used in season for the full Continental breakfast that is served daily. Convenient to all Cape attractions, the home is a relaxing getaway for the hurried traveler seeking a Cape Cod vacation. $75.

Bed and Breakfast Cape Cod #75
P. O. Box 341, West Hyannisport, 02672-0341
(508) 775-2772; FAX (508) 2884

An authentic 1830 Greek Revival host home with two bedrooms. One has a double bed and the other twins. The house was restored by the owners several years ago. There is a Jacuzzi on the ground floor in an atrium porch. This enclosed porch is comfortable for enjoying the full breakfast served by the hosts. The house is a mile from a lake and one and one-half miles from the ocean. No children under 10. $75.

Michigan

BELLAIRE

Grass River
Bed and Breakfast

5615 Grass River Road, 49615
(616) 533-6041

Situated 30 miles north of Traverse City, this home offers modern comfort in a natural environment. It is tucked in the woods of Antrim County along a chain of lakes, and the house is just steps from its dock on the Grass River. It is frequently visited by a variety of wildlife. Soothe your aches and pains away in the hot tub or relax in the glass sun room. Many activities and two ski resorts are just a few miles away.

Hosts: Harriett and Susan Beach
Rooms: 3 (PB) $85-95
Full Breakfast
Credit Cards: A, B
Notes: 2, 4, 5, 9, 11, 12, 13,

BLACK RIVER

Silver Creek Lodge
Bed and Breakfast

4361 US 23 South, 48721
(517) 471-2198

Spacious lodge and craft shop nestled on 60 tranquil acres that adjoin 5,200 acres of beautiful national forest. Step out the door and enjoy nature trails for hiking or cross-country skiing. Pick wild mushrooms or berries in season. View deer, turkey, and all forms of wildlife in a woodland setting where nature flourishes. No pets.

Hosts: Gladys and Larry Farlow
Rooms: 4 (SB) $45-55
Full Breakfast
Credit Cards: None
Notes: 2, 5, 8, 10, 11, 12

BLISSFIELD

H. D. Ellis Inn

415 Adrian Street, US 223, Blaney Park, 49836
(517) 486-3155

This restored two-story brick Victorian, circa 1883, is situated across the street from the famous Hathaway House Restaurant. All rooms feature telephones, cable TV, AM-FM radio, and private baths. Complimentary bicycles available, and the village of 3,200 has many antique and specialty shops. Try the excursion and dinner trains on the Erie and Kalamazoo, the oldest tracks west of the Alleghenies.

Rooms: 4 (PB) $60-70
Continental Breakfast
Credit Cards: None
Notes: 2, 3, 4, 5, 6, 8, 9, 10, 12

CADILLAC

Hermann's European Hotel

214 North Mitchell Street, 49601
(616) 775-2101; (800) 354-1523

Upstairs from a three-star European cafe. Seven unique rooms that reflect European tastes but have all the American comforts. Large continental breakfast served to your room with the daily paper. Affordable summer rates; corporate rates available.

Host: Hermann J. Suhs
Rooms: 7 (PB) $50-85

6 Pets welcome; 8 Children welcome; 9 Social drinking allowed; 10 Tennis available; 11 Swimming available; 12 Golf available; 13 Skiing available; 14 May be booked through travel agents.

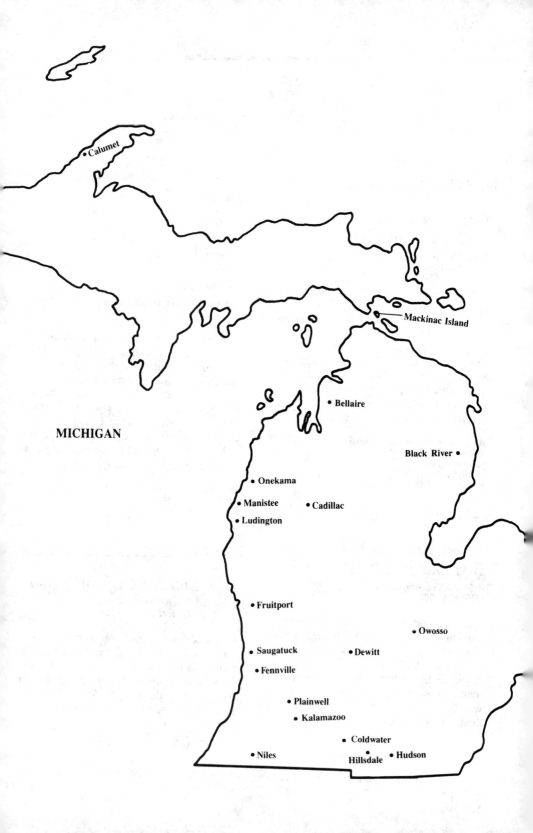

MICHIGAN

• Calumet

Mackinac Island

• Bellaire

Black River •

• Onekama

• Manistee   • Cadillac
• Ludington

• Fruitport

• Owosso

• Saugatuck   • Dewitt

• Fennville

• Plainwell

• Kalamazoo

• Coldwater

• Niles   • Hudson
         Hillsdale

Continental Breakfast
Credit Cards: A, B
Notes: 2, 3, 4, 5, 8, 9, 10, 11, 12, 13, 14

CALUMET

Calumet House

1159 Calumet Avenue, P. O. Box 126, 49913
(906) 337-1936

The Calumet House is on the scenic, historic Keweenaw Peninsula. The house was built by the Calumet and Hecla Mining Company, circa 1895. It features original woodwork and antique furniture. Breakfast is served in the formal dining room, which has the original butler's pantry. Near Michigan Technological University and Suomi College.

Hosts: George and Rose Chivses
Rooms: 2 (SB) $25-30
Full Breakfast
Credit Cards: None
Notes: 2, 5, 9, 10, 11, 12, 13

COLDWATER

Batavia Inn

1824 West Chicago Road, US 12, 49036
(517) 278-5146

This 1872 Italianate country inn with original massive woodwork and high ceilings offers a restful charm. Seasonal decorations are a speciality, and an in-ground pool is available for guests to enjoy in the summer. Bird watching and miniature golf are also available on the property. Guests are pampered with evening turndown and gourmet breakfast. Antique and discount shopping nearby. Recreation and acres of wildlife trails nearby.

Host: E. Fred Marquardt
Rooms: 5 (PB) $59-99
Full Breakfast
Credit Cards: None
Notes: 2, 5, 11

DEWITT

Griffin House

303 North Bridge Street, 48820
(517) 669-9486

Built in 1871 near the center of a quiet, historic country town, this home features comfort and hospitality. Easily accessed from US 27 and I-69, Dewitt is only 20 minutes from the Michigan State University campus, and minutes from Lansing airport and the new Outlet Shopping Mall to be completed this summer on US 27. Canoeing and golf are available. Many antique shops are nearby, and less than an hour's drive away. Enjoy breakfast and lively conversation with the hosts.

Hosts: Phyllis and Roger Griffin
Rooms: 3 (1 PB; 2 SB) $55-60
Full Breakfast
Credit Cards: None
Notes: 2, 9, 12

FENNVILLE

Hidden Pond
Bed and Breakfast

5975 128th Avenue, 49408
(616) 561-2491

Hidden Pond Bed and Breakfast is a quiet retreat set on 28 acres. Full gourmet breakfast included. Sunny breakfast porch, fire-

Hidden Pond

NOTES: Credit cards accepted: A Master Card; B Visa; C American Express; D Discover Card; E Diner's Club; F Other; 2 Personal Checks accepted; 3 Lunch available; 4 Dinner available; 5 Open all year; 6 Pets welcome; 8 Children welcome; 9 Social drinking allowed; 10 Tennis available; 11 Swimming available; 12 Golf available; 13 Skiing available; 14 May be booked through travel agents.

The Kingsley House

place, library, and 60-foot deck for guests' exclusive use. Behind the house is a ravine with a pond, the perfect spot to relax and watch the wildlife. This lovely retreat is near the beaches of Lake Michigan, the boutiques of Saugatuck, and the winery and cider mill in Fennville.

Hosts: Larry and Priscilla Fuerst
Rooms: 2 (PB) $64-170
Full Breakfast
Credit Cards: None
Notes: 2, 5, 9, 10, 11, 12, 13, 14

The Kingsley House

626 West Main Street, 49408
(616) 561-6425

This 1886 elegant Queen Anne Victorian was built for the prominent Kingsley family. The inn has been featured in *Glamour* and *Innsider* magazines and was selected to the list of "Top 50 Inns in America." Situated near Holland, Saugatuck, South Haven, Allegan State Forest, sandy beaches, and cross-country and downhill skiing. Bicycles are available for use. Beautiful surroundings, family antiques. Honeymoon getaway suites with whirlpool bath for two. Delicious full family-style breakfast served in the formal dining room.

Hosts: David and Shirley Witt
Rooms: 7 (PB) $75-125
Full Breakfast
Credit Cards: A, B, C
Notes: 2, 5, 9, 10, 11, 12, 13, 14

GRAND HAVEN

Village Park Bed and Breakfast

60 West Park Street, 49415
(616) 865-6289

Overlooking the welcoming waters of Spring Lake and Village Park where guests can picnic, play tennis, or use the pedestrian bike path and boat launch to enjoy Spring Lake with access to Lake Michigan. Relaxing common area with fireplace and decks. Historic setting of mineral springs health resort. Tradition continues with "Wellness Weekend" special package, including complimentary massage, use of exercise facility, programs on stress management, and creative visualization. Serving Grand Haven and Muskegon areas; Hoffmaster Park and Gillette Sand Dune Nature Center nearby.

Hosts: John and Virginia Hewett
Rooms: 6 (PB) $50-75 (excluding special packages)
Full Breakfast
Credit Cards: A, B
Notes: 2, 5, 8, 10, 11, 12, 13, 14

Village Park

GRAYLING

Borchers

101 Maple Street, 49738
(517) 348-4921

Borchers is a simple, cozy, affordable bed and breakfast situated on the beautiful AuSable River. The hosts endeavor to provide their guests with the comforts of home and the friendliness of small town life. Full breakfasts are served in the country kitchen that overlooks the river. On winter mornings a log will be in the fireplace, and lots of hot coffee, fresh breads, and unique entrees will be served. In the summer, relax and enjoy the covered porches. Canoe rental available on the premises.

Hosts: The Henrys and Hunters
Rooms: 6 (3 PB; 3 SB) $55-75
Full Breakfast
Credit Cards: A, B
Notes: 2, 5, 8, 9, 11, 12, 13

Shadowlawn Manor

HILLSDALE

Shadowlawn Manor Bed and Breakfast

84 Union Street, 49242-1332
(517) 437-2367

A brick Victorian built in 1863, this bed and breakfast has lots of gingerbread trim, spacious entrance hall, and a small iron fireplace that extends into the parlor and provides warm, even heat for the area. Rooms are in various period styles, including Victorian, turn-of-the-century, 1920s, and rattan-and-white wicker bedrooms. Five blocks from Hillsdale College and three blocks from downtown.

Host: Art Young
Rooms: 5 (2 PB; 4 SB) $50-60
Plus Breakfast
Credit Cards: A, B
Notes: 2, 5, 9, 11, 12, 14

HOLLAND

Dutch Colonial Inn

560 Central Avenue, 49423
(616) 396-3664

An award-winning Dutch colonial inn, built in 1928, offers elegant decor with 1930s furnishings and lovely heirloom antiques. All guests rooms have tiled private baths, some with a whirlpool for two. Honeymoon suites are available for that "special getaway." Attractions include excellent shopping, Hope College, bike paths, ski trails, and Michigan's finest beaches. Business people welcome; corporate rates available. Air conditioning. Open year-round with special Christmas touches. Dutch hospitality at its finest.

Hosts: Bob and Pat Elenbass; Diana Klunger
Rooms: 5 (PB) $65-125
Full Breakfast
Credit Cards: A, B, C, D
Notes: 2, 5, 10, 11, 12

HOMER

Grist Mill Inn

3130 East Main, 49245
(517) 568-4063

A late Victorian home in the heart of Michigan's antique country, only a few minutes away from Marshall, the "Williamsburg of the Midwest," and Allen, the self-styled antiques capital of Michigan.

6 Pets welcome; 8 Children welcome; 9 Social drinking allowed; 10 Tennis available; 11 Swimming available; 12 Golf available; 13 Skiing available; 14 May be booked through travel agents.

Grist Mill Inn

Featured in *The Great Country Inn of America Cookbook*, the inn is noted for its exceptional food and creative decorating. The newest edition, "Memories," has facilities for a series of workshops emphasizing quick and easy gourmet cooking and decorative arts.

Host: Judith Krupka
Rooms: 9 (PB) $55-95
Full Breakfast weekends; Continental Breakfast
   weekdays
Credit Cards: None
Notes: 2, 4, 5, 9, 12, 14

HUDSON

Baker Hill Bed and Breakfast

119 Tiger Drive, 49247
(517) 448-8536

Baker Hill was built in 1859 by one of historic Hudson's most prominent citizens. The home was a part of the Underground Railway. Country charm and hospitality prevail in this quiet and private setting. Hot tub, bicycles, swimming, walking, hiking, fishing, tennis, fine dining, antiques, and specialty shops are available. Eighteen

miles to the Michigan International Speedway. Situated 11 miles north of the Michigan-Ohio line, one block off I-27.

Hosts: Doug and Shirley Sprague
Rooms: 3 (SB) $45-60
Continental Breakfast
Credit Cards: None
Notes: 2, 5, 6, 8, 9, 10, 11, 12

Sutton's Weed Farm Bed and Breakfast

18736 Quaker Road, 49247
(517) 547-6302; (800) VAN FARM

Visiting this seven-gable Victorian farmhouse, built in 1873, is like going back to Grandma's. Filled with family antiques. Situated on 180 acres of woods, trails, wildlife, birds, etc. Ancient maple trees are still tapped for syrup to be enjoyed at the breakfast table. Good restaurants nearby.

Hosts: Jack and Barb Sutton
Rooms: 4 (SB) $65
Full Breakfast
Credit Cards: A
Notes: 2, 5, 8, 9, 10, 11, 12

KALAMAZOO

Stuart Avenue Inn

Bed and Breakfast
237 Stuart Avenue, 49007
(616) 342-0230

A full-service inn in two meticulously restored Victorian buildings in a registered historic district. Beautiful antiques and hand-printed wallpapers combine with modern amenities. Features more than an acre of gardens. Evening meals available on request. Near downtown, Western Michigan University, Kalamazoo College; 45 minutes from Lake Michigan. Ideal for business and pleasure travelers.

Hosts: The Casteels
Rooms: 16 (PB) $55-120
Continental Breakfast
Credit Cards: A, B, C, D, E
Notes: 2, 4, 5, 8, 9, 10, 11, 12, 13, 14

NOTES: Credit cards accepted: A Master Card; B Visa; C American Express; D Discover Card; E Diner's Club; F Other; 2 Personal Checks accepted; 3 Lunch available; 4 Dinner available; 5 Open all year;

LUDINGTON

Bed and Breakfast at Ludington

2458 South Beannue Road, 49431
(616) 843-9768

"Next to the Hesslund farm there was another creek with a log bridge. The creek began as a spring a bit farther west and was called Good Creek, as the water was so good to drink. Here, the teams were allowed to stop and rest and take a long, cool drink." Plus: 16 acres, hot tub, various trails, toboggan hill, skating pond, and big breakfasts. Ten percent discount for successive nights.

Hosts: Grace Schneider and Robert Schneider
Rooms: 3 (2 PB; 1 SB) $35-55
Full Breakfast
Credit Cards: None
Notes: 2, 5, 6, 8, 9, 10, 11, 12, 13, 14

MACKINAC ISLAND

Cloghaun

P. O. Box 203, 49757
(906) 847-3885

Cloghaun, a large Victorian home built in 1884, is close to shops, restaurants, and ferry lines. The name *Cloghaun* is Gaelic

Cloghaun

and means "land of little stones." Built by Thomas and Bridgett Donnelly to house their large Irish family, the Cloghaun represents the elegance and ambience of a bygone era. The house is still owned by their descendants and has undergone recent renovations to bring it back to its original elegance.

Hosts: James and Dorothy Bond
Rooms: 10 (8 PB; 2 SB) $50-95
Continental Breakfast
Credit Cards: None
Notes: 2, 8, 9, 10, 11, 12

Haan's 1830 Inn

Box 123, 49757
(906) 847-6244

Lovely restored Greek Revival home furnished with antiques and decorated from the period. In a quiet neighborhood three blocks from historic fort and 19th-century downtown. Dining room has 12-foot harvest table for breakfast of home-baked cakes and breads, plus cereals and fruit. A short ferry ride brings guests to this historic and beautiful island. Sightseeing, bicycling, horseback riding, fine dining, tennis, golf, and shopping nearby. Or sit on three porches and watch the horse-drawn carriages go by. Winter address: 1134 Geneva Street, Lake Geneva, Wisconsin 53147. Winter phone: (414) 248-9244.

Hosts: Nicholas and Nancy Haan; Vernon and Joy Haan
Rooms: 7 (5 PB; 2 SB) $73-108
Continental Breakfast
Credit Cards: None
Notes: 2, 8, 9, 10, 12

MANISTEE

1879 E. E. Douville House

111 Pine Street, 49660
(616) 723-8654

Victorian home with ornate, hand-carved woodwork, interior shutters, a soaring staircase, and elaborate archways with original pocket doors. Ceiling fans in every room. Lake Michigan beaches, fishing, golf, skiing, and historic buildings are nearby.

Hosts: Barbara and Bill Johnson
Rooms: 3 (SB) $40-50
Continental Breakfast
Credit Cards: None
Notes: 2, 5, 9, 10, 11, 12, 13

NILES

Yesterdays Inn Bed and Breakfast
518 North 4th Street, 49120
(616) 683-6079

This elegant Italianate brick home in the historic district has 12-foot ceilings, lace in the windows, antique bedsteads, classical music, and candlelight breakfasts on old china with home-baked goodies and homemade fruit sauces and syrups. Close to Lake Michigan beaches, Fernwood Nature and Art Center, Notre Dame University, and 15 minutes from the South Bend, Indiana airport.

Hosts: Elizabeth and Bob Baker
Rooms: 5 (3 PB; 2 SB) $50-65
Full Breakfast
Credit Cards: A, B, D
Notes: 2, 5, 8, 10, 12, 13, 14

ONEKAMA

Lake Breeze House
5089 Main Street, 49675-0301
(616) 889-4969

Two-story frame house on Portage Lake, where guests share the family bath, livingroom, and breakfast room. Each room has its own special collection of charming family antiques. Come relax and enjoy the back porch and the sounds of the babbling creek with a full breakfast. Reservations and deposit required.

Hosts: Bill and Donna Erickson
Rooms: 3 (SB) $55-65

Full Breakfast
Credit Cards: None
Notes: 2, 10, 11, 12, 13

OWOSSO

R&R Farm-Ranch
308 East Hibbard Road, 48867
(517) 723-3232; (517) 723-2553

A newly remodeled farmhouse from the early 1900s, the Rossmans' ranch sits on 150 acres overlooking the Maple River Valley. Rossman's large concrete circular drive and white board fences lead to stables of horses and cattle. Guests may use the family parlor, game room, and fireplace or stroll about the gardens and pastures along the river. Breakfast is served in the dining room or outside on the deck. Children and pets are welcome.

Hosts: Carl and Jeanne Rossman
Rooms: 2 (SB) $35-45
Continental Breakfast
Credit Cards: None
Notes: 2, 5, 6, 8, 13 (XC)

PLAINWELL

The 1882 John Crispe House Bed and Breakfast
404 East Bridge Street, 49080
(616) 685-1293

Museum quality Victorian elegance and elaborate original gaslight fixtures and plaster moldings complement this home's fine Victorian furnishings. Situated between Kalamazoo and Grand Rapids and within walking distance of some of Michigan's finest gourmet dining and antique districts, the two-and-one-half-acre parklike grounds on the banks of the Kalamazoo River offer a relaxing atmosphere for guests to enjoy.

Host: Ormand and Nancy Lefever
Rooms: 5 (3 PB; 2 SB) $55-65
Full Breakfast
Credit Cards: A, B
Notes: 2, 5, 10, 12, 13

NOTES: Credit cards accepted: A Master Card; B Visa; C American Express; D Discover Card; E Diner's Club; F Other; 2 Personal Checks accepted; 3 Lunch available; 4 Dinner available; 5 Open all year;

Rosemont Inn

SAUGATUCK

Rosemont Inn

83 Lakeshore Drive, P. O. Box 214, 49453
(616) 857-2637

This turn of the century Victorian home overlooking Lake Michigan offers 14 delightful rooms, each with a private bath and air conditioning. Nine rooms feature gas fireplaces, and there are three common rooms, two with fireplaces. There also are an outdoor heated pool and an in-door spa-pool and sauna. Public beach on Lake Michigan is across the street.

Hosts: Joe and Marilyn Sajdak
Rooms: 14 (PB) $55-135
Continental Breakfast
Minimum stay weekends: May 1-October 31: 2
   nights
Credit Cards: A, B, D
Notes: 2, 5, 8, 9, 10, 11, 12, 13, 14

Sherwood Forest Bed and Breakfast

938 Center Street, P. O. Box 315, 49453
(616) 857-1246

Surrounded by woods, this beautiful Victorian-style house was built in the 1890s. Each of the five bedrooms has a private bath, one with Jacuzzi, and queen-size beds, which add 20th century comforts to the traditionally furnished rooms. There is a heated swimming pool and patio, and the eastern shore of Lake Michigan and a public beach are less than a block away.

Hosts: Keith and Susan Charak
Rooms: 5 (PB) $75-105
Continental Breakfast
Credit Cards: A, B
Notes: 2, 5, 8, 9, 10, 11, 12, 13, 14

Twin Oaks Inn

227 Griffith, P. O. Box 867, 49453
(616) 857-1600

Built in 1860, this totally renovated building is now a charming old English bed and breakfast. Nestled at the foot of Hoffman Street hill, this inn offers queen or king-size beds, air conditioning, cable television, VCR, movies, outdoor hot tub, horseshoes, and bicycles. The common room features a fireplace and is the best place in the house to relax, socialize, or play games. Private parking lot. Only one block from Main Street. Many rooms accommodate more than two guests.

Hosts: Nancy and Jerry Horney
Rooms: 6 and a cottage (PB) $64-94
Full Breakfast weekends; Continental Breakfast
   weekdays
Credit Cards: A, B, D
Notes: 2, 5, 8, 9, 10, 11, 12, 13, 14

SOUTH HAVEN

Yelton Manor Bed and Breakfast

140 North Shore Drive, 49090
(616) 637-5220

An elegant, gracious Victorian minimansion on the sandy shore of beautiful Lake Michigan. The gorgeous rooms all have private baths, some with Jacuzzis. Plentiful common areas, two salons with fireplaces, cozy wing chairs, floral carpets, four-poster beds, lovely antiques, a wicker porch retreat, and a pampering staff set the tone for relaxation and romance. Enjoy wonder-

6 Pets welcome; 8 Children welcome; 9 Social drinking allowed; 10 Tennis available; 11 Swimming available;
12 Golf available; 13 Skiing available; 14 May be booked through travel agents.

Yelton Manor

ful breakfasts, day-long treats, and evening hors d'oeuvres. Guests will never want to leave!

Hosts: Elaine and Rob
Rooms: 11 (PB) $95-180
Full Breakfast
Credit Cards: A, B, C
Notes: 2, 5, 9, 11, 13

WEST BRANCH

The Rose Brick Inn
124 East Houghton Avenue, 48661
(517) 345-3702

A 1906 Queen Anne-style home with a graceful veranda, white picket fence, and cranberry canopy, the Rose Brick Inn is tucked in the center two floors of the Frank Sebastian Smith House, listed on Michigan's register of historic sites. It is on downtown Main Street in Victorian West Branch. Golf, hiking, biking, cross-country skiing, snowmobiling, hunting, shopping, and special holiday events await you year-round.

Host: Leon Swartz
Rooms: 4 (PB) $48-58
Continental Breakfast
Credit Cards: A, B
Notes: 2, 5, 8, 10, 11 (seasonal), 12, 13

The Rose Brick Inn

Minnesota

DULUTH

Barnum House Bed and Breakfast

2211 East Third Street, 55812
(218) 724-5434; (800) 879-5437

An elegant haven in Duluth's historic East End. Built in 1910, it is surrounded by stately mansions of historic and architectural significance and situated on a quiet cul-de-sac with wooded ravine and brook. Refreshing retreat for those seeking history, quality, and luxury. Museum-quality antiques throughout, king/queen antique bedrooms with fireplaces, verandas, and private baths. Barnum House provides breakfasts that are as distinctive as the guests. Whatever the season, indulge in a delicious full breakfast with fresh fruit, muffins and breads, main entree, and gourmet coffee or tea. Brochure and room pictures available.

Hosts: Dorothy and Dick Humes; Susan Watt
Rooms: 5 (PB) $95-115
Full Breakfast
Credit Cards: A, B
Notes: 2, 5, 10, 12, 13, 14

FERGUS FALLS

Bakketopp Hus

Rural Route 2, Box 187 A (Long Lake), 56537
(218) 739-2915

This contemporary rustic lake home is ten minutes from I-94. King and queen size beds, spa, fireplace, skylight, vaulted ceilings with use of natural woods, and windows to create a feeling of spaciousness. Furnished with antiques, it has country French canopy poster beds, decks on the lakeside, and flower garden patio. The state park is nearby, as well as nature, ski, snowmobile, and hiking trails. Antiques, restaurants, golf, and other recreation nearby. A relaxed retreat surrounded by woods and a hilltop view of the lake.

Hosts: Judy and Dennis Nims
Rooms: 3 (1 PB; 2 SB) $55-85
Full Breakfast
Credit Cards: None
Notes: 2, 5, 8, 9, 10, 11, 12, 13

HIBBING

Adams House Bed and Breakfast

201 East 23rd Street, 55746
(218) 263-9742

This English Tudor-style manor house is situated in the central area of Hibbing. There are many tourist and business areas in the immediate vicinity. Rooms are furnished with chintz and antiques, and the lounge with a television is for guests' use, as well as a kitchenette. A little bit of England in northern Minnesota.

Hosts: Merrill and Marlene Widmark
Rooms: 5 (1 PB; 4 SB) $37
Continental Breakfast
Credit Cards: None
Notes: 2, 5, 8, 9, 10, 11, 12, 13

LITTLE MARAIS

Stone Hearth Inn Bed and Breakfast

1118 Highway 61 East, 55614
(218) 226-3020

6 Pets welcome; 8 Children welcome; 9 Social drinking allowed; 10 Tennis available; 11 Swimming available; 12 Golf available; 13 Skiing available; 14 May be booked through travel agents.

Little Marais •

• Hibbing

Duluth •

Lutsen •

• Fergus Falls

MINNESOTA

Saint Paul •

Winona •

Spring Valley •

This 1889 homestead nestled on the shore of Lake Superior offers comfortable elegance. All guest rooms have Old World antiques and private baths. Some rooms have whirlpool tubs, fireplaces, and kitchens. Enjoy four seasons of activities while being treated to relaxed hospitality and North Shore serenity. Enjoy the cozy stone fireplace or the covered front porch. Breakfast of regional cuisine is served in the lakeside dining room. Hike from this bed and breakfast to another bed and breakfast along the Superior hiking trail. Also near downhill and cross-country skiing, golf, and mountain biking.

Hosts: Charlie and Susan Michels
Rooms: 7 (PB) $75-124
Full Breakfast
Credit Cards: A, B, C
Notes: 2, 3, 4, 5, 9, 10, 12, 13

LUTSEN

Caribou Lake
Bed and Breakfast
N514 County 38, P. O. Box 156, 55612-0156
(218) 663-7489

Experience the quiet beauty, spectacular view, and rosy sunsets from our modern log home and guest cabin. Guest suite features two queen beds and private sauna. The two-bedroom cabin has a fully equipped kitchen and fireplace. Gourmet breakfasts and private dining are offered. The area boasts some of the finest hiking and biking trails; golf, fishing, swimming, and downhill skiing are available. Canoe and boat rentals are also possible on the premises. *Minnesota Monthly* says, "It's like stepping into a Hallmark card."

Hosts: Leanne and Carter Wells
Rooms: 2 (2 PB) $85-110
Full Breakfast
Credit Cards: A, B
Notes: 2, 4, 5, 9, 11, 12, 13, 14

ST. PAUL

Chatsworth
Bed and Breakfast
984 Ashland Avenue, 55104
(612) 227-4288

Elegantly furnished Victorian home in a quiet residential neighborhood. Fifteen minutes from the airport. Near the governor's mansion and numerous restaurants and shops. Easy access to downtown St. Paul and Minneapolis. Two rooms with double whirlpool baths; licensed.

Hosts: Donna and Earl Gustafson
Rooms: 5 (3 PB; 2 SB) $63.90-106.50
Continental Breakfast
Credit Cards: None
Notes: 2, 5, 8, 9, 10, 11, 12, 13

Chatsworth

Prior's on Desoto
1522 Desoto Street, 55101-3253
(612) 774-2695

Delightful new home nestled among the trees in a quiet neighborhood five minutes from city center. Homey atmosphere, as

NOTES: Credit cards accepted: A Master Card; B Visa; C American Express; D Discover Card; E Diner's Club; F Other; 2 Personal Checks accepted; 3 Lunch available; 4 Dinner available; 5 Open all year; 6 Pets welcome; 8 Children welcome; 9 Social drinking allowed; 10 Tennis available; 11 Swimming available; 12 Golf available; 13 Skiing available; 14 May be booked through travel agents.

your home away from home. Parlor with fireplace and cathedral ceiling, private and shared baths, telephones, and television. Full gourmet breakfast, complete with homemade caramel rolls and scones. Dietary preferences are honored. Coffee and tea available anytime. Conveniently situated near I-35 East and state hiking and biking trails. Airport and train pick-up available for a small fee.

Hosts: The Priors
Rooms: 3 (2 PB; 1 SB) $55-69
Full Breakfast
Credit Cards: None
Notes: 2, 5, 8, 9, 10, 11, 12, 13, 14

University Club of St. Paul

420 Summit Avenue, 55102
(612) 222-1751

Circa 1912. Established to enhance literary, cultural, and social activities for the well-educated, this Tudor Revival club is modeled after the Cambridge and Oxford clubs in London. Fine English antiques and oil paintings of English landscapes decorate the interiors. In the Grill Bar, F. Scott Fitzgerald's initials can be found carved

beside those of other club members. There is a library, dining room, fireside room, conference room, and a fitness center. TV available.

Host: John Rupp
Rooms: 5 (PB) $45-85
Full Breakfast
Credit Cards: A, B, C
Notes: 2, 3, 4, 5, 8, 9, 10, 11, 12, 13

SPRING VALLEY

Chase's

508 North Huron Avenue, 55975
(507) 346-2850

It's life in the slow lane at this Second Empire mansion. It's flowers, birds, stars, and exploring this unglaciated area. Step back in time with a tour: Amish, Laura Ingalls Wilder, or caves. Enjoy the trails, trout streams, and bike trail.

Hosts: Bob and Jeannine Chase
Rooms: 5 (PB) $75
Full Breakfast
Credit Cards: A, B, D
Notes: 2, 8, 10, 11, 12

University Club of St. Paul

NOTES: Credit cards accepted: A Master Card; B Visa; C American Express; D Discover Card; E Diner's Club; F Other; 2 Personal Checks accepted; 3 Lunch available; 4 Dinner available; 5 Open all year;

WINONA

Carriage House Bed and Breakfast

420 Main Street, 55987
(507) 452-8256

Chase's

Indulge yourself at Winona's Carriage House Bed and Breakfast. Stay in one of the beautifully decorated rooms, each with its own special charm. Built in 1870, the Carriage House is on the Mississippi River. Enjoy a wonderful breakfast, free tandem bikes, carriage rides, and old-fashioned river town hospitality. AAA approved. Carriage rides available.

Hosts: Deb and Don Salyards
Rooms: 4 (2 PB; 2 SB) $60-85
Continental Breakfast
Credit Cards: A, B
Notes: 2, 5, 9, 10, 11, 12, 13, 14

6 Pets welcome; 8 Children welcome; 9 Social drinking allowed; 10 Tennis available; 11 Swimming available; 12 Golf available; 13 Skiing available; 14 May be booked through travel agents.

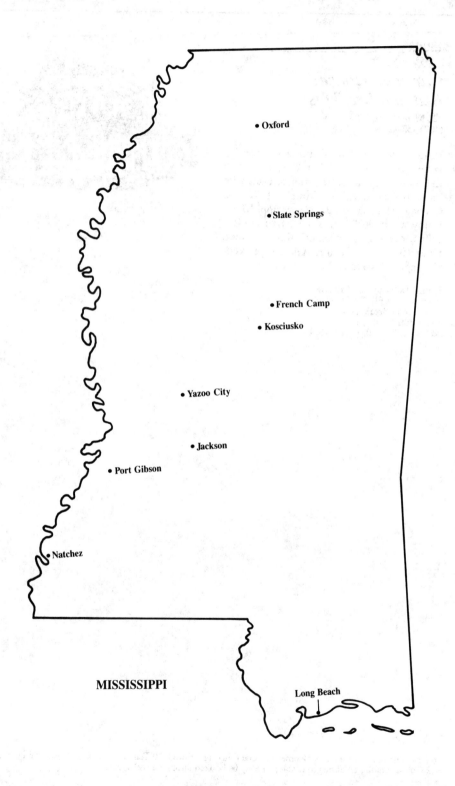

Oxford

Slate Springs

French Camp

Kosciusko

Yazoo City

Jackson

Port Gibson

Natchez

Long Beach

MISSISSIPPI

Mississippi

FRENCH CAMP

Lincoln Ltd. #59

P. O. Box 3479, Meridian, 39303
(601) 482-5483 information
(800) 633-MISS reservations
FAX (601) 693-7447

Enjoy the spacious view of forest and wildlife from the wide windows of this two-story log home. Built with chinked log walls, the home was reconstructed from two log cabins more than 100 years old. Here guests awake to a traditional country breakfast and air scented with cypress and sweet pine. The hosts share their historic home with southern hospitality and their personal collection of antique tables, books, and quilts. Four guest rooms with private baths. $53.

JACKSON

Lincoln Ltd. #50

P. O. Box 3479, Meridian, 39303
(601) 482-5483 information
(800) 633-MISS reservations
FAX (601) 693-7447

Circa 1888. Step through the door and back across 100 years into a graceful world of sparkling chandeliers and finely crafted furnishings in this 19th-century home. Mere moments away from the city's central business and government districts. Convenient to many of Jackson's finest shopping, dining, and entertainment opportunities. The bedrooms are individually

decorated, each accompanied by a fully modern private bath. Eleven guest rooms. $80-155.

KOSCIUSKO

Lincoln Ltd. #63

P. O. Box 3479, Meridian, 39303
(601) 482-5483 information
(800) 633-MISS reservations
FAX (601) 693-7447

One of the finest examples of Queen Anne architecture, this historic inn stands as a visual example of the lifestyle and culture of 1884. Four lovely bedrooms, furnished with antiques. Lunch and dinner are available by reservation. Breakfast included. $75.

LONG BEACH

Red Creek Colonial Inn

7416 Red Creek Road, 39560
(601) 452-3080 information; (800) 729-9670 reservations

This three-story, raised French cottage is situated on eleven acres of live oaks and magnolias. The 64-foot porch and six fireplaces add to the relaxing atmosphere of this circa 1899 brick-and-cypress home. English, French, Victorian, and country antiques; and the workable wooden radios and a Victrola are for guests' use. The inn is situated just one and one-half miles south of I-10 off Exit 28 and about five miles

NOTES: Credit cards accepted: A Master Card; B Visa; C American Express; D Discover Card; E Diner's Club; F Other; 2 Personal Checks accepted; 3 Lunch available; 4 Dinner available; 5 Open all year; 6 Pets welcome; 8 Children welcome; 9 Social drinking allowed; 10 Tennis available; 11 Swimming available; 12 Golf available; 13 Skiing available; 14 May be booked through travel agents.

from Beach Highway 90 in Pass Christian via Menge Avenue and Red Creek Road. Biloxi is about 20 minutes distant, and New Orleans is about an hour away.

Hosts: Daniel and Rebecca Peranich
Rooms: 7 (5 PB; 2 SB) $49-69
Continental Plus Breakfast
Credit Cards: None
Notes: 2, 5, 8, 9, 10, 11, 12, 13 ,14

MERIDIAN

Lincoln Ltd. #18

P. O. Box 3479, 39303
(601) 482-5483 information
(800) 633-MISS reservations
FAX (601) 693-7447

In one of Meridian's loveliest neighborhoods, this home is set among flowering shrubs and dogwood trees. The host and hostess have always been active in civic and cultural activities, both locally and within the state. Attractively furnished, it has two bedrooms with shared bath (for family or four people traveling together, only) or a double room with private bath. Full Mississippi breakfast. $55-70.

NATCHEZ

The Briars

P. O. Box 1245, 39121
(601) 446-9654; (800) 634-1818

Situated on a promontory overlooking the mighty Mississippi River, The Briars is one of the finest examples of early southern plantation-style architecture. Known historically as the residence where Jefferson Davis married Varina Howell in 1845, the home features 13 spacious bedrooms with private baths, cable TV in the main house, guest house, and pavilion. Guests may enjoy a delicious plantation breakfast served in the pavilion dining room, and enjoy the more than 1,000 azaleas that grace the flower gardens. AAA Four Diamond Award winner.

Clifton Heights

212 Linton Avenue, 39120
(601) 446-8047

Enjoy southern hospitality and a quiet evening at this turn-of-the-century Victorian home in the historic garden district of downtown Natchez. It features a full southern breakfast, pool, and TV. Guests can relax in this peaceful setting or can stroll down the street past many architectural marvels. Open year-round. Children welcome.

Dorsey House

305 North Pearl Street, 39120
(601) 442-5845

Experience the southern hospitality of Natchez with a personal touch. Guests can enjoy a big southern breakfast in the formal dining room and large rooms with private baths and fireplace. Situated in historic downtown Natchez.

Glen Auburn

300 South Commerce Street, 39120
(601) 442-4099; (800) 833-0170

Glen Auburn, a French Second Empire mansion in the center of antebellum Natchez, offers the overnight guest a taste of Victorian elegance. Recent restoration of this 1875 mansion has enhanced its outstanding original features, including Eastlake-style chandeliers, fine millwork, ornamental plaster, and stenciled ceilings. Guests may chose from four large suites in the main house, some with a Jacuzzi, or the eclectic carriage house. Just a short stroll to the Mississippi River, Natchez Under the Hill, or carriage rides through the historic downtown area. Open year-round.

Harper House

201 Arlington Avenue, 39120
(601) 445-5557

NOTES: Credit cards accepted: A Master Card; B Visa; C American Express; D Discover Card; E Diner's Club; F Other; 2 Personal Checks accepted; 3 Lunch available; 4 Dinner available; 5 Open all year;

Hosts Mr. and Mrs. John Warren invite visitors to experience Harper House. It features two guest rooms and an enjoyable continental breakfast. Children over 12 welcome.

Lincoln Ltd. #19

P. O. Box 3479, Meridian, 39303
(601) 482-5483 information
(800) 633-MISS reservations
FAX (601) 693-7447

This three-story mansion, circa 1832, features an outstanding semi-eliptical stairway. Horses once trod where a collection of priceless furnishings and fine paintings now reside. Listed on the National Register of Historic Places. Full breakfast served. Swimming pool on premises. Ten guest rooms. $70-125.

Lincoln Ltd. #46

P. O. Box 3479, Meridian, 39303
(601) 482-5483 information
(800) 633-MISS reservations
FAX (601) 693-7447

One of the finest examples of early southern Plantation-style architecture, this lovely home is situated on a promontory overlooking the Mississippi River. Abounding in history, the antique-filled rooms offer the guest time to relax and enjoy the very room where Jefferson Davis was married in 1845. All 13 bedrooms are spacious. Private baths available. Full breakfast is served. $105-135.

Lincoln Ltd. #69

P. O. Box 3479, Meridian, 39303
(601) 482-5483 information
(800) 633-MISS reservations
FAX (601) 693-7447

Once owned by the last territorial governor and the first U.S. governor of Mississippi, this home built in 1794 is situated in the heart of Natchez. Many of the rooms have

original 18th-century paneling and are furnished in period antiques. Enjoy the formal drawing room and eat a full plantation breakfast in the elegant dining room or cozy breakfast room. Five guest rooms and one suite available. $75-110.

Lincoln Ltd. #72

P. O. Box 3479, Meridian, 39303
(601) 482-5483 information
(800) 633-MISS reservations
FAX (601) 693-7447

An elegant Victorian mansion (circa 1880) furnished with antiques. Situated in the Natchez Historic District, it is within walking distance of several antebellum tour homes. Enjoy a full breakfast served in the formal dining room accompanied by fine crystal, silver, and china. Visit with the owners over wine and cheese or tea in the late afternoon and early evening. Features four guest rooms; shared or private baths available. $60-80.

Monmouth

P. O. Box 1736, 39121
(601) 442-5852; (800) 828-4531
FAX (601) 446-7762

Monmouth Plantation is a glorious return to the antebellum south. Rated "...one of the top 10 most romantic places in the U.S.A." by *Glamour* magazine and *USA Today*, this haven of tranquility awaits to enfold you in luxury and service. More than 25 landscaped acres, including pebble paths bursting with flowers, a white bridge gracing a small pond, Mississippi songbirds, and moss-draped oak trees. Guest accommodations are provided in the main house, slave quarters and cabins, and the carriage house —all meticulously rebuilt or restored. Special thoughts go into guest preparations, from the full breakfast, unique soaps and creams, luxurious robes, and the pralines and beverage that greet travelers upon arrival. AAA Four Diamond Award winner.

6 Pets welcome; 8 Children welcome; 9 Social drinking allowed; 10 Tennis available; 11 Swimming available; 12 Golf available; 13 Skiing available; 14 May be booked through travel agents.

Mount Repose

19 Homochitto, 39120
(800) 647-6742

A perfect example of an early plantation
house, Mount Repose was built on lands
granted to John Bisland by the Spanish
Crown in 1786. Still owned and occupied
by his descendants, it contains several treasured heirlooms.

Sweet Olive Tree Manor

700 Orleans, 39120
(800) 647-6742

This Victorian bed and breakfast, is just a
few blocks from the mighty Mississippi
River and other Natchez attractions.
Children 14 and up welcome. No pets.

The Turkey Feather

127 South Commerce Street, 39120
(601) 442-3434; (800) 647-6742

This charming bed and breakfast offers
guests a choice of four spacious suites,
kitchen appliances, and a tasty continental
breakfast. Children welcome.

Weymouth Hall

1 Cemetery Road, 39120
(601) 445-2304

The unique cubical form, clean lines, and
spectacular location of Weymouth Hall
make it one of the most impressive Greek
Revival mansions in the city. Situated on a
bluff overlooking the Mississippi River, it
provides guests with recessed porches, and
a delightful panorama of the "Mighty
Mississip" like none other. Completely furnished in period antiques, Weymouth Hall
is open year-round by reservation.

William Harris Hall

311 Jefferson Street, 3912
(800) 647-6742

Built by William Harris, an early Natchez
business man and civic leader in 1835, this
home is listed on the National Register of
Historic Places. Mr. Harris was also the
father of Confederate General Nathaniel
Harrison Harris. Reasonable rates.

OXFORD

Lincoln Ltd. #23

P. O. Box 3479, Meridian, 39303
(601) 482-5483 information
(800) 633-MISS reservations
FAX (601) 693-7447

Built in 1838, this lovely antebellum home,
made entirely of native timber, is on the
National Register of Historic Places.
Treasures abound here. "It's a homey
museum/showplace," says the hostess. In
an attic, 150 years of fashion are displayed
on mannequins. Guests can enjoy cakes
that are still warm and have a full breakfast
on the balcony on warm spring mornings.
Conveniently situated close to the
University of Mississippi and the William
Faulkner home. Downstairs filled with
antiques. Four guest rooms. $55-70.

PORT GIBSON

Oak Square Plantation

1207 Church Street, 39150
(601) 437-4350; (800) 729-0240

In the town Gen. U. S. Grant said was "too
beautiful to burn," this antebellum mansion
features heirloom antiques and canopied
beds. On the National Register of Historic
Places. Four Diamond rated by AAA.

Hosts: Mr. and Mrs. William Lum
Rooms: 10 (PB) $75-95
Full Breakfast

NOTES: Credit cards accepted: A Master Card; B Visa; C American Express; D Discover Card; E Diner's
Club; F Other; 2 Personal Checks accepted; 3 Lunch available; 4 Dinner available; 5 Open all year;

Credit Cards: A, B, C, D
Notes: 2, 5, 8, 9, 14

SLATE SPRINGS

Cedar Grove Mansion-Inn
2200 Washington Street, 39180
(800) 862-1300

Straight out of *Gone With the Wind* is this 1840 magnificently furnished inn with its four acres of gardens and its fountains, courtyards, gas lights, four-poster beds, and period antiques. The pool, Jacuzzi, and the terrace provide a spectacular view of the Mississippi River. Chosen by the book *Escape in Style* as one of the most romantic inns in the world, it is four-diamond rated by AAA and a national historic property.

Rooms: 18 (PB) $85-150
Full Breakfast
Credit Cards: A, B, C
Notes: 2, 5, 8 (over 5), 9, 10, 11, 12, 14

Cedar Grove Mansion Inn

Lincoln Ltd. #27
P. O. Box 3479, Meridian, 39303
(601) 482-5483 information
(800) 633-MISS reservations
FAX (601) 693-7447

Enjoy true southern hospitality in this Federal-style home. Here history combines with every modern amenity, including a hot tub and a swimming pool. Step back in time in an antique-filled bedroom, and

enjoy a full plantation-style breakfast in the formal dining room. A tour of the home and a welcoming beverage are included. There are 11 guest rooms. $75-115.

Lincoln Ltd. #32
P. O. Box 3479, Meridian, 39303
(601) 482-5483 information
(800) 633-MISS reservations
FAX (601) 693-7447

Situated on six landscaped acres, this outstanding home designed in the Federal style boasts exquisite milled woodwork, sterling silver door knobs, French bronze chandeliers, and a lonely ghost—all echoes of the past. Three lovely guest rooms are all furnished in antiques: a Mallard bed, a Heppelwhite tester, or a plantation-style room are yours to enjoy. A tour of the home, a plantation breakfast, and mint juleps are included. $85.

Lincoln Ltd. #35
P. O. Box 3479, Meridian, 39303
(601) 482-5483 information
(800) 633-MISS reservations
FAX (601) 693-7447

This home, circa 1873, was built as a wedding present from a father to his daughter. It is an interesting mixture of Victorian and Greek Revival architectural styles. All bedrooms are furnished with antiques and have private baths; some rooms are available with fireplace and television. From a rocking chair on the front gallery, enjoy a spectacular view of the Mississippi River and valley. A full plantation breakfast is included. Listed on the National Register of Historic Places. Six guest rooms. $75-130.

Lincoln Ltd. #36
P. O. Box 3479, Meridian, 39303
(601) 482-5483 information
(800) 633-MISS reservations
FAX (601) 693-7447

6 Pets welcome; 8 Children welcome; 9 Social drinking allowed; 10 Tennis available; 11 Swimming available; 12 Golf available; 13 Skiing available; 14 May be booked through travel agents.

This lavish antebellum mansion was built between 1840 and 1858 as a wedding present from a wealthy businessman to his bride. Guest will not soon forget the *Gone With the Wind* elegance of this place. Exquisitely furnished with many original antiques, it has beautiful formal gardens, gazebos, and fountains. Relax in the courtyard or in the pool and spa. Listed on the National Register of Historic Places. Its 17 guest rooms have private baths. $75-140.

VICKSBURG _____

Cedar Grove Mansion

2300 Washington Street, P. O. Box B, 39181
(800) 862-1300

Cedar Grove was built by John A. Klein as a wedding present to his bride. Since then, it has established itself as a well-known bed and breakfast throughout the South and the United States. The grounds, furnishings, and staff provide guests with comfort and enjoyment. All accommodations are furnished with period pieces and contain all modern conveniences.

Rooms: 20 (PB) $95-145
Full Breakfast
Credit Cards: A, B, C
Notes: 2, 5, 8, 9, 10, 11, 12

YAZOO CITY _____

Lincoln Ltd. #70

P. O. Box 3479, Meridian, 39303
(601) 482-5483 information
(800) 633-MISS reservations
FAX (601) 693-7447

Situated twenty miles from Yazoo City, guests can step back into history and walk among azaleas and spectacular day lilies. This manager's plantation home, built in 1860, has four bedrooms and is tastefully decorated with period antiques. It offers an intriguing oasis of privacy for those who wish to get away from the rush of life. Guests may relax in two gazebos and absorb nature's sounds and aromas or slip away to a cozy sitting room upstairs and enjoy a panoramic view of the entire front garden. A full plantation evening meal and breakfast are included. $90-110.

Missouri

BRANSON

Ozark Mountain Country Bed and Breakfast 101

Box 295, 65616
(800) 695-1546

An elegant early 1900s inn with seven uniquely furnished guest rooms. Features privates baths, air conditioning, and a parlor for guest use. A hearty breakfast is served. $65-80.

Ozark Mountain Country Bed and Breakfast 102-A

Box 295, 65616
(800) 695-1546

Situated four miles south of Kimberling City, this inn features a guest room loft, with bath on the main level. A full breakfast is served. No pre-teenagers. $50.

Ozark Mountain Country Bed and Breakfast 102-B

Box 295, 65616
(800) 695-1546

This log cabin guest house features a double bed and sleeper sofa, as well as a sleeping loft for children. A full breakfast is served. Air-conditioned. $10 per extra person. Open April through November. $50.

Ozark Mountain Country Bed and Breakfast 102-C

Box 295, 65616
(800) 695-1546

A little gingerbread log cabin with a queen bed, kitchenette, sleeping loft, and Franklin stove. A self-serve continental breakfast is provided. Air conditioning; open year-round. $60; $10 per extra adult; $5 per extra child.

Ozark Mountain Country Bed and Breakfast 103

Box 295, 65616
(800) 321-8594

"On a clear day you can see forever" from this high bluff overlooking Lake Taneycomo three miles south of Branson. The lakeview guest room has TV, private bath, and entrance from deck. A smaller room is also available with TV. School-age children welcome. Picnic table and grill available for guests. Full breakfast with choice of entrées. $50-85.

Ozark Mountain Country Bed and Breakfast 107

Box 295, 65616
(800) 695-1546

Two blocks from Table Rock Lake with easy access to Silver Dollar City, Table Rock Dam, and state park. Easy access to shows. Two guest areas available with

6 Pets welcome; 8 Children welcome; 9 Social drinking allowed; 10 Tennis available; 11 Swimming available; 12 Golf available; 13 Skiing available; 14 May be booked through travel agents.

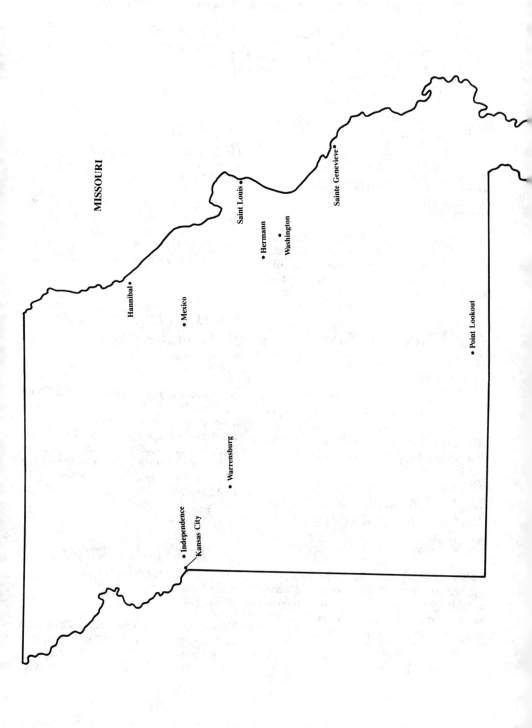

MISSOURI

Hannibal

Mexico

Saint Louis

Hermann

Washington

Sainte Genevieve

Point Lookout

Warrensburg

Independence

Kansas City

color TV, private bath, and private entrance. Sitting area, game table, refrigerator, cable TV. Special breakfast on weekends. $60-80.

Ozark Mountain Country Bed and Breakfast 118

Box 295, 65616
(800) 695-1546

Charming contemporary featuring a pool, hot tub, and three separate guest rooms. Rooms offer king or queen beds, private entrances, and many modern amenities. Group rates; discounts after third night. $70-90. $10 per night per extra guest.

Ozark Mountain Country Bed and Breakfast 121-A

Box 295, 65616
(800) 695-1546

Quaint farm home built in 1890 near Lampe, halfway between Silver Dollar City and Eureka Springs. Honeymoon Suite features a king bed, private entrance, private bath, garden room, and spa. Family Suite includes three twin beds and a private bath. Special country breakfast, hiking trails, air conditioning. Children welcome, $5 each. $50-75.

Ozark Mountain Country Bed and Breakfast 121-B

Box 295, 65616
(800) 695-1546

Hillside hideaway rustic retreat next to Grandpa's Farm. Two suites, each with private entrance and bath, livingroom, and bedroom with king-size bed. Wood stove and sleeping loft for children included. One

suite has a kitchenette. $65-70. $10 per extra adult; $5 per child.

Ozark Mountain Country Bed and Breakfast 124

Box 295, 65616
(800) 695-1546

This bed and breakfast offers easy access to Silver Dollar City and shows. Private entrance, bath with shower, sitting area, and patio. Marvelous view of the valley and Ozark Mountains. Full breakfast upstairs in dining room. Continental breakfast served in guest area. Children welcome. $45.

Ozark Mountain Country Bed and Breakfast 125

Box 295, 65616
(800) 321-8594

Six lakeview suites with private baths, private entrances, complete kitchenettes, and patio/deck. Color TV, air conditioning. Hearty continental breakfast. Rental boats available. Private dock. Group discounts available, as well as discounts after the third night. $78-95.

Ozark Mountain Country Bed and Breakfast 126

Box 295, 65616
(800) 695-1546

Just a mile from Silver Dollar City, this contemporary home with a view of Table Rock Lake features a sitting area for guests and bountiful breakfasts. Guest rooms feature private baths with queen bed or king-size waterbed, antique furnishings, and one with a hot tub and sun room. Air-conditioned. Children over four welcome. $55-75.

NOTES: Credit cards accepted: A Master Card; B Visa; C American Express; D Discover Card; E Diner's Club; F Other; 2 Personal Checks accepted; 3 Lunch available; 4 Dinner available; 5 Open all year; 6 Pets welcome; 8 Children welcome; 9 Social drinking allowed; 10 Tennis available; 11 Swimming available; 12 Golf available; 13 Skiing available; 14 May be booked through travel agents.

Ozark Mountain Country Bed and Breakfast 132

Box 295, 65616
(800) 321-8594

Seven miles southwest of Branson on a bluff above Lake Taneycomo, this private suite has easy access to nearby attractions. Features include sitting area, king bed, sleeper sofa, TV, and full breakfast delivered to your suite. Open April through October. $70.

Ozark Mountain Country Bed and Breakfast 133

Box 295, Branson, 65616
(800) 321-8594

Lake Taneycomo is practically on the doorstep of this new rustic cedar home. Some of the features include private entrance, private bath, TV, king and queen bed, whirlpool tub, kitchenettes, sleeper sofa, dining area, and great room. $60-75.

Ozark Mountain Country Bed and Breakfast 134

Box 295, 65616
(800) 321-8594

Try this famous early 1900s restored and decorated hotel in the historic district. Features include hearty breakfast in formal dining room, nine guest areas, antiques, and collectibles. Available April through December. $70-95.

Ozark Mountain Country Bed and Breakfast 135

Box 295, 65616
(800) 321-8594

This private cottage situated five miles south of Branson has a complete kitchen,

sitting area, and antiques. Other features include day bed, double bed, and both with shower. Infants allowed. Full breakfast in cottage. Open all year. $60.

Ozark Mountain Country Bed and Breakfast 140

Box 295, 65616
(800) 321-8594

These elegant contemporary guest rooms are above Lake Taneycomo, with easy access to nearby attractions. Rooms have sitting areas, lake views, private baths, king and queen beds, cable TV, private hot tub, kitchenette; two rooms with fireplace. The meeting/conference room is ideal for large families or groups. $70-80.

Ozark Mountain Country Bed and Breakfast 143

Box 295, 65616
(800) 321-8594

Situated just two blocks from 76 Country Boulevard, this private duplex apartment offers a fully equipped kitchen, TV, livingroom, dining area, air conditioning, and queen sleeper sofa. Two bedrooms, each with double bed, and private bath. $65. $15 extra adult; $10 extra children.

Ozark Mountain Country Bed and Breakfast 144

Box 295, 65616
(800) 321-8594

A contmporary home with a luxurious private suite. Situated three miles east of Branson, it is less than a mile from the golf course. Features a private deck, private entrance, private bath, and king waterbed with mirrored canopy. A full breakfast is served. $65; $5 extra child.

NOTES: Credit cards accepted: A Master Card; B Visa; C American Express; D Discover Card; E Diner's Club; F Other; 2 Personal Checks accepted; 3 Lunch available; 4 Dinner available; 5 Open all year;

Ozark Mountain Country Bed and Breakfast 153

Box 295, 65616
(800) 321-8594

Exclusive four bedroom log cabin adjoining Mark Twain National Forest. Features a chemical-free environment, with air conditioning, hot tub, and indoor sauna. A nutritious breakfast with natural foods is served next door. Three extra-long double beds and day bed. $60. $15 extra adult; $5 extra child.

Ozark Mountain Country Bed and Breakfast 158-A

Box 295, 65616
(800) 321-8594

Turn-of-the-century home with antiques and a parlor for guests. A hearty breakfast is served in the dining room, with two upstairs guest areas available. Two bedrooms feature extra-long double beds, sitting room, TV, bath. $55-75. $10 extra person.

Ozark Mountain Country Bed and Breakfast 158-B

Box 295, 65616
(800) 321-8594

Unhosted bungalow, with a hearty breakfast served at Heim House next door. Four guest rooms featuring accommodations from king- and queen-size beds to double beds and fireplaces. $55-95.

Ozark Mountain Country Bed and Breakfast 160

Box 295, 65616
(800) 321-8594

Charming Victorian inn situated five miles north of Branson. Seven guest rooms, three elegant suites, and four smaller rooms. Near hiking trails and landscaped gardens. Perfect for weddings, family reunions, and corporate retreats. $75-95. $10 extra person sharing a room.

Ozark Mountain Country Bed and Breakfast 162

Box 295, 65616
(800) 321-8594

Country-style home with antique furnishings. Features three main level guest rooms with queen beds and private baths. One lower level suite boasts a private entrance, king-size bed. sitting area, and private bath. $65-90.

Ozark Mountain Country Bed and Breakfast 163

Box 295, 65616
(800) 321-8594

This three-bedroom German-style "haus" features a master bedroom with king bed and adjoining bath, plus smaller bedrooms with queen and double beds that share a bath. Enjoy a spacious livingroom and complete, well-stocked kitchen. TV and air conditioning make this a very comfortable stay. $75-125.

CAMDENTON

Ozark Mountain Country Bed and Breakfast 203

Box 295, Branson, 65616
(800) 321-8594

This guest house is only 50 feet from Lake of the Ozarks. The master suite has adjoining bath. Another room shares a hall bath. Adults only. Smoking only on decks. Hearty continental breakfast served. $55.

6 Pets welcome; 8 Children welcome; 9 Social drinking allowed; 10 Tennis available; 11 Swimming available; 12 Golf available; 13 Skiing available; 14 May be booked through travel agents.

Ozark Mountain Country Bed and Breakfast 207

Box 295, Branson, 65616
(800) 321-8594

The two guest rooms come with a full hearty breakfast served in the dining room or on the shady deck. King and queen beds with shared bath or private bath option. Smoking on deck. Available all year. $45-80.

Ozark Mountain Country Bed and Breakfast 209

Box 295, Branson, 65616
(800) 321-8594

This 676-acre farm is eight miles northeast of Carthage. The four-story mansion, built between 1900 and 1904, contains 22 guest rooms filled with family heirloom antiques. Four guest rooms on the second floor. Continental breakfast. Pool and Ping-Pong tables. Tour of the home and grounds. $55.

Ozark Mountain Country Bed and Breakfast 227

Box 295, Branson, 65616
(800) 321-8594

This 1890s mansion filled with antiques permits its guests to return to the Victorian era. Five elegant guest rooms, each uniquely furnished. Private bath. Hearty home-made breakfast. $50-90.

Ozark Mountain Country Bed and Breakfast 225

Box 295, Branson, 65616
(800) 321-8594

This 10,000-square-foot Colonial-style mansion overlooks a private lake. It offers four guest rooms with four full baths. Country breakfast. Adults only. Guests can enjoy an indoor swimming pool and Jacuzzi spa as well as a game room with a pool table and a Ping-Pong table. Smoking only in pool room. $55.

Fifth Street Mansion

213 South Fifth Street, 63401
(314) 221-0445; (800) 874-5661

This historic 1858 Italianate mansion of lifelong friends of Mark Twain combines Victorian charm with contemporary comforts. Period furnishings, original fireplaces, stained glass, and old-fashioned hospitality abound. Walk to historic sites, shops, and restaurants. Inquire about special weekends.

Hosts: Donalene and Mike Andreotti
Rooms: 7 (PB) $60-90
Full Breakfast
Credit Cards: A, B, C, D
Notes: 2, 5, 8, 9, 10, 11, 12, 14

Ozark Mountain Country #202

Box 295, Branson, 65616
(417) 334-4720; (800) 695-1546

This authentic Victorian home is furnished with antiques. One guest room is on the main floor; three are upstairs. $35.

Birk's Gasthaus

700 Goethe Street, 65041
(314) 486-2911

NOTES: Credit cards accepted: A Master Card; B Visa; C American Express; D Discover Card; E Diner's Club; F Other; 2 Personal Checks accepted; 3 Lunch available; 4 Dinner available; 5 Open all year;

Romantic Victorian mansion. Two weekends a month you can be Agatha Christie and try to solve the mystery of the month.

Hosts: Elmer and Gloria Birk
Rooms: 9 (7 PB; 2 SB) $51.21-83.49
Full Breakfast
Credit Cards: A, B, C, D
Closed Dec. 23-Jan. 31
Notes: 2, 8 (over 16), 9, 10, 11, 12, 14

Ozark Mountain Country Bed and Breakfast 232

Box 295, Branson, 65616
(800) 321-8594

This bed and breakfast has two rooms, and children are welcome. Features include sitting area for guests, TV/VCR, deck overlooking lake and quaint village, and a queen waterbed for one room. Children under two stay for free. Three guest rooms. $45-90.

INDEPENDENCE

The House of Hoyt

626 North Delaware, 64050
(816) 461-7226

Every bedroom is decorated in a theme, from the Ralph Lauren Room to the Old World French Room, the Elaborate Italian Folk Art Room, and the spacious bridal suite done in Colonial American. A gourmet breakfast is served in the formal country French breakfast room, or outside in a private garden setting. Formal dinners are available in the spectacular formal dining room decorated with an 18th-century lighted chandelier and a 12-foot walnut Chippendale table.

Host: Martin Hoyt
Rooms: 4 (1 PB; 2 SB) $65-85
Full Breakfast
Credit Cards: A, B
Notes: 3, 4, 9, 10, 11, 14

Woodstock Inn Bed and Breakfast

1212 West Lexington, 64050
(816) 833-2233

Situated in the heart of historic Independence close to the Truman Library and home, historic mansions, sports stadiums, theme parks, and denominational centers of the Latter Day Saints. Eleven guest rooms are available, each with private bath, air conditioning, and tasteful furnishings. Two suites are handicapped accessible. Excellent food, private parking.

Hosts: Mona and Ben Crosby
Rooms: 11 (PB) $45-65
Full Breakfast
Credit Cards: A, B, C
Notes: 2, 5, 8, 9, 10, 11, 12, 14

INDIAN POINT AREA

Ozark Mountain Country Bed and Breakfast 116

Box 295, Branson, 65616
(800) 321-8594

This home on Indian Point, two miles from Silver Dollar City, is on Table Rock Lake. The home offers a large, carpeted, air-conditioned guest area that is great for families. Private entrance, patio overlooking the lake, large boat dock. Guests may secure a rental boat at dock; public launch is less than a mile from the home. The guest area has a queen bed, sitting area, and adjoining bath. Another small bedroom has a double bed. Full breakfast. Children welcome. From $50.

Ozark Mountain Country Bed and Breakfast 117

Box 295, Branson, 65616
(800) 321-8594

6 Pets welcome; 8 Children welcome; 9 Social drinking allowed; 10 Tennis available; 11 Swimming available; 12 Golf available; 13 Skiing available; 14 May be booked through travel agents.

This home offers a peaceful lakefront get-away three miles from Silver Dollar City. Amenities include full breakfast, private baths, king and queen beds, TV, view of Table Rock Lake, exclusive use of great room, private entrance, fireplace, and whirlpool. Children are welcome. Open all year, and discounts are available January and February. $50-90.

Ozark Mountain Country Bed and Breakfast 126

Box 295, Branson, 65616
(800) 321-8594

This contemporary home near Silver Dollar City has a view of Table Rock Lake. A full gourmet breakfast with homemade breads is featured. Children welcome. $50-75.

KANSAS CITY _____

Bed and Breakfast Kansas City

P. O. Box 14781, 66285
(913) 888-3636

Forty Victorian turn-of-the-century contemporary homes and three inns for great getaways. Accommodations near County Club Plaza, Kansas City, Independence or adjacent historic towns. All sizes of beds, all but two with private bath. Some with fireplace, Jacuzzi, pools, hot tubs. Accommodations also available in the country. Full breakfast. RSO Agent: Edwina Monroe. $40-125.

Milford House

3605 Gillham Road, 64111
(816) 753-1269

Milford House is a three-story red brick home combining Queen Anne and Dutch Colonial architecture, situated conveniently between the Plaza and Crown Center. The guest rooms, reached by climbing the 100-year-old spiral staircase, are furnished with antiques. Each guest room is equipped with cable TV. The livingroom is dominated by a 70-square-foot stained-glass window, which is a copy of a Tiffany landscape. The house is centrally heated and air-conditioned, and breakfast is a real eye-opener.

Hosts: Ian and Pat Mills
Rooms: 4 (PB) $70
Full Breakfast
Credit Cards: A, B, C
Notes: 2, 5, 9, 10, 14

KIMBERLING CITY AREA _____

Ozark Mountain Country Bed and Breakfast 102-A

Box 295, Branson, 65616
(800) 321-8594

This charming log home is four miles south of Kimberling City. Two guest rooms available. The room in the loft is decorated with antiques. Downstairs guest bath includes tub and shower. Full breakfast is served. Smoking only on deck. No preteenagers. $50-90.

Ozark Mountain Country Bed and Breakfast 102-B

Box 295, Branson, 65616
(800) 321-8594

Milford House

A log cabin with double bed plus sleeper sofa is at your disposal. There is also a sleeping loft for children, and you are entitled to a full breakfast. Open April through November. $50.

Ozark Mountain Country Bed and Breakfast 102-C

Box 295, Branson, 65616
(800) 321-8594

Gingerbread-style log cabin has queen bed, kitchenette, sleeping loft for three, Franklin stove, and continental breakfast is self-serve. Open all year. $60.

Ozark Mountain Country Bed and Breakfast 111

Box 295, Branson, 65616
(800) 321-8594

Victorian furnishings and unique decor adorn this house located near Kimberling City. Amenities include private entrance, bath with shower, king bed, sitting area, cable TV, lake view deck, and gourmet breakfast. Open all year. $50-65.

Ozark Mountain Country Bed and Breakfast 137

Box 295, Branson, 65616
(800) 321-8594

Situated near a golf course in Kimberling City, this bed and breakfast offers private entrances, private baths, deck, sitting area, TV/VCR, full breakfast, queen and double beds. Not suitable for children. Available all year. $60-125.

Ozark Mountain Country Bed and Breakfast 151

Box 295, 65616
(800) 321-8594

Private three-bedroom suite with private bath, queen bed, kitchen, livingroom, TV, and private entrance. $50-115. $10 extra adult; $5 extra child.

Ozark Mountain Country Bed and Breakfast 155

Box 295, 65616
(800) 321-8594

Probably the most unique bed and breakfast stay in the state! This 47-foot luxury yacht docked at Kimberling City features two state rooms, two baths, and a breakfast basket. Not suited for small children. $105-195.

LAMPE

Ozark Mountain Country Bed amd Breakfast 121

Box 295, Branson, 65616
(800) 321-8594

You can get a special country breakfast at this farm built in 1890 near Lampe. Features include a king bed, private entrance, hot tub, garden room, family suite, hiking trails, and deck. Children welcome; open year-round. $45-65.

MANSFIELD

Ozark Mountain Country Bed and Breakfast 233

Box 295, Branson, 65616
(800) 321-8594

This quaint bungalow with country Victorian decor and antiques is located near the Laura Ingalls Wilder home. Children are welcome, and a hearty country breakfast is served. $35-45.

6 Pets welcome; 8 Children welcome; 9 Social drinking allowed; 10 Tennis available; 11 Swimming available; 12 Golf available; 13 Skiing available; 14 May be booked through travel agents.

Ozark Mountain Country Bed and Breakfast 234

Box 295, Branson, 65616
(800) 321-8594

A stone's throw from the Wilder home, this contemporary-style home offers hiking trails, picnic area, fishing ponds, optional picnics and dinners, great room with cathedral ceiling, fireplace, games, and TV. Open all year. Delicious breakfasts. $60.

MEXICO

Hylas House Inn

811 South Jefferson, 65265
(314) 581-2011

Quality service and warm hospitality are the first priorities of this inn, featuring Italinate architecture, unique scroll work, mantels of cherubs, antique fireplaces, cherry wood, and white carpeting. Gourmet breakfast. One suite and three rooms with phones, stereo remote cable TV, and VCR. Popular with romantics. Beautifully decorated. Featured on TV.

Hosts: Tom and Linda Hylas
Rooms: 4 (2 PB; 2 SB) $65-95
Full Breakfast
Credit Cards: A, B,
Notes: 2, 4, 5, 9, 10, 11, 12, 14

OSAGE BEACH

Ozark Mountain Country Bed and Breakfast 228

Box 295, Branson, 65616
(800) 321-8594

Contemporary lakeside home features sitting area with fireplace. On the lower level there is a guest room with queen-size bed and private bath with shower. On the main level there are two guest rooms that share a hall bath with tub. Hearty breakfast. Smoking only on decks. $60.

OZARK

Ozark Mountain Country Bed and Breakfast 236

Box 295, Branson, 65616
(800) 321-8594

This rustic home built by Amish craftsmen is located 12 miles from Ozark and 20 miles from Springfield. Wooded surroundings include a view of the Mark Twain National Forest. Relax in spa on the deck at the end of each day or bring a book to cuddle up with next to the fireplace. Other features include queen bed, TV, huge bath tub and shower, antiques, upstairs loft room, and dressing area. Expect a bountiful breakfast. $50-85.

PARKVILLE-KANSAS CITY

Ozark Mountain Country Bed and Breakfast 245

Box 295, Branson, 65616
(800) 321-8594

This unique bed and breakfast is actually an earth shelter home on a farm near Kansas City. There are fish in the pond, and be sure to bring your swim suit for the heated indoor pool. Other amenities include patio, picnic table, lounge, quilts, antiques, great room, fireplace, piano, guest entrance, and parking. A full breakfast is served. $55-75.

POINT LOOKOUT

Cameron's Crag

Box 295, Branson, 65616
(800) 321-8594

The lodge is situated on 90 acres of Ozark woods between Bolivar and Humansville. Venture the outdoors on nature trails, fishing, or at swimming ponds. The lodge is open all year. Other features include a courtyard with picnic table, game table, piano, livingroom, TV/VCR/video library, and country breakfast. Three doubles with private bath. Two rooms with shared bath. $35-45.

Credit Cards: A, B, C, D
Notes: 2, 5, 8 (over six), 9, 14

STE. GENEVIEVE

Southern Hotel

146 South Third Street, 63670
(800) 275-1412

Step gently into the time when riverboats plied the mighty Mississippi River and weary travelers looked forward to the hospitality of this famous hotel. A graceful Federal building operated as a hotel since 1805, it has been well-known for the finest in accommodations, food, busy gambling rooms and the first pool hall west of the Mississippi. A total renovation has restored this magnificent inn.

Hosts: Mike and Barbara Hankins
Rooms: 8 (PB) $65-105
Full Breakfast
Credit Cards: A, B, D
Notes: 2, 5, 9

Southern Hotel

ST. LOUIS

Ozark Mountain Country Bed and Breakfast 241

Box 295, Branson, 65616
(800) 321-8594

This large two-story suburban home is complete with antiques, collectibles, homemade breads, and breakfast cakes. You have three rooms to choose from. $35-45.

Ozark Mountain Country Bed and Breakfast 242

Box 295, Branson, 65616
(800) 321-8594

Situated on the bluffs of the Mississippi River, this French Colonial home was built circa 1790. Completely and authentically restored, its features include a spacious solarium, antiques, quilts, dining room with working fireplace, private and shared baths, homemade breads and continental breakfast. Children are welcome, especially if they want to meet the resident cat. $45-60.

Ozark Mountain Country Bed and Breakfast 243

Box 295, Branson, 65616
(800) 321-8594

In the historic district of St. Charles, this 1840 inn is quaintly furnished with old quilts and late 1800s antiques. Guests have six rooms to choose from (four have private showers and entrances). Two rooms include a shared bath with claw foot tub and shower. Children over ten welcome. $50-75.

The Winter House

3522 Arsenal Street, 63118
(314) 664-4399

6 Pets welcome; 8 Children welcome; 9 Social drinking allowed; 10 Tennis available; 11 Swimming available; 12 Golf available; 13 Skiing available; 14 May be booked through travel agents.

This ten-room Victorian built in 1897 features pressed-tin ceiling in lower bedroom and a suite with balcony and decorative fireplace on second floor. Breakfast, served in the dining room using crystal and antique Wedgewood china, always includes freshly squeezed orange juice. Tea and live piano music are available by reservation. Fruit, candy, and fresh flowers are provided in bedrooms. Nearby attractions include a Victorian walking park on the National Register and the Missouri Botanical Garden. Within four miles are the Arch, Busch Baseball Stadium, the new Science Center, zoo, symphony, and Union Station. Walk to fine dining. Reservations required.

Hosts: Sarah and Kendall Winter
Room: 2 (PB) $60
Suite: 1 (PB) $75
Continental Breakfast
Credit Cards: A, B, C, D, E
Notes: 2, 5, 8, 9, 10, 11, 12, 14

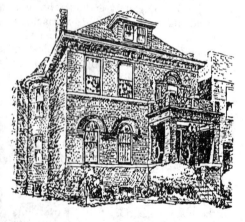

The Winter House

SHELL KNOB

Ozark Mountain Country Bed and Breakfast 128

Box 295, Branson, 65616
(800) 321-8594

Situated 28 miles from Eureka Springs and 28 miles from Silver Dollar City, this bed and breakfast has a deck that overlooks Table Rock Lake. Water activities include a pool, rowboat, swimming area in the lake, and complimentary cruises on the lake. Other features include private entrance, private bath, kitchenette, hot tub on deck, sitting area, and queen beds; children are welcome. Open year-round. $40-70.

Ozark Mountain Country Bed and Breakfast 129

Box 295, Branson, 65616
(800) 321-8594

This private suite is one-half block from Table Rock Lake near Shell Knob. At your disposal is a complete kitchen, dining area, sitting area, and queen sleeper sofa. Open all year. $60.

Ozark Mountain Country Bed and Breakfast 130

Box 295, Branson, 65616
(800) 321-8594

This contemporary bed and breakfast is situated two blocks from Table Rock Lake, where guests can enjoy boating. Other features include exclusive guest sitting room, queen or double bed, fireplace, TV, and hearty breakfast. Open year-round. $45-48.

SILVER DOLLAR CITY

Ozark Mountain Country Bed and Breakfast 122

Box 295, Branson, 65616
(800) 321-8594

This private guest cottage, built in the 1920s and recently refurbished, is situated one-half mile from Silver Dollar City on Highway 76. Great for special occasions. Bath with pedestal tub and separate shower. Dining area with ceiling fan; equipped kitchenette. Hearty continental breakfast in cottage. Air conditioning, private patio. Adults only. $60-80.

SPRINGFIELD

Ozark Mountain Country Bed and Breakfast 205

Box 295, Branson, 65616
(800) 321-8594

This Colonial-style home with antiques is situated in a quiet, rural area in southeast Springfield. Three guest rooms are available. Two upstairs rooms share a hall bath. The private suite has a sitting room with TV and fireplace, and a kitchen. Full breakfast in formal dining room. Airport pickup can be arranged. Two resident Yorkshire terriers. All guests can enjoy a Jacuzzi spa and exercise/game room. $40-70.

Ozark Mountain Country Bed and Breakfast 206

Box 295, Branson, 65616
(800) 321-8594

Take a step back in time! This 1894 mansion situated in Springfield's historic district has been redecorated with antiques and stained glass. The gathering room has a fireplace and game table. Seven distinctive guest rooms. Full gourmet breakfast. Weekday special, Sunday through Thursday. Children over eight welcome. Smoking only on veranda. $65-110.

Ozark Mountain Country Bed and Breakfast 211

Box 295, Branson, 65616
(800) 321-8594

This charming country home four miles south of Springfield is filled with antiques. Full country breakfast is served on antique china. Resident dogs and cats. No pre-teenagers. Whirlpool tub. One room has a queen canopy bed with adjoining bath and sitting room. $40-95.

SUNRISE BEACH

Ozark Mountain Country Bed and Breakfast 235

Box 295, Branson, 65616
(800) 321-8594

This elegant home with a spectacular view is on the quiet side of Lake of the Ozarks. Amenities include fresh flowers, swimming/fishing dock, gas grill, sitting area, spa, and a gourmet breakfast served overlooking the lake. Fishing trips, candlelight dinners, and cruiser excursions can be arranged to Tantara Resort. Also available is dinner at nearby Amish settlement. Open all year. $75-95.

TABLE ROCK LAKE

Ozark Mountain Country Bed and Breakfast 106

Box 295, Branson, 65616
(800) 321-8594

This bed and breakfast is situated one and one-quarter miles from a marina and swimming area and just up the hill from Table Rock Lake. Features include private baths, livingroom, TV, and sleeper sofa. A continental breakfast is served. $35-45.

Ozark Mountain Country Bed and Breakfast 131

Box 295, 65616
(800) 321-8594

6 Pets welcome; 8 Children welcome; 9 Social drinking allowed; 10 Tennis available; 11 Swimming available; 12 Golf available; 13 Skiing available; 14 May be booked through travel agents.

This suite on a bluff overlooking Table Rock Lake features two bedrooms with queen beds, two baths, kitchen, wood-burning stove, and a great room. $55-100.

Ozark Mountain Country Bed and Breakfast 154

Box 295, 65616
(800) 321-8495

This lovely bed and breakfast features a spectacular view of Table Rock Lake. A hearty breakfast is served in the dining room. A luxurious suite features a king bed, sitting area, TV, and fireplace. The two upstairs guest rooms offer queen and double beds, a common sitting area, and a library. $65-95. $10 extra person.

Ozark Mountain Country Bed and Breakfast 157

Box 295, 65616
(800) 321-8495

This bed and breakfast stay features a suite overlooking Table Rock Lake, with a king bed, TV, hot tub, private entrance, and bath. An additional rooms features a day bed (two twins). A full breakfast is served. Children over 12 welcome. $75-105.

WARRENSBURG

Cedarcroft Farm

431 SE "Y" Highway, 64093
(816) 747-5728; (800) 368-4944

Cedarcroft Farm offers old-fashioned country hospitality, country quiet, and country cooking in an antique-filled 1867 family farmhouse. Guests may explore the 80 acres of secluded woods, meadows, and streams and enjoy a full country breakfast.

Civil War re-enactor hosts demonstrate 1860s soldiers' life. Horseback riding and bike trails nearby.

Hosts: Sandra and Bill Wayne
Rooms: 2 (SB) $45-48
Full Breakfast
Credit Cards: A, B, D
Notes: 2, 5, 8, 9, 14

Ozark Mountain Country Bed and Breakfast 216

Box 295, Branson, 65616
(417) 334-4720; (800) 695-1546

An 1867 farmhouse features antiques, a parlor, and sitting room for guest use. A country breakfast is served. $40.

WASHINGTON

Washington House Bed and Breakfast

3 Lafayette Street, 63090
(314) 239-2417; (314) 239-9834

Washington House, built circa 1837, is situated in a National Historic District. This authentically restored inn on the Missouri River features river views, canopy beds, antiques, complimentary wine, and full breakfast. Washington House is in the heart of Missouri's wine country, only 45 minutes west of St. Louis.

Hosts: Chuck and Kathy Davis
Rooms: 4 (PB) $55-75
Full Breakfast
Credit Cards: None
Notes: 2, 5, 8, 9, 10, 11, 12, 14

WEST PLAINS

Ozark Mountain Country Bed and Breakfast 212

Box 295, Branson, 65616
(800) 321-8594

NOTES: Credit cards accepted: A Master Card; B Visa; C American Express; D Discover Card; E Diner's Club; F Other; 2 Personal Checks accepted; 3 Lunch available; 4 Dinner available; 5 Open all year;

This farm welcomes pets and has a stable for horses. Double beds with hall bath. Resident cat. Weekends only. $35-60.

Ozark Mountain Country Bed and Breakfast 219

Box 295, Branson, 65616
(800) 321-8594

This 100-year-old Colonial-style home offers many antiques, a library, and a gazebo. Three guest rooms share two hall baths with tub and shower. $55-60.

6 Pets welcome; 8 Children welcome; 9 Social drinking allowed; 10 Tennis available; 11 Swimming available; 12 Golf available; 13 Skiing available; 14 May be booked through travel agents.

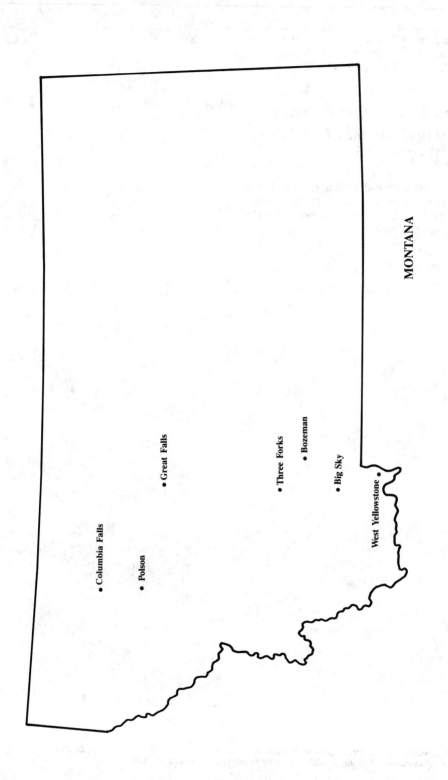

MONTANA

Columbia Falls

Polson

Great Falls

Three Forks

Bozeman

Big Sky

West Yellowstone

Montana

Voss Inn

BIG SKY

Lone Mountain Ranch

Box 160069, 59716
(406) 995-4644

Comfortable ranch cabin accommodations nestled in a secluded valley. Horseback riding, Yellowstone National Park interpretive trips, Orvis-endorsed fly-fishing program, kids' activities, nature hikes in summer. Cross-country skiing, sleigh-ride dinners in winter. Nationally acclaimed cuisine in the spectacular log dining lodge. All meals are included in the weekly rate.

Hosts: Bob and Vivian Schaap
Cabins: 23 (PB) $1075-1300/week
Full Breakfast
Credit Cards: A, B, D
Notes: 2, 3, 4, 8, 9, 10, 12, 13, 14

BOZEMAN

Voss Inn Bed and Breakfast

319 South Wilson, 59715
(406) 587-0982

This magnificently restored Victorian inn in the historic district offers elegant guest rooms with private baths. A delightful gourmet breakfast is served in the privacy of your room. Bozeman is 90 miles north of Yellowstone Park near skiing, fishing, hiking, and snowmobiling. Guided day trips are conducted into Yellowstone and the surrounding area by your host.

Hosts: Bruce and Frankee Muller
Rooms: 6 (PB) $55-70
Full Breakfast
Credit Cards: A, B
Notes: 2, 5, 8 (over 5), 9, 10, 11, 12, 13, 14

COLUMBIA FALLS

Turn in the River Inn

51 Penney Lane, 59912
(406) 257-0724; (800) 892-2474

Western hospitality and European elegance will be yours in this modern Craftsman farm house situated on the Whitefish River. Travelers can enjoy superb cuisine, relax-

Turn in the River Inn

NOTES: Credit cards accepted: A Master Card; B Visa; C American Express; D Discover Card; E Diner's Club; F Other; 2 Personal Checks accepted; 3 Lunch available; 4 Dinner available; 5 Open all year; 6 Pets welcome; 8 Children welcome; 9 Social drinking allowed; 10 Tennis available; 11 Swimming available; 12 Golf available; 13 Skiing available; 14 May be booked through travel agents.

ation, and respite in a perfect country surrounding. Private baths, a television
lounge, great room with a fireplace, music
room, hot tub, hiking, skiing, canoeing,
swimming, and bird watching.

Hosts: Judy and Don Spivey
Rooms: 3 (PB) $75-85
Full Breakfast
Credit Cards: A, B
Notes: 2, 3 (ask in advance), 4 (ask in advance), 5,
   6 (ask in advance), 8, 9, 10, 11, 12, 13, 14

GREAT FALLS

Sovekammer Bed and Breakfast

1109 3rd Avenue North, 59401
(406) 453-6620

The Sovekammer (Danish for sleep chamber) features eye-pleasing combinations of
color and antiques in an early 1900s home
in the historical downtown area. Situated
just one block from the world famous
C. M. Russell Museum, the inn is also a
perfect stop over between Yellowstone and
Glacier National Parks. Let the hosts treat
you to Danish hospitality in the middle of
Montana.

Hosts: Dean and Irene Nielsen
Rooms: 4 (PB) $55-65
Full Breakfast
Credit Cards: None
Notes: 2, 5, 8, 12, 13, 14

POLSON

Ruth's Bed and Breakfast

802 Seventh Avenue West, 59860
(406) 883-2460

There are two guest rooms with portable
bathroom facilities and one room in this
home in which bath and shower are shared.
Each room has a comfortable double bed and
television, with one room featuring a sofa that
will convert into an extra bed and one room
that will accommodate four people.

Host: Ruth Hunter
Rooms: 3 (SB) $28
Full Breakfast
Credit Cards: None
Notes: 2, 5, 8, 9, 10, 11, 12

THREE FORKS

Sacajawea Inn

5 North Main, P. O. Box 648, 59752
(406) 285-6515

The hotel was founded in 1910 by John
Quincy Adams to serve the travelers of the
Milwaukee Railroad and named after
Sacajawea, who guided the expeditions of
Lewis and Clark in the Three Forks area. On
the route between Yellowstone and Glacier
National Parks and within easy access of hiking, skiing, fishing, hunting, and golf. Graced
with rocking chairs, a large veranda welcomes you to a spacious lobby, fine dining,
and comfortable nostalgic rooms.

Host: Jane and Smith Roedel
Rooms: 33 (PB) $50-99
Continental Breakfast
Credit Cards: A, B, C, D
Notes: 2, 4, 5, 6 (limited), 8, 9, 12, 14

WEST YELLOWSTONE

Sportsman's High

750 Deer Street, 59758
(406) 646-7865; (800) 272-4227

This spacious country-style home with
wraparound porch is nestled on three acres
of aspen and pines. Spectacular views
await guests' arrival, only eight miles from
the west entrance of Yellowstone Park. The
moment you enter the front door, you are
treated like a friend. All five antique-filled
rooms are lovingly decorated with country
colors and fabrics. Feather pillows, terry-
cloth robes, and a hot tub are just some of
the amenities you will enjoy.

Hosts: Diana and Gary Baxter
Rooms: 5 (PB) $75-85 in-season; $65-75 off-
   season
Full Breakfast

NOTES: Credit cards accepted: A Master Card; B Visa; C American Express; D Discover Card; E Diner's
Club; F Other; 2 Personal Checks accepted; 3 Lunch available; 4 Dinner available; 5 Open all year;

Credit Cards: A, B
Notes: 2, 5, 10, 11, 12, 13, 14

WHITEFISH

Castle Bed and Breakfast

900 South Baker, 59937
(406) 862-1257

Enjoy one of three comfortable guest rooms in this home that is listed on the National Register of Historic Places. The Castle has unusual architecture and charm. Breakfasts are hearty and tempting, including homemade breads and freshly ground gourmet coffee to compliment the featured menu of the day. The Castle is just nine miles from the Big Mountain Ski Resort and 25 miles from Glacier National Park.

Hosts: Jim and Pat Egan
Rooms: 3 (1 PB; 2 SB) $63-98
Full Breakfast
Credit Cards: A, B, D
Notes: 2, 9, 10, 11, 12, 13

Sportsman's High

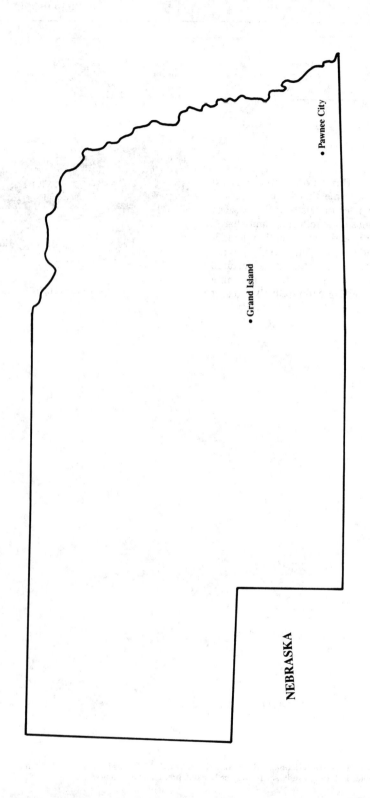

Nebraska

GRAND ISLAND

Kirschke House

1124 West 3rd Street, 68801
(308) 381-6851

Enjoy and experience yesterday today! This 1902 Victorian home is decorated in period antiques and furnishings. A wooden hot tub adds to the Old World charm in the lantern-lit brick wash house.

Host: Lois Hank
Rooms: 4 (SB) $45-55
Full Breakfast
Credit Cards: A, B
Notes: 2, 5, 9, 14

PAWNEE CITY

My Blue Heaven Bed and Breakfast

1041 5th Street, 68420
(402) 852-3131; (402) 852-9914

Conversation, relaxation, and a quiet place to sleep will be found here. There are three places to dine in Pawnee City in the evening. Arrangements can be made to tour the 15-building museum. Directions can be obtained to three lakes situated just 15 minutes away where guests can swim, fish, and water ski. Only a few blocks from shopping, two city parks, a sand greens golf course, municipal swimming pool, pet hospital, and airport. Two rooms are decorated with antiques, tatting, and quilts for your enjoyment.

Hosts: Duane and Yvonne Dalluge
Rooms: 2 (SB) $30-35
Full Breakfast
Credit Cards: A, B
Notes: 2, 5, 10, 11, 12

NOTES: Credit cards accepted: A Master Card; B Visa; C American Express; D Discover Card; E Diner's Club; F Other; 2 Personal Checks accepted; 3 Lunch available; 4 Dinner available; 5 Open all year; 6 Pets welcome; 8 Children welcome; 9 Social drinking allowed; 10 Tennis available; 11 Swimming available; 12 Golf available; 13 Skiing available; 14 May be booked through travel agents.

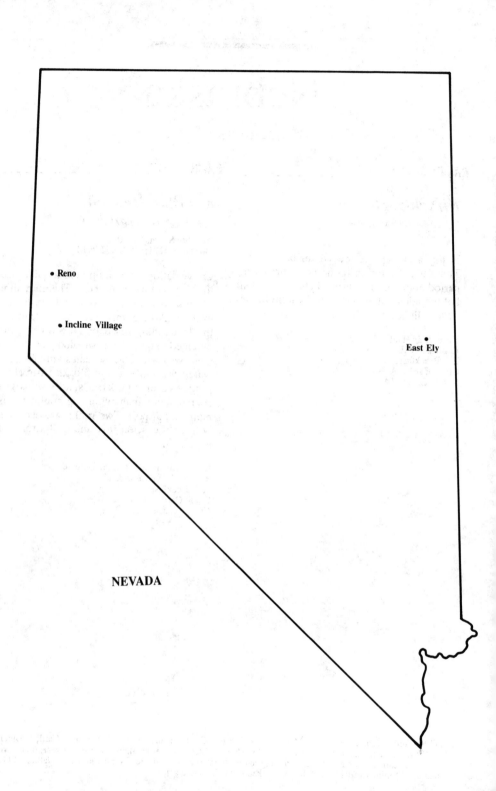

Reno

Incline Village

East Ely

NEVADA

Nevada

_____

Steptoe Valley Inn

P. O. Box 151110, 220 East 11th Street, 89315-1110
(702) 289-8687

A 1907 western store reconstructed (1990) to incorporate details of an elegant Victorian cottage. Private balconies overlook the Nevada Northern Railway Museum, mountains, spruce trees, the rose garden, and gazebo. Guests have use of the library, livingroom, dining room, and outside veranda. Weekend train excursions, golf, and tennis are nearby; Cave Lake State Park is 14 miles away. The Great Basin National Park is 70 miles away. Open June through September.

Hosts: Jane and Norman Lindley
Rooms: 5 (PB) $73.15-79.63
Full Breakfast
Credit Cards: A, B, C
Notes: 2, 10, 12, 14

INCLINE VILLAGE _____

Haus Bavaria

P. O. Box 3308, 89450
(702) 831-6122; (800) GO-TAHOE

Haus Bavaria is a European-style guest house built in 1980. Each of the five upstairs guest rooms opens onto a balcony offering a view of the surrounding mountains, while the livingroom, with its rustic wood paneling and collection of German bric-a-brac, retains the Alpine charm set in place by the original owners. Breakfast, served daily in the cozy dining room downstairs, includes freshly baked goods, seasonal fruits and juices, freshly ground coffee, and a selection of teas.

Host: Bick Hewitt
Rooms: 5 (PB) $70-90
Full Breakfast
Credit Cards: A, B, C
Notes: 2, 5, 9, 10, 11, 12, 13, 14

RENO _____

Bed and Breakfast: South Reno

136 Andrew Lane, 89511
(702) 849-0772

Situated just off Highway 395 in South Reno, the inn is decorated in Early American, including poster-queen beds and beamed ceilings. Landscaped lawns, patios, and decks surround a heated swimming pool. Facing the bed and breakfast are ranch lands, Mount Rose, and Slide Mountain for hiking, sleigh riding, and downhill skiing. Visit Lake Tahoe, Virginia City, or the many Reno casinos. The inn is twelve miles from the airport. Open all year.

Host: Caroline S. Walters
Rooms: 3 (1 PB; 2 SB) $64-74
Full Breakfast
Credit Cards: C
Notes: 2, 5, 8, 9, 10, 11, 12, 13, 14

NOTES: Credit cards accepted: A Master Card; B Visa; C American Express; D Discover Card; E Diner's Club; F Other; 2 Personal Checks accepted; 3 Lunch available; 4 Dinner available; 5 Open all year; 6 Pets welcome; 8 Children welcome; 9 Social drinking allowed; 10 Tennis available; 11 Swimming available; 12 Golf available; 13 Skiing available; 14 May be booked through travel agents.

NEW HAMPSHIRE

• Jefferson

• Franconia   Moultonborough
Stark Village •   •

                    Madison   Jackson
                              •
                    Bartlett •   • Glen   • Sugar Hill
North Woodstock •   North Conway •
                                      •
        Lyme •   Eaton Center

Wentworth •   • Campton
              • Rumney
                    • Holderness

                    • Mirror Lake
            Center Harbor
                    •
        • Enfield   • Meredith
                    • Laconia

• Claremont   • North Sutton   New Hampton •
              • Sutton Mills

                                        Dover •
        • Munsonville   • Henniker
                    • Hillsboro   Portsmouth •
                                      • Northwood
• Marlborough   Hampstead Hampton •
              • Wilton Center   Haverhill •
        Londonderry •
    New Ipswich •

New Hampshire

The English House

Box 162, 03216
(603) 735-5987

This home has been renovated and furnished to re-create an English country house. Afternoon tea, as well as a notable breakfast, is served to all guests. All breads, muffins, cakes, jams, jellies, and marmalades are homemade.

Hosts: Gillian and Ken Smith
Rooms: 7 (PB) $75
Full Breakfast
Minimum stay for foliage weekends and holidays: 2 nights
Credit Cards: A, B
Closed one week in mid-March
Notes: 2, 5, 8 (over 7), 9, 10, 11, 12, 13

The Country Inn at Bartlett

Route 302, P. O. Box 327, 03812
(603) 374-2353

A bed and breakfast inn for hikers, skiers, and outdoor lovers in the White Mountains of New Hampshire. Inn and cottage rooms, fireplaces, hearty breakfasts, outdoor hot tub. The warmth and friendly atmosphere of this inn makes it a memorable stay.

Host: Mark Dindorf
Rooms: 16 (10 PB; 6 SB) $28-48 per person
Full Breakfast
Credit Cards: A, B, C
Notes: 2, 5, 6, 8, 9, 10, 11, 12, 13, 14

The Notchland Inn

Hart's Location, 03812
(603) 374-6131

A traditional country inn where hospitality hasn't been forgotten. There are 11 guest rooms, all with working fireplaces and private baths. Gourmet dining, spectacular mountain views, hiking, cross-country skiing, and swimming are offered at this secluded mountain estate.

Hosts: John and Pat Bernardin
Rooms: 11 (PB) $47.50-83/person
Full Breakfast and Dinner
Credit Cards: A, B, C
Notes: 2, 4, 5, 10, 11, 12, 13, 14

Amber Lights Inn Bed and Breakfast

Rural Free Delivery 1, Box 828, 03223
(603) 726-4077

The newest bed and breakfast in the White Mountains, this lovingly restored 1815 Colonial offers a sumptuous six-course breakfast, homemade bread and muffins, queen country beds, hand-made quilts, and meticulously clean guest rooms. Hannah Adams dining room with a fireplace, guest library, and garden room. Hors d'oeuvres served nightly. Conveniently situated in Thornton between Loon Mountain and Waterville Valley. Murder mystery weekends available.

Hosts: Paul V. Sears and Carola L. Warnsman
Rooms: 5 (1 PB; 4 SB) $65-70
Full Breakfast

NOTES: Credit cards accepted: A Master Card; B Visa; C American Express; D Discover Card; E Diner's Club; F Other; 2 Personal Checks accepted; 3 Lunch available; 4 Dinner available; 5 Open all year; 6 Pets welcome; 8 Children welcome; 9 Social drinking allowed; 10 Tennis available; 11 Swimming available; 12 Golf available; 13 Skiing available; 14 May be booked through travel agents.

Credit Cards: A, B, C, D
Notes: 2, 5, 8, 9, 10, 11, 12, 13, 14

Mountain-Fare Inn
Mad River Road, P. O. Box 553, 03223
(603) 726-4283

The Mountain-Fare Inn is a comfortable, friendly home two hours from Boston, 15 minutes from Waterville Valley Resort, and 20 minutes from Franconia Notch. The White Mountains offer a peaceful retreat and New England's most alluring sports and recreation possibilities. The hosts make this vitality and excitement available to their guests.

Hosts: Susan and Nick Preston
Rooms: 8 (5 PB; 3 SB) $48-70
Full Breakfast
Credit Cards: None
Notes: 2, 4, 5, 8, 9, 10, 11, 12, 13, 14

New Hampshire Bed and Breakfast NH 116
329 Lake Drive, Guilford, CT 06437
(800) 582-0853

Situated just minutes from I-93, the Waterville Valley four-season resort area, the Franconia Notch State Park, and Plymouth. This large, white clapboard farmhouse has gables, a farmer's porch, and a warm hearth. You can enjoy the recreational activities in the White Mountains: hiking the marked Appalachian Mountain Club trails, bicycling, snowmobiling, swimming, picnicking, and an excellent selection of alpine and cross-country skiing. The large lawns feature volleyball and croquet sets. Guests are welcome to use the large country livingroom with fireplace, color cable TV with VCR, games, puzzles, and books. Enjoy a full breakfast and generous seasonal snacks. Eight guest rooms with private baths, three with shared bath. Children welcome. $40-70.

CENTER HARBOR

New Hampshire Bed and Breakfast NH 215
329 Lake Drive, Guilford, CT 06437
(800) 582-0853

Situated on 75 beautiful acres on Long Island in the center of Lake Winnipesaukee (connected by bridge). The house was built in the 1830s and was established as an inn in 1874. It is now run by a descendant of the original family. Guests enjoy the 75 acres of lawns, fields, and woods which run to the water's edge, either of two private beaches, the lakeside picnic area, and the large livingroom with fieldstone fireplace. A hearty country breakfast is served in the dining room. Children welcome. No pets. Open from the end of June through September. $45 for single; $50 for double.

CLAREMONT

Goddard Mansion Bed and Breakfast
25 Hillstead Road, 03743-3399
(603) 543-0603; (800) 736-0603
FAX (603) 543-0657

Delightful early 1900s English manor-style 18-room mansion on seven acres with panoramic mountain view. Expansive porches and tea house. Eight uniquely decorated

Goddard Mansion

guest rooms await. A full continental, natural food breakfast starts each day. Four-season activities nearby, including historical sites, antique shops, and excellent restaurants.

Hosts: Frank and Debbie Albee
Rooms: 8 (2 PB; 6 SB) $65-95
Full Breakfast
Credit Cards: A, B, D, E, F
Notes: 2, 5, 8, 9, 10, 12, 13

DOVER

New Hampshire Bed and Breakfast NH 410
329 Lake Drive, Guilford, CT 06437
(800) 582-0853

The charming 100-year-old Queen Anne Victorian offers a special experience for a traveler who wants more than the ordinary. A turned oak staircase and fretwork welcome guests to the turn-of-the-century era. Relax on the tree-shaded porch or enjoy the livingroom in all seasons. Located in the seacoast area, convenient to UNH, Portsmouth, Durham, and Maine. Two guest rooms furnished with antiques and a double bed share a full bath. Children over four welcome. $45-50.

New Hampshire Bed and Breakfast NH 412
329 Lake Drive, Guilford, CT 06437
(800) 582-0853

A large Victorian country home dating from the mid-19th century, this farm offers comfortable, spacious guest rooms in a rural setting. The inn is set among rolling fields with nature trails along the Cacheco River. Guests are welcome to use the antique-filled formal parlor and library. There are horseshoe pits and a volleyball net. Swimming, cross-country skiing, golf, and snowmobiling are available nearby. A full, home-cooked breakfast is complemented by fresh fruits and juices, home-

made muffins, breads, scones, and fresh brewed coffee, all served with a touch of Scottish hospitality. Near New Hampshire's seacoast and mountains, near Spaulding Turnpike. Downtown Dover is two miles away and Portsmouth is 15 minutes away. Five guest rooms share two antique baths and are furnished with antiques. Children welcome. $45-65.

The Inn at Crystal Lake

EATON CENTER

The Inn at Crystal Lake
Route 153, Box 12, 03832
(603) 447-2120; (800) 343-7336

Unwind in a restored 1884 inn in a quiet, scenic corner of the Mount Washington Valley. Eleven guest rooms have Victorian antiques and private baths. There's a parlor, TV-den/library, and cocktail lounge for guests enjoyment. Swim, fish, canoe, ski, skate, outlet shop, or just relax! Modified American Plan available.

Hosts: Walter and Jacqueline Spink
Rooms: 11 (PB) $60-110
Full Breakfast
Credit Cards: A, B, C, D
Notes: 2, 4, 5, 8, 9, 10, 11, 12, 13, 14

ENFIELD

Boulder Cottage
Rural Route 1, Box 257, Crystal Lake Road, 03748
(603) 632-7355

---

6 Pets welcome; 8 Children welcome; 9 Social drinking allowed; 10 Tennis available; 11 Swimming available; 12 Golf available; 13 Skiing available; 14 May be booked through travel agents.

A spacious turn-of-the-century home facing beautiful Crystal Lake, our inn is centrally situated in the Dartmouth-Sunapee region. in the Dartmouth-Sunapee region. Wake up to the breezes of the lake; enjoy a swim, a canoe or boat ride; or take a quiet walk along the shore of the lake. A full New England breakfast is served. Special rates for children and three-night stays. No pets.

Hosts: Barbara and Harry Reed
Rooms: 3 (1 PB; 2 SB) $50-60
Full Breakfast
Open May-November
Credit Cards: None
Notes: 2, 8, 9, 10, 11, 12, 14

FRANCONIA

Blanche's Bed and Breakfast
351 Easton Valley Road, 03580
(603) 823-7061

A sunny, century-old farmhouse restored to a glory it probably never had. Quiet, pastoral setting with views of the Kinsman Ridge. In the English bed and breakfast tradition, offering cotton linens, down comforters, comfortable beds, and a great breakfast that might include fresh fruit salad, spinach omelet, or blueberry pancakes (with pure maple syrup) and homemade muffins. Decorative painting throughout; working studio featuring unusual handmade floorcloths. Ask about the live folk music.

Hosts: Brenda Shannon and John Vail
Rooms: 5 (SB) $60
Full Breakfast
Credit Cards: A, B, C
Notes: 2, 4 (to groups), 5, 8, 9, 10, 11, 12, 13, 14

Bungay Jar Bed and Breakfast
P. O. Box 15, Easton Valley Road, 03580
(603) 823-7775

Secluded woodlands with spectacular mountain views, brook, and gardens make memorable this home built from an 18th-century barn. King or queen suites, private balconies, skylights, six-foot soaking tub, sauna, canopy bed. Two-story common area with fireplace for reading, music, and talk. Mountain gaze in the morning sun while breakfasting outside in summer. Small in scale, intimate. Hosts are a landscape architect, a patent attorney, and their young son.

Hosts: Kate Kerivan and Lee Strimbeck
Rooms: 6 (4 PB; 2 SB) $60-110
Full Breakfast
Credit Cards: A, B, C
Notes: 2, 5, 8, 9, 10, 11, 12, 13, 14

Bungay Jar

The Inn at Forest Hills
P. O. Box 783, 03580
(603) 823-9550; (603) 823-8701
FAX (603) 823-5555

Enjoy the majestic beauty and year-round attractions of the White Mountains of New Hampshire at a charming 19-room, 100-year-old Tudor Manor house. Eight comfortable, gracious rooms with either private or shared baths, sun-filled solarium, livingroom, dining room, and alpine room. All feature fireplaces for socializing in country casualness. Gourmet New England breakfast. A fine country inn.

Hosts: Joanne and Gordon Haym
Rooms: 8 (3 PB; 5 SB) $25-50
Full Breakfast
Credit Cards: A, B
Notes: 2, 4, 5, 9, 10, 11, 12, 13

NOTES: Credit cards accepted: A Master Card; B Visa; C American Express; D Discover Card; E Diner's Club; F Other; 2 Personal Checks accepted; 3 Lunch available; 4 Dinner available; 5 Open all year;

Lovetts' Inn by Lafayette Brook
Route 18, Profile Road, 03580
(603) 823-7761; (800) 356-3802

Lovetts' Inn is a sophisticated country inn and bed and breakfast that emphasizes excellent food and service. Situated at the head of Franconia Notch, it affords a great opportunity for sightseeing, hiking, walking, and photo trips. The area abounds with things to do: antiquing, summer theater, and exploring the unique trails and gorges in the notch. Cross-country ski trails are on the premises, and downhill skiing is available on nearby Cannon Mountain. Reserve early.

Hosts: Anthony and Sharon Avrutine
Rooms: 30 (22 PB; 8 SB) $40-146
Full Breakfast
Credit Cards: A, B, C
Notes: 2, 4, 5, 6 (limited), 8, 9, 10, 11, 12, 13 (XC), 14

New Hampshire Bed and Breakfast NH 105
329 Lake Drive, Guilford, CT 06437
(800) 582-0853

In a beautiful meadow setting, only ten-minutes from Franconia Notch, an unadorned, restored Victorian farmhouse. Built in 1887, it was considered haunted by some in the 1940s. Guests will appreciate the decorative painting, stenciling, and glazing. A full breakfast is served in the common room. Minutes from hiking and cross-country skiing on the Appalachian Trail. A day's trip to the attractions of the White Mountains, the Connecticut River Valley, and Vermont. Five guest rooms with shared baths. Children welcome. Dog in residence. No guest pets permitted. $60.

The Bernerhof Inn
P. O. Box 240, 03838
(603) 383-4414; (800) 548-8007

An elegant white Victorian set in the foothills of the White Mountains, the Bernerhof remains true to its European tradition. A Taste of the Mountains Cooking School, the inn's dining table, offers a changing menu of middle European favorites, while popular tap room offers lighter fare. Several rooms boast extra-large hot tubs for true relaxation.

Hosts: Ted and Sharon Wroblewski
Rooms: 9 (2 suites) $90-140
Full Breakfast
Credit Cards: A, B, C
Notes: 2, 3, 4, 5, 8, 9, 10, 11, 12, 13,

New Hampshire Bed and Breakfast NH 605
329 Lake Drive, Guilford, CT 06437
(800) 582-0853

Built by the Ordway family in 1850, this Greek Renaissance Italianate rests on gentle acreage on Main Street in Hampstead. This bed and breakfast boasts three stairways, five chimneys, hardwood floors with Oriental rugs, working wood stoves, and fireplaces. An expanded continental breakfast is served on the weekdays, and a full, hot, hearty breakfast is served in the formal dining room on weekends. Complimentary wine is offered on arrival, and the cookie jar is always full. Five-minutes to Sunset Lake, and 30 minutes from both Manchester and Nashua. Four accommodations are available. Children welcome. $60-90.

6 Pets welcome; 8 Children welcome; 9 Social drinking allowed; 10 Tennis available; 11 Swimming available; 12 Golf available; 13 Skiing available; 14 May be booked through travel agents.

HAMPTON

New Hampshire Bed and Breakfast NH 421

329 Lake Drive, Guilford, CT 06437
(800) 582-0853

This restored custom Cape is on five country acres, just over the Exeter line. The large sunny rooms are furnished with many antiques and lovely reproductions that are crafted by a descendent of Darby Field. Guests enjoy fresh fruit in air-conditioned guest rooms and comfortable cozy livingroom, or enjoy the breeze on the porch. A full country breakfast is served each morning. Three quiet rooms, two that have private baths and one that shares a bath, are air-conditioned and furnished with antiques. Limited smoking on porch. No small children. $65.

The Oceanside

365 Ocean Boulevard, 03842
(603) 926-3542

The Oceanside overlooks the Atlantic Ocean and its beautiful sandy beaches. Each of the ten rooms is tastefully and individually decorated, many with period antiques and all with private baths. The intimate cafe is open for breakfast during July and August and features homemade bread and pastries. At other times a complimentary continental breakfast is available. This gracious inn is in a less congested part of Hampton Beach within easy walking distance of restaurants, shops, and other attractions.

Hosts: Skip and Debbie Windemiller
Rooms: 10 (PB) $86-110
Continental Breakfast
Credit Cards: A, B, C, D
Closed mid-Oct.—mid-May
Notes: 8 (limited), 9, 10, 11, 12

HAVERHILL

Haverhill Inn

Route 10, 03765
(603) 989-5961

This gracious 1810 Colonial home is situated in the Haverhill Cornet Historic District. Enjoy hikes in the nearby White Mountains, take walks along country lanes, converse in the parlor, or choose a book and settle in by the fire. Four rooms, all of which have private baths and working fireplaces, are available.

Hosts: Stephen Campbell and Anne Baird
Rooms: 4 (PB) $75
Full Breakfast
Credit Cards: None
Notes: 2, 9, 10, 13

Haverhill Inn

HENNIKER

Meeting House Inn

35 Flanders Road, 03242
(603) 428-3228

The Meeting House Inn is a renovated 200-year-old country farmstead. Established in 1982, it is situated just south of Henniker at the base of Pat's Peak ski area. The inn seeks to provide a relaxed and cozy atmosphere, where special attention is paid to the individual comforts of the guests. Boasting six rooms, all with private baths, the Meeting House also features a delightful restaurant serving American cuisine.

Hosts: Bill and June Davis; Cheryl and Peter
    Davis-Bakke
Rooms: 6 (PB) $65-93
Full Breakfast
Credit Cards: A, B, C, D
Notes: 4, 5, 9, 10, 11, 12, 13

HOLDERNESS

The Inn on Golden Pond

Route 3, 03245
(603) 968-7269

An 1879 Colonial home situated on 50 wooded acres. Bright and cheerful sitting, breakfast, and game rooms. Close to major ski areas. Nearby is Squam Lake, the setting for the film *On Golden Pond*.

Hosts: Bill Webb and Bonnie Webb
Rooms: 9 (PB) $90-135
Full Breakfast
Minimum stay holidays
Credit Cards: A, B, C
Notes: 2, 5, 8 (over 12), 9, 10, 11, 12, 13, 14

INTERVALE

The Forest, A Country Inn

P. O. Box 37, Route 16A, 03845
(603) 356-9772; (800) 448-3534

Step into an era of old-fashioned charm and hospitality at this beautifully maintained 1890 Victorian inn set on 25 quiet wooded acres three miles from North Conway Village. The 11 lovely rooms, furnished with antiques, boast private baths. A romantic stone cottage built around 1900 is the honeymooner's hideaway. The guests-only dining room serves country breakfasts each morning. Enjoy the large screened veranda, heated outdoor pool, tennis, and 60 kilometers of cross-country ski trails at the door. AAA Three Diamond rated.

Hosts: Ken and Rae Wyman
Rooms: 11 (PB) $60-110
Full Breakfast
Credit Cards: A, B, C
Notes: 2, 5, 8, 9, 10, 11, 12, 13, 14

JACKSON

Ellis River House

Route 16, Box 656, 03846
(603) 383-9339; (800) 233-8309

A traditional bed and breakfast that boasts fine lodging and superb country dining in a turn-of-the-century farmhouse overlooking the spectacular Ellis River. Rooms with Jacuzzi are available. Fireplaces, antiques, minutes to all area attractions. Cross-country skiing from the door. Trout fishing on premises. Enjoy hiking, canoeing, swimming, and outlet shopping.

Hosts: Barry and Barbara Lubao
Rooms: 5 (SB) $47.20-141.60
Cottage: 1 (PB)
Suite: 1 (PB)
Full Breakfast
Credit Cards: A, B, C
Notes: 2, 4, 5, 6 (call), 8, 9, 10, 11, 12, 13, 14

Nestlebrook Farm

Dinsmore Road, 03846
(603) 383-9443

Escape into a Victorian past on a 65-acre estate. Seven elegant guest rooms, all of which have two-person Jacuzzis and some of which have parlor stoves, canopy beds, and fireplaces are also available. Intimate

Nestlebrook Farm

6 Pets welcome; 8 Children welcome; 9 Social drinking allowed; 10 Tennis available; 11 Swimming available; 12 Golf available; 13 Skiing available; 14 May be booked through travel agents.

pub, antiques, and fireplace gazebo. Horsedrawn sleighs, trolley rides, horseback riding, mountain bikes, rowboats, fishing, and Victorian pool. Savor the romance and step back in time at Nestlebrook Farm, a gingerbread country inn.

Hosts: Robert and Nancy Cyr
Rooms: 7 (PB) $95
Full Breakfast
Credit Cards: A, B, C
Notes: 5, 9, 10, 11, 12, 13, 14

New Hampshire Bed and Breakfast NH 109

329 Lake Drive, Guilford, CT 06437
(800) 582-0853

Situated on a birch-covered hill looking towards Mount Washington, this brand-new house has opened recently to rave reviews as a bed and breakfast. The home offers 18th-century antiques, textiles, and folk art, handmade quilts, designer sheets, fresh flowers, fruit baskets, and terrycloth robes. The full gourmet breakfast served on English bone china features sticky buns, shortbread, and fudge. Afternoon tea is served. The livingroom has a fireplace, TV, and VCR. The deck, hammock, and flower gardens provide splendid mountain views. Three guest rooms with private baths. One room has a private Jacuzzi and private deck looking towards Mount Washington. No pets. Children over 10 welcome. $50-95.

Paisley and Parsley

Box 572, Five Mile Circuit Road 16 B, 03846
(603) 383-0859

Small but charming bed and breakfast with a spectacular view of Mount Washington and the valley. Near ski trails and five downhill areas. Noted for superb hospitality and service, gourmet breakfasts, tea time, herb and perennial gardens. Rooms with private baths, telephones, and cable TV available, with one room featuring a

Paisley and Parsley

two-person whirlpool. Perfect for getaways, celebrations, and small meetings. Three- and four-day packages available.

Hosts: Bea and Chuck Stone
Rooms: 3 (PB) $50-125
Full Breakfast
Credit Cards: A, B
Notes: 2, 5, 8 (over 6), 9, 10, 11, 12, 13, 14

JEFFERSON

Applebrook Bed and Breakfast

Route 115A, 03583-0178
(603) 586-7713; (800) 545-6504

Taste the midsummer raspberries while enjoying panoramic mountain views from this old Victorian farmhouse. Bike, hike, fish, ski, go antiquing, or just relax in the sitting room by the goldfish pool or outdoor hot tub. Near Santa's Village and Six Gun City. Dormitory rooms available in addition to private guest rooms. Brochure available.

Hosts: Sandra J. Conley and Martin M. Kelly
Rooms: 10 (4 PB; 6 SB) $46-60
Dorm Rooms: $20/person
Full Breakfast
Credit Cards: A, B, D
Notes: 2, 4, 5, 6, 8, 9, 10, 11, 12, 13, 14

The Jefferson Inn

Route 2, Rural Free Delivery 1, Box 68A, 03583
(603) 586-7998; (800) 729-7908

NOTES: Credit cards accepted: A Master Card; B Visa; C American Express; D Discover Card; E Diner's Club; F Other; 2 Personal Checks accepted; 3 Lunch available; 4 Dinner available; 5 Open all year;

Situated among the White Mountains National Forest, the Jefferson Inn offers a 360-degree view. With Mount Washington nearby, the inn is an ideal location for hiking and cross-country and downhill skiing. Six golf courses nearby. Afternoon tea is served. Swimming pond. Two family suites available and a large family room

Hosts: Greg Brown and Bertie Koelewijn
Rooms: 13 (13 PB) $52-100
Full Breakfast
Minimum stay: 2 nights
Credit Cards: A, B, C, D
Closed November and April
Notes: 2, 8, 9, 10, 11, 12, 13, 14

New Hampshire Bed and Breakfast NH 125

329 Lake Drive, Guilford, CT 06437
(800) 582-0853

Built in 1896, this charming Victorian is nestled among the White Mountain National Forest and offers a 360-degree mountain view. Look across the Jefferson Meadows to Franconia Notch, Mount Washington, and the northern Presidential Range. See Mount Star King and Waumbek in back of the inn. Each room is furnished with period antiques and has a character of its own, such as the Victorian and Shaker rooms. Daily afternoon tea is served in the common room. The inn is ideally situated for hiking, golf, biking, fishing, canoeing, swimming, antiquing, alpine and Nordic skiing, skating, and snowshoeing. Right in town are Santa's Village and Six Gun City attractions. Ten guest rooms, five with private bath. A two-room suite with private bath accommodates families. Children welcome; no pets. $55-82.

LACONIA

New Hampshire Bed and Breakfast NH 237

329 Lake Drive, Guilford, CT 06437
(800) 582-0853

Spacious contemporary home on Lake Winnisquam with spectacular views of lake and mountains. Swimming, canoeing, fishing, and sunbathing on premises. Just 10 minutes to Lake Winnipesaukee attractions and Laconia's downtown area of shops and fine restaurants; 20 minutes to Gunstock Ski area; 30 minutes to White Mountains National Forest. Guests enjoy the great outdoors, the livingroom, and the large fieldstone fireplace in the dining area. A full breakfast is served each morning. Two guest rooms with private bath. Upstairs suite offers an antique double canopy bed, cable TV, refrigerator, and wet bar, a private sitting area, and a balcony-porch overlooking the lake and mountains. Children welcome. $65-85.

New Hampshire Bed and Breakfast NH 238

329 Lake Drive, Guilford, CT 06437
(800) 582-0853

In the local native American tongue, *Winnisquam* means "smiling water." One cannot help but smile at this beautiful setting. The serenity of the lake, mountains, and surrounding woodlands lifts one's spirit. This recently built contemporary was expertly designed and finished by the host. All of the wood finish is native oak and pine milled from trees where the house now stands. The two-story solarium greenhouse that overlooks the lake serves as a wonderful place to read or have a snack. Two sitting rooms have TVs, books, and board games; guests are welcome to use the canoe or sunfish sailboat. Full breakfast and three freshly decorated guest rooms are available. Resident dog, but no guest pets please. Children welcome. $60-85.

6 Pets welcome; 8 Children welcome; 9 Social drinking allowed; 10 Tennis available; 11 Swimming available; 12 Golf available; 13 Skiing available; 14 May be booked through travel agents.

LONDONDERRY

New Hampshire Bed and Breakfast NH615

329 Lake Drive, Guilford, CT 06437
(800) 582-0853

This large Colonial bed and breakfast home specializes in meeting the needs of family vacationers or business travelers. Just minutes from I-93 in a quiet New Hampshire town. Relax in the great room, enjoy the comforts of the fireplace in the family room, or sing songs around a piano in the formal livingroom. Enjoy a breeze on the all-season porch. Take a dip in the pool, play horseshoes, or barbecue the evening meal. Continental breakfast is served each morning. Two guest rooms share a bath. Infants and children over 10 are welcome. $45-50.

LYME

Dowd's Country Inn

5 Main Street, 03768
(603) 795-4712; FAX (603) 795-4220

Dowd's Country Inn is a picture perfect white Colonial built in the 1780s set on six acres with a tranquil pond frequented by ducks and resident turtles. Guests can enjoy afternoon tea with flaky scones and a homemade country breakfast served in the sun porch and the dining room. Twenty-three guest rooms offer their own private baths, and Dartmouth College, biking and hiking trails, and snowmobiling are all close by.

Hosts: Mickey and Tami Dowd
Rooms: 23 (PB) $55-110
Full Breakfast
Credit Cards: A, B, D, E
Notes: 2, 4, 5, 8, 9, 10, 11, 12, 13

Loch Lyme Lodge

Rural Free Delivery 278, Route 10, 03768
(603) 795-2141

Loch Lyme Lodge has been hosting guests since 1924. From May through September, the 25 cabins and rooms in the main lodge are open for the enjoyment of summer vacationers. During the fall and winter months, the main lodge, a farmhouse built in 1784, is open. Children are welcome at any season, and the emphasis is always on comfortable, informal hospitality.

Hosts: Paul and Judy Barker
Rooms: 4 (SB) $24-55/person
Full Breakfast
Credit Cards: None
Notes: 2, 3 (summer), 4 (summer), 5, 6 (summer),
    8, 9, 10, 11, 12, 13

Loch Lyme Lodge

MARLBOROUGH

Peep-Willow Farm

51 Bixby Street, 03455
(603) 876-3807

Peep-Willow Farm is a working Thoroughbred horse farm that also caters to humans. Situated on 20 acres with a view all the way to the Connecticut River Valley. Guests are welcome to help with chores or watch the young horses frolic in the fields, but there is no riding. Flexibility and serenity are the key ingredients to enjoying a stay here.

Host: Noel Aderer
Rooms: 3 (SB) $27.50-45
Full Breakfast
Credit Cards: None
Notes: 2, 5, 6 (by arrangement), 8, 9, 13 (XC), 14

NOTES: Credit cards accepted: A Master Card; B Visa; C American Express; D Discover Card; E Diner's Club; F Other; 2 Personal Checks accepted; 3 Lunch available; 4 Dinner available; 5 Open all year;

Thatcher Hill Inn

Thatcher Hill Road, 03455
(603) 876-3361

A rambling, revitalized 1794 country home on 60 acres of rolling meadows and woodlands in New Hampshire's quiet, uncrowded, and remarkably beautiful Monadnock Region, "the heart of New England." Antique-filled, immaculate, comfortable rooms; private baths. Wheelchair access. Leisurely buffet breakfasts. Enjoy nearby villages, back roads, ponds and streams, covered bridges, state parks, antique shops, maple syrup, fall foliage, and cross-country skiing.

Hosts: Marge and Cal Gage
Rooms: 7 (PB) $68-88
Full Breakfast
Credit Cards: A, B
Notes: 2, 9, 10, 11, 12, 13 (XC)

MEREDITH

New Hampshire Bed and Breakfast NH 211

329 Lake Drive, Guilford, CT 06437
(800) 582-0853

On the shore of Lake Winnipesaukee, four miles from the center of town, sits this beautiful turn-of-the-century home. Enjoy swimming, boating, canoeing, and badminton outside. Inside, relax on the screened porch or in front of the fireplace in the livingroom, overlooking the Ossipee Mountains and Lake Winnipesaukee. In town there are shops, galleries, antiques, and restaurants. In the Lakes Region, guests can enjoy such attractions as scenic train and boat rides, amusement centers, golf, tennis, and boat rentals. Full breakfast is served on the porch or on the 80-foot deck. Three guest rooms with shared bath. Children welcome; pets accepted. Open May, June, September, October. $55.

New Hampshire Bed and Breakfast NH 212

329 Lake Drive, Guilford, CT 06437
(800) 582-0853

The closest bed and breakfast to Meredith Bay Village. Just a short stroll to the Marketplace of shops, galleries, restaurants, and Lake Winnespesaukee. Situated on a quiet residential lane, it guarantees peaceful days and nights; yet guests are central to all activities of the Lakes Region. Minutes away from Winnespesaukee Scenic Railroad, the M.S. *Mount Washing-ton* cruise ship, Analee's Dolls Gift Shop and Museum, and Weirs Beach. Inside the inn, guests enjoy an Early American ambience of fluffy quilts, hand-stenciled walls and floors, antique furnishings, and a romantic brick fireplace in the guest parlor. A continental breakfast is served in the dining room; evening snacks feature seasonal beverages and freshly baked delights. Five guest rooms, two with private bath. Children welcome. Small pets permitted. $50-65.

MIRROR LAKE

Pick Point Lodge, Inc.

Windleblo Road, P. O. Box 220, 03853
(603) 569-1338

Pick Point's main lodge is situated on 113 acres of pine forest and one-half mile of the best shoreline that Lake Winnipesaukee offers. The nonsmoking main lodge rooms feature king beds, color cable TV and AM/FM radio. The lodge also features a game room, library, main livingroom, and 60-foot deck with a spectacular view of the lake. Other activities include tennis, beach, boats, dock space, walking trails, and cookouts.

Host: Dick Newcomb
Rooms: 2 (PB) $135
Full Breakfast
Credit Cards: None
Notes: 2, 10, 11, 12, 14

6 Pets welcome; 8 Children welcome; 9 Social drinking allowed; 10 Tennis available; 11 Swimming available; 12 Golf available; 13 Skiing available; 14 May be booked through travel agents.

MOULTONBOROUGH

Olde Orchard Inn

Route 1, Box 256, 03254
(603) 476-5004

The Olde Orchard Inn is a Colonial home situated on 12 acres with more than 100 apple trees. Each of the four lovely bedrooms has been decorated with needlework. A full country breakfast varies each day.

Host: Mary Senner
Rooms: 4 (PB) $60-70
Full Breakfast
Credit Cards: C
Notes: 2, 5, 9, 11, 13

MUNSONVILLE

New Hampshire Bed and Breakfast NH 505

329 Lake Drive, Guilford, CT 06437
(800) 582-0853

This 200-year-old house was used to house the workers from the mill across the road. The mill produced cotton and woolen fabrics and later became the Colony Mill Chair Company. Although the mill is no longer standing, the house stands near Granite Lake, a natural, spring-fed, sandy bottom, 212-acre lake that accommodates swimming, fishing, and boating. A full country breakfast is served each morning, and handmade quilts, afghans, stencils, and teddy bears adorn each guest room. Five rooms share two full bathrooms. Children welcome. $35-45.

NEW HAMPTON

New Hampshire Bed and Breakfast NH 240

329 Lake Drive, Guilford, CT 06437
(800) 582-0853

This 150-year-old antique-filled home with a converted barn is in the heart of the Lakes Region. Common rooms include the livingroom with a fireplace, den with TV and Nordic Track, and a pool room with pool table, piano, and stereo system. A hearty full breakfast is served, and wine will be offered, candy will be in your room, and fruit is always on the table. New Hampton, home to the co-ed prep school by the same name, is an easy stroll from the inn. Four rooms are available. Children welcome. $40-60.

New Hampshire Bed and Breakfast NH 545

329 Lake Drive, Guilford, CT 06437
(800) 582-0853

Built in 1790, this lovely farmhouse still possesses its early American charm. A classic red barn adjoins the house, and the grounds are bordered by stone walls, gardens, and fruit trees. In summer, guests can enjoy the fresh air on a screened porch full of white wicker furniture. In cooler seasons, guests may play Scrabble by the fire in the parlor or choose a book from the library. Breakfast is served in the keeping room by a crackling fire, and the inn is close to a myriad of activities in the Monadock area. Six guest rooms, two that share a bath and three that offer private baths, are available. Resident dog. Children over seven welcome. $45-65.

NEW IPSWICH

The Inn at New Ipswich

Porter Hill Road, P. O. Box 208, 03071
(603) 878-3711

Relax awhile in a graceful 1790 home amid fruit trees and stone walls. Cozy fireplaces, front-porch rockers, and large comfortable guest rooms furnished country-style. All

NOTES: Credit cards accepted: A Master Card; B Visa; C American Express; D Discover Card; E Diner's Club; F Other; 2 Personal Checks accepted; 3 Lunch available; 4 Dinner available; 5 Open all year;

rooms have private baths. Scrumptious hearthside breakfasts (with fresh eggs from the premises). Situated in the Monadnock region of New Hampshire. Hiking, band concerts, antique auctions, maple sugaring, apple picking, unsurpassed autumn color, and cross-country and downhill skiing. Children over eight welcome.

Hosts: Ginny and Steve Bankuti
Rooms: 5 (PB) $60
Suite: 1 (PB) $95 sleeps 4
Full Breakfast
Credit Cards: A, B
Notes: 2, 5, 8 (over 8), 9, 13

NORTH CONWAY

The Forest, A Country Inn

Route 16 A, 03845
(800) 488-3534

Step into an era of old fashioned charm and hospitality at this beautifully maintained 1890 Victorian inn set on 25 quiet, wooded acres three miles north of North Conway Village. Eleven lovely rooms with private baths are uniquely furnished with antiques. A romantic stone cottage built around 1900 that is a honeymooner's hideaway! The guests-only dining room serves country breakfasts each morning. Enjoy the large, screened veranda, heated outdoor pool, tennis, and 60 kilometers of cross-country ski trails at the door. AAA Three Diamond rated.

The Forest, A Country Inn

Hosts: Ken and Rae Wyman
Rooms: 11 (PB) $60-110
Full Breakfast
Credit Cards: A, B, C
Notes: 2, 5, 8, 9, 10, 11, 12, 13, 14

Nereledge Inn

River Road, P. O. Box 547, 03860
(603) 356-2831

This small 1787 house is a comfortable, casual bed and breakfast with English-style pub (with darts and draft beer). Close to all outdoor activities: hiking, fishing, climbing, canoeing, golfing, and skiing. Walk to village or to river. Reasonable rates include country breakfast with warm apple pie.

Hosts: Valerie and Dave Halpin
Rooms: 9 (4 PB; 5 SB) $59-85
Full Breakfast
Credit Cards: A, B, C
Notes: 2, 5, 8, 10, 11, 12, 13

The Victorian Harvest Inn

28 Locust Lane, Box 1763, 03860
(603) 356-3548; (800) 642-0749

The comfortably elegant 1853 inn is situated at the edge of quaint North Conway Village, featuring shops, outlets, and national forest trails. The large, country-Victorian decorated rooms all feature mountain views. Start a romantic adventure with a bounteous breakfast and hospitality as it was meant to be. Fireplace, in-ground pool, air conditioning. AAA Three Diamond award winner.

Hosts: Linda and Robert Dahlberg
Rooms: 6 (4 PB; 2 SB) $65-80
Full Breakfast
Credit Cards: A, B, C, D
Notes: 2, 5, 8 (over 10), 9, 10, 11, 12, 13, 14

NORTH SUTTON

Follansbee Inn

P. O. Box 92, 03260
(603) 927-4221; (800) 626-4221

6 Pets welcome; 8 Children welcome; 9 Social drinking allowed; 10 Tennis available; 11 Swimming available; 12 Golf available; 13 Skiing available; 14 May be booked through travel agents.

An authentic 1840 New England inn with white clapboard and green trim. Situated on peaceful Kezar Lake, with an old-fashioned porch, comfortable sitting rooms with fireplaces, and charming antique furnishings. Nestled in a small country village but convenient to all area activities (4 miles south of New London and 95 miles north of Boston). Private lakefront and pier with rowboat, canoe, paddle boat, and windsurfer for guests. Beautiful walk around the lake during all seasons.

Hosts: Dick and Sandy Reilein
Rooms: 23 (11 PB; 12 SB) $70-90
Full Breakfast
Credit Cards: A, B
Closed parts of November and April
Notes: 2, 4, 8 (over 10), 9, 10, 11, 12, 13, 14

NORTHWOOD

New Hampshire Bed and Breakfast NH 621

329 Lake Drive, Guilford, CT 06437
(800) 582-0853

This authentic 18th-century New England Colonial home is on 60 acres in a country setting. Enjoy the character of old beams, original fireplaces, early paneling, and wide-board floors. A full breakfast is served in the keeping room in front of the fireplace. Fields and woods surround the property, and horses graze in the pastures. A short walk down a country lane brings guests to a private beach on Jenness Pond, where they are welcome to swim. Three guest rooms furnished with antiques share a bath. Concord is 30 minutes away. Two resident dogs. Children welcome. $45-55.

PORTSMOUTH

The Bow Street Inn

121 Bow Street, 03801
(603) 431-7760

An attractive alternative for any sea coast tourist, the Bow Street Inn is also irresistible lodging for the traveling professional and visitor. Situated on the Piscataqua River in downtown Portsmouth, the inn's newly decorated and furnished rooms offer spectacular river views, rooftop views of Portsmouth, telephone, full bath, and color TV. Guests can also enjoy the sitting room and complimentary continental breakfast. The Bow Street Theatre is on the premises. You can walk across the city's classic liftbridge into Maine or enjoy the flower gardens at Prescott Park just blocks away. Other local attractions include ten restaurants within three blocks and access to waterfront decks and marina.

Hosts: Jann Bova
Rooms: 10 (PB) $89-129
Expanded Continental Breakfast
Credit Cards: A, B
Notes: 8, 9, 12

RUMNEY

New Hampshire Bed and Breakfast NH 248

329 Lake Drive, Guilford, CT 06437
(800) 582-0853

This 1790 Early American farmhouse and attached ell sits on 125 acres of beautiful fields and woodland, with views of the White Mountains. Gardens, a real sugar house, and a barn all add to the peaceful country setting. Guests will enjoy private sitting areas, games, books, and a full country breakfast in the dining room of the main house. Hiking, walking, or cross- country ski trails are available throughout the property. The sugar house is in operation during March and April of every year. Three guest rooms are available. Resident dog. Children welcome. $55-75.

NOTES: Credit cards accepted: A Master Card; B Visa; C American Express; D Discover Card; E Diner's Club; F Other; 2 Personal Checks accepted; 3 Lunch available; 4 Dinner available; 5 Open all year;

STARK VILLAGE

New Hampshire Bed and Breakfast NH 130
329 Lake Drive, Guilford, CT 06437
(800) 582-0853

Situated in historic Stark Village on the banks of the Upper Ammonoosuc River, this large, rambling white farmhouse has been restored and updated to offer guests a large livingroom with TV and fireplace, a country kitchen with antique wood stove, and a dining room where wonderful breakfasts are served. The inn borders the White Mountains National Forest and is three miles from the Nash Stream Valley Wilderness Area known for some of the best hunting and fishing in New Hampshire. Hiking, swimming, canoeing, bicycling, picnicking, hunting, fishing, cross-country skiing, snowmobiling, and skating are all available. Three guest rooms with private baths. Children welcome. No pets. $45.

SUGAR HILL

The Hilltop Inn
Sugar Hill Road, Box 9, 03585
(603) 823-5695; (800) 551-3084

An 1895 Victorian inn in the small village of Sugar Hill in the heart of the White Mountains near Franconia Notch. Peaceful and homey, filled with antiques, lots of porches, and a deck for sunsets and bird watching. Comfortable beds with handmade quilts and large country breakfasts. The Victorian dining room offers memorable fine dining. All rooms have private baths. AAA Three Diamond rating.

Hosts: Meri and Mike Hern
Rooms: 6 (PB) $60-110
Full Breakfast
Minimum stay holidays and fall foliage: 2 nights
Credit Cards: A, B, C, D
Notes: 2, 4, 5, 6, 8, 9, 10, 11, 12, 13

New Hampshire Bed and Breakfast NH 133
329 Lake Drive, Guilford, CT. 06437
(800) 582-0853

Situated on the eastern slope of Sugar Hill overlooking Franconia Notch, Mount Washington, and the Presidential Range. Relax on the porch in a comfortable rocker and enjoy views of expansive fields with a backdrop of Mount Washington's snow-capped peak. The surrounding White Mountains region offers year-round recreation and activities, and on-site tennis courts and a nearby golf course, available for guests to use. A full country breakfast is served each morning; and three guest rooms, all with private baths, are available. Centrally situated within a short drive to Franconia Notch State Park, the Robert Frost Homestead, Cannon Mountain Ski Area, and the New England Ski Museum. Resident dog. Children welcome. $65-80.

SUTTON MILLS

The Quilt House
Bed and Breakfast Marblehead and North Shore
P. O. Box 35, Newtonville, MA. 02160
(617) 964-1606; (800) 832-2632 outside MA

This is one of the prettiest bed and breakfasts in the area. It is a 130-year-old Victorian country house overlooking a quaint village. The hostess runs workshops on quilting, and there are many fine quilts throughout the house. Three guest rooms on the second floor share two baths. Situated ten minutes away from summer theater, excellent restaurants, fine shopping, and antiquing. Delicious full breakfast; children welcome. $45-55.

The Village House
Box 151, Grist Mill Road, 03221
(603) 927-4765

6 Pets welcome; 8 Children welcome; 9 Social drinking allowed; 10 Tennis available; 11 Swimming available; 12 Golf available; 13 Skiing available; 14 May be booked through travel agents.

The Village House is an 1857 country Victorian overlooking a quaint New England village. Recently redecorated, rooms are now outfitted with antiques and old quilts. The guest house, separated from the host's quarters, affords comfort, quiet and relaxation. Room rates include a full country breakfast. The Lake Sunapee area means access to downhill skiing at King Ridge and Mount Sunapee within minutes. Seasonal activities include boating, swimming, fishing, hiking, biking, and shopping.

Hosts: Peggy and Norm Forand
Rooms: 3 (SB) $50
Full Breakfast
Credit Cards: None
Notes: 2, 5, 9, 10, 11, 12, 13, 14

WENTWORTH

New Hampshire Bed and Breakfast NH 120

329 Lake Drive, Guilford, CT 06437
(800) 582-0853

This charming home built in the early 1880s is within an easy drive of both the Lakes Region and Franconia Notch, where guests can enjoy outdoor sports, shops, crafts and art galleries, theater, and fine restaurants. Wentworth offers three natural swimming holes, many hiking trails, fishing streams, and antique shops. The home itself is furnished with antiques. The pine-paneled recreation room is complete with an antique piano, games, an extensive library, and cable TV. Continental breakfast and afternoon teas are served. Six guest rooms, four with private bath. Two housekeeping cottages with kitchen unit, private livingroom with fireplace, and screened porch available. Children welcome. No pets. $60.

WILTON CENTER

Stepping Stones Bed and Breakfast

Bennington Battle Trail, 03086
(603) 654-9048

Stepping Stones is owned by a garden designer and weaver. The house is surrounded by pathways through extensive gardens. Breakfast may be served on the garden terrace in summer or in the solar garden year-round. Working looms, handwoven materials, and a crafts collection make for interesting furnishings. The cozy livingroom provides good reading, TV, and an atmosphere of civilized quiet.

Host: D. Ann Carlsmith
Rooms: 3 (1 PB; 2 SB) $45-50
Full Breakfast
Credit Cards: None
Notes: 2, 5, 6, 8, 9, 12, 13

New Jersey

AVON BY THE SEA

The Avon Manor Inn

109 Sylvania Avenue, 07717
(908) 774-0110

The Avon Manor Inn is a gracious turn-of-the-century home where you will always find a warm and friendly welcome for your special seaside getaways, vacations, and corporate events. Enjoy breakfast in the sunny dining room and ocean breezes on the full wraparound veranda. The large livingroom has a cozy fireplace for winter nights. Many antiques and family heirlooms make this a special retreat to experience the serenity and romance of yesteryear. Air-conditioned. Open year-round.

Hosts: Kathleen and Jim Curley
Rooms: 8 (4 PB; 4 SB) $50-100
Continental Breakfast weekdays; Full Breakfast holidays and weekends
Credit Cards: A, B, C
Notes: 5, 8 (well behaved), 9, 10, 11, 12, 14

The Avon Manor Inn

Cashelmara Inn

22 Lakeside Avenue, 07717
(908) 776-8727

Oceanside/lakefront Victorian inn where guests can enjoy views of the Atlantic from their beds. Rooms are decorated in beautiful Victorian antiques; a wicker-filled veranda overlooking the ocean makes a visit memorable. A suite with a fireplace is also available. Only 55 minutes from New York City and one hour from Philadelphia.

Host: Martin J. Mulligan
Rooms: 14 (PB) $80-157
Full Breakfast
Minimum stay summer weekends: 3 nights; holidays: 1 nights
Credit Cards: A, B, C
Notes: 2, 5, 8, 9, 10, 11, 12

The Sands Bed and Breakfast Inn

42 Sylvania Avenue, 07717
(908) 776-8386

The Sands is situated in a small Victorian town just seven houses from the nicest beach on the Jersey shore. The inn radiates warmth and hospitality. Each of the nine rooms has a paddle fan, and many have sinks and refrigerators. Spend an afternoon on the beautiful white sandy beach, which is just steps away. A lovely breakfast is served each morning in the family dining room or on the porch. A stay at the inn will make you feel relaxed and refreshed.

Host: Ana Suchecki
Rooms: 9 (SB) $50-70
Full Breakfast
Credit Cards: A, B
Notes: 2, 5, 11, 12

6 Pets welcome; 8 Children welcome; 9 Social drinking allowed; 10 Tennis available; 11 Swimming available; 12 Golf available; 13 Skiing available; 14 May be booked through travel agents.

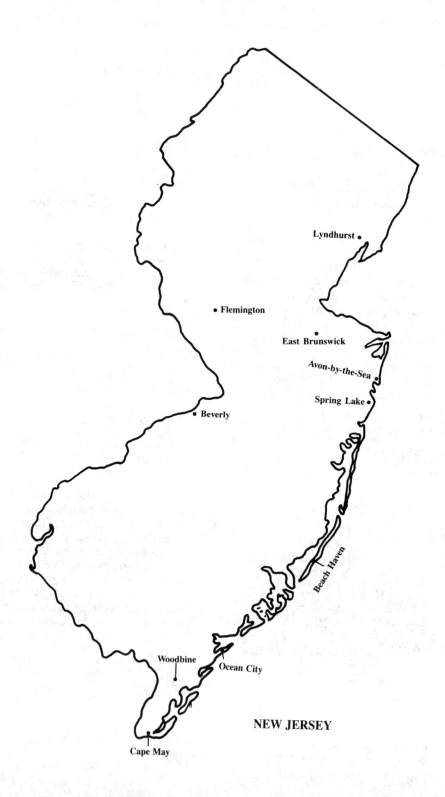

Lyndhurst •

• Flemington

• East Brunswick

Avon-by-the-Sea •

Spring Lake •

• Beverly

Beach Haven

Woodbine
•

Ocean City

NEW JERSEY

Cape May

BEACH HAVEN

Victoria Guest House

126 Amber Street, 08008
(609) 492-4154

Step back to the charm of the late 19th century. The gracious guest houses offer the warmth of a friendly atmosphere and the refreshment of a home away from home in the heart of beautiful Long Beach Island. Guests are only four houses from the beach and steps away from the heated pool. Bicycles, beach chairs, and badges are available. An expanded continental breakfast is served every morning, and lemonade and iced tea are offered in the late afternoon.

Hosts: Marilyn and Leonard Miller
Rooms: 17 (16 PB; 1 SB) $85-130
Expanded Continental Breakfast
Credit Cards: None
Notes: 2, 9, 10, 11, 12

BEVERLY

Historic Whitebriar Bed and Breakfast

1029 Cooper Street, Edgewater Park, 08010
(609) 871-3859

Whitebriar is a 17th-century farmhouse with a glass conservatory, pool, spa, farm animals, and gift shop 25 minutes from Philadelphia. Historic tours of Philadelphia are available upon request. New Jersey hunting tours and environmental retreats available with reservations. Only one hour from Jersey shores, two hours from New York City, and three hours from Washington. Rooms are furnished with antiques, doll houses and quilts. Breakfast is included, with lunch or dinner reservations available. This historic home is situated on the main street of Edgewater Park and backs up to historic Beverly National Cemetery. Tours available.

Hosts: Carole and Bill Moore, Carrie and Lizzie
Rooms: 4 (1 PB; 3 SB) $35-50
Continental or Full Breakfast
Credit Cards: C
Notes: 2, 3, 4, 5, 9, 11

CAPE MAY

The Abbey

34 Gurney Street at Columbia Avenue, 08204
(609) 884-4506

The Abbey consists of two restored Victorian buildings originally in the John McCreary family in the heart of Cape May's historic district. All rooms are furnished with period Victorian antiques and have private baths and small refrigerators. On-site or remote parking; beach chairs included. Afternoon tea served.

Hosts: Jay and Marianne Schatz
Rooms: 14 (PB) $90-185
Full Breakfast and Afternoon Tea
Minimum stay June 15-Sept. 30 and major holidays: 3-4 nights, weekends 2-4
Closed mid-December-March
Credit Cards: A, B, D
Notes: 2 (deposit), 8 (over 12), 9, 10, 11, 12

The Albert Stevens Inn

127 Myrtle Avenue, 08204
(609) 884-4717

Built in 1889 by Dr. Albert G. Stevens for his bride, Bessie, this Queen Anne Victorian home offers its guests a warm, restful visit. Just three blocks from the beach and shopping. A two-course hot breakfast is served each morning with a relaxing tea in the afternoon.

Hosts: Curt and Diane Diviney Rangen
Rooms: 8 (PB) $85-135
Full Breakfast
Credit Cards: A, B
Notes: 2, 4, 5, 9, 10, 11, 12, 14

Amanda's Bed and Breakfast #168

1428 Park Avenue, 21217
(410) 225-0001; (410) 383-1274

NOTES: Credit cards accepted: A Master Card; B Visa; C American Express; D Discover Card; E Diner's Club; F Other; 2 Personal Checks accepted; 3 Lunch available; 4 Dinner available; 5 Open all year; 6 Pets welcome; 8 Children welcome; 9 Social drinking allowed; 10 Tennis available; 11 Swimming available; 12 Golf available; 13 Skiing available; 14 May be booked through travel agents.

Built in 1840 and enlarged in 1900, this Victorian mansion retains the ambience and grandeur of the era. Enjoy elegance and comfort, period reproduction wallpapers, and the original furnishings of the Wilbraham family. Heated swimming pool available to guests. Seven accommodations, all with private baths. Full breakfast. $85-145.

Barnard-Good House

238 Perry Street, 08204
(609) 884-5381

The Barnard-Good House is known for its breakfasts, which were selected as number one by *New Jersey Monthly* magazine. The hosts continue to make them even better. Breakfast consists of four courses, all gourmet and homemade. This purple house caters to happiness and comfort. All rooms have private baths and air conditioning.

Hosts: Nan and Tom Hawkins
Rooms: 5 (PB) $94.16-126.26
Full Breakfast
Minimum stay weekdays and weekends in-season:
   3 nights; holidays in-season: 4 nights
Credit Cards: A, B (for deposit only)
Closed Nov. 15-Mar. 15
Notes: 2, 9, 10, 11, 12

Captain Mey's Inn

202 Ocean Street, 08204
(609) 884-7793

The Dutch heritage is evident, from the Persian rugs on table tops to Delft blue china to European antiques. Guests will marvel at the Eastlake paneling in the dining room, leaded-glass bay window, and the recently restored fireplace. The full country breakfast consists of homemade breads, cakes, egg dishes, meats, cheeses from Holland, fresh fruit, and jelly. The meal is served by candlelight with classical music. Cape May offers a beach, shops, fine restaurants, bicycling, walking and trolley tours, bird watching, boating, fishing, and gaslit streets.

Host: Milly LaCanfora
Rooms: 9 (6 PB; 3 SB) $95-165 in-season; $75-
   120 off-season
Full Breakfast
Credit Cards: A, B
Notes: 5, 8, 9, 10, 11

Colvmns by the Sea

1513 Beach Drive, 08204
(609) 884-2228

Elegant Victorian mansion overlooking the ocean in a historic landmark village. Large, airy rooms are decorated with antiques. Gourmet breakfast and snacks; complimentary bikes, hot tub, beach towels, and badges. Relaxing, enjoyable retreat for history buffs, bird watchers, and seashore lovers. Great restaurants nearby.

Hosts: Barry and Cathy Rein
Rooms: 11 (PB) $110-175
Full Breakfast
Credit Cards: None
Notes: 2, 7, 9, 10, 11, 12

Colvmns by the Sea

Mainstay Inn and Cottage

635 Columbia Avenue, 08204
(609) 884-8690

"The jewel of them all has got to be the Mainstay," says *The Washington Post.* Twelve large, comfortable, antique-filled rooms with private baths. Three parlors, spacious gardens, breakfast and tea daily. This former gentlemen's gambling house offers history, romance, and hospitality. Near shops, restaurants, historic attractions, and beaches.

Hosts: Tom and Sue Carroll
Rooms: 12 (PB) $95-175
Full Breakfast
Credit Cards: None
Notes: 2, 9, 10, 11, 12

The Mason Cottage

625 Columbia Avenue, 08204
(609) 884-3358

The Mason Cottage is an elegant Victorian seaside inn constructed in 1871 as the summer resident for a wealthy Philadelphia entrepreneur. The inn is French Second Empire with a curved roof; and it offers superior accommodations, including several suites with air conditioning and baths with whirlpool tub.

Hosts: Dave and Joan Mason
Rooms: 4 (4 PB) $75-145
Suite: 1 (PB)
Full Breakfast
Credit Cards: A, B
Notes: 2, 9, 10, 11, 12, 14

The Mission Inn

1117 New Jersey Avenue, 08204
(609) 884-8380; (800) 800-8380

A touch of California on the East Coast. A latticed open pergola or dining room for breakfast and enclosed studio offer relaxing ambience, with the beach and surf one-half block away. Spacious guest rooms contain king- and queen-size beds. Hollywood stars and Broadway show people stayed here. Restore yourself in this historic inn. All parking on-site. All baths private. Continental breakfast.

Hosts: Diane Fischer and Judith DeOrio
Rooms: 6 (4 PB; 2 SB) $60-135
Continental Breakfast
Credit Cards: A, B
Notes: 2, 9, 10, 11, 12, 14

The Queen Victoria

The Queen Victoria

102 Ocean Street, 08204
(609) 884-8702

The Wells family welcomes you as friends and treats you royally with unpretentious service and attention to detail. Three restored buildings, furnished with antiques, are in the center of the historic district. Nationally recognized for its special Christmas.

Hosts: Dane and Joan Wells
Rooms: 16 and 7 suites (PB) $65-210 plus tax
Full Breakfast
Credit Cards: A, B
Notes: 2, 5, 8, 9, 10, 11, 12

The Wooden Rabbit

609 Hughes Street, 08204
(609) 884-7293

Situated on one of the prettiest streets in Cape May, the Wooden Rabbit is nestled in the heart of the historic district and is surrounded by Victorian cottages, cool, shady trees, and brick walkways. Two blocks from beautiful sandy beaches, one block from Cape May's quaint shopping mall, and within easy walking distance of fine restaurants. Each guest room is air-conditioned and has a private bath, TV, and comfortably sleeps two to four persons. The Wooden Rabbit is also the home of the

6 Pets welcome; 8 Children welcome; 9 Social drinking allowed; 10 Tennis available; 11 Swimming available; 12 Golf available; 13 Skiing available; 14 May be booked through travel agents.

hosts, comfortable and casual folks, who look forward to sharing their home with you. Decor is country and relaxed. Children welcome.

Hosts: Greg and Debby Burow
Rooms: 3 (PB) $85-165
Full Breakfast
Credit Cards: A, B
Notes: 2, 5, 8, 9, 10, 11, 12

EAST BRUNSWICK

Amanda's Bed and Breakfast #273

1428 Park Avenue, 21217
(410) 225-0001; (410) 383-1274

Enjoy a charming and comfortable bed and breakfast experience in this spacious Cape Cod-style home nestled in the privacy of the East Brunswick suburbs. Sumptuous breakfasts served on the screened-in patio. Three guest rooms share a bath. $60.

FLEMINGTON

Jerica Hill— A Bed and Breakfast Inn

96 Broad Street, 08822
(908) 782-8234

Jerica Hill

Be warmly welcomed at this gracious country inn situated in the historic town of Flemington. Spacious, sunny guest rooms, livingroom with a fireplace, and a wicker-filled screen porch invite you to relax. Champagne hot-air balloon flights are arranged, as well as country picnic and winery tours. A delightful continental-plus breakfast is served, a fully stocked guest pantry is available at all times, and you can have a rental bicycle delivered to the inn. Corporate and midweek rates available. Featured in *Country Inns Bed and Breakfast* and *Mid-Atlantic Country*.

Host: Judith S. Studer
Rooms: 5 (PB) $70-100 plus tax
Expanded Continental Breakfast
Credit Cards: A, B, C
Notes: 2, 5, 9, 10, 11, 12, 14

FRENCHTOWN

The Hunterdon House

12 Bridge Street, 08825
(908) 996-3632

Built in 1864, the Hunterdon House is a true Victorian mansion notable for its Italianate style. There are seven large and lovely rooms, three featuring queen beds, one with a wood-burning fireplace and a two-room suite for honeymooners. Frenchtown is home to fine restaurants, antique shops, and art galleries, and is just minutes from historic Bucks County, Pennsylvania. Outdoor enthusiasts will enjoy river sports and hiking or biking along the 60-mile canal towpath.

Hosts: Stan and Karen Pugh
Rooms: 7 (PB) $110-145
Full Breakfast
Credit Cards: A, B, C, D
Notes: 2, 3, 5, 11, 12, 14

LYNDHURST

The Jeremiah J. Yereance House

410 Riverside Avenue, 07071
(201) 438-9457

NOTES: Credit cards accepted: A Master Card; B Visa; C American Express; D Discover Card; E Diner's Club; F Other; 2 Personal Checks accepted; 3 Lunch available; 4 Dinner available; 5 Open all year;

This 1841 house, a state and national landmark, is five minutes from the Meadowlands complex and 20 minutes from New York City. The guest rooms in the south wing include a front parlor with fireplace, a central hall, and a small but comfortable bedroom that adjoins the parlor and private bath. The north wing includes a common parlor with three bedrooms that share a bath.

Hosts: Evelyn and Frank Pezzolla
Rooms: 4 (1 PB; 3 SB) $55-75
Continental Breakfast
Credit Cards: C
Notes: 2, 5, 8 (over 12), 9, 10

OCEAN CITY

BarnaGate
Bed and Breakfast

637 Wesley Avenue, 08226
(609) 391-9366

This 1895 seashore Victorian, painted a soft peach with mauve and burgundy trim, is only three blocks from the ocean. The attractively furnished rooms have paddle fans, antiques, quilts and wicker accessories. Enjoy the homey atmosphere and sensitive hospitality, where privacy is respected, company offered. Near Cape May and 10 miles from Atlantic City.

Hosts: Lois and Frank Barna
Rooms: 5 (1 PB; 4 S2B) $50-70
Expanded Continental Breakfast
Credit Cards: A, B
Notes: 2, 5, 8 (over 10), 10, 11, 12

OCEAN GROVE

Cordova

26 Webb Avenue, 07756
(908) 774-3084 (summer); (212) 751-9577 (winter)

This century-old Victorian inn, situated in Ocean Grove and listed on the National Register of Historic Places, has a friendly atmosphere with Old World charm. This four-story structure situated one block from the beach boasts three porches, 14 guest rooms and two cottages. Continental breakfast, with kitchen; barbecue and picnic areas available to guests. Great for family gatherings. Saturday night wine and cheese parties. Weekly rates and mid-week specials. Near buses, trains.

Host: Doris Chernik
Rooms: 14 plus 2 cottages (3 PB; 13 SB) $31-56
Continental Breakfast
Credit Cards: None
Notes: None

Pine Tree Inn

10 Main Avenue, 07756
(908) 775-3264

A small Victorian hotel offering a quiet interlude for visitors to the Jersey Shore. It is truly a bed and breakfast adhering to the charm of an earlier time. All the rooms are equipped with sinks and have either private or shared baths. Well-mannered, chaperoned children over the age of 12 are welcome. The hosts love animals but unfortunately cannot accommodate them. For guest convenience, beach towels and bicycles are available upon request.

Hosts: Karen Mason and Francis Goger
Rooms: 13 (3 PB; 8 SB; 2 HB) $55-95
Continental Breakfast
Credit Cards: A, B
Notes: 2, 5, 9, 10, 11, 12

SPRING LAKE

Ashling Cottage

106 Sussex Avenue, 07762
(908) 449-3553

Under sentinel sycamores since 1877 in a storybook setting, Ashling Cottage, a Victorian seaside inn, has long served as a portal to an earlier time. A block from the ocean and just one-half block from a freshwater lake.

Hosts: Goodi and Jack Stewart
Rooms: 10 (8 PB; 2 SB) $60-135
Full Breakfast

6 Pets welcome; 8 Children welcome; 9 Social drinking allowed; 10 Tennis available; 11 Swimming available; 12 Golf available; 13 Skiing available; 14 May be booked through travel agents.

Ashling Cottage

Credit Cards: None
Closed January-March
Notes: 2, 8 (over 12), 9, 10, 11, 12

La Maison

404 Jersey Avenue, 07762
(908) 449-0969

Escape to a romantic French Victorian inn and discover the warm, European hospitality of "The House." La Maison is the smallest, most intimate bed and breakfast in the charming oceanside borough of Spring Lake. Tucked away on a quiet, tree-lined street close to the ocean, shops, restaurants, and the lake. Bedrooms are light and airy with Louis Philippe queen-size beds, en suite baths, cable television, and air conditioning. A wonderful breakfast, complimentary beverages, bicycles, and beach badges are included.

Host: Barbara Furdgna
Rooms: 8 (PB) $85-159
Continental Breakfast
Credit Cards: A, B, C
Notes: 2, 5, 8 (well behaved), 9, 10, 11, 12, 13, 14

Sea Crest by the Sea

19 Tuttle Avenue, 07762
(908) 449-9031

A lovingly restored 1885 Queen Anne Victorian bed and breakfast inn for ladies and gentlemen on seaside holiday. Ocean views, open fireplaces, luxurious linens, feather beds, and buttermilk scones. Candlelit breakfast and afternoon tea; an atmosphere to soothe your weary body and soul.

Hosts: John and Carol Kirby
Rooms: 12 (PB) $84-147
Full Breakfast
Credit Cards: A, B
Notes: 2, 5, 9, 10, 11, 12

WOODBINE

Henry Ludlam Inn

Cape May Country, 1336 Route 47, 08270
(609) 861-5847

This romantic circa 1760 home, voted "Best of the Shore 1991," offers enchanting rooms, unforgettable gourmet breakfasts, bedroom fireplaces, and fireside picnic baskets. Guests invest in memories here.

Hosts: Ann and Marty Thurlow
Rooms: 5 (3 PB; 2 SB) $75-95
Full Breakfast
Credit Cards: A, B, C
Notes: 2, 5, 9, 10, 11, 12, 14

NOTES: Credit cards accepted: A Master Card; B Visa; C American Express; D Discover Card; E Diner's Club; F Other; 2 Personal Checks accepted; 3 Lunch available; 4 Dinner available; 5 Open all year;

New Mexico

Adobe and Roses

1011 Ortega Northwest, 87114
(505) 898-0654

An adobe hacienda on two acres in Albuquerque's North Valley, featuring a casually elegant and spacious suite with private entrance, fireplace, piano, kitchen, and big windows overlooking the gardens and horse pasture. Also a two-bedroom, two-bath adobe guest house. A quiet, romantic place to visit.

Host: Dorothy Morse
Rooms: 2 (1 PB; 1 SB) $50-105
Full Breakfast
Credit Cards: None
Notes: 2, 5, 6, 8, 9, 10, 12, 13

B&B of New Mexico #402

P. O. Box 2805, Santa Fe, 87504
(505) 982-3332

Beautiful and large single-story adobe home with 18-inch thick walls, brick floors, and viga ceilings. Very private. Surrounded by alfalfa fields, yet close to Albuquerque. Private bath in both rooms. $60.

B&B of New Mexico #404

P. O. Box 2805, Santa Fe, 87504
(505) 982-3332

This dramatic pueblo-style home has magnificent mountain views and spectacular sunsets. A generous continental breakfast with freshly ground coffee is served in guests' room, on the patio, or in the dining area. One room with the king bed has a private deck and bath outside door. Twin beds in other room with private bath across livingroom. $55-60.

Las Palomas Valley Bed and Breakfast

2303 Candelaria Road, 87107
(505) 345-7228

Las Palomas ("the doves") will take visitors into the heart of the traditions of New Mexico. From the moment you drive onto our three-acre establishment you will feel as if you have stepped back in time. Situated in the heart of Albuquerque's historic North Valley. Enjoy a walk through the Rose Garden, pick your own fruit from the trees in our orchard, or play tennis on the private courts. All of the luxurious suites offer a private bath, cable television, and special add-on amenities. Within walking distance of the Rio Grande Nature Center and just a short drive from Coronado State Monument, the New Mexico Museum of Natural History, and other attractions.

Host: Lori Caldwell
Rooms: 8 (PB) $65-95
Full Breakfast
Credit Cards: A, B, C
Notes: 2, 4 (with advance notice), 5, 6, 8, 9, 10, 11, 12, 13, 14

Maggie's Raspberry Patch

9817 Eldridge Road, 87114

Maggie's, near the Rio Grande, has a heated pool and lots of flowers and fruit trees. The hostess makes all the jams and jellies served with the daily baked breads and full

6 Pets welcome; 8 Children welcome; 9 Social drinking allowed; 10 Tennis available; 11 Swimming available; 12 Golf available; 13 Skiing available; 14 May be booked through travel agents.

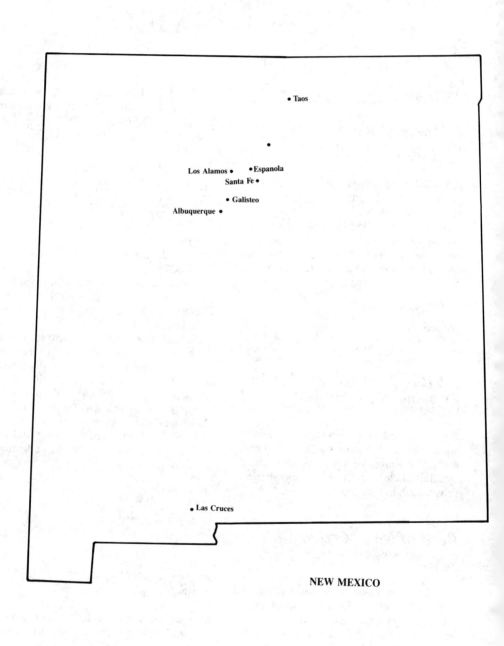

• Taos

•

Los Alamos • • Espanola
Santa Fe •
• Galisteo
Albuquerque •

• Las Cruces

NEW MEXICO

breakfasts. Guests are invited to the Berry Patch to lounge and watch the ducks, geese, and chickens feed and swim in the pond. There is a large suite for families, but privacy for couples. Jacuzzi available.

Host: Maggie Lilley
Rooms: 1 suite, 2 rooms (2 PB; 1 SB) $50-125
Full Breakfast
Credit Cards: None
Notes: 2, 5, 6, 8, 10, 12, 13, 14

W. E. Mauger Estate

701 Roma Avenue NW, 87102
(505) 242-8755

This wonderful 1897 Queen Anne Victorian on the National Register of Historic Places has eight unique accommodations with private baths, full breakfast, and afternoon refreshments. Within walking distance of Old Town, museums, zoo, Indian Center, shops, and restaurants. The beautiful front porch is furnished in wicker. Other features include indoor and outdoor dining rooms. Elegant, gracious, and affordable, this showplace is a must-see.

Hosts: Chuck Silver and Brian Miller
Rooms: 8 (PB) $65-105
Full Breakfast
Credit Cards: A, B, C, E, F
Notes: 2, 5, 6, 8, 9, 14

The Windmill Ranch

6400 Coors Boulevard NW, 87120
(505) 898-6864

W. E. Mauger Estate

Windmill Ranch is an old southwestern hacienda sitting amid ancient elms next to the Rio Grande. Tree-lined paths along the river provide beautiful scenery for those who wish to jog, bicycle, or simply enjoy a peaceful nature walk. With the mesa at your back and the Sandia Mountains in your eyes, you're only a stone's throw from the famous Indian petroglyphs, Albuquerque's Old Town, and Santa Fe.

Hosts: Margaret and Bob Cover
Rooms: 4 (PB) $65-95
Full Breakfast
Credit Cards: A, B
Notes: 2, 5, 9

CHAMA

B&B of New Mexico #250

P. O. Box 2805, Santa Fe, 87504
(505) 982-3332

This remote, fully modern cottage offers an unobstructed view of the Brazos Cliff situated in the foothills of the San Juan Mountains. Your only visitors will be the deer and the elk. Only seven miles from Chama and Cumbres/Toltec Railroad. You can either cook your meal or have pizza and sandwiches delivered. After your meal, take a hike or fish in the trout pond. Twin or double. $90-120.

CHIMAYO

Casa Escondida

P. O. Box 142, 87522
(505) 351-4805

Casa Escondida is a northern New Mexico-style adobe inn set on six acres of land in the historic village of Chimayo, situated on the magnificent "High Road" from Santa Fe to Taos. Six unique rooms, each with private Mexican tile baths, are tastefully decorated with American arts and crafts and antiques. Designed for intimacy and comfort. Gourmet breakfasts are a Casa Escondida specialty, as are warm beds and a welcoming atmosphere.

Hosts: Babette Landau and Irenka Taurek
Rooms: 6 (PB) $65-120
Full Breakfast
Credit Cards: A, B
Notes: 2, 5, 6, 8, 9, 13, 14

ESPANOLA

B&B of New Mexico #260

P. O. Box 2805, Santa Fe, 87504
(505) 982-3332

This simple, elegant adobe casita is nestled in the pine cliffs of northern New Mexico. It is filled with local handmade crafts and furniture. High-beamed ceiling, Talavera tile, pine floors, and a fireplace in the bedroom. The sleeping arrangements can be either a king bed or two twin beds. Situated near Española, halfway between Santa Fe and Taos. It is a short walk from the Chama River. The casita is detached from the main house to afford privacy. No kitchen. Full breakfast. $70.

Casa Del Rio

P. O. Box 92, 87532
(505) 753-2035

Casa Del Rio is a traditional adobe bed and breakfast set amid the pink cliffs of northern New Mexico on twelve acres of land along the Chama River and within a half hour of Santa Fe, Taos, and Los Alamos. Furnished in authentic southwestern style with hand-carved furniture and crafts. Viga and latilla ceilings and Talavara tile add to its charm. There are Arabian horses and fine wool sheep on the premises, and a tray of wake-up coffee is delivered to guests' rooms each morning.

Hosts: Eileen and Mel Vigil
Rooms: 2 (PB) $75-105
Full Breakfast
Credit Cards: A, B (to hold reservation only)
Notes: 2, 5, 9, 14

La Puebla House

Route 3, Box 172A, 87532
(505) 753-3981

La Puebla House is a ten-room traditional adobe with vigas and latillas, flagstone and brick floors. It is situated in a small Spanish village between Santa Cruz and Chimayo. This provides a lovely country setting from which to explore the many attractions of northern New Mexico. Nearby are Indian pueblos and ruins, the Santa Fe Opera, Taos, Abiqui, Ojo Caliente, and other small villages in the Espanola Valley.

Host: Elvira Bain
Rooms: 4 (1 PB; 3 SB) $50-75
Full Breakfast
Credit Cards: A, B
Notes: 2, 5, 6, 8, 9, 13

FARMINGTON

B&B of New Mexico #601

P. O. Box 2805, Santa Fe, 87504
(505) 982-3332

A traditional northern New Mexico adobe situated on the cliffside confluence of the San Juan and La Plata rivers on the outskirts of Farmington, this newly constructed bed and breakfast suite includes bedroom with queen bed, livingroom/dining room with two twin day beds, bathroom with Mexican tile shower, kitchen, and hot tub. $65-80.

FORT SUMNER/TAIBAN

B&B of New Mexico #301

P. O. Box 2805, Santa Fe, 87504
(505) 982-3332

This small guest house, near Fort Sumner beside the ghost town of Taiban, is truly the Little House on the Prairie. It is in the middle of Billy the Kid country. It has two bedrooms that can accommodate up to four

NOTES: Credit cards accepted: A Master Card; B Visa; C American Express; D Discover Card; E Diner's Club; F Other; 2 Personal Checks accepted; 3 Lunch available; 4 Dinner available; 5 Open all year;

people in the same party who share a bath. It is filled with antiques. Guided tours are available at night or on weekends. With advance notice and $10 per person, the host will grill lamb for dinner. $60.

GALISTEO

The Galisteo Inn

HC 75, Box 4, 87540
(505) 982-1506

Visit this 240-year-old adobe hacienda in the beautiful countryside of northern New Mexico, 23 miles southeast of Santa Fe. Enjoy the hot tub, sauna, pool, bicycles, and horseback riding. The dinners feature creative southwestern cuisine, nightly except for Monday and Tuesday. Reservations required for accommodations and dining.

Hosts: Joanna Kaufman and Wayne Aarniokoski
Rooms: 12 (8 PB; 4 SB) $90-165
Continental Breakfast
Credit Cards: A, B, D
Notes: 2, 3, 4, 9, 10, 11, 14

LAS CRUCES

B&B of New Mexico #506

P. O. Box 2805, Santa Fe, 87504
(505) 982-3332

Just 11 miles from Las Cruces at the foot of the Organ Mountains. Surrounded by U.S. government land, the area is quiet and beautiful. Horse boarding is available, and you can take your horse for a ride in the mountains. Owners speak German, French, Greek, Spanish, Arabic, and understand Italian. The home has a pool for guests. Two guest rooms are available: one has two twin beds and a private bath; the other has an atrium door that opens onto the deck surrounding the pool, double bed, private bath, and kitchenette. $50-60.

Lundeen Inn of the Arts

618 South Alameda Boulevard, 88005
(505) 526-3327

For those who appreciate meaningful living, the Inn of the Arts is definitely the place to start. The inn, along with the Linda Lundeen Art Gallery, is housed in a century-old adobe hacienda. The 15 guest rooms, all with private bath, gazebos, patios, and cozy alcoves, are representative of a southwestern artist, and some rooms have kiva fireplaces. Furnishings combine English and American antiques with traditional Mexican white walls and red brick floors. While staying at the inn, you can visit one of the many nearby attractions. The inn also schedules Indian dancing, southwest-style architectural seminars, and pottery making. A popular location for wedding ceremonies and honeymoon retreats.

Hosts: Jerry and Linda Lundeen
Rooms: 15 (PB) $45-85
Full Breakfast weekends; Continental weekdays
Credit Cards: A, B, C, D
Notes: 2, 5, 9, 10, 11, 12, 14

LOS ALAMOS

Casa del Rey

305 Rover Street, 87544
(505) 672-9401

Quiet residential area, friendly atmosphere. Situated in White Rock, minutes from Los Alamos and 40 minutes from Santa Fe. Excellent recreational facilities and restaurants nearby. The area is rich in Indian and Spanish history. In summer, breakfast featuring homemade granola and breads is served on the sun porch overlooking flower gardens, with views of the mountains.

Host: Virginia King
Rooms: 2 (SB) $40
Expanded Continental Breakfast
Credit Cards: None
Notes: 2, 5, 8 (over 7), 9, 10, 11, 12, 13

6 Pets welcome; 8 Children welcome; 9 Social drinking allowed; 10 Tennis available; 11 Swimming available; 12 Golf available; 13 Skiing available; 14 May be booked through travel agents.

PECOS

B&B of New Mexico #290

P. O. Box 2805, Santa Fe, 87504
(505) 982-3332

This historic three-bedroom log cabin, situated six miles above Pecos toward Cowels on State Road 63, is probably the most photographed in the canyon. Sitting on a natural rock foundation right on the river, and only 25 minutes from Santa Fe, it offers beautiful scenic trails, trout fishing at the doorstep, and a chance to reflect while sitting on the outdoor patio surrounded by the Sangre de Cristo Mountains. Continental breakfast. One bedroom has a fireplace and half-bath. A full bath is across the hall. The other bedroom has a queen bed and a single bed with a full bath. $70.

QUESTA

B&B of New Mexico #210

P. O. Box 2805, Santa Fe, 87504
(505) 982-3332

Large, cozy, rustic log home is waiting at the base of the Sangre de Cristo Mountains with three bedrooms, two baths, hot tub, and sauna. Area is quiet and restful with close access to Rio Grande. Wild river hiking, wilderness area, three major ski resorts, much wildlife, and shopping in Taos are all at your disposal. Continental breakfast, southwestern style. Rooms are queen, double, and single. $40-60.

RATON

Red Violet Inn

344 North 2nd Street, 87740
(505) 445-9778; (800) 624-9778

Red brick Victorian 1902 home on the Santa Fe Trail. A tea or coffee tray is served upon request. Classical music, highlighted by our great food and hospitality. Social hour from 5:30 until 6:30 P.M. Amtrak pick-up available. A theater and gallery are within walking distance, and fishing opportunities are only six miles away. Capulin Volcana is an hour away. Antique shops, golf, and bird watching.

Hosts: Ruth and John Hanrahan
Rooms: 4 (2 PB; 2 SB) $50-65
Full Breakfast
Credit Cards: A, B
Notes: 2, 3 (advanced notice), 4 (advanced notice),
    8 (over 8), 9, 10, 11, 12, 13, 14

SANTA FE

B&B of New Mexico #102

P. O. Box 2805, 87504
(505) 982-3332

Your own adobe casita. Ideally situated in a quiet historic neighborhood, short walk to plaza, surrounded by shops, restaurants, and galleries. Three separate casitas can accommodate between two to six people per casita. All the casitas have equipped kitchens and telephones. The first is elegant, newly restored, remodeled, and decorated. High-beamed ceilings, plastered walls, pine and tile floors, air conditioning, and a front courtyard. Two bedrooms. The second is in the back part of the first casita and also has high beamed ceilings, pine and tile floors. The third is a separate house with pine floors and Mexican tile. Large, well-equipped kitchen, livingroom and dining room, and two bedrooms. $85-$165.

B&B of New Mexico #104

P. O. Box 2805, 87504
(505) 982-3332

Large, two-story home with Spanish-tile roof in the Sangre de Cristo Mountains. Master bedroom has king-size bed, fireplace, sitting area, refrigerator, and private bath with room for a roll-away bed if needed. Second bedroom has queen bed and shares bath across the hall with twin bedroom. Home has pool table for guest use and an outside dog. $50-60.

B&B of New Mexico #105

P. O. Box 2805, 87504
(505) 982-3332

Beautiful two-story home less than one mile from the plaza. Large downstairs bedroom with queen bed, refrigerator, lots of closet space, private bath and shower. Upstairs room has twin bed, walls covered with watercolors, private three-quarter bath. Breakfast upstairs in dining room with view of hills filled with piñon trees. Livingroom has views of Sangre de Cristo Mountains, beamed ceiling, and kiva fireplace. Spanish tile in kitchen and hallways. $50-70.

B&B of New Mexico #107

P. O. Box 2805, 87504
(505) 982-3332

Pure Santa Fe! This new adobe-style home has high-beam and rough-sawn ceilings throughout, with foot-thick walls, saltillo-tile floors, Mexican tile in baths and kitchen, kiva fireplace, and vigas in the livingroom. One-half block to historic Canyon Road, one mile to the plaza. Both rooms are on the second floor and have private baths. One room has its own private portal and small refrigerator. The other has its own private sitting room with twin bed. $75 for two in either room; $90 for three in suite.

B&B of New Mexico #108

P. O. Box 2805, 87504
(505) 982-3332

Small, cozy adobe home two blocks from Canyon Road and five blocks from downtown plaza. Kiva fireplace in livingroom, enclosed courtyard in front. Door from guest room opens onto back garden area. Host very knowledgeable about activities in Santa Fe. Private full bath down the hall and king-size bed. $70.

B&B of New Mexico #110

P. O. Box 2805, 87504
(505) 982-3332

Beautiful pueblo-style home in the foothills of the Sangre de Cristo Mountains. Gorgeous sunsets and views of the city lights at night. Jogging trails behind the house. Very quiet except for the sounds of nature. Only 15 minutes to ski basin, 10 minutes to the plaza. Patio for sunning; livingroom and dining room have high-beamed ceiling with fireplace. Master bedroom has king bed, dressing area, walk-in closet, private bath, and views of the foothills. Smaller bedroom has twin beds, large closet, and private bath. Cat in residence. $65-80.

B&B of New Mexico #119

P. O. Box 2805, 87504
(505) 982-3332

From 1867 to 1890 this lovely old adobe was the Santa Fe Meat and Livestock Headquarters. Situated in the heart of the historic district five blocks from the plaza and one block south of Canyon Road. Parts of the home are believed to date prior to 1846. All of the outside and some of the inside walls are made of adobe, in some cases 30 inches thick; the ceiling of the livingroom has six inches of dirt on top in spite of the pitched roof. There is a parlor grand piano in the home that guests can use. The bunkhouse can sleep four in two queen beds sharing a bath (same party). Queen bed, private bath, and private library in the main house. $80.

6 Pets welcome; 8 Children welcome; 9 Social drinking allowed; 10 Tennis available; 11 Swimming available; 12 Golf available; 13 Skiing available; 14 May be booked through travel agents.

B&B of New Mexico #120

P. O. Box 2805, 87504
(505) 982-3332

This adobe casita has viga ceilings, separate bedroom, small livingroom with double sleeper/sofa, full bath, and kitchenette. Approximately one and one-half miles from the plaza. $70-$80.

B&B of New Mexico #127

P. O. Box 2805, 87504
(505) 982-3332

Beautiful, spacious adobe-style home in fashionable northeast Santa Fe, only one and one-fourth miles from downtown. Situated on a ridge above the city, this home offers a lovely view, spectacular sunsets, and walled back yard. Extensive decks provide summertime relaxation and privacy. Kiva fireplace and beamed ceiling in the den offer winter comfort. Glassenclosed hot tub feels great at the end of a long day. King bed with private bath. Twin beds with private bath next to main room. Breakfast features a variety of homemade breads served in the elegant dining room. $65-75.

B&B of New Mexico #128

P. O. Box 2805, 87504
(505) 982-3332

This is a delightful home on the east side, one-half block to Canyon Road and walking distance to town. It has hardwood floors and some antiques. Enjoy breakfast on its cheerful sun porch. Cable TV is available. There are two rooms to choose from. One is a master bedroom with a private bath and queen bed; the other has a full-size bed with private three-quarter bath. $75.

B&B of New Mexico #133

P. O. Box 2805, 87504
(505) 982-3332

Very private 150-year-old adobe casita plaqued by the Historic Santa Fe Foundation in the historic Bario De Analco near the oldest church. Entrance to private casita is framed by a giant wisteria. Sitting room with Taos day bed and pigskin furniture features kiva fireplace, vigas, flagstone and pine floor. Bedroom has Taos-style queen bed, McMillan bureau, and Spanish chair. Fully furnished kitchen with Mexican tile, full bath, southwestern art throughout. Courtyard and garden are adorned with apple, catalpa, and sumac trees. $95.

B&B of New Mexico #139

P. O. Box 2805, 87504
(505) 982-3332

This home begins with the hostess' music space and ends with the host's painting area. The bedroom corridor gives a warm welcome to visitors. The queen bedroom is a comfortable size and overlooks the garden; the single bedroom, though smaller, enjoys spaciousness of a mountain view and a wall of books that tempt a guest tired from tourist activities. Cat and dog are also on the premises. Both rooms share same bath. $50-65.

B&B of New Mexico #142

P. O. Box 2805, 87504
(505) 982-3332

Romantic guest suite in the heart of Santa Fe's historic eastside. This adobe residence is at the end of a narrow lane, secluded and quiet, surrounded by rock walls, coyote fence, and adobe walls, yet minutes to Canyon Road, galleries, shops, and restaurants. Features include sun-filled bedroom, queen four-poster bed, kiva fireplace, vigas, and clerestory windows so you can watch the stars. Also available are a cozy sitting room and cable TV, with both rooms opening onto a patio. $75.

B&B of New Mexico #145

P. O. Box 2805, 87504
(505) 982-3332

Decorated in Santa Fe style, this casita has a fully equipped kitchenette, TV, stereo, microwave, and king bed with convertible sofa. It only takes minutes to get to the Plaza, Santa Fe Ski Basin, and Ten Thousand Waves (a Japanese bath house). $70-80.

Canyon Road Casitas

652 Canyon Road, 87501
(505) 988-5888; (800) 279-0755

Situated in the historic district behind a walled private courtyard garden on Santa Fe's famous Canyon Road. Built around 1887, the accommodations include a suite with dining room, kitchen, and two separate beds. Fine amenities include duvets, down pillows, imported linens, custom toiletries, Pima cotton towels, guest robes, French-roast coffee, with complimentary wine and cheese upon check-in. The finest in southwestern decor, including kiva fireplace, hand-carved beds, vigas, latillas, original art, and hand-tiled private baths. Award-winner.

Host: Trisha Ambrose
Rooms: 2 (PB) $85-169
Continental Breakfast
Credit Cards: A, B, C, D, E
Notes: 2, 5, 8, 9, 14

Dunshee's

986 Acequia Madre, 87501
(505) 982-0988

A romantic adobe getaway in the historic east side, about a mile from the plaza. The suite includes a livingroom and bedroom with kiva fireplaces, antiques, folk art, fresh flowers, homemade cookies, refrigerator, private bath, and patio. Gourmet breakfast.

Host: Susan Dunshee
Room: 1 (PB) $88-99
Full Breakfast
Minimum stay weekends and holidays: 2 nights
Credit Cards: A, B
Notes: 2, 5, 8, 9, 13

El Paradero

220 West Manhattan, 87501
(505) 988-1177

Just a short walk from the busy plaza, this 200-year-old Spanish farmhouse was restored as a charming southwestern inn. Enjoy a full gourmet breakfast, caring service, and a relaxed, friendly atmosphere. The inn offers lots of common space and a patio for afternoon tea and snacks.

Hosts: Thom Allen and Ouida MacGregor
Rooms: 14 (10 PB; 4 SB) $50-130
Full Breakfast
Credit Cards: None
Notes: 2, 5, 6, 8 (over 4), 9, 10, 11, 12, 13, 14

El Paradero

---

6 Pets welcome; 8 Children welcome; 9 Social drinking allowed; 10 Tennis available; 11 Swimming available; 12 Golf available; 13 Skiing available; 14 May be booked through travel agents.

Jean's Place

2407 Camino Capitan, 87505
(505) 471-4053

A modest home and vibrational healing center, Jean's Place is situated in a quiet neighborhood just ten minutes from the town plaza. A deck above the patio overlooks the greenbelt, with views of the mountains on each side. Guests sleep on queen beds, and those attracted to crystals will enjoy the energy here. Dog and cat in residence.

Host: Jean Gosse
Room: 1 (PB) $40
Continental Breakfast
Credit Cards: None
Notes: 2, 5, 10, 11, 12, 13, 14

American Artists Gallery House

TAOS

American Artists Gallery House

P. O. Box 584, 87571
(505) 758-4446; (800) 532-2041

Charming southwestern hacienda filled with artwork by American artists. Gourmet breakfasts, adobe fireplaces, private baths, outdoor hot tub, and gardens. Magnificent view of mountains. Minutes from art galleries, museums, restaurants, St. Francis Assisi Church, and ski valley.

Hosts: Judie and Elliot Framan
Rooms: 6 (PB) $65-95

Full Breakfast
Credit Cards: A, B
Notes: 2, 5, 8, 9, 10, 11, 12, 13, 14

B&B of New Mexico #209

P. O. Box 2805, Santa Fe, 87504
(505) 982-3332

This two-story house on a quiet corner is near the plaza. Rooms are huge, with private baths on opposite sides of the house, one upstairs and one downstairs. The livingroom offers a stone fireplace. Artwork is displayed throughout the house. $85-95.

Casa Feliz

137 Beut Street, 87571
(505) 758-9790

Casa Feliz is an old, spacious home with much southwestern charm. The house itself, more than 100-years old, was the home of artist Rebecca Salisbury James, once married to photographer Paul Strand. Within easy walking distance of downtown restaurants and shops. Common areas include large sitting room with a fireplace, large breakfast room, also with a fireplace and a large enclosed yard. Many of the furniture pieces are handmade in southwestern style by local artists. An art gallery is also on the premises, featuring the work of local artists.

Host: Dianna Richey
Rooms: 4 (PB) $95-110
Full Breakfast
Credit Cards: A, B, C
Notes: 2, 3, 4, 5, 6, 8, 9, 11, 13, 14

Casa de Milagros Bed and Breakfast

P. O. Box 2983, 321 Kit Carson Road, 87571
(505) 758-8001; (800) 243-9334
FAX (505) 758-0127

Experience the rich flavors and textures of Taos in a turn-of-the-century adobe home, just a short walk from the Old Town Plaza.

NOTES: Credit cards accepted: A Master Card; B Visa; C American Express; D Discover Card; E Diner's Club; F Other; 2 Personal Checks accepted; 3 Lunch available; 4 Dinner available; 5 Open all year;

Eclectic decor and and friendly staff welcome you. Delicious gourmet breakfasts, featuring Helen's famous "Nirvana Crunch." Amenities include down comforters, fireplaces, cable television with free movie channel, outdoor hot tub, FAX machine, and cruelty-free soaps, shampoo, and moisturizer. Two cats and a dog on the premises.

Host: Helen Victor
Rooms: 6 (PB) $70-145
Full Breakfast
Credit Cards: A, B
Notes: 2, 5, 10, 11, 12, 13, 14

Orinda

Orinda Bed and Breakfast

Box 4551, Orinda Lane, 87571
(505) 758-8581

Surrounded by open meadows and towering elm trees, Orinda is a dramatic adobe estate that combines spectacular views and country privacy within walking distance to Taos Plaza. Enjoy a spacious two-bedroom suite with livingroom or a distinctive one-bedroom suite. Each has a kiva fireplace, Mexican-tiled bath, and private entrance. Healthy breakfasts are served in the huge, art-filled sunroom.

Hosts: Cary and George Pratt
Rooms: 3 (PB) $65-85
Continental Breakfast
Credit Cards: A, B
Notes: 2, 5, 8, 9, 10, 12, 13, 14

Salsa del Salto Bed and Breakfast Inn

P. O. Box 1468, El Prado, 87529
(505) 776-2422

Designed by world-renowned architect Antoine Predock, this beautiful home offers six guest rooms, each of which reflect the southwestern earth tones and pastel colors. All are decorated to tend to the guest's every need, with king-size beds, down comforters, furniture specially designed by local artisans for Salsa del Salto, and original paintings by Taos artists throughout the inn. As an added treat, all rooms have spectacular views of the mountains and mesas. Breakfast is a gourmet's delight. Hot tub, heated pool, and private tennis court.

Hosts: Dadou Mayer and Mary Hockett
Rooms: 8 (PB) $85-160
Full Breakfast
Credit Cards: A, B
Notes: 2, 5, 9, 10, 11, 14

6 Pets welcome; 8 Children welcome; 9 Social drinking allowed; 10 Tennis available; 11 Swimming available; 12 Golf available; 13 Skiing available; 14 May be booked through travel agents.

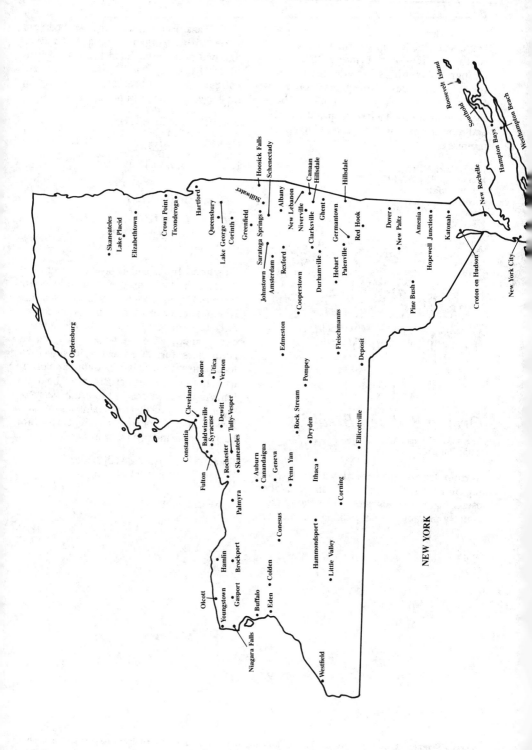

NEW YORK

Niagara Falls
Westfield
Olcott
Youngstown
Buffalo
Gasport
Eden • Colden
Hamlin
Brockport
Little Valley
Hammondsport •
Palmyra
Conesus
Corning
Ithaca •
Auburn
Canandaigua
Geneva
Penn Yan
Dryden •
Rochester
Skaneateles
Fulton •
Constantia
Baldwinsville
Syracuse
Cleveland
Tully • Vesper
Dewitt
Rock Stream •
Pompey
Rome •
Utica
Vernon
Ellicottville •
Deposit
Edmeston •
Fleischmanns •
Cooperstown •
Durhamville •
Rexford •
Amsterdam •
Johnstown •
Saratoga Springs •
Greenfield
Corinth
Lake George
Queensbury
Hartford
Ticonderoga •
Crown Point •
Elizabethtown •
Lake Placid
Skaneateles •
Ogdensburg •
Hoosick Falls •
Schenectady
Stillwater
Canaan
Hillsdale
Albany •
New Lebanon •
Niverville •
Clarksville •
Ghent
Germantown •
Hobart •
Palenville •
Red Hook •
Hillsdale •
Pine Bush •
Dover •
New Paltz •
Amenia •
Hopewell Junction •
Katonah •
Croton on Hudson •
New Rochelle •
New York City
Roosevelt Island
Southold
Peconic
Hampton Bays
Westhampton Beach

New York

Addison Rose
Bed and Breakfast

37 Maple Street, 14801
(607) 359-4650

A visit to the Addison Rose Bed and Breakfast will be remembered as "Victorian elegance in the heart of the country." This notable 100-year old Queen Anne "Painted Lady" sits among some of the Finger Lake's finest Victorian architecture. All rooms are furnished with period antiques, which invite relaxation and conversation. A full gourmet breakfast is served on fine china. Just minutes away from downtown Corning, museums, and wineries.

Hosts: Bill and Mary Ann Peters
Rooms: 3 (1 PB; 2 SB) $55-65 plus tax
Full Breakfast
Credit Cards: None
Notes: 2, 5, 9, 12

The American Country
Collection 097

4 Greenwood Lane, Delmar, 12054
(518) 439-7001

This elegant turn-of-the-century Victorian home is conveniently situated on the bus route and just a few minute's drive from all major area colleges, state buildings, and attractions. Four guest rooms, two with shared baths. All rooms have telephones and air conditioning. Children over 12 welcome. Continental breakfast. Guests can use the TV in the livingroom. Off-street parking is provided. $49-64.

Mansion Hill Inn

115 Phillip Street at Park Avenue, 12202
(518) 465-2038; (518) 434-2313
(800) 477-8171

This urban inn is nestled in a quiet residential neighborhood, within walking distance of the New York state governor's executive mansion and the state capitol complex. The Victorian-era buildings have been renovated with charm. Dinner is served with an American flair, rated Four Stars by the *Albany Times-Union* and *MetroLand Magazine*. Please request nonsmoking upon reservation. Handicapped accessible.

Hosts: Maryellen and Steve Stofelano, Jr.
Rooms: 14 (PB) $95-145
Full Breakfast
Credit Cards: A, B, C, E
Notes: 2, 3, 4, 6, 8, 9, 10, 11, 12, 13, 14

Mansion Hill Inn

NOTES: Credit cards accepted: A Master Card; B Visa; C American Express; D Discover Card; E Diner's Club; F Other; 2 Personal Checks accepted; 3 Lunch available; 4 Dinner available; 5 Open all year; 6 Pets welcome; 8 Children welcome; 9 Social drinking allowed; 10 Tennis available; 11 Swimming available; 12 Golf available; 13 Skiing available; 14 May be booked through travel agents.

ALTAMONT

The American Country Collection 045

4 Greenwood Lane, Delmar, 12054
(518) 439-7001

This 75-year-old refurbished Colonial is just 20 miles from the State Capitol. It is situated on 15 acres of well-groomed lawns, old shade trees, a swimming pool, barns, patio, and orchards. Business travelers find this location offers convenient access to both Albany and Schenectady. One third-floor suite has two bedrooms, livingroom, and private bath. One single room on the second floor shares the bath with the owner. Pets in residence. Children welcome. $35-60.

Pine Haven Bed and Breakfast

531 Western Avenue, 12203
(518) 482-1574

Pine Haven is a century-old Victorian home in the heart of Albany's prettiest area. Furnished with antiques, feather mattresses, and brass and iron beds, it has the ambience of Grandma's house. Situated on

Pine Haven

the main artery, it is served by bus lines in every direction, has off-street parking and is close to restaurants, theater, a bookstore, and other attractions.

Host: Janice Tricarico
Rooms: 4 double (SB) $64
Continental Breakfast
Credit Cards: None
Notes: 2, 5, 8 (over 12), 9, 14

AMENIA

Covered Bridge 2AMNY

P. O. Box 447 A, Norfolk, CT 06058
(203) 542-5944

Contemporary home set on three acres has been tastefully decorated with antiques and paintings from the owner's gallery. A full breakfast is served in the dining room. The house has central air conditioning. There are four guest rooms, two of which share a bath. Double, twin, queen, and king beds are available. $75-95 for rooms, or the house can be rented on a weekly basis.

AMSTERDAM

The American Country Collection 118

4 Greenwood Lane, Delmar, 12054
(518) 439-7001

The guest rooms in this brick Federal Colonial have wide-pine floors, fireplaces, and are decorated with a mix of antiques, country furniture, and treasures. The history of the house is preserved in photos and mementos displayed throughout the home. Guests are treated to afternoon tea served in the English tradition with light pastries and sweet cakes. Three guest rooms with shared bath. Parakeet in residence. Children welcome. Crib available. $35.

NOTES: Credit cards accepted: A Master Card; B Visa; C American Express; D Discover Card; E Diner's Club; F Other; 2 Personal Checks accepted; 3 Lunch available; 4 Dinner available; 5 Open all year;

AUBURN

Elaine's Bed and Breakfast and Inn Reservation Service

4987 Kingston Road, Elbridge, 13060
(315) 689-2082

Situated on Lake Owasco, this magnificent 1910 Adirondack cottage-lodge features two spacious rooms, excellent craftsmanship throughout, solid wood paneling, and built-ins. Each room has picture windows overlooking the lake and double French doors opening onto a large screened porch filled with antique wicker and hung with plants. Each room has private half-bath and shares a full bath. Fireplaces in bedrooms. The livingroom has a large fieldstone fireplace and an ever-changing view of the lake. Breakfasts are varied, with homemade hot casseroles, muffins, fruit, juice, coffee, and cold cereal. No children under 12. No pets. No credit cards. Winter rate, $65; after May 1, $75.

BALDWINSVILLE

Elaine's Bed and Breakfast and Inn Reservation Service

4987 Kingston Road, Elbridge, 13060
(315) 689-2082

Spacious, historic Colonial in the village. The home was built around 1845 and, in keeping with its character, is decorated with many antiques and collectibles. Four guest rooms available, one with private bath and working fireplace. The house is on two acres high on a hill, a short walk to stores and the picturesque Seneca River.

BALLSTON LAKE

The American Country Collection 009

4 Greenwood Lane, Delmar, 12054
(518) 439-7001

This renovated Second Empire Victorian is once again the focal point of the historic district of this tiny village. The home is divided into two sections. The rear bed and breakfast area has a private entrance, guest livingroom with fireplace, dining room, kitchen, and porch for afternoon refreshments. The second floor has three guest rooms and a bath. Rooms in this section are ideal for family gatherings and groups of four to six traveling together. Smoking outdoors only. No pets. Children over 11 welcome. Younger children permitted when entire bed and breakfast section is rented to one party. $65-110 rooms, seasonal; $150-175 for suite.

BALLSTON SPA

The American Country Collection 119

4 Greenwood Lane, Delmar, 12054
(518) 439-7001

This working farm and girls' summer riding academy is situated on 100 acres of rolling meadows and scenic farmland. Riding lessons are available in the indoor riding arena. A heated swimming pool on the premises is available for guest use. The three guest bedrooms, one with private bath, have air conditioning. There is also a full apartment on the lower level during off-season. Children welcome. Crib available, but guests should bring crib linens. Dogs and cats indoors; horses, ducks, geese, goats on the farm. $70-95 July-Aug.; $50-65 Sept.-June.

The American Country Collection 133

4 Greenwood Lane, Delmar, 12054
(518) 439-7001

Part of a modern home set back from the road on 2.9 acres, this self-contained three-room efficiency apartment is only 15-20 minutes from Saratoga. A fully furnished livingroom is the first thing guests see when they step through the private entrance, and the kitchen, which is within view of the livingroom, is fully equipped. The bedroom and full bath are off the hall. An abundant continental breakfast is self-catered. The bedroom has queen-size bed, and a fold-out queen sofa is in the livingroom. $55-95, seasonal.

BROCKPORT

Rainbow Hospitality B100

504 Amherst Street, Buffalo, 14207
(800) 373-8797

An 1850 Greek Revival historic landmark and recipient of the Gold Medallion Award in 1991. Nestled among sycamore, maple, and blue spruce trees in the historic district of Clarkson. Hand-painted lead glass foyer panels, 10-foot ceilings, large windows, and three working fireplaces all combine to welcome bed and breakfast travelers for a special time and fond memories. $50-60.

BUFFALO

Rainbow Hospitality B200

504 Amherst Street, 14207
(800) 373-8797

Charming turn-of-the-century Victorian in the heart of Buffalo's historic preservation area. The hosts, a writer and interior designer, recommend excellent area restaurants, boutiques, art galleries, and theaters.

Just minutes from downtowns revitalized and restored cultural and entertainment centers, the waterfront, and Peace Bridge leading north to Canada. Niagara Falls is only 18 miles to the north. Two easy going cats, Salem and Samantha, reside in this meticulously maintained city home. Three rooms, each with a private bath. $50-65.

Rainbow Hospitality B600

504 Amherst Street, 14207
(800) 373-8797

Comfortable center entrance three-story red brick Colonial offers travelers a choice of four bedrooms with shared bath. Tastefully decorated with antiques, wicker, and collections of rose and blue glass. Convenient to all locations in Buffalo, Niagara Falls, the universities, and shopping. $50.

Rainbow Hospitality B701

504 Amherst Street, 14207
(800) 373-8797

This gracious 100-year-old Queen Anne Victorian mansion is minutes from Buffalo's downtown-in-renaissance and cultural events. Near colleges, a major hospital, Allentown antique shops, Elmwood Avenue restaurants and boutiques. Niagara Falls is only 20 minutes away. The hosts offer four beautifully restored rooms, each representative of Buffalo's cultural history. Superb breakfast and pleasant surroundings.

CANAAN

Covered Bridge

P. O. Box 447, Norfolk, CT 06058
(203) 542-5944

This 1806 Federal Colonial set on more than three acres is on the National Register of Historic Places and has been an inn for 185 years. There is a sitting area with a TV and VCR, two dining rooms, where a full breakfast is served, and a large porch for guest use. Seven guest rooms with air conditioning and individual heat controls share three full baths. $65-85.

The Re Family Bed and Breakfast
4166 Split Rock Road, 13031
(315) 468-2039

This 100-year old early American farmhouse features a lodge-style den, country kitchen, side deck, 40-foot pool, barn, gardens, and grape arbors. Two guest rooms offer brass queen-size beds, each with orthopedic mattresses and pedestal sinks. Rooms have easy access to garden-style bathroom, with walk-in tile shower, tub, vanity with double sink, and full mirrored backwall. Enjoy a stress-free environment close to Syracuse and the beauty of Central New York.

Hosts: Joseph and Terry Re
Rooms: 3 (SB) $55-65
Continental Breakfast
Credit Cards: None
Notes: 2, 5, 8, 10, 11, 12, 13, 14

CANANDAIGUA

Lakeview Farm Bed and Breakfast
4761 Route 364, Rushville, 14544
(716) 554-6973

Hospitality and nature are at their best in this country home on the east side of Canandaigua Lake on 170 acres of woods, fields, and streams. A pair of lake-view bedrooms are furnished in family antiques, and share an upstairs sitting room. Enjoy the pond, beautiful ravine, and cross-country skiing. Only two minutes to public

beach and lakeside restaurant. Just 10 minutes to Canandaigua shops and restaurants. Air-conditioned.

Hosts: Betty and Howard Freese
Rooms: 2 (SB) $50-55
Full Breakfast
Credit Cards: C
Notes: 2, 5, 8 (older), 9, 11, 14

Nottingham Lodge Bed and Breakfast
5741 Bristol Valley Road, 14424
(716) 374-5355

Rural and mountainous, situated on Route 64 across from Bristol Mountain Ski Center. This English Tudor lodge has a common room two stories high, with balcony overlooking ski mountain, barnwood walls, and a cobblestone fireplace. Casual elegance. Three guest rooms with private baths; full gourmet breakfast. Ski packages are available. Bicycle tours available May through October.

Hosts: Bonnie and Bill Robinson
Rooms: 3 (PB) $60
Full Breakfast
Credit Cards: A, B, D
Notes: 2, 5, 8, 9, 11, 12, 13

CHAUTAUQUA LAKE

Plumbush—A Victorian Bed and Breakfast
Route 33, P. O. Box 864, Chautauqua, 14722
(716) 789-5309

Plumbush

Newly restored, circa 1865, Italian villa on a hilltop surrounded by 125 acres. Just one mile from Chautauqua Institution. Bluebirds and wildlife abound. Bicycles available; cross-country ski trail. Sunny rooms, wicker, antiques, and a touch of elegant charm. As seen in *Victorian Homes,* Summer 1991; *Innsider* magazine, May/June 1990; and *Victoria* magazine, August 1989.

Hosts: George and Sandy Green
Rooms: 4 (PB) $85
Full Breakfast
Credit Cards: A, B
Notes: 2, 5, 9, 10, 11, 12, 13, 14

Rainbow Hospitality C109

504 Amherst Street, Buffalo, 14207
(800) 373-8797

Gracious lakefront home tastefully furnished with antiques and Oriental rugs. The hosts are retired and have relocated to beautiful Chautauqua Lake from Connecticut. Special features include central air and an inviting in-ground swimming pool for the guests to enjoy. Convenient to Chautauqua Institution and all summer and winter activities. $65.

CHERRY PLAIN

Berkshire B&B Homes NY 3

P. O. Box 211, Williamsburg, MA 01096
(413) 268-7244

A 1790 Federal-style home surrounded by acres of woodlands and ponds. Swimming pond, trout stream, and hiking on 10 acres. Both full breakfast and gourmet dinner served. Three double bedrooms with private baths. Children over nine welcome. Animals in residence. $110.

Berkshire Bed and Breakfast Homes NY 6

P. O. Box 211, Williamsburg, MA 01096
(413) 268-7244

An 1830 Colonial on one acre. Antique and Victorian furnishings. Parlor and den with TV for guest use. View of fields. One queen with private bath; two double bedrooms and one single. Full breakfast. Children of all ages welcome. $50-95.

Covered Bridge 1CPNY

P. O. Box 447 A, Norfolk, CT 06058
(203) 542-5944

This 1790 Colonial, nestled in the New York Berkshires, is secluded yet minutes from Tanglewood and summer theaters. Hiking trails, cross-country skiing, and a pond for fishing and skating are available on the grounds. Enjoy a full breakfast and dinner, both made with natural foods. The four guest rooms, two with antique canopy beds, have private baths. The rate, including dinner, is $110.

CLEVELAND

Elaine's Bed and Breakfast and Inn Reservation Service

4987 Kingston Road, Elbridge, 13060
(315) 689-2082

On the north shore of Oneida Lake, you will find this circa 1820 white Colonial built by an early industrial baron. It has 6,000-square feet of living space. An open porch welcomes guests with antique wicker and a hammock. From the wide center hall, there is a large playroom with billiard table, jukebox, many musical instruments, and the owner's collection of prizes from showing his many antique automobiles. The

---

NOTES: Credit cards accepted: A Master Card; B Visa; C American Express; D Discover Card; E Diner's Club; F Other; 2 Personal Checks accepted; 3 Lunch available; 4 Dinner available; 5 Open all year;

family room features a large TV, stereo, and beautiful stained-glass leaded window behind the bar. All rooms have working fireplaces and private baths. There is a formal livingroom full of antiques, a large cheery dining room with a player piano and more than 1,000 rolls. As this is a musical inn, there is an organ and a nickelodeon. Also, year-round beach house with Jacuzzi has two bedrooms, livingroom, kitchen and deck. No pets. No children under 16. $125-165.

COLDEN

Back of the Beyond
7233 Lower East Hill Road, 14033
(716) 652-0427

A charming country mini-estate situated in the Boston Hills and ski area of western New York; 25 miles from Buffalo and 50 from Niagara Falls. Accommodations are a separate chalet with three bedrooms, one and one-half baths, fully furnished kitchen, dining/livingroom, piano, pool table, and fireplace. Stroll through the organic herb, flower, and vegetable gardens; swim in the pond; or hike the woods. Cross-country ski trails on the premises; commercial downhill slopes are only one mile away.

Hosts: Bill and Shash Georgi
Rooms: 3 (S1.5B) $60 plus tax
Full Breakfast
Credit Cards: None
Notes: 2, 5, 8, 9, 10, 11, 12, 13, 14

CONESUS

Conesus Lake Bed and Breakfast
2388 East Lake Road, 14435
(716) 346-6526; (800) 724-4841

Situated lakeside on beautiful Conesus Lake near Route 390. Unique European styling with private balconies and flower

boxes. Relaxing atmosphere includes large private boat dock, picnic facilities, free use of paddleboats and overnight boat docking with mooring whips. Each attractive bedroom features a queen bed and cable TV. Private bathroom and double whirlpool tub available. Near excellent restaurants. Weekly discount. Reservations suggested.

Hosts: Dale and Virginia Esse
Rooms: 3 (1 PB; 2 SB) $60-70
Full Breakfast
Credit Cards: A, B, D
Notes: 5, 9, 11, 12, 13

CONSTANTIA

Elaine's Bed and Breakfast Reservation Service
4987 Kingston Road, Elbridge, 13060
(315) 689-2082

Large, cozy, and warm farmhouse overlooks Oneida Lake. Three guest rooms and bath upstairs, and two rooms with private baths downstairs. Next to restaurant. All freshly remodeled and cheery.

COOPERSTOWN

The American Country Collection 014
4 Greenwood Lane, Delmar, 12054
(518) 439-7001

This Victorian cottage and restored barn are situated on 14 acres of meadows and hills. The barn features three first-floor rooms with private baths. The house has a two-bedroom suite and guest bath on the second floor. Wicker, timeless antiques, old photos, ceiling fans, and green plants tie each room to the past. Guests are welcome to sit by the fire in the common room. Children welcome. Two-night minimum on weekends, holidays, major festival activities. $68-77.

6 Pets welcome; 8 Children welcome; 9 Social drinking allowed; 10 Tennis available; 11 Swimming available; 12 Golf available; 13 Skiing available; 14 May be booked through travel agents.

The American Country Collection 128

4 Greenwood Lane, Delmar, 12054
(518) 439-7001

Enjoy this rural farmhouse set on 7.5 acres just outside of historic Cooperstown. Surrounded by a pond, sugar bush, hills, and meadows, this inn offers travelers a parlor room for relaxing or reading, an air-conditioned breakfast room, and an adjoining room with TV. Four bedrooms are available for guests. One room has a private bath, and the other three rooms share a full hall bath. Full country breakfast. Children over five welcome. Resident cat. $45-65.

The Inn at Brook Willow

Rural Delivery 2, Box 514, 13326
(607) 547-9700

An 1885 Victorian country home on 14 acres with a fine collection of antiques in the main house and three guest rooms in the "reborn barn." Fresh fruit, garden flowers, and a bountiful breakfast await each guest. Two fireplaces, fields, and meadows relax the traveler. Just five minutes to the Baseball Hall of Fame and Otsego Lake.

Hosts: Joan and Jack Grimes
Rooms: (PB) $55-75 (single rate upon request)
Minimum stay weekends and holidays: 2 nights
Full Breakfast
Credit Cards: None
Notes: 2, 5, 8, 9, 10, 11, 12, 13

The Phoenix on River Road

Rural Delivery 4, Box 360, 13326
(607) 547-8250

Once a Victorian hotel, the Phoenix has been completely remodeled into a charming French country inn, serving an expanded continental breakfast in what was once the tavern room. All rooms feature ceiling fans and private baths. The Phoenix is situated two miles from Cooperstown on Scenic River Road, near museums and cross-country ski trails.

Hosts: Meg and Jim Myers, Mary Dunkle
Rooms: 4 (PB)
Continental Breakfast
Credit Cards: A, B
Notes: 2, 5, 8, 9 ,10, 11, 12, 13 (XC), 14

CORINTH

The American Country Collection 151

4 Greenwood Lane, Delmar, 12054
(518) 439-7001

Guests are graciously invited to share a most unusual country inn at the gateway to the Adirondacks, only minutes away from the villages of Saratoga Springs, Lake George, and Lake Luzerne. Five rooms, all with private baths, and an access ramp for handicapped guests is available. Saratoga, the racetracks, Skidmore College, and SPAC are all within an easy drive. Breakfast features a fresh fruit platter, juice selection, muffins with jam, Belgian waffles with cinnamon apples or strawberry blend, coffee, and tea. $50-99. Seasonal.

CORNING

Delevan House

188 DeLevan Avenue, 14830
(607) 962-2347

The Phoenix on River Road

NOTES: Credit cards accepted: A Master Card; B Visa; C American Express; D Discover Card; E Diner's Club; F Other; 2 Personal Checks accepted; 3 Lunch available; 4 Dinner available; 5 Open all year;

Southern Colonial with home-like hospitality. Overlooking Corning. Quiet surroundings, outstanding accommodations, complimentary cool drink served on the beautiful screened porch. Free pick-up from and delivery to airport.

Host: Mary M. DePumpo
Rooms: 3 (1 PB; 2 SB) $55-85
Full Breakfast
Credit Cards: None
Notes: 2, 5, 8 (over 10), 9, 12, 13

CROTON-ON-HUDSON

Alexander Hamilton House

49 Van Wyck Street, 10520
(914) 271-6737

An 1889 Victorian home overlooking the Hudson with in-ground pool and antique furniture. Four rooms share two baths. The first-floor suite has queen bed, private bath, and sitting room with fireplace. The Bridal Chamber has king bed, fireplace, private bath with Jacuzzi, and skylights. An executive apartment with private bath, full kitchen, and private entrance is also available. Convenient to West Point and White Plains (12 miles) and New York City (30 miles).

Host: Barbara Notarius
Rooms: 6 (2 PB; 4 SB) $65-250
Full Breakfast
Credit Cards: A, B, C
Notes: 2, 5, 8, 9, 11, 12, 14

The American Country Collection 157

4 Greenwood Lane, Delmar, 12054
(518) 439-7001

Perfect for vacations, business travel, and romantic getaways, this stately Victorian home, circa 1889, is nestled on a cliff above the Hudson River, only a short walk from the picturesque village of Croton-on-Hudson. Luxurious without being ornate, this bed and breakfast offers two suites,

each with a private bath and fireplace, four rooms on the second floor that share two hall baths, and a third-floor suite with a whirlpool. Breakfast offers juice, deep-dish pancakes, stuffed French toast or eggs, coffee, or tea. Train station is within close proximity. Children welcome. Resident dog. $65-250.

CROWN POINT

The American Country Collection 095

4 Greenwood Lane, Delmar, 12054
(518) 370-4948

It took three years for a team of Italian craftsmen to complete this 18-room Victorian mansion, circa 1887, situated on five and one-half acres in the center of this small town. Carved woodwork, doors, and stair railing from oak, cherry, mahogany, and walnut grace the home. Two of the five guest rooms have private baths. In winter, breakfast is served in front of the fireplace in the dining room. Fort Ticonderoga and Fort Crown Point are nearby. Children welcome. $45-60.

DEPOSIT

The White Pillars Inn

82 Second Street, 13754
(607) 467-4191

The White Pillars Inn is "the perfect place to do nothing at all...but eat." For breakfast, try the French Toast Sampler, a baked apple in pastry served in a warm caramel sauce, or any one of seven overstuffed omelettes. Dining is truly an experience, with seafood and decadent desserts are a specialty. Magnificent floral arrangements, soothing sounds of soft jazz, and a bottomless cookie jar are just a few of the unexpected pleasures guests will find. The lav-

6 Pets welcome; 8 Children welcome; 9 Social drinking allowed; 10 Tennis available; 11 Swimming available; 12 Golf available; 13 Skiing available; 14 May be booked through travel agents.

ishly furnished inn evokes romance and privacy and kick-off-your-shoes relaxation amid elegant surroundings.

Host: Ms. Najla R. Aswad
Rooms: 5 (3 PD; 2 SB) $65-110
Full Breakfast
Credit Cards: A, B, C, D, E, F
Notes: 2, 3, 4, 5, 8, 9, 10, 11, 12, 13, 14

The White Pillars Inn

DEWITT

Elaine's Bed and Breakfast Reservation Service 1

4987 Kingston Road, Elbridge, 13060
(315) 689-2082

Near Shoppington, this fine, older Colonial is warmly furnished with some antiques. A large front guest room has an antique double bed, and a den with a sofa sleeper is available if necessary for family.

Elaine's Bed and Breakfast Reservation Service 2

4987 Kingston Road, Elbridge, 13060
(315) 689-2082

Dewitt adjoins Syracuse on the east. A nice comfortable home in a well-established residential area convenient to everything. Near highways, shopping, restaurants, and the university. Two rooms with double beds, one single, one and one-half baths. Many

antiques and original artworks. Hostess does weaving and has an antique business. Children and dogs welcome.

DOVER

Nutmeg B&B Agency 311

P. O. Box 1117, West Hartford, CT 06107
(203) 236-6698

Tucked just over the border from Kent, Connecticut, is this charming "Eyebrow" Colonial built in 1850. Guests can use the livingroom with TV, warm up by the wood-burning stove, lounge on the large front porch complete with wicker furniture, and enjoy the pool. All four guest rooms are on the second floor. Three rooms share a bath. The room with a private bath has a handsome double sleigh bed. All rooms have spectacular views of the surrounding countryside, a foliage lover's delight. Full breakfast. Children welcome. Pets in residence.

DOVER PLAINS

Covered Bridge 1DPNY

P. O. Box 447 A, Norfolk, CT 06058
(203) 542-5944

Genuine old farmhouse with a large sitting porch on which to relax and admire the views of the Connecticut hills. Enjoy a full farm breakfast in the sunny dining room or on the porch. Four beautifully appointed guest rooms, one with private bath, are decorated with the owner's collection of antique linens. There are three doubles and one room with twin beds. There is also a pool for guests to enjoy. $65-95.

The Mill Farm Inn

66 Cricket Hill Road, 12522
(914) 832-9198

NOTES: Credit cards accepted: A Master Card; B Visa; C American Express; D Discover Card; E Diner's Club; F Other; 2 Personal Checks accepted; 3 Lunch available; 4 Dinner available; 5 Open all year;

This 1850 rambling Colonial makes you feel like a welcomed guest. Enjoy panoramic views from the large sitting porch. The home is decorated with antique furniture and linens. The setting is real country, yet less than two hours north of New York City, near the Connecticut line.

Host: Margery Mill
Rooms: 4 (1 PB; 3 SB) $65-95
Full Breakfast
Closed February - March
Credit Cards: None
Notes: 2, 9, 10, 11, 12, 13

DRYDEN

Margaret Thacher's Spruce Haven Bed and Breakfast

9 James Street, Box 119, 13053
(607) 844-8052

This log home surrounded by tall spruce trees gives guests the feeling of being in the woods while enjoying the advantages of the village. On a quiet street, this warm and friendly home is within 12 miles of Ithaca, Cortland, lakes, golf, skiing, colleges, museums. Restaurants nearby. One night's deposit holds reservations.

Host: Margaret Thacher Brownell
Rooms: 2 (SB) prices on request
Full Breakfast
Credit Cards: None
Notes: 2, 5, 8, 10, 11, 12, 13

DURHAMVILLE

Elaine's Bed and Breakfast and Inn Reservation Service

4987 Kingston Road, Elbridge, 13060
(315) 689-2082

This stately old farm Colonial sits on its own quiet three acres in the country yet has easy access to all activities in the Oneida Valley: Sylvan Beach, Verona Beach, fishing, boating, Vernon Downs, antique shops

on Route 20, historic Fort Stanwix in Rome, Charlestown outlet shopping in Utica, and several nearby colleges. The interior is new and carpeted throughout. Four guest rooms share two full baths and have individual heat control. TV/VCR in livingroom. Check in is after 5:00 P.M. during the week as owner works in Rome. MasterCard and Visa. Children under five free. $45-65.

EDEN

Eden Inn Bed and Breakfast

8362 North Main Street, 14057
(716) 992-4814

The Eden Inn is situated on Route 62 in Eden, New York, roughly 17 miles southwest of Buffalo and six miles south of Hamburg. The inn features turndown service, wine and cheese (weekends). The solarium, which includes the common room and breakfast room, features a working fireplace. Each room is tastefully appointed with a theme in mind, such as The Menagerie, Amish Room, Train Room, and the Rose Suite (with a sitting room and private whirlpool bath.)

Hosts: Betsy and Chris Walits
Rooms: 4 (1 PB; 3 SB) $40-70
Continental Breakfast (weekdays); Full Breakfast (weekends)
Credit Cards: A, B (possibly)
Notes: 2, 5, 9, 13, 14

EDMESTON

Elaine's Bed and Breakfast Reservation Service

4987 Kingston Road, Elbridge, 13060
(315) 689-2082

Six varied guest rooms, two baths, above a fine restaurant. Great location in a tiny village.

6 Pets welcome; 8 Children welcome; 9 Social drinking allowed; 10 Tennis available; 11 Swimming available; 12 Golf available; 13 Skiing available; 14 May be booked through travel agents.

ELBRIDGE

Elaine's Bed and Breakfast Reservation Service

4987 Kingston Road, 13060
(315) 689-2082

Just 20 minutes west of Syracuse, seven minutes north of Skaneateles, and 12 minutes from Auburn, this remodeled ranch house offers peace and quiet on five acres in the country. The two guest rooms feature double beds and one and one-half baths. Handy to restaurants, antique shops, boutiques, art galleries, lake cruises, Syracuse University, highways, hospitals, and colleges. Ski areas only 30 minutes away. Summer theater 20 minutes away on Owasco Lake. Open year-round. Winter $35-45; summer $40-50 plus tax.

ELIZABETHTOWN

The American Country Collection 072

4 Greenwood Lane, Delmar, 12054
(518) 439-7001

This bed and breakfast, circa 1775, was a sawmill, a "dine and dance," a resident summer art school, and home of Wayman Adams, and since 1972, a summer residence for student classical musicians. It is situated on two and one-half acres bordered on two sides by the Bouquet River, a favorite fishing and swimming hole for the locals. Five guest rooms available, some with private bath. In summer, breakfast is served on the covered stone patio that overlooks the grounds. Small cottages also available. Well-behaved children welcome. Resident pets. $66-78.

Ilex Inn

ELLICOTTVILLE

Ilex Inn

6416 East Washington Street, P. O. Box 1585, 14731
(716) 699-2002; FAX (716) 699-5539

A turn of the century Victorian farmhouse furnished with antiques and period decor. Each guest room has a private bath. Guests can enjoy the hot tub, and are offered Turkish robes and warm towels. The elegant yet comfortable livingroom features a fireplace, cable TV, and video library. The upstairs sitting room and library gallery finds morning coffee, parlor games, and a lovely view. The innkeeper's double smoked ham or freshly squeezed orange juice may accompany pumpkin-ginger pancakes on holidays or weekends as an addition to a plentiful daily fare. Golf or ski packages available, canoe excursions, mountain bikes, feather beds and other amenities such as flannel bed sheets are available upon request.

Hosts: Bill and M.J. Brown
Rooms: 5 (PB) $75-145
Full Breakfast
Credit Cards: A, B
Notes: 2, 5, 9, 10, 11, 12, 13

NOTES: Credit cards accepted: A Master Card; B Visa; C American Express; D Discover Card; E Diner's Club; F Other; 2 Personal Checks accepted; 3 Lunch available; 4 Dinner available; 5 Open all year;

FAYETTEVILLE

Elaine's Bed and Breakfast Reservation Service

4987 Kingston Road, Elbridge, 13060
(315) 689-2082

Historic Italianiate brick house built in 1830 and 1954. Many antiques, wide plank floors upstairs, main livingroom with original pier mirror, walnut valances, fireplace, and light fixtures. Three rooms up; one down with private bath. $55-75 plus tax.

FLEISCHMANNS

The American Country Collection 161

4 Greenwood Lane, Delmar, 12054
(518) 439-7001

The inn, originally built in 1867 as a classic Victorian summer retreat for a local wealthy resident, is open year-round and situated at the entrance to the high peaks of the Catskill Mountains. The 10 guest rooms, six private baths and two with shared baths, and common areas are furnished with select antiques, wicker, brass, and country chintz. King, queen, double, and twin beds are available, Also offered are two efficiency apartments with private baths, twin beds, and a shared kitchen. Individual glycerin soaps and plenty of books are found in the rooms, and your host, a full-time innkeeper, says his aim is for guests for feel that the inn is their "country house" for as long as they are there. Full breakfast served 8:30 until 10 A.M. Resident cocker spaniel on the premises. $25-90. Discount price for children in separate room.

FRIENDSHIP

Rainbow Hospitality A300

504 Amherst Street, Buffalo, 14207
(800) 373-8797

Come away to the enchanted hills to a little town that time forgot. Enjoy the hospitality of Friendship in an elegant Queen Anne-style home built for the financier of the town. Guest can relax while surrounded by beautifully carved cherry woodwork, parquet floors, graceful curving walls, stained glass, leaded glass, and etched glass. Five rooms contain fireplaces designed specifically for the motif of each room. Two guest rooms have gas fireplaces. Surrounded by the Allegany Mountains, hiking, biking, cross-country skiing and more are nearby. Guests may treat themsleves to a wide variety of stress reductions through the host's holistic services. $55-65.

FULTON

Battle Island Inn

Rural Delivery 1, Box 176, Route 48 North, 13069
(315) 593-3699

Battle Island Inn is a pre-Civil War farm estate that has been restored and furnished with period antiques. The inn is across the

Battle Island Inn

road from a golf course that also provides cross-country skiing. Guest rooms are elegantly furnished with high back beds, TV, phones and private baths. Breakfast is always special in the 1840s dining room.

Hosts: Richard and Joyce Rice
Rooms: 6 (PB) $65-75
Full Breakfast
Credit Cards: A, B, C, D
Notes: 2, 5, 8, 9, 12, 13

GASPORT

Rainbow Hospitality G200

504 Amherst Street, Buffalo, 14207
(800) 373-8797

Charming, intimate country cottage nestled in Niagara's fruit belt. Furnished with antiques, this Cape Cod embraces a comfortable style and timeless good taste. Convenient to Lockport, Olcott, Niagara Falls, and Buffalo. Visitors feel right at home with the friendly proprietress, a traveled professional and an award-winning kite maker. A country breakfast featuring freshly baked scones and seasonal fruits will be served on the spacious deck or family dining room. Double or twin accommodations available. $50.

GENEVA

Elaine's Bed and Breakfast and Inn Reservation Service

4987 Kingston Road, Elbridge, 13060
(315) 689-2082

A freshly decorated, comfortable, clean, and convenient brick Federalist house offers first-floor room with private bath and double bed. The second floor features two guest rooms, one with a queen bed and one with a double that share a bath. Near historic Main Street, colleges, Cornell Experimental Agriculture Center, State Park on Seneca Lake. $50-60 plus tax.

GERMANTOWN

The American Country Collection 113

4 Greenwood Lane, Delmar, 12054
(518) 439-7001

Wonderful views of the Catskill Mountains and the Hudson Valley can be had from this 18-year-old home. The guest quarters include two bedrooms and a private bath. There is a family room with fireplace, piano, and TV. Breakfast is served on the porch or in the dining room. Guests are welcome to use the in-ground swimming pool. Children welcome. Crib available. No pets. Full breakfast on weekends; continental breakfast Tuesday through Thursday. $60 (Nov.1-May 30); $65 (June 1-Oct. 31).

The American Country Collection 144

4 Greenwood Lane, Delmar, 12054
(518) 439-7001

This cozy loft apartment is nestled on the eastern banks of the Hudson River among the gently rolling hills of Columbia County. The apartment is furnished with a mix of traditional furniture and antiques, ceiling fan, skylight, fully-equipped kitchen, double bed and full bath. Close to Clermont Historical Site and Park, Bard College, and the Hunter and Catamount ski areas. Infants allowed; play pens available. Breakfast available at guest's convenience. $95.

GHENT

The American Country Collection 082

4 Greenwood Lane, Delmar, 12054
(518) 439-7001

NOTES: Credit cards accepted: A Master Card; B Visa; C American Express; D Discover Card; E Diner's Club; F Other; 2 Personal Checks accepted; 3 Lunch available; 4 Dinner available; 5 Open all year;

This early 19th-century farmhouse is situated on 10 scenic acres of open fields, perfect for walking and picnicking. There is also a private one-acre pond for fishing and paddleboating and a miniature horse farm. The guest room on the second floor is air-conditioned and has a TV and private bath. The two-room suite on the third floor is air-conditioned and has a TV. Children welcome. Dog in residence. $60-70.

GREENFIELD

The American Country Collection 112

4 Greenwood Lane, Delmar, 12054
(518) 439-7001

It was an inn for British officers during the War of 1812, then a stagecoach stop in the 1820s before serving as part of the Underground Railroad before the Civil War. A rich sense of history is enhanced by Oriental rugs and fine antiques from Europe and the Middle and Far East. Five guest rooms, three with private baths. One room has a Jacuzzi. Children over 11 welcome. Pets in residence. $60-125, seasonal.

HAMLIN

Sandy Creek Manor House

1960 Redman Road, 14464-9635
(716) 964-7528

Feather pillows, Amish quilts, and quiet nights lull guests at this peaceful retreat. The 1910 English tudor is on six wooded acres with several perennial gardens beckoning you to "stop and smell the roses." Trout, bass, and salmon fishing in the backyard. The antique player piano is reminiscent of grandma's house. Just 30 minutes to Rochester, 90 minutes to Niagara Falls along the Seaway Trail.

Hosts: Shirley Hollink and James Krempasky
Rooms: 3 (SB) $40-60
Full Breakfast
Credit Cards: None
Notes: 2, 5, 6, 9, 10, 11, 12, 13, 14

HAMMONDSPORT

Blushing Rosé Bed and Breakfast

11 William Street, 14840
(607) 569-3402; (607) 569-3483
(800) 982-8812

The Blushing Rosé has served as a pleasant hideaway for honeymooners, anniversary celebraters, and romantic trysters alike. Whether guests spend their day driving, hiking, biking, or just relaxing, this is the ideal haven in which to end the day and a great place to start the day with a copious specialty breakfast. The village has shopping, dining, and great walking. Keuka Lake is just a few doors away; wineries are nearby, as is the Corning Glass and Watkins Glen.

Hosts: The Laufersweilers
Rooms: 4 (PB) $65-85
Full and Continental Breakfast
Credit Cards: None
Notes: 2, 5, 9, 10, 11, 12, 13

Blushing Rosé

6 Pets welcome; 8 Children welcome; 9 Social drinking allowed; 10 Tennis available; 11 Swimming available; 12 Golf available; 13 Skiing available; 14 May be booked through travel agents.

Gone with the Wind

Gone with the Wind on Keaka Lake

453 West Lake Road 54 A, Branchport, 14418
(607) 868-4603

The name paints the picture of this 1887 stone Victorian. Fourteen acres on a slight rise overlook a quiet lake cove adorned by an inviting gazebo. Feel the magic of total relaxation and peace of mind, enjoying the solarium hot tub, nature trails, three fireplaces, and delectable breakfasts. Private beach and dock.

Hosts: Linda and Robert Lewis
Rooms: 5 (SB) $65-95
Full Breakfast
Credit Cards: None
Notes: 2, 5, 10, 11, 12, 13

J. S. Hubbs Bed and Breakfast

17 Sheather Street, P. O. Box 366, 14840
(607) 569-2440; (607) 569-3629

Come and relax in this family home. This historic Greek Revival (inkbottle house) was built in 1840 and has been in the family for almost 100 years. It offers a suite, single, and double rooms with one private bath, three private half-baths and a shared shower. Situated one-half block from Keuka Lake and the village square.

Hosts: Walter, Linda, and John Carl
Rooms: 4 (1 PB; 3 SB) $62
Full Breakfast
Credit Cards: A, B
Notes: 5, 10, 11, 12

HAMPTON BAYS

House on the Water

Box 106, 11946
(516) 728-3560

Ranch house with two acres of garden on Shinnecock Bay. Quiet location. One mile to village, train, and bus. Seven miles to Southampton and Westhampton. Only 2 miles to ocean beaches. Bicycles, windsurfers, pedal boat, barbecue, beach lounges, and umbrellas. German, Spanish, and French spoken. Kitchen facilities.

Host: Mrs. Ute
Rooms: 2 (PB) $75-95
Full Breakfast
Minimum stay weekdays: 2 nights; weekends: 3
  nights; holidays: 4 nights
Credit Cards: None
Closed Nov. 1-May 1
Notes: 2, 9, 10, 11, 12, 14

House on the Water

HARTFORD

The American Country Collection 160

4 Greenwood Lane, Delmar, 12054
(518) 439-7001

Within a short drive of both Saratoga Springs and Lake George, this historic Colonial tavern offers a relaxed country atmosphere in a quiet, rural setting. A history buff's delight, this restored home was built in 1802 and "remodeled" in 1878. Two second-floor rooms and one first-floor room are available for guests and offer both private and shared baths. A bountiful, full

NOTES: Credit cards accepted: A Master Card; B Visa; C American Express; D Discover Card; E Diner's Club; F Other; 2 Personal Checks accepted; 3 Lunch available; 4 Dinner available; 5 Open all year;

breakfast is served each morning in the dining room and includes juices and cereals, homemade rolls, breads, muffins, eggs, bacon or sausage, and coffee and tea. $25-50.

HILLSDALE

The American Country Collection 106

4 Greenwood Lane, Delmar, 12054
(518) 439-7001

This inn is surrounded by 100 acres of meadows, woodlands, and an ancient cemetery. Built as a farmhouse around 1830, it was formerly the parsonage to the old church next door, then an inn with a somewhat dubious reputation during Prohibition. Four guest rooms, two with private baths. Breakfast is served on the screened porch or in the candlelit dining room. Children over 11 welcome. Two cats in residence. $90-95; two-night minimum stay on in-season weekends; three-night minimum stay on holiday weekends.

HOBART

Breezy Acres Farm Bed and Breakfast

Rural Delivery 1, Box 191, 13788
(607) 538-9338

"Better than home..." reads one entry in the guest book. That's because the hosts strive for excellence in every area. Individually decorated rooms, each with private, squeaky-clean bath. Bountiful, homemade breakfast. Five minutes from Scotch Valley Ski Center, and 30 minutes from Ski Windham. Spa, fireplace, pond for fishing and swimming, hunting, 300 acres for hiking, a deck surrounded by beautiful flower gardens, and a shady porch for relaxing.

Hosts: Joyce and David Barber
Rooms: 3 (PB) $50-60
Full Breakfast
Credit Cards: A, B
Notes: 2, 5, 9, 10, 11, 12, 13

HOMER

Elaine's Bed and Breakfast Reservation Service

4987 Kingston Road, Elbridge, 13060
(315) 689-2082

Homer is off I-81 just north of Cortland, between Syracuse and Binghamton. The first brick home built in 1834 in this picturesque village. Three cheerful guest rooms featuring either queen-size, full, or double beds. Cots are available for a third person in the room for $15. Wide plank floors, antiques. Open year-round. $40-70.

HOOSICK FALLS

The American Country Collection 068

4 Greenwood Lane, Delmar, 12054
(518) 439-7001

Beginning as a stagecoach inn in 1843, then as a stop for the Underground Railroad, this bed and breakfast is just 10 minutes from Bennington, Vermont, and in the center of beautiful Grandma Moses country. Six second-floor guest rooms, one with private bath. There's a sitting room with cable TV and an inviting hot tub and sauna. Children welcome. Well-behaved pets permitted occasionally. $50-65.

HOPEWELL JUNCTION

Covered Bridge 1HJNY

P. O. Box 447 A, Norfolk, CT 06058
(203) 542-5944

6 Pets welcome; 8 Children welcome; 9 Social drinking allowed; 10 Tennis available; 11 Swimming available; 12 Golf available; 13 Skiing available; 14 May be booked through travel agents.

This 1841 Georgian Colonial built for a prominent Dutch silversmith is set on six acres that include lovely perennial gardens and a pool. The house has six fireplaces with double livingrooms that are adorned with large, imported crystal chandeliers and a fabulous sun room that overlooks the grounds. The common rooms and the four guest rooms are all beautifully decorated with antiques, some of which the owners collected when they lived in France. A full country breakfast is served by the hostess, who attended the Culinary Institute of America. $85-140.

ITHACA

Rose Inn

Route 34 North, Box 6576, 14851-6576
(607) 533-7905; FAX (607) 533-4202

An elegant 1840s Italianate mansion on 20 landscaped acres. Fabulous circular staircase of Honduran mahogany. Prix fixe dinner served with advance reservations. Close to Cornell University. Twice selected by Uncle Ben's as one of the "Ten Best Inns in America." Mobil four-star. AAA approved.

Hosts: Sherry and Charles Rosemann
Rooms: 15 (PB) $100-160
Suites: $185-250
Full Breakfast
Credit Cards: A, B
Notes: 2, 4, 5, 8 (over 10), 9, 10, 11, 12, 13, 14

JAMESVILLE

Elaine's Bed and Breakfast Reservation Service

4987 Kingston Road, Elbridge, 13060
(315) 689-2082

Country atmosphere. High on a hill with a view for 35 miles, including three lakes, this owner-designed contemporary home offers the ultimate in peace and quiet. Only

15 minutes from downtown Syracuse or the university. Unique solarium full of plants and casual seating. Rear deck features a picnic table and a marvelous view. Two guest rooms share a bath with a skylight. House is ideal for a small family. $40-55.

JEFFERSONVILLE

The Griffin House

Rural Delivery 1, Box 178, Maple Avenue, 12748
(914) 482-3371

Beginning in 1895, ten master carpenters worked for five years with American Chestnut to create this masterpiece of woodwork. Nestled in the village of Jeffersonville (pop. 484) and within walking distance of shops and restaurants. In this home, noted for architectural excellence, guests will enjoy fine antiques, spacious bedrooms, and a full cooked breakfast with the hosts. The original settlement home (circa 1840) occupies a wooded setting beneath majestic hemlocks and radiant maples. Laundry Creek contributes a comforting symphony of sounds, and a kaleidoscope of colors. This two-room structure has evolved from homestead to playhouse, and the chicken compound has most recently been ressurected to display a selection of gifts and locally-made crafts.

Hosts: Irene and Paul Griffin
Rooms: 4 (2 PB; 2 SB) $75-95
Full Breakfast
Credit Cards: None
Notes: 2, 4, 5, 9, 10, 11, 12, 13

JOHNSTOWN

The American Country Collection 099

4 Greenwood Lane, Delmar, 12054
(518) 439-7001

This 100-year-old in-town home is situated on one-half acre of manicured lawns, vegetable and flower gardens, with an above-ground swimming pool. Two guest rooms, one bath shared with owners. Rooms are normally rented to one party traveling together. The bedrooms have lots of natural light and cross ventilation. There's a TV in the livingroom and den. No pets. Children over two welcome. $40.

KATONAH

The American Country Collection 155

4 Greenwood Lane, Delmar, 12054
(518) 439-7001

Dream away in this 16th-century Dutch Colonial farmhouse situated on 4 acres of woods, gardens, and maple sugarbush. A short climb up four steps brings guests to the master bedroom, which has a brass bed, free-standing fireplace, and private, hand-painted Portuguese tile bath. A small study with a desk and library connects to the bedroom and a common room. The third floor has two more bedrooms that share a bath. Across the street is a lovely pond for trout fishing or swimming. A full breakfast is served each morning. $50-75.

LAKE GEORGE

House on the Hill Bed and Breakfast

Route 28, Box 248, Warrensburg, 12885
(518) 623-9390; (800) 221-9390

The bed and breakfast romantic fling. An unforgettable experience for lovers. Nurture that special relationship. Coffee and freshly baked goodies in your room followed by a full sumptuous breakfast in the wraparound sunroom overlooking 176 scenic acres. Pristine cross-country trails. Air conditioning, satellite TV/VCR. Two-

night minimum stay. Special packages available. French and Italian spoken.

Hosts: Joe and Lynn Rubino
Rooms: 5 (1 PB; 4 SB) $65-95
Full Breakfast
Credit Cards: A, B
Notes: 2, 3, 4, 5, 8 (by arrangement), 9, 10, 11, 12, 13, 14

LAKE PLACID

South Meadow Farm and Lodge

HCR 1 Box 44, Cascade Road, 12946
(518) 523-9369; (800) 523-9369

Small farm on 75 acres, bordered by state land in the heart of the Adirondack High Peaks. Ski out the back door onto 50 kilometers of Olympic cross-country trails. Family-style lodging with full, hearty meals. Come visit year-round and share this lodge, the view, and Adirondack hospitality.

Hosts: Tony and Nancy Corwin
Rooms: 5 (SB) $70-90
Full Breakfast
Credit Cards: A, B, C
Notes: 2, 3, 4, 5, 8, 9, 13, 14

LEWISTON

Rainbow Hospitality S100

504 Amherst Street, Buffalo, 14207
(800) 373-8797

This chalet-style home is nestled in an apple orchard set back from the road in the country, yet conveniently situated to shopping and historic sites. Breakfast may be enjoyed on the deck or in the dining room overlooking a spacious yard on an 80-acre farm in the fruit belt of Niagara County. Just 15 minutes from Niagara Falls, Lewiston, Canada, shopping malls, and farmers' markets. $40-45.

6 Pets welcome; 8 Children welcome; 9 Social drinking allowed; 10 Tennis available; 11 Swimming available; 12 Golf available; 13 Skiing available; 14 May be booked through travel agents.

Rainbow Hospitality L211
504 Amherst Street, Buffalo, 14207
(800) 373-8797

Gracious Victorian minutes from the village of Lewiston and Artpark. The inn provides guests a breathtaking view of the Canadian shoreline at sunset. Just seven miles north of Niagara Falls. An abundance of antiques decorate the house, and guests may choose from four rooms. Wraparound porches and a quiet rural setting central to all historic landmarks, Canada, and the Falls. $65-99.

Rainbow Hospitality L240
504 Amherst Street, 14207
(800) 373-8797

This 100-year old Victorian set in a rural area boasts three guest rooms and a large family room with two shared baths and a full breakfast. Ample parking for boats and an extra-early breakfast for fishermen. Easy access to Lewiston, Youngstown, and Niagara Falls. $45-50.

Rainbow Hospitality L400
504 Amherst Street, 14207
(800) 373-8797

Attractive bungalow in th historic village of Lewiston. Large suites with private baths. Great for families; crib available for baby. Hostess speaks fluent Spanish and French. Within walking distance of Art Park, antique shops, and restaurants. Niagara Falls is just 10 minutes away. $55.

Rainbow Hospitality L500
504 Amherst Street, 14207
(800) 373-8797

Ranch-style home on more than two acres on the Lower Niagara River. Situated 10

minutes from the Lewiston-Queenston Bridge, and 20 minutes from Niagara Falls. Cathedral ceilings with beams in the livingroom, dining room, kitchen, and den. In-ground pool, two fireplaces, master suite has a private bath. Two other rooms with bath in the hall. $60-65.

LITTLE VALLEY

The Napoli Log Homestead
Rural Delivery #2, Box 301, 14755
(716) 938-6755; (716) 358-3926

This cedar log cedar home was built in 1988. It is furnished with Early American pieces handed down from five generations. Two rooms share a bath upstairs, and one room has a private bath. There is a cozy Victorian sitting room upstairs. The full breakfast of waffles and sausage, served with pure maple syrup or bacon and eggs, is included in the room rate. A convenient 20 minutes from Holiday Valley, Cockaigne, Allegheny State Park, Chautauqua Lake, and Amish settlement.

Hosts: Dean and Annette Waite
Rooms: 3 (1 PB; 2 SB) $40-50
Full Breakfast
Credit Cards: None
Notes: 2, 5, 6, 8, 13

LIVERPOOL

Elaine's Bed and Breakfast Reservation Service
4987 Kingston Road, Elbridge, 13060
(315) 689-2082

Victorian house filled with country charm and antiques. A 100-year old, three-story house overlooking the yacht club on Onondaga Lake. Conveniently situated next to antique and craft center. Just five minutes to downtown Syracuse, restaurants, shops, libraries, Johnson Park, and other attractions. One large guest room fea-

NOTES: Credit cards accepted: A Master Card; B Visa; C American Express; D Discover Card; E Diner's Club; F Other; 2 Personal Checks accepted; 3 Lunch available; 4 Dinner available; 5 Open all year;

tures a four-poster bed and bay window alcove, with table and chairs. Another guest room features a maple and pine antique bed, with matching chest and a collection of powder boxes and dresser jars. These rooms share a lovely modern tub and shower bath. Ideal for a party of four. Enjoy a full country breakfast. $45-65.

LIVINGSTON MANOR

Clarke's Place in the Country

Rural Delivery 2, Box 465 A, 12758
(914) 439-5442

In a unique, contemporary rustic home on top of Shandelee, in the heart of the Catskills, the great room features a wood-burning stove and a 20-foot cathedral ceiling. The interior has tongue-and-groove white pine throughout. A deep water pond on the premises offers year-round enjoyment. Extraordinary restaurants, exquisite antiques and cider mills nearby. Ask about the weekend gourmet cooking classes!

Hosts: Robert Clarke and Nan Clarke
Rooms: 2 (PB) $55-65
Full Breakfast
Credit Cards: A, B
Notes: 2, 5, 8, 9, 10, 11, 12, 13

R. M. Farm

Box 391, 12758
(914) 439-5511

Situated on a mountain slope with a panoramic view of the Catskill Mountains, R. M. Farm offers hospitality reminiscent of the days when life was sweet and slow. Enjoy swimming, fishing, hiking, or bird watching on this 260-acre preserve. Stay in bright, sunny rooms which are furnished in country antiques. Enjoy the full breakfast, featuring homemade bread and jam.

Hosts: Gina Molinet and Bob Runge
Rooms: 3 (SB) $50 plus tax

Full Breakfast
Credit Cards: None
Notes: 2, 5, 8, 9, 10, 11, 12, 13

LOCKPORT

Rainbow Hospitality G200

504 Amherst Street, Buffalo, 14207
(800) 373-8797

Charming, intimate country cottage nestled in Niagara's fruit belt. Furnished with antiques, this Cape Cod embraces a comfortable style and timeless good taste. Convenient to Lockport, Olcott, and only 40 minutes from Niagara Falls and Buffalo. The hostess is a traveled professional and award-winning kite maker. Fresh-baked scones, seasonal fruits, and country breakfasts will be served on the spacious deck or family dining room. $50.

Rainbow Hospitality LO400

504 Amherst Street, Buffalo, 14207
(800) 373-8797

Welcome to this working produce farm situated on Route 104, previously known as the "Million Dollar Highway," "Honeymoon Trail," and "Old Niagara Road." Four large guest rooms on the second floor, two with shared baths, await weary travelers. A hearty farm breakfast is served, and the menu varies from day to day. Just minutes away from first class restaurants and world famous scenic and historic tourist sites. $50.

Rainbow Hospitality LO500

504 Amherst Street, Buffalo, 14207
(800) 373-8797

The nation's centennial is reminiscent of this homes' ancestry. Antique furnishings, spacious guest rooms, and a host and hostess that lovingly share their collection of family heirlooms and history with guests.

6 Pets welcome; 8 Children welcome; 9 Social drinking allowed; 10 Tennis available; 11 Swimming available; 12 Golf available; 13 Skiing available; 14 May be booked through travel agents.

Convenient to Lockport, Amherst, and 40 minutes from Niagara Falls. The Erie Barge Canal Locks are minutes away, providing boat tours for guests water escursion to the days of a bustling barge community. $65-85.

NEW LEBANON

The American Country Collection 132

4 Greenwood Lane, Delmar, 12054
(518) 439-7001

This historic Colonial was built in 1797 for a preacher and his family. Nestled on 18 acres just outside of town, this country inn is convenient to Lenox, the Berkshires, the Capital District, and major ski areas. There is a suite on the first floor with a feather mattress, day bed with a trundle, and a private bath, and three rooms on the second floor share a bath. Rooms are light and airy with homemade quilts and period Colonial furniture. A full country breakfast is served each morning. $35-75, seasonal.

Covered Bridge

P. O. Box 447, Norfolk, CT 06058
(203) 542-5944

This 1797 Colonial farmhouse set on 18 acres offers a quiet country retreat but is close to all of the activities offered in the Berkshires. Guests may relax beside the fireplace in the livingroom, or enjoy the beautiful front porch with a view of the Taconic Hills. A full country breakfast is served in the dining room. There is a first-floor suite with a private bath and three guest rooms on the second floor that share a bath. $60-75.

NEW PALTZ

The American Country Collection 117

4 Greenwood Lane, Delmar, 12054
(518) 439-7001

Plan the day from the rambling lemonade porch of this immaculate Queen Anne Victorian in this tiny village near the Shawangunk Mountains. Three guest rooms, one with private bath. Guests in the master bedroom have a view of the solarium and the gardens from their indoor balcony. Children over 10 welcome. Two cats in residence. $70-80.

NEW ROCHELLE

The American Country Collection 152

4 Greenwood Lane, Delmar, 12054
(518) 439-7001

Set in a quiet suburban community, this gracious English Tudor features a manicured lawn and shrubs, and is surrounded by other homes which are some of the finest examples of Norman Tudor architecture in the Northeast. A large elm tree, one of the few that survived the great Dutch Elm disease, highlights the muted charm of this picturesque location not far from New York City and the Long Island Sound beaches. One third-floor room, which is air-conditioned in the summer, offers a king-size bed and private hall bath. A continental plus breakfast is served in the morning. Children over 10 welcome. $75.

Aaah! Bed and Breakfast #1, Ltd. BALD45-1

P. O. Box 200, 10108-0200
(212) 246-4000

Brownstone on a tree-lined street just opposite London Terrace. Second-floor studio walkup. The apartment has original ornate ceiling moldings. Three windows facing north fill the apartment with plenty of natural light. Round dining table and fold-out day bed are the major pieces of furniture. Many accent pieces make this studio with Pullman kitchen a very homey place. Continental breakfast. $80-100.

Aaah! Bed and Breakfast #1, Ltd. CHA

P. O. Box 200, 10108-0200
(212) 246-4000

West Side midtown two-bedroom apartment in a fourth-floor walkup that has been redone. New floors, walls, doors, appliances, windows, and sleeping for as many as eight. Continental breakfast. TV, air conditioning, and dishwasher. Unhosted. $160/night.

Aaah! Bed and Breakfast #1, Ltd. DAVI

P. O. Box 200, 10108-0200
(212) 246-4000

If guests are looking for romantic and charming surroundings, this studio apartment, filled with walls covered with miniature busts and other art, is suggested frequently. Its courtyard with trellises, trees, and a carriage house make it hard to to realize it is on restaurant row in New York City. Continental breakfast. Unhosted. $80-100.

Aaah! Bed and Breakfast #1, Ltd. DUNB32-CC1

P. O. Box 200, 10108-0200
(212) 246-4000

A gracious parlor-floor one-bedroom unit in a brownstone on 35th Street featuring 14-foot ceilings, a modern kitchen, tasteful furnishings, cable/color TV/VCR, air conditioning, and fireplace. Continental breakfast. Must be 18 or older. Unhosted. $120.

Bed and Breakfast Network of New York

134 West 32nd Street, Suite 602, 10001
(212) 645-8134

This reservation service represents more than 100 nonsmoking accommodations in New York City, both traditional homestays and entire furnished apartments. Most accommodations are in Manhattan's most exciting neighborhoods, such as Greenwich Village, Soho and the mid-upper East and West Sides. $50-90 hosted; $80-300 unhosted. Checks accepted for deposit, open year-round, children welcome and accommodations may be booked through a travel agent.

Bed and Breakfast U.S.A., Ltd. 37

Old Sheffield Road, South Egremont, MA 01258
(413) 528-2113

Three large studio apartments in a historic landmark town house on Riverside Drive (between 75th and 76th) in Manhattan. Romantically decorated with antiques, queen beds, comfortable sofas, dining areas, TVs, and kitchenettes. Monogrammed terry-cloth robes are provided in the oversize baths. The guest apartments give total privacy with the advantage of hosts nearby. Easy access to all public

6 Pets welcome; 8 Children welcome; 9 Social drinking allowed; 10 Tennis available; 11 Swimming available; 12 Golf available; 13 Skiing available; 14 May be booked through travel agents.

transportation. Walking distance to Lincoln Center and Columbus Avenue shops and eateries. Continental breakfast. No pets. Children welcome. $110-120.

Urban Ventures, Inc.
38 West 32th Street, #1412, 10001
(212) 594-5650; FAX (212) 947-9320

Urban Ventures is a reservation service that represents approximately 650 accommodations in New York City. Bed and breakfasts have hosts, offer breakfast and loan sweaters and umbrellas. Accepts Master Card, Visa, American Express, Discover and Diner's Club cards. Each accommodation is inspected and accurate descriptions are offered. Urban Ventures networks with other agencies in order to make reservations in other American cities, Canada, London, and Paris. $60-125.

Urban Ventures, Inc.
BRE000
P. O. Box 426, 10024
(212) 594-5650; FAX (212) 947-9320

The lucky new owners of this apartment have created a breathtakingly beautiful home. Two bedrooms, a queen and double, with private baths. Built-in mahogany closets, a terrace, garden, and delightful extras to discover. At East 29th off 3rd Avenue. $190-194.

Urban Ventures, Inc.
FAB111
P. O. Box 426, 10024
(212) 594-5650; FAX (212) 947-9320

An 1840 home in all its elegance. Original brick, fireplace, two baths, on a landmark street. A place to write home about! On West 22nd between 8th and 9th avenues. $115.

Urban Ventures, Inc.
HOW100
P. O. Box 426, 10024
(212) 594-5650; FAX (212) 947-9320

The sun sets on the balcony about the same time as the theater lights sparkle on. The room with private bath is in an apartment filled with theater memorabilia. The building has an exercise room with a sauna and a tiled roof garden. First class! West 55th Street and 8th Avenue. $75 single; $90 double; $115 as apartment.

Urban Ventures, Inc.
KIR100
P. O. Box 426, 10024
(212) 594-5650; FAX (212) 947-9320

Bed and breakfast on the 15th floor at 38th and Lexington gives guests views of penthouses. Very nice! Light, airy, twin-bed room in a fashionable building. $90 double; $125 as apartment.

Urban Ventures, Inc.
MAU003
P. O. Box 426, 10024
(212) 594-5650; FAX (212) 947-9320

Sitting on top of the world with Central Park and Lincoln Center at your feet. Open air concerts float up to your 27th-floor window. Wonderful Irish host. On West 62nd Street. $90-115.

NIAGARA FALLS

The Cameo Inn
4710 Lower River Road, Route 18F, 14092
(716) 745-3034

Just five miles north of Niagara Falls, this stately Queen Anne Victorian commands a

---

NOTES: Credit cards accepted: A Master Card; B Visa; C American Express; D Discover Card; E Diner's Club; F Other; 2 Personal Checks accepted; 3 Lunch available; 4 Dinner available; 5 Open all year;

majestic view of the lower Niagara River and Canadian shoreline. Lovingly furnished with period antiques and family heirlooms, the Cameo will charm guests with its quiet elegance. Here guests can enjoy the ambience of days past in a peaceful setting far from the bustle of everyday life. Three rooms with private or shared baths are available, as well as a three-room private suite the overlooks the river.

Hosts: Greg and Carolyn Fisher
Rooms: 4 (2 PB; 2 SB) $65-99
Full Breakfast
Credit Cards: A, B
Notes: 2, 5, 9, 10, 11, 12, 13, 14

Rainbow Hospitality NF110

504 Amherst Street, Buffalo, 14207
(800) 373-8797

Stately home close to the Falls and situated on a quiet street of lovely older homes. The hostess is a "transplanted" Southerner, and welcomes guests with a full cooked breakfast. Confortable and homey, enjoy the patio in summer and two guest rooms. $50.

Rainbow Hospitality NF200

504 Amherst Street, Buffalo, 14207
(800) 373-8797

Step back in time to the grandeur of yesteryear in this cross-gabled Queen Anne Victorian home. Built in 1906, this beautifully restored home boasts original light fixtures, oak woodwork and wainscoting, stained-glass windows, many family antiques, and friendly hospitality. Situated in the heart of the city of Niagara Falls, bus service and fine dining are within walking distance. Ample off-street parking. Full breakfast. $60-70.

Rainbow Hospitality NF500

504 Amherst Street, Buffalo, 14207
(800) 373-8797

Spend some quality time in this excellent bed and breakfast inn. Four guest rooms, combined with personal attention at a price that makes sense. Plenty of off-street parking. Within walking distance of the sights and sounds of Niagara Falls. A full breakfast is served. $55-65.

NIVERVILLE

The American Country Collection 079

4 Greenwood Lane, Delmar, 12054
(518) 439-7001

Beautifully preserved gingerbread and an old oak door with Venetian glass inserts detail this Italianate private home built in 1870. Two second-floor guest rooms share one bath. Normally rented to one party traveling together. Breakfast is served in either the elegant dining room with its original faux fireplace and crystal chandelier, or in the new solarium overlooking the garden. Adults only. No pets. $60 (Nov. 1-May 1); $70 (May 2-Oct. 31).

OGDENSBURG

The Salty Dog Bed and Breakfast

Route 2, Box 2, 13669
(315) 393-1298

The Salty Dog is situated on the St. Lawrence River, west of Ogdensburg at the gateway to the Thousand Islands. A double bedded mini-suite has a seating area with a twin hide-a-bed, and there is also a spacious queen bedroom. Each features its own lavatory and vanity. Swim and fish from the dock and beach. Boat mooring is available. The rolling lawn and spacious screened porch provide a great spot to

6 Pets welcome; 8 Children welcome; 9 Social drinking allowed; 10 Tennis available; 11 Swimming available; 12 Golf available; 13 Skiing available; 14 May be booked through travel agents.

The Salty Dog

watch the large ships plying the St. Lawrence seaway.

Hosts: Peggy and Bernard Sperling
Rooms: 2 (SB) $55-65
Full Breakfast
Credit Cards: None
Notes: 2, 5, 8, 9, 10, 11, 12, 13

OLCOTT

Bayside Guest House
P. O. Box 34, 1572 Lockport Olcott Road
(State Road 78), 14126-0034
(716) 778-7767; (800) 438-2192

Overlooking the harbor and marina, near Lake Ontario, this country-style Victorian home offers fishermen and travelers a comfortable, relaxed stay. Antiques and collectibles furnish this guest house. Great fishing and a county park within walking distance. Plenty of restaurants. Only 30 minutes from Niagara Falls, one hour from Buffalo. Dogs and cats on the premises.

Host: Jane M. Voelpel
Rooms: 5 (SB) $30
Continental Breakfast
Credit Cards: None
Notes: 2, 5, 6, 8, 9, 10, 12

PALENVILLE

Bed and Breakfast U.S.A., Ltd. 21
Old Sheffield Road, South Egremont, MA 01258
(413) 528-2113

A turn-of-the-century Queen Anne Victorian with large rooms. Distance is 18 miles to Woodstock, 10 miles to Hunter Mountain, 2 miles to horseback riding, 5 miles to Catskill Game Farm and North Lake, 8 miles to cross-country skiing, and a short walk to swimming or golf. Accommodations include a ground-floor suite with private entrance, private bath with whirlpool, fireplace, and a ladder to the loft; a room with a double bed and private bath; two other rooms with shared bath. Full breakfast. No pets. Children over four welcome. $55-125.

PENN YAN

The Wagener Estate Bed and Breakfast
351 Elm Street, 14527
(315) 536-4591

Centrally situated in the Finger Lakes, this bed and breakfast is in an historic 1796 home furnished with antiques and nestled on four acres. Hospitality, country charm, comfort, and an elegant breakfast await.

Hosts: Norm and Evie Worth
Rooms: 4 (2 PB; 2 SB) $60-70
Full Breakfast
Credit Cards: A, B, C
Closed Jan.-Feb.
Notes: 2, 9, 10, 11, 12

Bayside Guest House

PINE BUSH

Sunrise Farm

Rural Delivery 1, Box 433A
Bruyn Avenue, 12566-9801
(914) 361-3629

Sunrise Farm is a 30-acre certified organic farm featuring Scottish highland cattle, vegetables and fruit, lawns, flowerbeds, cross-country skiing and ice skating on a large pond. The guest room on the second floor has a ceiling fan and skylight. There is a wood-burning stove in the livingroom, where guests are welcome to join the hosts for tea and wine. Dinner is available by arrangement.

Hosts: Janet and Fred Schmelzer
Rooms: 1 (PB) $45
Full Breakfast
Credit Cards: None
Notes: 2, 4, 5, 8, 9, 11, 12

POMPEY

Elaine's Bed and Breakfast and Inn Reservation Service

4987 Kingston Road, Elbridge, 13060
(315) 689-2082

Charming, well-furnished, sparkling ranch flat on two acres, with a view of a sculptured garden. Guests may have the entire main floor. Two double bedrooms, a master bedroom opens to another, with a sleeper sofa for a family suite. One and one-half baths. Southeast of Syracuse in the country.

QUEENSBURY

The American Country Collection 126

4 Greenwood Lane, Delmar, 12054
(518) 439-7001

Original gingerbread accents this 100-year-old farmhouse on a working berry farm.

There's a comfortable country feeling here with family furnishings and mementos, patchwork quilts, and oak furnishings. Two guest rooms with private baths. One room has a whirlpool tub. Excellent location for outlet shopping, hot air balloon festival, Great Escape Amusement Park, and Lake George. Children over six welcome. Cat in residence. $50-65.

Crislip's Bed and Breakfast

Rural Delivery 1, Box 57, Ridge Road, 12804
(518) 793-6869

Situated just minutes from Saratoga Springs and Lake George in the New York Adirondack area, this landmark Federal home provides spacious accommodations, complete with period antiques, four-poster beds, and down comforters. The country breakfast menu features buttermilk pancakes, scrambled eggs, and sausages. The hosts invite guests to relax on the porches and enjoy the mountain view.

Hosts: Ned and Joyce Crislip
Rooms: 3 (PB) $55-75
Full Breakfast
Credit Cards: A, B, C
Notes: 2, 5, 8, 9, 10, 11, 12, 13

RED HOOK

The American Country Collection 115

4 Greenwood Lane, Delmar, 12054
(518) 439-7001

This home, built in 1821 in the Federal-style and restored in 1988, offers a ground-level suite with private entrance and bath, non-working fireplace, antique table and chairs, microwave, coffee maker, and small refrigerator. Breakfast, made with only the freshest organic ingredients, is served at the table in front of the two deep-silled windows that look out to two acres of trees, vegetable, and flower gardens. Children welcome. Port-a-crib available. No pets. $85.

6 Pets welcome; 8 Children welcome; 9 Social drinking allowed; 10 Tennis available; 11 Swimming available; 12 Golf available; 13 Skiing available; 14 May be booked through travel agents.

REXFORD

The American Country Collection 123

4 Greenwood Lane, Delmar, 12054
(518) 439-7001

An idyllic landscape of rolling hills, grassy fields, woodlands, and flowers surrounds this private suite set 800 feet back from a cul-de-sac on seven country acres. The suite includes a private bath, kitchenette, and separate entrance. Children school age and over welcome. No pets. Arrangements for guests' dogs may be made occasionally. Fixings for breakfast provided in kitchenette for leisurely breakfast at guests' convenience. $65; $85 during August; $200 weekly; $500 monthly.

RICHFIELD SPRINGS

Country Spread Bed and Breakfast

23 Prospect Street, P. O. Box 1863, 13439
(315) 858-1870

Built in 1893 and situated within the village limits directly on New York State Route 28. Convenient to many central Leatherstocking attractions, including antiquing, Cooperstown, opera, swimming, and boating. Guest rooms have a country decorated flair. Breakfast offers many delicious choices from Karen's kitchen. Families welcome. The hosts have two children. A casual respite with genuine and sincere hospitality. Rated and approved by the American Bed and Breakfast Association.

Hosts: Karen and Bruce Watson
Rooms: 2 (PB) $50-75
Full Breakfast
Credit Cards: A, B
Notes: 2, 5, 8, 9, 10, 11, 12, 14

Jonathan House

39 East Main Street, P. O. Box 9, 13439
(315) 858-2870

This 1883 house, a hybrid of the Eastlake and Stick styles, has three full floors and a tower room on the fourth level for a total of 17 rooms. The four bedrooms feature two private baths. It is elegantly decorated with antiques, fine paintings, and Oriental rugs. Breakfast is served in the dining room with bone china, linen, and English silver. MasterCard, Visa, and American Express accepted. $55-75.

ROOSEVELT ISLAND

Aaah! Bed and Breakfast #1, Ltd. BRI

P. O. Box 200, New York, 10108
(212) 246-4000; (800) 776-4001
FAX (212) 265-4346

Roosevelt Island, one of the safest places in Manhattan, is conveniently situated by tram across the East River just three and one-half minutes from midtown Manhattan. The island is filled with parks and beautiful promenades. Excellent views of Manhattan. The apartment itself is a duplex in a high-rise building with a doorman. It is tastefully and eclectically furnished in contemporary and antiques. The master bedroom has a private bath and air conditioning. TV/VCR, laundry service, elevator. Continental breakfast is served. Hosted. $60-75.

ROCHESTER

Woods-Edge

151 Bluhm Road, Fairport, 14450
(716) 223-8877

Woods-Edge is nestled among fragrant pines and wildlife only 20 minutes from downtown Rochester, near Exit 45 of I-90.

NOTES: Credit cards accepted: A Master Card; B Visa; C American Express; D Discover Card; E Diner's Club; F Other; 2 Personal Checks accepted; 3 Lunch available; 4 Dinner available; 5 Open all year;

Hideaway cabin is a romantically decorated private lodge with a large fireplace, queen bed, full kitchen, and private bath. Woods-Edge main house has two additional bedrooms with private baths. Rooms have wonderful old country pine against white walls and barn beams. Full breakfast is included. Children welcome; no pets.

Host: Betty Kinsman
Rooms: 3 (1 PB; 2 SB) $50-65 main house; $75-95 cabin
Full Breakfast
Credit Cards: None
Notes: 2, 5, 8, 9, 10, 12, 13, 14

Woods-Edge

ROCK STREAM

Reading House Bed and Breakfast

4610 Route 14, 14878
(607) 535-9785

A carefully restored 1820 home with spacious grounds, two ponds and a broad view of Seneca Lake. Enjoy 19th-century ambience, with today's comforts. Private baths, great breakfasts and a warm, relaxing atmosphere. Five miles north of Watkins Glen, close to wineries, colleges, the International Motor Speedway and most major Finger Lake attractions.

Hosts: Rita and Bill Newell
Rooms: 4 (PB) $50-55
Full Breakfast
Credit Cards: None
Notes: 2, 5, 9, 11, 12, 13 (XC)

ROME

Elaine's Bed and Breakfast and Inn Reservation Service

4987 Kingston Road, Elbridge, 13060
(315) 689-2082

On six acres near state Thruway, this 1840 Cape saltbox is warmly furnished with many antiques and crafts made by the hostess. Full country breakfast of guests' choice. Suite features double bed, sitting area, and private bath. Two other rooms with one double bed each share main bath. Cot available. Perfect stop-off from Route 90 about halfway between Boston and Toronto. $45-60.

Elaine's Bed and Breakfast Reservation Service

4987 Kingston Road, Elbridge, 13060
(315) 689-2082

This brick Victorian farmhouse built in 1857 features complete antique furnishings. Three guest rooms are upstairs; one room offers a double and single bed. Near Griffiss Air Force Base. Pool, 40 acres, gardens, hiking trails, cross-country skiing. Near downhill skiing area. Resident dog and cat.

ROOSEVELT ISLAND

Aaah! Bed and Breakfast #1, Ltd. BRI

P. O. Box 200, New York, 10108
(212) 246-4000; (800) 776-4001
FAX (212) 265-4346

Roosevelt Island, one of the safest places in Manhattan, is conveniently situated by tram across the East River just three and one-half minutes from midtown Manhattan. The island is filled with parks and beautiful promenades. Excellent views of Manhattan. The apartment itself is a duplex in a high-rise building with a doorman. It is tastefully and eclectically furnished in contemporary and antiques. The master bedroom has a private bath and air conditioning. TV/VCR, laundry service, elevator. Continental breakfast is served. Hosted. $60-75.

SARANAC LAKE

Elaine's Bed and Breakfast Reservation Service

4987 Kingston Road, Elbridge, 13060
(315) 689-2082

In the Adirondacks near Lake Placid are three bed and breakfasts. One rustic ranch has three double bed guest rooms; a stately old Colonial offers two large guest rooms. An updated Victorian has two guest rooms.

SARATOGA SPRINGS

The American Country Collection 107

4 Greenwood Lane, Delmar, 12054
(518) 439-7001

This cozy, restored Victorian cottage with gingerbread millwork was probably the caretaker's home for one of the nearby mansions on North Broadway. It is conveniently situated within walking distance of the downtown shops and Skidmore College. Two guest rooms share one bath with the owner. Rooms are comfortable and immaculately clean. Cat in residence. Children welcome. $55; $105 during jazz, racing season, college weekends.

The American Country Collection 153

4 Greenwood Lane, Delmar, 12054
(518) 439-7001

Situated just five miles from Saratoga, this four-year old Contemporary home is set in the woods across from a private country club. Two guest rooms on the second floor, one with two twin beds and the other with a double, share a bath. Each rooms has its own alcove with a sink, vanity, and walk-in closet. Another guest room on the first floor boasts a queen-size bed, private bath, and Jacuzzi. The livingroom has a TV and VCR, fireplace, two extra-large sofas, and a screened-in porch in the rear for reading or relaxing. Breakfast is continental-plus. $65-95.

The Inn on Bacon Hill

P. O. Box 1462, 12866
(518) 695-3693

A peaceful alternative where you come as strangers and leave as friends, just 10 minutes east of Saratoga Springs. The 1862 Victorian is situated in a quiet, pastoral setting with four air-conditioned bedrooms, featuring twin, full and queen beds. Enjoy beautiful gardens and gazebo, explore country lanes, or relax in comfortable guest parlor with an extensive library. Baby grand piano adorns a Victorian parlor suite. Innkeeping courses offered. Full country breakfasts included.

Host: Andrea Collins-Breslin
Rooms: 4 (2 PB; 2 SB) $65-135
Full Breakfast
Credit Cards: A, B
Notes: 2, 5, 9, 10, 11, 12, 13, 14

Six Sisters Bed and Breakfast

149 Union Avenue, 12866
(518) 583-1173

This beautifully appointed 1880 Victorian is on a historic, flower-laden boulevard in the heart of Saratoga Springs. Luxurious, immaculate rooms and suites offer king-size beds, private baths, and air conditioning. Antiques, Oriental carpets, hardwood

NOTES: Credit cards accepted: A Master Card; B Visa; C American Express; D Discover Card; E Diner's Club; F Other; 2 Personal Checks accepted; 3 Lunch available; 4 Dinner available; 5 Open all year;

floors, and Italian marble create a resplendent decor. The inn is close to Skidmore College, Convention Center, the racetracks, SPAC, downtown, museums, spa, antiques, and restaurants. SPAC discounts. The owner is a native of Saratoga eager to share local information. Recommended by *Gourmet*.

Hosts: Kate Benton and Steve Ramirez
Rooms: 4 (PB) $70-100
Full Breakfast
Credit Cards: None
Notes: 2, 5, 8 (over 10), 9, 10, 11, 12, 13, 14

The Westchester House

102 Lincoln Avenue, Box 944, 12866
(518) 587-7613

This gracious 1885 Queen Anne Victorian inn features elaborate chestnut moldings, antique furnishings, and up-to-date comforts. Enjoy the extensive library or play the baby grand piano. The charm and excitement, museums and racetracks, boutiques and restaurants of historic Saratoga are an easy walk from the Westchester House. After a busy day of sampling the delights of Saratoga, relax on the wraparound porch, in the old-fashioned gardens, or the double Victorian parlors, and enjoy a refreshing glass of lemonade.

The Westchester House

Hosts: Bob and Stephanie Melvin
Rooms: 7 (PB) $70-125
Continental Breakfast
Minimum Stay Weekends and Holidays: 2 nights
Credit Cards: A, B, C
Notes: 2, 5, 8 (over 12), 9, 10, 11, 12, 13, 14

SCHENECTADY

The American Country Collection 172

4 Greenwood Lane, Delmar, 12054
(518) 439-7001

Set in the heart of the city, this late Victorian-style home has been meticulously restored to its former charm and grace. Two guest rooms share a bath. One room features a queen-size bed, walnut armoire, desk, dresser, and wicker rocker. The other sports either a brass and iron bed with birdseye maple dresser and floral balloon shades, or one large room with a double bed. Children welcome; resident cat named Tuxedo. Offers full and continental breakfast. Close to Union College, General Electric, SUNY, and Saratoga Raceway. $35-45.

SKANEATELES

Cozy Cottage

4987 Kingston Road, Elbridge, 13060
(315) 689-2082 after 10:00 A.M.

Just four miles outside of a Finger Lakes village on a quiet country road, this remodeled ranch house sits on four and one-half acres and has two comfortable guest rooms sharing one and one-half baths with the hostess. Bask in the sun, hike or bike. Enjoy flowers, birds, and the orchard, and pick berries. Visit the village, stroll the scenic streets, browse in galleries and boutiques, take a cruise, launch your boat, and enjoy fine restaurants. Antique shops nearby. Syracuse just 20 minutes, Auburn just 15 minutes drive. Resident cat.

6 Pets welcome; 8 Children welcome; 9 Social drinking allowed; 10 Tennis available; 11 Swimming available; 12 Golf available; 13 Skiing available; 14 May be booked through travel agents.

Host: Elaine Samuels
Rooms: 2 (SB) $40-50
Continental Breakfast
Credit Cards: None
Notes: 2 (two weeks notice), 5, 6 (cats), 8 (over 10), 9, 11, 12, 13

Elaine's Bed and Breakfast and Inn Reservation Service

4987 Kingston Road, Elbridge, 13060
(315) 689-2082

Cute, clean, comfortable, convenient, cozy, congenial, casual country atmosphere in a newly remodeled ranch on five acres. Adults preferred. Two modest guest rooms, each with a firm double bed, share a new bathroom. The hostess can direct guests to almost any place in Onondaga County including Syracuse (12 miles), Auburn (9 miles), Skaneateles Village (4 miles). Resident cat. $40-50.

Elaine's Bed and Breakfast Reservation Service

4987 Kingston Road, Elbridge, 13060
(315) 689-2082

Elaine's offers three bed and breakfasts in this gorgeous historic village on the eastern shore of Finger Lakes. An executive ranch freshly remodeled and redecorated offers an antique-furnished guest room with a double iron bed and private bath. A sleeper sofa in the den can take two or more guests. Lakes, stores, restaurants, and cruise boats are within walking distance. Another freshly decorated ranch-style home offers two guest rooms with good double beds that share one and one-half baths. A pretty little ranch home on the edge of town offers two extra-long beds and private bath.

SOUTHOLD

Goose Creek Guesthouse

1475 Waterview Drive, 11971
(516) 765-3356

Goose Creek Guesthouse is a quiet Civil War-era bed and breakfast home nestled in the woods on the south side of Goose Creek. A country breakfast is served, featuring all homemade foods: granola, whole-wheat or cornmeal pancakes, the specialty apple rings, jams, jellies, and freshly baked bread. Farm-fresh eggs and homegrown or local fruits and vegetables are used. A continental breakfast is available if guests prefer.

Host: Mary Mooney-Getoff
Rooms: 4 (SB) $70-75
Full Breakfast
Credit Cards: None
Notes: 2 (deposit only), 5, 6, 8, 9, 10, 11, 12, 14

STEPHENTOWN

The American Country Collection 169

4 Greenwood Lane, Delmar, 12054
(518) 439-7001

A rural farmhouse built around the late-1700s and updated in the middle 1800s situated on two acres a lawn, trees, and gardens. Built with wide plank floors and furnished with a mix of antiques and collectibles, the three guest rooms on the second floor share a bath with another full bath on the first floor. Each room has two twin beds, with one converting into a king-size bed. There is also a studio apartment with a double bed and queen sofa bed, private bath, and private entrance on the first floor. A buffet-style breakfast is served from 8 until 10 a.m. and earlier upon request. Children welcome; crib available. Close to Brodie Mountain, Jiminy Peak, the Chatham Playhouse, and the Shaker Museum. $45-80.

STILLWATER

The American Country Collection 005
4 Greenwood Lane, Delmar, 12054
(518) 439-7001

This is a quiet retreat on 100 acres of rolling countryside, complete with mountain vistas. The circa 1800 barn has been transformed into an exquisite home. It is conveniently between Saratoga Lake and Saratoga National Historical Park. Two rooms and two second-floor suites, each with private bath. Breakfast is served in the dining room or on the deck overlooking the countryside. Children over nine welcome. Dog in residence. Sept. 1-June 30: suites $75 and rooms $65; July to two days before racing season: suites $95 and rooms $85; August (racing)/Jazz Fest/ Christmas-New Year's: suites $105 and rooms $95 (three-night minimum stay).

The American Country Collection 170
4 Greenwood Lane, Delmar, 12054
(518) 439-7001

A charming home in a tranquil setting, convenient to historic Saratoga Springs and neighboring a major thoroughbred breeding and training farm. An interior of white walls, natural woodwork, soft pastel accents, and walls of windows. Three guest rooms share a full bath. One bedroom is on the entrance level and features a queen-size bed. The two rooms on the lower level boast a brass double bed and a queen bed, respectively. Makings for a full breakfast are in the kitchen for guests to prepare as they choose. Children welcome only when entire house is rented. Close to Saratoga Springs Historical Park, Lake George, and the Saratoga Performing Arts Center. $65-80 (seasonal).

SYRACUSE—SEE ALSO ELBRIDGE AND JAMESVILLE

Elaine's Bed and Breakfast and Inn Reservation Service
4987 Kingston Road, Elbridge, 13060
(315) 689-2082

Convenient to Syracuse University and LeMoyne College, this delightful knotty pine basement apartment can sleep two and has a completely furnished eat-in kitchen and attractive shower-bath with many built-ins. The living/bedroom includes color TV, desk, easy chairs, game table, and much more. Patio and yard. Quiet dead-end street with a great view. Use of laundry for long-term guest. $65-75; long-term rates available.

Elaine's Bed and Breakfast Reservation Service-1
4987 Kingston Road, Elbridge, 13060
(315) 689-2082

This spacious Tudor built in 1920 offers three beautifully decorated guest rooms. An Art Deco room features a queen-size bed and private bath. A Victorian room has a double bed and shares a spacious vintage bath with a more traditional room that has a pair of twin beds, a sitting area, and TV.

Elaine's Bed and Breakfast Reservation Service-2
4987 Kingston Road, Elbridge, 13060
(315) 689-2082

Situated in the Eastside area near LeMoyne College and Syracuse University, this cute, customized Cape Cod has a newly redecorated first-floor guest room with a double bed, handmade chest, rocker, window seat, and private bath. An adjacent TV den can be a second guest room with a sofa bed. Both rooms are in a separate rear wing of the house.

6 Pets welcome; 8 Children welcome; 9 Social drinking allowed; 10 Tennis available; 11 Swimming available; 12 Golf available; 13 Skiing available; 14 May be booked through travel agents.

Elaine's Bed and Breakfast Reservation Service-3
4987 Kingston Road, Elbridge, 13060
(315) 689-2082

Nice ranch house situated 16 blocks from Syracuse University offers one queen and one single room, with a shared bath.

Elaine's Bed and Breakfast Reservation Service-6
4987 Kingston Road, Elbridge, 13060
(315) 689-2082

Situated on the western edge of the city, this three-year young, contemporary Cape is set on three acres. The guest area is on the second floor. One room has twin beds, and one has a double bed; both share a bath. Peaceful, quiet setting, yet quite handy to shopping, state fair, zoo, restaurants, Onondaga Community College, highways, and Syracuse University.

Elaine's Bed and Breakfast Reservation Service-7
4987 Kingston Road, Elbridge, 13060
(315) 689-2082

This wonderful large brick house has decor of many periods. Top floor features an executive or honeymoon suite with a king-size canopy bed, Jacuzzi, complete kitchen under an L-shaped mahogany bar, lovely sitting area with wood stove, skylight, round table, and leather chairs. A private marble bath, garage, and fresh flowers are only a few of the amenities found in this home. Three rooms on the second and first floors are furnished with antiques, and all offer private baths. Guest kitchen is stocked with snack foods, and breakfast is always served on beautiful china. $80-150.

TICONDEROGA

The American Country Collection 046
4 Greenwood Lane, Delmar, 12054
(518) 439-7001

This 52-acre farm offers year-round activities. Sleigh rides and cross-country skiing in winter, horsedrawn wagon rides in summer. Canoeing, fishing, and swimming are nearby. Three double-bed rooms on the second floor share a bath. The entire house is furnished with family antiques and treasures. Well-behaved children welcome. $40-50.

TULLY-VESPER

Elaine's Bed and Breakfast and Inn Reservation Service
4987 Kingston Road, Elbridge, 13060
(315) 689-2082

Just four scenic miles from Route 81, this owner-built raised ranch offers two double rooms plus a master bedroom suite with private bath. Full country breakfast. Close to Song Mountain downhill skiing, 20 minutes from Syracuse, Cortland, and Auburn in a quiet country setting with view of rolling hills. Guests may relax in front of a cozy fire in the Pennsylvania bluestone fireplace.

UTICA

The Iris Stonehouse Bed and Breakfast
16 Derbyshire Place, 13501-4706
(315) 732-6720; (800) 446-1456

In town, close to everything, this stately stone house with leaded-glass windows. A separate guest sitting room, and guest rooms with private and and shared baths. Full breakfast from the daily menu, central air, three miles from I-90, Exit 31 (NYS Thruway), one block off Genesee Street, three blocks from the North/South arterial and Routes 5, 8, and 12. Member of ABBA, with three-crown ratings.

Hosts: Shirley and Roy Kilgore
Rooms: 3 (1 PB; 2 SB) $45-60
Full Breakfast
Credit Cards: A, B, C
Notes: 2, 5, 12, 13, 14

WESTFIELD

Westfield House

East Main Road, Route 20, P. O. Box 505, 14787
(716) 326-6262

Westfield House was built in 1840 as part of the Granger homestead. In 1860 a Gothic Revival additional was built. A complete renovation was completed in 1988. The large common rooms have huge Gothic windows, and are furnished with antiques. A lovely carriage barn is full of unfinished furniture. There are several exceptional wineries in the area. Westfield is a national antique center.

Hosts: Betty and Jud Wilson
Rooms: 6 (PB) $60-85
Full Breakfast
Credit Cards: A, B
Notes: 2, 5, 9, 10, 11, 12, 13

The William Seward Inn

South Portage Road, Route 394, 14787
(716) 326-4151

Formerly the home of Lincoln's Secretary of State, this 1821 Greek Revival mansion features fourteen rooms with period antiques and private baths (four with Jacuzzi). Full gourmet breakfasts feature scrambled eggs with tarragon and cheese, amaretto French toast, and apple cinnamon pancakes. Comfortable elegance close to Westfield's wineries, boutique shops and national antique center. Minutes from world-famous Chautauqua Institution, Lily Dale, and both downhill and cross-country skiing.

Hosts: Jim and Debbie Dahlberg
Rooms: 14 (PB) $80-135
Full Breakfast
Credit Cards: A, B
Notes: 2, 4, 5, 8 (over 12), 9, 10, 11, 12, 13, 14

WESTHAMPTON BEACH

1880 House

2 Seafield Lane, 11978
(800) 346-3290

This 100-year-old country retreat is only 90 minutes from Manhattan on Westhampton Beach's exclusive Seafield Lane. A swimming pool and tennis court are on the premises, and it's only a short walk to the beach. The Hamptons offer numerous outstanding restaurants and shops. Indoor tennis is available locally, as is a health spa at Montauk Point.

Host: Elsie Pardee Collins
Rooms: 2 (PB) $100-200 (suites)
Full Breakfast
Minimum stay: 2 nights
Credit Cards: A, B, C
Notes: 2, 5, 9, 10, 11, 12, 14

WILLET

Woven Waters

HC 73, Box 193E, Cincinnatus Lake, 13863
(607) 656-8672

A beautifully renovated 100-year-old barn on the shores of a lovely private lake in south central New York. The rustic interior is accented with antiques and imported laces. Relax in the large comfortable livingroom with beamed cathedral ceiling and massive stone fireplace or on one of the porches overlooking the lake (one open, one enclosed).

Hosts: Erika and John
Rooms: 4 (SB) $58

6 Pets welcome; 8 Children welcome; 9 Social drinking allowed; 10 Tennis available; 11 Swimming available; 12 Golf available; 13 Skiing available; 14 May be booked through travel agents.

Full Breakfast
Credit Cards: A, B, D
Notes: 5, 9, 13, 14

WILSON

Rainbow Hospitality W200
504 Amherst Street, Buffalo, 14207
(800) 373-8797

Lovely lakefront bed and breakfast set in a small fishing town on Lake Ontario. Minutes from three marinas, two yacht clubs, and only 40 minutes from Niagara Falls. Hostess speaks German and welcomes guests with a full breakfast on weekends. $60.

YOUNGSTOWN

Rainbow Hospitality Y106
504 Amherst Street, Buffalo, 14207
(800) 373-8797

This 150-year old country manor home provides an idyllic country getaway. Situated just fifteen minutes north of Niagara Falls and 30 minutes from Buffalo. A spacious veranda overlooks the Lower Niagara River, and is the setting for leisurely morning meals, weather permitting. Guest rooms include Queen Anne furnishings and private suites. $65-80.

Rainbow Hospitality Y110
504 Amherst Street, Buffalo, 14207
(800) 373-8797

This large villa overlooks the Niagara River and Canada. The home, surrounded by scenic grounds, is less than 15 minutes from Niagara Falls. Huge rooms with fireplaces for relaxing after a day of sightseeing or theater events. Private/shared baths and either a porch or patio adjacent to each room. $65-150.

North Carolina

_____

Albemarle Inn

86 Edgemont Road, 28801
(704) 255-0027

A distinguished Greek Revival mansion with exquisite carved oak staircase, balcony, paneling, and high ceilings. Situated in beautiful residential area. On the National Register of Historic Places. Eleven spacious and comfortable guest rooms with TV, telephones, air conditioning, and private baths with claw foot tubs and showers. Delicious full breakfast served in the dining room or on the sun porch. Unmatched hospitality.

Hosts: Dick and Kathy Hemes
Rooms: 11 (PB) $75-110
Full Breakfast
Credit Cards: A, B
Notes: 2, 5, 8 (over 13), 9, 10, 11, 12, 14

The Black Walnut Bed and Breakfast Inn

288 Montford Avenue, 28801
(704) 254-3878

The Black Walnut is a turn-of-the-century shingle-style home in the heart of the Montford Historic District just minutes from downtown Asheville and the Biltmore Estate. The inn is decorated with a blend of antiques and traditional furniture. Amenities include large guest rooms with fireplace and TV, full breakfast featuring homemade breads and preserves, welcoming refreshments, use of all common areas, the grand piano, and air conditioning. Supervised children are welcome.

Host: Jeanette Syprzak
Rooms: 4 (PB) $65-95
Full Breakfast
Credit Cards: A, B, D
Notes: 2, 5, 8, 9, 10, 11, 12, 14

Blake House Inn

150 Royal Pines Drive, 28704
(704) 684-1847

Built in 1847, Blake House Inn is one of the area's finest surviving examples of French Gothic architecture. The house served as a field hospital for Confederate armies still active in western North Carolina near the close of the Civil War. The Blake House, named as one of the "Top 50 Inns in America," offers spacious bedrooms, all elegantly decorated with country antiques and family heirlooms. Full breakfast. Minutes to Biltmore Estate, the Blue Ridge Parkway, and other area attractions. Fireside dining Wednesday through Saturday and brunch on Sunday.

Hosts: Bob, Eloise, and Pati Roesler
Rooms: 5 (PB) $65-85
Full Breakfast
Credit Cards: A, B
Notes: 2, 3, 4, 5, 8 (over 12), 10, 11, 12, 13

Cairn Brae

217 Patton Mountain Road, 28804
(704) 252-9219

Cairn Brae is situated in the mountains above Asheville. Very private, on three acres of woods, but only 12 minutes from downtown. Guests have private entrance to livingroom with fireplace. Complimentary snacks are served on the terrace overlooking Beaverdam Valley. Beautiful views. Woodsy trails. Quiet and secluded.

6 Pets welcome; 8 Children welcome; 9 Social drinking allowed; 10 Tennis available; 11 Swimming available; 12 Golf available; 13 Skiing available; 14 May be booked through travel agents.

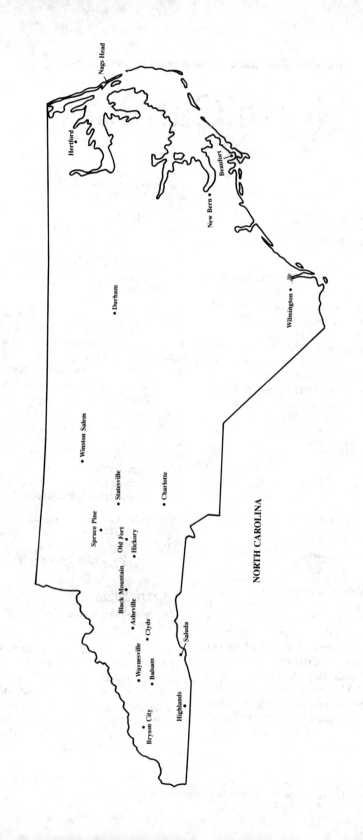

NORTH CAROLINA

Nags Head

Hertford

Beaufort

New Bern

Durham

Wilmington

Winston Salem

Statesville

Charlotte

Spruce Pine

Old Fort

Hickory

Black Mountain

Asheville

Clyde

Saluda

Waynesville

Balsam

Bryson City

Highlands

Hosts: Milli and Ed Adams
Rooms: 3 (PB) $80-95
Full Breakfast
Credit Cards: A, B
Closed December 1-March 31
Notes: 2, 8 (over 6), 9, 10, 11, 12, 14

BALSAM

Balsam Lodge Bed and Breakfast

P.O. Box 279, Valley Road, 28707
(704) 456-6528

Chose to stay in the charming turn-of-the-century main house or the restored Balsam Depot.

Hosts: Steven and Jennifer Kellam
Rooms: 7 (4 PB; 1 SB) $45-55
Continental Breakfast
Credit Cards: A, B
Notes: 2, 5, 9, 12, 13

BEAUFORT

Pecan Tree Inn

116 Queen Street, 28516
(919) 728-6733

Relive history in the historic town of Beaufort, the third-oldest city in North Carolina. At the Pecan Tree Inn guests are only a few blocks from wonderful restaurants and quaint shops. There are seven air-conditioned guest rooms, all with private baths. The bridal suite features a Jacuzzi for two and a king-size canopy bed. You will enjoy the freshly baked, homemade muffins, cakes, and breads along with choice of fruit, cereal, and beverages for breakfast. Beaufort's historic district is a leisurely walk from the inn.

Hosts: Susan and Joe Johnson
Rooms: 7 (PB) $65-115
Expanded Continental Breakfast
Credit Cards: A, B
Notes: 2, 5, 8 (over 12), 9, 10, 11, 12, 14

BLACK MOUNTAIN

Bed and Breakfast Over Yonder

431 North Fork Road, 28711
(704) 669-6762

This comfortable old mountain home, furnished with antiques, has views of mountains and the surrounding woods from its landscaped decks and terrace. Secluded on 40 acres, it is two miles from I-40 and Black Mountain, which has antique and craft shopping. Close to the Blue Ridge Parkway and Asheville's Biltmore Estate. The breakfast specialty is fresh mountain brown trout.

Host: Wilhelmina Headley
Rooms: 5 (PB) $42.20-64.80
Full Breakfast
Credit Cards: None
Closed December 1-May 14
Notes: 2, 7, 8, 9, 10, 11, 12, 14

BRYSON CITY

Folkestone Inn

101 Folkestone Lane, 28713
(704) 488-2730

Enjoy the romance of an Old World inn, the charm and nostalgia of the long-forgotten lifestyle of gracious country living. The inn is situated in the Great Smoky Mountains in Swain County, which is 86 percent parkland. Guests may hike, fish, sail, raft, or go horseback riding.

Hosts: Norma and Peter Joyce
Rooms: 9 (PB) $59-79
Full Breakfast
Credit Cards: None
Notes: 2, 5, 9, 10, 11

CHARLOTTE

The Homeplace

5901 Sardis Road, 28270
(704) 365-1936

NOTES: Credit cards accepted: A Master Card; B Visa; C American Express; D Discover Card; E Diner's Club; F Other; 2 Personal Checks accepted; 3 Lunch available; 4 Dinner available; 5 Open all year; 6 Pets welcome; 8 Children welcome; 9 Social drinking allowed; 10 Tennis available; 11 Swimming available; 12 Golf available; 13 Skiing available; 14 May be booked through travel agents.

The Homeplace

Restored 1902 country Victorian on two and one-half acres with garden gazebo and wraparound porch. Victorian elegance and old-fashioned charm with a full home-cooked breakfast. A quiet setting and unique experience for the traveler, business executive, or connoisseur of fine older homes.

Hosts: Peggy and Frank Dearien
Rooms: 4 (2 PB; 2 SB) $68-88 plus tax
Full Breakfast
Credit Cards: A, B, C
Notes: 2, 5, 14

CLYDE

Windsong: A Mountain Inn

120 Ferguson Ridge, 28721
(704) 627-6111

Enjoy a secluded, romantic interlude at this contemporary log inn high in the breath-taking Smoky Mountains. Though the inn is small and intimate, the rooms are large and bright, with high-beamed ceilings, pine log walls, and Mexican tile floors. Each room has a fireplace, oversize tub, separate shower, and private deck or patio. Guest lounge with billiards and wet bar. Full breakfast included. On 25 acres with pool, tennis, hiking, and lovable llamas. Newly added is the Pond House, a separate two-bedroom log suite with full kitchen. Near Maggie Valley. Closed in January.

Hosts: Donna and Gale Livengood
Rooms: 5 (PB) $90-95
Full Breakfast

Credit Cards: A, B
Closed January
Notes: 2, 9, 12, 14

DURHAM

The Blooming Garden Inn

513 Holloway Street, 27701
(919) 687-0801

An unexpected use of color transforms this restored 1892 Queen Anne-style home into a cozy, pleasant retreat in downtown historic Durham. Exquisite antiques, stained glass, and arts and crafts treasures from around the world add to your visiting pleasure. In addition to three guest rooms, two spacious luxury suites with Jacuzzis for two are available. A designated historic site.

Hosts: Dolly and Frank Pokrass
Rooms: 5 (PB) $75-140
Full Breakfast
Credit Cards: A, B, C
Notes: 2, 5, 8, 9, 14

HERTFORD

Gingerbread Inn and Bakery, Inc.

103 South Church Street, 27944
(919) 426-5809

This beautifully restored turn-of-the-century home is on the local historic tour and boasts a wraparound porch with paired columns. The comfortably furnished rooms are spacious, with queen or king-size beds and plush carpeting. All rooms are centrally air-conditioned and have color cable TV. The aroma of freshly baked gingerbread from the bakery entices you during your stay, and guests are offered a gingerbread boy or girl for the ride home.

Host: Jenny Harnisch
Rooms: 3 (PB) $47.70
Full Breakfast
Credit Cards: A, B
Notes: 2, 5, 8, 9, 12

NOTES: Credit cards accepted: A Master Card; B Visa; C American Express; D Discover Card; E Diner's Club; F Other; 2 Personal Checks accepted; 3 Lunch available; 4 Dinner available; 5 Open all year;

Gingerbread Inn and Bakery

HICKORY

Hickory Bed and Breakfast

464 7th Street, Southwest, 28602
(704) 324-0548; (800) 654-2961

This 1908 two-story Georgian-style house that sits on one and one-half acres surrounded by various trees and flowers offers a true a home away from home. Sit in the parlor, or curl up with a good book, or play a game in the library. Guests can sit by the pool and enjoy iced tea or lemonade with something freshly baked from the oven. Relax on the screened porch. The house is decorated with a country theme. A full country breakfast is offered.

Hosts: Bob and Suzanne Ellis
Rooms: 4 (PB) $55
Full Breakfast
Credit Cards: None
Notes: 2, 5, 10, 11, 12, 13, 14

HIGHLANDS

The Laurels:
Freda's Bed and Breakfast

Route 2, Box 102, 28741
(704) 526-2091

The Laurels, a unique bed and breakfast, is situated on seven acres in historic Horse Cove, two and one-half miles outside of Highlands. The half-acre pond is stocked with rainbow trout. Come in the afternoon and have an English tea. Two cozy fireplaces warm the cool evenings. The large English country breakfast features fresh fruit, bacon, ham, and eggs any way you want them. The hosts grind their own whole-wheat flour and make crunchy toast.

Hosts: Warren and Freda Lorenz
Rooms: 4 (PB) $50-60
Full Breakfast
Credit Cards: None
Notes: 2, 9

Phelps House
Bed and Breakfast Inn

Main Street, Route 1, Box 55, 28741
(704) 526-2590

Built in 1885, Phelps House has welcomed guests in downtown Highlands for over 100 years. Over 1,400 feet above sea level, Highlands is delightfully cool in summer and spectacularly beautiful in winter. Each room is individually decorated and furnished with antiques. A full country breakfast of hot cakes, eggs, bacon and homemade biscuits is included—guaranteed to prepare you for a hard day of relaxing. All meals available for groups of ten or more at special rates.

Host: Carol Williams
Rooms: 20 (PB) $49-59
Full Breakfast
Credit Cards: A, B
Notes: 2, 5, 8, 10, 11, 12, 13

NAGS HEAD

First Colony Inn

6720 South Virginia Dare Trail, 27959
(919) 441-2343; FAX (919) 441-9234

The Outer Banks' only historic bed and breakfast inn is a handsome shingle-style building with 18 dormers and one-quarter mile of wraparound verandas. Set in five acres, it boasts a private boardwalk to the ocean, a large secluded pool, and water views to the east and west. A sunny breakfast room, large sun deck, and elegant

6 Pets welcome; 8 Children welcome; 9 Social drinking allowed; 10 Tennis available; 11 Swimming available; 12 Golf available; 13 Skiing available; 14 May be booked through travel agents.

library complement the comfortable rooms, with king, queen, or twin beds, English antiques, remote control heat and air conditioning, tiled baths, telephones, kitchenettes or wet bars with microwaves, and the friendliest service on the beach. Honeymoons, small conferences, and weddings are specialties.

Hosts: The Lawrences
Rooms: 26 (PB) $120-200
Continental Breakfast
Credit Cards: A, B, D
Notes: 2, 5, 8, 9, 10, 11, 12, 14

First Colony Inn

NEW BERN

Harmony House Inn

215 Pollock Street, 28560
(919) 636-3810

This circa 1850 Greek Revival inn provides comfortable elegance in New Bern's historic district. Unusual spaciousness, antiques, a guest parlor, rocking chairs, and swings on the front porch, and a full breakfast add to guests' enjoyment. Near Tryon Palace, restaurants, and shops.

Hosts: A. E. and Diane Hansen
Rooms: 9 (PB) $80
Full Breakfast
Credit Cards: A, B, C
Notes: 2, 5, 8, 9, 10, 12, 14

New Berne House Inn

709 Broad Street, 28560
(800) 842-7688

Listed on the National Register of Historic Places and situated one block from Tryon Palace, New Berne House offers the charm and ambience of English country house decor. Guest rooms all have private baths, some with claw foot tubs and pedestal sinks. Antique beds piled with pillows; crisp eyelet sheets; fireplaces in some rooms. The inn is noted for its fine breakfasts, including southern specialties such as pralines 'n' cream waffles and peach French toast. The library features an interesting collection of books, and the Rose Parlor boasts a baby grand piano.

Hosts: Marcia Drum and Howard Bronson
Rooms: 7 (PB) $60-80
Full Breakfast
Credit Cards: A, B, C
Notes: 2, 5, 9, 10, 11, 12, 14

OLD FORT

The Inn at Old Fort

P. O. Box 1116, 28762
(704) 606-9384

Two-story Gothic Revival-style Victorian cottage, circa 1880. Situated on more than three and one-half acres overlooking the historic small town of Old Fort. Features rooms furnished with antiques; warm, friendly conversation; front-porch rockers; terraced lawn and gardens; and extended continental breakfast featuring freshly baked breads and fresh fruits.

Hosts: Chuck and Debbie Aldridge
Rooms: 4 (PB) $40-50
Expanded Continental Breakfast
Credit Cards: None
Notes: 2, 5, 8, 9, 10, 11, 12, 14

SALUDA

The Oaks

P. O. Box 1008, 28773
(704) 749-9613

A turreted Victorian home benefits from the mountain breezes. Rooms are decorated

The Oaks

in period furnishings, with many interesting antiques. The Oaks provides a warm and welcoming atmosphere. The surrounding porch offers a place to relax and mull before ambling down to the many antique and crafts shops on Main Street. Saluda is situated between Hendersonville and Tryon.

Hosts: Ceri and Peggy Dando
Rooms: 5 (PB) $55-85
Full Breakfast
Credit Cards: A, B
Notes: 2, 5, 9, 10, 12, 14

SPRUCE PINE

Ansley/Richmond Inn

101 Pine Avenue, 28777
(704) 765-6993

This lovely half-century-old "country elegant" inn, specializing in pampering guests, is nestled into the hills overlooking the town of Spruce Pine and the Blue Ridge Parkway just four miles to the south. Centrally situated for hiking, crafts, skiing, golf, and gem mining, the inn has seven luxurious rooms, all with private baths, and serves a full breakfast each morning and a complimentary glass of wine in the evening.

Hosts: Bill Ansley and Lenore Boucher
Rooms: 7 (PB) $55-75
Full Breakfast
Credit Cards: A, B
Notes: 2, 5, 8, 9, 10, 11, 12, 13, 14

STATESVILLE

Madelyn's Bed and Breakfast

514 Carroll Street, 28677
(704) 872-3973

Fresh flowers and homemade cookies await your arrival at Statesville's first bed and breakfast. It is a charming 1940s brick home filled with unique collections of family antiques, Raggedy Anns, iron dogs, and bottles. There are three lovely bedrooms with private baths, each with a different size bed to suit any traveler's needs. A full gourmet breakfast includes a choice of juice, fresh or baked fruit, bread, and entree. The house has central air conditioning.

Hosts: Madelyn and John Hill
Rooms: 3 (PB) $55-65
Full Breakfast
Credit Cards: A, B
Notes: 2, 5, 9, 10, 12, 14

Madelyn's

WAYNESVILLE

The Palmer House

108 Pigeon Street, 28786
(704) 456-7521

Built before the turn of the century, the Palmer House is one of the last of Waynesville's once numerous tourist homes. Within one block of Main Street.

6 Pets welcome; 8 Children welcome; 9 Social drinking allowed; 10 Tennis available; 11 Swimming available; 12 Golf available; 13 Skiing available; 14 May be booked through travel agents.

Relaxing environment, beautiful mountains, and good food. A home away from home.

Hosts: Jeff Minick and Kris Gillet
Rooms: 7 (PB) $50-60
Full Breakfast
Credit Cards: A, B, C, D
Notes: 2, 5, 8, 9, 10, 11, 12, 13

Market Street

WILMINGTON

Market Street Bed and Breakfast

1704 Market Street, 28403
(919) 763-5442; (800) 242-5442

Built in 1917, this elegant Georgian-style brick house is on the National Register of Historic Places. It is furnished with antiques and reproductions and features central air and paved off-street parking. Riverfront dining, shopping, and several beaches are only minutes away. A large side porch is available for rocking and relaxing. In the Mansion District, it is on U.S. Highways 17 and 74.

Hosts: Jo Anne and Bob Jarrett
Rooms: 3 (PB) $65-80
Full Breakfast
Credit Cards: A, B
Notes: 2, 5, 9, 10, 11, 12

WINSTON-SALEM

Wachovia Bed and Breakfast, Inc.

513 Wachovia Street, 27101
(919) 777-0332

Lovely rose-and-white Victorian cottage on a quiet street. Within walking distance of city center, Old Salem Historia, antique shops, and gourmet restaurants. A European-style bed and breakfast. Flexible check-in/check-out. No rigid breakfast schedule. Expanded continental breakfast—all you can eat. Complimentary wine.

Host: Carol Royals
Rooms: 6 (2 PB; 3 SB) $40-60
Expanded Continental Breakfast
Credit Cards: None
Notes: 2, 5, 8, 9, 12

NOTES: Credit cards accepted: A Master Card; B Visa; C American Express; D Discover Card; E Diner's Club; F Other; 2 Personal Checks accepted; 3 Lunch available; 4 Dinner available; 5 Open all year;

North Dakota

MCCLUSKY

Midstate Bed and Breakfast

Route 3, P.O. Box 28, 58463
(701) 363-2520

Country peace and quiet prevail at this easily found location alongside Highway 200. This newer home is situated on a working grain and livestock farm. The house features a private entrance to a complete lower level where guests stay. As a guest, the bedroom, bath, large TV lounge with fireplace, and kitchenette provide everything one needs. More than 4,500 acres available for those who only want to experience excellent hunting of upland game, waterfowl, and deer. Breakfast is served in a lovely plant-filled atrium.

Hosts: Grace and Allen Faul
Rooms: 3 (1 PB; 2 SB) $30
Continental or Full Breakfast
Credit Cards: None
Notes: 2, 5, 6 (call), 8, 10, 11

• McClusky

NORTH DAKOTA

Ohio

McNutt Farm II

6120 Cutler Lake Road, 43720
(614) 674-4555

Country bed and continental breakfast in rustic quarters for overnight travelers on a working farm in the quiet of the Blue Rock hill country. Only 11 miles from I-70, and 35 miles from I-77. Sixty miles from I-71. For those who wish to enjoy a longer stay, please ask about the log cabin by-the-week, two-weeks or weekend, or about the "cellar building" primitive bunk house with a porch and swing, overlooking pastures and forests. Hike, bicycle, bird watching, photograph, relax, or join in such farm chores as milking the cows, and feeding the horses and cattle. Visitors can even join the three Australian Blue Heeler dogs in a game of Frisbee. Next to The Wilds, 5,000-acre Blue Rock State Forest, the Muskingum River, and other local attractions.

Hosts: Patty and Don R. McNutt
Rooms: Suites 2 (SB) $30; Log Cabin (PB) $200-300; Carriage House (PB) $30, two-day minimum
Continental Breakfast
Credit Cards: A, B
Notes: 5, 6 (by arrangement), 8 (by arrangement), 11, 12

Prospect Hill
Bed and Breakfast

408 Boal Street, 45210
(513) 421-4408

Nestled into a wooded hillside, this Italianate Victorian town house was built in 1867 on Prospect Hill, Cincinnati's first suburb and now a national historic district. The bed and breakfast has been restored, keeping original woodwork, doors, hardware, and light fixtures. Each room is furnished with period antiques and offers fireplaces, skeleton keys, and spectacular views. Prospect Hill overlooks downtown and is only a 15-minute walk to Fountain Square or the Ohio River.

Host: Gary Hackney
Rooms: 3 (1 PB; 2 SB) $69-79
Full Breakfast
Credit Cards: A, B
Notes: 2, 5, 9, 11, 14

The Victoria Inn
of Hyde Park

3567 Shaw Avenue, 45208
(513) 321-3567; FAX (513) 321-3147

The Victoria Inn of Hyde Park is an elegantly comfortable bed and breakfast in the heart of one of Cincinnati's most charming neighborhoods. The award-winning inn,

Victorian Inn of Hyde Park

6 Pets welcome; 8 Children welcome; 9 Social drinking allowed; 10 Tennis available; 11 Swimming available; 12 Golf available; 13 Skiing available; 14 May be booked through travel agents.

OHIO

● Cleveland

● Northfield

Millersburg
●

● Worthington
● Danville

● West Milton

● Pickerington
● Blue Rock

● Circleville

● Laurelville

● Cincinnati

Stout
●

recognized by *Better Homes and Gardens* for outstanding renovation, is a perfect place to start business over breakfast or for a romantic getaway. Less than 15 minutes from downtown, the Riverfront, zoo, Mt. Adams, and local universities. It is the only area bed and breakfast with individual private room phones, on-site fax, copier, and in-ground pool.

Hosts: Tom Possert and Debra Moore
Rooms: 3 (3PB) $69-99
Full Breakfast
Credit Cards: A, B, C
Notes: 2, 5, 9, 10, 11, 12

CIRCLEVILLE

Castle Inn

610 South Court Street, 43113
(614) 477-3986; (800) 477-1541

Arches, battlements, towers, and plenty of stained glass adorn this romantic medieval castle completed in 1899 for a beautiful bride. All rooms feature Victorian antiques. Breakfast is served on English china in a museum-quality dining room overlooking the walled Shakespeare Garden. Occasional weekend events include murder mysteries and Elizabethan holidays.

Hosts: Sue and Jim Maxwell
Rooms: 6 (4PB; 2 SB) $55-85
Full Breakfast
Credit Cards: A, B
Notes: 2, 5, 8 (over 8), 11, 12, 14

Castle Inn

CLEVELAND

Notre Maison

Private Lodgings, Inc. A-1
P. O. Box 18590, 44118
(216) 321-3213

A lovely French chateau not far from the university hospitals and museums. Two guest rooms with private bath or a carriage house with private bath are available. $65-75.

Private Lodgings, Inc.

P. O. Box 18590, 44118
(216) 321-3213

A variety of accommodations including houses and apartments for rent in the greater Cleveland area. Near the Cleveland Clinic, Case Western Reserve University, major museums and galleries, Metro park system, downtown Cleveland business district, and some are near or on Lake Erie. No credit cards. $45-125.

DANVILLE

The White Oak Inn

29683 Walhonding Road, 43014
(614) 599-6107

This turn-of-the-century farmhouse in a rolling wooded countryside features fine gourmet dining in a relaxed atmosphere. Enjoy reading, board games, or just socializing in the common room with a fireplace and antique square grand piano. An outdoor enthusiast's haven, near the world's largest Amish population and Roscoe Village. Three rooms feature fireplaces.

Hosts: Yvonne and Ian Martin
Rooms: 10 (PB) $60-130
Full Breakfast
Credit Cards: A, B
Notes: 2, 4, 5, 9, 10, 11, 12, 14

6 Pets welcome; 8 Children welcome; 9 Social drinking allowed; 10 Tennis available; 11 Swimming available; 12 Golf available; 13 Skiing available; 14 May be booked through travel agents.

LAURELVILLE

Hocking House

18597 Laurel Street, P. O. Box 118, 43135
(614) 332-1655

The beautiful Hocking Hills region beckons. Caves, waterfalls, forests—spectacular scenery abounds. Sports nearby. All rooms feature private baths, antique furnishings, quilts and hand-crafted accessories. Walk to restaurants and more in this friendly little village in the hills of southeast Ohio.

Hosts: Max and Evelyn England; Jim and Sue Maxwell
Rooms: 4 (PB) $55-65 (winter discount)
Full Breakfast
Credit Cards: A, B
Notes: 2, 5, 8 (over 8), 11, 12, 14

MILLERSBURG

Adams Street Bed and Breakfast

175 West Adams Street, 44654
(216) 674-0766

This Victorian country home is in Holmes County, in the center of the world's largest Amish community. Amish quilts, and rugs abound, along with an oak-framed fireplace, library, homemade bread and air conditioning. One block from village shops. The host, who grew up Amish, recently retired as a reporter for the *Cleveland Plain Dealer,* and studied at Zona Spray Cooking School. Abigail Adams, resident cat, welcomes guests.

Host: Alma J. Kaufman
Rooms: 2 (SB) $45-55
Full Breakfast
Credit Cards: None
Notes: 2, 9, 10, 12

NORTHFIELD

The Inn at Brandywine Falls

8230 Brandywine Road, 44067
(216) 467-1812

Guests come again and again to this historic inn, surrounded by 33,000 acres of park land. The Greek Revival (1848) farmhouse and carriage barn are filled with period antiques. Linens are 100 percent cotton and freshly ironed. All baths are private, and the heating and air conditioning systems works well. The food is exceptional in quality, as well as presentation. Local, state and national writers have called the inn "Impeccable...a miracle...the perfect place."

Hosts: Katie and George Hoy
Rooms: 6 (6 PB) $75-165
Full Breakfast
Credit Cards: A, B, D
Notes: 2, 5, 8, 9, 11, 12, 13, 14

PICKERINGTON

Central House

27 West Columbus Street, 43147
(614) 837-0932

The Central House is a restored 1860s hotel, situated amidst many quaint shops in the historic Old Village of Pickerington. Each of the four guest rooms feature a private bath, and uniquely decorated with antiques of the period. A wholesome "from scratch" breakfast is served, with any special dietary needs cheerfully accommodated. Enjoy nearby parks, tennis, covered bridges, "backroading," or just relax and enjoy a good book and conversation.

Central House

NOTES: Credit cards accepted: A Master Card; B Visa; C American Express; D Discover Card; E Diner's Club; F Other; 2 Personal Checks accepted; 3 Lunch available; 4 Dinner available; 5 Open all year;

Hosts: Judy and Rob Wagley
Rooms: 4 (PB) $55-60
Full Breakfast
Credit Cards: A, B
Notes: 2, 5, 8, 10, 12

STOUT

100 Mile House

US 52, Box 4866D, 45684
(614) 858-2984; (800) 645-2051

Perhaps the most noted of estates in the southern Ohio area, this majestic mansion has all anyone could ask. The beautiful view of the Ohio River, lush green landscape and the birds singing while guests sit under their favorite tree add up to total relaxation. The 11-acre spread offers plenty of room for a nice walk, or you can bask in the sun while enjoying the junior Olympic-sized pool. One room features a private balcony.

Hosts: Jim and Barb Larter
Rooms: 3 (1 PB; 2 SB) $50-60
Full Breakfast
Credit Cards: None
Notes: 2, 5, 8, 9, 10, 11, 12

WORTHINGTON

A. M. House Bed and Breakfast

556 High Street, 43085
(614) 885-5580; (614) 885-5579

A restored turn-of-the-century Queen Anne home in the heart of Old Worthington, within walking distance of shops, restaurants, and New England-style village green. A. M. House has easy access to Columbus events and walking paths along the Olentangy River. Varied breakfast menus with special dietary needs considered. Enjoy porches and yard, TV in parlor. Discount for longer stay. Pet-free environment.

Hosts: Doug and Lee Buford; Colin and Robin Buford Wigney
Rooms: 4 (2 PB; 2 SB) $60-70
Full Breakfast
Credit Cards: None
Notes: 2, 5, 10, 11

6 Pets welcome; 8 Children welcome; 9 Social drinking allowed; 10 Tennis available; 11 Swimming available; 12 Golf available; 13 Skiing available; 14 May be booked through travel agents.

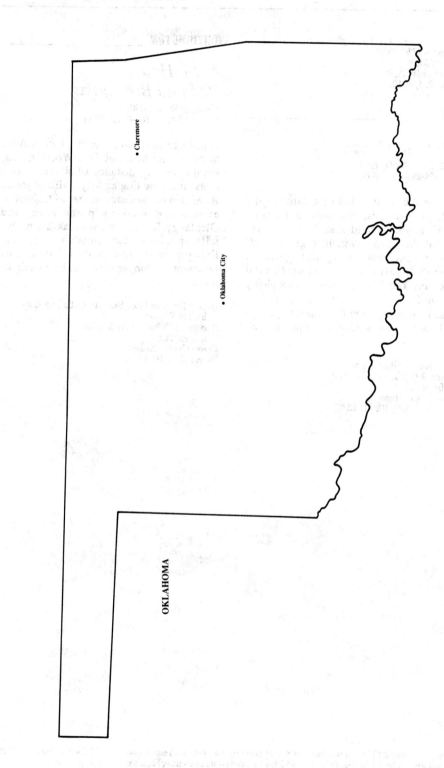

OKLAHOMA

• Claremore

• Oklahoma City

Oklahoma

Country Inn Bed and Breakfast

Route 3, Box 1925, 74017
(918) 342-1894

The hosts invite guests to this country retreat. Stay in charming barn-style guest quarters, separate from the main house. Enjoy the swimming pool, relax under a big shade tree with a cool drink, or take a country walk. A delightful continental breakfast is provided. Also, visit the on-premises quilt and craft shop. Nearby are J. M. Davis Gun Museum, Will Rogers Memorial, and horse racing at Will Rogers Downs during August and September.

Hosts: Leland and Kay Jenkins
Rooms: 2 (PB) $47
Suite: 1 (PB) $59
Full Breakfast
Credit Cards: None
Notes: 2, 5, 9, 11

Willow Way

27 Oakwood Drive, 73121-5410
(405) 427-2133

Willow Way is a wooded town retreat in English Tudor country-style, with antique decor and genuine charm. Established two-story stone with vaulted ceiling den and picture window, guests' favorite place for breakfast. Safe and comfortable with off-street parking. Quiet, situated near nature, the race track, Cowboy Hall of Fame, and other attractions. Three rooms with two private baths.

Hosts: Johnita and Lionel Turner
Rooms: 3 (2 PB; 1 SB) $50-80
Full Breakfast
Credit Cards: A, B
Notes: 2, 3, 5, 8, 9, 12

NOTES: Credit cards accepted: A Master Card; B Visa; C American Express; D Discover Card; E Diner's Club; F Other; 2 Personal Checks accepted; 3 Lunch available; 4 Dinner available; 5 Open all year; 6 Pets welcome; 8 Children welcome; 9 Social drinking allowed; 10 Tennis available; 11 Swimming available; 12 Golf available; 13 Skiing available; 14 May be booked through travel agents.

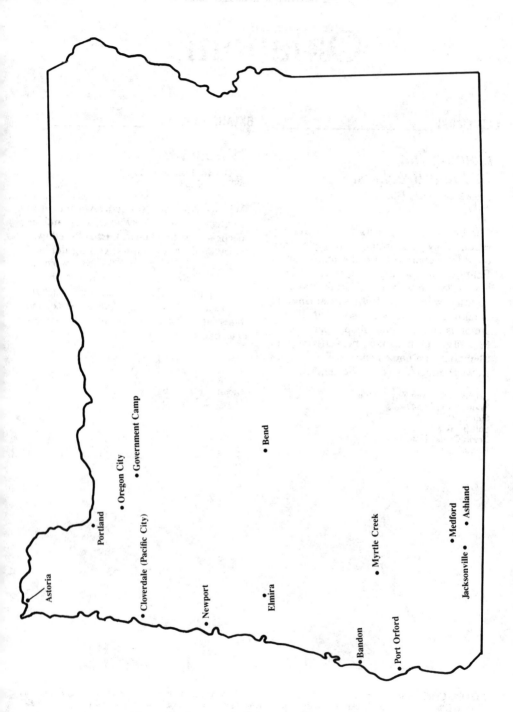

OREGON

Oregon

Cowslip's Belle

ASHLAND

Cowslip's Belle Bed and Breakfast

159 North Main Street, 97520
(503) 488-2901

The Cowslip's Belle has cozy down comforters and teddy bears to snuggle into, the
softest white linens to touch the skin, foam
baths to linger in, scrumptious breakfasts
to savor, and homemade smooth, creamy
chocolate truffles to melt in your mouth.
Just three blocks to restaurants, shops, and
theaters, this 1913 Craftsman bungalow
and carriage house is nestled in Ashland's
historic district. Voted one of the top 50
bed and breakfasts in the country by *Inn
Times*. Four rooms with private baths and
entrances. Special winter rates Nov. 1
through Feb. 12.

Hosts: Jon and Carmen Reinhardt
Rooms: 4 (PB) $55-110
Full Breakfast
Credit Cards: A, B
Notes: 2, 5, 9, 10, 11, 12, 13, 14

The Morical House

668 North Main Street, 97520
(503) 482-2254

A superbly restored 1880s farmhouse on
one and one-half acres of beautifully landscaped grounds, the Morical House offers
18th-century hospitality with 20th-century
comfort. Five gracious, air-conditioned
guest rooms, a bountiful breakfast menu
that changes daily, afternoon refreshments,
a putting green, unobstructed view of the
Rouge Valley, and Cascade Mountains.

Hosts: Pat and Peter Dahl
Rooms: 5 (PB) $85-115 seasonal
Full Breakfast
Credit Cards: A, B
Closed Jan. 15-30
Notes: 2, 8 (over 12), 10, 11, 12, 13, 14

Redwing

115 North Main Street, 97520
(503) 482-1807

The 1911 Craftsman-style home, with original lighting fixtures and beautiful wood-

Redwing

NOTES: Credit cards accepted: A Master Card; B Visa; C American Express; D Discover Card; E Diner's
Club; F Other; 2 Personal Checks accepted; 3 Lunch available; 4 Dinner available; 5 Open all year; 6 Pets welcome; 8 Children welcome; 9 Social drinking allowed; 10 Tennis available; 11 Swimming available; 12 Golf
available; 13 Skiing available; 14 May be booked through travel agents.

work, is nestled in Ashland's charming historic district. Each guest room enjoys its own distinctive intimacy and private bath. Relax on the front-porch swing and view the Cascade Mountains, or walk two blocks to Lithia Park or the nationally acclaimed Shakespearean Festival. In addition, downhill skiing, river rafting, salmon and steelhead fishing are all nearby.

Hosts: Mike and Judi Cook
Rooms: 3 (PB) $95
Full Breakfast
Credit Cards: None
Notes: 2, 5, 13

The Wood's House Bed and Breakfast Inn

333 North Main Street, 97520
(503) 488-1598; (800) 435-8260

In the historic district of Ashland four blocks from the Shakespearean theaters, 100-acre Lithia Park, restaurants, and shops, this 1908 Craftsman-style home offers six sunny and spacious guest rooms. Simple furnishings of warm woods, antique furniture, fine linens, watercolors, Oriental carpets, lace, leather, books, and private label amenities invite guests to relax in this comfortable, yet elegant, home. The half-acre terraced English gardens provide many areas for guests to relax, read, and socialize. Golf, swimming, hiking, biking, rafting, hot-air ballooning nearby.

Hosts: Françoise and Lester Roddy
Rooms: 6 (PB) $65-105
Full Breakfast
Credit Cards: A, B
Notes: 2, 5, 8, 9, 10, 11, 12, 13, 14

ASTORIA

Grandview Bed and Breakfast

1574 Grand Avenue, 97103
(503) 325-5555; (800) 488-3250
(800) 574-1574

Wonderful views of the Columbia River; close to the best maritime museum on the West Coast and other museums, churches, and Victorian homes. Tour domestic and foreign ships in port. Light, airy, three-story Victorian with hardwood floors.

Host: Charleen Maxwell
Rooms: 3 (PB) $39-88 plus tax
Suites: 3 (2 bedrooms, PB) $79-102 plus tax
Expanded Continental Breakfast
Credit Cards: A, B, D
Notes: 2, 5, 8 (over 10), 10, 11, 12, 14

BANDON

Lighthouse Bed and Breakfast

650 Jetty Road, Box 24, 97411
(503) 347-9316

Contemporary home situated on the beach across from the historic Bandon lighthouse. Unequaled jetty, lighthouse, and ocean views. Walk to Old Town, shops, galleries, and fine restaurants. In-room Jacuzzi available; fireplace, wood stove. A quiet, peaceful setting.

Hosts: Bruce and Linda Sisson
Rooms: 4 (PB) $80-115
Expanded Continental Breakfast
Credit Cards: A, B
Notes: 2, 5, 8 (over 12), 9, 10, 12, 14

Grandview

Farewell Bend

BEND

Farewell Bend Bed and Breakfast

29 Northwest Greeley, 97701
(503) 382-4374

Restored 70-year-old Dutch Colonial house. Four blocks from downtown shopping, restaurants, and Drake Park on the Deschutes River. In winter, ski Mount Bachelor. In summer, golf, whitewater rafting, fishing, and hiking. Complimentary wine or sherry. King beds, down comforters, handmade quilts, and terry-cloth robes.

Host: M. Lorene Bateman
Rooms: 3 (PB) $65-75
Full Breakfast
Credit Cards: A, B, C
Notes: 2, 5, 10, 11, 12, 13, 14

CLOVERDALE

Sandlake Country Inn

8505 Galloway Road, 97112
(503) 965-6745

A private, peaceful place for making marriage memories on the awesome Oregon coast. A shipwreck-timbered farmhouse built in 1894; old roses, private garden spa, and honeymoon suite (four rooms). The cottage has fireplace, Jacuzzi for two, and kitchen. Full breakfasts, bicycles, and croquet amid an exuberant country garden. One mile to the beach. "Togetherness Baskets" available. Wheelchair accessible.

Hosts: Margo and Charles Underwood
Rooms: 4 (PB) $65-100
Full Breakfast
Credit Cards: A, B
Notes: 2, 3, 4, 14

ELMIRA

McGillivray's Log Home Bed and Breakfast

88680 Evers Road, 97437
(503) 935-3564

West of Eugene, Oregon, guests will find the best of yesterday with the comforts of today. Situated on five wooded acres, this air-conditioned home has wheelchair access. The hearty breakfasts are often prepared on an antique wood-burning cook stove.

Host: Evelyn R. McGillivray
Rooms: 2 (PB) $50-70
Full Breakfast
Credit Cards: A, B
Notes: 2, 5

HOOD RIVER

Lincoln Street Lodging

1344 Lincoln Street, 97031
(503) 386-6166

This two-bedroom suite with queen-size beds offers a kitchenette, private entrance, and a view of the mountain and marina. Air-conditioned; all linens and breakfast fixings are provided. Off-street parking; a locked storage area near the staircase is perfect for storing spare luggage. In a quiet

6 Pets welcome; 8 Children welcome; 9 Social drinking allowed; 10 Tennis available; 11 Swimming available; 12 Golf available; 13 Skiing available; 14 May be booked through travel agents.

neighborhood near the river and windsurf-ing; mountain biking in Columbia Gorge National Scenic Area, one-half mile from downtown, with easy freeway access and train station nearby. Portland's Inter-national Airport is an hour away, and year-round skiing on Mount Hood, an hour away. Minmum reservation is three nights.

Hosts: Paul and Linda Keir
Suite: 1 (PB) $60
Continental Breakfast
Credit Cards: None
Notes: 2, 8, 9, 10, 11, 12, 13, 14

JACKSONVILLE

Jacksonville Inn

175 East California Street, 97530
(503) 899-1900

Jacksonville Inn offers eight air-condi-tioned rooms furnished with restored antiques and a historic honeymoon cottage furnished with everything imaginable. A lovely breakfast is provided. An award-winning dinner house featuring gourmet dining and more than 700 wines are in the 1861 vintage building.

Hosts: Jerry and Linda Evans
Rooms: 9 (PB) $80-175
Full Breakfast
Credit Cards: A, B, C, D, E
Notes: 2, 3, 4, 5, 8, 9, 10, 11, 12, 13, 14

MEDFORD

Waverly Cottage and Associated Bed and Breakfasts

305 North Grape, 97501
(503) 779-4716

This 1898 authentically restored Victorian is listed on the National Register of Historic Places. It is the most ornate Queen Anne-style cottage still standing in south-ern Oregon. Four adjacent suites of histori-cal merit have air conditioning, queen beds,

kitchens, livingrooms, climbing roses, appliances television, and VCR. Home away from home. One suite is handicapped accessible.

Hosts: David Fisse and Elaine Martens
Rooms: 6 (PB) $40-110
Continental Breakfast
Credit Cards: A, B, C, E, F
Notes: 2, 5, 6 (limited), 8, 9, 10, 11, 12, 13, 14

MOUNT HOOD

Falcon's Crest Inn

P. O. Box 185, 87287 Government Camp Loop
   Highway, Government Camp, 97028
(503) 272-3403; (800) 624-7384

Elegance "Mount Hood-style" features three rooms and two suites with private baths. Individually decorated with family heir-looms, in-room telephones, bed turndown service, morning refreshment tray, compli-mentary après-activity snacks. A full break-fast is served in the morning. Situated in the heart of a year-round recreation area, skiing, hiking, fishing, and horseback riding are all nearby. Corporate, private, and mystery par-ties are a specialty. Ski and holiday pack-ages available. Fine evening dining and spir-its available.

Hosts: Melody and Bob Johnson
Rooms: 5 (PB) $85-139
Full Breakfast

Waverly Cottage

Sonka's Sheep Station

Oceanfront bed and breakfast for book lovers. Each room is named after a different author and decorated individually. Some have fireplaces. Hot spiced wine is served in the library at 10 P.M. Dinner served nightly. Not suitable for young children.

Hosts: Ken Peyton and Charlotte Dinolt
Rooms: 20 (PB) $50-120
Full Breakfast
Credit Cards: A, B, C
Notes: 2, 4, 5, 9, 10, 11, 12

Credit Cards: A, B, C, D
Notes: 2, 4, 5, 9, 11, 12, 13, 14

MYRTLE CREEK

Sonka's Sheep Station Bed and Breakfast

901 Northwest Chadwick Lane, 97457
(503) 863-5168

The Sonka Ranch covers 400 acres along the picturesque South Umpqua River. This working ranch raises purebred Dorset sheep and markets fat lambs from 800 commercial ewes. Depending on the time of the year, guests can share ranch activities such as lambing, shearing, and haying. The working border collies always give demonstrations. Enjoy rural relaxing or visit local points of interest. More than just a bed and breakfast, this farm-stay promises a memorable visit.

Hosts: Louis and Evelyn Sonka
Rooms: 4 (3 PB; 1 SB) $50-60
Full Breakfast
Credit Cards: A, B
Closed Christmas holidays
Notes: 2, 8, 9, 14

NEWPORT

Sylvia Beach Hotel

267 Northwest Cliff, 97365
(503) 265-5428

OREGON CITY

Jagger House Bed and Breakfast

512 Sixth Street, 97045
(503) 657-7820

Furnished with antiques and reproductions, this carefully restored 1880 house has many special touches, including a garden gazebo, handmade folk art, the house jigsaw puzzle, and privacy. Oregon City, 12 miles south of Portland, is the Official End of the Oregon Trail, with five museums within two blocks of the inn. The innkeeper is an old-house fanatic and is very knowledgeable of local history and local walking tours.

Jagger House

---

6 Pets welcome; 8 Children welcome; 9 Social drinking allowed; 10 Tennis available; 11 Swimming available; 12 Golf available; 13 Skiing available; 14 May be booked through travel agents.

Host: Claire Met
Rooms: 3 (1 PB; 2 SB) $60-70
Full Breakfast
Credit Cards: A, B
Notes: 2, 5, 10, 11, 12, 13, 14

PORTLAND

John Palmer House

4314 North Mississippi Avenue, 97217
(503) 284-5893

Forty-five minutes from Columbia Gorge, Mount Hood, and wine country. One hour from the Pacific Ocean. This beautiful, historic Victorian can be a visitor's home away from home. Award-winning decor; gourmet chef. The hosts delight in providing the extraordinary. Dinner available. Wine sold on premises.

Hosts: Mary and Richard Sauter
Rooms: 7 (2 PB; 5 SB) $112.65
Full Breakfast
Credit Cards: A, B (6% service charge), C, D
Notes: 2, 4 (with notice), 5, 8, 9, 14

Pittock Acres Bed and Breakfast

103 NW Pittock Avenue, 97210
(503) 226-1163

This lovely 19-year-old contemporary with traditional, Victorian, and country furnishings is situated on a quiet country lane just five minutes from downtown Portland and within easy walking distance to historic Pittock Mansion. From the mansion grounds, walk beautiful forested trails to the zoo, Hoyt Arboretum, Washington Park, and the beautiful Japanese and Rose Gardens. Bus service is close by, as are fine restaurants, art galleries, and all major attractions and transportation.

Hosts: Linda and Richard Matson
Rooms: 3 (2 PB; 1 SB) $60-80 plus tax

Full Breakfast
Credit Cards: A, B, C, D
Notes: 2, 5, 8 (over 13), 14

PORT ORFORD

Home by the Sea Bed and Breakfast

P. O. Box 606, 97465-0606
(503) 332-2855; FAX (503) 332-7585

The hosts built this contemporary wood home on a piece of land overlooking a stretch of Oregon coast that takes your breath away. Queen Oregon myrtle woodbeds and cable TV are featured in both accommodations, which make ideal quarters for two couples traveling together. It's a short walk to restaurants, public beaches, historic Battle Rock Park, and the town's harbor. Amenities include a dramatic ocean view, direct beach access, full breakfast, laundry privileges, cable TV, and phone jacks in the rooms. No pets. No children. Brochure available.

Hosts: Alan and Brenda Mitchell
Rooms: 2 (PB) $65-75
Full Breakfast
Credit Cards: A, B
Notes: 2, 5, 9, 10, 12

Home by the Sea

NOTES: Credit cards accepted: A Master Card; B Visa; C American Express; D Discover Card; E Diner's Club; F Other; 2 Personal Checks accepted; 3 Lunch available; 4 Dinner available; 5 Open all year;

Pennsylvania

ADAMSTOWN

Adamstown Inn

62 West Main Street, 19501
(215) 484-0800; (800) 594-4808

Experience simple elegance at the
Adamstown Inn. A Victorian bed and
breakfast, resplendent with leaded glass
doors, chestnut woodwork and Oriental
rugs, situated in a small town brimming
with thousands of antique dealers and minutes from outlet shopping. Family heirlooms and handmade quilts appoint each
guest room. The master and front bedrooms
feature two-person Jacuzzis.

Hosts: Tom and Wanda Bermon
Rooms: 4 (PB) $65-90
Continental Breakfast
Credit Cards: A, B
Notes: 2, 5, 9, 10, 11, 12

Adamstown Inn

Spring House

AIRVILLE

Spring House

Muddy Creek Forks, 17302
(717) 927-6906

Built in 1798 of fieldstone, the house is
named for the pure spring it protects in the
tranquil pre-Revolutionary War river valley
village. Listed on the National Register of
Historic Places, and lovingly restored to
stenciled whitewashed walls, furnished
with antiques and art, the inn offers full
breakfast of local specialties, wine by the
fire or on the front porch, Amish-made
cheese, and caring hospitality. Horseback
riding, wineries, hiking, and trout fishing in
immediate area. Near Amish community
and a scenic railroad that follows Muddy
Creek and is under development.

Host: Ray Constance Hearne
Rooms: 5 (3 PB; 2 SB) $52-85
Full Breakfast
Minimum stay weekends and holidays: 2 nights
Credit Cards: None
Notes: 2, 5, 8, 9, 11, 12, 14

6 Pets welcome; 8 Children welcome; 9 Social drinking allowed; 10 Tennis available; 11 Swimming available;
12 Golf available; 13 Skiing available; 14 May be booked through travel agents.

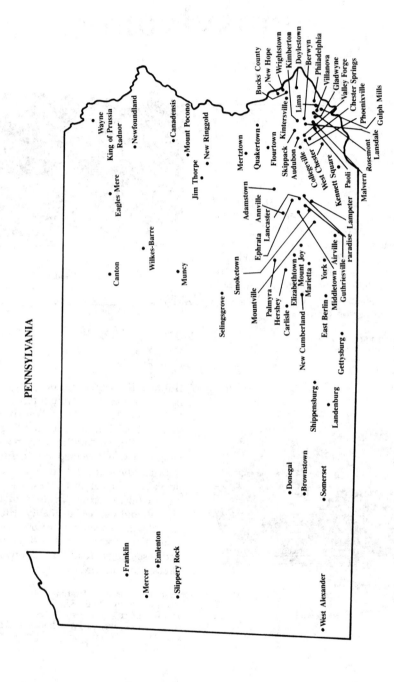

PENNSYLVANIA

West Alexander

Franklin
Mercer
Emlenton
Slippery Rock

Donegal
Brownstown
Somerset

Shippensburg
Landenburg

Gettysburg

New Cumberland
Carlisle
Hershey
Palmyra
Mountville

East Berlin
Elizabethtown
Mount Joy
Marietta
Middletown
Guthriesville
Airville
Paradise
Lampeter

York

Selingsgrove

Smoketown

Ephrata
Lancaster

Adamstown
Annville

Mertztown

Quakertown
Flourtown
Skippack
Audubon
Collegeville
West Chester
Kennett Square
Paoli
Malvern
Rosemont
Lansdale
Gulph Mills
Phoenixville
Chester Springs
Valley Forge
Gladwyne
Villanova
Philadelphia
Berwyn
Doylestown
Kimberton
Wrightstown
New Hope
Lima
Kintersville
Bucks County

Muncy

Wilkes-Barre

Canton

Eagles Mere

Wayne
King of Prussia
Radnor

Newfoundland

Canadensis
Mount Pocono
New Ringgold
Jim Thorpe

ANNVILLE

Hershey Bed and Breakfast Reservation Service

P. O. Box 208, Hershey, 17033-0208
(717) 533-2928

Victorian mansion built in 1860, 10 miles from Hershey, 18 miles from Harrisburg, and 2 miles from Indiantown Gap. All queen-size beds in ten guest rooms. Four of the rooms can accommodate four people. Children welcome. Full breakfast. Air conditioning, private bath. $50-70.

Swatara Creek Inn

Box 692, Rural Delivery 2, 17003
(717) 865-3259

An 1860 Victorian mansion in a country setting near Hershey and featuring 10 rooms with private baths, air conditioning, queen-size canopy beds, and a full breakfast served in the dining room. Sitting room and gift shop on the first floor. Restaurant within walking distance. Near Amish and outlet shops and Renaissance Faire at Mount Hope Winery. No pets.

Swatara Creek Inn

Rooms: 10 (PB) $50-70
Full Breakfast
Credit Cards: A, B, C, D, E
Notes: 2, 5, 8, 9, 10, 11, 12, 13, 14

AUDUBON

Benjamin Cox House

Bed and Breakfast of Valley Forge #0605
P. O. Box 562, Valley Forge, 19481-0562
(215) 783-7838; (800) 344-0123
FAX (215) 783-7783

This is an on-going restoration of a Federal-style, pointed stone farmhouse built in 1833. Highlights include five fireplaces, some of which work, original woodwork, stenciling, and antique furnishings. Breakfast is served in the keeping room in front of a working "walk-in" fireplace. Fragrances from the herb garden are an aromatic delight in spring and summer. Situated in a small suburb close to Valley Forge and an easy drive to the Brandywine area. Two guest rooms. $75.

Bonny Blue Farm— 1750 Farmhouse

Bed and Breakfast of Valley Forge #0800
P. O. Box 562, Valley Forge, 19481-0562
(215) 783-7838; (800) 344-0123
FAX (215) 783-7783

Situated on three acres of woodland and gardens, this stone farmhouse was built around 1750 on part of a William Penn land grant. Enjoy the warmth and hospitality of this Colonial home with an outdoor hot tub set near a four-square garden with roses, lavender, Medieval Elizabethan, and biblical gardens. Minutes from Valley Forge, one-half hour to Lancaster and Brandywine. Three guest rooms, three baths, one room with a king-size waterbed. $65-85.

NOTES: Credit cards accepted: A Master Card; B Visa; C American Express; D Discover Card; E Diner's Club; F Other; 2 Personal Checks accepted; 3 Lunch available; 4 Dinner available; 5 Open all year; 6 Pets welcome; 8 Children welcome; 9 Social drinking allowed; 10 Tennis available; 11 Swimming available; 12 Golf available; 13 Skiing available; 14 May be booked through travel agents.

BERWYN

Bed and Breakfast Connections #00243

P. O. Box 21, Devon, 19333
(215) 687-3565; (800) 448-3619 (outside PA)

This charming 1770 fieldstone farmhouse is in the picturesque countryside of Main Line Philadelphia near area universities, the Brandywine Valley, and Valley Forge Park. Two second-floor guest rooms with a shared bath are in the old part of the home. Each room has a four-poster canopied queen-size bed. Also available on the second floor is a large room with views of the pastures, canopied king-size bed, and private attached bath. A delicious breakfast is served in the breakfast nook. A turnout shed and pasture are available for a guest's horse. Resident dog. $85-110.

C. 1770 Country Farmhouse

Bed and Breakfast of Valley Forge # 0501
P. O. Box 562, Valley Forge, 19481-0562
(215) 783-7838; (800) 344-0123
FAX (215) 783-7783

This farmhouse features beamed ceilings, hand-stenciled walls, antique country furnishings, samplers, and local quilts. The oldest part is a restored 1770 tenant house. Set on five acres, there are pastoral views from every room. The guest room may have a canopy bed and fireplace, or a private stairway to the cozy den with fireplace. A hearty country breakfast will be served in a brick-floored sun room overlooking the gardens. Minutes from tennis and swimming. Resident Pomeranian. Three guest rooms with private bath. $85-110.

Hilltop Privacy

Bed and Breakfast of Valley Forge #1912
P. O. Box 562, Valley Forge, 19481-0562
(215) 783-7838; (800) 344-0123
FAX (215) 783-7783

This home is situated in a quiet wooded area. The guest quarters occupy the entire downstairs and include two bedrooms, family room with fireplace, hot tub solarium, and bar area with private entrance off the gardens. Other amenities include cable TV, refrigerator, phone, air conditioning, laundry facilities, use of the kitchen, and a breathtaking setting. Ingredients for breakfast are provided; self-serve at your leisure. Basic French and Dutch spoken. Weekly and monthly rates upon request. $65-70.

BRANDYWINE

Bed and Breakfast Connections #00358

P. O. Box 21, Devon, 19333
(215) 687-3565; (800) 448-3619 (outside PA)

Discover this tucked-away, quietly elegant manor house near the heart of the Brandywine Valley. With 36 acres, historic buildings, gardens, paths, and trails, each season is special at this bed and breakfast. Well-appointed rooms offer canopied king-size beds, queens, doubles, twins, and suites, five large country baths with showers. All rooms have TV, and most have private baths. A full country breakfast with homemade breads, muffins, croissants, and other goodies is served each morning. Concierge services are offered, and arrangements can be made for local activities. $75-110.

BROGUE

Bed and Breakfast Connections #00311

P. O. Box 21, Devon, 19333
(215) 687-3565; (800) 448-3619 (outside PA)

Lovingly restored, this late 1800s six-room guest house is nestled in the woods beside a meandering stream. Relax on the screen

NOTES: Credit cards accepted: A Master Card; B Visa; C American Express; D Discover Card; E Diner's Club; F Other; 2 Personal Checks accepted; 3 Lunch available; 4 Dinner available; 5 Open all year;

porch, and take in the beauty and serenity of this magnificent Susquehanna River estate that once was the home of Benjamin Franklin's grandson. Fish in the stream, swim in the old-fashioned swimming hole, bike or jog on the country roads, or wander through the grist mill that is being restored. Fine restaurants and a winery are nearby. Lancaster County attractions are within an easy drive. This is an ideal spot for business meetings, with phone and FAX available. $95.

BROWNSTOWN

1840 Pineapple Inn
Bed and Breakfast
50 Main Street, 17508
(717) 656-0566

The 1840 Pineapple Inn was built in 1840. The rooms have tall poster canopy beds with private baths. The inn is furnished with antiques. It retains the original wide-pine flooring, and three fireplaces. An antique shop is on premises. The hosts will be more than glad to share their knowledge of Amish country antique shops and local history with their guests.

Hosts: Mary and Bernie Peters
Rooms: 2 (PB) $65-75
Full Breakfast
Credit Cards: A, B
Notes: 5, 7, 8 , 9

BUCKS COUNTY

The Butler's House
Bed and Breakfast of Valley Forge #1906
P. O. Box 562, Valley Forge, 19481-0562
(215) 783-7838; (800) 344-0123
FAX (215) 783-7783

The original owners came to an unsettled wilderness of Bucks County in 1720, and built a stone dwelling to which a main formal house was added in 1840. A magnificent walk-in fireplace greets arriving guests. After a full day, guests can relax

next to a fire in the livingroom or in the library. The country kitchen has rustic stone walls, beehive oven, and hand-hewn beams. Seven guest rooms, all with private bath. $95-100.

Oak Farm
Bed and Breakfast
Bed and Breakfast of Valley Forge #1901
P. O. Box 562, Valley Forge, 19481-0562
(215) 783-7838; (800) 344-0123
FAX (215) 783-7783

This traditional 18th-century farmhouse is situated in the heart of Bucks County on ten wooded acres. Open-beamed ceilings and Oriental carpets throughout the 14 rooms contribute to its rustic charm and elegance. After a full day, guests can relax in the redwood hot tub, or on cool days relax by the fire. Breakfast can be enjoyed in the dining room or on the lovely sun porch. $95-125.

Upper Black Eddy
Bed and Breakfast
Bed and Breakfast of Valley Forge, #2302
P. O. Box 562, Valley Forge, 19481-0562
(215) 783-7838; (800) 344-0123
FAX (215) 783-7783

Welcome to peace and security in this 1820s farmhouse on 26 acres surrounded by hundreds of acres of wildlife preserve. Situated within minutes of the finest restaurants along the Delaware River and just 20 minutes to New Hope. Three antique-filled guest rooms. $115-135.

CANADENSIS

Brookview Manor
Bed and Breakfast Inn
Rural Route 1, Box 365, 18325
(717) 595-2451

6 Pets welcome; 8 Children welcome; 9 Social drinking allowed; 10 Tennis available; 11 Swimming available; 12 Golf available; 13 Skiing available; 14 May be booked through travel agents.

Situated on four picturesque acres in the Pocono Mountains, Brookview Manor offers eight guest rooms and suites uniquely appointed with country and antique furnishings. Enjoy the wraparound porch, hiking trails, fishing, and nearby skiing, golf, tennis, boating, and antiquing. A delicious full breakfast, afternoon refreshments, and warm hospitality are all included.

Hosts: Lee and Nancie Cabana
Rooms: 8 (6 PB; 2 SB) $65-145
Full Breakfast
Credit Cards: A, B, C, D
Notes: 2, 5, 8 (over 12), 9, 10, 11, 12, 13, 14

The Old Village Inn

Route 390, Skytop Road, 18325
(717) 839-0796

The most romantic little hotel in the heart of the Poconos. Turn-of-the-century country inn on five manicured acres with a stream. Suites or rooms, individually decorated with antiques. Full country breakfast served on the sun porch adjacent to the dining room. Dinner is available, also. Relax in front of the fire at the cozy, antique marble-topped bar. Accommodations have private baths, television, air conditioning, refrigerator, tea service and bedtime snacks. Honeymoon packages available.

Hosts: Jack and Donna Asure
Rooms: 9 (PB) $65-95
Full Breakfast
Credit Cards: A, B, C, D
Notes: 4, 5, 9, 10, 11, 12, 13, 14

CANTON

Mm-m Good

Rural Delivery 1, Box 71, 17724
(717) 673-8153

Situated in the center of the endless mountains of Pennsylvania, this bed and breakfast, featuring three rooms with double beds, has a large lawn with picnic tables under sugar maple trees. In the morning the host serves a full breakfast, including homemade muffins and rolls.

Hosts: Melvin and Irene Good
Rooms: 3 (SB) $23.50
Full Breakfast
Credit Cards: None
Notes: 2, 5, 8

CARLISLE

Line Limousin Farmhouse Bed and Breakfast

2070 Ritner Highway, 17013
(717) 243-1281

This 110-acre homestead has an eleven-room brick and stone home. It is only one and one-half miles from Exit 12 of I-81 and within close proximity to Dickinson College and many fine restaurants. Carlisle Fairgrounds, home of many fine automobile shows, are nearby. Furnishings inside the inn include antiques and a player piano that guests will enjoy. Hosts raise Limousin beef cattle, and guests may play croquet, bocce ball, or drive golf balls on two of the golf courses that border the farm.

Hosts: Robert and Joan Line
Rooms: 4 (2 PB; 2 SB) $50-60
Full Breakfast
Credit Cards: None
Notes: 2, 5, 8, 9, 12

CHALFONT

Bed and Breakfast Connections #00356

P. O. Box 21, 19333
(215) 687-3565; (800) 448-3619

Nestled in beautiful central Bucks County, this inn offers comfortable lodging on more than four handsomely landscaped acres. Thoughtful improvements by each successive owner have enhanced the property to its present state. Each room is tastefully furnished with period pieces reflecting a warm and relaxing atmosphere. There is a cozy fireplace to enjoy in the winter, and a patio and swimming pool to enjoy in the summer. Sleep in the luxury of a queen-

NOTES: Credit cards accepted: A Master Card; B Visa; C American Express; D Discover Card; E Diner's Club; F Other; 2 Personal Checks accepted; 3 Lunch available; 4 Dinner available; 5 Open all year;

size spindle-post bed, or choose the cozy twin-bed room. Private and semi-private baths. A full gourmet breakfast is served in the dining room. $65-95.

CHESTER SPRINGS

Bed and Breakfast Connections #00216

P. O. Box 21, Devon, 19333
(215) 687-3565; (800) 448-3619 (outside PA)

Complimentary wine or sparkling water await guests upon arrival at this lovely 1830s farmhouse with classic mid-century features. Two spacious guest rooms share a hall bath. While visiting, guests are invited to jog or walk a meandering trail or relax by the stream on this quiet ten-acre country retreat. A continental-plus breakfast is served in the dining room in front of the original fireplace and beehive oven. Resident cat. $65.

Springdale Farm

Bed and Breakfast of Valley Forge #1302
P. O. Box 562, Valley Forge, 19481-0562
(215) 783-7838; (800) 344-0123
FAX (215) 783-7783

A circa 1840 farmhouse on ten acres of lawns and woods perfect for biking, jogging, hiking, or just appreciating. Good location for Longwood Gardens and Brandywine area. An expanded continental breakfast is served in the formal dining room, with random width flooring, fireplace, and beehive oven. Guests may choose to stay in the Blue Room with a reading corner and windows on three sides, or Grandmother's Room with Early American pine furniture and rope bed. Enjoy fireplaces, porches, barbecue, patio, and chairs by the stream. $65-70.

COLLEGEVILLE

Fircroft

Bed and Breakfast of Valley Forge #1305
P. O. Box 562, Valley Forge, 19481-0562
(215) 783-7838; (800) 344-0123
FAX (215) 783-7783

Near Ursinas College. In 1838, this spacious Federal-style home with wraparound porch was built around the original 1769 homestead. The country kitchen has beamed ceiling and stained glass. A full country breakfast is served in the large formal dining room. Guest quarters are private and appealing. The bath has a flowered pedestal sink with gold fixtures and a claw foot tub. $65.

Victorian Elegance

Bed and Breakfast of Valley Forge #1904
P. O. Box 562, Valley Forge, 19481-0562
(215) 783-7838; (800) 344-0123
FAX (215) 783-7783

Skilled European and American craftsmen fashioned this 22-room Victorian mansion in 1897. Stained glass and fireplaces abound. A three-story winding chestnut staircase leads to the air-conditioned guest rooms that offer such touches as marble lavatory, ornate medicine cabinet, and built-in armoire of exotic woods. A full breakfast is served in the dining room. This elegant mansion is renowned for year-round house tours, weddings both in the mansion and in the gardens, small corporate meetings, dinners in the dining room, and the perfect setting for wedding pictures. Seven guest rooms, five with private bath. $75-85.

DONEGAL

Mountain View Bed and Breakfast

Mountain View Road, 15628
(412) 593-6349

6 Pets welcome; 8 Children welcome; 9 Social drinking allowed; 10 Tennis available; 11 Swimming available; 12 Golf available; 13 Skiing available; 14 May be booked through travel agents.

Historic 1850s farmhouse and barn with guest rooms furnished with 18th and early 19th-century American antiques. Spectacular view of the Laurel Mountain, and close proximity to Fallingwater, hiking, skiing, rafting, and mountain resorts. Antique shop on premises.

Hosts: Jerry and Lesley O'Leary
Rooms: 6 (3 PB; 3 SB) $75-125
Full Breakfast
Credit Cards: A, B, C, D, E
Notes: 2, 5, 9, 11, 12, 13, 14

DOYLESTOWN

Ye Olde Inn

Bed and Breakfast of Valley Forge #0803
P. O. Box 562, Valley Forge, 19481-0562
(215) 783-7838; (800) 344-0123
FAX (215) 783-7783

This pre-Revolutionary War farmhouse built of fieldstone and stucco is set on eight wooded acres in historic Bucks County. A wonderful stone fireplace in the lobby greets guests with warmth. Fifteen guest rooms, all with private baths. $80-110.

EAGLES MERE

Eagles Mere Inn

Mary and Sullivan Avenues, 17731
(717) 525-3273; (800) 426-3273

Eagles Mere Inn

This 1887 country inn with old-fashioned hospitality and outstanding food features a hearty breakfast and a five-course gourmet dinner included in the room rates. Called the "Last Unspoiled Resort," it offers the ultimate stress relief, peace and quiet, crystal clear mountaintop lake, swimming and boating, incredible waterfalls, hiking trails and vistas, trout fishing, golf, tennis, cross-country skiing, tobogganing, antique shops, wine-tasting weekends, and more. Featured as a special vacation spot in *Mid-Atlantic, Washingtonian,* and numerous travel articles.

Hosts: Susan and Peter Glaubitz
Rooms: 15 (PB) $120-175
Full Breakfast
Credit Cards: A, B
Notes: 2, 4 (included), 5, 8, 9, 10 , 11, 12, 13 14

Shady Lane: A Bed and Breakfast Inn

Allegheny Avenue, P. O. Box 314, 17731
(717) 525-3394

A picturesque mountaintop resort close to excellent hiking, swimming, and fishing. In a quiet Victorian town high in the Endless Mountains, the charming seven-bedroom inn offers all the conveniences and amenities of a home away from home. Explore the laurel path that surrounds the crystal-clear lake. Take a step back in time to the Eagles Mere gaslight era village shops. In winter, enjoy the famous Eagles Mere toboggan slide or some of the finest cross-country skiing. Mystery weekends. AAA and AB&BA approved.

Hosts: Pat and Dennis Dougherty
Rooms: 8 (PB) $65-100
Full Breakfast
Credit Cards: None
Notes: 2, 5, 8, 9, 10, 11, 12, 13, 14

EAST BERLIN

Bechtel Mansion Inn

400 West King Street, 17316
(717) 259-7760; (800) 331-1108

Magnificently restored Victorian mansion with quality period furnishings and hand-made quilts. Perfect setting for honeymoons and special occasions. Guest rooms are air-conditioned, with private baths. The mansion is on the western frontier of the Pennsylvania Dutch country. Excellent restaurants, golf courses, and antiques nearby. Convenient to York, Gettysburg, and Lancaster County. Situated in a national historic district approximately 100 miles from both Washington, D.C., and Philadelphia. Skiing just 18 miles away.

Hosts: Ruth Spangler; Charles and Mariam Bechtel
Rooms: 7 (PB) $82.50-110
Suites: 2 (PB) $125-135
Continental Breakfast
Minimum stay October weekends and holidays: 2
 nights
Credit Cards: A, B, C, D
Notes: 2, 5, 8, 9, 10, 12, 13, 14

Bechtel Mansion Inn

ELIZABETHTOWN

Hershey Bed and Breakfast Reservation Service

P. O. Box 208, Hershey, 17033-0208
(717) 533-2928

A luxurious getaway at a beautiful country estate home. Hobby farm with horses, Angus cattle, two fishing ponds, tennis court. Health room with hot tub. Full breakfast. Eight rooms with private bath. $60-85.

West Ridge Guest House

1285 West Ridge Road, 17022
(717) 367-7783

Tucked midway between Harrisburg and Lancaster, this European-type manor can be found four miles off Route 283 at Rheems-Elizabethtown Exit. Nine guest rooms, four in the main house and five in a separate guest house, which offers complete privacy. Private baths. Each room decorated to reflect a different historical style, featuring two fireplaces and some rooms open onto decks. Exercise room with hot tub, large social room, and dining area. Fish in one of two ponds, or travel 20 to 40 minutes to local attractions, such as Hershey Park, Lancaster County Amish farms, outlet shopping, Masonic homes, or Gettysburg. Gazebo and outdoor picnic area available. Full breakfast. Handicapped accessible.

Host: Alice P. Heisey
Rooms: 9 (PB) $60-85
Full Breakfast
Credit Cards: A, B, C
Notes: 2, 5, 8, 9, 10, 14

EMLENTON

Whippletree Inn and Farm

Rural Delivery 3, Box 285, 16373
(412) 867-9543

Whippletree Inn and Farm is a restored turn-of-the-century cattle farm. The house, barns and 100 acres of pasture sit on a hill above the Allegheny River and the town of Emleton. There is a pleasant trail leading down to the river. Guests are welcome to use the half-mile race track for horses, carriages and hiking. There are no horses for rent, but boarding for private horses is available.

Hosts: Warren and Joey Simmons
Rooms: 4 (2PB; 2 SB) $45-50
Full Breakfast
Credit Cards: None
Notes: 2, 5, 8, 11, 12

6 Pets welcome; 8 Children welcome; 9 Social drinking allowed; 10 Tennis available; 11 Swimming available; 12 Golf available; 13 Skiing available; 14 May be booked through travel agents.

EPHRATA

Clearview Farm Bed and Breakfast

355 Clearview Road, 17522
(717) 733-6333

A beautiful limestone farmhouse built in 1814, this bed and breakfast overlooks a large pond with a pair of swans. Beautifully restored and lovingly redecorated, it is surrounded by a well-kept lawn on 200 acres of peaceful farm land. A touch of elegance in Pennsylvania Dutch Country, it was featured in *Country Decorating Ideas.*

Hosts: Glenn and Mildred Wissler
Rooms: 5 (3 PB; 2 SB) $59-89
Full Breakfast
Credit Cards: A, B
Notes: 2, 5, 9, 10, 12

ERIE

Historic Zion's Hill at Carriage Hill Farm

9023 Miller Road, Cranesville, 16410
(814) 774-2971

An 1830 Colonial-style home situated on a knoll and surrounded by majestic maples. Beautiful farm setting provides security and nostalgia. Close to cross-country and hiking trails, bird sanctuary, sleigh rides, and carriage rides, and children's petting farm. Convenient to mall shopping, Presque Isle, and Pymatuming State Park. Excellent fishing, swimming, and boating areas, as well as cross-country downhill skiing.

Hosts: John and Kathy Byrne
Rooms: 5 (3 PB; 2 SB) $40-70
Continental Breakfast
Credit Cards: None
Notes: 2 (advance reservation), 5, 8, 9, 13 (XC), 14

FLOURTOWN

All About Town B & B in Philadelphia #0401

P. O. Box 562, Valley Forge, 19481-0562
(215) 783-7838; (800) 344-0123
FAX (215) 783-7783

Delightful one bedroom guest cottage offers the executive a place to unwind. Continental breakfast foods are provided in the kitchenette. Minimum stay is one week. $300 weekly.

FRANKLIN

Quo Vadis Bed and Breakfast

1501 Liberty Street, 16323
(814) 432-4208

A stately brick and terra cotta home, Quo Vadis (Whither Goest Thou?) is an eclectic Queen Anne built in 1867, and is in the historic district of Franklin. The high ceilings, spacious rooms, parquet floors and detailed woodwork display Victorian elegance. The furniture has been acquired by the same family over four generations. Quilts, embroidery and lacework are family handwork.

Hosts: Kristal and Stanton Bowmer-Vath
Rooms: 6 (PB) $60-70
Full Breakfast
Credit Cards: A, B, C
Notes: 2, 8 (over 11), 9, 10, 11, 12, 13 (XC), 14

GERMANTOWN

Bed and Breakfast Connections #0031

P. O. Box 21, Devon, 19333
(215) 687-3565; (800) 448-3619

NOTES: Credit cards accepted: A Master Card; B Visa; C American Express; D Discover Card; E Diner's Club; F Other; 2 Personal Checks accepted; 3 Lunch available; 4 Dinner available; 5 Open all year;

Circa 1885, this home offers several fascinations: its history, its antique furnishings, and its well-traveled host who lovingly cares for it. Two second-floor guest rooms with connecting baths are available; one offers a single canopied bed, and the other, a pair of twin beds. Each has been tastefully appointed and reflects the overall elegance of the home. The location of this home is ideal for a visit to historic Germantown or the interesting shops of Chestnut Hill. Resident dog. $25-35.

The Brafferton Inn

GETTYSBURG

Amanda's Bed and Breakfast #125

1428 Park Avenue, Annapolis, MD 21217
(301) 225-0001; (301) 383-1274

Situated on Oak Ridge, this restored Colonial offers a splendid view of the town. Enjoy the charm of a bygone era with the comforts of home-cooked breakfasts, cozy quilts, and country antiques. Rooms are decorated with Civil War accents. Nine rooms have private and shared baths. $79-99.

Amanda's Bed and Breakfast #214

1428 Park Avenue, Annapolis, MD. 21217
(301) 225-0001; (301) 383-1274

Split-level house five minutes from historic Gettysburg. Antiques, quiet setting, excellent breakfast. Two rooms share a bath. $50.

The Brafferton Inn

44 York Street, 17325
(717) 337-3423

This 1786 stone home is listed on the National Register of Historic Places. Enjoy the colonial antiques, stenciled decor, and full breakfast served near a primitive mural. Experience Gettysburg in the first house built in town. Featured in the February 1988 issue of *Country Living* magazine.

Hosts: Mimi and Jim Agard
Rooms: 10 (6 PB; 4 SB) $55-95
Full Breakfast
Credit Cards: A, B
Notes: 2, 4, 5, 8 (over 7), 9, 10, 11, 12, 13, 14

Goose Chase Bed and Breakfast

200 Blueberry Road, Gardners, 17324
(717) 528-8877

A restored 18th-century stone home on 25 tranquil acres among vast apple orchards. Air-conditioned for summer comfort, it is

Goose Chase

6 Pets welcome; 8 Children welcome; 9 Social drinking allowed; 10 Tennis available; 11 Swimming available; 12 Golf available; 13 Skiing available; 14 May be booked through travel agents.

handsomely furnished with handmade quilts, folk art, and carefully chosen American antiques. Wide-plank floors, Oriental rugs, stenciled walls, and deep-silled windows add to the charming atmosphere. Full breakfast is always served and afternoon refreshments are graciously offered. Summer swimming pool and walking trails are on the property. Just 15 minutes from Gettysburg Battlefield.

Host: Marsha Lucidi
Rooms: 5 (3 PB; 2 SB) $69-89
Full Breakfast
Credit Cards: A, B
Notes: 2, 5, 9, 11, 12, 13

Keystone Inn

Keystone Inn

231 Hanover Street, 17325
(717) 337-3888

Keystone Inn is a large late-Victorian brick house filled with lots of natural woodwork. The guest rooms are bright, cheerful, and air-conditioned. The soft pastels and ruffles give guests a warm welcome. Each room has a reading nook and writing desk. Relax with a book in Aunt Weasie's Library. Choose a breakfast from the full menu.

Hosts: Wilmer and Doris Martin
Rooms: 4 (2 PB; 2 SB) $59-75
Full Breakfast
Credit Cards: A, B
Notes: 2, 5, 8, 10, 11, 12, 13

The Tannery
Bed and Breakfast

449 Baltimore Street, P. O. Box 4565, 17325
(717) 334-2454

The Tannery has been in the Swope family since 1920. A Gothic structure built in 1868, the building has been completely refurbished over the last 10 years. It is named for the tannery that stood at the side of the property, and is convenient for touring the Gettysburg battlefield, within four blocks of the visitor's center, museums, shops and restaurants.

Host: Charlotte Swope
Rooms: 5 (PB) $65-85
Continental Breakfast
Credit Cards: A, B
Notes: 2, 5, 8, 9, 10, 12, 13

GLADWYNE

Glad Haven

Bed and Breakfast of Valley Forge #0202
P. O. Box 562, Valley Forge, 19481-0562
(215) 783-7838; (800) 344-0123
FAX (215) 783-7783

This spacious, air-conditioned Cape Cod Colonial home is situated on a large wooded lot. Fine furnishings, collectibles, art, and expanses of windows all contribute to the sunlit, cheerful atmosphere. The gourmet country breakfasts may be served in the formal dining room with its collection of blue glass, or in the sun room with its wicker and foliage. The adjoining terrace, gardens, lawn, reflecting pool and fountain enhance the feeling of privacy and rest. Four guest rooms with private baths. $55.

GULPH MILLS

The Barn at Rebel Hill
Bed and Breakfast

Bed and Breakfast of Valley Forge #0306
P. O. Box 562, Valley Forge, 19481-0562

NOTES: Credit cards accepted: A Master Card; B Visa; C American Express; D Discover Card; E Diner's Club; F Other; 2 Personal Checks accepted; 3 Lunch available; 4 Dinner available; 5 Open all year;

(215) 783-7838; (800) 344-0123
FAX (215) 783-7783

A home made from a barn, this fabulous, luxury barn offers an atmosphere of quiet taste to highlight a visit to this historic area. All guest rooms are situated off the spacious entrance hall. A full breakfast is served in the parlor or in the great room with a fireplace and antiques. In warm weather, lounge or dine on the upper deck overlooking the enclosed stone paddock, the rolling green hills, and pond. Close to Valley Forge, Philadelphia. An easy drive to Brandywine and Amish areas. Three guest rooms, each with a private bath. $85-95.

GUTHRIESVILLE

Burns 1805
Bed and Breakfast

Bed and Breakfast of Valley Forge #1503
P. O. Box 562, Valley Forge, 19481-0562
(215) 783-7838; (800) 344-0123
FAX (215) 783-7783

Lovely example of an early 19th-century Pennsylvania farmhouse overlooking a panoramic view of farm and woodland. It has been on Chester County day tours for many years. Share the special warmth and serenity of this lovely old house. Walk about on eight acres of hill, meadow, and hedgerow, or just enjoy the views from the porch. Close to the Amish/Lancaster area, and the Brandywine Longwood Garden area. Two guest rooms, each with a private bath. $45-75.

HERSHEY

Hershey Bed and Breakfast
Reservation Service

P. O. Box 208, 17033
(717) 533-2928

This reservation service offers personalized service in matching guests with just the right bed and breakfast inn or homestay in south central Pennsylvania. Be it a family vacation, a farm experience, business meetings or transfers, a honeymoon, or weekend getaway, here is help and knowledgeable advice. Renee Deutel, coordinator. $50-125.

Credit Cards: A, B, C
Notes: 2, 5, 8, 9, 10, 11, 12, 14

Hershey Bed and Breakfast
Reservation Service #1

P. O. Box 208, 17033-0208
(717) 533-2928

Lovely home near the Hershey Medical Center. One guest room with private bath and choice of full or continental breakfast. Air conditioning. Dog in residence. $50.

Hershey Bed and Breakfast
Reservation Service #2

P. O. Box 208, 17033-0208
(717) 533-2928

A former Milton Hershey Boys School, this large brick home is convenient to Hershey museums, park, rose gardens, Chocolate World, sports arena and stadium, theater, and outdoor recreations. Twelve guest rooms, one room with private bath, three shared bathrooms on the second level and one on the first floor. Continental breakfast. Resident cat. Handicapped accessible. Air conditioning. $54-59. Children $5 with parents in same room. Extra adults $10.

Hershey Bed and Breakfast
Reservation Service #3

P. O. Box 208, 17033-0208
(717) 533-2928

A log home dating from the 1700s on a lovely horse farm. Country roads for walking and biking, and fields and woods for

6 Pets welcome; 8 Children welcome; 9 Social drinking allowed; 10 Tennis available; 11 Swimming available; 12 Golf available; 13 Skiing available; 14 May be booked through travel agents.

hiking. One guest room with private half-bath and sitting room. Continental breakfast. Resident pets. $65. Children over six $10 additional charge.

Hershey Bed and Breakfast Reservation Service #4

P. O. Box 208, 17033-0208
(717) 533-2928

Countryside home offers one guest room with king bed and private bath. Resident cat. Full breakfast on weekends, continental during the week. Air conditioning. $55.

Hershey Bed and Breakfast Reservation Service #5

P. O. Box 208, 17033-0208
(717) 533-2928

Home near Hershey Motor Lodge offers three guest rooms with shared bath, plus a new suite with a private bath. Full breakfast. Children welcome. $55-75.

HUNTINGDON VALLEY

Bed and Breakfast Connections #00338

P. O. Box 21, Devon, 19333
(215) 687-3565; (800) 448-3619 (outside PA)

This fantasy cottage is an ideal spot for a quiet retreat from the hubbub of Philadelphia, yet just 30 minutes away. The combination greenhouse and potting shed shares a broad expanse of lawn with the main house. It is bordered on one side by a grape arbor and on the other side by a swimming pool. The in-room refrigerator is stocked with wine, cheese, and soft drinks, as well as all that is needed to fix your own hearty continental breakfast. Enjoy a fruit basket on arrival. There is air conditioning in the

warm weather and a fireplace for the cooler months. Horseback riding, tennis courts, and jogging trails nearby. $85.

HESSTON

Aunt Susie's Country Vacations

Rural Delivery 1, Box 225, 16647
(814) 658-3638

Experience country living in a warm, friendly atmosphere in a Victorian parsonage or a renovated country store and post office. All rooms are nicely furnished, with antiques and oil paintings. Raystown Lake is nearby for recreation; boating, swimming, and fishing are within three miles. Bring the family to the country.

Host: John Wilson
Rooms: 8 (2 PB; 6 SB) $45-50
Continental Breakfast
Credit Cards: None
Notes: 2, 5, 8, 9, 10, 11, 12

JIM THORPE

The Inn at Jim Thorpe

4 Broadway, 18229
(717) 325-2599; FAX (717) 325-9145

The Inn at Jim Thorpe rests in a lovely setting in the heart of historic Jim Thorpe. The elegant, restored guest rooms are complete with private baths, remote cable TV, and air conditioning. While in town, take a historic walking tour of Millionaire's Row; shop in fifty quaint shops and galleries; go mountain biking on the Northeast's best trails; raft the turbulent LeHigh River. It's all right outside the inn's door.

Host: David Drury
Rooms: 22 (PB) $65-125
Continental Breakfast
Credit Cards: A, B, C, D, E
Notes: 3, 4, 5, 8, 11, 12, 13, 14

NOTES: Credit cards accepted: A Master Card; B Visa; C American Express; D Discover Card; E Diner's Club; F Other; 2 Personal Checks accepted; 3 Lunch available; 4 Dinner available; 5 Open all year;

KENNETT SQUARE

Bed and Breakfast of Valley Forge #2001

P. O. Box 562, Valley Forge, 19481-0562
(215) 783-7838; (800) 344-0123
FAX (215) 783-7783

This brick ranch home in the Brandywine Valley offers an adjoining private entrance suite and a twin room in the main house. The kitchen is stocked for long-term guests, and a full breakfast is also served. $75.

Scarlett House Bed and Breakfast

503 West State Street, 19348
(215) 444-9592

Historic Victorian situated in the heart of Brandywine Valley. Four guest rooms are available, with air conditioning and antique furnishings. Several common areas include two spacious parlors with fireplaces, upstairs sitting area, and wraparound porch. Breakfast is served by candlelight in the dining room, or on the porch, depending on the weather. The fare includes fresh fruit, mushroom-shaped chocolate chip scones, homemade muffins, breads, and specialty coffees. Complimentary refreshments on arrival.

Host: Susan Lalli-Ascosi
Rooms: 4 (2 PB; 2 SB) $65-90
Continental Breakfast
Credit Cards: None
Notes: 2, 5, 9

KIMBERTON

Windmills

Bed and Breakfast of Valley Forge #2201
P. O. Box 562, Valley Forge, 19481-0562
(215) 783-7838; (800) 344-0123
FAX (215) 783-7783

This Dutch-style farmhouse was built in 1860 and grew into a rambling home that has been lovingly restored. The Netherlands influence is evident in the decor, food, and hospitality. A full European breakfast is served. The king/twin suite has a private entrance, deck, sitting room with access to a Jacuzzi. The queen rooms also share a sitting room. Enjoy the terrace, Jacuzzi, and Japanese gardens. Excellent location en route to Amish country. $65-75.

KING OF PRUSSIA

Tranquil Haven

Bed and Breakfast of Valley Forge #0201
P. O. Box 562, Valley Forge, 19481-0562
(215) 783-7838; (800) 344-0123
FAX: (215) 783-7783

This home is set in a peaceful, heavily wooded neighborhood and is decorated with both antique and modern furnishings. Sitting room with fireplace and color cable TV, laundry facilities, and in-ground pool. Gourmet breakfasts are served in the dining room or on the spacious screened porch overlooking the garden. Some French spoken. Two cats in residence. Three guest rooms with private baths. $45-60.

KINTNERSVILLE

The Bucksville House

Route 412 and Buck Drive
4501 Durham Road, 18930
(215) 847-8948

Country charm and a friendly atmosphere await the guests at this 1795 Bucks County registered historical landmark. Offering beautifully decorated rooms with many quilts, baskets, antiques and handmade reproductions. Enjoy the six fireplaces, air conditioning, gazebo, herb garden, and courtyard. Near New Hope, Peddler's Village and Nockamixon State Park. AAA Three Diamond approved.

Hosts: Barbara and Joe Szollosi
Rooms: 5 (PB) $85-125

6 Pets welcome; 8 Children welcome; 9 Social drinking allowed; 10 Tennis available; 11 Swimming available; 12 Golf available; 13 Skiing available; 14 May be booked through travel agents.

Full Breakfast
Credit Cards: A, B, C, D
Notes: 2, 5, 9, 11

Bucksville House

LAMPETER

Walkabout Inn
Bed and Breakfast
837 Village Road, P. O. Box 294, 17537
(717) 464-0707

This restored Mennonite home with
Australian hosts, features English gardens,
antiques, canopy beds, and fireplaces.
Candlelight breakfast includes homemade
pastries and tea from Down Under.
Specials include Amish dinner, tours, and
antique auctions. Romantic honeymoon
and anniversary suites are available, as are
coupons for local restaurants and attractions.

Hosts: Richard and Margaret Mason
Rooms: 5 (PB) $79-125
Full Breakfast
Credit Cards: A, B, C
Notes: 2, 4, 5, 8, 9, 10, 11, 12, 13, 14

LANCASTER

Bed and Breakfast
of Valley Forge #0303
P. O. Box 562, 19481-0562
(215) 783-7838; (800) 344-0123
FAX (215) 783-7783

The inn, circa 1735, is a splendid fieldstone
manor, perfectly situated overlooking picture postcard fields. Minutes from all the
attractions of Lancaster County, including
antiques and Amish farms. Eight rooms
with private baths. Full breakfast. $65-140.

Candlelite Inn
2574 Lincoln Highway East, Ronks, 17572
(717) 299-6005

Surrounded by Amish farmlands, this
1920s farmhouse offers four clean, quiet
guest rooms, sitting room with TV, central
air/heat, phone, and country breakfast. Two
rooms have private half-baths. Full baths
are shared. It is close to all attractions.
There is also an antiques and collectibles
shop on the premises.

Host: David W. Simpson
Rooms: 4 (SB) $55-65
Full Breakfast
Credit Cards: A, B, D

Hershey Bed and Breakfast
Reservation Service #1
P. O. Box 208, Hershey, 17033-0208
(717) 533-2928

Country farmhouse, circa 1817, situated on
a working dairy farm near Hershey,
Lancaster, and Harrisburg at Exit 20. Two
guest rooms with shared bath, plus a cottage that sleeps four with private bath. Full
breakfast. $55.

Hershey Bed and Breakfast
Reservation Service #2
P. O. Box 208, Hershey, 17033-0208
(717) 533-2928

Farmhouse inn, circa 1738, nestled on 12
acres of farmland in Lancaster County.
Situated just off Route 283 between Lancaster and Harrisburg. Three guest rooms
with private or shared bath. Continental
breakfast. Resident cat. $75-95.

NOTES: Credit cards accepted: A Master Card; B Visa; C American Express; D Discover Card; E Diner's
Club; F Other; 2 Personal Checks accepted; 3 Lunch available; 4 Dinner available; 5 Open all year;

Hershey Bed and Breakfast Reservation Service #3

P. O. Box 208, Hershey, 17033-0208
(717) 533-2928

Historic Civil War brick house situated near Routes 30 and 501. Seven guest rooms, including family suites, with private or shared bath. Continental breakfast. $75-85; $95 for family of four with private bath.

Homestead Lodging

Homestead Lodging

184 East Brook Road, Smoketown, 17576
(717) 393-6927

Come to this beautiful Lancaster County setting, where guests hear the clippity-clop of Amish buggies go by and can experience the sights and freshness of our farmlands. Clean country rooms provide a homey atmosphere, and an Amish farm is adjacent to our property. There is a large grassy area and a creek to enjoy. Within walking distance of restaurants and within minutes of farmers' markets, quilt, antiques and craft shops, outlets, auctions, and museums.

Hosts: Robert and Lori Kepiro
Rooms: 5 (PB) $28-49
Continental Breakfast
Credit Cards: A, B
Notes: 2 (deposit only), 5, 8, 9, 10, 11, 12

The King's Cottage, A Bed and Breakfast Inn

1049 East King Street, 17602
(800) 747-8717

Traditionally styled elegance, modern comfort, and warm hospitality in Amish country. King and queen beds, private baths, gourmet breakfasts, and personal service create a friendly atmosphere at this award-winning Spanish-style mansion. Relax by the fire and enjoy afternoon tea in the library while chatting with innkeepers about directions to restaurants or attractions. Special Amish dinners or personal tours arranged. Near farmers' markets, Gettysburg, and Hershey. On the National Register of Historic Places. AAA and Mobil-listed excellent.

Hosts: Karen and Jim Owens
Rooms: 7 (PB) $100-120
Full Breakfast
Credit Cards: A, B, D
Notes: 2, 5, 9, 10, 11, 12, 14

The King's Cottage

Lincoln Haus Inn Bed and Breakfast

1687 Lincoln Highway East, 17602
(717) 392-9412

Centrally situated in Lancaster County. A suburban home, built in 1915, with distinctive hip roofs. Front porch for sitting and double lawn swings for relaxing. Inside are natural oak woodwork and gleaming hard-

6 Pets welcome; 8 Children welcome; 9 Social drinking allowed; 10 Tennis available; 11 Swimming available; 12 Golf available; 13 Skiing available; 14 May be booked through travel agents.

wood floors. Antique furniture and rugs are throughout the house. The hostess, a member of the Old Order Amish church, serves a full breakfast family-style in her shining, homey dining room. Her specialty is to be a great hostess.

Host: Mary K. Zook
Rooms: 5 plus apartment (PB) $43-70
Full Breakfast
Credit Cards: None
Notes: 2, 5, 8, 14

O'Flaherty's Dingeldein House

1105 East King Street, 17602
(717) 293-1723; (800) 779-7756

O'Flaherty's Dingeldein House is the former residence of the Armstrong family of the floor tile fortune. Since its original construction in 1912, portions have been added, and other owners have included the Leath family, founders of the Strasburg Railroad Museum. Each of the air-conditioned guest rooms has been individually decorated and has a unique personality. Available are several common areas with fireplaces, a spacious porch, and beautiful landscaped gardens.

Hosts: Jack and Sue Flatley
Rooms: 4 (2 PB; 2 SB) $60-70
Full Breakfast
Credit Cards: A, B, D
Notes: 2, 5, 8, 12

Vogt Farm Bed and Breakfast

1225 Colebrook Road, 17547
(717) 653-4810

Vogt Farm guests are treated like friends by the hosts of this bed and breakfast. The guest rooms are decorated with antiques and other family treasures. Guests are welcome to enjoy the fireplace in the livingroom, cozy porches, and air conditioning. Breakfast is served at 8:30 A.M. weekdays, and 8:00 A.M. on Sunday in the large farm kitchen. Air-conditioned, spacious yard, three porches, animals.

Rooms: 3 (SB) $55
Full Breakfast
Credit Cards: A, B, C, D
Notes: 2, 5, 8, 12

LANDENBERG

Cornerstone Bed and Breakfast

Rural Delivery 1, Box 155, 19350
(215) 274-2143

To understand history is to live it. Charming 18th-century country inn with canopy beds, fireplaces in bedrooms, private baths, and antiques galore situated minutes from Brandywine Valley museums and gardens: Longwood, Winterthur, Hagley.

Hosts: Linda and Marty
Rooms: 5 (PB) $75-130
Full Breakfast
Credit Cards: A, B, C, D
Notes: 2, 5, 8, 9, 10, 11, 12

LANSDALE

Bed and Breakfast of Valley Forge #0703

P. O. Box 562, 19481-0562
(215) 783-7838; (800) 344-0123
FAX (215) 783-7783

This circa 1880 carriage house is completely private. It has a 1940s jukebox, wood-burning stove, and kitchenette. Outside is an enclosed private patio with a swing and pool. Full breakfast. $75.

LIMA

Amanda's Bed and Breakfast #279

1428 Park Avenue Annapolis, MD 21217
(301) 225-0001; (301) 383-1274

This bed and breakfast is a large 19th-century country manor house. Built in 1856, it has been on the National Register of Historic Places since 1971. More than three-fourths of the land is covered with luxuriant growth. Eight guest rooms, all with private baths, are available. $85-125.

LITITZ

Alden House

62 East Main Street, 17543
(717) 627-3363; (800) 584-0753

Fully restored 1850 town house situated in the heart of the town's historic district. All local attractions are within walking distance. Relax at the day's end one one of three spacious porches, and watch Amish buggies or experience a whiff of fresh chocolate from the local candy factory. Home of the nation's oldest pretzel bakery. Family suites, off-street parking, Amish dining and bicycle storage available. Antiques abound in this area, as well as local handmade quilts. Enjoy old-fashioned hospitality.

Host: Gloria Adams
Rooms: 7 (5 PB; 2 SB) $65-95
Continental Breakfast
Credit Cards: A, B
Notes: 2, 5, 8 (over 6), 9

MALVERN

Eaglesmere

Bed and Breakfast of Valley Forge, #0702
P. O. Box 562, Valley Forge, 19481-0562
(215) 783-7838; (800) 344-0123
FAX (215) 733-7783

This 21-sided contemporary home is nestled on a wooded cul-de-sac. It boasts three cathedral ceilings, exposed beams, and walls of windows overlooking Great Valley and Valley Forge Mountain. A gourmet breakfast is served in the dining room or on one of four decks. The enormous lower level contains the guest quarters. Preheated beds, bath gels, bathroom toe warmers, and thick terry-cloth robes are provided for your pleasure. Two guest rooms with private bath. Also a Jacuzzi, sauna, and billiards table for guests to enjoy. $75-85.

Eaglesmere

MARIETTA

The River Inn

258 West Front Street, 17547
(717) 426-2290

Restored home, circa 1790, situated in National Historic District of Marietta. Centrally situated, along Susquehanna River, near Lancaster, York, and Hershey attractions. Decorated with antiques and reproductions, this home offers three cozy guest rooms. When weather permits, breakfast is served on the screened porch. In the winter, warm your body with the six fireplace throughout the home. Enjoy the herb and flower gardens. Owner can provide guided boat fishing on river. Air conditioning, cable TV.

Hosts: Joyce and Bob Heiserman
Rooms: 3 (PB) $60-70
Full Breakfast
Credit Cards: A, B, D
Notes: 2, 5, 9, 14

6 Pets welcome; 8 Children welcome; 9 Social drinking allowed; 10 Tennis available; 11 Swimming available; 12 Golf available; 13 Skiing available; 14 May be booked through travel agents.

MERCER

Magoffin Inn

129 South Pitt Street, 16137
(412) 662-4611

Visit the Magoffin Inn and be reminded of
a gentler, quieter era. The house, a Queen
Anne Victorian, was built in 1884 by Dr.
Montrose Magoffin. It boasts nine guest
rooms for weary travelers and is completely furnished in antiques. Other amenities
include cable TV and working fireplaces.

Host: Jacque McClelland and Judy Forrester
Rooms: 9 (PB) $60-100
Full Breakfast
Credit Cards: A, B, C
Notes: 2, 3, 4, 5, 8, 10, 11, 12

MERTZTOWN

Longswamp Bed and Breakfast

Rural Delivery 2, Box 26, 19539
(215) 682-6197

This 200-year-old home, furnished with
antiques and every comfort, is set in gorgeous countryside, yet is close to Reading,
Kutztown, Allentown, and Amish country.
Delicious, bountiful breakfasts draw raves
from guests.

Hosts: Elsa and Dean Dimick
Rooms: 10 (6 PB; 4 SB) $63-79.50
Full Breakfast
Credit Cards: A, B
Notes: 2, 5, 8, 9, 10, 11, 12, 13

MIDDLETOWN

Hershey Bed and Breakfast Reservation Service

P. O. Box 208, Hershey, 17033-0208
(717) 533-2928

Gracious home set on nine acres of land
with a deck facing the woods. Just 10 minutes from Hershey Park and local attractions. Two guest bedrooms with shared
bath. Full breakfast. $50.

MOUNT AIRY

Bed and Breakfast Connections #00321

P. O. Box 21, Devon, 19333
(215) 687-3565; (800) 448-3619 (outside PA)

This 12-room stone home features
Scandinavian decor and carved woodwork.
The quaint shops and restaurants of
Chestnut Hill are only a short walk away.
Accommodations in this turn-of-the-century Victorian are on the third floor.
Hand-stenciled walls, handwoven fabrics,
and lace curtains make it an inviting home
away from home. On weekends, a full
gourmet breakfast is served and afternoon
tea is available in the parlor. A
continental-plus breakfast is provided during the week. Resident cats. $50-60.

MOUNT JOY

Cedar Hill Farm

305 Longenecker Road, 17552
(717) 653-4655

Cedar Hill Farm

Green Acres Farm

This 1817 stone farmhouse sits in a quiet area overlooking a stream. The charming bedrooms have private baths and are centrally air-conditioned. The farm is situated near Amish farms and Hershey. Other attractions are nearby farmers' markets, antique shops, and interesting country villages. Gift certificates available.

Hosts: Russell and Gladys Swarr
Rooms: 5 (PB) $60-65
Continental Breakfast
Credit Cards: A, B, C, D
Notes: 2, 5, 8, 9, 10, 11, 12

Green Acres Farm Bed and Breakfast

1382 Pinkerton Road, 17552
(717) 653-4028; FAX (717) 653-2840

This 160-acre farm has pony cart rides, trampoline, swings, kittens, chickens, goats and hogs. The house is furnished in antiques and is air-conditioned. A full farmer's breakfast is served. There is also an efficiency house next door, rented by the week, that sleeps 12.

Hosts: Wayne and Yvonne Miller
Rooms: 10 (5 PB; 5 S2B) $45-55
Full Breakfast
Credit Cards: A, B
Notes: 2, 5, 6, 8, 9, 10, 11, 12

Rocky Acre Farm

1020 Pinkerton Road, 17552
(717) 653-4449

Come relax, enjoy farm life in a peaceful community. A 200-year old stone house, which was used as a station for the Underground Railroad. Start the day with a farmer's breakfast, milking a cow, or feeding the calves. Guests may even discover a calf being born. Boating and fishing is also available in the creek. The farm is for children of all ages. Enjoy the cats and dogs and a wake up call by the rooster. Guests will find a warm welcome here at Rocky Acre Farm. Visitors have been enjoying this hospitality for more than 25 years.

Hosts: Galen and Eileen Benner
Rooms: 8 (5 PB; 3 SB) $45-55
Full Breakfast
Credit Cards: None
Notes: 2, 5, 8, 10, 12, 13

MOUNT POCONO

Farmhouse Bed and Breakfast

HCR 1, Box 6 B, 18344
(717) 839-0796

"Where the Honor of Our House is Hospitality." An 1850 homestead on six manicured acres. Separate cottage and two suites in house, all with fireplace. Farm-style breakfast complete with original country recipes prepared by the host, a professional chef. Enjoy bedtime snacks fresh-

Farmhouse

6 Pets welcome; 8 Children welcome; 9 Social drinking allowed; 10 Tennis available; 11 Swimming available; 12 Golf available; 13 Skiing available; 14 May be booked through travel agents.

ly baked each day. Antiques adorn each room, with cleanliness being the order of the day. Accommodations have private baths, queen beds, TV, phones, and air conditioning.

Hosts: Jack and Donna Asure
Rooms: 3 (PB) $75-95
Full Breakfast
Credit Cards: A, B, D
Notes: 5, 9, 10, 11, 12, 13

MUNCY

The Bodine House

307 South Main Street, 17756
(717) 546-8949

Built in 1805 and situated in the National Historic District of Muncy, the Bodine House offers guests the opportunity to enjoy the atmosphere of an earlier age. The comfortable rooms are furnished with antiques, and candlelight is used in the livingroom by the fireplace, where guests enjoy refreshments. Three blocks from town center, movies, restaurants, library, and shops.

Hosts: David and Marie Louise Smith
Rooms: 4 (3 PB; 1 SB) $50-75
Full Breakfast
Credit Cards: A, B, C
Notes: 2, 5, 8 (over 6), 9, 10, 11, 12, 13, 14

The Bodine House

NEW CUMBERLAND

Hershey Bed and Breakfast Reservation Service

P. O. Box 208, Hershey, 17033-0208
(717) 533-2928

An 11-room limestone farmhouse that sits on three acres high on a hill overlooking Yellow Breeches Creek. Legend has it that this house was part of the Underground Railroad. Each guest room has a double bed and comfortable seating with good lighting. One room has a private bath; two rooms share a bath. Two rooms have large porches to enjoy in good weather. Antique furnishings throughout. Full breakfast. $65-70; $15/additional person.

NEWFOUNDLAND

Buena Vista

P. O. Box 195, Route 447, 18445
(717) 676-3800

Come and relax in rural northeastern Pennsylvania. High above the valley floor, the inn overlooks the village of Newfoundland. The buildings began as a Maravian farm in the 1800s, and have been converted to a country inn. The location in the Lake Wallenpaupack watershed region offers natural beauty and ample opportunities for recreation, shopping and dining. A pool is situated on the property. Breakfast is served, and other meals can be made available. Reservations required.

Hosts: Dave and Denise Keevil
Rooms: 25 (13 PB; 12 SB) $35-45
Full Breakfast
Credit Cards: A, B
Notes: 2, 5, 8, 11, 12, 13

White Cloud

Rural Delivery 1, Box 215, 18445
(717) 676-3162

NOTES: Credit cards accepted: A Master Card; B Visa; C American Express; D Discover Card; E Diner's Club; F Other; 2 Personal Checks accepted; 3 Lunch available; 4 Dinner available; 5 Open all year;

This is a meatless, natural foods inn and restaurant with 45 acres of woodland, tennis court, pool, library, and meditation room. Situated three miles south of Newfoundland on Route 447. Specialties are peace, quiet, and good food.

Host: George Wilkinson
Rooms: 20 (7 PB; 13 SB) $37.75-63.50
Full Breakfast
Credit Cards: A, B, D
Notes: 2, 3, 4, 5, 6, 8, 9, 10, 11, 12, 13, 14

NEW HOPE—SEE ALSO WRIGHTSTOWN

Aaron Burr House

80 West Bridge Street, 18938
(215) 862-2343

This vintage village Victorian inn sits atop a residential tree-lined street in New Hope's historic district. Named for the U.S. vice president who sought a safe haven in Bucks County in 1804, Aaron Burr House offers today's business and pleasure travelers similar refuge. Three Diamonds, AAA approved.

Hosts: Nadine and Carl Glassman
Rooms: 6 (PB) $100-160
Continental Breakfast
Minimum stay weekends: 2 nights; holidays: 3 nights
Credit Cards: C
Notes: 2, 5, 8, 9, 10, 11, 12, 13, 14

Ash Mill Farm Country Bed and Breakfast

P. O. Box 202, 18928
(215) 794-5373

Circa 1790 Manor house on 11 sheep-filled acres just minutes from Peddler's Village and New Hope. Full gourmet breakfast and afternoon tea served to the sounds of Mozart and Brahms. Enjoy the fireplace in winter or our flowered patio in summer. Walking paths abound through the nurseries, where berries, bunnies and deer abound. Discounts for stays of more than four days and during mid-week. Beautifully furnished rooms, cited by *Gourmet* and *Family Circle* magazines.

Hosts: Patricia and Jim Auscander
Rooms: 6 (4 PB; 2 SB) $85-125
Full Breakfast
Credit Cards: A, B, C
Notes: 2, 5, 9, 10, 12, 14

Wedgwood Inn of New Hope

111 West Bridge Street, 18938
(215) 862-2570

Voted Inn of the Year by readers of inn guidebooks, this historic inn, on two acres of landscaped grounds, is steps from the village center. Antiques, fresh flowers, and Wedgewood china are the rule at the inn, where guests are treated like royalty. AAA Three Diamonds. Also offers seminars for those interested in innkeeping.

Hosts: Carl A. Glassman and Nadine Silnutzer
Rooms: 12 (10 PB; 2 SB) $70-160
Continental Breakfast
Credit Cards: C
Notes: 2, 5, 8, 9, 10, 11, 12, 13, 14

The Whitehall Inn

Rural Delivery 2, Box 250, 18938
(215) 598-9745

Experience a 1794 estate with fireplaces in rooms, heirloom sterling, European crystal and china. Afternoon high tea, chamber music, velour robes, chocolate truffles. Swimming pool on premises, dressage horses, roses, and the legendary four-course candlelight breakfast featured in *Bon Appetit, Gourmet,* and *Food and Wine.*

Hosts: Mike and Suella Wass
Rooms: 6 (4 PB; 2 SB) $120-170
Full Breakfast
Minimum stay weekends: 2 nights; holidays: 3 nights
Credit Cards: A, B, C, D, E, F
Notes: 2, 5, 8 (over 12), 9, 10, 11, 12, 13, 14

6 Pets welcome; 8 Children welcome; 9 Social drinking allowed; 10 Tennis available; 11 Swimming available; 12 Golf available; 13 Skiing available; 14 May be booked through travel agents.

NEW RINGGOLD

Windmill Farm
Rural Delivery 1, Box 95, 17960
(717) 386-4701

Windmill Farm is situated 35 miles north of Allentown, one mile off Route 309 in the beautiful Blue Mountain area. Guests will enjoy the coziness of a four-room cottage, beautifully furnished with all facilities provided, including bath, bedroom towels, and linens. A fully equipped kitchen is provided for guests to use. Golf, swimming, horseback riding, Hawk Mountain, the Appalachian Trail, and other historical sites are nearby.

Hosts: Peter and Jenny Beck
Rooms: 4 cabins (PB) $35 per day
Credit Cards: None
Notes: 2, 8, 9, 10, 11, 12

NEWTOWN SQUARE

Bed and Breakfast Connections
P. O. Box 21, Devon, 19333
(215) 687-3565; (800) 448-3619 (outside PA)

Built in 1715, this pre-Revolutionary farmhouse overlooking Ridley Creek State Park has been faithfully restored and carefully maintained by the resident innkeepers. The old hearth and bake oven are still in use, as well as a restored fireplace with a mantel of orange chestnut. The dining room is a fine example of Federal period craftsmanship, and dates back to 1826. The largest guest room has a canopied double bed, working fireplace and attached private bath. A large spinning wheel occupies a corner of the pleasant twin bedroom, and the light and airy double room features a built-in desk. These two rooms share a bath. Resident cat. $70-105 fall-winter; $70-90 spring-summer.

PALMYRA

Hershey Bed and Breakfast Reservation Service
P. O. Box 208, Hershey, 17033-0208
(717) 533-2928

Situated on the edge of town surrounded by one acre of country pleasures is this circa 1825 Georgian-style farmhouse. A warm "down home" atmosphere prevails throughout, offering simple hospitality and comfort away from the hustle and bustle of the city. The six air-conditioned rooms offer private baths and cozy informal comfort. A full breakfast is served from 8:00 to 9:30 A.M., and afternoon or early evening refreshments provide a relaxing break from the day's activities. $65.

PAOLI

The General's Inn
Bed and Breakfast of Valley Forge #0701
P. O. Box 562, Valley Forge, 19481-0562
(215) 783-7838; (800) 344-0123
FAX (215) 783-7783

This inn has been in service since 1745. It is authentically restored and furnished; and air-conditioned. Eight complete suites, three with fireplaces and one with Jacuzzi. The first floor is an upscale restaurant and lounge open to the public for lunch and dinner. A continental breakfast is served in the dining room. No pets; no children under 12. $85-135.

The Great Valley House
Bed and Breakfast of Valley Forge #0203
P. O. Box 562, Valley Forge, 19481-0562
(215) 783-7838; (800) 344-0123
FAX (215) 783-7783

Situated on four acres, this 15-room stone farmhouse, built in 1692, is the second oldest in the state. It is one of the 100 oldest in the country. The original flooring, exposed beams, hand-wrought hinges, and fireplaces add to the charm. An English breakfast is served in front of the walk-in fireplace in the kitchen. Each of the three guest rooms is hand-stenciled, accented with handmade quilts, air-conditioned, furnished with antiques, TV, and radio. Refrigerator, coffee pot, and microwave are provided for guests. Swimming pool. $70-75.

PARADISE

Maple Lane Guest House

505 Paradise Lane, 17562
(717) 687-7479

In the heart of Amish country in Lancaster County, guests will find this working dairy farm with winding stream and woodland. Clean, comfortable, air-conditioned rooms have TV, canopy and poster beds, handmade quilts, wall stenciling, and antiques. Close to all the Pennsylvania Dutch attractions such as farmers' markets, outlets, historic sites, and excellent restaurants. See the dairy in operation.

Hosts: Edwin and Marion Rohrer
Rooms: 4 (2 PB; 2 SB) $45-60
Continental Breakfast
Minimum stay weekends and holidays: 2 nights
Credit Cards: None
Notes: 2, 5, 8, 10, 12

PHILADELPHIA

Bed and Breakfast Connections #00108

P. O. Box 21, Devon, 19333
(215) 687-3565; (800) 448-3619 (outside PA)

This charming town house is situated just off Rittenhouse Square on a lovely city street. The focal point of magnificently appointed guest rooms is the massive walnut antique double bed beautifully adorned with a Marsailles spread. Select a book,

make a cup of hot tea from the electric kettle, and curl up on the Hide-a-bed sofa to rest from the day's activities. All the comforts of home are here, including a small refrigerator tucked behind closet doors. Private adjoining bath. Private entrance. Gourmet continental breakfast. Resident cats. $70-75.

Bed and Breakfast Connections #00111

P. O. Box 21, Devon, 19333
(215) 687-3565; (800) 448-3619

This historic registered row home provides generous third-floor guest quarters and is convenient to the University of Pennsylvania, Drexel University, the Civic Center, and Children's Hospital. At one end of the third floor, guests will find a bedroom that can accommodate a family with its two twin beds and a double. The sitting room is at the opposite end of the hall and is perfect for relaxing in front of the TV or curling up with a book. Private bath. Laundry facilities and refrigerator space are available. $45-55.

Bed and Breakfast Connections #00114

P. O. Box 21, Devon, 19333
(215) 687-3565; (800) 448-3619 (outside PA)

This 1811 historic registered town house was purchased as a shell and has been interestingly renovated and decorated to retain much of its original charm. Its Society Hill address is right in the hub of historic Philadelphia, and close by are the attractions of New Market Square and South Street. The original "tight winder" stairs lead to the third-floor guest room that is tastefully, yet simply, furnished. One large room has a fireplace, settee, and double bed with a private adjoining bath, and a second room with a double and private

6 Pets welcome; 8 Children welcome; 9 Social drinking allowed; 10 Tennis available; 11 Swimming available; 12 Golf available; 13 Skiing available; 14 May be booked through travel agents.

adjoining bath is available also. A full breakfast is served in the kitchen, where the original exposed beams add to the warmth and charm of the home. $50-60.

Bed and Breakfast Connections #00122

P. O. Box 21, Devon, 19333
(215) 687-3565; (800) 448-3619 (outside PA)

Complete third-floor privacy awaits the guest in this town house situated on Antique Row within walking distance of the historic district. Simply, yet tastefully, furnished, this guest room is bright and inviting with double bed accommodations, TV, and phone. Sliding glass doors lead to a deck where guests can relax and enjoy the city skyline and the beauty of the patio gardens below. With a private adjoining bath and full breakfast, this accommodation could not be more perfect for the business traveler or the long term guest. $45-55.

Bed and Breakfast Connections #00147

P. O. Box 21, Devon, 19333
(215) 687-3565; (800) 448-3619 (outside PA)

Built between 1805 and 1810 and redone after the Civil War in Federalist style, this charming Society Hill town house saw further renovation when its current owners bought it as a shell some 20 years ago. The creative host has done much of the renovation himself, finding unusual artifacts in old churches and homes in the city that have created a unique and inviting atmosphere. The second-floor bedroom offers a color TV, phone jack, and individual thermostat with a private hall bath. On the third floor there are two more rooms, one with a trundle bed and a queen-size bed and the other with a double bed. All rooms have an individual thermostat, TV, and private bath. Continental breakfast is served in the pleas-

ant kitchen in the winter or on the patio in the warm months. Two-night minimum stay on weekends. $75-80.

Bed and Breakfast Connections #00152

P. O. Box 21, Devon, 19333
(215) 687-3565; (800) 448-3619 (outside PA)

A comfortably furnished room provides pleasant accommodations in a friendly homestyle atmosphere at a surprisingly affordable price. This row house, on a quaint historic registered residential block is situated within walking distance of the University of Pennsylvania, Children's Hospital, and the Civic Center. The historic sites and museums of Center City are just ten minutes away and easily accessible with public transportation. The spacious third-floor room includes an antique oak double bed and armoire. A private hall bath with an old-fashioned tub and shower is available. Full breakfast. $45-55.

Bed and Breakfast Connections #00156

P. O. Box 21, Devon, 19333
(215) 687-3565; (800) 448-3619 (outside PA)

Conveniently situated two blocks from the Italian Market and two blocks from Antique Row, this home offers private third-floor accommodations. The double bedded guest room furnished with antiques and collectibles has a sitting room and a private attached bath. A large collection of books is available for guests to enjoy during their stay. The hosts are fluent in Portuguese and French, and have a deep interest in music. Breakfast is a hearty continental with delicious pastries, fresh fruit, and coffees and teas from nearby bakeries and markets. $45-55.

NOTES: Credit cards accepted: A Master Card; B Visa; C American Express; D Discover Card; E Diner's Club; F Other; 2 Personal Checks accepted; 3 Lunch available; 4 Dinner available; 5 Open all year;

All About Town B & B in Philadelphia #1914

P. O. Box 562, Valley Forge, 19481-0562
(215) 783-7838; (800) 344-0123
FAX (215) 783-7783

The second-floor suite has a view of Rittenhouse Square, and the location is readily accessible to all Philadelphia historical sites and events. $85.

All About Town B & B in Philadelphia #2002

P. O. Box 562, Valley Forge, 19481-0562
(215) 783-7838; (800) 344-0123
FAX (215) 783-7783

The third floor is a charming apartment area with full kitchen that offers a family a truly private area. Old fashioned porches shade the house, one in the front, the other off the kitchen.

Chestnut Hill Bed and Breakfast

All About Town-B&B in Philadelphia #1907
P. O. Box 562, Valley Forge, 19481-0562
(215) 783-7838; (800) 344-0123
FAX (215) 783-7783

This home is a lovely renovated old stone schoolhouse. The atmosphere exudes the warmth and welcome of a cozy fire on a cold day. Its location in the historic area of Chestnut Hill in Philadelphia reminds one of the early days of this great nation. There are three guest rooms sharing two full baths. A full beakfast is served. $70.

Country Inn the City

All About Town-B&B in Philadelphia #0206
P. O. Box 562, Valley Forge, 19481-0562
(215) 783-7838; (800) 344-0123
FAX (215) 783-7783

This 12-room country inn in the historic area of Philadelphia is a restored, circa 1769, guest house within Independence National Historic Park. All rooms are individually decorated and have private baths, telephones, TV, and period furniture. An enclosed parking garage is next door. Continental breakfast is served weekdays and a full breakfast on weekends. Walk to restaurants and the major historic sites in Philadelphia . $95-140.

Historic Philadelphia Bed and Breakfast

All About Town-B&B in Philadelphia #2203
P. O. Box 562, Valley Forge, 19481-0562
(215) 783-7838; (800) 344-0123
FAX (215) 783-7783

This circa 1811 certified historic home is situated near Society Hill. Guests have access to the city while also enjoying a historic atmosphere. Two guest rooms with private bath. Full breakfast. $65.

La Reserve Bed and Breakfast of Center City

1804 Pine Street, 19103
(215) 735-1137; (215) 735-0582
(800) 354-8401

Known by many as Center City Bed and Breakfast and by all as "The Grand Dame of Philadelphia," this 140-year old town house reflects the elegance of the city's historic past while offering a warm and cozy retreat in a hustling modern city. The suites feature king or queen beds and a private bath, while the other bedrooms have double or twin beds with shared baths. Sip a glass of wine or sherry in the drawing room or play the grand piano. La Reserve is close to several national monuments, including the Liberty Bell, Congress Hall, and the U.S. Mint, as well as the Philadelphia Museum of Art and Rodin Museum.

---

6 Pets welcome; 8 Children welcome; 9 Social drinking allowed; 10 Tennis available; 11 Swimming available; 12 Golf available; 13 Skiing available; 14 May be booked through travel agents.

Host: Bill Buchanan
Rooms: 7 (3 PB; 4 SB) $40-80
Full Breakfast
Credit Cards: A, B
Notes: 2, 8, 10, 14

Marietta's Bed and Breakfast

All About Town-B&B in Philadelphia #1401
P. O. Box 562, Valley Forge, 19481-0562
(215) 783-7838; (800) 344-0123
FAX: (215) 783-7783

This turn-of-the-century elegant town house has high ceilings and is furnished throughout with antiques and artwork. Ideally situated for access to Center City, Rittenhouse Square, and an elegant shopping area. Good restaurants abound. $75.

Society Hill Bed and Breakfast

All About Town-B&B in Philadelphia #0104
P. O. Box 562, Valley Forge, 19481-0562
(215) 783-7838; (800) 344-0123
FAX (215) 783-7783

This town house was built about 1805 and renovated in the Federal style during the post-Civil War era. Four guest rooms with private bath, individual thermostat control for heat and air conditioning, and TV. Full breakfast. During warm weather, breakfast may be served on the patio. One and one-half blocks to Independence Hall. If guests stay over a Saturday night, there is a two-night minimum. $80.

The Spite House

All About Town-B&B in Philadelphia #0801
P. O. Box 562, Valley Forge, 19481-0562
(215) 783-7838; (800) 344-0123
FAX (215) 783-7783

This historically certified home is associated with the Museum Council of Philadelphia and Delaware Valley, and the Historical Society of Pennsylvania. This is one of the "spite houses," so called because it was built, according to legend, with its back to its neighbors. Full breakfast served. The first floor houses the kitchen, with its Victorian oak oval table and wash stand. The second level features the parlor with grand piano and dining room and butler's pantry with original soapstone sink and dumbwaiter. In Mount Airy amid the Lutheran Seminary, Spring Garden College, and the Coombs College of Music. Near train station. $60-65.

Spruce Garden Bed and Breakfast

All About Town-B&B in Philadelphia #0205
P. O. Box 562, Valley Forge, 19481-0562
(215) 783-7838; (800) 344-0123
FAX (215) 783-7783

Guest quarters are a private first-floor suite in an 1840 town house ideally situated in Center City Philadelphia. A full breakfast is served in the second-floor dining area. The guest suite consists of two bedrooms, two bathrooms, and a sitting room for reading, TV, or cards. If both rooms are rented at the same time, the occupants must be relatives or good friends, as guests must pass through one bedroom to get out or enter the other. $60-65.

Trade Winds Bed and Breakfast

All About Town-B&B in Philadelphia #0101
P. O. Box 562, Valley Forge, 19481-0562
(215) 783-7838; (800) 344-0123
FAX (215) 783-7783

NOTES: Credit cards accepted: A Master Card; B Visa; C American Express; D Discover Card; E Diner's Club; F Other; 2 Personal Checks accepted; 3 Lunch available; 4 Dinner available; 5 Open all year;

This historically certified town house was built in 1790. Two third-floor guest rooms are elegantly appointed with collectibles and Old World antiques. Each room has color cable TV, phone, central air conditioning, and the twin room has a refrigerator. A full breakfast is served on the French Empire table in the dining area. For special occasions, guests may consider a very large second-floor guest room with antique brass bed, fireplace, color cable TV, phone, private bath, air conditioning. Situated on the Washington Square/Society Hill border. Six blocks to Independence Hall and one block to South Street. Public tennis courts across the street. $65 for rooms; $100 for fireplace suite.

Trinity Bed and Breakfast

All About Town-B&B in Philadelphia #2101
P. O. Box 562, Valley Forge, 19481-0562
(215) 783-7838; (800) 344-0123
FAX (215) 783-7783

This home is one of four situated in a small court in the lovely and quiet Rittenhouse Square section within the bustle of the city. Guests have access to all the attractions of the city and still enjoy a private retreat after a day of sightseeing. $75.

Washington Square Bed and Breakfast

All About Town-B&B in Philadelphia #1601
P. O. Box 562, Valley Forge, 19481-0562
(215) 783-7838; (800) 344-0123
FAX (215) 783-7783

Built in the 1830s, this three-story Colonial town house is situated on one of Society Hill's narrow, cobblestone streets just blocks from Independence Hall. A wisteria-covered patio with a bubbling fountain welcomes guests in the summer. In the winter, a Franklin stove in the guests' parlor warms them. $60.

PHOENIXVILLE

Manor House

Bed and Breakfast of Valley Forge #0301
P. O. Box 562, Valley Forge, 19481-0562
(215) 783-7838; (800) 344-0123
FAX (215) 783-7783

Built in 1928 by a British executive, this English Tudor home stands on a lovely sycamore-lined street. It boasts a massive slate roof and original red oak flooring and stairway. The spacious livingroom and cozy den both have fireplaces. Gourmet breakfasts are served in the formal dining room or on the brick-floored screened porch overlooking the garden. Complimentary bedtime beverage and snack in the room. Five guest rooms, three with private bath. $45-70.

Tinker Hill Bed and Breakfast

Bed and Breakfast of Valley Forge #0210
P. O. Box 562, Valley Forge, 19481-0562
(215) 783-7838; (800) 344-0123
FAX (215) 783-7783

This contemporary house on two and one-half acres is in a private, wooded area. Two-story glass-walled livingroom. Guest rooms are separated from the suite and overlook the woods. Hot tub on the deck, swimming pool. Full breakfast. $60-65.

POCONO MOUNTAINS

Nearbrook Bed and Breakfast

Rural Delivery 1, Box 630, Canadensis, 18325
(717) 595-3152

Meander through rock garden paths and enjoy the roses, woods, and stream at Nearbrook. A hearty breakfast is served on the outdoor porch. The hosts will join guests for morning conversation to help

6 Pets welcome; 8 Children welcome; 9 Social drinking allowed; 10 Tennis available; 11 Swimming available; 12 Golf available; 13 Skiing available; 14 May be booked through travel agents.

find trails for good hiking and to describe other areas of interest. A friendly informality encourages guests to play the upright piano and enjoy the many games. Restaurant menus, maps, and art lessons are available.

Hosts: Barbara and Dick Robinson
Rooms: 3 (1 PB; 2 SB) $45
Full Breakfast
Credit Cards: None
Notes: 2, 5, 8, 10, 11, 12, 13

Victoria Ann's Bed and Breakfast

Bed and Breakfast of Valley Forge #1502
P. O. Box 562, Valley Forge, 19481-0562
(215) 783-7838; (800) 344-0123
FAX (215) 783-7783

Built in 1860 on Millionaire's Row. Once guests step inside, they feel as if they have stepped back into time with all the delightful charms of antiques, lace, and elegant chandeliers of day gone by. Enjoy an air of leisurely 19th-century opulence, beautiful Victorian porches, garden terraces, and spacious rooms. Close to white-water rafting, swimming, walking, hunting, good restaurants, winter sports, and walking. $85-145.

QUAKERTOWN

Sign of the Sorrel Horse

243 Old Bethlehem Road, 18951
(215) 536-4651

Built in 1749 of stone, near Lake Nockamixon in Bucks County, as a stagecoach stop. Secluded on five manicured acres. A gracious country inn with five antique-filled rooms, each with private bath. Includes sherry and fruits in the common area and fine gourmet dining. Swimming pool. Garden weddings are a speciality. Near New Hope's Peddlers Village. Received food and wine DiRona award 1992. AAA Three-Star rated.

Hosts: Monique Gaumont-Lanvin and Jon Atkin
Rooms: 5 (PB) $85-125
Continental Breakfast
Credit Cards: A, B, C
Notes: 4, 9, 11, 13

RADNOR

Bed and Breakfast Connections #00220

P. O. Box 21, Devon, 19333
(215) 687-3565; (800) 448-3619 (outside PA)

This home-within-a-barn offers privacy, a refreshing night's sleep, and a delicious breakfast. The two-story entrance hall and stairway welcome guests to this 19th-century bank barn and its exposed post-and-beam construction. One room has a king bed, private bath, and dining area. Another room has twin beds and private bath. Both rooms have refrigerators. Breakfast is served in the room or in the great room with fireplace surrounded by English antiques and Japanese prints. Close to Gulph Creek, near the Schuylkill Expressway, Valley Forge/King of Prussia, and 20 minutes from downtown Philadelphia. Resident cat. $80-90.

Main Line Estate

Bed and Breakfast of Valley Forge #2601
P. O. Box 562, Valley Forge, 19481-0562
(215) 783-7838; (800) 344-0123
FAX (215) 783-7783

This expansive English Tudor, built in 1969, is surrounded by three and one-half acres of original grounds belonging to two estates owned by the brothers who made a local German beer. The spacious guest rooms can be reached privately by a back staircase. A full breakfast is served in the country French kitchen. Greenhouse, swimming pool, cabana, and tennis court. Washer/dryer, baby equipment, and cable TV available. $75.

NOTES: Credit cards accepted: A Master Card; B Visa; C American Express; D Discover Card; E Diner's Club; F Other; 2 Personal Checks accepted; 3 Lunch available; 4 Dinner available; 5 Open all year;

ROSEMONT

Conestoga Bed and Breakfast

Bed and Breakfast of Valley Forge #1802
P. O. Box 562, Valley Forge, 19481-0562
(215) 783-7838; (800) 344-0123
FAX (215) 783-7783

The hosts of this bed and breakfast inherited the home they were raised in. Guests have the privilege of the entire house. The interior of this 1890 home has been restored and furnished. Fully equipped kitchen, livingroom, dining room, sun room, two bedrooms, and bath. TV, on-site parking, grill, furnished patio. The kitchen is stocked with breakfast foods. $100 nightly.

SELINSGROVE

The Blue Lion Inn

350 South Market Street, 17870
(717) 374-2929

Experience a night in an authentic plantation home more than 150 years old. Situated in the heart of the Susquehanna Valley, known for its antique shops, farmers markets, picturesque landscapes, and beautiful fall foliage. Antique furnishings, gourmet breakfast and warm and friendly hospitality add to the atmosphere. A few blocks from Susquehanna University, and convenient to Bucknell University in Lewisburg.

Hosts: Kent and Marilyn Thomson
Rooms: 4 (PB) $52.50-62.50
Full Breakfast
Credit Cards: A, B, C
Notes: 2, 8, 9

SHIPPENSBURG

Wilmar Manor Bed and Breakfast

303 West King Street, 17257
(717) 532-3784

A friendly Victorian guest house, elegantly decorated with antiques offers serenity and beautifully unusual rock gardens. Stroll down Main Street of this historic village in the midst of the quiet Pennsylvania countryside.

Hosts: Wilton and Marise Banks
Rooms: 6 (2 PB; 4 SB) $45-60
Full Breakfast
Credit Cards: None
Notes: 2, 5, 8, 11, 12, 13

SKIPPACK

Highpoint Victoriana

Bed and Breakfast of Valley Forge #1908
P. O. Box 562, Valley Forge, 19481-0562
(215) 783-7838; (800) 344-0123
FAX (215) 783-7783

Dutch Colonial Victorian five-acre farmette consists of a barn with vintage cars and fields that serve as a Christmas tree farm. The house has been carefully restored and modernized in authentic keeping with the Victorian atmosphere. It is filled with lovely antiques. Enjoy a lovely wraparound porch in the summer, and a wood-burning stove to warm beside in the winter. Four guest rooms. $65-70.

SLIPPERY ROCK

Applebutter Inn

666 Centreville Pike, 16057
(412) 794-1844

This charming, original 1844 farmhouse was restored, renovated and now provides 11 beautifully appointed rooms with antiques and decorator linens. Breakfast is served and the adjacent Wolf Creek School Cafe. Breakfast and luncheon fare is prepared and served in the quaint atmosphere of a one-room schoolhouse, recently restored to its original state.

Hosts: Gary and Sandra McKnight
Rooms: 11 (PB) $69-115

6 Pets welcome; 8 Children welcome; 9 Social drinking allowed; 10 Tennis available; 11 Swimming available; 12 Golf available; 13 Skiing available; 14 May be booked through travel agents.

Full Breakfast
Credit Cards: A, B, C
Notes: 3, 4, 5, 10, 11, 12, 13

Applebutter Inn

SMOKETOWN

Old Road Guest Home

2501 Old Philadelphia Pike, 17576
(717) 393-8182

Situated in a small town that is nestled in the rolling Amish farmlands of the Pennsylvania Dutch country. Surrounded by a spacious, shaded lawn, with easy parking. There are comfortable air-conditioned rooms and "top of the line" mattresses. Ground floor rooms are available. Near the finest restaurants and the most popular attractions. Come enjoy this home.

Hosts: David and Marian Buckwalter
Rooms: 6 (3 PB; 3 SB) $ 28-35
Credit Cards: None
Notes: 2, 5, 8

SOMERSET

The Heart of Somerset

130 West Union Street, 15501
(814) 445-6782

A beautifully refurbished home built circa 1839. Antiques fill every room, and the wooden oak floors have been restored to their original beauty. Edison electric light fixtures grace the lower level, and each room is decorated differently, with eyelet comforters and pillow shams to enhance

that romantic feeling of the Victorian era. The Heart is a most restful getaway in the beautiful Laurel Highlands ski and biking country.

Hosts: Phyllis and Hank Vogt
Rooms: 6 (4 PB; 2 SB) $35-85
Continental Breakfast
Credit Cards: A, B, C, D
Notes: 2, 5, 9, 12, 13

STRASBURG

The Decoy

958 Eisenberger Road, 17579
(717) 687-8585

Situated in Amish farm country, the Decoy has a spectacular view. Formerly and Amish home, it features five guest rooms and serves a country breakfast. Strasburg is a great area for shopping, with wonderful crafts store, outlets, and for quilters, an ideal place to buy fabric or a quilt frame.

Hosts: Debby and Hap Joy
Rooms: 5 (PB) $40-60
Full Breakfast
Credit Cards: None
Notes: 2, 5, 8, 9, 11, 12

VALLEY FORGE

Bed and Breakfast of Valley Forge #0304

P. O. Box 562, 19481-0562
(215) 783-7838; (800) 344-0123
FAX (215) 783-7783

This private guest cottage is situated on a peaceful, 20-acre, pre-Revolutionary War farmstead, where horses and sheep graze and swans glide across a pond. $100.

Bed and Breakfast of Valley Forge #0904

P. O. Box 562, 19481-0562
(215) 783-7838; (800) 344-0123
FAX (215) 783-7783

NOTES: Credit cards accepted: A Master Card; B Visa; C American Express; D Discover Card; E Diner's Club; F Other; 2 Personal Checks accepted; 3 Lunch available; 4 Dinner available; 5 Open all year;

Completely private accommodations are offered in this 12-room old stone Colonial filled with antiques and country comfort. Terrace and grill are available for guest use. $90.

Bed and Breakfast of Valley Forge #1909

P. O. Box 562, 19481-0562
(215) 783-7838; (800) 344-0123
FAX (215) 783-7783

Behind an ivy-covered, circa 1770 house and beyond the barn is the cottage that formerly housed the master of the hounds of the old Valley Forge Hunt. Enjoy the view of the Valley Forge National Historical Park. $85-100.

Country Charm

Bed and Breakfast of Valley Forge #1203
P. O. Box 562, 19481-0562
(215) 783-7838; (800) 344-0123
FAX (215) 783-7783

This Colonial farmhouse is on three acres of an original William Penn land grant, and dates from the 1700s. The outbuildings include a smokehouse, springhouse, and outhouse. The home is cozy, comfortable, and furnished in traditional country style appropriate to the home's age, complete with antiques, quilts, and hand stenciling. A full breakfast is served in the cheerful dining room. $60-65.

Deep Well Farm

Bed and Breakfast of Valley Forge #0804
P. O. Box 562, 19481-0562
(215) 783-7838; (800) 344-0123
FAX (215) 783-7783

This 18th-century fieldstone farmhouse has 16-inch thick walls and exposed beams overhead. Originally it was part of Gen. Anthony Wayne's estate. The two and one-half acres accommodate a horse barn and a

pond where geese gather. The bedrooms are spacious and comfortable, cooled by ceiling fans. A full breakfast is served in the country dining room or kitchen. A parrot and two horses reside. One mile to Valley Forge Park; one-half mile to Valley Forge Music Fair. $45-65.

Valley Forge Mt. Bed and Breakfast

Box 562, 19481
(215) 783-7838; (800) 344-0123
FAX (215) 783-7783

George Washington had headquarters here. Centrally situated between Philadelphia, Lancaster County, Reading outlets, and Brandywine Valley. French Colonial on three wooded acres adjacent to Valley Forge Park. Air conditioning, complimentary breakfast, guest room telephone, TV, VCR, computer, printer, FAX, two fireplaces. Bridle and hiking trail. Finest shopping, antiquing, restaurants, cross-country skiing, horseback riding, golf within minutes. California king and single/sitting room with private bath. Double/sitting room with private bath.

Host: Carolyn Williams
Rooms: 2 (PB) $45-65
Full Breakfast
Credit Cards: A, B, C, E
Notes: 2, 3, 5, 6, 7, 8, 9, 10, 11, 12, 13, 14

VILLANOVA

English Regency

Bed and Breakfast of Valley Forge #1903
P. O. Box 562, Valley Forge, 19481-0562
(215) 783-7838; (800) 344-0123
FAX (215) 783-7783

This home, featured on house tours, is situated on one and one-half acres in an elegant, quiet, wooded area. It is furnished with antiques, art, and Oriental rugs. The two guest rooms are beautifully appointed and includes a graceful canopy bed, leather

6 Pets welcome; 8 Children welcome; 9 Social drinking allowed; 10 Tennis available; 11 Swimming available; 12 Golf available; 13 Skiing available; 14 May be booked through travel agents.

wing chair and private bath. Weekdays, breakfast is self-serve continental. On weekends, a full breakfast is served. Central air conditioning. $75-80.

WAYNE

Fox Knoll

Bed and Breakfast of Valley Forge #0904
P. O. Box 562, Valley Forge, 19481-0562
(215) 783-7838; (800) 344-0123
FAX (215) 783-7783

Completely private accommodations in this 12-room old stone Colonial filled with antiques and country comfort. The guest entrance leads from the terrace to a spacious and charming room with areas for eating, sitting, and sleeping. The kitchenette is fully equipped and stocked for breakfast, or join the hosts in the country dining room. The stone terrace with grill and umbrella are for guests' use. Other amenities include a large stone fireplace, TV, and stereo. A cheerful bedroom with sitting room in the main house is also available. $65-90.

Woodwinds

Bed and Breakfast of Valley Forge #1309
P. O. Box 562, Valley Forge, 19481-0562
(215) 783-7838; (800) 344-0123
FAX (215) 783-7783

This newly remodeled home sits on two acres on a quiet, wooded street, surrounded by gardens, lawns, and trees. The light, comfortable guest room is up a short, private flight of stairs separated from the hosts' quarters. A continental breakfast is served in the formal dining room or on the terrace. Just one-half block from the main line train station and the Paoli local to Philadelphia. $65-75.

WEST ALEXANDER

Saint's Rest Bed and Breakfast

77 Main Street, P. O. Box 15, 15376
(412) 484-7950

Earl and Myrna invite guests to visit this beautiful gingerbread-style Victorian home situated one minute from I-70 east or west. Fifteen minutes from Oglebay Park, Jamboree USA, and Wheeling Downs dog track. Saint's Rest stands on Old National Road. Fresh flowers, homemade muffins, a welcome-in drink, and good beds are just some of the guests' comments about this friendly home away from home.

Hosts: Myrna and Earl Lewis
Rooms: 2 (PB) $60 plus tax
Continental Breakfast
Credit Cards: None
Notes: 2, 5, 8, 9

WEST CHESTER

The Bankhouse Bed and Breakfast

875 Hillsdale Road, 19382
(215) 344-7388

An 18th-century "bankhouse" nestled in a quiet country setting with view of pond and horse farm. Rooms charmingly decorated with country antiques and stenciling. Offers

The Bankhouse

NOTES: Credit cards accepted: A Master Card; B Visa; C American Express; D Discover Card; E Diner's Club; F Other; 2 Personal Checks accepted; 3 Lunch available; 4 Dinner available; 5 Open all year;

a great deal of privacy, with private entrance, porch, sitting room/library, and air conditioning. Near Longwood Gardens, Brandywine River Museum, and Winterthur. Easy drive to Valley Forge, Lancaster, and Philadelphia. Canoeing, horseback riding, biking, walking/jogging trails offered in the area. Also, luscious country breakfast and afternoon snacks.

Hosts: Diana and Michael Bove
Rooms: 2 (1 PB; 1SB) $65-85
Full Breakfast
Credit Cards: None
Notes: 2, 5, 9, 12, 13

Bed and Breakfast Connections #00352

P. O. Box 21, Devon, 19333
(215) 687-3565; (800) 448-3619 (outside PA)

Picture a majestic 1850 farmhouse with a wraparound porch sitting atop the highest point in beautiful Chester County. The original landowner was the founder of West Chester, and since then it has been the site of an Arabian horse farm and the summer home of a wealthy family who owned the house for 95 years before they sold it to the hosts. Four guest rooms are available; two suites offer a private bath, and two rooms on the second floor share a hall bath. A full farm-style breakfast is served each morning, and guests are invited to join the hostess for tea in the grand entry room in front of the crackling fire. Attractions, such as Longwood Gardens, Winterthur, and the historic Brandywine Valley, are within a short drive. $100-135.

Bingham House

Bed and Breakfast of Valley Forge #0204
P. O. Box 562, Valley Forge, 19481-0562
(215) 783-7838; (800) 344-0123
FAX (215) 783-7783

This modern farmhouse situated on property deeded from William Penn features Early American furnishings and antiques collected and inherited over the years. In

West Chester, one-half hour to Brandywine Valley, Valley Forge, and Amish country, as well as all businesses along the Route 202 corridor from King of Prussia to Wilmington. Guests have access to a refrigerator, microwave, grill, washer/dryer, phone, TV, and VCR. $55-65.

WILKES-BARRE

Ponda-Rowland Bed and Breakfast Inn and Farm Vacations

Rural Route 1, Box 349, Dallas, 18612
(717) 639-3245

Large, scenic farm in the mountains. Farm animals. This 30-acre wildlife refuge offers ponds, hiking, canoeing, swimming, cross-country skiing, ice skating. State park, game land, fishing, horseback riding, antiquing, restaurants, downhill skiing, county fairs nearby. Museum-quality country antiques. Circa 1850 timberframe (post-and-beam) double plank construction. Large stone fireplace. Satellite TV. Awarded Gold Seal of Approval by *Bed and Breakfast Worldwide*. Featured in *B&B/Unique Inns of Pennsylvania*. Member of ABBA and PAII.

Hosts: Jeanette and Clifford Rowland
Rooms: 3 (PB) $50-80
Full Breakfast
Credit Cards: A, B
Notes: 2, 5, 8, 9, 11, 13, 14

WRIGHTSTOWN

Hollileif Bed and Breakfast Establishment

677 Durham Road (Route 413), 18940
(215) 598-3100

An 18th-century farmhouse on five and one-half acres of Bucks County countryside with romantic ambience, gourmet breakfasts, fireplaces, central air condition-

6 Pets welcome; 8 Children welcome; 9 Social drinking allowed; 10 Tennis available; 11 Swimming available; 12 Golf available; 13 Skiing available; 14 May be booked through travel agents.

Hollileif

ing, and private baths. Gracious service is combined with attention to detail. Each guest room is beautifully appointed with antiques and country furnishings. Enjoy afternoon refreshments by the fireside or on the arbor-covered patio. Relax in a hammock in the meadow overlooking a peaceful stream. View a vibrant sunset and wildlife. Close to New Hope.

Hosts: Ellen and Richard Butkus
Rooms: 5 (PB) $80-120
Full Breakfast
Credit Cards: A, B, C
Notes: 2, 5, 9, 14

YORK

Amanda's
Bed and Breakfast #105

1428 Park Avenue, Annapolis, MD 21217
(301) 225-0001; (301) 383-1274

This 1836 restored brick Colonial is on three acres of manicured lawns with trees, shrubs, and flowers. This farmhouse with a fireplace has an antique shop on the premises. Three guest rooms with two shared baths. Just 20 minutes from Lancaster and a little more than an hour from Baltimore. $60.

Smyser-Bair House
Bed and Breakfast

30 South Beaver Street, 17401
(717) 854-3411

A magnificent 12-room Italianate town house in the historic district, this home is rich in architectural detail and contains stained-glass windows, pier mirrors, and ceiling medallions. There are three antique-filled guest rooms and a two-room suite. Enjoy the warm hospitality, walk to the farmers' market, historic sites, and antique shops. Eight blocks from the York Fairgrounds; near Lancaster and Gettysburg.

Hosts: The King Family
Rooms: 4 (1 PB; 3 SB) $60-80
Full Breakfast
Credit Cards: A, B
Notes: 2, 5, 8, 9, 12, 13, 14

Rhode Island

BLOCK ISLAND _____

The Barrington Inn

Beach Avenue, P. O. Box 397, 02807
(401) 466-5510

On peaceful, picturesque Block Island, the
inn is situated just 12 miles off the coast of
Rhode Island. Bright, cheerful corner guest
rooms have lovely water views. Two
housekeeping apartments are also available. Within walking distance of the beach,
restaurants and shops.

Hosts: Joan and Howard Ballard
Rooms: 6 (PB) $50-145
Continental Breakfast
Credit Cards: A, B
Notes: 2, 8 (over 12), 9, 10, 11

The Blue Dory Inn

Box 488, 02807
(401) 466-5891; (800) 992-7290

The Victorian age is alive and well at the
Blue Dory. Situated on Crescent Beach,
this delightful year-round inn offers an
opportunity to revisit a period of time that
has long since gone by. The inn is filled
with antiques and turn of the century decor,
yet has all the modern comforts.

Hosts: Ann and Ed Loedy
Rooms: 14 (PB) $55-245
Continental Breakfast
Credit Cards: A, B, C, F
Notes: 2, 5, 8, 9, 10, 11, 14

BRISTOL _____

Rockwell House Inn

610 Hope Street, 02809
(401) 253-0040

Federal-style home built in 1809 is situated
in the heart of the historic Waterfront
District. Large and inviting guest rooms
with king-size beds and fireplaces are
available for guests, and a casual yet elegant decor with period antiques and stenciling throughout adds to the house's charm.
Breakfast is served on the porch or in the
candlelit dining room, and afternoon tea
and sherry are served. Two rooms with private baths and two rooms with a shared
bath are available, with turn down service.
The harbor, antiquing, museums, boating,
tennis, and golf are nearby. Walk to the
America's Cup Hall of Fame and
Narragansett Bay.

Hosts: Debra and Steve Krohn
Rooms: 4 (2 PB; 2 SB) $65-90
Continental Breakfast
Credit Cards: A, B, C
Notes: 2, 5, 9, 10, 11, 12, 14

CHARLESTOWN_____

One Willow by the Sea

1 Willow Road, 02813-4162
(401) 364-0802

Enjoy hospitality year-round in a peaceful
South County shoreline community. Guest
comfort is a priority. Wake to birds, sunshine, and sea breezes. A delicious gourmet
breakfast is often served on the sun deck.
Explore the miles of beautiful sandy beaches, salt ponds, wildlife refuges—a birder's
paradise. Windsurf, swim, bike, or fish;
many sports activities are here. Restaurants, theaters, live music, antique shows,
craft fairs, historic New England, and
Narragansett Indian landmarks nearby.

6 Pets welcome; 8 Children welcome; 9 Social drinking allowed; 10 Tennis available; 11 Swimming available;
12 Golf available; 13 Skiing available; 14 May be booked through travel agents.

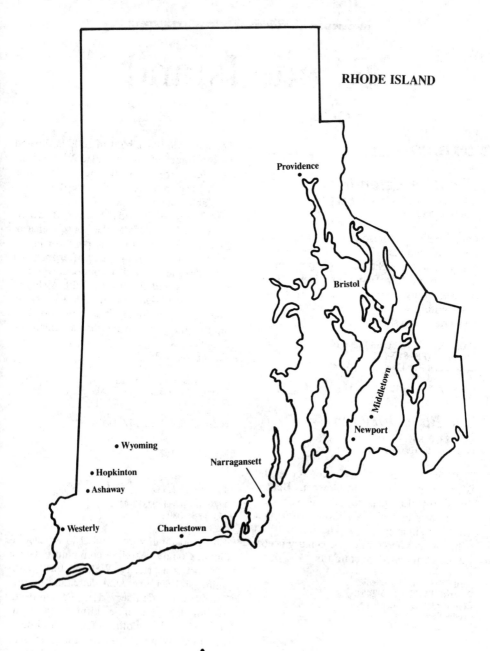

RHODE ISLAND

Providence

Bristol

Middletown

Newport

Wyoming

Narragansett

Hopkinton

Ashaway

Westerly

Charlestown

Block Island

Providence, Newport, Block Island, and Mystic are a short drive. Host speaks French.

Host: Denise Dillon Fuge
Rooms: 4 (SB) $45 off-season; $55 in-season
Full Breakfast
Credit Cards: None
Notes: 2, 5, 8, 10, 11, 12, 14

KINGSTON

Hedgerow Bed and Breakfast

P. O. Box 1586, 02881
(401) 783-2671; (800) 738-2671

Lovely Colonial in Kingston, one-half mile from the University of Rhode Island campus. Handy for trips to Newport, Block Island, and the Rhode Island beaches, Mystic aquarium and seaport. Happy hour and full breakfast are included. Beautiful gardens and a tennis court on the premises for guests to enjoy.

Hosts: Ann and Jim Ross
Rooms: 4 (SB) $55-60 plus tax
Full Breakfast
Credit Cards: D
Notes: 2, 5, 8, 9, 10, 11, 12, 14

MIDDLETOWN

Lindsey's Guest House

6 James Street, 02840
(401) 846-9386

Situated one mile from Newport's famous mansions, Cliff Walk, and Tennis Hall of Fame. Lindsey's is a split-level home with large yard, deck, and off-street parking. Just a 10-minute walk to beaches and Norman Bird Sanctuary.

Hosts: Anne
Rooms: 3 (1 PB; 2 SB) $45-80
Continental Breakfast
Credit Cards: A, B
Notes: 2, 5, 8, 9, 10, 11, 12, 14

NARRAGANSETT

Bed and Breakfast Inns of New England RI-905

329 Lake Drive, Guilford, CT 06437
(800) 582-0853

Enjoy the elegance of a circa 1884 ocean-front Victorian summer estate on the National Register of Historic Places overlooking the ocean and set on two acres. Guests may explore the grounds, play croquet, sunbathe on the ocean beach, swim, and relax on the sun porch or patio. The eight guest rooms have a variety of bed sizes, and are furnished with antiques and collectibles; and many have ocean views. All rooms have private baths. Children over 10 are welcome. Resident dog, but no guest pets, please. $60-125, seasonal.

Ilverthorpe Cottage

41 Robinson Street, 02882
(401) 789-2392

Lacy touches, hand-carved moldings, and stenciled walls are found throughout this 1896 Victorian "cottage" a convenient three blocks from the beach. Travel to Newport for a day of mansion touring, sailing, and shopping, or take the ferry to nearby Block Island. Whatever their pleasure, guests will enjoy the sumptuous gourmet breakfast each morning.

Hosts: Jill, Chris, and John Webb
Rooms: 4 (2 PB; 2 SB) $70-75
Full Breakfast
Credit Cards: None
Notes: 2, 8, 9, 10, 11, 12, 14

The Old Clerk House

49 Narragansett Avenue, 02882
(401) 783-8008

NOTES: Credit cards accepted: A Master Card; B Visa; C American Express; D Discover Card; E Diner's Club; F Other; 2 Personal Checks accepted; 3 Lunch available; 4 Dinner available; 5 Open all year; 6 Pets welcome; 8 Children welcome; 9 Social drinking allowed; 10 Tennis available; 11 Swimming available; 12 Golf available; 13 Skiing available; 14 May be booked through travel agents.

Enjoy country comfort in this Victorian home. Twin, double, and king-size beds, with private baths, color TV, and air conditioning available. Full home-cooked breakfast is served in the plant-filled sun room. Situated only one block from the beach, movie theater, library, and fine restaurants. Just 10 minutes to Block Island. Tennis courts only three blocks away, and 18 miles to Newport. The guest livingroom offers basic cable TV, VCR, and stereo. Off-street parking available.

Host: Patricia Watkins
Rooms: 2 (PB) $65-85
Full Breakfast
Credit Cards: None
Notes: 2, 5, 9, 10, 11, 14

The Richards

144 Gibson Avenue, 02882
(401) 789-7746

Gracious accommodations in an 1884 historic manse. Relax by the fire in the library or in your guest room with fireplace. Enjoy a leisurely full breakfast with homemade muffins, strudels, blintzes. The hostesses' special touches will spoil you—down comforters, canopy beds, flowers from the gardens.

Hosts: Steven and Nancy Richards
Rooms: 4 (2 PB; 2 SB) $55-85
Full Breakfast
Minimum stay weekends: 2 nights; holidays: 3 nights
Credit Cards: None
Notes: 2, 5, 8 (over 12), 9

Stone Lea

40 Newton Avenue, 02882-1368
(401) 783-9546

Built circa 1884, this rambling Victorian estate is situated on two magnificent oceanfront acres at the mouth of Narragansett Bay. One of a handful of summer homes built during the peak period of high society in Narragansett. Waves crashing along the rocky shoreline may be seen and heard

from most rooms. English antiques and collections of Victorian china clocks, miniature cars, and model ships are incorporated into the decor.

Hosts: Carol and Ernie Cormier
Rooms: 4 (PB) $60-100 off-season; $85-125 in-season.
Full Breakfast
Credit Cards: A, B
Notes: 2, 5, 8 (over 10), 9, 10, 11, 12, 14

NEWPORT

Bed and Breakfast of Rhode Island

38 Bellvue Avenue, P. O. Box 3291, 02840
(401) 849-1298

Bed and Breakfast of Rhode Island is a reservation service that serves all of Rhode Island, including Block Island and southeastern Massachusetts. The 120 bed and breakfasts range from the small one-room homestays to the large 19-room inns. In-season rates apply May through October with rates from $55-95 for shared baths and $95-225 for private baths. Off-season rates apply November-April. Rooms with shared baths are $45-75, and rooms with private baths are $60-225.

Rooms: 400 (PB and SB) $55-225
Full and Continental Breakfast
Credit Cards: A, B, C
Notes: 2, 5, 6, 8, 9, 10, 11, 12, 14

Bellevue House

14 Catherine Street, 02840
(401) 847-1828

Built in 1774, Bellevue House was converted into the first summer hotel in Newport in 1828. Situated on top of Historic Hill, off the famous Bellevue Avenue and three blocks from the harbor. The house retains a combination of ideal location, colonial history, nautical atmosphere, and Victorian charm.

NOTES: Credit cards accepted: A Master Card; B Visa; C American Express; D Discover Card; E Diner's Club; F Other; 2 Personal Checks accepted; 3 Lunch available; 4 Dinner available; 5 Open all year;

Hosts: Joan and Vic Farmer
Rooms: 8 (6 PB; 2 SB) $65-110, plus tax
Continental Breakfast
Credit Cards: None
Closed November-April
Notes: 2, 8 (over 12), 9, 10, 11, 12, 14

Cliffside Inn

2 Seaview Avenue, 02840
(401) 847-1811; (800) 845-1811

Perfect site on a quiet, tree-lined street removed from the hubbub of downtown, yet just one block from Cliff Walk (the city's famous seaside walking trail), two blocks from the beach, and a short stroll from the Newport mansions. Built in 1880 as a summer getaway for Gov. Thomas Swann of Maryland, the cottage became the site of Saint George's School in 1897. The inn was later owned by well-known Newport artist Beatrice Turner. Guest bedrooms have private bath. Conference facilities available.

Hosts: Annette and Norbert Mede
Rooms: 12 (PB) $115-225
Full Breakfast
Credit Cards: A, B, C, D, E
Notes: 2, 5, 9, 10, 14

Hydrangea House Inn

16 Bellevue Avenue, 02840
(800) 945-4667

This small inn in the heart of Newport's walking district pays attention to detail and to comfort. Guest rooms are sumptuously decorated with antiques, fine fabrics, and original works of art. Rooms have private baths and air conditioning. Included is a gratifying three-course buffet breakfast each morning. *The Boston Globe* said of this inn, "In a city known for its lodging, the Hydrangea House is not to be missed!" AAA approved.

Rooms: 6 (PB) $89-139
Full Breakfast
Credit Cards: A, B
Notes: 2, 5, 8, 10, 11, 12, 14

Jenkins Guest House

206 South Rhode Island Avenue, 02840
(401) 847-6801

This home was built on a quiet side street in a residential area of Newport when the hosts married. A three-minute walk to the beach; 15 to downtown; 10 to mansions. Yachting activities, boutiques, and shopping. Plenty of parking on grounds.

Hosts: David and Sally Jenkins
Rooms: 2 (SB) $60
Continental Breakfast
Credit Cards: None
Open April 1-Nov. 1
Notes: 2, 8, 9, 10, 11, 12

On the Point

102 Third Street, 02840
(401) 846-8377

This comfortable 100-year old Victorian is in one of Newport's most charming historic areas. Relax in comfortable, beautifully furnished accommodations with king-size beds. Rooms feature either private of shared baths. Enjoy a wonderful homemade continental breakfast in antique wicker surroundings. Newport's best restaurants are within walking distance. Public tennis courts are just around the corner. The hosts have excellent knowledge of Newport Colonial history.

Hosts: Sheila and George Perry
Rooms: 2 (PB) $55-105
Continental Breakfast
Credit Cards: None
Notes: 5, 8, 9, 10, 11, 14

Pilgrim House Inn

123 Spring Street, 02840
(401) 846-0040; (800) 525-8373

This Victorian inn, with its comforts and elegance, is two blocks from the harbor in the midst of the historic district. A livingroom with fireplace, immaculate rooms, and wonderful atmosphere awaits.

6 Pets welcome; 8 Children welcome; 9 Social drinking allowed; 10 Tennis available; 11 Swimming available; 12 Golf available; 13 Skiing available; 14 May be booked through travel agents.

Breakfast on the deck overlooking Newport's harbor. Just outside the door are the mansions, shops, and restaurants.

Hosts: Pam and Bruce Bayuk
Rooms: 10 (8 PB; 2 SB) $49.50-137.50
Continental Breakfast
Credit Cards: A, B
Closed January
Notes: 2, 8 (over 12), 9, 10, 11, 12, 14

Stella Maris Inn

91 Washington Street, 02840
(401) 849-2862

An elegant historic inn situated on the water in downtown Newport, the Stella Maris was built in 1861 from Connecticut redstone with French Victorian design. Four rooms have working fireplaces. The inn is tastefully furnished with period antiques, and a large porch overlooks the gardens and harbor. Homemade muffins and breads are a specialty.

Hosts: Dorothy and Ed Madden
Rooms: 8 plus cottage (PB) $75-150
Full Breakfast
Credit Cards: None
Notes: 2, 5, 8, 9, 10, 11, 12

PROVIDENCE

State House Inn

43 Jewett Street, 02908
(401) 785-1235

In the center of a quiet and quaint neighborhood, the State House Inn is a 100-year-old building newly restored and renovated into a country bed and breakfast. Situated just minutes from downtown Providence and the many local colleges and universities, the inn brings country living to the big city.

Hosts: Frank and Monica Hopton
Rooms: 10 (PB) $75-105
Full Breakfast
Credit Cards: A, B, C
Notes: 5, 8, 9, 14

WESTERLY

Nutmeg B&B Agency #507

P. O. Box 1117, West Hartford, CT. 06107
(203) 236-6698

Situated five minutes from the beach, this renovated 1920 summer home is by a salt-water pond that looks out to the ocean. Originally a working farm, it provides the perfect quiet getaway. One guest room has two double beds, many windows, and a private bath with shower. The second guest room has a canopy double bed, private deck with a view of the water, and a private bath with a tub. For the family getaway, two summer cottages are also available, one with three bedrooms and the other with six. Continental breakfast. Children welcome. Pets in residence.

Woody Hill
Bed and Breakfast

149 South Woody Hill Road, 02891
(401) 322-0452

The hostess, a high school English teacher, invites guests to share this reproduction Colonial home, with antiques and gardens. Visitors may snuggle under quilts, relax on the porch swing, visit nearby Newport and Mystic, or swim in the pool or at beautiful ocean beaches. Westerly has it all!

Host: Ellen L. Madison
Rooms: 3 (1 PB; 2 SB) $50-90
Full Breakfast
Credit Cards: None
Notes: 2, 5, 8, 9, 10, 11, 12,

WYOMING

The Cookie Jar
Bed and Breakfast

64 Kingstown Road, 02898
(401) 539-2680

NOTES: Credit cards accepted: A Master Card; B Visa; C American Express; D Discover Card; E Diner's Club; F Other; 2 Personal Checks accepted; 3 Lunch available; 4 Dinner available; 5 Open all year;

The heart of this home, the livingroom, was built in 1732 as a blacksmith's shop. The original ceiling, hand-hewn beams, and granite walls remain today. The country property includes a barn, a swimming pool, 50 fruit trees, grapevines, a flower garden, and an acre of grass. The hosts offer friendly homestyle living just a short drive from the beaches, the University of Rhode Island, Mystic, and Providence.

Hosts: Dick and Madelein Sohl
Rooms: 3 (1 PB; 2 SB) $55-60
Full Breakfast
Credit Cards: None
Notes: 2, 5, 8, 9, 11, 12, 14

6 Pets welcome; 8 Children welcome; 9 Social drinking allowed; 10 Tennis available; 11 Swimming available; 12 Golf available; 13 Skiing available; 14 May be booked through travel agents.

Bennettsville •

Myrtle Beach •

Georgetown •

McClellanville

Charleston

SOUTH CAROLINA

South Carolina

TwoSuns Inn
Bed and Breakfast

1705 Bay Street, 29902
(803) 522-1122; (800) 532-4244
FAX (803) 522-1122

A prince of an inn in an antebellum brigadoon. Southern charm abounds historic Beaufort, the film site for *Prince of Tides*, and informal elegance characterizes this 1917 grand home right on the bay. Visit the quaint downtown, enjoy a carriage ride, or bicycle through the historic waterfront community. Relax in this newly restored home, complete with weavings, period decor, collectibles, full handicapped facilities, and business amenities.

Hosts: Carrol and Ron Kay
Rooms: 5 (PB) $88-108 (seasonal)
Full Breakfast
Credit Cards: A, B, C, E
Notes: 2, 5, 9, 10, 11, 12, 14

BENNETTSVILLE

The Breeden House Inn

404 East Main Street, 29512
(803) 479-3665

Built in 1886 as a wedding present for the original owner's bride, the romantic Breeden House is a beautifully restored Southern mansion on two acres that includes a carriage house. Listed on the National Register of Historic Places, the inn is 20 minutes off I-95; a great halfway point between Florida and New York. A

haven for antique lovers. Pool, goldfish pond, and cable TV. Indoor and outdoor sitting areas including a wraparound front porch, rockers, and swings. The comfortable surroundings will capture your interest and inspire your imagination. Near museums and antique shops. Bicycles available.

Hosts: Wesley and Bonnie Park
Rooms: 7 (PB) $50-55
Full Breakfast
Credit Cards: A, B, D
Notes: 2, 5, 11, 14

CHARLESTON

Ann Harper's
Bed and Breakfast

56 Smith Street, 29401
(803) 723-3947

This circa 1870 home is situated in Charleston's historic district. Two rooms with connecting bath and sitting area with TV. The owner is a retired medical technologist and enjoys serving a full breakfast.

Host: Ann D. Harper
Rooms: 2 (PB) $60-70
Full Breakfast
Minimum stay: 2 nights
Credit Cards: None
Notes: 2, 5, 8 (over 10), 9, 10, 11, 12

Ashley Inn
Bed and Breakfast

201 Ashley Avenue, 29403
(803) 723-1848; FAX (803) 723-9080

Stay in a stately, historic (circa 1835) home. Elegant, but warm and hospitable,

NOTES: Credit cards accepted: A Master Card; B Visa; C American Express; D Discover Card; E Diner's Club; F Other; 2 Personal Checks accepted; 3 Lunch available; 4 Dinner available; 5 Open all year; 6 Pets welcome; 8 Children welcome; 9 Social drinking allowed; 10 Tennis available; 11 Swimming available; 12 Golf available; 13 Skiing available; 14 May be booked through travel agents.

the Ashley Inn offers seven intimate bedrooms featuring canopy beds, private baths, fireplaces, and air conditioning. Delicious breakfasts are served on the grand columned piazza overlooking a beautiful Charleston garden or in the formal dining room. Relax with afternoon sherry or tea and cookies after touring nearby historic sites, or enjoying the complimentary touring bicycles. Simple elegance in a warm and friendly home noted for true southern hospitality.

Hosts: Bud and Sally Allen
Rooms: 7 (PB) $59-98
Full Breakfast
Credit Cards: A, B
Notes: 2, 5, 8, 9, 10, 11, 12

Brasington House Bed and Breakfast

328 East Bay Street, 29401
(803) 722-1274

Elegant accommodations in a splendidly restored Greek Revival Charleston single house furnished with antiques. Centrally located in Charleston's beautiful historic district, four lovely, well-appointed guest rooms with central heat and air conditioning include private baths, telephones, cable TV, and tea-making services. King, queen, and twin beds are available. Included is a bountiful family-style breakfast, wine and

Brasington House

cheese served in the livingroom, liqueurs and chocolates available in the evening, and off-street parking.

Host: Dalton K. Brasington
Rooms: 4 (PB) $89-98
Full Breakfast
Credit Cards: A, B
Notes: 2, 5, 9, 10, 11, 12

Cannonboro Inn Bed and Breakfast

184 Ashley Avenue, 29403
(803) 723-8572; FAX (803) 723-9080

The Cannonboro Inn lies at the heart of a section of Charleston's historic district. This circa 1850 historical single house shares Ashley Avenue with the antebellum Lucas and Weckinburg mansions and former U.S./Confederate arsenal grounds. Shaded by crepe myrtles and palmettos, guests enjoy a full breakfast served in a formal dining room or on a columned piazza overlooking a Low Country garden. The parlor welcomes guests to visit, read, or play games; complimentary sherry served in the afternoon and complimentary bicycles provided for touring.

Hosts: Sally and Bud Allen
Rooms: 6 (PB) $69-98
Full Breakfast
Credit Cards: A, B
Notes: 2, 5, 9, 10, 11, 12

Country Victorian Bed and Breakfast

105 Tradd Street, 29401-2422
(803) 577-0682

Rooms have private entrances and contain antique iron and brass beds, old quilts, oak and wicker antique furniture, and braided rugs over the heart-of-pine floors. Homemade cookies will be waiting. The house, built in 1820, is within walking distance of restaurants, antique shops, churches, art galleries, museums, and all points of historical interest. Parking and bicycles are available. Many extras.

NOTES: Credit cards accepted: A Master Card; B Visa; C American Express; D Discover Card; E Diner's Club; F Other; 2 Personal Checks accepted; 3 Lunch available; 4 Dinner available; 5 Open all year;

Host: Diane Deardurff Weed
Rooms: 2 (PB) $65-85
Continental Breakfast
Credit Cards: None
Notes: 2, 5, 8, 9, 10, 11, 12, 14

Country Victorian

1837 Bed and Breakfast and Tea Room

126 Wentworth Street, 29401
(803) 723-7166

Accommodations in a wealthy cotton planter's home and brick carriage house, now owned by two artists. Centrally situated in the historic district within walking distance of boat tours, Old Market, antique shops, restaurants, and main attractions. Full gourmet breakfast is served in the formal dining room or on our outside piazzas. Visit with others while enjoying such specialities as sausage pie, eggs Benedict, ham omelettes, and home-baked breads (lemon, apple spice, banana, and cinnamon swirl). Afternoon tea is served. Verandas, rockers and southern hospitality.

Hosts: Sherri Weaver and Richard Dunn
Rooms: 8 (PB) $59-99
Full Breakfast
Credit Cards: A, B, C
Notes: 2, 5, 9, 10

The Hayne House

30 King Street, 29401
(803) 577-2633

The Hayne House, circa 1755, is in the heart of the Charleston historic district one block from the Battery, which overlooks the Charleston Harbor and Fort Sumter. A treasury of good books, art, and antiques provide guests all they need to step back in time. No TV. Parlor, grand piano in livingroom, sherry on the piano, fireplaces throughout, Charleston garden with eating area, rockers, swing, jogging, back porch.

Rooms: 5 (3 PB; 2 SB) $45-95
Continental Breakfast
Credit Cards: A, B
Notes: 2, 5, 9, 10, 11, 12

Historic Charleston Bed and Breakfast

43 Legare Street, 29401
(803) 722-6606

A reservation service for private historic homes, carriage houses, mansions, and plantations in or near Charleston. This port city is one of the most historical in the United States, with many cultural activities offered. All bed and breakfasts offered have private baths, TV, and air conditioning. Many have lovely gardens, patios, or porches. Most locations are within walking distance of restaurants, shops, museums, and other historic sites. Beaches are ten miles away.

Host: Charlotte Fairey
Rooms: 70 (PB) $60-140
Continental and Full Breakfast
Credit Cards: A, B, C
Notes: 2, 5, 9, 10, 11, 12

Indigo Inn

1 Maiden Lane, 29401
(803) 577-5900

The Indigo Inn is a 40-room property done in 18th-century antiques and antique repro-

6 Pets welcome; 8 Children welcome; 9 Social drinking allowed; 10 Tennis available; 11 Swimming available; 12 Golf available; 13 Skiing available; 14 May be booked through travel agents.

ductions. The quiet, traditional property surrounds a beautiful courtyard in the center of the quadrangle. An excellent location, private on-premises parking, and delicious hunt breakfast are just a few of the reasons travelers should visit.

Host: L. B. Deery
Rooms: 40 (PB) $75-125
Continental Breakfast
Credit Cards: A, B, C, D
Notes: 2, 5, 6, 8, 9, 10, 12, 14

King George Inn and Guests

32 George Street, 29401
(803) 723-9339

The King George Inn is a 200-year-old (circa 1790s) Federal-style historic house in the downtown historic district. There are four stories in all, with three levels of lovely Charleston porches. All rooms have fireplaces, ten-foot ceilings, and six-foot windows. All rooms have original lovely wide-planked hardwood floors, original oak doors, old furnishings, and many antiques. A minute's walk to shopping and restaurants and a five-minute walk to the Historic Market. Maps and brochures of historic sights and dining information is available. On-site parking. Come visit the past!

Hosts: Jean, B. J., Lynn, and Mike
Rooms: 8 (PB) $60-85
Continental Breakfast, seasonal
Credit Cards: A, B
Notes: 2, 5, 6 (limited), 8, 9, 10, 11, 12, 13 (water)

Rutledge Victorian Inn

114 Rutledge Avenue, 29401
(803) 722-7551

A century-old Italianate-style Victorian house in Charleston's downtown historic district. The house is quaint but elegant: a beautiful round decorative porch, 12-foot ceilings, eight to ten-foot doors and windows, fireplaces everywhere! The private or shared baths are modern. Air conditioning and TV. A 10- to 20-minute walk to all tours and historic sites. Help with tours.

Come and "set a spell" on an old rocker and feel the history around you.

Hosts: Jean, Lynn, B. J., and Mike
Rooms: 7-10 (5 PB; 5 SB) $45-90, seasonal
Continental Breakfast
Credit Cards: A, B
Notes: 2, 5, 6 (restricted), 8, 9, 10, 11, 12

Rutledge Victorian Inn

Villa de La Fontaine Bed and Breakfast

138 Wentworth Street, 29401
(803) 577-7709

Villa de La Fontaine is a columned Greek Revival mansion in the heart of the historic district. Built in 1838, it boasts a garden with fountain and terraces. It has been restored to impeccable condition and furnished with museum-quality furniture and accessories. The hosts are retired A.S.I.D. interior designers and have decorated the rooms with 18th-century American antiques. Several of the rooms feature canopy beds. Breakfast is prepared by a master chef who prides himself on serving a different menu every day. Off-street parking.

Hosts: William Fontaine and Aubrey Hancock
Rooms: 4 (PB) $100
Suites: 2 (PB) $165
Full Breakfast
Minimum stay weekends: 2 nights; holidays: 3 nights
Credit Cards: A, B, C
Notes: 2, 5, 8 (over 11), 9, 10, 11, 12, 14

NOTES: Credit cards accepted: A Master Card; B Visa; C American Express; D Discover Card; E Diner's Club; F Other; 2 Personal Checks accepted; 3 Lunch available; 4 Dinner available; 5 Open all year;

DILLON

Magnolia Inn Bed and Breakfast

601 East Main Street, Highway 9, 29536
(803) 774-0679

Southern hospitality abounds as one enters the Magnolia Inn's magnificent foyer. Relax and make yourself at home in the "duck" library or Victorian parlor. Mornings are filled with the savory aromas of breads, pastries, pecan-apple pancakes, breakfast casseroles, fresh fruits, coffee, or tea. Breakfast is served in the formal dining room or on the second-floor summer porch. Four guest rooms are available—the Azalea, the Camellia, the Dogwood, and the Wysteria. The Magnolia Inn is easily accessible from I-95.

Hosts: Jim and Pam Lannoo
Rooms: 4 (3 PB; 1 SB) $35-50
Full Breakfast
Credit Cards: A, B
Notes: 2, 5, 8, 9, 10, 11, 12

GEORGETOWN

1790 House

630 Highmarket Street, 29440
(803) 546-4821

Meticulously restored, this 200-year-old plantation-style inn is in the heart of historic Georgetown. Spacious, luxurious rooms with fireplaces and central air and heat. Stay in the the Rice Planters Room, the beautiful honeymoon cottage with Jacuzzi, or one of the other lovely rooms. Walk to shops, restaurants, and historic sights. Just a short drive to Myrtle Beach and Grand Strand—a golfer's paradise.

Hosts: John and Patricia Wiley
Rooms: 6 (PB) $65-125
Full Breakfast
Credit Cards: A, B, C
Notes: 2, 5, 9, 10, 12, 14

MCCLELLANVILLE

Laurel Hill Plantation

8913 North Highway 17, P. O. Box 190, 29458
(803) 887-3708

Laurel Hill faces the Intracoastal Waterway and the Atlantic Ocean. Porches provide a scenic view of marshes and creeks. The house is furnished in country and primitive antiques that reflect the Low Country lifestyle. Situated 30 miles north of Charleston, 60 miles south of Myrtle Beach.

Hosts: Jackie and Lee Morrison
Rooms: 4 (PB) $65-75
Full Breakfast
Credit Cards: None
Notes: 2, 5, 9, 14

MYRTLE BEACH

Brustman House

400 25th Avenue South, 29577
(803) 448-7699; FAX (803) 626-1500

Only two minutes from the beach, this Myrtle Beach bed and breakfast offers three luxurious rooms with private baths, and a fully equipped suite that sleeps up to eight persons. Afternoon tea, wine and freshly baked sweets are served. Guests can enjoy a game of croquet or badminton or can stroll the rose garden leading to a wooded glade. Tennis, golf, water sports, and discount shopping nearby. Breakfast is a healthy fare, with ten-grain buttermilk pancakes a specialty. Coffee is also a house brand, organically grown and naturally low in caffeine.

Host: Dr. Wendell C. Brustman
Rooms: 4 (PB) $50-80
Full Breakfast
Credit Cards: A, B, D
Notes: 2, 5, 9, 10, 11, 12, 14

6 Pets welcome; 8 Children welcome; 9 Social drinking allowed; 10 Tennis available; 11 Swimming available; 12 Golf available; 13 Skiing available; 14 May be booked through travel agents.

SOUTH DAKOTA

Rapid City

Custer

South Dakota

Custer Mansion Bed and Breakfast

35 Centennial Drive, 57730
(605) 673-3333

This historic 1891 Victorian Gothic home features country charm and western hospitality with clean, quiet, comfortable accommodations and a home-cooked full breakfast. Central to all Black Hills attractions, such as Mount Rushmore. Recommended by *Bon Appetit* and *G.M.C. Friends* magazines.

Hosts: Mill and Carole Seaman
Rooms: 6 (2 PB; 2 SB) $45-75
Full Breakfast
Credit Cards: None
Notes: 2, 5, 8, 10, 12, 13, 14

Custer Mansion

Abend Haus Cottage and Audrie's Cranbury Corner Bed and Breakfast

Rural Route 8, Box 2400, 57702
(605) 342-7788

The Black Hills "inn place." Ultimate in charm and Old World hospitality, this country home and five-acre estate is surrounded by thousands of acres of national forest. Situated 30 miles from Mount Rushmore and seven miles from Rapid City. Each quiet, comfortable suite and cottage has a private entrance, bath, hot tub, patio, cable TV, and refrigerator with free trout. Trout fishing, biking, and hiking available on property.

Hosts: Hank and Audry Kuhnhauser
Rooms: 6 (PB) $85
Full Breakfast
Credit Cards: None
Notes: 2, 5, 9, 10, 11, 12, 13

NOTES: Credit cards accepted: A Master Card; B Visa; C American Express; D Discover Card; E Diner's Club; F Other; 2 Personal Checks accepted; 3 Lunch available; 4 Dinner available; 5 Open all year; 6 Pets welcome; 8 Children welcome; 9 Social drinking allowed; 10 Tennis available; 11 Swimming available; 12 Golf available; 13 Skiing available; 14 May be booked through travel agents.

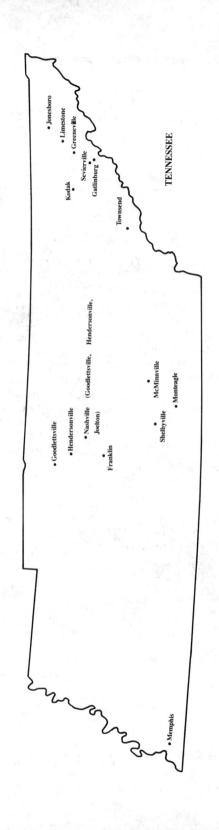

TENNESSEE

Jonesboro
Limestone
Greeneville
Kodak
Sevierville
Gatlinburg
Townsend

(Goodlettsville, Hendersonville,

Goodlettsville
Hendersonville
Nashville
Joelton
Franklin
McMinnville
Monteagle
Shelbyville

Memphis

Tennessee

CHATTANOOGA (SEE ALSO FT. OGLETHORPE, GEORGIA)

Bed and Breakfast About Tennessee

P. O. Box 110227, Nashville, 37222-0227
Information: (615) 331-5244; Reservations: (800)
458-2421 (U.S.); FAX (615) 833-7701

Visitors to the new Tennessee Aquarium will want to see this nearby suite. Queen bedroom with private bath, sitting room, and small kitchen. Children welcome. Swimming pool on the premises. Just eight miles from the airport, and only three miles from the University of Tennessee at Chattanooga. $85-100.

CLARKSVILLE

Bed and Breakfast About Tennessee

P. O. Box 110227, Nashville, 37222-0227

Carothers House

Information: (615) 331-5244; Reservations:
(800) 458-2421 (U.S.); FAX (615) 833-7701

Just 30 minutes from Nashville this spacious guest house sits beside a large beautiful pool on a manicured lawn. Perfect for honeymooners and anniversaries. $125. Main house has a suite of rooms, perfect for singles with a bedroom, sitting room, and bath. $75. Dinner provided at extra cost.

COOKEVILLE

Bed and Breakfast About Tennessee

P. O. Box 110227, Nashville, 37222-0227
Information: (615) 331-5244; Reservations:
(800) 458-2421 (U.S.); FAX (615) 833-7701

This guest house, situated on Center Hill Lake, features one bedroom and a private bath. $75.

FRANKLIN

Bed and Breakfast About Tennessee

P. O. Box 110227, Nashville, 37222-0227
Information: (615) 331-5244; Reservations:
(800) 458-2421 (U.S.); FAX (615) 833-7701

Just three miles from Franklin is this garden suite with a private bath for four persons. $68. The Santa Fe Suite welcomes a maximum of four guests, with private bath and spa. $88. $10 per extra adult.

NOTES: Credit cards accepted: A Master Card; B Visa; C American Express; D Discover Card; E Diner's Club; F Other; 2 Personal Checks accepted; 3 Lunch available; 4 Dinner available; 5 Open all year; 6 Pets welcome; 8 Children welcome; 9 Social drinking allowed; 10 Tennis available; 11 Swimming available; 12 Golf available; 13 Skiing available; 14 May be booked through travel agents.

Carothers House Bed and Breakfast
4301 South Carothers Road, 37064
(615) 794-4437; (800) 327-8492

This cheerful log home in a wooded setting is just minutes from Nashville. Civil War historic area, antique stores, Galleria mall, unique restaurants, and limousine service. Two enclosed lofts and two suites, all of which have private baths. Private outdoor spa available. Relaxing porch, stone fireplace. Full business amenities. Just one mile from I-65 at the Franklin exit. Many historical buildings and activities. Wedding arrangements. Host is a Tour Tennessee promotion member.

Host: John Reitmeier
Rooms: 4 (PB) $68-108
Full Breakfast
Credit Cards: A, B
Notes: 3, 4, 5, 8, 9, 14

GATLINBURG

Bed and Breakfast About Tennessee
P. O. Box 110227, Nashville, 37222-0227
Information: (615) 331-5244; Reservations: (800) 458-2421 (U.S.); FAX (615) 833-7701

Stately plantation house built in 1840. Greek Revival in structure, with a panoramic view of lakes and mountains. Large special chambers with private baths, fireplaces, and antiques. A gourmet breakfast is served. $120.

Bed and Breakfast About Tennessee
P. O. Box 110227, Nashville, 37222-0227
Information: (615) 331-5244; Reservations: (800) 458-2421 (U.S.); FAX (615) 833-7701

Large log home on a golf course. Four bedrooms with private baths, one with two double beds. Great room with fireplace, log gazebo, and Jacuzzi. Tennis courts and a deck overlooking mountain streams. Full breakfast. $90. $10 per extra adult.

Bed and Breakfast About Tennessee
P. O. Box 110227, Nashville, 37222-0227
Information: (615) 331-5244; Reservations: (800) 458-2421 (U.S.); FAX (615) 833-7701

High on a hilltop above Gatlinburg, this secluded stay features hiking, skiing, horseback riding, and ice skating. Antiques and cable TV. Four guest rooms with private baths. View Mt. LeConte from the deck. Chosen the best in the state. $100.

Butcher House in the Mountains
1520 Garrett Lane, 37738
(615) 436-9457

Cradled 2,800-feet above the city of Gatlinburg, directly across from Mt. Le Conte, the second-highest mountain in the Smokies, Butcher House in the Mountains is only minutes from downtown Gatlinburg. The spacious cedar and stone chalet is elegantly furnished with many museum-quality antiques. Guests are treated to unique gourmet breakfasts, which are original creations of the innkeeper. One will feel pampered when served from fine china, crystal, and goldware. Highest AAA rating. A+ rating from the American Bed and Breakfast Association.

Rooms: 5 (PB) $69-95
Full Breakfast
Credit Cards: A, B, C
Notes: 2, 5, 9, 10, 12, 13

GOODLETTSVILLE (SEE ALSO NASHVILLE)

Woodshire Bed and Breakfast
600 Woodshire Drive, 37072
(615) 859-7369

NOTES: Credit cards accepted: A Master Card; B Visa; C American Express; D Discover Card; E Diner's Club; F Other; 2 Personal Checks accepted; 3 Lunch available; 4 Dinner available; 5 Open all year;

Family antiques, homemade preserves, southern hospitality—all these just 15-20 minutes from Nashville's universities, museums, Parthenon, Opryland, and many country music attractions. Private entrance, use of screened porch, continental breakfast. Country atmosphere with urban conveniences. A mid-1800s reconstructed log cabin is also available.

Hosts: John and Beverly Grayson
Rooms: 2 (PB) $50 (couple); $40 (single)
Log Cabin: $70
Continental Breakfast
Credit Cards: None
Notes: 2, 5, 8, 10, 11, 14

GREENEVILLE

Oak Hill Farm Bed and Breakfast

Route 1, Box 342 A, 37743
(615) 639-2331 (days); 639-5253 (nights)

A replica of an old farm house situated on the highest hill in the surrounding area, with views of the Appalachian and Cumberland Mountains. A quiet setting only three miles from Greeneville, and seven miles from I-81. A country breakfast is served, dinner may be served on request, and a swimming pool is available.

Hosts: Marie and Bill Guinn
Rooms: 3 (1 PB; 2 SB) $60-150
Full Breakfast
Credit Cards: A, B, C
Notes: 2, 4, 5, 8, 9, 11, 12

JONESBOROUGH

The Inn at Sheppard Springs

1208 Highway 81 North, 37659
(615) 753-6471

Sheppard Springs is a charming two-story traditional country farmhouse (circa 1860), situated less than five miles from historic Jonesborough—home of the National Storytelling Festival. Three comfortable and spacious homespun rooms with private

bath and air conditioning await, surrounded by 12 rolling acres with gardens to visit and the ever-present birds and critters. A deck and porches are on the premises, and guests determine the amount of personal privacy.

Host: Sheila A. Sheppard
Rooms: 3 (PB) $70-100 ($35 extra per adult)
Full Breakfast
Credit Cards: None
Notes: 2 (Traveler's checks or money orders), 5, 9, 10, 11, 12, 13

Bed and Breakfast About Tennessee

P. O. Box 110227, Nashville, 37222-0227
Information: (615) 331-5244; Reservations: (800) 458-2421 (U.S.); FAX (615) 833-7701

A restored 1900s home in a quiet neighborhood features antiques and beautiful decor. Just four miles from the University of Tennessee campus; near Smoky Mountain sites. Lunch and dinner by appointment. One twin room and one double room share a bath. $45-60.

KODAK

Grandma's House

P. O. Box 445, 37764
(615) 933-3512; (800) 676-3512

Situated at the base of the Great Smoky Mountains in Dumplin Valley, this two-story Colonial-style house combines antique charm with modern-day comfort. Three guest rooms, each with a private bath, are decorated in antiques and country

Grandma's House

themes. Hosts are both native East Tennesseans with lots of down-home friendliness. A loosen-your-belt breakfast is served, and snacks are always on hand. Murder mysteries available January through March.

Hosts: Charlie and Hilda Hickman
Rooms: 3 (PB) $65
Full Breakfast
Credit Cards: A, B
Notes: 2, 5, 12, 14

LEBANON

Bed and Breakfast About Tennessee

P. O. Box 110227, Nashville, 37222-0227
Information: (615) 331-5244; Reservations: (800) 458-2421 (U.S.); FAX (615) 833-7701

This Cape Cod-style home, just 19 miles from Nashville, features a fully equipped kitchen, king bedroom with Jacuzzi, cable TV, double sink, and separate shower. Close to antique shopping. $100.

LIMESTONE

Snapp Inn Bed and Breakfast

Route 3, Box 102, 1990 Davy Crockett Road, 37681
(615) 257-2482

Snapp Inn

The hosts welcome guests into this gracious 1815 Federal home furnished with antiques and set in farm country. Enjoy the mountain view from the full back porch or play a game of pool or horseshoes. Close to Davy Crockett Birthplace Park. Just a 15-minute drive to historic Jonesborough or Greeneville. Third person in room at no extra charge.

Hosts: Dan and Ruth Dorgan
Rooms: 2 (PB) $40-50
Full Breakfast
Credit Cards: None
Notes: 2, 5, 6, 8 (one child only), 9, 11, 12, 14

LOUDON

Bed and Breakfast About Tennessee

P. O. Box 110227, Nashville, 37222-0227
Information: (615) 331-5244; Reservations: (800) 458-2421 (U.S.); FAX (615) 833-7701

This 1865 antebellum plantation home has a grand entrance, nine working fireplaces, and is listed on the National Registry. Features a beautiful swimming pool, gazebo, and arbor. Five bed rooms with private baths. Generous breakfast. $100.

The Mason Place Bed and Breakfast

600 Commerce Street, 37774
(615) 458-3921

The Mason Place, nestled in a quaint Civil War setting along the Tennessee River, is a lovely, impeccably restored plantation home, circa 1865. Tastefully decorated throughout with comfortable period antiques, original chandeliers, delightful feather beds, and ten working fireplaces. Three acres of lawn and gardens, Grecian swimming pool, gazebo, and wisteria-covered arbor. Overflowing with charm and character, the Mason Place is near Knoxville, the Smoky Mountains, I-75, and I-40. No children, please.

NOTES: Credit cards accepted: A Master Card; B Visa; C American Express; D Discover Card; E Diner's Club; F Other; 2 Personal Checks accepted; 3 Lunch available; 4 Dinner available; 5 Open all year;

Hosts: Bob and Donna Siewert
Rooms: 5 (PB) $88
Full Breakfast
Credit Cards: None
Notes: 2, 5, 9, 10, 11, 12

MCMINNVILLE

Falcon Manor
Bed and Breakfast
Faulkner Springs Road, 37110
(615) 668-4444

"Where elegance and history go hand in hand" describes this 1896 Victorian mansion, which is listed on the National Register of Historic Places. Filled with period antiques. Experience the friendly warmth of this fine old house. Rock on the peaceful gingerbread veranda, shaded by giant trees. Situated half-way between Nashville and Chattanooga off I-24, and 90 minutes from Opryland and Rock City. One hour from the Jack Daniel's Distillery, 30 minutes from four state parks. McMinnville is known as the "nursery capital of the world" and the home of America's second-largest cave. Opens May 1993.

Hosts: George and Charlien McGlothin
Rooms: 5 (2 PB; 3 SB) $60-75
Continental Breakfast
Credit Cards: A, B
Notes: 2, 5, 8 (over 12), 14

MEMPHIS

Bed and Breakfast
About Tennessee
P. O. Box 110227, Nashville, 37222-0227
Information: (615) 331-5244; Reservations: (800) 458-2421 (U.S.); FAX (615) 833-7701

Situated just 25 minutes from downtown Memphis, three rooms with private baths, beautifully appointed, generous breakfast, genial hosts, and picturesque surroundings.

The surprise is the enormous enclosed room with a heated pool, waterfalls, sprays, flora, and large hot tub. Breakfast can be served in this surrounding if desired. $90.

B&B in Memphis #D-0302
P. O. Box 41621, 38174-1621
(901) 726-5920; FAX (901) 725-0194

Gracious southern living on the "Mighty Mississippi" epitomizes this open and airy garden condo beautifully decorated with antiques and Oriental furnishings. Two guest rooms, each with its own private bath, continental breakfast served in full view of the river, and a thoroughly engaging southern hostess all take you back to a more gentle time of grace and elegance. The Wonders Series world class exhibitions are within walking distance; great jazz and blues on famous Beale Street. $115.

B&B in Memphis #G-1900
P. O. Box 41621, 38174-1621
(901) 726-5920; FAX (901) 725-0194

This friendly host couple travels extensively in bed and breakfasts. Enjoy breakfast on the screened porch in fashionable Germantown. Spacious guest room with antique pineapple twin beds, private bath, and use of office area for business travelers. Privacy, comfort, and congeniality for only $62.29.

B&B in Memphis #M-0400
P. O. Box 41621, 38174-1621
(901) 726-5920; FAX (901) 725-0194

Charming studio apartment in award-winning midtown high-rise offers large livingroom with Stearnes and Foster double sleeper, dining/work area, sleeping alcove

6 Pets welcome; 8 Children welcome; 9 Social drinking allowed; 10 Tennis available; 11 Swimming available; 12 Golf available; 13 Skiing available; 14 May be booked through travel agents.

(twin bed), full bath with shower, fully equipped kitchen with microwave, and ample closet space. Cable TV, VCR, and one complimentary video. FAX and secretarial services available. Unhosted. Minimums may apply. Weekly and monthly rates available. $84.94.

B&B in Memphis #M-1200

P. O. Box 41621, 38174-1621
(901) 726-5920; FAX (901) 725-0194

Lovely gardens, lush trees, and scampering squirrels are all right in the heart of the city. Professionally decorated host home in the historic Hein Park near Rhodes College and the zoo. Choice of upstairs suite (double and single beds) with shower and wet bar, or downstairs guest room with king-size bed, cable TV, VCR, and private bath. Popular hostess teaches English at a local college and travels extensively. $67.95.

MONTEAGLE

Adams Edgeworth Inn

Box 340, Monteagle Assembly, 37356
(615) 924-2669; FAX (615) 924-3236

A friendly 10-room 1896 mountain inn in the Monteagle Assembly National Historic District, the southern Chautauqua. Enjoy rope hammocks, wicker rockers, and gingerbread porches; delve into plentiful books and magazines by the cheerful library fire; or experience the refreshing waterfalls and pools along the many nearby trails. The University of the South at Sewanee is six miles away.

Hosts: Wendy and David Adams
Rooms: 11 (PB) $55-150
Continental Breakfast
Credit Cards: A, B
Notes: 2, 3, 4, 5, 8 (call), 9, 10, 11, 12, 14

NASHVILLE

Bed and Breakfast About Tennessee

P. O. Box 110227, Nashville, 37222-0227
Information: (615) 331-5244; Reservations: (800) 458-2421 (U.S.); FAX (615) 833-7701

Accommodations in private homes or inns convenient to local points of interest. Continental breakfast served each morning. Guests fill out a questionnaire upon request for reservations. Then a compatible host is carefully selected to assure a pleasant experience for both the guest and the host. Accommodations in Nashville, Gatlinburg, Memphis, Lynchburg, Knoxville, Chattanooga, Jackson, Columbia, and other Tennessee cities.

Bed and Breakfast About Tennessee

P. O. Box 110227, Nashville, 37222-0227
Information: (615) 331-5244; Reservations: (800) 458-2421 (U.S.); FAX (615) 833-7701

Beautiful spacious lakefront home, with a canopy bed in the master bedroom, fireplace, double Jacuzzi, and private bath. $125. King room with double Jacuzzi and private bath; $100. Twin bedroom and private bath; $95. Double bedroom with private bath; $75. All rooms have a lake view and boat dock. Fishing allowed from the dock. Well traveled hosts that love to entertain.

Bed and Breakfast About Tennessee

P. O. Box 110227, Nashville, 37222-0227
Information: (615) 331-5244; Reservations: (800) 458-2421 (U.S.); FAX (615) 833-7701

Suite of rooms by a lake, with swimming, boat dock, and beautiful gardens. Near

---

NOTES: Credit cards accepted: A Master Card; B Visa; C American Express; D Discover Card; E Diner's Club; F Other; 2 Personal Checks accepted; 3 Lunch available; 4 Dinner available; 5 Open all year;

homes of several country music stars. Gracious hosts. $100 per night; two night minimum stay.

Bed and Breakfast About Tennessee

P. O. Box 110227, Nashville, 37222-0227
Information: (615) 331-5244; Reservations: (800) 458-2421 (U.S.); FAX (615) 833-7701

This restored 1900s home features a large double downstairs private bath and a beautiful view of the hills. $75.

Bed and Breakfast About Tennessee

P. O. Box 110227, Nashville, 37222-0227
Information: (615) 331-5244; Reservations: (800) 458-2421 (U.S.); FAX (615) 833-7701

This restored 1900 home is just minutes from the downtown area in a beautiful older neighborhood. Two double rooms with a shared bath. $60-67.50.

Bed and Breakfast About Tennessee

P. O. Box 110227, Nashville, 37222-0227
Information: (615) 331-5244; Reservations: (800) 458-2421 (U.S.); FAX (615) 833-7701

A quiet country home on 116 acres of pasture and wooded area near Nashville, but secluded. Close to Nashville attractions. One double room with shared bath, fireplace, antiques, and a triple room with shared bath, fireplace, and antiques. A full country breakfast is served. $40-50.

Chateau Graeme

2200 Lebanon Road, 37214
(615) 883-1687

Large 1880s Country Victorian private home on eight acres, situated just minutes from Opryland USA, the Opryland Hotel and the historic Hermitage, home of Andrew Jackson. Spacious bedrooms with private baths and 12-foot ceilings. Breakfast is served in the formal dining room among treasured antiques, or informally on the front porch, surrounded by 100-year old trees.

Hosts: Marion and George Kelley
Rooms: 3 (PB) $50-60
Full Breakfast
Credit Cards: A, B, C, D, E
Notes: 2, 5, 8, 14

SAVANNAH

Bed and Breakfast About Tennessee

P. O. Box 110227, Nashville, 37222-0227
Information: (615) 331-5244; Reservations: (800) 458-2421 (U.S.); FAX (615) 833-7701

This comfortable home on the Tennessee River is furnished with family antiques. Near the Shiloh Battlefield, it is a nice way to get away from the city. Water sports available. Dinner is extra. $70.

SEVIERVILLE

Blue Mountain Mist Country Inn

1811 Pullen Road, 37862
(615) 428-2335

This inn is a new Victorian-style farmhouse with a big wraparound porch overlooking rolling hills, with the Great Smoky Mountains as a backdrop. Furnished with country antiques, Grandmother's quilts, and old photographs, this inn provides a homey atmosphere. Just minutes from the Great Smoky Mountains National Park, Gatlinburg, and Dollywood. Five romantic country cottages recently added.

6 Pets welcome; 8 Children welcome; 9 Social drinking allowed; 10 Tennis available; 11 Swimming available; 12 Golf available; 13 Skiing available; 14 May be booked through travel agents.

Hosts: Norman and Sarah Ball
Rooms: 12 (PB) $79-115
Cottages: 5 (PB) $125
Full Breakfast
Credit Cards: A, B
Notes: 2, 5

Milk and Honey Country Hideaway

2803 Old Country Way, 37862
(615) 428-4858

Near Gatlinburg and Pigeon Forge, this charming two-story cedar home has six bedrooms, each furnished with antiques and decorated in Country Victorian. The parlor, which has a large stone fireplace, usually filled with aromas of freshly baked desserts coming from the kitchen. The surrounding area has much to offer in the unparalleled beauty of the Great Smoky Mountains National Park. Off-season rates and group discounts available.

Hosts: Gary and Cathey McFarland
Rooms: 6 (4 PB; 2 SB) $65-97
Full Breakfast
Credit Cards: A, B
Notes: 2, 5, 12, 13, 14

SHELBYVILLE

Bed and Breakfast About Tennessee

P. O. Box 110227, Nashville, 37222-0227
Information: (615) 331-5244; Reservations: (800) 458-2421 (U.S.); FAX (615) 833-7701

The best kept secret in Tennessee! Beautiful country inn situated in the pretty rolling hills of middle Tennessee. Swimming pool on the premises. Lunch and dinner extra. $65-120.

Bottle Hollow Lodge

P.O. Box 92, 111 Gobbler Ridge Road, 37160
(615) 695-5253

Nestled in the foothills of middle Tennessee, Bottle Hollow Lodge serves up peace and quiet along with traditional southern hospitality. Area attractions include the Tennessee Walking Horse National Celebration, the Jack Daniel Distillery and the University of Tennessee Space Institute. During a stay, enjoy the sights or simply relax by the fire and enjoy a breathtaking view of the valley.

Hosts: Pat and Jim Whiteside
Rooms: 5 (one suite, PB) $85-150
Full Breakfast
Credit Cards: A, B, F
Notes: 2, 3 (by request), 4 (by request), 5, 8 (case-by-case basis), 9, 10, 12, 14

TOWNSEND

Bed and Breakfast About Tennessee

P. O. Box 110227, Nashville, 37222-0227
Information: (615) 331-5244; Reservations: (800) 458-2421 (U.S.); FAX (615) 833-7701

This 100-year old home is situated on several acres of land near Cades Cove, Gatlinburg, and Knoxville. Host speaks many languages. One double room with rollaway bed and fireplace, king room, and twin room available. Shared bath. $60-70.

Richmont Inn

220 Winterberry Lane, 37882
(615) 448-6751

Situated on the "peaceful side of the Smokies," this Appalachian barn is beautifully furnished with 18th-century English antiques and French paintings. Breathtaking mountain views, graciously appointed rooms with sitting areas, wood-burning fireplaces, spa tubs for two, and balconies. French and Swiss cuisine are served at breakfast with flavored coffees, and gourmet desserts by candlelight in the

Richmont Inn

evenings. The Smoky Mountains, arts/crafts shops, outlet shopping, historic Cades Cove, and golf are all nearby. "A special place for couples."

Hosts: Susan and Jim Hind
Rooms: 10 (PB) $85-130
Full Breakfast
Credit Cards: None
Notes: 2, 5, 12

Texarkana •

• Fort Worth   • Canton   Jefferson •

Granbury •   • Tyler

• Glen Rose   • Ennis

Center •

• Leander

• Johnson City

• Fredericksburg   • Brenham
                         • Burton

• Gonzales   • Houston

• San Antonio   Columbus •

• Rio Medina   Galveston

TEXAS

Texas

Heartland Country Inn
Bed and Breakfast Retreat

Route 2, Box 446, 77833
(409) 836-1864

Two-story home overlooking a spectacular view on 158 acres. Large porches to enjoy hilltop breezes, rolling hills and lakes. Fourteen bedrooms tastefully furnished in antiques, comfortable king, queen or twin beds with private baths. All you can eat country breakfast featuring eggs, bacon, sausage, potatoes, grits, pancakes, fresh fruit, biscuits, muffins and juice. Experience a delightful step back in time that provides a gentler lifestyle with elegance.

Host: Shirley Sacks
Rooms: 15 (7 PB; 8 SB) $65-110
Full Breakfast
Credit Cards: None
Notes: 2, 3 (groups), 4 (groups), 6, 8, 9, 14

Long Point Inn

Route 1, P. O. Box 86-A, 77835
(409) 289-3171

Texas hospitality on a 175-acre cattle ranch describes this bed and breakfast. Situated on one of the officially designated scenic highways of Texas, the historic La Bahia Road, which was one of the bluebonnet trails of Washington County, the inn is in the county voted by readers of *Texas Highways* as the most scenic county in Texas for spring flowers. A luxury home copied inside and out from Old World chalets and featured as the "Prettiest Place in the Country" in *Farm and Ranch Living*, June 1988.

Hosts: Bill and Jeannine Neinast
Rooms: 3 (2 PB; 1 SB) $79.50-90.10
Full Breakfast
Credit Cards: C
Notes: 2, 5, 8, 9

Long Point Inn

Bed and Breakfast
Country Style

P. O. Box 1101, 75103
(800) 725-2899

Reservation service for 32 bed and breakfasts in the Canton area. Catering only to First Monday Trade Days—the largest and oldest flea market in the world. Featured in several travel magazines, including *National Geographic*.

Hosts: Vic and Marti Weatherholt
Rooms: 52 (25 PB; 27 SB) $50-80
Full Breakfast
Credit Cards: A, B, C
Notes: 2, 5, 14

NOTES: Credit cards accepted: A Master Card; B Visa; C American Express; D Discover Card; E Diner's Club; F Other; 2 Personal Checks accepted; 3 Lunch available; 4 Dinner available; 5 Open all year; 6 Pets welcome; 8 Children welcome; 9 Social drinking allowed; 10 Tennis available; 11 Swimming available; 12 Golf available; 13 Skiing available; 14 May be booked through travel agents.

Pine Colony Inn

CENTER

Pine Colony Inn

500 Shelbyville Street, 75935
(409) 598-7700

Situated in a quiet east Texas town, this inn sits just west of the Sabine River which runs between Texas and Louisiana. Only a few miles from Toledo Bend, it is a popular spot for bass fishing. Group gatherings welcome.

Hosts: Regina Wright and Marcille Hughes
Rooms: 12 (8 PB; 4 SB) $27-55
Full Breakfast
Credit Cards: A, B
Notes: 2, 5, 8, 9, 10, 11, 12, 14

COLUMBUS

The Gant Guest House

936 Bowie Street, Box 112, 78934
(409) 732-5135; (409) 732-2190

Whether an overnight traveler, staying for a week, or getting away for a weekend, guests find a charming and unusual atmosphere in this restored German cottage. Built about 1870, The Gant House retains the original wall painting and stenciling. One bedroom was copied for the Texas Room in the DAR Museum of Washington, D.C. Completely furnished in antiques, The Gant House offers two bedrooms with double beds, a hall sitting room, dining room,

modern kitchen and bathroom with tub-shower, and central heating and air conditioning.

Owner: Laura A. Rau
Host: R.F. (Buddy) Rau
Rooms: 2 (PB) $65-95
Continental Breakfast
Credit Cards: None
Notes: 2, 5, 9, 10, 11, 12

Magnolia Oaks

634 Spring Street, 78934
(409) 732-2726

This 1890 Victorian jewel sits amidst giant magnolias near the historic courthouse and Stafford Opera House. The gingerbread porches, summer room, 14-foot ceilings, fireplaces, stained glass windows, garden arbor, fountain and herb garden offer total relaxation. Three rooms feature king beds, one with Jacuzzi. Magnolia Oaks is one mile off I-10 connecting Houston and San Antonio. Wildflowers and antiques are abundant. Complimentary afternoon tea. The hosts often entertain with guitar and piano.

Hosts: Nancy and Bob Stiles
Rooms: 6 (PB) $80-95
Full Breakfast
Credit Cards: None
Notes: 2, 5, 9, 10, 11, 12,

ENNIS

Raphael House

500 West Ennis Avenue, 75119
(214) 875-1555

Six exquisite bedrooms with private baths set in a beautifully restored 1906 Neoclassical mansion appointed with original antiques, rich wall coverings, and luxurious fabrics. Amenities include oversize beds with down comforters and pillows, claw foot tub with scented soaps and bubble baths, afternoon refreshments, and turn-down service. Situated in a National Register historic district just 35 minutes from

NOTES: Credit cards accepted: A Master Card; B Visa; C American Express; D Discover Card; E Diner's Club; F Other; 2 Personal Checks accepted; 3 Lunch available; 4 Dinner available; 5 Open all year;

Dallas and 15 minutes from Waxahachie and lots of antiques.

Host: Danna Cody
Rooms: 6 (PB) $58-95
Full Breakfast
Credit Cards: A, B, C, E
Notes: 2, 3, 4, 5, 9, 10, 11, 12

Raphael House

FORT WORTH

Miss Molly's Hotel

109 1/2 West Exchange Avenue, 76106
(817) 626-1522

Situated in the Fort Worth Stockyard's Historic District. Miss Molly's was once a respectable boarding house, but later became a popular "bawdy house." Eight rooms filled with historic Old West antiques highlighting the personalities of former customers: gunslingers, cowboys, oil men, railroad men, cattle men ... An elegant "Madame's Room," complete with draped ceiling and unique private bath, honors the former popular madame, Miss Josie. Horseback riding, restaurants, saloons, shopping, and the world's largest honky tonk, Billy Bob's Texas, are all within walking distance. Reserved parking.

Hosts: Susan and Mark Hancock
Rooms: 8 (1 PB; 7 SB) $68-125
Continental Breakfast
Credit Cards: A, B, C, D
Notes: 2, 5, 8, 9, 14

FREDERICKSBURG

Country Cottage Inn

249 East Main Street, 78624
(512) 997-8549

Fredricksburg's two most historic homes (the Chester Nimitz Birthplace and Kiehne House) form this inn. Thick limestone walls, handcut beams and woodwork, and mellow stone fireplaces are in both homes. Both are on the National Register of Historic Places. Enjoy complimentary wine, large continental breakfasts, king-size beds, old fans, room refrigerators, microwaves, bathrobes, giant whirlpool tubs, tubside candles, and wood-burning fireplaces.

Host: Ms. Jeffrey Webb
Rooms: 7 (PB) $70-105
Continental Breakfast
Credit Cards: A, B
Notes: 2, 5, 8, 9, 10, 11, 12

Landhaus Bed and Breakfast

P. O. Drawer E, 78624
(210) 997-4916

This bed and breakfast is a charming 1883 restored home on 40 acres in the heart of Texas Hill Country, approximately eight minutes northeast of Fredericksburg on Rural Route 1631. There are four bedrooms, one large bath with shower tub, modern kitchen, den, and livingroom. The house has central heat and air, two cast-iron wood-burning stoves, a microwave oven, dishwasher, TV, and telephone. Hiking, jogging, biking, fishing permitted. Not far from Lyndon Baines Johnson Ranch and Boyhood Home, Nimitz Museum, Enchanted Rock, and many other historic sites, shopping, and excellent restaurants.

Hosts: Monty and Maria McDonald
Rooms: 4 (SB) $95
Full Breakfast (self-serve)
Credit Cards: None
Notes: 2, 5, 8 (under 1 and over 13), 9, 14

6 Pets welcome; 8 Children welcome; 9 Social drinking allowed; 10 Tennis available; 11 Swimming available; 12 Golf available; 13 Skiing available; 14 May be booked through travel agents.

GALVESTON

Hazlewood House

1127 Church Street, P. O. Box 1326, 77550
(409) 762-1668

Romantic Victorian home with three rooms to choose from with private baths, and a Jacuzzi suite. Antique furnishings, Oriental carpets, and fine tapestries throughout. Wine and cheese on arrival; morning coffee and a hearty continental breakfast are served on fine china, crystal, and silver. Near the beach, historical tours, musicals, museums, and trolley.

Host: Pat Hazlewood
Rooms: 3 (PB) $55-125
Continental Breakfast
Credit Cards: A, B
Notes: 2, 5, 9, 10, 11, 12, 13, 14

The Queen Anne Bed and Breakfast

1915 Sealy Avenue, 77550-2312
(409) 763-7088; (800) 472-0930

This home is a four-story Queen Anne Victorian built in 1905. Stained-glass windows, beautiful floors, large rooms, pocket doors, 12-foot ceilings with transom doors, beautifully redecorated in 1991. Walk to historic shopping district, restaurants, 1886 opera house, museums, and the historic homes district. A short drive to the beach. A visit to Queen Anne is to be anticipated, relished, and remembered.

Hosts: John McWilliams and Earl French
Rooms: 4 (SB) $85-125
Full Breakfast
Credit Cards: A, B
Notes: 2, 5, 9, 10, 11, 12, 13

GLEN ROSE

Inn on the River

205 Southwest Barnard Street, 76043
(817) 897-2101

This 1919 inn on the Paluxy River near the town square is a designated Historic Texas Landmark. The 19 rooms and three suites are individually designed, and all have private baths. The Great Blue Heron Meeting House was added in 1990. The entire inn was renovated in 1993, and features a new but traditional elegant decor. Handicapped accessible. This area of Texas is noted for its scenic hills, rivers, Dinosaur Valley State Park, Fossil Rim Wildlife Conservation Center, and Texas Amphitheater.

Hosts: Nancy and Michael Rosenthal
Rooms: 22 (PB) $80-140
Full Breakfast
Credit Cards: A, B, C, D
Notes: 2, 4, 5, 9, 10, 11, 12, 14

GONZALES

Saint James Inn

Bed and Breakfast Hosts of San Antonio
166 Rockhill, San Antonio, 78209
(512) 824-8036

This inn is a Greek Revival home built in 1914. One hour from San Antonio, Austin, and Victoria, it has three rooms. For breakfast, enjoy fruit, fresh pastries, homemade jams, juices, and other surprises with freshly brewed coffee or tea. Each room is unique, with antiques and fresh flowers; and there are porches on which to enjoy the breeze, church bells, and birds. No pets. Children over 12 only. $65.

GRANBURY

Dabney House Bed and Breakfast

106 South Jones, 76048
(817) 579-1260; (817) 823-6867 (evenings)

Built in 1907, this house boasts its original hardwood floors, trimwork, beveled glass, stained glass and various light fixtures. Craftsman-style one-story situated seven blocks from the historic Downtown Square. Candlelight romance packages available with dinner by reservation only. Special occasion baskets available by request for $12. TV and VCR available in the common room, with tours available Thursday through Saturday. Pecan waffles are a specialty of the house.

Hosts: John and Gwen Hurley
Rooms: 4 (2 PB; 2 SB) $ 60-90
Full Breakfast
Credit Cards: A, B, C
Notes: 2, 4 (by reservation only), 5, 9, 10, 12, 14

HOUSTON

Durham House Inn Bed and Breakfast

921 Heights Boulevard, 77008
(713) 868-4654

Durham House is a faithfully restored Queen Anne Victorian on the National Register of Historic Places. Situated in central Houston, just 10 minutes from downtown, Durham House is convenient for business travelers and tourists. Guests may use the backyard gazebo, the player piano, or the solarium. Walk and jog on the boulevard.

Host: Marguerite Swanson
Rooms: 6 (5 PB; 1 SB) $60-85
Full Breakfast
Credit Cards: A, B, C
Notes: 2, 5, 8, 10, 11, 12, 14

Durham House Inn

The Highlander

607 Highland Street, 77009
(713) 861-6110

A tranquil oasis only five minutes from downtown. Choose from luxurious rooms or whimsical delights. The gracious hospitality includes afternoon tea, bedside snacks, and a lovely full breakfast. Longtime residents of Houston, the hosts can assist in planning guests' visit. Only one block to metro bus, near both I-45N and I-10W, this location is convenient to everything. Here southern charm and Christian hospitality combine to make memories beautiful.

Hosts: Arlen and Georgie McIrvin
Rooms: 4 (2 PB; 2 SB) $60-75
Full Breakfast
Credit Cards: A, B, C, D
Notes: 2, 5, 8, 11, 14

Robin's Nest

4104 Greeley, 77006
(713) 528-5821; (800) 622-8343

History, comfort, convenience, and tastebuds make a stay at Robin's Nest memorable. The rooms are spacious and airy, furnished in eclectic Victorian. The atmosphere is relaxed and easy. Situated in a vibrant neighborhood in the inner city, among Houston's five major museums, downtown, theater district, medical center, and major sporting events. Individual tours for registered guests.

Host: Robin Smith
Rooms: 3 (PB) $75
Full Breakfast
Credit Cards: A, B
Notes: 2, 3, 4, 5, 8, 9, 10, 11, 12, 14

JEFFERSON

McKay House Bed and Breakfast Inn

306 East Delta Street, 75657
(903) 665-7322

6 Pets welcome; 8 Children welcome; 9 Social drinking allowed; 10 Tennis available; 11 Swimming available; 12 Golf available; 13 Skiing available; 14 May be booked through travel agents.

Jefferson is a riverport town from the frontier days of the Republic of Texas. It has historical mule-drawn tours, 30 antique shops, boat rides on the river, and a narrow gauge train. The McKay House, a recently restored 1851 Greek Revival cottage, offers period furnishings, cool lemonade, porch swings, fireplaces, and a full gentleman's breakfast. Hospitality abounds, and Victorian nightclothes are provided.

Owners: Peggy and Tom Taylor
Innkeeper: Alma Anne Parker
Rooms: 7 (PB) $70-125
Full Breakfast
Credit Cards: A, B
Notes: 2, 5, 9, 12, 14

JOHNSON CITY

Hoppe's Guest House
Bed and Breakfast Hosts of San Antonio
166 Rockhill, San Antonio, 78209
(512) 824-8036

This charming, turn-of-the-century restoration in a quiet neighborhood provides two bedrooms, one with a queen-size bed and the other with a double bed. The rooms share a bath. $55.

LEANDER

Trail's End Bed and Breakfast
12223 Trail's End Road, # 7, 78641
(512) 267-2901

This bed and breakfast is situated in the country on six acres of beautiful Texas hill country. Elegant, but comfortable, the two guest rooms upstairs are large, featuring double mahogany beds, a sofa and bath in each, with one opening to the upper porch. The guest house is down the hill a short distance, and will sleep six or more. The breakfasts are delicious.

Hosts: JoAnn and Tom Patty
Rooms: 2 (PB-main house) $68.90; 4 (SB-guest house) $100.90
Full Breakfast
Credit Cards: None
Notes: 2, 3 (advanced request), 4 (advanced request), 5, 8, 11, 12, 14

RIO MEDINA

Haby Settlement Inn
Bed and Breakfast Hosts of San Antonio
166 Rockhill, San Antonio, 78209
(512) 824-8036

Cottage in beautiful rural setting lovingly restored has one bedroom, bath, livingroom with sleeper sofa, dining room, and kitchen. Adults only. $65.

SAN ANTONIO

Adams House Bed and Breakfast
231 Adams Street, 78210
(210) 224-4791; FAX: (210) 223-5125

Experience the gracious hospitality of Adams House. Built in San Antonio in 1902 in what is now known as the King William Historic District, Adams House is a reflection of southern tradition. This soaring, two-story house gracefully wears the beauty and charm of another era. A visit will be steeped in history, with all the modern accommodations and comforts to make the stay pleasant and memorable.

Hosts: Harold Fuchs and Betty Mays Lancaster
Rooms: 4 (PB) $60-85
Full Breakfast
Credit Cards: A, B, C
Notes: 2, 5, 8 (over 12), 9, 12, 14

Alan's Guest House
Bed and Breakfast Hosts of San Antonio
166 Rockhill, 78209
(512) 824-8036

NOTES: Credit cards accepted: A Master Card; B Visa; C American Express; D Discover Card; E Diner's Club; F Other; 2 Personal Checks accepted; 3 Lunch available; 4 Dinner available; 5 Open all year;

Situated in the King William area, Alan's Guest House has all the modern conveniences. Loft bedroom with twin beds, downstairs bedroom with double bed and private bath. Sofa bed in livingroom and full kitchen with continental breakfast provided. Original portion of home was built in 1871. Two bicycles are available. $70-100.

Beauregard House Bed and Breakfast

Bed and Breakfast Hosts of San Antonio
166 Rockhill, 78209
(512) 824-8036

This charming Victorian home was built in 1910 with hardwood floors and furnishings appropriate to the era. Downstairs room has queen bed, private bath and entrance. The two upstairs guest rooms have king beds and private baths. Breakfast is served in the dining room, on the tree-shaded backyard deck, or on the spacious front porch, whichever the guest prefers. $60-75.

Beckman Inn and Carriage House

222 East Gunther Street, 78204
(210) 229-1449

This charming Victorian is in the heart of San Antonio in the King William district. The beautiful wraparound porch welcomes guests to this cozy home, and guest rooms are colorfully decorated and feature antique Victorian queen-size beds and private baths. Stroll on the scenic river walk or ride the trolley to enjoy all the festivities.

Hosts: Betty Jo and Don Schwartz
Rooms: 5 (PB) $80-120
Continental Breakfast
Credit Cards: A, B
Notes: 2, 5

Bed and Breakfast Hosts of San Antonio #6

166 Rockhill, 78209
(512) 824-8036

This restored turn-of-the-century Victorian offers an upstairs bedroom with and adjoining bath. A second upstairs bedroom has a double bed and private hallway bath. Each guest room opens onto its own private porch. A continental breakfast is served in the dining room or on the porch. Close to the Ten Cent Trolley and VIA bus that takes you to the Alamo, River Walk, the Old Market, and many other downtown attractions. $60.

Bed and Breakfast on the River

Bed and Breakfast Hosts of San Antonio
166 Rockhill, 78209
(512) 824-8036

Restored Victorian right on the river in downtown. All rooms feature queen beds and private baths. Some rooms have adjoining sitting room overlooking the river. Special continental breakfast is provided. The host, Dr. Zucht, is a licensed hot air balloon pilot who can arrange for charter flight for guests or anyone visiting San Antonio. $99.

The Bonner Garden

Bed and Breakfast Hosts of San Antonio
166 Rockhill, 78209
(512) 824-8036

This bed and breakfast is a large Italian-style villa in the Monte Vista area. Stroll in the garden, relax on the rooftop, or swim in the beautiful pool surrounded by flowers and shrubs in full bloom. Three guest rooms with private bath in the main house and a private detached studio. This was the home of Mary Bonner, renowned artist. Call for current rates.

6 Pets welcome; 8 Children welcome; 9 Social drinking allowed; 10 Tennis available; 11 Swimming available; 12 Golf available; 13 Skiing available; 14 May be booked through travel agents.

Buttercup
Bed and Breakfast

Bed and Breakfast Hosts of San Antonio
166 Rockhill, 78209
(512) 824-8036

Spacious guest cottage centrally situated on
one acre in a quiet Alamo Heights neighborhood. Just two blocks to shopping center, VIA bus to downtown in minutes.
Airport transportation is provided.
Landscaped grounds and extensive play-
ground equipment make this home ideal for
children of all ages. Private cottage consists
of one bedroom with twin beds and adjoining bath, second bedroom with double bed
and sitting area. Private bath in hallway.
Hosts provide a special breakfast in the cottage kitchen for guests to serve themselves.
Guests may use the kitchen and game room
with pool table. $115.

Chabot Reed House

403 Madison, 78204
(512) 223-8697

The Chabot Reed House is an 1876
Victorian house situated one block from the
Riverwalk in the King William Historical
District in downtown San Antonio. A special treat is staying in the Carriage House
where two guest suites are located.
Luxurious, yet comfortable; bold and colorful with an appropriate sense of history and
sophistication. Private and romantic, the
Carriage House is situated on the lovely
landscaped grounds to the side of the main
house. Guests are welcomed in the manor
house as well.

Hosts: Sister and Peter Reed
Rooms: 5 (4 PB; 1 SB) $95-105
Full Breakfast
Credit Cards: None
Notes: 2, 5, 8 (over 12), 9, 14

Cross Mountain Ranch

Bed and Breakfast Hosts of San Antonio
166 Rockhill, 78209
(512) 824-8036

This modern upstairs guest house in the
northwest hills of San Antonio set on more
than two acres provides a livingroom, bedroom, kitchen, dinette, and full bath.
Central heat and air conditioning. Children
are welcome. Pets permitted outside. $60.

Falling Pines
Bed and Breakfast

300 West French Place, 78212
(210) 733-1996; (800) 880-4580

Falling Pines is in the Monte Vista Historic
District, one mile north of downtown San
Antonio. Construction on the home began
in 1911 under the direction of famed architect Atlee Ayres. Pine trees, not native to
San Antonio, tower over the mansion on an
acre park-like setting. Brick and limestone
construction, a green tiled roof and shuttered windows enhance a magnificent limestone archway entree and veranda on the
front facade. The entry level features six
rooms of a quarter-cut oak paneling, wood
floors, Oriental carpets, fireplace, and a
tiled solarium, where breakfast is served.
Spacious and elegant guest rooms are on
the second level, while the third level is
entirely the 2,000-square foot Persian
Suite, which commands a grand view of
downtown San Antonio and nearby beer
baron Koehler Mansion.

Hosts: Grace and Bob Daubert
Rooms: 4 (PB) $67-97
Full Breakfast
Credit Cards: None
Notes: None

The Gatlin House

Bed and Breakfast Hosts of San Antonio
166 Rockhill, 78209
(512) 824-8036

This beautifully restored turn-of-the-century Victorian home is furnished with lovely
antiques. The first upstairs bedroom has a
queen bed and adjoining private bath; the
second has a double bed and private hall-

way bath. Each bedroom opens onto its own private porch. Continental breakfast. One-half block from Ten Cent Trolley and VIA bus. $60.

Linden House

Bed and Breakfast Hosts of San Antonio
166 Rockhill, 78209
(512) 824-8036

Twelve blocks north of downtown, this house was built in 1902 by Judge Linden, a colorful character with a peg leg who rode posse with the best of them to pursue notorious criminals and bandits in South Texas. The present owners offer four second-floor bedrooms, each with adjacent private bath. A generous continental breakfast is served in the coffee room. TV is available. Airport transportation. Convenient to downtown, only two blocks from the Ten Cent Trolley to downtown. Older children welcome. $60.

Naegelin Bed and Breakfast

Bed and Breakfast Hosts of San Antonio
166 Rockhill, 78209
(512) 824-8036

Situated in the La Vaca historic district of San Antonio and adjacent to all downtown attractions, this Colonial brick home with Corinthian columns was built in 1910 and carefully restored and furnished in Victorian style. A special continental breakfast is served in the dining room. Four guest rooms, one with private bath. $55-70.

Norton Brackenridge House

230 Madison, 78204
(512) 271-3442

This is an 80-year-old fully restored home in the King William historic district, the oldest historic district in Texas. It is a two-story house with Corinthian columns, and verandas on the front and back. It is decorated with Victorian antiques and has private entrances and baths, central air and heat, fans in all rooms. A full gourmet breakfast is served on the veranda or in the dining room.

Host: Nancy Cole
Rooms: 5 (PB) $75-95
Full Breakfast
Credit Cards: A, B, C, D
Notes: 2, 5, 7, 14

Nunez Home

Bed and Breakfast Hosts of San Antonio
166 Rockhill, 78209
(512) 824-8036

The Nunez Home is near all downtown San Antonio attractions. Our European guests have been very appreciative of this charming couple's knowledge of San Antonio and enjoy being welcomed as true friends into their restored family Victorian Home. They have an upstairs bedroom with a double bed and a single bed with a private bath in the hallway. Airport transportation upon request. $35-45.

The Ogé House on the Riverwalk

209 Washington Street, 78204
(800) 242-2770; FAX (512) 226-5812

Step back to an era of elegance and romance in this historic antebellum mansion shaded by massive pecans and oaks, graciously situated on more than an acre of beautifully landscaped nature along the banks of the famous San Antonio Riverwalk. The inn, beautifully decorated with antiques, has large verandas, nine fireplaces and a grand foyer. All rooms have either queen or king beds, private baths, air conditioning, telephones, and TV. Dining, entertainment, convention center, trolley, and the Alamo are only steps away.

Hosts: Patrick and Sharrie Magatagan
Rooms: 10 (PB) $125-195

6 Pets welcome; 8 Children welcome; 9 Social drinking allowed; 10 Tennis available; 11 Swimming available; 12 Golf available; 13 Skiing available; 14 May be booked through travel agents.

Continental Breakfast
Credit Cards: A, B, C
Notes: 2, 5, 9, 12, 14

Summit Haus I and II

Bed and Breakfast Hosts of San Antonio
166 Rockhill, 78209
(512) 824-8036

These two renovated 1920s residences—side by side—are in the historic Monte Vista area. The main residence provides a suite with king-size bed and a full bath, with a double bed in the adjoining sun room. The cottage has two large bedrooms, one with a king-size bed and the other with a double bed. Summit Haus I is furnished with German Biedermier antiques, crystal, linens, porcelains, and antique Persian and Turkish rugs. Summit Haus II is furnished with French and English antiques. $70.

Terrell Castle
Bed and Breakfast

Bed and Breakfast Hosts of San Antonio
166 Rockhill, 78209
(512) 824-8036

Terrell Castle was built in 1894 as the residence of Edwin Holland Terrell, who served as ambassador to Belgium in the early 1890s. A full breakfast is served in the dining room. No charge for children under six. A variety of rooms and suites are available on the second and third floors of this mansion, which was inspired by the beauty of the castles and chateaux of Europe. $70-100 plus tax.

TEXARKANA

Mansion on Main

802 Main Street, 75501
(903) 792-1835

"Twice as Nice," the motto of Texarkana (Texas and Arkansas) USA, is standard practice at the Mansion on Main. The 1895 neoclassical Colonial, surrounded by 14 tall columns, was recently restored by the owners of the McKay House, a popular bed and breakfast in nearby Jefferson. Six chambers vary from the Governor's Suite to the Butler's Garret. Guests enjoy southern hospitality, period furnishings, fireplaces and a gentleman's breakfast. Just 30 miles away rests the town of Hope, the birthplace of President Bill Clinton.

Hosts: Carolyn and Bill White
Owners: Peggy and Tom Taylor
Rooms: 6 (PB) $55-125
Full or Continental Breakfast
Credit Cards: A, B
Notes: 2, 5, 12, 14

TYLER

Mary's Attic
Bed and Breakfast

413 South College, 75702
(903) 592-5181; FAX (903) 592-3846

A two-bedroom, two-bath 1920 bungalow restored and furnished with English and American antiques on the brick streets in the historic part of Tyler. Apartment annex features three bedrooms, one bath, a fully furnished kitchen and children are welcome. The continental breakfast features homemade sweet rolls and breads. Refrigerator stocked with complimentary cold drinks, juice, and fresh fruit tray. No pets. No children.

Rooms: 2 (PB) $75
Continental Breakfast
Credit Cards: A, B, D
Notes: 2, 5

WIMBERLEY

Coleman Canyon Ranch

Bed and Breakfast of Wimberley
P. O. Box 589, 78676
(512) 847-9666; (512) 847-2837

NOTES: Credit cards accepted: A Master Card; B Visa; C American Express; D Discover Card; E Diner's Club; F Other; 2 Personal Checks accepted; 3 Lunch available; 4 Dinner available; 5 Open all year;

Relax on the front porch swing or hike over this Hill Country ranch. Find fossils in the creek bed, or watch deer from the rear deck. Two bedrooms, two baths, livingroom, dining room, kitchen, and a library are available for guest use. A full breakfast is included. Situated four miles north of Wimberley Square. Two-night minimum stay holidays and market day weekends. Special dietary needs can be met with advance notice. $100.

J.R. Dobie House

Bed and Breakfast of Wimberley
P. O. Box 589, 78676
(512) 847-9666; (512) 847-2837

This restored, historic cottage is furnished with comfortable antiques: 1890s charm combined with 1990s comfort. Enjoy the wood-burning fireplace, with wood provided by the hosts. Cable TV, telephone, a full kitchen, private bath, central heat and air, and picnic facilities are provided. $85.

Wide Horizon

Bed and Breakfast of Wimberley
P. O. Box 589, 78676
(512) 847-9666; (512) 847-2837

Situated on Ranch Road 12 south of the Blanco River, this bi-level home offers two very private accommodations, each with private entrance and bath. The Southwest Suite has a wet bar, color TV, and king-size bed. The Antique Suite has a private sitting room with a hide-a-couch, and a large bedroom with antique double beds. Relax on the large deck that spans the width of the house. No pets. $85.

6 Pets welcome; 8 Children welcome; 9 Social drinking allowed; 10 Tennis available; 11 Swimming available; 12 Golf available; 13 Skiing available; 14 May be booked through travel agents.

UTAH

- Salt Lake City
  - Park City
- Sandy
  - Midway

- Saint George

Utah

MIDWAY

Schneitter Family Hotel at the Homestead Resort

700 North Homestead Drive, 84049
(801) 654-1102; (800) 327-7220

The original Schneitter Family Hotel at the historic Homestead Resort. Eight Victorian "adults only" rooms individually appointed with antiques, linens, and special amenities. Adjacent solarium and whirlpool. The AAA Four Diamond resort offers golf, swimming, horseback riding, tennis, elegant dining, sleigh rides, cross-country skiing, snowmobiling, and complete meeting facilities.

Host: Britt Mathwich
Rooms: 8 (PB) $89-105
Continental Breakfast
Credit Cards: A, B, C
Notes: 2, 3, 4, 5, 9, 10, 11, 12, 13, 14

PARK CITY

The Imperial Hotel

221 Main Street, P. O. Box 1628, 84060
(801) 649-1904; (800) 669-UTAH (reservations)

Listed on the National Register of Historic Landmarks, this 1904 hotel is a finely restored property reminiscent of a bygone era. Each room is decorated with turn-of-the-century antiques and appointments, yet boasts cable TV, telephones and beautifully tiled baths with Roman tubs. Guests may relax in the intimate parlor, unwind in the Jacuzzi, or socialize in the art gallery/pub on the ground floor.

Hosts: Marianne and Ted Dumas
Rooms: 10 (PB) $52-160
Continental Breakfast
Credit Cards: A, B, C
Notes: 2, 5, 8, 9, 10, 11, 12, 13, 14

Imperial Hotel

The Old Miners' Lodge

615 Woodside Avenue, Box 2639, 84060
(801) 645-8068; (800) 648-8068
FAX (801) 645-7420

A restored 1893 miners' boarding house in the national historic district of Park City, with ten individually decorated rooms filled with antiques and older pieces. Close to historic Main Street, with the Park City ski area in its back yard. The lodge is "more like staying with friends than at a hotel!"

Hosts: Hugh Daniels, Jeff Sadowsky, Susan Wynne
Rooms: 10 (PB) $45-180
Full Breakfast
Minimum stay Christmas: 4-6 nights; US Film: 4 nights; Art: 2 nights
Credit Cards: A, B, C, D
Notes: 2, 5, 8, 9, 10, 11, 12, 13, 14

NOTES: Credit cards accepted: A Master Card; B Visa; C American Express; D Discover Card; E Diner's Club; F Other; 2 Personal Checks accepted; 3 Lunch available; 4 Dinner available; 5 Open all year; 6 Pets welcome; 8 Children welcome; 9 Social drinking allowed; 10 Tennis available; 11 Swimming available; 12 Golf available; 13 Skiing available; 14 May be booked through travel agents.

Old Miners' Lodge

SAINT GEORGE

Seven Wives Inn

217 North 100 West, 84770
(801) 628-3737; (800) 484-1084 (code 0165)

The inn consists of two adjacent pioneer adobe homes with massive hand-grained moldings framing windows and doors. Bedrooms are furnished in period antiques and handmade quilts. Some rooms have fireplaces; two have whirlpool tubs. Swimming pool on premises.

Hosts: Donna and Jay Curtis; Alison and Jon
    Bowcutt
Rooms: 12 (PB) $45-100
Full Breakfast
Credit Cards: A, B, C, E
Notes: 2, 5, 8, 9, 10, 11, 12, 14

SALT LAKE CITY

The Anton Boxrud Bed and Breakfast Inn

57 South, 600 East, 84102
(801) 363-8035; (800) 524-5511

The Anton Boxrud is a charming restored Victorian inn situated in the historic district of Salt Lake City. A hearty breakfast, and guests are on their way to Utah's many cultural events and renown outdoor activities. During the summer months, visitors are welcome to join the hosts on the veranda for evening hors d'oeuvres and great conversation. Just a few minute's walk to many downtown attractions.

Hosts: Mark Brown and Keith Lewis
Rooms: 6 (3 PB; 3 SB) $49-108
Full Breakfast
Credit Cards: A, B, C
Notes: 2, 5, 8, 9, 10, 11, 12, 13, 14

The Spruces Bed and Breakfast

6181 South 900 East, 84121
(801) 268-8762

The inn is set amid many tall spruces and has four suites furnished with folk art and southwestern touches. The largest suite has three bedrooms, a livingroom, and kitchen. Easy access to ski resorts, restaurants, hospitals, and shopping. Originally built in 1907 and renovated in 1985.

Hosts: Karl and Susan Lind
Rooms: 4 (PB) $50-90
Continental Breakfast
Credit Cards: A, B, C
Notes: 2, 5, 8, 9, 10, 11, 12, 13, 14

Seven Wives Inn

SANDY

Mountain Hollow Inn

10209 South Dimple Dell Road, 84092
(801) 942-3428

Situated on a secluded two-acre estate just minutes away from Alta, Brighton, Snowbird, and Solitude ski resorts. Close to

---

NOTES: Credit cards accepted: A Master Card; B Visa; C American Express; D Discover Card; E Diner's Club; F Other; 2 Personal Checks accepted; 3 Lunch available; 4 Dinner available; 5 Open all year;

downtown Salt Lake City, restaurants, hiking and mountain biking. Relax in the ten-person outdoor hot tub; play pool, Ping-Pong, or snooker in the game room. Watch a movie in front of the fireplace. Rooms for small business conferences. Spend a vacation or romantic interlude resting and relaxing among the trees.

Hosts: Doug and Kathy Larson
Rooms: 10 (1 PB; 9 SB) $58-150
Continental Breakfast
Credit Cards: A, B
Notes: 2, 5, 10, 11, 12, 13, 14

6 Pets welcome; 8 Children welcome; 9 Social drinking allowed; 10 Tennis available; 11 Swimming available; 12 Golf available; 13 Skiing available; 14 May be booked through travel agents.

Alburg

North Troy

Derby Line

Jeffersonville

Hyde Park

Lyndon

Essex Junction

Stowe

Burlington

Waterbury

Shelburne

Moretown

Waitsfield

Barre

Northfield

Vergennes

Warren

Middlebury

Randolph

Chelsea

Shoreham Village

Post Mills

Gayesville

VERMONT

Brandon

Rutland

Woodstock

Shrewsbury

Wallingford

Windsor

Middletown Springs

Ludlow

Dorset

Weston

Manchester Center

Chester

Manchester

Bellows Falls

West Townshend

Arlington

Putney

Bennington

Vermont

ALBURG

Thomas Mott
Bed and Breakfast

Blue Rock Road, Route 2, P. O. Box 149B, 05440
(802) 796-3736; (800) 348-0843

Open all year and hosted by Patrick J. Schallert, M.A., this completely restored 1838 farmhouse offers four rooms, all with private baths, that overlook Lake Champlain. A full view of the Green Mountains can be enjoyed from this beautifully restored bed and breakfast, and guests are less than an hour from Burlington and the Island of Montreal. Lake activities for all seasons; Sno-Springers & Vast; game room with bumper pool and darts. Approved AAA, AB&BA, *Yankee* magazine; and the National B&B Association. Complimentary Ben and Jerry's ice cream. Lawn games and R&R.

Host: Patrick J. Schallert, M.A.
Rooms: 4 (PB) $50-70
Full Breakfast
Credit Cards: A, B, D
Notes: 2, 3, 4, 5, 8 (over 6), 9, 10, 11, 12, 13, 14

ARLINGTON

The Inn on
Covered Bridge Green

Rural Delivery 1, Box 3550, 05250
(802) 375-9489

Unwind in country elegance at this two-century-old farmhouse and former home of

Norman Rockwell. Stroll across the green from the front porch to enjoy river activities on the Battenkill. A gourmet breakfast is served.

Hosts: Anne and Ron Weber
Rooms: 5 (PB) $110-165 plus tax
Full Breakfast
Credit Cards: None
Notes: 2, 5, 8, 9, 10, 11, 12, 13

BARRE

Woodruff House

13 East Street, 05641
(802) 476-7745; (802) 479-9381

Large 1883 Victorian home situated on a quiet park close to downtown shops and restaurants. Barre is the Granite Center of the World. Great scenery, fantastic fall foliage. Halfway between Boston and Montreal, off I-89. Like coming home to Grandma's.

Hosts: Robert and Terry Somaini and Katie
Rooms: 2 (PB) $55-65
Full Breakfast
Credit Cards: None
Notes: 2, 5, 8 (over 11), 12, 13

BELLOWS FALLS

Blue Haven Christian
Bed and Breakfast

Rural Delivery 1, Box 328, 05101
(802) 463-9008

This bed and breakfast has been called "a most peaceful escape" and "a benchmark

NOTES: Credit cards accepted: A Master Card; B Visa; C American Express; D Discover Card; E Diner's Club; F Other; 2 Personal Checks accepted; 3 Lunch available; 4 Dinner available; 5 Open all year; 6 Pets welcome; 8 Children welcome; 9 Social drinking allowed; 10 Tennis available; 11 Swimming available; 12 Golf available; 13 Skiing available; 14 May be booked through travel agents.

bed and breakfast facility." The 1830 schoolhouse reflects a gentler time, with thoughtful attention to modern needs. Enjoy breakfast in a wood-warmed farm kitchen, sample tea time treats, and cozy up to the stone hearth fireplace in the ruddy pine common room. The hostess loves to bake and keeps guests eager for breakfast. Immaculately clean, AAA approved.

Host: Helene Champagne
Rooms: 6 (4 PB; 2 SB) $58-85
Full Breakfast (weekends, holidays) Continental
    Breakfast (midweek)
Credit Cards: A, B, C
Notes: 2, 4, 5, 8, 9, 10, 11, 12, 13, 14

The Schoolhouse Inn

Bed and Breakfast Marblehead and North Shore
P. O. Box 35, Newtonville, MA 02160
(617) 964-1606; (800) 832-2632
FAX (617) 332-8572

Situated in the scenic countryside of the Connecticut River Valley, this country inn was formerly a schoolhouse for almost a century before its renovation to a residence. The common room has original wide floorboards and a magnificent stone fireplace. There are five guest rooms, sharing three baths. Each room is beautifully decorated and has a goose-down comforter for cold nights. A full country breakfast is served on weekends, continental mid-week. $60-75, seasonal.

BENNINGTON

The American Country Collection #041

4 Greenwood Lane, Delmar, NY 12054
(518) 439-7001

The peaceful sounds of Brahms, Bach, or Mozart play softly in the background. Guest rooms are scented with fresh flowers, mints, lovely linens, and towels. There is a stream in the rear of the property and a

large front porch for rocking. Braided rugs cover wide plank floors, with each room highlighted by antiques, pretty curtains, and country touches. All six bedrooms, two with private baths, feature new mattresses and window fans, and there is a wood-burning stove on a brick hearth in the common room on the first floor. A full gourmet breakfast is served. Children 12 and over welcome. Near Bennington College, Southern Vermont College, and Prospect Mountain. $60-90 (seasonal).

Molly Stark Inn

1067 East Main Street, 05201
(800) 356-3076

A true country inn with an intimate atmosphere, this 1890 Victorian home is situated on the main road through a historic town in southwestern Vermont and welcomes visitors year-round. Decorated and tastefully furnished with antiques, country collectibles, braided rugs on gleaming hardwood floors, and patchwork quilts on the beds. Guests are invited to use the wraparound front porch with rocking chairs; the den and parlor with wood-burning stoves are most inviting on those cool Vermont nights. Clean and affordable. Champagne dinner packages available, too.

Host: Reed Fendler
Rooms: 6 (2 PB; 4 SB) $60-80
Full Breakfast
Credit Cards: A, B, C, D
Notes: 2, 4, 5, 8, 9, 14

BRANDON

The Gazebo Inn

Route 7, 25 Grove Street, 05733
(802) 247-3235

Circa 1865, listed on the National Register of Historic Places. Relax by the wood-burning stove, out back in the gazebo, or on the porch. Relish a hearty breakfast, then

NOTES: Credit cards accepted: A Master Card; B Visa; C American Express; D Discover Card; E Diner's Club; F Other; 2 Personal Checks accepted; 3 Lunch available; 4 Dinner available; 5 Open all year;

enjoy a short walk to a picturesque village. Great bike loops, antiquing, crafts shops, skiing, and much more just minutes from the doorstep. Comfortable rooms with private baths await. Reservations and walk-ins are welcome.

Hosts: Janet and Joel Mondlak
Rooms: 4 (PB) $55-75
Full Breakfast
Credit Cards: A, B, C
Notes: 5, 8, 9, 10, 11, 12, 13, 14

HIVUE Bed and Breakfast Tree Farm

Rural Route 1, Box 1023
High Pond Road, 05773-9704
(802) 247-3042

Centrally situated for Vermont day trips, this 76-acre wildlife habitat and primitive tree farm boasts incredible views of the Pico, Killington, and Green Mountains. A four-season splendor. A hearty country breakfast is served.

Hosts: Wini and Bill Reuschle
Rooms: 3 (PB) $50
Full Breakfast
Credit Cards: None
Notes: 2, 5, 8, 9, 10, 11, 12, 13

Rosebelle's Victorian Inn

31 Franklin Street, Route 7, 05733
(802) 247-0098

This elegantly restored Victorian structure is listed on the National Register of Historic Places. Six spacious rooms with semi-private and private baths, full country breakfast, afternoon tea, and candlelight dining available to guests. Only minutes to Killington, Pico, and Sugarbush downhill and cross-country skiing. A true four-season inn with much to offer.

Hosts: Ginette and Norm Milot
Rooms: 6 (2 PB; 4 SB) $60-70 weekends; $50-65 midweek.
Full Breakfast
Credit Cards: A, B, C
Notes: 5, 8 (over 15), 10, 11, 12, 13

BROOKFIELD

Green Trails Country Inn

By the Floating Bridge, 05036
(802) 276-3412; (800) 243-3412

Cozy, relaxing, informal, like going home to Grandma's. Home-cooked meals at hearthside, guest rooms decorated with quilts and antiques. Hiking and biking, with vistas. In winter enjoy horse-drawn sleigh rides, cross-country skiing (34 km. tracked trails), and fireside friendship. "The epitome of a country inn"—NBC's "Today." Bed and breakfast or Modified American Plan available.

Hosts: Pat and Peter Simpson
Rooms: 15 (9 PB; 6 SB) $68-80
Credit Cards: None
Closed April
Notes: 2, 4, 8, 9, 10, 11, 12, 13, 14

BURLINGTON

Howden Cottage Bed and Breakfast

32 North Champlain Street, 05401
(802) 864-7198

Howden Cottage offers cozy lodging and warm hospitality in the home of a local artist. Situated in downtown Burlington, the house is convenient to shopping, Lake Champlain, movies, night spots, churches, and some of Burlington's best restaurants.

Host: Bruce Howden
Rooms: 3 (1 PB; 2 SB) $45-79
Continental Breakfast
Credit Cards: A, B
Notes: 2, 5, 9, 10, 11, 12, 13

CHELSEA

Shire Inn

8 Main Street, 05038
(802) 685-3031

6 Pets welcome; 8 Children welcome; 9 Social drinking allowed; 10 Tennis available; 11 Swimming available; 12 Golf available; 13 Skiing available; 14 May be booked through travel agents.

An 1832 historic brick Federal, "Very Vermont" inn. Eighteenth-century accommodations with 20th-century bathrooms. Small and intimate; some rooms have working fireplaces. Chef-owned and operated, with five-course dining available. Centrally situated; 30 miles north of Woodstock/Queeche; 34 miles to Hanover and Dartmouth; 30 miles south of Montpelier.

Hosts: Jay and Karen Keller
Rooms: 6 (PB) $65-95
Full Breakfast
Minimum stay weekends and holidays: 2 nights
Credit Cards: A, B
Notes: 2, 4, 5, 8 (over 6), 9, 10, 11, 13

CHESTER

The Hugging Bear Inn and Shoppe

Main Street, 05143
(802) 875-2412

Bed, breakfast, and bears in this charming Victorian home on the village green. The shop has over 3,500 bears, and guests may "adopt" a bear for the night as long as he's back to work in the shop by 9 A.M. the next morning. Puppet show often performed at breakfast; breakfast music provided by an 1890 music box. Two lovable cats in residence. A magical place to visit!

Hosts: The Thomases
Rooms: 6 (PB) $75-95
Full Breakfast
Minimum stay weekends: 2 nights; holidays: 2-3 nights
Credit Cards: A, B, C, D
Notes: 2, 5, 8, 9, 10, 11, 12, 13

The Inn at Long Last

Main Street, P. O. Box 589, 05143
(802) 875-2444

A warm and welcoming inn where all the rooms have individual themes, where the decor is highly personal, and where the staff hospitality is exceptional. Gardens,

tennis courts, food, and theme weekends that draw raves. Modified American plan meals.

Host: Jack Coleman
Rooms: 30 (25 PB; 5 SB) $160
Full Breakfast
Credit Cards: A, B
Notes: 2, 4, 8, 9, 10, 12, 13, 14

DERBY LINE

Derby Village Inn

46 Main Street, 05830
(802) 873-3604

A charming old Victorian mansion situated in the quiet village of Derby Line. Five airy rooms, each with private bath. Nestled within walking distance of the Canadian border and the world's only international library and opera house. The nearby countryside offers year-round recreation: downhill and cross-country skiing, water sports, cycling, fishing, hiking, golf, snowmobiling, sleigh rides, antiquing, and most of all, peace and tranquility.

Hosts: Tom and Phyllis Moreau
Rooms: 5 (PB) $50-60
Full Breakfast
Credit Cards: A, B, D
Notes: 2, 5, 8, 9, 10, 12, 13

DORSET

Marble West Inn

Dorset West Road, 05251
(800) 453-7629

Marble West Inn is an elegant country inn, with beautiful polished floors, Oriental rugs and eight individually decorated guest rooms with private baths. Throughout the inn antiques, architecture and preserved features of the Greek Revival Building remind its guests of yesteryear. The original building is 150 years old. Afternoon refreshments welcome you, and a full breakfast prepares guests for travel plans.

NOTES: Credit cards accepted: A Master Card; B Visa; C American Express; D Discover Card; E Diner's Club; F Other; 2 Personal Checks accepted; 3 Lunch available; 4 Dinner available; 5 Open all year;

Hosts: June and Wayne Erla
Rooms: 8 (PB) $90-150
Full Breakfast
Credit Cards: A, B, C, F
Notes: 2, 4, 5, 9, 10, 11, 12, 13

EAST MIDDLEBURY

The Annex

Route 125, 05740
(802) 388-3233

Just five miles south of Middlebury, the Annex is nestled in the cozy village of East Middlebury. An 1830 Greek Revival house, it was originally built as an addition to the Waybury Inn. It is now privately owned and operated by T. D. Hutchins. The country village of East Middlebury lies at the edge of the National Forest, with hiking, skiing, and antique hunting the doorstep.

Host: T. D. Hutchins
Rooms: 6 (4 PB; 2 SB) $50-75
Continental Breakfast
Credit Cards: None
Notes: 2, 5, 8, 9, 10, 11, 12, 13

ESSEX JUNCTION

The Amos Bliss House

143 Weed Road, 05452
(802) 899-4577

Formerly known as Varnums, this charming farmhouse is the oldest home in town. Built in 1792, it was originally used as a stagecoach stop. Guests can enjoy antiques, a cool swim in the summer and a cozy chat in front of a wood stove during winter. Situated 20 minutes from Burlington Airport, 30 minutes from the Shelburne Museum, and less than an hour from Stowe and Sugarbush ski areas. Stunning view of the Green Mountains.

Hosts: Todd and Sheila Varnum
Rooms: 2 (SB) $75
Full Breakfast
Credit Cards: None
Notes: 2, 5, 10, 11, 12, 13

FAIRFAX

The American Country Collection #149

4 Greenwood Lane, Delmar, NY 12054
(518) 439-7001

This intimate, family-run country home is nestled on 400 spectacular acres in the rural countryside of Northern Vermont, just a short drive from Lake Champlain and Burlington. Children are free to romp and play in the fenced-in area, and everyone can enjoy the heated pool and wooded trails. Four guest rooms offer queen-size beds and shared baths. A Jacuzzi is available to all guests. Resident pets include a dog and two cats. Complimentary pony rides available. $45-75.

GAYESVILLE

Cobble House Inn

Box 49, 05746
(802) 234-5458

The inn sits secluded on a hilltop overlooking the Green Mountains, and the White River flows along the boundary, offering swimming and fishing. Each room is decorated in antiques and country furnishings, and there is a dining room that features northern Italian cuisine prepared by the chef/owners. Complimentary afternoon hors d'oeuvres are served. Dinner is available by reservation. A host of sports, including biking, swimming, tubing, skiing, and golf are available to help work off the day's meals.

Hosts: Beau and Phil Benson
Rooms: 6 (PB) $80-100
Full Breakfast
Credit Cards: A, B, C
Notes: 3, 4, 5, 8, 9, 11, 12, 13

6 Pets welcome; 8 Children welcome; 9 Social drinking allowed; 10 Tennis available; 11 Swimming available; 12 Golf available; 13 Skiing available; 14 May be booked through travel agents.

HARTLAND

The American Country Collection #163

4 Greenwood Lane, Delmar, NY 12054
(518) 439-7001

Guests at this hillside retreat are greeted on the first level and shown downstairs to their own private section of the house featuring a common room with a sofa that can be used as a double bed, wood-burning stove, and generous views of the tranquil Vermont highland scenery. A continental breakfast is served. On either side of the common room is a guest room, each with private bath. Close to Woodstock, Dartmouth College, Ski Killington, and Quechee Gorge. Children over seven welcome. Resident cat. $55-65. Additional guests stay $20 each.

HYDE PARK

Fitch Hill Inn

Rural Free Delivery Box 1879, Fitch Hill Road, 05655
(802) 888-5941; (802) 888-3834

Affordable elegance on a hilltop overlooking Vermont's highest mountain in the beautiful Lamoille River Valley. Ten miles north of famous Stowe, the historic Fitch Hill Inn, circa 1795, offers four tastefully antique-decorated rooms, all of which have views. There are four common livingroom areas and more than 200 video movies for guests to enjoy. Ungroomed cross-country ski trails begin on the property, and there are also nature trails to explore. A full gourmet breakfast is served, and dinners are available at a modest price. Packages available. AAA rated.

Host: Richard A. Pugliese
Rooms: 4 (SB) $50-60
Full Breakfast
Credit Cards: A, B
Notes: 2, 4, 5, 9, 10, 11, 12, 13, 14

JACKSONVILLE

The American Country Collection #165

4 Greenwood Lane, Delmar, NY 12054
(518) 439-7001

Built in 1840, this warm country inn is nestled in the heart of southern Vermont, convenient to both local ski areas and to those of northern Massachusetts. There are three guest room and two full baths. Rental of all three rooms results in shared bath accommodations. King, queen, and double beds are available. A full breakfast is served at 8:30 A.M. unless by prior arrangement. Children welcome; crib available. Near North River Winery, Stone Soldier Pottery, Molly Stark State Park, and other attractions. $45-65.

JEFFERSONVILLE

Sterling Ridge Inn

Junction Hill Road, P. O. Box 5780, 05464
(802) 644-8265; (800) 347-8266

This quiet, elegant rural inn is near Mount Mansfield, Stowe, Smuggler's Notch and the Lamoille River. Enjoy cross-country skiing, mountain and back-road biking, canoeing, and hiking packages on this beautiful scenic property. Groups and families find this ideal environment perfect for getting together.

Hosts: Susan and Scott Peterson
Rooms: 8 (4 PB; 4 SB) $55-65
Full Breakfast
Credit Cards: A, B
Notes: 2, 3, 4, 5, 8, 9, 10, 11, 12, 13, 14

LUDLOW

The Andrie Rose Inn

13 Pleasant Street, 05149
(802) 228-4846; (800) 223-4846

NOTES: Credit cards accepted: A Master Card; B Visa; C American Express; D Discover Card; E Diner's Club; F Other; 2 Personal Checks accepted; 3 Lunch available; 4 Dinner available; 5 Open all year;

Elegant circa 1829 country village inn at the base of Okemo Ski Resort. Enjoy fireside cocktails with complimentary hors d'oeuvres. Lavishly appointed, antique-filled guest rooms, all with private baths, fine linens, and down comforters. Some rooms boast whirlpool tubs and skylights. Indulge yourself in one of the luxury suites featuring marble fireplaces, canopy beds, and oversize whirlpool tubs. Family suites also available. Savor delectable breakfasts and epicurean dinners. Use inn bikes to tour back roads. Minutes from lakes, theaters, golf, tennis, hiking, downhill and cross-country skiing.

Hosts: Rick and Carolyn Bentzinger
Rooms: 10 (PB) $95-115
Suites: $185-250
Full Breakfast
Credit Cards: A, B, C
Notes: 2, 4 (weekends and holidays), 5, 9, 10, 11, 12, 13, 14

The Andrie Rose Inn

LYNDON

Branch Brook Bed and Breakfast

South Wheelock Road, P. O. Box 143, 05849
(802) 626-8316; (800) 572-7712

Restored 1850 house in northeast Vermont. An attractive livingroom, dining room, and library are available for guest use. Situated one-half mile off I-91 at exit 23. Burke Mountain Ski area is eight miles for both downhill and cross-country skiing. Hiking, biking, and swimming are available. A

complete breakfast prepared on an English AGA cooker is served in the dining room.

Hosts: Ted and Ann Tolman
Rooms: 5 (3 PB; 2 SB) $55-70
Full Breakfast
Credit Cards: A, B
Notes: 2, 5, 8, 9, 12, 13

MANCHESTER CENTER

The Inn at Ormsby Hill

Historic Route 7A, Rural Route 2,
P. O. Box 3264, 05255
(802) 362-1163

This splendid, restored manor house is situated on more than two acres overlooking the Green Mountains. Listed on Vermont's Register of Historic Places, the inn offers five guest rooms, all of which have private baths, four with fireplaces, and four with whirlpools. Rates include full breakfast. Many excellent places for lunch and dinner are nearby. Manchester is a four-season resort community with a full assortment of sports and cultural activities.

Hosts: Nancy and Don Burd
Rooms: 5 (PB) $90-165
Full Breakfast
Credit Cards: A, B, C
Notes: 2, 9, 10, 11, 12, 13, 14

Manchester Highlands Inn

Box 1754 AD, Highland Avenue, 05255
(802) 362-4565; (800) 743-4565
FAX (802) 362-4028

Discover Manchester's best-kept secret, a graceful Queen Anne Victorian inn on a hilltop overlooking town. Front porch with rocking chairs, large outdoor pool, game room, and pub with stone fireplace. Rooms individually decorated with feather beds, down comforters, and lace curtains. Gourmet country breakfast and afternoon snacks are served.

Hosts: Robert and Patricia Eichorn
Rooms: 15 (PB) $85-125
Full Breakfast
Credit Cards: A, B, C
Notes: 2, 5, 8, 9, 10, 11, 12, 13, 14

6 Pets welcome; 8 Children welcome; 9 Social drinking allowed; 10 Tennis available; 11 Swimming available; 12 Golf available; 13 Skiing available; 14 May be booked through travel agents.

MIDDLEBURY

The Annex

Route 125, 05740
(802) 388-3233

This 1830 Greek Revival home was originally built as an annex to the Bob Newhart "Stratford Inn." The annex features four rooms with private baths and two that share a bath. The decor is a blend of country, antiques, and handmade quilts. A warm and homey atmosphere welcomes guests.

Host: T. D. Hutchins
Rooms: 6 (4 PB; 2 SB) $50-75
Continental Breakfast
Credit Cards: None
Notes: 2, 5, 8, 9, 10, 11, 12, 13

Brookside Meadows Country Bed and Breakfast

Rural Delivery 3, Box 2460, 05753-8751
(802) 388-6429; (800) 442-9887 reservations

Attractive and comfortable home in rural setting just two and one-half miles from village center. All rooms have private baths. Two-bedroom suite has livingroom and wood stove. Spacious lawns and perennial gardens. Best downhill and cross-country skiing. Many excellent restaurants in town. Near Shelburne Museum. Quiet rest and relaxation at foot of Green Mountains.

Hosts: Linda and Roger Cole
Rooms: 3 (PB) $75-85
Suite: $145.80-156.60
Full or Continental Breakfast
Credit Cards: A, B
Notes: 2, 5, 8 (over 5), 9, 10, 11, 12, 13, 14

MIDDLETOWN SPRINGS

The American Country Collection #147

4 Greenwood Lane, Delmar, NY 12054
(518) 439-7001

This large Victorian home, currently listed on the National Historic Register, is filled with antiques and a vast music box collection. Guests can relax on the wraparound porch or in the parlor while enjoying a newspaper, hot tea, and freshly baked scones. The six guest rooms, all with private baths, feature queen and twin beds. Two of these rooms are in the annex next door. Full breakfast; dinner served by reservation only. Near Wilson Castle, Lake St, Catherine, Ski Killington, Green Mountain College, and many other attractions. $55-65. Extra bed $20.

Priscilla's Victorian Inn

52 South Street, 05757
(802) 235-2299

Priscilla's Victorian Inn is an 1870 Victorian house listed on the National Register of Historic Places. The inn was built by the inventors of the Grays horsepower machinery and is filled with music boxes, phonographs, and Victorian memorabilia. Breakfast is served on large porches overlooking an English garden. Close to Lake Saint Catherine, boat rentals, and trout fishing. A 30-minute drive to Manchester, surrounded by some of the prettiest scenery in Vermont.

Hosts: Doyle and Priscilla Lane
Rooms: 6 (PB) $65
Full Breakfast
Credit Cards: A, B
Notes: 2, 3, 4, 5, 8

MORETOWN

Camel's Hump View

P. O. Box 720, 05660
(802) 496-3614

Camel's Hump View is a unique old-style country inn dating back to 1831, with the Mad River to the east and Camel's Hump Mountain to the west. Warm up by the glowing fire in the winter or enjoy cattle grazing in the fields during the summer. The inn can accommodate 16 guests and serves hearty country meals from our gardens. Skiing, golf, fishing, horseback riding, and hiking are all available.

Hosts: Jerry and Wilma Maynard
Rooms: 8 (1 PB; 7 SB) $50-60
Full Breakfast
Credit Cards: None
Notes: 2, 4, 5, 10, 11, 12, 13

Camel's Hump View

NEWPORT

The American Country Collection #148

4 Greenwood Lane, Delmar, NY 12054
(518) 439-7001

With views of Lake Memphramogog, this charming Cape Cod sits on a hillside in northeastern Vermont. Remarks the owner, "I love my home and want my guests to enjoy it, too." Breakfast, which includes produce of the freshest organic quality, homemade baked goods, and bacon or sausage made from animals of chemical free ancestry, is served in the lakeview dining room or on the side deck in the morning sun. Two second-floor guest rooms share a bath. One room features a double and single bed, while the other sports a sofa that coverts into a double bed. Resident cat. $50.

NORTHFIELD

Northfield Inn

27 Highland Avenue, 05663
(802) 485-8558

This lovely 24-room turn-of-the-century home has been fully restored to its original grand style of Victorian elegance, and luxuriously decorated with period antiques. Guest accommodations include private baths, brass and wood-carved beds with European feather bedding, and other romantic surroundings. Relax with soft music on the porch while savoring the lovely gardens and birdsong. Charming villages, mountain views, and walks through forest trails add to the natural beauty of the area. Experience the wonder of hearing your own heartbeat.

Hosts: Aglaia and Alan Stalb
Rooms: 11 (6 PB; 2 SB) $75-85
Full Breakfast
Credit Cards: A, B
Notes: 2, 3, 4, 5, 9, 10, 11, 12, 13

NORTH TROY

Rose Apple Acres Farm

Rural Route 2, Box 300, East Hill Road, 05859
(802) 988-4300

Our turn-of-the-century farmhouse has three large guest rooms and panoramic mountain views. Experience peace and quiet on 52 acres of fields, woods, ponds, and gardens. Hiking, cross-country skiing, and snowshoeing can be enjoyed on the premises. Horse-drawn carriage and sleigh rides are offered. The hosts raise Jersey cows, Lincoln long wool sheep, Alpine goats, and Belgian horses. Fine restaurants nearby. Just four hours from Boston or Quebec City and two hours from Montreal.

Hosts: Jay, Cam, and Courtney Mead
Rooms: 3 (1 PB; 2 SB) $42-52
Continental Breakfast
Credit Cards: C
Notes: 2, 5, 9, 10, 11, 12, 13, 14

6 Pets welcome; 8 Children welcome; 9 Social drinking allowed; 10 Tennis available; 11 Swimming available; 12 Golf available; 13 Skiing available; 14 May be booked through travel agents.

POST MILLS

The Lake House Inn — A Spiritual Garden

P. O. Box 65, Route 244, 05058
(802) 333-4025

A delightfully cozy country inn, specializing in spiritual retreats and workshops. An 1865 ballroom and barn and English country gardens on the shores of Lake Fairlee. Ideal for relaxing, communing with nature, and just enjoying the peaceful village setting. Specializing in English country garden weddings, retreats, romantic weekends, and vacations with or without the children. In the heart of bicycle country, rental bikes are available with advanced arrangement.

Host: Betty Pemberton
Rooms: 12 (2 PB; 10 SB) $79-89 plus tax
Full Breakfast
Credit Cards: None
Notes: 2, 3, 4, 5, 6 (by special arrangement), 8, 9 (no hard liquor), 10, 11, 12, 13, 14

PUTNEY

Hickory Ridge House

Rural Route 3, Box 1410, 05346
(802) 387-5709

Gracious 1808 Federal brick manor surrounded by rolling fields and woods on a quiet country road near Putney village. Six working fireplaces (four in bedrooms), original tamarack wide-board floors, antique furnishings throughout, and perennial gardens. Area offers fine crafts and music, antiques, hiking, cross-country skiing, boating, and swimming. Just two miles from I-91 and the Connecticut River. Handicapped accessible.

Hosts: Jacquie Walker and Steve Anderson
Rooms: 7 (3 PB; 4 SB) $45-80
Full Breakfast
Credit Cards: A, B
Notes: 2, 5, 8, 9, 11, 13

RANDOLPH

Placidia Farm Bed and Breakfast

Rural Delivery 1, Box 275, 05060-9413
(802) 728-9883

Six miles north of Randolph on 81 acres with mountain views, pond, and brook. Hand-hewn log home with private apartment for bed and breakfast guests. Deck for enjoying the view. TV, stereo, books, and games.

Host: Viola A. Frost-Laitinew
Apartment: 1 (PB) $75-80
Full Breakfast
Credit Cards: None
Notes: 2, 5, 8, 9, 10, 11, 12, 13

RUTLAND

The Inn at Rutland

70 North Main Street, 05701
(802) 773-0575

The inn is a beautiful restored 1890s mansion filled with unique period details. This Victorian bed and breakfast has 11 old-fashioned, comfortable guest rooms with updated private baths, TVs, and phones. Guests are sure to enjoy our cozy, fire-placed common rooms after a busy day of sightseeing or skiing. A delicious continental breakfast and afternoon snack is included. Near Killington and Pico ski areas. Corporate and off-season rates.

The Inn at Rutland

Hosts: Amber and Mark Quinn
Rooms: 11 (PB) $65-150
Continental Breakfast
Credit Cards: A, B, C, D
Notes: 2, 5, 8 (over 10), 9, 10, 11, 12, 13

SHELBURNE

The Inn at Shelburne Farms

Shelburne Farms, 05482
(802) 985-8498

The Inn at Shelburne Farms offers turn-of-the-century elegance, contemporary cuisine, and some of the most beautiful lake and mountain views anywhere in the world. Original furnishings and decor in its 24 bedrooms and spacious common rooms recall the grandeur and gracious hospitality of another era. First built in 1899 by William Seward and Lila Vanderbilt Webb, Shelburne House is now owned by Shelburne Farms, a non-profit environmental education organization.

Rooms: 24 (17 PB; 7 SB) $100-230
A la carte Breakfast Menu
Credit Cards: A, B, C, E
Notes: 2, 3, 4, 8, 9, 10, 11, 12

SHOREHAM VILLAGE

Shoreham Inn and Country Store

P. O. Box 182, 05770
(802) 897-5861; (800) 255-5081

On the Village Green close to the college town of Middlebury and Fort Ticonderoga, this family-run inn, circa 1790, offers good food, great location, and excellent lodging. Close to all seasons' activities in Vermont! Call or write for free activities map and travel directions.

Hosts: Cleo and Fred Alter
Rooms: 11 (SB) $70
Full Breakfast
Credit Cards: B
Closed Nov.
Notes: 2, 4, 8, 9, 10, 11, 12, 13, 14

SHREWSBURY

Buckmaster Inn Bed and Breakfast

Lincoln Hill Road, 05738
(802) 492-3485

Historic country inn that was originally a stagecoach stop stands on a knoll overlooking a typical red barn scene and picturesque valley. The charm of a center hall, grand staircase, and wide-pine floors show off family antiques. Wood-burning fireplaces, a library, huge porches, dining room, and country kitchen with wood-burning stove are special favorites of guests. Near ski areas, eight miles southeast of Rutland, near Cuttingsville.

Hosts: Sam and Grace Husselman
Rooms: 3 (2 PB; 1 SB) $40-60
Full Breakfast
Credit Cards: None
Notes: 2, 5, 8, 10, 11, 12, 13

Shoreham Inn and Country Store

STOWE

The American Country Collection #091

4 Greenwood Lane, Delmar, NY 12054
(518) 439-7001

Contemporary alpine-style private home nestled into the side of the Worcester Mountain Range just six miles from Stowe. The second floor is entirely for guests' use;

6 Pets welcome; 8 Children welcome; 9 Social drinking allowed; 10 Tennis available; 11 Swimming available; 12 Golf available; 13 Skiing available; 14 May be booked through travel agents.

the two guest rooms share a bath. One room may be rented with private bath. Breakfast is served in the elegant country kitchen in front of the wood-burning stove. Couples only. $65; $75-95 during foliage, with a two-night minimum stay.

Butternut Inn at Stowe

2309 Mountain Road, 05672
(800) 3BU-TTER

Award-winning inn on eight acres of beautifully landscaped grounds alongside a mountain stream. Cottage gardens, pool, antiques, afternoon tea, collectibles. All rooms have private baths. Close to sleigh rides, downhill and cross-country skiing, summer hiking, golf, tennis, and horseback riding. Described as one of the "best bed and breakfasts in the northeast" by *Skiing* magazine. Honeymoon and anniversary packages available. Enjoy real "Texas" hospitality in Vermont.

Hosts: Jim and Deborah Wimberly
Rooms: 18 (PB) $90-140
Full Breakfast
Credit Cards: A, B
Notes: 9, 10, 11, 12, 13, 14

The Gables Inn

Mountain Road, Rural Route 1, Box 570, 05672
(802) 253-7730

Classic country inn with 17 beautifully appointed rooms in an 1860s farmhouse. New carriage house suites have queen beds, fireplaces, Jacuzzis, and TV. Outdoor hot tub and pool; sitting room and den. Hearty country breakfasts and candlelight dinners. Minutes from seasonal attractions and Stowe village. Smoke-free bedrooms and dining room.

Hosts: Sol and Lynn Baumrind
Rooms: 17 (PB) $75-125 summer; $110-180
  Modified American Plan winter
Full Breakfast
Credit Cards: A, B, C
Notes: 2, 3 (summer), 4 (winter), 5, 8, 9, 10, 11,
  12, 13, 14

The Inn at the Brass Lantern

717 Maple Street, 05672
(802) 253-2229; (800) 729-2980

A traditional Vermont bed and breakfast country inn in the heart of Stowe. Award-winning restoration of an 1810 farmhouse and carriage barn overlooking Mount Mansfield, Vermont's most prominent mountain. The inn features period antiques, air conditioning, handmade quilts, planked floors, and private baths. Some rooms have fireplaces and most have views. An intimate inn for house guests only. AAA Three-Diamond inn. Special packages include honeymoon, gourmet dining out, skiing, golf, air travel, sleigh and surrey rides, and more.

Host: Andy Aldrich
Rooms: 9 (PB) $65-120
Full Breakfast
Credit Cards: A, B, C
Notes: 2, 5, 9, 10, 11, 12, 13, 14

Spruce Pond Inn

1250 Waterbury Road, 05672-9716
(802) 253-4236; (800) 283-1853

This cozy country inn features six comfortable guest rooms, one with fireplace, a large living room with fieldstone fireplace, complimentary afternoon tea, and a large dining room serving some of Stowe's finest cuisine by Chef Patrick Miller.

Hosts: Larry, Patrick, and Susan Miller
Rooms: 6 (PB) $45-120
Full Breakfast (winter-fall); Continental Breakfast
  (summer)
Credit Cards: A, B
Notes: 2, 4, 5, 9, 10, 11, 12, 13, 14

VERGENNES

Strong House Inn

82 West Main Street, 05491
(802) 877-3337

Comfortable, elegant lodging in an 1834 Federal-style home listed on the National Register of Historic Places. Perfectly situated in the heart of the Lake Champlain Valley with fine views of the Green Mountains and Adirondack ranges, the area offers some of the finest cycling in Vermont. Nearby lake, hiking, golf, and Shelburne. The inn offers eight rooms, five with private baths and three with working fireplaces. A full country breakfast is included, and dinner is available on request.

Host: Mary Bargiel
Rooms: 8 (5 PB; 3 SB) $55-130
Full Breakfast
Credit Cards: A, B, C
Notes: 2, 3, 4, 5, 8, 9, 11, 12, 13, 14

WAITSFIELD

The Inn at the Round Barn Farm

RR1, Box 247, East Warren Road, 05673
(802) 496-2276

This is the inn that lives in your imagination. A place that is rich in history, elegant, luxurious, and charming, without the least bit of pretension. Offering ten dream-like guests rooms, visitors can relax by a roaring fireplace, enjoy steam showers, Jacuzzi, and canopied beds so comfortable guests will feel like they are sleeping in a big hug. A truly caring staff will help make the time in the picture perfect Mad River-Sugarbush Valley all you ever dreamed of. Sports and recreation are nearby, as well as Ben and Jerry's Ice Cream Factory. AAA approved. Three Diamonds.

Hosts: Jack and Doreen, Simko, and Alison Duckworth
Rooms: 10 (PB) $90-155
Full Breakfast
Credit Cards: A, B, C
Notes: 2, 5, 10, 11, 12, 13, 14

Mountain View Inn

Rural Free Delivery, Box 69, Route 17, 05673
(802) 496-2426

Mountain View Inn, a small country inn, circa 1826, has seven guest rooms, each with private bath, accommodating two people. The rooms are decorated with stenciling, quilts, braided rugs, and antique furniture. Meals are served family-style around an antique harvest table. Good fellowship is enjoyed around the wood-burning fireplace in the livingroom.

Hosts: Fred and Susan Spencer
Rooms: 7 (PB) $64.80-75.60
Full Breakfast
Minimum stay weekends: 2 nights
Credit Cards: None
Notes: 2, 4, 5, 8, 9, 10, 11, 12, 13, 14

Newtons' 1824 House Inn

Route 100, Box 159, 05673
(802) 496-7555

Enjoy relaxed elegance in a perfect country setting on the Mad River. Six guest rooms, all with private baths. Classical music, Oriental rugs, fireplaces, sun porch. Gourmet breakfast with breakfast souffles and freshly squeezed orange juice. Stroll on 52 acres near the Mad River. Even a private swimming hole. Featured in the *Los Angeles Times*, *Glamour* magazine, and *Travel & Leisure*. AAA rated three Diamonds.

Hosts: Nick and Joyce Newton
Rooms: 6 (PB) $75-115
Full Breakfast
Credit Cards: A, B, C
Notes: 2, 5, 9, 10, 11, 12, 13, 14

Valley Inn

Rural Route 1, Box 8, Route 100, 05673
(802) 496-3450; (800) 638-8466

This is a recipe for a great Vermont vacation: take an exceptional country inn situated in a lovely New England village, add cozy bedrooms, stir in conversation around a warm fire, add excellent meals and a sauna, mix in nice people, and season with vacation packages to taste. Dinner is served during the ski season. Come try a Valley Inn-terlude.

6 Pets welcome; 8 Children welcome; 9 Social drinking allowed; 10 Tennis available; 11 Swimming available; 12 Golf available; 13 Skiing available; 14 May be booked through travel agents.

Hosts: The Stinson Family
Rooms: 20 (PB) $40-70
Full Breakfast
Credit Cards: A, B, C, D
Notes: 2, 5, 8, 9, 10, 11, 12, 13, 14

The Waitsfield Inn

Route 100, P. O. Box 969, 05673
(802) 496-3979

This gracious 1820s restored colonial inn is situated in the heart of the beautiful Mad River Valley. The inn offers spectacular skiing minutes away from Sugarbush and wonderful hiking, shopping, antiquing, and much more. Relax in one of the 14 rooms, all of which are beautifully appointed with antiques, quilted beds, and private baths. Enjoy a full breakfast, and let the "Innspired" hosts make the stay a memorable one.

Host: Steve and Ruth Lacey
Rooms: 14 (PB) $50-115
Full Breakfast
Credit Cards: A, B, C, D
Notes: 2, 5, 8, 9, 10, 11, 12, 13, 14

WALLINGFORD

The American Country Collection #055

4 Greenwood Lane, Delmar, NY 12054
(518) 439-7001

This restored 1840 Colonial farmhouse listed on the National Register of Historic Places is situated on 20 acres of pastures and woods. The Gothic-style barn, a Vermont landmark, is often painted by artists. Swimming, fishing, and canoeing on the premises; golf, tennis, and horseback riding nearby. Five guest rooms, all with private baths. Children over ten welcome. Pets in residence. $65-85. Rates slightly higher during foliage season. Two-night minimum stay during foliage season.

WARREN

The Sugartree, A Country Inn

Rural Route 1, Box 38, Sugarbush Access Road, 05674
(802) 583-3211; (800) 666-8907

Featuring ten romantic rooms furnished with brass, white iron, canopy beds, quilts, and antiques, this bed and breakfast is a true haven for those looking to get away. Situated less than one mile from the base of Sugarbush Mountain, here guests can enjoy spectacular views and a cozy gathering room with a fireplace. Close to all activities, including cross-country and downhill skiing, golf, tennis, horseback riding, and canoeing. Unwind with an afternoon refreshment in the gazebo. Enjoy a delicious breakfast featuring homemade breads, butters, and syrups.

Hosts: Frank and Kathy Partsch
Rooms: 10 (PB) $40-124
Full Breakfast
Credit Cards: A, B, C, D
Notes: 2, 5, 9, 10, 11, 12, 13, 14

The Sugartree

West Hill House Bed and Breakfast

West Hill Road, Rural Route 1
P. O. Box 292, 05674
(802) 496-7162

Location, location! Just one mile from Sugarbush Ski/Summer Resort, Cross-Country Center (golf course designed by Robert Trent Jones, Sr.), restaurants, and activities galore, yet off the beaten path, West Hill House boasts both country charm and idyllic setting. An intimate, restored farmhouse, circa 1862, offering quiet privacy, gorgeous mountain views, cozy guest rooms, fireplace, BYOB wet bar, and spacious porch with rockers. Mornings bring sounds of soft music and a hearty, delicious breakfast. Relaxed, friendly, affordable.

Hosts: Nina and Bob Heyd
Rooms: 4 (2 PB; 2 SB) $60-90
Full Breakfast
Credit Cards: A, B
Notes: 2, 3 (picnic), 4 (groups), 5, 8 (over 9), 9, 10, 11, 12, 13, 14

WATERBURY

Grünberg Haus Bed and Breakfast

Rural Route 2, Box 1595, Route 100 S., 05676
(802) 244-7726; (800) 800-7760

Hand-built Austrian chalet secluded in a mountainside forest. Year-round fireplace, BYOB pub, sauna, Jacuzzi, tennis court, hiking, cross-country ski trails, and chickens. Guest room opens onto a balcony with a dramatic view of the mountains. Memorable, musical breakfasts, such as ricotta-stuffed French toast, maple-poached pears, and pumpkin apple streusel muffins. Innkeepers entertain at fireside grand piano. Just minutes from Stowe, Sugar-bush, Mad River Glen, and Bolton Valley ski areas in the hometown of Ben & Jerry's Ice Cream.

Hosts: Christopher Sellers and Mark Frohman
Rooms: 10 (5 PB; 5 SB) $55-125
Full Breakfast
Credit Cards: A, B, C, D, F
Notes: 2, 3, 4, 5, 8, 9, 10, 11, 12, 13, 14

Inn at Blush Hill

Blush Hill Road, Box 1266, 05676
(802) 244-7529; (800) 736-7522

A circa 1790 restored Cape on five acres with beautiful mountain views. The inn has four fireplaces, a large sitting room, and lots of antiques. It is situated across from a golf course, and all summer sports are nearby. Enjoy skiing at Stowe, Sugarbush, and Bolton Valley, only minutes away. Adjacent to Ben and Jerry's Ice Cream Factory. Afternoon refreshments served. Packages available.

Hosts: Gary and Pam Gosselin
Rooms: 6 (2 PB; 4 SB) $50-115
Full Breakfast
Credit Cards: A, B, C, D, F
Notes: 2, 5, 8, 9, 10, 11, 12, 13, 14

Grünberg Haus

WATERBURY CENTER

The Black Locust Inn

Rural Route 1, Box 715, 05677
(800) 366-5592

Circa 1832 farmhouse set on a hill graced with black locust trees and looking to the Green Mountains and Camel's Hump. Antiques, old beds, lace curtains, Laura Ashley wallpapers, and Oriental rugs on polished hardwood floors. In the large livingroom there are movies, books, music, games, and magazines. Wine and cheese are served in the afternoon. Comfort, wonderful breakfasts, and a relaxed atmosphere are the inn's number-one amenities.

Hosts: Anita and George Gajdos
Rooms: 6 (PB) $65-100
Full Breakfast
Credit Cards: A, B, D
Notes: 2, 5, 9, 10, 11, 12, 13, 14

WESTON

1830 Inn on the Green

Route 100, 05161
(802) 824-6789

Colonial building built in 1830 as a black-smith/wheelwright shop, situated in the center of town overlooking the delightful village green. Parlor with fireplace, slate terrace overlooking the gardens and pond. Furnished with traditional and family antiques.

Hosts: Sandy and Dave Granger
Rooms: 4 (PB) $60-80
Full Breakfast
Credit Cards: A, B
Notes: 2, 5, 9, 10, 11, 12, 13

The Wilder Homestead Inn and 1827 Craft Shoppe

Rural Route 1, Box 106 D, 05161
(802) 824-8172

An 1827 brick home listed on the National Register of Historic Places. Walk to shops, museums, and summer theater. Crackling fires in common rooms, canopy beds, down comforters. Rooms have original Moses Eaton stenciling and are furnished with antiques and reproductions. Weston Priory nearby.

Hosts: Peggy and Roy Varner
Rooms: 7 (5 PB; 2 SB) $60-95
Full Breakfast
Minimum stay weekends: 2 nights; holidays: 2-3 nights
Credit Cards: A, B
Notes: 2, 5, 8 (over 6), 9, 10, 11, 12, 13, 14

WEST TOWNSHEND

The American Country Collection #093

4 Greenwood Lane, Delmar, NY 12054
(518) 439-7001

Steeped in history, this farmhouse built in 1773 is reputed to be the oldest standing house in West River Valley. There are several out-buildings and a duck pond on the inn's five acres. Three guest rooms with private baths offer such amenities as hand-made crafts and quilts, fresh towels, sweets in the bedchambers, and a tour of the small but historic property. Near covered bridges, flea markets, auctions, antiquing, factory outlet shopping, hiking, boating, fishing, swimming, and canoeing. Children welcome. Cat in residence. Choice of full or continental breakfast. $55-60.

Windham Hill Inn

Rural Route 1, Box 44, 05359
(802) 874-4080

Circa 1825 farmhouse and barn situated at the end of a dirt road high in the mountains on 160 acres. Spectacular views, hiking trails, cross-country skiing. Summer outdoor programs and concerts in the white barn. The 15 guest chambers have been recently updated and redecorated (king and queen beds), some with hand-made solid cherry canopy beds. Hosts have an old-fashioned shoe collection. Wonderful candlelit dinners with six courses on fine china and antique silverware. Warm, caring innkeepers. A true country experience; designated an inn of distinction for being judged one of the ten best inns in the nation on three occasions. Handicapped accessible.

NOTES: Credit cards accepted: A Master Card; B Visa; C American Express; D Diner's Club; F Other; 2 Personal Checks accepted; 3 Lunch available; 4 Dinner available; 5 Open all year;

Hosts: Ken and Linda Busteed
Rooms: 15 (PB) $160-180 Modified American
    Plan
Suite: $225
Full Breakfast
Credit Cards: A, B, C
Closed April 1-May 15; November 1-Thanksgiving
Notes: 2, 10, 11, 12, 13, 14

WINDSOR

Juniper Hill Inn

Rural Route 1, Box 79, 05089
(802) 674-5273

Pamper yourself in this elegant but informal inn with antique-furnished guest
rooms, all with private baths and some with
working fireplaces. Sumptuous candlelight
dinners and hearty full breakfasts are
served. Cool off in the outdoor pool or visit
antique shops, covered bridges, museums,
and craft shops. Only 20 minutes to
Woodstock and Quechee in Vermont and
Hanover, New Hampshire. A perfectly
romantic inn.

Hosts: Rob and Suzanne Pearl
Rooms: 16 (PB) $80-120
Full Breakfast
Credit Cards: A, B
Closed November 1-15
Notes: 2, 4, 9, 10, 11, 12, 13, 14

WOODSTOCK

Canterbury House

43 Pleasant Street, 05091
(802) 457-3077

A 100-year-old village home just east of
the village green. This bed and breakfast,
furnished with authentic Victorian
antiques, has seven rooms with private
baths. Livingroom with TV and stereo.
Within walking distance of shops and
restaurants. Full breakfast in dining room.
Guest rooms have air conditioning and
fresh flowers. Bicycles provided summer
and fall.

Hosts: The Houghs
Rooms: 7 (PB) $75-135
Full Breakfast
Credit Cards: A, B
Notes: 2, 5, 8, 9, 10, 11, 12, 13, 14

The Charleston House

21 Pleasant Street, 05091
(802) 457-3843

This circa 1835 Greek Revival home has
been authentically restored. Listed in the
National Register of Historic Places.
Furnished with antiques combined with a
hospitality reminiscent of a family home-
coming. Situated in the picturesque village
of Woodstock, "one of the most beautiful
villages in America."

Hosts: Barb and Bill Hough
Rooms: 7 (PB) $100-145
Full Breakfast
Credit Cards: A, B
Notes: 2, 5, 8 (over 9), 9, 10, 11, 12, 13, 14

6 Pets welcome; 8 Children welcome; 9 Social drinking allowed; 10 Tennis available; 11 Swimming available;
12 Golf available; 13 Skiing available; 14 May be booked through travel agents.

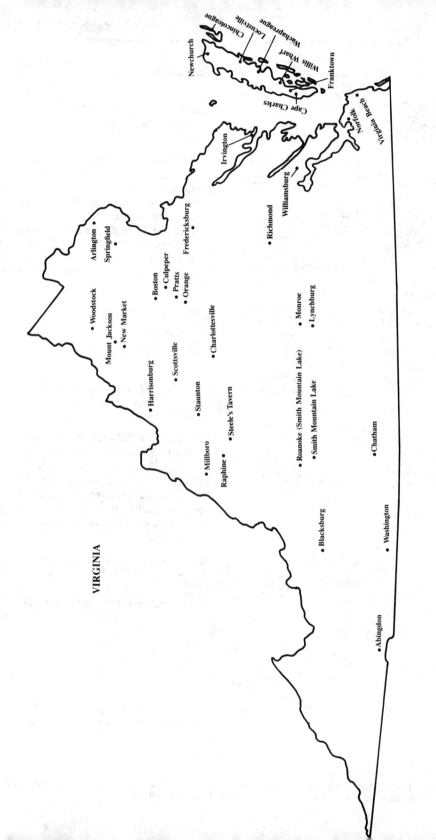

VIRGINIA

Newchurch
Chincoteague
Locustville
Wachapreague
Willis Wharf
Franktown
Cape Charles
Norfolk
Virginia Beach

Irvington

Williamsburg

Richmond

Arlington
Springfield

Fredericksburg

Boston
Culpeper
Pratts
Orange

Woodstock

Mount Jackson
New Market

Monroe
Lynchburg

Charlottesville

Harrisonburg

Scottsville

Staunton

Steele's Tavern

Millboro

Raphine

Roanoke (Smith Mountain Lake)
Smith Mountain Lake

Chatham

Blacksburg

Washington

Abingdon

Virginia

Maplewood Farm Bed and Breakfast

Route 7, Box 461, 24210
(703) 628-2640

Maplewood's home, built around 1880, is a beautifully renovated farmhouse surrounded by maples. This tranquil 66-acre horse farm has wooded hiking trails and a lake stocked for fishing. The inn offers two guest rooms with private baths and a two-bedroom suite; delightful breakfasts are served in the Garden Room or outside on the deck. Overnight stabling is available to guests traveling with horses. Close to the Barter Theatre and Virginia Creeper Trail.

Hosts: Doris and Jennie Placak
Rooms: 3 (PB) $70
Full Breakfast
Credit Cards: None
Notes: 2, 4, 5, 8, 9, 10, 11, 12, 14

ARLINGTON_____

Memory House

6404 North Washington Boulevard, 22205
(703) 534-4607

Charming, ornate 1899 Victorian fully restored with period antiques, wall stenciling, prize-winning handicrafts, and collectibles. Relax on front porch wicker or in double parlors. Tasty continental-plus breakfast. Conveniently situated for touring Washington, D. C. One block from the subway; three blocks from I-66 (Exit 69).

Memory House

Share in the old-fashioned comfort and friendship of Memory House.

Hosts: John and Marlys McGrath
Rooms: 2 (1 PB; 1 SB) $75
Continental Breakfast
Credit Cards: None
Notes: 2, 5, 10, 11, 14

BLACKSBURG _____

L'Arche Bed and Breakfast

301 Wall Street, 24060
(703) 951-1808

An oasis of tranquility just one block from the Virginia Tech campus, L'Arche Bed and Breakfast is an elegant turn-of-the-century Federal Revival home situated among terraced gardens in downtown Blacksburg. Spacious rooms have traditional antiques, family heirlooms, handmade quilts and private baths. Delicious full breakfasts feature homemade breads, cakes, jams and jellies.

Host: Vera G. Good
Rooms: 4 (PB) $75

NOTES: Credit cards accepted: A Master Card; B Visa; C American Express; D Discover Card; E Diner's Club; F Other; 2 Personal Checks accepted; 3 Lunch available; 4 Dinner available; 5 Open all year; 6 Pets welcome; 8 Children welcome; 9 Social drinking allowed; 10 Tennis available; 11 Swimming available; 12 Golf available; 13 Skiing available; 14 May be booked through travel agents.

Full Breakfast
Credit Cards: None
Notes: 2, 5, 10, 12

Per Diem Bed and Breakfast

401 Clay Street Southwest, 24060
(703) 953-2604; (800) 272-4707

Situated one block from Virginia Tech's campus and a five-minute walk to the stadium, Coliseum, and downtown Blacksburg, this lovely bed and breakfast offers two guest houses with fully equipped kitchens and comfortable living areas that are connected to the main house by a large covered porch. Antiques, Appalachian crafts and quilts, Oriental rugs, and original art are displayed. A beautifully landscaped courtyard includes a large heated swimming pool, patios, decks, and gardens. The guest houses are equipped with cable TV, phones, and air conditioning.

Host: Jo Pat Huggins
Rooms: 6 (4 PB; 2 SB) $65-75
Full Breakfast
Credit Cards: A, B
Notes: 2, 5, 9, 10, 11, 12, 14

BOSTON

Pickett's Harbor

P. O. Box 97 AA, Cape Charles, 23310
(804) 331-2212

Pickett's Harbor

Nestled in pines and dogwoods in a back yard of 27 acres on Virginia's eastern shores, on secluded and marvelous wide beaches for guests, seagulls, pelicans, and herons. A Colonial home (big house, little house, and kitchen) with cupboards, doors, and floors made from old barn rafters. Fireplaces, antiques, and reproductions. All rooms and the porch face the Chesapeake Bay. Country breakfast served overlooking the bay. Late afternoon beverage served. Central air.

Hosts: Sara and Cooke Goffigon
Rooms: 6 (2 PB; 4 SB) $65-110
Full Breakfast
Credit Cards: None
Notes: 2, 5, 8, 10, 11, 12, 14

Thistle Hill Bed and Breakfast

Route 1, P. O. Box 291, 22713
(703) 987-9142

Situated on a hillside on the morning side of the Blue Ridge Mountains, Thistle Hill offers modern amenities in a rural park-like setting. Two cottages, one with a fireplace, and the main house are cozily decorated with antiques and collectibles. Relax in the hot tub or wander through the lawns and woods. Enjoy afternoon tea in the gazebo and a hearty, savory breakfast in the morning. Picnics and candlelight dinners by arrangement.

Hosts: Charles and Marianne Wilson
Rooms: 4 (PB) $95-135
Full Breakfast
Credit Cards: A, B, C, D
Notes: 2, 3, 4, 5, 8, 9, 14

CAPE CHARLES

Amanda's Bed and Breakfast #122

1428 Park Avenue, Baltimore, MD 21217
(410) 225-0001; (410) 383-1274

Lovely, quiet, rural setting along the Chesapeake Bay featuring unspoiled land, abundant wildlife, game birds, miles of private beach, and nature's most fabulous sunsets. This two-story brick home has a great view of the bay and is decorated with antiques, reproductions, and collectibles. Three rooms with private baths. Full breakfast. $75-85.

Amanda's Bed and Breakfast #138

1428 Park Avenue, Baltimore, MD 21217
(410) 225-0001; (410) 383-1274

Restored 1910 Colonial Revival. Just steps from a public beach on the bay. Enjoy and relax on one of the porches, sample the cool breezes off the bay, or bike through the historic town. Set your own pace and explore. Four guest rooms and one cottage. Full breakfast. $65-75.

Nottingham Ridge

Nottingham Ridge Bed and Breakfast

28184 Nottingham Ridge Lane, 23310
(804) 331-1010

This lovely home reflects the beauty and charm of Virginia's historical Eastern Shore. Private secluded beach on the Chesapeake Bay bordered by tall trees, sand dunes, and abundant wildlife. Enjoy breakfast on the porch watching boats and birds or spectacular sunsets. Cooler times are spent in the den by a crackling fire. Featured activities include biking, fishing,

tennis, golf, running, bird watching, crabbing, swimming, and sightseeing. Visitors to Nottingham Ridge can look forward to an informal, relaxed atmosphere with emphasis on the small details that create a memorable stay.

Hosts: Bonnie Nottingham and M. S. Scott
Rooms: 3 (PB) $75-90
Full Breakfast
Credit Cards: None
Notes: 2, 5, 8 (over 8), 9, 10, 11, 12, 14

CHARLOTTESVILLE

Alderman House

Guesthouses Bed and Breakfast
P. O. Box 5737, 22905
(804) 979-7264; FAX (804) 293-7791

This large, formal Georgian home is authentic in style and elegant in decor. It was built by the widow of the first president of the University of Virginia in the early 1900s and is about one mile from the university. Breakfast is served with true southern hospitality. Guests may choose a room with a four-poster bed or one with twin beds, each with adjoining private bath. Air conditioning. $68-100.

Auburn Hill

Guesthouses Bed and Breakfast
P. O. Box 5737, 22905
(804) 979-7264; FAX (804) 293-7791

An antebellum cottage situated on a scenic farm, which was once part of the original Jefferson Plantation. The main house was built by Jefferson for one of his overseers. Just six miles east of the city, it is conveniently located near Monticello and Ash Lawn. The cottage has a sitting room with a fireplace, bedroom with a four-poster bed, and connecting bath and shower. During the summer guests are invited to use the pool. Scenic trails, walks, and views. Air conditioning. $80-125.

6 Pets welcome; 8 Children welcome; 9 Social drinking allowed; 10 Tennis available; 11 Swimming available; 12 Golf available; 13 Skiing available; 14 May be booked through travel agents.

Balla Machree

Guesthouses Bed and Breakfast
P. O. Box 5737, 22905
(804) 979-7264; FAX (804) 293-7791

A separate suite in an architect-designed contemporary home, this superb lakefront location offers complete privacy for guests. About ten miles west of town, this suite overlooks a 250-acre lake with excellent fishing. The cozy quarters have a private entrance, large brick fireplace, and comfortable bedroom with iron frame and double bed with private adjoining bath. Tennis is available, but please bring proper shoes! Golf, riding, hiking, fishing, and canoeing are nearby, or you can simply enjoy the magnificent mountain view. Continental breakfast materials in the suite. Air conditioning. $80-100.

Boxberry

Guesthouses Bed and Breakfast
P. O. Box 5737, 22905
(804) 979-7264; FAX (804) 293-7791

An English country cottage setting just a few miles west of Charlottesville, Boxberry has lovely gardens and a spacious terrace for guest use, or enjoy the garden view from the cheerful sun room. The guest room has a queen bed and private adjoining bath. Full breakfast; air conditioning. $60-80.

Boxwood Lane Farm

Guesthouses Bed and Breakfast
P. O. Box 5737, 22905
(804) 979-7264; FAX (804) 293-7791

Virginia country living at its best describes this lovely bed and breakfast. A boxwood-lined path leads to the gracious front door of this 19th-century manor house just 15 miles south of Charlottesville and 15 miles from the Blue Ridge Parkway. There is a fine collection of contemporary paintings in this tastefully appointed home of a designer and an architect. This home has lovely surroundings, country walks past gardens, ponds and unusual plantings; a pool is available for summer enjoyment. There are two large guest rooms, one with a queen-size bed and the other a double bed. Both rooms offer private baths, air conditioning, and full breakfast. $80-100.

Carrsbrook

Guesthouses Bed and Breakfast
P. O. Box 5737, 22905
(804) 979-7264; FAX (804) 293-7791

Peter Carr built this estate home in 1798 using many of the architectural innovations of his uncle and guardian, Thomas Jefferson, including 15-foot ceilings and Jefferson's characteristic way of hiding stairways. Private entrance to the suite is from a large patio overlooking a formal boxwood garden with the deepest hand-dug well in Albermarle County. Downstairs is the sitting room with a pull-out sofa, adjacent bath, and small refrigerator. Upstairs is a bedroom with a king-size bed. Listed on the National Register of Historic Places. Air conditioning. $68-100.

Chathill

Guesthouses Bed and Breakfast
P. O. Box 5737, 22905
(804) 979-7264; FAX (804) 293-7791

A delightful country house in a rural setting only a few minute's drive from Charlottesville and the University of Virginia. Accommodations consist of a large paneled room with fireplace and sofa bed in the sitting area, a queen bed, and adjoining bath. During the summer, visitors can enjoy the swimming pool and the informal gardens. Air conditioning. $68-100.

Clifton, The Country Inn

Route 13, Box 26, 22901
(804) 971-1800

A Virginia historic landmark, Clifton is among the few remaining large plantation properties in Albermarle County. On 48 secluded acres with walking trails, private lake, lap pool, tennis courts, and croquet pitch. All rooms feature wood-burning fireplaces, private baths, large sitting areas, canopy or four-poster beds. Just five minutes to Charlottesville.

Host: Craig and Donna Hartman
Rooms: 14 (PB) $178-193
Full Breakfast
Credit Cards: A,B, C
Notes: 2, 4, 5, 8, 9, 10, 11, 12, 13

Cottage Grove

Guesthouses Bed and Breakfast
P. O. Box 5737, 22905
(804) 979-7264; FAX (804) 293-7791

This quaint country cottage offers beautiful views from two porches. The cozy guest room has an antique double bed and private hall bath. Another bedroom with a queen bed and private adjacent bath is available for a minimum of two nights. $60-80.

Ingleside

Guesthouses Bed and Breakfast
P. O. Box 5737, 22905
(804) 979-7264; FAX (804) 293-7791

A farm that has been in the same family for several generations, Ingleside lies on 1,250 acres of rolling pasture backed by steep, wooded mountains. The house was built around 1840 of bricks made from the farm's red clay. Accommodations consist of a large, antique-furnished room with double bed, fireplace, and adjacent bath. A tennis court is available for guest use. Air conditioning. $60-80.

The Inn at the Crossroads

Guesthouses Bed and Breakfast
P. O. Box 5737, 22905
(804) 979-7264; FAX (804) 293-7791

Built in 1820 as a tavern on the historic James River Turnpike, the inn continues its long tradition, offering a quiet respite for the weary traveler. A four-story brick building with a long front porch, it is situated on five acres overlooking pastures and the foothills of the Blue Ridge Mountains and is convenient to Monticello and Charlottesville, as well as the James River and Skyline Drive. $69.

Meander Inn

Guesthouses Bed and Breakfast
P. O. Box 5737, 22905
(804) 979-7264; FAX (804) 293-7791

A 75-year-old Victorian farmhouse on 50 acres of pasture and woods skirted by hiking trails and traversed by the Rockfish River. The inn offers five queen or twin bedrooms, some with private bath. A full country breakfast is served. Guests may enjoy the hot tub, wood-burning stove, player piano, deck, or front porch. Wintergreen Resort and Stoney Creek golf and tennis facilities are available to guests. Air conditioning. $60-80.

Millstream

Guesthouses Bed and Breakfast
P. O. Box 5737, 22905
(804) 979-7264; FAX (804) 293-7791

A lovely, large house about 20 minutes north of Charlottesville up a long driveway lined with old box bushes. The house, with a brick English basement, was built before the Civil War and enlarged in 1866. There are two guest rooms, each with private bath. Guests may enjoy the fireplace in the library or the mountain views from the livingroom. A full breakfast is served in the kitchen, which has hand-hewn exposed beams. Air conditioning. $50-80.

6 Pets welcome; 8 Children welcome; 9 Social drinking allowed; 10 Tennis available; 11 Swimming available; 12 Golf available; 13 Skiing available; 14 May be booked through travel agents.

Silver Thatch Inn

Northfields

Guesthouses Bed and Breakfast
P. O. Box 5737, 22905
(804) 979-7264; FAX (804) 293-7791

This gracious home is on the northern edge
of Charlottesville. The guest room is furnished with twin beds and has a TV, private bath, and air conditioning. Another
bedroom is available with a double four-
poster bed and private hall bath. A full
gourmet breakfast is served. $60-68.

Piney Mountain

Guesthouses Bed and Breakfast
P. O. Box 5737, 22905
(804) 979-7264; FAX (804) 293-7791

This contemporary home on the side of a
mountain is in a wooded setting with spectacular views of the valley. There are several levels of deck, a hot tub, and a pool. The
lower-level suite has a sitting room with
fireplace and two bedrooms with queen
beds sharing a bath. On the main level
there is a queen room with a private hall
bath. Upstairs is a room with twin beds and
an adjoining bath. Guests may choose a
continental or full breakfast. Children over
12 welcome. $68-100.

The Rectory

Guesthouses Bed and Breakfast
P. O. Box 5737, 22905
(804) 979-7264; FAX (804) 293-7791

This charming home in a small village five
miles west of Charlottesville was a church
rectory. It is furnished in lovely antiques
and has an English garden in the back. The
guest room overlooking the formal rose
garden has its own entrance, twin beds, and
adjoining full bath. Air conditioning.
$60-80.

Rolling Acres Farm

Guesthouses Bed and Breakfast
P. O. Box 5737, 22905
(804) 979-7264; FAX (804) 293-7791

A lovely brick Colonial home in a wooded
setting on a small farm, this guest house
has two bedrooms with a hall bath upstairs.
One room has a double bed, and the other
has twin beds. The house is furnished with
many Victorian pieces. Air conditioning.
$60-80.

Silver Thatch Inn

3001 Hollymead Drive, 22901
(804) 978-4686

Silver Thatch Inn is a rambling white clapboard home that dates from 1780. With
three dining rooms and seven guest rooms,
it is a sophisticated retreat on the outskirts
of Charlottesville. Silver Thatch's modern
American cuisine uses the freshest of ingredients, and all sauces are prepared with
fruits and vegetables. The menu features
grilled meats, poultry, and game in season,
and there are always vegetarian selections.
The inn provides a wonderful respite for
the sophisticated traveler who enjoys fine
food and a quiet, caring atmosphere.

Hosts: Vince and Rita Scoffone
Rooms: 7 (PB) $105-125
Continental Breakfast
Credit Cards: A, B
Notes: 2, 4, 5, 8, 9, 10, 11, 12, 13, 14

Sweetwater Farm

Guesthouses Bed and Breakfast
P. O. Box 5737, 22905
(804) 979-7264; FAX (804) 293-7791

A working fish farm 28 miles south of
Charlottesville, this well-thought-out contemporary home with a traditional southern
farmhouse feel has a spacious deck overlooking a four-acre lake. Two guest rooms,
one with a queen bed and one with twin
beds, share a connecting bath. Air conditioning. Relax and enjoy the abundant
wildlife of the area. A full breakfast is
served. "Fee fishing" available in stocked
pond. Reasonable rates.

Woodstock Hall

Guesthouses Bed and Breakfast
P. O. Box 5737, 22905
(804) 979-7264; FAX (804) 293-7791

A few miles west of Charlottesville,
Woodstock was built about 1757 and 1808
and served as an 18th-century inn. Now
listed as a Virginia landmark and with the
National Register of Historic Places, the
inn has been restored and furnished with
period pieces. Four guest rooms are available, each with private bath and fireplace.
Afternoon tea and a full breakfast are
served. Guests may use the Federal parlor,
keeping room, and patio. $95-130.

CHATHAM

House of Laird Bed and Breakfast

335 South Main Street, P. O. Box 1131, 24531
(804) 432-2523

A small-town setting where the amenities
of a less-hurried time are still preserved.
The century-old Greek Revival is in a
grove of 200-year-old oaks. Professionally,
lovingly restored and decorated, all rooms

have private baths, fireplaces, and canopied
beds. Antiques, Oriental rugs, imported
moldings, and fabrics. Full breakfast on
period china and silver. Afternoon tea.
Complimentary wine and snack bar.
Central heat/air. Heated towels. Monitored
security system. Guest centered. Historic
hospitality.

Hosts: Mr. and Mrs. Ed Laird
Rooms: 4 (PB) $40-80
Full Breakfast
Credit Cards: A, B
Notes: 2, 5, 9, 14

CHINCOTEAGUE

The Main Street House Bed and Breakfast

4356 Main Street, P. O. Box 126, 23336
(804) 336-6030

Collections of antiques, wildlife art, and
carvings weave a story of the lives and
experiences of your hosts in this tastefully
decorated 100-year-old Victorian home.
Quiet, cozy, and relaxing are the words
here. The rooms are air-conditioned and
have paddle ceiling fans. Small refrigerators and terry-cloth robes add to your convenience. Our screened porch is perfect for
viewing lovely sunsets and enjoying afternoon refreshments. Only minutes from the
beach.

Hosts: Dennis and Kathy Holland
Rooms: 2 (SB) $55-75
Full Breakfast
Credit Cards: None
Notes: 2, 9

Miss Molly's Inn

4141 Main Street, 23336
(804) 336-6686

A charming Victorian inn on the bay two
miles from Chincoteague National Wildlife
Refuge and Assateague National Seashore.
All rooms are air-conditioned and furnished with period antiques. Room rate

6 Pets welcome; 8 Children welcome; 9 Social drinking allowed; 10 Tennis available; 11 Swimming available;
12 Golf available; 13 Skiing available; 14 May be booked through travel agents.

Miss Molly's Inn

incudes full breakfast and a traditional English afternoon tea. Marguerite Henry stayed here while writing *Misty of Chincoteague*.

Hosts: Barbara and David Wiedenheft
Rooms: 7 (5 PB; 2 SB) $69-135
Full Breakfast
Credit Cards: None
Closed: January 1-February 12
Notes: 2, 8 (over 10), 9, 11, 12

The Watson House

4240 North Main Street, 23336
(804) 336-1564

The Watson House has been tastefully restored with Victorian charm. Nestled in the heart of Chincoteague, the house is within walking distance of shops and restaurants. Each room has been comfortably decorated, including air conditioning, private baths, and antiques. A full, hearty breakfast and afternoon tea are served in the dining room or on the screened porch. Enjoy free use of bicycles to tour the island. Assateague National Wildlife Refuge is two minutes away, offering nature trails, surf, and Chincoteague's famous wild ponies.

Hosts: David and Jo Anne Snead; Tom and Jacque Derrickson
Rooms: 6 (PB) $55-99
Full Breakfast
Credit Cards: A, B
Notes: 2, 8 (10 and over), 9, 10, 11, 12, 13

CULPEPER

Fountain Hall Bed and Breakfast

609 South East Street, 22701-3222
(703) 825-8200; (800) 476-2944

Built in 1859, this grand bed and breakfast is within walking distance of historic downtown Culpeper. The inn is furnished with antiques and warmly welcomes business and leisure travelers. It offers one twin, two double, and three queen-size beds, and area activities and attractions include wineries, historic battlefields, antique shops, Skyline Drive, tennis, swimming, golf, and more.

Hosts: Steve, Kathi, and Leah-Marie Walker
Rooms: 5 (PB) $50-115
Continental Breakfast
Credit Cards: A, B, C, D
Notes: 2, 5, 8 (supervised), 9, 10, 11, 12, 13, 14

Fountain Hall

FRANKTOWN

Amanda's Bed and Breakfast #150

1428 Park Avenue, Baltimore, MD 21217
(410) 225-0001; (410) 383-1274

This charming 1895 Victorian home is in a setting of old maples, loblolly, white pines, dogwood, magnolia, and azaleas. The library is filled with volumes of books, many of them historical. Guests may also use the piano. Afternoon tea is served. Three rooms with private baths. Full breakfast. $65-75.

La Vista Plantation

FREDERICKSBURG

La Vista Plantation

4420 Guinea Station Road, 22408
(703) 898-8444

This lovely 1838 Classical Revival home is just outside historic Fredricksburg. On ten quiet acres, the grounds present a fine balance of mature trees, flowers, shrubs, and farm fields. The pond is stocked with bass. Choose from a spacious apartment that sleeps six with a kitchen and a fireplace or a formal room with a king mahogany rice-carved four-poster bed, fireplace, and Empire furniture. Homemade jams and farm-fresh eggs for breakfast.

Hosts: Michele and Edward Schiesser
Rooms: 2 (PB) $85
Full Breakfast
Credit Cards: A, B
Notes: 2, 5, 8, 9, 14

Richard Johnston Inn

711 Caroline Street, 22401
(703) 899-7606

This nine-room bed and breakfast, originally constructed in 1787, still reflects the grace and charm of a past era while providing all the amenities necessary for today's traveller. Whether you prefer the elegance of Victorian or Queen Anne, or the rustic charm of an old summer kitchen, you'll find that the Richard Johnson Inn is the perfect retreat. The inn is in the heart of historic Fredericksburg, where museums, antique shops, and restaurants abound. Conveniently situated within two blocks of Amtrak.

Host: Susan Thrush
Rooms: 7 and 2 suites (PB) $85-130
Continental Breakfast
Credit Cards: A, B, C
Notes: 2, 5, 9

The Spooner House Bed and Breakfast

1300 Caroline Street, 22401
(703) 371-1267

A lovely two-room suite with private bath and private entrance in a 1794 Federal-style home within Fredericksburg's National Historic District. Breakfast served with a morning newspaper at the guests' convenience in their private quarters. Complimentary tour of the Rising Sun Tavern next door to the Spooner House. Within walking distance of attractions, museums, restaurants, Amtrak, and shopping.

The Spooner House

6 Pets welcome; 8 Children welcome; 9 Social drinking allowed; 10 Tennis available; 11 Swimming available; 12 Golf available; 13 Skiing available; 14 May be booked through travel agents.

Hosts: Peggy and John Roethel
Rooms: 1 suite (PB) $85
Continental Breakfast
Credit Cards: None
Notes: 2, 5, 9, 10

HARRISONBURG

Joshua Wilton House Inn and Restaurant

412 South Main Street, 22801
(703) 434-4464

The Joshua Wilton House is a Victorian mansion built by Joshua Wilton in 1888. The house was renovated in 1987 and turned into an inn and restaurant. The rooms feature private baths and queen-size beds. All rooms are decorated in period antiques, and the restaurant features four lovely dining rooms, a lounge, bar, and terraced gardens.

Hosts: Craig and Roberta Moore
Rooms: 5 (PB) $100
Full Breakfast
Credit Cards: A, B
Notes: 2, 4, 5, 9, 10, 11, 12, 13

IRVINGTON

Bed and Breakfast of Tidewater Virginia

P. O. Box 6226, Norfolk, 23508
(804) 627-1983

Originally a 19th-century boarding school, this is now an inn with nine guest rooms and assorted livingrooms, dining rooms, and screened porches. There is something for everyone here: side trips to historic houses, mainly Stratford Hall, for history buffs and numerous activities for sports enthusiasts. A special country breakfast is served. Most rooms offer private baths. $50-65.

LOCUSTVILLE

Amanda's Bed and Breakfast #143

1428 Park Avenue, Baltimore, MD 21217
(410) 225-0001; (410) 383-1274

This 18th-century Colonial is near Wachapreague and just one mile from the ocean. Quiet and comfortable. Water sports nearby. One room with double bed and private bath. Continental breakfast. $68.

LYNCHBURG

Langhorne Manor

313 Washington Street, 24504-4619
(804) 846-4667; (800) 851-1466

Share the comforts, delights, and heritage of this home, a 27-room antebellum mansion built circa 1850. The spacious bedrooms and suites feature massive antiques, family heirlooms, private baths, and central air conditioning. Enjoy hearty homemade breakfasts with freshly ground coffee, then stroll around the architecturally magnificent historic neighborhood of Diamond Hill. Call about the "feel better" weekends of aerobic walks, biking, massage, and herbal cooking.

Host: Jaynee Acevedo
Rooms: 4 (PB) $70-95
Full Breakfast
Credit Cards: C
Notes: 2, 4, 5, 8, 9, 10, 11, 12, 13, 14

Lynchburg Mansion Inn Bed and Breakfast

405 Madison Street, 24504
(804) 528-5400; (800) 352-1199

Return to a finer yesterday in our 9,000-square foot Spanish Georgian mansion, restored with your every comfort in mind. King beds, fireplaces, private bathrooms,

TV, telephones, air conditioning, lavish linens and turn down service. Breakfast is served on fine china, with silver and crystal. Enjoy beautiful gardens, and relax on the veranda. Situated on a half-acre downtown, along a brick-paved street in turn-of-the-century neighborhood listed on the National Register.

Hosts: Bob and Mauranna Sherman
Rooms: 4 (PB) $89-109
Full Breakfast
Credit Cards: A, B, C
Notes: 2, 5, 14

The Madison House Bed and Breakfast
413 Madison Street, 24504
(804) 528-1503

Lynchburg's finest Victorian bed and breakfast (1880) boasts a magnificent, authentic interior decor. Spacious, elegantly appointed guest rooms graced with antiques, private baths, plush robes, and linens. Full breakfast served on antique Limoges and Wedgewood china; fresh-perked cinnamon coffee and afternoon high tea included. Central air, telephones, off-street parking. Near colleges, Appomattox, Poplar Forest, fine restaurants.

Hosts: Irene and Dale Smith
Rooms: 3 and 1 suite (PB) $70-95
Full Breakfast
Credit Cards: A, B
Notes: 2, 5, 9, 10, 11, 12, 14

Thistle Hill Bed and Breakfast
Route 1, P. O. Box 291, 22713
(703) 987-9142

Situated on a hillside on the morning side of the Blue Ridge Mountains, Thistle Hill offers modern amenities in a rural park-like setting. Two cottages, one with a fireplace, and the main house are cozily decorated with antiques and collectibles. Relax in the hot tub or wander through the lawns and woods. Enjoy afternoon tea in the gazebo

and a hearty, savory breakfast in the morning. Picnics and candlelight dinners by arrangement.

Hosts: Charles and Marianne Wilson
Rooms: 4 (PB) $95-135
Full Breakfast
Credit Cards: A, B, C, D
Notes: 2, 3, 4, 5, 8, 9, 14

MILLBORO

Fort Lewis Lodge
HCR 3, Box 21A, 24460
(703) 925-2314

Mountain forests teeming with deer and wild turkey; glistening river runs cool and clear. These are the gifts nature bestowed on Fort Lewis. The lodge's large gathering room and 12 guest rooms with wildlife art and handcrafted furniture are cozy and downright comfortable. For dinner and breakfast you'll feast on meals of homemade everything in a magnificently restored 19th-century grist mill.

Hosts: John and Caryl Cowden
Rooms: 12 (10 PB; 2 SB) $120-130 Modified American Plan
Full Breakfast
Credit Cards: A, B
Notes: 2, 3, 4, 8, 9, 11, 12, 14

Fort Lewis Lodge

MONROE

"St. Moor" House
High Peak Road, Box 136, Route 1, 24574
(804) 929-8228

6 Pets welcome; 8 Children welcome; 9 Social drinking allowed; 10 Tennis available; 11 Swimming available; 12 Golf available; 13 Skiing available; 14 May be booked through travel agents.

614   Mount Jackson, VA

Warm Virginia Hospitality seasoned with a British touch welcomes you at this lovely house. It sits among large trees facing majestic High Peak Mountain, near peach and apple orchards. Nature lovers can enjoy strolling the acres of fields, woodlands, and pastures where cows and horses graze. This serene spot offers a scrumptuous full breakfast and cathedral ceilings. Advanced registration only.

Hosts: Jean and John Camm
Rooms: 3 (2 PB; 1 SB) $59-65
Full Breakfast
Credit Cards: None
Notes: 2, 5, 8, 9, 13

MOUNT JACKSON

Amanda's Bed and Breakfast #181
1428 Park Avenue, Baltimore, MD 21217
(410) 225-0001; (410) 383-1274

An 1830 Colonial homestead on seven acres overlooking the George Washington Mountains. Some bedrooms have wood-burning fireplaces, and the antique furniture is for sale. Pool on premises. Area activities include craft fairs, hiking, fishing, tennis, and horseback riding. Five rooms with private baths. Two guest cottages. Full breakfast. $65-85.

A Touch of Country

NEWCHURCH

Amanda's Bed and Breakfast #210
1428 Park Avenue, Baltimore, MD 21217
(410) 225-0001; (410) 383-1274

This historic country inn offers elegant lodging and gourmet dining in the tradition of a small French inn. Near Chincoteague and Assateague National Seashore and Wildlife Refuge. Only a 15-minute drive to one of the most beautiful beaches on the eastern shore. Five guest rooms. Continental breakfast. $85-135.

NEW MARKET

A Touch of Country
9329 Congress Street, 22844
(703) 740-8030

Come relax at this restored 1870s home where a warm, friendly, atmosphere awaits you. Daydream on the porch swings or stroll through town, with its antique shops, gift shops, and restaurants. Rest in one of six bedrooms decorated with a country flavor. In the morning enjoy a down-home country breakfast. Near caverns and battlefields.

Hosts: Jean Schoellig and Dawn Kason
Rooms: 6 (PB) $60-70
Full Breakfast
Credit Cards: A, B
Notes: 2, 5, 8 (over 12), 9, 10, 11, 12, 13, 14

NORFOLK

Bed and Breakfast of Tidewater Virginia
P. O. Box 6226, 23508
(804) 627-1983

This bed and breakfast is a spacious third-generation home on a tree-lined street in old Ghent where your world-traveled host-

NOTES: Credit cards accepted: A Master Card; B Visa; C American Express; D Discover Card; E Diner's Club; F Other; 2 Personal Checks accepted; 3 Lunch available; 4 Dinner available; 5 Open all year;

ess grew up. A short drive to Old Dominion University, Chrysler Museum, medical complex, and the Norfolk Naval Base. Rooms have four-poster beds, and a private porch overlooks an enchanting patio and garden offering privacy and tranquility. Two guest rooms are available; one offers a private bath. Full breakfast. $55-65.

Bed and Breakfast of Tidewater Virginia #1
P. O. Box 6226, Norfolk, 23508
(804) 627-1983

Just two houses from the beach in a town designated as a "historic district," this 1910 house has been lovingly restored by its owners. There are French, English, and American antiques throughout, with an antique brass bed in one room and a four-poster bed in another guest room. Four guest rooms are available. Full breakfast and afternoon tea served. $60-70.

Bed and Breakfast of Tidewater Virginia #2
P. O. Box 6226, 23508
(804) 627-1983

Casual sophistication for adults in a warm, historic inn-like atmosphere describes this delightful turn of the century cottage. Just two blocks from the beach and fishing pier, it features six rooms, two with private baths. Full breakfast served. $65-80.

Bed and Breakfast of Tidewater Virginia
P. O. Box 6226, 23508
(804) 627-1983

Near I-64, this contemporary house features a solarium and an open kitchen in the middle of the house. Comfortable and unique, this bed and breakfast features two

rooms, one with twin beds and the other a double. Both rooms offer a private bath. Full breakfast. $55-65.

Bed and Breakfast of Tidewater Virginia Reservation Service
P. O. Box 6226, 23508
(804) 627-1983

Norfolk boasts the world's largest naval base, the famed Chrysler Museum, and MacArthur Memorial. It is a cultural hub in which top-rated opera, symphony, and stage productions abound. There are miles of scenic beaches to explore on the Chesapeake Bay and the Atlantic Ocean. Old Dominion University, Eastern Virginia Medical School, and Virginia Wesleyan College are conveniently nearby. Town and beach homes, inns, and apartments are available. Now offering Bed and Breakfast Dockside. Charters available. $55-150.

ORANGE

The Holladay House
155 West Main Street, 22960
(703) 672-4893; (800) 358-4422
FAX (703) 672-3028

The Holladay House, circa 1830, is a restored Federal-style home that has been in the Holladay family since 1899. The large, comfortable rooms are furnished with family pieces, and each one features its own sitting area. Breakfast is normally served to guests in their own rooms. Surrounded by a residential neighborhood on three sides, the Holladay House is two blocks from the center of the historic town of Orange and just 90 minutes from Richmond or Washington, D. C.

Hosts: Pete and Phebe Holladay
Rooms: 6 (4 PB; 2 SB) $75-120
Full Breakfast

6 Pets welcome; 8 Children welcome; 9 Social drinking allowed; 10 Tennis available; 11 Swimming available; 12 Golf available; 13 Skiing available; 14 May be booked through travel agents.

Credit Cards: A, B
Notes: 2, 5, 8, 9, 10, 14

PRATTS

Colvin Hall
Bed and Breakfast

HCR 03, Box 30G (Route 230 East) Madison
County, 22731
(703) 948-6211

Relaxation and romance await you at this
1870 country retreat on more than seven
acres. The inn offers working fireplaces
and firewood, air conditioning, swimming,
and a hearty breakfast. Close to
antique/craft shops, Skyline Drive,
Montpelier, hiking, and wineries. Rooms
include a queen canopy bed with fireplace
and private bath, king bed with fireplace
and private bath, and twin beds with shared
bath. Situated in the central Virginia
Piedmont between Charlottesville and
Culpeper. A true bed and breakfast experience.

Hosts: Sue and Dave Rossell
Rooms: 3 (2 PB; 1 SB) $60-85
Full Breakfast
Credit Cards: A, B
Notes: 2, 5, 9, 11, 13

RAPHINE

Oak Spring Farm
and Vineyard

Route 1, Box 356, 24472
(703) 377-2398

Newly restored 1826 plantation house on
40 acres filled with antiques, family treasures, and other items reflecting 26 years of
worldwide military service. There are modern conveniences on this working farm and
vineyard. Three rooms available, all with
private baths. You can expect spectacular
views, woods to walk in, and exotic animals in the pasture, along with peace and
quiet. Convenient to I-81 and I-64 halfway
between historic Lexington and Staunton.

Hosts: Pat and Jim Tichenor
Rooms: 3 (PB) $63-73
Continental Breakfast
Credit Cards: A, B
Notes: 2, 5, 9, 10, 11, 12, 13

RICHMOND

Bensonhouse of
Williamsburg, Virginia

2036 Monument, 23220
(804) 353-6900

Representing seven carefully selected private homes, inns, and cottages situated in
close proximity to Colonial Williamsburg.
Selections include a beautiful reproduction
of an 18th-century Connecticut tavern, with
a queen bed in the bedroom, private bath,
and fireplace. There are also two charming
Colonial cottages, with queen beds in the
bedrooms and private baths (one has a
Jacuzzi); and one of these cottages has a
fireplace.

Rooms: 7 (PB) $65-125
Continental Breakfast
Credit Cards: A, B, C
Notes: 2, 5, 8, 9, 11, 12, 14

The Emmanuel Hutzler
House

2036 Monument Avenue, 23220
(804) 353-6900; (804) 355-4885

This large Italian Renaissance-style inn has
been totally renovated in the past three
years and offers leaded-glass windows, coffered ceilings, and natural mahogany raised
paneling throughout the downstairs, as well
as a large livingroom with a marble fireplace for guests' enjoyment. There are four
guest rooms on the second floor, each with
private bath. The suite has a four-poster
queen bed, love seat, and wing chair. The
two queen rooms have a sitting area and
private baths. The largest room has a marble fireplace, four-poster mahogany bed,
antique sofa, dresser, and a private bath
with shower and Jacuzzi.

NOTES: Credit cards accepted: A Master Card; B Visa; C American Express; D Discover Card; E Diner's
Club; F Other; 2 Personal Checks accepted; 3 Lunch available; 4 Dinner available; 5 Open all year;

Hosts: Lyn M. Benson and John E. Richardson
Rooms: 4 (PB) $89-135
Full Breakfast
Credit Cards: A, B, C, D
Notes: 2, 5, 9, 10, 11, 12, 14

ROANOKE—SEE ALSO
SMITH MOUNTAIN LAKE

The Manor at Taylor's Store
Route 1, Box 533, Smith Mountain Lake, 24184
(703) 721-3951; (800) 248-6267

Explore this secluded, historic 120-acre estate conveniently situated near Smith Mountain Lake, Roanoke, and the Blue Ridge Parkway. The manor has six guest suites with extraordinary antiques and Oriental rugs. Guests enjoy all luxury amenities, including central air conditioning, hot tub, fireplaces, private porches, billiard room, exercise room, guest kitchen, movies, and six private, spring-fed ponds for swimming, fishing, and canoeing. A lovely gazebo overlooks the ponds for picnics. A full "heart healthy" gourmet breakfast is served in the dining room with panoramic views of the countryside.

Hosts: Lee and Mary Lunn Tucker
Rooms: 6 (4 PB; 2 SB) $70-100
Cottage: 1 (PB)
Full Breakfast
Credit Cards: A, B
Notes: 2, 3, 5, 8, 9, 10, 11, 12, 13, 14

SANDBRIDGE

Bed and Breakfast of Tidewater Virginia
P. O. Box 6226, Norfolk, 23508
(804) 627-1983

A delightful suite on the first floor of the builder/owner's home offers a combination livingroom/bedroom with a queen-size bed and a queen-size sleeper sofa. Across the street from the Atlantic Ocean, which guests can enjoy from a picture window and the rear door, a lovely flower and herb garden can be explored and enjoyed. Guest room has a private entrance. Hostess provides beach chairs and a bicycle for guests to use. Private bath and refrigerator. Continental breakfast. $85, plus $5 per child.

SCOTTSVILLE

High Meadows Vineyard and Mountain Sunset
Route 4, Box 6, Route 20 South, 24590
(804) 286-2218; (800) 232-1832

Enchanting 19th-century European-style auberge with tastefully appointed, spacious guest rooms, private baths, period antiques. Two-room suites available. Several common rooms, fireplaces, and tranquility. Pastoral setting on 50 acres. Privacy, relaxing walks, gourmet picnics. Virginia wine tasting and romantic candlelight dining nightly. Virginia Architectural Landmark. National Register of Historic Places.

Hosts: Peter, Sushka, and Mary Jae Abbitt
Rooms: 12 (PB) $90.52-172.42
Full Breakfast
Minimum stay weekends and holidays: 2 nights
Credit Cards: A, B
Closed December 24-25
Notes: 2, 4, 6, 8, 9, 10, 11, 13, 14

High Meadows Vineyard

6 Pets welcome; 8 Children welcome; 9 Social drinking allowed; 10 Tennis available; 11 Swimming available; 12 Golf available; 13 Skiing available; 14 May be booked through travel agents.

SPRINGFIELD

Bonniemill Bed and Breakfast

7305 Bonniemill Lane, 22150
(703) 569-9295

Stay in a quiet, residential neighborhood convenient to the nation's capitol. The Jacuzzi Suite has a four-poster queen-size bed, TV, VCR, compact disc player, and double whirlpool. The Victorian Suite features an antique bed and armoire, floral wallpaper, and rich draperies. Lynn and Dave run their health, fitness and nutrition business from their home. Lynn also does interior decorating, and her touch is evident throughout. Feel free to use the bicycles, Lifecycle, and gas grill.

Hosts: Lynn and David Tikkala
Rooms: 2 (PB) $60-75
Full Breakfast
Credit Cards: None
Notes: 2, 5, 9, 10, 12

Renaissance Manor Bed and Breakfast and Art Gallery

2247 Courthouse Road, 22554
(703) 720-3785

Designed to resemble Mt. Vernon (25 miles away) in architecture, decor, and charm. Features ten-foot ceilings, hardwood floors, canopied king-size beds, fireplace, claw foot tubs, and unlimited hospitality. Formal courtyard with gardens, gazebo, and a windmill. Local artists work reasonably priced. Afternoon tea and homemade expanded breakfast. On a winding country road four miles off I-95 between Fredericksburg and Washington D. C. Near the Potomac and Rappahonnock rivers, historic battlefields, antique shops, and wineries.

Rooms: 4 (2 PB; 2 SB) $55-95
Continental Breakfast

Credit Cards: None
Notes: 2, 5, 8, 9, 14

STAUNTON

Ashton Country House

1205 Middlebrook Road, 24401
(703) 885-7819

The Ashton Country House, circa 1860, is a Greek Revival brick home situated on twenty peaceful acres at the outskirts of Staunton. Each of the four spacious guest rooms features a private bath and a queen or double bed. Mornings begin with a hearty breakfast that is often accompanied by live piano music. Convenient to historic attractions and fine restaurants.

Hosts: Sheila Kennedy and Stanley Polanski
Rooms: 4 (PB) $65-80
Full Breakfast
Credit Cards: None
Notes: 2, 5, 9, 10, 11, 12

Frederick House

Frederick and New Streets, P. O. Box 1387, 24401
(703) 885-4220; (800) 334-5575

A small hotel and tea room in the European tradition. Large, comfortable rooms or suites, private baths, cable TV, air conditioning, telephones, and antique furnishings. Across from Mary Baldwin College. Convenient to fine restaurants, shopping, museums, and the Blue Ridge Mountains.

Hosts: Joe and Evy Harman
Rooms: 14 (PB) $45-110
Full Breakfast
Credit Cards: A, B, C, D, E
Notes: 2, 3, 4, 5, 8, 9, 10, 11, 12, 13, 14

Kenwood

235 East Beverley Street, 24401
(703) 886-0524

Spacious, restored 1910 Colonial Revival brick home adjacent to Woodrow Wilson Birthplace and Museum. Filled with period furniture and antiques, Kenwood offers comfortable accommodations in a relaxed atmosphere. Just two miles west of the I-81 and I-64 intersection, near the Museum of American Frontier Culture, Skyline Drive, Blue Ridge Parkway, Statler Brothers Museum, Monticello. Four guest rooms with queen beds, private baths, air conditioning, full breakfast.

Hosts: Liz and Ed Kennedy
Rooms: 4 (2 PB; 2 SB) $55-70
Full Breakfast
Credit Cards: A, B
Notes: 2, 5, 8, 9, 10, 11, 12

The Sampson Eagon Inn

238 East Beverley Street, 24401
(800) 597-9722

Situated in the Virginia historic landmark district of Gospel Hill, this gracious, circa 1840, town residence has been thoughtfully restored and transformed into a unique inn offering affordable luxury and personal service in an intimate, inviting atmosphere. Each elegant, spacious, air-conditioned room and suite features private bath, sitting area, canopy queen bed, and antique furnishings. Adjacent to the Woodrow Wilson Birthplace and Mary Baldwin College, the inn is within two blocks of downtown dining and attractions.

Hosts: Laura and Frank Mattingly
Rooms: 4 (PB) $75-90
Full Breakfast
Credit Cards: None
Notes: 2, 5, 9, 10, 11, 12, 13, 14

The Sampson Eagon Inn

STEELE'S TAVERN

The Osceola Mill Country Inn

State Route 56, 24476
(703) 377-6455; (800) 242-7352
FAX (703) 377-6455

Unique and gracious, yet unpretentious, the inn consists of a restored 1840s grist mill and miller house, and the 1870 mill store, now an exquisite honeymoon cottage. In the heart of the Shenandoah Valley and Blue Ridge area, with 14 colleges and major attractions nearby, "The Mill" delivers an ambience like grandma's house and can keep vacationers busy for weeks on end.

Host: Paul Newcomb
Rooms: 12 (PB) $89-119
Cottage $139-169 (discount for extended stays)
Full Breakfast
Credit Cards: None
Notes: 2, 4 (weekends only), 5, 8, 9, 11, 12, 13, 14

VIRGINIA BEACH

Angie's Guest Cottage

302 24th Street, 23451
(804) 428-4690

Situated in the heart of the resort area, one block from the ocean. Large beach house that guests describe as "cute, clean, comfortable, and convenient." All rooms are air-conditioned; some have small refrigerators and private entrances. Breakfast is served on the front porch, and there is also a sun deck, barbecue pit, and picnic tables.

Host: Barbara G. Yates
Rooms: 6 (1 PB; 5 SB) $48.18-67.89
Continental Breakfast
Minimum stay in season: 2 nights
Credit Cards: None
Closed October 1-April 1
Notes: 8, 9, 10, 11, 12

The Burton House/ Hart's Harbor House

9 and 11 Brooklyn Street, 23480
(804) 787-4560

The Burton House and Hart's Harbor House are two Victorians, side-by-side, in a seaside fishing village. Both are fully air-conditioned when needed. Guests can enjoy biking, fishing, and boating. Bikes are provided, and rental boats are available. Enjoy a generous country breakfast and afternoon tea or coffee. Quiet, affordable elegance. Cabins are also available; close to the marina. Guests should feel free to bring their own boats. Brochure available upon request.

Hosts: Pat, Tom, and Mike Hart
Rooms: 10 (PB) $65-75 plus tax
Cabins: 4 (PB) $40-50 plus tax
Full Breakfast
Credit Cards: A, B
Notes: 2, 5, 8 (over 12), 10, 11, 12, 14

The Burton House

WACHAPREAGUE

Amanda's Bed and Breakfast #271

1428 Park Avenue, Baltimore, MD 21217
(410) 225-0001; (410) 383-1274

Antiques, family heirlooms and working fireplaces await you at this bed and breakfast. Situated in the historic Church Hill District. Beautiful period furniture,
canopied beds, large armoires, crystal chandeliers, and hospitality that will make your stay a pleasant one. Five rooms with private and shared baths. $75-160.

WASHINGTON

Caledonia Farm

Route 1, Box 2080, Flint Hill, 22627
(703) 675-3693

Beautifully restored 1812 stone home and romantic guest house on farm adjacent to Shenandoah National Park. This historic landmark listed on the National Register of Historic Places offers splendor for all seasons in Virginia's Blue Ridge Mountains. Skyline Drive, wineries, caves, historic sites, superb dining. Fireplaces, air conditioning, bicycles. Only 68 miles to Washington, D.C.

Host: Phil Irwin
Rooms: 2 plus suite (1 PB; 2 SB) $80-140
Full Breakfast
Credit Cards: A, B, D
Notes: 2, 3, 5, 8 (over 12), 9, 10, 11, 12, 13, 14

WILLIAMSBURG

Amanda's Bed and Breakfast #253

1428 Park Avenue, Baltimore, MD 21217
(410) 225-0001; (410) 383-1274

This Flemish bond brick home was one of the first homes built on Richmond Road after the restoration of Colonial Williamsburg began in the late 1920s. The house features 18th-century decor, and the owner's apple collection is evident throughout. Four rooms with private baths. Continental-plus breakfast. $65-95.

Indian Springs

330 Indian Springs Road, 23185
(804) 220-0726; (800) 262-9165

NOTES: Credit cards accepted: A Master Card; B Visa; C American Express; D Discover Card; E Diner's Club; F Other; 2 Personal Checks accepted; 3 Lunch available; 4 Dinner available; 5 Open all year;

Memorable hospitality awaits you at this quiet wooded retreat. Indian Springs is three blocks from Colonial Williamsburg. Charming guest suites include king feather beds, private baths, and private entrances. The veranda overlooking a shady ravine is a bird watcher's haven. Awake to a full breakfast featuring freshly ground coffees and muffins baked daily. Enjoy our game room, study, and gardens.

Hosts: Kelly and Paul Supplee
Rooms: 4 (PB) $63-85
Full Breakfast
Credit Cards: None
Notes: 2, 5, 8, 9, 10, 11, 12

Liberty Rose Bed and Breakfast

1022 Jamestown Road, 23185
(804) 253-1260

This delightful old Williamsburg home is showcased on a wooded hilltop near the historic area. A charming blend of the 18th century, Country French, and Victorian antiques. Guest rooms include claw foot tubs, marble showers, papered walls, and queen beds. Fireplaces, chocolate chip cookies, in-room television and VCRs, and delicious breakfasts. Awarded the highest rating by the American Bed and Breakfast Association (ABBA).

Hosts: Brad and Sandi Hirz
Rooms: 4 (PB) $100-155
Full Breakfast
Credit Cards: A, B
Notes: 2, 5, 12, 14

Newport House

710 South Henry Street, 23185-4113
(804) 229-1775

Newport House was designed in 1756 by Peter Harrison. It is furnished totally in the period, including four-poster canopy beds. Each room has a private bathroom. The full breakfast includes authentic Colonial period recipes. Only a five-minute walk from the historic area (as close as you can get).

The host is a former museum director and author of many books on Colonial history. Enjoy colonial dancing in the ballroom every Tuesday evening.

Hosts: John Millar
Rooms: 2 (PB) $90-120
Full Breakfast
Credit Cards: None
Notes: 2, 5, 8, 10, 11, 12, 14

Newport House

The Travel Tree 9

P. O. Box 838, 23187
(800) 989-1571

Treat yourself to a four-poster, queen-bedded room with sitting area and private bath. Add the adjoining room with antique double bed for a family suite, and enjoy all that Williamsburg has to offer. Near Busch Gardens and four miles from the historic area. $75.

The Travel Tree 10

P. O. Box 838, 23187
(800) 989-1571

Rest safe and secure tucked under the eaves of a one-and-one-half-story cottage in a charming wooded setting. Sleep upstairs in a queen-size brass bed; relax downstairs in the sitting room with fireplace and Pullman kitchen. With sofa bed downstairs, accommodates four. One and one half baths. One mile from the historic area. $105.

The Travel Tree 133

P. O. Box 838, 23187
(800) 989-1571

Luxuriate in this home away from home in a spacious room complete with king-size bed, dining alcove, private bath, and private entrance. Or select the economical queen-bed room with a lovely wooded view, or the pleasant twin-bed room, furnished with Oriental accents and adjacent Shared bath. Three miles from the historic area. $55-75.

The Travel Tree 139

P. O. Box 838, 23187
(800) 989-1571

Relax in an airy, inviting room with private entrance, private bath, kitchenette, and patio doors leading to the lawn. Or choose the gracious suite furnished with 18th- and 19th-century antiques, a four-poster double bed, sitting area with fireplace, breakfast room, and private bath. Only one mile from the restored area. Roll away bed available. $70-95.

The Travel Tree 517

P. O. Box 838, 23187
(800) 989-1571

Enjoy the ambience of a lovely Colonial Revival home furnished with turn-of-the-century antiques and country charm. Double, twin, or king-size beds available. Four blocks from the historic area. $70.

The Travel Tree 605

P. O. Box 838, 23187
(800) 989-1571

Walk to the historic area after starting the day with the companionship of fellow guests at breakfast. The lovely guest rooms, each in Colonial decor, will charm you, from the first-floor suite with fireplace to the quaint third-floor dormered room. All have queen beds and private baths. Five blocks from the historic area. $70-100.

Williamsburg Sampler Bed and Breakfast

922 Jamestown Road, 23185
(804) 253-0398; (800) 722-1169

This bed and breakfast is an elegant 18th-century plantation-style, six-bedroom brick Colonial, richly furnished with antiques, pewter, and samplers. Internationally known as a favorite for honeymoons, anniversaries, or romantic getaways. The hosts return guests to an era when hospitality was a matter of pride and fine living was an art. Lovely rooms with four-poster king/queen-size beds plus private baths. Skip-lunch breakfast. Close to all major attractions. Personalized gift certificates available. AAA rated Three Diamonds.

Hosts: Helen and Ike Sisane
Rooms: 4 (PB) $85-100
Full Breakfast
Credit Cards: A, B
Notes: 2, 5, 9, 10, 11, 12, 14

WILLIS WHARF

Amanda's Bed and Breakfast #145

1428 Park Avenue, Baltimore, MD 21217
(410) 225-0001; (410) 383-1274

NOTES: Credit cards accepted: A Master Card; B Visa; C American Express; D Discover Card; E Diner's Club; F Other; 2 Personal Checks accepted; 3 Lunch available; 4 Dinner available; 5 Open all year;

Eighty-year-old country farmhouse with wraparound porch and gazebo by a stream. Near a freshwater pond, bird watching, photographic scenes, and guided tours. Amenities include outside swings, hammock, play gym, and bicycles. Relaxed family atmosphere. Four rooms with shared and private baths. Full breakfast. $60-75.

WOODSTOCK

The Inn at Narrow Passage

U.S. 11 South, 22664
(703) 459-8000

Historic log inn with five acres on the Shenandoah River. Colonial-style rooms, most with private baths and working fireplaces. Once the site of Indian attacks and Stonewall Jackson's headquarters, the inn is now a cozy spot in winter with large fireplaces in the common, living, and dining rooms. In spring and summer, fishing and rafting are at the back door. Fall brings the foliage festivals and hiking in the national forest a few miles away. Nearby are vineyards, caverns, historic sites, and fine restaurants. Washington, D. C. is 90 miles away.

Hosts: Ellen and Ed Markel
Rooms: 12 (10 PB; 2 SB) $55-95
Full Breakfast
Credit Cards: A, B
Notes: 2, 5, 8, 9, 10, 11, 12, 13, 14

6 Pets welcome; 8 Children welcome; 9 Social drinking allowed; 10 Tennis available; 11 Swimming available; 12 Golf available; 13 Skiing available; 14 May be booked through travel agents.

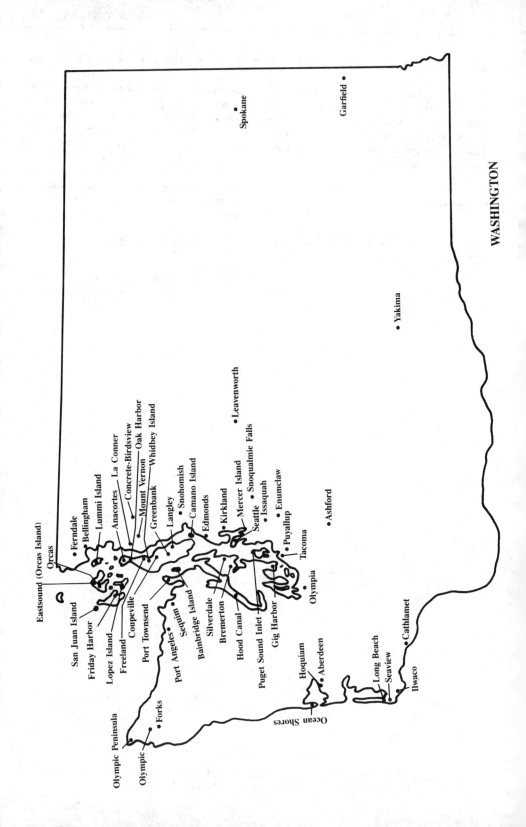

WASHINGTON

Garfield •

Spokane
•

Yakima
•

Leavenworth •

Ashford •

Eastsound (Orcas Island)
Orcas
• Ferndale
• Bellingham
Lummi Island
Anacortes La Conner
Concrete-Birdsview
Mount Vernon Oak Harbor
Greenbank Whidbey Island
Langley
• Snohomish
Camano Island
Edmonds
• Kirkland
Mercer Island
Seattle • Snoqualmie Falls
• Issaquah • Enumclaw
• Puyallup
Tacoma

San Juan Island
Friday Harbor
Lopez Island
Freeland
Coupeville
Port Townsend

Port Angeles •
Sequim
Bainbridge Island
Silverdale
Bremerton
Hood Canal
Puget Sound Inlet
Gig Harbor
Olympia

Hoquiam
• Aberdeen

Long Beach
Seaview •
Ilwaco

Cathlamet •

Ocean Shores

Olympic Peninsula
Olympic
• Forks

Washington

Anacortes

Pacific Bed and Breakfast Agency
701 Northwest 60th Street, Seattle, 98107
(206) 784-0539

This restored Victorian turn-of-the-century home features fine antiques, Oriental carpets, a library, colorful flower gardens, three fireplaces, and an outdoor hot tub. Views of Puget Sound can be seen from two rooms and the shared bathrooms. Intimate in size with warm hospitality. $60-105.

Albatross Bed and Breakfast

5708 Kingsway West, 98221
(206) 293-0677

Across from the Skyline Marina, this 1927 Cape Cod-style home with a large viewing deck offers king and queen-size beds, and all rooms feature a private bath. Skyline Marina offers charter boats, a deli, and fine dining. Nearby are Washington Park and ferries to the San Juan Islands and Victoria, B. C. Free transportation to and from the ferries and Anacortes airport. Sailboat cruises and bicycles available. AAA approved.

Hosts: Barbie and Ken
Rooms: 4 (PB) $75-85
Full Breakfast
Credit Cards: A, B, D
Notes: 2, 5, 12, 14

Growly Bear

37311 State Road 706, 98304
(206) 569-2339

Experience a bit of history and enjoy a mountain stay at a rustic homestead house built in 1890. Secluded location near Mount Rainier National Park. Listen to Goat Creek just outside the window; indulge in fresh pastries from the Sweet Peaks Bakery.

Host: Susan Jenny
Rooms: 2 (1 PB; 1 SB) $50-80
Full Breakfast
Credit Cards: A, B, C
Notes: 2, 5, 9, 13, 14

Growly Bear

Bombay House

8490 Beck Road, 98110
(206) 842-3926; (800) 598-3926

NOTES: Credit cards accepted: A Master Card; B Visa; C American Express; D Discover Card; E Diner's Club; F Other; 2 Personal Checks accepted; 3 Lunch available; 4 Dinner available; 5 Open all year; 6 Pets welcome; 8 Children welcome; 9 Social drinking allowed; 10 Tennis available; 11 Swimming available; 12 Golf available; 13 Skiing available; 14 May be booked through travel agents.

The Bombay House is a spectacular 35-minute ferry ride from downtown Seattle. The house was built in 1907 and sits high on a hillside in the country overlooking Rich Passage. Widow's walk; rustic, rough-cedar gazebo; masses of gardens exploding with seasonal color. Watch the ferry pass and see the lights of Bremerton in the distance. Just a few blocks from the beach, a country theater, and fine dining. A great spot for the Seattle business traveler or vacationer.

Hosts: Bunny Cameron and Roger Kanchuk
Rooms: 5 (3 PB; 2 SB) $55-125
Continental Breakfast
Credit Cards: A, B, C
Notes: 2, 5, 9, 10, 11, 12, 14

Pacific B&B Agency Bainbridge Island-1

701 Northwest 60th Street, Seattle, 98107
(206) 784-0539

This special country inn invites guests to sit on the wraparound porch, enjoy the beautiful flower gardens, the gazebo, or snuggle up by the crackling fire in the fireplace. A stay here will renew and refresh spirits. Built for a ship's captain, this lovely bed and breakfast offers nice views over the water, three bedrooms with private baths, and two bedrooms that share a bath. Legendary country breakfast. $65-95.

Pacific B&B Agency Bainbridge Island -2

701 Northwest 60th Street, Seattle, 98107
(206) 784-0539

This Bainbridge accommodation is on a beautifully landscaped acre enclosed by a forest on both sides. Guests can relax on comfortable wicker furniture and look out at the rose garden after a day of sightseeing or exploration. Perfect for honeymooners and couples. The cookie jar is always deep, a new snack is served on the table next to

the sofa every day, and the bedroom has a queen-size bed with a wonderful new mattress and a private bath. $85.

Pacific B&B Agency Bainbridge Island-3

701 Northwest 60th Street, Seattle, 98107
(206) 784-0539

In this traditional, but not overly formal bed and breakfast, guests can relax in a new English-shingled cottage. Two large private rooms are only a short stroll from the beach. Both rooms have queen-size beds, private baths, large windows, telephones, and TV. Near the quaint towns of Rolling Bay and Winslow. $75.

BELLINGHAM

Bellingham

Pacific Bed and Breakfast Agency
701 Northwest 60th Street, Seattle, 98107
(206) 784-0539

Decorated with stained glass and etchings crafted by the hostess, this restored Victorian overlooking the bay is a great getaway spot. The two guest rooms have private baths. The hosts are more than happy to give advice to sightseers if needed. Guests are assured a warm, friendly welcome at this bed and breakfast. $42-57.

Loganita by the Sea

2825 West Shore Drive, 98265
(206) 758-2651

Near Billingham, only 15 minutes off I-5 to the ferry, then a nine minute ferry ride to Lumni Island. *Journal American* describes the inn as "The most romantic bed and breakfast getaway in western Washington." All private baths, spa, fireplaces, and a private sandy beach. Irresistible location; San

NOTES: Credit cards accepted: A Master Card; B Visa; C American Express; D Discover Card; E Diner's Club; F Other; 2 Personal Checks accepted; 3 Lunch available; 4 Dinner available; 5 Open all year;

Juan Island view. Lovely hideaway by the sea on bucolic Lumni Island.

Hosts: Ann and Glen Gossage
Rooms: 5 (PB) $85-175
Full Breakfast
Credit Cards: A, B
Notes: 8, 9, 14

North Garden Inn

1014 North Garden, 98225
(800) 922-6416 (US); (800) 367-1676 (Canada)

North Garden Inn is an 1897 Queen Anne Victorian on the national register. Many of the guest rooms have splendid views of Bellingham Bay. The inn features two studio grand pianos in performance condition and is situated close to shopping, fine dining, and Western Washington University.

Hosts: Frank and Barbara DeFreytas
Rooms: 8 (winter) 10 (summer) (PB) $64-74
Full Breakfast
Credit Cards: A, B, D
Notes: 2, 5, 9, 10, 12, 13, 14

BREMERTON

Willcox House

2390 Tekiu Road, 98312
(206) 830-4492

Overlooking Hood Canal and the Olympic Mountains is a place where time rests. Life is paced by the slow, steady hand of nature. It is quiet enough to hear the birds sing. Deer amble through the gardens. Saltwater beaches and good books wait for quiet companions. Willcox House is an elegant

Willcox House

10,000-square-foot mansion built in 1936 with landscaped grounds, private pier, and beach. Five guest rooms, all with private baths and magnificent views of the Hood Canal and Olympic Mountains.

Hosts: Cecilia and Philip Hughes
Rooms: 5 (PB) $100-165
Full Breakfast
Credit Cards: A, B
Notes: 2, 3, 4, 5, 9, 11, 12, 14

CAMANO ISLAND

Willcox House Bed and Breakfast

1462 Larkspur Lane, 98292
(206) 629-4746

Built in 1985, this two-story house with a wraparound covered porch is furnished with family antiques and named for an early 1900s children's illustrator, Jessie Willcox Smith. The rooms overlook the Puget Sound where snow geese and trumpet swans migrate each fall. Mount Baker looms in the distance. Gourmet breakfasts are served in a peaceful country setting on an island one hour north of Seattle connected by bridge to the mainland, close to picturesque towns.

Hosts: Madelyn and Joe Braun
Rooms: 4 (1 PB; 3 SB) $55-65
Full Breakfast
Credit Cards: A, B
Notes: 2, 5, 8, 9, 10, 11, 12, 13

CATHLAMET

The Gallery Bed and Breakfast at Little Cape Horn

4 Little Cape Horn, 98612
(206) 425-7395; FAX (206) 425-1351

Large contemporary home with picture windows overlooking the majestic Columbia River ship channel. Private bath. Fishing, wind surfing, and pleasant walk-

6 Pets welcome; 8 Children welcome; 9 Social drinking allowed; 10 Tennis available; 11 Swimming available; 12 Golf available; 13 Skiing available; 14 May be booked through travel agents.

ing; deer, bald eagles, hummingbirds, hawks, and water birds. Beautiful mature cedar and fir trees; very restful surroundings. Friendly hosts enjoy guests. Two cats and a Labrador retriever will greet visitors.

Hosts: Carolyn and Eric Feasey
Rooms: 3 (1 PB; 2 SB) $70-80
Full or Continental Breakfast
Credit Cards: C
Note: 2, 5, 6, 8 (over 10), 12, 14

CONCRETE-BIRDSVIEW

Cascade Mountain Inn

3840 Pioneer Lane, 98237
(206) 826-4333

The inn is close to the Skagit River, Baker Lake, and the North Cascades National Park, just off Highway 20 in a pastoral setting. Easy access to hiking, fishing, and sight-seeing in one of the nation's most scenic mountain areas. Full cooked country breakfast. AAA rated Three Diamonds.

Hosts: Ingrid and Gerhard Meyer
Rooms: 6 (PB) $84
Full Breakfast
Credit Cards: A, B
Notes: 2, 5, 9, 14

COUPEVILLE

The Inn At Penn Cove

702 North Main Street, P. O. Box 85, 98239
(206) 678-8000

The Inn at Penn Cove, two historic Victorian homes, is just north of Highway 20 in the heart of Coupeville. Kineth House's three guest rooms have private baths, one with Jacuzzi. Three additional rooms are available in Gillespie House. Full breakfast and afternoon tea is served. Area attractions include historic Coupeville and Ebey's Landing, Deception Pass, Penn Cove, specialty shops, fine restaurants and bicycling and kayaking nearby.

Hosts: Gladys and Mitchell Howard
Rooms: 6 (4 PB; 2 SB) $60-125

Full Breakfast
Credit Cards: A, B, C, D
Notes: 2, 5, 8, 14

EASTSOUND, ORCAS ISLAND

Kangaroo House

Box 334, 98245
(206) 376-2175

Restful 1907 home on Orcas Island, gem of the San Juans. Period furnishings, extensive lawns, and flower gardens. Gourmet breakfasts. Walk to village shops, galleries, and restaurants. Panoramic view of the islands from Moran State Park.

Hosts: Jan and Mike Russillo
Rooms: 5 (2 PB; 3 SB) $65-100
Full Breakfast
Credit Cards: A, B
Notes: 2, 5, 8, 9, 10, 11, 12, 14

Turtleback Farm Inn

Route 1, Box 650 (Crow Valley Road), 98243
(206) 376-4914

This meticulously restored farmhouse has been described as a "marvel of bed and breakfastmanship, decorated with country finesse and a sophisticated sense of the right antiques." Seven bedrooms with private baths. Award-winning breakfasts.

Hosts: William and Susan Fletcher
Rooms: 7 (PB) $65-150
Full Breakfast
Credit Cards: A, B
Notes: 2, 5, 9, 10, 11 (nearby), 12, 14

EDMONDS

Harrison House

210 Sunset Avenue, 98020
(206) 776-4748

New waterfront home with sweeping view of Puget Sound and the Olympic Mountains. Many fine restaurants within walking distance. Guests spacious rooms have a private bath, private deck, TV, wet

NOTES: Credit cards accepted: A Master Card; B Visa; C American Express; D Discover Card; E Diner's Club; F Other; 2 Personal Checks accepted; 3 Lunch available; 4 Dinner available; 5 Open all year;

bar, telephone, and king-size bed. The University of Washington is nearby.

Hosts: Jody and Harve Harrison
Rooms: 2 (PB) $40-55
Continental Breakfast
Credit Cards: None
Notes: 2, 5, 9, 10, 11, 12, 13

ENUMCLAW

Stillmeadow Bed and Breakfast

46225 284th Avenue, Southeast, 98022
(206) 825-6381

In Enumclaw, "the gateway to Mt. Rainier," this 1940s Tudor farmhouse sits on five tranquil acres by a rushing creek. Two charming rooms, both featuring private baths, can be enjoyed, as well as a generous continental breakfast, books and music. Thirty minutes from Crystal Mountain and Mt. Rainier for skiing and hiking. Scenic bicycling and golf nearby.

Hosts: Miles and Sue Nelson
Rooms: 2 (PB) $50-60
Continental Breakfast
Credit Cards: None
Notes: 2, 5, 10, 11, 12, 13

FERNDALE

Anderson House Bed and Breakfast

2140 Main Street, P. O. Box 1547, 98248
(206) 384-3450

Whatcom County's most famous inn. Dave and Kelly Anderson have restored this landmark to its original 1897 charm. All rooms tastefully decorated in 1890s motif. If this is a guests first bed and breakfast experience, Anderson House is a perfect choice. Guests from 43 states and 25 countries have left words of praise. Stay where the book authors stay!

Hosts: Dave and Kelly Anderson
Rooms: 4 (PB) $49-79
Full Breakfast

Credit Cards: A, B, C, D
Notes: 2, 5, 9, 10, 12, 13, 14

Slater Heritage House Bed and Breakfast

1371 West Axton Road, 98248
(206) 384-4273

Come and spend a night in another era! This completely restored Victorian home is less than one mile off I-5. Close to the largest shopping mall in the Pacific Northwest, guests have easy access to mountains, water, or golfing. Only 12 miles from Canada. The inn offers four lovely bedrooms with queen-size beds and private baths. Guests will find an atmosphere of nostalgia and comfort. A full country breakfast is included in the room rate.

Host: Rickie Prink
Rooms: 4 (PB) $52-65
Full Breakfast
Credit Cards: A, B, C, E
Notes: 2, 5, 12

FORKS

Miller Tree

P. O. Box 953, 98331
(206) 374-6806

A 1917 farmhouse on three park-like acres, this original homestead is within 20 minutes of three beautiful Pacific beaches and the famous Olympic National Park Hot

Anderson House

6 Pets welcome; 8 Children welcome; 9 Social drinking allowed; 10 Tennis available; 11 Swimming available; 12 Golf available; 13 Skiing available; 14 May be booked through travel agents.

Rain Forest. With six rooms on the second floor, two large common rooms, a hot tub, full country breakfasts, and a make-your-self-at-home atmosphere, a warm welcome has been extended to travelers and fishermen for eight years.

Hosts: Ted and Prue Miller
Rooms: 6 (2 PB; 4 SB) $50-60
Full Breakfast
Credit Cards: A, B
Notes: 2, 5, 6, 8 (over 8), 9

FREELAND

Cliff House
5440 Windmill Road, 98249
(206) 331-1566

On Whidbey Island, a setting so unique there is nothing anywhere quite like Cliff House. In a private world of luxury, this stunning home is yours alone. Secluded in a forest on the edge of Puget Sound, the views are breathtaking. Stone fireplace, spa, miles of driftwood beach. King-size feather bed, gourmet kitchen. Also The Snug and Enchanting Seacliff cottage.

Hosts: Peggy Moore and Walter O'Toole
Rooms: 2 (PB) $155-325
Continental Breakfast
Minimum stay: 2 nights
Credit Cards: None
Notes: 2, 5, 9, 12

Seacliff Cottage
5440 Windmill Road, 98249
(206) 321-1566

With its warm country feeling, this pretty cottage invites guests. Forget the outside world and ease into a private hideaway, with a fireplace, a petite kitchen, and bedroom, featuring a luxurious queen-size bed. There is even a window seat for daydreaming as guests watch the passing parade of ships and seabirds. Near the beach, where visitors will discover a fine spot for picnicking, as well as the occasional sea lion, seal, or pod of killer whales.

Hosts: Peggy Moore and Walter O'Toole
Rooms: 2 (PB) $155-325
Continental Breakfast
Minimum stay: 2 nights
Credit Cards: None
Notes: 2, 5, 9, 12

FRIDAY HARBOR

Tucker House
260 B Street, 98250
(206) 378-2783; (800) 792-8210

Victorian home with three cottages featuring private baths, queen beds, TVs and off-street parking. The deck has a built-in Jacuzzi, with the setting in a quiet, residential area very relaxing. Close to all restaurants, gift shops, charter fishing, whale watching boats, scuba diving and sailing. Reservations suggested. Gift certificates available.

Hosts: Skip and Annette Metzger
Rooms: 5 (3 PB; 2 SB) $65-105
Full Breakfast
Credit Cards: A, B, D
Notes: 2, 5, 6, 8, 9, 10, 11, 12, 14

GARFIELD

Garfield
Pacific Bed and Breakfast Agency
701 Northwest 60th Street, Seattle, 98107
(206) 784-0539

This beautiful guest home was built as a Classical Revival house in 1898 and offers two guest rooms, one with a double bed and the other with two twin beds. There is a large shared bathroom with a huge claw foot soaking tub. Breakfast might include juices, flapjacks with local organic red wheat, homemade jams, maple syrup, home-baked breads, and other delights prepared on an old-fashioned wood-burning stove. $60.

NOTES: Credit cards accepted: A Master Card; B Visa; C American Express; D Discover Card; E Diner's Club; F Other; 2 Personal Checks accepted; 3 Lunch available; 4 Dinner available; 5 Open all year;

GIG HARBOR

Orchard

Pacific Bed and Breakfast Agency
701 Northwest 60th Street, Seattle, 98107
(206) 784-0539

This lovely bed and breakfast was built in 1984 on three acres of rural land between Gig Harbor and Bremerton, 90 minutes from Seattle. The large guest room features a double bed and a private bath, and welcomes guests to relax in the two-person whirlpool tub. Views of Mount Rainier can be seen from the living and dining rooms. What a perfect spot for a quiet country getaway! $75.

GREENBANK

Guest House Cottages

3366 South Highway 525, 98253
(206) 678-3115

A couple's romantic retreat, this AAA Four Diamond-rated bed and breakfast hideaway offers storybook cottages in cozy settings on 25 acres. Fireplaces, VCRs, in-room Jacuzzis, kitchens, feather beds, country antiques, and wildlife pond are all amenities guests can enjoy. Pool, spa, peace, and pampering. Voted "Best place to kiss in the Northwest." Near the winery. No pets, no children.

Hosts: Don and Mary Jane Creger
Rooms: 6 (PB) $135-255 (high season)
Continental Breakfast
Credit Cards: A, B, C, D
Notes: 2, 5, 9, 11, 14

HOOD CANAL

Hood Canal Waterfront Victorian

Pacific Bed and Breakfast Agency
701 Northwest 60th Street, Seattle, 98107
(206) 784-0539

This bed and breakfast offers three guest rooms, a charming atmosphere of genteel living, and sloping grounds leading to the beach. Enjoy a home-cooked breakfast and a relaxed friendly environment just right for getaways. $55-65.

Waterfront Hood Canal

Pacific Bed and Breakfast Agency
701 Northwest 60th Street, Seattle, 98107
(206) 784-0539

This cozy bed and breakfast offers guests total privacy. There are two bedrooms, one with queen bed and the other with a double bed; both share a bath. A wall of windows allows guests to take in the ever-changing view. Guests can snuggle up in front of the tall stone fireplace or take the elevator to a private beach where oysters can be gathered. Hosts are not on location to serve breakfast; the full kitchen will have everything that is needed. $125 and up.

Waterfront Mansion Hood Canal

Pacific Bed and Breakfast Agency
701 Northwest 60th Street, Seattle, 98107
(206) 784-0539

Experience the grandeur of a bygone time and the opulence of the rich and famous in the 1930s at this premier bed and breakfast inn. Built in 1936, this inn is on several acres of waterfront property and features a combination of Art Deco, the architecture of Northern China, seasoned with northwestern flair. There are five guest rooms with private baths, towel warmers, clothes steamers, down comforters, and hair dryers. $110-165.

6 Pets welcome; 8 Children welcome; 9 Social drinking allowed; 10 Tennis available; 11 Swimming available; 12 Golf available; 13 Skiing available; 14 May be booked through travel agents.

HOQUIAM

Pacific B&B Agency HO-1

701 Northwest 60th Street, Seattle, 98107
(206) 784-0539

A historic 20-room mansion is offered to visitors on the southern tip of the Olympic Peninsula only two hours from Seattle and minutes to the Pacific Ocean. The mansion is filled with a fascinating array of antiques. Five bedrooms with queen beds share three baths. A full and delicious breakfast is served in the large, formal dining room. Recommended by the *Los Angeles Times*. $65.

ILWACO

Inn at Ilwaco

120 Williams Street NE, 98624-0922
(206) 642-8686

The inn, a 1928 New England/Georgian-style church lovingly transformed into a gracious bed and breakfast with a 120-seat wedding chapel/playhouse. Cozy guest rooms nestled under eaves and dormers. Generous and informal parlor with library. Eclectically furnished, some old, some new, some antiques and country touches. Occupies hillside site overlooking historic port town where the Columbia River meets the ocean. Nearby are 28 miles of sandy beach, working lighthouses, museums, and three nationally acclaimed restaurants.

Host: Laurie Blancher
Rooms: 9 (7 PB; 2 SB) $55-80
Full Breakfast
Credit Cards: A, B
Notes: 2, 5, 8, 9, 10, 11, 12, 14

Kola House
Bed and Breakfast

P. O. Box 646, 98624
(206) 642-2819

This beautiful home, built in 1919, offers a view of the bay and Astoria. Suite has a fireplace and sauna, with a pool table and hot tub also available for guests to enjoy. TVs are in every room, and fishing grounds, museums, and shopping opportunities are within walking distance. This is a quiet town, but close to the beach and activities in Long Beach. Four rooms sleep two, and the suite, which features a hide-away bed, sleeps three. The guest house sleeps five, with roll-away beds available to accommodate groups.

Host: Linda Luokkala
Rooms: 5 (PB) $65-75
Full Breakfast
Credit Cards: A. B
Notes: 2, 5, 9, 12

ISSAQUAH

Issaquah

Pacific Bed and Breakfast Agency
701 Northwest 60th Street, Seattle, 98107
(206) 784-0539

This lovely log inn is situated in peaceful seclusion, nestled in woods filled with evergreens. With a gazebo in back, this get-away is perfect for family gatherings and small weddings. Hosts offer four guest rooms, two with private baths, for their visitors. Comfortable brass queen beds, cozy wall coverings, country charm, and antiques all add to the wonderful feeling of being made welcome and treasured. $65.

KIRKLAND

Shumway Mansion

11410 99th Place Northeast, 98033
(206) 823-2303

Overlook Lake Washington from this award-winning, 23-room mansion dating from 1909. Seven individually decorated guest rooms with private baths. Variety-filled breakfast. Complimentary use of athletic club. Short distance to all forms of shopping; 20 minutes to downtown Seattle. Water and snow recreation close at hand.

Hosts: Richard and Salli Harris
Rooms: 8 (PB) $65-92
Full Breakfast
Credit Cards: A, B, C
Notes: 2, 5, 10, 11, 12, 13, 14

Shumway Mansion

LA CONNER

Pacific B&B Agency - LA-1
701 Northwest 60th Street, Seattle, 98107
(206) 784-0539

This charming house was built in 1979 as a replica circa 1900 home. Three guest rooms are featured in this home where visitors have total privacy since the host is next door and not in the guest house. The host will come over to prepare breakfast for guests in the mornings. Enjoy the lovely views over the fields, meadows, and mountains. $50-75.

Pacific B&B Agency - LA-2
701 Northwest 60th Street, Seattle, 98107
(206) 784-0539

Guests can relax and enjoy themselves in this beautiful Victorian-style country inn.

The hosts offer 10 guest rooms with private baths, telephone, TV, and some with fireplaces and wonderful views. The honeymoon suite features a Jacuzzi. Guests are invited to enjoy the outdoor hot tub. $55-150.

The Rainbow Inn
P. O. Box 15, 98257
(206) 466-4578

This beautifully restored 1908 farmhouse is one half mile from the historic fishing village of La Conner, with panoramic views of the rich Skagit Valley farmlands, the Cascade Mountain Range, and Mount Baker. There are eight guest rooms with private or shared baths, and a deck with a gazebo and hot tub. A hearty gourmet breakfast is served, featuring fresh, locally grown produce.

Hosts: Sharon Briggs and Ron Johnson
Rooms: 8 (5 PB; 3 SB) $75-95
Full Breakfast
Credit Cards: A, B
Notes: 2, 5, 9, 12, 13

The Rainbow Inn

6 Pets welcome; 8 Children welcome; 9 Social drinking allowed; 10 Tennis available; 11 Swimming available; 12 Golf available; 13 Skiing available; 14 May be booked through travel agents.

Ridgeway Bed and Breakfast

1292 McLean Road, 98273
(206) 428-8068; (800) 428-8068 (US and Canada)

A 1928 yellow brick Dutch Colonial farmhouse built on the "Ridgeway" from the historic waterfront town of La Conner. Situated in the heart of the rich Skagit Valley, where daffodils, tulips, and iris fields paint the landscape. The large windows in the home offer and open and airy view of the mountains and farm fields in every direction. Stroll by the more than 10,000 bulbs in the personal display gardens, and enjoy homemade dessert by the fireplace. Wake up to coffee, tea, or hot chocolate to sharpen one's appetite for the hearty farm breakfast. Quiet smoke-free guest rooms with king or queen beds. An orchard, flowers, and two acres of lawn are here for guest enjoyment. Come home to the farm and let the hosts pamper.

Hosts: Louise and John Kelly
Rooms: 5 (2 PB; 3 S2B) $70-90
Full Breakfast
Credit Cards: A, B, C
Notes: 2, 5, 8, 9, 11, 12, 13

The White Swan Guest House

1388 Moore Road, 98273
(206) 445-6805

The White Swan

The White Swan is a "storybook" farmhouse built in 1898 on the Skagit Flats, home of the famous Tulip Festival. This Victorian home is full of country antiques, the smell of chocolate chip cookies, and is just six miles from the historic waterfront town of La Conner. A separate Honeymoon Cottage with full kitchen facilities is also available. In the spring and summer guests can visit the acre of fruit trees and English gardens, and in winter watch the migrating snow geese, swan, and eagles from the window. Just one hour north of Seattle.

Host: Peter Goldfarb
Rooms: 4 (1 PB; 3 S2B) $75-125
Continental Breakfast
Credit Cards: A, B
Notes: 2, 5, 8, 9

LANGLEY

Eagles Nest Inn

3236 East Saratoga, 98260
(206) 321-5331

The inn's rural setting on Whidbey Island offers a sweeping view of Saratoga Passage and Mount Baker. Casual elegance abounds. Relax and enjoy the wood stove, spa, library, and bottomless chocolate chip cookie jar. Canoeing available. Write or call for brochure. AAA rated Three Stars.

Hosts: Nancy and Dale Bowman
Rooms: 4 (PB) $85-105
Full Breakfast
Minimum stay holiday weekends: 2 nights
Credit Cards: A, B
Notes: 2, 5, 10, 14

Log Castle

3273 East Saratoga Road, 98260
(206) 221-5483

Situated on Whidbey Island, 30 miles north of Seattle. Log lodge on secluded beach. Big stone fireplace, turret bedrooms, panoramic views of Puget Sound and the Cascade Mountains. Norma's breakfast is legendary. Watch for bald eagles and Orca whales from the widow's walk.

Hosts: Senator Jack and Norma Metcalf
Rooms: 4 (PB) $80-105
Full Breakfast
Minimum stay holidays: 2 nights
Credit Cards: A, B, D
Notes: 2, 5, 8 (over 11), 10

LEAVENWORTH

All Seasons River Inn Bed and Breakfast

8751 Icicle Road, 98826
(509) 548-1425

Put the phone and the world on hold, and come relax in this peaceful setting at the base of the Cascade Mountains. Nestled in evergreens overlooking the Wenatchee River, all rooms are spacious with antique decor, private baths, and riverfront decks. In the evening, enjoy a scrumptuous dessert in the guest livingroom or upstairs TV room, play one of several games in the game room, or listen to the relaxing sounds of the waters below the decks. Awaken to the hearty breakfasts that guests say lasts them all day. Enjoy hiking, biking, rafting, cross-country skiing, or fishing, all within a mile from the home, or swim at the private beach. Once guests have been here, they will want to return again and again.

Hosts: Kathy and Jeff Falconer
Rooms: 5 (PB) $90-115
Full Breakfast
Credit Cards: A, B
Notes: 2, 5, 9, 10, 11, 12, 13, 14

Haus Rohrbach Pension

12882 Ranger Road, 98826
(509) 548-7024

A bed and breakfast inn in the time honored tradition of an Alpine European Pension, with outstanding views and genuine hospitality. Three luxurious suites are recommended for that special occasion. Hiking, biking, fishing, skiing and shop-

ping in the nearby Bavarian theme village are just some of the activities guests will enjoy. Year-round hot tub and summer swimming pool.

Hosts: Robert and Kathryn Harrild
Rooms: 12 (8 PB; 4 SB) $65-145
Full Breakfast
Credit Cards: A, B, C, D
Notes: 2, 5, 8, 9, 10, 11, 12, 13, 14

Leavenworth

Pacific Bed and Breakfast Agency
701 Northwest 60th Street, Seattle, 98107
(206) 784-0539

This peaceful country inn is situated in a town that has taken on a Bavarian atmosphere with German stores, shops, restaurants, and flowers everywhere. Enjoy the wonderful views, hot tub, pool, and the continental breakfast. Some rooms have private baths. $55-85.

Pine River Ranch

19668 Highway 207, 98826
(509) 763-3959

An exceptional inn, perfect for special getaways or family retreats, the Pine River Ranch offers spacious, beautifully decorated rooms that will pamper travelers with wood stoves, decks, and sunny sitting areas. A deluxe suite offers romantic seclusion with a claw foot tub, wet bar, breakfast nook, and entertainment center. Private cottages are ideal for families. Fabulous food, hot tubs, stream fishing, private ski trails,

Pine River Ranch

and lots of friendly farm animals are but a few of the features on premises. In the Lake Wenatchee Area, a 200-acre valley with a million-dollar view.

Hosts: Mary Ann and Michael Zenk
Rooms: 4, plus guest cottages (2 PB; 2 SB) $65-95
Full Breakfast
Credit Cards: A, B
Notes: 2, 5, 9, 10, 11, 12, 13, 14

Run of the River
Bed and Breakfast

9308 East Leavenworth Road
P. O. Box 285, 98826
(509) 548-7171; (800) 288-6491

Run of the River, a log bed and breakfast inn on the Icicle River, is surrounded by a wildlife and bird refuge. All rooms have hand-hewn log furniture, high cathedral pine ceilings, and private baths. From the decks, enjoy the Cascade view. Mountain bikes available at no extra charge. Running and biking trails right from the inn. Bountiful country breakfasts.

Hosts: Monty and Karen Turner
Rooms: 5 (PB) $90-140
Full Breakfast
Credit Cards: A, B, C
Notes: 2, 5, 9, 10, 11, 12, 13, 14

LONG BEACH

Pacific B&B Agency LB-1

701 Northwest 60th Street, Seattle, 98107
(206) 784-0539

A three to four hour drive will take visitors to this lovely but often undiscovered spot of the state where the Columbia River meets the Pacific Ocean. The best beach-combing, clam digging, salmon fishing, and relaxation can be found here. This historic inn offers 12 rooms that are furnished in antiques as a reminder of a gentler time. Five rooms have private baths. $60-145.

Scandinavian Gardens Inn
Bed and Breakfast

Route 1, Box 36, 98631-9801
(206) 642-8877

Enjoy a touch of Scandinavia with affordable excellence. A deluxe inn with four rooms and a honeymoon suite, each decorated in a different country style. Imported queen beds, private baths, indoor spa and sauna and living and social rooms with fireplaces. Innkeepers dress in costume. Buffet-style breakfast with Scandinavia specialties. Just a 10-minute walk to the beach and panoramic views from the half-mile board walk. A 15-minute walk from downtown to shops and restaurants.

Hosts: Mike and Gail Sonnenberg
Rooms: 5 (PB) $65-110
Continental Breakfast
Credit Cards: A, B
Notes: 2, 5, 9, 12, 14

LOPEZ ISLAND

MacKaye Harbor Inn

Route 1, Box 1940, 98261
(206) 468-2253

The ideal beachfront getaway. Lopez's only bed and breakfast on a low-bank sandy beach, perfect for beach-combing, kayaking, rowing, and biking. This 1927 Victorian home has been painstakingly restored. Guests are pampered in comfortable elegance. Eagles, deer, seals, and otters frequent this Cape Cod of the Northwest. Commendations from *Sunset*, *Pacific Northwest Magazine*, the *Los Angeles Times*, and *Northwest Best Places*.

Hosts: Mike and Robin Bergstrom
Rooms: 5 (1 PB; 4 SB) $69-109
Full Breakfast
Credit Cards: A, B
Notes: 2, 5, 9, 12, 14

Pacific B&B Agency LI-1

701 Northwest 60th Street, Seattle, 98107
(206) 784-0539

At the first stop by the ferry, relax at this Victorian waterfront inn with lovely antiques, a restaurant on the premises, and all the charm of a tranquil setting. Grand sunsets, sandy beaches, tidal pools, and beachcombing. Watching the eagles and other wildlife will keep guests busy. Bring a kayak, bicycles, windsurfing, or fishing gear. Five guest rooms, one with private bath. $75-115.

LUMMI ISLAND

The Willows Inn

2579 West Shore Drive, 98262
(206) 758- 2620

Established in 1911 by the hostesses' grandparents, The Willows is an island landmark. On the sunset side of the island, it boasts a private beach and a spectacular view of the San Juan Islands. Noted for fine dining and award-winning gardens, The Willows is a most peaceful and romantic destination. Ten minutes from I-5 near Bellingham and a 75-minute ferry ride to this quiet little island.

Hosts: Victoria and Gary
Rooms: 7 (5 PB; 2 SB) $95-135
Full Breakfast
Credit Cards: A, B
Notes: 2, 4, 9, 11

MERCER ISLAND

Pacific B&B Agency MI-2

701 Northwest 60th Street, Seattle, 98107
(206) 784-0539

A spacious contemporary home with special features. The livingroom will surprise you with two grand pianos and an organ. Several rooms with various bed sizes. Have a home-cooked gourmet breakfast on the sunny patio or around the inviting round dining room table. Listed in Seattle's Best Places. $65 and up.

Waterfront Cottage

Pacific Bed and Breakfast Agency
701 Northwest 60th Street, Seattle, 98107
(206) 784-0539

There is no better way to experience the Northwest than here. In the summer, swim or watch the boats go by while sipping a cool drink on the lanai. Two bedrooms, that sleep up to five guests. Kitchen, food provided, privacy, and only five miles to downtown Seattle. Make reservations early. $95. $20 extra person. Two night minimum.

MOUNT RAINIER AREA

Country Inn

Pacific Bed and Breakfast Agency
701 Northwest 60th Street, Seattle, 98107
(206) 784-0539

Originally built in 1912, this inn was restored in 1984 and features eleven guest rooms with queen beds. The hand-made quilts, antiques, Tiffany lamps, and stained-glass windows all add to the comfort of this bed and breakfast. There is also a critically acclaimed restaurant that serves delicious food in a relaxed, genteel fashion by a big stone fireplace. $65-105.

Jasmer's Guesthaus Bed and Breakfast

30005 State Road 706 E, 98304
(206) 569-2682

Jasmer's Guesthaus is a perfect balance of pampering and privacy. A love nest. Upstairs is an all-wood interior, angled ceilings, king-size bed, wood stove, and

6 Pets welcome; 8 Children welcome; 9 Social drinking allowed; 10 Tennis available; 11 Swimming available; 12 Golf available; 13 Skiing available; 14 May be booked through travel agents.

antiques. Downstairs, a heartwarming bubble bath/shower, and kitchen. The cabin on Big Creek has a complete kitchen, bath, two bedrooms, wood stove, deer, bird feeders, a seasonal hot tub, and a perfect setting of restful solitude. Come! See! Smell! Relax among the noble works of nature. Near Mount Rainier National Park and open all year.

Hosts: Tanna and Luke Osterhaus
Rooms: 2, plus 5 cabins (PB) $65-125
Continental Breakfast
Credit Cards: A, B
Notes: 2, 5, 9, 11, 13, 14

OAK HARBOR

A Country Pillow
419 East Troxel Road, 98277
(206) 675-8505

Experience a quiet, romantic getaway in this warmly decorated country home. Built in 1940 on four and one-half acres of secluded woodlands, beachfront and meadows, guests can enjoy the breathtaking view of Puget Sound against the backdrop of Mt. Baker and the Cascade Mountains. Smell the aroma of the salt sea air and natural flora of the region, and be soothed by the natural stream running into the sea. Beautiful Deception Pass Bridge and its hiking trails are only five miles away.

Hosts: Jenny and Jim Toland, Doris and Bob Foster
Rooms: 3 (SB) $65-75
Continental Breakfast
Credit Cards: None
Notes: 5, 11, 12, 13

OCEAN SHORES

Pacific B&B Agency Ocean Shores-1
701 Northwest 60th Street, Seattle, 98107
(206) 784-0539

A bed and breakfast inn situated right on the ocean offers five bedrooms, all of which feature private baths. Enjoy a full breakfast in the dining room overlooking the everchanging scenery of the water and the seagulls. Take a dip in the hot tub after a long walk on the beach. Hospitality is the word here, and the hostess will see to it that visitors have a fine stay. $55-80

OLYMPIA

Harbinger Inn
1136 East Bay Drive, 98506
(206) 754-0389

Completely restored national historic landmark. View of East Bay marina, Capitol, and Olympic Mountains. Ideally situated for boating, bicycling, jogging, fine dining, and business ventures. A Northwest Best Place.

Hosts: Marisa and Terrell Williams
Rooms: 4 (1 PB; 3 SB) $60-85
Continental Breakfast
Credit Cards: A, B, C
Notes: 2, 5, 8 (over 12), 9

OLYMPIC

Pacific B&B Agency Olympic-1
701 Northwest 60th Street, Seattle, 98107
(206) 784-0539

With an unobstructed view over the water, this private two-bedroom cottage with double and twin beds invites guests to linger. Right next door to a state park, visitors can rent a boat and enjoy the lovely water, or relax in the privacy of the cottage, nicely furnished and decorated in country-style. Breakfast will be served in the morning on a tray to eat outside or in, depending on the weather. Minimum stay of two nights on the weekends. $85.

OLYMPIC PENINSULA

Pacific B&B Agency Olympic Peninsula-1

701 Northwest 60th Street, Seattle, 98107
(206) 784-0539

This is where a splendid historic lodge is offered. Majestically situated in a picturesque setting with the finest views ever offered from a lodge, the gravel lobby of this home with its imposing stone fireplaces gives a quiet elegance and charm of yesteryear. Cocktails by the fire, an elegant dinner in the restaurant, and a refreshing dip in an indoor pool all add up to great vacation experience. European-style bath in the lodge. Two-night minimum stay on weekends. $55-100.

ORCAS

Pacific B&B Agency OI-1

701 Northwest 60th Street, Seattle, 98107
(206) 784-0539

A large two-story log inn welcomes guests with seven bedrooms, all with private baths. Most of the rooms have views of the water. Rustic and comfortable, this inn is newly built and has a restaurant on the premises. Breakfast will be delivered in a basket to enjoy in the privacy of the room. $85, winter rates available.

PORT ANGELES

Anniken's Bed and Breakfast

214 East Whidbey Avenue, 98362
(206) 457-6177

Enjoy a wonderful view of the harbor and the mountains of Olympic National Park from our Scandinavian-style home, decorated in blues, whites, and wood tones. Two comfortable rooms with double beds share a bath and enjoy a lofty sitting room. High, light, and homey characterizes the guest quarters. Anniken's is just five minutes from Victoria ferries or the Park Visitor Center. A homemade breakfast always includes fresh fruit and gourmet coffee.

Hosts: Robert and Ann Kennedy
Rooms: 2 (SB) $50-60
Full Breakfast
Credit Cards: A, B
Notes: 2, 5, 10, 11, 12, 13

Pacific B&B Agency Port Angeles-1

701 Northwest 60th Street, Seattle, 98107
(206) 784-0539

Uniquely European in style, this comfortable and magnificent English-style Tudor house was built in 1910 and restored to serve as an inn. Five guest rooms with a view of the water are available. Full breakfast. Wonderful antiques are throughout this lovely old house. Two-night minimum stay on weekends. Two blocks to downtown and restaurants. $85 and up.

PORT TOWNSEND

Ann Starrett Mansion Victorian Bed & Breakfast Inn

744 Clay Street, 98368
(206) 385-3205; (800) 321-0644

Situated on a bluff overlooking the Olympic Mountains, the Cascades, Puget Sound, and historic Port Townsend. The house is renowned for its Victorian architecture, free-hanging staircase, frescoed domed ceiling with a solar calendar, and sumptuous breakfasts. AAA Three Diamonds.

Hosts: Edel and Bob Sokol
Rooms: $65-125
Full Breakfast
Credit Cards: A, B, C, D
Notes: 2, 5, 9, 10, 11, 12, 14

---

6 Pets welcome; 8 Children welcome; 9 Social drinking allowed; 10 Tennis available; 11 Swimming available; 12 Golf available; 13 Skiing available; 14 May be booked through travel agents.

1892 Castle

Pacific Bed and Breakfast Agency
701 Northwest 60th Street, Seattle, 98107
(206) 784-0539

The castle sits on a hill with commanding
marina views. It features rooms with private baths and Victorian decor, and lovely
gardens. The landmark mansion is on the
National Register of Historic Places and
was totally restored in 1973. Enjoy splendid luxury while in Port Townsend.
Continental breakfast. $75-150.

The Grand Dame

Pacific Bed and Breakfast Agency
701 Northwest 60th Street, Seattle, 98107
(206) 784-0539

The most photographed house in Port
Townsend, this great Victorian was built in
1889 by a wealthy contractor for his wife
as a wedding present. It features a spiral
freestanding staircase that is one of the
finest in existence. Special frescoes in the
dome will delight guests. Most of the
rooms on the second floor have a wonderful view of the water and the mountains.
Five bedrooms on the second floor, and
four bedrooms on the carriage level.
Healthy breakfast is served on fine china.
$60, shared bath. $70-135, private bath.

Lizzie's Victorian Bed and Breakfast

731 Pierce Street, 98368
(206) 385-4168

An 1888 Victorian mansion within walking
distance of shops and restaurants. The inn
is decorated in antiques and some original
wallpaper. Parlors are comfortable retreats
for reading or conversation. Gateway to the
Olympic Mountains, San Juan Islands, and
Victoria.

Hosts: Bill and Patti Wickline
Rooms: 8 (5 PB; 3 SB) $50-89

Full Breakfast
Credit Cards: A, B, D
Notes: 2, 5, 8 (over 10), 9, 10, 11, 12

Quimper Inn

1306 Franklin Street, 98368
(206) 385-1060

This 1888 mansion in the historic Uptown
District offers lovely water and mountain
views. Four comfortable bedrooms, plus a
two-room suite with a sitting room and
bath. Antique period furniture, lots of
books and two porches for relaxation.
Within walking distance of downtown,
shops, and restaurants. A wonderful breakfast is served.

Hosts: Ron and Sue Ramage
Rooms: 5 (3 PB; 2 SB) $65-120
Full Breakfast
Credit Cards: A, B
Notes: 2, 5, 9, 10, 12

Sequiem Victorian

Pacific Bed and Breakfast Agency
701 Northwest 60th Street, Seattle, 98107
(206) 784-0539

A fine bed and breakfast inn, one-half mile
from the beach, on Dungeness Spit, a quiet,
peaceful area, yet only minutes from Port
Townsend, Port Angeles, or the Victoria
ferry. Remember that this area is the
"Banana Belt" of the region, with less rain-
fall. A favorite beverage and morning
paper will be delivered to the door in the
morning. A full breakfast will be served
downstairs. Four bedrooms, two that share
a bath, and two that offer private baths, are
available. $55-85.

Trenholm House Bed and Breakfast

2037 Haines, 98368
(206) 385-6059

Step back in time and enjoy the warmth
and comfort of an 1890 Victorian farm-

NOTES: Credit cards accepted: A Master Card; B Visa; C American Express; D Discover Card; E Diner's
Club; F Other; 2 Personal Checks accepted; 3 Lunch available; 4 Dinner available; 5 Open all year;

house inn. Built by shipbuilder Howard Trenholm, the house has been maintained in almost original condition and is furnished in country antiques. The aroma of freshly brewed coffee will awaken the senses as a gourmet breakfast is being prepared. What a great way to greet the day!

Hosts: Michael and Patrice Kelly
Rooms: 6 (2 PB; 4 SB) $59-89
Full Breakfast
Credit Cards: A, B
Notes: 2, 5, 9, 10, 11, 12, 14

PUGET SOUND INLET

Pacific B&B Agency Puget Sound Inlet-1

701 Northwest 60th Street, Seattle, 98107
(206) 784-0539

Near the water, a delightful Victorian farmhouse with a rolling lawn down to the water's edge. Furnished with antiques and three bedrooms to choose from, this is a favorite of weekenders. A great breakfast is served in the morning. Shared bath. $60-75.

PUYALLUP

Hart's Tayberry House Bed and Breakfast

7406 80th Street East, 98371
(206) 848-4594

Tayberry's bed and breakfast is a Victorian house with stained-glass, an open stairway, and tin ceiling in the kitchen. The romantic atmosphere sweeps visitors back to an age of charm and history. Old-fashioned hospitality welcomes the crowd-weary traveler with a cheerful room, bath, and breakfast. Owners share rich history and places of interest with guests.

Hosts: Sandy Hart Hammer; Ray and Donna Hart
Rooms: 3 (1 PB; 2 SB) $40-60
Full Breakfast

Credit Cards: None
Notes: 2, 5, 9, 10, 11, 12, 13

SAN JUAN ISLANDS

Friday Harbor

Pacific Bed and Breakfast Agency
701 Northwest 60th Street, Seattle, 98107
(206) 784-0539

This is a floating inn, a restored 60-foot wooden sailboat that offers guests two staterooms, one with a queen bed and private bath, the other with a double bed, two bunk beds, and shared bath. The hosts will provide a full seaman's breakfast that might be served on the deck in fair weather or in front of a roaring fire in the parlor. Have a totally different experience here! $85.

Orcas Island Country Inn

Pacific Bed and Breakfast Agency
701 Northwest 60th Street, Seattle, 98107
(206) 784-0539

This is a beautiful country inn nestled in a valley with fine views of meadows and mountains. The inn offers eight guest rooms that have private baths with claw foot tubs, and antique furnishings. Guests can enjoy a gourmet breakfast in a charming, elegant atmosphere. $65-135.

Waterfront Country Inn

Pacific Bed and Breakfast Agency
701 Northwest 60th Street, Seattle, 98107
(206) 784-0539

Built before 1888, this inn used to serve as a meeting place for the townspeople, barber shop, general store, post office, and jail. Now as a popular getaway, it offers guest rooms with and without private baths, hand-carved beds, marble-topped dressers, and a collection of period memorabilia. No pets, please. $60-84.

6 Pets welcome; 8 Children welcome; 9 Social drinking allowed; 10 Tennis available; 11 Swimming available; 12 Golf available; 13 Skiing available; 14 May be booked through travel agents.

SEATTLE

Bellevue Place Bed and Breakfast

1111 Bellevue Place East, 98102
(206) 325-9253

Bellevue Place is in the Landmark District of Capitol Hill. Our 1905 "storybook" house with leaded glass and Victorian charm is close to Broadway restaurants and stores, Volunteer Park, and a 20-minute walk to downtown Seattle. Parking is available.

Hosts: Gunner Johnson and Joseph C. Pruett
Rooms: 3 (SB) $75-85
Continental Breakfast
Credit Cards: A, B, C
Notes: 5, 14

Chambered Nautilus

Chambered Nautilus

5005 22nd Avenue Northeast, 98105
(206) 522-2536

This charming 1915 Georgian Colonial perched high on a hill is furnished with antiques, Persian rugs, a grand piano, two fireplaces, and a library with more than 2,000 books. Six spacious bedrooms, four with porches, have private or shared baths. Full, award-winning breakfasts. Close to downtown, biking and walking trails, and the University of Washington campus.

Hosts: Bunny and Bill Hagemeyer
Rooms: 6 (4 PB; 2 SB) $75-97.50
Full Breakfast
Credit Cards: A, B, C, E, F
Notes: 2, 5, 9, 10, 11, 12, 13, 14

Chelsea Station Bed and Breakfast Inn

4915 Linden Avenue North, 98103
(206) 547-6077

For a quiet, comfortable, and private accommodation, nothing beats Chelsea Station. With Seattle's rose gardens at the doorstep, guests can breathe in the restorative calm. Walk Greenlake's exceptional wooded pathways, then try a soothing cup of tea or a nap in the afternoon. That's the style at Chelsea Station, and guests are welcome to enjoy it. Member Washington Bed and Breakfast Guild.

Hosts: Dick and Marylou Jones
Rooms: 5 (PB) $59-109
Full Breakfast
Minimum stay holidays: 3 nights
Credit Cards: A, B, C, D, E
Notes: 2, 5, 9, 10, 11, 12, 14

The Downtown Hotel

Pacific Bed and Breakfast
701 Northwest 60th Street, 98107
(206) 784-0539

Built in 1928 and recently remodeled, this lovely European-style hotel offers comfortable room with double or twin beds. Walk to the waterfront, scores of fine restaurants, Pike Place Market, the Kingdome, Amtrak station, and the convention center. Many of the original fixtures, such as the mahogany door and tiling, were left. Personal service, friendly staff, and professional help is at guests' beck and call. Continental breakfast. Parking available. $60.

Pacific B&B Agency BA-1

701 Northwest 60th Street, 98107
(206) 784-0539

NOTES: Credit cards accepted: A Master Card; B Visa; C American Express; D Discover Card; E Diner's Club; F Other; 2 Personal Checks accepted; 3 Lunch available; 4 Dinner available; 5 Open all year;

Here is the private apartment with everything: private entrance, livingroom with TV, phone, private bath, queen bed, equipped kitchen. Maid service, chocolates on the pillow, fresh flowers, and a warm welcome. One block to bus lines and a 15-minute ride to downtown. Close to University of Washington area. $45.

Pacific B&B Agency BA-2

701 Northwest 60th Street, 98107
(206) 784-0539

All the comforts of home can be found in this two-bedroom cottage in a quiet neighborhood. One bedroom features a 1925 antique bedroom set, and the second room offers twin beds. The cottage sleeps up to six, and is comfortably furnished with brass and oak accents. Close to Greenlake, the university, parks, the zoo, beaches, marinas, shops, and restaurants. Children welcome. $85, monthly rates available.

Pacific B&B Agency BA-4

701 Northwest 60th Street, 98107
(206) 784-0539

A new home, Northwest-style, offers a private suite of two rooms with sliding glass doors to a private patio. Private bath, queen bed. Kitchenette with breakfast supplies provided. Occasionally breakfast is served upstairs in the dining room. Close to Greenlake and restaurants. $55.

Pacific B&B Agency BA-5

701 Northwest 60th Street, 98107
(206) 784-0539

For families or business groups, nothing compares to the comfort of ones own house. Guests may take over the whole house, or just rent one room, but will always receive great value staying here. Close to Greenlake, shops, and restaurants,

and just minutes from downtown via the freeway. Two bedrooms are available, but sleeping accommodations can be made for up to 10 guests. No pets. Free off-street parking. $45.

Pacific B&B Agency BA-6

701 Northwest 60th Street, 98107
(206) 784-0539

For families or business groups, nothing compares to the comfort of ones own home. Rent the entire guest house, or just one room for a great value. Close to Greenlake, shops, restaurants, and only minutes to downtown. Two bedrooms can sleep up to 10; children welcome. Fully equipped kitchen includes staple foods galore. Two TVs, two VCRs, movies, play things for the kids, and many other surprises. $50 and up.

Pacific B&B Agency BE-1

701 Northwest 60th Street, 98107
(206) 784-0539

This large family home on Beacon Hill was built in 1910 with fine woodwork, beamed ceilings, built-ins, a tiled fireplace in the parlor, huge windows, and decks that take advantage of the wonderful views of Elliott Bay, the Olympic Mountains, and the skyline. Four guest rooms and two large bathrooms are offered. Fine antiques, Navajo weavings, and artwork from Latin American countries will delight guests. At breakfast time, enjoy the specialties of this inn: Mexican and Latin American dishes, or American, if you desire. $35-45 and up.

Pacific B&B Agency Bellevue-1

701 Northwest 60th Street, 98107
(206) 784-0539

6 Pets welcome; 8 Children welcome; 9 Social drinking allowed; 10 Tennis available; 11 Swimming available; 12 Golf available; 13 Skiing available; 14 May be booked through travel agents.

This wonderful contemporary home offers a private suite with two bedrooms, a livingroom, one full bath, and a private entrance. Have a full breakfast served upstairs in the dining room. Visitors are also welcome to use the hot tub in the back. An urban oasis at its finest. One mile from the center of Bellevue, this guest home will be a comfortable retreat after a day of sightseeing or business. $50-55.

Pacific B&B Agency Bellevue-2

701 Northwest 60th Street, 98107
(206) 784-0539

Hospitable retired hosts offer guests two bedrooms, with a livingroom, private bath, kitchenette, private entrance, and a tasty breakfast. Handy location. Fine views of the lake. $50-55.

Pacific B&B Agency CH-2

701 Northwest 60th Street, 98107
(206) 784-0539

Here is a true Victorian built in 1890 with stained-glass windows, fine period furniture, original woodwork, and an ambience that is unequaled. The hostess makes guests feel right at home. All the little touches that provide that special bed and breakfast experience are here. Breakfasts are legendary. $60-65.

Pacific B&B Agency CH-4

701 Northwest 60th Street, 98107
(206) 784-0539

An elegantly furnished traditional brick house with a lovely garden and covered patio is on a tree-lined street in an exclusive, residential neighborhood. Within a few minutes from the University of Washington, downtown, theaters, shopping,

and the convention center. On the bus lines. Breakfast is served in the formal dining room. Children welcome.

Pacific B&B Agency CH-5

701 Northwest 60th Street, 98107
(206) 784-0539

A large turn-of-the-century home that looks like a castle has been lovingly restored. The location is handy to everything in the city, only 12 blocks from downtown. The guest rooms are on the first floor and have private baths. Guests may help themselves to the library with a wonderful window seat to lounge, read, watch TV, or sit and plan a day's activities. $40-45; $10 surcharge for one-night stays.

Pacific B&B Agency CH-6

701 Northwest 60th Street, 98107
(206) 784-0539

A spacious Victorian greets its visitors with warm hospitality. From the second floor guests will have a great view of the city, the Space Needle, the Sound, and the Olympic Mountains. Walk to restaurants, shops, action on Broadway, and art museum. Two guest rooms share a bath. Home-cooked breakfast served in the dining room by an experienced hostess. Some Spanish, Norwegian, and Indonesian spoken. $40-75.

Pacific B&B Agency CH-8

701 Northwest 60th Street, 98107
(206) 784-0539

This grand house was built in 1912 for the astonishing sum of $100,000. It has 14,000 square feet and features a ballroom, a billiard room, several huge public rooms, and an impressive entry hall. The second-floor guest rooms feature antiques, Old World charm, original tile baths with pedestal sinks and showers. There are five grand pianos in the house. Continental breakfast is served in the formal dining room. Within walking distance of shops, restaurants, parks, and gardens. $65-125.

Pacific B&B Agency CH-10

701 Northwest 60th Street, 98107
(206) 784-0539

A gracious brick building in the Georgian style welcomes guests in a convenient location on Capitol Hill. Walk to restaurants, bus lines, a fine city park, and other attractions. Spacious rooms on the first floor with sitting areas and queen beds. Enjoy breakfast on the patio or in the dining room. $55-75.

Pacific B&B Agency CH-12

701 Northwest 60th Street, 98107
(206) 784-0539

Private entrance, private bath, double bedroom, all in this wonderful brick home. Guests may have as much privacy as they want. Self-catered breakfast is in the refrigerator. Visiting relatives love this spot, because of its convenience to the city, 10 to 15 minutes to downtown, or the bus lines. The hosts are young professionals, most interested in making every stay as pleasant as possible. So close to the University of Washington, one could even walk there. A fine garden is available for guests to enjoy. $60.

Pacific B&B Agency CH-14

701 Northwest 60th Street, 98107
(206) 784-0539

Near Broadway on Capitol Hill where one can walk to restaurants, shops, and bus lines. This fine old house is kept in the style of its time, and the antiques compliment the house. A full breakfast will be served on heirloom china and silverware. Two guest rooms share a bath. $45 and up.

Pacific B&B Agency MAG-2

701 Northwest 60th Street, 98107
(206) 784-0539

Situated just two miles northwest of downtown, this stay offers a quiet street and a private bedroom with a double bed, a single bed and a private bath. Full breakfast is served, and there is a lovely view of Seattle from the patio where breakfast is served. $50-70.

Pacific B&B Agency QA-1

701 Northwest 60th Street, 98107
(206) 784-0539

A beautiful professional facility in an impressively restored building with a comfortable, relaxed atmosphere. Guests wish they could stay longer to enjoy the proximity to downtown, the fine antiques, the window seat, the wicker furniture, and great breakfasts that are served in the formal dining room. Four bedrooms, some with private baths. $65-75.

Pacific B&B Agency QA-6

701 Northwest 60th Street, 98107
(206) 784-0539

On lower Queen Anne, only two blocks from the Seattle Center and all the restaurants and shops there, this stay offers guests delightful alternatives to motels. Stay in these fine studio apartments, with queen-size beds, TV, phones, and kitchenettes. $45-50.

6 Pets welcome; 8 Children welcome; 9 Social drinking allowed; 10 Tennis available; 11 Swimming available; 12 Golf available; 13 Skiing available; 14 May be booked through travel agents.

Pacific B&B Agency QA-10

701 Northwest 60th Street, 98107
(206) 784-0539

In a private home atmosphere, guests enjoy a cozy one-bedroom suite on the second floor, private entrance, phone, TV, full kitchen, on a bus line. See the downtown skyscrapers from the bedroom windows and enjoy a lovely view of Capitol Hill. A second suite is on the garden level, with a private entrance, full bath, and kitchen. No breakfast is served. $45-50.

Pacific B&B Agency QA-12

701 Northwest 60th Street, 98107
(206) 784-0539

If there ever was the ultimate lodging for travelers, this must be it. The setting is Queen Anne Hill, the most desirable location in the city. Private suite with private bath, a European kitchen, private entrance, TV, phone, queen bed, and security system. The large deck lets visitors drink in the great view of Puget Sound and the Olympic Mountains. Ideal for honeymooners, business travelers, and visiting relatives. $75.

Pacific Bed and Breakfast Agency-TNN-WASHINGTON

701 Northwest 60th Street, 98107
(206) 784-0539

Part of the Bed and Breakfast National Network, Pacific Bed and Breakfast Agency offers bed and breakfast not only in Washington, but also in many other cities and states across the country. The members of this network adhere strictly to the standards set by TNN, such as getting to know the hosts personally, having an established cancellation and refund policy, and following a thorough inspection and approval process for all properties rented.

This is because each member of the network is dedicated to ensuring guests' comfort, pleasure, and personal needs while they are staying at one of these "homes away from home."

Salisbury House

750 Sixteenth Avenue East, 98112
(206) 328-8682

An elegant turn-of-the-century home on Capitol Hill, just minutes from Seattle's cultural and business activities. Gracious guest rooms with private baths. A well-stocked library and wraparound porch invite relaxation. In a historic neighborhood with parks, shops, and restaurants.

Hosts: Mary and Cathryn Wiese
Rooms: 4 (PB) $74-88
Full Breakfast
Credit Cards: A, B, E
Notes: 2, 5, 8 (over 12), 9, 10, 11, 12

Seattle Pacific

Pacific Bed and Breakfast Agency
701 Northwest 60th Street, 98107
(206) 784-0539

A downtown location on a lake, just minutes from sightseeing attractions. Pamper yourself on a houseboat. Features a queen-size bed, privacy, kitchen, breakfast foods, new mahogany and brass accents, gleaming wood floors, deck to relax on, and a sauna. Sleeps up to four. Super location and views. Experience the romance of the water. $95. $20 extra person.

The Shafer-Baillie Mansion

907 14th Avenue East, 98112
(206) 322-4654; FAX (206) 329-4654

A quiet and livable atmosphere, Shafer-Baillie Mansion is the largest estate on historic Millionaire's Row in Seattle's Capitol Hill. Having recently undergone a facelift, guests will enjoy new luxury services and

NOTES: Credit cards accepted: A Master Card; B Visa; C American Express; D Discover Card; E Diner's Club; F Other; 2 Personal Checks accepted; 3 Lunch available; 4 Dinner available; 5 Open all year;

surroundings that are second to none. A TV and refrigerator are in every room, and a gourmet continental breakfast is served between 8:30 A.M. and 9:30 A.M. with a morning newspaper. Eleven suites, most with private baths.

Host: Erv Olssen
Rooms: 11 (8 PB; 3 SB) $55-115
Continental Breakfast
Credit Cards: A, B, C
Notes: 2, 5, 8, 10, 12, 13, 14

Wallingford

Pacific Bed and Breakfast Agency
701 Northwest 60th Street, Seattle, 98107
(206) 784-0539

Private suite with a queen-size bed, private entrance, livingroom, and kitchen in a private home, which is on the busline. Situated only three miles from the downtown core of the city and conveniently near the University of Washington and the people-oriented University District. This home is ideal for longer stays for the person who is looking for comfortable private lodgings. $45-50.

SEAVIEW

Gumm's Bed and Breakfast Inn

P. O. Box 447, 98644
(206) 642-8887

A lovingly restored example of northwest Craftsman architecture with a turn-of-the-century ambience, this home features a large living room with a great stone fireplace. A sun porch offers a warm spot for casual conversation or reading. The four guest rooms are all uniquely decorated with special thought to comfort.

Host: Mickey Slack
Rooms: 4 (2 PB; 2 SB) $65-75
Full Breakfast
Credit Cards: A, B
Notes: 2, 5, 8, 9, 10, 12

SEQUIM

Greywolf Inn

177 Keeler Road, 98382
(206) 683-5889

Hidden in a crescent of towering evergreens, this northwest country estate is just a scenic two hour drive from Seattle. Ideally located in the sunny Dungeness Valley, Greywolf is the perfect starting point for the light adventure of the Olympic Peninsula. Enjoy hiking, fishing, bicycling, windsurfing, golf, and sightseeing. Relax on the broad decks or take a meandering wooded walk, relax by the fire with a good book, then retire to one of Greywolf's cozy, comfortable theme rooms for the perfect ending to an exciting day.

Hosts: Peggy and Bill Melang
Rooms: 6 (PB) $50-90
Full Breakfast
Credit Cards: A, B, C
Notes: 2, 3 (picnic), 5, 8 (over 10), 9, 11, 12, 13

Seabreeze Beach Cottage

SILVERDALE

Seabreeze Beach Cottage

16609 Olympic View Road Northwest, 98383
(206) 692-4648

Challenged by lapping waves at high tide, this private retreat will awaken the five senses with the smell of salty air, a taste of fresh oysters and clams, views of the Olympic Mountains, the exhilaration of sun, surf, and sand. Spa at water's edge.

6 Pets welcome; 8 Children welcome; 9 Social drinking allowed; 10 Tennis available; 11 Swimming available; 12 Golf available; 13 Skiing available; 14 May be booked through travel agents.

Host: Dennis Fulton
Rooms: 2 (PB) $119-149
Continental Breakfast
Credit Cards: A, B
Notes: 2, 5, 6, 8, 9, 11, 12, 14

SNOQUALMIE FALLS

Snoqualmie Falls

Pacific Bed and Breakfast Agency
701 Northwest 60th Street, Seattle, 98107
(206) 784-0539

Situated at the side of the spectacular Falls, this new inn offers guests unequaled comfort, privacy, and style in each of the 90-plus rooms. Curl up in front of the wood-burning fireplace or relax in a personal spa. Each room has a private bath. A library, country store, and fine restaurant await guests. Hiking, biking, skiing, golf, wineries, and fishing are nearby. $150-450.

SNOHOMISH

Pacific B&B Agency Sno-1

701 Northwest 60th Street, Seattle, 98107
(206) 784-0539

This beautifully restored Victorian country estate was built in 1884. Crowning the crest of a hill overlooking Snohomish, with a panoramic view of the Cascades, Mount Rainier, and the Olympics, the accommodation offers a quiet serenity and relaxed atmosphere. Guests are encouraged to linger in the sun-filled parlors, stroll the beautiful gardens, or just relax and swim in the heated pool. Guest rooms are tastefully decorated with antiques, handmade quilts, and unique beds. $55 and up.

SPOKANE

Spokane

Pacific Bed and Breakfast Agency
701 Northwest 60th Street, Seattle, 98107
(206) 784-0539

Enjoy this fine, restored 1891 Victorian featuring hand-carved woodwork, tin ceilings, and an open, curved staircase. A cheerful fire in the parlor will warm guests in the winter, while the wraparound porch is a nice place to relax on a warm day. Period furniture decorates the guest rooms, and a wonderful home-cooked breakfast is served in the mornings. The host will gladly assist and advise sightseers. $45 and up.

Spokane-2

Pacific Bed and Breakfast Agency
701 Northwest 60th Street, Seattle, 98107
(206) 784-0539

Situated in an attractive suburb, this bed and breakfast offers guests a quiet, relaxing place to unwind and enjoy. This home features a livingroom-bedroom combination, queen-size bed, private bath, TV and a private deck overlooking a picturesque garden. A gourmet breakfast is served with the morning news. Golf course and shops are nearby. $45-55.

TACOMA

Cottage in the Woods

Pacific Bed and Breakfast Agency
701 Northwest 60th Street, Seattle, 98107
(206) 784-0539

Situated on 15 forested acres, this hidden cottage will be equally suitable for long or short stays, honeymoons, anniversaries, or getaways. Overlooking a salmon stream and next to a golf course, it affords guests total privacy. Hosts live on the property and are available to assist guests with sightseeing plans, but will honor the privacy guests seek. One room has a freestanding fireplace on a hearth, brass bed, and kitchenette where breakfast is self-catered. $65.

NOTES: Credit cards accepted: A Master Card; B Visa; C American Express; D Discover Card; E Diner's Club; F Other; 2 Personal Checks accepted; 3 Lunch available; 4 Dinner available; 5 Open all year;

Tacoma Tudor

Pacific Bed and Breakfast Agency
701 Northwest 60th Street, Seattle, 98107
(206) 784-0539

This cozy bed and breakfast is situated next
door to the Victorian Guesthouse. Enjoy
friendly hospitality and comfort in this
home with country-style decor. Guests
should allow themselves to be pampered
here. $45 and up.

Victorian Guesthouse

Pacific Bed and Breakfast Agency
701 Northwest 60th Street, Seattle, 98107
(206) 784-0539

This lovely guest house is near the university on a tree-lined street, away from busy-
ness of downtown. Mount Rainier and
Commencement Bay are nearby. While
relaxing in the parlor, the innkeeper can
help guests with sightseeing plans. The
guest house offers clean, comfortable guest
rooms furnished with country antiques. $40
and up.

WESTPORT

Pacific B&B Agency WE-1

701 Northwest 60th Street, Seattle, 98107
(206) 784-0539

A small, lovely town on the ocean where
the salmon fishing is the greatest. If guests
are not into fishing, there are many other
activities to enjoy. Stay in this historic
mansion situated on eight acres, two blocks
from the ocean, with the peacefulness you
desire. Chose from five guest rooms, all
with private baths, lace curtains, antiques,
and fine period furnishings. Don't forget to
take a long soak in the large hot tub on the
grand cedar deck under the gazebo. Also
enjoy the barbecue and picnic areas, badminton, volleyball, and horseshoes. $45
and up.

WHIDBEY ISLAND

Oak Harbor

Pacific Bed and Breakfast Agency
701 Northwest 60th Street, Seattle, 98107
(206) 784-0539

At this bed and breakfast guests can enjoy a
fresh complete Northwest breakfast,
including salmon or mussels prepared in
the hostess's sunlit kitchen. Spend the day
searching out the treasures of Whidbey
Island and spend the evening refreshing in
the hot tub while enjoying the outside view.
The hosts offer three wonderful, cozy guest
rooms to guests when they are ready to
retire for the evening. $65-95.

Whidbey-3

Pacific Bed and Breakfast Agency
701 Northwest 60th Street, Seattle, 98107
(206) 784-0539

Situated on a quiet cove along wooded
shores, this turn-of-the-century country inn
offers guests the charm and comfort of
rooms and cottages. Some guest rooms are
furnished with antiques. The cottages with
kitchenettes are suitable for family getaways. Guests are invited to enjoy the
charm of the big stone fireplace in the parlor and the breathtaking views over the
water. $55-95.

Whidbey-4

Pacific Bed and Breakfast Agency
701 Northwest 60th Street, Seattle, 98107
(206) 784-0539

This new and splendidly built waterfront
inn offers a great getaway location. All
rooms have lanais, queen beds, whirlpool
bath for two, wood-burning fireplaces, and
are beautifully decorated. Restaurant with
award-winning cuisine is on the premises.
$135 plus.

6 Pets welcome; 8 Children welcome; 9 Social drinking allowed; 10 Tennis available; 11 Swimming available;
12 Golf available; 13 Skiing available; 14 May be booked through travel agents.

Whidbey-5

Pacific Bed and Breakfast Agency
701 Northwest 60th Street, Seattle, 98107
(206) 784-0539

This bed and breakfast is a spacious, modern beach home decorated with comfortable homey antiques, including a beautiful diamond-tufted leather love seat with matching wing-backed chairs. Guests can sit back, enjoy a crackling fire, watch the 52-inch TV, or enjoy a game of pool. The breathtaking view of the Olympic Mountains, Puget Sound, and the San Juan Islands will encourage guests to linger and sip freshly ground coffee while savoring the view. $65-95.

YAKIMA

Yakima

Pacific Bed and Breakfast Agency
701 Northwest 60th Street, Seattle, 98107
(206) 784-0539

This stately English Tudor mansion was built in 1929 and is surrounded by beautiful grounds, formal hedges, a variety of trees, flowers, and a garden pool. Each room is furnished with antiques from the early 1800s and has a color TV. The bridal suite features a king-size bed, private bath, bar with refrigerator, microwave oven, and a bottle of champagne. $65-125.

West Virginia

CHARLESTON

Brass Pineapple

1611 Virginia Street East, 25311
(304) 344-0748

In 1910, E. C. and Clara Bauer built a marvelous brick home with lots of stained glass, oak paneling, and Italian marble. That house is now the Brass Pineapple Bed and Breakfast. This elegant home is an eclectic blend of styles. A full or continental breakfast and afternoon tea are served by candlelight. The goal is to provide guests with all the comforts of home, where they can be a private or a social as they choose.

Host: Sue Pepper
Rooms: 4 (PB) $75-90
Full Breakfast or Continental Breakfast
Credit Cards: A, B, C
Notes: 2, 5, 8 (over 6), 10, 11, 12, 14

CHARLES TOWN

Gilbert House
Bed and Breakfast

P. O. Box 1104, 25414
(304) 725-0637

An American treasure, the Gilbert House, circa 1760, is a magnificent stone house listed on the Historic American Buildings Survey and the National Register of Historic Places. The house is richly decorated with European antiques, some of which came from royal courts of Europe and were collected or inherited by the hosts. Situated in the Middleway Historic District, near Antietam, Harpers Ferry and Washington, D. C.

Hosts: Jean and Bernie Heiler
Rooms: 3 (PB) $70-150
Full Breakfast
Credit Cards: A, B, C
Notes: 2, 5, 9, 10, 11, 12, 14

LOST CITY

Kathleen's

P. O. Box 83, 26810
(304) 897-6787

A completely renovated 19th-century farmhouse. The amenities here include three full baths, central heat and air, outside deck, patio, and wraparound front porch. Situated on a hill that provides an excellent view of the Lost River Valley and surrounding mountains, it caters to couples and families. Special family extended-stay rates available. Situated near the George Washington National Forest and Lost River State Park.

Host: Kathleen Funkhouser
Rooms: 4 (1 PB; 3 SB) $65-80
Full Breakfast
Credit Cards: None
Notes: 2, 5, 8, 9, 10, 11

MARTINSBURG

Amanda's
Bed and Breakfast #282

1428 Park Avenue, Baltimore, MD 21217
(410) 225-0001; (410) 383-1274

Restored 19th-century Federal-style stone farmhouse surrounded by acres of rolling pasture and woods. The seven-foot windows provide lots of light and give each room a remarkable view. Visit nearby Harpers Ferry, Antietam Battlefield, and

6 Pets welcome; 8 Children welcome; 9 Social drinking allowed; 10 Tennis available; 11 Swimming available; 12 Golf available; 13 Skiing available; 14 May be booked through travel agents.

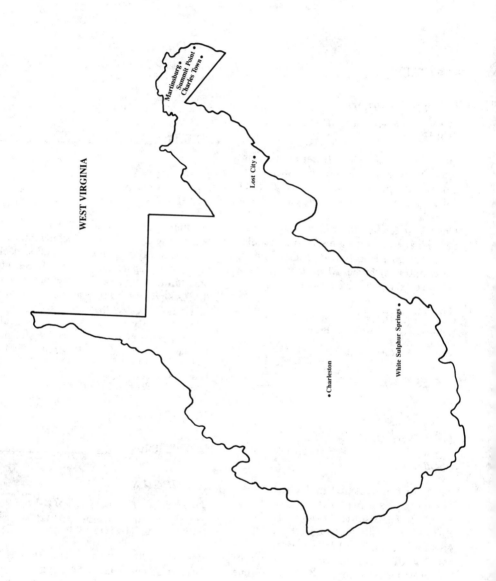

WEST VIRGINIA

Martinsburg •
Summit Point •
Charles Town •

Lost City •

White Sulphur Springs •

• Charleston

more. Three guest rooms with private and shared baths. Full breakfast. $85-100.

Aspen Hall
405 Boyd Avenue, 25401
(304) 263-4385

A majestic 18th-century limestone mansion situated on a four-acre estate in a pleasant West Virginia village. Its spacious rooms with high ceilings are furnished with an accumulation of objects from centuries past. The bedchambers have canopy beds and private baths. Tea is served on the terrace on summer afternoons or in the parlor in cooler weather. The country breakfast is a delicious surprise each morning here where hospitality is a matter of pride and calories are ignored.

Hosts: Gordon and Lou Anne Claucherty
Rooms: 5 (PB) $110
Full Breakfast
Credit Cards: A, B
Notes: 2, 5, 9, 10, 11, 12, 14

Boydville, The Inn at Martinsburg
601 South Queen Street, 25401
(304) 263-1448

1812 stone plantation mansion in a 14-acre private park, once part of the Lord Fairfax Grant. Original wallpaper and woodwork. High ceilings, great porch with rockers. National Register of Historic Places. Built by Gen. Elisha Boyd, War of 1812 hero, it was a retreat for Stonewall Jackson and Henry Clay. Just off I-81, 90 minutes from Washington, D. C., in the heart of Civil War country.

Hosts: LaRue Frye; Bob Boege; Carolyn Snyder; Pete Bailey
Rooms: 6 (PB) $100-125
Continental Breakfast
Credit Cards: A, B
Notes: 2, 5, 9, 10, 11, 12, 13, 14

SUMMIT POINT

Amanda's Bed and Breakfast #114
1428 Park Avenue, Baltimore, MD 21217
(410) 225-0001; (410) 383-1274

In the quaint village of Summit Point near Harpers Ferry. Decorated with a cheery mixture of old and new. Old-fashioned hospitality for the crowd-weary traveler. Many activities in the area, including hiking, bicycling, and sightseeing. Two rooms with private baths. Continental breakfast. $70.

Countryside
P. O. Box 57, 25446
(304) 725-2614

Countryside is in a charming village near historic Harpers Ferry, decorated with items old and new, including quilts, baskets, books, and collectibles. Guests are welcomed with a cheerful room, bath, and breakfast amid lovely rural scenery. This inn specializes in romantic getaways, featuring a breakfast tray brought to the guests' rooms.

Hosts: Lisa and Daniel Hileman
Rooms: 2 (PB) $53-68.90
Continental Breakfast
Credit Cards: A, B
Notes: 2, 5, 8, 12

WHITE SULPHUR SPRINGS

The James Wylie House Bed and Breakfast
208 East Main Street, 24986
(304) 536-9444

Situated in a circa 1819 Georgian Colonial house, this bed and breakfast is situated in a small-town setting ten blocks from the Greenbrier Resort and nine blocks from historic Lewisburg. Large, spacious rooms

NOTES: Credit cards accepted: A Master Card; B Visa; C American Express; D Discover Card; E Diner's Club; F Other; 2 Personal Checks accepted; 3 Lunch available; 4 Dinner available; 5 Open all year; 6 Pets welcome; 8 Children welcome; 9 Social drinking allowed; 10 Tennis available; 11 Swimming available; 12 Golf available; 13 Skiing available; 14 May be booked through travel agents.

offer comfort in this historical home. A log cabin guest house offers accommodations as well. The Wylie House has been given excellent reviews in a national golf magazine, *Mid-Atlantic Country* magazine, and statewide newspapers.

Hosts: Cheryl and Joe Griffith
Rooms: 4 (PB) $65-120
Full Breakfast
Credit Cards: A, B, C
Notes: 2, 5, 8, 9, 10, 11, 12, 13

James Wylie House

Wisconsin

ALBANY

Albany Guest House

405 South Mill Street, 53502
(608) 862-3636

Enjoy a restored, spacious block house in
the heart of south central Wisconsin's
Swiss communities. Swing or rock among
the flowers on the front porch or stroll
through the two acres of lawn and gardens.
Bike, hike, or ski the Sugar River Trail;
canoe, tube, or fish the river; or light the
fireplace in the master bedroom and relax.
Visit the huge farmers' market on the state
capitol square only 30 miles north, or discover the nearby virgin prairie.

Hosts: Bob and Sally Braem
Rooms: 4 (PB) $50-68
Full Breakfast
Credit Cards: None
Notes: 2, 5, 8, 9, 11, 12, 13

BARABOO

Pinehaven
Bed and Breakfast

E13083, Highway 33, 53913
(608) 356-3489

This home is nestled in a pine grove, with a
beautiful view of the Baraboo bluffs.
Rooms feature queen and twin beds, and air
conditioning. Breakfasts may include coffee cakes, breads, egg dishes, meats, fruit,
and juices. Belgian draft horses are kept at
the farm site, with wagon and sleigh rides
available, weather permitting. Take a stroll
through the inviting surroundings. Fine
restaurants and numerous activities abound
in the area. Ask about the guest house.

Hosts: Lyle and Marge Getschman
Rooms: 4 (PB) $55-65
Full Breakfast
Credit Cards: A, B
Notes: 2, 5, 8 (over 5), 9, 10, 11, 12, 13

CEDARBURG

Stagecoach Inn

West 61 North 520, Washington Avenue, 53012
(414) 375-0208

The Stagecoach Inn is a historic, restored
1853 stone building of Greek Revival style.
Its 13 cozy rooms offer stenciled walls and
antique furnishings, central air and private
baths. Suites with large whirlpool baths are
available. Situated in the heart of historic
Cedarburg, the inn also features an on-
premises pub with a 100-year-old bar and a
chocolate shop. Located in the historic district near shops and restaurants.

Hosts: Liz and Brook Brown
Rooms: 13 (PB) $65-95
Continental Breakfast
Credit Cards: A, B, C
Notes: 2, 5, 9, 10, 11, 12, 13, 14

CHETEK

The Lodge at Canoe Bay

W16065 Hogback Road, 54728
(800) 568-1995

The ultimate in relaxation. Secluded, luxurious lodge features soaring cedar ceilings
and a massive fieldstone fireplace. Set by a
pristine lake in a 280-acre oak, aspen and

6 Pets welcome; 8 Children welcome; 9 Social drinking allowed; 10 Tennis available; 11 Swimming available;
12 Golf available; 13 Skiing available; 14 May be booked through travel agents.

WISCONSIN

Minoqua

Chetek

Ellison Bay
Ephraim

Merrill

Hudson

Sturgeon Bay

River Falls   Eau Claire

Stevens Point

La Farge

Baraboo

Cedarburg

Viroqua

Madison

Fort Atkinson

Whitewater

Albany

maple forest. Every amenity, including large private whirlpools and nature trails.

Hosts: Dan and Lisa Dobrowolski
Rooms: 8 (4 PB; 4 SB) $59-129
Continental Breakfast
Credit Cards: A, B, D
Notes: 2, 5, 11, 12, 13, 14

EAU CLAIRE

Fanny Hill Inn and Dinner Theatre
3919 Crescent Avenue, 54703
(715) 836-8184; (800) 292-8026

On a bluff overlooking the Chippewa River Valley, Fanny Hill is the perfect setting to "get away from it all." Each of the seven guest rooms has a private bath and is tastefully decorated with antiques and curiosities. The unique combination of scenic beauty, gracious fine dining, hilarious live theatre, and warm Victorian atmosphere will make guests' stay a pleasure.

Host: Dennis Heyde
Rooms: 7 (PB) $69-139
Continental Breakfast
Credit Cards: A, B, C, D, E
Notes: 2, 4, 5, 9, 12

Otter Creek Inn
2536 Highway 12, 54701
(715) 832-2945

This spacious country Victorian inn features double whirlpools in three of the four guest rooms. The magnificent decor and area antiques combine with warm hospitality and a crackling fire in the lounge to create a memorable retreat. Enjoy breakfast in bed, stroll the wooded one-acre lot, explore the creek, peek at the Whitetail deer in the backyard, or dine and shop at one of 30 restaurants and malls located just five minutes away.

Hosts: Randy and Shelley Hansen
Rooms: 4 (PB) $59-119
Continental Breakfast
Credit Cards: A, B, C
Notes: 2, 5, 9, 10, 11, 12

ELLISON BAY

Wagon Trail Resort Restaurant and Conference Center
1041 Highway 22, 54210
(414) 854-2385

Wagon Trail's homestyle hospitality begins with comfortable year-round accommodations, from a large Scandinavian lodge to secluded vacation homes and cozy bayside cottages. Tensions melt in the indoor pool, sauna, and whirlpool. Homemade specialties and a delectable buffet distinguish the restaurant, while Grandma's Swedish Bakery serves famous pecan rolls and other Scandinavian treats. Miles of groomed hiking trails and ski trails criss-cross 200 acres of wooded acres. Swimming and fishing areas and a complete marina and bait shop accent a half-mile of shoreline.

Hosts: Mike and Miriam Dorn, Bob and Jewel Ovradrik
Rooms: 81 (PB) $69-229
Full Breakfast
Credit Cards: A, B, C, D, E
Notes: 2, 3, 4, 5, 8, 9, 10, 11, 12, 13, 14 (groups only)

EPHRAIM

French Country Inn of Ephraim
3052 Spruce Lane, P. O. Box, 129, 54211
(414) 854-4001

Originally built as a summer cottage in 1912, the house now serves as a comfortable European-style bed and breakfast featuring seven guest rooms in summer and four in winter. A large stone fireplace and spacious common rooms add to the friendly atmosphere. Situated in the village of Ephraim in Wisconsin's famous Door County, the house has a peaceful garden setting. Enjoy Lake Michigan in summer and cross-country skiing in winter. Beautiful sunsets all year long.

Host: Walt Fisher
Rooms: 7 summer (2 PB; 5 SB) $52-79; 4 winter (SB) $45-55
Continental Breakfast
Credit Cards: None
Notes: 2, 5, 9, 10, 11, 12, 13

FORT ATKINSON

The Lamp Post Inn Bed and Breakfast
408 South Main Street, 53538
(414) 563-6561

Take a step back in time to our beautifully restored 1880s Victorian home, just six blocks from the famous Fireside Playhouse. The house is furnished in period antiques, and features five phonographs. Warm, cozy rooms make guests feel at home, with air conditioning available for warm summer nights. The area offers antique shops, bike trails, museums, shopping, river cruises and horsedrawn sleds. Special diets can be accommodated. "Come a stranger, and leave a friend."

Hosts: Debbie and Mike Rusch
Rooms: 3 (2 PB; 1 SB) $60-85 plus tax
Full Breakfast
Credit Cards: None
Notes: 2, 5, 8, 9, 10, 11, 12, 13

HUDSON

Phipps Inn
1005 Third Street, 54016
(715) 386-0800

Described as the "Grand Dame" of Queen Anne houses in historic Hudson, this 1884 Victorian mansion offers authentic furnishings and cozy suites, some with fireplaces and whirlpools. Guests enjoy three parlors, two porches, a baby grand piano, and lavish and leisurely breakfasts in bed or served in the elegant dining room. Only 30 minutes from Minneapolis/St. Paul. A romantic retreat.

Hosts: Cyndi and John Berglund
Rooms: 6 (PB) $79-159
Full Breakfast weekends; Continental Breakfast weekdays
Credit Cards: A, B
Notes: 2, 5, 9, 11, 12, 13, 14

LA FARGE

Trillium
Route 2, Box 121, 54639
(608) 625-4492

A cozy, private cottage is fully furnished on this family farm. Complete with kitchen, stone fireplace, and a porch overlooking the gardens and orchard, the cottage faces out over woods and fields. It is in Wisconsin's largest Amish community, near rivers, state parks, historical sites, and bike trails.

Host: Rosanne Boyett
Cottage: 1 (PB) $52-65
Full Breakfast
Credit Cards: None
Notes: 2, 5, 8 (under 12 stay free), 9, 10, 11, 12, 13

MADISON

Annie's Bed and Breakfast
2117 Sheridan Drive, 53704
(608) 244-2224

When travelers want the world to go away, come to Annie's Bed and Breakfast. This quiet little inn on Warner Park offers a beautiful view and deluxe accommodations. Enjoy the romantic gazebo surrounded by butterfly gardens, the lily pond by the terrace for morning coffee, followed by a sumptuous breakfast. The guest rooms are cozy with antiques, gorgeous quilts, and down comforters. Double Jacuzzi is available. Convenient to everything.

Hosts: Anne and Larry Stuart
Suites (2 rooms each): 2 (PB) $75-95
Full Breakfast
Credit Cards: A, B, C
Notes: 2, 5, 8 (over 12), 9, 10, 11, 12, 13 (XC)

MERRILL

Candlewick Inn

700 West Main Street, 54452-4376
(715) 536-7744; (800) 382-4396

The ambience of yesteryear is truly reflected in this classic Victorian Prairie-style home built by a lumber baron in the early 1880s. Recently restored to its original elegance, this four-season inn radiates all the warmth and charm of the Victorian era. It includes fine antiques, handmade quilts, oak and mahogany woodwork, collectibles, and gift shop, all combining to create a romantic masterpiece. Conveniently situated in a historic district of Merrill, the inn provides easy access to shops, museums, antiques, and restaurants.

Host: Dan Staniak
Rooms: 5 (3 PB; 2 SB) $50-95
Full Breakfast
Credit Cards: A, B
Notes: 2, 5, 10, 11, 12, 13, 14

MINOCQUA

Whitehaven Bed and Breakfast

1077 Highway F, 54548
(715) 356-9097

Whitehaven is a gracious, rustic inn reminiscent of the northwoods retreats of yesteryear. Romantic arched doorways and

windows grace the inn. Secluded on 12 acres against the pristine shores of beautiful Whitefish Lake, enjoy the many waterfowl who frequent the lake, including loons and eagles. Breakfast is served in the screened porch overlooking the lake, or in the great room, with a fieldstone fireplace. With private baths installed in May of this year, two spacious bedrooms boast antiques and handmade quilts.

Hosts: Ronald and Anita White
Rooms: 2 (1 PB; 1 SB) $50-55
Full Breakfast
Credit Cards: None
Notes: 2, 5, 9, 11, 12, 13

RIVER FALLS

Knollwood House Bed and Breakfast

N8257 950th Street, Knollwood Drive, 54022
(715) 425-1040; (800) 435-0628

A mini-resort situated 45 minutes from the Mall of America, 15 minutes from the Great River Road and five minutes from the Kinnickinnic Trout Stream. Eighty acres of beautiful Wisconsin countryside. Cozy 1886 brick farmhouse, family heirlooms, outdoor pool, hot tub, cross-country skiing/hiking trails, golf, flowers and fish ponds. A relaxing atmosphere.

Hosts: Jim and Judy Tostrud
Rooms: 3 (SB) $60-125
Full Breakfast
Credit Cards: None
Notes: 2, 5, 9, 10, 11, 12, 13

STEVENS POINT

Dreams of Yesteryear Bed and Breakfast

1100 Brawley Street, 54481
(715) 341-4525

This Queen Anne home is architect designed, rich in history and listed on the

National Register of Historic Places. The restoration of this house was featured in *Victorian Homes Magazine*. Antique-appointed rooms with twin to king-size beds await you, as well as formal and informal gardens. All this and more, located two blocks from historic downtown, the Wisconsin River and the Green Circle hiking trails. The hosts are pleased to tell you stories of their house and community.

Hosts: Bonnie and Bill Maher
Rooms: 4 (2 PB; 2 SB) $55-75
Full Breakfast
Credit Cards: A, B, D
Notes: 2, 3 (nearby), 4 (nearby), 5, 8 (over 12), 9, 10, 11, 12, 13, 14

STURGEON BAY

The Scofield House Bed and Breakfast

908 Michigan Street, P. O. Box 761, 54235
(414) 743-7727

Described as "Door County's most elegant bed and breakfast." Authentic bed and breakfast in a turn-of-the-century restored Victorian Queen Anne house, circa 1902. Prominent home of Sturgeon Bay Mayor Bert Scofield. Very ornate interior with inlaid floors and ornamented woodwork. Six guest rooms, each with private bath. Some with double whirlpool, fireplaces, color TV/cable, VCR/stereo. Free movie library. High Victorian decor throughout with fine antiques. Air-conditioned. Full gourmet breakfast and afternoon complimentary sweet treats and teas. Call or write for brochure. Gift certificates available.

Hosts: Bill and Fran Cecil
Rooms: 6 (PB) $69-180
Full Breakfast
Credit Cards: None
Notes: 2, 5, 9, 10, 11, 12, 13

White Lace Inn

16 North 5th Avenue, 54235
(414) 743-1105

The White Lace Inn is a romantic getaway featuring three restored turn-of-the-century homes surrounding lovely gardens and a gazebo. The 15 wonderfully inviting guest rooms are furnished in antiques with four-poster and Victorian beds, in-room fireplaces in some rooms, and double whirlpool tubs in others.

Hosts: Bonnie and Dennis Statz
Rooms: 15 (PB) $66-148
Continental Breakfast
Credit Cards: A, B, C
Notes: 2, 5, 9, 10, 11, 12, 13

VIROQUA

Viroqua Heritage Inn Bed and Breakfast

220 East Jefferson Street, 54665
(608) 637-3306

Memories are made at this restored 1890 Queen Anne Victorian. Elegant yet warm, comfortable and romantic. Antique furnishings, baby grand piano previously owned by Coleen Moore (silent movie star), fireplace, hardwood floors, Oriental rugs, porch swings, plush robes, and concession area. Abundant breakfasts are served at the guest's convenience. Situated in beautiful southwestern Wisconsin, recreational opportunities include bicycle trails, state parks, golf, fishing, historic sites, fairs, auctions, and murder mystery weekends. Come enjoy!

Host: Nancy Rhodes-Seevers
Rooms: 4 (1 1/2 SB) $45-65
Full Breakfast
Credit Cards: A, B, C, D
Notes: 2, 5, 8, 9, 10, 11, 12, 13, 14

WHITEWATER

The Greene House Country Inn and Guitar Gallery

Route 2, Box 214, Highway 12, 53190-9412
(414) 495-8771; (800) 468-1959 (outside Wisconsin)

NOTES: Credit cards accepted: A Master Card; B Visa; C American Express; D Discover Card; E Diner's Club; F Other; 2 Personal Checks accepted; 3 Lunch available; 4 Dinner available; 5 Open all year;

Unique Country Inn: "Soft Rock Cafe" atmosphere abounds, as guitars and other stringed instruments decorate the inn. Restaurant open weekends for travelers with hearty appetites. Enjoy this wonderful outdoor recreation area with bike trails, horseback riding, cross-country skiing and hiking. Just north of Lake Geneva, two hours north of Chicago, an hour south of Milwaukee, and one hour east of Madison.

Hosts: Lynn and Mayner Greene
Rooms: 4 (SB) $49-79
Full Breakfast
Credit Cards: A, B, C, D
Notes: 2, 3, 4, 5, 8, 9, 10, 11, 12, 13, 14

WYOMING

- Cody
- Wilson
- Jackson Hole
- Lander
- Riverton
- Laramie
- Cheyenne

Wyoming

Adventurer's Country Bed and Breakfast

3803 I-80, South Service Road, 82009
(307) 632-4087

This bed and breakfast is situated on Raven Cry Ranch, on a knoll above I-80, surrounded by 102 acres of prairies and green pasture. The expansive front lawn, tree-lined adobe courtyard with flower-filled gardens and large comfortable front porch welcomes guests to this southwestern-style ranch home. A cozy library complete with fireplace, TV, videos, games and books are available for guests' enjoyment. The ranch is also home to horses, chickens, geese, cats, whippet and greyhound competition dogs.

Hosts: Chuck and Fern White
Rooms: 4 (PB) $50-70
Full Breakfast
Credit Cards: None
Notes: 2, 3, 4, 5, 6, 8, 9, 10, 11, 12

A. Drummond's Ranch Recreation Bed and Breakfast

399 Happy Jack Road, 82007
(307) 634-6042

Quiet, tranquil retreat conveniently situated between Cheyenne and Laramie in the Laramie Range, the scenic bypass for I-80. Adjacent to state park and five miles to national forest; fishing, hiking, rock climbing, cross-country skiing. Bring a horse or mountain bicycle and train at 7,500 feet. Boarding for horses and family pets. Just get away from cars and crowds. Outdoor hot tub. Added touches: Flowers in room, terry-cloth robes for guests during stay; beverages, fresh fruit, and homemade snacks always available. Reservations required.

Hosts: Kent and Taydie Drummond
Rooms: 3 (1 PB; 2 SB) $60-80
Full Breakfast
Credit Cards: None
Notes: 2, 3 & 4 (advance notice), 6, 8, 9, 13 (XC), 14

Trout Creek Inn

Yellowstone Highway 14, 16, 20 West, 82414
(307) 587-6288

This inn features clean, comfortable deluxe rooms, featuring tub and showers and kitchens, but the real value is outside in the beautiful mountain valley Teddy Roosevelt said was "the best in the world." Horseback riding, a private stream, pond fishing, and a pool. A photographer's and hiker's paradise.

Hosts: Bert and Norma Sowerwine
Rooms: 21 (PB) $55-65
Full or Continental Breakfast
Credit Cards: A, B, C, D, F
Notes: 2 (for deposit only), 5, 6, 8, 9, 10, 11, 12, 13, 14

NOTES: Credit cards accepted: A Master Card; B Visa; C American Express; D Discover Card; E Diner's Club; F Other; 2 Personal Checks accepted; 3 Lunch available; 4 Dinner available; 5 Open all year; 6 Pets welcome; 8 Children welcome; 9 Social drinking allowed; 10 Tennis available; 11 Swimming available; 12 Golf available; 13 Skiing available; 14 May be booked through travel agents.

JACKSON HOLE

Fish Creek Bed and Breakfast

2455 Fish Creek Road, Box 366, 83014
(307) 733-2586

In Jackson Hole, this beautiful log home is situated on the banks of Fish Creek in an exclusive and secluded location. Guests are offered gourmet breakfasts, private fly fishing, guided skiing and wildlife viewing 15 minutes from Jackson and the Jackson Hole Ski Area. National park and forest are close by, as well as over 50 restaurants and other activities. Outdoor hot tub. Owners are 40-year residents of the area.

Hosts: Putzi and John Harrington
Rooms: 4 (PB) $85-105
Full Breakfast
Credit Cards: A, B
Notes: 2, 9, 10, 11, 12, 13

Teton Tree House

P. O. Box 550, 83014
(307) 733-3233

A classic bed and breakfast inn on a forested mountainside hosted by warm, on-the-premises innkeepers. Rooms are large, with excellent beds, and most feature decks with wonderful views. The great room has a sweeping staircase, fireplace, piano, and walls of books. Hosts are local guides and travelers who delight in sharing information. Mentioned in the *New York Times* and *National Geographic* magazine.

Hosts: Chris and Denny Becker
Rooms: 5 (PB) $90.95 - 133.75
Full Breakfast
Credit Cards: A, B
Notes: 2, 5, 8, 9, 10, 12, 13, 14

LANDER

The Highland Rose

2900 U.S. Highway 287 North, 82520
(307) 332-7727

Peaceful 100-year old ranch house with views of the Wind River Range and ranch life. French antiques and western art decorate the interior, and guests can feast on homemade breads at brunch or sample complimentary liqueur in the evening. A paradise for hikers, fishermen, hunters, and skiers. Activities include the Indian Museum and shops, llama trips, and bronze foundry tours. The Tetons and Yellowstone National Park are only two hours away.

Host: Chantal T. Peranteaux
Rooms: 4 (SB) $53
Continental Breakfast
Credit Cards: B
Notes: 2, 3, 5, 6, 9, 10, 11, 12, 13, 14

LARAMIE

Annie Moore's Guest House

819 University Avenue, 82070
(307) 721-4177

Restored Queen Anne home with six individually decorated guest rooms, four with sinks. Large, sunny, common livingrooms, second-story sun deck. Across the street from the University of Wyoming; two blocks from the Laramie Plains Museum; six blocks from downtown shops, galleries, and restaurants. Just 15 minutes from skiing, camping, biking, and fishing in uncrowded wilderness areas. House cat in residence. "Hospitality is our specialty."

Annie Moore's

Hosts: Ann Acuff and Joe Bundy
Rooms: 6 (SB) $50-60
Continental Breakfast
Credit Cards: A, B, C, D
Notes: 2, 5, 9, 12, 13, 14

RIVERTON

Cottonwood Ranch Bed and Breakfast
951 Missouri Valley Road, 82501
(307) 856-3064

Visit the Cottonwood Ranch Bed and Breakfast, and enjoy western hospitality on a working ranch. Established in 1937, the host raises corn, oats, malting barley, alfalfa, cattle and occasionally lambs. His wife, Judie, a former caterer, writes cooking columns. The ranch is situated just 15 minutes from Riverton, and a three-hour drive will take guests to Yellowstone or Jackson Hole. Closer yet are Wind River Indian Reservation and Hot Springs State Park, situated only an hour away. The ranch also offers good fishing and swimming at nearby lakes, rivers, and streams.

Cottonwood Ranch

Hosts: Judie and Earl Anglen
Rooms: 3 (SB) $40-50
Full Breakfast
Credit Cards: None
Notes: 2, 3 (on occasion), 4 (on occasion), 5, 6 (outdoors only), 8 (supervised), 9 (on occasion), 10, 11, 12

YAKIMA

'37 House
4002 Englewood Avenue, 98908
(509) 965-5537

An inn of extraordinary elegance, the '37 House was built in 1937 by one of Yakima's first fruit-growing families. The warm and gracious atmosphere invites guests of all ages to sit by one of three large hearth fireplaces or roam across more than two acres surrounding the house. With a total of 7,500 square feet, the '37 House offers a variety of overnight accommodations, with each room boasting its own special charm. Guests can find special touches of the 1930s everywhere—roomy walk-in closets, window seats tucked under sloping eaves, built-in desks with lots of cubby holes, shuttered windowpanes and fully tiled baths. Dessert before bed is included in every overnight stay.

Host: Beatrice McKinney
Rooms: 6 (PB) $65-120
Full Breakfast
Credit Cards: A, B, C
Notes: 2, 5, 10, 14

6 Pets welcome; 8 Children welcome; 9 Social drinking allowed; 10 Tennis available; 11 Swimming available; 12 Golf available; 13 Skiing available; 14 May be booked through travel agents.

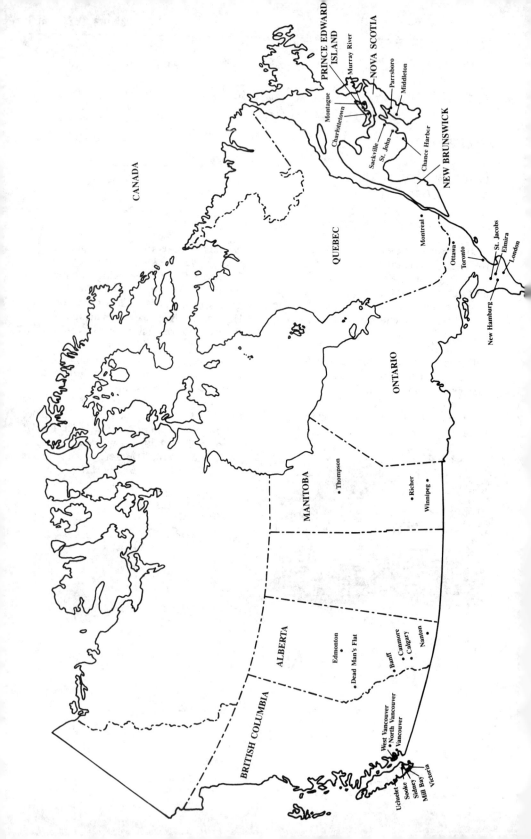

Alberta

Alberta Bed and Breakfast

P. O. Box 15477, MPO, Vancouver, BC, V6B 5B2
(604) 944-1793

Beautiful large home in a quiet crescent offers two guest rooms, a queen and twin and one guest bath. An adjoining sitting room with a lovely view of the mountains through the skylight is available for guest use.

CALGARY

Alberta Bed and Breakfast

P. O. Box 15477, MPO, Vancouver, BC, V6B 5B2
(604) 944-1793

Multi-level home has a family room with a fireplace and a cedar-lined hot tub. Guest room features a double bed and private bath.

CANMORE

Alberta Bed and Breakfast

P. O. Box 15477, MPO, Vancouver, BC, V6B 5B2
(604) 944-1793

Twenty minutes from Banff, this large modern home offers four guest rooms. A spacious honeymoon room has a queen bed, private balcony, large ensuite bath with Jacuzzi and the first morning's breakfast is served in your room. Three other guest rooms of double, twin and two double beds share two bathrooms. Hosts have a daughter, and children are welcome.

Cougar Creek Inn

P. O. Box 1162, T0L 0M0
(403) 678-4751

Quiet, rustic cedar chalet with mountain views in every direction. Grounds border on Cougar Creek and back onto land reserve area. There is hiking out your back door with wildlife often spotted. Hostess is an outdoor enthusiast with a strong love for mountains; she can assist in making plans for local hiking, skiing, canoeing, mountain biking, and backpacking. Barbecue, bonfire pit, private entrance. Fireplace, sitting room with TV, games, private dining and serving area, sauna.

Host: Patricia Doucette
Rooms: 4 (S2B) $55-60 Canadian
Full Breakfast
Credit Cards: None
Notes: 2 (for deposit), 3, 5, 8, 9, 10, 11, 12, 13

DEAD MAN'S FLAT

Alberta Bed and Breakfast

P. O. Box 15477, MPO, Vancouver, BC, V6B 5B2
(604) 944-1793

Situated twenty miles from Banff and twenty minutes to Kananaskis Village, this large home offers three guest rooms, one with a double bed and two with queen size beds. Each room features a private bath. The resident feline welcomes guests.

NOTES: Credit cards accepted: A Master Card; B Visa; C American Express; D Discover Card; E Diner's Club; F Other; 2 Personal Checks accepted; 3 Lunch available; 4 Dinner available; 5 Open all year; 6 Pets welcome; 8 Children welcome; 9 Social drinking allowed; 10 Tennis available; 11 Swimming available; 12 Golf available; 13 Skiing available; 14 May be booked through travel agents.

EDMONTON

Alberta Bed and Breakfast

P. O. Box 15477, MPO, Vancouver, BC, V6B 5B2
(604) 944-1793

This home is within walking distance of the famous West Edmonton Mall, the largest entertainment and shopping mall on Earth. Three large guest rooms are offered, two with double beds, the other with a single and one guest bath. Travelers are invited to use the sauna, deck, and hot tub.

Haus Alpenrose

629 9th Street, P. O. Box 723, T0L 0M0
(403) 678-4134

Haus Alpenrose is a small, rustic lodge in the town of Canmore, the very heart of the Canadian Rockies. The Alpenrose is built in a Bavarian chalet style, with a recreational lodge for the outdoor enthusiast. It offers rooms for two to four people, with private or shared bathrooms, kitchen access, and a large lounge. Hosts speak German and French. The Alpenrose is also home to the Canadian School of Mountaineering, where hiking and climbing trips and courses are offered in the summer, cross-country skiing and ice-climbing instruction in the winter. Close to Banff National Park, Kananaskis Provincial Park, and Assiniboine Provincial Park.

Hosts: Ottmar and Ulrike Setzer
Rooms: 9 (4 PB; 5 SB) $55-65, seasonal
Full Breakfast
Credit Cards: A, B
Notes: 5, 8, 9, 10, 11, 12, 13, 14

NANTON

Timber Ridge Homestead

P. O. Box 94, T0L 1R0
(403) 646-5683 (summer); (403) 646-2480 (winter)

Timber Ridge Homestead is a rustic establishment in the beautiful foothills of ranching country about 70 miles southwest of Calgary. There are good, quiet horses to help you explore the abundant wildflowers, wildlife, and wonderful views of the Rockies. Good, plain cooking, if guests want it.

Hosts: Bridget Jones and family
Rooms: 3 (SB) $25 Canadian
Full Breakfast
Credit Cards: None
Notes: 2, 3, 4, 8, 9

NOTES: Credit cards accepted: A Master Card; B Visa; C American Express; D Discover Card; E Diner's Club; F Other; 2 Personal Checks accepted; 3 Lunch available; 4 Dinner available; 5 Open all year;

British Columbia

Gabriela's Bed and Breakfast

2242 Park Crescent, V3J 6T2
(604) 469-7105

Gabriela's Bed and Breakfast is a comfortable, spotless German home located 20 kilometers from Vancouver. Enjoy the guest room, with a king-size bed, private bath and guest lounge, fireplace, toy box, TV, and magazines. A nutritious gourmet breakfast is served. Cribs and high chairs are available. Situated in a quiet, residential area, with a large, private backyard. German and English spoken here.

Host: Gabriela Butz
Rooms: 1 (PB) $70 (US)
Full Breakfast
Credit Cards: None
Notes: 2, 5, 8, 9, 10, 11, 12, 14

MILL BAY

Pine Lodge Farm Bed and Breakfast

3191 Mutter Road, V0R 2P0
(604) 743-4083

A charming pine lodge built on a 30-acre farm overlooking ocean and islands. Walking trails, farm animals, and deer and magnificent arbutus trees add to the paradise-like setting. Antique-filled lodge with stained-glass windows features cozy bedrooms with private bathrooms, furnished with beautiful antiques. Honeymoon cottage with a hot tub is available. Enjoy a full breakfast with homemade jams, and then browse through a spectacular collection of antiques. Featured in *Country Living* and on CBS television.

Hosts: Cliff and Barbara Clarke
Rooms: 8 (PB) $65-95
Full Breakfast
Credit Cards: A, B
Notes: 2, 5, 9, 14

NORTH VANCOUVER

Laburnum Cottage Bed and Breakfast

1388 Terrace Avenue, V7R 1B4
(604) 988-4877

Set on half an acre of award-winning English gardens, nestled against a forest, yet only 15 minutes from downtown Vancouver. Each of the upstairs guest rooms in the main house has a private bath, decor, featuring delicate wallpapers, stunning antiques, and invitingly warm colors complemented by magnificent garden views. Breakfasts are jolly occasions in the big farmhouse-style kitchen near the cozy Aga cookers where all enjoy a full three or four-course meal.

Hosts: Delphine and Margot Masterton
Rooms: 3, plus 2 cottages (PB) $95-125
Full Breakfast
Credit Cards: A, B
Notes: 2, 5, 8, 10, 12, 14

Old English Bed and Breakfast Registry

P. O. Box 86818, V7L 4L3
(604) 986-5069; FAX (604) 986-8810

6 Pets welcome; 8 Children welcome; 9 Social drinking allowed; 10 Tennis available; 11 Swimming available; 12 Golf available; 13 Skiing available; 14 May be booked through travel agents.

The Old English Bed and Breakfast Registry is a professional reservation service that represents 45 bed and breakfast homes in the Greater Vancouver area, as well as Victoria and Vancouver Island. Each home has been personally inspected and will provide guests with a friendly, hospitable, and relaxing stay in the area. All prices include breakfast and free parking. Visa and MasterCard accepted. Open all year. $65 and up.

Old English Bed and Breakfast 1

P. O. Box 86818, V7L 4L3
(604) 986-5069

Guests can lay back, put their feet up, and enjoy tranquility at the end of the day in this elegant bed and breakfast. The guest room is built into the rocky evergreen slopes, looking out through tall cedar and fir to the Pacific, sailing ships, tiny islands —a scene that may alter your life forever. Find the suite lovingly decorated with an assortment of finery that reflects both Canada and the Orient. Situated just 20 minutes from downtown Vancouver. Elizabeth has two rooms available. One queen bed sitting room with private bath, and a private patio deck. The other room features a king-size bed, sitting room, private bath, and private patio deck. $105-115.

Old English Bed and Breakfast 3

P. O. Box 86818, V7L 4L3
(604) 986-5069

This gracious home with a Victorian air is situated on a quiet tree-lined street in the lovely Kerrisdale area of Vancouver. Your queen-size bedroom has a private four-piece bathroom. There is a small sitting room with a fireplace adjoining your bedroom. The hostess, Lydele, will serve breakfast in the intimacy of your own room, on the sun deck, or in the dining room. Just 12 minutes from the airport and downtown Vancouver. Bus service is nearby. $65.

Old English Bed and Breakfast 4

P. O. Box 86818, V7L 4L3
(604) 986-5069

This North Vancouver Bed and Breakfast is charm plus. Guests have a ground-level studio suite with queen bed, potbelly fireplace, TV, and patio. Beautifully decorated in old country style. Barb, the hostess, will leave food to prepare at guests' convenience, or they are invited to enjoy breakfast with the family. Only 15 minutes to downtown. $65.

Old English Bed and Breakfast 5

P. O. Box 86818, V7L 4L3
(604) 986-5069

Receive the royal treatment at Giselle's bed and breakfast in North Vancouver. This bed and breakfast is nestled on a very large lot that has a natural, parklike setting. Accommodations consist of three rooms, one with private bath and large Jacuzzi. Each room is equipped with TV and telephone. Giselle will bring coffee and the morning paper to start the day before breakfast is served. $65-75.

Pacific Bed and Breakfast Agency NVAN-1

701 Northwest 60th Street, Seattle, WA 98107
(206) 784-0539

NOTES: Credit cards accepted: A Master Card; B Visa; C American Express; D Discover Card; E Diner's Club; F Other; 2 Personal Checks accepted; 3 Lunch available; 4 Dinner available; 5 Open all year;

One acre of seclusion a short 10-minute ride over the Lions Gate Bridge from downtown. At the end of a dead-end street with a creek running through the award-winning English gardens and a fountain. This Tudor house is furnished with antiques with a distinctly British influence and offers a queen room with private bath, a twin room with shared bath, and two private cottages. Breakfast is served in the oversize kitchen around a big table and will surely include some special surprises and a different elegant setting every morning. German and French spoken. $85-105 Canadian.

Sue's Victorian Guest House

152 East 3rd, V7L 1E6
(604) 985-1523

This lovely, restored 1904 nonsmoking home is just four blocks from the harbor, seabus terminal, and Quay market. Centrally situated for restaurants, shops, and transportation. The decor is ideal for those who appreciate that loving-hand touch, Victorian soaker baths (no showers), and are happy to remove outdoor shoes at the door to help maintain cleanliness. Each room is individually keyed and offers a TV, phone, fan, and video player. Situated in the restaurant district. There is a guest refrigerator. Minimum stay is three nights in busy seasons; long-term stays encouraged. Two resident cats.

Host: Sue Chalmers
Rooms: 3 (1 PB; 2 SB) $55-60
Continental Breakfast
Credit Cards: B
Notes: 2 (deposit only), 5

Weston Lake Inn Bed and Breakfast

813 Beaver Point Road, Rural Route 1, V0S 1C0
(604) 653-4311

Nestled on a knoll of flowering trees and shrubs overlooking beautiful Weston Lake, this exquisite country bed and breakfast is a serene adult getaway. Down quilts, fresh bouquets, a fireside lounge, hot tub, wonderful breakfasts, and warm hospitality. Recommended in *Northwest Best Places*, the *Vancouver Sun*, and the *Seattle Times*. Salt Spring Island, near Victoria, has a mild climate, exceptional beauty, and a large population of artists and artisans.

Hosts: Susan Evans and Ted Harrison
Rooms: 3 (PB) $80-100
Full Breakfast
Credit Cards: A, B
Notes: 2, 5, 9, 10, 11, 12, 14

SIDNEY

Graham's Cedar House Bed and Breakfast

1825 Landsend Road, Rural Route 3, V8L 5J2
(604) 655-3699; FAX (604) 655-1422

Spectacular West Coast home on acreage where tall trees and magnificent ferns surround the house. Relish the peace and quiet, walk among the trees, or to the beach. Enjoy either the romantic executive suite or a one or two-bedroom apartment for up to six people. All rooms feature a private bath, private entrance, patio, deck, and TV. Breakfast is served at guests' convenience. Close to Butchart Gardens, Victoria, marinas, the U.S., and Canadian ferries.

Hosts: Dennis and Kay Graham
Rooms: 3 (PB) $65-85
Full Breakfast
Credit Cards: B
Notes: 2, 5, 9, 10, 12, 14

SOOKE

Ocean Wilderness

109 West Coast Road, Rural Route 2, V0S 1N0
(604) 646-2116

6 Pets welcome; 8 Children welcome; 9 Social drinking allowed; 10 Tennis available; 11 Swimming available; 12 Golf available; 13 Skiing available; 14 May be booked through travel agents.

This bed and breakfast features seven guest rooms on five wooded acres of oceanfront, with a breathtaking view of the Straits of Juan de Fuca, the Olympic Mountains, and forest. The original log house serves as a dining room and common area for the inn. The large, beautifully decorated guest rooms feature private baths, Persian carpets, and bed canopies in the new wing. A silver coffee service with a miniature vase of flowers is delivered to guest room doors with a gentle wake-up call. A full breakfast is served daily, and dinner can be arranged. The hot tub, tucked in a little Japanese gazebo, is a popular respite for weary vacationers. Book time for a private soak. Ocean wilderness is located 30 miles from Victoria on West Coast Road (Highway 14) and is open year-round. Book direct or through a travel agent.

Host: Marion Paine
Rooms: 7 (PB) $75-150 US
Full Breakfast
Credit Cards: A, B
Notes: 2, 4 (by arrangement), 5, 6 (by arrangement), 8 (by arrangement), 9, 12, 14

UCLUELET

Burley's

1078 Helen Road, Box 550, V0R 3A0
(604) 726-4444

A waterfront home on a small drive-to island at the harbor mouth, offering single, double, and queen, water or regular beds, and TV in friendly Ucluelet. Enjoy the open ocean, sandy beaches, lighthouse lookout, nature walks, charter fishing, diving, fisherman's wharves, whale watching and sightseeing cruises, or later, the exhilarating winter storms. A view from every window. No pets. Adult oriented. French Aussi.

Hosts: Ron Burley and Micheline Riley
Rooms: 6 (S4B) $40-50
Full Breakfast
Credit Cards: A, B
Notes: 5, 10, 11, 12

VANCOUVER

AB & C Bed and Breakfast Agency, Ltd.

4390 Frances Street, Vancouver, V5C 2R3
(604) 298-8815; FAX (604) 298-5917

Professional reservation service featuring modern cabins to well-appointed mansions and private homes. Guest rooms have single, twin, double, queen or kings beds. Only 15 minutes to most major attractions. Friendly hosts welcome guests.

Rooms: 135 (80 PB; 55 SB) $60-135 (CDN)
Full Breakfast
Credit Cards: A, B
Notes: 5, 8, 10, 11, 12, 13, 14

Kenya Court Guest House

2230 Cornwall Avenue, V6K 1B5
(604) 738-7085

Ocean-view suites on the waterfront, in a gracious heritage building minutes from downtown Vancouver. Across the street is Kitsilano Beach Park, a swimming beach with tennis courts. It's an easy walk to Granville Island, the planetarium, and interesting shops and restaurants. All the suites are large and tastefully furnished. Breakfast is served in a glass solarium with a spectacular view of English Bay.

Host: D. M. Williams
Suites: 4 (PB) $85-110
Full Breakfast
Credit Cards: F
Notes: 2, 5, 8 (over 12), 9, 10, 11, 12, 13

Pacific Bed and Breakfast Agency VAN-1

701 Northwest 60th Street, Seattle, WA 98107
(206) 784-0539

A gracious 1920 Colonial that offers guests two bedrooms, one with two twin beds, one with a double bed, and a shared bathroom. Enjoy the sun deck, garden, den, and private breakfast room. Take a walk down the

NOTES: Credit cards accepted: A Master Card; B Visa; C American Express; D Discover Card; E Diner's Club; F Other; 2 Personal Checks accepted; 3 Lunch available; 4 Dinner available; 5 Open all year;

quiet tree-lined street or take the bus to the many attractions in the area. The host is a longtime resident and is available to assist guests with sightseeing plans. $50-55 U.S.

Pacific Bed and Breakfast Agency VAN-2

701 Northwest 60th Street, Seattle, WA 98107
(206) 784-0539

With a view of Kitsilano Beach, the North Shore Mountains, English Bay, and downtown Vancouver, this guest house is in the best location for a peaceful, cozy getaway. This guest house features large, tastefully decorated rooms with king, queen, or twin beds, and private entrances. Breakfast may consist of gourmet coffees, juices, fruits, croissants, fresh breads, cereal, or for the hearty eaters eggs and bacon, served in a glass-enclosed solarium. $65-100 Canadian.

Pacific Bed and Breakfast Agency VAN-3

701 Northwest 60th Street, Seattle, WA 98107
(206) 784-0539

This Tudor house is furnished with antiques with a distinctly British influence and offers guests a guest room with a queen-size bed with a private bath, or one with twin and double beds, as well as two private cottages. Breakfast is served in the oversize kitchen and will include some special surprises and a different elegant setting every morning. Grouse Mountain and other attractions are nearby. $65-75 Canadian.

Pacific Bed and Breakfast Agency VAN-4

701 Northwest 60th Street, Seattle, WA 98107
(206) 784-0539

This cozy country heritage guest home features three private rooms with sitting area, cable TV, and private bath. Enjoy the full farm breakfasts in the morning and take a dip in the large outdoor heated pool or soak in the whirlpool. $40-55 U.S.

The West End Guest House

1362 Hard Street, V6E 1G2
(604) 681-2889; FAX (604) 688-8812

This heritage house was constructed in 1906 and was occupied by one of the city's first photographers. Today, the West End Guest House offers the informal ambience of a fine country inn, the amenities of a small luxury hotel, and the excitement of its surroundings, such as shopping on Robson Street, a walk in Stanley Park, a peak at the zoo, possibly a splash at the Whale Show, or a romantic gaze at a sunset on English Bay. Rooms include a bathroom, TV, telephone, off-street parking, bathrobes and slippers, full breakfast, use of two bikes, and a sun deck with wicker furniture where on a hot summer day iced tea is served. Sherry is provided year round in front of the fireplace.

Rooms: 7 (PB) $95-175
Full Breakfast
Credit Cards: A, B, C, D
Notes: 2, 5, 10, 11, 12, 13

VICTORIA

Battery Street Guest House

670 Battery Street, V8V 1E5
(604) 385-4632

This newly renovated guest house, built in 1898, offers bright, comfortable rooms centrally located within walking distance to downtown. The bed and breakfast is only one block from Beacon Hill Park and the ocean. A full, hearty breakfast is served by a Dutch hostess.

6 Pets welcome; 8 Children welcome; 9 Social drinking allowed; 10 Tennis available; 11 Swimming available; 12 Golf available; 13 Skiing available; 14 May be booked through travel agents.

Host: Pamela Verduyn
Rooms: 6 (2 PB; 4 SB) $35-55
Full Breakfast
Credit Cards: None
Notes: 2, 5, 8, 10

The Beaconsfield Inn

998 Humboldt Street, V8V 2Z8
(604) 384-4044

Experience Victoria's most highly
acclaimed inn, only four blocks from the
inner harbor and downtown shopping
attractions. Twelve luxurious rooms, featuring antique furnishings, goosedown
comforters, crackling fireplaces and private
bathrooms with claw foot or Jacuzzi tubs.
Innkeeper's gourmet breakfast and evening
social hour served complimentary. Rated
three stars by *Northwest Best Places*, and
chosen by *Special Places* and *Best Places
to Kiss*. A dazzling example of the bed and
breakfast experience. "Simply the finest
accommodations in Victoria."

Host: Bill McKechnie, owner
Rooms: 12 (PB) $80-198
Full Breakfast
Credit Cards: A, B
Notes: 2, 5, 8, 9, 10, 11, 12, 14

Elk Lake Lodge Bed and Breakfast

5259 Pat Bay Highway, Route 17, V8Y 1S8
(604) 658-8879

Originally built in 1910 as a monastery and
chapel, Elk Lake Lodge has been maintained as a bed and breakfast since 1975.
Guests are warmly welcomed and made
comfortable in large bedrooms, a beautiful
sitting room, outdoor hot tub and back
patio. The Elk Lake area offers a public
beach, picnic areas, walking and biking
paths, fishing and boating areas and is only
10 minutes from downtown Victoria.
Accommodations also include king and
queen-size beds, fresh flowers, and delicious breakfasts.

Hosts: Marty and Ivan Musar
Rooms: 5 (3 PB; 2 SB) $75-90

Full Breakfast
Credit Cards: A, B
Notes: 5, 9, 10, 11, 12, 14

Garden City Bed and Breakfast Reservation Service

660 Jones Terrace, V82 2L7
(604) 479-1986; FAX (604) 479-9999

No reservations fee charged. Catering to
every need whether on vacation, honeymoon or special itinerary. Doreen's attention to detail ensures the best possible
accommodations in Victoria, or the many
locations on Vancouver Island. Majestic
heritage homes, cozy, demure cottages, and
seaside views are examples of the many
choices available. Family-owned since
1985.

Host: M. Doreen Wensley
Rooms: 150 (70 PB; 80 SB) $55-190
Full Breakfast
Credit Cards: A, B, C, E
Notes: 5, 6, 8, 10, 11, 12, 13, 14

Pacific Bed and Breakfast Agency VIC-A

701 Northwest 60th Street, Seattle, WA 98107
(206) 784-0539

A turn-of-the-century home one block to
the beach and a grand beach walk. It offers
three bedrooms, one with a private bath and
fireplace, favorite with honeymooners. The
spacious livingroom and dining room welcomes guests to sit back and relax with
German hostess. She will fix a memorable
breakfast. Discover the wonderful Beacon
Hill Park close by. On a bus line. $60-75
Canadian.

Pacific Bed and Breakfast Agency VIC-B

701 NW 60th Street, Seattle, WA 98107
(206) 784-0539

NOTES: Credit cards accepted: A Master Card; B Visa; C American Express; D Discover Card; E Diner's Club; F Other; 2 Personal Checks accepted; 3 Lunch available; 4 Dinner available; 5 Open all year;

An elegant, refined small inn with ten bedrooms. Only two blocks to the harbor and within walking distance of everything. All rooms have private baths and decks. The breakfasts are either served to you in the dining room or in your own room. Ideal for a honeymoon, anniversary, or that special weekend. Unequalled comfort and charm with original art by the premier artists of Victoria. $100-160 Canadian.

Pacific Bed and Breakfast Agency VIC-C

701 Northwest 60th Street, Seattle, WA 98107
(206) 784-0539

Cordova Bay. Here is luxury at a modest cost. This lodge features oversize rooms with private baths, refrigerators, and TV. Some rooms have kitchenettes. This residential area is 15 minutes from Victoria and close to Butchart Gardens, airport, and ferries. A delicious full breakfast is served. Golfing, skiing, water skiing, fresh and salt water fishing, swimming, and walking are just some of the activities waiting. $55-75 Canadian.

Pacific Bed and Breakfast Agency VIC-D

701 Northwest 60th Street, Seattle, WA 98107
(206) 784-0539

Lakefront mansion. Turn-of-the-century mansion on 17 acres with frontage on a large lake. Built by prominent architect Samuel McClure, this special guest home features waterfront garden paths to enjoy while watching the graceful swans. Tennis court and billiard room with a magnificent antique table. Visit the famous Forest Open Air Museum. Three distinctively decorated guest rooms share a bath. $135 and up (CDN).

Pacific Bed and Breakfast Agency VIC-F

701 Northwest 60th Street, Seattle, WA 98107
(206) 784-0539

An exceptional house situated on half an acre overlooking Portage Inlet. This house is three miles from the inner harbor and is furnished with antiques. Many views are available in this guest home featuring five bedrooms. Two rooms have private balconies, and all rooms have private baths. A sumptuous gourmet breakfast is provided to start the day's activities. $80-100 Canadian.

Pacific Bed and Breakfast Agency VIC-2

701 Northwest 60th Street, Seattle, WA 98107
(206) 784-0539

The hostess of this wonderful bed and breakfast is dedicated to her guests and shows this dedication in everything she does, from the welcome drink to the delicious breakfasts. This two-story house, built in 1885, features a high ceiling, fireplaces, charm, and fine antiques. One room has a private bath, the others share a bath. Breakfast will be served on fine china in the formal dining room. $65-100.

Pacific Bed and Breakfast Agency VIC-4

701 Northwest 60th Street, Seattle, WA 98107
(206) 784-0539

This guest home was built in 1899. It is now restored and offers three bedrooms with shared bath. Antiques fill the house and complement the original woodwork fireplaces, floors, and fittings. A memorable, full breakfast changes from day to day. $70-80 Canadian.

6 Pets welcome; 8 Children welcome; 9 Social drinking allowed; 10 Tennis available; 11 Swimming available; 12 Golf available; 13 Skiing available; 14 May be booked through travel agents.

Portage Inlet House Bed and Breakfast

993 Portage Road, V8Z 1K9
(604) 479-4594

A delightful waterfront home just 10 minutes from city centre. Situated on an acre that overlooks beautiful Portage Inlet. Because Portage Inlet House does not use any insecticides, there is a multitude of birds and animals that live within the "Acre of Paradise." Organic food served. Guest rooms feature private baths, TV, private entrances, and parking spots. The inn is licensed and insured; check-in time is 3 until 6 P.M. Children welcome. There is a seven day cancellation policy.

Hosts: Jim and Pat Baillie
Rooms: 4 (3 PB; 2 SB) $55-95
Full Breakfast
Credit Cards: A, B, E
Notes: 5, 8, 9, 10, 11, 12, 14

Rose Cottage

3059 Washington Avenue, V9A 1P7
(604) 381-5985

Rose Cottage is a large, attractive 1912 Victorian-style home situated on a quiet street. Robert and Shelley work very hard to create a warm, fun, and informal atmosphere with lots of sharing between guests and hosts. Shelley serves a four-course breakfast that sustains one all morning. Robert has sailed and traveled extensively; he loves stimulating conversation over breakfast or on the porch watching a sunset. Their information about the area will guide guests to the best of Victoria.

Hosts: Robert and Shelley Bishop
Rooms: 3 (S2B) $55-75 Canadian
Full Breakfast
Credit Cards: A, B
Notes: 2, 5, 8, 9, 10, 11, 12, 14

Wellington Bed and Breakfast

66 Wellington Avenue, V8V 4H5
(604) 383-5976

Situated less than a block from the scenic Pacific Ocean bordered by a panoramic walkway, three blocks from beautiful Beacon Hill Park, this 1912 inn offers you a taste of true Victorian hospitality. All rooms have private baths, walk-in closets, large windows, king or queen beds, and are wonderfully appointed. The quiet, tree-lined street allows for a restful sleep, and the breakfasts are a delight.

Hosts: Inge and Sue Ranzinger
Rooms: 3 (PB) $60-75 US
Full Breakfast
Credit Cards: A
Notes: 2, 5, 9, 10, 11, 12, 14

WEST VANCOUVER

Beachside Bed and Breakfast

4208 Evergreen Avenue, V7V 1H1
(604) 922-7773; (800) 563-3311
FAX (604) 926-8073

Stay in a quiet, beautiful waterfront home in one of the finest areas in Vancouver. A lovely beach is at the doorstep. Situated just minutes from downtown, Stanley Park, Horsehoe Bay ferries, and North Shore attractions. Its southern exposure affords a panoramic view of the city, harbor, and Alaska Cruise ships. A hearty home-baked breakfast is served in the seaside dining room. Close to fishing, sailing, wilderness hiking, skiing, antiques, shopping, and excellent restaurants.

Hosts: Gordon and Joan Gibbs
Rooms: 3 (PB) $95-150 Canadian
Full Breakfast
Credit Cards: A, B
Notes: 2, 5, 9, 10, 11, 12, 13, 14

NOTES: Credit cards accepted: A Master Card; B Visa; C American Express; D Discover Card; E Diner's Club; F Other; 2 Personal Checks accepted; 3 Lunch available; 4 Dinner available; 5 Open all year;

Manitoba

RICHER

Geppetto

Bed and Breakfast of Manitoba
533 Sprague Street, R3G 2R9
(204) 783-9797

Enjoy your stay in a quiet and attractive
modern home with country-style hospitality. Outdoor activities include bird-watching, horseshoes, fishing in stocked trout
pond, 27-hole golfing. Situated 45 minutes
from Falcon Lake Beach; 25 minutes from
Steinbach shopping center and Mennonite
Heritage Village. $45.

THOMPSON

Anna's Bed and Breakfast

Bed and Breakfast of Manitoba
533 Sprague Street, R3G 2R9
(204) 783-9797

Open all year, Anna and Robert invite
guests to share their comfortable home and
warm Dutch hospitality. Pickup at airport
and train station. Completely private quarters and private bath. Come and enjoy the
heart of the north! $30-45.

WINNIPEG

Alego

Bed and Breakfast of Manitoba
533 Sprague Street, R3G 2R9
(204) 783-9797

Walk in Fraser's Grove Park along the Red
River. Frequent bus service, restaurants,
and shopping nearby. Convenient to Bird's
Hill Park, Rainbow Stage, beaches, and
museums. Full breakfast. $30-40.

Andrews

Bed and Breakfast of Manitoba
533 Sprague Street, R3G 2R9
(204) 783-9797

Relax in the privacy of the rustic sitting
room beside the fireplace with country and
western stereo music, VCR, and TV. Enjoy
breakfast and summer evenings in the gazebo, overlooking Assiniboine River in this
beautiful neighborhood near downtown.
Close to jogging path, hospitals, and restaurants. Quick access to the airport, Via Rail,
and bus depot. $30-55.

Bannerman East

Bed and Breakfast of Manitoba
533 Sprague Street, R3G 2R9
(204) 783-9797

Come and enjoy this lovely Georgian
home, evening tea, quiet walks in St. Johns
Park or along the Red River. Close to
Seven Oaks Museum, planetarium, concert
hall, and Rainbow Stage. $40.

Belanger

Bed and Breakfast of Manitoba
533 Sprague Street, R3G 2R9
(204) 783-9797

Enjoy the relaxing atmosphere in this special home built in 1900. Sitting room adjacent to guest bedroom. Can accommodate a
family of four. $40.

6 Pets welcome; 8 Children welcome; 9 Social drinking allowed; 10 Tennis available; 11 Swimming available; 12 Golf available; 13 Skiing available; 14 May be booked through travel agents.

Brite Oakes
533 Sprague Street, R3G 2R9
(204) 783-9797

Relax in this spacious home, located on park-like grounds near the Red River. Close to St. Vital Park, the University of Manitoba, good restaurants, and the St. Vital Shopping Center. Easy access to The Mint, St. Boniface, and downtown. English, French and Polish spoken.

Drenker
Bed and Breakfast of Manitoba
533 Sprague Street, R3G 2R9
(204) 783-9797

Enjoy a private and pleasant stay in this quiet, neat home. Situated in old St. Boniface, it is within a short walking distance of the Forks, the St. Boniface Hospital, and downtown. Near museum, Manitoba Theatre Centre, concert hall, and paddlewheel boats. $45.

Ellie
Bed and Breakfast of Manitoba
533 Sprague Street, R3G 2R9
(204) 783-9797

This downtown accommodation in a peaceful neighborhood is near good bus service, two major hospitals, the zoo, convention center, concert hall, museums, Theatre Centre, planetarium, the Forks, bus depot, and Via Rail. $45-47.

Fillion
Bed and Breakfast of Manitoba
533 Sprague Street, R3G 2R9
(204) 783-9797

Situated in a nice community setting close to the Trans-Canada Highway city route. Nearby attractions include the mint, St. Vital Mall, Fun Mountain Waterslide, Tinkertown, outdoor pool, and bicycle path. $40.

Hawchuk
Bed and Breakfast of Manitoba
533 Sprague Street, R3G 2R9
(204) 783-9797

Situated on the banks of the Red River, this beautiful Tudor home has English gardens and a riverbank walkway. Top off the day with a paddlewheel boat dinner cruise. English, German, and French spoken. For an additional charge, a full-course dinner is available. $69.

Hillman
Bed and Breakfast of Manitoba
533 Sprague Street, R3G 2R9
(204) 783-9797

Cozy private sitting room, full breakfast of guests' choice. Situated downtown, close to bus route, airport, Polo Park, planetarium, concert hall, and Theatre Centre. $45.

Hillside Beach Resort
Bed and Breakfast of Manitoba
533 Sprague Street, R3G 2R9
(204) 783-9797

A beautiful resort area to "get away from it all" summer or winter. Come for the weekend. Winter cross-country skiing, summer water skiing, boating, fishing, beaching, cycling, evening walks, or just relaxing.

Johnson
Bed and Breakfast of Manitoba
533 Sprague Street, R3G 2R9
(204) 783-9797

Situated in a quiet residential area with a very private yard for sunbathing. Private kitchen available. near two public swimming pools, Assiniboia Downs Racetrack, shopping centers, and Living Prairie Museum. Children welcome. $40.

NOTES: Credit cards accepted: A Master Card; B Visa; C American Express; D Discover Card; E Diners Club; F Other; 2 Personal Checks accepted; 3 Lunch available; 4 Dinner available; 5 Open all year;

McCormack

Bed and Breakfast of Manitoba
533 Sprague Street, R3G 2R9
(204) 783-9797

Come for a relaxing stay in this quiet, quaint, and cozy home. Guests can enjoy use of the livingroom and TV. In Ft. Garry near the Pembina Highway, there is easy access to excellent city transit service to downtown and the University of Manitoba. Near golf course, Crescent Park, and Ft. Whyte Nature Center.

Narvey

Bed and Breakfast of Manitoba
533 Sprague Street, R3G 2R9
(204) 783-9797

This quiet, attractive, comfortable home in the River Heights area offers a family room, garden, and good hospitality. Excellent bus service city-wide. Close to downtown, Assinboine Park and Zoo, the Forks, Grant Park, and Polo Park shopping malls. $32-42

Paulley

Bed and Breakfast of Manitoba
533 Sprague Street, R3G 2R9
(204) 783-9797

Quiet, comfortable, and relaxing, and within walking distance of the Convention Center, Manitoba Archives, tourist bureau, shopping, direct bus route to the Via Rail, the historic Forks site, and three hospitals. A mere one block south of the Trans-Canadian Highway. $30-40.

Preweda

Bed and Breakfast of Manitoba
533 Sprague Street, R3G 2R9
(204) 783-9797

Enjoy complete privacy in lower level with a spacious and attractive sitting lounge. Excellent transit service and public library. Quick access to the Mint, the Forks, downtown, Osborne Village, and St. Boniface Hospital. $45.

Southern Rose Guest House

Bed and Breakfast of Manitoba
533 Sprague Street, R3G 2R9
(204) 783-9797

Experience the charm of decades past with a touch of southern hospitality. Enjoy morning breakfast and a newspaper in the formal dining room or on the wraparound cedar sun deck. Boasting a red brick exterior, warm woods, burnished brass trim, leaded glass a flickering fireplace and live greenery. Play horseshoes or relax in a redwood hot tub. Close to Polo Park shopping mall, The Forks, Casino, restaurants, zoo, airport, the Winnipeg convention center and bicycle routes. Guest pick-up for an additional charge. $30-45.

Selci

Bed and Breakfast of Manitoba
533 Sprague Street, R3G 2R9
(204) 783-9797

Very private facilities in this private home can accommodate a family of four. A warm welcome to guests, and quick access to the Trans-Canada Highway. $30-40.

Siemens

Bed and Breakfast of Manitoba
533 Sprague Street, R3G 2R9
(204) 783-9797

Warm hospitality and quiet relaxation! Can accommodate a family of five. Close to the express bus route, Unicity Mall, Assiniboina Downs, shopping, restaurants, and recreation. $38-40.

6 Pets welcome; 8 Children welcome; 9 Social drinking allowed; 10 Tennis available; 11 Swimming available; 12 Golf available; 13 Skiing available; 14 May be booked through travel agents.

Stony Mountain: The Golden Pine Log Cabin

Bed and Breakfast of Manitoba
533 Sprague Street, R3G 2R9
(204) 783-9797

For a taste of the country, for quiet relaxation in rustic surroundings, this is the place. These adventurous hosts with multiple interests will make every stay unforgettable. Quick access to beaches, airport, Polo Park and Garden City shopping. Visit the annual folk festival and Lower Ft. Garry. $30-40.

Tidmarsh

Bed and Breakfast of Manitoba
533 Sprague Street, R3G 2R9
(204) 783-9797

This attractive older home is situated in the quiet, tree-lined River Heights area. Guest sitting room on mezzanine floor with tea and coffee making facilities. Choose breakfast from an ample menu. Close to Polo Park shopping center, the Forks, and casino. Enjoy the English-style hospitality. $40-42.

Zonneveld

Bed and Breakfast of Manitoba
533 Sprague Street, R3G 2R9
(204) 783-9797

Enjoy a relaxed atmosphere in this unique three-story home with a beautiful oak interior. Excellent transit service, near downtown, will pick up at the airport. Quick access to the Forks, zoo, hospital, and Dainavert museum. $30-40.

NOTES: Credit cards accepted: A Master Card; B Visa; C American Express; D Discover Card; E Diners Club; F Other; 2 Personal Checks accepted; 3 Lunch available; 4 Dinner available; 5 Open all year;

New Brunswick

The Mariner's Inn

Mawhinney Cove Road, Box 645, Rural Route 2,
  EOG2HO
(506) 659-2619

Experience the Bay of Fundy feeling at The Mariner's Inn. Relax and make yourself at home in one of its nine tastefully appointed rooms, with private bath. From the cedar deck there is an inspiring view of the Bay of Fundy, one of the richest marine environments in the world. Pamper yourself with sauteed-in-butter Chance Harbor scallops, or baked Atlantic salmon. Like memories of The Mariner's Inn, guests will savor the taste for a long time.

Hosts: Matthew and Valerie Mawhinney
Rooms: 9 (PB) $55-75
Continental Breakfast
Credit Cards: A, B
Notes: 4, 8, 9

SACKVILLE

The Different Drummer

P. O. Box 188, 82 West Main Street, E0A 3C0
(506) 536-1291

Welcome to The Different Drummer Bed and Breakfast. Here guests can enjoy the comforts and conveniences of modern living in a restful and homey atmosphere. Attractive bedrooms are furnished much as they would have been at the turn of the century, and they all have private baths. In the large parlor and adjacent sun room, guests can chat, browse through a well-stocked library, watch color TV, or just relax. A continental breakfast is served each morning; enjoy home-baked bread, muffins, local honey, freshly ground coffee, and berries in season.

Hosts: Georgette and Richard Hanrahan
Rooms: 8 (PB) $48-51

The Different Drummer

Expanded Continental Breakfast
Credit Cards: A, B
Notes: 5, 8, 9, 10, 11, 12, 13

ST. ANDREWS

Pansy Patch

59 Carleton Street, EOG 2XO
(506) 529-3834

A New Brunswick architectural landmark, Pansy Patch is a comfortable, inviting bed and breakfast combined with an antique

6 Pets welcome; 8 Children welcome; 9 Social drinking allowed; 10 Tennis available; 11 Swimming available; 12 Golf available; 13 Skiing available; 14 May be booked through travel agents.

shop and rare out-of-print book shop. The
four guest rooms, tastefully furnished with
antiques, look out over the terraced gardens
toward the Bay of Fundy. In addition to
memorable breakfasts, evening meals are
available with advance notice. The delightful village of St. Andrews is one of the
most picturesque in the Maritimes.

Host: Kathleen Lazare
Rooms: 4 (S2B) $75 (Canadian)
Full Breakfast
Credit Cards: A, B, C
Notes: 2, 4, 9, 10, 11, 12, 14

Nova Scotia

Fairfield Farm Inn

10 Main Street, Highway 1 West, B0S 1P0
(902) 825-6989

A Three Star inn, this Annapolis Valley
farmhouse has been completely restored
and furnished in period antiques to enhance
its original charm. The five bedrooms feature king or queen-size beds and ensuite
private bathrooms. Bordered by the
Annapolis River and Slocum Brook, the
property offers excellent bird watching and
walking trails. Museums, recreational facilities, boutiques, and restaurants are only a
short walk from Fairfield Farm. The inn is
situated on a 75-acre fruit and vegetable
farm, famous for luscious cantaloupes.

Hosts: Richard and Shae Griffith
Rooms: 5 (PB) $50-65 Canadian
Full Breakfast or Continental Breakfast
Credit Cards: A, B, C
Notes: 3, 5, 9, 10, 11, 12, 13, 14

Confederation Farm

RR 3, B0M 150
(902) 254-3057

Make a country visit Nova Scotia-style at
Confederation Farm. Situated five miles
west of Parrsboro on Highway 209, guests
can enjoy the beach, clam digging, and the
historic harbor of Diligent River. Modern
accommodations in addition to homemade
bread and seafood. Special rates for children. Come relax in a friendly haven.
Visitors love the beauty of the village.

Hosts: Mr. and Mrs. Robert Salter
Rooms: 4 (SB) $40
Full Breakfast
Credit Cards: None (cash accepted)
Notes: None

6 Pets welcome; 8 Children welcome; 9 Social drinking allowed; 10 Tennis available; 11 Swimming available;
12 Golf available; 13 Skiing available; 14 May be booked through travel agents.

Ontario

BAYSVILLE

Burton's Bed and Breakfast
Box 70, P0B 1A0
(705) 767-3616

A beautiful four-generation brick home, situated in the heart of picturesque Baysville near the Muskoka River. The area features antique and crafts shops, Algonquin Park, and a Muskoka artisan studio tour each September.

Hosts: Robert and Shirley Burton
Rooms: 3 (SB) $40-50
Full Breakfast
Credit Cards: None
Notes: None

BRACEBRIDGE

Century House
Bed and Breakfast
155 Dill Street, P1L 1E5
(705) 645-9903

The hosts invite you to this charming, air-conditioned, restored century-old home in the province's premier recreational lake district, a two-hour drive from Toronto. The breakfasts are creative and generous. Waffles with local maple syrup are a specialty. Century House is close to shopping, beaches, and many craft studios and galleries. Enjoy the sparkling lakes, fall colors, studio tours, and winter cross-country skiing. An aloof cat and a friendly dog are residents here.

Hosts: Norman Yan and Sandy Yudin-Yan
Rooms: 3 (SB) $45-50 Canadian
Full Breakfast
Credit Cards: None
Notes: 2, 5, 7 (restricted), 8, 10, 11, 12, 13

Riverview
Bed and Breakfast
420 Beaumont Drive, Rural Route 4, P1L 1X2
(705) 645-4022

Spacious old farmhouse on more than three acres overlooking the Muskoka River. Close to all seasonal amenities of the district. Cross-country skiing from the door all winter. Open year-round.

Hosts: Ruth and Len Yeo
Rooms: 3 (SB) $25 per person
Continental Breakfast
Credit Cards: None
Notes: 13 (XC)

Treasured Moments
Bed and Breakfast
74 Toronto Street, Box 1567, P1L 1V6
(705) 645-7282

Large, two-story turn of the century home located less than blocks from the Muskoka River and downtown Bracebridge. Easy access to the delights of Muskoka.

Hosts: Joyce and Wayne Campbell
Rooms: 3 (SB) $35-50
Full Breakfast
Credit Cards: None
Notes: None

ELMIRA

Teddy Bear
Bed and Breakfast Inn
Rural Route 1, N3B 2Z1
(519) 669-2379

Relax and enjoy the hospitality of this gracious and elegant inn, enhanced with Canadiana and quilts. In the Old Order Mennonite countryside close to St. Jacobs, Kitchener-Waterloo's markets, museums, Stratford, Elora, Fergus, and Guelph. Spacious deluxe bedrooms, private or shared bathrooms, TV lounge, craft shop. Cross-country skiing, golf, boating, hiking, tours, and much more are nearby. Sumptuous continental breakfast, or full breakfast on request. Seminar and private dining facilities are available.

Hosts: Vivian and Gerrie Smith
Rooms: 3 (1 PB; 2 SB) $45-65
Continental or Full Breakfast
Credit Cards: A, B, C
Notes: 2, 4, 5, 8, 12, 13

GRAVENHURST

Allen's Bed and Breakfast

581 David Street East, P1P 1H9
(705) 687-7368

Comfortable home on a quiet street featuring central heat and air, TV sitting room, and large screened porch with access to the garden. Close to Gull Lake Park, beach, bus and railway station, downtown shopping, summer theater, Bethune Memorial House, and RMS Segwun cruises. Open May through Thanksgiving; winter by reservation.

Host: Karen Allen
Rooms: 3 (1 PB; 2 SB) $35-50
Full Breakfast
Credit Cards: None
Notes: None

Cunningham's Bed and Breakfast

175 Clairmont Road, P1P 1H9
(705) 687-4511

Country living in town. Modern two-story home on a cul-de-sac, electrically heated, family room with cable TV. Walk to RMS

Segwun, Bethune House, Opera House, restaurants, shops, bus, train, and parks. Cross-country skiing nearby. No pets. Open May through October. Winter by chance.

Hosts: Leona (Lee) and David Cunningham
Rooms: 3 (SB) $30-50
Full Breakfast
Credit Cards: None
Notes: 13 (XC)

Huelands Bed and Breakfast

191 Royal Street, P1P 1T6
(705) 687-4493

This three-story brick home is only a short walk to downtown shopping, theaters, Bethune House, Gull Lake Park, RMS Segwun cruises, and the bus and train station. Open may through October. Other months by reservation.

Host: Mary Montgomery
Rooms: 3 (SB) $25-40
Full Breakfast
Credit Cards: None
Notes: None

Milnes' Bed and Breakfast

270 Hotchkiss Street, M1P 1H7
(705) 687-4395

Two-story home on a shady street. Centrally located close to shops, restaurants, and all Gravenhurst attractions. No pets.

Hosts: Marg and John Milne
Rooms: 3 (SB) $25-40
Full Breakfast
Credit Cards: None
Notes: None

HUNTSVILLE

Dee Dee's Bed and Breakfast

832 Riverlea Road, Rural Route 2, P0A 1K0
(705) 789-1497

6 Pets welcome; 8 Children welcome; 9 Social drinking allowed; 10 Tennis available; 11 Swimming available; 12 Golf available; 13 Skiing available; 14 May be booked through travel agents.

Spacious modern home in the rolling countryside on the Muskoka River. Only a short drive from all of Huntsville's year-round amenities. Features a patio dock, swimming, diving, fishing, free boating, horseshoes, pool table, workout room, and TV. Dine in the Muskoka Room. No pets.

Host: Dolores Bartlett
Rooms: 2 (SB) $40-55
Full Breakfast
Credit Cards: None
Notes: 11

LONDON

Chiron House

398 Piccadilly Street, N6A 1S7
(519) 673-6878

Recall the comfort and elegance of an earlier time in this turn-of-the-century home, lovingly maintained and furnished in period style with modern amenities discreetly added. Within walking distance of theater, restaurants, and shopping. Convenient to University of Western Ontario and airport. Suite with whirlpool available. Visa accepted. $44-55.

Clermont Place

679 Clermont Avenue, N5X 1N3
(519) 672-0767
FAX (519) 672-2445

A modern home, situated in a park like setting with an outdoor pool. Central heat and air conditioning. Three attractive rooms and a four-piece bath. A full Canadian breakfast is served in the dining room or by the pool. Tennis courts are located less than a block away, and a public golf course rests only five minutes away. Close to the University of Western Ontario and University Hospital in North East London.

Hosts: Doug and Jacki McAndless
Rooms: 3 (SB) $40-45
Full Breakfast
Credit Cards: B
Notes: 3, 4, ,5 ,9, 10, 12, 14

NEW HAMBURG

The Waterlot

17 Huron Street, N0B 2G0
(519) 662-2020

The Waterlot opened in the fall of 1974, and from the onset it has been committed to quality of ambience and service. Two large and comfortably appointed rooms share a memorable marbled shower, bidet, water closet, wet vanity, and sitting area. The inn is one of Ontario's finest dining establishments. This bed and breakfast offers quality and service in a memorable lodging.

Rooms: 3 (1 PB; 2 SB) $65-85
Continental Breakfast
Credit Cards: A, B, C
Notes: 2, 3, 4, 5, 9, 10, 11, 12, 13

OTTAWA

Ottawa Bed and Breakfast

488 Cooper Street, K1R 5H9
(613) 563-0161

Travelers to Ottawa have the opportunity to participate in the bed and breakfast style of accommodation like nowhere else. This professional reservation service offers an economical alternative to run-of-the-mill hotels and motels. The hosts are residents who are happy to meet you, share their comfortable home, and provide you with helpful advice about our beautiful city. City stays feature stately older homes, well maintained, with large air-conditioned rooms. These homes are furnished with antiques and boast lovely gardens and patios. In the suburbs experience homes featuring private baths, in-ground swimming pool and use of recreation facilities. Our country home offers restored structures, built in 1867 on a 150 acre farm. Rates include, single, $40; double, $50; en suite, $64; and triple, $70. All amounts shown are based on Canadian currency.

NOTES: Credit cards accepted: A Master Card; B Visa; C American Express; D Discover Card; E Diner's Club; F Other; 2 Personal Checks accepted; 3 Lunch available; 4 Dinner available; 5 Open all year;

Constance House
Bed and Breakfast

62 Sweetland Avenue, K1N 7T6
(613) 235-8888

Constance House is a prime example of modest (1895) Victorian scale housing. The original intent was to provide warmth and comfort for family living. Today, after an extensive award-winning renovation, it once again exudes those much desired qualities, offering them to travelers from around the world. With a little help from your hosts, Esther and Nickolas, your visit to Ottawa will be enjoyable and truly memorable.

Host: Esther M. Peterson
Rooms: 4 (1 PB; 3 SB) $52-90
Full or Continental Breakfast
Credit Cards: A, B, C, E,
Notes: 2, 5, 8, 9, 10, 11, 12, 13

Gasthaus Switzerland Inn

89 Daly Avenue, K1N 6E6
(613) 237-0335; (800) 267-8788
FAX (613) 594-3327

Unique, traditional Swiss hospitality in the heart of Canada's capital. Enjoy a friendly Swiss breakfast in this bed and breakfast which boasts 21 rooms, each with private bath, central air conditioning, TV, and telephone. Limited free parking. AAA approved.

Hosts: Josef and Sabina Sauter
Rooms: 25 (21 PB; 4 SB) $64-88
Full Breakfast
Credit Cards: A, B, C, E
Notes: 5, 9, 10, 11, 12, 13, 14

Rideau View Inn

177 Frank Street, K2P 0X4
(613) 236-9309; (800) 268-2082
FAX (613) 231-6842

This inn is a large Edwardian home with seven well-appointed guest rooms furnished in that period. Though situated on a quiet street, it is within easy walking distance of all major attractions, shops, and fine restaurants. Guests are encouraged to enjoy the home, take a stroll along the famous Rideau Canal, or play tennis on nearby public courts. A hearty breakfast is provided each morning to help you on your way.

Host: George Hartsgrove
Rooms: 7 (SB) $58-66
Full Breakfast
Credit Cards: A, B, C, F
Notes: 5, 8, 10, 13, 14

OWEN SOUND

Sunset Farms
Bed and Breakfast

Rural Route 6, N4K 5N8
(519) 371-4559

This is the seventh year of welcoming guests to this large and unique home, which reflects an early Canadian farmhouse. Features include an open Quebec-type kitchen with antique brick floor and cozy wood stove. Comfortably furnished with antiques, attractive decor, and friendly atmosphere, offering a quiet respite from city life. Situated in the heartland of Grey and Bruce Counties, ideally situated for day trips throughout the Georgian Bay and Tobermory areas. The nearby Beaver Valley boasts some of the most spectacular fall colors in Ontario. Enjoy a complimentary evening beverage. Fresh, homemade garden treats and breads at breakfast. An adorable dog and friendly cat complete the scene. Reservations recommended.

Hosts: Bill and Celie Moses
Rooms: 4 (SB) $45-60
Full Breakfast
Credit Cards: None
Notes: 5, 8, 9, 10, 11, 12, 13

PORT SYDNEY

Stone Cottage

Rural Route 1, P0B 1L0
(705) 385-3547

6 Pets welcome; 8 Children welcome; 9 Social drinking allowed; 10 Tennis available; 11 Swimming available; 12 Golf available; 13 Skiing available; 14 May be booked through travel agents.

Restored century home on 30 acres of pine forest on the North Muskoka River. Decorated and furnished in Canadiana. Features swimming, boating, fishing, and fun-golf on the property; cross-country skiing in winter. Just minutes from live theater, Pioneer Village, and boat cruises.

Hosts: Joanne and Bill Chalmers
Rooms: 3 (SB) $35-60
Full Breakfast
Credit Cards: None
Notes: 8 (over 10), 11, 12, 13

ROCKPORT

The Houseboat "Amaryllis" Bed and Breakfast

Box C-10, K0E 1V0
(613) 659-3513

Located between Gananoque and Brockville on 1,000 Islands Parkway, the 100-foot, double-deck houseboat "Amaryllis" is situated on its own island in the middle of the 1,000 Islands region. Originally built in 1920 as a private hunting and fishing lodge to float around the St. Lawrence and Rideau Rivers, it has a unique atmosphere of comfort and relaxation. Available for small groups, seminars and meetings, as well, gourmet meals are available for overnight guests.

Hosts: Pieter and Karin Bergen
Rooms: 4 (PB) $75-105
Full and Continental Breakfast
Credit Cards: None
Notes: 2, 3, 4, 8, 9, 10, 11, 12

ST. JACOBS

Jakobstettel Guest House, Inc.

16 Isabella Street, N0B 2N0
(519) 664-2208; FAX (519) 664-1326

Turn-of-the-century estate Victorian home, completely renovated. Has 12 individually decorated guest rooms with private baths. Library, lounge for all guests, and open kitchen all day and evening for coffee, tea,

juice, and cookies. Outdoor pool, tennis court, horseshoe pits, bikes, and walking trail. Within a few blocks of more than 80 retail shops, this is a shopper's delight.

Host: Elle Brubaeker
Rooms: 12 (PB) $105-150
Continental Breakfast
Credit Cards: A, B, C
Notes: 2, 3 (by arrangement), 4 (by arrangement, for groups), 5, 8, 10, 11, 14

TORONTO

Downtown Toronto Association of Bed and Breakfast Guesthouses

P.O. Box 190, Station B, M5T 2W1
(416) 690-1724
FAX (416) 690-5730

Toronto's oldest professional booking service representing private homes. All hosts are active in the arts or hospitality industry, and proudly feature distinctive homes in great locations, with access to 24-hour transit. Full gourmet breakfasts are provided, with special requests cheerfully accommodated. All homes are nonsmoking. Rates: $45-75. A $10 surcharge for one-night stays.

VANKOUGHNET

Heron Blue Bed and Breakfast

Rural Route 3, Bracebridge, P1L 1X1
(705) 645-2746

Modern two-story home in a private country setting overlooking a small pond. Cross-country skiing, walking trails, and a river nearby. Only a 30-minute drive to Minden or Bracebridge. No pets.

Hosts: Catherine and Robert Elliott
Rooms: 2 (SB) $35-45
Full Breakfast
Credit Cards: None
Notes: 13 (XC)

NOTES: Credit cards accepted: A Master Card; B Visa; C American Express; D Discover Card; E Diner's Club; F Other; 2 Personal Checks accepted; 3 Lunch available; 4 Dinner available; 5 Open all year;

Prince Edward Island

CHARLOTTETOWN

An Island Rose
285 Kinlock Road, Rural Route 1, C1A 7J6
(902) 569-5030

Rural ocean setting with a superb view of Northumberland Strait. Seven minutes from downtown, or beautiful Bellevue Cove with its beaches and clam digging. Three tastefully decorated rooms, one with a queen bed, half-bath and balcony, one with a queen bed and one with two twins. Guest lounge with a balcony. Bicycles available, and a two-bedroom self-contained apartment is also available.

Hosts: Nora and Steve Stephenson
Rooms: 3 (1.5 PB; 2 SB) $40-50
Continental Breakfast
Credit Cards: None
Notes: 2, 9, 10, 11, 12

MONTAGUE

Partridge's Bed and Breakfast
Panmure Island, Rural Route 2, C0A 1R0
(902) 838-4687

Partridge's Bed and Breakfast is near Panmure Island Provincial Park, where lifeguards patrol one of the most beautiful beaches on Prince Edward Island. One house has three bedrooms with private baths and is wheelchair accessible. The other house has two bedrooms with shared bath and another bedroom with private bath. Seal cruises, plays, tennis, golf, and horseback riding within 20 miles. Canoe, rowboat, and bicycles free for guests. Laundry and kitchen for guests.

Host: Gertrude Partridge
Rooms: 7 (5 PB; 2 SB) $40-50
Full Breakfast
Credit Cards: B
Notes: 6, 8, 9, 11, 14

MURRAY RIVER

Bayberry Cliff Inn Bed and Breakfast
Rural Route 4, Little Sands, C0A 1W0
(902) 962-3395

Situated on the edge of a 40-foot cliff, the inn consists of two converted post-and-beam barns decorated with antiques and marine art. Stairs to the shore allow for swimming, tubing, snorkeling, and beachcombing. Seal boat tours and bird watching tours nearby, as well as fine restaurants and craft shops. A honeymoon suite with private bath is available.

Hosts: Nancy and Don Perkins
Rooms: 8 (1 PB; 3 SB) $35-70
Full Breakfast
Credit Cards: A, B
Closed October 1 - May 1
Notes: 2, 8, 9, 11, 14

---

6 Pets welcome; 8 Children welcome; 9 Social drinking allowed; 10 Tennis available; 11 Swimming available; 12 Golf available; 13 Skiing available; 14 May be booked through travel agents.

Quebec

A B&B Downtown Network 1

3458 Laval Avenue, H2X 3C8
(514) 289-9749; FAX (514) 287-7386

Downtown turn-of-the-century home. This restored Victorian home features a marble fireplace, original hardwood floors, and a skylight. The host offers two charmingly decorated double rooms, and grandma's quilt in the winter. Guests can bird watch on the balcony or have a challenging game of Trivial Pursuit in the evening. Full breakfast. $35-55 Canadian.

A B&B Downtown Network 2

3458 Laval Avenue, H2X 3C8
(514) 289-9749; FAX (514) 287-7386

Be in the heart of everything! The big bay window of this 90-year-old restored home overlooks the city's most historic park. Original woodwork and detail add to the charm of this nine-room home, where a double and triple are offered. The neighborhood is famous for is excellent "bring your own wine" restaurants, and the host knows them all. Full breakfast. $35-75 Canadian.

A B&B Downtown Network 3

3458 Laval Avenue, H2X 3C8
(514) 289-9749; FAX (514) 287-7386

Downtown double off Sherbrooke Street. This antique-filled apartment on Drummond Street is tastefully decorated and only two minutes to the Museum of Fine Arts and all shopping. Mount Royal Park is nearby, and McGill University is just two blocks. The hosts pamper guests with a gourmet breakfast and invite them to join them for a sherry in the evening. One double room, shared bath. $55 Canadian.

A B&B Downtown Network 4

3458 Laval Avenue, H2X 3C8
(514) 289-9749; FAX (514) 287-7386

Downtown, in the heart of the Latin Quarter. Enjoy the superb location of this restored traditional Québecoise home. The host, active in the restaurant business, offers two sunlit doubles and one triple with a bay window opening onto a typical Montreal scene. The privacy of this tastefully furnished home is perfect for first or second honeymoons. Shared bath, full breakfast. $55-75 Canadian.

A B&B Downtown Network 6

3458 Laval Avenue, H2X 3C8
(514) 289-9749; FAX (514) 287-7386

When traveling to Quebec City, stop at this landmark home built in 1671, facing the beautiful St. Lawrence River. The hostess, a blue-ribbon chef, offers guests a memorable breakfast featuring "Quiche Floriane." For an unforgettable stay, guests are invited to experience the warmth and hospitality of a typical Québecoise home. Two enchanting doubles. Full breakfast. $55 Canadian.

A B&B Downtown Network 7

3458 Laval Avenue, H2X 3C8
(514) 289-9749; FAX (514) 287-7386

This Old Montreal landmark offers eight guest rooms and one suite. Decorated with a combination of antiques and contemporary pieces, the guest rooms are spacious and air-conditioned. All have private baths in marble, some with Jacuzzi. In winter, snuggle before a crackling fire with a good book. Within strolling distance of Notre Dame church, fine restaurants, shops, and museums. Enjoy the richness of Montreal's heritage. Full gourmet breakfast. $75-95 Canadian.

Bed and Breakfast à Montréal

P. O. Box 575, Snowdon Station, H3X 3T8
(514) 738-9410

These bed and breakfasts are in the finest private homes and condo apartments, carefully selected for their comfort, cleanliness, and convenient locations downtown or just minutes away. Many are within walking distance of Old Montreal and the Convention Centre. All of the hosts are fluent in English. They'll enhance every visit with suggestions, outgoing personalities, and delicious breakfasts. Stay long enough to visit Old Montreal, the lively Latin Quarter, the Underground City, Botanical Gardens, Mount Royal Park, and St. Joseph's Oratory, among other sights. Coordinator: Marian Kahn.

Brigette's Bed and Breakfast

Bed and Breakfast à Montréal
P. O. Box 575, Snowdon Station, H3X 3T8
(514) 738-9410

The hostesses' love of art and antiques is obvious in this fabulous three-story town house. Fireplace, cozy livingroom, and view of the city's most historic park all add to the charm of this home. One double with brass bed, duvet, antique pieces, and your own bathroom. Experience the nearby "bring your own wine" restaurants. $50-70 Canadian.

Jacky's Bed and Breakfast

Bed and Breakfast à Montreal
P. O. Box 575, Snowdon Station, H3X 3T8
(514) 738-9410

This interior designer hostess has created warmth and charm in an elegant downtown condo apartment, with treasures collected in India and New Mexico. The guest room has a queen-size bed and private bathroom facilities. Sherbrooke St., the Museum of Fine Arts, and the city's best shops are just a couple of minutes away.

Joanne's Bed and Breakfast

Bed and Breakfast à Montreal
P. O. Box 575, Snowdon Station, H3X 3T8
(514) 738-9410

This marvelous three-story home dates from 1873 and offers a ground-floor suite, double bedroom, livingroom with fireplace, and private bathroom. Two smaller doubles are on the third floor. An oakwood spiral staircase is the centerpiece. Ample sitting area welcomes you. Situated in the fashionable Westmount section of the city, not even 10 minutes to downtown. $60-80 CDN.

Johanna's Cottage Bed and Breakfast

Bed and Breakfast à Montreal
P. O. Box 575, Snowdon Station, H3X 3T8
(514) 738-9410

This elegant hostess invites guests to share her bright, airy, two-story home, filled with European style. An avid gardener, she is

6 Pets welcome; 8 Children welcome; 9 Social drinking allowed; 10 Tennis available; 11 Swimming available; 12 Golf available; 13 Skiing available; 14 May be booked through travel agents.

pleased when guests take delight in her work. One double with private bathroom is offered in this Westmount home. Only five minutes to downtown.

Martha's Bed and Breakfast

Bed and Breakfast à Montréal
P. O. Box 575, Snowdon Station, H3X 3T8
(514) 738-9410

From Martha's house walk to Montreal's hockey arena, the Forum, or the city's most elegant shopping complex, Westmount Square. Stenciled glass windows, original woodwork and detail, and smart period furnishings are just some of the features of this bed and breakfast. $50-70 Canadian.

Le Jardin D'Antoine

2024 Rue Saint Denis, H2X 3K7
(514) 843-4506; (514) 281-1491

A warm atmosphere and a cozy room await you. Take advantage of a private inner court to have breakfast in the morning, or just relax at the end of a busy day. All rooms are fully air-conditioned, and feature a telephone, TV, and private bathroom.

Host: Antoine Giardina
Rooms: 14 (PB) $50-79
Full Breakfast
Credit Cards: A, B, C
Notes: 5, 6, 8, 14

NEW CARLISLE WEST

Bay View Farm

Box 21, 337 Main Highway, Route 132, G0C 1Z0
(418) 752-2725; (418) 752-6718

Situated on Route 132 between New Carlisle and Bonaventure on the rugged and beautiful Baie de Chaleur coastline of Quebec's Gaspé Peninsula. Seaside accommodations include five comfortable guest rooms. Full country breakfast is made from fresh farm and garden produce. Additional light meals by arrangement. Handicrafts on display. August Bay View Folk Festival, museums, historic sites, Fauvel Golf Course, beaches, lighthouse, hiking, bird watching. Breathtakingly beautiful panoramic seascapes. Tranquil and restful environment.

Host: Helen Sawyer
Rooms: 5 (1 PB; 4 SB) $35
Full Breakfast
Credit Cards: None
Notes: 3, 4, 5, 8, 10, 11, 12, 13

QUEBEC CITY

Gîte-Québec

3729, Avenue Le Corbusier
Sainte-Foy, G1W 4R8
(418) 651-1860

Gîte-Québec Bed & Breakfast arranges accommodations in private homes offering comfortable rooms, a complete breakfast, and warm hospitality. All listings have been personally inspected for their comfort and cleanliness. All are convenient to the city's attractions through excellent public transportation. Prices are $60-70 Canadian with a $15 deposit per person required. Call or write for a brochure and reservation form.

Bay View Farm

Puerto Rico

Parador Martorell, Inc.
Ocean Drive 6-A, P. O. Box 384, 00773
(809) 889-2710; FAX: (809) 889-4520

This small, family inn situated in the northeast portion of the island, rests only a block
from the ocean and 45 minutes from Isla
Verde Airport. Featuring modern rooms,
breakfast is served on the patio, with
restaurants, golf, and tennis nearby.

Host: Oscar Rivera
Rooms: 10 (4 PB; 6 SB) $58.85-74.90
Full Breakfast
Credit Cards: A, B, C
Notes: 8, 9, 10, 11, 12, 13, 14

6 Pets welcome; 8 Children welcome; 9 Social drinking allowed; 10 Tennis available; 11 Swimming available;
12 Golf available; 13 Skiing available; 14 May be booked through travel agents.

Virgin Islands

_____

Raintree Inn, Inc.

Box 566, Cruz Bay, 00831
(809) 776-7449; (800) 666-7449
FAX (809) 776-7449

This budget priced guest house is situated
in Cruz Bay Town, just a short walk from
the dock, restaurants, stores, and buses to
national park beaches. Three spacious, air-
conditioned efficiency apartments sleep up
to six people, with eight air-conditioned
guest rooms, and private baths, that sleep
up two. Fifty percent deposit required, with
a 30 day cancellation notice. Tropical
courtyard and a prize-winning restaurant,
The Fish Trap.

Hosts: Lonnie Willis and Clare Hartnett
Rooms: 11 (PB) $60-111
No Breakfast
Credit Cards: A, B, C, D
Notes: 4, 5, 8, 9, 10, 11, 14

NOTES: Credit cards accepted: A Master Card; B Visa; C American Express; D Discover Card; E Diner's
Club; F Other; 2 Personal Checks accepted; 3 Lunch available; 4 Dinner available; 5 Open all year; 6 Pets welcome; 8 Children welcome; 9 Social drinking allowed; 10 Tennis available; 11 Swimming available; 12 Golf
available; 13 Skiing available; 14 May be booked through travel agents.